Daniel Webster

DANIEL WEBSTER

The Man and His Time

ROBERT V. REMINI

W·W·NORTON & COMPANY·NEW YORK·LONDON

The text of this book is composed in New Caledonia with the display set in Caslon Openface and Garamond Light Condensed. Composition and manufacturing by the Maple-Vail Book Manufacturing Group. Genealogy chart by Gina Webster. Book design by Marjorie J. Flock.

Library of Congress Cataloging-in-Publication Data

Remini, Robert Vincent, 1921–
Daniel Webster : the man and his time / Robert V. Remini.
p. cm.
Includes bibliographical references and index.
ISBN 978-0-393-31849-4
1. Webster, Daniel, 1782–1852. 2. United States—Politics and government—1815–1861. 3. Legislators—United States—Biography. 4. United States. Congress. Senate—Biography. I. Title.
E340.W4R36 1997
328.73'092—dc21
[B]   97-24371
CIP

W. W. Norton & Company, Inc., 500 Fifth Avenue, New York, N.Y. 10110
http://www.wwnorton.com
W. W. Norton & Company Ltd., 10 Coptic Street, London WC1A 1PU
3 4 5 6 7 8 9 0

For Ruth
Who made it all possible

Contents

Illustrations follow pages 254 and 542

Preface

DURING the years I spent researching and writing my biography of Henry Clay I was constantly amazed to discover how few Americans knew who Clay was.

"The greatest Speaker in the history of the United States House of Representatives," I ventured in an effort to help.

"Really," came the reply.

"The Great Compromiser," I continued, hoping it would stir a memory of something learned years ago.

"Is that so."

"The Missouri Compromise," I offered in desperation.

"Sorry."

After I completed my Clay biography and decided to attempt the life of Daniel Webster, I was delighted to get a better response from friends and acquaintances when they asked about my next project.

"Daniel Webster! Oh, yes, I know him."

"You do. That's great."

"Yes, he wrote the dictionary!"

Alas. Noah Webster is someone vastly different from Daniel Webster, although they were contemporaries.[1]

So few Americans really know the history of this nation and the men and women who figured prominently in its development—except for Presidents, notorious criminals, and other exotics. Such important individuals of the early nineteenth century as Clay, Webster, John C. Calhoun, Thomas Hart Benton (not the artist), and others are slowly disappearing from the country's collective memory, and it is a great pity.

This biography of Daniel Webster therefore seeks to remind its readers of a truly major figure in the history of this nation. Moreover, it attempts to encom-

---

1. Noah Webster was twenty-four years older. Webster himself liked to tell the story about a small boy who was asked if he'd like to meet the renowned statesman. "Is it that Mr. Webster who made the spelling-book, and set me so many hard lessons," the boy asked; "if so, I never want to see him as long as I live." Charles Lanman, *The Private Life of Daniel Webster* (New York, 1852), p. 144. Noah Webster published an elementary spelling book, *A Grammatical Institute of the English Language, Part I,* in 1783, supplemented with a grammar in 1784 and a reader in 1785.

pass in a single volume his many extraordinary careers. He was a statesman, one of the five greatest senators in the history of the United States Congress, a magnificent orator (arguably the best the nation ever produced), an excellent secretary of state, an outstanding lawyer, and an important contributor to the constitutional development of the United States.

His political career traversed much of the first half of the nineteenth century, roughly from the War of 1812 to the eve of the Civil War. One of the most dynamic eras of American history, those years brought into view a phenomenal number of heroic individuals who took over from the Founding Fathers and by their efforts stretched the nation from ocean to ocean and shaped it into an industrial and democratic society. This is the so-called Age of Jackson, a period in our history I personally define, although not all historians would agree, as beginning with the emergence of Andrew Jackson into the national consciousness and concluding with the death of Daniel Webster in 1852.

The men of the Jacksonian era grappled with, argued over, dodged, and sometimes settled many questions left unresolved by the Founders. Slavery was the one problem they knew how to keep from escalating into bloody civil war but could not solve. And in a very real sense, with the deaths or retirements of these statesmen the country lost whatever chance it had to keep the North and South from submitting the question to the test of arms.

Webster both reflected the spirit of the age and opposed it. He was an ardent nationalist, and his words still soar with a majesty of language that conveys a sense of the true beauty and wonder of this country. All his life he was a Federalist: in his thinking, in his behavior, in his political style. From time to time he changed the name of his political affiliation, moving from Federalist to National Republican to Whig, but his ideas of government and the relationship of the governed to the central authority did not significantly change over the span of his seventy-year life, although he did come to acknowledge the ever-increasing presence of advancing democracy. An ardent advocate of capitalism, he believed in the right of property and the need of the government to protect it, in the merits of labor, and in the importance of business and industry to the growth and life of the nation. But he was an elitist and as such did not fit into the world of the early 1800s as it evolved more and more into a democratic society.

While researching and writing my studies of the lives of Jackson and Clay, I found them personally appealing in different ways, and therefore I can appreciate why contemporaries idolized them. But in preparing this biography, I came to understand why so many men in his own time disliked Daniel Webster. I learned that he was untrustworthy, particularly when it came to money or the demands of his ambition. This, I believe, was his greatest defect of character. He used people. He used them to enrich himself and to obtain their assistance to advance his several careers. John Quincy Adams observed this flaw and despised him for it. Daniel Webster, he said, had a "rotten heart."[2] Others,

2. Adams, *Memoirs*, XI, 20.

like Edward Everett, recognized but overlooked the defect because of his genius.

With Webster there was also a thin veil of hauteur in his manner whenever he dealt with individuals whom he regarded as his intellectual or social inferiors. He was a snob about many things: his New England breeding, his education, his legal, linguistic, and literary talents, the fact that he represented the state where the struggle for liberty first occurred and that he was the foremost constitutional authority in the United States, the recognized "Defender of the Constitution."

But if Webster's faults were many and grievous, and they were, his talents and his contributions to this nation were far greater. And they have endured.

Having said all this, I must confess to a deep admiration for this extraordinary man. Added to all his other talents as orator, lawyer, and constitutionalist, I found it quite remarkable that he could move easily and surefootedly from managing the affairs of state, whether diplomatic or political, to composing a literary or historical oration, to writing critical reviews of scientific and humanistic books, to arguing a case before the Supreme Court of the United States at the same time he was fighting off attacks of nullifiers and secessionists in Congress. He had "intellect stamped on his face in clearer characters than any man I ever saw," wrote George Templeton Strong, a distinguished New York lawyer.[3] Small wonder contemporaries called him the "Godlike Daniel."

But whether men hated or admired him, all agreed (and I include myself) on the majesty of his oratory, the immensity of his intellectual powers, and the primacy of his constitutional knowledge. No one else at the time could articulate the history of the United States or its certain and monumental destiny that Americans felt at the time. No one could explain its institutional life or the pride the American people took in what they and their forebears had accomplished since the arrival of English settlers on these shores. The lyricism and beauty of his language when describing nature or the marvels of his country sometimes approached genuine literature. In this book I have tired to include enough examples of his writings and speeches for readers to reach their own conclusions in the matter. But it must be remembered that his oratory and style of writing— the florid language, the historical and classical allusions, and the slower tempo of the whole—are no longer fashionable, and they must be read in perspective, in the context of his own time.

I found it interesting that in 1850, when Webster was working on the six-volume edition of his *Works* with his editor, Edward Everett, he said that he did not wish to see included "any life, written in a very popular air, or attempted to be enlivened by variety of incident & anecdote." A "temperate & chaste manner of composition . . . would be the more gratifying to me."[4] Well, I confess I have tried to enliven this text with a "variety of incident & anecdote." As for a

3. Allan Nevins and Milton Halsey Thomas, eds., *The Diary of George Templeton Strong* (New York, 1952), I, 147.
4. DW to Everett, January 8, 1851, in *PC*, VII, 192.

"temperate & chaste manner," I have my own opinion, but readers will have to decide for themselves.

As the biographer of both Jackson and Clay, two men Webster sharply differed with at times, I can only hope that as I round out my personal "Great Triumvirate," he himself will not be too dissatisfied with what I have written.

Acknowledgments

I HAVE BEEN researching the Jacksonian era in American history since 1947, and over the years I have received guidance and assistance from countless historians, librarians, and archivists, as well as friends and private individuals who owned important historical documents. They are too numerous to list here, but they know who they are, and I trust they also know how indebted I am to them.

Still, I would be very remiss not to single out several individuals and institutions that have helped me enormously in the preparation of this biography of Daniel Webster. First of all, I must thank the members of the History Department of the University of Richmond who invited me to assume the Douglas Southall Freeman Chair of American History at their institution. The chair included enough research funds for me to purchase the fourteen volumes of *The Papers of Daniel Webster,* expertly edited by Charles M. Wiltse and his associates. The entire collection of Webster's manuscripts had been previously released on forty-one reels of film, together with a *Guide and Index* (Hanover, N.H., 1971). Collectively these works stand as a lasting memorial to Webster's statesmanship.

I am also very grateful to Senator Bob Smith of New Hampshire for his kindness in permitting me to inspect the Webster desk that he now occupies in the U.S. Senate and for the excellent tour he provided of the present chamber and its several adjourning rooms where the two parties caucus and where senators can escape the prying eyes of spectators and reporters. John B. Odell of the Senate's Commission on Art provided a considerable amount of information about the Webster desk. Pictures of the desk used in this book were obtained through the help of Tom Evans of the National Graphic Center. I also wish to extend my thanks to Senator Patrick J. Leahy of Vermont, who kindly allowed me to view Webster's "wine room," which has been expanded and redecorated by Mrs. Leahy and is now the senator's "hideaway" in the Capitol.

My friend Donald A. Ritchie, associate historian of the Senate, informed me of not only the existence of Webster's "wine room" but the location of valuable documentary material in the Senate library. He also conducted me on a tour of the Capitol, which he calls his "Blood on the Floor" tour, and showed me rooms and passageways in the building that I never dreamed existed.

Diane K. Skvarla, curator of the Senate, assisted my search for Webster material in the curator's care, and Scott M. Strong, administrator of the Senate curator's office, guided me through the Isaac Bassett Papers. His excellent index to these papers saved me countless hours of hunting through the material.

I owe a very special salute to a very special lady, Joan A. Scolponeti, secretary of the Marshfield Historical Commission, who, upon hearing about my project, offered to supply me with maps, articles, photographs, and all manner of information about Webster and especially about his home, Marshfield. I cannot thank her enough. Together with her colleagues on the commission—Anne Philbrick Hall, Betty Bates, Cynthia Krusell, and James Cantwell, president of the Daniel Webster Preservation Trust—she took me on an extended and most informative tour of the Marshfield property. Thanks to Betty Bates, I discovered why Webster suffered so much from his "catarrh" during each summer and fall when he returned to Marshfield.

Anne M. Ostendar, the archivist at Dartmouth, aided me in my search for information on Webster's career at the college. And Barbara Krieger, archives assistant, gave me invaluable help in compiling the genealogy for the Webster, Bachelder, and Fletcher families, as well as aid in the selection of portraits available at Dartmouth. She also hunted through the records of the college in an attempt to find evidence of Webster's academic performance at the school.

As usual my friend John McDonough at the manuscript division of the Library of Congress constantly alerted me to new and old material relating to Webster at the library, and Jeffrey M. Flannery went out of his way on several occasions to render assistance in obtaining documents at the library and in deciphering them. I am very grateful to him. Beverly Cox, curator of exhibitions at the National Portrait Gallery in Washington, expedited my efforts in locating and obtaining copies of many of the photographs used in this book.

I am especially grateful to Dr. Bernard H. Adelson, professor of clinical medicine at Northwestern University, who spent many hours examining Webster's medical records and providing me with information that significantly changed my understanding of the causes of Webster's final illness and death. I am also grateful to his assistant, Arlene Ponto, R.N., for her indispensable help.

Pearl Hanig performed the heroic task of copyediting this behemoth, and my appreciation is unbounded for all the errors, contradictions, and repetitions she uncovered. She is an absolute wonder.

James L. Mairs, the ever-genial and obliging editor at W. W. Norton, who is also a valued friend, made many helpful suggestions and criticisms toward improving the content of this book.

Lastly, I want to say that fundamental to my life and work as a historian and writer was my marriage in 1948 to Ruth Theresa Ann Kuhner, who ever since has been the inspiration for all my books, and so to her I dedicate this biography.

THE WEBSTER FAMILY

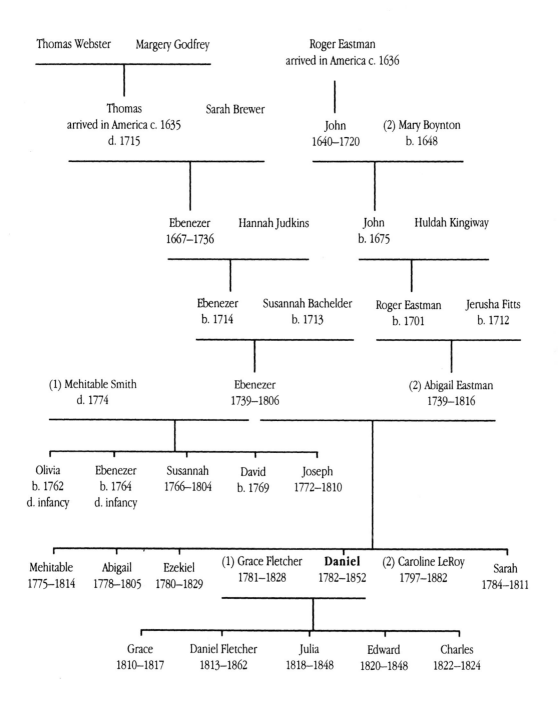

Thomas Webster   Margery Godfrey

Roger Eastman
arrived in America c. 1636

Thomas
arrived in America c. 1635
d. 1715

Sarah Brewer

John
1640–1720

(2) Mary Boynton
b. 1648

Ebenezer
1667–1736

Hannah Judkins

John
b. 1675

Huldah Kingiway

Ebenezer
b. 1714

Susannah Bachelder
b. 1713

Roger Eastman
b. 1701

Jerusha Fitts
b. 1712

(1) Mehitable Smith
d. 1774

Ebenezer
1739–1806

(2) Abigail Eastman
1739–1816

Olivia
b. 1762
d. infancy

Ebenezer
b. 1764
d. infancy

Susannah
1766–1804

David
b. 1769

Joseph
1772–1810

Mehitable
1775–1814

Abigail
1778–1805

Ezekiel
1780–1829

(1) Grace Fletcher
1781–1828

Daniel
1782–1852

(2) Caroline LeRoy
1797–1882

Sarah
1784–1811

Grace
1810–1817

Daniel Fletcher
1813–1862

Julia
1818–1848

Edward
1820–1848

Charles
1822–1824

Chronology of Webster's Life 1782–1852

1782 *January 18*   Born in Salisbury, New Hampshire
1784 *January*   Moved to Salisbury Lower Village
1786 Witnesses flooding of the Merrimack River
      Tutored by Thomas Chase and later by James Tappan and William Hoyt
1796 *May 25*   Enters Phillips Exeter
      December–January   Withdraws from Phillips Exeter
1797 *Winter*   Teaches school in Salisbury
      February   Studies with Dr. Samuel Wood in Boscawen
      Spring   Studies Greek with David Palmer, a Dartmouth senior
      August   Enters Dartmouth and rooms in college dormitory
1799 *May*   Offers to help finance his brother's education
      July 12   Helps found Federal Club at Dartmouth
      Temporarily manages the town's newspaper, the *Dartmouth Gazette*
1799–1800   Family moves to the Elms Farm, Salisbury, later renamed Franklin
1800 *Winter*   Teaches school in Salisbury
      July 4   Delivers Independence Day address in Hanover
      Elected president of United Fraternity
1801 *August 26*   Graduates from Dartmouth
      August   Begins study of law with Thomas W. Thompson
1802 *January*   Teaches school at Fryeburg Academy in Maine
      September   Returns to Salisbury and resumes legal studies
1804 *July 17*   Joins his brother in Boston
      July 20   Enters law office of Christopher Gore as a student
      November 5   Takes three-week trip to New York with Taylor Baldwin
1805 *Winter*   Refuses offer to be county clerk of the Hillsborough County Court of Common Pleas, New Hampshire
      February   Publishes anonymously "An Appeal to the Old Whigs of New Hampshire"

March   Admitted to practice before the Suffolk Court of Common Pleas in Boston

March 25   Leaves Boston

April   Opens law office in Boscawen

September 3   Argues his first case in court

1806   *April 22*   Ebenezer Webster, Daniel's father, dies

August 26   Gives State of Literature address to the Phi Beta Kappa Society of Dartmouth College

Writes articles and reviews for the Boston *Monthly Anthology*

1807   *May*   Admitted as counselor in the superior court of New Hampshire

September   Opens law office after moving to Portsmouth

1808   *May 29*   Marries Grace Fletcher in Salisbury

1810   *April 29*   Daughter Grace Fletcher Webster born

July 3   Appointed chairman of Portsmouth Committee to write memorial in support of Federalist candidates

1811   *June 26*   Appointed to three-man committee to revise New Hampshire's criminal code

1812   *June 18*   War declared against Great Britain

July 4   Speaks before Washington Benevolent Society of Portsmouth and attacks administration's war policy

August 5   Writes Rockingham Memorial, the definitive statement of New England Federalism, and raises specter of disunion

October 7   Nominated for Congress on Federalist ticket

November   Elected to lower house of Congress

1813   *May 24*   Takes his seat in House of Representatives

May 25   Pays respects to President Madison

June 10   Introduces five resolutions to look into origins of war

June 21   Resolutions passed. Webster delivers them to President Madison

July 23   Son Daniel Fletcher Webster born

November   Helps Rockingham Bank in Portsmouth obtain charter

December 22   Home in Portsmouth destroyed by fire

1814   *January 14*   Speaks against enlistment bill

January 14   Admitted to practice before U.S. Supreme Court

March 12   Argues first case before Supreme Court

April 6   Gives first important speech attacking embargo and gains recognition in Congress as a powerful speaker

1814   *August 24*   British burn Capitol and White House

August 29   Reelected to Congress

September 10   Chairman of safety committee and signs notice calling for massing of troops to protect Portsmouth from invasion

December 9   Opposes conscription bill

December 15   Hartford Convention begins

December 24   Treaty of Ghent signed ending War of 1812

1815   *January 8*   Battle of New Orleans

1816   *March 14*   Votes against chartering Second Bank of the United States

      April 25   Abigail Eastman Webster, Daniel's mother, dies

      April   Challenged to a duel by John Randolph

      August 16   Moves from Portsmouth to Boston but continues as representative from New Hampshire

1817   *January 23*   Daughter Grace Fletcher Webster dies

      September 19   Appears for plaintiff in the *Dartmouth College* case before the New Hampshire superior court

1818   *January 16*   Daughter Julia born

      March 10   Argues *Dartmouth College* case before U.S. Supreme Court

1819   *February 2*   Wins *Dartmouth College* case

      February 22   Argues *McCulloch* v. *Maryland* case before U.S. Supreme Court

      March 7   Wins *McCulloch* v. *Maryland* case

      December 3   Chairs Boston committee opposing expansion of slavery

1820   *March 6*   Missouri Compromise enacted

      July 20   Son Edward born

      Summer   Conducts John C. Calhoun on a tour of Boston

      October 16   Elected a delegate to Massachusetts Constitutional Convention

      November 15   Massachusetts Constitutional Convention convenes

      December 22   Delivers Plymouth oration

1821   *December 31*   Son Charles born

1821–1824   Argues cases before Spanish Claims Commission

1822   *Spring*   Elected to Massachusetts General Court and attends for a few days in May and June

      November   Elected as a Federalist from Boston to lower house of Congress

      Recognized as head of the American bar

1823   *February 4*   Argues *Steamboat* case before U.S. Supreme Court

      March 2   Wins *Steamboat* case

      August   Receives honorary degree from Dartmouth

      December 1   Takes his seat in House of Representatives

1824   *January 19*   Praises Greek independence in House

      February 4   Argues *Gibbons* v. *Ogden* before U.S. Supreme Court

      February   Fails to reform judiciary

      April 1–2   Delivers antitariff speech in House

      September   Discovers Marshfield

      November   Reelected to House of Representatives

      November   Presidential election indecisive and goes to the House of Representatives

      December 9–19   Visits Madison and Jefferson

      December 19   Son Charles dies

1825   *January–February*   Assists election of Adams to presidency
        February 21   Challenged to a duel by John Randolph
        February   Challenge withdrawn
        June 17   Delivers Bunker Hill oration
        June 25–July 28   Visits Niagara Falls
        December 22   Assists in extinguishing a fire at the Library of Congress
1825–1826   Fails once again to reform judiciary
        January 3   His mouthpiece, *Massachusetts Journal,* begins publication
        August 2   Delivers eulogy for John Adams and Thomas Jefferson
        November 6   Reelected to House of Representatives
1826–1828   Assists in efforts to reelect Adams as President
1827   *January 6*   Elected director of BUS
        June 7   Elected to U.S. Senate
        December 17   Takes his seat as senator from Massachusetts
1828   *January 21*   Wife Grace Fletcher Webster dies
        May 13   Votes for Tariff of 1828
        November   Andrew Jackson elected President
        December 16–17   Libel suit against Theodore Lowell, Jr., ends with the jury deadlocked
1829   *April 10*   Brother, Ezekiel, dies
        December 12   Marries Caroline Le Roy
1830   *January 20*   Replies to Senator Robert Y. Hayne in debate over sale of public lands and switches the debate away from public lands
        January 26   Makes second reply to Hayne
        April 26   Votes for Indian removal
        Summer–autumn   Prosecutes John Francis Knapp in murder trial
1832   *January 25*   Votes again confirmation of Van Buren as minister to England
        April 23   Purchases house and property in Marshfield, Massachusetts
        May 25–28   Speaks in defense of a bill to recharter the Second Bank of the United States
        July 11   Attacks Jackson veto of the Bank bill
        November   Jackson reelected President
        November 24   South Carolina nullifies tariffs
        December 17   Denounces nullification
1833   *January 16*   Reelected to U.S. Senate
        February 8–16   Defends Force Bill
        February   Opposes compromise tariff
        March 2   Compromise Tariff of 1833 enacted
        Spring–1834   Rumor of Jackson-Webster alliance
        May–July 20   Tours New York, Ohio, and Pennsylvania
        October 1   Taney orders government deposits removed from BUS
        December 21   Requests BUS "refresh" his retainer
1834   *March 28*   Votes to censure Jackson and Taney; rumors of alliance with Jackson end

Spring   Whig party forms

May 7   Denounces Jackson's Protest message

1835   *January 21*   Nominated for President by caucus of the Massachusetts legislature

July 6   John Marshall dies

1836   *January 22*   Attacked by John Quincy Adams

March 15   Fails to block Roger B. Taney confirmation as chief justice

November   Van Buren elected President

1837   *January 24–26*   Argues *Charles River Bridge* case before Supreme Court

February 14   Loses *Charles River Bridge* case

March 17   Onset of financial panic

May 10   New York banks suspend specie payments

May–July   Tours Kentucky, Ohio, Illinois, Missouri

1838   *March 12–13*   Attacks subtreasury bill

1839   *January 17*   Reelected to U.S. Senate

May 18   Sets sail for Europe

June 2   Arrives in Liverpool

June 6   Arrives in London

June 17   Meets Queen Victoria

July 18   Delivers speech to Royal Agricultural Society at Oxford

August 5   Dines with Queen Victoria

August 6–September 20 (?)   Tours England, Wales, and Scotland

September 24   Daughter Julia marries Samuel Appleton Appleton in London

October 19   Visits Paris

October 29   Dines with King Louis Philippe at St.-Cloud

November 2   Returns to London

November 22   Departs for New York

December 28   Arrives in New York Harbor

1840   *February 10*   Grandson Daniel Fletcher Webster, Jr., born

March–October   Campaigns for Harrison

November   Harrison elected President

December 1   Invited to join cabinet

December 11   Accepts office of secretary of state

1841   *February 22*   Resigns Senate seat

February   Assists Harrison in writing of inaugural address

March 5   Confirmed as secretary

March 20   Purchases house in Washington

Spring–summer   Attempts to win release of Alexander McLeod, accused of murder in the *Caroline* incident

April 4   Harrison dies

August 8   Suffers riding accident

September 11   Cabinet resigns, except Webster

November 7   Slaves revolt aboard *Creole*

December   British send Lord Ashburton to America to settle several disputes, principally the boundary between the United States and Canada

1842   *April 2*   Ashburton arrives at Annapolis

August 9   Webster-Ashburton Treaty signed

August 20   Senate ratifies treaty

September 30   Defends himself in speech in Faneuil Hall

1843   *May 8*   Writes instructions for China mission

May 8   Resigns as secretary of state

June 17   Delivers second Bunker Hill oration

1844   *February*   Argues and loses *Girard* case

February 7   Granddaughter Grace Fletcher Webster dies

November   James K. Polk elected President

1845   *January 16*   Reelected to Senate

March 1   Texas annexed

September 10   Joseph Story dies

1846   *February 9–29*   Charged with official misconduct

May 13   War declared against Mexico

June 9   Investigating committee dismisses charges of misconduct

June 15   Oregon Treaty ratified

July 30   Walker Tariff enacted

August 8   Wilmot Proviso introduced

1847   *January*   Argues *License* case before Supreme Court

March 6   Loses *License* case

April 28–May 29   Tours Virginia, the Carolinas, and Georgia

September 29   Claims credit for Wilmot Proviso

September 30   Endorsed for President by Massachusetts Whig convention

January 23   Son Edward dies

1848   *January 24*   Argues *Luther* v. *Borden* case before Supreme Court

March 10   Votes against ratification of the Treaty of Guadalupe Hidalgo ending Mexican War

March 23   Denounces Mexican War in Senate speech

April 28   Daughter Julia dies

June 9   Loses nomination of Whig party for President to Zachary Taylor

November   Taylor elected President

December   Argues *Passenger* case before Supreme Court

1849   *January*   Wins *Luther* v. *Borden* case

February 7   Wins *Passenger* case

1850   *March 7*   Delivers speech in Senate favoring compromise

July 9   Taylor dies

July 17   Delivers his last speech in the Senate

July 23   Confirmed as secretary of state in President Millard Fillmore's cabinet

September 20 Compromise of 1850 enacted

December 31 Writes Hülsemann letter

1850–1851 Condemned for efforts to enforce Fugitive Slave Law

1851 *February 26* Signs Convention for Settlement of Claims against Portugal

May 12–June 2 Tours New York

June 10 Writes instructions for Japan mission

July 4 Give principal address at laying of cornerstone of new Capitol in Washington

July 10 Negotiates treaty of amity and commerce with Costa Rica

September 10 Aids rescue of Louis Kossuth and his associates

November 13 Apologies to Spain over filibuster attack against Cuba

December 5 Kossuth arrives in New York

1852 *January 7* Speaks at banquet honoring Kossuth and causes breach with Austria

February 23 Lectures before the New-York Historical Society on the importance of history

March 20–April 2 Argues and wins the *India rubber* case in U.S. Circuit Court in Trenton, New Jersey, his last important case

May 8 Sustains severe head injury

June 16 Signs Convention for the Mutual Delivery of Criminals with Prussia

June 21 Loses nomination of Whig party for President to Winfield Scott

July 9 Given gargantuan reception in Boston

July Mishandles fishing dispute with Britain and denounced in Senate

June–September Bungles dispute with Peru over Lobos Islands

October 21 Signs last will and testament

October 24 Dies at Marshfield

October 29 Funeral and burial at Marshfield

Abbreviations and Short Titles Used in the Notes

Adams, *Memoirs*   Charles Francis Adams, ed., *Memoirs of John Quincy Adams* (Philadelphia, 1874–1877), twelve volumes

ASPFR   American State Papers, Foreign Relations

Benton, *Thirty Years' View*   Thomas Hart Benton, *Thirty Years' View* (New York, 1968) two volumes

BM   British Museum, London

Calhoun Papers   W. Edwin Hamphill et al., eds., *The Papers of John C. Calhoun* (Columbia, S.C., 1963–), twenty-two volumes

Clay *Papers*   James F. Hopkins et al., eds., *The Papers of Henry Clay* (Lexington, Ky., 1959–), eleven volumes

Curtis, *Webster*   George Ticknor Curtis, *Life of Daniel Webster* (New York, 1870), two volumes

Fuess, *Webster*   Claude Moore Fuess, *Daniel Webster* (Boston, 1930), two volumes

Harvey, *Reminiscences*   Peter Harvey, *Reminiscences and Anecdotes of Daniel Webster* (Boston, 1877)

Hone, *Diary*   Philip Hone, *The Diary of Philip Hone, 1828–1851*, ed. Allan Nevins (New York, 1927), two volumes

IB Papers   The Isaac Bassett Papers on deposit: Office of the Senate Curator, U.S. Capitol

LC   Library of Congress

March, *Webster*   Charles W. March, *Daniel Webster and His Contemporaries* (New York, 1852)

McGrane, ed., *Correspondence of Biddle*   Reginald C. McGrane, ed., *The Correspondence of Nicholas Biddle Dealing with National Affairs, 1807–1844* (Boston, 1919)

MHS   Massachusetts Historical Society

Microfilm Edition   Charles M. Wiltse, ed., *The Microfilm Edition of the Papers of Daniel Webster* (Hanover, N.H., 1970), forty-one reels

NA   National Archives

PC   Charles M. Wiltse et al., eds., *The Papers of Daniel Webster, Correspondence* (Hanover, N.H., 1974–1986), seven volumes

PD Kenneth E. Shewmaker et al., eds., *The Papers of Daniel Webster, Diplomatic, 1841–1843, 1850–1852* (Hanover, N.H., 1983, 1987), two volumes

PLBP Alfred S. Konefsky and Andrew J. King, eds., *The Papers of Daniel Webster, Legal Papers, the Boston Practice* (Hanover, N.H., 1983)

PLFP Andrew J. King, ed., *The Papers of Daniel Webster, Legal Papers, Federal Practice,* (Hanover, N.H., 1989), three volumes

PRO Public Record Office, London

PS Charles M. Wiltse et al., eds., *The Papers of Daniel Webster, Speeches and Formal Writings* (Hanover, N.H., 1986), two volumes

Remini, *Clay* Robert V. Remini, *Henry Clay: Statesman for the Union* (New York, 1991)

Remini, *Jackson II, III* Robert V. Remini, *Andrew Jackson and the Course of American Freedom, 1822–1832* (New York, 1981); *Andrew Jackson and the Course of American Democracy, 1833–1845* (New York, 1984)

RG Record Group

Richardson, *Messages and Papers* J. D. Richardson, *Compilation of Messages and Papers of the Presidents* (Washington, D.C., 1908), twenty volumes

Story, *Life and Letters* William W. Story, ed., *Life and Letters of Joseph Story* (New York, 1851), two volumes

Ticknor, *Life* George Ticknor, *Life, Letters, and Journal of George Ticknor* (Boston and New York, 1909), two volumes

Van Buren, *Autobiography* John C. Fitzpatrick, ed., *Autobiography of Martin Van Buren* (Washington, D.C., 1920)

Van Tyne, ed., *Letters of Webster* C.H. Van Tyne, ed., *The Letters of Daniel Webster* (New York, 1902)

W&S The National Edition of *The Writings and Speeches of Daniel Webster* (Boston, 1903), eighteen volumes

Webster, ed., *Private Correspondence* Fletcher Webster, ed., *The Private Correspondence of Daniel Webster* (Boston, 1857), two volumes

Wiltse, *Calhoun, I, II, III* Charles M. Wiltse, *John C. Calhoun, Nationalist, 1782–1828, John C. Calhoun, Sectionalist, 1829–1839, John C. Calhoun, Secessionist, 1840–1850* (Indianapolis and New York, 1944–1951), three volumes

DANIEL WEBSTER

1

The Godlike Daniel and Black Dan

THAT VOICE. It mesmerized. It dazzled. And it rang out like a trumpet. Never shrill, never unpleasantly loud, but deep, dark, with a roll of thunder in it, tempered by a richness of tone and powered by a massive chest that sent it hurtling great distances, even in the open air, it turned "on the harps of the blessed" and shook "the earth underground." Under perfect control, it never broke however high it was driven to convey an emotion or emphasize a point. For a typical three-, four-, or even five-hour oration it usually needed some form of lubrication to be fired up and ready to perform. But once it started to function, it sang out like music in clear and sonorous cadences and swelled and diminished on command. Nobody who heard it ever forgot it. One carried the sound of it to the grave.[1]

And that look. It hypnotized. It riveted. It could wither miscreants with a single glance. Large, deep-socketed black eyes peered out from a "precipice of brows" and glowed like coals in a furnace waiting for the annoyance or offense that would bring them to full heat.

"He gave me that black look," reported Isaac Bassett, a Senate page, "whenever I did something he did not like," and while "his voice was majestic, his eye was almost superhuman." On one occasion Bassett remembered being asked by Senator Webster one rainy day to go and get a "hack." The boy failed in his search, whereupon "Webster just looked at me. But what a glance! I would rather endure anything than another such glance. I felt like sinking through the floor. Then Webster said, 'Go—and—get—that hack.' It is needless to say the carriage was found."

A Congregational minister in New Hampshire recalled looking down at his congregation one Sunday and seeing Webster sitting in the first pew. He fixed

1. Curtis, *Webster*, I, 249 note; Stephen Vincent Benét, *The Devil and Daniel Webster* (New York, 1937), pp. 14–15.

"such great, staring black eyes upon me," said the minister, "that I was frightened out of my wits."[2]

Webster had the same effect on other senators as well. Once Stephen A. Douglas of Illinois, the Little Giant, as he was called, tried to move forward a bill in which he was interested.

"We have no such practice in the Senate, sir," intoned Webster in his deep, solemn voice, fixing his eye on the mover without rising from his seat.

Douglas tried a different tack but did not get very far.

"That is not the way we do business in the Senate, sir," Webster repeated "still more derisively and sternly." Horace Greeley, editor of the New York *Tribune,* who was sitting in the Senate chamber, saw the Little Giant's reaction and reported that if Douglas "did not quiver under the eye and voice of Webster, then my eyesight deceived me,—and I was very near him."[3]

A man of swarthy complexion, with bushy eyebrows and hair as black as the feathers of a raven, a "craglike face," a stern countenance, small hands and feet, a mouth like a mastiff, and a stare that locked a listener in an inescapable embrace—that was Daniel Webster, "Black Dan."

One contemporary claimed to have seen many of the great men of the age—King George, Sir Robert Peel, Lord Palmerston, Daniel O'Connell, François Guizot, Henry Clay, and John C. Calhoun—"yet not one of these approached Mr. Webster in the commanding power of their personal presence. There was a grandeur in his form, an intelligence in his deep dark eye, a loftiness of his expansive brow, a significance in his arched lip, altogether beyond those of any other human being I ever saw." He stood five feet ten inches and weighed 190 pounds in his prime. "He was physically the most splendid specimen of noble manhood my eyes ever beheld," declared Senator George F. Hoar of Massachusetts.[4]

Some thought him ugly. Webster was taking a trip from Baltimore to Washington by coach one day when the driver suddenly turned to him and said, "Now, sir, tell me who are you!"

"I am Daniel Webster, member of Congress from Massachusetts," came the reply.

"What!" exclaimed the coachman, grasping his passenger warmly by the hand. "Are you Webster? Thank God! Thank God! You were such a deuced ugly chap, that I took you for some cut-throat or highwayman."[5]

2. IB Papers, Box 1, Folder B, p. 54; Box 20, Folder B, p. 38D; Box 33, Folder D, p. 71.

3. Horace Greeley, *Recollections of a Busy Life* (New York, 1868), p. 251.

4. Thomas Carlyle to a friend, June 24, 1839, quoted in Curtis, *Webster,* II, 21; George F. Hoar, *Autobiography of Seventy Years* (New York, 1905), I, 142; S. G. Goodrich, *Recollections of a Lifetime* (New York, 1856), II, 411–412; Dr. John Jeffries, "An Account of the Last Illness of the Late Honourable Daniel Webster," *American Journal of the Medical Sciences,* New Series, XXV (January 1853), p. 110. Dr. Jeffries said that Webster's appearance "was peculiarly imposing, and the expression of his features, more particularly of his eye, was, perhaps, more powerful than that of any other man." Ibid.

5. Lanman, *Private Life of Daniel Webster,* p. 96. Lanman served as Webster's private secretary from June 1851 to October 1852.

A poet later wrote a short story about him entitled "The Devil and Daniel Webster." The story tells how Black Dan argues a case in New Hampshire before a jury handpicked by the devil. The devil, called Scratch, confronts Webster, his "eyes glowing like a fox's deep in the woods." "Black Dan" stares back at Scratch, and "his eyes were glowing too." Both argue their case before this jury of hardened criminals, and Black Dan wins. From that day to this, claims the poet, the devil "hasn't been seen in the state of New Hampshire."[6]

Ralph Waldo Emerson insisted that the American people regarded Webster "as the representation of the American Continent."[7] Indeed they did. They saw him as the nation's best image of itself from whose mind and mouth came the most glorious images of this country's heroic past. In their respect and admiration they dubbed him "the Godlike Daniel."

He might be "the Godlike" to many, but to others he remained "Black Dan," one of the greatest intellects "God ever let the Devil buy."[8]

This strange, compelling, extraordinary man emerged from the rocky slopes of New England. His lineage in America stretched back over four generations. Approximately sixteen years after the Pilgrims fell on their knees at Plymouth to give thanks for their safe passage across the Atlantic Ocean, a young Scot by the name of Thomas Webster—the name means a male weaver—was brought to this country from England[9] around 1636 by his widowed mother, who had subsequently remarried.[10] Margaret (or Margery) Webster Godfrey first settled in Ipswich, Massachusetts, before moving with her teenage son to the coast at Hampton, New Hampshire.

The son came "thither from, or thro' Mass," wrote Daniel Webster about his ancestor, "tho he may have come by way of Piscataqua."[11] One of Thomas's five sons, Ebenezer,[12] became a tolerable Indian fighter and guide for Captain John Gilman and was one of several grantees of the town of Kingston. Of

6. Benét, *Devil and Daniel Webster*, pp. 36, 61. Douglas Moore composed a one-act folk opera based on this story.

7. Emerson, *The Complete Works of Ralph Waldo Emerson* (Cambridge, Mass., 1904), XI, 221.

8. Quoted in Irving Bartlett, *Daniel Webster* (New York, 1978), p. 3. The New York *Mirror*, October 1, 1831, claimed that if you saw Webster "in some solitary place" at night, you would not know whether he was "a demi-god or a devil."

9. George Curtis says that the family originally came from Scotland but probably emigrated to America from England. Standing on the walls of Quebec for the first time as an adult, Peter Harvey reported, Daniel Webster said that he cast "an imaginary glance over the broad extent of that dominion, thought of the magnitude of the power that governed half a civilized globe by her superior intellect. And I was proud . . . that the blood of the Englishman flowed in my veins!" Curtis, *Webster*, I, 2; Harvey, *Reminiscences*, pp. 144–145.

10. H. J. Raymond, "Memoir of Daniel Webster" states that Thomas, born in 1632, emigrated from Norfolk, England, in 1656 and settled in Hampton, New Hampshire. In Lyman, *The Public and Private Life of Daniel Webster* (Philadelphia, 1852), I, 7.

11. Fragment of an "Autobiography," written in 1829, in *PC*, I, 3. Fuess, *Webster*, I, 5, says that Thomas Webster's father, also named Thomas, died in Ormsby, near Yarmouth, England, in 1634.

12. Born in 1667, married Hannah Judkins in July 1709. Lyman, *Public and Private Life of Webster*, I, 7.

Ebenezer's nine children, the eldest boy, also named Ebenezer, eked out a scant living as a farmer and freeholder but had the good fortune to marry Susannah Bachelder, a descendant of the Reverend Stephen Bachelder, the first settled clergyman in New Hampshire and "a man of some notoriety, in his time, in the County of Rockingham." Susanna possessed all the fortitude and vitality her husband lacked. She added great strength to the Webster lineage. Their eldest son, and the third generation of Ebenezers, was born on April 22, 1739, in Kingston. This Ebenezer was Daniel Webster's father.[13]

He served with some distinction in the French and Indian War in a company of Rangers commanded by Major Robert Rogers. He participated in the invasion of Canada, led by Sir Jeffrey Amherst, and rose to the rank of captain. At the conclusion of the war in 1763 the twenty-four-year-old Ebenezer,[14] together with a group of other men, obtained a grant of a township of land from the royal governor of New Hampshire, Benning Wentworth, which they called Stevenstown (to honor their leader, Colonel Ebenezer Stevens) but which was later changed to Salisbury. This township was located near the center of New Hampshire where two steams converge to form the Merrimack River. It stretched nine miles along the west bank of the river and extended in a southwesterly direction.[15]

As his portion of the land grant Ebenezer Webster chose a section of some 225 acres at the extreme northern end of the town along a stream he called Punch Brook. There in 1764 he built a log cabin for himself and his family along with a small gristmill that he shared with his neighbors. The house was perched on a rugged hill some three miles west of the Merrimack River. His nearest "civilized neighbor" to the north lived in Montreal![16]

Ebenezer Webster and his family endured many hardships in the isolated wilderness of New Hampshire: brutal winters with mountains of snow that lasted sometimes from November to April, marginal land, no roads to reach the outside world, and the constant terror of midnight raids by hostile Indians who took offense at his intrusion into their country. Brown and black bears, gray wolves, and lynxes also challenged his claim to the land.

Not surprisingly, Ebenezer Webster looked as rugged as the country that surrounded him: tall, standing a little over six feet, full-chested, and hairy, with piercing black eyes under bushy eyebrows, a helmet of jet black hair, and large, indeed very prominent, features, including a bulging forehead and "a Roman nose." But to his son Daniel, Ebenezer was "the handsomest man I ever saw," with the exception of his brother, Ezekiel.[17] The father resembled no other

13. "Autobiography" in *PC*, I, 4.

14. At the age of twelve or fifteen, according to Daniel Webster, Ebenezer lived with the family of Colonel Ebenezer Stevens. "Autobiography," in *PC*, I, 4.

15. Harvey, *Reminiscences*, pp. 2–3.

16. Thomas H. Pettengill to Professor Sanborn, January 14, 1853, in Webster, ed., *Private Correspondence*, I, 60. "Autobiography," in *PC*, I, 5.

17. Ezekiel "was an improved edition of his father, in form and features, and had such a form as a statuary . . . might select for a model. His complexion was some shades lighter than that of his father

Webster. Most Websters had light complexions and sandy hair and tended to be slender. Not Ebenezer. Said his son: "No two persons looked more unlike than my father, & either of his brothers." Ebenezer took after his mother's side of the family in both appearance and personal characteristics. "This woman," declared Daniel Webster about his grandmother, "had black hair, & black eyes, & was, besides, as my father, who was her eldest son, has told me, a person of uncommon strength of character."[18]

Susannah Bachelder Webster's uncommon strength of character manifested itself many times in her son. At the age of fourteen Ebenezer ran away from a tyrannical master to whom he had been apprenticed, and this strength of character no doubt sustained him throughout the years as he struggled to survive in the remote wilderness of Salisbury.

Commentators frequently mentioned his decisiveness. As an adult he headed a committee to choose a new clergyman for the town, and when a dispute arose over a minor doctrinal point that delayed the ordination, he stood before the members of the church council selected to perform the ordination and barked, "Gentlemen, the ordination must come on *now*, and, if you cannot assist, we must try to get along without you." That outburst settled the matter. The ordination proceeded without further delay. For when Ebenezer spoke, his words had the ring of authority, which his son believed resulted from his "early soldiership."[19] Firm, possibly rigid, and certainly decisive whenever he rendered judgment, Ebenezer Webster struck his fellow citizens as resolute and determined, an extremely strong-minded man.[20]

As the town grew, he served his community at different times as selectman, town clerk, highway surveyor, coroner, and judge.[21] Throughout his life he held important local positions, and he charged only three or four shillings a day for his services.

Ebenezer had no formal education, although he could read and write. Indeed some of the earliest records of Salisbury are in his handwriting. "He had in him," Daniel remembered years later, "what I collect to have been the character of some of the old Puritans. He was deeply religious, but not sour. On the contrary, good-humored, facetious, showing even in his age, with a contagious laugh, teeth all as white as alabaster, gentle, soft, playful, and yet having a heart

---

or brother. The form of his head and face was essentially Grecian . . . his eyes large, dark, and brilliant." Webster said his brother had "the finest human form that ever I laid eyes on." Thomas H. Pettengill to Sanborn, January 14, 1853, DW to R. M. Blatchford, May 3, 1836, in Webster, ed., *Private Correspondence*, I, 61; II, 228. Pettengill's letter includes a detailed summary of Ezekiel's life.

18. "Autobiography," in *PC*, I, 4; Thomas H. Pettengill to Sanborn, January 14, 1853, DW to R. M. Blatchford, May 3, 1836, in Webster, ed., *Private Correspondence*, I, 58, II, 228.

19. Curtis, *Webster*, I, 3, note 2.

20. Thomas H. Pettengill to Sanborn, January 14, 1853, in Webster, ed., *Private Correspondence*, I, 59–63.

21. In 1791 he was chosen judge of the Court of Common Pleas for the county of Hillsborough, a post that he held until 1805. Lyman, *Public and Private Life of Webster*, I, 10.

in him that he seemed to have borrowed from a lion." Daniel Webster loved his father very deeply. In fact he idolized him.[22]

With the outbreak of the American Revolution Captain Webster assembled nearly two hundred men from the township and marched forward into battle with troops from other New Hampshire towns.[23] He commanded these troops at Bennington, and at White Plains, and he was present at West Point at the moment of Benedict Arnold's defection. He stood guard at General George Washington's headquarters the night of Arnold's treason. The general reportedly said to him, "Captain Webster, I believe I can trust *you.*" As someone who revered George Washington above all other statesmen, Daniel Webster took enormous pride in what the general had said to his father. "I should rather have it said upon my father's tombstone that he had guarded the person of George Washington, and was worthy of such a trust, than to have emblazoned upon it the proudest insignia of heraldry that the world could give!"[24]

Years later at a tavern in Concord, General John Stark, the hero of the Bennington fight, peered at Ebenezer's son and then, with all the candor of age fortified by several stiff drinks, said, "Daniel, your face is pretty black, but it isn't so black as your father's was with gunpowder at the Bennington fight."[25] Daniel later recorded that it was the last time he ever saw General Stark, and he took it as a high compliment that he resembled his father.[26]

Ebenezer and his first wife, Mehitable Smith, a Kingston girl, had five children, only three of whom survived to maturity.[27] When Mehitable died in March 1774, she left an eight-year-old girl, Susannah, and two small boys, David and Joseph. In need of another helpmate Ebenezer consulted his brother's wife. She told him to take a look at Abigail ("Nabby") Eastman, a seamstress of good character, who was visiting her relatives in Salisbury. A meeting took place, and in August 1774, five months after Ebenezer's first wife died, the two were married by Parson Jonathan Searle. When the couple entered his cabin, Ebenezer turned to his bride and said, "These, Nabby, are my children."[28]

22. Harvey, *Reminiscences,* p. 8; DW to Blatchford, May 3, 1846, in Webster, ed., *Private Correspondence,* II, 229.

23. Ebenezer wrote a pledge and persuaded eighty–four neighbors to sign it, stating: "We do solemnly engage and promise that we will, to the utmost of our power, at the risk of our lives and fortunes, with arms, oppose the hostile proceedings of the British fleets and armies against the United American Colonies." Harvey, *Reminiscences,* p. 6.

24. Curtis, *Webster,* I, 4 note 2; Harvey, *Reminiscences,* p. 6.

25. Curtis, *Webster,* I, 248–249.

26. "Autobiography" in *PC,* I, 5.

27. These five included Olle or Olive, born January 28, 1762, and died in infancy; Ebenezer, born July 16, 1764, also died young; Susannah, born October 25, 1766, married John Colby of Boscawen, and died on March 23, 1804; David, born May 1, 1769, married Rebecca Huntoon, had a large family, and moved to Canada; and Joseph, born March 25, 1772, and died January 20, 1810. Curtis, *Webster,* I, 5 note 1; Fuess, *Webster,* I, 8–9 and note 2. David moved to Canada, but Susannah and Joseph lived all their lives in or near Salisbury.

28. Fuess, *Webster,* I, 9.

Abigail was a "spinster lady," long past the usual marital age for a woman in the colonial era. Born on July 19, 1737, she was thirty-seven at the time of her wedding. She was dark-complexioned, stout, and decidedly plain, an appearance that may account for her prolonged spinsterhood.[29] But she was described as a woman of "clear and vigorous understanding," tender and self-sacrificing.[30] "She was a woman of more than ordinary intellect, & possessed a force of character which was felt throughout the humble circle in which she moved," wrote one of her sons.[31] Of Welsh origin, she was descended from Roger Eastman, who migrated to America in 1636 and settled in Salisbury, Massachusetts. Her father, Major Roger Eastman, lost a leg fighting the French and together with his wife, Jerusha Fitz, Nabby's mother, also Welsh, came to live with their newly acquired son-in-law and died many years later in the Webster home.

During the next ten years Abigail bore Ebenezer five children. First, two girls: Mehitable, later an unmarried schoolteacher, born in 1775, and then Abigail, born in 1778, who later married William Haddock. The first son, Ezekiel, called Zeke by the family, arrived on March 11, 1780. Two years later Daniel was born on January 18, 1782, the same year as Martin Van Buren, John C. Calhoun, and Thomas Hart Benton, three men who were to have a profound effect upon his life. The youngest child, Sarah, born in 1784, later married a cousin, Ebenezer Webster.[32]

Just three months prior to Daniel's birth, Lord Cornwallis surrendered his army to General George Washington at Yorktown, Virginia. To all intents and purposes the American Revolution ended with this surrender, and now a free people, numbering slightly fewer than three million and scattered geographically over more than a thousand miles from north to south, had to form a government that would protect their newly acquired freedom.

Webster, Van Buren, Calhoun, Benton, and many others of their generation helped shape and direct the government they inherited from the revolutionary generation. They all were men of ferocious ambition, and none more so than Black Dan, whose ambition was instilled in him at an early age by his mother.

Not much is known about Abigail Webster except that she wanted her two sons to "excel" in whatever careers they chose. "Her anticipations went beyond the narrow sphere in which their lot seemed to be cast. The distinction attained by both, & especially by the younger may well be traced in part to her early promptings & judicious guidance."[33]

---

29. However, Charles Lanman, Webster's private secretary, claims she was "a woman not only of superior intellect, but of the warmest affections, and remarkably beautiful." Lanman, *Private Life of Webster*, p. 12.

30. Curtis, *Webster*, I, 7.

31. "A Biographical Memoir of the Public Life of Daniel Webster with a Few Anecdotes of his Parentage, Education and Early Life," by Ezekiel Webster, Everett Papers, MHS.

32. Fuess, *Webster*, I, 14. The two boys were named after the mother's brothers.

33. "A Biographical Memoir," Everett Papers, MHS.

Daniel's birth, in the midst of a bleak New Hampshire winter, took place in a frame house, built by his father, near the spot where the original log cabin stood.[34] (When birth in a log cabin became a distinct political advantage during the 1840s, Daniel lamented his misfortune in missing out on his opportunity. But he always boasted that his older brothers and sisters enjoyed the privilege.[35]) The house was a single-story four-room affair with a high gabled roof, a single chimney, a window on either side of the front door, and three other windows at each end. The kitchen was at the rear of the house.

Two years later, in January 1784, the family moved three miles east to Salisbury Lower Village. They moved into a larger house in a much better location in a valley at the bend of the Merrimack River. Still part of Salisbury, it was later incorporated into the township of Franklin. Ebenezer purchased it from the Call family, who Daniel later remembered had suffered frightful cruelties from Indian attacks just a few years earlier. The house had two stories with a garret, and it was here that young Daniel grew up.[36]

From the house, on clear days, the rugged peaks of Mount Kearsarge and Mount Ascutney could be seen to the west and the White Mountains to the northeast. High hills surrounded the Webster farm, some of them crowned with wooded summits, others showing rocky heads of gray granite. A small alluvial plain stretched half a mile on the western side of the Merrimack River on which the Webster house stood. When skillfully cultivated, this plain could be extremely productive. "This is a very picturesque country," observed Daniel many years later. "I really think this region is the true Switzerland of the United States."[37]

Daniel's earliest memory of growing up in this valley—and it was a very vivid impression, he claimed—occurred in 1790, when he was eight. A steady downpour of rain pelted his house for two days, and the river rose and overflowed its banks, sending tons of water cascading over the meadowland. A huge barn, fifty by twenty feet, belonging to a Mr. G. and filled with hay and grain and sheep and chickens, floated majestically downstream under the eyes of the Webster family. "We were all busy in preparing to fly to the mountains," Daniel

34. "Some of my older brothers and sisters were born in the first house erected by my father which was a log cabin," Webster wrote to Edward Everett, who was preparing a biographical sketch. "Before my birth, he had become able to build a small frame house, which several persons now living will remember. . . . This house, in its turn, gave way to a much larger one, which now stands on the spot, and which was built by those who purchased the property of my father. I have recently repurchased this spot." DW to Everett, October 18, 1851, in Webster, ed., *Private Correspondence,* II, 480–481.

35. "It did not happen to me to be born in a log cabin," said Daniel Webster in a speech in Saratoga in 1840, "but my elder brothers and sisters were born in a log cabin, raised among the snow drifts of New Hampshire. . . . Its remains still exist. I make it an annual visit; I carry my children to it to teach them the hardships endured by the generations that have gone before them." *National Intelligencer,* August 27, 1840.

36. DW to Millard Fillmore, July 13, 1852, in *W&S,* XVIII, 536; Curtis, *Webster,* I, 5.

37. DW to Mrs. Louisa Hosmer Cheney, September 29, 1845, quoted in Fuess, *Webster,* I, 19.

wrote, "so soon as our house should manifest a disposition to follow Mr. G's barn."[38] Fortunately the house stood its ground.

Unlike his brother, Ezekiel, who was robust and enjoyed the heavy labor of working a farm, Daniel was a rather sickly child, not much given to physical exertion. He did of course work the fields, plowing them, raking them, and hoeing them, but he never mowed them. "Somehow I could never learn to hang a scythe," he later recalled, and he complained to his father. Hang it to suit yourself, said Ebenezer, whereupon Daniel hung it on a tree and said, "There, that's just right." His father laughed and told him to leave it there. "I had not wit enough" to learn to hang a scythe, Daniel later admitted. "My brother Joe used to say that my father sent me to college in order to make me equal to the rest of the children."[39]

At different times in his early life Daniel's parents despaired of his life. On one occasion Ebenezer turned to his wife with his son in his arms and said, "We must give him up; we never can raise this child." Abigail said nothing. She simply took Daniel into her arms, "and her tears fell fast upon his face as she pressed him to her bosom." There was no further talk of giving him up. At another time, concerned that he would develop rickets, she rode on horseback to the Boar's Head at Hampton Beach in the hope that seabathing would help him. She traveled to the coast alone, carrying Daniel in her arms. "There was a mother for you!" Daniel proudly boasted to a friend years later.[40]

But despite his "sickly nature," the child inherited his father's constitution as well as his frame and physical appearance, and he survived a good twenty-two years longer than his more robust older brother.[41]

Because of his physical limitations as a child, Daniel read a great deal. In later life he could not remember who taught him to read—he naturally supposed that it was his mother[42]—and in fact he read the Bible at such an early age that he never knew a time when he could not read Holy Scripture.[43] His father encouraged his reading habits and frequently read to him. "My father had a sonorous voice," Daniel later claimed, "an untaught yet correct ear, and a keen perception of all that was beautiful or sublime in thought. How often after the labors of the day, before twilight had deepened into obscurity, would he read to me his favorite portions of the Bible, the Book of Job, the Prayer of Habakkuk, and extracts from Isaiah!"[44]

38. "Autobiography," in *PC*, I, 6.

39. DW to Richard Blatchford, May 3, 1846, in Webster, ed., *Private Correspondence*, II, 228; Lanman, *Private Life of Webster*, p. 20.

40. Harvey, *Reminiscences*, pp. 397, 317.

41. "I was by much the most slender and feeble of the family in early life; but have yet outlived them all, and no one of them, I think, attained my present age [fifty-nine]." Diary, January 18, 1839, in Harvey, *Reminiscences*, p. 9.

42. DW to Tappan, February 26, 1851, in Lanman, *Private Life of Webster*, p. 12.

43. "A Biographical Memoir," Everett Papers, MHS.

44. "Conversations with Charles Lanman," in *W&S*, XIII, 572.

Ebenezer tried to give the boy the best education available in this remote area. The neighbors regarded two of his instructors, Thomas Chase and James Tappan, as mediocre at best.[45] The first, Chase, took on Daniel as a student when the lad was three or four years of age.[46] Chase "read tolerably well & wrote with a fair hand; but spelling was not his *forte.*" Tappan was hardly better.[47] "Something that was called a school," remembered Ezekiel years later, "was kept for two or three months in the winter by some itinerant pedagogue,— often a wretched pretender, claiming only to teach a little reading, writing & cyphering,—& wholly incompetent to give any valuable assistance to a clever youth in learning either."[48] When it came to reading, the boy "generally could perform better than the teacher." Tappan later stated that "Daniel was always the brightest boy in the school, and Ezekiel the next: but Daniel was much quicker at his studies than his brother. He would learn more in five minutes than another boy in five hours."[49]

As for writing, Daniel found it "laborious, irksome & repulsive," so much so that his instructors warned him that his fingers were "destined for the plough tail." What education Daniel actually acquired during these early years, recalled Ezekiel, "was derived from the judicious & experienced father, & the strong-minded, affectionate, & ambitious mother."[50]

Later one of his teachers, William Hoyt, an austere man, turned out to be an exceptional teacher. He was "a good reader, and could teach boys, and did teach boys that which so few masters can, or will do, to read well themselves," declared Daniel. Hoyt had been a printer in Newburyport and kept a dry goods shop in Salisbury, where Daniel remembered buying a small cotton pocket handkerchief with the Constitution of the United States printed on both sides. He was about eight at the time. He sat down under an elm tree and "read and re-read" it. "From this I first learned either that there was a constitution, or that there were thirteen states. I remember to have read it, and have known more or less of it ever since."[51]

All his teachers remembered Daniel's phenomenal memory. Tappan, for example, once offered a jackknife to the student who could memorize the greatest number of verses in the Bible over the weekend. Daniel outdistanced every other student in the class. He recited some sixty or seventy verses before Tappan stopped and awarded him the prize. But Daniel pro-

45. Curtis, *Webster*, I, 14.

46. DW to Tappan, in the Gloucester *News,* February 26, 1851.

47. In 1851 Tappan, still living, wrote to Webster, who said that the teacher "boarded at our house." DW to Tappan, February 26, 1851, in Lanman, *Private Life of Webster,* p. 14.

48. "A Biographical Memoir," Everett Papers, MHS. Charles Lanman later imagined Daniel "tramping on his way to school, carrying a little tin pail with his dinner, and in the other his spelling-book." DW to Tappan, February 26, 1851, in Lanman, *Private Life of Webster,* p. 13.

49. Lanman, *Private Life of Webster,* p. 15.

50. "A Biographical Memoir," Everett Papers, MHS.

51. Lyman, *Public and Private Life of Webster,* I, 199; Curtis, *Webster,* I, 7; memorandum dictated by Webster to Richard Blatchford, October 29, 1850, in *W&S,* XVIII, 398.

tested. He had learned several more chapters, he insisted.[52]

Early on the boy developed a real passion for reading, and thanks to the efforts of Thomas W. Thompson, a local lawyer, the Reverend Thomas Worcester, and his father, the neighborhood acquired a small circulating library that enabled Daniel to sample the *Spectator* and portions of Joseph Addison's *Criticism upon Chevy Chase*. He was particularly fond of poetry. "As far back as I can recollect," he declared at a later time, "I had a great passion for poetry, and devoured all I could command." At the age of ten or twelve he memorized whole passages from Alexander Pope's *An Essay on Man* and Dr. Isaac Watts's *Psalms and Hymns*. He especially admired the *Psalms and Hymns*. "No other poetry has since appeared to me so affecting." Virtually to the day he died Daniel could "repeat, almost literally, the devotional lines I was then so fond of." As an adult he littered his speeches with "quotations from the old English poets, but also verses from the old Sternhold and Hopkins hymn-book which he had studied in the Salisbury meeting-house." So few books were available that for Daniel to read each book several times "was nothing." He even memorized the poetry and anecdotes in the almanac.[53]

Toward the end of his life a friend asked him if the many quotations he employed in his speeches from the classics and English literature took a great deal of research. Mostly, he replied, "I learned those things when young, & laid them up & have now only to fetch them out."[54]

When the school was located near his house, Daniel naturally found it easy to attend. But when it moved to a distant district, he had to travel two and a half to three miles in the dead of winter to reach it. When the school moved still farther away, Ebenezer boarded his son with a neighboring family so that he could attend classes regularly. This "extra care" Daniel received "originated in a conviction of the slenderness & frailty of my constitution."[55]

Once around 2:00 A.M. in midwinter, when he had risen from bed to check the exact wording of a poem, he inadvertently let fall from his candle a spark that started a fire. Fortunately the other members of the family awoke immediately to his cries for help, and the fire was soon extinguished. "The house was saved by my father's presence of mind," Daniel later confessed. "While others went for water, he seized every thing movable which was on fire, and wrapped them up in woollen blankets. My maternal grandmother, eighty years of age, was sleeping in the room."[56]

In addition to reading, Daniel loved sports. Reading and sports became his

52. Lanman, *Private Life of Webster*, pp. 15–16; Harvey, *Reminiscences*, p. 18.

53. "Conversations with Charles Lanman," in *W&S*, XIII, 577; "A Biographical Memoir," Everett Papers, MHS; Poore, *Reminiscences*, II, 174.

54. DW to Reverend Thomas A. Merrill, January 10, 1851, in *W&S*, XVIII, 412; Nathaniel Sawyer to Alphonso Taft, August 23, 1851, in *PC*, VII, 269. Charles Lanman says that even in his old age Webster could "recite long narratives out of the old book" he had read. Lanman, *Private Life of Webster*, p. 18.

55. "Autobiography ," in *PC*, I, 6.

56. "Conversations with Charles Lanman, in *W&S*, XIII, 578–579; Curtis, *Webster*, I, 8.

two delights in life, and he never outlived them. Though sickly and frail as a youth, he always managed to find the energy to amuse himself in games of one kind or another with his brothers and sisters whenever they could afford the time from their assigned chores. He liked to pitch quoits, skate on the frozen river during the winter, and wrestle with his older brother. He and Zeke became close friends. For his brother Ezekiel, "Daniel had not only the most devoted affection, but the most exalted respect."

On one occasion Ebenezer assigned the two boys a specific task that they neglected to do. Annoyed, the father turned to them and demanded a reason for their failure.

"What have you been doing, Ezekiel?"

"Nothing, sir," came the reply.

"Well, Daniel, what have *you* been doing?"

"*Helping Zeke, sir,*" the boy happily responded.[57]

Another companion was "a certain battered old British soldier and sailor" who had deserted at Bunker Hill and moved to New Hampshire, where he settled on the Webster farm. The old soldier taught the boy the art of angling, a pastime that Daniel enjoyed immensely to the end of his life.[58]

Daniel later remembered a scene in which he was in the fields with his father when Abiel Foster, a congressman, called and came into the field to speak with Ebenezer. When the visitor had left, the father summoned Daniel and said, "My son, that is a worthy man, he is a member of Congress, he goes to Philadelphia, and gets six dollars a day, while I toil here. It is because he had an education, which I never did. If I had had his early education, I should have been in Philadelphia in his place. . . . Now I must work here."

"My father," the boy responded, "you shall not work. Brother and I will work for you, and wear our hands out, and you shall rest." Then young Daniel broke down and wept.

"My child," Ebenezer declared, "it is of no importance to me. I now live but for my children. I could not give your elder brothers the advantages of knowledge, but I can do something for you. Exert yourself, improve your opportunities, learn, learn, and when I am gone, you will not need to go through the hardships which I have undergone, and which have made me an old man before my time."[59]

The following May 25, 1796, Ebenezer took his young son, then fourteen years of age, to Exeter and deposited him in the Phillips Academy, over which Dr. Benjamin Abbot presided.[60] The boy had never been so far away from home

57. Lanman, *Private Life of Webster,* p. 20.

58. Harvey, *Reminiscences,* p. 10; Curtis, *Webster,* I, 10.

59. DW to Richard Blatchford, May 3, 1846, in Webster, ed., *Private Correspondence,* II, 229.

60. Samuel Lyman claims that Ebenezer acted on Thompson's and Abigail's urging. Thompson's recommendation was based on Daniel's phenomenal memory. When Daniel arrived, Abbot had him read from the Bible, and he gave such a good account of himself that the principal pronounced him fully "qualified to enter this institution." *Public and Private Life of Webster,* I, 201, 205.

before, and the change "overpowered" him. He joined ninety boys who had seen more, done more, and knew more than he. The experience terrified him, but he quickly set about adapting himself to this new environment. Since he had arrived late in the academic year, he was assigned to the lowest class. He studied English grammar, writing, and arithmetic. He fairly mastered the grammar over a six-month period, and then, after a short break at home, he began the study of Latin, reciting his lessons to the twelve-year-old Joseph Stevens Buckminster, who had completed his work at Exeter but was too young to enter college.[61] Daniel's other instructors included Peter Oxenbridge Thacher and Nicholas Emery. "I am proud to call them both masters," he later wrote.[62]

Daniel did not distinguish himself as a scholar, despite his passion for reading. Other students read more and knew more, he later admitted, "but so much as I read I made my own. When a half hour or an hour, at most, had elapsed, I closed my book, and thought over what I read. If there was any thing peculiarly interesting or striking in the passage, I endeavored to recall it, and lay it up in my memory, and commonly could effect my object." This ability to concentrate on and remember what he read proved enormously valuable to him throughout his life. "Thus greater credit was given me for extensive and accurate knowledge than I really possessed," he modestly confessed.[63]

One classmate, James Bingham, claimed that when Daniel arrived at Exeter, he had "an independent air and was rather careless in his dress and appearance." Nor did he "join much in the plays and amusements of the boys of his age, but paid close attention to his studies."[64] The adult Daniel Webster dressed and behaved similarly. Many contemporaries commented on his aloofness and his incorrect and inappropriate "costume," especially when arguing before the Supreme Court.[65]

According to his own lights, young Daniel made tolerable progress in most subjects he took at Exeter—all except one. Difficult as it is to believe, he later claimed that he "could not make a declamation. I could not speak before the School." Many a speech he memorized and repeatedly rehearsed in his room to impress his tutors and the other students. Alas, when the day arrived to deliver the declamation before the entire school and all eyes turned toward him when his name was called, he could not rise from his seat. He sat there paralyzed. Several instructors frowned their displeasure; others smiled. Buckminster "pressed and entreated," but "I never could command sufficient resolution."

61. "A Biographical Memoir," Everett Papers, MHS; Lanman, *Private Life of Webster,* p. 23.

62. "Autobiography," in *PC,* I, 8–9.

63. J. W. McGaw to Professor Sanborn, November 16, 1852, in Webster, ed., *Private Correspondence,* I, 51.

64. Bingham to Sanborn, November 25, 1852, in ibid., I, 55.

65. Hone, *Diary,* II, 523. Not that Webster was "unsocial," but his conversation, said one congressman, was always "marked with cool deliberation." John Wentworth, "Congressional Reminiscences: Adams, Benton, Calhoun, Clay, and Webster," Charles Cleaver, *Early Chicago Reminiscences,* Fergus Historical Series, no. 24 (Chicago, 1882), p. 34.

When the assembly was dismissed, Daniel went back to his room "& wept bitter tears of mortification."[66]

It is possible that he exaggerated what had happened, or he may have deliberately misstated the case in an attempt to show how limitations can be overcome or to emphasize the distance he had traversed as an adult when he achieved national recognition as the country's greatest orator. Whatever the truth, it seems clear that Daniel Webster did not make his mark as a speaker during his brief stay at Exeter.

Once during his residence at the school he and another boy walked ten miles to Rye Beach to see the ocean. They arrived just before sunset, and Daniel looked at the sea in wonder and amazement. "I saw the ocean for the first time that I remember," he said. He stood transfixed. "I remember distinctly the impression made upon me at that time—a sensation such as has never since come to me, much as I have looked at, and love to look at, the sea." The sea became an obsession with him to the end of his life.[67]

Determined to justify his father's faith in him, Daniel made a special effort to improve his grades. In the beginning "he was at the foot of his class," and the other boys laughed at him. But with a diligence that became a hallmark of his work habits as a lawyer he "mastered the principles and philosophy of the English grammar in less than four months." Then, one day, Nicholas Emery, an assistant tutor, turned to the class and said, "Daniel Webster, gather up your books and take down your cap." Terrified that he was about to be expelled, Daniel obeyed. "Now, sir," said Emery, "you will please report yourself to the teacher of the *first class;* and you, young gentlemen, will take an affectionate leave of your class-mate, *for you will never see him again.*"[68]

As a matter of fact Daniel, now promoted to the first class, was about to return home for good, although Emery did not know it. His father came to fetch him in December 1796. Just why Daniel left Exeter after a stay of only nine months is not exactly clear. It may have been for financial reasons or the always precarious state of his health and the fact that the family wanted him closer to home in the event of a sudden illness. Or although it seems unlikely, it may have been that the family did not want him to continue to suffer the discomfort and embarrassment he felt in the company of boys who ridiculed his "rustic manners and unfashionable raiment."[69] It was reported that he knew no more about holding a knife and fork "than a cow does about holding a spade."[70] If he did suffer acute embarrassment because of his dress and manners, then it might

66. March, *Webster,* p. 12. This work was originally published as *Reminiscences of Congress* (New York, 1850) and later retitled *Daniel Webster and His Contemporaries;* "Autobiography," in *PC,* I, 9; Lanman, *Private Life of Webster,* p. 24.

67. Harvey, *Reminiscences,* p. 346.

68. Lanman, *Private Life of Webster,* p. 25.

69. J. W. McGaw to Professor Sanborn, November 16, 1852, in Webster, ed., *Private Correspondence,* I, 50.

70. Fuess, *Webster,* I, 34.

explain why he failed to speak when called upon to give a declamation before a school assembly. In any event young Daniel did form lasting friendships with some of the boys at Exeter, including Leverett Saltonstall and James Bingham. He also knew Lewis Cass, who subsequently served as territorial governor of Michigan, minister to France, secretary of state, secretary of war and who won the Democratic nomination for President in 1848.[71] Later on Daniel came to know other distinguished Exeter alumni, such as Edward Everett, Jared Sparks, and George Bancroft.[72]

In February 1797 his father took him to the Reverend Dr. Samuel Wood, minister of the adjoining town of Boscawen, for private instruction. Wood lived only a half dozen miles from the Webster farm. Daniel boarded with the family, and the entire charge for instruction and board *"was but one dollar per week. We pay much dearer now for much less,"* he later allowed.[73] As they rode along together, Ebenezer indicated to his son that he intended to send him to college, a prospect that "thrilled my whole frame," Daniel recorded in 1829. The father repeated to him that he lived only for his children and that he would do all in his power for his son. "I remember that I was quite over come—& my head grew dizzy. The thing appeared to me so high, & the expense & sacrifice it was to cost my father so great, I could only press his hands, & shed tears. Excellent, excellent Parent! I cannot think of him, even now, without turning child again."[74]

It should be noted that Daniel was a very emotional young man, easily given to tears. A close associate said that "he was beyond all question as much a man of feeling as a man of intellect." Several letters written a little later show the emotional attachments he formed to several of his male and female friends. He remained intensely emotional all of his life, although he successfully hid it except from family and closest intimates.[75]

To prepare Daniel for college, the Reverend Dr. Wood set him to work translating Virgil and Cicero. The young man rather enjoyed Cicero. "With what vehemence, did I denounce Cataline! with what earnestness struggle for Milo!"[76] But sometimes he skipped off to the woods to hunt and fish. On one occasion Wood scolded him for neglecting his studies and as punishment assigned one hundred lines of Virgil for his next recitation. Daniel stayed up all night to fulfill the assignment, and when the recitation hour arrived, he reeled off the hundred lines without difficulty, whereupon Wood congratulated him.

71. Cass also gave Webster considerable trouble during the negotiations of the Webster-Ashburton Treaty. See chapter 33.

72. Although Webster's association with Exeter as a student was limited, he was elected a trustee in 1835 and remained a member of the board until his death in 1852. However, he was recorded as attending only two meetings of the board: one in 1836, another in 1838. Fuess, *Webster*, I, 38.

73. March, *Webster*, p. 13.

74. "Autobiography," in *PC*, I, 9–10.

75. Lanman, *Private Life of Webster*, pp. 86–87. Lanman was Webster's private secretary in the 1850s.

76. "Autobiography," in *PC*, I, 10.

"But I have a few more lines that I can recite," Daniel insisted.

"Well, let us have them." The boy easily recited another hundred.

"Very remarkable," said the astonished reverend, "you are a smart boy."

"But I have another, and five hundred of them, if you please."

The good doctor was flabbergasted. Anxious to get away, Wood exclaimed, "You may have the whole day, Dan, for pigeon shooting."[77]

In the spring he began Greek grammar under the direction of David Palmer, a Dartmouth senior, also residing with Wood, but he failed to make much progress with it. Years later, after Daniel had become a renowned orator, he lamented the fact that he never mastered Greek. "Would that I had pursued Greek, till I could read and understand Demosthenes in his own language!"[78]

But while living in Boscawen, he did discover a circulating library, and he found time to read many of its volumes. He especially remembered reading *Don Quixote* in an inferior translation. Inferior or not, Daniel could not put it down. "It is literally true that I never closed my eyes till I had finished it; nor did I lay it down for 5 minutes; so great was the power of that extraordinary book on my imagination."[79]

Sometime during the summer of 1797 Wood suddenly turned to his pupil and said, "I expected to keep you till next year—but I am tired of you, & I shall put you into College next month." Wood himself was not much of a scholar, probably as good as or not much better than most clergymen in New England at that time. So with a curt dismissal he sent off his charge to college "miserably prepared, both in Latin & Greek."

Thus, at the age of fifteen, as he was about to enter Dartmouth College, Daniel's education consisted of limited studies in a few schools and a number of books he had read in the circulating libraries at Salisbury and Boscawen, the first six books of the *Aeneid*, Cicero's four orations against Cataline, a fair amount of Latin grammar, a little Greek grammar, the four Gospels of the Greek New Testament, English grammar, some arithmetic, some of Addison's prose and Pope's poetry, the devotional poetry of Dr. Watts, a poor translation of *Don Quixote*, and practically no geography or history.[80]

But most important of all, he had acquired a tremendous love of reading. He became a voracious reader for the rest of his life, and that love and that voraciousness made a great deal of difference in the person Daniel Webster became. To a very large extent, therefore, his early education was self-imposed.

77. Lanman, *Private Life of Webster,* p. 26

78. "Autobiography," in *PC,* I, 10; DW to Reverend Merrill, January 10, 1851, in Webster, ed., *Private Correspondence,* II, 412.

79. "Autobiography," in *PC,* I, 10.

80. Curtis, *Webster,* I, 24–25.

2

Dartmouth

DANIEL WEBSTER was a very lucky young man. Not only did he have a father who loved him very much and whom he apparently idolized, but his father, by his own account, wanted to do everything possible to advance his son's education, including mortgaging the farm if necessary. Moreover, Ebenezer understood the value of an education, especially for Daniel, who it was generally agreed could never make a living as a farmer. He therefore sent his son to college, something few of Daniel's distinguished contemporaries enjoyed.[1]

But before leaving home for Dartmouth, Daniel got his first taste of teaching. In 1797, shortly after he left Exeter, he taught school briefly in Salisbury. There may have been twenty pupils in his class[2] who studied English grammar and Latin with him. There is no record of his performance as a teacher, and six months later he took off for Dartmouth.

Dartmouth College, in Hanover on the extreme western border of New Hampshire, was the only institution of higher learning in the state at this time. The Reverend Dr. Samuel Wood, pastor of the Congregational Church at Boscawen, was a graduate, and Ebenezer Webster had served on a state committee in 1789 that had recommended a forty-two-thousand-acre grant of land to Dartmouth. The school was also easily accessible to Daniel since a road connected Hanover with Salisbury and Boscawen.

The college consisted of a collection of buildings around a large quadrangle situated in a little village near the banks of the Connecticut River and surrounded by pine forests and the foothills of the New Hampshire mountains. Dartmouth Hall, a three-story Georgian building topped by an imposing dome, included a dormitory, classroom space, and the library. The obligatory chapel

---

1. Andrew Jackson repeatedly expressed regret over his lack of education, and one of his earliest biographers said that "his ignorance was a wall round about him—high, impenetrable. He was imprisoned in his ignorance, and sometimes raged round his little, dim enclosure like a tiger in his den." Henry Clay said that his lack of education "remained one of his weak points through life." James Parton, *Life of Andrew Jackson* (New York, 1861), III, 699, and *Famous Americans of Recent Times* (Boston, 1867), pp. 51–52.

2. I am inferring this number from the letter he wrote three years later, when he took up teaching a second time. "My school increases fast enough," he wrote. "Instead of twenty, I have fifty." DW to James Hervey Bingham, February 5, 1800, in *PC*, I, 29.

stood directly to the south, as did the president's house. Students "bathed" and swam in the river and played football on the common adjacent to the hall.[3]

Dartmouth had been founded as an eleemosynary school for Indians in 1769 by the Reverend Eleazar Wheelock. It was named for William Legge, the earl of Dartmouth, a benefactor of the school. Over the years its primary mission had all but disappeared. Initial support for the institution came from English benefactors and occasionally from provincial and later local and state sources. But by the time Daniel arrived in Hanover the school depended mainly on student tuition, which ranged from twenty to thirty dollars a year. John Wheelock, son of the founder, now presided over the college and ruled it with a firm hand that brooked no violation of a strict code of discipline. Humorless, somber in manner and appearance, devoid of real intellectual interest or strength, given to insipid sermons in a strangulated voice, Wheelock governed a college of about 150 students and a faculty of less than half a dozen, not including young tutors who were barely out of Dartmouth themselves.[4]

To enter Dartmouth, Daniel was required to pass examinations proving that he could write the English language and translate English into Latin, that he was versed in Virgil, Cicero's select orations, the Greek Testament, and that he had an understanding of the fundamental rules of arithmetic. He was also required to post a bond of three hundred dollars for payment of college bills and other miscellaneous items.

For Daniel's examination a neighbor made him a new suit "of blue clothing—coat, vest and pantaloons." Unfortunately it rained on the day of the examination, and the blue dye began to run. Daniel presented himself before his examiners looking not only like *"Black* Dan" but *"blue* Dan" as well. Demonstrating great presence of mind, he said to them, "Thus you see me, as I am, if not entitled to your approbation, at least to your sympathy." He told them what books he had read and answered their questions "without embarrassment and to his best ability." He was then directed to report to the president's office at a particular time when he would be informed of the results.

Probably he did reasonably well in English, but he barely passed Greek, Latin, and arithmetic. What made the difference in gaining his admission, other than the sympathy his examiners no doubt felt, was the very strong recommendation written by Dr. Wood. When he finally appeared before President Wheelock, he found the four examiners also present. Happily he was informed that he had been admitted.[5]

So in August 1797 the fifteen-year-old Daniel entered the institution. He was a few years younger than most of the other undergraduates, but apparently

3. Kate Ball Powers et al., eds., *The Autobiography of John Ball* (Glendale, Calif., 1925), p. 18.

4. See New Hampshire General Court, *Documents Relative to Dartmouth College* (Concord, N.H., 1816); David M'Cure, *Memoirs of Reverend Eleazar Wheelock* (Newburyport, Mass., 1811); and Frederick Chase, *A History of Dartmouth College* (Concord, N.H., 1891), 2 vols.

5. Lyman, *Private and Public Life of Webster,* I, 219–221; Herbert Darling Foster, "Webster and Choate in College: Dartmouth under the Curriculum of 1796–1819," *Dartmouth Alumni Magazine,* XIX (April 1927), p. 510.

that caused no problem. When he appeared at the school, looking swarthy and peering around at his new surroundings under dark "overhanging brows," some might have thought that Dartmouth still operated as an eleemosynary school for Indians. In fact the first time Webster walked down the aisle at chapel a few of the students actually believed he was an Indian. Black Dan soon became his nickname.

The curriculum at Dartmouth from 1796 to 1819 required freshmen to take Latin and Greek classics, arithmetic, English grammar, rhetoric, and the elements of criticism; sophomores to study Latin and Greek classics, logic, arithmetic, geography, geometry, trigonometry, algebra, conic sections, surveying, mensuration of heights and distances, and belles lettres; juniors to take Latin and Greek classics, geometry, natural and moral philosophy, and astronomy; and seniors "Metaphysics, Theology & Natural and Politic Law." The curriculum also stated that "the study of Hebrew and other oriental languages as also of the French language is recommended to the students." In addition, members of all classes in rotation "shall declaim before the officers in the chapel on every Wednesday at two o'clock in the afternoon." Seniors were to hold a forensic disputation in the chapel on the first Wednesday of every month immediately following the declamations. All students were required to attend these exercises.[6]

At this time Dartmouth was reputedly deficient in modern languages as well as "mathematics and the exact sciences." Some reports even claimed that in every department the teaching was "exceedingly meagre." Professors "went mostly by the book. The question was always what does the book say." Any expression of doubt was treated "as an unreasonable presumption." For purpose of recitation students were seated alphabetically, and since instructors tended to call on those students seated close to them, those at the end of the alphabet were frequently overlooked.[7]

Despite the alleged mediocre teaching, Daniel adjusted himself to Dartmouth a lot better than he had at Phillips Exeter. For his freshman and sophomore years he continued his studies of Latin and Greek and struggled through Pike's *Arithmetic and Algebra*—"a miserable book," in the opinion of George Ticknor, a professor at Harvard—and spent a lot of time catching up to the level of his peers in this subject. Of course he indulged his passion for English literature, but later he thought that his college reading was "too miscellaneous." What aided his efforts was his great ability to concentrate on the matter before him, committing the most interesting or striking parts of it to memory. His powers of mental concentration and total recall helped him at Dartmouth to become a most informative conversationalist and speaker.[8]

6. Foster, "Webster and Choate," p. 511. Foster quotes from the curriculum as stated in the "Laws to be observed by the members of Dartmouth College," enacted by the trustees on February 9, 1796.

7. Powers et al., eds., *Autobiography*, pp. 17, 24.

8. J. W. McGaw to Professor Sanborn, November 16, 1852, in Webster, ed., *Private Correspondence*, I, 44–45. Curtis, *Webster*, I, 27 and note 1.

For his first three years at Hanover Daniel roomed in the college dormitory, but in his senior year he moved to a private residence. He paid a total college bill of $88.34 for three years' room rent, four years' tuition and incidentals, interest, and a commencement tax. His room rent averaged $4 a year, and board at the college commons came to $1 a week. Like most other undergraduates, he delayed payment of his college costs, and not until the eve of graduation did he settle what he owed—an unfortunate habit that he practiced for the rest of his life. When he settled his debt with the college, he was forced to borrow $26 from a man named Lang, a storekeeper and moneylender, and this too became another unfortunate habit. Of the $88.34 college bill, he paid Dartmouth a total of $59.89 for tuition, room, and board for his four-year education. "No wonder," as one historian has remarked, "there were those who loved her!"[9]

Daniel completed his first two years at Dartmouth acceptably but without great distinction. He delivered an occasional address, as was required, but none of them immediately marked him as a budding orator. He also wrote a little poetry, which showed all the distinguishing characteristics of a sixteen-year-old undergraduate. But young Daniel kept working at his writing and speaking. He was also beginning to get some sense of direction to his life. He joined the United Fraternity, one of the two important literary societies on campus. Not only did this society provide a superior library where Daniel could gratify his love of reading, but it became a place where he started the process of honing his skills as a debater and public speaker. He learned to organize his thoughts in private meditation, either in his room or on walks, and then he committed them to paper just before he was scheduled to speak. As a consequence he always spoke with great clarity, precision, and ease, demonstrating a strong grasp of his subject, which invariably impressed his listeners.

When he spoke, he hardly moved. Everything he did was prolonged and deliberate. Only slowly would he work himself up to an outburst of emotional feeling, and then his arms would begin to swing through the air as his oratory became more vivid and vigorous. By the time he completed his college career he had acquired a reputation as the best speaker on campus. In these new surroundings he had obviously completely overcome his Exeter shyness and reluctance to speak. Never again did he have that problem. He had shown that through persistence and hard work a natural talent could be enhanced and finally sharpened into a remarkable skill.

In the same way he worked on his writing. He produced essays and several more poems, which got better as he matured. In his poetry what emerged as noteworthy was a genuine competence in descriptive verse. There is a tradition that he wrote and recited one of his poems in class about a battle between an English and a French warship that amazed both the professor and the other members of the class. Fifty-four years later one classmate remembered the incident with such clarity that he said he could still hear the French ship's cannon

9. Foster, "Webster and Choate," p. 516. Foster took his information from accounts contained in the treasurer's office.

roar and see her as she disappeared beneath the waves.[10]

Webster further developed his writing skill by submitting pieces to the town's small weekly newspaper, the *Dartmouth Gazette,* recently founded by Moses Davis in 1799. Daniel unhesitatingly offered his services. "Having seen your Proposals for printing a Newspaper," he wrote to Davis, ". . . I have presumed to come forward, and cast in my mite, to increase, if not to enrich your weekly repast. Should you think the productions of my puerile pen worthy of a place in your new 'vehicle of Knowledge,' you may depend on a number weekly. Since I am unable to treat any subject with that knowledge and accuracy it deserves, you will permit me as a compensation for want of abilities, to range the whole field of nature in order to collect those productions, which fortune may throw in my way." He signed his letter "Icarus"[11] and enclosed an essay on "Hope."[12] Davis must have been impressed or desperate, for he accepted the offer and published both the letter and essay. A flood of Websterian productions followed over the next several months, and true to his promise, Daniel ranged over a wide assortment of topics from hope and fear to deception and the horror of war. He frequently included some poems and selections from literary works and contemporary literature.[13]

Daniel later described his efforts for the *Gazette* as "foolish." He probably did not remember them exactly but simply presumed that they must have been sophomoric, if not worse. Nonetheless these "foolish" pieces added to his writing experience and no doubt gave him a heightened sense of accomplishment, even if they appeared without any mention of his name. Daniel's literary interest and ability won him the appointment to superintend the newspaper when Davis absented himself from town, for which he received enough money to pay for his board for a full year.[14]

What is particularly remarkable was the fact that Daniel could keep up his studies and write a great number of articles for the newspaper. This was not mindless toil but labor that required intense intellectual effort. What it demonstrated, even at this early age, was his extraordinary capacity for intense, concentrated work.

In the spring of 1799 during his sophomore year Daniel became con-

10. Curtis, *Webster,* I, 32.

11. In Greek mythology Icarus escaped from Crete using artificial wings. But he flew so high that the sun melted the wax that fastened the wings to him, and he fell into the sea and was drowned.

12. DW to Moses Davis, August 27, 1799, in *PC,* I, 26.

13. These pieces and other contributions under the "Icarus" pseudonym appeared in the *Gazette* on August 27, October 21, 28, November 25, December 2, 9, 1799, February 17, 24, April 21, 28, December 6, 13, 1800, February 21, 1801, July 10, August 7, 1802.

14. Webster regularly deprecated his early efforts at both writing and speaking. Of these published addresses, he expressed the hope that they would be forgotten. "They were in very bad taste," he admitted in 1829. "I had not then learned, that all true power, in writing, is in the ideas, not in the style; and error, into which the *Ars Rhetorica,* as it is usually taught, may easily lead stronger heads than mine." "Autobiography" in *PC,* I, 10. With the money he earned from the *Gazette* he paid his board. Foster, "Webster and Choate," p. 516.

science-stricken about his older brother's situation. The brothers had a strong "mutual attachment to each other," and Daniel's reliance on "his elder brother's judgment was unbounded; his reliance upon his wisdom and counsel was without limit." Unlike Daniel, Ezekiel was a healthy and robust lad who labored all day in the fields and helped his father run the farm. He was presumed to be less competent for academic study, and his father had decided to keep him home. Actually he was the equal of his more celebrated brother in intellectual power. On one occasion their father supposedly remarked, "Ezekiel could not tell half he knew; but Daniel could tell more than he knew." The older brother was very timid, the younger "bold and fearless as a lion."[15]

As Daniel recognized, Ezekiel's prospects for the future were not very promising. So, when he went home during his May vacation, Daniel raised the subject with his brother. They talked the night away. Ezekiel actually resented the role assigned him, that of following in his father's footsteps as a farmer and providing for his mother and sisters after his father died. He had "aspirations beyond his condition," Daniel insisted, yet without any schooling he could never hope to attain them.[16]

As the brothers talked, they finally settled on a plan, which Daniel presented to their father in the morning. They proposed that Zeke be sent to school and eventually college, late as it was—he was twenty at the time—to begin academic work. Daniel spoke with great conviction and earnestness. He told his father how unhappy he was over Zeke's prospects. "For myself, I saw my way to knowledge, respectability, & self protection," he later wrote, "but as to him, all looked the other way." Daniel offered to teach and take care of his own expenses, even delay finishing his college education, if Ezekiel could be sent to school.

Ebenezer Webster stared at his son and perhaps even marveled at the young man's ability to plead his cause. Actually he needed little convincing since as he said repeatedly, he lived only for his children. To put both his boys through college, he replied, was his greatest desire, even if it took everything he owned. What better way for a man to spend his money. Yes, he was willing to run the risk, but since this was a serious matter involving their mother and sisters, they must first give their consent. If they agreed, then he would trust "to Providence & get along as well as he could."[17]

Ebenezer explained the matter to his wife without disguising their economic situation. The farm had been mortgaged to help pay for Daniel's education, and if Ezekiel also went to college, it would take everything they had. Her decision, then, involved her financial resources for the rest of her life and the lives of their unmarried daughters.

"Well," Abigail responded, "I will trust the boys."[18] She was as ambitious

15. Harvey, *Reminiscences*, p. 14.

16. Ibid., pp. 10–11.

17. "Autobiography" in *PC*, I, 11.

18. Curtis, *Webster*, I, 34.

for her sons as Ebenezer, probably more so. The sisters also agreed.

That settled the matter. By the time Daniel returned to Dartmouth his brother had started school at the local academy, where he stayed for two terms. Like his younger brother, Zeke then went to reside with Dr. Wood to prepare for college, and he finally entered Dartmouth in March 1801, six months before Daniel was graduated.[19]

Ebenezer Webster could not meet the expenses for the education of both his sons and as agreed, Daniel helped out. He taught school in Salisbury during the winter of 1800.[20] He had also earned a year's board by managing the *Dartmouth Gazette*. Meanwhile, in 1799, the family exchanged houses with Daniel's sister Abigail and her husband, William Haddock, and moved across the road to a place called the Elms Farm because of the many excellent elms in the vicinity.

Daniel's deep devotion to his brother can be readily seen by the letters he wrote to Zeke after his return to Dartmouth. He attempted to boost his brother's morale and encourage his sense of self-worth. In the future, he instructed Zeke, when you write, say to me, "I am superior to you in natural endowments; I will know more in one year, than you do now, and more in six than you ever will." But be assured, he cautioned, "your great puissance shall never insure you a victory without a contest."[21]

During his four years at Dartmouth Webster made a large number of friends, few of whom remained close to him after graduation. These friends included his former classmate at Exeter James Hervey Bingham,[22] whom he described as "the friend of my heart, the partner of my joys, griefs, and affections, the only participator of my most secret thoughts,"[23] George Herbert,[24] to whom he wrote one of his earliest poems while at Dartmouth, and Habijah

19. Ibid., 35–36.

20. This was the second time Daniel taught school. "I have fifty [pupils], and shall have more; five English grammarians, I mean students in English, and two Latin Scholars." DW to James Hervey Bingham, February 5, 1800, in *PC*, I, 29.

21. Daniel to Ezekiel, April 25, 1800, in *W&S*, XVII, 83. Once Ezekiel began school, Daniel asked him for full details about the subjects he was taking, where he boarded, the number of students at the academy, and everything pertaining to his course of study.

22. Later Bingham practiced law, became cashier of a bank, moved to Cleveland in 1845, and was appointed a clerk in the Interior Department in Washington in 1847. He died in 1859, age seventy-eight. George T. Chapman, *Sketches of the Alumni of Dartmouth College* (Cambridge, Mass., 1867), p. 103.

23. DW to Bingham, February 11, 1800, in *W&S*, XVII, 80. Several of his letters are addressed to Bingham as "Dearly Beloved" and end by "expressing my eternal attachment, to my dearest J.H.B." See for example DW to Bingham, May 18, 1802, in *PC*, I, 38, 42. There is no question that Daniel Webster was a man of great sentiment and affection to those close to him. As the two men matured, they grew apart, but in 1849 Bingham wrote Webster, possibly to ask for an appointment, and the great man responded: "My Dear old Classmate, Room-mate, and Friend,—It gives me very true pleasure to hear from you. . . . Years have not abated my affectionate regard. . . . You are still James Hervey Bingham . . . and I am the same Daniel Webster." Unfortunately Webster said he did not expect to have any influence with the incoming administration. Bingham to DW, February 4, 1849, in Webster, ed., *Private Correspondence*, I, 56–57.

24. Herbert was a year ahead of Webster and later practiced law, served in the Massachusetts legislature, and died at the age of forty-one in 1820. Chapman, *Sketches of Alumni of Dartmouth*, p. 101.

"Henry" Welt Fuller, whom he called "Barrister Fuller."[25] Other friends included Joseph Warren Brackett, who graduated in 1800, and Samuel Ayer Bradley, who was graduated in 1799.[26]

Daniel was genuinely liked by his peers. He was "humorous, always companionable and pleasant."[27] And it meant a great deal to him to have their approbation. He also had a number of female friends in Hanover, whom he mentions in his letters. There was Fanny, whom he considered a "sister," and Mary, the daughter of Professor Bezaleel Woodward, and Sally and Sophia and a "Miss O." Daniel Webster was always a very romantic and passionate man. To what extent he seriously pursued these young ladies, especially Mary—"la bonne," as he called her—cannot be determined from the record. There are numerous hints in his letters and poems that his desire for love could lead to something serious.

In his junior year he mentioned to Bingham that another classmate was fighting off the impulse to marry. "What does he hint at here?" Daniel asked. "How should he know that I was just about to (try to) be married? My amour, you very well know, had not commenced the last time I wrote to him." This "amour" may have been Sally, for not much later, after his intentions about marriage got him nowhere, Daniel wrote again to Bingham and told him that while he was walking down the street with a friend, "we perceived a chaise, containing a gentleman and lady . . . ; judge my surprise, when I saw, as the carriage passed me, that its fair inhabitant was no other than SALLY! The chaise drove so fast I only had time to bow and blush, and receive a smile and a look as the carriage passed on." He dashed to the tavern, hoping to find her there. But no. She was nowhere to be seen. "So Sally you see is gone; yes, gone! gone!"[28]

Daniel discussed his romantic inclinations quite frankly with his closest friend. But he was intensely ambitious, and marriage could upset whatever plans he might be contemplating for the future. Besides, Sally apparently had her own plans, and they did not include Daniel Webster. Problems with the opposite sex gave him many troublesome moments for the rest of his life. In Washington he later developed a reputation of being something of a philanderer.

Apart from anything else was his physical appearance. The black-haired, heavy-browed Daniel was sickly, thin, and pale. His many illnesses made him seem undersized, even puny and immature, hardly a catch for an intelligent and attractive young girl. His failure to make headway with any of the girls who caught his eye sometimes roused him to peevishness. On one social occasion "a Miss . . . made a very saucy remark" and Daniel favored her with a glance that if looks could reveal his displeasure, then "I fancy she repented what she had said."

25. Fuller practiced law and served as a probate judge in Kennebec County and as a member of the Massachusetts legislature. He died at the age of fifty-seven in 1841. Ibid., p. 103.

26. Brackett moved to New York, where he practiced law and was elected an alderman, while Bradley, a bachelor, practiced law in Fryeburg, representing it in the Massachusetts legislature from 1813 to 1818. Ibid., p. 99, 95.

27. N. Shattuck to Sanborn, December 27, 1855, in Webster, ed., *Private Correspondence*, I, 67.

28. DW to Bingham, February 5, 11, 1800, June 14, 1801, in W&S, XVII, 79–80, 90.

So these attachments at Dartmouth during his junior and senior years were probably one-sided infatuations. Most of the young women he met in Hanover apparently saw nothing exceptional in him and made no effort to encourage his attentions. Daniel revealed a little of his annoyance when he proclaimed that "if there were to be a new edition of human nature, I think it would be found expedient to give the girls stronger ribs and a thicker pericardium. I say a plague to the girls, if they cant keep their little beaters at home."[29]

Daniel's interest in girls did help improve his appearance, at least in his dress. For the first two years of his residence in Hanover he usually wore home-spun, which was all he could afford. But during his junior and senior years he suddenly developed a greater consciousness about his appearance. He became more "fastidious in his attire," according to one report, and started dressing better than most Dartmouth undergraduates. But good clothes and fashionable dress can cost a great deal of money. In order to buy the fancy trousers, shirts, and stockings, Daniel had to borrow funds, a practice he later developed into an art as he struggled to satisfy his burgeoning desire for the finer things in life.[30]

If Daniel had difficulty attracting the serious attention of pretty girls, he had no trouble meeting the approval of his classmates. For one thing he had become a skillful conversationalist. He could enthrall a small group with stories, anecdotes, and jokes, much of it acquired through his extensive—he called it "miscellaneous"—reading.[31] He was so popular with his classmates that they admitted him to their literary fraternity shortly after his arrival at Dartmouth, and he was the only freshman, and the only sophomore, elected to office in the society. By his senior year he had become president of the United Fraternity.

His peers also enjoyed his growing talent as an orator, and his reputation soon extended beyond the confines of the campus into Hanover itself. To celebrate the twenty-fourth anniversary of the Declaration of Independence, the townspeople invited him to deliver an oration. He was then eighteen years old and a junior at the college. It was a mark of the high regard the locals had for Daniel's talents that they extended this invitation to him. He had begun to win the acclaim and attention that throughout his life meant so much to him and fired his best efforts.

When Daniel stepped to the podium on July 4, 1800, in Hanover, New Hampshire, and delivered himself of his prepared speech, he moved to a new and exciting stage in his developing career. He had come quite a distance since 1796, when he entered Phillips Exeter and found himself unable to speak in public and "perform the exercise of declamation, like the other boys." Now he was the honored orator of Hanover about to engage the emotions and intellect of his audience in a celebration marking the day of national freedom. He confidently stepped to the speaker's position and began:

29. DW to Bingham, December 28, 1800, February 5, 1800, January 17, 1801, September 10, December 8, 1801, DW to Fuller, January 26, 1801, in *W&S*, XVII, 85, 79, 87, 89, 90, 99.

30. Fuess, *Webster*, I, 58; Bartlett, *Webster*, pp. 24–25.

31. "Autobiography" in *PC*, I, 10.

COUNTRYMEN, BRETHREN, AND FATHERS, ... Nothing less than the birth of a nation, nothing less than the emancipation of three millions of people, from the degrading chains of foreign dominion, is the event we commemorate.

Twenty four years have this day elapsed, since United Columbia first raised the standard of Liberty, and echoed the shouts of Independence!

Those of you, who were then reaping the iron harvest of the martial field, whose bosoms then palpitated for the honor of America, will, at this time, experience a renewal of all that fervent patriotism, of all those indescribable emotions, which then agitated your breasts. As for us ... we now most cordially unite with you to greet the return of this joyous anniversary, to hail the day that gave us Freedom, and hail the rising glories of our country!

It was a splendid beginning. It was oratory in the grand manner, and the crowd loved it. They shouted and applauded and enjoyed every extravagant phrase, every patriotic allusion. Daniel went on to say that he would not attempt a lecture on civil government because of his age and lack of experience. Instead he gave an overview of colonial history that culminated in the Declaration of Independence. "It was then, ye venerable patriots, it was then you stretched the indignant arm, and unitedly swore to be free!" Great men came forth to do battle for freedom, many of whom were no more. We must "pause, for a moment," said Daniel, "to drop the tear of affection over the graves of our departed warriors." He then singled out his hero, George Washington, for special mention.

With hearts penetrated by unutterable grief, we are at length constrained to ask, where is our Washington? where the hero, who led us to victory—where the man, who gave us freedom? Where is he, who headed our feeble army, when destruction threatened us, who came upon our enemies like the storms of winter; and scattered them like leaves before the Borean blast? Where, O my country! is thy political saviour? where, O humanity! thy favorite son? ... The lamentations of the American people will answer, "alas, he is now no more—the Mighty is fallen!"

Daniel then described the convulsions in Europe that had produced Napoleon, the knavery of French demands for money as the price for peace, the attacks on American shipping, the steady descent of Europe into the abyss of war. "But Columbia stoops not to tyrants; her sons will never cringe to France. ... Let the sons of Europe be vassals; let her hosts of nations be a vast congregation of slaves; but let us, who are this day free, whose hearts are yet unappalled, and whose right arms are yet nerved for war, assemble before the hallowed temple of Columbia Freedom, and swear, to the God of our Fathers, to preserve it secure, or die at its portals!"[32]

The crowd cheered wildly as Daniel concluded. His oration was full of bluster and bombast, florid effusions and rhetorical excesses, but it was just what the occasion called for, and the audience demonstrated its appreciation. Those present remembered especially "his large, black, piercing eye, peering out under dark, overhanging brows; his broad, intellectual forehead; the solemn tones of his voice" and the "earnestness" with which he threw himself into his subject,

32. W&S, XV, 475–484.

"evincing the sincerity of his belief that the cause he advocated was that of truth and justice."

Later he regarded these early attempts at oratory as an embarrassment. Indeed they cannot begin to compare with his more mature efforts, even those just a few years away. But this initial Fourth of July address contained several noble sentiments, nobly expressed. That such wondrous thoughts and ringing phrases should come from the mouth of an eighteen-year-old stirred many in the crowd to speculate about what heights this dark-faced young man might rise to. A number of them requested printed copies of the oration, and his friend Moses Davis published it.

But a critic of considerable reputation at the time, one Joseph Dennie, reviewed it, and although he praised some parts as "vigorous and eloquent," he thought other parts "were mere *emptinesses.*"

That stung. But the truth of it hit Daniel forcibly. He vowed "from that time forth there would be no *emptiness*" in his written and spoken efforts."[33]

Daniel vowed to check not only content but style as well. He took time and care in preparing his speeches, and if possible, he took even greater care in readying them for publication. Few of his contemporaries reworked what they had written for oral presentation. Henry Clay gave fabulous speeches but never bothered to review them before publication. As a result his addresses elicit little attention today because they seem antiquarian, relatively tame, and sometimes ponderous while Daniel Webster's speeches still command a reading public.

After July 4, 1800, there could no longer be any doubt in anyone's mind who heard this address that Daniel Webster was a born orator. On campus he received unbounded acclaim. He had become someone to know. And Daniel reveled in it. He delighted in the recognition and adulation his speaking talents elicited.

Daniel's Fourth of July oration also revealed his own personal political commitment. He was a Federalist, like his father and many other New Hampshire farmers, who supported the party of George Washington, Alexander Hamilton, and John Adams. He believed that the Federalist party attracted into its ranks more than "two thirds of the talent, the character, and the property of the nation." The attack on France in the oration was only one indication of his political allegiance. The Federalist party distrusted and feared French radicalism. The French Revolution had unleashed a "reign of terror," and Federalists shivered at the thought and prospect of Jacobin doctrine polluting American soil. Trumpeted Daniel in his oration: "[N]either a supercilious, five-headed Directory, nor the gasconading pilgrim of Egypt [Napoleon] will ever dictate terms to sovereign America."[34]

The speech also commended President John Adams on "the virtuous man-

33. "Conversations with Professor C. C. Felton," in *W&S*, XIII, 582; Brown Emerson to Professor Sanborn, November 19, George Farrar to Sanborn, November 25, 1852, in Webster, ed., *Private Correspondence*, I, 52–53.

34. DW to John Porter, June 4, 1802, in *W&S*, XVII, 115, XV, 482, 483.

ner" in which he had conducted his administration. "The firm, the wise, the inflexible Adams," asserted Daniel, was a "worthy successor" to the beloved Washington. But the young man made no mention—it would have been inappropriate—of the fact that Adams was running for reelection in 1800 against the candidate of the Republican party, Thomas Jefferson. Whereas Federalists agreed with Alexander Hamilton about the need for a strong central government with sound credit and currency managed by a national bank in order to safeguard the nation's newly won liberty, Republicans opposed a powerful, controlling, and centralized governmental authority as a danger to individual freedom, and they supported the states in all their rights and prerogatives. Republicans also questioned the legitimacy of a national bank, arguing that the Constitution did not empower the government to create such an institution. On the whole they favored strict construction of the Constitution, while the Federalists, again following Hamilton's philosophy, believed that the Constitution should be interpreted as loosely as needed to provide for the nation's safety and welfare.

Of particular importance in Daniel's developing commitment to the Federalist party was his role in founding the Federal Club at Dartmouth. He and eight other classmates signed the constitution for this society on July 12, 1799. Their purpose was the "improvement in political information" as well as the acquisition of "useful knowledge," and its members were expected to be "Philanthropists, Gentlemen and Scholars."[35]

When the presidential election of 1800 ended in the defeat of John Adams and the Federalist party, Daniel reacted as expected. "Two things I can't say I like," he informed his friend George Herbert, "Jefferson's election to the Presidency, and Hamilton's letter. Of the two I prefer the former." He was offended by the publication of Hamilton's scathing letter of denunciation concerning the "Public Conduct and Character of John Adams." The letter unintendedly aided Jefferson's election, and Daniel pronounced it an "absurdity."[36]

Daniel gave several other orations during his final year at Dartmouth, of which his funeral oration for a classmate, Ephraim Simonds, was the most remarkable for its unaffected directness, compelling emotion, and strong religious feeling. Daniel had been raised in the Presbyterian faith and at an early age taught to say his prayers, read his Bible, and attend Sunday services. It was part of his cultural and intellectual baggage, but it was nothing that profoundly affected him. He understood the role and importance of religion in New England and accepted and believed it without question. He frequently spoke about the value of religion and incorporated many religious themes into his speeches, but he never felt the commitment toward the Presbyterian Church that Andrew Jackson did, nor did he experience Henry Clay's religious conversion. "When

35. Constitution of the Federal Club, in *PC*, I, 25–26.

36. DW to Herbert, January 7, 1801, ibid., I, 31. "Jefferson's Presidency which now seems certain," Daniel wrote to James Bingham, "sets not very well on our stomachs." DW to Bingham, December 28, 1800, in *W&S*, XVII, 84.

Hamilton strongly disapproved some of Adams's actions as President and wrote this letter to promote the election of Adams's running mate, Charles Cotesworth Pinckney.

the pride of science, the pageantry of philosophy, the wily arts of cunning and subterfuge, and the parade of hypocrisy all vanish away," he declared at Simonds's funeral, "religion then, like a protecting seraph, shields her votary from harm, drives from his presence the pale, terrifying spectres of death and despair, and serenely lays him to repose in the bosom of Providence."[37]

During his senior year Daniel also wrote a number of essays in which his argument for the acquisition of the Floridas forecasts his later strong nationalist sentiments. He worried about the safety of American commerce in the West if the Floridas, New Orleans, and the most southerly stretch of the Mississippi River remained a Spanish possession. The United States, he wrote, would be reduced to seizing Florida by force or surrendering American rights of commerce. He therefore recommended a convention of some sort with the Spanish king by which the Floridas would be ceded to the United States.[38]

He worried as well about the possibility of civil strife in the nation. The party rivalry, local disturbances in the several states, especially in the South and in Pennsylvania, and the lack of leaders to replace the dead Washington and the "worn down" Adams frightened Daniel. "In my melancholy moments," he noted to a friend, "I presage the most dire calamities. I already see, in my imagination, the time when the banner of civil war shall be unfurled; when Discord's hydra form shall set up her hideous yell, and from her hundred mouths shall howl destruction through our empire; and when American blood shall be made to flow in rivers, by American swords!" With piercing imaginative insight Daniel foresaw what would come to pass sixty years later.[39]

By the time the nineteen-year-old Daniel graduated from Dartmouth in August 1801, he had done a great deal of speaking and writing, all of which gave him tremendous experience and training on which he could build for the future. He was the best orator in the college, and although his style was excessively florid and conspicuously self-serving, he had learned how to convey emotion and sentiment so as to stir an audience and at times even move them deeply. In the ensuing years he learned the value of simplicity and directness, and he would delete dozens of words and sentences in order to sharpen and define better what he wanted to say. He also developed a writing style that emphasized the orderly and logical presentation of his arguments, a talent that immensely aided him as a lawyer later on. Most important, he learned how to edit his writing before publication, especially his speeches, so that a reader could almost hear him pronounce the words on the page. And he always strove for "the greatest effort of power in the tersest and fewest words." He demanded of himself precision and clarity of thought. "My style," he later revealed to his private secretary, "was not formed without great care and earnest study of the best authors. I have labored hard upon it, for I early felt the importance of expression to thought. I have rewritten sentence after sentence, and pondered long upon each alteration.

37. *W&S*, XV, 487–493. See also his oration on opinion, which he gave to commemorate the anniversary of the United Fraternity. Ibid., XV, 494–504.

38. Ibid., XV, 485–486.

39. DW to James Hervey Bingham, February 5, 1800, in *PC*, I, 28.

For, depend upon it, it is with our thoughts as with our persons—their intrinsic value is mostly undervalued, unless outwardly expressed in an attractive garb."[40]

Daniel did remarkably well at Dartmouth, and in a class of thirty he was one of twelve who won election to Phi Beta Kappa.[41] "My College life was not an idle one," he later commented.[42] If anything, he read too indiscriminately, "for nothing is more dangerous to the mind than indiscriminate indulgence in books."[43] By dint of hard work, a virtue he frequently extolled in his speeches, he could be proud of what he had accomplished, although mathematics and Greek, as he said, gave him trouble; still, he graduated toward the top of his class and therefore expected to take a prominent role in the commencement exercises.

Unfortunately, it did not work out that way. There were usually four principal orations given, two in English and one each in Latin and Greek. Three of these were assigned, and one, the Valedictory, was decided by the graduating class and was considered the most important. Naturally, as a young man of immense pride and ambition, Daniel wanted the Valedictory, and because of his accomplishments and popularity, he had every reason to expect to get it. But previous classes had quarreled over their selection of a valedictorian, so the faculty decided to choose all four orators. Unfortunately the faculty decided that Daniel's high rank in class disqualified him for the Valedictory oration, "which, for this occasion, they ranked as the fifth of the academic honors."[44] So they offered him a choice of delivering a poem in English or an oration in English on the fine arts.

Daniel rejected the offer. Reading a poem did not rank among the important appointments, and giving an oration on the fine arts consigned him to a secondary role in the program. So he asked to be excused from any participation in the event and, as a consequence, received his diploma without special recognition.[45]

Several of his friends also excused themselves to protest faculty interference with their right to choose their own valedictorian. They wanted Daniel as their speaker, and no one else would do. Angry and bitter, he decided to oblige them. He delivered an oration before them to commemorate the anniversary of the United Fraternity just a few days before their commencement.

40. "Conversations with Lanman," in *W&S*, XIII, 564–565.

41. Chapman, *Sketches of Alumni of Dartmouth*, p. 106. Unfortunately, as far as can be determined at this time, Dartmouth does not hold undergraduate academic records before about 1830 or student registers before 1862. There was no fire that might account for their disappearance. In 1985 the college instituted a records management program, but no grade registers for the early period turned up. Barbara L. Krieger, an archivist at the college, does not believe the records exist on campus, although she holds out hope that they might turn up in someone's attic or barn. Krieger to author, March 25, 1996.

42. "Autobiography," in *PC*, I, 10.

43. "Conversations with Lanman," in *W&S*, XIII, 579.

44. Nor could he give the Latin oration despite his proficiency since there were superior scholars more entitled than he to give it.

45. Curtis, *Webster*, I, 41–42.

He chose "Opinion" as his subject. In it he surveyed the importance of opinion on politics, philosophy, religion, and education, taking sideswipes at Hume, the Edict of Nantes, the conquests of Pizarro and Cortez, the Stuarts and Bourbons, Tom Paine and Mary Wolstonecraft, the "unsexed authoress of the 'rights of Woman.' " Revealing his conservative bent, Daniel warned against new ideas that challenge the wisdom of ages and bring about "a wicked laxity of principle." That man is a child of God, he said, and has rights "essential and intransferable" is an incontestable truth. Yet "these newfangled rights of man" theories presume to have "just as much meaning as the substantial forms of Aristotle." They are taught "amidst the orgies of a civil feast, and propagated at the mouth of the cannon, and point of the bayonet" and have shaken Europe to its foundation. A man, he continued, who keeps himself free of these aberrations is truly great. If he has a single trait of excellence in his character, it is his "dependence on his own exertions, and rejection of the phantasms of Opinion." He believes in himself and what he is about. "Self-collected," he stands as a bulwark in the "iron front of war."

As we leave Dartmouth and "step into a new scene in the drama," Daniel pontificated, "let us endeavor to collect principles" that do not lead into the mazes of opinion but direct us in a path of truth. "Let neither tergiversation nor seduction attach us to the systems of those opinionated visionaries, who mistake the fantastic dreams of their own minds for the oracles of philosophy."

Both a Federalist and a conservative, with strong feelings against the radical ideas propagated by the French Revolution, Daniel extolled the virtues of self-esteem and self-reliance. "Persevere in industry and improvements," he told his audience, and you will succeed. Enduring principles about man obtained from ancient philosophy and the Christian religion must not be overthrown or compromised by the modern suppositions of science or political theory. The greatness of an individual is totally internal and rests on natural endowments and hard work. "The laurels of fame" are won by a "life of labor and contemplation."[46]

Such was the oration Daniel might have given at the commencement had he been chosen. That he received his diploma on August 26, 1801, without recognition or distinction rankled. In fact it was later reported that in an outburst of passion and fury he tore up his diploma and flung it "to the winds." "My industry may make me a great man," he allegedly exclaimed, "but this miserable parchment can not!"[47]

An unlikely story. Even so, months later the sting of rejection still tormented him. "You will see the propriety of apologizing as much as possible for the sterility of Commencement," he wrote his friend Bingham. "Tell people it is because they discouraged genius."[48]

46. Oration on Opinion, 1801, *W&S*, XVII, 494–504.

47. Lanman, *Private Life of Webster*, p. 29.

48. DW to Bingham, September 22, 1801, in *W&S*, XVII, 94. Webster told Rufus Choate that "no disappointment of his whole life ever affected him more keenly." Edward Parker, *Reminiscences of Rufus Choate* (Buffalo, 1972), p. 270, quoted in Fuess, *Webster*, I, 51, note 1.

3

"School Keeping" and the Law

DARTMOUTH had a tremendous impact on Webster. Besides helping him grow intellectually, it made him a more social creature, albeit a bit of a snob. He could be cold and aloof with strangers or those not his social or intellectual equal, a characteristic that remained constant throughout his life, but among his peers he became a delightful companion, witty, charming, generous, and fun to have as a friend and confidant.

Webster loved Dartmouth all his life, despite the blow to his pride at graduation. He returned to his alma mater as often as possible. As he said in his famous peroration in the *Dartmouth College* case, "there are those who love it." And he certainly was one.

Salisbury was quite a letdown after Hanover. Gone were the good friends, the stimulating conversation, the agreeable young ladies, the opportunities for public discourse, and the outlet that the *Dartmouth Gazette* provided for his essays and poetry. Now he had to make a living and decide on a career. But which one? Books were his passion, but he could never support himself on his writing. He might return to teaching, but what future did that hold for an ambitious young man? There was the ministry and medicine, but those callings did not remotely interest Webster. And there was the law. But the law did not particularly attract him either, or so he said, not the way books and the world of ideas did.

At the age of nineteen he needed to make a decision, but his mind was filled with uncertainty. His father, concerned about his future, urged him to take up the law. Other friends and neighbors may have made the same suggestion. The alternative, as he certainly knew, was the plow, and that possibility neither he nor his father could abide. Probably what determined his final decision was the presence in Salisbury of a very able lawyer with a reasonably good law library and an outstanding local reputation who soon became a trustee of Dartmouth. And because the office was next door to the Elms Farm, he could live at home and save money while he studied law. All things considered, the legal profession seemed the wisest and best career he could make, so with a wistful sigh, since he was backing into a profession rather than embracing it eagerly, Daniel Webster chose law as his profession and entered the law office of Thomas W. Thompson. "I fell into a law office," he revealed to a friend, "pretty much by casualty," and, considering how long it would take to win admission to the bar, my "prospects are not very flattering." Most of his classmates at Dartmouth were also inclined to the law, he commented, "but I believe we have all mistaken our talents." None, he thought, had the "brilliancy . . . penetration and judgment" to make a great career in the profession.[1]

Not a very auspicious way to begin a career, but Webster honestly expressed how he felt. To make it a little more agreeable, he tried unsuccessfully to talk his bosom friend James Bingham into moving nearby to Concord to study law so that they could regularly get together. Concord had many attractions, according to Webster, including a fine town library and the opportunity for gainful employment three months out of the year. "And the ladies of Concord are very learned," he wryly added.[2]

The study of law in the early nineteenth century usually involved entering the office of a resident attorney, reading a prescribed list of lawbooks, and whenever possible, receiving some instruction and help from the attorney himself. In return the student performed various clerical chores, such as copying documents, writing writs, and attending to minor affairs of the office. Frequently it included menial duties, like sweeping the floor and cleaning the office.

Webster began his studies with Thompson on a diet of Vattel, Burlamaqui, Montesquieu, and Hume. After that he commenced an inquiry into the principles of municipal and common law. By the end of the year he had read not only Vattel and the other works but Robertson and three volumes of Blackstone. Studying alongside him was the affable and slightly older Daniel Abbott, who was devoted to one of Webster's pet peeves, David Hume. Nevertheless the two men remained lifelong friends. Abbott later recalled that Webster read voraciously books on law and history, but "more the latter than the former." Whenever the reading became so boring and unbearable that he needed to get away, Webster went fishing or hunting or riding. An "excellent shot," he hunted partridges, "quails," and squirrels.[3] He confessed that he disliked a good deal of what he read and really learned little and forgot much. To vary his boring lawbooks, he turned to Shakespeare, Milton, or some other literary favorite. But nothing gave him greater pleasure than curling up with his "new-found friend" tobacco and delving into one of the available classics.

> Come, then, tobacco, new-found friend,
> Come, and thy suppliant attend
>   In each dull, lonely hour;
> And though misfortunes lie around,
> Thicker than hailstones on the ground,
>   I'll rest upon thy power.

1. DW to Nathaniel Coffin, October 3, 1801, in *W&S*, XVII, 95.

2. DW to Bingham, September 10, 1801, ibid., XVII, 91.

3. George Abbott to Sanborn, February 5, 1853, in Webster, ed., *Private Correspondence*, I, 64.

Unfortunately his newfound friend repeatedly made him sick so he had to "dismiss" the fellow—temporarily. Later he frequently found pleasure in smoking a cigar. "Smoking inspires wisdom," he pontificated.[4]

His social life in Salisbury was virtually nil. "I see no ladies," he joked with Bingham; "they are scarce articles with us. The *Damas* are all at Charlestown. Do give my love to some of them, for you know my heart always overflows with affection for the sex."[5] So whenever possible during this period of legal training he liked to revisit Dartmouth, the scene of his earliest triumphs. He could always find friends and amusements in Hanover to brighten his life.

On one occasion Webster found himself alone in the law office—Thompson had gone to Boston and Abbott to Salem—and he was asked to bring an action of trespass for breaking a violin. It seems the plaintiff was playing his violin at a husking as girls skipped over husks when a "surly creature" came up to him, snatched his violin out of his hands, and smashed it against the wall. "For the sake of having plump witnesses," the bemused Webster wrote, "the plaintiff will summon all the girls to attend the trial at Concord." At another time a man demanded a "remedy" against his neighbor "whose lips were found damage feasant on his, the plaintiff's, wife's cheek." Webster was not certain about the law concerning kissing and said he needed guidance and would write to Barrister Fuller![6]

Webster remained in Thompson's office until mid-January, when he was forced to leave on account of his father's financial need. He knew as early as late October that he might have to abandon his law studies, and this, he said, mortified him beyond words. The expenses involved in Ezekiel's continuing education and the fact that Daniel no longer provided an income necessitated his departure. He simply had to find employment. Either that or his brother would have to leave Dartmouth. The thought of interrupting his law career depressed Webster because he wanted to complete his studies as soon as possible and begin earning a respectable living. "I never was half so much dispirited as now. Though I make myself easy as I can, yet I am really very unpleasantly circumstanced." But he had no other choice. Since he had experience teaching, the thought immediately occurred to him to return to it. Fortunately, just about this time, through his college friend Samuel A. Bradley, he received from Judah Dana,[7] a Dartmouth graduate of the class of 1795, an invitation on behalf of the trustees of Fryeburg Academy in Maine "to keep school" in Fryeburg at a salary of $350 per annum. When the letter reached him after a twenty-day delay in the mail, Webster immediately accepted it, although he stipulated in his acceptance that he could take the post for only two quarters. "My prospects and engage-

4. DW to Bingham, September 10, 22, October 26, 1801, in *W&S*, I, XVII, 91, 92–93, 98; DW to Ezekiel Webster, November 4, 1802, in *PC*, I, 43.

5. DW to Bingham, December 8, 1801, in *W&S*, XVII, 101.

6. DW to Bingham, October 26, 1801, ibid., XVII, 95–98. No word on the outcome of these actions.

7. On Dana, see Dr. James A. Spalding, "The School and College Life of Judah Dana of the Class of 1795," in *Dartmouth Alumni Magazine*, IX (February 1917), pp. 155–166.

ments will not allow a longer absolute engagement," he responded. In arranging his departure, he decided to accompany Robert Bradley, a prosperous Fryeburg farmer, on his return home, but because of the delay in receiving Dana's letter and the poor roads, he did not think he could arrive in Fryeburg by the first of January but hoped to be there by the fifth or sixth of the month. So he packed his bags, took his departure from family, Thompson, and friends, mounted his horse, and rode the relatively short distance across the border to Fryeburg.[8]

Fryeburg was a typical New England village, new but growing. Already it was crowded with merchants, doctors, and lawyers. Once the hunting grounds of the Pequawket Indians but now clear of their presence, Fryeburg sat beneath the Pequawket Mountains through which the Saco River twists. A broad, elm-lined avenue marked its center with imposing houses behind white picket fences standing on either side, all built by the prosperous farmers and lumbermen of the town. Here, in a small square one-story building, stood Fryeburg Academy, where Webster began his "school keeping." He found the town most agreeable with a "pretty little society" and a goodly number of men of "information and conversable manners." He had the good fortune to board with James Osgood, register of deeds of Oxford County, paying $1.75 a week for board. Osgood's son later remembered that "he was always dignified in his deportment. He was usually serious, but often facetious." From the moment of his arrival Webster was treated with great kindness and made to feel welcome. "Nothing here is unpleasant," he told Bingham, and Osgood offered to share recording fees with him if he would copy deeds into the register. "I greedily seized on so tempting an offer," admitted Webster, since it meant twenty-five cents for each deed he copied. On a long winter evening he figured he could copy two deeds, and if he devoted four nights a week to the task—"the *ache* is not yet out of his fingers," he later recalled—he could make $2. And $2 paid his board. That together with his $350 salary provided a comfortable living of about $500 or $600.[9]

Jacob McGaw, another recent Dartmouth graduate, also resided in the Osgood home, and Judah Dana lived across the street with his wife, the grand-daughter of Dartmouth's founder. Webster spent a great deal of time with the Danas—"I have exalted ideas of his lady," Webster playfully noted—and Mrs. Dana's sister, Abigail, was expected momentarily. The presence of this company guaranteed a pleasant society, full of spirited conversation and congenial companionship.[10]

On Wednesday and Saturday afternoons he invariably went fishing alone,

8. DW to Bingham, October 26, December 8, 1801, in *W&S*, XVII, 97, 98; DW to Dana, December 26, 1801, *Microfilm Edition*, F2/86.

9. DW to Bingham, February 25, 1802, in *PC*, I, 36; DW to Bingham, May 18, 1802, Samuel Osgood to Sanborn, December 5, 1852, in Webster, ed., *Private Correspondence*, I, 110, 58; DW to Thomas Merrill, June 7, 1802, in *W&S*, XVII, 116; "Autobiography," in *PC*, I, 12; March, *Webster*, p. 17. March claims Webster saved his $350 salary. Ibid., p. 16.

10. DW to Fuller, May 3, 1802, in *W&S*, XVII, 106; DW to Bingham, February 25, 1802, in *PC*, I, 36.

"with rod in hand, and a copy of Shakespeare in his pocket."[11] To add to his pleasure, he found another circulating library, where he borrowed Blackstone's *Commentaries*, "[the John] Adams defence of the American Constitutions, Mosheims Ecclesiastical History, Goldsmith's history of England . . .[and] Mr Ames' celebrated speech, on the British Treaty, & committed it to memory." To amuse himself and friends, he continued writing poetry and essays.[12]

There is little documentation concerning Webster's career as a schoolmaster in Fryeburg, although the secretary of the academy's Board of Trustees later stated that Webster was "a very good scholar for one of his years." He was twenty. When he arrived at the school and entered the classroom, he undoubtedly tried to give the students the impression of authority and maturity. Slender, weighing less than 120 pounds, and pale with prominent cheekbones, Black Dan looked very intense and grave. There was nothing particularly prepossessing about him except his large, full black eyes peering intently from under the dark canopy of his overhanging brow. His students probably never forgot those searching, steady dark beacons. No one did.[13]

Later his private secretary asked about his appearance when he began teaching at Fryeburg. "Long, slender, pale, and all eyes," Webster responded; "indeed, I went by the name of *all eyes* the country round."[14]

One of the duties of "all eyes" as preceptor was to present the "semi-annual exhibition" performance to show off the talents of the pupils and the coaching ability of their teacher. Apparently the exhibition went off handsomely, and the trustees of the school expressed their pleasure by voting Webster a five-dollar bonus.[15]

On the day of the exhibition a letter arrived from Hanover informing him that his brother, Ezekiel, was ill in Hanover. Webster was also told that a young man in Salisbury, engaged to his oldest sister, was on the verge of death and wished urgently to see him to reveal something important to him alone. Under the circumstances he could hardly wait for the spring break to return to New Hampshire. Pride of accomplishment added to his excitement. He was anxious to place "the first earnings of my life, in my brother's hands, for his College expenses." So, on the first day of the spring break in May, Webster took his quarter salary, mounted his horse, and rode straight over the hills to Hanover. Happily he found his brother fully recovered. Then with enormous satisfaction he turned over the money he had earned.

While in Hanover, he visited old Dartmouth friends, who seemed genuinely happy to see him. Webster also looked up Fanny and kissed her (nobody else, he said), Mary Woodward, who shook his hand, and Sophia, who may have been

11. Lanman, *Private Life of Webster*, p. 32.

12. March, *Webster*, p. 17; "Autobiography," in *PC*, I, 12–13.

13. McGaw to Sanborn, November 16, 1852, in Webster, ed., *Private Correspondence*, I, 50; Harvey, *Reminiscences*, p. 26; Curtis, *Webster*, I, 52, 53.

14. Lanman, *Private Life of Webster*, p. 31.

15. Harvey, *Reminiscences*, p. 27.

the mysterious "Miss O." But he did not visit another mysterious lady who signed her letters "C. D." This may have been a serious romance, at least as far as the lady was concerned, a romance that he apparently terminated. Some indication of their relationship can be found in one of her letters to him, written the previous February. It went as follows:

My Dear friend: Hanover Feb 25th 1802
      Suffer me once more to address and ask you if you have entirely forgotten one whose anxiety to hear from you makes her completely unhappy. not *[sic]* one syllable have I heard from you since your letter of Nov 20th accepting *[sic]* by accident, that you was at Fryeburg had an earthquake shook the house to its foundations am confident I should have had more command of my feelings than I had when in a large circle of company was asked if I knew that you had taken the Academy at Fr.g. I affected composure however and answered in the negative. . . .
      When your Brother left here I was preparing for my journey to Connecticut it is now six weeks since I have had every thing in readiness to set off. . . .
      Do not forget one who thinks of you with the same tender friendship a friendship which causes her to go so far from you with the greatest reluctance but in so doing follows your better judgment yours with
the truest affection
CD

Just how serious this relationship had been, or who she was, cannot be determined, although it should be noted that the letter was preserved. Apparently the young lady had designs on Webster, and at one point in the letter she mentions a rejected rival suitor with the initials AB, possibly to make him jealous, possibly to indicate that she was now available. "I three weeks since had an interview with AB," she wrote. "He makes the same professions as usual. In a decisive manner told him our acquaintance must cease . . . it is needless to relate all that he said but let his conduct be what it will in future I feel myself perfectly free as if I had never seen him."

Webster had embarrassed and perhaps humiliated her when he left for Fryeburg without even telling her. Obviously he wanted no more of her. So her attempt here to excite jealousy in him, if that indeed was her purpose, failed. In any event, at his urging, she left for Connecticut "with the greatest reluctance."[16]

After two or three days at Hanover Webster then shot over to Salisbury to find out what his sister's fiancé wished to say to him. Unfortunately by the time he arrived the young man had died. Webster never did discover what it was that seemed to prey on the young man's mind. "If he had done me any injury," he told Bingham, "for which he wished forgiveness, God knows I heartily forgive him. Peace to him!"[17]

Having accomplished all his missions, Webster returned immediately to his

16. "CD" to Webster, February 25, 1802, *Microfilm Edition*, F2/114. There are no other letters to or from C. D. in the Webster papers. I am grateful to Jeffrey M. Flannery, manuscript reference librarian, and Ronald H. Gephardt, an editor of the Letters of the Delegates of the Continental Congress project at the Library of Congress, for their assistance in reading and interpreting this letter.

17. "Autobiography," DW to Bingham, February 25, May 18, 1802, in *PC*, I, 12, 36, 38–39.

"school keeping" and deed copying, suffering through bad roads and worse taverns on his route from Salisbury to Fryeburg. On his return he was surprised and absolutely delighted to find that the trustees were so pleased with his performance in the classroom that they asked him to stay on at the academy. In return they would increase his salary to five or six hundred dollars, provide a house to live in, and a bit of land to cultivate, and arrange for a clerkship in the Court of Common Pleas. It was a tempting offer, one Webster seemed unable to refuse. "What shall I do?" he asked Bingham. Say "Yes, Gentlemen," and settle down to spend the rest of my life in "a kind of comfortable privacy?" Or should I return to a profession "where my living must be squeezed from penury" and where "my moral principle" would be "continually at hazard?" He had talents—many of them. That much he knew, and he felt responsible for the use of those talents and said he would not "pervert" or hide them. His father gently tried to persuade him to pursue the law. But Ebenezer did not dictate or plead. In fact the "delicacy with which this wish is expressed," Webster reported, "gives it more effect than it would have in the form of a command." His friends also urged him to return to his studies in Salisbury so that he might more effectively develop his talents. To cap it all off, Thompson offered him free tuition.[18]

Having no great attachments in Fryeburg, as he did in Salisbury, and taking the course of least resistance, Webster opted to return to the study of law. On balance he knew that the legal profession offered many more possibilities for a career of distinction and recognition than schoolkeeping. And Webster hungered for prominence and appreciation.

Ezekiel came to Fryeburg in September, and the brothers took a short trip through lower Maine before returning to Salisbury. Ezekiel continued on to Dartmouth while Daniel reentered Thompson's law office.

It was back to the boring lawbooks, and although Thompson was a fine lawyer and an admirable man, he had no sense about how to assist Daniel's education. He simply did things the "old way," which meant starting Daniel off with the most difficult works available. Presumably the challenge would either confirm Webster's commitment to the law or drive him from it. Thompson handed him *Coke on Littleton* and let him struggle through it as best he could.

Webster found it impossible. But he hit upon a solution to his problem when he happened to take up Espinasse's *Law of Nisi Prius* and found he could understand it. He thrust Coke to one side and worked his way through the easiest, plainest, and most intelligible writers he could find. No young man of twenty can understand Coke, he later remarked, and it is folly to set him upon such an abstract and technical treatise. "Why disgust & discourage a boy, by telling him that he must break into his profession, thro such a wall as this?" Sometimes he despaired.[19] Coke and similar books of this ilk, he lectured, written in a hard, mean, and didactic style and "interspersed on every page with

18. DW to Bingham, May 10, 1802, ibid., I, 40.
19. "Autobiography" in ibid., I, 13.

the mangled pieces of murdered Latin, and as perfectly barren of all elegance as a girl's cheek is of beard; you see I can't keep entirely off the girl's cheek"—all these account for the mortality in the profession. Who wants a career in such a profession? "The morality of the profession is, too, a matter of doubt." Any lawyer who preserves his integrity unspotted "deserves a place in the calendar of saints."

In these moments of genuine depression, especially in the beginning when wrestling with Coke, he doubted he could ever master the law. And he almost changed him mind and went back to schoolkeeping. Fortunately Espinasse rescued him, and he resolved to stick it out. He would become a lawyer despite everything. This would be the profession to which he would devote himself. "O blindness! stupidity! infatuation! nonsense! folly!" he cried.[20]

For diversion from reading these dreadful tomes he turned to the Latin classics—Cicero, Sallust, Caesar, and Horace—and to memorizing large chunks of Cicero's orations. He also translated some of Horace's poetry, which was later published, and tried his hand at Juvenal but found his style troublesome. He fished and rode and hunted, all without a companion. He loved the solitude, always did and always would. When alone, he would sometimes sing, or rather chant, from the old Sternhold and Hopkins hymnbook in his deep voice "without a particle of melody." He found that solitude stimulated thought, refreshed his mind, provided those flights of fancy that frequently induced bright new ideas or allowed him to imagine himself a nationally acclaimed orator, writer, and statesman. No doubt about it. Daniel Webster was an incorrigible romantic.[21]

Otherwise his life in Salisbury was the same as it had been before his sojourn in Fryeburg. "We are all here just in the old way," he remarked to his brother, "—always behind and lacking—boys digging potatoes with frozen fingers, and girls washing without wood. I shall not stir from the Office again till winter that I know of—nor then unless I go for you."[22] He sounded very disheartened.

But further misery awaited him. Early in December 1802 he contracted a bad case of the measles "once more." His head throbbed, his eyes ached, and his heart beat faster. His lips were parched, and his fingers cold as ice. After a two-week period of torment he began a slow recovery. "Lovers, I have heard it said, are apt to write with trembling hand," he told Bingham, once he felt well enough to lift pen to paper. "If that circumstance alone be sufficient to constitute one, I am as valiant a lover as ever made a vow." Not only did his hand tremble as he wrote, but "my brain dances with twice as much giddiness as ever." Of course he wanted sympathy from his many friends, especially the girls. "Do

20. DW to Thomas Merrill, January 4, 1803, in *W&S*, XVII, 129–130. In another letter Webster told a friend that if he studied law, he must say good-bye to meeting any author who pretends to "elegance of style or sweetness of observation. The language of the law is dry, hard, and stubborn as an old maid." DW to Cook, January 14, 1803, in *W&S*, XVII, 131.

21. "Autobiography," in *PC*, I, 13–14; Poore, *Reminiscences*, p. 174; March, *Webster*, p. 20.

22. DW to Ezekiel Webster, November 4, 1802, in *PC*, I, 43.

mention this grievance to the ladies whom we love and ask of them a remedy."[23]

During his convalescence Webster had many solitary moments in which to contemplate his future. He thought about girls, naturally, and even "thought as how 'twould be well enough to tie one's self up fast to some one of the Virgins, but, & but, & but—and so I concluded it would *not* be well enough." In "this little Mary matter," he confessed to his classmate Thomas Merrill (and she was not Mary Woodward), "I feel *serious* (don't laugh) but *moderate*. The *object* I think worth an effort, but then I have no notion of dying in event of failure. I am not yet quite deep enough in the suds to resolve, either to succeed or else in despair to depart in hemp or fueling steam. Hanging or drawing has still more terrors to me than a *refusal*." For that reason—namely, to visit with, if not pursue, suitable females—he decided to go to the next Dartmouth commencement.

If I should go to Commencement with a design *of doing any thing* I foresee that I shall be likely to get into scrapes. In pursuit of Miss Ma-y I shall I know at that initial time . . . jog against *other Misses*. For instance, I may be found with *Mis-conduct*, then up will come *Mis-Fortune*, then the *Mis*-takes will hang round me; the world, uncharitable, will say I'm running after *Mis*-chief, & in the meantime Miss Ma-y will be distant from me [torn] the pale. . . . You are the only man or woman to whom I have opened my heart in this business, & my felicity is that you are incapable of betraying a friend.[24]

He also disliked, maybe even loathed his situation in Salisbury. "You know what conditions I live here," he wrote to Merrill, "—no perquisites & no tuition. To live in some Commercial Town is at present my ardent wish." But how to escape? He could turn to his friends for help, but that idea was distasteful. He could return to his former employment and "keep school," possibly in Boston. But everyone told him that keeping school would consume all his time each day and leave nothing for other pleasures. "So Adieu to school keeping! Well, what next? Why, next, I will—will—will—I don't know what I will, finally—& there is a very wise conclusion for you!"[25]

It even crossed Webster's mind that he should migrate south and see where destiny led. Or Vermont, where he might worm his way into "some Man's family." And all this because of his poverty. He hated his poverty. He said he could give a lecture on poverty and how to endure it. "Some men are born with a silver spoon in their mouths," he sighed, "and others with a wooden ladle!" Still, he would "utter no pathetic exclamations against poverty, because that is not the best way to be rid of it." But he certainly would embrace with a passion any opportunity that came along to free him from his bondage.[26]

23. DW to Jacob McGaw, December 18, 1802, in *PC*, I, 44; DW to Bingham, December 21, 1802, in *W&S*, XVII, 127.

24. DW to Samuel Ayer Bradley, June 30, 1803, in *PC*, I, 45; DW to Thomas Abbot Merrill, August 3, 1803, *Microfilm Edition*, F2/232. See DW to Fuller, December 21, 1802, in *W&S*, XVII, 126, where Webster mentions "Mary W." and then refers to "the other Mary."

25. DW to Bradley, June 30, 1803, in *PC*, I, 45.

26. DW to Bradley, June 30, September 24, 1803, in *PC*, I, 45, 46, 47; DW to Bingham, October 6, 1803, in Webster, ed., *Private Correspondence*, I, 145.

His intense poverty as a boy and young adult permanently scarred Daniel Webster, and for the remainder of his life he was constantly grasping after money and pursuing the interest and support of those who had it. But instead of learning the necessity of frugality and the importance of saving some of what he earned, he regularly indulged his ever-expanding appetite for all the luxuries and comforts that had been denied him in his youth.

In the meantime he returned to his books and the dull life of Salisbury. His thoughts about escaping to Vermont had some basis in reality since his father had an important suit pending before the state's supreme court and Ebenezer's lawyer was a Dartmouth graduate and trustee who might agree to allow Daniel to read in his office. Failing that, he might try his luck in Massachusetts, where some "acquaintance" in Boston might give him a helpful boost to his career.[27]

By the winter of 1803–1804 Webster had clearly decided to leave Salisbury and pursue his fortune elsewhere. Boston became more and more attractive to him as "the Capital of New England" and could provide many advantages. Despite his declared aversion to the law—and he did hate reading Coke, Blackstone, and Hale—he knew in his heart that the law carried the key to future monetary success. In this country at least. England, he asserted, produced a Locke, a Newton, a Pope, and a Sir Joshua Reynolds, which this country would not produce, at least not in the immediate future. "But Mansfields and Kenyons, I believe, we shall rear in the next age; and the reason of the difference is that eminence will be sought with more ardor in the lucrative professions, than in the abstract sciences and the fine arts."[28]

Law was clearly the lucrative profession. Much as he loved to write essays, compose orations, read the classics of English and Latin literature, write witty letters,[29] many of which are delightfully self-deprecating, Webster was practical enough to accept an important fact of American life. He had been poor all his life. He and his brother regularly discussed their limited finances in their letters to each other and how much distress they suffered because of their lack of funds. Above all else Daniel Webster wanted to "live comfortably," and he was hell-bent on achieving that goal.[30]

So he turned back to "that prince of the laws, Sir Edward Coke," gritted his teeth, and wrestled mightily with the pronouncements and principles of that mind-numbing "prince." If any "difficulty arises between him and me, as no doubt there will be," Webster joked, "my master T. [Thompson] is ready to appear in character of empire." He would serve the law and serve it faithfully and as well as his abilities allowed. After all, he declared, virtually anyone can become a lawyer. "Accuracy and diligence are much more necessary to a lawyer,

27. DW to James Hervey Bingham, October 6, 1803, in *PC*, I, 47–48.

28. DW to Bingham, May 18, 1803, in *W&S*, XVII, 137.

29. Throughout his life Webster frequently resorted to wit in his letters to friends and in his speeches. He also joked about his obvious talents. "Good-bye. You will never have another such an interesting letter as this. Two prodigies come not in one age." DW to Bingham, June 18, 1804, ibid., XVII, 176.

30. DW to Ezekiel Webster, June 10, 1804, in *PC*, I, 55.

than great comprehension of mind, or brilliancy of talent." To be a great lawyer, one "must first consent to be only a great drudge." So he would become a drudge. No matter. He meant to be a great lawyer.[31]

To relieve the tedium, Webster also took an increasingly active role in politics, no doubt with the encouragement and urging of his mentor, Thomas W. Thompson, who had served as postmaster of Salisbury from 1798 until Republicans removed him in 1802. A Federalist to the bone, like his father and brother, Webster abhorred the politics and principles of the Republican-Democratic party, dominated by Thomas Jefferson, James Madison, and a host of other southerners. That party had even "infected" New Hampshire and several other New England states. The rising power of these "democrats," as he called them, worried and frightened Webster. His brother was even more alarmed. "Democracy has triumphed in New Hampshire," Zeke lamented. "In my opinion there is not a nook or corner in the United States that will not be revolutionized. The contagion of democracy will pervade every place and corrupt every generous and manly sentiment. It cannot be successfully resisted."[32]

The brothers and a good many other Federalists in New England agreed that one factor involved in the "contagion" was the clause of the Constitution that stipulated that three fifths of the slaves would be counted with whites in determining representation in the lower house of Congress. This clause provided southern states with a disproportionate amount of political power over the rest of the country, Webster argued, and if New England was ever to regain a position of equality with southern states, the clause had to be repealed.

To effect this alteration of the Constitution, the Massachusetts legislature took up a proposition to initiate action. William Ely sponsored the proposal, and Daniel Webster, at that time a Boston law student, enlisted in the good fight by offering Ely his editorial support.[33] And when Thompson and other New Hampshire Federalists met in Concord to organize a more energetic and resourceful Federalist party to fight the democratic surge in their state, they formed a central committee to help provide useful propaganda for newspapers. At Thompson's behest, the central committee asked Webster to lend his pen to the cause. The young man unhesitatingly agreed and one of his productions, entitled "An Appeal to the Old Whigs of New Hampshire," appeared anonymously in February 1805. It was his first political essay.

In the spring 1805 election in New Hampshire a bruising contest developed between the Federalist John Taylor Gilman and the Republican John Langdon,

31. Ibid., DW to Merrill, November 11, 1803, in W&S, XVII, 148–149.

32. Ezekiel Webster to DW, June 17, 1804, in ibid., XVII, 174–175.

33. On the three-fifths clause Webster wrote a short piece that was published in the Boston *Repertory* on October 2, 1804, in which he ridiculed the justice and fairness of the clause. If Virginia's property could provide added representation in Congress, why not New Hampshire's? "The slave, like the ox," he wrote, "is so much property—a mere marketable article." The Republicans ask for our support, to unite with the majority party, and to provide votes for the very measures about which we complain. "If Virginia smite one cheek, you must not only offer the other, but to save her trouble, you must smite it yourself."

and since Webster supported Gilman, he responded instantly to the urging of Gilman's friends to write his "Appeal." In a single day and night he "did the deed," although it was later mistakenly credited to William Plumer. "I have had the pleasure of seeing [it] kicked about under many tables," Webster laughingly informed Bingham. "But you are one of the few who know the author of the 'Appeal to the Old Whigs'! Keep the precious secret."[34]

In his nine-page "Appeal," Webster declared that "we are fallen on evil times." The arts that cheat us of our political rights are at work to "beguile us of our understandings. Extraordinary dangers impose extraordinary duties." In the contest before us, he continued, we know from past history that "Mr. Gilman has been the most esteemed, when men are tranquil, dispassionate, and united. Mr. Langdon's fate seems ever to have been, to set the ocean of politics into a rage, and then to float himself on the surface." Like the successful lawyer he hoped to become, Webster then attempted to prove his case by linking Langdon to the radical, "Jacobin" cause. But, he said, when the excesses of the Reign of Terror of the French Revolution horrified Americans, Langdon and his Republican friends "put off the appelation [*sic*] of Jacobins, and called themselves Democrats." He further linked Langdon to a quarrel with the sainted Washington over the treaty-making power; he also connected him with opposition to the ratification of the Constitution. "Show me the man who persevered in hostility to the Federal Constitution, and I will shew you a friend of Mr. Jefferson and his Administration. Or shew me the personal enemy of Washington, and I will shew you a man who now calls himself a Republican." And he cataloged other "crimes" against the benign rule of Presidents Washington and Adams.

Do we prefer the enemy of Washington, to his friend? . . . Do we prefer such a Government as the mercy of Jacobinism may hereafter bestow on us, to the National Constitution? . . . Is peace less desirable than the sword? [If so,] we will go to the polls, and there renounce our regard for the Constitution—renounce the character of Freemen—renounce our veneration for Washington—renounce our interest—renounce our duty—and renounce our Faith!

But if we should choose to support the opposite Ticket . . . a united, vigorous, persevering effort, may do much. If it cannot prevent the final catastrophe, it may at least delay it—delay it, a few years, till the remnant of the Fathers, who achieved our Revolution, shall be carried to peaceful graves, and their presence no longer reproach the apostacy of their sons!

An Old Whig[35]

It was a quarrelsome but powerfully argued diatribe against the Republicans (and Langdon, in particular) and demonstrated Webster's continuing skill in writing politically exciting and commanding prose. He had developed into a

---

34. *W&S*, XV, 522–531, and note on p. 523. Webster's letter to Bingham was dated 1806, and in it he says it took him two days to write the "Appeal." In his Autobiography he says it took him "a single sitting of a winter's day and night."

35. Webster, "An Appeal to the Old Whigs of New Hampshire" (February 1805), in *W&S*, XV, 522–531.

most competent polemicist. What is remarkable about this youthful tract is that in many passages one can hear a voice behind the prose. The great Websterian rhetoric of the future was already in evidence. It is also interesting that he chose to keep his authorship of the piece a "precious secret." He was a young man still finding his way, and he probably wished to play it safe and not offend anyone who might later prove useful in helping him advance his career.

The spring election ended disastrously for the Federalists, and Webster's "Appeal" had little effect. Langdon won by a majority of 3,751, and the Republicans captured both houses of the legislature.[36]

The year before this political upheaval occurred in New Hampshire,[37] young Webster definitely made up his mind to complete his legal studies someplace other than Salisbury. He needed the experience of a larger milieu, even if he ultimately chose to practice as a country lawyer. He simply had to get out of Salisbury, this *"vale of tears,"* as he called it.[38] Friends recommended Portsmouth, and he himself initially considered New York City or Albany, but he finally settled on Boston. His brother, after completing his education at Dartmouth, had moved to Boston, thanks to the help Daniel had provided through a friend, Dr. Cyrus Perkins, who was leaving a teaching position in Boston and proposed that Ezekiel take his place.[39] After his move Ezekiel urged his brother to join him. *"Come,"* he wrote. "It is the most easy thing in the world for a young fellow of any enterprise or ability to support himself here very handsomely without descending to any business incompatible with the situation of the gentleman." It is a cosmopolitan city, Ezekiel argued, and one cannot help learning many valuable things. He sweetened his offer by offering to provide room and board in exchange for tutoring some eight students in his school in Latin and Greek. Another such offer might never come again, he added.[40]

Webster decided to accept Ezekiel's proposition even though as a Latin scholar he could not compare with his brother. At one time they had read Juvenal together, but Webster never did master the style of the great classicist so as to read him with any ease and pleasure.[41] Still he figured he could get by.

He arrived at his brother's school on Short Street (later renamed Kingston Street) on July 17, 1804. After settling in at Mrs. Whitwell's boardinghouse on Court Street, Webster attempted to get himself placed in a legal office. But because he knew no lawyer in Boston and had no letters of introduction, he failed in his quest. In desperation he decided on a daring move. On July 20, together with a friend, Samuel A. Bradley, he audaciously went to the Scollay Building on Tremont Street and presented himself at the office of Christopher

36. Lynn Warren Turner, *The Ninth State: New Hampshire's Formative Years* (Chapel Hill and London, 1983), p. 220.

37. Ibid., p. 219.

38. DW to Ezekiel Webster, May 5, 1804, in *PC*, I, 52.

39. "Autobiography," ibid., I, 15.

40. Ezekiel Webster to DW April 4, 1804, ibid., I, 53.

41. "Autobiography," ibid., I, 13.

Gore, a distinguished and wealthy Federalist and lawyer, who had been appointed by President Washington as the first U.S. attorney for Massachusetts and had recently returned from Great Britain, where, since 1796, he had served as a commissioner under the Jay Treaty to settle American claims for spoliations by British cruisers during the wars of the French Revolution. Gore had no clerk. And Webster knew it. So he and Bradley decided to go to Gore's office and introduce themselves. It was a risky ploy, but Webster figured he had nothing to lose.

Gore, the quintessential gentleman, agreed to see the young man. By this time Bradley "had already disappeared," apparently the victim of a "faint heart." Gore's "habitual courtesy of manners" put Webster at ease and gave him the courage to speak. If nothing else, Webster knew how to speak. "I had a tongue in my head," he explained to Bingham, and he used it persuasively and with infinite grace. What followed came *"trippingly* on the tongue." He began with an apology for appearing without an appointment. He had acted, he said, out of a belief in Gore's reputation for "kindness & generosity of character." He was a simple country lad who had studied law for two years and had come to Boston to study for another year, "to work & not to play." Webster then identified Federalists in New Hampshire whom he knew and who knew Gore, such as Gore's classmate Oliver Peabody. He admitted that he had not brought any letters of introduction but swore he could get them to prove his trustworthiness. Then he got to the point. He had heard, he went on, that Gore had no clerk, and he wished to apply for the position and to be Gore's pupil.

Gore smiled. He invited Webster to take a seat. He "spoke kind words," and they conversed for about a quarter of an hour. Gore admitted that what Webster had suggested was completely reasonable and did not require an apology. He went on to say that he did not wish to fill his office with clerks and intended to take on only one or two. With that Webster rose to leave.

Gore also rose. "My young friend," he said, "you look as if you might be trusted—you say you come to study, & not to waste time—I will take you, at your word. You may as well hang up your hat, at once, go to the other room, take your Book, & set down to reading it—& write, at your convenience, to N. Hamp. for your letters."[42]

Webster staggered from the room in a state of disbelief and exultation. Then it dawned on him what had happened. There had opened up to him a brilliant, new world of opportunity, a world of books and study and "men, & things" that could lead him to fortune and fame if he had the wit and will to take advantage of these opportunities in the limited time available to him. As it turned out, he remained in Gore's office from July 1804 to March 1805. And he put the time to excellent use. He attended the state supreme court in August

42. Ibid., I, 15–16; DW to Bingham, August 4, 1804, in *W&S*, XVI, 185; Harvey, *Reminiscences*, pp. 32–34. An amusing aspect of this interview was the fact that Gore did not catch Webster's name when introduced. "I had been in the office a week or so before Mr. Gore knew the name of his clerk!!!" DW to Bingham, August 4, 1804, in *W&S*, XVI, 185.

and reported every one of its decisions; the same with the U.S. circuit court. He kept a journal listing the books he read. "His chief study, however, was the Common Law, and more especially that part of it which related to the science of Special Pleading." He gobbled down Ward's *Law of Nations*, Viner's *Title of Pleadings*, Bacon's *Elements of Common Law*, Abbott on shipping, and even Vattel, for the third time in his life. He read "Puffendorf's Latin History of England, Giffords Juvenal, Boswell's Tour to the Hebrides, Moore's Travels, & many other miscellaneous things." "From that day to this," he declared in 1829, "the forms & language of special Pleas have been quite familiar to me. I believe I have my little abstract yet."[43]

Webster also remembered sitting in the office one day deep in the study of one of his lawbooks on maritime law when a gentleman, dressed in a plain gray outfit, came in and asked for Gore. Webster explained that his mentor was out at the moment. The gentleman then inquired about what the young man was reading, and Webster held out his book and showed it to him. "Well, I read that book too when I was a boy," the gentleman remarked, and proceeded to talk about ships, insurance, freights, prize money, "and other matters of maritime law," which "put me up to all I knew," Webster later recounted, "& a good deal more."[44]

The inquiring gray-coated gentleman turned out to be none other than Rufus King, a delegate to the Constitutional Convention, U.S. minister to Great Britain, Federalist candidate for the vice presidency in 1804, and a once and future U.S. senator. Little did either of them know at the time that they were destined within ten years to serve in Congress together, and on the most intimate terms.

As the young man had said, being Gore's clerk and pupil opened up to him a fantastic new world of "men, & things." And one of the "things" that came into his hands were letters President Jefferson had written to a state representative. All of a sudden Webster realized that the legal profession might be a worthy one for him after all. One good reason for his change of attitude was Christopher Gore himself. A few months later Webster told a friend that the urbane Gore was "a deep and various scholar. Since I left John Wheelock, I have found no man so indefatigable in research. He has great amenity of manners, is easy, accessible, and communicative, and, take him all in all, I could not wish a better preceptor."[45]

This eager, wide-eyed twenty-two-year-old postulant of the law studied not only Gore, his style and his work habits, but every legal mind and practitioner who came within his sights. And he jotted down in his journal their physical and intellectual characteristics, their style, and their "different modes of argumentation." He obviously meant to imitate the best of what he observed.

43. "Autobiography," in *PC*, I, 16–17; March, *Webster*, p. 20.
44. "Autobiography," in *PC*, I, 17; March, *Webster*, pp. 20–21.
45. DW to Merrill, November 30, 1804, in *W&S*, XVII, 194.

And there was Boston. He loved Boston, "this marvellous town," he called it, "full of every thing of every sort." Just imagine, he wrote Bingham, "a large room in the third story of a brick building" in the center of town, "a sea-coal fire, and a most enormous writing-table with half a cord of books on it." Then imagine "your most obedient, with his back to the fire, and his face to the table, writing by candlelight, and you will precisely see a 'happy fellow.'"Unfortunately his friendships did not extend very far in Boston because he could not afford them. "A young man who has a fortune to spend, is not a proper companion for another who has a fortune to make," he said. But to drive off moments of "gloom," he sometimes played "backgammon with the girls."[46]

In late summer, with Gore's approval, Daniel filled in for his brother at school while Ezekiel returned to Hanover to receive his diploma from Dartmouth. One of the pupils he met was Edward Everett, who later became one of his closest friends.

At the boardinghouse he met other interesting figures, including a wealthy and eccentric gentleman by the name of Taylor Baldwin, who took a "fancy" to the young man and invited him to be his companion on a "pleasure trip to the Hudson River."[47]

Webster attracted the attention of the well-off in part because he was such a lighthearted spirit. A sense of fun animated his words and actions, as his surviving letters to his friends attest. He was a person others found congenial, and that trait may explain Gore's readiness to accept him as a clerk and student. He was also well read, ferociously intelligent and well informed on many subjects, making him an excellent conversationalist.

Because of his continuing poverty and his hunger for the "better things" that wealth could provide, Webster took advantage of every opportunity that placed him in the company of men of property. He had learned a good deal from Baldwin about "the world at large and matters and things in general."[48] So, when he received the invitation to accompany Baldwin on his trip, he accepted with enthusiasm and sincere gratitude.

Gore had no objections to his absence and may have encouraged him to see more of the outside world. In any event, at twenty-seven minutes past twelve o'clock on Monday, November 5, election day—the day President Jefferson and his running mate, George Clinton of New York, crushed the Federalist ticket of Charles Cotesworth Pinckney and King in Massachusetts and then went on to pile up a majority of electoral votes to win a second term in office[49]—Webster

46. DW to Bingham, August 4, 1804, January 2, 1805, DW to Merrill, November 30, 1804, in *W&S*, XVII, 185, 198, 194.

47. Fuess, *Webster*, I, 79.

48. Lyman, *Public and Private Life of Webster*, II, 16.

49. Jefferson received 162 votes to Pinckney's 14. In New England only Connecticut voted for Pinckney. Groaned Webster: "And there went abroad over all the land an evil spirit, and it deluded many. Oh, Good old mother Massachusetts!" DW to Ezekiel Webster, November 15, 1804, in *PC*, I, 64.

and Baldwin took off on their pleasure jaunt. And they did it in the grand manner. They journeyed "in a hackney coach, with a pair of nimble trotters, a smart coachman before, and a footman on horseback behind. There's style for you!" wrote the approving Webster in a letter to Bingham.[50] They went by way of Worcester and Springfield and then headed for Saratoga, "the resort of the well, as well as the sick—of the gay, the rich and the fashionable," where they were to take the waters and generally enjoy themselves. They delighted in the assembly rooms, the billiard tables, and the taverns, where they consumed a fair amount of wine, for which Webster had already acquired a lively taste, thanks to the generosity of Christopher Gore. Then it was down to Albany, which Webster found dirty but with a few handsome buildings.

This was Webster's first excursion outside New England, and it proved to be quite an adventure. He had never seen so many different sorts of people as he encountered in New York, especially in Albany: "Greek & Jew—Englishman & Dutchman, Negro & Indian. Quite a mixture. Almost every body however speaks English occasionally," he informed his brother, "tho' I have heard them talk among themselves in a lingo which I never learned, even at the Indian charity school." Webster also met some distinguished New Yorkers: the "Patroon," Stephen Van Rensselaer, Abraham Van Vechten, and the Schuylers. He rather liked, nay, loved, meeting these wealthy and influential New Yorkers, and they him.

The couple returned to Boston by way of Hudson, New York (where Webster "oiled" his feathers), and then proceeded to Hartford, Connecticut, and Providence, Rhode Island, where he met two old friends, and after "cooing and chattering" with them "fluttered into Boston."

The two men arrived back at Mrs. Whitwell's boardinghouse at 1:00 P.M. on Wednesday, November 28, their trip having lasted a little more than three weeks. Naturally all of Webster's expenses had been paid by his companion, and when he arrived at the boardinghouse, "I put my hand in my pocket, and found one hundred and twenty dear delightfuls!" What a splendid conclusion to a splendid trip! "I'm so proud to have a dollar of my own," he exclaimed.[51] This incident marked the real beginning of Webster's long career of accepting gifts from friends and wealthy admirers. After a while he grew to expect them as his due.

Shortly after returning to Boston, Webster took a quick trip to Salisbury to see his father, who had been ill. One night Ebenezer had been "taken with a violent pain in his side, which terminated in a pleurisy fever." The doctor bled him, as was usual, and thus gave Ebenezer some relief, but it was several days

50. DW to Bingham, January 2, 1805, in W&S, XVII, 198.

51. DW to Ezekiel Webster, November 15, 1804, in PC, I, 63–64; DW to Bingham, January 2, 1804, DW to Habijah ("Henry") Fuller, March 10, 1805, in W&S, XVII, 198–200. Webster's sister Sally heard that her brother had received seven dollars a day for his companionship. "We should all be willing to give as much to see you in this town," she wrote him, "if we had the change as handy as you have in Boston." Sally Webster to DW, December 21, 1804, in W&S, XVII, 196.

before he could move, even to have his bed made or the sheets changed. Finally the fever abated, and he was able to walk. He had kept this worrisome news from his sons until he had recovered. But the information no doubt distressed the two men, especially when they learned that their mother was also in "very poor" health.[52]

Ebenezer had long expected to have his sons back in Salisbury and since the previous summer had begun through the good offices of Timothy Farrar, the chief justice of the state's superior court, to advance his younger son's name for the post of county clerk of the Hillsborough County Court of Common Pleas, a post he hoped Daniel would be willing to take. As a lay justice himself of the county Court of Common Pleas Ebenezer had every expectation that his appeal on his son's behalf would be given favorable consideration. Indeed, when Ebenezer first brought up the matter, the son indicated that he was interested.[53] What made the post particularly attractive was the fact that it carried an annual salary of fifteen hundred dollars, which "seemed to me," Webster later recalled, "very great," as indeed it was. "Its possession would make the family easy."[54]

In January the appointment came through, and Ebenezer immediately notified his son "that the prize was won. I certainly considered it a great prize, myself," Webster admitted, "& was ready to abandon my profession for it; not that I did not love my profession, & not that I did not hate the clerkship, & all clerkship[s]." But the money was a tremendous temptation, and the illnesses of his parents seemed to dictate that he must accept it. So he went to Gore and announced his decision.

Gore spoke quietly to his student. It was indeed a signal honor that had been offered, no doubt intended as a mark of confidence, he began, and therefore Webster must write a respectful letter declining it.

The unanticipated words startled Webster. "This was a shower bath, of ice water," he declared.

Gore continued. Webster had almost completed his studies and would soon be admitted to the bar and no doubt would become very successful in his practice. To accept a post that was precarious at best, was dependent on the will of others, and could at any time be taken from him and given to someone else made no sense. Even if it were permanent, it would go nowhere. Webster would remain a clerk for the remainder of his life and sit with a "pen behind his ear." Is that what he aspired to?

For the moment Webster could barely comprehend what was being said to him.

"Go on," commanded Gore, "& finish your studies; you are poor enough, but there are great[er] evils than poverty; live on no man's favor; what bread you do eat, let it be the bread of independence; pursue your profession, make

52. Ebenezer Webster to his sons, October 6, 1804, in *W&S*, XVII, 187–188.

53. DW to Farrar, July 12, 1804, DW to Ezekiel Webster, June 10, 1804, in *PC*, I, 57, 55.

54. "Autobiography," in *PC*, I, 19; Harvey, *Reminiscences*, pp. 35–36; March, *Webster*, pp. 22–23.

yourself useful to your friends, & a little formidable to your enemies, & you have nothing to fear."[55]

Wise words. They struck the young man with such force that he overcame the temptation to reach out for instant "riches." In that moment he made his decision. He would finish his studies. He later blessed the day that Gore had spoken to him.

Then it hit him. What would he say to his father? The old man counted on the office to "make us all, easy & comfortable." His health was bad and growing worse. His sons were gone. This office would bring Daniel home and give Ebenezer a degree of happiness in the final days of his life. The news, the young man worried, would come like a "thunderbolt."

Still, it had to be done. Webster found a country sleigh—its being midwinter a stage coach would not venture into New Hampshire—and in two or three days arrived at the Elms Farm. He almost lost heart as he entered his father's house. But fortifying himself with "an air of confidence, success, & gaiety," he strode inside.

His father looked much more feeble than the last time he had seen him, but Ebenezer received his son with "manifest joy." As the old man babbled about how kind the chief justice had been in conferring such an honor on the family, Daniel "felt as if I could die, or fly. I could hardly breathe." But he carried it off as best he could.

As the words tumbled from his mouth, their meaning suddenly dawned on Ebenezer. "Do you intend to decline this Office?" the shocked father asked.

"Most certainly," the son replied. "I cannot think of doing otherwise. I should be very sorry if I could not do better at present, than to be Clerk, for fifteen hundred Dollars a year, not to speak of future prospects! I mean to use my tongue, in the Courts, not my pen; to be an actor, not a register of other men's actions. I hope yet, Sir, to astonish your Honor, in your own Court, by my professional attainments."[56]

The old man stared at his son. His eyes, still black as jet, flashed for a moment. He rocked his chair. Then he spoke. "Well, my son, your mother has always said that you would come to something, or nothing, she was not sure which. I think you are now about settling that doubt for her."

That was the end of it. Ebenezer never said another word about the matter. For he undoubtedly knew, as did Daniel, that the young man had come of age, had matured, had taken charge of his life.

Daniel stayed a week before returning to Boston. He promised to return as soon as he won admission to the bar.[57]

But winning admission proved more difficult than he anticipated. The

55. "Autobiography," in PC, I, 19–20; March, Webster, p. 23; Lanman, Private Life of Webster, p. 36.

56. "Autobiography," in PC, I, 20–21; Harvey, Reminiscences, pp. 39–42; March, Webster, pp. 24–25; Lanman, Private Life of Webster, p. 37.

57. "Autobiography," in PC, I, 21; Harvey, Reminiscences, pp. 41–42; Lanman, Private Life of Webster, pp. 37–38.

general requirement for admission involved three years of study. Usually the candidate's teacher registered with the secretary of the bar association the date when the study began. But Webster had read law with several teachers, and none had reported that fact to the association. Since he wished admission to both the Suffolk, Massachusetts, and the Hillsborough, New Hampshire, bars, Webster needed statements from Thomas W. Thompson and Judah Dana that he had studied with them.

It would be an outright fabrication to claim that he had studied law with Dana, but that is not what Webster asked him to do. "Circumstances exist," he wrote Dana, "which render it desirable to me to be able to show that during the eight months in which I instructed in the Fryeburg Academy I considered myself destined for the profession of the law, and had access to the library of a practitioner. If you can *salvo honore* [save honor] say this of me, it would gratify me that you should." Webster readily admitted that "a 'student at law' I certainly was not unless 'Alan Ramsay's Poems' and 'Female Quixotism' will pass for law books." He acknowledged that he did not expect Dana to "certify" him as being a "student of any thing during the time I loitered away in your country, pursuing rather my male and female friends than any books." But, he went on, "you would really oblige me by writing a line and stating in it, if you can, that while I was within the academy six hours in the day, you understood me to have made choice of the law as a profession and that I had access to your library."[58]

Dana not only agreed to the request but embroidered it. "On your arrival," he wrote, "you informed me that, as you had commenced; you intended to pursue the Study of the Law: and wished for the use of my Library—during said term, and you had access to the same—and I expect that you devoted the principal part of your leisure hours, while you were at Fryeburg to the Study of the Law."[59] Dana distorted the truth, but he understood the young man's plight and was happy to accommodate him.

Thompson also responded with a generous statement and apologized for being "criminally negligent" in not informing the association of Webster's study with him. To make amends, he wrote a circular letter to each member of the bar in the county "propounding you for admission."[60]

Once these letters arrived, Gore petitioned the court in Boston to waive the additional year required for all those who lacked a Harvard degree. It was granted, and in March 1805 Gore introduced his pupil to the judges of the Suffolk Court of Common Pleas, made a short speech commending his student's diligence and knowledge of the law, and moved for Webster's admission to the bar, to which the judges immediately agreed.

The young man remembered every word of what Gore said. It carried a prediction. Webster swore it would not go unfulfilled.[61]

58. DW to Dana, December 26, 1804, *Manuscripts* (Summer 1959), p. 33.

59. Dana to Webster, January 18, 1805, in *PC*, I, 67.

60. Thompson to Webster, October 17, 1804, ibid., I, 61.

61. "Autobiography," ibid., I, 19. Webster seemed reluctant to reveal what Gore had said—modesty?—but most likely Gore predicted a distinguished career in the law for his student.

4

Portsmouth

$\mathbb{A}$ S HE HAD PROMISED, Webster returned home immediately. He left Boston on March 25, 1805, "with a good deal of regret" and headed directly for Amherst, New Hampshire, where the court was sitting, to pick up his father and accompany him back to the Elms Farm. He now had to decide where to practice. Naturally the family wanted him to settle in Salisbury, but he preferred Portsmouth. The idea of beginning his legal career in "the vale of tears" greatly distressed him. But when he found his father extremely ill, increasingly feeble, and "little fit to be left by all his sons," Webster resolved to stay with his father during his lifetime. So "partly through duty, partly through necessity, and partly through choice," he decided at the age of twenty-three to set up his practice in Boscawen, six miles south of Salisbury, where he could hurry back to the Elms in an emergency.[1]

Boscawen was a typical New England town of fourteen hundred residents, rather picturesque, quite hospitable, and built along a main street that paralleled the west bank of the Merrimack River. It was a town Webster knew well, having studied there many years before under Dr. Wood. Webster rented an office and a room—"a red store with stairs upon the outside"—from Joel French, a local merchant and town officer, and paid about fifteen dollars a year.[2]

He practiced law in Boscawen for the next two years, operating what he called "a shop in this village for the manufacture of Justice writs." He struggled to make a living, mostly collecting bills, and vowed that he would leave the place as soon as possible. His near contempt for Boscawen showed in the general air of superiority he exhibited, and it gained him something of a reputation for haughtiness and arrogance.[3] "When I commenced practice," he later commented, "I was without fortune or friends. I went into an interior town in New Hampshire, hired two rooms of a broken merchant and paid him nine shillings a week, made my own fire and bed and brushed my own boots and lived almost

1. DW to Bingham, May 4, 1805, in *W&S*, XVII, 206.

2. Harvey, *Reminiscences*, pp. 42–43.

3. When William Plumer first met Webster in August 1810, he had the same impression. "His manners are not pleasing—being haughty, cold, and overbearing." William Plumer, "Reminiscences of Daniel Webster," in *W&S*, XVII, 547.

literally for two years on bread and milk, and for a whole time went not into a single party. I had little to do; and only a small library which I read over and over on the principle of *multum non multa.*"[4]

Webster tried to get away as much as possible. He attended numerous courts around the state in pursuance of his practice, sharing a bed at the taverns he frequented, as was the custom. He even journeyed to Boston and Fryeburg. He later asserted to Josiah Quincy that to be successful in the law, "a young man should cultivate as much as possible an early intercourse with Courts—those even of the lowest grade—he should engage, in their discussions, and as often as possible appear as an advocate in them. This habituates him to self confidence to attack and defence,—to readiness of elocution and facility of investigation." This is precisely what Webster did. A young man just starting out, he declared, must "look forward to reward at Twenty years distance and to work for it, as though it was within his immediate grasp. This is the spirit, which ensures elevation."[5]

On Tuesday, September 3, 1805, Webster first addressed a jury as a full-fledged lawyer, and his father sat on the bench.[6] It was a civil suit argued in the Court of Common Pleas for the county of Grafton, then held in Plymouth. The elder Webster congratulated his son on "a creditable performance; one about which there was nothing to regret." "He never heard me a second time," Daniel lamented. No doubt Ebenezer took great delight in listening to his twenty-three-year-old son argue his position, and in a voice of unsurpassed sonority. One report claimed that the young man astonished everyone in the room by his "eloquence, learning and powers for reasoning."[7]

On the whole, once he began to plead cases of criminal[8] and civil law on a regular basis, Webster enjoyed a modest degree of success, and in May 1807 he was admitted as counselor in the superior court of New Hampshire. Within a relatively short time he developed a style and manner in addressing the court that were most individual and very appealing to his listeners. When he began to speak, his voice was low, his massive head sunk upon his chest, eyes fixed upon

4. Conversation between Webster and Josiah Quincy, in a letter from Quincy to Josiah Quincy, Jr., February 4, 1827, Quincy, Wendell, Holmes, Upham Papers, MHS.

5. Conversation between Webster and Josiah Quincy, in a letter from Quincy to Josiah Quincy, Jr., February 4, 1827, Quincy, Wendell, Holmes, Upham Papers, MHS.

6. The case Webster argued before his father is believed to have involved an action founded on a tavern bill of twenty-four dollars, of which seventeen dollars were recovered by Webster for his client. Fuess, *Webster,* I, 87–89. Webster also argued—unsuccessfully—against the celebrated and formidable Jeremiah Mason. To win his case, Mason found that he did not have an easy time of it. Webster "examined his witnesses, and shaped his case with so much skill" that Mason had "to exert every faculty" he possessed. Curtis, *Webster,* I, 77, note.

7. Harvey, *Reminiscences,* p. 43; Lyman, *Public and Private Life of Webster,* II, 21.

8. Claude Fuess claims that one of Webster's earliest cases involved his defense of a man charged with murder. Having been assigned to the case by the court, Webster based his defense on the argument against capital punishment. The jury rejected his argument and brought in a guilty verdict, whereupon the murderer was hanged on August 12, 1806, before a crowd of ten thousand people—or so it was reported. Fuess, *Webster,* I, 89.

the floor, and his feet moving incessantly, backward and forward, in a shuffling motion "as if trying to secure a firmer position." Soon the voice swelled and filled the room, his head now erect, his eyes "black as death." The voice, ah, "no lion in Africa ever had a voice like him." And he had the look of a lion to match, a heavy, not a sleepy, look. Black Dan in all his majesty "overpowered" those who heard him. "They all said—lawyers and judges and people—that they never heard such a speech, or anything like it. They said he talked like a different creature from any of the rest of them, great or small,—and there were men there that were not small." As he spoke, "[h]is whole countenance was radiant with emotion." And the listening audience sat transfixed.[9]

But with it all he always remembered whom he was addressing. For different audiences, he provided different styles. His voice, his manner, his words always accorded with what his audience could handle. "I remembered that I had my bread to earn," he later remarked, "by addressing the understanding of common men—by convincing juries—and that I must use language perfectly intelligible to them. You will therefore find, in my speeches to juries, no hard words, no Latin phrases, no *fieri facias;* and that is the secret of my style, if I have any."[10]

Webster's speaking skills, apart from his courtroom performances, brought him considerable attention in Boscawen and surrounding communities, including Concord, soon to become the capital of the state, and he was invited in 1806 to give the Independence Day address before the "Federal Gentlemen of Concord and its Vicinity." What he delivered was a well-constructed, relatively short address, one that bespoke the young man's intense national pride, one that warned of external dangers, one that raged particularly over the depredations of American commerce by Great Britain and France, currently locked in the mortal combat of the Napoleonic Wars.

If an angel should be winged from heaven on an errand of mercy to our country, the first accents which would glow on celestial lips would be, "Beware! Be cautious! Be wise! You have everything to lose; you have nothing to gain!" We live under the only government that ever existed, which was formed by the deliberate consultations of the people. Miracles do not cluster. That which has happened but once in six thousand years, cannot be expected to happen often. Such a government, once destroyed, would leave a void to be filled, perhaps for centuries, with evolution and tumult, riot and despotism.

Here then, for perhaps the first time, was one of the great themes that Webster was to repeat in countless speeches in the future—namely, the necessity of preserving the miraculous government of the United States that had been brought into existence through the suffrage of the people. If it were destroyed, it might not happen again for centuries. "As a land power, Great Britain can never be formidable to this country. Her navy is her weapon, and in the use of that she will continue to harass us, until she finds us able and disposed to resist

9. New York *Tribune,* quoted in Harvey, *Reminiscences,* pp. 46–50.
10. "Conversations with Felton."

her." Nor did Webster forget France in his general condemnation. "Ambition is the never-dying worm which feeds and fattens in the bosom of the Gaul. To an eagerness for personal distinction is also added a thirst for national glory, unheard of since the days of Rome, and unequalled, perhaps, even by the Romans. . . . How much further the power of France may be extended . . . is impossible to determine. No friend, however, of the human race, can wish to see it extended further."[11]

His expanding reputation as a speaker brought an invitation from his alma mater to address the Phi Beta Kappa Society of Dartmouth College on August 26, 1806. For his subject he chose "The State of Literature." So busy had he been prior to the address that much of it, he insisted, was written "on the road." Although he had undoubtedly polished the piece by the time it was published, it still showed the unbecoming marks of hasty composition and shallowness of thought. But he made some interesting points. He started off by acknowledging this nation's "inordinate ambition to accumulate wealth." "The love of gold," he said, "is the ruling passion." This passion for wealth and pursuit of politics—two of Black Dan's own personal demons—are "impediments to the advancement of literature." How then can it flourish and grow? Government must of necessity intervene. "It is the duty, and in a great measure in the power of Government, to enlarge and liberalize this passion, to induce the individual to embrace public, as well as private views, and blend his own interest with the best interests of the community." In short, it was up to the government to aid an individual in legitimizing his passion for money by blending it with the interests of the community.[12]

Other than the satisfaction his speaking performances provided him, Webster had no real outside pleasures in Boscawen, no social life to speak of, although there was a young schoolmistress by the name of Grace Fletcher who caught his fancy. With the possible exception of Miss Fletcher, his greatest enjoyment came from reading history and writing reviews and essays, a few of which were published in the Boston *Monthly Anthology*. His first article for the *Anthology* was "Original Criticism. First Canto of Terrible Tractoration," followed by "The French Language." He also wrote several reviews of books, including Tunis Wartman's *Treatise on Political Economy*, the first volume of Johnson's *New York Reports*, and Edward Lawe's *Treatise on Pleading*. Of his own poetry he wrote little, but this, he said, "I mean to reform."

Although the law provided little real enjoyment for him, the world of books constantly excited his interest. He bought books from a dealer in Boston whenever he could scrape up the money, and he continued to hone his writing skills,

11. *W&S*, XV, 537–547.

12. Ibid., XV, 575–582. Some of Webster's admirers apparently could not get enough of his oratory. Cyrus Perkins, a trustee of the college, chided him for refusing to allow the publication of his address. "It is [not] a thing," Perkins wrote him, "I think good to die with the breath which gave it utterance and be blown away by the wind—you *must* not persist in a refusal." Perkins to Webster, September 3, 1806, in *PC*, I, 84. It was finally published in 1809.

even though he later contended that these literary efforts were "not worth looking up, or remembering."[13]

Still, books and writing could not earn his living. His profession was the law, and if he expected to get ahead and make a name for himself, there was only one way to do it: study. In a letter to his friend Bingham, he emphasized the need to study and repeated some of the things he had said in his Phi Beta Kappa address:

Study is truly the grand requisite for a lawyer. Men may be born poets, and leap from their cradle painters; nature may have made them musicians, and called on them only to exercise, and not to acquire, ability. But law is artificial. It is a human science to be learnt, not inspired. . . . To make a lawyer, application must do as much as if nature had done nothing. The evil is, that an accursed thirst for money violates everything. We cannot study, because we must pettifog. . . . The love of fame is extinguished; every ardent wish for knowledge repressed; conscience put in jeopardy, and the best feelings of the heart indurated, by the mean, money-catching, abominable practices, which cover with disgrace a part of the modern practitioners of the law. The love of money . . . has taken root deeply, and I fear will never be eradicated. While this holds everything in its grip, America will produce few great characters. We have no patronage for genius; no reward for merit. . . . Money is the chief good; every eye is on it; every heart sighs for it.[14]

No one understood this craving for money better than Daniel Webster. Although he hated the idea of having to pursue it, he was determined to have it and the recognition of success that went with it. But that took study and effort and determination, all three of which he believed he could and would provide. Not surprisingly, starting in 1805, he became associated with banking interests in the state, first with the Coos Bank and later with the Concord Bank.[15] In time—several years down the road—bankers, businessmen, and merchants took his measure, especially those of his talents that they could employ, and welcomed him into their fold.

Webster's other interest, besides money and books and writing, was politics, Federalist politics. In fact politics was supremely important to him. With Jefferson's Republican party riding high Webster feared for the political future of his state and his party. When his former law instructor Thomas W. Thompson was elected to the Ninth Congress, Webster began a regular correspondence with him, and they exchanged political information. Thompson informed his student about national affairs, and Webster kept his teacher abreast of local and state developments. The Napoleonic Wars had begun, and the United States found it increasingly difficult to protect its trade and preserve its neutrality. This regular exchange of letters provided Webster with invaluable background information and a "feel" for national politics that served him well when he later entered

13. DW to Bingham, January 19, 1806, in W&S, XVII, 220; "Autobiography," in PC, I, 21. Excerpts from "Original Criticism. First Canto of Terrible Tractoration" can be found in Van Tyne, ed., Letters of Webster, pp. 19–21.

14. DW to Bingham, January 19, 1806, in W&S, XVII, 222.

15. DW to Bingham, May 4, 1805, DW to Ezekiel Webster, April 30, 1804, "Autobiography," in PC, I, 69, 68, 21. In 1808 Webster became a stockholder of the so-called lower Concord Bank.

Congress himself. He was enormously grateful, he told Thompson, for "the thousand small incidents, private anecdotes, &c which happen at the theatre of national business" and could not be obtained by reading the newspapers. "The chit chat of a Congressional party is a very important business, when transported from the Potomac to the Merrimac [*sic*]." Thompson reported on the divisions that seemed to be breaking out between the President and several leading members of the Republican party, such as John Randolph of Roanoke. "Randolph has made a violent attack upon the President [in Congress] & treated Madison . . . with ineffable contempt. It has been conjectured that Randolphs object is to prepare the way for Munroe [*sic*] to the Presidential chair."

The news delighted Webster. "I hope the division in the democratic party will create the possibility" of Federalists' joining the Randolph faction to form a majority party. Still, there was something to be said for remaining a minority. "I consider a minority the place where a great politician is made. In the history of parliamentary warriors we find no distinguished combatants who did not learn their art of political fencing by exercising against a superior enemy." As it turned out, Webster himself would get a considerable amount of training in the "art of political fencing" when he went to Congress and had to face such a formidable "enemy" as Andrew Jackson and his horde of Democrats.

Webster was especially pleased to hear about Jefferson's developing problems with Great Britain over the protection of American commerce. If the President failed to initiate some action during this session of Congress, Webster predicted, it will "put a period to the popularity of the administration. If the cities are awakened, they will awaken the country. The nation may cease to sleep, and the paltry politicians who govern it, may be shaken from their seats."[16]

It is probable in view of Webster's intense ambition for place that in writing these letters to his mentor, he thought a great deal of joining him one day as a congressman. He liked excitement and already missed the hectic life in Boston. Washington might prove even more exciting. But any thought of removal to the capital or anywhere else had to wait of course until his obligations at home had been resolved.

Then it happened. On April 22, 1806, his father, Ebenezer, died at the age of sixty-seven after a long illness.[17] He died, Webster later recorded, "after a life of exertions, toil, and exposure; a private soldier, an officer, a legislator, a judge, every thing that a man could be, to whom learning never had disclosed her 'ample page.' "

Webster closed the old man's eyes, remembering only "a white forehead, a tinged cheek, a complexion as clear as heavenly light!" Webster deeply loved, admired, and respected his father. He felt obligated to stay home as long as his father lived, yet he left no record of his own personal reaction to Ebenezer's

16. Thompson to DW, January 10, January 29, February 14, March 5, 1806; DW to Thompson, March 5, 15, 1806, in *PC*, I, 74–83.

17. Ebenezer had already buried his first wife, Mehitable, and three children, the infants Olle or Olivia and Ebenezer and then, in 1804, the thirty-eight-year-old Susannah.

passing. In his "Autobiography" Webster simply writes, "He died in April 1806, & lies in the burial ground, in his own field, just at the turn of the road beneath the shadow of a tall pine." Perhaps the memory of his loss was too painful to say more.[18]

A way of escape had now opened up. Ezekiel Webster had begun the study of law in Boston and upon completion planned to return to Salisbury. Webster desperately needed and wanted to leave his situation in Boscawen and reestablish himself in a larger and more congenial area. What the brothers finally decided to do satisfied both their ambitions and salved Daniel's conscience about his family. Once admitted to the bar, Ezekiel would take over his brother's practice and look after the family farm and their mother, while Daniel would move to Portsmouth, which could provide greater opportunities for his particular needs and special interests and talents.

Ezekiel was admitted to the bar in September 1807, moved back home, and seemed to enjoy his new life as country squire and legal adviser and attorney to the community. Life on the farm in a small town provided him with immense pleasure, everything that his brother could not abide. He became the family anchor and a person of enormous support to Daniel, with whom he frequently collaborated on legal matters. He no sooner arrived back home than Daniel shot out of town and headed for Portsmouth.[19]

No longer the state capital, which it had been in colonial times until revolutionary patriots moved the capital inland, Portsmouth retained its preeminence among New Hampshire communities. The state's largest city and only harbor, it flourished because of its lively commercial trade. Wharves and warehouses, stuffed with molasses, rum, coffee, tea, spices, silk, cloth, and many other useful and luxury items, fringed its shoreline to receive the bounties from China and India and other exotic places. Stately mansions, elegantly furnished, dotted every street, their owners, wealthy shipowners and retired sea captains. Nestled around Market Square stood the Old State House, the Assembly House, and numerous shops. For Webster Portsmouth could rival Boston in benefits and opportunities. Although staunchly Jeffersonian in its politics, the town had a reasonably good Federalist tradition and a commitment to conservative principles. Webster thought that in this city his real career could surely begin, one that would quickly bring him the recognition and rewards he so desperately craved.[20]

Now in his element, Webster could hardly wait to announce his practice and start meeting congenial townsfolk. Prior to his arrival he had asked Nathaniel Adams, a clerk of the superior court, to help him find suitable quarters. Adams complied by setting him up at the home of Mrs. John Wardrobe, who charged him five dollars a week for room and board and a sitting room that he

18. "Autobiography," in *PC*, I, 21.

19. There is some evidence that Webster actually moved in late August 1807, but in his "Autobiography" he says it was September 1807. *PC*, I, 21.

20. Maurice G. Baxter, *One and Inseparable: Daniel Webster and the Union* (Cambridge, Mass., and London, 1984), pp. 22–23; Fuess, *Webster*, I, 94–97.

would share with other boarders. "Washing will be an additional expence," Adams informed him, "which you can easily procure in the neighborhood." Adams also arranged to have Webster set up his practice over William H. Wilkins's dry goods shop at sixty-six dollars per annum.[21]

One of the first things Webster did after arriving in Portsmouth and settling in at Mrs. Wardrobe's house was to visit the Old North Church, whose sexton was the Reverend Dr. Joseph Buckminster, the father of Webster's Latin "tutor" at Phillips Exeter and one of the founders of the Boston *Monthly Anthology* to which Webster had contributed several articles. Presumably this connection with the son afforded Webster his initial introduction and an entrée into Portsmouth society. He soon became "very intimate" with Buckminster's family, especially its young females. One of them, Eliza,[22] said that he "riveted her attention" when he first came into the Old North Church and sat in the pew next to her. She described him as slender and rather fragile-looking. His "large eyes and massive brow seemed very predominant above the other features, which were sharply cut, refined, and delicate. The paleness of his complexion was heightened by hair as black as the raven's wing." To help this frail young man gain strength, Dr. Buckminster prescribed sawing wood. Before breakfast the two of them regularly took a long two-handed saw outside, and then, working both ends in unison, they sawed away for half an hour. And, said Eliza, no matter how "disagreeable in itself, Mr. Webster appeared at our breakfast, afterward, with his genial humor unimpaired."[23]

From this beginning Webster slowly built a circle of friends around him, "of which he was the life and soul." He charmed all he met. The young people particularly liked his marvelous sense of humor and his playacting. He frequently entertained his friends by looking out the window at strangers walking down the street and then concocting "the most humorous imaginary histories" about them. Jeremiah Mason, with whom he regularly tangled on the circuit and who soon became a very close friend, commented that "there was never such an actor lost to the stage as he would have made had he chosen to turn his talents in that direction."[24]

But as sociable and agreeable as Webster could be with intimates, "outsiders" frequently found him cold and remote and his conversation with them "marked by cool deliberation." In repose he looked solemn, even morose at times, with a built-in pout. His dark eyes set in a dark face seemed to discourage familiarity. Not that he was uncivil. He never said a word to which anyone could take the least personal offense.[25] On the other hand, his close friends saw none of this. With them he was all wit and charm, laughter and fun.

21. Adams to Webster, June 9, 1807, in *PC*, I, 94–95.

22. Eliza Buckminster Lee became an intimate friend, for whom Webster wrote his "Autobiography."

23. "Sketch of Mrs. G. F. Webster by Mrs. E. Buckminster Lee, January 23, 1856," in Webster, ed., *Private Correspondence*, I, 438–439.

24. Ibid., I, 439.

25. Wentworth, "Congressional Reminiscences," p. 34.

Webster's decision to link himself immediately with the Buckminster family may have been very deliberately and carefully plotted. As he did in his law cases, he prepared himself well in advance before making his move. His purpose? Marriage.

Marriage had been on his mind for some time. He thought he needed a wife, and he wanted a wife. "You husbands, happy race," he said in a letter to a friend, have a wife, and a wife "is like a burning-glass, which concentrates every ray of affection that emanates from a husband's heart."[26] He was now twenty-five and a half years of age; he had a profession and had been active in pursuing it for two years. Most of his friends and college classmates had married, had settled, and were raising families. On the matter of love, he lamented to Bingham in 1806, "I can at present say nothing only that I am not married, and seriously am inclined to think I never shall be. The example of my friends sometimes excites me, and certain narratives I hear of you, induce me to inquire why the deuce the female flesh and blood was not made for me as well as others; but reasons, good or bad, suppress hope and stifle incipient resolution." A year after writing this doleful letter he still lacked a wife but may have met a likely prospect. "I rejoice that you have so comfor[table] a cage," Webster joked with Thomas Merrill. "A Bird you cannot but find eas[ily]. [Your] friend W. has neither cage nor bird. How[ever he] lives in hopes."[27]

No doubt the "bird" Webster had in mind when he wrote this letter was Grace Fletcher, a cousin of the Buckminsters', and the young schoolmistress he had first met in Salisbury.[28] Born on January 16, 1781, in Hopkinton, making her a year and two days older than Webster, the young lady was the daughter of the Reverend Elijah Fletcher and Rebecca Chamberlin Fletcher of Hopkinton. After her father's death her mother married another clergyman, the Reverend Christopher Paige. Not surprisingly, Grace was "sincerely and deeply religious." She was also well educated (Atkinson Academy) for her sex and time, cultivated, intelligent, reasonably attractive, and, at the age of twenty-seven, verging on spinsterhood. Although physically and emotionally delicate, she had about her a quiet dignity and composure that put everyone at ease. She was imperturbable and just as calm in a fashionable salon as in her own quiet parlor. She had come to Salisbury to visit her elder sister, Rebecca, who was married to Israel Webster Kelly, the county sheriff.

Webster had first met Grace in church in Salisbury. She caught his attention because she was wearing a tight-fitting dress and looked "like an angel." When she returned home, she told her sister that she saw "some one, a man with a black head, who looked as if he might be somebody." Their slight acquaintance developed over the next few months into a friendship, and one of Grace's cousins noted that she was trying to "entertain" Webster by playing checkers. The family

26. DW to Jacob McGaw, January 12, 1807, in W&S, XVII, 223–224.

27. DW to Merrill, March 8, 1807, in PC, I, 93.

28. James W. Paige, Grace Fletcher's half brother, referred to Eliza Buckminster as Cousin Eliza. Paige to Webster, December 19, 1824, in PC, I, 369.

thought "him a young man of great promise, but we girls think him rather awkward and verdant."[29]

Once Webster had spotted his "bird" and thought about living with her in a "comfor[table] cage," he knew that because religion was supremely important to her, she would never permit him to court her unless he joined the church. Without a moment's hesitation he obliged. On August 8, 1807, he wrote out a confession of faith and sent it to the pastor of the Salisbury Congregational Church, the Reverend Thomas Worcester, an action that surely implies his growing interest in Grace as a wife.

In the confession Webster summarized his beliefs, and they were fully in accord with the conservative Calvinist doctrines of the Congregational community. After affirming his belief in the existence of God, who created and governs the world, the divinity of Christ, and the authority of Scripture, he added: "I hold it my duty to believe, not what I can comprehend, or account for, but what my Maker teaches me. . . . I believe in the utter inability of any human being to work out his own Salvation, without the constant aids of the spirit of all grace. . . . Although I have great respect for some other forms of worship, I believe the Congregational mode, on the whole, to be preferable to any other."

Having proved his worthiness by this confession, Webster was duly admitted to the church just prior to his removal to Portsmouth. Although he often worshiped at other churches as he grew older, especially the Episcopal Church, he ended his days usually attending Congregational services. He expressed little preference for forms of worship and rather disliked "abstruse reasoning" from the pulpit. He wanted "plain, pungent preaching, which arraigned the sinner as guilty before a holy God and a holy law." Abstruse reasoning made him uneasy. The clergy should return to the simplicity of the Gospels, he pontificated, and "preach more to individuals and less to the crowd." Too many clerics take their text from St. Paul "and preach from newspapers." When they do, "I prefer to enjoy my own thoughts rather than to listen."

But he did like to sing, especially the devotional hymns of Dr. Watts, which he had learned by heart as a boy. Frequently, when alone, he would burst forth with "Welcome, Sweet Day of Rest" or any number of other hymns. He liked them so much that at parties he would end the evening by leading the company in one of Dr. Watts's inspiring songs.[30]

Before Webster departed for Portsmouth, he and Grace may have come to some agreement about their future. By this time they had known each other for several years. Once he was settled in Portsmouth, his friendship and intimacy

29. "Sketch of Mrs. G. F. Webster," in Webster, ed., *Private Correspondence*, I, 440; IB Papers, Box 20, Folder B, p. 38.

30. DW to Worcester, August 8, 1807, in *PC*, I, 95–96; Harvey, *Reminiscences*, pp. 395, 409; Lyman, *Public and Private Life of Webster*, II, 247. Webster's commitment to Christianity was based on a simple logical argument: The Gospels are true history or a fraud; Christ was what he professed to be or an impostor. "There is no other alternative." His spotless life in "earnest enforcement of the truth," His suffering and death in its defense "forbids us to suppose that he was suffering an illusion of the heated brain." Ibid., II, 246.

with the Buckminster family added to his worthiness and suitability to a woman like Grace Fletcher. That her cousins, Eliza particularly, highly approved of him meant a great deal to Grace. It is very likely that by the fall of 1807, if not sooner, Grace and Daniel had agreed to marry, once he established himself in Portsmouth.[31]

The earliest-known letter Webster wrote to Grace may have been written shortly before he left Boscawen. It is reproduced here in full.

Dear G.   [September?] 4, 1804
    I was fortunate enough [to] be at home Sunday morning, 6 o'clock, after rather a *solitary* ride. The Country from Cambridge to Dunstable is really, as I tho't, much more pleasant, than from Dunstable to Concord. I have not yet seen your friends, but I understand from Mr [Israel Webster] Kelly that they are well. By Mr [Daniel] A[bbott] I send you a small piece of velvet, for the aforesaid 5 pence.
    Early in the week after next, I hope to see y[ou] all. Give my love to all the friends & excuse a scrawl written in a Court hours. Yours entirely—
                                        D.W.[32]

Not a particularly romantic letter but one appropriately decorous and proper to a decorous and proper young lady. No other letter to Grace survives for this period, but the courtship, however conducted, continued for the next several months.

Anxious to marry as soon as his finances would allow, Webster turned his attention to improving his situation but found himself constantly out of pocket. He pettifogged, to use his own term, by selling writs in town, and he appealed for help from his brother and friends and chased every penny he could spot. "There is no money here, within my reach," he moaned. "I have sued any body I could."[33]

By the following spring Webster's situation had begun to improve enough for him to hope that a marriage date could be set. His legal reputation had grown steadily, and he had become active in politics, which no doubt increased his business. "I am earning a small living," he informed Bingham in May 1808, which involved about as much business as he had a right to expect as a relative newcomer to the city, and he had started to acquire a library. But "I . . . have long been convinced that I never shall be rich."[34]

Rich or not, he and Grace, with her family's consent, decided to marry. It is impossible to judge the degree to which they genuinely loved each other at this moment, but in time each developed a deep commitment to the other. At the moment Webster was desperate to get married. At his age he knew he should be married. It was expected of him. And he was probably lonely. Sentimental and romantic, he undoubtedly idealized his feelings toward Grace. But quietly and unostentatiously, as the years passed, his affections ripened into a profound love

31. Fuess, *Webster,* I, 100 and note 3.
32. DW to Grace Fletcher, [September?] 4, 1807, in *PC,* I, 97–98.
33. DW to Ezekiel Webster, December 16, 1807, ibid., I, 98.
34. DW to Bingham, May 5, 1808, in *W&S,* XVII, 230.

for Grace and their children. All his life he craved affection, and Grace fulfilled his needs completely. She loved him deeply and was devoted to him. It is rather remarkable that within the small circle of his family and intimate friends he possessed the extraordinary ability to attract boundless devotion.

Without breathing a word to anyone in Portsmouth, he left town, presumably to visit his family in Salisbury. On Sunday, May 29, 1808, Daniel and Grace were married in the home of her sister, Rebecca, "in the middle west room" by the Reverend Thomas Worcester.[35] If they followed the traditional form, the couple stood before the minister, with the witnesses on either side, and joined hands. They then recited a brief exchange of vows.[36]

The two returned to Portsmouth, where Webster temporarily rented a house—137 Vaughan Street—from his friend Jeremiah Mason. This residence had a lovely garden in back and was centrally located across the street from the Assembly House, not far from the business center of town. Not much later Webster purchased a modest wooden residence for six thousand dollars. It was on the northwest corner of Court and Pleasant streets, about two blocks from Market Square. It rose two stories with a gambrel roof, twin chimneys, and two windows on either side of the front door. A fence with carved posts at the entranceway separated the house from the street. Here the Websters resided until the building burned in 1813. Shortly thereafter the family moved to a third house, a two-story, four-room structure on High Street.[37]

Married, settled, with a growing—however slowly—legal practice, Webster lived nine years, save one month, in Portsmouth, and "they were very happy years," he later recorded. Grace tended to his every need. "She not only lived in his shadow," remembered Eliza Buckminster, "but her pulses seemed to 'beat double' with his and her life." The circle of friends about Webster became more intimate with Grace's arrival "and was held by more powerful attractions." During these Portsmouth years of his late twenties and early thirties Webster's health markedly improved. He actually looked robust, and the sickly pallor of his youth, caused by his many illnesses, completely disappeared. More and more he resembled his father as his complexion darkened. His hairline receded slightly, making his bulging forehead ever more prominent. His dark, deep-set eyes and jet black hair gave him an appearance of leonine fierceness when his emotions flared during extended political debate or intense legal pleading. He now had a bearing and a presence and a manner that could strike awe in all who saw and heard him. His progress in the legal profession now began to move swiftly forward.[38]

Webster set up his office on the west side of Market Street, just a few doors

35. In his "Autobiography," Webster says that he was married on June 24, 1808, but the records of the Salisbury church give the date as May 29. "Autobiography," in *PC,* I, 21; "Sketch of Mrs. G. F. Webster," in Webster, ed., *Private Correspondence,* I, 439–440; Fuess, *Webster,* I, 101 and note 1.

36. Jack Larkin, *The Shaping of Everyday Life, 1790–1840* (New York, 1988), p. 63.

37. Fuess, *Webster,* I, 101–103.

38. "Sketch of Mrs. G. F. Webster," in Webster, ed., *Private Correspondence,* I, 438, 440–441.

from the square, in the second story of a dry goods store. The office had "less furniture and more books" than usual, and it opened onto a small inner room that provided Webster with a degree of privacy. By chaise and by sleigh he followed the superior court around the state, visiting many towns in all six counties, further sharpening his legal and speaking skills. Courtrooms became scenes of dramatic conflict when the combatants showed power in their reasoning and force in their declamations. At such moments farmers from surrounding countryside hastened into court to hear the harangues and register their dismay or approval. It was a wonderful form of entertainment and education; few others existed at the time. Webster's striking ability to think rapidly on his feet, to respond to arguments with telling wit and clearly focused rebuttal won him a reputation that during the next few years nudged him into the front ranks of the state's legal profession. Over the following decade he handled more than seventeen hundred cases. And withal he met with a fair amount of success.[39]

To a very large extent Webster was propelled headlong to distinction by the excellence of his opponents in court, especially Jeremiah Mason.[40] Repeatedly during these Portsmouth years he jousted with Mason, sustaining one legal pounding after another, pounding he could still feel twenty-five years later.[41] But he learned from the blows. He learned to duck and feint and maneuver.

Mason, fourteen years Webster's senior, was a huge bear of a man, standing six feet seven inches and massively built. "If there be in the country a stronger intellect," asserted the admiring Webster, "if there be a mind of more native resources, if there be a vision that sees quicker or sees deeper into whatever is intricate, or whatever is profound, I must confess I have not known it." Before a jury Mason used no rhetoric, no gestures, no ornamentation whatever. But each word he spoke "was the embodiment of pure reason, the expression of irresistible logic." The evidence he presented invariably crushed "the intellect of his hearer into conviction." A consummate master of common law, Mason stood at the head of the New Hampshire bar. Webster learned a great deal about pleading from this man. "He had a habit," reported the younger man, "of standing quite near to the jury, so near that he might have laid his finger on the foreman's nose; and then he talked to them in a plain conversational way, in short sentences, and using no word that was not level to the comprehension of the least educated man on the panel. This led me to examine my own style, and I set about reforming it altogether."

It proved to be an important lesson. Webster could still sink into bombast at times; Mason demonstrated the value of simplicity. Webster often appeared haughty, cold, and overbearing; the folksy, congenial Mason showed him how to

39. *PLBP,* I, 185ff.

40. Some of these eminent barristers included, besides Mason, Edward Livermore; Jeremiah Smith, judge of the superior court and governor of the state; William King Atkinson, attorney general of the state; George Sullivan, another attorney general; and Samuel Dexter. March, *Webster,* p. 27.

41. DW to Mason, February 27, 1830, in *W&S,* XVII, 489.

charm a jury. Webster occasionally prepared his cases in haste, relying on language and delivery; Mason taught him the overwhelming primacy of facts and their lucid presentation in any litigation.

A story was told of a client who wished to retain Webster but found him already committed to the other side. Webster told the litigant to retain Mason.

"What do you think of Mr. Mason?" the litigant asked.

"I think him second to no man in the country," Webster replied.

The downcast client went to Mason and asked him what he thought about Webster's ability, since Webster would argue the other side.

"He's the very devil in any case whatever," responded Mason, "and, if he's against you, I beg to be excused."[42]

With his reputation as an extremely competent lawyer steadily growing he was soon earning two thousand dollars a year, a not inconsiderable sum in the early nineteenth century, even though Webster later thought it insignificant.[43] What made it seem insignificant was his habitual indebtedness. "Property was something which Webster could acquire," commented one man, "but never retain." His debts accumulated faster than he could pay them. He regularly speculated in land, not always successfully, and he developed extravagant tastes for food, drink, and "things" that invariably emptied his pockets. Like his father, he had no sense of thrift, no Yankee sense of frugality. He had gone through Dartmouth on loans; he borrowed constantly; he always seemed to be in need. Worse, he developed an attitude of indifference toward paying back what he owed. One debt piled on top of another. He became constitutionally incapable of meeting or facing financial obligations.[44]

His carelessness with money can be demonstrated by a story about how he and Mason, who "carried their families with them" and boarded together during one court session, put up a small shed to keep a carriage they shared. At the end of the session the landlord said the shed had to be removed to provide room for some other purpose during the summer.

"Well," said Webster, "remove it when you please. . . . If it is worth anything to you you are welcome to it." But, he added, you had best speak to Mason since he shared ownership of the shed.

The landlord thanked Webster for his "liberality." Then he went to Mason.

"You may take down the shed," said Mason, "and sell the materials either at auction or private sale, and account to me for the proceeds."

William Plumer, a leading Republican politician and self-taught lawyer who later became Webster's close friend, thought this story a "fair sample of Webster's carelessness and Mason's prudence; of Webster's liberality, and Mason's thrift." Webster thought nothing of a few boards and joists; Mason deemed them

42. March, *Webster*, pp. 27–28, Lanman, *Private Life of Webster*, pp. 38–39; Fuess, *Webster*, I, 108.

43. Charles March says Webster's Portsmouth clients were not rich and his fees not large, "nor were persons so litigious as in places less civilized by intelligence." March, *Webster*, p. 28.

44. Fuess, *Webster*, I, 104–106, 118; *PC*, VII, 348 editorial note.

92

DANIEL WEBSTER

of financial worth. Mason was attentive to his interests, said Plumer; Webster was not.[45]

"The impudent dog that he is," chuckled his friend Jeremiah Smith, "he does not know the value of money, and never will." Then, with a shrug, Smith added: "No matter; he was born for something better than hoarding money-bags."[46] It was that attitude of Smith's, and other friends, bankers, and business-men, who indulged Black Dan's financial recklessness that eventually created a spiral of indebtedness from which he never escaped.

One obvious way of improving both his financial and professional situation in New Hampshire did not escape Webster's notice. Politics held out many enticing prospects, especially the likelihood of expanding his reputation and with it his practice. Moreover, by 1810 he had become known as "the best speaker at the bar,"[47] so the value of taking a more active part in politics became increasingly compelling. The Federalists desired and needed his voice and pen, and the Republicans feared that he could do them great harm. In the past he had contributed a few pamphlets and speeches to the political debate, but not until he finally established himself in Portsmouth, and not until the political situation in Europe and in the country worsened, did he finally rouse himself to greater efforts on behalf of his conservative and Federalist beliefs.

Like most Federalists, Webster greatly admired Great Britain. Not its monarchical system, with its "Kings, Lords, and Commons, however nicely adjusted their relative powers," but rather "the free municipal organization of her commonalty" that made the nation prosperous and saved it "from those dangerous revulsions" so frequent in other European countries. France, he thought, had suffered from the absence of "an organic development of democracy in the form of municipal corporations. There was no breakwater," he argued, "between the rage of ignorant, impoverished, turbulent masses, and the rashness of dreamy, hot-headed theorists." The world was constantly plagued by "turbulent masses" and "hot-headed theorists," resulting in tyrants like Napoleon. To put it simply, "The path to despotism leads through the mire and dirt of uncontrolled democracy."[48] And the tyranny of a dictator like Napoleon could engulf the world.

The times are such I am surprised at nothing. [If] before I rise from my Table, I should [learn] that Buonapartte [was in] London, it would not astonish me. I am persuaded that a great revolution is taking place, not only in Europe but through the world. Society is deeply shaken every where. The minds of men are flying from all steadfast principles. . . . Principles are called prejudices, & duty, scrupulosity. Where all this will

45. Plumer, "Reminiscences of Webster," in W&S, XVII, 547–548. Plumer had been a Federalist but deserted to the Republican party. See Lynn W. Turner, William Plumer of New Hampshire, 1759–1850 (Chapel Hill, 1962), pp. 177–201.

46. Plumer, "Reminiscences of Webster," in W&S, XVII, 547.

47. Ibid., XVII, 546.

48. "Conversations with Lanman," in W&S, XIII, 565–566; DW to Bingham, May 18, 1802, in Webster, ed., Private Correspondence, I, 112.

end, you and I cannot tell. May we at all times have grace to say, with honest and sincere hearts, "Father in Heaven, th[y will be] done."[49]

Looking at his own country, Webster shivered with fear for the future. "Indeed I fear that our Country is growing corrupt at a rate, which distances the speed of every other. . . . The course towards total depravity is swift." And as history has proved over and over, once private morality falls, public virtue falls with it.[50]

All that was beautiful and noble and just in Europe was being overwhelmed by the "mighty torrent of French power." And the United States itself might soon fall prey to this French malignancy. Just look at what had happened in the last few years. The Napoleonic Wars had brought repeated disasters to this country in the seizure of American ships and cargoes, actions that threatened to cripple New England commerce. On November 21, 1806, Napoleon issued the Berlin Decree, which declared a blockade of Great Britain. Less than two months later Britain responded by issuing an order-in-council that barred all shipping from French coastal trade. Napoleon retaliated with the Milan Decree, promising to seize any foreign vessel that obeyed the British order. Then he ordered the seizure of American ships in French harbors.

Caught between these decrees and orders-in-council, American ships were stopped, searched, and seized, and when the USS *Chesapeake*, on its maiden voyage in June 1807, refused the demand of the British frigate *Leopard* to search the ship for deserters, the *Leopard* opened fire, killing three Americans. After being boarded and after four of her sailors had been removed, the crippled *Chesapeake* returned to port.

Furious, President Jefferson ordered British warships out of U.S. ports on July 12. Congress went further by passing the Embargo Act of 1807, which prohibited all vessels, foreign as well as American, from leaving the country.

The reaction in New England came swiftly and explosively. Merchants howled their pain as their commerce sank to its knees. Large coastal cities like Portsmouth suffered tremendous losses. With the state capital already moved to Concord and now the embargo cutting off its financial lifeblood, Portsmouth faced inevitable ruin.

Since 1808 was a presidential election year with James Madison running on the Republican ticket, Webster, like many others, saw the splendid opportunity that had opened up to them of reclaiming New Hampshire for the Federalist party. They were especially keen to win all the state offices as well as the congressional slate, and they knew that they could ill afford to bungle their chance.

Enraged and energized by recent events, Webster became more politically involved in this election than he had ever been before. His party welcomed his revitalized commitment and assigned him various tasks, including contacting his friends and clients and soliciting their support. "We have felt a good deal of

49. DW to Merrill, March 8, 1807, in *PC*, I, 92–93.
50. Ibid.; "Conversations with Charles Lanman," in *W&S*, XIII, 566.

alarm here about the Election—& are taking some pains to wake up our folks," he informed Samuel Smith, a leading manufacturer in Peterborough. "I am requested to write to you, & most devoutly to solicit your attention to the subject. The Federalists must be roused, or we shall lose the Election. *You must see to all the Towns around you.* . . . I am requested to urge the importance of this Election upon your consideration in the most urgent manner."[51]

He wrote many more letters in this vein and seemed obsessed with the need to stir every Federalist to action and drive out every Republican who held a state office. Since the embargo provided the best instrument to defeat Republicans, Webster focused on that "criminal act" to excite the electorate. He set about composing a pamphlet entitled "Considerations on the Embargo Laws." In it he argued at length the illegality of the law and used language that southerners later employed to express their anger with the federal government.

The states, he began, came together and formed a Union under the Constitution, surrendering some (but not all) of their powers in the process. The government so formed possesses delegated, limited powers, and those powers not expressly delegated to the central government are reserved to the states and the people. Is the power to lay an embargo expressly delegated? No. But what of the power to regulate commerce with foreign powers? "To regulate," Webster lectured, ". . . could never mean to destroy," and the embargo of 1807, which is "an unlimited suspension of commerce," will surely "produce the total annihilation of all the commerce of the country." The administration has resorted to it as "an Instrument of War. Its avowed object is, to reduce the powers of Europe to the necessity of complying with our terms." It is making war by embargo, and that is clearly unconstitutional.

American commerce, he went on, was not endangered by either the French decrees or British orders-in-council. Jefferson said that the safety of our ships, cargoes, and seamen prompted him to act as he did, but he is a liar. "The motive assigned for laying the Embargo, was never the true motive." It was intended as an act of war against Britain as a means of taking sides with France against England.

It is not material to consider, whether this partiality for France arises from the fear or the love of her. That it exists is certain. The administration party are perpetually singing the praises of the French Emperor. They rejoice in his successes, and justify and applaud his most enormous acts of injustice and oppression. Even when he marched his army to Spain, overturned its Government, traitorously dethroned its sovereign, and murdered one of its Princes, subjugated its provinces, and placed a plundering and bloodthirsty creature of his own on the throne of the last branch of the ill-fated House of Bourbon, they burst forth in exclamations of rapturous and unhallowed joy, at the progress of successful guilt and violence. They even blasphemed Heaven, and mocked it with diabolical gratitude, when they thanked God that the world was blessed with this detestable tyrant, and that society was like to regain its ancient peace and dignity under his iron sway!

51. DW to Smith, March 6, [1808], in *PC*, I, 101–102.

"Such is the Embargo," Webster thundered; "such the doubts of its constitutionality; such its obvious causes." And what will be its consequences? Destruction of our trade and war with Great Britain.[52]

The pamphlet was widely distributed, and its highly charged language undoubtedly had a tremendous influence on those who read it, given New England's spreading economic woes. It also enhanced Webster's reputation within the Federalist party. The state responded as expected by giving all seven of its electoral votes to the Federalist candidate for President, Charles Cotesworth Pinckney. To be sure, the margin of Federalist victory was slim—probably six hundred votes. Still, it proved very comforting to someone like Webster who had campaigned so vigorously for the past several months. The party also carried its congressional slate. With the exception of Vermont, all New England voted for Pinckney. Unfortunately the South and Middle Atlantic states went almost solidly for Madison, and he was elected to succeed Jefferson.[53]

This election was a good start for a rejuvenated Federalist party, even though the Republicans still hung on in Portsmouth. The victory, however, resulted more from the successful campaigning of such men as Daniel Webster than from the economic consequences of the embargo.[54] But the party still had a distance to go. The state elections the previous March had produced an overwhelming majority for the popular Republican governor, John Langdon, and more active young Federalists of the Webster caliber were needed if the party was ever to regain the statehouse.

The statehouse did come back into Federalist control in 1809, when Webster helped seat his friend Chief Justice Jeremiah Smith in the governor's chair.[55] Even more important, the Federalists won majorities in both the lower and upper houses of the legislature. Unfortunately Langdon returned the following year and unseated Smith. No doubt the repeal of the Embargo Act by the Nonintercourse Act[56] in the final days of Jefferson's administration helped Langdon in his election. Despite this Federalist loss, the two parties remained vigorous and fairly evenly matched for the next seven years.

For Webster the maintenance of Federalist strength and ascendancy required continued party involvement and activity. And he did his part. When he

52. "Considerations on the Embargo Laws, [July], 1808," in *W&S*, XV, 564–574.

53. Madison received 122 total electoral votes to Pinckney's 47. New York cast 6 of its votes for George Clinton. Arthur Schlesinger, Jr., and Fred Israel, eds., *History of American Presidential Elections* (New York, 1967), I, 246.

54. Turner, *The Ninth State*, p. 241. The antiembargo propaganda aroused voters, two thirds of whom were Federalists.

55. Webster and his friends induced Smith to resign from the bench. Why Smith would give up a secure nonpolitical position to risk a contest against a popular governor is not clear. Obviously Webster and his friends were very persuasive. Smith defeated Langdon by 369 votes. Turner, *The Ninth State*, p. 250.

56. The Nonintercourse Act of 1809 reopened trade with all countries except France and Britain. The act further declared that trade would be resumed with France and Britain once those countries repealed their decrees and orders-in-council.

heard that Boscawen might slip into Republican hands, he wrote his brother and urged his total commitment to the cause. "This will never do," he scolded. "Make Boscawen 'toe the mark' once more, as nobly as last year. I will not think you will fail in this Respect."[57]

He watched over other towns as well, alerting the faithful to the dangers of becoming apathetic. On July 3, 1810, he was appointed chairman of a four-member committee in Portsmouth to draft a communication to Federalist committees all over the state urging "influential men" to aid with "zeal & activity" the election of Federalists to Congress by all "honorable means" within their power. The memorandum was dated August 1, 1810, and its author warned that the "imperial Democrats in the next Congress, unless they are checked by a respectable federal minority, will, beyond doubt, have recourse to another Embargo, or some measure equally pernicious." Make no mistake. "The result of the election will depend on the labours of the several town Committees." Be sure that "every sound political man" does his duty.[58]

In addition to composing this memorandum, Webster wrote articles for the newspapers whenever he could afford the time from his law practice. For example, on February 24, 1810, he wrote a piece entitled "Look to the Money Chest!!!" for the Federalist sheet the Portsmouth *Oracle,* in which he contrasted the financial allowances to the secretary of state and his deputy by the Republican and Federalist administrations. Much of the material for this scathing attack on Republicans was obtained from his former law tutor Thomas W. Thompson, who had become New Hampshire's treasurer.[59]

Webster's assaults on New Hampshire Republicans and the Madison administration had gained such intensity and verbal firepower that many now regarded him as the voice of the Federalist party in the state. And because the Nonimportation Act forbade trade with Great Britain, New Englanders kept up their complaints against the administration, which Webster translated into written protests that soon attracted the attention of Federalists in surrounding states. Then, on May 1, 1810, Congress replaced the Nonimportation Act with Macon's Bill No. 2. This bill removed all trade restrictions but provided that if either France or Britain revoked its edicts, the President could reimpose nonintercourse against the other belligerent.

On April 29, 1810, at half past eleven in the evening and just two days before the passage of the Macon bill, Webster's first child, Grace Fletcher Webster, was born. The child was later described as having "uncommon intelligence, with a brilliant red and white complexion, and deep-set eyes, and hair as black as her father's." To the mother the child seemed close to God. She once said to a friend, "I wish I could feel the presence of God as little Grace seems to feel it." The family circle now complete with the arrival of this infant, the twenty-

57. DW to Ezekiel Webster, March 2, [1810], in *PC,* I, 116.
58. [To Federalist Committees in New Hampshire], in ibid., I, 119–120.
59. Thompson to Webster, February 17, 1810, ibid., 114–115.

eight-year-old Webster doted on the child, and she added immense joy and satisfaction to his life.[60]

The birth of his daughter necessarily refocused his attention on his legal practice, particularly as he again found himself short of cash. Notes came due, clients failed to pay him, and he frequently sent out appeals to family and friends for help. "If you have a dollar," he begged Ezekiel, "you must send it. . . . Whatever money you send me, or whosoever, I will replay at Amherst. This you may be sure of. If you can & will furnish me with some present aid, you need not go to Boston to see about the other two notes, until we meet at Amherst." Ezekiel bailed his brother out as often as possible. Indeed the two brothers frequently worked together, and Ezekiel looked after not only family affairs but their other legal business outside Portsmouth.

Because of Webster's increased reputation as a lawyer, the lower house of the New Hampshire legislature appointed him, together with Jeremiah Mason and John Goddard, to revise the state's criminal code and prepare police laws for the regulation of the prison in Charlestown. The three men were paid for their work, but the resulting revised code was never adopted, no doubt because of controversy over the revision and the disposition of documents used by the commissioners.[61] But Webster's appointment to this commission constituted a signal honor and surely indicated that not only Federalists but Republicans as well entertained enormous respect for both his political and his legal skills.

That esteem prompted the Federalists to invite him to address the Washington Benevolent Society on Independence Day 1812. They could not have made a better choice because no one else could speak more forcefully about all the momentous events that had occurred over the past year than Black Dan. For example, Napoleon had tricked Madison into believing that he would lift his decrees and the President had witlessly played into his hand by reimposing trade restrictions against Great Britain; then a group of young, nationalistic congressmen called War Hawks had conspired in Washington to force Madison to ask Congress for a declaration of war; finally Madison had capitulated to the pressure.[62] Congress declared war against Great Britain on June 18, 1812. With virtually all New England in arms *against* this war Webster was called upon to articulate its wrath so that the entire country would understand that the region wanted no part of it.

The society purposely took the name of George Washington in order to assert its contention that Federalists, not Republicans, were the true heirs of the first President's legacy, that they revered, practiced, and endeavored to

60. Curtis, *Webster,* I, 85; "Sketch of Mrs. G. F. Webster," in Webster, ed., *Private Correspondence,* I, 441.

61. Samuel Sparhawk to Webster, June 26, 1811, Peter Thacher to Webster, July 6, 1811, in *PC,* I, 124–125 and editorial note.

62. His message to Congress listed seizure of American ships, impressment of seamen, and Indian raids along the frontier instigated by Great Britain as the reasons for going to war.

perpetuate his principles, something Jefferson, Madison, and their minions had betrayed. There were many such societies throughout New England, all Federalist, and the members of these associations now proclaimed themselves the "Friends of Peace." Thus, while the Republicans planned to hold patriotic celebrations in Portsmouth on July 4 to fire up public enthusiasm for the war, the Federalists meant to denounce it in the name of liberty.

On July 4, 1812, an immense crowd turned out for the Republican rally. At the same time the Washington Benevolent Society marched through the streets escorted by the "Gilman Blues" to the Reverend Mr. Ballou's meetinghouse. There they heard an invocation, the reading of Washington's Farewell Address, and then Black Dan himself.

"It is in the power of every generation," Webster began, "to make themselves, in some degree, partakers in the deeds, and in the fame of their ancestors, by adopting their principles, and studying their examples. Wherever history records the acts of men, the past has more or less influence on the present."

Not a particularly rousing beginning when it is read, but it must be remembered that the only version of the address extant is the one later printed as corrected and amended by Webster. Like Washington, he took great care over what appeared in print over his name. And because he was such a fine, thoughtful, and painstaking writer, he altered the printed address so that its intellectual content would immediately seize the attention of the reader.

"We come to take counsel of the dead," he continued. "From the tumults and passions that agitate the living world, we withdraw to the tomb, to listen to the dictates of departed wisdom." We come to listen to the sainted Washington. Then Webster went on to extol the first President's virtues and services, especially his policy of neutrality and the fact that when an embargo was imposed during his administration, it was "legitimately" limited to sixty days.

Here was another theme that Webster was to play repeatedly in his speeches and writings in the future. A free country had been established under the Constitution, thanks in large measure to the wisdom, the genius, and the patriotism of George Washington. The first President played the essential role in creating a permanent Union, and that must never be forgotten.

To Webster, George Washington epitomized everything a head of state should be; the "Father of His Country" always remained Black Dan's personal hero, his beau ideal. Furthermore, in taking counsel from the dead, Webster asserted in this speech his absolute commitment to and reverence for the values and principles received from the past. Those values and principles must never be forgotten, neglected, or replaced, he said. We forget them at our peril.

Then he struck another important theme in his thinking. "The Federal Constitution was adopted for no single reason so much as for the protection of commerce." Americans should never forget that commerce formed the central basis for the establishment of the Union under the Constitution. Its protection must be preserved. If it is destroyed, our free government will fall with it. And that protection was unlike a convict who is "committed to the safe-keeping of his jailer. It was not for close confinement. It was for encouragement, for protection and manly defence." Now we have a war "professedly commenced for the defence of the commercial interest," but "the voice of the whole mercantile interest is . . . against the war, which is declared to be undertaken, at so much hazard of blood and treasure, for their benefit."

What can be done? What does duty dictate? At this point Webster pronounced his unwavering commitment to the Union, even though he knew there were many voices raised throughout New England calling for immediate secession.

> With respect to the war, in which we are now involved, the course which our principles require us to pursue cannot be doubtful. It is now the law of the land, and as such we are bound to regard it. Resistance and insurrection form no parts of our creed. The disciples of Washington are neither tyrants *in* power, nor rebels *out*. If we are taxed, to carry on this war, we shall disregard certain distinguished examples, and shall pay. If our personal services are required, we shall yield them to the precise extent of our Constitutional liability. At the same time, the world may be assured that we know our rights, and shall exercise them. We shall express our opinions on this, as on every other measure of government, I trust without passion—I am certain without fear. We have yet to learn that the extravagant progress of pernicious measures abrogates the duty of opposition, or that the interest of our native land is to be abandoned, by us, in the hour of her thickest dangers, and sorest necessity. By the exercise of our Constitutional right of suffrage, by the peaceable remedy of election, we shall seek to restore wisdom to our councils, and peace to our country.

> Nor will we shut our eyes to the prospect of an alliance with the French tyrant. "French brotherhood is an idea big with horror and abomination." We will never allow the "unhallowed hosts" of France to "profane the ground where the bones of New England's ancestors lie enshrined. There is no common character, nor can there be a common interest, between the Protestants, the Dissenters, the Puritans of New England, and the Papists, the Infidels, the Atheists of France; or between our free, republican institutions, and the most merciless tyranny that ever Heaven suffered to afflict mankind."[63]

This last remark surely hit his audience with such force that it roared its approval. Indeed, when it was printed in the Portsmouth *Oracle* on July 11, the reporter who heard it declared that Webster delivered it "in a more impressive and eloquent manner than we ever witnessed on a similar occasion." The address went through two editions, other newspapers in New England reprinted it, and Federalists throughout the region expressed their astonishment at its power and truth. They marked in their memories the name of this thirty-year-old man and predicted his imminent rise to national prominence.

By this time Webster had learned the secret of oratory—or so he later

63. "Address at Portsmouth," in *W&S*, XV, 583–998. It is interesting that the address concludes with the words "when they [the sons of New England] shall, for the last time, behold the light of that sun, or look on the verdure of these fields, it shall not be with the eyes of slaves and subjects of an impious despotism." Some of the expressions of this address appear in later speeches, most notably his second reply in the famous Webster-Hayne debate in 1830.

claimed. It is said, he declared, that " 'he is a man of talent that can make a thing move.' And after all, say I, he is an orator that can make me think as he thinks, and feel as he feels."[64] That criterion is precisely what Daniel Webster met— over and over.

Webster was immediately appointed the Portsmouth delegate to a meeting of Rockingham County Federalists scheduled to convene in Brentwood on August 5. But before he left for Brentwood, Webster received an indication that he might be placed on a committee to prepare a memorial to the President, so he decided to draft a memorial ahead of time and bring it with him to the convention. As anticipated, he was chosen chairman of the committee to draw up the document with four other men, one of whom was his former tutor Thomas W. Thompson. The committee approved his draft with slight changes and reported it to the floor of the convention.

To a constantly cheering group of delegates he read what was to be called the Rockingham Memorial. It proved to be the "ultimate statement of New England Federalism." It was restrained, carefully worded not to sound disrespectful of the President, and very effective. It detailed the commercial suffering of New England, denied any grievance over impressment, and asked for the reasons that had led to a declaration of war. It carefully but respectfully dismissed the reasons Madison had cited in his message to Congress, insisting that the French had been just as guilty as the British with regard to seizures, confiscations, and burnings. It also noted that unlike the French, the British had recently rescinded their orders-in-council. "Give us but to see," Webster pleaded, "that this war hath clear justice, necessity, and expediency on its side, and we are ready to pour out our treasure, and our blood in its prosecution."

He went on to raise the specter of disunion. If disunion did come, he warned, it will someday happen "when one portion of the country undertakes to control, to regulate, and to sacrifice the interest of another." It was a frightening but real apprehension on the part of Black Dan. "We shrink from the separation of the states, as an event fraught with incalculable evils."[65]

The memorial, later signed by more than fifteen hundred citizens of Rockingham County, was quoted extensively not only in New England papers but up and down the Atlantic coastline. The Boston, New York, and Philadelphia press gave it a national audience. Later on southerners also took notice. As far as Federalists were concerned, Daniel Webster had reached national eminence. It was only necessary now to send him forth as the party's spokesman to the seat of the central government.

Over the past few months he had articulated what many most sincerely believed in New England, and he had articulated it powerfully and clearly because he believed in it profoundly. This nation, according to Webster, had created a miracle in the form of free government based on the Constitution,

64. DW to Reverend John Brazer, November 10, 1828, in Webster, ed., *Private Correspondence*, I, 465.

65. *PS*, I, 3, 6–17.

which had been established primarily to protect commerce. George Washington was the hero who made it happen, and the Federalist party was and is the means by which it can be preserved. It would be preserved through peace and commerce. The Republicans had shattered both, and the nation now stood in grave peril.

Federalists in New Hampshire and elsewhere who read and thought about what Webster had written concluded straightaway that this young man belonged in Washington, where his voice might help restore sanity to the national councils. Although he was virtually skipping to the top of the party hierarchy without the necessary apprenticeship at the state level, nevertheless, for the good of the country, for the preservation of all those principles the Federalists so dearly loved, he had to be elevated.

Accordingly the Rockingham Convention placed Webster in nomination for a congressional seat. When Jeremiah Smith first mentioned the possibility of his nomination to Webster, the young man refused it. He said he was poor and must attend to his business as a lawyer. But the next day he changed his mind. He would not decline a seat in Congress if elected, he declared. "As to the law, I must attend to that too—but honor after all is worth more than money."[66]

Two months later, on October 7, the state Federalist convention meeting in Gilmanton officially nominated Webster as one of six candidates to represent New Hampshire in the lower house of the U.S. Congress. Since Madison was the Republican candidate for a second term, the convention denounced him and "his" war, drew up appropriate resolutions, and gave its support for President to De Witt Clinton, the so-called Peace Candidate, who had been nominated in New York and endorsed by many Federalists, even though he was a Republican. Clinton, they thought, stood a better chance of winning against Madison than any man in their own party.

The campaign proved nastier than usual. On October 13, 1812, the *New Hampshire Gazette,* a Republican sheet, labeled Timothy Pickering, secretary of state under both Washington and Adams, a "Benedict Arnold." Webster immediately jumped in and offered to represent Pickering in a libel suit. A suit was duly filed but later dropped.[67]

With the exception of Vermont, Clinton captured all New England. New Hampshire voters balloted on a statewide basis, and of 34,800 votes cast, Clinton took 20,386. All six elected candidates for Congress running at large were Federalists. Webster received 18,597, right behind Roger Vose of Walpole, who placed first with 18,611. It was a sweep for the party, the first of an unbroken string of victories that continued for the next four years.[68]

Although Clinton also captured New York and New Jersey, he failed to take

66. Plumer, "Reminiscences of Webster," in *W&S*, XVII, 547.

67. DW to John Pickering, October 15, 1812, in *PC*, I, 133. John Pickering was Timothy's son.

68. Turner, *The Ninth State*, pp. 275–277; Lynn Warren Turner, "The Election of 1812," in Schlesinger and Israel, eds., *History of American Presidential Elections*, I, 261–262; Lyman, *Public and Private Life of Webster*, II, 45; Fuess, *Webster*, I, 146–147.

Pennsylvania and consequently lost the election. The South stood solidly behind Madison, and together with Vermont and Pennsylvania the total of its votes gave him a narrow victory in the electoral college. The final tally was 128 to 89.

President Madison had not bothered to respond to Webster's memorial. Now he would hear his voice in Congress. And it would be frequent and quarrelsome and aggravating.

5

Congress

WEBSTER set out for Washington by "mail coach" in May and headed for Boston, Hartford, New Haven, and then the "very long" and tedious journey to New York by stagecoach. He traveled only a few miles a day. The roads were poor; the coach was cramped and uncomfortable; the food and lodging along the way were frequently abysmal. In 1813 it usually took almost a week just to get from Boston to New York, depending on the weather and road conditions, but by the 1830s that time had been reduced to a day and a half and cost ten to twelve dollars. When the railroad arrived by the 1840s, it took only half a day. A fully loaded stagecoach would have nine passengers riding inside on three seats and one passenger riding outside next to the driver.[1] The journey could be and frequently was a nightmare.

When Webster entered the House of Representatives[2] on May 24, 1813, at the start of the special session of the Thirteenth Congress, the nation had been at war for almost a year, and the war to date had been a disaster. General William Hull led an invasion of Canada that stalled and turned tail with the fall of Michilimackinac on July 17, 1812. He returned to Detroit and then unwisely surrendered to an inferior force of British soldiers and their Indian allies out of fear for the safety of the city's inhabitants.[3] Other invasions proved equally disastrous when American troops refused to cross the border, citing constitutional principles. American ships lost control of Lake Champlain after first achieving early naval victories. Then, on June 1, 1813, the frigate USS *Chesapeake* departed Boston and once at sea sustained murderous cannon fire from a British frigate. The captain of the *Chesapeake,* James Lawrence, and many crewmen on board were killed. The ship was seized and sailed to Halifax. The British blockaded the entire eastern coast from New York southward but ex-

---

1. Lyman, *Public and Private Life of Webster,* II, 45–46; Larkin, *Everyday Life,* pp. 205, 223, 225.

2. Webster was one of six congressmen at large from New Hampshire. The others were Bradbury Cilley of Nottingham, William Hale of Dover, Samuel Smith of Peterboro, Roger Vose of Walpole, and Jeduthun Wilcox of Orford.

3. For the miliary history of this war, see Donald R. Hickey, *The War of 1812: A Forgotten Conflict* (Urbana, Ill., 1989) and Reginald Horsman, *The War of 1812* (New York, 1969).

cluded New England in the hope of encouraging that section to secede from the Union.[4]

Napoleon's retreat from Moscow also added to the gloomy war news for the Madison administration. Thus, when the Russian czar offered to mediate a peace accord between the United States and Great Britain, Madison jumped at the chance. Once again he acted rashly and in haste. Without waiting to discover Britain's reaction to the proposal he rushed to accept it.

The special session of Congress began on May 24, and Webster arrived in Washington on Saturday, May 22. What he saw as he approached the city profoundly disappointed him. "The general appearance of this Country," he reported, is most discouraging. "It has not the wealth nor the People which I expected. From Baltimore to this place, the whole distance, almost, you travel thro woods, & in a worse road than you ever saw." A few "plantations" appear "tolerable well;—all the rest is a desert." He never believed he could see such wretched roads. It truly shocked him.[5]

Midsummer discomfort had already descended upon Washington by the time Webster arrived, and with few trees or shady groves to protect an unwary visitor the intense heat and humidity of the place quickly became oppressive. In many places the swampy terrain added to the misery. The smell of the city frequently caused nausea because of the garbage littering the streets near the center of town. A city of vast distances laid out in a grid of streets and diagonal avenues looked empty and desolate. Government buildings were spotted at great distances from one another, with the Capitol and the President's House located a mile apart and connected by an avenue so muddy during bad weather as to be virtually impassable.[6]

Webster found living accommodations at Crawford's Hotel in nearby Georgetown, where he enjoyed the companionship of his former law instructor Christopher Gore, who had been appointed senator of Massachusetts to fill a vacancy caused by the resignation of James Lloyd, and Senator Rufus King of New York, whom Webster had met in Gore's office. The following month Jeremiah Mason, recently elected to the Senate by the New Hampshire legislature to fill a vacancy, joined this congenial group. They frequently commiserated with one another about the strength of their Republican opposition. Federalists numbered only 68 men in the House and 10 in the Senate, compared with the

---

4. "Let this war terminate as it may," wrote Representative Nathaniel Macon to Joseph H. Nicholson, "it must produce an effect either to raise or lessen the national character, if the latter, it will be almost fatal to the navigating and commercial interest, neither of which can be maintained without an established reputation to defend their rights." Macon to Nicholson, January 8, 1814, Nicholson Papers, LC.

5. DW to Samuel Ayer Bradley, May 28, 1813, in *PC*, I, 141.

6. Constance McLaughlin Green, *Washington: Village and Capital, 1800–1878* (Princeton, 1962), Wilhelmus Bogart Bryan, *A History of the National Capital* (New York, 1914), and James S. Young, *The Washington Community, 1800–1828* (New York, 1966) provide excellent information on Washington during the early nineteenth century. See also John W. Reps, *Washington on View: The Nation's Capital since 1790* (Chapel Hill and London, 1991).

Republican majority of 114 and 26. King clearly stood at the head of his party and would run for President in the next election on the Federalist ticket. His opinions, advice, and influence counted for a great deal, and Webster assiduously cultivated his friendship.

When the dark-faced young representative arrived for the first day of the first session of the Thirteenth Congress, he found that "some friend" had reserved a seat for him. Immediately to his left sat Joseph Lewis and Daniel Sheffey, both from Virginia, and to his right Timothy Pitkin of Connecticut and William Gaston from North Carolina. As he looked around the elliptically shaped chamber with its fluted Corinthian pillars draped with velvet, he could spot any number of distinguished colleagues, some of whom he verbally confronted and challenged in the years to come.

Unquestionably the most important person in the room was the Speaker, Henry Clay of Kentucky. Seated in the heavily ornate Speaker's chair on a dais under a canopy fit for an Eastern potentate, Clay had fashioned his office into the most powerful position in Washington after the President. He had been born in Virginia, studied law with Chancellor George Wythe, and moved to Lexington, Kentucky, where he quickly emerged as his state's most promising politician. On the first ballot of the first day of the Twelfth Congress he had been elected Speaker. A War Hawk intent on driving the Madison administration into war with Great Britain, he and his fellow War Hawk congressmen from the South and West had contrived to coerce Madison into capitulating to their demands. Tall, cadaverous, fair-haired, with a high forehead, a prominent, slightly arched, and protruding nose, small blue-gray eyes, and a wide mouth that looked like a long slash across his face, he exuded a manner that was friendly, congenial, and authoritative. When he spoke, and he did so rather frequently, as was quite novel for a Speaker, he regaled the members with a repertory of gestures that any professional actor would envy. He shrugged, grimaced, and twisted "his features, & indeed his whole body in the most dreadful scowls and contortions." He spoke with his entire body: arms, legs, torso, head, and hands. And his voice. "Whoever heard one more melodious," commented one man. "There was a depth of tone in it, a volume, a compass, a rich and tender harmony, which invested all he said with majesty." His voice, remembered George Bancroft, "was music itself." And what he said frequently reduced his audience to tears or uncontrolled fits of laughter. He was by turns eloquent, often dramatic, sometimes playful, witty, and, when necessary, devastating. A social animal, he drank, gambled, swore, attended parties with a woman on each arm, and fascinated both sexes. "When I look upon his manly & bold countenance, & meet his frank & eloquent eye," wrote Edward Bates, a future representative from Missouri and attorney general in the Lincoln administration, to his wife, "I feel an emotion little short of enthusiasm in his cause." Everyone admired Henry Clay; few could resist his seductive personal appeal.[7]

7. William Plumer, Jr., to William Plumer, Sr., February 12, 1820, in Everett Somerville Brown, ed., *The Missouri Compromises and Presidential Politics, 1820–1825* (St. Louis, 1926), pp. 8–9;

John C. Calhoun also decorated the roster of this Congress, but he had little seductive appeal. Still, what a formidable mind he possessed: cold, hard, analytical, brilliant, simply irresistible. The force and power of his arguments in debate flattened his opponents. Unlike Clay, who brought his entire body into play when he spoke, Calhoun hardly moved at all. There was no need; "it would have been out of place." His words provided all the action necessary. They were terse, clear, and direct. His arguments were elaborately constructed, profoundly deliberate, totally analytical. His style was chaste yet vigorous, his logic close and compelling. Unlike Clay's voice, which was "soft as a lute or full as a trumpet," a voice of "wonderful modulation, sweetness, and power," Calhoun's voice was sharp, reedy, somewhat nasal, and he spoke quickly in near-staccato fashion "but with such a clear enunciation that every word was distinctly heard."[8] Born in South Carolina, educated at Yale, trained in the law, and a zealous nationalist, Calhoun served a brief term as a South Carolina legislator before coming to Congress in 1811 as a War Hawk. He provided Clay with enormous moral and verbal support in bringing about a declaration of war.

Both these worthies were to play long and important roles not only in the history of the nation but in Webster's development as a politician and statesman. They were not the only ones. A rather large number of distinguished men graced the Thirteenth Congress in 1813. They included William H. Crawford of Georgia, soon to become secretary of war and then secretary of the treasury; John Forsyth of Georgia; Timothy Pickering of Massachusetts; John W. Taylor of New York; Nathaniel Macon of North Carolina; Langdon Cheves of South Carolina; Felix Grundy and John Sevier of Tennessee; and James Barbour and Philip P. Barbour of Virginia. Others, who were less distinguished but whose careers one way or another later impacted on Webster's, included George M. Bibb and William T. Barry of Kentucky and Abner Lacock, Charles Ingersoll, and Samuel Ingham of Pennsylvania. Many years later Webster remembered back to these days and the pleasure he derived from talking to the ancients in Congress whose memories of the past went back beyond the Revolution, men like Pickering, John Findlay of Pennsylvania, and James Schureman of New Jersey. Deeply enamored of the nation's colonial and revolutionary past, Webster could not learn enough about those distant times. "I was young and eager to learn; they had well-stored memories, and were willing to talk." The memory of those days stayed with him to the end of his life. "Oh, I shall never hear such story-telling again!" he exclaimed.[9]

Because he had enormous confidence in his ability to move an audience

---

"Anecdotes of Henry Clay," Manuscript Department, Filson Club, Louisville, Kentucky; George Bancroft, "A Few Words about Henry Clay," *Century Magazine*, VIII (July 1885), p. 480; Bates to Julia Bates, February 25, 1828, Edward Bates Papers, Virginia Historical Society, Richmond; Remini, *Clay*, passim.

8. Nathan Sargent, *Public Men and Events* (Philadelphia, 1874), II, 34; Benton, *Thirty Years' View*, II, 98; Remini, *Clay*, p. 514.

9. DW to Richard M. Blatchford, February 4, 1849, in *W&S*, XVIII, 296.

and command its attention and interest, Webster undoubtedly expected to create enough riveting yet powerful sounds in the House to win a position of leadership. The Federalists did not have many orators in their arsenal to send up against the likes of Clay and Calhoun. Daniel Webster therefore might be just the man they needed to generate the right amount of firepower and become the party's spokesman in the House.

The first few days of the session involved listening to the President's message and carving it up and delivering its pieces to several committees. Madison reported that the Treasury was empty and that additional taxes were necessary to prosecute the war. The House resolved itself into a Committee of the Whole and heard Speaker Clay deliver a "furious speech" over the manner in which the war had been waged by Great Britain. Webster was chosen to sit on the Foreign Relations Committee, no doubt in the belief that he could create little mischief, especially since Clay's chief henchman, Calhoun, chaired the committee.[10]

Over the next several weeks Webster watched what was going on around him, and he waited. "The time for us to be put on the stage and moved by the wires, has not yet come," he commented. "I suppose the 'show' is now in preparation, and at the proper time the farce of legislating will be exhibited." He could not be sure that the "Democrats"—or "Demos," as he regularly called the opposition—would "hang together" or that taxes would not be opposed. "But before any thing is attempted to be done here, it must be arranged."[11]

It must be arranged! He knew how the science and the art of politics were played. He might come from one of the less important states in terms of political influence and lack legislative and parliamentary experience, but that did not mean he was a novice to the ways of seasoned politicians. He understood the game very well. The trouble was he could not play it very well.

Webster was never a good legislator. No bills of any moment ever bore his name. His forte was oratory, and that was what his party expected of him. Little more.[12]

On May 26, like a dutiful new member of Congress, Webster hied himself to the White House to "make my bow to the President." And as he had been by the city of Washington, he was unimpressed by what he saw. "I did not like his looks, any better than I like his Administration," Webster admitted to Edward Cutts, senator from New Hampshire. The features on the President's face clearly registered "Embargo, Non-Intercourse & War." Webster went to only one "levee" during these early weeks. It involved bowing to Dolley and President Madison, "if he comes in your way," and mixing with the foreign ministers, heads "and tails of departments," members of Congress, and army and navy personnel.

10. DW to Ezekiel Webster, May 26, 1813, DW to Samuel A. Bradley, May 28, 1813, Charles March to DW, May 31, 1813, in *PC*, I, 141–143; *Annals of Congress*, 13th Congress, 1st Session, p. 109ff. Webster's brother, Ezekiel, thought the President's message "very warlike." Ezekiel Webster to DW, June 5, 1813, in *PC*, I, 145.

11. DW to Bingham, June 4, 1813, in *W&S*, XVII, 233.

12. Wentworth, "Congressional Reminiscences," pp. 36–37.

"You stay from five minutes to an hour, as you please; eat and drink what you can catch, without danger of surfeit, and if you can luckily find your hat and stick, then take French leave; and that's going to the 'levee.' "[13]

Webster made his House debut on June 10, when he introduced a series of five resolutions that had the potential of embarrassing the President in his conduct of foreign affairs. He wanted specific information about when and under what circumstances the administration had first learned about Napoleon's supposed intention of revoking the Berlin and Milan decrees. Some congressmen believed that Madison had known as early as 1811 and had kept it secret for fear that Great Britain might respond by revoking its orders-in-council and thus remove the pretext for war. Had Madison withheld this information? Had the nation been tricked into declaring war?[14]

A four-day debate over the resolutions ensued, during which Webster himself spoke only briefly. He did not deliver any set speech, as such, when he presented them. He probably thought it best to bide his time and wait until the big guns of the House on both sides had exhausted their arguments and then step in and blast away at the administration in a heroic effort.[15]

If that was his plan, he miscalculated. Calhoun rightly viewed the resolutions as a possible rallying point for the opponents of the war. Indeed the resolutions were printed in the New York *Evening Post* and the New York *Spectator*, both with favorable editorial comments.[16] Calhoun therefore wisely decided to get rid of this nuisance by letting the resolutions pass unamended.[17] On June 21, just at the moment when Webster had risen to speak, some of the chief "Demos" "manifested a disposition" to vote for the resolutions "just as they were." Wisdom dictated that he keep his mouth shut, and so the young man on the eve of his first intended oratorical triumph slumped back into his seat and watched as his resolutions passed one by one.[18] Perhaps as compensation, he,

13. DW to Cutts, May 26, 1813, in *PC*, I, 139; DW to Bingham, June 4, 1813, in *W&S*, XVII, 234.

14. *Annals of Congress*, 13th Congress, 1st Session, pp. 149–151.

15. Webster clearly states that he had prepared to give "a little speech." DW to Ezekiel Webster, June 28, 1813, in *W&S*, XVII, 236. The New York *Evening Post* confirmed this intention on June 25, 1813. And there are "Notes and Memoranda for a Speech on My Resolutions," printed in *Century Magazine*, L (July 1895), pp. 468–471. Webster said that Congressmen Alexander C. Hanson, Thomas P. Grosvenor, Thomas J. Oakley, Joseph Pearson, and several others "made excellent Speeches." DW to March, June 21, 1813, in *W&S*, XVI, 22.

16. The *Post* article appeared on June 14, and the *Spectator's* on June 16. And "a friend" very considerably had them forwarded to the New York *Commercial Advertiser* for publication; Webster also asked Charles March to send copies of the newspaper for distribution around the Portsmouth, Concord, and Boston areas. DW to Charles March, June 10, 1813, in *W&S*, XVI, 20. Webster himself delighted in the attention his resolutions had elicited. "Already do our Citizens bow with respect to *The Mover of the Resolutions*," he wrote. DW to Charles March, June 14, 1813, in *PC*, I, 150.

17. Calhoun informed Webster that he and his friends would vote for the resolutions. "They have acted very strangely," commented Webster. DW to Charles March, June 21, 1813, in *PC*, I, 151; *Calhoun Papers*, I, 169–177.

18. *Annals of Congress*, 13th Congress, 1st Session, pp. 307–311.

along with John Rhea of Tennessee, were selected by the Speaker to "carry the Resolutions to the Palace."[19]

Webster delighted in what he believed was intense embarrassment by the "Palace" over the course of recent events. "There cannot be much sleep in the White-house about this time," he remarked.[20] He and Rhea dutifully attended the President. "I found him in his bed, sick of a fever," a nightcap on his head and his wife, Dolley, watching over him. Webster handed the President his resolutions with bemused satisfaction that "he will find *no relief* from my prescription." Madison said little as he took the document. "He merely answered that they would be attended to." The young man came away from the "Palace" convinced that "poor Madison," as he called him, "does not know what to do. . . . Never was man sinking faster."[21]

Despite Webster's lost opportunity to deliver his maiden speech on the House floor, he did impress his colleagues enough to win a place on an important Federalist committee. It was, he noted, "a kind of Committee to superintend our concerns," or steering committee, and included such notables as Timothy Pickering of Massachusetts, Thomas P. Grosvenor and Thomas J. Oakley of New York, and William Gaston of North Carolina, among others, for a total of thirteen.[22]

During the weeks Webster waited for Madison's response he suffered with the heat and humidity of a particularly bad Washington summer and found himself "getting out of sorts." For a New England man any congressional session that lasted into July boded ill. "So late is the period of the Session, so hot the season, so languid is everybody" that nothing important can be done. He finally "determined not to remain here more than ten days," he informed his brother on July 4, although he did feel obliged "in decency" to wait for Madison's report in order to see if "supplementary questions are necessary."[23] He finally made up

19. Ibid., p. 311; DW to Jedidiah Morse, June 28, 1813, in *PC*, I, 154. Rhea had requested that the President provide a copy of the orders-in-council which is probably why Clay included him as a messenger to carry the resolutions to Madison.

20. DW to Charles March, June 10, 1813, in *PC*, I, 148. It is interesting that Webster referred to the President's House—which is what it was usually called—as the White House. This letter is one of the earliest, but not *the* earliest, known reference to the mansion as the White House. A few days later he again referred to "the little occupant of the great White House." DW to Charles March, June 14, 1813, in *PC*, I, 150. See Remini, "Becoming a National Symbol: The White House in the Early Nineteenth Century," in Frank Freidel and William Pencak, eds., *The White House: The First Two Hundred Years* (Boston, 1994) pp. 23–24.

21. DW to Ezekiel Webster, June 28, 1813, in *W&S*, XVII, 236; DW to Charles March, June 24, 28, 1813, in *PC*, I, 152, 153.

22. The others were William Reed of Massachusetts, William Baylies of Massachusetts, Elisha R. Potter of Rhode Island, Timothy Pitkin of Connecticut, Richard Stockton of New Jersey, Henry M. Ridgely of Delaware, Alexander C. Hanson of Maryland, and Daniel Sheffey of Virginia. See DW to Ezekiel Webster, July 4, 1813, in *PC*, I, 155. Earlier Webster had described Grosvenor and Oakley as "very good fellows" who could be relied on "to give us a lift. Hanson is a hero," he added. DW to Charles March, June 7, 1813, in *W&S*, XVI, 19.

23. DW to March, July 6, 1813, in *W&S*, XVI, 24; DW to Ezekiel Webster, July 4, 1813, in *PC*, I, 155.

his mind to depart Washington on Sunday, July 11, but when he heard that Madison would have the report ready no later than Monday, the twelfth, he decided to wait a few days longer.[24]

The President submitted his report on the appointed day. It was written by Secretary of State James Monroe, whose biographer has aptly described it as a "carefully woven fabric of equivocation and evasion" that did not even begin to answer Webster's questions. Naturally the report denied prior knowledge of French intention to revoke the decrees. The whole messy business had been fabricated by the French, it read. Since the report was secret, the Federalist press lost a wonderful opportunity to shoot it full of holes for its "equivocation and evasion" and hold the administration up to public scorn.[25] After reading it, Webster referred to the document as "Munroes [sic] Jesuitical answer."[26]

Webster deserted Washington while Congress still debated a tax bill that the President deemed essential for the prosecution of the war. He felt both disappointed that there had not been a full-scale "general battle" on the conduct of the war and bored by the debates over disputed House elections in Virginia and Tennessee. Not a few times he wrote to friends, "We have done noth'g today, of any importance."[27]

Webster could take little pride in his initial experience as a United States congressman. He had said and done nothing of particular moment. His resolutions brought him some attention, enough to win a place on his party's steering committee, but that hardly set him apart in as meaningful a way as he might have hoped. His partisan Federalist political stance was always in evidence, and in every instance he voted as his party expected. In that sense he was no different from any number of his colleagues. Webster would have a long way to go in ensuing sessions to reach the level of involvement in congressional business his ambition had already set.

It is interesting and instructive that nowhere in his personal correspondence did Webster mention the fact that his wife was pregnant with their second child and due to deliver in July. He made no mention of this in connection with his anxiety to leave Washington. Surely it had something to do with his haste and concern about getting home. His silence was no doubt due to the delicacy and circumspection in which most men in the early nineteenth century discussed their home life. Anything dealing remotely with sex or "female concerns" was simply not permissible in personal correspondence. In any event, his second child, Daniel Fletcher Webster, was born at half past eight o'clock in the morning, on July 23, 1813, approximately ten days after he left Washington. Fletcher, as the family called the boy, was the only child (of an eventual total of five) to survive the father.

24. DW to March, July 10, 1813, in W&S, XVI, 25.

25. For the report, dated July 12, 1813, see ASPFR, III, 608–612, and Harry Ammon, James Monroe (New York, 1971), p. 321.

26. DW to Richard Stockton, July 23, 1813, in PC, I, 156.

27. DW to March, June 8, 9, 11, 15, 28, July 6, 1813, in W&S, XVI, 19–21, 23, 24.

Throughout the remainder of the summer and fall the young congressman devoted himself to the needs of his family and his law practice. He rode a four-county circuit during his stay at home, attending the courts of common pleas and the superior court of judicature. Because of his expected and probably extended absences in Washington, and in order to protect his law practice, he had taken Timothy Farrar, Jr., son of Chief Justice Timothy Farrar of the New Hampshire Court of Common Pleas, as a partner on March 24, 1813. The twenty-five-year-old Farrar had read law and clerked with Webster and proved to be an able associate.

Webster also helped obtain the incorporation of the Rockingham Bank in Portsmouth. He had a lively interest in banking almost from the moment he entered the legal profession, and this interest never abated despite some difficult and embarrassing moments he experienced in serving the needs of banks. He actively campaigned for the incorporation among his friends in the New Hampshire legislature, assuring them that a favorable action would "gratify the inclinations, & promote the interest, of the most active, *useful & zealous* men in this place; on whom we are chiefly to rely hereafter."[28] In November 1813 the Rockingham Bank received its charter.

Returning to Washington for the second session of the Thirteenth Congress, which began on December 6, Webster arrived three weeks late, on December 28.[29] The first news to greet him on his arrival was word that Portsmouth had suffered a catastrophic fire on December 22 and that his house was one of 108 residences consumed in the blaze. When the fire began, a neighbor by the name of Perry spotted flames on the roof of the Webster house, and he rushed into the house and seized Grace by the hand.

"Mrs. Webster, don't be agitated—don't be alarmed, Mrs. Webster."

"I am not alarmed, Mr. Perry," she responded. "Why should I be? What's the matter?"

"Don't be alarmed, Mrs. Webster—for Heaven's sake, don't be alarmed," Perry insisted, "there is no danger."

"Danger of what," cried the startled lady.

"My dear madam [,] don't be alarmed, *but your house is all on fire, and the roof must be falling in by this time.*"[30]

Fortunately Grace and the children escaped harm and found shelter in the home of Senator Jeremiah Mason. But the Webster house, uninsured and valued at six thousand dollars, plus his library and personal belongings, was totally consumed in the blaze. This so-called Great Fire occurred at seven-thirty in the evening in a barn belonging to the Woodward family, on the corner of Church and Court streets, just back of Webster's residence. Fanned by a light wind, the flames spread rapidly and destroyed some 272 buildings, including private

28. DW to Thomas W. Thompson, [October 1813], in *PC*, I, 157–158.
29. *Annals of Congress*, 13th Congress, 2d Session, p. 812.
30. March, *Webster*, p. 41 note.

homes, shops, and service stores. Not until five the following morning was the fire finally extinguished.[31]

Only the safety of his family "compensated" Webster for this staggering emotional and financial blow. "When I found nothing lost but house and property," he later remarked to Isaac P. Davis, a Boston businessman and close friend, "you may well imagine how much I felt relieved from distress." Webster's first inclination, naturally enough, was to drop everything and rush home, but Grace suspected as much, and in her first letter to him after the fire she advised against it. She and the children were well and in good hands. He should remain in Washington.[32]

So he stayed—and grumbled about one thing or another. If it was not the conduct of the war, the idiocy of the Madison administration, the threat of conscription, the imposition of a new embargo, or the likelihood of new taxes, then it was life generally in Washington. "You know, pretty well, the pleasures of a winter here," he commented to one friend, tongue in cheek. "Every other day rain—every day, mud. Our business, to sit in our places. Our amusement;—to read the Newspapers."[33]

He also took a more active role in the House debates. With all the negative things he recorded about Washington at least there was controversy, "controversy enough to keep the spirits alive, & we have some good speaking. It seems to be a talking season," he added. And who knew better than Daniel Webster how to talk, how to rouse an audience, even a partisan one? With a war on, with one American military disaster following another, with the possibility of another invasion of Canada, with a newly enacted embargo that forbade all exports, with the need for money becoming desperate, and with the call for higher taxes ever echoing around the halls of Congress, there was plenty of controversy, which the Federalists exploited at every opportunity.[34]

Webster took his seat on Wednesday, December 29, and after the New Year's break moved for a discussion of the President's response to his resolutions.[35] Calhoun and his committee reluctantly agreed, but the House modified Webster's motion and finally referred the entire question to the Committee of the Whole.[36]

Webster's initial speeches during this session were not of a particularly high caliber.[37] Good and well received, indeed, but unexceptional, even though many of his Federalist friends assured him that they were just grand and should be

31. Curtis, *Webster,* I, 115–116; Fuess, *Webster,* I, 119–120. Initially Grace stayed with Mrs. Mason, whose husband was also in Washington, but a few weeks later she decided to stay with her brother-in-law, Ezekiel, in Boscawen.

32. DW to Davis, January 6, 1814, in *W&S,* XVII, 238.

33. DW to ?, February 11, 1814, in *PC,* I, 164.

34. Ibid.

35. *Annals of Congress,* 13th Congress, 2d Session, pp. 824–825.

36. Ibid.

37. Ibid., pp. 824, 904, 932, 940, 1121, 1223, 1893, 1943, 1966.

published without any change. "No member before ever rivetted the attention of the House so closely, in his first speech," reported one enthusiast. "Members left their seats where they could not see the speaker, face to face, and sat down, or stood on the floor fronting him. All listened attentively and silently," and when he finished, "many went up and warmly congratulated the orator."[38] Even the distinguished chief justice of the United States, John Marshall, was impressed. "At the time when this speech was delivered, I did not know Mr. Webster," he reportedly said, "but I was so much struck with it, that I did not hesitate then to state, that Mr. Webster was a very able man, and would become one of the very first statesmen in America, and perhaps the very first."[39]

His enlistment speech did show some sparkle, but even he admitted to Ezekiel that it was "not exactly what it ought to be. I had not time. I had no intention of speaking till nine o'clock in the Morning, & delivered the thing about 2—I could make it better—but I dare say you think it would be easier to make a new one than to mend."[40]

He gave the enlistment speech on Friday, January 14. Two things troubled him particularly when he spoke: the apparent determination of the administration to attempt another ill-advised invasion of Canada and the new embargo, which had been passed during Webster's absence.

The defence of our own territory seems hitherto to have been regarded as an object of secondary importance—a duty of a lower order than the invasion of the enemy. The army raised last year was competent to defend the frontier. To that purpose the Government did not see fit to apply it. It was not competent, as the event proved, to invade with success the provinces of the enemy. To that purpose, however, it was applied. The substantial benefit which might have been obtained, and ought to have been obtained, was sacrificed to a scheme of conquest, in my opinion a wild one, commenced without means, prosecuted without plan or concern and ending in disgrace. Nor is it the inland frontier only that has been left defenceless. The seacoast has been, in many places wholly exposed.

Here Webster cited several examples of conditions along the Atlantic seaboard. When we were urged to declare war, he continued, this was not what was promised. "This is not the harvest of greatness and glory, the seeds of which were supposed to be down with the declaration of war."

Who is to blame? "When we ask, sir, for the causes of these disappoint-

38. March, *Webster*, pp. 34–36. March also says that the speech "displayed cautious regard for facts, a philosophical moderation of tone, a fullness of knowledge, and an amplitude of historical illustration which astonished the House." Ibid.

39. Joseph Story to DW, January 23, 1831, in Curtis, *Webster*, I, 110 note 1. Curtis seems to think Marshall's statement resulted from Webster's remarks on introducing his resolutions. But the record shows that "in offering these resolutions, it was not his [Webster's] intention, he said, to enter into any discussion or argument, or to advance any proposition whatever." *Annals of Congress*, 13th Congress, 1st Session, p. 149. It is much more likely that Marshall's statement referred to Webster's speech in the second session. All of Webster's remarks in the first session are extremely brief. See ibid., pp. 149–150, 163, 169, 170.

40. DW to Ezekiel Webster, January 30, [1814], in *PC*, I, 160–161.

ments, we are told that they are owing to the opposition which the war encounters in this House and among the people. All the evils which afflict the country are imputed to Opposition." He paused for a moment as the great head turned from side to side to draw in his audience on both ends of the chamber. Then he possibly surprised his listeners with an obvious political truism. "What possessor of political power," he said with a sneer, "ever yet failed to charge the mischiefs resulting from his own measures, upon those who had uniformly opposed those measures?"

"Utterly astonished at the declaration of war," he went on, "I have been surprised at nothing since. Unless all history deceives me, I saw how it would be prosecuted when I saw how it was begun. There is in the nature of things an unchangeable relation between rash counsels and feeble execution."

And one of the most feeble and rash acts of the administration, he thundered, was the recent reenactment of the embargo. Do you think Massachusetts or any other northern state would have ratified the Constitution, he asked, if it had known that such monstrous legislation would be enacted in the future?

Let any man examine our history, and he will find that the Constitution of the country owes its existence to the commerce of the country. Let him inquire of those who are old enough to remember, and they will tell it to him. The idea of such a compact, as is well known, was first unfolded in a meeting of delegates [the Mount Vernon Convention of 1785] from different States, holden for the purpose of making some voluntary agreements respecting trade, and establishing a common tariff. . . . The faith of this nation is pledged to its commerce, formally and solemnly. I call upon you to redeem that pledge, not by sacrificing, while you profess to regard it, but by unshackling it and protecting it and fostering it, according to your ability, and the reasonable expectations of those who have committed it to the care of Government. In the commerce of the country the Constitution had its growth; in the extinction of that commerce it will find its grave.[41]

Webster polished this speech and several others on the resolutions as best he could, given the limitations on his time, and had them reprinted and distributed where they would do the most good, especially among his constituents in Portsmouth. "I enclose you a few creatures called speeches," he wrote to Ezekiel. "Give them, in my name, to those you think proper, Feds or Demos."[42] To his happy surprise his enlistment speech was widely reprinted in pamphlet form throughout New Hampshire and generally elicited favorable comments. Readers liked the strong New England flavor of the speech and his powerful allusions to the Constitution. Already he had established himself as knowledgeable in understanding the fundamental instrument of the nation's government. Already he had staked his claim to a preeminent position in Congress in interpreting the Constitution. In time he would stand supreme as the great "Defender of the Constitution."

41. *Annals of Congress*, 13th Congress, 2d Session, pp. 940–941, 942, 943–944, 950.
42. DW to Ezekiel Webster, January 30, [1814], in *PC*, I, 160–161

6

The Supreme Court

$\mathbb{S}$HORTLY after arriving back in Washington in the winter of 1813–1814, Webster descended to the basement of the Capitol building and entered what was then the Supreme Court to argue his first case. The distinguished architect and surveyor of public buildings Benjamin Latrobe had designed this semicircular room and placed it directly underneath the Senate chamber. The attractive vaulted ceiling, described as an "umbrella vault" or "half a pumpkin shell," braced by a series of archways supported the floor above. It was a small, severely decorated room dimly lit by three windows on the east wall. In front of these windows in an arcade formed by three arches supported by Doric colonnades was a raised bench for the seven justices of the United States Supreme Court.[1]

At 11:00 A.M. the justices entered the room and donned their long black silk robes in full view of their audience. They sat on raised mahogany chairs; below them stretched the bar. Facing the justices were four counsel tables with two chairs behind each table for lawyers authorized to plead before the High Court. Visitors sat in rows of benches behind the lawyers and around the arch supports and along the arcade. Parties of women frequently sauntered into the Court after visiting the gallery of the representatives. For the most part these visitors were wives of government and foreign officials. Because of the cramped conditions of the room, the ladies remained but a short time unless the arguments were particularly exciting or an important case was under review. Indians also visited, dressed "in their native costume, their straight black hair hanging in plaits down their tawny shoulders, with mockassins [sic] on their feet, rings in their ears and noses, and large plates of silver on their arms and breasts."[2] Usually they came to the capital to meet with their "Great Father" in the White House. Possibly they looked in on the Court in an effort to familiarize themselves with American justice.

The crowd in attendance, both male and female, invariably expected enter-

1. *The Supreme Court Chamber, 1810–1860* (Washington, 1993), p. 7; Charles Warren, *The Supreme Court in United States History* (Boston, 1922), I, 457–458; Maurice G. Baxter, *Daniel Webster and the Supreme Court* (Boston, 1966), p. 17.

2. Baxter, *Webster and the Supreme Court*, p. 17; Warren, *Supreme Court*, I, 458.

tainment. They wanted the lawyers to dazzle them with their knowledge and oratorical skill. From his very first appearance in this court Webster knew what was expected and tried to please. He tried a little too hard, as he later conceded. "When I was a young man," he recalled, "and for some years after I had acquired a respectable degree of eminence in my profession, my style was bombastic and pompous in the extreme. Some kind friend [Jeremiah Mason, no doubt] was good enough to point out that fact to me, and I determined to correct it, if labor could do it. Whether it has been corrected or not, no small part of my life has been spent in the attempt." This applied to both his verbal and his written presentations. Any writer, he said, needs to learn "how to *scratch out.*" A "very large part of my life has been spent in 'scratching out.' "[3]

A reporter for the Court studied Webster's style and stated that in preparing his briefs, Black Dan carefully weighed "the fitness and import of every word." Moreover, he verified every quotation and paid particular attention to punctuation. The "literary character" of his legal arguments was just as "critically attended to," as were his formal speeches and orations.[4]

The Court held its regular session from the first Monday in February to early March. It normally heard arguments from 11:00 A.M. until 2:00 P.M., and this constituted one sitting. Three sittings were considered the maximum for any one lawyer to argue his case, although the Court did not set any time limit. Webster rarely needed more than one sitting to present his argument. When he did take two sessions, his brief invariably involved constitutional issues.[5]

When the justices entered, the chief justice, John Marshall took his seat in the center of the raised bench, and his six associates, in order of seniority, placed themselves on either side of him. Marshall, a tall, gaunt man with a small head, disheveled hair, and bright black eyes, was by no means a distinguished jurist. A warm, good-humored Virginian, he had had only two years of formal education and later some legal training under the learned George Wythe at the College of William and Mary. Despite his many limitations as a lawyer, he had a sharp, analytical mind, a retentive and spacious memory, and a superb prose style. As chief justice he excelled in unifying the Court, and he invariably delivered the Court's decision. Of the constitutional decisions rendered by the Marshall Court, he wrote more than half. Of more than eleven hundred cases tried before him, he dissented in only eight, and in just one case dealing with a constitutional issue.[6]

Unquestionably the greatest legal mind on the court at this time belonged to Associate Justice Joseph Story. Mild-mannered, a compulsive conversational-

3. Lyman, *Public and Private Life of Webster,* II, 285–286.

4. Ibid., II, 288.

5. Introduction, *PLFP,* Part I, xxv.

6. Herbert Alan Johnson, "John Marshall, 1755–1835," in Leon Friedman and Fred L. Israel, eds., *The Justices of the United States Supreme Court, 1789–1978: Their Lives and Major Opinions* (New York, 1980), I, 285–303. See also Albert Beveridge, *The Life of John Marshall* (Boston, 1916–1919), 4 vols.

ist, with fine features, a head "white as a snow bank, below middle-size, of light and airy form . . . and polished and courtly in his manners," Story looked older than his years because of his "baldness and glasses." Born in Massachusetts in 1779, educated at Harvard, where he later taught, he quickly rose to prominence as a lawyer. Welcomed by Marshall to the Court in 1811, Story joined the chief justice in support of national interests. Story's opinions, unlike Marshall's, reflected his great scholarship by the myriad use of legal commentaries and previous judicial opinions to help buttress his position. He and Webster later formed a team as well, with Story assisting the congressman in drafting legislation and Webster assisting the justice in the preparation of a criminal code for enactment by Congress.[7]

The other justices included Bushrod Washington, William Johnson, Brockholst Livingston, Thomas Todd, and Gabriel Duvall. Washington, a nephew of the first President's, tended to support Marshall and Story in protecting property rights and supporting increased power for the central government. Livingston, appointed by Jefferson in 1807 to oppose the prevailing Federalist opinion of the Marshall Court, fell under the chief justice's influence and, like Story, proved to be a major disappointment to the President who had appointed him. Todd frequently absented himself from the Court because of illness and family matters, and although a Jeffersonian, he too quickly fell victim to Marshall's compelling personality and domination. Duvall, who was appointed by President Madison and was another follower of Marshall and Story's, has the distinction and reputation of being one of the least important justices in the entire history of the Court. Clearly this High Court decided law pretty much as John Marshall dictated. And it did not take many years before Marshall himself came under the spell of Websterian eloquence. In some respects the two men were much alike. Both were Federalists and greatly revered George Washington, both held similar economic viewpoints, and both contributed substantially to the development of the nation's political and economic strength.

The court session began when the chief justice nibbed his pen. He always wrote with a quill, never the "barbarous invention of steel pens," after which he pulled up the sleeves of his gown and nodded to the counsel who was to address him, "as much as to say, 'I am ready; now you may go on.' "[8]

Webster was admitted to practice before the High Court on January 14, 1814. Almost immediately he took a liking to Marshall and said so in his correspondence. "There is no man in the Court that strikes me like Marshall," he informed his brother, Ezekiel. "He is a plain man, looking very much like Colonel Adams, & about 3 inches taller. I have never seen a man of whose intellect I had a higher opinion." Mutual admiration soon typified the ongoing relationship

7. Warren, *Supreme Court*, I, 467–468, 470. See also R. Kent Newmyer, *Supreme Court Justice Joseph Story* (New York, 1985), James McClellan, *Joseph Story and the American Constitution* (New York, 1971), and Gerald T. Dunne, *Justice Joseph Story and the Rise of the Supreme Court* (New York, 1970).

8. Harvey, *Reminiscences*, p. 142.

between the chief justice and the young representative, for as it turned out, Webster invariably argued the side more agreeable to Marshall and the Court's majority. The young man quickly and shrewdly discerned the chief justice's influence on the other members of the Court and consequently pitched his legal arguments directly at him. Just as quickly he took Story's measure and tailored his arguments accordingly.[9]

Webster's great forte lay in arguing for an appellant. He loved to retell the case to the court, and he did it with enormous emotional vigor and clarity, "weaving the law into the fabric of the facts." Like most truly distinguished lawyers, he cut immediately to the heart of the case and reduced the details and the law to a few apparently simple premises. Once he had shed his bombastic style, he learned first to master all the facts relative to his case and then to present them to the court in as simple and straightforward a manner as possible. "His style rested on demonstrating a total mastery of facts and law, history and philosophy."[10]

By the time Webster appeared before the Supreme Court he had come to understand that the common law was "both evolutionary in its process and inductive in its method." Law involved fixed rules drawn from principles and precedent. Similar cases must be decided in similar manner. A judge, according to Webster, could not "indulge his own discretion or inclination." Once judges indulge their "inclination," he said, "then *men* govern, and rule us, and *not the law.*"[11]

Webster also distinguished between common law, which had developed slowly over time, and public law, which he considered a new development, an American development, because only in America did there exist written constitutions that specifically limited legislative power. What he meant, of course, and what it subsequently became was constitutional law. And because legislatures tended more and more to infringe on private rights, act out of passion, and concern themselves too often with winning popular approval, the courts, acting through "reason and the rule of law," must then, of necessity, step in and decide the constitutional validity of these legislative enactments.[12]

In arguing before the Supreme Court, Webster made a clear distinction between those cases involving private and those involving public law. And he usually informed the Court which cases he thought concerned private rights and which public rights. Judges could not indulge their inclinations in private law, but they could make public law because public law came from a written constitution. It had not evolved; it was not inductive; its method was deductive. In arguing cases involving public law, Webster urged the Court to draw sharp distinctions between federal and state authority and between legislative and

9. Introduction, *PLFP,* Part I, xxiii–xxv.

10. Ibid., Part I, xxv, xxvi.

11. Quoted in ibid., Part I, xxvii.

12. Ibid., Part I, xxviii.

judicial powers. The system of federalism and the separation of powers were his principal weapons.[13]

So, over a period of many years of study and practice, he mastered the mysteries of the common law, helped interpret public law, and then combined these skills with his powerful speaking talents to serve his clients rather handsomely as well as advance his own economic and political fortunes and the welfare of the nation as a whole.[14]

When Webster debuted before the justices of the Supreme Court during the February term, it was the beginning of what became a very long association with the tribunal in this room. From 1814 to his death in 1852 he appeared before the Court in virtually every session. He argued 223 cases during those thirty-eight years—25 involving constitutional issues—and won approximately half of them.[15] He initially took Supreme Court cases largely to supplement his income, but he soon discovered that his views of the Constitution could be enormously decisive in shaping the extent of federal jurisdiction.

Throughout his career in Washington Webster regularly descended from either the House or Senate chamber to plead before the justices. It was not uncommon for him to deliver a speech in Congress and then immediately proceed to the floor below to argue an important case. And once his reputation as an advocate and "Defender of the Constitution" had been established, particularly after the *Dartmouth College* case, the galleries of the Congress and the small chamber of the Supreme Court swelled to overflowing with visitors whenever he was scheduled to speak.

Webster's appearance before the Supreme Court began modestly and involved admiralty cases on appeal. On March 12, 1814, he presented his first prize case from Massachusetts, *The Grotius*,[16] and won a rehearing and extra time for his clients in a decision rendered by Justice Washington. The following year the Court reversed the decision of the lower court. On March 14 he argued the second prize case from New Hampshire, *The St. Lawrence*,[17] for two of the claimants and sought a reversal of the lower court judgment while another lawyer, named Irving, represented the remaining claimants.[18] Justice Livingston handed down the Court's decision against the clients represented by Irving but agreed to allow more time for Webster's clients to prove their case. Unfortunately neither of the clients could come up with additional evidence, and the final judgment, delivered by Justice Story during the following term, went against them.[19]

13. Ibid., Part I, xxix.

14. Ibid., Part I, xxvi.

15. Ibid., III, Part II, 1046–1066. Webster also argued seventy-six cases from 1813 to 1852 before lower federal courts. Ibid., 1069–1071.

16. 8 Cranch 456. Webster argued the case with Samuel Dexter, who had been his role model ten years earlier. Webster's argument can be found ibid. on pages 458–459.

17. 8 Cranch 434.

18. The Court normally limited representation in a case to two lawyers for each side.

19. 9 Cranch 420.

"In one case I charged a N. Yorker 300 Dls," Webster jubilantly informed his brother, "—& in two other cases, 100 Ds each. So much for prize causes & c."[20] Shortly after that he argued his first appeal of any importance in the case, *The Town of Pawlet* v. *Clark et al.*[21] He and Timothy Pitkin, a representative from Connecticut, presented the case for the plaintiffs on an appeal from the Vermont Circuit Court, while a man named Sheperd represented the defendants. The case involved a dispute over a colonial land grant between citizens of the same state whose claims emanated from grants of different states. On March 10, 1815, Justice Story delivered the majority opinion.[22] He sided with Webster and Pitkin and not only affirmed the rights of the town of Pawlet but agreed with them on the constitutional issue that what applied to the original thirteen states also applied to those states like Vermont that had been admitted to the Union after the adoption of the Constitution.[23]

By this time one thing seemed clear. These cases put the Court on notice that an important counselor had arrived, for they demonstrated Webster's "mastery of technical exposition and emotional appeal," his clarity of explanation, and his sharply focused argument. He emphasized logic, not rhetoric, in his presentations. And his successful courtroom style soon became the style of other lawyers for virtually the remainder of the century.[24]

His early successes before the Supreme Court were matched, according to some observers, by his success in forcing the Madison administration to reverse its policy regarding the embargo and to ask Congress for a repeal of the despised law. Napoleon had already abdicated, the allies had occupied Paris, and the liberated Continental nations had begun again to trade with Great Britain. It therefore made little sense to continue the embargo, and Madison capitulated to the inevitable. The President alerted his friends in Congress, and they dutifully switched sides with him. In the House Calhoun had privately opposed the embargo when it was enacted but had reluctantly gone along with it. Now, as chairman of the Committee on Foreign Relations, he reported a bill to repeal the law at the same time that he defended the administration's change of attitude resulting from the new conditions prevailing in Europe.[25] With hardly a murmur of opposition the bill passed.

Webster gloated. He seized the opportunity to ridicule publicly the administration's general ineptness. In addition, he congratulated his party on a victory well fought. On Wednesday, April 6, 1814, he rose in the House and delivered a speech described as "a florid benediction over the restrictive system," one that

20. DW to Ezekiel Webster, March 28, 1814, in *PC*, I, 167.

21. 9 Cranch 295.

22. Ibid. Webster's argument can be found on pages 314–320. Justice Johnson wrote a concurring opinion.

23. Fuess, *Webster*, I, 191.

24. Webster's argument runs from page 438 to 439 in 8 Cranch; *PLFP*, Part I, 4–5.

25. *Calhoun Papers*, I, 243–249.

elicited extraordinary attention from both Federalists and Republicans. Obviously, in his very first term in Congress he had emerged as an important speaker and leader of the Federalist party.[26]

"Mr. Chairman," he said, "I am happy to be present . . . and to act a part in the funeral ceremonies" of this dreadful and destructive restrictive system, the embargo.

The occasion, I think, will justify a temperate and moderate exultation on the part of those who have constantly opposed this system of politics, and uniformly foretold its miserable end. I congratulate my friends on this triumph of their principles. . . . Sir, a Government which cannot administer the affairs of a nation without producing so frequent and such violent alterations in the ordinary occupations and pursuits of private life, has, in my opinion, little claim to the regard of the community.

Throughout the speech Webster repeatedly accused Republicans of pursuing a policy rooted in the mistaken belief that American interests were necessarily joined to the French cause. Napoleon is not our friend, Webster insisted. He closed the Continent to imports, and what did we do but turn around and help him by restricting our own trade with this despicable embargo?

It is the true policy of government to suffer the different pursuits of society to take their own course, and not to give excessive bounties or encouragements to one over the another. This, also, is the true spirit of the Constitution. It has not, in my opinion, conferred on the Government the power of changing the occupations of the people of different States and sections, and of forcing them into other employments. It cannot prohibit commerce any more than agriculture; nor manufactures any more than commerce. It owes protection to all. I rejoice that commerce is once more permitted to exist; that its remnant, as far as this unblessed war will allow, may yet again visit the seas, before it is quite forgotten that we have been a commercial people. I shall rejoice still further, when I see the Government pursue an independent, permanent, and steady system of national politics; when it shall rely for the maintenance of rights and the redress of wrongs on the strength and resources of our own country, and break off all measures which tend, in any degree, to connect us with the fortunes of a foreign Power.[27]

When he ended, Federalists rushed over, virtually in a body, to congratulate him on his skillful verbal decapitation of the administration's embargo policy. The Republicans made no attempt to defend what they had done and by their downcast appearances showed their embarrassment. They had a "melancholy gloom over their faces," and Webster's speech only deepened their gloom. "His speech," remarked Nathaniel Macon of North Carolina to his friend Joseph H. Nicholson, "contained a good deal of bitter. . . . Those who voted the embargo so very lately, and those or him who recommended it, must I think, feel a little sore under Websters rubs. . . . I have not for a long time seen the feds look in so good humor, they have all a smile on their countenances, and look at each other,

---

26. Wiltse, *Calhoun, Nationalist*, pp. 91, 98.
27. "On the Repeal of the Embargo," in *W&S*, XIV, 35–46.

as if they . . . are the wise men not only of this nation, but of the world."[28]

Perhaps Webster had the brightest smile of all. He had capped this victory with a speech so forceful and so deliciously sarcastic that everyone in Congress took note and agreed that a potent new force had arrived in Washington.

With the repeal of the embargo Congress concluded its main business for this session and adjourned. Webster scurried home as fast as he could. No doubt he was anxious to assess the damage to his house and its impact on his family. He also needed to get home because he faced reelection to Congress to be held in New Hampshire in late August.

Over the next several months he moved his family to a rented house and diligently attended to his law business to reduce the debts he faced because of the fire and his extended absence from his regular legal practice. Most likely around the time of his return to Portsmouth he started toying with the idea of giving up his seat in Congress and moving to another state, like Massachusetts, where he could earn more money. The urge to remove became stronger with each passing month.

Meanwhile the Federalists meeting together at Concord on June 22, 1814, renominated Webster with great enthusiasm. They expressed their pride in his record as a representative and asked him to head what they called the American Peace Ticket in the August election.

Republicans attacked the ticket as unpatriotic and aimed their biggest salvos at Webster. Isaac Hill, the editor of the *New Hampshire Patriot*, was particularly vitriolic, accusing Black Dan of hindering the war effort and aiding and abetting the enemy. "Of all the men in the State, he is the fittest to be the tool of our enemy; and if he has not already been rewarded he probably expects some portion of 'secret service money' for prating long and loud about *French influence,* about the justice and magnanimity of Britain, and the wickedness and corruption of the American government."[29]

Despite these stinging blasts from a hostile press, Webster and the rest of his ticket won a clear victory on election day, Monday, August 29. Still, the accusations against him of behavior bordering on treason continued over the next few months and years and indeed hounded Webster for the remainder of his life.

Just four days before the New Hampshire election a British army commanded by General Robert Ross invaded Washington and on August 25, 1814, put it to the torch. The White House, the Capitol, and many other public and private buildings were set ablaze. Any resistance or opposition to the invasion brought a response in the form of lighted torches. Newspapers throughout the country reported the outrage felt by the American people over this "barbarous conflagration" of their capital city by the British. "The hate with which *we* have always said *Great Britain* regarded us, is now exhibiting by a Goth-like war,"

28. Macon to Nicholson, April 6, 1814, Nicholson Papers, LC. "The fed Senators are almost constantly in the House today, they look as well pleased as their brethren of this House." Ibid.

29. *Patriot,* July 5, 19, 25, August 2, 1814.

editorialized one newspaper. "How could a nation eminently civilized, conduct itself at Washington with as much barbarity as the old banditti of *Attila*, and *Genseric?* Is not this act of attrocious vengeance *a crime against all humanity?*"[30] The press reported that some two million dollars in property were lost during the destruction before the British withdrew and that the justice of the peace William Thornton had to appoint a guard at the White House and other public buildings to "prevent plunderers who were carrying off articles to the amount of thousands of dollars."[31]

The attack on Washington coincided with several other raids along the coast in what appeared to be an all-out frontal assault on the United States to bring the war to an end. Blockade, invasion, and coastal raids formed a pattern, and the Portsmouth naval station seemed a likely target for a raid, if not outright seizure.

On Saturday, September 10, 1814, Webster, as chairman of a safety committee, signed and had printed a notice by the Portsmouth Committee of Defense calling for the massing of troops on the parade grounds in Portsmouth to help protect the town, with every man instructed to bring such arms as he had in his possession. In the future Webster cited this call every time he was accused of urging disunion.

However, much of New England resisted the war effort in every possible way, condemning the administration for policies that had brought havoc and near ruin to the most prosperous section of the nation. Even Webster believed that "the Govt could not, if it would, protect N England. Indeed its inability so to do is already sufficiently manifest." Finally, on October 5, 1814, a special session of the Massachusetts legislature summoned a convention to meet in Hartford, Connecticut, on December 15 to consider appropriate action. Some hoped it would lead to secession.[32]

At first Webster was a little confused about the date for the convention, and in a letter to William Sullivan of Massachusetts, who subsequently attended the convention, he expressed his obvious interest, if not enthusiasm, for the projected meeting and regretted that so many months would pass before it convened. "We are not a little disappointed today," he explained, "in finding that your proposed Convention is put off till next *August*. What can be the reason of so much delay? You perceive now that there is no hope of Peace. I am perfectly confident . . . that the Govt could not, if it would, protect N England."[33]

Clearly he believed that the central government cared nothing for New England's interests, and therefore it was up to the six states in the region to take

30. *Niles' Weekly Register,* September 10, December 31, 1814.

31. *National Intelligencer,* August 31, September 7, 1814; *Niles' Weekly Register,* September 10, 1814.

32. "Notice of Portsmouth Committee of Defence," September 10, 1814, DW to William Sullivan, October 17, [1814], in *PC,* I, 169–170; *Columbian Centinel,* October 12, 1814.

33. DW to Sullivan, October 17, [1814], in *PC,* I, 170.

action themselves, just as Kentucky and Virginia had done to protest the Alien and Sedition Acts in 1798. Webster hated the war and wanted to see it end. But he was contemptuous of the administration's ability to do anything to bring about peace.

Webster delayed until October his return to Washington for the special session on September 19 called by the President. Approaching the capital by stagecoach, he was shocked by the sight of the ruined city that stretched out before him: the White House in virtual ruins, its walls blackened; the Capitol gutted; and the Treasury and War Department buildings severely damaged. Gone too were the books and documents contained in the Library of Congress. Thomas Jefferson offered to sell his library to replace what had been lost, and the government accepted the offer. Within a year Jefferson's books began arriving in Washington and were stored in the Post Office building. It soon became apparent that the cost of repair, replacement, and rebuilding of the capital would be astronomical, and some wondered if it might not be a good idea to move it to a less vulnerable place, somewhere farther inland like Lancaster, Pennsylvania, or even Cincinnati, Ohio. But the residents of the District strongly protested such suggestions and were echoed in the press. "We cannot find language to express our abhorrence and astonishment at the suggestion," cried the *National Intelligencer.* Congress "dare not sanction" such a move.[34]

President and Mrs. Madison took up residence in the Octagon House on New York Avenue, just a block or two away from the gutted White House. Congress was obliged to hold its sessions in the Post Office building while work began on a brick structure on the site of the present Supreme Court building. This temporary "Brick Capitol" was completed by the start of the Fourteenth Congress in December 1815, with the Senate chamber on the first floor and the House of Representatives on the second floor. It was to serve until December 1819, at which time the new Capitol would be ready for occupancy.[35]

Also dispossessed on account of the torching of the city, the Supreme Court moved into a private house on Capitol Hill and for the next two years held its sessions in this residence. After that the Court made do with a rather makeshift room in the unrestored Capitol. Webster no longer enjoyed the luxury of simply descending to the floor below to plead before the Court—not until 1819, when it moved back to its old chambers prior to the fire.[36] It was during this interim period in the makeshift chamber that Webster argued his most famous case, *Trustees of Dartmouth College* v. *William H. Woodward,* more popularly known as the *Dartmouth College* case.

Webster found living quarters at Crawford's Hotel in Georgetown, the ostensible headquarters of the Federalist party in Washington. Senators Rufus King of New York and Christopher Gore of Massachusetts lived there, as did

34. September 2, 1814.
35. Green, *Washington,* pp. 63–67; Bryan, *History of the National Capital,* I, 631–637.
36. Bryan, *History of the National Capital,* I, 632.

Senator Jeremiah Mason of New Hampshire, who had a room next to Webster's. This group frequently met in the evening in Mrs. King's and Mrs. Gore's private parlor. Webster usually messed with Gore and was described by observers as "very amusing, talking gayly, and as if no care rested upon him. Everywhere he was liked as a social companion." Within his own social circle he was the most gregarious, amusing, and delightful companion to have at a dinner party. He regaled his friends with anecdotes that had them laughing hysterically or listening intently as he recounted a dramatic incident, and then he would top off the evening by leading everyone in a medley of popular songs.[37]

The Federalists naturally expected Webster to help lead them in debate, and he readily responded to the opportunity. He, William Gaston of North Carolina, and Alexander C. Hanson of Maryland pretty much headed the Federalist attacks in the House. Almost upon the first moment of his arrival for the third session of the Thirteenth Congress Webster charged right in to berate the administration and its policies. When he spoke to the full House, some listeners found him at times too theatrical, but his style changed as need required. He could be immensely eloquent and dramatic and speak in the grand manner, or he could assume a "very deliberate conversational manner, and with the peculiar exactness of phraseology, which marked him as a public debater to the end of his life. He did not fail then, any more than afterward, to command the attention of the House."[38] When he rose to speak, even though he was only in his early thirties, he awed his listeners by his physical appearance and of course his voice. His dress drew particular attention: blue coat with brass buttons, black pants, white vest and tie. He rarely wore anything else.

Money was desperately needed by the government to prosecute the war, and an increase in direct taxes had been put forward as a remedy that Webster felt compelled to oppose. But his thinking and words in a speech delivered on October 24 were so tortured and misleading that the *National Intelligencer* reported that he would vote for an increase.[39] This he immediately contradicted. What he wished to say was that he would neither approve nor obstruct passage of the new taxes. He would simply "hold himself not to approve, without reason, the course pursued."[40] He admitted that perhaps "a fuller tone of opposition would have better suited my own feelings, but I did not wish to jostle agt. those [Federalists], who had felt it their duty to take a different course" because of "circumstances & the peculiar state of public opinion in their Districts." Moreover, these Federalists needed the central government to help their districts defend themselves against possible invasion. So it became incumbent upon him "to touch lightly—& to leave the way open for Federalists to vote either way,

---

37. Curtis, *Webster,* I, 135–136, quoting George Ticknor.

38. George Ticknor's "Recollections," quoted ibid., I, 136.

39. October 25, 1814.

40. *Annals of Congress,* 13th Congress, 3d Session, pp. 464–465; *National Intelligencer,* October 27, 1814.

without ceasing to be Federalists." He consulted with his brother, now a member of the New Hampshire legislature, who warned him that "most of these taxes, I apprehend will operate very injuriously upon New England."[41]

Webster decided to vote for the whiskey tax but no other. He said he was anxious to see the whiskey tax pass because "it will stop distillation in New England;—a practice which is drawing upon our sources of life, & rendering us far less independent than we otherwise should be upon others for *bread*."[42] (For a man who had developed a keen taste for alcohol this decision would in no way affect his own sources of supply.) He predicted that the tax bills—including a land tax[43] which was raised from three to six million—would pass the House without his support, and indeed they did by a large majority in late December. Webster shook his head in dismay. "Almost every thing is taxed which can be thought of."[44]

Another fiscal matter occasioned by the desperate condition of the Treasury involved the National Bank. The First National Bank had been chartered in 1791. Proposed by Alexander Hamilton in the Washington administration, it had been strongly opposed by both Jefferson and Madison as unconstitutional. It passed over their objections, but its charter had expired in 1811. As the nation entered the war, it did not have the necessary financial backing of the National Bank, and the strongest state banks, principally in New England, refused to come to the administration's financial rescue. With each passing month the fiscal situation became increasingly untenable. Many Republicans, but not all, now agreed with the Hamiltonian position that the Bank was indeed constitutional and must be rechartered, so in 1813 Secretary of the Treasury Alexander Dallas proposed a new bank with a capitalization of fifty million (mostly in United States stock), with an obligation to loan the government, when needed, up to thirty million and with presidential authority to suspend specie (gold or silver) payment of bank notes when necessary.

One Republican to disagree with the Dallas plan was John C. Calhoun. He wanted a reduced capitalization, less responsibility by the Bank to lend to the government, and a provision requiring specie payments.[45] Webster agreed with Calhoun and led the opposition to the bill. The bill was reported out of committee on December 24. Webster had gone to Baltimore for Christmas but was hurriedly summoned to return by his friends. In a speech delivered on January 2, 1815, he said that he too favored smaller capitalization, but he also wanted the expunging of the Bank's loan obligation to the government and a definite

41. DW to [Timothy Farrar, Jr.?], October 30, 1814, DW to Ezekiel Webster, October 30, 1814, Ezekiel Webster to DW, October 29, 1814, in *PC*, I, 174–175, 176, 173.

42. DW to Ezekiel Webster, October 30, 1814, ibid., I, 175–176.

43. It was this tax particularly about which he had difficulty making up his mind, and he asked his brother for advice. See DW to Ezekiel Webster, October 20, 1814, in Van Tyne, ed., *Letters of Webster*, p. 52.

44. DW to [William F. Rowland?], January 11, 1815, in *PC*, I, 181.

45. *Calhoun Papers*, I, 254–259; Wiltse, *Calhoun, Nationalist*, pp. 95–96.

commitment to specie payments. Without such restrictions he feared a torrential outpouring of worthless bank notes. Instead of a national bank the nation would be saddled with another department of government formed for the sole purpose of supplying paper money. Such a consequence would be ruinous to the nation, both at home and abroad. The speech had such "great force" and displayed such "an amount of knowledge of the history and philosophy of finance" that it "astonished even those who thought most highly of his abilities."[46]

Now allied on this one issue, Webster, the Federalist, and Calhoun, the Republican, who normally acted as an administration spokesman, watched the bill go down to defeat on a tie vote.[47] No sooner was the vote announced than Calhoun walked across the floor where Webster stood, held out both hands, and announced that they must prepare a new bill. The young New England leader assured Calhoun that his support would not be withheld.[48] A new bill that provided for a real specie-paying bank was reported on January 6, and Webster and his friends voted for it. On January 7, 1815, it passed by a very large majority.[49]

Webster predicted that the President would sign it, but he was mistaken. On January 30 Madison sent a vigorous veto message to Congress, declaring that the measure did not meet the requirements of the government and could "not be relied on during the war to provide a circulating medium nor to furnish loans or anticipations of the public revenue." Interestingly, he posed no constitutional objection.[50] The issue of structuring a workable and acceptable bank bill remained, and it therefore carried over to the next Congress.

A far more "dreadful" war measure was proposed by James Monroe, acting in his capacity as secretary of war, in attempting to address the problem of enlistments in the national service. The army needed to be enlarged, and Monroe suggested raising an additional eighty thousand men and *conscripting* another forty thousand. A draft! One such had never been proposed before, and the idea to some sounded despotic. It was "usurpation" pure and simple, cried Webster. If such a bill is attempted, he warned, "it will cause a storm such as was never witnessed before."[51] But the government was desperate. It had no money, and its army was slowly evaporating. In addition, many states had refused the government's repeated requests to free a portion of their militias to serve in the

46. Curtis, *Webster*, I, 142; *Annals of Congress*, 13th Congress, 3d Session, pp. 1014–1023; March, *Webster*, pp. 46–47.

47. The vote was eighty-one yeas and eighty nays, whereupon the Speaker, Langdon Cheves of South Carolina, voted nay and then declared that the bill was lost by a tie.

48. Curtis, *Webster*, I, 142–143. Curtis claims that Calhoun burst into tears as he spoke; that sounds most uncharacteristic. Nevertheless Curtis declares that Webster was his authority for the statement. Ibid., I, 143 note.

49. *Annals of Congress*, 13th Congress, 3d Session, p. 173ff.

50. Richardson, *Messages and Papers*, I, 540–542; *Annals of Congress*, 13th Congress, 3d Session, pp. 189–191.

51. DW to Ezekiel Webster, October 30, November 29, 1814, in *PC*, I, 174, 177.

national army. To achieve the desired military increase, Monroe proposed four plans. The first would divide the entire white male population into groups of twenty-five, each one of which would be "compelled" to furnish one able-bodied recruit for national service. A second plan would draft a portion of the state militias, while the third and fourth permitted substitutions for service, lowered the enlistment age from twenty-one to eighteen, and doubled the land bounty for volunteers.[52]

The Senate passed the plan conscripting detachments of the state militias while the House preferred the scheme of dividing the population into groups. Webster fumed. The law, if enacted, "will be a dead letter in New England," he said. "Indeed the Bill is as weak and ridiculous, as it is wicked & violent."[53]

The debate over enacting what Webster called a "draft from new created classes" triggered several heated exchanges in the House, with Republicans arguing the Hamiltonian position of the implied powers clause of the Constitution. Webster could not abide this argument, particularly since it invoked supposedly Federalist principles, and on December 9 he rose to add his voice to those in opposition.

He straight off condemned the intended legislation as a clear violation of the Constitution. Not a single power of Congress could be found to justify its passage. "The question," Webster contended, "is nothing less than whether the most essential rights of personal liberty shall be surrendered, and despotism embraced in its worst forms."[54]

Is this, sir, consistent with the character of a free government? Is this civil liberty? Is this the real character of our Constitution? No, sir, indeed it is not. The Constitution is libelled, foully libelled. The people of this country have not established for themselves such a fabric of despotism. . . . Where is it written in the Constitution, in what article or section is it contained, that you may take children from their parents, and parents from their children, and compel them to fight the battles of any war in which the folly or the wickedness of government may engage it? . . . If the Secretary of War has proved the right of Congress to enact a law enforcing a draft of men out of the militia and into the regular army, he will at any time be able to prove, quite as clearly, that Congress has power to create a Dictator.[55]

He went on at length in this vein. Only toward the tail end of it did he suggest what recourse those who opposed the measure might be driven to take. "The operation of measures thus unconstitutional and illegal ought to be prevented by a resort to other measures which are both constitutional and legal." He then invoked the Jeffersonian-Madisonian doctrine of interposition! "It will be the solemn duty of the State Governments to protect their own authority over their own militia, and to interpose between their citizens and arbitrary

52. *Annals of Congress,* 13th Congress, 3d Session, p. 482.
53. DW to Ezekiel Webster, December 22, [1814], in *PC,* I, 178.
54. *PS,* I, 20, 21.
55. Ibid., I, 24, 27.

power. These are among the objects for which the State Governments exist; and their highest obligations bind them to the preservation of their own rights and the liberties of their people."

Surely the listening members of the House recognized in these words the arguments of the Kentucky and Virginia Resolutions, written in 1798 by Jefferson and Madison to attack the Alien and Sedition Laws passed in the John Adams administration. And they were amazed at the man who uttered them. It had become a topsy-turvy world. Republicans were arguing Hamiltonian dogma, and Federalists were citing Jeffersonian precepts. It was astonishing to all what politics could do to turn everything around.

Webster ended the speech with a jolting admission that there was much loose talk about New England's attitude toward the Union and what it might do in the foreseeable future. Within a few days the delegates to the Hartford Convention would meet to determine an appropriate course of action, and there was much popular speculation about what might happen. Webster knew that this concern preyed on the minds of the other representatives, and he faced it squarely as he closed his speech.

Allusions have been made, sir, to the state of things in New England, and, as usual, she has been charged with an intention to dissolve the Union. The charge is unfounded. She is much too wise to entertain such purposes. She has had too much experience, and has too strong a recollection of the blessings which the Union is capable of producing under a just administration of government. It is her greatest fear, that the course at present pursued will destroy it, by destroying every principle, every interest, every sentiment, and every feeling which have hitherto contributed to uphold it. Those who cry out that the Union is in danger are themselves the authors of that danger.[56]

Fortunately the congressional record did not report this address. In a single sentence it merely mentioned that he had spoken. Webster wrote out his speech but decided against publication. "Upon the most wise reflection," he informed his brother, "I have laid it up in the drawer."[57] The printed speech would not live up to the expectations of his Federalist friends who heard it, he added.

A weak excuse but a wise move. In view of his later reputation as the great defender of the Union who ripped into the arguments of southerners when they spoke of leaving the Union in order to preserve individual rights and freedoms, Webster would have a hard time explaining this speech away. But it should be remembered that interposition is not secession, although such action could easily lead to disunion if the federal government resisted with force.

Those southerners who heard him and remembered his words later mocked his "hypocrisy" in pretending that their arguments were not essentially his as spoken in this debate. In future years, especially when his name was mentioned as a possible presidential candidate, his opponents diligently searched the record for any other statement supporting the theory of interposi-

56. Ibid., I, 31.
57. DW to Ezekiel Webster, December 22 [1814], in *PC*, I, 178.

tion. Several times he was queried directly by "interested parties" about his involvement with the Hartford Convention. The following letter is one example of his response.

Dear Sir

I have recd your letter, & very cheerfully answer its inquiry. I was not a member of the Hartford Convention, and had no agency in it, nor any correspondence with any of its members. If you will refer to the Journal of Congress, & to the dates of the proceedings relative to that Convention, you will find, My Dear Sir, that I was in my seat in the House of Representatives in Congress, which was before any proposition to hold such a Convention was brought forward, & that I remained in that seat, until after the Convention had met & dissolved.[58]

Later he was forced to prepare a formal statement attesting to his noninvolvement in the Hartford Convention.

It is interesting—and instructive—that any number of distinguished figures in the antebellum era resorted to interposition when it suited their purposes. They included, among many others, Jefferson, Madison, Calhoun, and Daniel Webster.

It would have been even more "interesting" had the conscription bill passed. Surely it would have caused a national "storm such as was never witnessed." But it did not pass. It failed in the Senate. "I believe," commented Webster, "some of its friends had become frighted [sic]."[59] And with good reason. Conscription seemed so alien to the American character and spirit that it might conceivably have brought about the collapse of the government, as some, like Webster, predicted. He had another speech on the issue ready to go but decided to bide his time. "If a good occasion presents," he remarked, "I will shoot one little gun more . . . this session."[60]

Although he had warned of dire consequences if the war continued—"this Government will almost cease to exist—& dwindle to nothing"—there can be no doubt that the young congressman remained committed to the Union— deeply committed. And he believed New Hampshire shared that commitment. "All the reflecting men in the nation know how important New England is to the Union; & all reflecting men in New England feel that the Union is also important to her." If New England maintains its religious, social, and literary institutions, he argued, and *"reforms her morals,"* it will have the best guarantee of prosperity and lasting happiness.[61]

While the debates on these various measures reverberated through Congress in what was described as one of the stormiest sessions in memory, delegates to the Hartford Convention gathered to determine a course of action. Fortunately the more radical of the group never captured control of the convention.

58. DW to a Mr. Lawrence, [no date], in Van Tyne, ed., *Letters of Webster,* p. 50.

59. DW to [William F. Rowland?], January 11, 1815, in *PC,* I, 181.

60. DW to Ezekiel Webster, January 22, 1815, in *W&S,* XVII, 250.

61. DW to [William F. Rowland?], January 11, 1815, in *PC,* I, 181; DW to Ezekiel Webster, November 20, 1814, in *W&S,* XVI, 31.

More moderate and conservative voices predominated, and the final results of the gathering did not threaten secession. Rather it put forward a series of constitutional amendments that a committee would presently bring to Washington. These amendments included, among others, repealing the three-fifth slave representation clause (Article I, Section 2) and requiring a two-third vote in Congress for the admission of new states, for the enactment of nonimportation legislation, and for the enactment of a declaration of war. It also forbade any state from furnishing two successive chief executives, and it limited the President to a single term. These amendments showed a distinct bias in favor of New England and against other sections of the country.[62]

Because the deliberations of the convention were held behind closed doors, many people around the country presumed that the delegates plotted to separate from the Union. Some irate Americans even accused the delegates of treason, and the convention soon acquired a distinctly offensive odor that tarnished the reputation not only of the attending members but of the entire Federalist party. And the publication of the proposed list of amendments to the Constitution did not alter that conclusion. More and more the delegates were accused of taking advantage of a weakened nation suffering military losses and diminished revenues to force their selfish demands upon the American people.

Webster's immediate response to the amendments when they arrived in Washington on January 10 missed recognizing that the proceedings at Hartford could possibly prove fatal to his party. He did not seem to understand the bitterness many people around the country felt over New England's self-centered concern for its own needs and interests. On the contrary, he found the demands "moderate, temperate & judicious. The Federalists who belong in the middle & southern states, are very highly gratified," he declared.[63]

But not for long. On Tuesday, February 4, 1815, word arrived in Washington that an enormous British invasion force had been defeated—triumphantly defeated—at New Orleans by a ragtag collection of American militiamen, army regulars, pirates, a Negro battalion, and Indians under the command of General Andrew Jackson of Tennessee. The gloom in Washington and around the country because of the war and all its hardship and suffering dissolved in an instant, replaced by shouts of joy and thanksgiving. It was hard to believe. More than two thousand British soldiers killed, wounded, and captured while only a dozen American casualties were reported. It was fantastic. Who would ever believe that frontiersmen had destroyed the army of the greatest power in the world? "ALMOST INCREDIBLE VICTORY!" trumpeted the *National Intelligencer.* "Enemy . . . beaten and repulsed . . . with great slaughter. The Glorious News . . . has spread around a general joy, commensurate with the brilliance of this event, and the magnitude of our Victory."[64]

62. See Linda Kerber, *Federalists in Dissent* (New York, 1970).
63. DW to [William F. Rowland?], January 11, 1815, in *PC,* I, 181.
64. February 7, 1815.

Nine days later came more stunning news. On Christmas Eve 1814 the American delegates in Ghent, Belgium, had concluded a peace treaty with their British counterparts ending the War of 1812. Never mind that the terms of the treaty basically reaffirmed the *status quo ante bellum.* The country had escaped a hideous and needless war with its boundaries intact and its honor vindicated. Its independence had been reestablished, thanks to Andrew Jackson and his valiant soldiers at New Orleans.[65]

Men ran through the streets of Washington crying, "Peace! Peace!" Groups of people paraded from one public building to another to shout their congratulations and gratitude. Amid these celebrations the representatives from the Hartford Convention with their constitutional amendments in hand quietly slipped out of town.

"Who would not be an American?" demanded *Niles' Weekly Register.* *"Long Live the republic! . . . Last asylum of oppressed humanity."*[66]

The congressional session ended happily on March 3, 1815, but Webster had already left for home—he had a habit of arriving late and leaving early—in order to appear in the "February court." As he had earlier said, he had no intention of spending "another winter in this Great Dismal."[67]

The conclusion of the Thirteenth Congress confirmed in the minds of most observers that the thirty-two-year-old Daniel Webster had emerged as an important leader of the Federalist party, one of its best and most persuasive spokesmen, and a political force to be reckoned with in the future. In addition, he had taken fairly well-defined positions on several issues that would continue to face the nation. He had opposed tariffs because they were harmful to his agrarian and commercial constituents. Manufacturers needed protective tariffs, but in 1815 New Hampshire did not have a preponderant number of manufacturers. Webster had also favored a strong national bank structured along conservative lines that guaranteed specie payments. A bank regularly issuing worthless paper to a ailing government, he argued, would very quickly bankrupt the country. By and large his thinking rested principally on Federalist notions going back to Alexander Hamilton but infused with a degree of Jeffersonian agrarianism.

It was an old man's creed, more or less. Even Webster conceded that. He said that "though young," he possessed "antiquated notions; and that, to be useful, he ought to have been with generations that had gone by."[68]

"To be useful." Not many months later he proved to be very useful indeed.

65. On the negotiations at Ghent, see Remini, *Clay,* pp. 94–122.

66. March 4, 1815.

67. DW to Ezekiel Webster, January 22, 1815, DW to Moody Kent, December 22, [1814], in *W&S,* XVII, 250, XVI, 32.

68. Speech on the National Bank bill, February 28, 1816, in *W&S,* XIV, 76.

7

The Dartmouth College *Case*

W ITH HIS reputation rapidly expanding outside the narrow confines of his congressional district in New Hampshire Webster seriously thought of moving to a larger and more influential area. Money was a consideration. Money was *always* a consideration. As he later explained, "I could carry my practice in New Hampshire no further; I could make no more of it; & its results were not competent to the support of my family."[1]

At the moment he could not decide whether to move to Boston or New York City or Albany. He inclined toward Boston but worried about its future financial strength. "Our New England prosperity and importance," he explained to his brother, "are passing away. This is fact. The events of the times, the policy of England, the consequences of our war, and the Ghent Treaty, have bereft us of our commerce, the great source of our wealth. If any great scenes are to be acted in this country within the next twenty years, New York is the place in which those scenes are to be viewed."[2]

So he hesitated. But there was another consideration for holding fast. On August 29, 1814, just the year before, he had been reelected to Congress. Another year remained in his current term. He could resign of course, but that would interrupt the real progress he had made in becoming an important leader of the Federalist party. With the war now over, with the country on the brink of industrial development, with so many troublesome issues still to be resolved, like the National Bank, Webster was not ready to pull out of Congress and start over in another state.

So he spent the remainder of 1815 attending to his law practice. Then something momentous happened. During the summer he received a letter from John Wheelock, the rather crusty president of Dartmouth College who had succeeded his father, Eleazar, the founder of the college. Over the past few years Wheelock had been having trouble with his increasingly-independent Board of Trustees, and this letter introduced Webster into what became the celebrated *Dartmouth College* case.

1. "Autobiography," in *PC*, I, 23.
2. DW to Ezekiel Webster, March 26, 1816, ibid., I, 196.

The struggle between the trustees and the president came to a head over a theological dispute, Congregationalism versus Presbyterianism, in which Wheelock took the Presbyterian position and the trustees the Congregational side. It developed because of the religious revival spreading across the country during the first several decades of the nineteenth century, the so-called Second Great Awakening. At Dartmouth the religious revivalists clashed with the religious conservatives, like Wheelock, and this schism split both the faculty and student body. The trustees, staunch Congregationalists and Federalists, sided with the anti-Wheelock faction of the faculty and student body and subsequently limited the president's authority. In addition, they rejected two of his nominees to fill vacancies on the board and elected two men hostile to him. To complicate matters, Wheelock published a pamphlet[3] attacking the trustees and then appealed to the state legislature to intervene on his behalf and appoint a committee to look into his charges. The trustees counterattacked by removing Wheelock and naming the Reverend Francis Brown to the presidency. The legislature responded in June 1815 by appointing an investigating committee.[4]

In what had now become a public free-for-all Wheelock then turned to Webster to represent him in the legal proceedings, and apparently—although his actions seemed uncertain and confused—the young lawyer consented. In a letter dated August 5 Wheelock asked Webster to attend the first meeting of the investigating committee, and he enclosed a twenty-dollar retaining fee.[5] Webster did not respond, did not appear at the meeting of the committee, but pocketed the fee.[6] When Webster failed to appear, Wheelock and his friends naturally assumed that the trustees had won him over. Infuriated, they accused him of treachery. Josiah Dunham threatened him with political reprisals. "Unless you can extricate yourself from this unpleasant affair, it will be *unpleasant for you.* If great men will manage thus, the Lion's Skin must be stript off."[7]

Finding most Federalists siding with the trustees, Wheelock turned for help to Republicans, who had long been concerned about the Federalist influence on the state's only institution of higher learning. The Republicans quickly decided that their interests coincided with those of Wheelock. What had developed in a relatively short time was not simply a contest between a president and trustees or between Congregationalism and Presbyterianism but a political contest between Federalists and Republicans to shape the state's educational future. The Republicans recognized and feared that without legislative control the institution would become a training school for "aristocratic leaders" with Federalist inclinations. And underlying the entire conflict was the question of Dartmouth's auton-

---

3. *Sketches of the History of Dartmouth College . . . from the Year 1779 to the Year 1815* (1815).

4. Baxter, *Daniel Webster & The Supreme Court,* p. 65ff.

5. Wheelock to Webster, August 5, 1815, in *PC,* I, 188.

6. Webster claimed that the letter asking him to attend did not arrive in time. Besides, he had other commitments. DW to [Josiah Dunham], August 25, 1815, ibid., I, 192.

7. Dunham to Webster, August 16, 1815, in *PLFP,* I, 22.

omy since it had received a royal charter from the governor of New Hampshire in 1767.[8]

Both political parties in the state now girded themselves for the next election. Isaac Hill, the Republicans' leading journalist in New Hampshire, portrayed the venerable Wheelock as the victim of a plot by the clergy, lawyers, college trustees, and Federalists of New England to perpetuate their aristocratic interests and dying party in the religious and educational institutions of the country. The Republicans chose as their gubernatorial candidate William Plumer, an ex-Federalist himself, and claimed that he represented religious freedom and the rights of all denominations.[9]

The Federalists repeatedly fumbled the political ball in their effort to find a suitable candidate to run against Plumer. They discarded the regular nominee, John Gilman, who had been around for years, and tried several other possibilities before throwing their support to James Sheafe, the richest merchant in the state. It was a nomination born of desperation, and it went down to shattering defeat in March 1816. Plumer received 52.95 percent of the vote in the second-largest total ever cast in a New Hampshire contest. In addition, the Federalist party lost every branch of the government except the judiciary. Obviously desertions from the ranks because of the taint of treason and the Dartmouth excitement had ravaged the Federalist party in the state and threw its future into serious doubt.[10]

As usual, Webster had delayed returning to Washington. He had waited until his party found a gubernatorial candidate. He did not reach the capital until early February and took his seat on February 7. He became immediately aware—frankly startled—by the vast changes occasioned by the end of the war and the great victory at New Orleans. A spirit of nationalistic pride, a sense that the nation had reached the threshold of tremendous economic expansion that would be "revolutionary" in its impact on all sections of the country, now pulsated through Congress. Leading the way, President Madison called for a new approach that would bind the country together and stimulate its financial growth. He urged the passage of a new national bank, a protective tariff, and the possibility of federally sponsored public works. These internal improvements, as they were called, would be essential to the inauguration of a market economy. Henry Clay, now back from his mission abroad and again elected Speaker, threw all his energies into backing Madison's summons. "We had become the scorn of foreign powers, and the contempt of our own citizens," he cried in one House speech. That must not and will not happen again, not if the nation builds up "the whole physical power of the country." His floor manager, as before, John C. Calhoun, argued long and effectively for a broad interpretation of the Constitution that would allow this nationalistic program to be enacted into law. A number

8. The charter stipulated that there would be a board of twelve trustees and a president.

9. *New Hampshire Patriot*, February 13, 20, 27, 1816.

10. Turner, *Plumer of New Hampshire*, pp. 234–239.

of Federalists were intrigued by the possibilities of this "market revolution," while many conservative Republicans reacted in horror.[11]

The secretary of the treasury Alexander J. Dallas and Calhoun concocted a bill that provided a twenty-year charter for a national bank with a thirty-five-million-dollar capital stock of which the government would purchase one fifth with specie, Treasury notes, or government stocks, and the rest would be offered for public sale. This quasi-public institution would be run by a twenty-five-member board of directors to which the government would appoint one fifth and the stockholders the other four fifths. Into this bank the government would deposit all its funds. The bank would issue notes acceptable as legal tender. It would collect taxes for the government and transmit government funds without cost. In return for this generous charter the Bank would pay the government a bonus of a million and a half dollars in three installments over a four-year period.[12]

On returning to Washington, and without wasting any time, Webster jumped into the acrimonious debate that had developed over the administration's nationalistic program, in particular the chartering of this new bank. As he had the year before, he objected to the large capitalization. He much preferred ten million, the size of the original bank suggested by Hamilton. He also objected to investing the government with the appointment of five directors of the bank. Such a close relationship between the government and the bank could prove fatal. He could foresee collusion, corruption, and all manner of other horrible evils.[13]

The currency question also disturbed him because weak state banks outside New England had been paying taxes with depreciated paper. Throughout the war only New England banks had redeemed their paper with gold and silver. In a speech on February 28, 1816, Webster said he believed this situation needed to be corrected if the currency of the United States was to be equitable and sound. "The power of the Government must be exercised in some way," he insisted, "and that speedily, or evils would result, the extent of which he would not attempt to describe."[14]

In a rousing address to his colleagues Speaker Clay repudiated his earlier opposition to a national bank and tried to calm the fears of many Republicans concerning the measure's constitutionality. Circumstances produced by the war convinced him that Congress did in fact have the power to initiate this legislation, something Webster never doubted.

But there were other problems, and on February 28 the New Englander detailed his great concerns about the currency. He said he would rather no bank

11. Remini, *Clay*, p. 135ff; *Annals of Congress*, 14th Congress, 1st Session, pp. 776–778.

12. Ralph C. H. Catterall, *The Second Bank of the United States* (Chicago, 1903), pp. 10–21.

13. Webster gave this particular speech on March 14, 1816. *Annals of Congress*, 14th Congress, 1st Session, pp. 1212–1213.

14. Ibid., pp. 1091–1094.

at all to one that allowed millions of depreciated paper to float freely around the country and be used to pay debts owed to the government.[15]

Despite his objections the Second Bank of the United States (BUS) passed the Congress with many Federalists—but not Webster—voting for it. "Indeed," declared Black Dan, "Federal votes carried it."[16] Madison signed the bill on April 10, 1816, with the Bank scheduled to go into operation in January 1817. But Calhoun also worried about the currency, and while the bill still lay on the President's desk, he introduced legislation in line with Webster's objections and, for several weeks, with Webster's help, deftly guided the debate. Even so, the bill went down to defeat on April 25 by a vote of sixty to fifty-nine. A single vote made the difference.

That single vote tormented Webster. He could not bear it. He had to do something, so he consulted Calhoun, and on the following day, April 26, he introduced three resolutions requiring that after February 1, 1817, all debts, duties, and taxes owed to the United States must be paid in legal tender (gold or silver) or Treasury notes or notes of the BUS.[17] In presenting these resolutions, Webster spoke with great feeling and determination. A Boston merchant pays duties in specie or cash notes, he argued, which are at least 20 percent more valuable than the notes offered by a Baltimore merchant. He went on:

> Such monstrous inequality and injustice are not to be tolerated. Since the commencement of this course of things, it can be shown that the people of the Northern States have paid a million of dollars more than their just proportion of the public burdens. . . . But it is not merely the inequality and injustice of this system, if that may be called system which is rather the want of all system, that need reform. It throws the whole revenue into derangement and endless confusion. It prevents the possibility of order, method, or certainty in the public receipts or disbursements. This mass of depressed paper, thrown out at first in loans to accommodate government, has done little else than embarrass and distress government. It can hardly be said to circulate, but it lies in the channel of circulation, and chokes it up by its bulk and its sluggishness.[18]

To Webster's great delight his resolution requiring legal tender for all government revenues after February 1817 passed overwhelmingly with a two-thirds vote. He took enormous pride in the outcome, later contending that his efforts helped establish a truly sound and efficient system of banking and currency in the United States during a period of tremendous industrial expansion.[19]

Another important nationalistic issue advanced by the administration and supported by Clay, Calhoun, and other Republicans was the tariff. Advocates of

15. Remini, *Clay,* p. 140ff.; *Annals of Congress,* 14th Congress, 1st Session, pp. 1091–1094. See also his speech on April 5; ibid., pp. 1339, 1341–1343.

16. DW to Samuel Ayer Bradley, April 21, 1816, in *PC,* I, 197. It passed the House on March 14 by a vote of eighty to seventy-one. It is interesting that Webster voted against the bill and subsequently became the Bank's attorney. *Annals of Congress,* 14th Congress, 1st Session, p. 1219.

17. Ibid., p. 1440.

18. Ibid., pp. 1440–1449.

19. The vote was seventy-nine to thirty-five. Ibid., pp. 1450–1451.

such a bill argued that the nation must build an independent domestic economy and not rely, as it had in the past, in the imports of foreign nations. Manufactures were essential to industrial growth, future prosperity, and national security, but they could never survive if Europe continued to dump its goods on American markets and undersell domestic products. The defense of national freedom demanded protective tariffs. Only a self-sufficient economy could guarantee a strong Union and a prosperous people.

The House Ways and Means Committee reported a tariff bill on March 20, 1816, that followed fairly closely the recommendations of the treasury secretary. But where Secretary Dallas had suggested a 33⅓ percent duty on cotton products and 28 percent on woolens, the committee lowered both to 25 percent. Massachusetts had a high concentration of woolen and cotton manufactures, and its representatives dutifully demanded a return to the higher schedule. Other representatives wanted similar considerations and proposed increased duties on a wide variety of commodities, including iron, sugar, gunpowder, hemp, and sailcloth.[20]

As the representative of a state whose principal concern was commerce, Webster was not especially interested or supportive of protective rates on manufactures. He could understand the nationalistic argument for a tariff hike, but his seafaring constituents would not be directly affected, unless of course their carrying trade was diminished by reduced imports. However, during the 1815 and 1816 congressional sessions he had made the acquaintance of Francis Cabot Lowell, one of the leading textile manufacturers in the country. They passed several weeks in Washington together. "I was much with him," wrote Webster in his "Autobiography," "& found him full of exact practical knowledge, on many subjects." No doubt the young representative heard a great deal from Lowell about his industry's needs and how much he looked to the government for a liberal policy when considering tariff legislation.[21]

Not surprisingly, therefore, Webster proposed on Saturday, March 23, that the cotton duty be raised and fixed at 30 percent for two years, then lowered to 25 percent for the next two years and leveled off thereafter at 20 percent.[22] Clay objected to the proposal because a longer period might be needed to obtain the desired economic benefit of the legislation, so he moved to restore the original figures.

Webster stood his ground. He had "conversed with those well informed on the subject," he insisted in his response on the following Monday, and understood that although many manufacturers would be satisfied with higher rates for a one-year period, he had proposed two years to accommodate those who needed a higher rate. He said the basic question was how far the country was bound to support these "institutions." At the moment he was not prepared to

20. Ibid., pp. 1233–1234, 1257ff.
21. "Autobiography," in *PC*, I, 23.
22. *Annals of Congress*, 14th Congress, 1st Session, pp. 1271–1272.

say whether the government was obliged to adopt permanent protection. The people had a right to expect relief from the dangers to which sudden changes of events exposed manufactures. But the government also had the right to say whether such relief should be permanent or not and the right to reduce protective duties when and if it thought proper. What he did oppose was a "changing and fluctuating policy," and therefore he had offered his motion in order to provide a duty "so moderate as to insure its permanency and be still an adequate one." His object, he claimed, "was to protect the manufacturers permanently." Calhoun sided with Webster against Clay on this issue—the two men had become something of a team—and argued that a permanent duty of 20 percent once reached would provide ample protection.[23] A vote immediately followed this debate and Clay's substitute motion went down to defeat, forty-seven to sixty-one, and Webster's was approved by a "large majority."[24]

But Webster also voted to reduce rates for iron, wool, and sugar, so he hardly qualified as an advocate of the protective system. As he said, his immediate object was the protection of manufacturers. When the tariff bill came up for a third reading and final passage on April 8, the highly eccentric John Randolph of Roanoke tried to block its passage by indulging in a three-hour harangue against a protective policy for manufacturers. The Speaker frequently interrupted in an effort to move to a vote, faulting Randolph for deliberately delaying House business. Randolph shot back: "I labor under two great misfortunes—one is, that I can never understand the honorable Speaker; the other is, that he can never understand me."[25]

Hothead that he was, Randolph also sparred with Webster over the sugar duty and got so provoked that he challenged the New Hampshire representative to a duel! He claimed his "feelings" had been insulted. The challenge was as ridiculous as Randolph himself, and Webster simply brushed it aside.

Sir
    For having declined to comply with your demand yesterday, in the House, for an explanation of words of a general nature used in debate, you now "demand of me that satisfaction which your insulted feelings require & refer me to your friend (Mr——[Thomas B. Robertson] I presume, as he is the bearer of your note) for such arrangement as are usual."
    This demand, for explanation, you, in my judgment, as a matter of right, were not entitled to make on me; nor were the temper & style of your own reply to my objections to the Sugar Tax of a character to induce me to accord it as a matter of courtesy.
    Neither can I (under the circumstances of this case) recognize in you a right to call me to the field to answer what you may please to consider an insult to your feelings. It is unnecessary for me to state other & obvious considerations growing out of this case. It is enough that I do not feel myself bound, at all times & under any circumstances, to accept, from any man, who shall choose to risk his own life, an invitation of this sort; altho' I shall

23. Ibid., pp. 1271–1272.
24. Wiltse, *Calhoun, Nationalist,* p. 119; *Annals of Congress,* 14th Congress, 1st Session, pp. 1272–1273.
25. Cited in Remini, *Clay,* p. 138 note 13.

be always prepared to repel in a suitable manner the aggression of any man who may presume upon such a refusal.[26]

Mutual friends intervened, and the dispute was amicably settled without further fuss. Webster had not kept a copy of his written reply to the challenge, so he wrote a gracious note to Randolph and asked for one. He received an equally gracious response.

Apr. 30. 1816

Sir
    Your polite & friendly note was put into my hands this morning. . . . Accept my acknowledgments for the terms in which that request is made & believe me with very high respect & regard
    Your obedient Servt.

John Randolph of Roanoke[27]

The Tariff of 1816 won final approval in the House on April 8, but Webster was not present to record his vote, and he offered no explanation. Possibly he was torn about which side to take. His position on the issue could best be defined as "ambivalent."[28] It came down to the fact that he would support protection for his friends in shipping and manufacturing, but that was his limit. At least for the moment.

One other minor issue developed during this first session of the Fourteenth Congress that later generated an uproar. Colonel Richard M. Johnson, the reputed slayer of the Indian chieftain Tecumseh, complained that each session dragged on because congressmen were paid by the day and consequently stretched out the length of each session in order to increase their earnings. Clay assigned him and Webster with others to investigate the matter. The subsequent report of the committee recommended changing the compensation for House members from six dollars a day to fifteen hundred dollars per annum. Most members, even those who subsequently voted against it, supported the report. Ever ready to increase his own income, Webster spoke in favor of the bill, claiming that two months were sufficient for House business—that is, if every member paid attention to what was being said on the floor. He noted the papers and letters strewn on desks monopolizing the attention of each representative. "If, in any way, the attention of the House could be fixed on the speaker," Webster argued, "there would be an end to long speeches; for he defied any man to address any assembly of this sort, and address them long, if that attention was fixed on him. They would cease to speak when they ceased to have anything to say on anything or subject under debate." He allowed that under normal circumstances and proper controls "a session of two months in a year was perfectly adequate to the ordinary business of legislation." He ended by declaring that he did not much care whether the House increased or decreased the com-

26. DW to Randolph, [April 1816], copy, in *PC*, I, 198.
27. DW to Randolph, [April 30, 1816], Randolph to DW, April 30, 1816, ibid., I, 197–198.
28. Baxter, *Webster and the Supreme Court*, p. 65.

pensation, but he contended that the mode of compensation could be "benefi-
cially changed." With little vocal opposition the bill passed on March 19, eighty-
one to sixty-seven.

Then "all hell broke loose." The electorate cried out its disgust over this
blatant theft of public money and threatened retribution at the ballot box in the
fall elections against all those responsible.[29] Fortunately Webster would not seek
another term since by this time he had decided to move to Boston. As it turned
out, fully two thirds of the House and half the members of the Senate were
expelled from office during the fall election. Even a number of those who voted
against the bill were defeated! It is interesting to speculate on what might have
happened had Webster chosen to remain in New Hampshire and seek another
term.[30]

As Webster prepared to depart from Washington in late April, he pondered
gloomily about the course of American political history over the last several
months. He frankly did not quite comprehend what was happening. The nation
rejoiced over its escape from near disaster with Great Britain, the administration
delighted in its newfound popularity in guiding the country to a successful
conclusion of the war, and a new, intense, nationalistic furor seemed to grip
every American, including New Englanders. But what of parties and principles?
To Webster's consternation Federalists frequently sounded and acted like Republicans, while Republicans sounded and acted as though they had abandoned
the philosophy of Jefferson for that of Hamilton. It hardly made any sense.
"There are strange things happening here as well as elsewhere," he confided to
Samuel Bradley. "Whether all our party distinctions are not breaking up, I
cannot say. Appearances are very much in favor of such a supposition. Many
Federalists voted for the Bank. Indeed Federalist votes carried it. On the *Tariff*
Federalists as well as Democrats were much divided. The manufacturing interest has become a *strong distinct party.* This you may rely on. In short, I believe
we are all to be thrown into new forms, & new associations."[31]

Indeed. Webster had the wit to realize that something profound was happening in the operation of the political system and that there had begun to
emerge a new wealthy class of Americans who would have a deep, lasting, and
important influence on the way the system functioned in the future. As a matter
of fact the party structure had already come unglued because of the war and its
impact on Federalist ranks. Suspicions of treason continued to circulate about
the Hartford Convention, and slowly but inevitably those suspicions destroyed
the Federalist party. Principles about the powers of government and their limits
no longer generated sharp distinctions. As Webster said, the voting record in

---

29. *Annals of Congress,* 14th Congress, 1st Session, pp. 1133, 1174; Remini, *Clay,* p. 144; C. Edward
Skeen, "*Vox Populi, Vox Dei:* The Compensation Act of 1816," *Journal of the Early Republic,* VI
(Fall 1986), pp. 253–274.

30. Remini, *Clay,* pp. 145–146. The Compensation Act was repealed by the House on March 19,
1816, and the per diem allowance to each congressman was raised from six to eight dollars.

31. DW to Bradley, April 21, 1816, in *PC,* I, 197.

Congress this past session made it difficult to distinguish a Federalist from a Democrat. The future seemed to belong to the Republican party with no organized opposition to challenge its supremacy.

In fact an entirely new generation of men had arrived on the political scene to manage national affairs. Gone were the great patriots of the Revolution who fought and won independence for the American people and then committed their beliefs and principles to a written record for all to see and affirm. The Declaration of Independence and the Constitution stated precisely and clearly their philosophy of government. But these Founding Fathers were dead or in retirement. Would their heirs and successors match their devotion to the public good, the common weal? Would their successors possess the virtue of the revolutionary generation? Webster had his doubts. He wrote at this time that some good men may be willing to sacrifice their interests and take office for the sake of the people they serve, but there will be many more who struggle for office "from motives of gain and selfishness." And while the "tumult of elections discourage public spirit and wear out patriotism," it will "in no degree abate the eagerness of self-interest, or mitigate the fury of party."[32]

The fury of party! Just as George Washington, John Adams, and many other Founders had predicted. These great men regarded parties as an evil, as a blight that corrupted everything connected with it, as a threat to the safety of the Republic, as nothing more than factions of vicious self-seekers locked together in pursuit of their own greedy ends. Like these Founders, Webster also regarded party spirit as "the most tremendous engine of mischief ever wielded against the liberties of a free people."[33]

But Webster was living with the dead party prejudices of dead men. The new leadership in the Republican party understood the value and purpose of party structure. These leaders had no record of achievement in the colonial or early national periods of American history. They had neither fought in the Revolution nor participated in any of the conventions that shaped the form of government for the states or the central authority. These new leaders necessarily looked to the party to advance their interests and those of their constituents. They did not see parties as evil; they saw them as a positive good.

The most perceptive of this new breed was Martin Van Buren, who was just beginning to direct and control the Republican organization in New York controlled by the Albany Regency. Short, fair-complexioned, with light yellowish red hair and small, brilliant eyes, he exuded charm and good manners to everyone he met. Possessing unsurpassed skills as a political manipulator, he was known as the Little Magician or the Red Fox of Kinderhook, denoting his birthplace. Van Buren argued that parties were essential for the stable and orderly running of the government. A two-party system, he contended, holding

---

32. A review by Webster of the "Extraordinary Red Book" and published in the *North American Review* (December 1816), reprinted in *W&S*, XV, 8.

33. *W&S*, XV, 8.

different principles and openly contending against each other, provides the people with a choice of direction they wish their government to take, and this in turn acts as a check upon the abuse of power by any one party and results in safeguarding the liberty of all.[34]

None of this made much sense to Webster. He had seen too many instances of corruption, of indifference to the common good, of political hacks concerned solely with office seeking to have the Van Buren faith in party structure. Unlike the New Yorker, he relied on his own superior talents as a lawyer and orator to make his way in the political world.

But Webster did see, however dimly, a new world beginning that would completely recast the forces and ideas that would dominate the nation for the next century and beyond. A market revolution had begun to evolve that would ultimately transform American society from an agrarian to an industrial economy. And Webster himself would play an important role in that transformation.

In one sense the market revolution began with the end of the War of 1812. Politically it began with the election of 1816, which saw the virtual disappearance of the Federalist party on the national level and the total triumph of the Republican party. The Federalists did manage to put forward a presidential candidate to stand against James Monroe, the nominee of the Republicans, but it was a one-sided contest. Their candidate, Rufus King of New York, never had a chance, and never again did the Federalists offer the nation a presidential nominee. With the Republican party in sole control of the government a newspaperman dubbed the years of Monroe's administration the "Era of Good Feelings."[35]

Despite the euphemism, political feelings in every part of the nation continued to be as lusty and combative as before. Men of different opinions and principles crowded into the single party and fought their battles over issues as Republicans, calling those who disagreed with them "Federalists" and "aristocrats" or "Jacobins" and "democrats." Such a system could not go on indefinitely. Van Buren, for one, hated it because a one-party system did in fact generate corruption and misconduct in office. A one-party system, to his mind, smacked of dictatorship. Only a two-party system guaranteed balance, stability, honesty, and efficiency in government. According to Van Buren, what the nation needed was a new restructuring of the party system.[36]

Not only did the Federalists take a savage beating at the polls in the national election, but they suffered great losses in the states as well. In New Hampshire the Republicans swept the state. But by that time Webster had already moved to Boston.

A removal had been on his mind for many months, in fact years. Furthermore, the ties he had to New Hampshire had been coming apart, one after

34. Richard Hofstadter, *The Idea of Party* (California, 1969), passim.

35. George Dangerfield, *Era of Good Feelings* (New York, 1963), passim.

36. Robert V. Remini, *Martin Van Buren and the Making of the Democratic Party* (New York, 1959), passim.

another. He had little contact with his relatives, save Ezekiel. His father had already passed away, and on April 25, 1816, his mother, Abigail Eastman Webster, died in Boscawen. Ezekiel, with whom she had been living, had informed him of her illness, and Webster responded by asking his brother to tell her, if still alive, that "I pray for her everlasting peace and happiness, and would give her a son's blessing for all her parental goodness. May God bless her, living or dying!"[37] On April 28 Abigail was buried in Salisbury by the side of her mother and her husband.[38]

At first Webster considered moving to New York City or Albany. But he was a New Englander. His roots went deep into its soil, into its culture and lifestyle. So too Grace Fletcher Webster. And he knew Boston and had friends in the area. He therefore rejected New York and decided to relocate in Boston.

At the time of his mother's death Webster was already involved in the arrangements for his removal. In June he went with his wife to see about a house in Boston, and he took one of his former law students, Alexander Bliss, into his office, which he set up on Court Street near the Old State House. Bliss, a Yale graduate, was expected to run the office while Webster attended to his legal affairs in Washington and elsewhere. Almost immediately upon his return to Portsmouth Webster packed and shipped his library to Bliss and asked him to have the books properly shelved in the office in time for his arrival. Then on "the 16. of August I left Portsmouth forever." He, his wife, his six-year-old daughter, Grace, and his three-year-old son, Fletcher, arrived in Boston on the same day, and for the next three weeks stayed at Mrs. Hannah Delano's boardinghouse, after which they moved into a four-story brick and stone house on Mount Vernon Street in a fashionable part of town at the summit of Beacon Hill and took up "house-keeping in a house of Mr J. Mason."[39]

Boston meant opportunity, a better and more fashionable life, a wealthier, more discriminating, more cultivated, and better-educated society in which to display his verbal skills and legal talent. Webster was no stranger to Boston. He knew its narrow, twisted streets, the noise, the congestion; he also knew the names, the wealth, and the habits of the most distinguished families, and he understood what he must accomplish to become part of Boston's highest society. He wanted to live well and fraternize with important people and represent them as their lawyer in advancing principles and ideas they all espoused. Most important, he wanted to count them as his friends.

The Boston elite also knew Webster, had known him long before he arrived on Court Street to set up his law practice. He had established a reputation as a leader of the New Hampshire bar. Many of his more important cases before the U.S. Supreme Court, the U.S. Circuit Court, and the New Hampshire Supreme Court were observed in Boston, and his talents had been duly noted and com-

37. DW to Ezekiel Webster, April 11, 1816, in *W&S*, XVII, 257.

38. Ezekiel Webster to Charles Brickett Haddock, April 29, 1816, ibid., XVII, 257.

39. "Autobiography," DW to Bliss, June 27, 1816, in *PC*, I, 23–24, 200.

mented upon. Moreover, his role as a leader of the Federalist party in Congress and his speeches and record in the House of Representatives were particularly well known and regularly applauded.[40] His reputation as a distinguished orator also preceded him so that when he appeared in court in Boston to plead a case or give a speech, a huge crowd came out to hear him. He was already something of a celebrity in 1816, so his settling in Boston came off without any difficulty whatsoever. He immediately found his proper place.

In addition to everything else, there was the man himself and what he stood for. His literary pretensions, his knowledge of history, language, and the classics, his pride of ancestry, his conservatism, his reliance on and reverence for reason, his appreciation of religion, his defense of property rights, and his respect for the accomplishments of the "wellborn" were among the virtues the Boston aristocracy most admired in him. Quite simply, he belonged. He was Boston to his fingertips without having been born there. Once settled, he attended the Brattle Square Church,[41] not far from his law office, where the younger Joseph Buckminster was pastor until his early death, succeeded briefly by Edward Everett and then by John Gorham Palfrey, all of them Unitarians who took a less dismal view of human frailties than the more traditional Puritans. Webster also purchased a pew in St. Paul's Episcopal Church, perhaps to touch all possible social bases within the community. He also sought and won membership in some of Boston's most prestigious cultural societies, such as the Boston Athenaeum, the American Antiquarian Society in Worcester, and the American Academy of Arts and Sciences. Within a very few years he was one of the city's preeminent intellectual and cultural leaders.

And some even thought he looked like a Bostonian. Said Eliza Buckminster: "He was now thirty-five years old, and certainly in the perfection of all the powers of body and mind. The majestic beauty of his countenance was never more striking than at this period."[42]

Webster's first years in Boston were mainly spent building his law practice, and he quickly found employment arguing in the local courts of Suffolk and the surrounding counties of Essex, Middlesex, Plymouth, and beyond. When he first arrived, there seemed to be little room for another lawyer "in the upper class of the legal fraternity." After all, there was Dexter, Prescott, Sullivan, Shaw, Gorham, and many others. But he walked straight into this "distinguished company," and "none dared to question his right to be there."[43] He was a regular pleader in the First Circuit Court of the United States as well as the U.S. Supreme Court.

---

40. "At the close of the fourteenth Congress," wrote a contemporary, "the three names most distinguished in it—Webster, Clay, Calhoun—occupied, almost exclusively, the minds of all men. There was nothing, seemingly, beyond the scope of their ambition or attainment. They had but to form a triumvirate, and divide the world between them." March, *Webster,* pp. 54–55.

41. Although Webster attended other churches, he never officially left the Brattle Square Church. Harvey, *Reminiscences,* p. 396.

42. "Sketch of Mrs. G. F. Webster," in *W&S,* XVII, 442.

43. Lanman, *Private Life of Webster,* p. 44.

And although he tended to be more the corporate lawyer, he argued criminal and civil cases as well.

He prospered from the day he arrived. Within the first two months he acquired James Otis, Samuel Hubbard, George Crowninshield, and Harrison Gray Otis as clients. Francis Cabot Lowell, George Cabot, John Brooks, and others consulted him, and in 1819 John Jacob Astor retained him. Shipowners, manufacturers, insurance firms, mercantile companies, businessmen of every type engaged his services. Within a month of his arrival he had earned close to two thousand dollars and by the start of the year following his arrival in Boston he was approximating fifteen thousand dollars per annum, a pretty hefty income in those days. Within two years "his income from his professional practice was greater than that of any lawyer of his time, or any that had preceded him." Still, it was never enough. Indebtedness constantly plagued him. His uninsured and mortgaged house in Portsmouth had burned, and his housekeeping on Mount Vernon Street set him back a good deal. Grace economized as much as possible during these early years. For example, like most Americans at the time, she used candles sparingly. The Webster household probably had no more than one or two candlesticks at the most and therefore had their evening meal at a very early hour, 3:00 or 4:00 P.M.[44] Still his borrowing invariably outpaced his income. There were long-standing creditors in New Hampshire and New York and several new ones in Massachusetts. Fortunately benefactors such as Nathaniel A. Haven of Portsmouth and Charles March of New York City, both wealthy businessmen, readily came to his rescue when needed. Moreover, the Boston Associates, men like Lowell, Nathan Appleton, Thomas H. Perkins, and others who had founded the Boston Manufacturing Company in 1813 and other subsidiary enterprises, singled Webster out after his arrival in their city as their special and favored friend whose financial needs they would meet. The money they lent Webster was supposed to be repaid in time, of course, but they did not hound him. For his part Webster understood his obligation and its implications. "If I can be of any use to you at W. or can contribute any thing to your information or amusement," he wrote Nathaniel Haven in late 1816, "I hope you will permit me." As it developed, once his career as a Massachusetts congressman began, he was able to provide the Associates with "federal legislative and banking influence, avenues of federal redress, and even federal financial support."[45]

Like many others of his generation, Webster speculated in land; "overspeculated" is probably a better way to put it. It was the easiest and quickest road to great wealth, and Webster never ceased to search for it. He held substantial

44. "Memorandum of Mr. Webster's Professional Fees for Two Years, 1818 and 1833," in *W&S*, XVII, 291–292; Larkin, *Everyday Life*, p. 136.

45. "Memorandum of Mr. Webster's Professional Fees for Two Years, 1818 and 1833," in *W&S*, XVII, 291–292; March, *Webster*, p. 58; DW to Haven, November 9, 1816, in *PC*, I, 203–204; Fuess, *Webster*, I, 209–210; Carl E. Prince and Seth Taylor, "Daniel Webster, the Boston Associates, and the U.S. Government's Role in the Industrializing Process, 1815–1830," *Journal of the Early Republic*, II (Fall 1982), pp. 283, 285; Robert F. Dalzell, Jr., *Enterprising Elite: The Boston Associates and the World They Made* (Cambridge, Mass., 1987), p. 48.

property in New Hampshire, some of which he shared with his brother, and some came as payment for his legal services. Not all his speculations proved profitable, and frequently he had to mortgage what he had acquired to creditors. In one letter to Ezekiel he asked his brother to come to Boston to discuss the possible sale of some of his property. "I have a chance of being able to make some disposition of some real estate, say 6 or 8 thousand Dls. . . . I want you to bring with you such proof or estimates of value as you may have."[46]

But Webster's principal source of income came from his growing law practice. And it grew because he quickly rose to the head of the Massachusetts bar. His main strength as a lawyer, according to several of his contemporaries, was his firm "knowledge of general principles." He could never be faulted for misquoting Blackstone or any of the other titans of the law. And when opposing lawyers wrongly cited these legal giants, Webster quickly pounced on them and forced them to retract their statements. In his later years, having the great maxims of the law and the important decisions of the past firmly stored in his retentive mind, he seldom consulted authorities. He trusted his past knowledge and readily assumed—sometimes mistakenly—that his opinion in a case must in fact be the law.[47]

Also, in building his argument before a jury or a panel of judges, Webster made sure that they understood the point of law involved, that it was the only point worth considering, and that they must base their decision upon it.

In addition to everything else, Webster excelled in cross-examination. In one case the signature of a bank president, a Mr. Tufts, came into question. Webster cross-examined the bank's cashier.

"You say you think this is not Mr. Tufts' signature. What means had you of knowing Mr. Tufts' signature?"

"I was cashier of the bank of which he was president, and used to see his signature in all forms," replied the witness.

"And you think that is not his signature?" asked Webster. "Please to point out, if you will, where there is a discrepancy."

"I do not know as I can tell," the witness responded.

"But a sensible man can tell why he thinks one thing is not like another."

The witness examined the note in dispute. "Well," he said, "in the *n* the top used to be closed."

"Gentlemen of the jury," cried Webster, "you hear: the top was closed. Go on."

"The *s* at the end of his name was usually kept above the horizontal line; this is below."

"Well; any other?"

"Not any other."

Then Webster reached over and picked up one of about forty genuine Tufts

46. DW to Ezekiel Webster, [May 25, 1817], in *PC*, I, 210.

47. Harvey, *Reminiscences*, pp. 79–80.

signatures available to him, his eyes glinting with wicked amusement. He turned to the jury and showed the document to them. Every one of the peculiarities denied by the witness as characteristic of Tufts' handwriting could be found in the signature.

The witness paled. He "looked chapfallen, and took his seat; and nearly all the witnesses were floored in the same way."[48]

An even more celebrated instance involved Elijah P. Goodridge, a respectable member of the community, who charged Levi and Laban Kenniston and others with assault and robbery. He claimed that on the night of December 19, 1816, along the road between Exeter and Newburyport the accused shot him through his left hand, beat him, and stole a large sum of money. By adroit cross-examination Webster, counsel for the defendants, convinced the jury that Goodridge had faked the robbery to evade creditors and had meant to shoot a hole through his coat but accidentally wounded his hand. The defense was conducted with a boldness and skill rarely witnessed in Essex County, and despite the mass of evidence against them, the Kennistons were acquitted.[49]

Sometimes Webster harangued the jury for four hours. And held them "breathless under his spell." Josiah Quincy said that when Black Dan spoke, the words were sometimes "no more than the libretto of an opera; but, with Webster behind them, they seemed to sweep away all adverse testimony, and to render an acquittal by acclamation a simple necessity." In this particular instance Webster was defending James Prescott, a probate judge, in an impeachment action before the Massachusetts senate. "To have heard the noble effort made in his behalf by Daniel Webster marked an epoch in the lives of those present. It gave me," Quincy confessed, "my first idea of the electric force that might be wielded by a master of human speech."[50]

Although Webster's life in Boston now centered on the law, he still had the final session of the Fourteenth Congress to attend. Despite the fact that he no longer lived in New Hampshire, he remained the duly elected representative from the Portsmouth district until March 3, 1817. He could have, and should have, resigned, but he needed the money and had cases to plead before the Supreme Court that, representative or not, would take him to Washington. So he and Grace put their children in the care of the widow of Samuel Webber, former president of Harvard College, and set off for Washington on Monday, November 11, 1816.

When Webster left Boston, he was concerned about his daughter because of a "tumor" on her neck. At first he and his wife thought it was the mumps, but it had lasted too long for mumps. "It has for some days appeared to be better," he observed, "& we believe it is going off."[51]

48. Ibid., pp. 93–94.
49. Webster's argument in the case can be found in W&S, X, 173–193.
50. Josiah Quincy, *Figures of the Past* (Boston, 1883), pp. 42–43.
51. DW to Jeremiah Mason, October 29, 1816, in W&S, XVI, 35–36.

In Washington, where they arrived on November 30 after spending a week in Philadelphia, the Websters found lodging near the Capitol and formed a mess with Jeremiah Mason and his wife. Grace Webster told her half brother, James W. Paige, who subsequently became a prosperous merchant and partner with Nathan Appleton, that the ruins of the Capitol were "more splendid than I had imagined." She had hoped to attend the "little Presbyterian Church" that morning, but her husband was too indisposed to go out.[52]

They had hardly gotten settled in Washington than they received word that their daughter, Grace, was desperately ill. William Sullivan wrote and said that the child had a blister on her chest, coughed often at night, every twenty or thirty minutes or so, and that the leeches that had been applied to her back did nothing but increase her debility. "Your poor little girl is very sick," he warned Webster. "It is certainly very proper that Mrs. W. should come home. I should not think your presence indispensable, unless your own feelings demand it."[53]

Daniel and Grace left immediately. Although he had important business in court—he paid little attention to the affairs of Congress—he immediately arranged to return home and arrived back in Boston on January 15. The following week, on January 23, the child lay dying, and Webster reached down and drew her toward him. "A smile of singular love and sweetness passed over her countenance and her life was gone," recounted Eliza Buckminster. Little Grace died of tuberculosis. "Mr. Webster turned away from the bed, and great tears coursed down his cheeks."[54] In a few days he notified his brother, who had lost his own seven-year-old daughter, Mary, six months earlier from the same disease. Tuberculosis was a dreadful killer of the young in the early nineteenth century. But it could and did strike any age. No generation was immune.

Boston Sunday [January 26, 1817]

Dear Ezl.
Our dear little daughter has followed yours. She died on Thursday Evening, at 11 oclock—& was interred yesterday. Her death, tho' I thought it inevitable soon, was rather sudden when it happened. Her disease, the consumption, had not apparently obtained its last stages. She had suffered very little—the day of her death she was pretty bright, in the forenoon, tho weak. In the afternoon she grew languid, & drowsy. She however desired her friends to read & talk to & with her untill a few minutes before eleven, when her countenance suddenly altered, & in five or six minutes she expired.
Mrs. W. tho' in great affliction, is in tolerable health. Our little boy is very well. Tomorrow Morning I set out on my return to Washington.[55]

No doubt Webster suffered a great deal that winter. But he was a very private person, and unlike Henry Clay or Andrew Jackson, he tried not to show his feelings, not to anyone. He was obliged to return to Washington to appear in court, and he went about his business as though nothing had happened. But he

52. Grace Webster to Paige, December 1, 14, 1816, in Van Tyne, ed., *Letters of Webster,* p. 72.

53. Sullivan to DW, January 9, 1817, in *PC,* I, 208.

54. "Sketch of Mrs. G. F. Webster," in *W&S,* XVII, 442.

55. DW to Ezekiel Webster, [January 26, 1817], in *PC,* I, 209–210.

rarely attended the sessions of Congress, although he voted when necessary. He should have resigned. "For my part, my dear Sir," he wrote to Associate Justice Joseph Story, "I am very glad to find myself so near the close of the short period of my public engagements. And tho' I would willingly fill up the little remnant with some effort for the general good I shall see the sun go down on the third of March with unusual cheerfulness."[56]

March 3, 1817, marked the end of the Fourteenth Congress. The following day, March 4, James Monroe took his oath of office as President of the United States. "On the rising of Congress & the Court," Webster later remembered, "I came back to Boston, & entered with diligence, on the labors of my profession."[57]

At the time he did not realize how much "diligence" he would have to exert to prepare for a particular case awaiting his attention. It was one of the most important and celebrated cases in American history, *Trustees of Dartmouth College* v. *William H. Woodward.*

With the Republican victory at the polls in the fall of 1815 Governor Plumer and the legislature worked out a bill that took control of Dartmouth College and changed its governance. The bill increased the Board of Trustees from twelve to twenty-one and authorized the governor and a state executive council to fill the additional slots. It created a separate board of twenty-five overseers to monitor the operation of the trustees, including the appointment of the president and the faculty. Finally, it renamed the college Dartmouth University with what would be separate colleges of law, medicine, arts, politics, and theology. The bill passed the legislature on June 28, 1816, and Governor Plumer signed it.[58] The college, in effect, would be converted from a private to a state institution.

The original twelve trustees—that is, the college trustees—now faced a totally new situation, one they had never anticipated. By their actions they had helped create a monster poised to devour them. Now they had to contend with the state's legislative and executive authorities and a board of overseers, not simply with a crusty old president. In protest they refused to attend meetings of the new board, whereupon the legislature passed another statue reducing a quorum vote in any action from eleven to nine. Thereafter the new trustees— that is, the university trustees—simply disregarded the dissidents. They dismissed President Brown and restored Wheelock. But because of Wheelock's ill health, the office was temporarily conferred on his son-in-law, William Allen.

The college trustees, the Federalists, and their friends were horrified at the course of events. "We have satisfactory evidence," raged Reuben D. Mussey to Leverett Saltonstall, "that democracy intends to pour her poison into our literary fountains and to train up our youth for her own purposes." Worse, "the other institutions of New England are to be *regenerated* to 'pure republicanism,' and

56. DW to Story, December 9, 1816, in *W&S*, XVI, 37.

57. "Autobiography," in *PC*, I, 24.

58. Turner, *Plumer of New Hampshire*, p. 240ff.

the world is to be astonished at the hugeness of our universities. . . . The College will become democratic, and a set of devoted sycophants, how literary, you may easily imagine, will be put in the place of some of the best men for a literary Seminary unless the stubborn arm of democracy can be arrested."[59]

The college trustees decided to fight back. They refused to recognize the legality of the state's action. Dartmouth was a private institution. Without their consent the governance of the institution could not be changed legally. They subsequently dismissed the secretary-treasurer of the college, William H. Woodward, a nephew of John Wheelock's and probably one of the authors of the bill that converted Dartmouth into a university. They also brought suit on February 8, 1817, in the state's superior court against Woodward to recover the charter, seal, and records of the college.[60]

Although he had moved to Massachusetts, Webster had kept himself informed of developments at Dartmouth. As he said, "I am willing to be considered as belonging to the cause and to talk about it, and consult about it." But any number of Dartmouth friends and alumni wanted him to do more. Jeremiah Smith, former chief justice of the superior court, who was to represent the college trustees, wrote to him and insisted that he "must take some part in the argument of this college question." Despite some hesitation and doubt, he decided to help. He wrote to Jeremiah Mason, who was also to argue for the college trustees, and asked for a look at the authorities he and Smith meant to cite in their arguments.[61] When the case was argued before the three-man superior court—all recently appointed by Governor Plumer after a reorganization of the judicial system—the state's attorney general, George Sullivan, and Ichabod Bartlett represented Woodward against Mason and Smith.

The court met and heard arguments in May and September. Webster attended during the September proceedings, took notes, and spoke before the court on the authorities cited by Sullivan and Bartlett. According to one reporter, he dazzled the court with his oratory "by the genius and eloquence of his soul, of sublime sentiment and feeling."[62] Among other things he invoked the historical recollection of Caesar's murder by senators as they reiterated stab upon stab before great Caesar fell lifeless to the floor.

But Woodward sneered at these theatrics. "D. W. drowned the whole audience in their common tears—and among the rest tears of repentance were shed by zealous advocates of the laws."[63] But Webster's eloquence, the imagery of Caesar's murder, and the fine arguments of Mason and Smith did the trustees little good. On November 6, 1817, the three Republican judges found for the

59. Mussey to Saltonstall, July 18, 1816, in *PLFP*, I, 39–40.

60. Baxter, *Webster and the Supreme Court*, pp. 70–71.

61. DW to Mason, September 4, 1817, in *PC*, I, 213.

62. Salem *Gazette*, quoted in Charles Warren, "An Historical Note on the Dartmouth College Case," *American Law Review*, XLVI (September–October 1912), p. 668.

63. Woodward to Plumer, October 2, 1817, Plumer Papers, cited in Baxter, *Webster and the Supreme Court*, p. 74.

defendant by declaring that Dartmouth was a public institution subject to state regulation.[64] Obviously this "biased" decision had to be reversed, and the trustees immediately appealed to the United States Supreme Court.

Without question Webster wanted to argue the case before the High Court and have full responsibility for handling it. He fully appreciated the impact of his pleading before the New Hampshire court and how effective it might be before an "impartial" panel of justices, especially one like John Marshall. Because he knew that Mason[65] and Smith did not wish to travel to Washington to make the appeal, he wrote to President Francis Brown, whom the college trustees still regarded as the true president of the school, with the presumption that Brown "would wish my attention to this cause." He would need help in the task, "some distinguished Counsel," and he mentioned, as his personal choice, Joseph Hopkinson, a prominent lawyer and Federalist congressman from Pennsylvania and author of "Hail Columbia!," whom he had known as a colleague in the House.[66] He then stated his fee: one thousand dollars. "I doubt whether I could do it, for a much less sum. Mr Hopkinson will be very competent to argue it, alone, & probably would do so for something less;—tho' no counsel, of the first rank, would undertake this cause at Washington probably under six or seven hundred dollars. . . . As my arrangements must be made soon, let me hear from you as quick as possible."[67]

Most probably Webster knew that both Brown and the trustees were extremely anxious for him to plead their case before the Supreme Court because he contacted Hopkinson the day after he wrote to Brown and invited his assistance. Hopkinson responded with enthusiasm. "I . . . enlist most cheerfully and heartily, under your banner, in the cause you mention—whether on business or pleasure, in social or professional intercourse, I know none with whom I would prefer to associate."[68] For his services Hopkinson later received five hundred dollars, none of which came from Webster's fee.

President Brown and the trustees happily agreed to Webster's offer and his financial terms, and immediately thereafter Webster contacted Mason and Smith and asked to see their notes and briefs. The arguments put forward by these gentlemen before the New Hampshire high court laid the foundation for Webster's case.

Between them Mason and Smith contended that the action of the state wrongly intruded upon the rights of a private corporation, violated due process, and ran afoul of the contract clause of the U.S. Constitution. Webster knew that he was expected to put forward the argument worked out by his predecessors,

64. See the various documents in *PLFP,* I, 40ff.

65. Mason had resigned from the U.S. Senate on June 16, 1817.

66. Among his many accomplishments, Hopkinson had successfully defended Associate Justice Samuel Chase in his impeachment trial before the U.S. Senate in 1805.

67. DW to Brown, November 15, 1817, in *PLFP,* I, 81.

68. Hopkinson to DW, November 20, 1817, ibid., I, 82.

but what troubled him was the realization that although the case turned on the contract clause, it limited his argument to a federal constitutional issue and not the meaning of the state's constitution as well. He unquestionably wanted to argue that the actions taken by the New Hampshire legislature violated the state's constitution and common law. But such arguments, according to the Judiciary Act of 1789, could not be made on an appeal from a state court directly to the Supreme Court. They would first have to come up through the lower federal courts. Only the issue of New Hampshire's violation of the U.S. Constitution could be considered by the Supreme Court on a direct appeal.[69] Because of such limitations, Webster rightly worried that the Supreme Court might choose to hand down a narrow reading of the contract clause, the scope of which was still uncertain, and thereby side with the state against the college. "I am sorry our College cause goes to W[ashington] on *one* point only," he informed Mason. "What do you think of an action in some court of U.S. that shall raise all the objections to the Acts in question?"[70]

Mason agreed with Webster's reasoning and set about preparing what were called cognate cases that later came before the circuit court of Portsmouth.[71] Meanwhile Webster prepared his brief for the Supreme Court while the state, acting through the trustees of the university it had recently created, hired a group of lawyers who proved totally unequal to the task. One of them, John Holmes, a former Federalist, like Governor Plumer, was incompetent. A political hack, more bluster than anything else, he presumed he could simply present the state court's decision and be done with it. Another, William Wirt, a brilliant lawyer, had just been appointed U.S. attorney general in the Monroe administration and was so overwhelmed by his new duties that he never gave the *Dartmouth* case the attention it required.[72]

Webster remained in Boston into the new year because his wife was pregnant and about to deliver. Their second daughter, Julia, was born on January 16, 1818. Webster hoped to hurry down to Washington around the first of February but had to change his plans when he was retained in another case that required his immediate presence.[73] He finally set out in late January and arranged to meet with Hopkinson in Philadelphia to prepare their final arguments.

Webster had expected to argue the *Dartmouth* case in February, but the

---

69. Webster explained this in his letter to Charles Marsh and Francis Brown, December 8, 1817, in *PLFP,* I, 87–88.

70. DW to Mason, December 8, DW to Smith, December 8, 1817, in *PLFP,* I, 85, 86–87, and note 27, p. 85.

71. These cases included *Hatch* v. *Lang, Pierce ex dem., Lyman* v. *Gilbert,* and *Marsh* v. *Allen.* They were argued in May 1818. The college wished to move them along speedily; the state did not.

72. The university also retained Salma Hale, a university trustee, as cocounsel but he had not yet been admitted to the bar. Hale hired Wirt. Wirt argued nine cases between February 3 and February 16, and he was much too fatigued to take on the *Dartmouth* case.

73. DW to Mason, January 9, 1818, DW to Jeremiah Mason, January [23], 1818, in *PC,* I, 216–217. The case was *United States* v. *Bevans.*

Supreme Court did not hear it until March, giving him plenty of time to prepare.[74] He planned to speak on all the points raised in the lower court if he could
get away with it. If objections arose, he would simply tell the Court that the
actions on the various points were already in train or about to be.[75]

A good deal of attention, if not quite excitement, had developed in Washington over the *Dartmouth* case, and although Webster did not pack the courtroom, a fair number of lawyers dropped by to hear him. Since a state law might
be in jeopardy, they rightly figured that the case could be important. And Wirt
was always worth a visit. Even Webster admitted that. "Wirt is a man of a good
deal of ability," he wrote. "He is rather more of a lawyer than I expected."
Webster also sized up Holmes perfectly. "As to Holmes, if he shines no more in
court than in Congress, he will not shed much light. . . . I never knew a man so
completely disappoint all expectation. Men of all sorts take a pride to gird at
him."[76]

On the afternoon of March 9, 1818, the clerk of the Supreme Court opened
the record in the *Dartmouth College* case. That meant that argument would
begin the following day. At 11:00 A.M. on March 10 Webster rose to speak for
the plaintiffs.[77]

Dressed in his usual blue coat with brass buttons, black pants, white vest
and tie—"not remarkably correct in his costume, nor graceful in his movements," commented one friend, who thought he should always wear a black suit
on such formal occasions—he began slowly and quietly. His tone was conversational, hardly more. Some strained to hear him. It was his usual style whether
addressing a vast audience or a small collection of jurists or jurymen. His right
hand invariably rested on the papers on his desk; the left hand hung free. The
rhythm of his speech would then pick up speed, his right hand would gesture,
and many times his left hand would work itself behind his back. If he became
agitated, the right hand would swing through the air in great looping gestures, a
signal that he was in the middle of a performance.[78]

Webster spoke for four straight hours, not unusual by Supreme Court
standards of the time. Much of what he said in the first hours was technical and
concerned with English common law regarding charitable corporations. But
it soon became obvious that this case had greater importance than originally
supposed. "The pecuniary, & personal & political interests in it were of no small

74. He even had time to dine with President Monroe. DW to Mason, February 22, 1818, in *PLFP*, I, 99.

75. DW to Brown, February 14, 1818, ibid., I, 96.

76. DW to Mason, February 22, 1818, ibid., I, 98.

77. The official account of the case can be found in 4 Wheaton 518ff. See also G. Edward White, *The Marshall Court and Cultural Change, 1815–1835*, Vols. III and IV, *The Oliver Wendell Holmes Devise History of the Supreme Court of the United States* (New York, 1988), pp. 174–180, 612–628, Francis Sites, *Private Power and Public Gain* (New York, 1972), and John C. Sterling, *Daniel Webster and a Small College* (New York, 1965).

78. Hone, *Diary*, II, 523.

magnitude," recalled Justice Story a few years later. "But the extent, to which the principles involved in it touched the rights of property, private & charitable as well as the extent, to which a claim to exercise legislation over literary & other corporations as a part of State Sovereignty could be maintained with reference to the prohibitions of the Constitution of the U. States gave it an importance so paramount, that every other consideration seemed at the moment to be no significance."[79]

The charter for the college, granted in 1769 on the application and request of the Reverend Eleazar Wheelock, who had already founded the school on his own property and at his own expense, Webster argued, established a private corporation. The school was an educational corporation, not a municipal corporation, and its rights could not be abrogated without its consent. "The case before the Court is clearly that of an eleemosynary corporation. It is, in the strictest legal sense, a private charity." He then expounded on the rights of corporations under the common law.

These rights, he continued, are protected by the U.S. Constitution. He referred to the Court's decision in *Fletcher* v. *Peck* that a contract is a compact, and he further argued that a "grant of corporate powers & privileges is as much a *contract* as a grant of land." And contracts were protected under the Constitution. Article I, Section 10 declares: "No State shall . . . pass any . . . Law impairing the Obligation of Contracts . . . ."

This case falls within the true meaning of this provision of the Constitution as expounded in the decisions of this Court; that [the] Charter of 1769, is a *contract,* a *stipulation,* an *agreement;* mutual in its considerations, express & formal in its terms, & of a most binding & sacred nature. That the acts in question [of the legislature] *impair* this contract, has already been sufficiently shewn. They repeal & abrogate its most essential parts.

It has been repeatedly stated, he went on, that the legislature, of *"necessity,"* must have power to regulate such corporations because of the abuses that might arise that cannot be remedied by the ordinary courts of law. "But this is only another instance of that habit of supposing extreme cases, & then of reasoning from them, which is another refuge of those who are obliged to defend a cause, which, upon its own merits is indefensible." Let me state "that it is not pretended that there was here any such case of necessity."[80]

He paused. Then he began his peroration. And he pulled out all stops. He never spoke with greater intensity or more control of himself and his language.

This, Sir, is my case. It is the case, not merely of that humble institution, it is the case of every college in our Land! It is more. It is the case of every eleemosynary institution throughout our country—of all those great charities founded by the piety of

79. Unsigned, undated document in Joseph Story's handwriting, Webster Papers, LC. The document was not written in 1818 because it also refers to the *Steamboat* case and *Ogden* v. *Saunders.* Most likely it was written in 1827 or shortly thereafter.

80. Webster's brief is reprinted in *PLFP,* I, 119–153.

our ancestors, to alleviate human misery, and scatter blessings along the pathway of life! It is more! It is, in some sense, the case of every man among us who has property of which he may be stripped, for the question is simply this: Shall our State Legislatures be allowed to take that which is not their own, to turn it from its original use, and apply it to such ends or purposes as they in their discretion shall see fit?

Again Webster paused. He had built his audience to the emotion level he needed. Then he let fly his most carefully worked-out conclusion. And he looked straight at Chief Justice Marshall.

Sir, you may destroy this little institution; it is weak, it is in your hands! I know it is one of the lesser lights in the literary horizon of our country. You may put it out! But, if you do so, you must carry through your work! You must extinguish, one after another, all those greater lights of science which, for more than a century, have thrown their radiance over our land!

It is, sir, as I have said, a small college. And yet *there are those who love it*!

At this point Webster's own feelings had become so engaged that he broke down. "His lips quivered; his firm cheeks trembled with emotion; his eyes were filled with tears; his voice choked; and he seemed struggling to the utmost, simply to gain that mastery over himself which might save him from an unmanly burst of feeling." There followed a series of broken sentences in which he spoke of his own affection for the college mixed with remembrances of his mother and father and brother and all the difficulties and deprivations through which he and they had journeyed. There was not a sound in the room. Everyone believed his sentiments sincere. Not in any way had they been faked.

Then he shook himself. He lowered his head. After a few moments to steady himself he looked up at Marshall and continued: "Sir, I know not how others may feel"—and he turned and looked at Wirt and Holmes and Hale, and the university trustee—"but, for myself, when I see my Alma Mater surrounded, like Caesar in the senate-house, by those who are reiterating stab after stab, I would not, for this right hand, have her turn to me, and say, *Et tu quoque, mi fili! And thou too, my son!*"

What a peroration! There was deathlike silence. Virtually the entire audience dissolved in tears. The spectators had been "wrought up to the highest excitement," remembered Justice Story years later. They were completely drained. Even Marshall, who had bent over the bench to catch each whispered word, reacted, "his eyes suffused with tears." Many wept uncontrollably. "Many betrayed the most agitating mental struggles; many were sinking under exhausting efforts to conceal their own emotions."[81]

---

81. This peroration is not included in the brief or what appeared in the Supreme Court reports. They were written down some thirty-five years later by Chauncey A. Goodrich, a professor at Yale and a spectator in the court, and published in a book by Rufus Choate. The quotations used here come directly from Goodrich, as quoted in Curtis, *Webster*, I, 170–171. Several years after the fact Justice Story also recorded his impressions of Webster's conclusion, and his account tends to corroborate what Goodrich wrote. See *PLFP*, I, 153–154; Samuel G. Brown, ed., *The Works of Rufus Choate* (Boston, 1862), I, 187–188; unsigned, undated document in Joseph Story's handwriting,

Even the opposing cocounsel was impressed. Salma Hale wrote to Governor Plumer and said that the speech was "as good as any I have ever heard. Webster . . . appeared himself to be much affected—and the audience was silent as death." His "argument was able and his peroration eloquent."[82]

All Washington buzzed with accounts of his achievement. Nothing like it had ever been heard before in the courtroom of the United States Supreme Court. People could talk of nothing else.[83]

Later Justice Story tried to recount for the record what had happened and why it so captivated and moved the Court and the spectators. "The argument was supposed to have been exhausted; & it was thought scarcely possible to give it" added novelty or force. But Webster surprised everyone.

He began by unfolding the facts in brief but exact manner, for which he is so remarkable; & arriving at the points, for which he meant to contend, he first presented them in their general bearing & aspect; & then proceeding to the more minute analysis, he brought out with singular felicity & clearness all the various learning, from juridical authorities, from historical archives, from parliamentary debates, from elementary writers, which could illustrate & fortify his grounds.

His speech has been published, Story continued, but nothing written can convey "the form, the principles, the manner & the expression, the glowing zeal, the brilliant turns of diction, the spontaneous bursts of eloquence, the polished language of rebuke . . . the sparkling eye, the quivering lips, the speaking gesture, the ever changing, & ever moving tones of the voice, which add such strength & pathos, & captivating enchantments to the Orator, as his words flow rapidly on during actual delivery." As Webster continued, he "kindled into more energetic action, & . . . scintillated at every step." We watched, commented Story, "the struggle of the giant to relieve that incumbent pressure of his thoughts, to deliver out the stirring workings of his soul, & to uproot the very foundation of the opposing argument."

It was a relief when he paused. We needed "some short internal repose from the intense stretch of thought by which the mind was irresistibly driven."[84]

Webster Papers, LC; John W. Black, "Webster's Peroration in the Dartmouth College Case," *Quarterly Journal of Speech*, XXIII (1937), pp. 636–642; Baxter, *Webster and the Supreme Court*, pp. 83–85; Sterling, *Webster and a Small College*; Charles M. Wiltse, "Webster and a Small College," *Dartmouth Alumni Magazine*, LXVI (1974), pp. 14–15. See also White, *Marshall Court*.

82. Hale to Plumer, March 24, 1818, in *PLFP*, I, 174.

83. Louis McLane to John J. Mulligan, March 15, 1818, in *PLFP*, I, 172. "Websters argument was said to be the ablest ever delivered in this Court," reported Eleazar Wheelock to William Allen, the new president of the recently formed Dartmouth University. Prepare for the worst, he advised. Ibid., I, 155.

84. "[There was] in his whole air & manner, in the fiery flashings of his eye, the darkness of his contracted brow, the sudden & flying flushes of his cheeks, the quivering & scarcely manageable movements of his lips, in the deep guttural tones of his voice, in the struggle to suppress his own emotions, in the almost convulsive clenchings of his hands without a seeming consciousness of the act, there was in these things what gave to his oratory an almost superhuman influence. There was a

And the peroration! It was almost unbearable.

When Webster ceased speaking, it was some minutes before anyone dared break the silence. "The whole seemed but an agonizing dream, from which the audience was slowly & almost unconsciously awakened."[85]

Webster was extremely pleased with his performance—and rightly so. The imagery of Caesar's assassination had triggered a strong response when he first used it before the New Hampshire court, and he knew it carried an emotional wallop. But his arguments, despite Story's laudatory remarks, could be challenged. Hale said he was "unfair, for which he deserved . . . castigation."[86] Was Dartmouth truly a private institution? Was there no way for a state to initiate controls of corporations chartered within its jurisdiction? In addition, Webster's mention of New Hampshire's violation of its constitution was irrelevant.

Fortunately the opposing counsel did not seriously challenge him or any of his contentions. Holmes opened for the defendant the following day and questioned the Court's jurisdiction because the parties did not live in different states. He denied that Dartmouth was a private institution and its charter a contract as envisioned by the Constitution. Education was a public matter, he declared, and subject to state regulation. He tried to be funny and even resorted to a frequently used allusion to Arthur St. Clair, once the governor of the Northwest Territory who suffered a devastating defeat at the hands of the Indians, but these feeble attempts at wit "were heard . . . with disgust." Hale remarked that Holmes had performed "below our moderate expectations." Webster took delight in reporting that Holmes "gave us three hours of the merest stuff that was ever uttered in a county court."[87]

Wirt performed better but still far below par.[88] He denied that the contract clause applied. Charters for public corporations for purposes of public policy, he contended, must be subject to legislative authority so that they can be modified or revoked as circumstances and the needs of society dictate.[89] In his peroration he spoke of the many services Wheelock had provided the college during his long tenure as president. The proof of his success, Wirt argued, was the eloquence just heard by his pupil Daniel Webster. Wheelock had recently

---

solemn grandeur in every thought, mixed up with such pathetic tenderness & refinement, such beautiful allusion to the past, the present & the future, such a scorn of artifice & rancor, such an appeal to all the moral & religious feelings of man, to the love of learning & literature, to the persuasive precepts of the law, to the reverence for justice, to all that can exalt the understanding & purify the heart, that it was impossible to listen without increasing astonishment at the profound reaches of the human intellect." Unsigned, undated document in Joseph Story's handwriting, Webster Papers, LC.

85. Ibid.

86. Hale to William Plumer, [Jr.], March 24, 1818, in *PLFP*, I, 174.

87. DW to Mason, March 13, 1818, Webster Papers, LC.

88. "He is a good deal of a lawyer," Webster reported to Mason, "and has very quick perceptions, and handsome power of argument; but he seemed to treat this case as if his side could furnish nothing but declamation." DW to Mason, March 13, 1818, in *PLFP*, I, 170.

89. Wirt's argument is summarized in 4 Wheaton 606–615.

died,[90] and Wirt spoke eloquently of his "cruel persecution, dismissal, & death of a broken heart." Then he whirled around and shouted at Webster, *"et tu Brute."*[91]

Joseph Hopkinson, Webster's associate, concluded the case on March 12 by directly challenging the arguments put forward by Holmes and Wirt. He reiterated many of Webster's contentions, especially the insistence that New Hampshire had violated the Constitution by depriving the college trustees of their rights under the charter.[92]

Since both sides were anxious to have a decision as quickly as possible, Holmes asked whether the Court would render a decision this term. Marshall replied that the Court could not treat legislation by a state lightly and that no judgment would be announced this term. Actually there was a difference of opinion in the Court, something Marshall liked to resolve before going public with a decision, and some of the judges had not yet made up their minds. Webster believed that Marshall and Washington favored the college, Duvall and Todd the university. That left Story, Livingston, and Johnson not yet decided.[93] Each side therefore set about trying to win over the holdouts by publishing what it thought most supportive of its position.

From the beginning of the case the conflict had been public, and popular opinion meant a great deal to both the college and university forces. Early on, after the verdict in the state court, Isaac Hill had attempted to publish in pamphlet form the arguments of counsel, and he wrote to Webster on December 16, 1817, requesting a copy of his brief to the New Hampshire court. Webster brushed him off with a reminder that the case was still pending and that it would be improper to publish his arguments. But once the Supreme Court had heard the case, Webster decided in the spring of 1818 to print copies of his argument. "All the nonsense is left out"—namely, the peroration—he told Mason. He purposely left out his peroration because it embarrassed him. It lacked legal reasoning.[94] In time his speech was seen by many distinguished and influential lawyers and jurists. Yet understandably what has been remembered over the years and become part of the folklore of this country is the peroration, not the argument.

For its part the university side published and distributed the decision of the New Hampshire superior court.[95]

90. Thereupon the university's trustees conferred the presidency on Wheelock's son-in-law, William Allen, who had been acting president.

91. Hale to Plumer, March 24, 1818, in *PLFP,* I, 174–175. "From this you will perceive how much the speakers of our highest court of law are indulged in their flights," Hale added.

92. 4 Wheaton 615–624.

93. Webster also believed that Story "will be with us in the end." DW to Sullivan, March 13, DW to Mason, March 13, and DW to Smith, March 14, 1818, in *PLFP,* I, 169, 170, 171.

94. DW to Mason, April 23, 1818, in *PC,* I, 224.

95. Hill to DW, December 16, 1817, DW to Hill, December 27, 1817, in *PLFP,* I, 88–89. Webster sent Story five copies of his argument. See DW to Story, September 9, 1818, in *PC,* I, 227–228. Not

Disappointed with the presentation of its case before the Supreme Court, the university wished to have the Court hear new arguments and new "facts" regarding Dartmouth's founding and establishment. To that end it hired William Pinckney, a flamboyant but masterful pleader, to replace the incompetent Holmes. Webster was not anxious to reargue the case—how could he duplicate, much less improve, on his performance in March?—and hoped the cognate cases moving through the lower courts would at least widen the legal area within which to maneuver in the event that the Supreme Court did order a reargument. But he really wanted to be done with the case. It had gone on too long, and he had grown weary of it. Besides, it cost him a great deal of money because of the time involved. When the Court adjourned in March, he returned immediately to Boston to resume his normal legal practice.[96]

For his part Pinckney made preparations to appear before the Supreme Court at its February term, and Webster supposed he would succeed in his effort, "altho I do not think it by any means certain." Webster also believed that during the course of the summer Story had been won over to his side—he certainly courted him as much as possible during the intervening months—but he acknowledged that "not a word has as yet fallen from any Judge on the cause." Even when he arrived in Washington to attend the 1819 February term, he had no idea what the justices would do. "They keep their own counsels," he commented.[97]

The court session officially began on Monday, February 1, 1819, but not until Tuesday did its business commence. As the justices filed in to take their

---

surprisingly two articles appeared in Hill's *New Hampshire Patriot* on February 10 and March 24, 1818, accusing Webster of handling ten thousand dollars worth of stock in the fraudulent Yazoo land sale for a private estate and diverting four thousand dollars of it for his use.

96. What time Webster spent on the Dartmouth matter for the remainder of 1818 had to do principally with preparing for publication of a complete record of the case. He made himself responsible for the collection and preparation of the arguments of all the attorneys and judges, while his associate Timothy Farrar, Jr., took care of the printing. But the task took on a life of its own and made many demands on Webster's time. He found he had to "examine, compare, correct, & edit" a mountain of material. He badgered Hopkinson to write up his speech in his own style and manner. Unfortunately Hopkinson did not spend enough time on his effort, and Webster rebuked him for it. "I am quite disappointed about your Speech. Please, pray, to *return* me the notes—possibly I may do something with them. I will do the best for you I can either by writing out a reply from your notes & from my own wits—or stating that you did make a good reply. Let me have the *notes* by return mail." The notes from Wirt and Holmes were worse. "They are poor & meagre," he commented. He also asked Mason and Smith for their briefs so that the world would "know where I borrowed my plumes." Ichabod Bartlett submitted material that disparaged the trustees and used slang. "50 or 60 pages!" Webster groaned. "Good Heavens!—and all slang!—do get it abridged," he instructed Farrar. Because of all the problems, not only in obtaining acceptable briefs from the various attorneys and judges involved but in finding a suitable printer, the *Report of the Case of the Trustees of Dartmouth College against William H. Woodward* did not appear in print until August 1819. But as he fully expected, it earned Webster a great deal of notoriety and acclaim. DW to Story, [March 25, 1819], DW to Hopkinson, March 22, April 23, 1819, DW to Mason, April 10, 1819, DW to Farrar, May 18, [1819], in *PC*, I, 251, 253–254, 258–259, 255, 260; DW to Farrar, February 1, 1819, in *PLFP*, I, 225.

97. DW to Farrar, February 1, 1819, in *PLFP*, I, 225.

respective places, Pinckney prepared to rise and ask for a reargument.[98] But Marshall never gave him a chance to speak. He announced that the justices had formed their separate opinions during the summer, and he proceeded immediately to read the majority decision. What he read turned out to be one of the most important and influential decisions in the history of the Supreme Court. And Webster could not have been more delighted.

"In a very long, & reasoned" decision Marshall found for the plaintiffs by declaring that the royal charter was a contract that created a private, not a public, corporation and therefore was not subject to the state's regulatory power. In fact any contract between a state and a private entity safeguarded the private entity from legislative interference. Eleazar Wheelock had founded the college, and private donors had contributed to its operation. The rights of these and subsequent donors and the trustees acting on their behalf were protected under the contract clause of the Constitution. New Hampshire's actions toward Dartmouth, he concluded, impaired the obligation of a contract and constituted a misuse of power. He therefore reversed the decision of the state court.[99]

Of the six[100] justices only one, Justice Duvall, dissented, but he wrote no opinion. Both Justices Story and Washington wrote concurring opinions, and Story tried to provide a loophole for the states by suggesting that in the future contracts should include clauses that specifically granted legislatures the power to alter or amend them.[101]

The importance of this decision became more and more apparent as the nation continued to develop into an industrial society. According to this very broad reading of the Constitution, states were severely limited in their authority over corporations, thereby allowing private entrepreneurs considerable leeway in their operations. In effect it helped promote economic expansion over the next several decades by protecting corporate activities from interference by local legislatures. Like *Fletcher* v. *Peck,* rendered in 1810, it also asserted the supremacy of national authority over state authority.

Marshall borrowed heavily from Webster in writing this decision, but the basic arguments had been developed by Jeremiah Mason. Webster could not take credit for them, or did he. What he had done was present Mason's ideas in a logical sequence and then top them off with an emotional plea. But nowhere in Marshall's decision is there evidence that the emotional plea counted for much. It was Webster's logical orderliness that attracted Marshall. It is unlikely that anything Webster said really influenced the chief justice. No doubt Marshall

98. There is some belief that Pinckney did not plan to ask for the reargument until the following week and in fact may not have been present when the new term began. But Webster specifically notes his presence in his letter to Mason, February 4, 1819, ibid., I, 227.

99. DW to Farrar, February 2, [1819], in *PLFP,* I, 225; 4 Wheaton 624–654.

100. Only six justices participated. Justice Thomas Todd was absent. Because of illness, family problems, and other reasons, he frequently missed Supreme Court sessions.

101. 4 Wheaton 666–713.

knew all along what he wanted to decide. Webster simply provided him with the material he needed.

Webster took one final step. To block Pinckney's attempt to bring up the cognate cases and use them to reargue the entire Dartmouth matter once again, he asked the court to enter judgment *nunc pro tunc* as of the 1818 session, which meant that any action on the cognate cases would have to be determined in the light of the *Dartmouth* decision. Wirt objected, but the Court agreed with Webster, and in the subsequent hearings before the U.S. circuit court in Portsmouth the cognate cases were all decided in favor of the college. The university ceased operations, and the college trustees regained control of the school.[102]

Webster learned a great deal from studying the Marshall decision that held him in good stead for the future. He said it was "reasoned out from step to step." Hereafter, when arguing cases involving constitutional interpretations, he would rely on logic and historical evidence to prove his case. He would begin with a major premise and from it draw out his conclusions deductively, introducing historical facts and legal precedents for documentation.[103] He also learned a great deal from studying Story's concurring opinion. Only an argument firmly grounded in the law could impress Story, and in the future Webster made every effort to oblige him. In fact these two men had become relatively close in their relationship. Webster nurtured that friendship by sending to the justice from time and time English newspapers and any new lawbooks that came to hand.[104]

Small wonder he played such a commanding role in helping the justices reach decisions involving constitutional law. Small wonder many people began calling him the Great Expounder of the Constitution.

Webster rushed news of the decision to New Hampshire, and he tried to be modest about what had been accomplished. We must prevent "the Newspapers from triumphing too much, on the result of the cause," he told Timothy Farrar. "It is our true wisdom to enjoy our victory with moderation. It is great indeed—& needs no flourish of trumpets to usher in the annunciation of it. On all accts a moderate & dignified course becomes us."[105]

But others could not wait to blow the trumpets in Webster's praise. And they blasted away for years. His associate Hopkinson wrote to President Francis Brown of Dartmouth College and said: "I would have an inscription over the door of your building. 'Founded by Eleazar Wheelock, Refounded by Daniel Webster."[106]

102. *PLFP,* I, 236–237.

103. *PLFP,* I, 224.

104. See, for example, DW to Story, [March 1819], in *W&S,* XVI, 46, and DW to Story, April 3, [1820], in *PC,* I, 271–272.

105. DW to Farrar, February 7, 1819, in *PLFP,* I, 228.

106. Hopkinson to Brown, February 2, 1819, in *PC,* I, 301. This suggestion was later followed when the college mounted a bronze tablet with this inscription at the entrance of Webster Hall. Furthermore, the trustees asked Mason, Smith, Hopkinson, and Webster to sit for their portraits by Gilbert Stuart; this in addition to their fees. These portraits now hang in the Dartmouth library on the second floor.

8

Nationalism and Conservatism

WEBSTER'S legal reputation soared as a result of the *Dartmouth College* case. At first observers in Washington doubted its importance, figuring it was a minor matter about a small college and would not interest anyone but a few locals in New Hampshire. But not long afterward the full impact and significance of the case became enormously apparent to both the legal and political worlds.

At a dinner party a number of years later Webster himself said that the *Dartmouth College* case was the "turning point in his career." It established his national reputation as a constitutional lawyer and orator and marked him as a man destined for even greater triumphs.

Webster involved himself in two other cases of national importance at this time: *Sturges v. Crowninshield*[1] and *McCulloch v. Maryland.*[2] He argued for Crowninshield in its initial hearing before a federal court in Massachusetts but did not represent him when the case went to the Supreme Court. In this decision Marshall, again speaking for the majority, struck down an 1811 New York bankruptcy law as a violation of the contract clause of the Constitution because it included debts contracted before the statute's passage. Webster had long championed federal enactment of a bankruptcy law as essential to the building of an national economy. The failure of the central government to pass such a law[3] prompted the states to step in and address the problem themselves.

It is not certain why Webster did not argue the case before the Supreme Court—possibly because of his overcrowded schedule—but if he had, ironically, he would have found himself, as Crowninshield's attorney,[4] pleading for the state's bankruptcy law and against the application of the contract clause to this

1. 4 Wheaton 122. See also White, *The Marshall Court*, pp. 633–641, 929–932.

2. 4 Wheaton 316. See also White, *The Marshall Court*, pp. 541–567, and Gerald Gunther, ed., *John Marshall's Defense of McCulloch v. Maryland* (New York, 1969).

3. Federalists passed a national bankruptcy law in 1800, but Republicans repealed it four years later.

4. He had received a fee of $320 from Crowninshield. *PLFP*, I, 298 note 5.

case. The decision was reached on February 17, 1819, approximately two weeks after the *Dartmouth* decision.

He played a far more important role in the *McCulloch* case, the effect of which reverberated politically for the next several decades. The case centered on the legality of the National Bank, enacted by Congress in 1816. The questions involved included the old chestnut about its constitutionality and a new chestnut about the rights of the states over branches of the Bank established within their borders without their consent.

When the First National Bank was established in 1791, both Madison and Jefferson challenged its constitutionality. The Constitution created a government with delegated powers, and what was not delegated was reserved to the states and the people. Nowhere in the document did it say that Congress could create a bank. It was therefore unconstitutional, according to this states' rights interpretation. Alexander Hamilton disagreed and in his famous opinion of 1791 convinced President Washington that Section 8 of Article I of the Constitution applied in this instance because it specifically empowered Congress to "make all Laws which shall be necessary and proper" for the execution of the delegated powers.

The charter of the First Bank ended in 1811, and the Second Bank of the United States (BUS) began its existence in 1816. The Second Bank immediately established eighteen branches in the leading cities throughout the nation. Captain William Jones, onetime secretary of the navy, was chosen to head the BUS and promptly demonstrated his ineptness by repeatedly violating the terms of the charter, speculating in the Bank's stock, and permitting state banks to overtrade and inflate the currency. He also engaged in the crooked operations of the Baltimore branch. He was replaced in 1819 by Langdon Cheves of South Carolina, a former congressman and Speaker of the House.[5]

Hostility toward the Bank existed in every state, and when its new president called in loans and foreclosed mortgages to rectify the mistakes of his predecessor, he helped precipitate the Panic of 1819 and the severe depression that followed in its wake. In their outrage and anger many states either laid heavy taxes on the branches within their borders or used their taxing power to keep the Bank from crossing their borders.

The Baltimore branch was particularly notorious, and in 1818 Maryland taxed it. James W. McCulloch, the cashier of this branch, refused to pay the tax, and the state brought action against him. The state won its case in the lower courts, but the Bank appealed to the Supreme Court on a writ of error for a reversal of the judgment.

The court heard arguments during its February 1819 term. Arguments took place from February 22 to March 3, with Webster, William Pinckney, and William Wirt (his opponents in the *Dartmouth* case), appearing for the Bank and Luther Martin, Walter Jones, and Joseph Hopkinson (the latter Web-

5. Catterall, *Second Bank*, pp. 10–21, 30–49.

ster's ally in the *Dartmouth* case) representing Maryland.[6]

Webster opened. And his presentation was masterful. He argued from basic principles in a lucid and succinct presentation. Most of the time he looked straight at Marshall and seemed to address himself directly and solely to the chief justice. He argued deductively and centered his remarks on the two basic questions: the Bank's constitutionality and the power of the state to tax it.

He began by noting Hamilton's opinion and pointing out that virtually every Congress and executive since the passage of the first bank bill had enacted such legislation on the assumption of the government's legal power to do so. Individuals have objected, he allowed, but not "the courts of law." He then discussed the necessary and proper clause and declared that "the true view of the subject is, that if it be a fit instrument to an authorized purpose, it may be used, not being specifically prohibited." A bank, he went on, is a proper instrument for the government in the collection and disbursement of revenue. Congress had duties to perform and therefore a right to the means by which those duties could be executed.

Next he turned to the question of the state's taxing power. He distinguished between powers granted the central government and those reserved to the state governments. When questions about their powers arise between these two entities, it is important to know on what *principle* these questions can be decided. In this case the principle is clear, he declared. The Constitution is "the *supreme law of the land* and controls all state legislation and their constitutions." The only question remaining is whether Maryland could legally tax an institution created by the central government. Then Webster struck hard:

> If the States may tax the bank, to what extent shall they tax it, and where shall they stop? An unlimited power to tax involves, necessarily, a power to destroy; because there is a limit beyond which no institution and no property can bear taxation. . . . If the States may tax, they have no limit but their discretion; and the bank, therefore must depend on the discretion of the State governments for its existence. This consequence is inevitable.

The power to tax involves a power to destroy! Marshall stared down at the lawyer and surely took note of what he had just heard. The idea of a state's destroying the work of Congress was repugnant to everything he believed and argued.

Webster struck again. Can a state tax the property of the government? The operations of custom houses? The proceedings of the federal courts? To hold that Maryland may tax a national bank means that every law of the government is subject to the "revision and control of the State legislatures."[7]

It was a powerful statement and had a telling effect upon the jurists. Although it was relatively short and very sweeping in its coverage, the statement laid the groundwork on which Wirt and Pinckney could further build the Bank's case. Webster's argument regarding the constitutionality of the Bank rightfully

6. The Court dispensed with its general rule of allowing only two attorneys to argue each side.

7. *W&S*, XV, 262–267.

belonged to others, starting with Hamilton, but the argument about the power to tax being a power to destroy belonged to him.

Opposing counsel followed immediately, and they necessarily attacked the legality of Congress's action. The national government was a government of delegated powers; what was not delegated was reserved to the states and the people. That was clearly stated in the Tenth Amendment. Since the document did not grant Congress the power to create a bank, any such action—especially now in 1819, when many state banks existed to serve the government—was unconstitutional. In 1791 only a few banks had existed, and the government had needed help with its fiscal operations. Under those circumstances the constitutionality of the First National Bank could be granted. But not now, not with so many private banks ready to assist Congress in its fiscal responsibilities.

Marshall and his colleagues listened, but as deeply committed nationalists they were not convinced.

Hopkinson sought to drive home an important point when he reminded the Court that the Bank could open branches in any state without that state's permission. Can a bank, in effect, disregard the sovereignty of states? Can it march in, without a by-your-leave, without any local authorization whatsoever, and set up shop? He also defended the right of the states to tax a corporation, such as the BUS, that was privately owned. The government subscribed to only one fifth of the Bank's stock; the rest belonged to private stockholders. The BUS, then, was a private, profit-making corporation and subject to state authority when it operated within the borders of the state.

Luther Martin, something of a windbag—he "delights in amplitude," wrote Hopkinson[8]—spoke for three days without making much of an impression other than his long-windedness. But Pinckney overwhelmed the Court with his eloquence. He too spoke for three days, but what he said and how he said it could not have been better, nor could it have been matched, even by Webster. Unquestionably at this stage of his career Pinckney was supreme as a practitioner before this Court. Webster could merely approach him. Only when Pinckney died three years later could he replace him.

Pinckney expanded on the necessary and proper clause and developed at length the implied powers interpretation of the Constitution. The Constitution, he maintained, came from the people, it was adopted by the people within their respective states, and it acts directly on the people by means of powers communicated directly from them.[9]

The response from the audience was rhapsodic. Even Justice Story admitted its compelling power. "I never, in my whole life, heard a greater speech," he wrote; "it was worth a journey from Salem to hear it; his elocution was excessively vehement, but his eloquence was overwhelming. . . . He spoke like a great statesman and patriot, and a sound constitutional lawyer." Beyond any other

8. Hopkinson to DW, April 19, 1819, in PC, I, 258.
9. 4 Wheaton 377–400.

man he had even seen or heard, Story credited Pinckney with "the power of elegant and illustrative amplification."[10]

So forceful, so compelling, so persuasive, so precisely on the mark of the Court's thinking in general had been the contentions of the Bank's counsel that the decision was handed down four days later, on March 7, 1819. It was unanimous, and it was another landmark decision that would have a powerful and lasting influence on the constitutional and political history of the country.

Marshall read the Court's opinion. Not only did it settle the meaning of the necessary and proper clause of the Constitution, but he broadly defined the powers belonging to the federal government. He affirmed the right of Congress to incorporate a bank and in the process picked up on Pinckney's contention that the Constitution resulted from the action of the American people. The government "is, emphatically, and truly, a government of the people." It "emanates from them," and "its powers are granted by them, and are to be exercised directly on them, and for their benefit."[11] Congress has the right to incorporate a bank by virtue of its right to make all laws necessary and proper to achieve the best interests of the people. Although the authority to grant bank charters was not among its enumerated powers, several other clauses, such as those involving war, commerce, and taxes, imply it. "Let the end be legitimate," he proclaimed, "let it be within the scope of the constitution, and all means which are appropriate, which are plainly adapted to that end, which are not prohibited, but consistent with the letter and spirit of the constitution, are constitutional."[12]

Turning to the question of Maryland's right to tax the bank, Marshall picked up on Webster's argument. "The power to tax involves the power to destroy," he held. If a state can tax the Bank, it can tax other agencies created by the federal government, and that would defeat the ends to which the people had created a government in the first place. Thus the Maryland tax was null and void, and the ruling of the lower court overturned.[13]

This was such a broad and sweeping interpretation of the powers of the national government that almost nothing seemed beyond federal control and involvement unless specifically prohibited by the Constitution. Many, including Jefferson and Madison, objected to it, and Andrew Jackson later denied that Marshall's decision ended the argument about the Bank's right to exist.

Webster of course thoroughly approved all of Marshall's arguments. "The opinion in the Bank cause," he remarked to Justice Story, "is universally praised. Indeed I think it admirable. Great things have been done this Session."[14] And Webster shared personally in the glory and benefit from those great things. The BUS was so delighted with his work that its president wrote and congratulated

10. Story to Stephen White, March 3, 1819, in Story, *Life and Letters*, I, 325.

11. 4 Wheaton 401, 404, 405.

12. 4 Wheaton 421.

13. 4 Wheaton 431–432.

14. DW to Story, [March 25, 1819], in *PLFP*, I, 246.

him. "I have been directed by the Directors of the Bank of the United States to present to you their respectful thanks for your very able and successful exertions on the part of the Bank ... and ask your acceptance of an additional fee of Fifteen Hundred Dollars which the Cashier of the Office at Boston has been directed to pay."[15]

Initially the BUS had given Webster a five-hundred-dollar retainer. This additional money helped the young lawyer overcome some of the reservations he had held about the Bank when its charter had been first argued in Congress. Already a stockholder[16] in the Bank, he was to increase his holdings in succeeding years and enjoy an excellent relationship with Nicholas Biddle when that distinguished gentleman assumed the presidency of the BUS in 1823, after Cheves resigned. Webster regularly received a retainer from the Bank following the *McCulloch* decision and later served on its board of directors.[17]

Webster was anxious to return to Boston at the conclusion of the February term. "A month is as long as Washington wears well," he advised Mason.[18] Pleading before the Supreme Court increased his fame, but pleading before the courts in and around Boston swelled his purse, and he always had need to attend to that worthy effort.

During his stay in Washington Webster took particular notice of the debates in Congress over the question of the admission of Missouri into the Union as a slave state. Missouri was the first area totally west of the Mississippi River to seek admission into the Union. That it wished to enter as a slave state troubled many in the North, who worried about the continued expansion of an institution they regarded as an abomination. Consequently Representative James Tallmadge, Jr., of New York proposed an amendment to the enabling act that would prohibit the further introduction of slaves into the territory and free those born in Missouri upon reaching the age of twenty-five. In effect the amendment would ultimately make Missouri a free state.[19]

Southerners howled their opposition. The Northwest Ordinance already forbade slavery north of the Ohio River. Now Congress, if the Tallmadge amendment passed, would further restrict their "peculiar institution" in the territory of the Louisiana Purchase. Once this happened, there was no telling where the restrictions would end. The Constitution protected slave property, stormed southern congressmen; any attempt to abrogate that right by limiting its extension into the territories could threaten the continued existence of the Union.

15. Langdon Cheves to DW, April 2, 1819, ibid.

16. "I have a few shares in the Bank, but they have not stood in my name long enough to give me a right to vote in this Election [of Directors]," he wrote. DW to James Lloyd, December 20, 1819, in *PC*, I, 267.

17. DW to James Lloyd, December 20, 1819, Webster Papers, Harvard University Library; DW to Biddle, January 6, 1825, January 26, 1827, Biddle Papers, LC.

18. DW to Mason, February 23, 1819, in *W&S*, XVI, 52.

19. For an excellent account of the question, see Glover Moore, *The Missouri Compromise* (Lexington, Ky., 1953).

The nation watched apprehensively as this momentous issue played out in Congress. Many New Englanders for various reasons demanded future restrictions on slavery, and in Boston a meeting took place in December 1819 in the State House for the purpose of expressing those opinions. Still present in Boston at the time, Webster attended the meeting and took a leading role in the proceedings. Naturally he spoke. According to the *Columbia Centinel* of December 4, he presented a historical "sketch" of the subject (his usual technique), argued the legality of the amendment, and, in a brief peroration, reported the newspaper, advocated the amendment's "expediency with his usual force and precision." Apparently his speech made a very positive impression on the crowd, and on December 3 he was appointed to chair a committee[20] to draw up a memorial to Congress protesting the introduction of slavery into incoming states. The resulting memorial clearly bore the marks of Webster's hand, for it principally offered historical and legal reasoning and little moral or humanitarian justification. It does begin by calling slavery a "great evil" and continues by declaring that if this institution is ever to be arrested, then the good work must begin immediately. "The happiness of unborn millions rests" on what Congress decides and does. As one might expect from Webster, the memorial then swings straightaway into a discussion of the constitutional right of the government to prohibit slavery in new states and includes an elaborate discourse on the necessary and proper clause of the Constitution. After that comes an even longer historical summary of actions taken in the past leading to the Northwest Ordinance of 1787, the admission of new states after the ratification of the Constitution, and the terms by which the nation acquired the Louisiana Territory. Not until the final paragraphs does it return to the question of slavery's evil.

The laws of the United States have denounced heavy penalties against the traffic in slaves, because such traffic is deemed unjust and inhuman. We appeal to the spirit of these laws; we appeal to this justice and humanity. We ask whether they ought not to operate, on the present occasion, with all their force? We have a strong feeling of the injustice of any toleration of slavery. Circumstances have entailed it on a portion of our community which cannot be immediately relieved from it without consequences more injurious than the suffering of the evil. But to permit it in a new country, where yet no habits are formed which render it indispensable, what is it, but to encourage that rapacity, fraud, and violence against which we have so long pointed the denunciations of our penal code? What is it, but to tarnish the proud fame of the country? What is it, but to throw suspicion on its good faith, and to render questionable all its professions of regard for the rights of humanity and the liberties of mankind?[21]

Webster took pride in his handiwork and immediately sent a copy of it to Senator Rufus King of New York, who led the restrictionists in the Senate. In the meantime Maine, the northern district of Massachusetts, petitioned for

20. The committee consisted of Webster, George Blake, Josiah Quincy, James T. Austin, and John Gallison.
21. "Memorial to Congress on Restraining the Increase of Slavery," December 15, 1819, in *W&S*, XV, 55–72, and *PS*, I, 267–271.

admission as a separate state in the Union, and Congress worked out a compromise bill that admitted Maine as a free state and Missouri as a slave state, thereby maintaining voting equality in the Senate. As part of this compromise it also adopted an amendment offered by Senator Jesse B. Thomas prohibiting the extension of slavery in the territory of the Louisiana Purchase north of 36°30′, with the exception of Missouri. Congress passed the Missouri Compromise, and President Monroe signed it on March 6, 1820.[22]

Webster's local involvement in the Missouri question not only signaled his continuing interest in politics but reminded proper Bostonians that he could and should be employed more directly in their public affairs. For his part Webster still preferred to expand his legal practice and devote all this time to that effort, but he never lost interest in state and national affairs. He really wanted a career that allowed him both to practice law and to engage in politics, unlike other statesmen at the time who tended to emphasize one profession or the other.

He needed a thriving law practice not only because of his lifestyle but because his family was constantly expanding. Another son was born to the Websters at 9:00 A.M. on July 20, 1820, and given the name Edward.

But politics could never be put aside indefinitely, and Webster kept his presence known in the political world, particularly on the national level. During his several visits to Washington to plead before the Supreme Court he visited and socialized with his old colleagues in Congress—those who had survived the bloodletting caused by the Compensation Act—and took the opportunity to call on President Monroe. "I have been once at Mrs. Monroe's, it was very full," he informed his friend Mason. "I have dined with the President. His style of life exceeds his predecessors."[23]

Monroe was anxious to pursue a policy of "amalgamation" of the two political parties when he took office and thereby bring about a true "Era of Good Feelings." His appointments to office were meant to reflect that policy, a policy someone like Martin Van Buren of New York regarded as destructive of the meaning and purpose of politics.[24]

George Sullivan, a Federalist congressman, endorsed Monroe's amalgamation policy and urged the President to select for his cabinet both Federalists and Republicans, but not those of the older generation. He suggested younger men, especially Federalists who were not scarred from old battles and would welcome a new era of harmony and "good feelings." He particularly mentioned Daniel Webster for the office of attorney general. But Monroe did not think Webster was ready for such an "advanced step" and appointed William Wirt instead.[25] Despite this rejection, Webster voted for Monroe in the election of

22. *Annals of Congress*, 16th Congress, 1st Session, pp. 1588–1590; Remini, *Clay*, p. 184.

23. DW to Mason, February 22, 1818, in *PC*, I, 218.

24. Dangerfield, *Era of Good Feelings*, passim; Remini, *Van Buren*, pp. 12–29.

25. Harry Amon, *James Monroe: The Quest for National Identity* (New York, 1971), pp. 357, 377.

1820 as one of Massachusetts's presidential electors.[26] The Federalist party put forward no candidate. It was moribund.

When Monroe took his celebrated tour of the northern states in the late spring of 1817, Webster had no visible involvement, but when, in the summer of 1820, the secretary of war, John C. Calhoun, toured the North to inspect forts and arsenals, Webster went out of his way to be hospitable toward his former congressional colleague when he arrived in Boston. They visited the arsenal at Watertown together. They drove around Boston all day, *"tête-à-tête* in a phaeton, and they understand one another," reported Webster's friend George Ticknor. Webster entertained the secretary in his new home at 37 Somerset Street[27] and invited a select number of guests. After dinner a group of young lawyers of the town came to the house and were introduced to the secretary. They all had the distinct impression that Webster favored Calhoun as the next President.[28]

If Webster appeared to be reemerging as a political figure by serving as an elector in the presidential election of 1820 and publicly sporting himself in public in the company of the secretary of war, his appearance on October 2 in Faneuil Hall to deliver a speech on the tariff surely left no doubt that he was moving very quickly in that direction.

Talk of raising tariff rates by Congress had prompted the calling of a meeting by a group of wealthy shipowners and merchants. Knowing Webster's commitment to free trade, they invited him to give the main address. He readily agreed, and his appearance in Faneuil Hall marked the first time in his career he addressed an audience in this most historic building. In his speech, reported by the Boston *Daily Advertiser* on October 11, 1820, he said everything these commercial businessmen wanted to hear. He absolutely opposed government action to raise tariff rates simply to protect infant industries. He had nothing against manufactures, he insisted, but a system of government protection inevitably leads "the people to too much reliance on government." And once government gets involved and offers help by way of tariffs and subsidies and special favors, it will be called upon for relief when these industries face distress. Government should leave men to their own "discretion" to work out their own problems by their own skill and hard work. That way men will employ their capital and labor in such occupations they find the most profitable.

The wealthy merchants of Boston thought his presentation of laissez-faire doctrines was superb, especially the clarity and drive by which he had presented them. So delighted were they that some of them even began discussing the possibility of lifting him to public office, where his conservative ideas could be put to better use.

26. But he would not vote for the Vice President, Daniel D. Tompkins, who was an alcoholic. Instead he voted for an old friend, Richard Stockton of New Jersey. DW to Mason, November 12, 1820, in *PC*, I, 278.

27. He moved to Somerset Street in November or December 1819. "Autobiographical Notes," in *W&S*, XIII, 549.

28. Quoted in Curtis, *Webster,* I, 176–177.

However, Webster's new political career in Massachusetts finally emerged when the state agreed to hold a convention in 1820 to modernize and liberalize its constitution. Over the past several years, and particularly with the admission into the Union of new states whose constitutions provided universal white male suffrage, demands swelled in the older states to heed the democratic wave and provide their citizens with a greater degree of equality, particularly in the operation of government. The masses—that is, white adult males—had been stirred, and they wanted both the vote and the right to hold office.

This democratic surge developed alongside the rise of nationalism, the industrial revolution, the transportation revolution, the market revolution, and the expansion of the country westward. Improved standards of living and rising expectations, among other things, encouraged ordinary citizens to demand a greater say in their political affairs.

In Massachusetts these stirrings sent shivers up the spines of all conservatives, including Webster. The great danger obviously was the threat to property and the balanced government that had been so carefully crafted for the state in 1780 by such revolutionary patriots as John Adams, Sam Adams, and others. Still, these demands for reforms could not be ignored, particularly now that the district of Maine had been detached from the state, necessitating a revision of the system of representation. So the legislature on June 16, 1820, called for a referendum to be held on August 21 in town meetings on revising the constitution. Only about 18,000 turned up to vote, but 11,756 approved the idea while 6,593 disapproved. On October 16 the people elected delegates to attend the convention scheduled to meet on November 15 in the State House. All in all the turnout for these two meetings proved disappointing to reformers. Apathy on the part of the electorate seemed to be the rule.

Conservatives understood the need for them to participate in the convention and prevent the "radical" reformers from inflicting deadly harm to the commonwealth. They also recognized the need to include their best men if they expected to hold their advantages provided by the original constitution. Federalists were rapidly declining in number throughout the state. All the more reason for putting forward their most articulate, intelligent and respected colleagues. Suffolk County, which included Boston, held a meeting to select its forty-six delegates, and among the men chosen were such conservative luminaries as Isaac Parker, Lemuel Shaw, Josiah Quincy, and Daniel Webster.[29] When the convention met on November 15, other worthy Federalists in attendance included former President John Adams, Justice Joseph Story, Leverett Saltonstall, and Samuel Hoar. Republicans, who outnumbered the Federalists, included such men as Henry Dearborn, Levi Lincoln, and James T. Austin.

The convention of 490 delegates, representing nearly three hundred towns, opened on November 15 with a salute to John Adams when they selected him

29. Merrill D. Peterson, *Democracy, Liberty, and Property* (Indianapolis and New York, 1966), pp. 4, 6, 18.

to preside. But the eighty-five-year-old statesman declined the honor, and Isaac Parker, the chief justice of the commonwealth, replaced him.

In organizing its proceedings, the convention agreed to divide the constitution into ten parts, each one of which would be assigned to a committee to consider alterations and bring back a report. The huge number of participants of the convention necessitated this approach, but it also gave the chairman of each committee considerable authority, if he was skillful, in shaping the report (including recommendations) and the direction of debate when the report came before the entire convention. Expert parliamentarians could, in effect, manipulate the final outcome of the proceedings. And the conservatives tended to have more experience and ability in this regard. They could and did dance circles around the radicals by virtue of their parliamentary deftness. They saw to it that considerable time went into the discussions on "Rules & Orders." "You laugh a little, I know," Webster remarked to Mason at the conclusion of the convention, "at our early debates about Rules & Orders &c." But the "rules & orders brought us out, at last. Without them there is reason to think we might have come badly off."[30] All things considered, however, the convention proved to be, in the opinion of one distinguished historian, "a model of deliberative conduct by a body of nearly five hundred men."[31]

Webster appears to have been one of the prime movers of this convention. Thirty-eight at the time, highly regarded and quite vocal during important moments of the many debates, he regularly consulted with other leading delegates and developed tactics and a strategy best suited to protecting conservative interests. He had learned the all-important need in politics for compromise and was prepared at every stage of the proceedings to negotiate concessions when necessary. As he said in one speech, "Mutual concession and accommodation . . . can alone accomplish the purpose of our meeting."[32]

He chaired several committees. One that provoked lively debate on the floor concerned the requirement that elected officials of the state must take an oath of loyalty to the Christian religion. This was something the radicals wanted to abolish in the name of religious freedom. Webster's committee brought to the floor the recommendation that the oath be abolished, and the chairman spoke in its favor on December 4 in the most convoluted and extraordinary speech imaginable.

The state, he declared, had a right to require such an oath, just as it had a right to require age, property, and residence qualifications to hold office. No man had a right to public office; therefore the people can regulate it "by any rules which they may deem expedient." However, "the *expediency* of retaining" the oath was another matter. Since ninety-nine out of every hundred inhabitants in Massachusetts profess belief in the Christian Church, it is reasonable to

30. DW to Mason, January 12, 1821, in *PC*, I, 280.

31. Peterson, *Democracy*, p. 6.

32. Speech on apportioning senatorial districts, in *W&S*, V, 24.

assume that those who do believe will be elected to office, "and none others." That being the case, the oath ought to be abolished. Personally he did not feel one way or another. He was prepared to retain the oath, but he was also prepared to abandon it because other parts of the constitution recognize "in the fullest manner the benefits which civil society derives from those Christian institutions which cherish piety, morality and religion." Although some thought he was trying to be "funny," actually he was attempting to satisfy both sides: the so-called radicals by recommending abolition and the conservatives by demonstrating the right of the state to require a religious test oath.[33] The recommendation was subsequently adopted by the convention.

He also chaired committees of lesser importance, including one that would affect the administration of Harvard and another concerning Boston's form of government, but he played a truly pivotal role in two issues vital to his conservative friends: legislative apportionment and the independence of the judiciary.

Henry Dearborn, son of President Jefferson's secretary of war, attempted to bring about the abolishment of apportionment on the basis of tax assessments and base it instead on population. Under the 1780 constitution representatives for the lower house of the legislature were divided by districts according to population, and for the upper house by the amount of taxable property. Dearborn and other Republicans, including Henry Childs and Levi Lincoln, denounced the present system of representation in the upper house as aristocratic and archaic. They wanted both houses divided by districts according to population and therefore put forward a resolution to that effect.

When the resolution carried without difficulty, the conservatives, in frightened alarm, scrambled to undo the damage. A motion to reconsider passed, and the conservatives then carted out their biggest guns, including the venerable John Adams and Leverett Saltonstall, to blast away at this "radical" revision of a time-honored system of representation. Story also spoke and delivered a lucid and learned speech, although one totally lacking in eloquence or fire. Something else was needed, and Webster rose on December 15 to provide it.[34] His address proved to be one of the high points of the convention.

The question involved two considerations: Should the legislative branch have any other check besides establishing two houses, and if so, what should it be? As for the first problem Webster denied that there was much check in having two houses because the members of each were chosen at the same time and were "actuated by the same feelings and interests," usually party. Nor could the judiciary provide help because of "legislative encroachment." As for an additional check he favored a property-based senate—not as "a check on the people,

---

33. *Journal of Debates and Proceedings in the Convention of Delegates, Chosen to Revise the Constitution of Massachusetts* (Boston, 1853), pp. 160–163. This *Journal* was derived from reports published in the Boston *Daily Advertiser* at the time and reprinted in 1853. Unfortunately not everything said was reported in the newspaper. Webster's address on this subject is also reprinted in *W&S*, V, 4–7.

34. *Journal of Debates*, p. 278ff. A recent and more convenient reprinting of Webster's address can be found in *PS*, I, 62–81.

but on the House of Representatives." This does not limit the power of the people, he continued, only the authority of their agents. If it is wise to give the house of representatives power to check the senate, then "some difference of character, sentiment, feeling, or origin" must exist in the senate to control the house. Age will not provide the difference, or "double election"—that is, choosing electors who chose the senators. In the present constitution property provided the difference. Whether this be the best mode is not the question, he declared. The question is "whether this be better than no mode."

The Republicans had demanded "authority" to support the idea of a property requirement. Webster obliged and shoveled it at them, spadeful after spadeful. He cited Grotius, Harrington, Aristotle, Bacon, and Raleigh. Harrington, he claimed, proved "that power *naturally* and *necessarily* flows from property," that government founded on property is legitimate, while government based on the disregard of property "is founded in injustice, and can only be maintained by military force." When property is centered in one class of people and power in another, balanced government, so beloved of the Founding Fathers, so essential to a republic, is impossible. Both property and power must be integral to any government. "Our own immortal Revolution was undertaken, not to shake or plunder property, but to protect it."[35]

The speech forcefully buttressed conservative beliefs and concerns. It also won over the other delegates, and the property basis for the senate was retained. The qualification was not abolished until twenty years later.

Although Webster spoke with great effect on retaining this qualification, he was singularly silent when the convention debated broadening the franchise to provide universal manhood suffrage. Here again property was the present requirement for voting: an estate valued at two hundred dollars or an annual income from a freehold of at least ten dollars. But the convention did not abolish it. Elimination of the requirement had minimum support among the delegates and generated little debate. Like Webster, many delegates had grave reservations about universal manhood suffrage, so the convention substituted a taxpaying requirement instead.[36]

Webster came alive again when the role of the judiciary arose for consideration. Joseph Story presented the committee's report and, among other recommendations, argued in favor of strengthening the independence of the judiciary. Here Webster really dazzled his listeners when he spoke on December 30 because the judiciary and its importance were close to his heart.

An independent judiciary, he lectured, was absolutely "essential to the preservation of private rights and public liberty." The plan and theory of constitutional government are to restrain the legislative, and other departments as well, whenever constitutional limits are breached.

Webster was particularly incensed over the question of removing judges

35. *W&S*, V, 8–25.

36. *Journal of Debates*, p. 246ff.

from office. The committee had recommended a two-third vote of each house of the legislature, but the opposition demanded a simple majority. Webster foresaw much mischief if the convention acceded to this demand. Removal would become a very easy technique for controlling the judiciary. "If the legislature may remove judges at pleasure, assigning no cause for such removal," he declared, will it not retain those judges who approve the constitutionality of their acts and remove those who do not? Nothing is as important to the individual as the "upright administration of justice. . . . We look to the judicial tribunal for protection against illegal or unconstitutional acts, from whatever quarter they may proceed. The courts of law, independent judges, and enlightened juries, are citadels of popular liberty, as well as temples of private justice."[37]

Story was ecstatic. "Our friend Webster," he informed Mason a few weeks later, "has gained a noble reputation. He was before known as a lawyer; but he has now secured the title of an eminent and enlightened statesman. . . . The whole force of his great mind was brought out," not only with this issue but with several others, and "he commanded universal admiration. He always led the van, and was most skillful and instantaneous in attack and retreat." On the whole, Story concluded, "I never was more proud of any display than his in my life."[38]

Unfortunately the convention would not consent to the two-third recommendation of the committee, so Webster and his conservative friends maneuvered approval of a substitute requiring the legislature to show cause for removal and provide a hearing for the accused.

Only once in the course of the convention did Webster explode in a torrent of emotional language, and that occurred when a gentleman from Worcester declared that the delegates were forging chains and fetters for the people of Massachusetts.

"Chains *and* fetters!" shouted Webster, as he jumped to his feet.

This convention of delegates, chosen by the people within this month, and going back to the people divested of all power within another month, yet occupying their space of time here in forging chains and fetters for themselves and their constituents! "Chains *and* fetters." A popular assembly, of four hundred men, combining to fabricate those manacles for the people—and nobody but the honorable member from Worcester with sagacity enough to detect the horrible conspiracy, or honest enough to disclose it! . . . Sir, there are some things too extravagant for the ornament and decoration of oratory . . . and I am persuaded that a little reflection would have persuaded the honorable member, that when he speaks of this assembly as committing outrages on the rights of the people, and as forging chains and fetters for their subjugation, he does as great injustice to his own character as a correct and manly debater, as he does to the motives and intelligence of this body.[39]

By and large conservatives were relatively pleased with the approval of fourteen amendments adopted by the convention when it adjourned on January

37. *W&S*, V, 30, 31–32.

38. Story to Mason, January 21, 1821, in Story, *Life and Letters*, I, 395–396.

39. March, *Webster*, pp. 63–64.

9.[40] Although a distinct minority, they managed to hold off the worst designs of the "radicals" and preserve "our best institutions."[41] It happened because of their mastery of parliamentary debate and a "vast preponderance of talent and virtue and principle."[42]

And few demonstrated greater talent than Daniel Webster. He knew it, and everyone else knew it too. His reputation surged enormously on account of the convention.

Whether he realized it or not, his political career had begun once again.

40. When the amendments were submitted to the people, only nine of the fourteen were approved.

41. Webster said they had to contend with "a good deal of inflamable matter, & some *radicalism.*" DW to Mason, January 12, 1821, in *PC,* I, 280.

42. Story to Mason, January 21, 1821, in Story, *Life and Letters,* I, 395.

9

The Plymouth Oration

MIDWAY through the proceedings of the constitutional convention Webster took time out to attend the bicentennial anniversary of the landing of the Pilgrims on Plymouth Rock and deliver an oration in commemoration of this historic event.

Earlier in the year a group of men had formed the Pilgrim Society and, knowing Webster's reputation for public speaking, asked him to address the great mass of people expected to attend the celebration. Although his mind was presently occupied with ideas and language for the delegates of the constitutional convention, he understood the importance of the invitation and its probable impact on all New England, so he readily accepted. He knew that what he said would be heard throughout the state and beyond because of its historic importance, and he did not wish to lose such a golden opportunity to enhance his reputation. It meant of course that for several days he had to turn his thoughts away from the convention—this may explain his silence on several major issues discussed in the convention—and devote countless hours to the undertaking. But the labor was well worth the cost in time and effort, and Webster applied himself with unusual energy.

For such events he always prepared himself very carefully, especially in researching the appropriate facts and the historical background. Frequently, as on this occasion, his preparation was so thorough that he hardly looked at his notes when he gave the address, and at this time he spoke for one hour and fifty minutes nonstop.

The address, which he called "The First Settlement of New England," was actually the first of his mature orations. An oration, such as this, was distinct from his usual political addresses and legal pleadings. Webster's several Fourth of July speeches in past years had been the efforts of a young man beginning to learn the great art of public speaking. He himself thought those efforts juvenile. And they were, even though they served a most important purpose in his development. The Phi Beta Kappa address had been a literary lecture, nothing more. And the speech before the Washington Benevolent Society of Portsmouth in 1812 had been a political discourse.[1] Here in Plymouth, Massachusetts, in 1820

1. Curtis, *Webster,* I, 190.

he was asked, in effect, to speak to the origins of the nation, its basic foundations. Nothing short of an effort worthy of Edmund Burke could suffice.

After Webster had toiled many days and hours on the preparation of this oration, he and his wife left Boston to travel the forty-odd miles to Plymouth in the company of Professor George Ticknor of Harvard and five other friends.[2] Ticknor was especially good to have along. A Dartmouth alumnus, class of 1807, widely traveled in Europe, where he absorbed the new German scholarship, appointed to the Smith professorship of French and Spanish and an added professorship of belles lettres, and withal a brilliant scholar, Ticknor became one of Webster's most fervent admirers.[3]

The group left on Thursday, December 21, at "half past eight precisely" and took the entire day to reach Plymouth. Along the way they met fifty or sixty people, most of whom Webster knew, headed in the same direction. If it had not crossed his mind earlier that the celebration would attract thousands of New Englanders, he knew now. Plymouth was the place from which they all originated or liked to think they had. It represented a beginning, the realization of a dream to be free. Anyone who thought that he or she descended from the Pilgrims—and there were many, even then—felt a keen obligation to be present at this momentous event.[4]

Driving down from Boston, Webster had seemed distracted and uninterested in his surroundings. His companions thought that the convention had wearied him or that he was apprehensive about the speech he would deliver the following day. But once they stopped off for dinner, reported Ticknor, "we had a merry time, and Mr. Webster was as gay as anyone."

When they reached the hill that opened a view of Plymouth Bay to them, "it was like coming upon classic ground, where every object was a recollection and almost a history." The town itself now hid "the little spot" the Pilgrims had "consecrated by their first footsteps." The group hurried out of their carriage to see where the first boatload had landed. And there it was: the "blessed rock." It was already surrounded by a crowd of strangers who had arrived in the afternoon, "and a cannon was mounted on it to fire a forefathers' salute to-morrow morning." Then the group walked over to the mound where King Massasoit had come the following spring to assure the Pilgrims of his friendship.[5]

A little later, as they surveyed the town, they could see that it was in a festive mood: All the houses and even individual rooms were lighted as if a party were under way in every one of them, and a crowd lounged about "to see the curiosities." A musical band paraded up and down the streets, followed by "the crowd and rabble," and it serenaded the many strangers who had arrived from

2. These friends included Mr. and Mrs. I. P. Davis, a Miss Russell, Frank Gary, Miss Stockton, and Miss Mason. Ticknor, *Life*, I, 328.

3. For further details, see David B. Tyack, *George Ticknor and the Boston Brahmins* (Cambridge, Mass., 1967).

4. Ticknor, *Life*, I, 328.

5. Ibid.

great distances to participate in the bicentennial. The patriarchs of Plymouth greeted Webster on his arrival with appropriate words of how it was their great good fortune that he should come and deliver the principal address.[6]

The next morning, Friday, December 22, the day of the principal celebration, Webster, Ticknor, and the others went to the Registry Office to examine records going back to 1623. They saw the handwriting of William Brewster, who led the Pilgrims aboard the *Mayflower* to Plymouth, and all the documents "that gave us, as it were, a more distinct ancestry than any other people on the globe." Then they walked to the cemetery where rested the "bones of *one* of the Pilgrims of 1620," the only one who had lived long enough "into settled times that it was safe to bury him with a gravestone."[7]

Like the consummate actor he was, Webster next went to the old First Church, where he was to deliver the oration, to check out the facilities. Ticknor accompanied him. Webster climbed the pulpit where he was expected to speak but found it "inconvenient," perhaps too confining or too remote from the audience. He came down and experimented with several other places before deciding to take his position at the deacon's seat, immediately under the pulpit. He had a table brought in and covered with a green baize cloth. Everyone with him thought the arrangement inappropriate until the audience began to arrive later and they realized it would serve the purpose precisely.[8]

That afternoon a procession of selectmen, clergy, a few other distinguished guests, and Webster marched through the streets to the meetinghouse. It was a relatively large church, a square wooden structure, and held approximately twelve hundred people on the ground level and another three hundred in the gallery. The people who had come from all over New England and elsewhere packed the hall. They knew about Webster's reputation as a speaker, especially what he had said in the *Dartmouth* case, and they expected something similarly appropriate and similarly grand and moving and exhilarating.

The ceremonies began with a hymn, prayers, and an ode written especially for the occasion, after which President John Thornton Kirkland of Harvard College introduced the speaker with a few brief remarks. Then Webster took his place at the dean's station. He wore "small clothes" with black silk stockings, buckled shoes, and a silk gown. After a moment he began.

"Let us rejoice that we behold this day," he exclaimed in the exquisite voice that never failed to enthrall his audience.

Let us be thankful that we have lived to see the bright and happy breaking of the auspicious morn, which commences the third century of the history of New England. . . . It is a noble faculty of our nature which enables us to connect our thoughts, our sympathies, and our happiness with what is distant in place or time; and, looking before and

6. Ibid., 329.

7. Ibid., 330. See Paul D. Erickson, "Daniel Webster's Myth of the Pilgrims," *New England Quarterly*, LVII (March 1984), pp. 44–64.

8. Curtis, *Webster*, I, 192–193, quoting from a reminiscence written especially for him by Ticknor.

after, to hold communion at once with our ancestors and our posterity. Human and mortal although we are, we are nevertheless not mere insulated beings, without relation to the past or the future. . . . We live in the past by a knowledge of its history; and in the future by hope and anticipation.

It was a flawless beginning that immediately caught up his audience in the flow of his thinking and the magnificent surge of his language. "We have come to this Rock," he continued, "to record here our homage for our Pilgrim Fathers; our sympathy in their sufferings; our gratitude for their labors; our admiration of their virtues; our veneration of their piety; and our attachment to those principles of civil and religious liberty, which they encountered the dangers of the ocean, the storms of heaven, the violence of savages, disease, exile, and famine, to enjoy and to establish."

This is the spot, he cried, where the first scene of our history occurred, where the homes and churches of New England were first laid, where Christianity and civilization began in a wilderness, "peopled by roving barbarians." It awes and inspires us. *"The genius of the place,"* he declared, brought forth free institutions, moral patterns of behavior, principles of imperishable truth and beauty, commercial success, and an abiding love of liberty.

Who would wish that his country's existence had otherwise begun? Who would desire the power of going back to the ages of fable? Who would wish for an origin obscured in the darkness of antiquity? Who would wish for other emblazoning of his country's heraldry, or other ornaments of her genealogy, than to be able to say, that her first existence was with intelligence, her first breath the inspiration of liberty, her first principle the truth of divine religion?[9]

This repetition of questions—Who would wish, who would desire, etc.—in a long cluster was typical of Webster's style and has been a time-honored technique for public speakers. It rarely fails to have an impact. The first part of the cluster usually contains short, staccatolike sentences followed by a final sentence of greater length that summarizes the essential point the speaker wishes to make. Such a technique engages the audience in a rhythm and forward motion that increase excitement until the release at the end of the cluster. At political rallies it can create a near frenzy of response from the audience. Webster used it sparingly in his speeches—perhaps two or three times in a two-hour address—and he separated the clusters from one another by a fair distance so that the audience did not become jaded and less responsive each time he used it.[10]

"This Rock," he asserted, "soon became hallowed in the esteem of the Pilgrims and these hills grateful to their sight." No longer would they till the soil of England or traverse the seas around it. "But here was a new sea, now open to

9. *W&S*, I, 181–198.

10. At political rallies Henry Clay later used the technique of repeated questions to rouse his audience and get them to join in with a vocal response. For example, he would ask: Did he need to explain his position on national issues? "No," the crowd roared back at him. Did he need to explain his position on any measure before Congress? Again, "no." And on and on. See Remini, *Clay*, p. 541.

their enterprise, and a new soil, which had not failed to respond gratefully to their laborious industry, and which was already assuming the robe of verdure."

Soon the Pilgrims had other reasons that bound them to their chosen land: children; the graves of relatives and friends; the common heritage of their history. Webster focused on their commitment to the supremacy of the British crown but also on their repugnance to "an entire submission to the control of British legislation."

There followed a long disquisition on the causes of the American Revolution. "I have dwelt on this topic," he said, "because it seems to me, that the peculiar original character of the New England Colonies . . . have a strong and decided influence on all their subsequent history, and especially on the great event of the Revolution." Unlike the colonies of ancient Greece and Rome or even the British West Indies, the New England colonies developed free institutions and their own culture. They did not merely imitate the past.

The gift of New England to the rest of the nation, he claimed, has been that its farms, houses, villages, and churches adorn the immense extent of land from the Atlantic to the Ohio and Lake Erie and stretch along the Allegheny "beyond the Miamis, and toward the Falls of St. Anthony." Two thousand miles from Plymouth Rock may now be found "the sons of the Pilgrims, cultivating smiling fields, rearing town and villages, and cherishing, we trust, the patrimonial blessings of wise institutions, of liberty and religion. The world has seen nothing of this." But, he predicted, in less than thirty years "the sons of the Pilgrims will be on the shores of the Pacific."

He spoke of the free school system that New England had devised for its citizens, of the great internal improvements erected in the country following the Revolution, of the republican form of government resting on "laws which regulate the descent and transmission of property." He noted the improvement in science, in literature, and "in the elegant as well as the useful arts."

He spent considerable time reminding everyone of the importance of "respect for property." The character of the nation's institutions was determined by the fundamental laws of property. And the property was all freehold. The true principle of a free and popular government is simply this: to give to all "an interest in its preservation; to found it, as other things are founded, on men's interest." At this point he was repeating much of what he had said in the convention about property, even to quoting Harrington and citing the history of foreign nations to make his point.[11] No matter. He felt very strongly about this point and insisted that government, to be stable and successful, must make certain that those who desire its continuance should be more powerful than those who are indifferent to it or who desire its dissolution.

This power cannot always be measured by sheer numbers, he insisted.

---

11. During this speech Webster showed off his considerable knowledge of history, including ancient history. And of course the discussion of ancient history allowed him to quote from the works of the classics, including one of Cicero's celebrated orations. And this long ten-line quotation was given *in Latin*.

Majorities cannot always be trusted. Numbers are a most important consideration, of course, but education, wealth, and talent also count. Universal suffrage cannot exist alongside inequality of property. The propertyless, in such a situation, would look at property as "its prey and plunder" and turn to "violence and revolution." It should be apparent, then, "to be part of political wisdom to found government on property" and allow for its distribution so as to interest the great majority of society in the support and protection of the government. "This is, I imagine, the true theory and actual practice of our republican institutions."[12]

Here was the essence of Webster's political philosophy. Property lies at the very root of man's efforts to establish government, devise laws, initiate moral and social codes, and lead a useful and productive life. It is the touchstone of civilization.

Then he brought up the question of slavery. It might have seemed inappropriate at this time and on this occasion, but it mattered a great deal to Webster, and he would not duck it or put a good face on it. The sons and daughters of the courageous Pilgrims needed to hear his views, he thought, as uncomfortable as they might be. And at this point his face darkened, his voice hardened, and he grew visibly angry. He spoke "with a power of indignation such as I never witnessed on any other occasion," reported George Ticknor.[13]

I deem it my duty on this occasion to suggest, that the land is not yet wholly free from the contamination of a traffic, at which every feeling of humanity must for ever revolt,—I mean the African slave-trade. Neither public sentiment, nor the law, has hitherto been able to put an end to this odious and abominable trade.[14] At the moment when God in his mercy has blessed the Christian world with a universal peace, there is reason to fear, that, to the disgrace of the Christian name and character, new efforts are making for the extension of this trade by subject and citizens of Christian states, in whose hearts there dwell no sentiments of humanity or of justice, and over whom neither the fear of God nor the fear of man exercises a control. . . . If there be, within the extent of our knowledge or influence, any participation in this traffic, let us pledge ourselves here, upon the rock of Plymouth, to extirpate and destroy it. It is not fit that the land of the Pilgrims should bear the shame longer. I hear the sound of the hammer, I see the smoke of the furnaces where manacles and fetters are still forged for human limbs.

Audibly roused, his arms constantly gesturing toward his audience, his body swaying from side to side, Webster resorted once again to the technique of the repeated phrase. "Let that spot be purified, or let it cease to be of New England. Let it be purified, or let it be set aside from the Christian world; let it be put out of the circle of human sympathies and human regards, and let civilized man henceforth have no communion with it." It was a blessed and noble utterance, and it fell, for the most part, on receptive ears.

He closed by stating that we in the present generation must leave for the

12. *W&S*, I, 198–215.

13. Curtis, *Webster*, I, 193.

14. The importation of slaves from Africa had been abolished by Congress in 1808. But the slave trade within the United States of course continued.

generations to follow some proof that we hold the blessings transmitted from our fathers in the highest estimation, that we are committed to good government, to civil and religious liberty, to the task of enlarging and improving the hearts of men. As he spoke his final words, Webster extended his arms as though to embrace his entire audience.

Advance, then, ye future generations! We would hail you, as you rise in your long succession, to fill the places which we now fill, and to taste the blessings of existence where we are passing, and soon shall have passed, our own human duration. We bid you welcome to this pleasant land of the fathers. We bid you welcome to the healthful skies and the verdant fields of New England. We greet your accession to the great inheritance which we have enjoyed. We welcome you to the blessings of good government and religious liberty. We welcome you to the treasures of science and the delights of learning. We welcome you to the transcendent sweets of domestic life, to the happiness of kindred, and parents, and children. We welcome you to the immeasurable blessings of rational existence, the immortal hope of Christianity, and the light of everlasting truth![15]

His head bowed as he concluded. The audience sat transfixed. It knew it had heard something "godlike." Ticknor, a discerning commentator, recounted that he had never been "so excited by public speaking before in my life. Three or four times I thought my temples would burst with the gush of blood." The miracle of it all was the fact that Webster had spoken without looking at the notes on the table yet had strung together a "collection of wonderful fragments of burning eloquence, to which his manner gave tenfold force."

Webster really did not need any notes. He had a phenomenal memory—total recall, as a matter of fact—and he had thought long and hard about what he would say. When Ticknor left the hall, he admitted that he was afraid to go near Webster. "It seemed to me as if he was like the mount that might not be touched, and that burned with fire." Webster seemed "god-like." "I was beside myself, and am so still."[16]

Soon a great many people referred to the orator as the godlike Daniel Webster. "Godlike" seemed to be the only appropriate way to refer to this extraordinary man. Word of his stunning performance at Plymouth quickly spread through New England and beyond, and the appellation, "godlike" spread with it.

Ticknor rushed back to his quarters to write down his impression of the oration. "Yet I do not trust myself about it, and . . . I have not the least confidence in my own opinion. His manner carried me away completely; not, I think, that I could have been so carried away if it had been a poor oration. . . . It *must* have been a great, a very great performance, but . . . I cannot be sure till I have read it, for it seems to me incredible."[17]

Like most great orators and public speakers, Webster knew instinctively

15. *W&S*, I, 215–226; Ticknor's quote can be found in Curtis, *Webster*, I, 193.
16. Ticknor, *Life*, I, 330.
17. Ibid., 329–330.

that he had given the finest performance of his life. "I never saw him at any time when he seemed to me to be more conscious of his own powers, or to have a more true and natural enjoyment from their possession." In those 110 minutes he could see the reaction of his words on his audience; he could feel its response; he sensed its emotional involvement. Everything he had said stirred his listeners, and they never forgot the experience. They relived it in their minds many times. In time they embellished the memory, as most people will. They felt as though they had been present at one of the truly great moments in New England history, present when Daniel Webster spoke with the sublime language of the "godlike."

When Webster returned to his lodgings, "all the principal people then in Plymouth" crowded around him. They shook his hand and congratulated him on his incredible accomplishment. "But there was something about him very grand and imposing at the same time." There still lingered around him an aura, a sense of the supernatural fire that burned within him. It was almost frightening.

At the public dinner later in the day Webster moved among the guests seemingly unmoved by the "great enthusiasm around him," enthusiasm that he himself had generated. He was distant, unapproachable. He seemed to be "above it all." The same thing occurred at the ball. "He was agreeable to everybody and nothing more."

But when he returned to his lodgings that night, his mood changed, and he was "as frolicsome as a school-boy, laughing and talking, and making merry" with his wife and the friends who had accompanied him to Plymouth. They "frolicked" until two o'clock in the morning.[18]

As word of his stupendous performance shot out across New England, many asked for more particulars about what he had said. The more they heard, the more they demanded further details. The officers of the Pilgrim Society approached Webster and requested that he prepare his address for publication. He said he would but advised them that the press of his law business would keep him from the preparation for several months—"a more distant day" was the way he put it. Normally he tried to publish his speeches as quickly as possible, and perhaps he was being truthful about the delay, at least in part. Another part may be that although he planned all along to publish it, he needed extra time to polish it to a hard, shining finish. It was as though he expected to be read long after he died. He intended his published works to be literary gems, and to accomplish that end, he gave them considerable care.[19]

Another reason for delaying publication had to do with his concern for

---

18. Curtis, *Webster*, I, 193, quoting Ticknor.

19. Unlike Henry Clay, who had to be heard and seen for someone to get any real feeling for the excellence of his speeches. Clay could not be bothered with polishing his work, important though it might be. He was careless about what he let the public read, and he paid a heavy political price for his laziness and indifference. See Remini, *Clay*, passim. Webster, on the other hand, sounded impressive both in person and in print. His speeches will always be read and appreciated because for most of his life he worked diligently to improve his literary style. Even today one does not need to be a descendant of the Pilgrims or a New Englander or to have lived there to sense the splendor of the Plymouth oration.

repetition. Some of what he said in Plymouth he had said during the constitutional convention. Since his convention speech had recently been printed, he probably wanted to avoid comparisons and therefore delayed submitting the final version of his address to the officers of the Plymouth Society for several months. He finally wrote the officers in May 1821 advising them that for the first time he at last had enough "leisure" to look over his address and begin to prepare it for publication. Actually he had been working on it from time to time over the past year, and a considerable portion of the oration was ready. Within the next few weeks he finished it. He left its printing to the Pilgrim Society, and it appeared in the late autumn of 1821.[20]

In preparing this speech for publication, Webster expanded it considerably. Much of what was printed, Ticknor reported, was never delivered at the old First Church. This was a constant complaint from those who heard him speak, no matter what the occasion. Rarely did the printed version of any of his speeches match what he actually said. Still, the fire, enthusiasm, learning, and majesty of the original Plymouth oration were excellently recaptured in print, thanks to his untiring efforts to make it as alive on the printed page as it had been when he delivered it.

He was proud of the final product and distributed it widely among friends, local and national leaders, distinguished statesmen, and anyone else he wanted to impress. One response he received must surely have delighted him. Former President John Adams, to whom Webster made reference in the address, wrote and thanked him for sending him a copy. Adams pronounced the discourse "the effort of a great mind, richly stored with every species of information. If there be an American who can read it without tears, I am not that American. It enters more perfectly into the genuine spirit of New England, than any production I ever read." Webster's remarks about the Greeks, Romans, colonization, and the slave trade, Adams continued, "are sagacious, profound, and affecting, in a high degree. Mr [Edmund] Burke is no longer entitled to the praise 'The most consummate Orator of modern times.' " Daniel Webster has a better title to it. "This Oration will be read five hundred years hence with as much rapture, as it was heard; it ought to be read at the end of every Century, and indeed at the end of every year, for ever and ever."[21]

What a commendation! What a tribute! And from what a source! Webster could ask for nothing finer. And Adams was right about the oration's longevity. The work became a literary classic, sections of which were memorized and repeated in classrooms throughout New England and wherever the New England presence was felt. The Plymouth oration set a new standard. It was totally original and became the model for all commemorative speeches for generations to come.

The great chancellor of New York James Kent, who virtually created equity

20. DW to Samuel Davis, May 14, 1821, in *PC*, I, 285.

21. Adams to DW, December 23, 1821, in ibid., I, 297–298.

jurisdiction in the United States, also sent Webster his compliments. "The reflections, the sentiments, the morals, the patriotism, the eloquence, the imagination of this admirable production," he wrote, "are exactly what I anticipated: elevated, just & true. I think it is also embellished by a Style distinguished for purity, taste & simplicity."[22]

Twenty-five years later Amos Lawrence, who heard many of Webster's great speeches, insisted that Webster never surpassed the Plymouth oration. "It is a model and a text for the youth of our country," he said.[23]

Indeed. And not only for the youth of the country. In a very real sense Daniel Webster had begun to provide the American people with something they did not have at this time, something they desperately needed: a history of their origins as a nation. No qualified historian had yet produced a work that would begin to teach Americans about their past. The first volume of George Bancroft's *History of the United States* did not appear until 1834[24] and was not completed until 1874, when he brought out the tenth and final volume, reaching 1789. Consequently for decades Webster's many speeches and orations served as the nation's history, a history glowing with feeling and sentiment and poetic imagery. Small wonder that they were taught and memorized in school. And not only in New England but around the country. In a very real sense Daniel Webster gave the American people their past.

At the age of forty-one he now sat at the top of the legal and literary American worlds. Between his plea before the Supreme Court in the *Dartmouth College* case and his Plymouth oration he had achieved such distinction and recognition as to win national and international attention.

22. Kent to DW, December 29, 1821, in *W&S*, XVII, 319.

23. William E. Lawrence, ed., *Extracts from the Diary and Correspondence of the late Amos Lawrence* (Boston, 1856), p. 208.

24. Lilian Handlin, *George Bancroft: The Intellectual as Democrat* (New York, 1984), p. 248.

10

An Expanding Reputation

WEBSTER returned to Boston and immediately plunged into a backlog of law cases awaiting his attention. One of the most important involved claimants against Spain and developed out of the Adams-Onís Treaty by which the United States acquired Florida.

Under orders from the War Department, General Andrew Jackson had pursued the Seminole Indians into Spanish-held Florida. The Indians had repeatedly crossed the border and attacked American settlements in Georgia. Florida also provided refuge for runaway slaves. But instead of just subduing the Indians, Jackson seized Florida and sent the Spanish governor fleeing to Cuba. The hot-tempered general believed that his action was Monroe's real intention.[1] Worse, he executed two British subjects accused of aiding and abetting the Indians in their raids against American settlers. President Monroe's cabinet, almost to a man, favored punishing Jackson for his unauthorized war against Spain. But John Quincy Adams, the secretary of state, defended him and ultimately won Monroe over to the position of pressuring Spain into selling Florida. At the same time Henry Clay, in the House of Representatives, tried and failed to win Jackson's censure.[2]

Secretary Adams convinced the Spanish that their best interests lay in relinquishing the territory to the United States. In the Adams-Onís Treaty of 1819 Spain not only agreed to the sale but surrendered its claim to Oregon while the United States gave up all claim to Texas. In addition, the western boundary of the Louisiana Purchase was defined. Finally, the United States assumed five million dollars' worth of American claims against Spain incurred for the most part during the period of the Napoleonic Wars. Although the treaty was signed in 1819, its ratification was delayed until February 22, 1821.

A great many New England shippers, merchants, and insurance companies[3] made claims under the terms of the treaty, and Webster's reputation as an eminent lawyer attracted an enormous number of these claimants. He consequently spent most of 1821 attending to the preparation of cases to be argued

1. On the dispute over Jackson's authority to seize Florida see Remini, *Jackson*, I, 341ff.

2. Remini, *Clay*, pp. 161–168.

3. Some of these companies were headquartered in Philadelphia as well as Boston.

before a three-man Spanish Claims Commission set up to adjudicate the claims.[4] The commissioners—Hugh Lawson White of Tennessee, Littleton W. Tazewell of Virginia, and William King of Maine—held their first organizational meeting in June and their first hearings in September 1821, but Webster held off appearing before them in order to observe how the guidelines operated in practice and what evidence the commissioners accepted.

Not only did his law practice prosper as a result of these cases, but he made many friends among the well-to-do families of merchants and shippers in Boston and many other coastal cities along the eastern seaboard, especially after he won judgments in their favor.[5]

Because of his booming business, his law associate Alexander Bliss wanted more spacious quarters and talked Webster into moving to a new location at the corner of Court and Tremont streets. "I confess I have been unwilling to move," Webster explained to Bliss, "but as you seem to prefer it, I am disposed to submit." He simply asked for his own room and accommodations for his associate and their law students.[6]

In maintaining this relatively large practice, Webster found himself constantly shuttling back and forth to Washington to appear before state courts, federal courts, the Supreme Court, and the Claims Commission. This proved very wearing on the family. The children frequently cried for him, and his wife, again pregnant and none too well, needed a great deal of support to help her get over her depression following the death of her mother in July 1821. Her letters to him, while he was away, bespeak her gentleness and her all-consuming devotion to her husband and children.

Bordenton Sunday Morning

10 O'clock

I hope ere this hour, my dear Husband, you are almost at the end of your journey. You are first, and last, and always in our hearts, and on our minds. I say *ours* for Julia's bonny hazel eye has often filled with tears since we parted and she could hardly enjoy the luxury of a nice bedroom and delightful bed because dear Papa was in the steamboat and her apprehensions for your safety are very great. I comforted her and quieted her fears, by our own safety, and by the beauty, and brightness, and stillness, of the night, which on your account was a cause of great joy and thankfulness to me.

The morning tho' warm, is delightful! A calm tranquility, a sort of sacred stillness, seems to pervade everything around, on a Sabbath morning in the country.

Mrs. [Joseph] H[opkinson] wishes me to tell you that I hear the "church going-bell" tho' I follow the example of the family and stay at home, and she hopes the children hear it also as one of them tho't it a strange village without a church—it must have been one of Puss' remarks.[7]

---

4. Some 1,859 claims were brought before the commission during its three-year life span. Of these, Webster filed approximately 125 of them. He also participated in another 100 cases for Philadelphia Insurance Companies. See *PLFP,* II, 179.

5. Webster had broad discretion in handling these cases, and he was usually paid 5 percent of the proceeds from the claims up to twenty thousand dollars. *PLFP,* II, 200.

6. DW to Bliss, February 9, [1821], in *PC,* I, 281–282.

7. Grace Webster to DW, [June 6, 1824], in Van Tyne, ed., *Letters of Webster,* pp. 548–549.

Sometimes Grace signed her letters to her husband "Your affectionate Mother G. W."[8]

Despite the pain he knew it caused his family, Webster regularly left home for weeks and sometimes months on end. Just the trip alone to the capital could consume the better part of a week. In one letter written in 1822 he explained to Joseph Story that he left Boston on the mail stagecoach on Saturday noon, December 29, and arrived in New Haven on Sunday at three in the afternoon. Several friends accompanied him. They remained in New Haven for the remainder of Sunday and then set out again in an "accommodation stage-coach" on Monday for New York, which they reached early in the evening of the same day. In New York they found a new line of stagecoaches, called the Union line, which gave the group an entire coach for forty dollars and allowed it to make its own schedule. So on Tuesday, New Year's Day at three or four in the afternoon they headed toward Philadelphia, stopped off for the night in New Brunswick, and arrived in Philadelphia in time to dine on Wednesday, January 2. Then it took another day to get to Washington.[9]

While he was on the road to Washington, Grace gave birth to their fifth child, Charles, at half past twelve on December 31, 1821, just two days after Webster's departure. Surely it distressed him to leave when his wife was so close to delivery, but he felt he had no choice. The faithful Eliza Buckminster wrote and assured him that Grace was "remarkably well" and that "the babe grows finely and seems to be as contented with this world as any one can be who has had as little experience of its changes." Grace sat up for half an hour each day and received callers regularly. All the other children were well, but each time Eliza went to the nursery, Edward would cry out, *"papa gone."* He "wants to come down stairs to find you," Eliza explained. Webster's second letter from New York had just arrived, and Eliza reported that Grace "thanks you for writing so often, and hopes soon to hear of your having crossed the Susquehannah in safety."[10]

During this hectic period in his life Webster involved himself in a number of legal cases of national and sometimes international importance. In cases involving national issues he naturally favored the authority of the central government in the exercise of its powers, particularly those he deemed exclusive. He also stoutly defended judicial rights. And he noticed that ever since Jefferson's attack on the judicial branch of the government in the famous impeachment trial of Associate Justice Samuel Chase in 1805 there had been growing complaints against the Supreme Court every time Marshall and his colleagues rendered decisions that seemed to endanger state sovereignty or individual rights.

The *McCulloch* decision was a case in point. John Taylor of Caroline published his very influential book *Construction Construed, and Constitutions Vin-*

8. See, for example, Grace Webster to DW, January 16, March 13, 1824, ibid., pp. 547–548.

9. DW to Story, January 3, 1821, but actually 1822, in *PC*, I, 299.

10. Buckminster to DW, January 4, 1822, ibid., I, 300.

dicated, followed by *Tyranny Unmasked* and *New Views of the Constitution,* in which he excoriated Marshall's interpretation of the Constitution and denied the validity of appeals from state courts to the Supreme Court.[11] President Andrew Jackson, in his famous veto of the Bank bill in 1832, later denied that Marshall's *McCulloch* decision was binding on the President or Congress.[12]

The attack on the authority of the Court outraged Webster. It infuriated him that the Supreme Court virtually stood alone in defending judicial authority. "More Courts & Judges," he snorted, are needed "for the purpose of enabling them better to defend themselves & their jurisdiction. In all the attacks on the judiciary the Judges of the S Court alone, & unaided, have been obliged to fight the battle." He therefore advocated two yearly sessions of the Supreme Court and eliminating the need for the justices to ride the circuit.[13] "A larger corps of Judges would afford more strength & stability" to the legal system, he contended.[14]

Webster frequently appeared before the U.S. First Circuit Court of Appeal, happily presided over by his close friend Associate Justice Joseph Story, whose thinking, like Marshall's, closely resembled Webster's. One case he argued before Story, *La Jeune Eugénie,*[15] brought international attention. This case involved an action against a French-owned schooner engaged in the slave trade in violation of U.S. law that had been seized and brought into Boston Harbor. Basically the case centered on the tricky question of maritime search and seizure practices in the attempt to suppress the international slave trade. Webster and the U.S. attorney, George Blake, argued on behalf of the United States and the captors of the schooner.

Webster's basic premise contended that the slave trade constituted piracy and was contrary to the law of nations because it violated natural law. He did not deny that the institution of slavery might under certain circumstances be legal and a trade in slaves might, under these circumstances, also be legal. But the traffic practiced in this case, he said, "preyed upon the innocent and the free to make them slaves, for no crime or offense. That it was merely a barbarous, unauthorized, private, piratical warfare, carried on against Africans to make them slaves." Since most nations had enacted laws against this trade, it must therefore be judged contrary to the law of nations.[16]

11. John Taylor, *Construction Construed and Constitutions Vindicated* (Richmond, 1820); *Tyranny Unmasked* (Washington, 1822); *New Views of the Constitution of the United States* (Washington, 1822).

12. Richardson, *Messages and Papers,* II, 1144–1145.

13. Supreme Court judges, according to the Judiciary Act of 1789, were required to participate in each of the three circuit courts of appeal. It was called riding the circuit and was quite burdensome. A court of appeal consisted of two Supreme Court judges and the district court judge where the case was tried.

14. DW to Mason, December 29, 1823, in *PLFP,* III, 360.

15. 26 Federal Cases 832.

16. *W&S,* XV, 280.

Webster already had become active on the issue of the slave presence in America. In 1817 the American Colonization Society was formed for the purpose of transporting manumitted slaves to Africa. The society attracted southern support among those who wished to get rid of former slaves by shipping them to Liberia. Bushrod Washington was its first president, and founding members included such slaveowners as Secretary of the Treasury William H. Crawford, Henry Clay, and Andrew Jackson. Webster contributed his "own little mite" to the cause and allowed his name to be added to the initial list of contributors, although frankly, he admitted, "I cannot, conscientiously very confidently recommend the cause of this Society as being a great attainable good."[17]

Story agreed on all points with Webster in the case of *La Jeune Eugénie* and found for the government, but on appeal the decision was reversed on the ground that the slave trade could be construed as piracy only when the law of the nation owning the property condemned it as such.[18]

A case of more national significance, *Cohens* v. *Virginia*[19] involved the question of a lottery. The U.S. Congress had authorized a lottery in the District of Columbia, and Philip and Mendes Cohen sold tickets in Virginia in violation of state law and were convicted. Here was another instance of growing antagonism toward the federal judicial authority because the state denied the Supreme Court's jurisdiction by virtue of the Eleventh Amendment to the Constitution, which said that the judicial power of the United States could not be construed to extend to any suit against a state by citizens of another state or subjects of a foreign country. Virginia openly challenged the *McCulloch* decision and also denied the right of Congress to authorize a lottery in a state that forbade it by law.

Marshall regarded the *Cohens* case as a direct assault on his Court and himself personally. It provided him with the opportunity to reassert federal judicial power and blast away at the presumption of states to question federal authority. In one of his most contrived decisions—and that is saying a great deal in light of his long judicial record—Marshall upheld the authority of the Supreme Court to review decisions of the state courts. Moreover, he asserted that the federal courts, not state courts, held the final authority in matters involving constitutional interpretation. The Eleventh Amendment did not apply in this case because it could not prevent federal courts from deciding legitimate federal questions, even when a state was a party to the dispute.

Marshall steered away from the question of Virginia's noncompliance by holding that the lottery statute applied only to the District of Columbia.

This is where Webster entered the case. He had not argued the question of jurisdiction, which was really the important issue. He now argued for the state of Virginia on the question of merit. Was the congressional law applicable to the state of Virginia? Webster responded with a resounding negative. Con-

17. DW to Story, August 6, 1822, in *PC*, I, 313.
18. 10 Wheaton 66.
19. 6 Wheaton 264. See also White, *The Marshall Court*, pp. 504–524.

gress had established the lottery in the District of Columbia, not Virginia or any other state, and the legislation in question could not be construed, he insisted, to force sale throughout the Union in contravention of state statutes. "Every act of legislation must be limited by its subject matter," he declared, "and there is . . . nothing to show that this municipal power is to be carried beyond the City [of Washington]. It may be exercised within the City alone, and Congress has not said . . . that it is to be exercised in other parts of the Union." There was no conflict between the local laws established by Congress for the District and those of the states. "A law cannot exceed the authority of the lawgiver."[20]

Three days later the Court in a unanimous opinion agreed with Webster. It was not in the mind of Congress, Marshall decreed, to permit the sale of lottery tickets beyond the limits of the District. The "law cannot be construed to embrace it."[21] It may be that Marshall yielded on the question to avoid giving the states any further cause for complaint about judicial authority. Besides, the important matter of the Court's jurisdiction had been upheld. So Virginia lost the case on the jurisdictional question but, thanks in part to Webster's efforts, won it on the merits.[22]

By late winter 1822 Webster was finally acknowledged as the unquestioned head of the American bar pleading before the Supreme Court. Only the death of William Pinckney, who rightfully commanded the admiration of all who ever heard him argue a case, made it possible.

The two men greatly respected each other, although the relationship got off to a shaky start. It was the "nearest I ever came to a downright row," Webster admitted. Pinckney's flamboyant manner, extreme dress, and general behavior did not comport with "a gentleman of his breeding and culture and great weight as a lawyer," Webster angrily remarked. Pinckney rather regarded himself as God's gift to the legal profession, and he expected proper deference. During one of their earliest encounters in the Supreme Court he treated Webster with unbridled contempt. "He pooh-poohed, as much as to say it was not worth while to argue a point that I did not know anything about; that I was no lawyer." Everyone in the courtroom, including Chief Justice Marshall, noticed his improper behavior. "It was very hard for me to restrain my temper," recalled Webster. As the two men started to leave the courtroom following the adjournment, Pinckney threw his cloak over his arm and picked up his riding whip and gloves.

Webster walked up to him. "Can I see you alone in one of the lobbies?" he said very calmly but deliberately.

The great man turned around and with all the hauteur he could summon for the occasion replied, "Certainly." He obviously thought that the young man intended to beg his pardon for daring to argue a case against him.

20. 6 Wheaton 434–437.

21. 6 Wheaton 447.

22. Warren, *Supreme Court*, II, 11.

They moved into a nearby anteroom. It was empty, and Webster shut the door and locked it. Pinckney looked astonished, not knowing what to expect.

"Mr. Pinckney," exclaimed the younger man, "you grossly insulted me this morning, in the court-room; and not for the first time either. In deference to your position and to the respect in which I hold the court, I did not answer you as I was tempted to do, on the spot."

Pinckney tried to say something in rebuttal, but Webster cut him short.

"You know you did: don't add another sin to that; don't deny it; you know you did it, and you know it was premeditated." By this time Webster had raised the volume of his voice, and his dark eyes flashed angrily. "It was deliberate," he repeated; "it was purposely done; and, if you deny it, you state an untruth."

Mouth agape, Pinckney stared at his attacker.

"Now I am here to say to you, once for all, that you must ask my pardon, and go into court to-morrow morning and repeat the apology, or else either you or I will go out of this room in a different condition from that in which we entered it."

Again Pinckney tried to respond. Again Webster interrupted him.

"No explanations, admit the fact, and take it back. I do not want another word from you except that. I will hear no explanation; nothing but that you admit it, and recall it."

Pinckney "trembled like an aspen leaf," or so Webster remembered. Once more he attempted an explanation.

"There is no other course," said Webster in his deepest and most threatening voice. "I have the key in my pocket, and you must apologize, or take what I give you."

Finally Pinckney "humbled down." He could see that Webster meant him bodily harm if he did not apologize. There was a moment of silence. Then the older man straightened himself to his full height and spoke in a clear voice. "You are right; I am sorry; I did intend to bluff you; I regret it, and ask your pardon."

"Enough," responded the vindicated young man. "Now, one promise before I open the door; and that is, that you will to-morrow morning state to the court that you have said things which wounded my feelings, and that you regret it."

"I will do so," Pinckney replied.

With that Webster unlocked the door and walked out.

The next morning, after the Court had been called to order, Pinckney rose and apologized for offending the opposing counsel. It took everyone in the room by surprise. "From that day, while at the bar," Webster declared, "there was no man, who treated me with so much respect and deference as Mr. William Pinckney."[23]

The end of their relationship came in February 1822. Pinckney and Webster, as opposing counsel, were arguing the case of *Ricard* v. *Williams,* and Pinckney had just harangued the Court for *"nine hours"* when he suffered a

23. Harvey, *Reminiscences,* pp. 119–124.

stabbing pain in his chest. Webster was about to begin his reply when Pinckney suddenly rose, his cloak wrapped around him, and asked the Court's and Webster's permission for an adjournment to another day. He could not continue; he was ill but needed to hear Webster's argument. Both the Court and Webster cheerfully acquiesced, and then Webster hurried to his side. Pinckney admitted to a severe chill, "a sort of ague shock," he thought.

Webster helped him adjust his cloak and drove him home. A week later, on February 25, 1822, Pinckney died of a heart attack.[24]

"Poor Pinckney!" lamented Attorney General William Wirt. "He died opportunely for his fame. It could not have risen higher."[25]

To everyone in the Court it seemed altogether fitting that Pinckney should leave the judicial scene after a nine-hour defense against the pretender to his preeminent position. Now there was no one to challenge Daniel Webster's place at the head of the American bar.

24. Harvey, ibid., p. 124; DW to Bliss, February 19, 1822, in *PC*, I, 306.

25. Wirt to Francis W. Gilmer, May 9, 1822, in John P. Kennedy, *Memoirs of the Life of William Wirt* (Philadelphia, 1849), II, 138.

11

The Steamboat *Case*

ATTORNEY GENERAL William Wirt sighed. Daniel Webster, he said, has been "reaping laurels in the Supreme Court, while I have been— sighing. . . . North of the Potomac, I believe to a man, they yield the palm to Webster."[1]

Carrying his palm proudly and publicly, Black Dan returned to Boston when the Supreme Court adjourned its February session. Before he left Washington, he naturally visited his many friends in Congress and heard a great deal of talk about the approaching presidential election. "There is much stir and buzz about Presidential candidates here," he declared.[2] Even in this early era the election of the President took precedence over all other national issues, and the various candidates were discussed and assessed years before the actual election took place. Monroe's second term in office was to expire in two years, and several possible contenders to replace him had already begun to scramble for support in order to win the nomination of the Republican party, the only viable national party. Traditionally that party chose its candidate at a caucus of congressmen, but now complaints arose over this method because a caucus nomination automatically provided election since no other national party existed to contest it. Thus the right of the people to select their President in a free election had been eradicated by default. Many, including leading politicians in Washington, insisted that the caucus system had outlived its usefulness and had to be abandoned in favor of some other method of nomination. One possibility was nominations by states. But the most conservative wing of the Republican party, paradoxically called Radicals, strenuously disagreed. It insisted on the traditional form because it believed it had the votes to nominate the secretary of the treasury, William H. Crawford, a big, hulking, very personable man who had used his office and its patronage to build a small army of supporters in Congress and across the nation. Crawford had graciously yielded the nomination to Monroe in 1816 in the hope that he would have a clear field in 1824. But he miscalculated. Not only did Monroe fail to support him publicly, as he expected, but Crawford now faced a growing number of rivals, each of whom condemned the

1. Wirt to Francis W. Gilmer, May 9, 1822, in Kennedy, *Memoirs of Wirt*, II, 138. Wirt also remarked that Littleton W. Tazewell held the palm south of the Potomac because of sectional pride.
2. DW to Story, January 14, 1822, in *PC*, I, 302.

caucus as outdated and sought nomination as a favorite son from his respective state.[3]

During his stay in Washington Webster heard much talk about the already crowded field of possible contenders. Henry Clay had numerous friends, said Webster, and means to run. Then there was talk of John C. Calhoun, the secretary of war, whom Webster seemed to prefer; John Quincy Adams, the secretary of state; William Lowndes of South Carolina, who had been nominated for President by his state in December 1821; and even De Witt Clinton, the once and future governor of New York, who had come close to winning the presidency in 1812 in a run against James Madison.

One would presume that Webster would be attracted to the secretary of state by virtue of background, education, sectional identification, and connection with Massachusetts. But he heard many complaints about Adams from his brother. "I never did like John Q Adams," Ezekiel told him, nor did a lot of other people in New Hampshire. In their minds he was an apostate, and they actually called him that. He had deserted the Federalist party and gone over to the "Democrats." Obviously he could not be trusted. There was only one way Ezekiel would support Adams: if "a very objectionable rival whose election I should not prefer" ran against him. Still, Zeke had to admit that it would be difficult to take New England away from Adams, despite his lack of personal attractiveness. "It seems to be in some degree a matter of necessity to support him—if any man is to be taken from the land of the *Pilgrims*."[4]

A brilliant secretary of state, arguably the greatest in American history, self-absorbed, self-demanding, ever dour, and ever critical of any and all who came within visual range, Adams had not a political bone in his body, and although he desperately wanted the presidency, he would not lift a finger to obtain it. Not so the other candidates. A great deal of politicking went on in Washington over the next two years, and the stakes increased as everyone scrambled to identify the winning contender. Since it might take a little while before all the candidates came forward and allowed their names to be offered, the shrewdest politicians waited to see what might develop in the ensuing months. "I think it clear there is to be a *warm* contest for the Presidency," Webster explained to his friend Jeremiah Mason, "& my expectation is, that after sifting out sundry candidates, having less support, the final struggle will be between Crawford & Calhoun." But would the other candidates abide by a caucus decision if one were held? And what about the people? "Whether the *People*," Webster continued, "may not interfere, before the time comes, & make a President of somebody else, I know not."[5]

Despite the obvious danger of eliminating the electorate from the presidential process, the Radicals kept up a drumbeat of demands that Republican

3. James F. Hopkins, "The Election of 1824," in Schlesinger, and Israel, eds., *History of American Presidential Elections*, I, 349–381.

4. DW to Story, January 14, 1822, DW to Ezekiel Webster, January 13, 1822, Ezekiel Webster to DW, January 28, 1822, in *PC*, I, 301–302, 304.

5. DW to Mason, March 23, 1822, ibid., I, 311.

congressmen meet in caucus and choose their party's nominee. That was the traditional method, that was the method that had brought the country Presidents Jefferson, Madison, and Monroe, and it must not be abandoned in favor of an untried and potentially uncontrollable system of state nominations.

If national politics seemed to be confused, the politics of Massachusetts was not much better. The Federalist party still functioned in the Bay State but had recently suffered a serious splintering. The first election of the mayor of Boston under the new city form of government—the change elevated Boston from town to city—provoked a series of disagreements during the winter of 1821–1822. The squabbling centered on the question of building materials in Boston—that is, whether bricks and stone should be used exclusively in construction to help prevent fires, or whether wood, which was less expensive, should be permitted.[6] Ordinary citizens—the so-called middling class, composed largely of a rising class of capitalists, younger entrepreneurs, and craftsmen—banded together and named themselves the Middling Interest. They demanded the repeal of the statute in order to permit the building of wooden structures. In the election for Boston's first mayor as a city the Federalists nominated U.S. Senator Harrison Gray Otis. The Middling Interest group chose its candidate without any regard for party and decided to run Representative Josiah Quincy, a staunch Federalist whose hatred of Republicanism sometimes embarrassed his party because his actions and words in Congress had been so outrageous. Quincy would not bow to the decision of the Federalist caucus that had outvoted his supporters and selected Otis as the party's candidate. Not only did he stay in the race, but he invited Republican support.[7]

Webster was appalled. "We are in a deplorable state here," he complained to Joseph Story. "Nothing seems practicable, but to go forward, & support Mr. O—and probably be *beaten*. Mr. Q has opposed the City from the beginning! He now wraps himself up in mystery, & importance—none of his old friends can *get audience* with him. . . . There will be a *vigorous* effort made for Mr. O.—let the event be what it will."[8] The upshot of this "deplorable state" disappointed both Otis and Quincy. Neither candidate won a majority in the election, and both men withdrew in favor of another Federalist, John Phillips, who subsequently became mayor.[9]

By this time the Federalists had realized how weak their position had become. They recognized that their political days in Boston were numbered unless they found more attractive candidates to place before the electorate. Naturally they thought of Webster. A few of them, especially those close to Black Dan, even approached him about succeeding Otis as U.S. senator. But he refused. "I had resolution enough to decline," he informed Joseph Hopkinson.

6. The law also specifically denied the right to build any structure more than ten feet in height.

7. Ronald P. Formisano, *The Transformation of Political Culture: Massachusetts Parties, 1790s–1840s* (New York, 1983), pp. 182–185.

8. DW to Story, [April 6, 1822], in *PC*, I, 312.

9. Formisano, *Transformation*, p. 186.

But most probably he declined because he worried about getting a reputation for "overreaching" at this early stage of his career and residence in the Bay State. Already some people had accused him of being "as ambitious as Caesar. He will not be outdone by any man, if it is within the compass of his powers to avoid it."[10] Besides, out of a sense of duty to the party, he had agreed to run for the lower house of the Massachusetts General Court in the spring election, and his name headed the list of "regular" Federalist candidates. He won his election rather handily and took his seat in the house of representatives on May 30, representing a Boston district. But he lacked any enthusiasm for the position. "I intend," he said, "to discharge my two-year duty, if I live & enjoy health, punctually & assiduously, & then consider that I have discharged my debts."[11]

A sense of duty may have impelled him to accept this apparently onerous assignment, but he probably wanted an immediate entry into Massachusetts politics, and this was as good and as easy and quick a way as any to start the process. He served a very short time, and it would be his only service in a state office. He attended the first session from late May to early June and did nothing of note.

Then Congressman Benjamin Gorham of Boston announced he would not seek reelection, and a meeting of Federalist delegates held in Concert Hall on October 17 unanimously chose Webster to represent the district in the next Congress. They took this action without first gaining his consent because he was out of town. "We beg you to be assured," read the letter of notification from the committee, "that in the performance of this duty, we experience a peculiar satisfaction, which will be greatly enhanced by the knowledge of your consent to conform, upon this occasion, to the wishes of your friends."[12]

Much as he might wish to reenter politics at this level, Webster needed an understanding about his financial situation before he accepted the nomination. He had a very lucrative law practice that a congressional career would substantially reduce. If the elite of Boston wanted his services in Congress, it would have to pay for it. It would have to provide some tangible evidence of its willingness to help him ease the financial burden a four-, five-, or six-month stint in Washington would involve.

As a matter of fact, ever since his arrival in Boston he had personally benefited from the support of the business community. The Boston Associates had been particularly generous and on December 7, 1821, even allowed him to buy four shares, costing one thousand dollars apiece, in the Merrimack Manufacturing Company, "an association for the purpose of manufacturing and printing cotton." This was a privilege granted to few others. It was a modest number of shares, to be sure, but it demonstrated the group's confidence in him and his future and its readiness to provide for his financial needs. These Boston Associ-

10. Wirt to Judge Carr, February 1, 1824, in Kennedy, *Memoirs of Wirt,* II, 164.

11. DW to Hopkinson, November 13, 1822, in *PC,* I, 318.

12. Committee to DW, October 18, 1822, in ibid., I, 317.

ates became his financial patrons and were repeatedly invited to contribute to his campaigns with loans or outright gifts.[13]

That same confidence was now expressed a year later to win Webster's acceptance of a congressional nomination. Only now subscriptions would be raised on his behalf. And so it began. On and off for the next thirty years Nathan Appleton, Abbott Lawrence, and hundreds of others, principally in Massachusetts and New York, regularly raised subscriptions for Webster to supplement his income. It was a mutually beneficial arrangement.[14]

Two days before his nomination the Middling Interest chose Jesse Putnam to replace Gorham. To strengthen Putnam's chances for success, the Republicans decided against naming their own candidate and endorsed Putnam. But the ploy failed. Webster had acquired such an outstanding reputation in so many areas—in August 1823 Dartmouth conferred on him the degree of L.L.D. in recognition of his "literary, scientific and professional eminence"[15]—that he won a stunning victory in the November election. He polled 2,638 to Putnam's 1,557, as reported in the Boston *Advertiser* on November 5. Clearly he was the popular favorite of his district, and the triumph must surely have given him great pleasure—and perhaps thoughts of higher office to come in the near future.

But the Eighteenth Congress would not begin its first session until December 1823. That was more than a year away. In the meantime he resigned from the Massachusetts house and turned back to his huge law practice.

One case in particular that had the makings of an exceptionally important matter involved a New York statute granting a monopoly over the operation of steamboat traffic in New York waters. It grew out of the fact that Robert Fulton had invented a steam-propelled vessel, the *Clermont*, that in 1807 successfully sailed the Hudson River upstream. Fulton and his partner, Robert R. Livingston, then acquired a monopoly from the New York legislature to operate steamboat traffic in the waters surrounding the state.[16]

The right of New York to confer this monopoly was soon challenged by the would-be competitors of Fulton and Livingston. In the case *Livingston and Fulton v. Van Ingen* the state's highest court in 1812 affirmed the right of the

13. In 1813 the Boston Manufacturing Company was formed to manufacture textiles and it in turn created the Merrimack Manufacturing Company. Stockholders of the Boston company were then permitted to buy stock in the Merrimack company and collectively were known as the Boston Associates. The company started to produce cloth in 1823. Two years later it built three additional mills. The first dividend of one hundred dollars per share was declared in 1825. The company then widened and deepened the Pawtucket Canal. It also built a machine shop and provided housing for the workers of its mills. Nathan Appleton, *Introduction of the Power Loom, and Origin of Lowell,* (Lowell, Mass., 1858), pp. 20, 22, 25; Dalzell, *Enterprising Elite,* pp. 4, 48.

14. For more details on other ways such money was raised, see below chapters 35 and 41.

15. The recently elected president of Dartmouth, Bennet Tyler, to DW, August 23, 1823, in *PC*, I, 331. In 1824 both Harvard and Columbia universities conferred honorary law degrees on Webster. Chapman, *Sketches of Alumni of Dartmouth,* p. 106.

16. White, *The Marshall Court,* and Maurice G. Baxter, *The Steamboat Monopoly, Gibbons v. Ogden, 1824* (New York, 1972); Wheaton J. Lane, *From Indian Trail to Iron Horse: Travel and Transportation in New Jersey, 1620–1860* (Princeton, 1939); Beveridge, *Life of John Marshall;* and Edward S. Corwin, *The Commerce Power versus States Rights* (Princeton, 1936).

state to grant the monopoly. In one of the three opinions delivered, Chief Justice James Kent ruled that the state retained its power over commerce unless it conflicted with national authority. The case in question concerned traffic from New York City to Albany, purely intrastate in nature, and therefore involved only the state's jurisdiction. Thereafter the monopolists used this ruling to fight off other possible competitors.

That is, until Aaron Ogden, a New Jersey lawyer, began running a steamboat from New York City to New Jersey under a license acquired from Livingston and Fulton. Ogden's former partner, Thomas Gibbons, decided to challenge not only Ogden's exclusive rights to ply this traffic but also New York's authority to grant the monopoly. In 1818 Gibbons purchased a steamboat and under a federal coasting license began ferrying passengers from Manhattan to Elizabeth-Town Point, New Jersey.

Ogden sued, and Chancellor Kent promptly issued an injunction against Gibbons. Several legal actions later the case finally went up to the New York Court of Errors. Once it reached the court of errors there was no doubt that the case would eventually wind up in the Supreme Court of the United States. At this juncture Gibbons wrote to Webster and asked for his help. If the decision in the court of errors went against him, Gibbons wrote, "I shall carry it before the Supreme Court . . . where I shall wish your services associated with Mr. Wirt the Attorney General." Webster accepted the invitation and a five-hundred-dollar retainer from Cornelius Vanderbilt, one of Gibbons's associates. Later he received an additional one thousand dollars.[17]

The progress of the case through the court of errors was slow, and the impatient Gibbons, ill with diabetes, desperately wanted a favorable decision as soon as possible. "I feel a deep concern in this question," he admitted, "and I want very much to get a decision that will contravene the uncontitunality [*sic*] of the Laws of New York. The monopolists under these Laws are very vexatious to many citizens in this section of the 2 States."[18]

After the court of errors found in Ogden's favor, Webster had hoped to bring the case before the Supreme Court in its 1822 term, but the unexpected death of William Pinckney, one of Ogden's attorneys, made that impossible. Webster wrote to Gibbons, expressing his disappointment. "I most devoutly wish it were in my power to invent some mode of hastening the trial," he declared, "but I do not see that it is." It is simply "beyond human effort." He counseled Gibbons to be patient. "I see no remedy but patience." But Gibbons continued to pester him, and he faulted the Court for not acting with dispatch on such an important issue. "There is something wrong with our Judiciary," he

---

17. Wirt received an equal amount. Thomas Gibbons to DW, December 13, 1819, receipt, dated February 28, 1821, DW to William (son of Thomas) Gibbons, February 18, 1824, William Gibbons to DW, March 8, 1824, in *PLFP*, I, 259–260, 261, 288, 291. William Gibbons thought that "Webster like all the Lawyers is unreasonable in relation to Money Matters. . . . It would not be a matter of surprise to me if he had the opinion of the Judges in his possession & meant to delay it until the matter of the fees was settled. I do not like the course he has taken in this matter." William to Thomas Gibbons, February 13, 1824, ibid., 289.

18. Gibbons to DW, April 2, 1821, ibid., I, 263.

snapped, "that this important tribunal should convene but once in a year. I entreat you to press on to the trial, or death will take from me the pleasure of rejoicing with you on the event."[19]

The 1823 term of the Supreme Court also proved impossible, and shortly after that term ended, Justice Brockholst Livingston died and was replaced by Smith Thompson of New York. Thompson's New York connection gave Webster pause, particularly when word circulated that the new justice favored the monopoly. But Thompson arrived at the Court too late to participate in the case when it finally and at long last came up for adjudication in the February term of 1824. Webster learned of it on January 1, and he told Gibbons it was case number 29 and "will therefore be a very early cause. Very probably it will come on the first week of the Court."[20]

And so it did. The case was argued from February 4 to 9, and Webster led off in a two-and-a-half-hour assault against the monopoly. William Wirt also defended Gibbons's position, while Thomas J. Oakley, attorney general for New York, and Thomas A. Emmet, a distinguished lawyer and general counsel to the monopolists, represented Ogden. Wirt declared that Emmet's "whole soul is in the cause, and he will stretch all his powers. Oakley is said to be one of the first logicians of the age."[21]

Webster provided the Court with the principal argument for Gibbons. He rose from his seat, looked squarely at Chief Justice Marshall and waited. "I can see the chief justice as he looked at that moment," Webster later reminisced.[22] At eleven o'clock or thereabouts on February 4 Marshall nibbed his quill, yanked up his sleeves, looked down at Webster, and nodded. The great case began.

Webster started off by stating almost immediately his major premise: "that the power of Congress to regulate commerce,[23] was complete and entire, and to a certain extent, necessarily exclusive; that the acts [of the New York legislature in initiating this monopoly] in question were regulations of commerce, in a most important particular; and affecting it in those respects, in which it was under the exclusive authority of Congress." Then he assured the Court that he did not mean to imply that "*all* regulations" affecting commerce belonged exclusively to Congress. But in this case New York did in fact intrude into the exclusive domain of the federal government.[24]

He went on to remind the Court that its usual "mode of reasoning" in adjudicating important questions, such as this, involved determining which pow-

19. DW to Gibbons, May 9, 1821, February 21, March 2, 1822, Gibbons to DW, January 14, 1823, ibid., I, 263–265, 266, 268.

20. DW to Gibbons, January 2, 1824, ibid., I, 270. The old chestnut about Webster's being unprepared when Marshall unexpectedly called up the case ahead of time and spending the entire night prior to his appearance boning up on the case is disproved by this letter.

21. Wirt to Judge Carr, February 1, 1824, in Kennedy, *Life of Wirt*, II, 164.

22. Harvey, *Reminiscences*, p. 142.

23. Article I, Section 8 of the Constitution states that Congress shall have power "to regulate Commerce with foreign Nations, and among the several States, and with the Indian Tribes."

24. 9 Wheaton 9.

ers were conferred exclusively by the Constitution, which by prohibitions on the states, and which "from the nature of the powers themselves." From the nature of the thing, he said, the power "ought to be considered exclusive." What we are dealing with in this instance are laws by the state of New York to set up "a *monopoly.*" Now, surely, the Constitution "never intended to leave with the States the power of granting monopolies, either of trade or of navigation; and, therefore, that as to this, the commercial power was exclusive in Congress."

Webster took cognizance of the fact that the Constitution does not say that the power of Congress over commerce was exclusive. Nor does it define exactly the powers of Congress; it enumerates them, "and where the power was general . . . the extent of the grant must be judged . . . by the nature of the power."[25] By this argument Webster would give to the Supreme Court the right to decide which congressional powers "by their nature" were exclusive, something states' righters would find totally unacceptable. And southerners could be expected to explode in rage or even threaten to secede from the Union if the Court, as a remote example, determined that slavery fell under the exclusive control of Congress. Simple legislation by the Congress, then, could wipe out the South's "peculiar institution" throughout the United States.

Having made his point, Webster wisely moved into discussing the history of the problem of regulating commerce, and he went back to the period of the Articles of Confederation, when states bitterly quarreled with one another over trade barriers and other matters, disputes that led to the calling of the Constitutional Convention so that this problem, among others, might be solved. At that convention, and in the subsequent state conventions to ratify the Constitution, declared Webster, no "man speaks of a general *concurrent* power, in the regulations of foreign and domestic trade, as still residing in the States." The object of the Constitution "was to take away such power." Had it not done so, the Constitution "would not have been worth accepting."[26]

Webster very properly faced the question of concurrent power—namely, the right of both the states and the Congress to legislate in certain areas. Both exercised the power to tax. Surely states could regulate trade within their borders, and as Thomas Emmet, the lawyer for Ogden, later pointed out, they had frequently legislated on interstate matters, such as quarantine laws and trade with Indians.[27]

But Webster would have none of this. He stared at Marshall as he drove home his argument. "The people intended in establishing the constitution," he lectured, "to transfer, from the several States to a general government those high and important powers over commerce." Webster stated this as fact, as though it were incontrovertible. Typically and shrewdly he pitched his argument to emphasize those views of constitutional power and their source that Marshall

25. 9 Wheaton 10–11.

26. 9 Wheaton 13–14.

27. In *Cooley* v. *Board of Wardens* in 1852 Chief Justice Roger B. Taney declared that some areas of commerce require national uniformity and therefore a uniform rule that only Congress could provide, while others permitted some degree of state action.

dearly believed and loved. The people, said Webster, not the states, established the Constitution. They transferred power away from the states and handed it over to the national government in order that their rights would be more faithfully and properly protected.

From the very nature of the case, he went on, "these powers must be *exclusive.*"

Exclusive? That was a bold, daring, and questionable (some said reckless) but original assertion. Once the Constitution won ratification, Webster continued, the commerce of the states constituted a *"unit,"* a unit of the United States, "complete, entire, and uniform. Its character was to be described in the flag which waved over it, E PLURIBUS UNUM. Now, how could individual States assert a right of concurrent legislation, in a case of this sort, without manifest encroachment and confusion?"[28]

As a matter of fact, he explained, this "supposed *concurrent* power in the States" seemed incomprehensible to him. The states, it had been argued, have power to pass legislation regulating commerce but only until such time as Congress shall pass other laws controlling the operation of trade, at which point the state laws must yield. "What sort of *concurrent* powers were these, which could not exist together?" To his mind monopolies of trade or navigation, embargoes, navigation laws, and the "countervailing laws," as against foreign states, belong exclusively to Congress. Can states grant monopolies of trade? Can New York shut its ports to all but its own citizens? Can it refuse admission of ships from foreign countries? If so, then we are back to the dreadful days under the Articles of Confederation, when government became nothing more than a loose association of quarrelsome states. We must not return to those unhappy days. The national government should not seek to operate where states can function with more advantage to the community, and states should not encroach on ground that the public good and the Constitution reserve to the exclusive control of Congress.

"This doctrine of a *general* concurrent power in the States, is insidious and dangerous," Webster exclaimed. If it is admitted, states will legislate where Congress has not made "a *plenary* exercise of its power." But Congress has acted. It acted in February 1793 by regulating coastal trade and fisheries. Are the states then left free to do whatever Congress has left undone? What Congress has left undone, Webster protested, is as much a part of the system as the part in which it has acted.

If, for the sake of argument, the states may legislate until Congress annuls their laws by the exercise of its legitimate power, then we have set up a system of "perpetual hostility" between the national and state governments. One sovereign power acts, and another sovereign power abrogates it—"and all this under the idea of *concurrent* legislation!" What nonsense!

The people of New York, Webster quietly continued, have a right to be protected against this monopoly. That is one reason they agreed to the Constitu-

28. 9 Wheaton 13–14.

tion. Here again Webster reiterated his contention that the people agreed to the Constitution, rejecting what other public figures of the day contended—namely, that the states brought the Constitution into being. Webster not only believed this truth but liked to think that the members of the Supreme Court also believed it. In addition, he held that the people brought the Constitution into existence in order to protect commerce from the vagaries, uncertainties, and even hostility at times of state legislation.

Thus, said Webster, if the national government cannot protect its citizens in commercial regulations, then the promises held out to the people by the Constitution could not be fulfilled. But the framers clearly meant the power to regulate to be exclusive, and this was known and understood in the state ratifying conventions. It needs to be reaffirmed.[29]

Now, Gibbons legally operated his steamboat in New York waters under the first section of a federal licensing law passed in February 1793. The license was granted to Gibbons's steamboat to be employed in carrying on the coasting trade. "Words could not make this authority more express," Webster thundered. Gibbons had a right to operate from New Jersey to New York, a *"right"* that belonged to him as a citizen of the United States.[30]

Chancellor James Kent[31] in the New York Court of Errors declared[32] that this federal license merely certified American ownership, but Kent assumed that Congress "had *not yet acted,* in such a way as to confer a *right* on the appellant." But it had acted, and Gibbons had the "right to navigate freely the waters of the United States, and to carry on the coasting trade," no matter what individual state laws might restrict or forbid. And no one can doubt the constitutional validity of the government's licensing law. Federal law is supreme under the Constitution when it conflicts with state laws. Moreover, Congress need not expressly rule New York's laws invalid. The mere passage of the licensing law voided the monopoly grant.

Webster then launched into his final argument.

There was, lastly, that provision of the constitution which gives Congress power to promote the progress of science and the useful arts, by securing to authors and inventors, for a limited time, an exclusive right to their own writings and discoveries. Congress had exercised this power, and made all the provisions which it deemed useful or necessary. The States might, indeed, like munificent individuals, exercise their own bounty towards authors and inventors, at their own discretion. But to confer reward by exclusive grants, even if it were but a part of the use of the writing or invention, was not supposed to be a power properly to be exercised by the States. Much less could they, under the notion of conferring rewards in such cases, grant monopolies, the enjoyment of which should be essentially incompatible with the exercise of rights holden under the laws of the United States.[33]

29. 9 Wheaton 16–18.

30. 9 Wheaton 26, 28.

31. Webster never mentioned Kent by name.

32. *Ogden* v. *Gibbons,* 17 Johnson 488.

33. 9 Wheaton 31

Webster's argument[34] rested on a very broad basis. He started with what he regarded as "self-evident" propositions drawn from "the nature of the Union." He defined the relationship between state and federal authority under the commerce clause, and he asserted the supremacy of federal over state law.[35]

As Webster returned to his seat after this long exposition, he must have felt confident that he had scored heavily with Marshall and most of the other members of the Court. He showed this confidence in a letter to his former colleague Joseph Hopkinson. "There is *no doubt* but the decision will be *against* the New York monopoly. . . . Be assured the result is certain."[36]

Ogden's counsel, Oakley and Emmet, struck back hard by maintaining that states had indeed concurrent power over commerce. Such laws dealing with transportation, Indians, lighthouses, quarantine laws, and many other issues had been exercised in the regulation of commerce, not as exercises of the police power or the need to protect public health, as Webster had insisted. Were states expected to wait until Congress acted in each area of concern before these matters could be attended?[37]

In responding to Oakley and Emmet, William Wirt concluded the case for Gibbons on February 9 by reiterating the exclusive power argument. But he also suggested the possibility of the divisibility of the commerce power with the states as an alternative, and he probably had Webster's help in constructing this possibility in order to counteract the strong statements of Oakley and Emmet.[38] Some subjects, like commerce, he admitted, by their very nature, were so complex and indefinite as to consist of many branches. One or more branches might be given exclusively to Congress—for example, those that occupied "higher branches" (whatever that meant)—while others could be "left open to the States." His "learned associate," he added, had not meant to suggest that *all* branches of commerce were exclusive. However, the branch dealing with navigation, "which prescribes the vehicles in which commerce shall be carried on," is most definitely exclusive.[39]

Marshall handed down the Court's unanimous decision a little more than three weeks later, on March 2.[40] The decision has always been regarded as a classic statement of American nationalism. Its implications were and are so wide-reaching as to stretch the power of the national government beyond anything ever imagined by the Founders. With the nation advancing toward an age of industrialization it opened up new areas in which the Congress might act to

34. For a critical analysis of Webster's argument see Howard Mann, "The Marshall Court: Nationalization of Private Rights and Personal Liberty from the Authority of the Commerce Clause," *Indiana Law Journal*, XXXVIII (1963), 193–214.

35. *PLFP*, III, 289–290.

36. DW to Hopkinson, February 14, [1824], ibid., I, 288.

37. 9 Wheaton 33–159.

38. Baxter, *Webster and the Supreme Court*, pp. 201–202. The Court later accepted this alternative in 1852.

39. 9 Wheaton 165, 180–181.

40. The decision can be found in 9 Wheaton 187–221.

regulate the national economy. With transportation involving turnpikes, bridges, canals, and, within a few years, railroads, with manufacturers establishing new routes with these vehicles to distribute their products, and with a market revolution changing the way the nation conducted its financial business, the decision would give the federal government enormous latitude in assisting or hindering these operations. It can even constitute the authority for civil rights and personal liberty legislation.[41]

Marshall plucked his text directly from Webster's brief. He offered a loose interpretation of the Constitution and warned of the dangers inherent in a narrow reading of the enumerated powers of Congress. He spent considerable time examining the meaning of commerce and ended up defining it very broadly. But he would not go as far as to say that commerce, as understood in the Constitution, was the exclusive domain of Congress. No doubt he worried about the public reaction it would bring, particularly in the South, and he could not disregard the recent virulent attacks upon the judiciary. So he ducked away from it. He allowed the states the power to regulate interstate commerce and to pass laws dealing with the health, safety, and welfare of its citizens, provided they did not conflict with congressional law. But he would not say whether the states could act in areas reserved to the central government in the absence of congressional legislation. Still, the strong implication is that he accepted Webster's belief that congressional power over many areas was exclusive whether Congress had acted or not.[42]

As for the case at hand, Marshall ruled that Gibbons had a right under the Coasting Act of 1793 to transport passengers aboard his steamboat from New York to New Jersey, a clear example of interstate commerce. Consequently the laws of New York establishing monopoly rights for Fulton and Livingston conflicted with an act of Congress and were therefore unconstitutional, null and void. Thus Marshall used the coasting act, not the commerce clause that he had just defined so broadly, to strike down the monopoly. He ruled on the narrowest basis possible and so delayed a more comprehensive judgment about when and under what circumstances a state may act and share authority in regulating commerce.

For the remainder of the decision Marshall seemed to be stewing in the juice of the coasting act and probably misconstrued its meaning as he had other federal laws in cases brought before him, such as *Marbury* v. *Madison*. Not that Gibbons cared. He got the decision he had long dreamed of obtaining.

Justice Johnson handed down a concurring opinion, but unlike Marshall, he held the New York laws invalid because of Congress's exclusive power over commerce. Coasting Act or no, the New York laws violated the Constitution and were therefore invalid.[43]

As he grew older, Webster liked to believe that the *Steamboat* decision

41. Baxter, *Steamboat Monopoly,* passim.
42. Baxter, *Webster and the Supreme Court,* pp. 204–205.
43. 9 Wheaton 232–232.

came directly from his argument. And he delighted in his victory. "The argument is a pretty good one," he boasted, "and was on a new question. It has been often observed that the opinion of the court, delivered by Chief Justice Marshall, follows closely the track of the argument. He adopts the idea, which I remember struck him at the time, that, by the Constitution, the commerce of the several States has become a unit."[44] He was even more expansive in reminiscing with Peter Harvey. "The two arguments that have given me the most satisfaction were the argument in the 'steamboat case,' and the Dartmouth College argument." And oh, he said, "I think I never experienced more intellectual pleasure than in arguing that naval question to a great man who could appreciate it, and take it in; and he did take it in, as a baby takes in its mother's milk."[45]

Which is nonsense. Had Marshall taken in his argument like a baby taking mother's milk, as Webster claimed, he would have ruled that the commerce clause gave Congress exclusive jurisdiction. And he did no such thing. He annihilated the monopoly with a coasting license, nothing more. Still, the best part of the decision, the long opening section about the comprehensive powers of the central government and the necessity of reading the Constitution in the broad context of national needs and concerns, came directly from Webster's argument. And it was this section that captured immediate attention. The coastal statute was soon forgotten. All that anyone knew was that Gibbons had authority to operate his steamboat, New York's monopoly laws had been struck down, and Marshall had trumpeted the authority of the national government. This is what the people remembered. Small wonder, then, that twenty years later Webster boasted about his contribution to an important early decision by the Supreme Court.

Indeed it is rather remarkable that of the eight most celebrated constitutional cases decided by the Marshall Court from 1801 to 1824—to wit, *Marbury v. Madison, Fletcher v. Peck, Martin v. Hunter's Lessee, Trustees of Dartmouth College v. Woodward, Sturges v. Crowninshield, McCulloch v. Maryland, Cohens v. Virginia,* and *Gibbons v. Ogden*[46]—Webster played an important role in five of them. With the Supreme Court handing down decisions based largely on Webster's arguments a great many people deferred without question to his understanding and interpretation of the basic law of the land. The real meaning of the Constitution could be learned from reading his briefs.

Not much later Black Dan, the "godlike," was hailed, celebrated, and universally recognized as the "Great Expounder and Defender of the Constitution."[47] By this time it almost seemed as though the Constitution meant whatever Daniel Webster said it meant.

---

44. DW to Edward Everett, October 30, 1851, in *W&S*, XVIII, 482.

45. Harvey, *Reminiscences*, pp. 140, 142.

46. The *Marbury* case established judicial review, the *Fletcher* case held a state law unconstitutional for the first time, and the *Martin* case upheld the right of the Supreme Court to overrule decisions of state courts.

47. Ben: Perley, Poore, *Perley's Reminiscences of Sixty Years in the National Metropolis* (Philadelphia, 1886), I, 146.

12

"The Demosthenes of America"

THE FIRST session of the Eighteenth Congress began on December 1, 1823, and Webster arrived in Washington, to the surprise of those who knew his previous record, on November 26, bringing with him his wife and children. They had had a "pleasant and agreeable" journey to the capital of nearly two weeks. They had stopped off for several days in New York to visit friends and paused again in Princeton and Philadelphia before continuing on their way south.[1]

The family quickly settled in Washington, and Webster thought that his wife liked the city "tolerably well." At first their evenings were sometimes "not a little lonesome." Parties for the first month or so were "not yet numerous," he confessed. In fact they attended only two, one at the home of General Jacob Jennings Brown and one at the home of the secretary of state, John Quincy Adams. The drawing room at the White House would be opened on New Year's Day, and that, he believed, would surely provide additional opportunity for social intercourse.[2]

As it turned out, Grace and Daniel spent "a very splendid New Year" at the White House, although Grace was offended that "nothing is said of the ladies" in the account that appeared the following day in the Washington *National Intelligencer.* "That, certainly, was a capital omission," Webster commented with a smirk.[3]

Although he had been absent from Congress for nearly seven years, he had returned for court appearances so often that it seemed to many that he had never been away. Because his eloquence and legal acumen had been on frequent display during the past six years, he enjoyed a respectable following of admirers. But performance before the Supreme Court was not the same as one before the members of Congress. It would be a challenge to repeat in the House of Representatives the technical mastery and skill that he regularly demonstrated in court.

But he had no fear. Rather, he wanted and needed to remind his colleagues

---

1. DW to Jeremiah Mason, November 20, 30, DW to Ezekiel Webster, November 20, 1823, in *PC,* I, 333–335.

2. DW to Mrs. George Blake, December 20, 1823, ibid., I, 341.

3. DW to Mrs. Langdon Elwyn, January 2, 1824, in *W&S,* XVII, 337.

in the House that he was no novice just starting out. He craved a quick reestablishment of his credentials as a leader and spokesman of his party—or what was left of the Federalist party. He desired a surefire reminder to the House members that Daniel Webster had once been a force to be reckoned with and was now back to reassert that prominence. He had to return with a splash, with a speech on a great issue that would reclaim his former position as a major figure in American politics.

And there was an issue waiting for him on his return, waiting just for him. Long before he left Boston for Washington, he knew what the subject of his "maiden" speech as a Massachusetts congressman before the Eighteenth Congress would be, and he had already started to prepare for it. Unquestionably it accounts for his early arrival in the capital. He needed extra time to settle himself and his family in Washington and complete the research and writing for this inaugural speech.

He chose Greek independence as his topic. It was an issue that would capture the attention of the American people and most likely the nations of Western Europe.

For centuries Greece had been a subjugated nation of the Ottoman Empire, but in 1821 it flared into open revolt against the Turks and looked to the West for support and assistance. Recognizing Americans' identification with the freedom-seeking Greek people, because of both their own past struggle for freedom and their indebtedness to the heritage of ancient Greece, Webster realized he could direct that romantic national sentiment to his own advantage by giving a speech that could not only win popular attention and acclaim but restore his standing among his colleagues in Congress.

Because Edward Everett, a professor of Greek literature at Harvard and recently returned from a visit to Greece, had published several articles about his experiences in the *North American Review,* Webster wrote to him and invited his help on the preparation of his intended speech. He said he felt "a great inclination to say or do something" on behalf of the Greeks "if I know what to say or to do. If you can readily direct me to any sources, from which I can obtain information that is already public, respecting their affairs, I would be obliged to you so to do."[4]

Everett immediately and enthusiastically responded. He promised to send another article he had in preparation as soon as he finished it,[5] whereupon Webster offered one of his law students in his office in Boston to help copy the article if that could speed things along. Thus began what proved to be a very lasting and profitable friendship between the two men. Everett, a tall, impressive-looking intellectual who had trained for the ministry but abandoned it for an academic career at Harvard, provided Webster with lifelong loyalty and

---

4. DW to Everett, November 16, [1823], in *PC,* I, 332–333.

5. "Life of Ali Pacha," published in the January 1824 issue of the *North American Review,* IX, 106–140.

devotion. The two men were alike in that their reasoning was always "logical and luminous" and their words gave evidence of "careful study." A man of self-discipline and dignity, a superb orator second only to Webster himself, Everett was later "seduced" by Black Dan into the political world, but he never got very far because he unfortunately gave people the impression that he was an "intellectual icicle."[6]

Webster counseled with a great many people about the subject of his proposed speech and in the process learned that President Monroe intended in his initial address to Congress to include "strong expressions of sympathy for the Greeks." However, because this message would also take "pretty high ground as to *this Continent*"—that is, it contained a warning to European nations against future involvement in the Western Hemisphere—Monroe "is afraid of the appearance of interfering in the concerns of the *other continent* also." So for the next several weeks Webster diligently sought to master the details of the Greek Revolution while he prepared his speech. He worried a little that "some other Gentleman may anticipate me, in this business," but he worried more about his command of the subject. "My real difficulty is *ignorance*," he confessed to Everett.[7]

An "uncommonly large" number of House members also arrived early in Washington and provided a quorum on the first day of the session. Anticipation of exciting political events prompted their early return. The town was swarming with presidential candidates and their friends looking for support, and everyone conjectured and commented on whether the Republican party would hold a caucus to choose its candidate and thereby wipe away (supposedly) all need for an election the following year. Since the Federalist party no longer functioned as a contending national party, the field was wide open to any candidate the Republicans (or Democrats, as Webster preferred to call them) could agree upon. The friends of Crawford, as expected, demanded the traditional congressional caucus as the nominating instrument, but the friends of the other candidates insisted that "King Caucus is dead" and deserved immediate burial.

Webster agreed. "One thing I hold to be *material*," he told his brother, Ezekiel, "—get *on without a Caucus*. It will only require a little more pains. It is time to put an end to *Caucuses*. They make great men little, & little men great."[8] Still, as long as the senator from New York Martin Van Buren had anything to say about it—and he had a great deal to say as an important leader of the Crawford faction—a caucus would be summoned in due course, and all responsible and loyal Republicans were expected to attend. But rumors circulated that Crawford was seriously ill and might not survive. Indeed he had suffered a

6. Paul A. Varg, *Edward Everett: The Intellectual in the Turmoil of Politics* (London and Toronto, 1992), pp. 16–18; Poore, *Perley's Reminiscences*, pp. 80–81; Ronald F. Reid, *Edward Everett, Unionist Orator* (Westport, Conn., 1990), pp. 24–25. Everett first met Webster when he attended the private school in Boston where Ezekiel Webster taught.

7. DW to Everett, November 28, [1823], December 6, 1823, in *PC*, I, 335–336, 339.

8. DW to Ezekiel Webster, December 4, [1823], ibid., I, 337.

devastating stroke that left him partially paralyzed, speechless, and almost sightless. This information was withheld from the public for months while the Radicals forged ahead with their plans to convene a caucus.

Not only had Crawford's rumored illness changed the political scene, but the number and identity of the presidential candidates had also changed. Now, in addition to Adams, Clay, Crawford, and Calhoun, General Andrew Jackson, the "Hero of the Battle of New Orleans," had been nominated by the legislature of his home state of Tennessee, which had elected him to the Senate in order to improve his presidential prospects. Extremely slender, weighing 145 pounds at most, and slightly round-shouldered, Jackson stood six feet tall and had strong cheekbones, a lantern jaw, cold, steely blue eyes, and a long, straight nose. He, his friends, and his supporters denounced the caucus as a violation of the right of the American people, not a Republican caucus, to select their own President. But Webster expressed it best when he said that caucuses only diminish great men. *"The true source of power is the People,"* he lectured his brother. "The Democrats are not Democratic enough. They are real aristocrats. Their leaders wish to govern by a combination among themselves, & they think they have a fee simple in the people's suffrages. Go to the *People,* & convince them that their pretended friends, are a knot of self-interested jobbers, who make a trade of patriotism, & live on popular credulity."[9]

Like many others, Webster recognized that the presidential election could very well end up in the House because of the number of nominated candidates. Winning an electoral majority, as required by the Constitution, could be all but impossible. If that occurred, then the House of Representatives would choose the President from among the three men with the highest votes in the electoral college. Webster was certain it would occur that way. "I remain of the opinion *the choice must come to the House.*"[10]

If that happened, the final choice would be made in the chamber built since the destruction of the Capitol by the British during the War of 1812. The building still needed a good deal of work before its total completion, but enough had been done by December 1819 to permit the House and Senate to occupy their respective chambers.

The new Capitol building stood on a twenty-two-acre plot on a hill and ran a length of 352 feet. Senators assembled on the second floor of the north wing of the structure, and House members in the south wing. The House chamber formed a semicircle and stretched 96 feet across at its widest and 60 feet at the highest part of the domical ceiling. It resembled a Greek theater and boasted twenty-six enormous columns topped by Corinthian capitals to support the dome. Henry Clay, having been elected Speaker once again, sat in a chair under an imposing statue of "Liberty" supported by an American eagle and Roman fasces. Down below, on the first floor of the structure, the Supreme Court

9. Ibid.; Remini, *Jackson,* II, 9, 51–54, 63; Hopkins, "The Election of 1824," I, 349–369.
10. DW to Ezekiel Webster, December 4, [1823], in *PC,* I, 338.

once more heard arguments and rendered decisions. This location made it very convenient for Webster to hop down whenever he needed to attend the proceedings of the *Steamboat* case during the fall term of 1824.

As Webster entered the glittering House chamber, he recognized only a few faces that had served with him in the past, but he knew several from his many visits to the capital, and he soon met other members who would play an important role in the nation's future. Samuel A. Foote of Connecticut, Louis McLane of Delaware, John Forsyth of Georgia, Edward Livingston of Louisiana, Henry R. Warfield of Maryland, the "Patroon" Stephen Van Rensselaer of New York, Willie P. Mangum of North Carolina, James Buchanan of Pennsylvania, James Hamilton, Jr., and George McDuffie of South Carolina, Sam Houston of Tennessee, and John Randolph of Virginia were a few of the more prominent names that significantly influenced history, but of this group, only Forsyth and Randolph had served with Webster earlier.

Speaker Clay assigned the chairmanship of the Judiciary Committee to Webster in recognition of his unchallenged distinction in the law.[11] And Webster took the assignment very seriously in an effort to reform the judicial system and bring it fully into the nineteenth century. The addition of new states admitted since the war—Indiana, Mississippi, Illinois, Alabama, Maine, and Missouri—placed great burdens on the circuit courts of appeal and obliged the Supreme Court justices to travel great distances to cover their respective circuits. The number of sessions of the Supreme Court itself also seemed inadequate to the needs of the country. As an earlier member of the House Webster had sponsored a bill drafted by Justice Story to reform the system by expanding the jurisdiction of federal courts as well as reorganizing the circuits, but it ultimately failed to win passage. Some of his old Federalist friends wanted to relieve the justices of the Supreme Court from circuit duty, others wished to increase the size of the court, and not a few states' rights champions desired not only to deprive the Court of its appellate jurisdiction over cases decided in state courts but also to require more than a majority to invalidate state statutes.

Webster asked Story for his opinion on the disadvantages of increasing the membership of the Court to nine. Some of the disadvantages he thought obvious, such as "the difficulty of commanding the attention of nine men to a cause, particularly as in cases of equity and admiralty, where evidence is to be examined." Yet he found himself singularly unable to make as strong a case against nine members as he had when the idea was first suggested to him.[12]

Finally, after many hours of discussion, Webster and his committee took a very middle-of-the-road position that pleased virtually no one. In February 1824 he presented to the House the committee's recommendation that four justices be added only for western circuit duty. These four would not sit on the Supreme Court. The committee also suggested lengthening the terms of the Supreme

11. And apparently at the urging of William Plumer, Jr., of New Hampshire, who had been the previous chairman. Plumer, "Reminiscences of Webster," in *W&S*, XVII, 547.

12. DW to Story, January 4, 1824, ibid., 339.

Court to help relieve its congested docket. The House hardly noticed the bill except for a few desultory efforts by states' righters to amend it by weakening the authority of the Court that Webster easily squelched. The House then turned to other more pressing matters and never even voted on the bill during this session.[13]

It was a wretched bill and deserved the fate it received. With an expanding nation the Supreme Court needed to be cut free from the circuit. But Webster hated to lose the justices to the important business conducted on the circuits. He especially hated to see Story eliminated from the First Circuit. In addition, a larger Court seemed mandatory, but opponents feared that if the Court grew with each new batch of states, it would become in time unmanageable.

This proved again that Webster was no legislator. Here was a question close to his interests and needs, yet he lacked the legislative skill to bring about a workable solution. As John Wentworth noted, Black Dan could give a fine speech on a particular subject, but not much else in the way of leadership to win passage of important legislation.[14]

Despite this failure, most observers acknowledged his preeminence in judicial matters, and they also noted that Webster and Story had formed a close and rewarding friendship. The two men served each other's needs, but it was difficult for outside observers to figure which one was the mentor or if they were equals. "I fear Judge Story is but the wretched tool of Mr. Webster," complained a former Federalist, Louis McLane, to Martin Van Buren. But Theodore Parker probably had a more accurate appraisal: "Mr. Webster was in the habit of drawing from that deep and copious well of legal knowledge, whenever his own bucket was dry. Mr. Justice Story was the Jupiter Pluvius from whom Mr. Webster often sought to elicit peculiar thunder for his speeches, and private rain for his own public tanks of law."[15]

Although Webster attended to his multiple duties as a new member of the Massachusetts House delegation and chairman of the Judiciary Committee, his thoughts were focused almost entirely on his upcoming speech on Greek independence. He planned his moves very carefully—right from the moment he decided to make the issue his first important speech of the session.

On Monday, December 8—a week after the House had convened and six days since the announcement by the President of the soon-to-be-celebrated Monroe Doctrine[16]—Webster rose on the floor and, after presenting a petition

13. *Annals of Congress,* 18th Congress, 1st Session, pp. 915–916, 2514–2541, 2619. At the next session the House was too busy electing a new President to be bothered with reforming the judiciary, and Webster did not even call up his bill for a vote. Baxter, *Webster and the Supreme Court,* pp. 229–232.

14. Wentworth, "Congressional Reminiscences," pp. 36–37.

15. Quoted in R. Kent Newmyer, "A Note on the Whig Politics of Justice Joseph Story," *Mississippi Valley Historical Review,* XLVIII (1961), p. 487.

16. "I look on the [Monroe Doctrine]," said Webster on the floor of the House, "as forming a bright page in our history. . . . It does honor to the sagacity of the government. . . . It elevated the hopes, and gratified the patriotism of the people." March, *Webster,* pp. 73–74.

from Massachusetts woolen manufacturers to increase the duty on foreign woolen goods by 12½ percent, introduced the following resolution: "*Resolved, that provisions ought to be made, by law, for defraying the expense incident to the appointment of an Agent or Commissioner to Greece, whenever the President shall deem it expedient to make such appointment.*"[17]

It was a modest enough proposal, and in offering it, he assured the House that he did not wish "in any manner" to commit the members in this or any of the "political contests" of Europe. But if the President's statement in his message was true, that the domination of Turkey over Greece had terminated, then Congress ought to act on the subject, at least with some expression relating to the sufferings and sacrifices of a "heroic people," sacrifices and suffering that ought to "excite the sympathy of every liberal minded man in Europe as well as in this country." He did not expect the resolution to be acted upon immediately but simply that it should lie on the table for the "deliberate reflection" of the members. Later he would deliver a full-fledged speech in support of his resolution.[18]

Not everyone in Congress appreciated Webster's resolution. The irascible John Randolph of Roanoke termed the idea of interference regarding Greece and Latin America as nothing more than "Quixotism." Other congressmen worried about the loss of trade with Turkey if the resolution passed. Secretary of State John Quincy Adams, the principal author of the Monroe Doctrine, also took exception to the resolution because of the nation's traditional policy of nonintervention in European affairs. Upon being pressed, Adams later told Webster that he opposed the measure and did not wish to see it acted upon by Congress. Webster in response said that he had spoken to Secretary of the Navy Samuel L. Southard and Secretary of War John C. Calhoun, both of whom encouraged him to offer the resolution. And President Monroe himself said he had no objection to it.[19]

For the next several weeks Webster worked diligently on his Greek liberation speech and on January 19, 1824, delivered it before a crowded, expectant, and excited audience of congressmen and distinguished visitors and townspeople.[20]

He began by noting the many benefits humankind had acquired from ancient Greece. "This free form of government, this popular assembly, the common council held for the common good—where have we contemplated its earliest models?" Even the columns, the architecture, the ornamentation of this Capitol building in which Congress has assembled "all remind us that Greece has existed, and that we, like the rest of mankind, are greatly her debtors."

17. *Annals of Congress,* 18th Congress, 1st Session, pp. 805–806.

18. Ibid., p. 806.

19. Adams, *Memoirs,* VI, 240.

20. In preparing for this speech, Webster wrote more than thirty pages of notes, which are in the New Hampshire Historical Society. He claimed to have studied the proceedings of all the European congresses from that of Paris in 1814 to that of Laibach in 1821. See *Microfilm Edition,* F4/3871.

But he came to speak of modern Greece, not of the ancient world, and no one can deny, he continued, that the great political question of today is that between "absolute and regulated governments," between government without control and a constitutional system that "restrains sovereign discretion" and asserts that society has the right to voice its wishes in the enactment of laws that are to regulate society.

Unfortunately a new era had arisen in the world in which doctrines are promulgated wholly subversive of the "general liberties of mankind," in particular, the formation in Paris in 1815 of the Holy Alliance among Russia, Prussia, and Austria. The members of this alliance promise to observe the rules of "justice and Christianity" in their dealings with other nations. But it is based on two overriding principles. The first is "that all popular or constitutional rights are held . . . as grants from the crown." Society has no rights of its own; its only duty can be expressed in a single word, *"submission."* The second principle is the right of the Holy Alliance to interfere forcibly in the affairs of other states, a right to control nations that dare desire a change of their own government. These allied powers profess that revolutions by oppressed peoples must be suppressed; colonies that establish independence must be returned to their "legitimate" sovereigns.

"Is it not proper for us, at all times," Webster asked, "is it not our duty, at this time, to come forth, and deny, and condemn, these monstrous principles? Where, but here . . . are they likely to be resisted?" Our system of government, as everyone knows, was founded on "principles utterly hostile to the new code." It is therefore right and appropriate that we voice our concern for the "preservation of those salutary principles."

Then he confronted the dilemma and asked the questions that were to face future generations many times over. "What can *we* do? Are we to go to war? Are we to interfere in the Greek cause, or any other European cause? Are we to endanger our pacific relations? Certainly not." Fortunately there is something called "moral cause." Public opinion of the civilized world is rapidly gaining an ascendancy over "mere brutal force," he said. "It is already able to oppose the most formidable obstruction to the progress of injustice and oppression; and as it grows more intelligent and more intense, it will be more and more formidable."

The Greeks, in their efforts to win their independence, have suffered daily misery on account of the despotism, anarchy, slavery, and religious persecution imposed by the Turks. "In the whole world, Sir, there is no such oppression felt as by the Christian Greeks." Their case is unique. Nothing exists or has existed quite like it. The Greek Revolution has been "discouraged, discountenanced, and denounced" solely because it *"is a revolution."*

It may now be asked, perhaps, whether the expression of our own sympathy, and that of the country, may do them good? I hope it may. It may give them courage and spirit. It may assure them of public regard, teach them that they are not wholly forgotten by the civilized world, and inspire them with constancy in the pursuit of their great end.

At any rate, Sir, it appears to me that the measure which I have proposed is due to our own character, and called for by our own duty. When we shall have discharged that duty, we may leave the rest to the disposition of Providence.

The Greeks, he concluded, address the civilized world with a pathos not to be denied. They stretch out their arms to the Christian communities of the world, "beseeching them, by a generous recollection of their ancestors, by the consideration of their desolated and ruined cities and villages, by their wives and children sold into an accursed slavery, by their blood, which they seem willing to pour out like water, by the common faith, and in the name, which unites all Christians, that they would extend to them at least some token of compassionate regard."[21]

The chamber rang with shouts and applause as he concluded. It was a deeply moving speech, beautifully structured, logically compelling, and incomparably delivered.

Webster had one strong ally in the House, despite the many reservations cited by several other congressmen. The Speaker himself joined in support of the resolution. The resolution, Clay declared, "asks us to speak a cheering word to the Greeks. Gentlemen had only to say yes or no." But he slowly worked himself into a passion and finally resorted to sarcasm to chastise a newly elected representative from New Hampshire, Ichabod Bartlett, who expressed reservations over the resolution. The young man, who had once argued the *Dartmouth College* case for Woodward, warned that the United States could hardly interfere in European affairs if it denied Europe's right to interfere in the affairs of the Western Hemisphere. In passing, he said that Webster seemed to be "running tilts with windmills," like Don Quixote.

Clay, who delighted in making sport of hapless politicians, decided to teach Bartlett a lesson, perhaps in an effort to enlist Webster's aid in his bid for the presidency. He not only rebuked the young man but dared the other representatives to vote against the resolution. "Go home, if you dare; go home, if you can to your constituents," he bellowed, "and tell them that you voted it down—meet, if you *dare*, the appalling countenances of those who sent you here . . . and tell them . . . that the spectres of cimetars and crowns, and crescents . . . alarmed you, and that you suppressed all the noble feelings prompted by religion, by liberty, by national independence, and by humanity."[22]

Bartlett jumped to his feet to "repel the charge of personality . . . cast by the honorable Speaker" as "unjust, ungenerous, untrue." At least, he snapped, Webster's speech had been "an intellectual treat," but Clay's insinuations were gratuitous and offensive. However young and inexperienced he might be, Bartlett said, "when I feel the need for lessons on the subject of political integrity, I feel myself of age to select my own instructor."

It was a particularly nasty exchange, and a few observers speculated on

21. *Annals of Congress,* 18th Congress, 1st Session, 1104–1111.

22. Ibid., pp. 1113–1114.

whether or not the quarrel might go further and lead to something violent. Fortunately that did not happen.[23]

Toward the end of the debate Webster himself took notice of Bartlett's allusion to Don Quixote and tilting at windmills. "Sir, if I should happen in my course to meet with a *wind-mill*, why, sir, I must take a tilt with it, whether it be large or small, unless, indeed, I should conclude to have a little patience, and to wait a while, till the motion and the noise shall die of themselves, for a slight puff is generally soon over."[24]

It was a delightful put-down. Not with a bludgeon, like Clay's, but with a sharp stiletto. It was "the happiest specimen of sarcastic wit I ever witnessed in the House," commented another representative. The applause that rocked the chamber amounted "to positive uproar and disorder."[25]

The debate terminated on January 26, and the House chose not to take any action. Clay's interference did not help, but Webster himself inclined to the belief that Adams's opposition "was the most formidable obstacle." The resolution ought to have been adopted and could have been, he claimed, "but for several reasons, which the Public will never know."[26] Still, his speech had an impact, captured national attention,[27] as he had planned, and was generally hailed as a triumph. "I am quite satisfied with that," he declared.[28]

The Washington *National Intelligencer* brought out its own version of his speech the next day, but not until the end of January did Webster finish revising it for publication. It received very favorable attention. "The universal praise [for it] is no louder than is deserved," Jeremiah Mason told him. "In my opinion, your first speech [since returning to Congress] is the best sample of Parliamentary eloquence & statesmanlike reasoning, that our Country can show."[29]

Indeed. Other congressmen, notably Henry Clay, might provide greater verbal fireworks in debate, and John C. Calhoun, after his return to Congress, might exhibit a more "abstract" and "metaphysical" cast to his speeches, but none could compare with Webster in "Parliamentary eloquence & statesmanlike reasoning."

Reasoning! One House colleague reminisced:

Compared to Clay, Webster has greater power of reasoning, and less native eloquence than the great Western orator. Webster acts directly on the understanding; Clay

23. Ibid., pp. 1104, 1170–1178, 1201–1202. For a more complete discussion of this exchange, see Remini, *Clay*, pp. 222–225.

24. *W&S*, XIV, 84.

25. Plumer, "Reminiscences of Webster," in *W&S*, XVII, 551.

26. DW to Mason, February 15, 1824, in *PC*, I, 354.

27. "Your views of the character, object, and extent of the Holy Alliance have particularly attracted public attention for their strength and novelty in many particulars." Joseph Hopkinson to DW, February 1, 1824, in *W&S*, XVII, 343. Writing from Boston, Henry A. S. Dearborn said it "has been received with general approbation & applause." Dearborn to DW, May 4, 1824, in Van Tyne, ed., *Letters of Webster*, p. 104.

28. DW to Mason, February 15, 1824, in *PC*, I, 354.

29. Mason to DW, February 1, 1824, ibid., 351.

on the understanding through the passions. In acquired knowledge, in taste, in professional attainments and political science, Webster has the advantage; but in popular address, in the skillful adaptation of means to ends, in the contagious enthusiasm which leaves no time for hesitation or doubt, in promptness, in confidence of power or success Clay possesses advantages over every person I ever saw, in the management of a popular assembly. Webster is generally grave, earnest, and argumentative.[30]

Charles March, a New York merchant, formerly of New Hampshire, declared that Clay's style lacked "dignity, elevation, gravity," that his speeches were too colloquial, too "disfigured by provincialisms." No scholar and with little acquaintance with the classics, Clay had no knowledge of "how grandly to express a grand idea." But he knew how to express passionate appeals passionately. He was pure theater. "As a popular speaker, he has had hardly an equal, certainly, no superior."[31]

Webster himself agreed pretty much with these evaluations. He had appeared in court on numerous occasions with Clay and admitted that "often, before beginning my argument, I have had to labor hard to do away with the effect and impression of his. Some of the most laborious acts of my professional life have consisted in getting matters back to the starting point, after Clay had spoken. The fact is, he was no lawyer. He was a statesman, a politician, an orator, but no reasoner."[32]

Calhoun, on the other hand, used axioms instead of imagery. Brevity of expression, severe simplicity of manner, yet graced with a power of thought few contemporaries could match: these best described his style. And his words were so well chosen and so appropriate that his speeches did not require any other ornamentation.[33]

Webster, unlike his two colleagues, also fired the enthusiasm of the international community, especially in this speech on Greek independence.[34] Copies of it became available throughout the entire English-speaking world, and it was translated into Spanish and Portuguese and circulated through South America. In London Henry A. S. Dearborn asserted that it was reprinted in Greek and "distributed all over Greece. I am happy," Dearborn informed Webster, "that the Demosthenes of America has taken the lead in encouraging and animating the countrymen of his great prototype."

Webster himself later admitted that his Greek speech had special meaning for him. "I think I am more fond of this child than of any of the family," he declared.[35]

Another, and more immediate, issue in the Eighteenth Congress provoked

30. Plumer, "Reminiscences of Webster," in *W&S*, XVII, 551.

31. March, *Webster*, p. 272.

32. Harvey, *Reminiscences*, pp. 217–218.

33. March, *Webster*, p. 272.

34. Webster had encouraged Edward Everett to send a copy of his speech "to any friend on the other side of the Atlantic." DW to Everett, February 13, [1824], in *PC*, I, 352.

35. Dearborn to DW, May 4, 1824, in Van Tyne, ed., *Letters of Webster*, p. 104; Curtis, *Webster*, I, 205.

Webster into delivering a second major speech. The tariff question not only set off a series of heated disputes among congressmen whenever raised but ultimately forced Webster into a reversal of his earlier position on the issue.

Technically the first protective tariff, passed in 1816, established duties on such important articles as woolen and cotton goods and iron products. As one committed to free trade, Webster opposed the bill, except for certain items[36] required by the merchants of his constituency. Nevertheless it won passage with the support of the West and the manufacturing interests of the Northeast. The South and the shipping interests of the Northeast, such as those Webster represented, vehemently opposed it. But the rates imposed by this tariff proved insufficient, and agitation for increased protection gained strength, particularly after the Panic of 1819. With the market revolution taking hold and more and more capital finding its way into manufacturing, important voices were heard in defense of the protective system. Mathew Carey, head of the Pennsylvania Society for the Encouragement of Manufactures, wrote an important book entitled *Essays on Political Economy,* and Hezekiah Niles, editor of the Baltimore paper *Niles' Weekly Register,* began a campaign to raise the rates on imported goods. But the man most responsible for advocating and advancing a higher tariff through congressional legislation was Henry Clay.

Clay had a vision of this nation's future greatness, and he believed that Congress had a duty to assist in its achievement. Because of the industrial revolution, the transportation revolution, and other momentous economic changes rapidly developing since the end of the 1812 War and speeding the country toward industrialization, the government had an obligation to aid this phenomenon wherever possible. Clay believed that a national program of public works to improve internal transportation, a sound banking system to provide stable credit and currency, and protective tariff duties to encourage domestic manufacturers and prevent the dumping of European goods on the American market would transform his vision into reality. He called this vision an American System, a system that would create a powerful industrial nation and make all its people living in every section of the land prosperous.[37]

So as Speaker Clay stacked the Committee on Manufactures with protectionists who reported a bill to the House in 1824 to increase the ad valorem rates on many articles, both raw materials and manufactured products. Most particularly, the bill substantially raised the general level of protection. The South denounced it as a device by which the government became a partner in enriching northern manufacturers at the expense of southern farmers. Why? Because southern farmers sold their cotton on an open market at a price determined by the laws of supply and demand but were forced to buy on a closed market where prices on manufactured goods were determined by tariff laws that

---

36. Such items as sailcloth, iron, and hemp.

37. For an extended discussion of Clay's American System, see Remini, *Clay,* pp. 210–233, and Maurice Baxter, *Henry Clay and the American System* (Lexington, Ky., 1995), passim.

virtually extinguished foreign competition. Accordingly many of them regarded protection as unconstitutional.

Clay spoke in favor of the tariff bill on March 30, 1824, beginning at 11:00 A.M. He continued until 3:30 P.M. and completed the speech the following day. In it he deliberately and astutely moved the debate from the question of individual duties to the importance of protection as a policy to bind the country together by comprehending all the great diversity of economic interests within the nation: agricultural, commercial, navigational, and manufacturing. "The cause is the cause of the country," he cried. The bill proposes "mutual concession" and compromise. All will ultimately benefit. Neither side wins or loses. "I invoke that saving spirit of mutual concession under which our blessed Constitution was formed, and under which alone it can be happily administered."[38]

A noble and mighty speech. Unfortunately Clay distinguished between those he called the friends of an "American policy" and those who were friends of a "foreign policy." And that stirred Webster into giving a response. Although he had solicited opinions from friends and his Boston constituents when the committee reported the bill, he probably had not intended to enter the debate. He admitted that the speeches of those favoring the bill had been impressive, especially on the need to protect domestic industry and raise farm prices. Then Clay spoke "a great deal of *nonsense*," and Webster felt obliged to respond. "I was not expecting to speak," he informed Jeremiah Mason, and was not ready to do so. In fact "I had but one night to prepare."[39]

And it showed. The ideas contained in his speech were well taken, but even he admitted that "as a *speech*" it was "clumsy, wanting in methods, & tedious." Still, he permitted its publication a month after delivery, having had the time to revise it to his satisfaction, because he realized that its ideas were important and worthy of widespread distribution.[40]

Like Clay, he needed two days for his rebuttal. He started on Thursday, April 1, and completed his address the following day. To start, he chided Clay for the distinction between an American and a foreign policy. After all, Clay's so-called American System had never been tried before. How is it American when those who oppose it follow the traditional form of employing American capital and labor to sustain the entire population? "With me," Webster said, "it is a fundamental axiom . . . that the great interests of the country are united and inseparable; that agriculture, commerce, and manufactures will prosper together or languish together." What Clay proposes will benefit only one of these three without regard for the consequences that may befall the other two. Webster called such legislation "dangerous." It was his opinion that Great Britain and other European nations were moving away from the mercantilism that had

38. *Annals of Congress*, 18th Congress, 1st Session, pp. 1962–2001.

39. DW to Nathan Appleton, January 12, 1824, DW to Mason, April 19, 1824, in *PC*, I, 347–348, 357. Webster does not name Clay specifically as talking nonsense but implies it.

40. DW to Jeremiah Mason, April 19, 1824, ibid., I, 357.

helped trigger the American Revolution and toward a policy of free trade. "In fine, Sir," Webster continued, "I think it is clear, that, if we now embrace the system of prohibitions and restrictions, we shall show an affection for what others have discarded, and be attempting to ornament ourselves with cast-off apparel."

He then discussed at length the economic conditions of the country following the Panic of 1819. Unlike Clay, who described the country as verging on national ruin, Webster had a more optimistic view and claimed the country had never rested on a more secure economic foundation. What Clay proposed would advance manufacturing interests through government support, not allow its natural development to operate through the laws of political economy. Webster was particularly effective in pointing out some of Clay's inconsistencies, faulty reasoning, and lapses in logic. Clay spoke as though manufactures constituted the only form of industry, whereas Webster insisted that commerce, navigation, farming, and a wide variety of artisan endeavors also made up domestic industry. "There is no foundation for the distinction which attributes to certain employments the peculiar appellation of American industry; and it is, in my judgment, extremely unwise to attempt such discriminations."

In elaborating his case favoring free trade, Webster quoted from *The Question concerning the Depreciation of Our Currency Stated and Examined* by William Huskisson, the president of the British Board of Trade.[41] Now that the world had returned to a state of peace, and commerce had resumed its normal operations, "all see," Webster insisted, ". . . that in this day of knowledge and of peace, there can be no commerce between nations but that which shall benefit all who are parties to it." He cited many examples to document a general sense that this age favored freedom of "commercial intercourse" and "unrestrained individual action." Nations had yielded their outmoded ideas of monopoly and restriction, just as they had yielded other prejudices, however slowly and reluctantly. In the long run they could not withstand the general tide of public and international opinion.

It is important to note that Webster never responded to Clay's insistence that Congress had the constitutional power to enact a protective tariff, a point vociferously denied by southerners. He actually did believe that Congress had the indisputable constitutional authority to raise revenue.

Webster concluded with these words: "Sir, I will detain you no longer. There are some parts of this bill which I highly approve; there are others in which I should acquiesce; but those to which I have now stated my objections appear to me so destitute of all justice, so burdensome and so dangerous to that interest which has steadily enriched, gallantly defended, and proudly distinguished us, that nothing can prevail upon me to give it my support."[42]

41. Later Huskisson told Webster "how greatly struck he had been with your speech on the tariff, wh[ich] he had read with the greatest pleasure." John Evelyn Denison to DW, July 11, 1826, ibid., II, 124.

42. *Annals of Congress*, 18th Congress, 1st Session, pp. 2026–2068. It can also be found in *W&S*, V, 94–149, and *PS*, I, 114–160.

Reading this speech today, one can only agree with its author that his efforts were "tedious"—excessively tedious. But then the tariff question, as he said, "is a tedious disagreeable subject." His great speeches devoted to patriotic and heroic themes can be read today with enormous profit and enjoyment. But this tariff speech is simply boring, probably because he had no fixed economic ideas and considered the tariff a matter of expedience and not of principle. He could hardly be expected to wax lyrical on such a topic. Still, his speech served its purpose in rebutting Clay's arguments. And in the opinion of some historians, it rang truer than his protectionist speeches[43] after he switched his position three years later, as he did, because a large and important segment of his constituency had in the interim completed the move from commerce and shipping to manufactures.

In the great Webster-Hayne debate in 1830 Hayne referred to this early tariff speech and said that Webster, "on that the proudest day of his life, like a mighty giant bore away upon his shoulders the pillars of the temple of error and delusion, escaping himself unhurt, and leaving its adversaries overwhelmed in its ruins." In its place, Hayne declared, Webster "erected to free trade a beautiful and enduring monument."[44] No question but that the Demosthenes of America had delighted southerners with his persuasive arguments.

What surprised everyone was Webster's apparent mastery of his subject. He really seemed to know what he was talking about. But it was a delusion. His facts came from the opinions and arguments of the many New England businessmen he canvassed prior to his speech, as well as from British free traders, and he simply repeated them in his speech. As a matter of fact Webster frequently gave misleading impressions about the extent of his knowledge, although he really was a very learned man and possessed an extraordinary memory of almost everything he had ever read. But he was also adept at intellectual deception. As he told his son Fletcher a few years later, "If, on a given occasion, a man can, gracefully, and without the air of a pedant, show a little more knowledge than the occasion requires, the world will give him credit for eminent attainments. It is an honest quackery. I have practised it, and sometimes with success."[45]

This 1824 speech was one of them. He knew that something was expected of him, far more than he could possibly deliver, and he gave the speech despite the fact that he had "very little hope" that it would make a difference. "The House, or a majority of it—are apparently *insane*—at least I think so. Whether any thing can be done to moderate the disease, I know not."[46]

As he anticipated, the House passed the bill, but the margin was close, 107 to 102. It took all of Clay's skill as Speaker and political tactician to win passage.[47]

43. Perhaps because only in this speech did he allow himself "the luxury of argument uncoerced by pressure from his constituents." *PS*, I, 114.

44. *Register of Debates*, 21st Congress, 1st Session, p. 49.

45. DW to Fletcher Webster, January 15, 1836, in Webster, ed., *Private Correspondence*, II, 16.

46. DW to [Edward Everett], February 13, [1824], in *PC*, I, 352.

47. For a discussion of Clay's tactics in winning passage, see Remini, *Clay*, pp. 228–233.

In the vote the middle states and the Northwest voted solidly for it, the South and Southwest solidly against, with New England split. Webster voted against the bill, as did a majority of New England representatives. A month later the bill by a wide margin, with amendments that Webster approved, whipped through the Senate, and President Monroe signed it into law on May 25, 1824.[48]

In the midst of the debate over the tariff the Radical friends of Secretary Crawford in Congress called on their colleagues to attend a caucus to be held on Saturday, February 14, in the evening in the House chamber. The summons appeared in the *National Intelligencer* and was signed by eleven congressmen. Although more than half the members of Congress had already signed a statement declaring that they would not attend a caucus, and although a number of people knew or suspected that Crawford was desperately ill, his supporters, led by Senator Martin Van Buren of New York, went ahead with the caucus anyway. Only sixty-six congressmen showed up. It was a dismal showing, and despite the demands of loud voices from the gallery that the caucus disband, Van Buren proceeded with the balloting. To the surprise of none, and to the accompaniment of "heavy groans in the Gallery," Crawford received sixty-two votes, Adams two, and there was one vote apiece for Jackson and Nathaniel Macon of North Carolina. Albert Gallatin, secretary of the treasury under Jefferson, was then nominated for the vice presidency.[49]

The caucus proved two things: first, that it should never have been held—"King Caucus" really was dead—and second, that the great Jeffersonian-Madisonian Republican party was badly split. Crawford was now the supposed official candidate of the Republican party, but as Webster said, "the measure is more likely to *hurt* than to *help* Mr. Crawford." Indeed it did. The friends of the other candidates knew their men could not obtain sufficient votes for a nomination so they not only stayed away but publicly denounced the caucus system as undemocratic and an affront to every intelligent voter in America.[50]

Webster saw the likely consequence. "This is an awful intimation of what will be the consequence, if the Election should come into the H. of R., and I fully believe it must come there." Many agreed. But which of the many candidates would end up in the House election? Webster thought Adams, Crawford (provided he won New York), and either Clay or Jackson. He believed that the Pennsylvania convention scheduled to meet on March 4 would nominate Jackson over Calhoun, and if that happened, then "Mr. Calhoun will be no longer a

48. Webster voted for this amended bill when it came back from the Senate. *Annals of Congress,* 18th Congress, 1st Session, p. 2674. The vote was 125 to 66. At one point Webster thought that "a mortal blow" had been struck "on the tariff principle. If it were not for instruction and other nonsense, two thirds nearly of our House would be against it." DW to Ezekiel Webster, April 18, 1824, in *W&S,* XVII, 350.

49. William Plumer, Jr., to William Plumer, February 5, 9, 16, May 2, 1824, in Brown, ed., *Missouri Compromises,* pp. 96, 98, 100, 117; Stephen Van Rensselaer to Solomon Van Rensselaer, February 15, 1824, in Mrs. Catharina V. R. Bonney, *A Legacy of Historical Gleaning* (Albany, 1875), p. 410.

50. Chase C. Mooney, *William H. Crawford, 1772–1834* (Lexington, Ky., 1974), pp. 249–268; Remini, *Van Buren,* pp. 46–50.

candidate." That is precisely what happened. The election of 1824 was reduced to four Republican candidates: Adams, Jackson, Clay, and Crawford. Calhoun withdrew as a presidential candidate and accepted the nomination for the second slot.[51]

Jackson's mounting acceptance by the people for the presidency caught everyone by surprise. Few figured that his nomination by the Tennessee legislature amounted to more than a respectful gesture of gratitude for his heroic efforts at New Orleans. But almost at once his popularity among the masses became obvious, and the defection of Pennsylvania from Calhoun was a clear indication of it. "The truth is," declared Webster, "he is the people's candidate in a great part of the southern and western country." Webster also thought that Adams's chances had improved over the last few months but that Jackson would most likely give him trouble.

The appearance in Washington of the newly elected senator from Tennessee took everyone by surprise. "General Jackson's manners," Webster told his brother, "are more presidential than those of any of the candidates." He actually looked and behaved like a President, like the leader of a great nation. "He is grave, mild, and reserved," Webster observed. "My wife is for him decidedly."[52]

But would the electors take Jackson's candidacy seriously? Would congressmen if the election ended in the House? Increasingly Webster thought that Adams would win the presidency, especially when it became common knowledge in late spring that "Mr. Crawford is *sick—very sick.*"[53]

Crawford's candidacy was also weakened by the appearance of a series of letters signed "A. B." in the Washington *Republican,* accusing the secretary of mismanaging public funds. Rumor had it that Senator Ninian Edwards of Illinois was the mysterious author of the "A. B. letters," but he denied it in testimony before a House committee.

The Radicals waited until Edwards had been appointed minister to Mexico and had left for his post before they launched an attack upon him and accused him of lying. When he heard the charge, Edwards admitted his perjury but repeated his accusations against Crawford. A House committee of investigation was then appointed by Speaker Clay to investigate the charges, and he named Webster, John Randolph, Edward Livingston of Louisiana, John W. Taylor of New York, John Floyd of Virginia, Duncan McArthur of Ohio, and George W. Owen of Alabama. Webster hated the appointment but could think of no excuse to escape it.[54] Most of the members were committed to one or another presiden-

51. DW to Mason, February 15, 1824, in *PC,* I, 353. Clay agreed with Webster, adding that he thought Adams and Jackson would be carried into the House with himself as the third candidate, if he carried New York. Clay to J. D. Godman, March 6, 1824, in the Gilder Lehrman Collection, Morgan Library, New York.

52. DW to Ezekiel Webster, March 14, April 18, 1824, in *W&S,* XVII, 347, 350, DW to Ezekiel Webster, February 22, 1824, in Webster, ed., *Private Correspondence,* I, 346; Grace Webster to James W. Paige, January 6, 1824, Paige Papers, MHS.

53. DW to Ezekiel Webster, June 5, [1824], in *W&S,* XVI, 88.

54. Plumer, "Reminiscences of Webster," in ibid., XVII, 552.

tial candidate. Not so Webster.[55] Could the investigation then be fair? According to Senator Rufus King of New York, it depended "upon the firmness and incorruptible integrity of Webster, who told him he was determined there should be a thorough investigation of the subject."[56] As a result, every time Webster entered the House chamber he was "surrounded by Crawford's friends who were seen one after the other, taking him aside and engaged with him in long conversations, doubtless on the subject of his report."[57]

Webster took a very jaundiced view of Edwards's perjury and ended up intent on censuring the minister. In this he failed. But the final report of the committee, which Webster and the House clerk carried to President Monroe on June 21, cleared Crawford of the charges. Nothing had been "proved to impeach the integrity of the Secretary, or to bring into doubt the general correctness and ability of his administration of the public finances." Monroe was prepared to revoke Edwards's commission but accepted his resignation instead, and "Mr. Edwards . . . disappeared from the federal political theatre."[58]

Secretary Adams, whose ambition for the presidency equaled that of any of the other candidates, kept a close watch on these proceedings and spoke regularly with several members of the committee, who reported to him the attitudes and reactions of the other members. On reading the report of the committee, he believed that there was a partiality toward Crawford motivated in large measure by the "personal impulses of interest and ambition in the breast of Mr. Webster, to catch the prospect of advancement in the event of Crawford's election." Adams seemed to be particularly interested in Webster's behavior and faulted him for his "secret and most improper intimation" to Monroe that the committee would censure Edwards.

Adams developed a distinct dislike, if not outright hatred, for Daniel Webster. His diary is filled with critical comments about the man, and he rarely missed an opportunity to find fault. He simply did not trust the congressman, and this report only strengthened his conviction that Black Dan was treacherous and that no faith could be placed in anything he said or did.

One of the committee members, John W. Taylor, told Adams that from Webster's conduct in the committee he had no doubt that Black Dan "is a thorough-going political partisan of Mr. Crawford," a view that could be proved by his "movements in concert with other persons" to build a case against Edwards and exonerate Crawford. Taylor had spoken with others, and they too were frankly "alarmed at this new and extensive *federal* organization for Crawford."[59]

---

55. Undoubtedly the reason Clay appointed him.

56. "King plainly told Webster that it depended upon him whether this affair should be laid open in all its true colors, or smothered as it has been twice before." Adams, *Memoirs*, VI, 317.

57. Plumer, "Reminiscences of Webster," in *W&S*, XVII, 552.

58. *ASPFR*, V, 80; Benton, *Thirty Years' View*, I, 36. The full report of the committee is in *ASPFR*, V, 79–80, and the examination of witnesses and copies of relevant documents can be found on pages 80–146.

59. Adams, *Memoirs*, VI, 392, 391.

A month prior to Taylor's conversation with the secretary, another Massachusetts representative, John Reed, had spoken to Adams and informed him that there was a "systematic effort" to unite the old Massachusetts Federalist party behind Crawford.[60] Why Crawford and not Adams? For the simple reason that Adams was an "apostate," having deserted the Federalist party for the opposition, and apostate Federalists were anathema. In addition, Federalists feared that Adams's "prejudices against them were so strong, that in the event of my election," recorded Adams, "they would be altogether prescribed." Naturally Adams denied that he would be partisan if elected. "I should be the President not of a section, nor of a faction, but of the whole Union," he pontificated.[61]

Several days later Reed again spoke to Adams. In the interim he had consulted with Webster and asked his House colleague to see Adams. Webster declined. Reed told Adams that Webster feared not only proscription but that such excellent men as his friends Jeremiah Mason and Joseph Hopkinson would be excluded from public office. Adams responded that he knew that both men were highly qualified for office and "never, under any circumstances, would I be made the instrument of a systematic exclusion of such men from it." In the privacy of his diary Adams reported that various "lures" had been held out to Webster to get him to unite with the Crawford faction. How successful they had been he did not know.[62]

It was true that Webster did concern himself with how the different candidates would treat Federalists if they were elected. He mentioned his concern several times in his letters. What disturbed him was the fact that the events of the past winter "have very much mixed up Federalists with some or other of the parties." A few Federalists try to keep up the old distinctions but find it most difficult to do, he declared. "Of Mr. Crawford's friends, the *South* are liberal, & the *North* are not." That was Webster's biggest complaint against Crawford: "the company he keeps, at the North." It "is my strongest objection to him." Webster undoubtedly had Van Buren and his northern Radicals in mind. Van Buren regarded Monroe's policy of showing goodwill toward Federalists and conferring political favors on them as a horror. The President seemed to be attempting an "amalgamation" of parties, and Van Buren wanted the old divisions between parties preserved and nurtured. Only through a party system in which Federalists and Republicans were openly arrayed against each other could there be effective government, he maintained.[63]

As for the New Englander John Quincy Adams, Webster had had a slight change of mind after speaking with Reed and others. "Mr. Adams, I think, sees also that *exclusion* will be a very doubtful policy. And in truth I think a *little* better of the kindness of his feeling towards us, than I have done.[64]

60. Reed himself was a Federalist representing a congressional district that was mainly Republican. He professed to be friendly toward Adams.

61. Adams, *Memoirs*, VI, 312, 313.

62. Ibid., 315–316.

63. Remini, *Van Buren*, pp. 12–42.

64. DW to Mason, May 9, 1824, in *PC*, I, 358–359.

By the time Webster was ready to return home—"I am homesick—homesick—homesick," he told a friend[65]—he felt thoroughly exhausted. The investigation had kept him in Washington weeks after Congress had adjourned, and he therefore sent his family ahead of him so that they could escape the blistering heat of the capital. For the last six months, in addition to his duties as a representative, he had argued the *Steamboat* case before the Supreme Court (and several other cases) and had appeared regularly before the Spanish Claims Commission to present the claims of the many litigants he represented. He had been attending to this Spanish claims business since 1821, and when the commission finally completed its work on June 8, 1824, he was awarded approximately $1,850,000 for his clients, who constituted the commercial elite of New England, especially the shipping interests, insurance underwriters, and merchants of Boston. Of the $5,000,000 awarded by the commission, Webster's clients received a little less than a third of the total amount. Since his fees turned out to be around $70,000, a fantastically large sum of money for 1824, Webster wanted desperately to get home to begin collecting what was owed him. Those fees, in terms of their value today, come approximately to $1,000,000.[66]

Although he had had many personal and profession expenses in connection with the Spanish claims and had spent many long hours during the past three years working on them, Daniel Webster was well paid for his efforts. In 1824, at the age of forty-three, he was a very rich man.

But money slipped through his fingers as fast as he could earn it.

65. DW to Blake, June 16, 1824, in *W&S*, XVII, 353.

66. *PLFP,* II, 265–266; John J. McCusker, *How Much Is That in Real Money: A Historical Price Index for Use as a Deflator of Money Values in the Economy of the United States* (Worcester, 1992), pp. 327, 332.

13

The Bunker Hill Oration

FOR THE next month, after his return to Boston, Webster happily set about collecting his fees. Within a two-week period he collected close to fifty thousand dollars, and within a month approximately sixty thousand.[1] The rest of it came dribbling in over the next several months.

One professional matter to engage his attention involved a request from Noah Webster, the famed lexicographer, to introduce a petition to Congress requesting that copies of his *Dictionary of the English Language* be imported into the United States free of duty for five years. The book had been printed in England because no printer in America could "hazard the expense of types" for such a costly work until its probable sales became clearer. If the sales proved sufficient in the five-year period, the author contended, he would then procure the necessary types to print the work in the United States. He had gone to England not only to have his book printed but to complete his lexicographical study, which he subsequently published in 1828 under the title *An American Dictionary of the English Language*.

As requested, the congressman introduced the petition on December 27, 1824, and a bill to that effect passed Congress on March 3, 1825.[2] To Noah Webster's delight, his work won immediate success in the United States upon publication.

For the month of August the congressman and his family vacationed at Sandwich on Cape Cod, which had become a favorite summer residence for them. But on their way back to Boston they passed a farm in Marshfield owned by Captain John Thomas, and Grace Webster took an immediate fancy to it. She was struck by the quiet beauty of the place, its lovely house, and the fact that the 160-acre farm was only a mile away from the ocean. Thomas and his family warmly greeted the renowned congressman and invited him to spend a few days as their guest. These few days went so well, and the two families proved so compatible, that the Websters returned each summer to visit with the Thomas family, perhaps little aware that eight years hence the house and

1. *PLBP,* II, 265.

2. Noah Webster to DW, October 16, 1824, in *PC,* I, 365–366. Noah Webster also asked that his *Synopsis of Languages* be included in the petition.

farm would become Webster's permanent residence.[3]

For the remainder of the summer and fall the approaching presidential election engaged Webster's complete attention and much of his correspondence. He himself had been nominated for a second term in the House, but he apparently did nothing to advance his candidacy. By this time his reputation was such as to guarantee election. In fact a Republican meeting in Boston on October 11 also nominated Webster, further blurring the lines that separated the state's rival parties. Naturally the Federalists gave him total support, and the elite of Boston, so heavily in his debt, would consider no one else. Some of them even talked about elevating him to the U.S. Senate.

As early as the spring of 1824 Webster figured out who the three candidates would be to go into the House election for President. Crawford, despite his illness, had the backing of a relatively well-oiled machine (with Treasury patronage) as well as the support of the Radical faction of the Republican party. Unless he died suddenly, he would surely enter the House contest. Then General Jackson had proved to be more popular among the masses and among his colleagues in Washington than anticipated, and he now appeared to be a very viable candidate because of strong southern and western support. The third likely candidate was John Quincy Adams because he would probably garner all the electoral votes of New England. Despite his past "apostasy" and the continued hatred of him by many Federalists, no other candidate could rival his hold on New England. He was, after all, an Adams.[4] As for Clay, few gave him much hope. The West once belonged exclusively to him; now he had to divide it with Jackson.

That the election would land in the House troubled Webster. In the absence of a "very prominent, & highly distinguished" statesman, "local considerations, personal considerations, & a hundred other *small* considerations" will have undue influence, he said. The result could be the "diminution of the weight & authority of the Executive Magistrate" and the devolution of more and more authority on the Congress. "I am fearful," he worried, "the President's Office may get to be thought too much in the gift of the Congress."[5]

Webster maintained a strict neutrality during the presidential contest. John C. Calhoun, the very efficient and energetic secretary of war, probably was Webster's original choice for the presidency. The congressman regarded Calhoun as a nationalist, not as the southern sectionalist he later became, and as a man who would not be indifferent to New England's needs. He did not differ with him on constitutional issues, and most important, Webster admired Calhoun's intellectual prowess. He believed him to be "a true man."[6] But when the

3. Curtis, *Webster*, I, 220–221.

4. DW to Jeremiah Mason, April 19, 1824, DW to William Gaston, September 8, 1824, in *PC*, I, 363; Arthur B. Darling, *Political Changes in Massachusetts, 1824–1848* (New Haven, 1925), p. 41.

5. DW to William Gaston, September 8, 1824, in *PC*, I, 363.

6. DW to George Ticknor, [January 25, 1825], ibid., II, 16.

South Carolinian withdrew his bid for the presidency after Pennsylvania had dumped him in favor of Jackson, choosing to run instead for the vice presidency, Webster switched to a neutral position. Now he had no strong feelings about any of the candidates.

In the fall election Massachusetts voters were offered two electoral tickets: one pledged to Adams that comprised Republicans and some Federalists, and the other an "unpledged" ticket consisting mostly of Federalists. In his own election Webster received a "nearly unanimous" endorsement by his constituents. Of 5,000 votes cast, he garnered 4,990—a result "without precedent in the annals of our political contests," claimed Charles March.[7] In the presidential contest, as far as can be determined from sketchy returns, Adams won 30,687 popular votes in Massachusetts, and Crawford 6,616. Nothing is recorded for the other two candidates.[8]

Throughout the nation the election ended with Jackson showing a plurality of 152,901 popular votes, Adams 114,023, Crawford 46,979, and Clay 47,217. In the all-important electoral college Jackson again had a plurality of 99 votes, Adams 84, Crawford 41, and Clay 37. No one had a majority, and therefore the election had to be decided in the House of Representatives. As Webster had predicted, Jackson, Adams, and Crawford were the three top candidates.[9] No question about it, the coming winter in Washington during the second session of the Eighteenth Congress would prove very exciting.

Webster left for the capital in late November and on December 3 found quarters at Mr. McIntire's house on Pennsylvania Avenue. It was a new, quite spacious house, and the other lodgers "seem to be good people." He had a large room to himself in the front and an inner one for "retreat." And he had his servant Charles Brown as "a man Friday."[10]

During this period Webster met four young Englishmen who were touring the country: John Evelyn Denison, the future earl of Derby, Stuart Wortley, and the future Lord Taunton. He and Story socialized a good bit with these men, and they stimulated Webster's desire to go abroad, possibly as minister to Great Britain. Denison in fact became the congressman's regular correspondent after his return home.

Ever the partygoer, Webster dined out quite often during this session and frequently had dinner with his friend George Ticknor and his wife, Anna Eliot Ticknor, whenever they were at home. Ticknor would also invite one or two other guests, such as Joel Poinsett, minister to Mexico in 1825; Henry Clay; Senator Littleton W. Tazewell of Virginia; Langdon Cheves, the former Speaker of the House; Edward Livingston and his wife; and General Lafayette,[11] who

---

7. March, *Webster,* p. 70. Webster had no opposition of any consequence.

8. Schlesinger and Israel, eds., *History of Presidential Elections,* I, 409.

9. Curtis, *Webster,* p. 220; Schlesinger and Israel, eds., *History of Presidential Elections,* p. 409.

10. DW to Mrs. Webster, December 4, 6, 1824, in *W&S,* XVII, 355–356.

11. New Englanders nicknamed Lafayette Lafe.

was touring the United States to universal applause. These dinners were very pleasant, said Ticknor, "for Mr. Webster was generally very animated, and there was no want of excitement among the rest of them."[12]

It so happened that Thomas Jefferson had invited Professor Ticknor many times to visit him at Monticello in order to obtain his advice about defining the course of studies at the University of Virginia ,which Jefferson had founded and of which he was extremely proud. Ticknor and Edward Everett had been working on a plan for reform that would raise academic standards at Harvard, reforms that emphasized specialization. Since Ticknor had occasion to visit Washington in the late fall of 1824, he finally accepted Jefferson's invitation. He happened to mention his plans to Webster, appointed an overseer at Harvard in 1822, who immediately asked to join him. Ticknor wrote to Jefferson and inquired if Webster might accompany him on the visit. Jefferson responded: "Whether Mr. Webster comes with you, or alone as suits himself, he will be a welcome guest. His character, his talents and principles, entitle him to the favor and respect of all his fellow-citizens, and have long ago possessed him of mine."[13]

So, on Thursday, December 9, Ticknor, his wife, and Webster set off to Fredericksburg Landing, where they stayed for the night. At dinner the landlord "dropped his knife and fork with astonishment, as he was carving a very nice turkey, when he understood that he was talking with Mr. Webster of Massachusetts." But astonished or not, he did not hesitate to inform Webster that whether Congress had the power under the Constitution to pass internal improvements or not, he wished it would do so. The two men had "a great argument" over the question.

The group soon understood the landlord's interest in internal improvements. As they continued their journey, they found the roads almost impassable. But Webster hardly noticed. He was in high spirits. He "was very amusing," recalled Ticknor, "telling stories to keep our spirits up, singing scraps of old songs, and making merry like a boy."[14] Such agreeable company and his keen anticipation of the meeting with the great author of the Declaration—never mind that Jefferson was a Republican who had signed the infamous embargo bill—brought out the most spirited and jovial in Webster.

Because President Monroe had alerted former President Madison of the Ticknor visit to Jefferson, the trio decided to stop at Montpelier on their way to Monticello and pay their respects. Madison, now seventy-three years old, informed the group that it would be most welcome and sent his coachman to guide them to his home.

Madison and Webster knew each other quite well and were "evidently well pleased to see each other again," despite the "strain" that had existed between them during the late war. Indeed the former President went out of his way to

12. Ticknor to William H. Prescott, January 16, 1825, in Ticknor, *Life*, I, 348.
13. Curtis, *Webster*, I, 222–223.
14. Ibid., I, 223.

"be agreeable to Mr. Webster." Later, since he was enjoying himself so much, Webster quietly informed Ticknor that he did not want to depart the next day as planned, so they extended their stay to two days.

Madison regaled his company with many "capital stories," told gracefully and with "great freedom" and effect. But he avoided current politics. Webster was so much impressed by the former President's conversation that "it had fully confirmed him in an opinion he had for some time entertained, that Mr. Madison was 'the wisest of our Presidents, except Washington.' " Interestingly, Henry Clay had the identical opinion of Madison.[15]

Webster probably hated to leave the former President, so delightful had been his visit. He later told the Ticknors "that without intending any compliment to his companions, he would say that he had not felt so free from care and anxious thought, as he did then, for five years."[16]

The thirty-two miles separating Montpelier from Monticello took Webster and his friends more than a day to travel. They were about to start up from Charlottesville to Jefferson's home when Webster received a letter from his wife that immediately transformed "his appearance and manner the moment he read it." Grace informed him that their son Charles was ill of a "lung fever." The child had had a heavy cold for more than a week when suddenly he "was taken in very great distress—every breath was a groan." The doctor was summoned, applied "Emetics and other medicines," which helped, and bled Charles with leeches. The next morning the child was better. The boy turned to his mother and asked: "Where is Papa I [miss] him, why don't he come home." Grace confessed that "this has been a very long fortnight since you left. It seems as [if] you had been gone long enough to return."[17]

Webster had planned to stay only a few days at Monticello before visiting Richmond and Norfolk, but the news from home forced him to change his plans. He intended now to proceed directly to Washington after seeing Jefferson and hurrying on to Boston if Charles's condition worsened.

The group had expected to stay at Monticello only a few days, but a heavy downpour prevented their departure, and they remained for five days.

The visit, as Webster recounted, "was not unpleasant." Jefferson, now eighty-one, came out on horseback to meet them on the road and greeted them warmly. He looked "straighter, and freer from the debility of age" than Webster had expected. And he, like Madison, showed them every courtesy and conversed freely and naturally. Although he had "regular habits and fixed hours for every thing," he was "very attentive to Mr. Webster, and plainly liked to talk with him."

Webster was most respectful of the former President and constantly introduced subjects about the past that stirred the great man into reminiscing about

---

15. Ibid., I, 223–224; Ticknor to W. H. Prescott, December 16, 1824, in Ticknor, *Life,* I, 347; Remini, *Clay,* p. 524.

16. Curtis, *Webster,* I, 224.

17. Ibid., 224; Grace Webster to DW, December 19, 1824, in *PC,* I, 368.

the Revolution and the men who had led it. Like Madison, he avoided talking about present-day politics, except to say that he felt "much alarmed at the prospect of seeing General Jackson, President. He is one of the most unfit men, I know of for such a place. He has very little respect for Laws or Constitutions." Rather than current politics, Jefferson much preferred to provide "early anecdotes of Revolutionary times—French society—politics—& literature, such as they were when he was in France—and Genl. Literature, & the Va. University."[18]

Webster thoroughly enjoyed Jefferson's company, and his partisan Federalist hostility faded under the Virginian's great charm "and force of his intellect." He especially enjoyed the anecdotes and, in the course of their conversation, provided a few of his own. One, in particular, vastly amused the former President. It seems that when he began his law practice, Webster took the case of a blacksmith that proved very difficult, forcing him to spend fifty dollars for books to help him understand the legal point in question. Webster won the case, but he took a financial loss. He received only fifteen dollars as his fee. Years later Aaron Burr asked him for a legal opinion on the very point involved in the blacksmith's case. Webster had ready answers. As he spoke, his client interrupted him. Had he been involved in such a case before? Burr asked. He rather suspected that Webster had argued the other side. Webster admitted knowledge of the point in question and proceeded to make Burr "pay enough to cover all his work for the blacksmith and something moreover for Mr. Burr's suspicions that he had been of counsel for the opposite party." Webster added: "Mr. Burr, no doubt, thought me a much more learned lawyer than I was, and, under the circumstances of the case, I did not think it worth while to disabuse him of his good opinion of me."[19]

Nothing pleased Jefferson more than to talk about the University of Virginia. They all rode over to inspect the institution, and Ticknor admitted that the buildings were "more beautiful than anything architectural in New England, and more appropriate to an university than can be found, perhaps, in the world." The campus included ten houses for professors, 108 apartments for students, four dining areas, four lecture rooms, and a rotunda with "a magnificent room for a library." Jefferson commented at one point that "when I can neither read nor ride, I shall desire very much to make my bow." Since Jefferson had invited comments and suggestions for improving his university, Webster suggested that the military exercises required by the rules of the university be practiced with guns made of wood, rather than the usual firearms. It proved to be a wise recommendation.[20]

18. DW to Joseph Hopkinson, December 31, DW to Jeremiah Mason, December 29, 1824, in *PC*, I, 381, 379; Curtis, *Webster*, I, 224. See also the notes about this visit that Webster and Ticknor dictated to Mrs. Ticknor at an inn where they spent their first night after leaving Monticello. In it Webster provides a very detailed description of Jefferson's physical appearance. *W&S*, XVII, 364–373. They are also printed in *PC*, I, 370–377.

19. *PS*, I, 237; Curtis, *Webster*, I, 225.

20. Ticknor, *Life*, I, 348; Curtis, *Webster*, I, 225.

Webster was extremely anxious to get back to Washington to obtain late word of his son's condition. He also wanted to check on what Congress was about. Once the storm passed, the company thanked their host for his hospitality and hurried away. Throughout the return journey Webster felt depressed and anxious about what the news from home might be.

His worse fears were realized. On December 19, after a particularly bad night, Charles had died at 7:00 A.M., just shy by days of his third birthday. It was the very day the group had left Monticello.

The news devastated poor Webster. He recollected later that he had been away from home when Charles was born, visiting with Joseph Hopkinson, and now he was absent again when he died, visiting with Thomas Jefferson. "I know that my presence at home could not have altered the course of things," he lamented to Edward Everett. "The loss I feel, heavily, but I hope not to be too much depressed by it. The oftener you call & see Mrs W. the more she & I shall be obliged to you."[21]

Charles's death hit Grace hard. Her cousin Eliza Buckminster stayed with her and offered as much comfort as possible, but the loss of a second child deeply affected her. On December 31 she wrote her husband: "This my dear Husband, is dear little Charles' birthday! but where is he! in his bed of darkness—every thing looks bright and gay, but cannot bring joy to the heart of a mother who mourns the untimely death of a beloved child."[22]

Webster sent her several "lines" he had composed in an attempt to assuage his own grief.

> My son, thou wast my hearts delight
> Thy morn of life was gay & cheery:
> That morn has rushed to sudden night.
> Thy fathers house is sad & dreary
>
> I held thee on my knee, my son!
> And kissed thee laughing, kissed thee weeping:
> But ah! thy little day is done,—
> Thou'rt with thy angel sister sleeping. . . .
>
> Dear Angel, thou art safe in Heaven:
> No prayers for thee need more be made
> Oh! let thy prayer for those be given,
> Who oft have blessed thine infant head
>
> My Father, I beheld thee born,
> And led thy tottering steps with care;
> Before me risen to Heaven's bright morn
> My Son! My Father! Guide me there—[23]

21. DW to Jeremiah Mason, December 31, DW to Everett, December 31, 1824, in *PC*, I, 382, 380–381. For a description of Charles's final hours, see James William Paige to DW, December 19, 1824, ibid., I, 369.

22. Grace Webster to DW, December 31, 1824, in Van Tyne, ed., *Letters of Webster*, p. 553.

23. Lines on the Death of His Son Charles, in *W&S*, XVII, 376–377.

Grace responded gratefully and affectionately for his gift of poetry, which she pronounced "very beautiful." Then she continued:

It makes me think of Edwards reflections on dear little Charles—tho' he saw him committed to the silent tomb he always speaks of him as alive, if any one mentions him as dead, Edward say[s] no, he is not dead he is alive in a beautiful place where he has everything he wants. The poor fellow was at first inconsolable. I never saw a child so much affected at such an event. He wept till it seemed as tho' his little heart would break. Among other things which seemed to renew his grief was the little waggon—he said he had no one now to help him drag the waggon. Dr [John C.] W[arren] was here and saw Neddy's grief, and he tried to console him by describing the pleasures of the place to which the dear child had gone, and Edward smiled and said he would not cry any more—and the idea that Charles has every thing he wants has perfectly satisfied him. Is it not more rational than those who are older? I feel that he is."[24]

Fortunately Grace herself had the consolation of her religion to help her through the ensuing days, but she suffered deep depression for many months afterward. She did not leave the house except to go to church. "O my husband," she wrote in late January, "have not some of our brightes[t] hopes perished! our fairest f[l]owers are indeed 'blossoms gathered for the tomb.' "[25]

In many ways Grace was a pathetic soul. Extremely insecure, suffering from a near-total sense of inadequacy, and always self-deprecating in her letters to her husband, she relied almost totally on Webster. She even called him her "lord and master." "You will perhaps say I am unusually humble," she confessed, "but these are not the feelings of an *hour* or a *day* they are *habitual.*"[26] She begged him to write at least every other day during this trying period, and he did make every effort to comply with her wishes. Virtually bringing up the children by herself, like the wives of so many statesmen at this time, she frequently felt overwhelmed by the burden. "I have lost the art [of] managing children," she complained to her husband, "and Julia requires a wiser head than mine, and a better heart I fear. She is very peculiar in her temper and feelings. I think it would be for her good to go from her Mother—but doubt if I could be happy without her."[27] Poor Grace was a very troubled woman.

In the weeks following the death of his son Webster found it very difficult to concentrate on business in Congress, even though a great deal regarding the presidential election was happening around him. The House prepared to make the final selection, and the voting was to take place in early February.

Webster only slowly allowed himself to get caught up in the intense lobbying for the several candidates by their respective supporters. But once he stirred himself to concentrate on matters immediately before him, he went on to play a vital role in the outcome of the House election.

Everyone assumed that he would prefer Adams because of the candidate's

24. Grace Webster to DW, January 10, 1825, in *PC*, II, 5.
25. Grace Webster to DW, January 22, 1825, ibid., II, 15.
26. Grace Webster to DW, February 21, 1825, in Van Tyne, ed., *Letters of Webster,* pp. 562–563.
27. Grace Webster to DW, March 10, 1825, in *PC*, II, 38.

identification with New England. But Webster had reservations. He enjoyed cordial but not intimate relations with Adams in Washington and for a time had avoided direct involvement in the general election the previous fall. But as the moment of decision neared, he began sending out ever-stronger signals about his future hopes and ambitions. He was "panting for the mission to London," reported William Plumer, who relayed this desire to Adams. Unfortunately the secretary did not respond favorably.[28] "I have known for the last eight months his wish to succeed Mr. Rush at the Court of London," recorded Plumer, ". . . but he is not very likely to get the appointment."[29] Plumer spoke to Adams again on January 17, but the secretary sourly replied that Webster "might be gratified hereafter but not immediately."[30]

As the House election approached, Webster was forced to abandon his neutrality. He was the head of the Federalist party in Congress and after Henry Clay the ablest man in the House. Other Federalists began turning to him for advice and counsel. His opinion was valued highly and could easily influence the final outcome, particularly in states where the delegations were split and in states with but a single representative. He could not remain passive in this election and hope to retain his preeminent position among the other members of his party. He had to become actively involved.

But whom to choose? With hardly a second thought he discarded Jackson as unqualified, a mere "military character," he said.[31] Crawford had the support of the states' rights Radicals, like Van Buren and John Randolph of Roanoke, as well as a veritable army of appointees, but he was desperately ill. The stroke had left him paralyzed and virtually sightless.[32] A sightless paralytic as President? Never. Like him or not, Adams had to be Webster's choice.

All things considered, it would not be a bad choice for him to make. At least he would not have to justify his vote to his constituency as he would if he voted for either of the other two candidates. They would understand his decision and would no doubt approve overwhelmingly.

Webster began to see Adams regularly around the middle of January. On one occasion he brought along his Massachusetts colleague in the House John Reed, also a Federalist. Adams noted their visit in his diary but did not elaborate on their conversation except to say that Webster claimed that there were persons who pretended to know how a member would vote in the House election by the manner in which he put on or took off his hat.[33] If this was meant to be funny, its humor sailed right over Adams's head.

28. Adams, *Memoirs*, VI, 442.

29. Plumer, "Reminiscences," in *W&S*, XVII, 553.

30. Adams, *Memoirs*, VI, 469.

31. DW to Jeremiah Mason, December 29, 1824, in *PC*, I, 378.

32. Although few in Washington knew Crawford's exact condition, reports abounded that his health was precarious. "You see nothing now in the papers respecting the health of Mr. Crawford," said Clay. "The truth is it is extremely precarious; he is greatly reduced, almost blind in one eye, and the other also affected." Clay to Peter B. Porter, April 26, 1824, in Clay, *Papers*, III, 825.

33. Adams, *Memoirs*, VI, 471–472.

Once Webster got involved in the contest, he proved to be very energetic. Troubled by the many disaffections of Federalists in New Jersey to Jackson, he began an active correspondence with leaders in that state to woo them over to Adams. Lucius Horatio Stockton, leader of the Adams forces in New Jersey, helped organize a meeting to instruct the state's delegation in the House to cast its vote for the secretary, and the proceedings of that meeting were sent to Webster for his information and use.[34]

Webster also kept careful tabs on Henry Clay's movements. As Speaker Clay would unquestionably have become President had he not been eliminated from the race by totaling the lowest number of electoral votes. Now he stood in the difficult—some said unenviable—position of possibly deciding the election by throwing his support to one of the three remaining candidates. Naturally all the political managers hounded him with pleas to turn to their particular man. "A main inquiry is," Webster informed his brother, Ezekiel, "in what direction Mr Clay & his friends will move." He suspected—a suspicion that mounted each day—that they would ultimately opt for Adams. His suspicions were realized on January 24, when Clay and the Kentucky delegation openly declared for the New Englander. That day the Ohio delegation also declared for Adams. With this announcement Webster had "no doubt of Mr Adams election. Probably he will be chosen [on] the first ballot." He guessed that the secretary would garner all six New England states plus Kentucky, Ohio, Missouri, Illinois, Louisiana, Maryland, and New York, which would give him thirteen states and the bare minimum required for election. "At any rate," he declared, "his final election is as certain as such event well can be."[35]

But were all the states on Webster's list certain to go for Adams? If he did not win all thirteen, and the House was required to keep balloting, there was no telling what might happen. Senator Van Buren, manager of the Crawford forces, prayed there would be repeated balloting. A deadlock between Adams and Jackson could conceivably end with Crawford's election.

At this point Webster's influence began to show itself. In a battle royal among three Republican candidates the Federalists might hold the balance of power. If they used their numbers among the several delegations wisely, they could gain many advantages.

So for the next several weeks Webster conferred with House Federalists and plotted strategy. His activities were noticed and commented upon, especially by the friends of Jackson and Crawford. Samuel D. Ingham, a Pennsylvania Jacksonian, wrote a letter to his constituents—published three months later in the Washington *National Intelligencer*[36]—in which he accused Webster of activities that showed a "bias" in favor of Adams. When he read the letter, Webster expressed contempt for this sort of snooping and reporting. "I have

34. Stockton to DW, January 11, 1825, in *PC*, II, 8–9.
35. DW to Joseph Hopkinson, January 29, 1825, in ibid., II, 17.
36. April 30, 1825.

great repugnance to appear in the Newspapers on such subjects. This habit of writing about what individual members said, or did, seems to me to be a very undignified & improper proceeding."[37]

On another occasion prior to the House election Webster sauntered over to William Plumer in his seat in the House and after a few pleasantries, as recorded by Plumer, "said we must act with firmness and with moderation supporting Mr. Adams, but not quarreling with General Jackson. If Adams succeeded all was well; if Jackson, the North by not quarreling with him would come in for her share in the Administration." Not that he was seeking anything for himself, he assured Plumer.

But what about the mission to England? Plumer asked. "It would perhaps be idle to shoot my arrow at so high a mark but—"and at that point their discussion was interrupted with a call for adjournment. Webster broke away with the comment that they would talk again and that it was very important they act together.[38]

One matter that concerned them all was the possibility that Adams would discriminate against Federalists in the awarding of the patronage. Perhaps by arrangement, perhaps not, Henry R. Warfield of Maryland, a Federalist, wrote a letter to Webster that confronted the problem head-on. Warfield pointed out that of Maryland's nine-man delegation in the House, all but he had declared their preference. "The awful responsibility of the vote of that state may devolve to me," he moaned. "Now Sir I am oppressed with this difficulty." The Federalists, with whom he regularly spoke, he continued, have "constantly expressed their apprehensions that should Mr. Adams be the President, he will administer the government on party considerations—that the old Land marks of party distinction will be built up—that an exclusion of all participation in office will be enforced with regard to those who have hitherto been denominated Federals." He concluded his letter by stating that "I shall feel particularly obliged if you will give me your candid opinion on those points."[39]

Webster received Warfield's letter the same day it was written. He immediately drafted a reply and then took both letters to Adams. In his response Webster stated that he would give Adams his vote in the election "cheerfully & steadily." But, he went on, "I should not do so, if I did not believe that he would administer the Government on liberal principles, not excluding Federalists." What was important was whether "a particular political name . . . is, of itself, to be regarded as a cause for exclusion." He ended his letter by again assuring Warfield that Adams would be just and liberal toward Federalists and Republicans.[40]

The fact that Webster called on the secretary the very day Warfield's letter

37. DW to Joseph Hopkinson, May 2, 1825, in *PC*, II, 45. The article appeared in the newspaper on April 30.

38. Plumer, "Reminiscences of Webster," in *W&S*, XVII, 553.

39. Warfield to DW, February 3, 1825, in *PC*, II, 18.

40. DW to Warfield, February 5, 1825, ibid., II, 21–22.

was written increases the suspicion that Warfield and Webster may have hatched this plot to draw their victim out on this most important question.

Slowly and carefully Adams read Warfield's letter and the draft of the response. Should he send his letter? Webster asked. Another Federalist, Representative John Lee, had also conveyed similar feelings as Warfield's. It was a matter of utmost urgency.

The sharp-witted Adams recognized immediately the inference that he could show a proper "disposition" toward the Federalists by "conferring some one prominent appointment upon a person of that party." Did that mean an appointment to a cabinet position? Adams asked.

Certainly not, Webster responded, "but to an appointment of a Judge."

Adams nodded. He liked the "general spirit" of Webster's answer and said he should consider it as "one of the objects nearest to my heart to bring the whole people of the Union to harmonize together." He added that undoubtedly Jackson and Crawford would pursue the same principle.

Webster then mentioned that he had also spoken to General Stephen Van Rensselaer, one of the thirty-four representatives from New York, whose vote, like that of New York itself, could be crucial. Van Rensselaer, the Patroon, was a kindly, very pious old man who was deeply concerned about the election.

Van Rensselaer, having "similar sentiments to his own," said Webster, had come to him for advice. Black Dan had urged him to speak to Adams. As a matter of fact, Webster continued, the general would call on the secretary the following morning at eleven o'clock. Adams thanked the congressman for the information, and on that note Webster departed.

The next day Van Rensselaer appeared on schedule. He expressed the same concerns as Warfield's, and Adams repeated to him what he had said to Webster the night before. Van Rensselaer then expressed his "complete satisfaction" with the answer.[41]

Adams had done well. So had Webster. Two crucial states ultimately voted for Adams, and that outcome resulted in no small measure from Webster's efforts.

Election day in the House fell on Wednesday, February 9. A heavy snowfall blanketed the city. When Van Rensselaer reached the Capitol, he was met by Henry Clay, who hustled him into the Speaker's private office, where Webster was waiting. They were taking no chances with the pious old man and plied him with arguments that the election turned on his vote. They said they feared the collapse of the government. Worse, they feared what it would mean in terms of the general's large New York estate.[42]

When they finally released him, Van Rensselaer staggered to his seat in the House, "in tears literally," muttering how "the vote of N. York . . . depended

41. Adams, *Memoirs*, VI, 492–493.
42. Van Buren, *Autobiography*, p. 152.

upon him" and "if he gave it to A. he could be elected most probably on the first ballot."[43]

At noon the two houses of Congress met together, counted the electoral ballots for President, and announced that no one had won a majority, whereupon the Senate withdrew to permit the House to proceed with determining the next President. The Speaker took his place at the podium, directed a roll call, and appointed Webster and John Randolph as tellers. On the very first ballot Adams took thirteen states, and with it the presidency; Jackson won seven states, and Crawford, four. The long agony had finally ended.

In recognition of the fact that he was "the leader of the House," Webster chaired a committee that informed Adams of his election.[44] Following protocol, he asked the President-elect when it might be convenient for him to receive the committee to announce his selection officially. Adams designated noon the following day.

The committee trooped to Adams's residence on February 10 and performed their duty. The President-elect reminded them that once before the House had made the final selection and on that occasion Thomas Jefferson had prepared a written statement. Following this "tradition," Adams read his own acceptance and handed it to Webster, who reported it to the House, where it was duly noted and filed.[45]

A man of incredible political ineptitude, Adams then chose Henry Clay as his secretary of state. The announcement startled Washington. The friends of Jackson cried out their horror over this "corrupt bargain," as they called it. For weeks there had been talk that Clay and Adams had reached an agreement, a bargain, in which Clay would throw his support in the House to Adams in return for appointment as secretary of state. Now the rumor had become reality. Clay desperately wanted the position because it traditionally led to the presidency, and more than anything else in the world he lusted after this office.

Jackson in disgust and anger resigned his seat in the Senate and returned to his home in Tennessee, where he immediately began the long campaign to win the presidency in 1828. He felt cheated. He believed the nation had been betrayed by conniving, corrupt politicians. Shortly thereafter a coalition began to form among hostile Republicans intent on frustrating any attempt Adams might make to initiate important legislation.

There could be no doubt where Webster would stand. He was absolutely confident that "Mr. Adams will pursue an honorable, liberal, magnanimous policy." And "unless the Administration has friends, its enemies will overwhelm it." The true course at present, he informed his brother, "is to maintain the Administration,—& give [it] a fair chance." For himself, Webster said, he had

43. Louis McLane to Mrs. McLane, February 9, 1825, McLane Papers, LC.

44. Poore, *Perley's Reminiscences*, p, 78. The other members were Joseph Vance of Ohio and William Archer of Virginia.

45. Adams, *Memoirs*, VI, 502, 505.

no real hopes of appointment in the new administration, particularly after he
had learned that the mission to England, the one position he desired, had gone
to Rufus King. "Everybody is willing I should remain as I am," he declared.[46]

Webster had kind things to say about King, and he wished him well. However, he could not resist mentioning that the appointee was "a little too much
advanced in life, perhaps to be expected to remain long in the situation." He
proved to be correct. King retired as minister to England in 1827 and died
shortly thereafter.[47]

Before the session ended, Webster had a brush with near disaster in the
form of another challenge to fight a duel—and from the same man! John Randolph. "After brooding in silence for nearly a year," Randolph decided to seek
satisfaction. This strange-looking six-foot-tall man with a small, round head and
a high-pitched, thin voice that could ring "like the shrill scream of an angry
vixen" suddenly acted out his anger.[48] His grievance went back to what had
happened in the House eight months earlier, when he and Webster served
on the committee investigating charges brought against Crawford by Ninian
Edwards. Randolph claimed that he persuaded the committee to give Crawford
an opportunity to respond to Edwards's charges, a claim Webster had denied.
The only matter that called for explanation, said Webster on the House floor,
was whether Randolph intended to infer that the majority of the committee
wished to deny Crawford the "fullest opportunity to answer the charges against
him." Randolph had snapped back: "I have stated as clearly as I could . . . the
facts as they occurred." Other members of the committee agreed with Webster.
Furious over "the castigation given him by Webster" and the others, and egged
on by many members who said that he was "a disgraced and degraded man" if
he did not demand satisfaction, he finally resorted to a challenge, his usual wont
when his anger had been sufficiently roused.[49]

The House was in session on February 21, 1825, when Senator Thomas
Hart Benton of Missouri delivered the challenge. Webster was sitting on a sofa
in back of the members' seats. With some formality Benton handed Webster the
note. Webster read it, folded it very deliberately, paused a moment, opened, and
read it again as though he could not believe the note's contents. He slowly ran
his hands over his massive brow and then muttered a few words to Benton. The
senator bowed and departed. What was said was not reported. Webster sat for a
few minutes more and then moved back to his House seat.[50]

William Plumer of New Hampshire, who had watched the encounter, later
asked Webster about it and what he intended to do. Webster showed Plumer

46. DW to Jeremiah Mason, February 14, 1825, DW to Ezekiel Webster, February 16, 1825, DW to
Edward Everett, February 23, 1825, in *PC*, II, 24, 25, 33.

47. DW to [John Denison], May 2, 1825, in ibid., II, 44.

48. Poore, *Perley's Reminiscences*, p. 68.

49. *Register of Debates*, 18th Congress, 2d Session, pp. 56–58; Plumer, "Reminiscences of Webster,"
in *W&S*, XVII, 553, 555.

50. Plumer, "Reminiscences of Webster," in *W&S*, XVII, 553.

the challenge and the answer he had written but not yet sent. The challenge demanded satisfaction for Webster's language that had impugned Randolph's veracity.

Webster's answer stated that whatever he had said had been said by him in the House in the discharge of his duties, for which he could not be held accountable on a dueling ground. However, if Randolph was convinced that Webster had said what was false, the New Englander "would readily make any reasonable satisfaction." Obviously he did not regard a duel, possibly to the death, as reasonable. At this point mutual friends intervened to soothe Randolph's injured feelings, he subsequently withdrew the challenge, and the matter ended. It is likely that Benton played the leading role in bringing about the amicable resolution to the dispute. In any event both Webster and Randolph agreed to keep the dispute secret, an undertaking that in Washington, even in 1824, was virtually impossible.[51]

But Webster had now become one of Randolph's favorite targets in the House.[52] Among other things the Virginian called the New Englander "a vile slanderer." One day, while speaking "with great freedom of abuse of Mr. Webster," he was informed that Mrs. Webster was present in the gallery. It did not faze him in the least. He kept right on spewing forth his venom. "He had not the delicacy to desist" until he had "fully emptied the vials of his wrath."[53]

The Eighteenth Congress dribbled to an end with discussions about the Cumberland Road, the Chesapeake and Delaware Canal, and a crimes bill for certain offenses against the United States that Webster, as chairman of the Judiciary Committee, reported to the full House. With Justice Story's considerable help, Webster had essentially shaped the committee's bill and spoke convincingly for its passage with an extraordinary display of legal and constitutional law. It won both House and Senate approval, and on March 3, 1825, President Monroe signed it in one of his last acts before leaving office. The new law filled gaps in federal jurisdiction and carried stiff penalties for many crimes.[54]

Of the several short speeches he gave in Congress during this session, Webster commented on a bill to extend the Cumberland Road, or National Road, as it was frequently called, from Wheeling in Virginia on the Ohio River to Zanesville, Ohio. The speech marked the public recognition that his nationalism now encompassed economic expansionism and that he fully endorsed Henry Clay's American System. President Madison had vetoed such a bill,[55] questioning its constitutionality. Webster did not agree. Road construction, he believed, would help provide a stronger and more united nation, which would

51. Ibid., 554.

52. Randolph had many targets, including John Quincy Adams, Henry Clay, John Holmes, and Edward Livingston. He pronounced Livingston "the contemptible and degraded of beings, whom no man ought to touch, unless with a pair of tongs." Poore, *Perley's Reminiscences*, p. 69.

53. Ibid.

54. *Register of Debates*, 18th Congress, 2d Session, pp. 150–158, 165–168, 335ff.

55. Webster had voted for the bill; he also voted to override the veto.

benefit all sections of the country, not simply the states through which the roads traversed. Speaking on January 18, 1825, before a packed house, he said he "wished to bring to the discussion a right feeling—that is, a feeling truly national."

This would be Webster's fundamental appeal for the rest of his life: the creation of a national, as opposed to a sectional or state, "feeling." As questions and issues that threatened the life of the Union arose over the next three decades, Webster rose to speak as an American who cared first and foremost about the good of the entire country—not Massachusetts and not New England.

When the National Road was initially authorized in 1806, he had declared, "Congress had virtually said to the people of the West" that it "should be carried on till it reached them all; and though it might not have said this in any formal act, yet it had virtually been given out in the speeches made on this floor. The people consider it as under pledge; and the present bill, in carrying on the road for eighty miles, does but carry Congress eighty miles further towards the redeeming of its pledge."[56]

But because of mounting concern about the constitutional question, the road only crept along with small allotments of money. It finally got to Vandalia, Illinois, in 1838 before halting altogether because of an economic depression and the competition of railroads.

Western settlers read with interest and appreciation the speech Webster gave before the House. Representative Joseph Vance of Ohio wrote to him shortly after the session ended to tell him about the wonderful reaction his speech on internal improvements had received among westerners. "Permit me to say that with our people no man in this nation stands on more elevated grounds."

What made the letter even more interesting was Vance's intimation that his constituents looked upon Webster as a likely future candidate for the presidency. "From the interest you took during the last congress in favour of some of the important measures of the West, you have not only a claim on the gratitude of this people, but are entitled to know the political feelings of this section of the union, both as it respects yourself personally, as well as those growing out of the late Presidential Election."[57]

No doubt Webster himself had long ago started to think about the possibility of someday winning the White House. Intensely ambitious all his life, never missing an opportunity to advance his interests, whether financial or political, and supremely confident of his ability to lead the country, especially to a greater awareness of its national purpose and destiny, he began to receive encouraging letters from various individuals from western and New England states. He modestly acknowledged some of these letters, but he had the good sense to try to conceal his true feelings. He usually waved off these tributes with a

56. *Register of Debates*, 18th Congress, 2d Session, pp. 249–252.
57. Vance to DW, March 29, 1825, in *PC*, II, 39.

comment about waiting to see what the future might bring.

When the Eighteenth Congress adjourned in March, Webster busied himself with his cases in the Supreme Court[58]—his appearances before the court attracted an increasingly large number of spectators—and then headed for home via Philadelphia and New York, where he stopped off to do some politicking. In Philadelphia he met with his old friend Joseph Hopkinson, and they talked about the state of the Federalist party and what they might expect from the new administration. Webster had in mind the writing of a history of the Federalist party from its origins through the Madison administrations. What he wanted was a work that would record the character and the principles of the party and its achievements. Since the materials for such a project were readily available at the time, he thought that the opportunity should not be missed to prepare such a work. He suggested as the writer Robert Walsh, Jr., whom he later contacted and finally got him to agree to do it.

Moving on to New York, he visited Jonathan Goodhue, a wealthy merchant, with whom he continued his discussion about the proposed history and how it would be subsidized. A private subscription seemed the best way to handle it, and after Webster returned home, he wrote and told Goodhue that he expected twenty men in the Boston area to contribute fifty dollars each. If twenty more in New York would contribute the same amount, they could launch the project. "This is all we wish," he declared. He wanted only a few individuals involved, and only "those of the most confidential character." About four thousand dollars were raised for Walsh to get him started, with the understanding that five thousand more would result from the sale of the book.

Webster also spoke with both Goodhue and Hopkinson about the recent presidential election, "in which he had taken a considerable share." He assured them that Adams would follow an "honorable course" in dealing with their party. It would appear that Webster meant to keep the interests of his party constantly before President Adams and gain the recognition, if he did not have it already, that he was its leader and spokesman.[59]

Unquestionably all these efforts were intended to help Webster move farther along the road to the White House. The history of the Federalist party would clarify and explain the principles on which he based his political career, principles the people would recognize as having imperishable value for the future of the nation. It was not enough to stand on a reputation of oratorical greatness. It was not enough to rest on his legal and constitutional superiority. He needed his opinions on important issues broadcast far and wide. A history would help, but he also needed a mouthpiece. Not surprisingly the *Massachusetts Journal*, whose chief purpose lay in promoting the political ambitions of

---

58. "While Congress remained in session," he told his brother, "I could not pay any attention to my business in the Court. In that I am now engaged." DW to Ezekiel Webster, March 8, 1825, ibid., II, 38.

59. Goodhue diary with its entry on April 1, 1825, quoted in *PC*, II, 47; DW to Goodhue, May 7, 1825, ibid., II, 48.

Daniel Webster, was founded shortly thereafter. It began publication on January 3, 1826, under the editorship of David L. Child. It ended in 1831.

Word of the project to write a history of the Federalist party eventually leaked to the press, which named Webster as the "instigator" of the idea.[60] But whether the implication that it was intended to advance his cause, or Walsh lost interest, or the subscriptions were never raised, the intended historical work, as far as can be determined, never materialized.[61]

Webster politicked in other areas as well. Through his brother and others he regularly intruded into New Hampshire's elections. He tried to get his brother elected to Congress but failed. Ezekiel lost by more than four thousand votes. Then he tried to win election to the U.S. Senate for his friend Jeremiah Mason and wrote a letter that was shown to the President asking that Adams "exercise influence" with his friends in the New Hampshire legislature. "I declined," reported Adams in his diary, "from a conviction that such interference would be not correct in principle, and unavailing in result—there being not the remotest chance of Mason's election. Webster himself ought to have seen this."[62]

Indeed. Webster frequently saw only what he wanted to see. In that sense his level of competence as a politician fell far below what it needed to be. In reaching for the presidency, he was reaching beyond his grasp, unless he could enlist the support of those more skillful in the political game than he.

The election of 1824 had split the nation into various factions, and disagreements among them had been exacerbated by the results of the House election in 1825. Many of Clay's friends deeply regretted that he had accepted the cabinet position because it "involved the awkward necessity of an explanation." And no matter how good the explanation, there lingered a suspicion, "and suspicion, they knew, often produced results as fatal to character as proven criminality."[63]

In an effort to bring about political harmony among these factions in Massachusetts, Webster gave a speech in Faneuil Hall on April 3. He told his audience that the "sentiment" that had brought about the meeting was an attempt to end factionalism and restore "union and conciliation." Differences of political opinion, he allowed, could be useful, "but these are very different things from organized and systematic party combination." New parties might arise in response to changing circumstances, but that was no reason to perpetuate "angry reflections on past differences." A new administration had commenced, one he believed rested on "the most liberal and conciliatory principles," as indicated by Adams's inaugural address. He did not believe there was a "corrupt bargain" and

60. *New Hampshire Patriot* for August 1, 1825, quoted ibid., II, 47.

61. There may have been difficulty raising money in New York because of the suspicion that the history was intended to "disparage the well earned fame of Col [Timothy] Pickering or Genl [Alexander] Hamilton." Webster vehemently denied this when he heard it. "It was to subserve no man's cause, nor to depress, on the other hand, any man's character," he told Goodhue, "that I wished the history of the Administration of the Govt. to be written." DW to Goodhue, July 30, 1825, ibid., II, 65.

62. Adams, *Memoirs*, VII, 14.

63. March, *Webster*, p. 72.

said that Clay's appointment had come about because of his talent and public service. He insisted that "a new era has arisen" and "if . . . we waste our strength in mutual crimination and recrimination concerning the past, we shall" do ourselves irreparable harm. Under the circumstances, therefore, with an approaching state election, he endorsed the formation of a "Union" ticket that would offer the electorate both Republicans and Federalists for governor and state senators.[64]

A Union ticket did in fact win the election but not without opposition from an all-Federalist slate of candidates, demonstrating that any attempt to create a party of amalgamated factions still ran into stiff resistance.

After tending to his legal business in Boston for the next month, Webster decided to go off with his son Fletcher on a short fishing trip on the Marshpee River in Barnstable County, where he could combine relaxation with a bit of work. He loved to fish for trout, and with the help of a local angler at Sandwich he found some of the best spots to cast his line. He was also good at the sport. In a single day he caught twenty-six trout each weighing over seven pounds. He said he had learned to follow this simple rule: *"careful & thorough* fishing of the difficult places, which others do not so fish."[65]

While on this brief vacation, when not fishing, Webster completed the composition of his famous Bunker Hill address, a speech that not only markedly swelled his national reputation but fully established his international reputation as well.[66]

Boston wished to commemorate the fiftieth anniversary of the Battle of Bunker Hill—the commemoration to take place on June 17, 1825—and an association had been formed to consider some "honorable and durable monument to the memory of the early friends of American Independence."[67] Webster had been elected president of the association, succeeding the first president, Governor John Brooks, who had died. The board of trustees unanimously agreed to ask Webster to deliver an appropriate address on the occasion of the laying of the cornerstone of the "honorable and durable monument." To add to the commemorative mood, General Lafayette, then touring the country to great acclaim, had accepted an invitation to be present at the ceremonies. A number of surviving participants of the battle would be present, and undoubtedly thousands would jam their way into the area around the monument.

Webster had doubts about whether he should give the address. The presence of revolutionary soldiers did not trouble him because he believed he knew how to talk to these men. His father and his father's friends had fought in the

64. *PS*, I, 170–174.

65. DW to Henry Cabot, June 4, 1825, in *PC*, II, 51–52.

66. In a letter to Webster written from France on December 28, 1825, Lafayette said, "Your Bunker Hill has been translated in French and other languages, to the very great profit of European readers." in Webster, ed., *Private Correspondence*, I, 400.

67. Webster's Bunker Hill oration can be found in *W&S*, I, 237–254. The design for the monument was crafted by the sculptor Horatio Greenough.

war, and Webster knew them and had spoken openly and freely to them. Several times he had conversed with General Stark, who teased him about his swarthy complexion. But the presence of Lafayette unnerved him. Before this icon he did not wish to appear or sound unworthy.

The other trustees assured him that the public expected him to do the honors. No one else could speak so well, and the country's great heroes deserved great oratory. So he agreed to do it.

It can be imagined what pressure and anxiety he experienced as he composed the address. During his fishing trip with Fletcher he frequently looked distracted and acted most peculiarly, as though his thoughts were a thousand miles away. He would let his line run carelessly down the stream, or he would hold his rod so that the hook did not reach the water. Several times his son alerted him to his hook hanging on a twig or caught in the long grass of the river. A few minutes later Webster stood staring at the overhanging trees. Then he advanced one foot, extended his right hand, and said in a loud voice, "Venerable men. . . ." His mind had become completely focused on the composition of the address.[68]

Day after day he worked feverishly on it. But it did not satisfy him. "I did the deed this morning, i.e. I finished my speech," he informed George Ticknor, "and I am pretty well persuaded it is a speech that will *finish* me, as far as reputation is concerned. There is no more tone in it than in the weather in which it has been written; It is 'perpetual dissolution and thaw.' "[69]

Fortunately the awful inclement weather that Bostonians had experienced in June changed abruptly. People prayed that June 17 would be a sunny day. "The Lord will not permit it to rain on that day," intoned one old man in Andover. Sure enough, the designated day for the ceremony dawned bright and clear and balmy. At dawn the roar of cannon summoned the citizenry to Bunker Hill. The previous day's showers had settled the dust and cooled the air. It was perfect.

The whole city came alive. People poured into the town from surrounding counties and beyond. The fact that Lafayette would be present brought out more than twenty thousand people. "Everything that has wheels and everything which has legs used them to get to Boston." A procession formed at the State House and headed toward Charlestown across the river. The honored veterans rode in carriages escorted by a military corps, followed by a military band, the Masonic fraternity in white aprons, blue scarfs, and banners, and Webster and the other trustees of the Bunker Hill Association. Lafayette rode in an open barouche, saluting the thousands who lined the streets and screamed his name. Churches opened their doors along the route, and women could be seen at the windows waving their handkerchiefs.

At the foot of the hill a stage had been erected for the orator and the trustees. Seats for the ladies present extended in a semicircle on each side of the

68. Fletcher Webster's note to a letter his father wrote him on June 12, 1847, in Webster, ed., *Private Correspondence*, II, 257.

69. DW to Ticknor, [June 15?, 1825], in *PC*, II, 54.

stage, which formed an amphitheater of sorts. Above them places had been reserved for the veterans. The people crowded around and behind them, finding seats as best they could.

A cannon sounded to signal the arrival of the procession. The cornerstone was laid on the other side of the hill with Lafayette assisting the operation. Those clustered near the stage could not see the cornerstone laying, but they could hear the "dirge to the memory of the dead" that followed. After about an hour the members of the procession came around the hill and took their designated places.

The veterans, their chests covered with badges and medals, were escorted by very young soldiers in brilliantly colored uniforms. Lafayette refused to sit in a pavilion for the governor, his staff, and distinguished guests. "No," he said, "I belong there among the survivors of the Revolution."

The ceremony began. Perfect silence accompanied the chaplain of Prescott's regiment, Joseph Thaxter, as he offered his thanksgiving. His aged voice shook as he spoke. Then the band played as the audience sang a hymn to the tune of "Old Hundred."

Now it was Webster's turn. He rose as the audience settled down to hear him. He looked magnificent. He bore himself with great dignity, as though he appreciated the fact that his physical appearance and mien would add to the solemnity of the occasion. "What a figurehead was there for the Ship of State!" wrote one observer. "No man . . . could be so great as this looked, and now he looked his very greatest." This commentator was at a loss for words, so he enlisted the aid of poets: "The front of Jove himself; an eye like Mars, to threaten and command." Below that, the "Atlantean shoulders, fit to bear the weight of mightiest monarchies." And if so, then those shoulders could also bear "the weight of that mightiest of republics, which was to throw them in the shade."

Webster began. But hardly had he opened his mouth when a sudden crash could be heard. Several women screamed. Men scrambled over seats and barriers that had collapsed and in their haste pulled down the awning protecting the ladies up front. Confusion ensued. "Some of the ladies almost fainted from alarm." Marshals, guards, and constables tried to restore order and shouted at the people to stay calm and in their places.

"It is impossible, sir, to restore order," one marshal informed Webster.

"Nothing is impossible, sir; let it be done."

With that Webster stepped forward and thundered a command to the other marshals. *"Be silent yourselves, and the people WILL obey!"* The marshal stared at him as Webster's piercing black eyes renewed his demand.[70]

The crowd quieted. Order was restored. The silence returned, and Webster began again. The great voice rolled out over the crowd and was distinctly heard by all. "Whether speaking in the open air, or under a roof," recorded one listener,

---

70. Quincy, *Figures of the Past,* pp. 115–116; George Ticknor's account of the occasion in Curtis, *Webster,* I, 248–249.

"he could make himself heard to a great distance, apparently without effort, and without being unpleasantly loud to those who were near him." This was partly due, suggested the listener, to the quality of his voice, which was naturally and properly placed. Also, he had a huge chest that could power his miraculous instrument. The sounds projected by Webster enveloped listeners. One felt engulfed in an uninterrupted stream of vocal music.[71]

As he spoke, he stared out at the crowd. Suddenly he experienced something like an anxiety attack or stage fright, but it was momentary and made the adrenaline flow faster and no doubt heightened his speaking effectiveness. "I never desire to behold again the awful spectacle of so many human faces all turned toward me," he remembered hours later. "As I looked at them, a strange idea came into my mind. I thought of what Effie Deans said, in contemplating her execution, that there would be 'seas of faces' looking up at her. There was, indeed, a sea of faces before me at that moment."[72]

He regained his composure after a few opening sentences and settled down to give one of the best-remembered orations of his life.

"We are among the sepulchres of our fathers," he intoned in big, fat, juicy sounds. "We are on ground, distinguished by their valor, their constancy, and the shedding of their blood. . . . We are Americans. We live in what may be called the early age of this great continent."

He then went on to trace the early history of the nation and how British contempt for American freedom had brought about the Revolution. At that point he paused. He looked at the veterans and addressed them directly.

VENERABLE MEN! you have come down to us from a former generation. Heaven has bounteously lengthened out your lives, that you might behold this joyous day. You are now where you stood fifty years ago, this very hour, with your brothers and your neighbors, shoulder to shoulder, in the strife for your country. Behold how altered! . . . God has granted you this sight of your country's happiness, ere you slumber in the grave. He has allowed you to behold and to partake the reward of your patriotic toils; and he has allowed us, your sons and countrymen, to meet you here, and in the name of the present generation, in the name of your country, in the name of liberty, to thank you!

But, alas! you are not all here. Time and sword have thinned your ranks. . . . [O]ur eyes seek for you in vain amid this broken band. . . . You lived at least long enough to know that your work has been nobly and successfully accomplished. You lived to see your country's independence established, and to sheathe your swords from war. . . .

The 17th of June saw the four New England colonies standing here, side by side, to triumph or to fall together; and there was with them from that moment to the end of the war, what I hope will remain with them for ever, one cause, one country, one heart.

Webster continued for several more minutes praising these heroes in the most extravagant language at his command. "Fortunate, fortunate man! with what measure of devotion will you not thank God for the circumstances of your extraordinary life. . . . Heaven saw fit to ordain, that the electric spark of liberty

71. Curtis, *Webster*, I, 249 note.

72. Quincy, *Figures of the Past*, pp. 117–118.

should be conducted, through you, from the New World to the Old; and we, who are now here to perform this duty of patriotism, have all of us long ago received it in charge from our fathers to cherish your name and your virtues."

He continued by outlining the fantastic developments in the country over the past fifty years, how the nation had grown in size, in productivity, and especially in advancing the cause of liberty. He closed with a noble utterance:

> Those who established our liberty and our government are daily dropping from among us. The great trust now descends to new hands. . . . We can win no laurels in a war for independence. Earlier and worthier hands have gathered them all. . . . But there remains to us a great duty of defence and preservation, and there is open to us, also, a noble pursuit, to which the spirit of the times strongly invites. Our proper business is improvement. Let our age be the age of improvement. . . . Let us cultivate a true spirit of union and harmony. . . . Let us act under a settled conviction, and an habitual feeling, that these twenty-four States are one country. . . . Let our object be, OUR COUNTRY, OUR WHOLE COUNTRY, AND NOTHING BUT OUR COUNTRY. And, by the blessing of God, may that country itself become a vast and splendid monument, not of oppression and terror, but of Wisdom, of Peace, and of Liberty, upon which the world may gaze with admiration for ever![73]

As he concluded, the audience, with one voice, let out a great shout of praise that went on minute after minute. "The address brought tears into the eyes of many," reported George Ticknor, "and bowed down the heads of the veterans themselves to conceal their emotion." The former governor of Virginia, James Barbour, turned to Ticknor and exclaimed, "If that address had been delivered in Virginia, I should say that the person who made it was sure of the first prize in the national lottery."[74]

The applause, shouting, and cheering continued until exhaustion set in. Hundreds of people charged the platform and surrounded Webster and told him what his address had meant to them. Surely Webster knew from these expressions and the wave upon wave of spontaneous delight that had erupted from the crowd that he had scored a tremendous success. Whatever doubts he may have entertained about his ability to do justice to the occasion should have been swept away with the noise of approval that engulfed him.

Those still seated marveled at what they heard. They sat stunned. Those all over the country and abroad who read the speech, after Webster had edited and polished it,[75] recognized that it had emanated from the nation's, if not the world's, greatest living orator, bar none.

There were other great speakers in the country at that time, but none in Webster's class. Henry Clay is a good example. He was a superb speaker and a better debater than Webster. But Clay's speeches, for the most part, dealt solely with current issues, and he gave no thought or time to editing them for the

73. *W&S*, I, 235–254.

74. Curtis, *Webster*, I, 249.

75. The address was published almost immediately. Webster gave it to the Bunker Hill Association, and the copyright was sold for three hundred dollars to Hilliard & Gray. Ibid., 250.

enjoyment of later generations. Not only did Webster care about what he left behind as a record of his oratorical prowess, but unlike others, he frequently gave speeches that dealt with timeless themes and, like the present circumstance, with a glorious moment in the nation's history. He commemorated those events and the lives of the individuals who had contributed to the establishment of the Republic. And he never failed to sound the nationalist chord of union, of "our country, our whole country, and nothing but our country."

Added to the overall impact of the oration was the magnificent physical presence of "the Godlike" himself. He stood before his audience looking as grand and impressive as the events he narrated.

Here was another oration that instructed Americans about their past. It was history vividly and majestically presented, and like the Plymouth oration in 1821, it was taught and memorized in schools throughout the nation.

These great orations did much to dispel the belief around the country that New England was an isolated region of secessionists, a land of penny-pinching Yankees, conniving traders, and puritanical ministers preaching hellfire sermons to self-righteous bigots. Webster, in the course of his lifetime, helped convince a skeptical nation at large that nationalism, not self-interest and certainly not secession, dominated the New England soul.

When the tumult finally subsided, a dinner was served to four thousand guests under a pavilion on the summit of the hill. Many toasts were made, among them Webster's and Lafayette's, but little could be heard because of the noise and confusion of feeding so many people at once.

That evening Webster held a reception at his home on Summer Street, and Josiah Quincy claimed that "there was never a more brilliant and interesting private party given in Boston."[76] Colonel Israel Thorndike, a shipowner reputed to be the richest man in New England, lived next door, and he cut through the brick walls that separated the two houses to create a passageway so that the many guests attending the party could have more breathing space and more room to socialize. Both houses were brilliantly illuminated, and a band played outside.

Webster and his wife received their guests and the ecstatic comments about the address "with great dignity and simplicity," said Quincy. Grace reveled in the adulation shown her husband but had the good sense not to show it. She displayed not "the slightest symptom of vanity or elation." Everyone spoke approvingly about the unassuming serenity of their hosts in the midst of unstinting praise.

Only in America could republican virtues flourish so successfully, thought Quincy. Only in America could the "intellect of the community" live in one house and be "backed by its purse" living right next door.[77]

76. Quincy, *Figures of the Past*, p. 117.

77. Ibid., pp. 117–118.

14

The "Godlike Daniel"

DANIEL and Grace took a much-needed rest after the Bunker Hill ceremonies by visiting Niagara Falls. Accompanied by their friends Joseph
Story and his wife, Sarah, and Eliza Buckminster, they traveled across the countryside by coach and, when they reached the Erie Canal, on boat.[1] They left
Boston on June 25 at nine in the morning, stopped off to pay their respect to
Governor Levi Lincoln, visited a Shaker village near Lebanon Spring, hastily
toured Albany, and explored the Catskill Mountains. They stopped for two hours
at Auburn, New York, to visit the state prison, the largest in the United States,
whose reputation for modern methods of incarceration attracted international
attention. They finally arrived at Niagara a little after sunset on Wednesday, July
13, after spending the better part of two days in the "very pretty village" of
Buffalo.[2]

Like most people who have seen the great falls, Webster was clearly overwhelmed by the staggering beauty of this natural phenomenon. He wrote a very
long letter describing in minute detail what he saw to his friend Mrs. George
Blake, who also lived on Summer Street and whose husband was the U.S.
attorney for Massachusetts and Webster's frequent fishing and hunting companion. Much of the description is matter-of-fact and technical, but occasionally his
emotions commanded his language. "As we stood to-day at noon, on the pro-
jecting point of Table Rock," he narrated, "we looked over into this abyss, and
far beneath our feet, arched over this tremendous aggregate of water, foam, and
vapor, we saw a perfect and radiant rainbow. This ornament of heaven does not
seem out of place, in being half-way up the sheet of the glorious cataract. It
looked as if the skies themselves paid homage to this stupendous work of nature." But he knew his words could not do the falls justice. "It must be seen," he
said; "it is something which speaks to the senses; no description can set it forth."[3]

The party left the falls on Sunday, July 17, for Rochester, then went on to
Syracuse to see the famous saltworks, after which they stopped at Schenectady

1. The Erie Canal was not completed until October 1825.

2. Joseph Story to William Pettyplace, July 14, 1825, in Story, *Life and Letters*, I, 467–468.

3. DW to Mrs. Blake, July 15, 1825, in *PC*, II, 385–392. See also Story's letters about the trip in
Story, *Life and Letters*, I, 449–481.

and proceeded through Bennington to Brattleboro in Vermont to take the most direct stage route to Boston. They arrived back home on Thursday, July 28.

By that time "the country was ringing with the power of the oration" at Bunker Hill.[4] James Madison wrote Webster that the address "merits all the praise which has been bestowed on it; and I tender you many thanks for the pleasure it has afforded me."[5] The only serious complaint about the oration that Webster heard was its failure to mention slavery.[6] Other than that there was nothing but universal applause. In giving splendid voice to the pride and love the American people felt for their revolutionary past, he had achieved a stature as an orator that no one else even approached for the remainder of his life.

The family spent the rest of the summer and early fall in Sandwich on Cape Cod, where they stayed at a boardinghouse. Webster filled his days with fishing, swimming, and tramping through the marshes to hunt. It helped refresh him after the rather exhausting, albeit exhilarating, trip to Niagara Falls.

However, he did not neglect his legal work. It had grown tremendously because of his steadily expanding eminence and reputation as a speaker and party leader and, of course, the success of his Spanish claims cases.[7] And the money came rolling in and rolling right out again. More and more he relied on Alexander Bliss, his associate, to handle day-to-day operations.

Webster decided to take his family to Washington to attend the first session of the Nineteenth Congress, and they arrived in the capital shortly before the first of December. They joined the mess at John Coyle's on Capitol Hill, where George Blake and his wife also resided. Fletcher remained in school in Boston and stayed with Dr. Sewall.[8] Because Webster lived close to the Library of Congress, he helped put out a fire that broke out in the library on December 22. In reporting the near disaster, the newspapers noticed his presence, but they did not mention that his efforts gave him an awful headache.[9]

Like so many previous sessions—and many more to come—the first session of the Nineteenth Congress produced more talk and little action. It was a *"talking"* winter," Webster reported.[10] And the talk continued into the spring, when the members adjourned. He enjoyed the praise he received from his colleagues who had read his Bunker Hill address, and as several representatives, both

4. George Ticknor, quoted in Curtis, *Webster,* I, 250.

5. Madison to Webster, August 12, 1825, in Webster, ed., *Private Correspondence,* I, 396.

6. See a letter from "Acacius" to Webster, July 1825, in *PC,* II, 66–69.

7. Inevitably Webster's success with the Spanish claims attracted clients with claims against France and other European countries. Five wealthy New Yorkers, for example, solicited his help. See Frederick de Payster, Charles King, George Griswold, Philip Kearney, and Elisha Tibbits to DW, April 12, 1826, in *PC,* II, 101–102.

8. DW to Ezekiel Webster, January 29, 1826, in *W&S,* XVII, 402.

9. Grace Webster to Mrs. Ticknor, December 24, 1825, in Curtis, *Webster,* I, 257.

10. "Upon the whole," Webster reported toward the end of the session, "it has not been a session in which we have dispatched many concerns of great moment." DW to Denison, May 3, 1826, ibid., I, 270.

John C. Calhoun, who together with Clay and Webster constituted the celebrated Great Triumvirate, possessed a sharp, analytical mind. His dark, staring eyes, excellently portrayed here by George P. A. Healy, riveted his audience with their intensity. (Courtesy of the National Portrait Gallery, Washington, D.C.)

Henry Clay, the greatest Speaker in the history of the House of Representatives, rivaled Webster in his ambition to win the presidency. Unfortunately the two men would not cooperate with one another and both suffered as a consequence. This daguerreotype was taken during the final years of his life. (Courtesy of the National Portrait Gallery, Washington, D.C.)

Thomas Hart Benton, President Jackson's principal spokesman in the Senate, whose sometimes aimless, nonsensical, and protracted oratory alternately outraged and amused Webster. Portrait by Ferdinand T. L. Boyle. (Courtesy of the National Portrait Gallery, Washington, D.C.)

The dour, dyspeptic-looking John Quincy Adams was one of Webster's bitterest critics. He kept an almost daily account of his own thoughts and activities and ceaselessly recorded Black Dan's shortcomings and moral failings. Portrait by George Caleb Bingham. (Courtesy of the Library of Congress)

Grace Webster regarded Andrew Jackson as the most presidential-looking of the four candidates running in the 1824 election. This portrait of him certainly bears out that opinion. (Courtesy of the Office of the Curator, the White House)

The mass resignation of Jackson's cabinet in 1831 was ridiculed in this popular cartoon. The four members of the cabinet who resigned their office are represented by the rats scurrying from Jackson's "Falling House." (Courtesy of the Tennessee State Library and Archives, Nashville)

Daniel Webster had this portrait painted by Chester Harding shortly after he debated Robert Y. Hayne in 1830. Harding heard the debate and said "he could not keep his seat" and stood "on tiptoe from beginning to end." Like Sarah Goodridge, Harding enjoyed a close relationship with Webster and painted him several times. (Courtesy of the Hood Museum of Art, Dartmouth College, gift of T. M. Evans)

Webster addresses the Senate in this lithograph by James M. Edney, dressed in his customary garb of brass-buttoned, blue dress-coat, a buff waistcoat, and a high cravat. (Courtesy of the Graphic Arts Collection, U.S. Senate)

Webster's historic desk (desk XXIX) in the U.S. Senate is the only one of its kind in the chamber. Among other things it is smaller and raised at the base to appear of equal height with the desks of other senators. (Courtesy of the U.S. Senate Commission on Art)

Interior of Webster's desk where the names of the senators who have occupied the desk, starting with Webster, have been carved into the wood, some by the senators themselves. (Courtesy of the U.S. Senate Commission on Art)

Self-portrait of Sarah Goodridge at age forty-two. She painted Webster and members of his family many times and had a very close relationship with him. (Courtesy of the Museum of Fine Arts, Boston, gift of Miss Harriet Sarah Walker)

This watercolor-on-ivory miniature of Webster by Sarah Goodridge was painted around the time that she visited Webster in Washington following the death of his first wife. (Courtesy of the Massachusetts Historical Society)

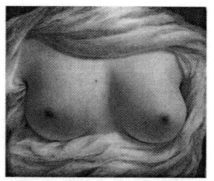

"Beauty Revealed," a self-portrait by Sarah Goodrich, was presented by her to Webster and inscribed "1828" on a paper backing. This miniature watercolor on ivory, along with Goodridge's easel and paint box, was passed down by members of the Webster family and sold in 1981. (From the collection of Gloria Manney, courtesy of the Metropolitan Museum of Art in New York)

Federalists and "democrats," agreed, "no man is listened to in debate with such attention. No man is so certain to convince his hearers and no man is so sure to carry the house with him." He "expresses himself with great strength and power in the most simple unadorned language," said one critic. "He would I think in any age and in any country be denominated a great man."[11]

The Nineteenth Congress began with the reading of President Adams's first message, a breathtakingly original and imaginative paper that proposed a program of national development that horrified states' rights advocates. Rooted in the ideas of Henry Clay's American System, the message recommended the building of a vast system of federally sponsored public works, such as roads, canals, bridges, and harbor and waterway installations; the exploration of the northwestern coast; the creation of a national university and an astronomical observatory; and the establishment of a uniformed standard of weights and measures. It also announced that a congress of Latin American countries had been proposed to meet in Panama to deliberate on matters of mutual concern. The United States had been invited to attend, and Adams had accepted the invitation. He stated that he would shortly name the ministers to represent the United States in Panama.[12]

The friends of William Crawford, led by Senator Van Buren, gasped when they heard these proposals. Strongly committed to the most conservative states' rights principles of the Republican party, they regarded the message as an affront. "The message of the President," sputtered Senator Nathaniel Macon, "seems to claim all the power to the federal Government."[13] Southern slaveholders, as a group, frantically worried about what the congress in Panama might do. The very idea of U.S. ministers sitting in the same room with black Haitians and possibly discussing the slavery question infuriated them. They simply would not have it. "An issue has been fairly made, as it seems to me," stormed Vice President Calhoun, "between *power* and *liberty*."[14] Back in Tennessee Andrew Jackson hated the idea of the conference. "The moment we engage in confederations, or alliances with any nation," he cautioned, "we may from that time date the down fall of our republic."[15]

As a consequence the message went a long way toward furthering party realignment. The old republicans of the Jeffersonian persuasion were lining up behind Andrew Jackson and restructuring their organization to include the supporters of Crawford and Calhoun. They even attracted some Federalists who were captivated by Jackson's charisma and popular appeal. As Senator Thomas Hart Benton of Missouri later noted, the message "went to the construction of

11. John Davis to George Bancroft, January 29, 1826, in *PC*, II, 80–81.

12. Richardson, *Messages and Papers*, II, 878–879, 881–882.

13. Macon to B. Yancey, December 8, 1825, in Edwin M. Wilson, *The Congressional Career of Nathaniel Macon* (Chapel Hill, 1900), p.76.

14. Calhoun to Jackson, June 4, 1826, in *Calhoun Papers*, X, 110.

15. Jackson to John Branch, March 3, 1826, Branch Family Papers, Southern Historical Collection, University of North Carolina, Chapel Hill.

parties on the old line of strict . . . construction of the constitution."[16]

Once Adams sent to the Senate for confirmation the nominations of John Sergeant of Pennsylvania and Richard C. Anderson of Kentucky to attend the Panama Congress, a heated debate immediately erupted. Webster watched the furor with keen interest, and he recognized at once what was happening. "The importance of the matter [of Panama] arises mainly from the *dead set* made against it, in the opposition. I am afraid my friend Calhoun organized & arranged the opposition. *He expected to defeat the measure.*" For his part, Clay suspected Van Buren as the organizer and arranger.[17] Fortunately for the administration, these "conspirators" failed in their efforts to scuttle the nominations, and on March 14, 1826, Sergeant and Anderson won confirmation.

The opposition in the House added its bit of nastiness by calling on the President to submit all the papers relating to the mission. Adams delayed responding, and the House retaliated by engaging in a long, acrimonious debate over the appropriations for the mission. Webster led the administration forces in defending the proposed bill and described the Panama Congress as an attempt to create a great "American family of nations," which indeed was one of its purposes. Not until April 22, 1826, did the House finally pass the appropriations bill, 134 to 60. The Senate gave its approval on May 3 by a vote of 23 to 19, and the President signed it on May 4.[18] Unfortunately this victory ended in defeat for the administration when Anderson died on his way to the conference and Sergeant did not arrive in Panama until after the conference had adjourned.

The voting on the Panama question showed that the administration commanded a majority in both houses of Congress, but it also showed the presence of a well-organized minority ready to oppose any measure put forward by the administration. The northeastern states and Kentucky regularly supported the President, but Louisiana, Tennessee, and Alabama, said Webster, do whatever Andrew Jackson and his henchmen decree. The Crawford men in Georgia lean toward General Jackson, but North Carolina and Virginia appear divided. Pennsylvania and New Jersey, he reported, seem to have gotten over their Jackson craze, and if New York and New England remain "steady," the administration forces could hold their own. "The truth is," he informed Jeremiah Mason, "that Mr. Adams will be opposed, by all the Atlantic States, south of Maryland. *So would any other northern man.* They will never acquiesce in the administration of any President on our side [of] the Potomac. . . . The perpetual alarm, which is kept up on the subject of negro slavery has its object. It is to keep the South united, & all jealous of the North."[19]

16. Benton, *Thirty Years' View*, I, 54.

17. DW to Jeremiah Mason, March 27, 1826, in *PC*, II, 98; Clay to Peter B. Porter, February 22, 1825, Porter Papers, Buffalo Historical Society; Clay to Francis Brooke, February 20, 1826, in Clay, *Papers*, V, 117–118.

18. *Register of Debates*, 19th Congress, 1st Session, pp. 461, 291.

19. DW to Mason, March 27, 1826, in *PC*, II, 99.

Sadly, the beast of sectionalism had reared its hoary head, and even Webster fell victim. As far as he could see, the politics of the present and possibly the future centered predominantly on sectional rivalry. And slavery was one of the motivating forces behind it.

Webster also suffered defeat after an apparent victory when he attempted to reform the federal judiciary system. As chairman of the Judiciary Committee he felt a keen responsibility not only to improve and update a system that had been virtually in place since the passage of the first Judiciary Act in 1789[20] but to make certain that the judicial process extended to every part of a rapidly expanding country. The docket of the Supreme Court was overloaded, the backlog of cases mounted each year, and although many western states had been added to the Union, the number of federal courts had remained virtually unchanged.[21]

In preparing the reform bill, Webster, as usual, consulted with Joseph Story. He told Story that he would like to appoint three or four circuit judges in the West and a circuit judge "contingently" in the East. His object: to require all Supreme Court judges to perform some circuit duty, with the other circuit judges taking up the slack. To this end he would add two western judges to the Supreme Court. "Is this a right object?" he asked Story. "If it be, tell me how I shall accomplish it. . . . Pray sit down, think, and write." He also sought advice from his friend in New Hampshire Jeremiah Mason. He sped up his work schedule because he wanted to have a bill ready for the House to consider early in the new year.[22]

Less than two weeks later he went to see President Adams and invited his counsel. He said that the one question dividing the committee concerned increasing the number of justices to sit on the Supreme Court. Some members wanted two additional seats; others opted for three. Adams wisely reminded Webster that adding three would produce ten justices resulting in many tie votes. Webster agreed. Then he mentioned that some members of the committee and others in the House feared the consequence of appointing western judges to the Supreme Court. They feared "the judge-breaking temper now prevailing in some parts of the Western county." Adams assured him that this spirit was subsiding and that such judges as John McLean of Ohio, the present postmaster general, and Senator Hugh Lawson White of Tennessee, could fill the post admirably. Again Webster agreed and said he would urge the committee to increase the court by two justices unless the committee resisted and insisted on three.

As Webster rose to leave, Adams pointedly invited him "to come and spend

20. Reform of the Judiciary Act of 1789 had been enacted in 1801, but it was repealed in 1802.

21. There were twenty-four states in 1825. Of federal courts, apart from the Supreme Court, there were thirty district courts and seven circuit court. All the circuit courts were located in the East, save one: the circuit for Ohio, Kentucky, and Tennessee. Each of the seven circuit courts was presided over by one of the seven justices of the Supreme Court.

22. DW to Story, December 26, 1825, in *W&S*, XVII, 412–413.

the evening with me whenever it might suit his leisure and convenience."[23]

Within a week Webster reported the new bill. Three more western circuits were created to be manned by three additional justices to the Supreme Court.[24] The ten justices would be distributed among ten circuits to encompass the entire country. The House opened debate on the bill in early January 1826, and Webster gave a spirited speech in its favor, declaring that despite some limitations, he believed that this bill, and only this bill, could pass Congress.[25]

Not true, cried the opposition, led by Charles F. Mercer of Virginia. The Supreme Court should be smaller, not larger, he declared, and it should be relieved of its circuit duties. That way the logjam in the High Court would be broken.[26]

Webster stood his ground. He yielded nothing. He remained in absolute control of his bill. And it passed the House overwhelmingly, once the Panama mission had cleared.[27]

But the Jacksonians did not give up. In the Senate Martin Van Buren interrupted his busy schedule in organizing the new Jackson party and steered a similar judicial bill through the upper house. It differed from the House bill, however, in one respect: It included Kentucky and Ohio in one western circuit and Indiana, Illinois, and Missouri in the other. Webster's bill linked Kentucky with Missouri and Ohio with Indiana and Illinois. Van Buren's object was to block the appointment of Adams's postmaster general, John McLean of Ohio, to the Supreme Court; this could be done because the High Court already had a member from Kentucky. He convinced the Senate not to yield on the distribution of the circuits. Nor would Webster's committee yield. Van Buren accused Webster of "Yankee craft" and told his political machine in New York, the Albany Regency, that "unless they can have a Judge in Kentucky (who is already appointed) and one in Ohio also, they wish to defeat the bill, in hopes of getting a better one next year. The great object is to get McLean out of the Post Office which can only be effected by his promotion, as they dare not displace him." It was obvious to Van Buren and a good many others that the reason the administration wanted to get rid of McLean was his underhanded support of Jackson.[28]

The Senate not only held to its own bill but refused to discuss the question with the House in conference. Many Jacksonians, of course, were dead set against giving Adams the opportunity of appointing three new justices. So the bill died. Although he himself would have compromised with the Senate

23. Adams, *Memoirs*, VII, 83–84.

24. "I was for two judges," Webster told Joseph Story, "but a majority of the committee were for three." December 31, 1825, in *W&S*, XVII, 400.

25. *Register of Debates*, 19th Congress, 1st Session, pp. 872–880. Webster spoke on January 25, three weeks after the bill had been introduced.

26. Ibid., pp. 890–892.

27. Ibid., pp. 1148–1149.

28. Van Buren to Benjamin F. Butler, May 15, 1826, Van Buren Papers, LC. President Jackson appointed McLean to the Supreme Court in 1829.

on that one issue, Webster's committee would not.[29]

Adams and Webster suffered still another defeat over the administration's treatment of the Indians, an issue that developed when Georgia renewed its efforts to despoil the Creek Nation. The President negotiated a treaty with the tribe by which the Creeks would cede their land in Georgia with the exception of a strip west of the Chattahoochee River. The governor of the state, George M. Troup, strenuously objected to the exception and threatened to use his militia if the terms of the treaty were carried out. In the House Webster warned against resisting the execution of a treaty of the United States. "If we have bound ourselves by any treaty to do certain things," he declared, "we must fulfil such obligations. . . . For myself, the right of the parties in this question shall be fully and fairly examined, and none of them with more calmness than the rights of Georgia."[30]

Not that Webster had any great sympathy for the Indians and their way of life or culture. He told George Ticknor that "I am a total unbeliever in the new doctrines about the Indian languages. I believe them to be the rudest forms of speech; and I believe there is as little in the languages of the tribes as in their laws, manners, and customs, worth studying or worth knowing. All this is heresy, I know, but so I think."[31]

The Senate, with its stronger contingent of Jacksonians, appointed a committee headed by Thomas Hart Benton to investigate the Adams-Troup conflict, and as expected, the committee's final report faulted the government for its unwarranted interference in Georgia's internal affairs. The southern states were determined to exercise total control over the Indians living within their borders, and they turned to Jackson in the approaching presidential contest to help them achieve their goal.[32]

One unpleasant event occurred during the session when John Randolph, now a member of the Senate, gave a particularly vicious speech in which he contrasted the alliance between Adams and Clay as "the coalition of Blifil and Black-George."[33] Vice President Calhoun did nothing to stop him, and so, Webster reported, "he talks on, for two, four, & sometimes *six* hours at a time; saying whatever occurs to him, on all subjects." In rage Clay called him out, and the duel took place across the Potomac in Virginia on April 8, 1826. Fortunately neither man was hurt, although Clay put a bullet through Randolph's coat very near his hip.[34]

29. DW to Jeremiah Mason, May 2, 1826, in *PC*, II, 106. Webster supposed that the opposition "did not wish to give so many important appointments to the President." No doubt he was correct. DW to Story, May 8, 1826, in *PC*, II, 113.

30. *Register of Debates*, 19th Congress, 2d Session, pp. 937–938, 1034–1036, 1046–1048.

31. DW to Ticknor, March 1, 1826, quoted in Curtis, *Webster*, I, 260.

32. Robert V. Remini, *The Election of Andrew Jackson* (New York, 1963), pp. 75–76.

33. These two scoundrels are characters in Henry Fielding's novel *Tom Jones*.

34. DW to John Denison, May 3, 1826, in *PC*, II, 107. For a detailed account of the duel, see Remini, *Clay*, pp. 292–295.

Although this first session of the Nineteenth Congress ended with no decisions on questions of "great moment," to use Webster's expression, one pivotal
event had begun to take shape that would have a profound effect on the future:
the realignment of political parties. Out of a four-faction contest in 1824 some
semblance of a two-party system was beginning to emerge: the administration
forces and the friends of Andrew Jackson.

The Jacksonians during this winter session had initiated a systematic assault
on the administration, opposing virtually every measure put forward by the
President and his supporters. They also began organizing their forces, winning
recruits from the various personal factions that had existed since the 1824 election. Some recruits joined because they recognized that General Jackson had
widespread support among the masses. Moreover, they believed he had been
"cheated" of the presidency by a "corrupt bargain" between "Blifil and Black-
George" in the House election. These opponents, to Webster's disappointment,
included Calhoun and his friends. They also included the states' rights supporters of William H. Crawford because of the horror they felt over the proposals by
the President in his December 6 message to Congress. Adams's program of
internal improvements, if enacted, would grievously violate the Constitution,
according to these conservatives, and further consolidate the central government. And stupidly the President, in his message, had invited Congress to enact
his program and not be "palsied by the will of our constituents."[35]

Politicians shook their heads in disbelief over this blunder. Adams sounded
like an elitist, an autocrat who despised republican institutions. Some opponents
even predicted that the presidential election in 1828 would undoubtedly be
"considered by the sound planters, farmers & mechanics of the country, as a
great contest between the *aristocracy* and democracy of America."[36]

If so, Webster's position could never be in doubt. He had been fighting for
years against "democrats" in his effort to preserve and protect the great principles of the Federalist party. Not only did he support the administration, but he
commanded its forces in the House. He dined regularly with Adams and Clay,
gave his advice, listened to their suggestions, and carried them out as best he
could in Congress. Clay frequently asked Webster in the name of the President
to perform some legislative service. "We really desire that you should . . . take
up Mr. H's resolution and pass it for him to day" went one such request. It would
tend to "spur" the Senate into action, Clay continued, and the "Senate wants a
spur."[37] According to the President, Webster had consulted with Clay from
almost the first day he had arrived in Washington in December.[38]

Webster's preeminent position as the administration's leader in Congress

35. Richardson, *Messages and Papers*, II, 866–968, 872, 879, 882.

36. Edward P. Gaines to Andrew Jackson, [1826], Jackson Papers, LC.

37. Clay to DW, no date, Clay, *Papers*, V, 81–82. Clay was referring to James Hamilton's resolution
concerning the Panama mission.

38. Adams, *Memoirs*, VII, 73.

delighted his constituents in Boston. "I have an idea," remarked the chief justice of the state, Isaac Parker, "that you have become . . . the Premier in the House of Commons."[39] Of course, Webster saw to it that his efforts were brought to the attention of his constituents as well as to important individuals around the country and abroad. His speeches were regularly dispatched from his office.[40] He also considered touring the West to advance the administration's cause (and his own), and he apparently discussed it with Congressman Francis Johnson of Kentucky. On returning home in May, Johnson wrote to tell him that "you are enquired after by the people, with interest—your rising, and conspicuously rising popularity in this country" has even alarmed the opposition, and they "*belabor* you very much" in an effort to put you down with accusations that "you were of the Hartford Convention. . . . Your course in Congress and your doctrine are admired and approved, and should you make the contemplated visit to this Country next summer, you will meet with many friends, whom you never saw. Your speech has silenced all opposition to the Panama Mission."[41]

As his sense of his role as a leader increased, Webster began a regular correspondence with Federalists in other sections of the nation to encourage their support of the administration and turn away from the Jacksonians. He told them that Adams's "feelings & purposes are extremely good. Be assured," he wrote to William Gaston, a Federalist and former member of Congress from North Carolina, "there is nothing in him of narrowness, or illiberality, or local prejudice. The South, I very much fear, means to quarrel with him, right or wrong." Webster really resented the fact that the friends of Jackson, as one of the reasons for their opposition, charged "*a tendency, in Mr Adams, to stand well with Federalists,*" as though any number of Federalists had not joined the opposition. Even after Congress had adjourned, Webster remained at his desk writing his old party friends, trying to convince them not to turn to the general.[42]

With the adjournment of Congress in early May, Webster also delayed his departure for home to attend to some legal matters. It meant suffering the heat and humidity that had started to rise in the capital, but he had no choice. He usually argued five cases before the High Court during its February session, although this term he argued seven. He also had business dealings with the Bank of the United States. Nicholas Biddle, the president of the BUS, had engaged him as a consultant and attorney and later arranged his election as a director of the Bank.[43] By 1825 Webster's income had taken a decided climb upward. Even

39. Parker to DW, February 12, 1826, in *PC*, II, 84.

40. See, for example, James Madison to DW, March 27, 1826, and John Marshall to DW, April 3, May 20, 1826, ibid., II, 100, 114.

41. Johnson to DW, July 7, 1826, ibid., II, 122.

42. DW to Gaston, May 31, 1826, ibid., II, 117.

43. Biddle to DW, January 2, 1827, ibid., 145. Webster feared he could not render much assistance as a director because he did not reside in Philadelphia. But he accepted the post under the supposition that "once or twice a year is as often as you desire the presence of the distant Directors." DW to Biddle, January 6, 1827, ibid., II, 146.

so, his youthful apprehension about money never subsided. He was especially conscious of anyone who might try to take advantage of him. "Several persons have written me to be concerned in their causes," he informed his associate Alexander Bliss, "whom I have referred to you, telling them that *I am retained when I am* RETAINED. I do not learn whether any of them have deposited the needful." Depositing the "needful" was expected of both the high and low, and more than once he had to remind Nicholas Biddle that his retainer needed to be "renewed or *refreshed* as usual."[44]

For the most part Webster rather liked Biddle and everything he possessed: name, position, money, education, taste, literary interests, and intelligence. A strikingly handsome man with an oval-shaped face, high forehead, fair complexion, and a distinctly aristocratic bearing, Biddle was born into a well-to-do Philadelphia family and graduated from Princeton at the age of fifteen. He practiced law and won election to the Pennsylvania legislature before being appointed by President Monroe to the Bank's board of directors. In 1823 he was elevated to the position of president. Passionate about classical art, he helped introduce and advance the Greek Revival in American architecture in the antebellum era. Webster had a devoted friend in Nicholas Biddle, who came to his financial aid on numerous occasions.

The congressman finally returned to Boston in late May in order to get back in time for the second week of the sitting of the circuit court. When he arrived, he learned that James Lloyd had resigned his seat in the U.S. Senate, and it was "intimated" to him that he could succeed Lloyd if he wished. "But my impression at present is against it," he told Henry Clay, "& I believe for very good reasons." One good reason was the fact that it was a vacancy to complete Lloyd's term, whereas Elijah Hunt Mills's term in the U.S. Senate was to expire the next March and his replacement would be elected by the legislature for six years. Clay responded immediately and assured him that "you acted wisely, for yourself and the Country, in deciding to remain where you are." There would be obvious advantages if Webster took a Senate seat, but some too would be "lost by your leaving the House. You could not have taken, during the whole of the first Session of your Service in the Senate, the strong and commanding ground which you now occupy in the house."

To replace Lloyd, the legislature ultimately chose a merchant, Nathaniel Silsbee, whom Webster described as "well disposed" (presumably toward the Adams administration), well informed, and quite "respectable." However, Webster did not expect him to participate very much in Senate debates.[45]

As for his own situation, Webster would simply bide his time, continue his role as leader of the administration forces in the House, and attend to his lucrative law practice. And like everyone else in the country, he looked forward to the celebrations that were to be held all over the country on July 4 to mark the fiftieth anniversary of the signing of the Declaration of Independence.

44. DW to Biddle, December 21, 1833, Biddle Papers, LC.
45. DW to Clay, June 8, 1826, Clay to DW, June 14, 1826, in *PC*, II, 118–119.

That great day arrived to the cheers, parades, speeches, barbecues, and other festive ceremonies that helped a grateful nation commemorate its liberation from Great Britain. Then came the shattering news that two revolutionary leaders and former Presidents of the United States, John Adams and Thomas Jefferson, had died, and remarkably, both on July 4, 1826. It was, declared some, as though a sign had been sent from on high to remind Americans that there once strode across the land two mighty statesman and that their kind would probably never appear again. The shock was overwhelming. Suddenly joy had turned to grief. Public and private buildings were draped in black crepe; black stripes bordered newspaper columns; the churches opened their doors to mourners and kept them open throughout the day, and preachers gave long, heartrending sermons about these two extraordinary statesmen and what they had contributed to the freedom and happiness of the nation.

Naturally the city council of Boston decided that a eulogy should be delivered, one in a public forum. And the members never doubted who would provide it. Daniel Webster was their unanimous choice, and they invited him to deliver it on August 2 in Faneuil Hall. The time for the preparation of such a commemoration was short, so short in fact that Webster himself was unsure if he could do it. But Joseph Story and others insisted that he was the only man in the country capable of doing these two remarkable men full justice. "My own judgt," wrote Story, "is that you must & ought to deliver it." He went on to say that it should be a *"State affair,"* not "a mere council affair," so as to give "a dignity to the occasion, which would make it felt in other states as well as abroad."[46]

Webster had personally known both statesmen, having worked with Adams in the Massachusetts constitutional convention of 1820 and having visited Jefferson at Monticello in 1824. Nevertheless he immediately began researching the lives of the two men and the events in which they had been intimately involved. He spoke to those who had known them and who had lived through the Revolution. He corresponded with some, notably Timothy Pickering, who had served as Adams's secretary of state and had a letter from Adams recollecting events at the time the Declaration of Independence was written and adopted. Unquestionably Webster recalled the many anecdotes told by Jefferson about the Revolution during his visit in 1824. And most probably he researched the collections in the Massachusetts Historical Society.[47]

Webster labored long and hard on his eulogy, especially in gathering his material, and the results, in the minds of many, surpassed the Plymouth and Bunker Hill orations. He had mastered his material so thoroughly that by the time he was ready to compose the eulogy the words came pouring out of him in one great rush. He later told Millard Fillmore that he "wrote that speech one morning before breakfast, in my library, and when it was finished my paper was wet with my tears."[48]

46. Story to DW, July 11, 1825, ibid., II, 127.

47. Timothy Pickering to DW, July 19, 1826, ibid., II, 127.

48. Curtis, *Webster*, I, 276.

He took the composition to his friend George Ticknor and read it to him. Ticknor had nothing but praise for what he had heard. But not much later doubts arose in Webster's mind. The day before he was to deliver the address he sent for Ticknor, who found him pacing his room in great agitation. He had invented two speeches by an opponent of the Declaration, as well as John Adams's response to them, and they troubled him. He could not tell whether they were the best or the worst part of the eulogy. But Ticknor reassured him. Obviously this speech meant a great deal to Webster, and he wanted it as near perfect as possible. The President of the United States would be present, among other notables, and when published, the eulogy could markedly advance his presidential ambitions.

The day scheduled for the commemoration turned out to be bright and sunny. It could not have been better. People by the thousands crowded into Faneuil Hall to hear him, and they filled it long before the ceremonies began. They numbered about four thousand. An immense throng also congregated outside the building and the marketplace surrounding it in the hope of gaining admittance. The hall, for the first time, had been draped in mourning. The audience sat quietly, and "the scene was very solemn." A large platform was erected for the dignitaries and settees were positioned throughout the hall.[49]

At eleven o'clock a procession formed in the senate chamber of the State House, where Webster, President Adams, the governor, lieutenant governor, the mayor, and other city officials had gathered. They proceeded directly to Faneuil Hall. "The streets from the State-House to the hall were thronged with a greater concourse of people than I ever witnessed in Boston," observed Adams in his diary. After they had arrived in the hall, the doors were closed.[50]

But the crowd outside had expected to be let in once the procession had entered, and they grew "so tumultuous and noisy that the solemnities were interrupted. The police in vain attempted to restore order." Thereupon Webster stepped to the front of the platform and in a voice easily heard over the uproar shouted a command: "*Let those doors be opened*. The power and authority of his manner were irresistible," reported George Ticknor, "the doors were opened, though with difficulty . . . but after the first rush, every thing was quiet, and the order during the rest of the performance was perfect."

The Reverend Charles Lowell gave the prayer, followed by a "funeral symphony, anthem, and dirge." Then Webster rose to deliver the eulogy. He was dressed conservatively and, as usual, wore "an orator's gown." His manuscript lay on a small table beside him, but not once did he need to refer to it, so thoroughly had he mastered what he would say. Then he began.[51] "This is an unaccustomed spectacle. For the first time, fellow-citizens, badges of mourning shroud the column and overhang the arches of this hall. These walls, which were consecrated, so long ago, to the cause of American liberty, which witnessed her

49. Ibid., 275.
50. Adams, *Memoirs*, VII, 139–140.
51. Curtis, *Webster*, I, 275.

infant struggles . . . proclaim, now, that distinguished friends and champions of that great cause have fallen. It is right that it should be thus. Extraordinary occasions demand extraordinary notice."[52]

He went on to speak for several minutes in general terms about the impact Adams and Jefferson had had on their country and its inhabitants. Then he noted how similar they were: both lawyers, both early friends of independence, both members of the committee that drew up the Declaration of Independence, both ministers abroad, and both elected Vice President and President of the United States.

He continued with a detailed discussion of the life of Adams and a less detailed narrative of Jefferson's, stopping at the moment they arrived at the Continental Congress and were assigned the duty of composing the Declaration. Then he launched into an analysis of the document and rightly declared that it contained no new ideas, no novel explanation of why the colonies should be free and independent. Jefferson merely repeated what most Americans already knew and understood, said Webster, and then listed a catalog of grievances that gave that instrument "its character of direct and pointed accusation." The writing of the Declaration, he continued, "belongs to [Jefferson] clearly and absolutely." But Adams also played a vital role. He "had no equal." He "was our colossus on the floor." Said Jefferson: "John Adams . . . not graceful, not elegant . . . yet he came out with a power, both in thought and of expression, which moved us from our seats."

How typical, Webster commented. The eloquence of Adams "resembled his general character. . . . It was bold, manly, and energetic; and such the crisis required." At this point Webster strayed into exalting the attributes and value of eloquence. But then, he declared, patriotism becomes eloquent ("the eloquence of action") when words lose their power and rhetoric fails. "The clear conception, outrunning the deductions of logic, the high purpose, the firm resolve, the dauntless spirit, speaking on the tongue, beaming from the eye, informing every feature, and urging the whole man onward, right onward to his object—this, this is eloquence; or rather it is something greater and higher than all eloquence, it is action, noble, sublime, godlike action."[53]

By this time Webster had worked himself up to fever pitch. As he pronounced the words "It is action, noble, sublime, godlike action," he stamped his foot repeatedly on the stage, "his form seemed to dilate, and he stood, as that whole audience saw and felt, the personification of what he so perfectly described. I never heard him," reported George Ticknor, "when his manner was so grand and appropriate."[54]

That last phrase—"noble, sublime, godlike"—caught everyone's notice, especially the word "godlike," and when Americans around the country read the passage, they were so moved that they applied the word to Webster himself.

52. *PS*, I, 238. The last sentence of that opening was included in the manuscript written by Webster but not in the printed version that subsequently appeared.

53. Ibid., I, 243–256.

54. Quoted in Curtis, *Webster*, I, 275.

Thereafter he was known to many as the Godlike Daniel.

But the best part of the eulogy followed. In a flight of pure fancy, but a flight based on Webster's research into what had been said concerning the Declaration at the convention, he invented a debate between an opponent of the document and Adams.

"Let us pause!" said the opponent. "This step, once taken, cannot be re-traced. This resolution, once passed, will cut off all hope of reconciliation. For ourselves, we may be ready to run the hazard; but are we ready to carry the country to that length? Is success so probable as to justify it? Can we rely on the constancy and perseverance of the people?"[55]

When the opponent finished his harangue, said Webster, John Adams rose to rebut it.

"Sink or swim, live or die, survive or perish," Adams responded, "I give my hand and my heart to this vote. It is true, indeed, that in the beginning we aimed not at independence. But there's a Divinity which shapes our ends. The injustice of England has driven us to arms; and independence is now within our grasp.

"The war, then, must go on," Adams argued. We must fight it through. And if the war must continue, why put off longer this Declaration of Independence? This measure will strengthen us. It will give us character abroad. The nations will then treat with us, as they can never do while we acknowledge ourselves subjects, in arms against our sovereign.

"If we fail, it can be no worse for us. But we shall not fail. The people, the people, if we are true to them, will carry us and will carry themselves, gloriously, through this struggle."

Webster went on for several more minutes playing the part of Adams as he argued the cause of independence. The audience sat spellbound, not uttering a sound. Then he concluded Adams's reply with these words:

Through the thick gloom of the present, I see the brightness of the future, as the sun in heaven. We shall make thus a glorious, an immortal day. When we are in our graves, our children will honor it. They will celebrate it with thanksgiving, with festivity, with bonfires, and illuminations. On its annual return they will shed tears, copious, gushing tears, not of subjection and slavery, not of agony and distress, but of exultation, of gratitude, and of joy. Sir, before God, I believe the hour is come. My judgment approves this measure, and my whole heart is in it. All that I have, and all that I am, and all that I hope, in this life, I am now ready here to stake upon it; and I leave off as I began, that live or die, survive or perish, I am for the Declaration. It is my living sentiment, and by the blessing of God it shall be my dying sentiment, Independence, *now*, and INDEPENDENCE FOR EVER.[56]

The wholly imaginary response by Adams enraptured those who heard it at the time and those who read it later. The passages immediately went into

55. The first two sentences of this opening argument by the opponent was later inserted in the printed version of the eulogy by Webster. *PS,* I, 256.

56. Ibid., I, 257–259.

schoolbooks "as specimens of English and eloquence" and as the noblest defense of the Declaration ever heard. In no time people believed that Adams had actually spoken these words, and Webster received countless letters asking where he had found it. Ticknor said that it had "such an air of truth and reality about it, that only a genius like Mr. Webster's, perfectly familiar with whatever relates to the Revolution, and imbued with its spirit, could have written it."[57]

Webster continued his eulogy by tracing the careers of Jefferson and Adams through their presidencies. He alluded to their political disagreements but rightly said that this was neither the time nor place to discuss them. Apparently he did not know that Adams and Jefferson had resolved their differences in their old age in an exchange of letters.

For his conclusion Webster turned away from the somber tone of a eulogy and returned to his familiar theme about the greatness and wonder of the American nation. "This lovely land, this glorious liberty, these benign institutions, the dear purchase of our fathers, are ours; ours to enjoy, ours to preserve, ours to transmit. Generations past and generations to come, hold us responsible for this sacred trust." He concluded:

> If we cherish the virtues and the principles of our fathers, Heaven will assist us to carry on the work of human liberty and human happiness. Auspicious omens cheer us. Great examples are before us. Our own firmament now shines brightly upon our path. WASHINGTON is in the clear, upper sky. These other stars have now joined the American constellation; they circle round their centre, and the heavens beam with new light. Beneath this illumination let us walk the course of life, and at its close devoutly commend our beloved country, the common parent of us all, to the Divine Benignity.[58]

Not a sound was heard as he finished. It was too solemn an occasion. He had spoken for two and a half hours, according to President Adams. Strangely, in his diary, the President said nothing about the quality of the eulogy or about Webster's delivery. It may be that he was so deeply moved that he could not find the words to describe his feelings. He simply wrote that while delivering the discourse, Webster "held the whole assembly mute."[59]

But later the orator was deluged with praise. Of the many letters he received, that of the secretary of the treasury, Richard Rush, was fairly typical. Many parts of the eulogy, explained Rush, "thrilled me. I read them to my family, and they thrilled them too. The speech . . . made my hair rise. . . . Nothing in Livy's ever moved me so much."[60]

Until the day he died, Webster continued to receive inquiries and compliments on this eulogy. By that time everyone acknowledged that when it came to expressing the people's deepest sentiments and personal feelings about their nation, Daniel Webster was indeed "godlike."

57. Ticknor, quoted in Curtis, *Webster*, I, 275–276.

58. *PS*, I, 260–271.

59. Adams, *Memoirs*, VII, 140

60. Rush to DW, August 30, 1826, quoted in Curtis, *Webster*, I, 280.

15

Election to the Senate

THE ADULATION heaped on Webster following this great eulogy unfortunately fed his arrogance and sense of intellectual superiority. His heightened feeling of self-worth further stimulated his desire for higher office. And while New England might understand and forgive him his pretensions, few others outside this region had much patience for it, particularly during this age of developing democracy.

The political world in the United States was undergoing profound changes by the middle of the 1820s, set in motion by many factors: the market revolution following the War of 1812, which inaugurated the nation's rush toward creating an industrialized society; the widening of the franchise that virtually provided universal white male suffrage, which began with the arrival in the Union of new western states with liberalized constitutions and continued with the electoral changes undertaken by the older eastern states at a series of constitutional conventions; and the collapse and slow demise of the Federalist party.

The growth of democracy constitutes one of the most important developments in American history during this antebellum era. The doctrines of republicanism were slowly giving way to democratic principles. This phenomenon accounted in large measure for Andrew Jackson's extraordinary showing in the 1824 presidential election, despite his threadbare credentials as a public servant. In the minds of many he typified the ordinary citizen. In an age when the "common man" had the vote he would necessarily attract the support of the masses. And Daniel Webster would not. Apart from everything else, he was a Federalist, a member of a discredited national party, a party generally regarded as aristocratic and elitist.

Only one party, the Republican party, effectively functioned on the national level. It had been badly split among several factions that had supported different candidates for the presidential election of 1824. However, following the House election of 1825, several of the factions joined together to form a coalition. The Clay and Adams factions had united to constitute the administration party, while the Crawford and Calhoun factions showed a growing disposition to link up with the Jacksonians to form an opposition. As Clay himself told Webster, "we really have in the Country no other than a Republican party. Names may be gotten up or kept up in particular States for local or personal purposes, but at this time there are but two parties in the Union, that of the Administration and the Opposition."[1]

Federalists, without a functioning national organization and unwilling to surrender their political principles, looked to both the administration and opposition parties in the hope of identifying which one would welcome them and provide them with greater incentives to join. Federalists, particularly in New Hampshire and probably in the rest of New England, "are generally, not by any means universally,—inclined to support the administration," Ezekiel Webster told his brother. But the administration men, he continued, "cannot expect, that when [Federalists] have been proscribed through the whole year—that they will, on election day sneak up to the ballot-boxes & vote for those, who denounce and proscribe them. Can they expect us to put our shoulders to the wheel with a halter about our necks . . . *marked & badged* by *them,* as outcasts, & aliens of the commonwealth?"[2]

Webster tried to reassure his brother by informing him that he had recently spoken to a leading Adams supporter and warned him "in the plainest manner" that Federalists would not support Adams's appointments "unless they are consulted in mak'g them; &, generally, that *they* must either agree to act with the Federalists, or expect the Federalists to act *agt.* them."[3]

As a long-time Federalist who had joined the administration party (the National Republican party, as it was now called), Webster had a twofold duty: to encourage Federalists to unite with him behind Adams and Clay and to convince the Adams government to show Federalists in tangible ways, like the dispensing of the patronage, that they were welcome and that their political "sensibilities" would be respected. To a very large degree what Webster wanted was an "amalgamation" of the two groups, such as President Monroe had advocated, in which "former distinctions are to be done away—former animosities to be forgotten."[4]

What made fusion difficult was the fact that Federalists did not abandon their name. Those who sided with the administration called themselves Federalist supporters of Adams. Even Webster kept using the name. But unlike many Federalists who could not bear to call themselves Republican or National Republican under any circumstances, Webster faced the reality of the present situation and tried to find ways to overcome it. "I have made so many sacrifices of feelings," he sighed, ". . . that they come easy to me."[5]

An "amalgamation," such as Webster desired, was precisely what Martin Van Buren and his faction railed against. They hated the notion of amalgamating principles, as though that could be done. "In all the states the divisions between

1. Clay to DW, November 10, 1826, in Clay, *Papers,* V, 889.

2. Ezekiel Webster to DW, July 27, 1826, in *PC,* II, 153.

3. DW to Ezekiel Webster, February 9, 1827, in Van Tyne, ed., *Letters of Webster,* p. 121.

4. Ezekiel Webster to DW, July 27, 1826, in *PC,* II, 153; John W. Taylor to Edward Everett, May 18, 1827, Everett Papers, MHS.

5. DW to Adams, June 30, 1827, in *PC,* II, 225–227.

Republican and Federalists is *[sic]* still kept up and cannot be laid aside whatever the leaders of the two parties may desire," Van Buren explained to Thomas Ritchie, editor of the Richmond *Enquirer* and leader of a Virginia political machine called the Richmond Junto. We need, he continued, a "revival of old party distinctions. We must have party distinctions and the old ones are the best of which the nature of the case admits." Van Buren desperately sought a revival of the two-party system, and what he hoped to do was bring about a renewal of Jefferson's old Virginia-New York political alliance.[6]

The profound changes occurring in the country at this time influenced not only the political world with respect to party development and allegiance but also the positions politicians took on the leading issues of the day compared with those they had held previously. Many of them completely reversed themselves by the 1820s, and they included Daniel Webster.

Webster had allied himself with the National Republican party, which had based its goals and purposes on Clay's American System. That involved support for federally sponsored internal improvements, a strong banking system, and protective tariffs. In the past Webster had steadily opposed protective tariffs. But now, as a result of the market revolution, Massachusetts was no longer exclusively a commercial and maritime state. Manufacturers had grown steadily over the past ten years, especially in the woolen industry, and they were suffering great financial losses because of foreign competition. So they complained to Webster, their representative in Congress, and urged him to do something about it.

Convinced of the justice of their demand, Webster by the fall of 1826 had slowly begun to reverse his own free market stand. Not only did this reversal make him a closer ally of Clay's, but it obliged him to seek converts among other representatives. He wrote to John C. Wright of Ohio and explained his position. Woolen manufactures faced extinction because of the low prices of imported woolen cloth and the high price of domestic wool. "It always seemed to me that the tax on foreign wool was injudicious; and although I remain fully of opinion that the Tariff is, in general, high enough, &, in relation to some articles, decidedly *too high,* I yet feel that Congress, by the late act, did undertake to give a certain degree of *'Protection'* to the woolen manufactures, which they have not realized, in consequence of the high duty on the raw material. On this account, I think . . . some alteration may be expedient."[7]

It should be pointed out that Webster was seeking reelection to his House seat in the fall and his reversal on the tariff started at the same time. Obviously he could use the support of manufacturers. He could also use the support of administration Republicans, and in his efforts to bring about an amalgamation he believed his election could be a means to that end.

6. Remini, *Van Buren*, pp. 12–29; Van Buren to Ritchie, January 13, 1827, reprinted in its entirety in Robert V. Remini, ed., *The Age of Jackson* (New York, 1972), pp. 5–6.

7. DW to John C. Wright, October 12, 1826, in *PC*, II, 133.

Progress of sorts toward amalgamation occurred when Webster received the caucus nomination for a third term as the U.S. representative from the Boston district. It came at a meeting on November 5 of Republicans and Federalists in which Webster would have received a unanimous nomination save for the fact that some Jacksonian Republicans and Federalists were "very industrious *to prevent the re-election of the present incumbent from appearing to be the Act of the Republican Party.*" Nevertheless he won the nomination, and that was all that mattered. But in the fall election the Jacksonians put up another Boston lawyer, Henry Barney Smith, to run against him. The nomination of Smith worried Webster because, as he told a friend, "we have here a Jackson *paper,*" the Boston *Statesman,* "& a Jackson *party.*"

He worried needlessly. Despite their organization and propaganda machine, the Jacksonians took a terrible drubbing at the polls by running a candidate against a man many believed had brought nothing but distinction and honor to their city. Webster received 1,545 votes to Smith's 98. For Webster personally, this election marked the end of his identification with the Federalist party.[8]

A few weeks later Webster headed back to Washington to participate in the last session of the Nineteenth Congress. He took lodgings at Mr. McIntire's house on Pennsylvania Avenue. "It is a new house," he informed his wife, "& the *people* seem to be good people. I have a large room, in front, to myself, & a very comfortable lodging room," what he called his "outer room, & an inner one for retreat." No other congressmen lodged at McIntire's, although Webster had invited the Patroon, Stephen Van Rensselaer, to join him, probably with the idea of influencing his vote in Congress. But Van Rensselaer had declined.[9]

In returning to Congress, Webster intended not only to influence the votes of friends and fellow former Federalists but to advance a legislative program of his own. High on his list were "some alteration" of the tariff to help the woolen manufacturers of Massachusetts and another attempt to reform the judiciary system. He also believed it "my duty to bring forward the Bankrupt Bill, as soon as possible." As he had remarked to one representative a short while earlier, "I hope you will aid therein."[10]

One of the first things he noticed upon returning to Washington was the very visible presence of a Jackson party. Small wonder. The Tennessee legislature had nominated Jackson for President the year before, and the campaign for the election of 1828 had already begun. Other states were now jumping on the bandwagon. In Nashville a committee was formed of Jackson's close friends and other distinguished men in the community to direct the campaign. Ezekiel alerted Webster to the fact that Jacksonians were "perfectly organized" in New Hampshire. They were "vigorous & unceasing" in their efforts "to gain friends

8. DW to Clay, November 6, 1826, ibid., II, 139.

9. DW to Grace Webster, December 4, 6, 1826, Van Rensselaer to DW, October 26, 1826, ibid., II, 141, 142, 138; Curtis, *Webster,* II, 20.

10. DW to John C. Wright, October 12, 1826, in *PC,* II, 133.

in every town in the state" and "by means of pamphlets—speeches—& Newspapers to address the passions—feelings, & prejudices of the voters." What Ezekiel described was characteristic of the activities of Jacksonians in nearly every other state.[11]

But the most important development in the structuring of the Jackson party occurred in the winter of 1826–1827. Senator Van Buren met privately with Vice President Calhoun in December 1826 at the home of William H. Fitzhugh of Virginia, and they agreed to join forces to defeat Adams and elect Jackson in 1828. To initiate the creation of the party, Van Buren told Calhoun that he would write to Thomas Ritchie and bring him and the Richmond Junto into this new coalition, thereby reviving the Virginia–New York alliance. To provide propaganda, the *United States Telegraph* under its very capable editor, Duff Green, was established in Washington with financial support coming from many members of the Nashville Central Committee and Jackson himself. With this series of alliances the Jackson party, soon to be known as the Democratic party, included the Crawford, Calhoun, and Jackson factions and rooted its doctrinal beliefs in the states' rights philosophy of Thomas Jefferson.

By this time Calhoun had shed his earlier nationalistic commitments. When the price of cotton declined, following passage of the Tariff of 1824, Calhoun became a strong opponent of protection and an active and vocal supporter of free trade and states' rights. Like Webster, he reversed himself.[12]

As the congressional session began, Webster remained relatively quiet in the debates of this short session. Perhaps he hoped to spend more time silently influencing individual members of the House to support the measures of the administration instead of preparing elaborate speeches in the expectation of winning their votes by oratory. If so, he was no match for the political skills and cunning of Senator Van Buren, who now had the Vice President as an active agent in helping defeat those measures in the Senate.

The new woolens bill, introduced early in the session, was a case in point. Compared with his all-out assault on the Tariff of 1824, Webster remained relatively mute and inconspicuous during the debate on this bill. However, he did send the letter he had received from a constituent on the plight of woolen manufacturers to the editors of the administration newspaper in Washington, the *National Intelligencer,* edited by Joseph Gales and William W. Seaton, who published it in early February 1827. Quietly but effectively Webster helped drive the bill through the House on February 10.[13]

Three days later the bill arrived in the Senate. Like Webster, Van Buren kept his own counsel during the debates because Pennsylvania regarded Jackson as a protectionist while the South saw him as a free trader. It was best to be

11. DW to Ezekiel Webster to DW, January 27, 1827, ibid., II, 151; Remini, *Election of Jackson,* ch. 3.

12. Van Buren, *Autobiography,* pp. 513–514; Van Buren to Ritchie, January 13, 1827, in Remini, ed., *Age of Jackson,* pp. 3–7; Wiltse, *Calhoun,* II, 285ff.

13. Wiltse, *Calhoun,* II, 350.

"noncommittal." He conveniently absented himself when the vote came on the final version of the woolens bill. A tie resulted, and the Vice President struck it down.

Nor did Webster have much luck with bankruptcy legislation. In December 1826, as chairman of the Judiciary Committee, he reported a bill for the establishment of a uniform system of bankruptcy. As it so happened, between January 18 and 20 he was involved in a case before the Supreme Court, *Ogden* v. *Saunders*,[14] over the insolvency issue. He and William Wirt argued for the defendant, Webster insisting that the bankruptcy power belonged exclusively to the national government under the contract clause of the Constitution. It was not, he declared, a concurrent power, as held by the Court in *Sturges* v. *Crowninshield*.[15]

Meanwhile the Senate considered the bankruptcy bill, and during the debate individual senators frequently made reference to the arguments going on below them in the Supreme Court. On the final vote the Senate rejected the bill. Shortly thereafter the Supreme Court, by a vote of four to three, disagreed with Webster and held that the states could pass bankruptcy laws, provided they did not impair future contracts.[16] For whatever solace it provided, both Marshall and Story sided with Webster.[17] But the decision spelled doom for a national insolvency law.[18] Not until 1898, despite several attempts, did Congress finally legislate a permanent bankruptcy law.[19]

Because Webster was so involved in court cases—he argued sixteen cases before the Supreme Court in 1827—and in efforts to build the administration party, he only halfheartedly pressed for a judiciary bill. Congress discussed it briefly before turning to other matters, and it ended like Webster's previous efforts. Not until 1837 did a judiciary bill finally become law.

Throughout the congressional session Webster met with Clay on a fairly regular basis. They talked mainly about appointments, party strategy, and the prospects of the administration's winning reelection in 1828. Toward the close of the session, with Webster getting ready to return to Boston, they held a special strategy session about what needed to be done during the spring and summer to get the campaign moving in the right direction. They had to find more newspapers to rally behind Adams and they had to encourage state legislatures, where dominated by National Republicans, to pass resolutions supporting the adminis-

14. This case involved a New York insolvency law.

15. The Ogden case can be found in 12 Wheaton 213. *Sturges* v. *Crowninshield* (1819) invalidated a retroactive insolvency law. 4 Wheaton 122.

16. *Register of Debates*, 19th Congress, 2d Session, p. 76ff, 577. 12 Wheaton 213.

17. Gabriel Duvall was the third dissenter. This was the only case in which Marshall dissented on an important constitutional question. In the second decision, or reargument, which came two weeks later, Justice William Johnson joined Marshall, Story, and Duvall to form a new majority, and they ruled that New York's insolvency laws could not apply to a citizen of another state.

18. Baxter, *Webster and the Supreme Court*, p. 119.

19. For example, a bankruptcy law was passed in 1841 but repealed two years later.

tration and its program. New York and Pennsylvania were two important states with huge electoral votes. These two states were pivotal. Clay figured that Pennsylvania would turn away from Jackson because of his free trade views. As for New York, they faced a real problem. De Witt Clinton and Martin Van Buren, who cordially disliked each other, were the two power brokers of the state, and both supported Jackson. Unless the National Republicans mounted a strong campaign, that state would surely be lost. Clay and Webster agreed—and that was the word the New Englander used—that he, Webster, would stop off in Pennsylvania and New York, visit the local Republican leaders, and encourage them to speed up their efforts to combat the Democrats. In addition, both Webster and Clay recognized the need to offset the obvious North-South alliance taking shape under Van Buren's skillful direction by allying protectionists in New England with those in the middle Atlantic states and the West. Their possible engine for this alliance would be the meeting in Harrisburg on July 30, 1827, of farmers and manufacturers called by the Pennsylvania Society for the Promotion of Manufactures and the Mechanic Arts. This meeting was expected to demand congressional action for the protection of domestic industry. Obviously such a meeting could be an excellent vehicle to advance the interests of the administration. But, as Clay reminded Webster, "we must keep the two interests of D[omestic] M[anufactures] & I[nternal] I[mprovements] allied, and both lead to the support of that other great & not less important interest of Navigation."[20]

Webster remained in Washington after Congress had adjourned to complete his responsibilities before the High Court. In late March he headed home, stopping off for a few days in Baltimore to visit friends. But he was politicking from the first moment he left the capital.

He found the climate in Baltimore fairly friendly toward the administration. Even so, supporters "need to be waked up and excited," he wrote. Maryland was also important if National Republicans hoped to cement an alliance between the middle Atlantic states and New England. "No pains," he added, "should be spared to obtain its vote." But he faced a problem that seemed endemic to the National Republican party when compared with the Democratic party, and Webster voiced it precisely: "Our friends, however, need organization, system & action. You know how these things can be, or must be, accomplished." First off, you need newspapers to provide adequate propaganda. Then you need committees to raise money, and organize rallies, parades, and barbecues to stir popular interest in the goals and accomplishments of the party. "Can you set them in motion?" he asked Charles Miner, a Federalist Representative from

20. DW to Clay, May 7, 1827, Clay to DW, June 7, 1827, in PC, II, 197, 216. In his diary President Adams gloomily recorded Van Buren's recent tour through Virginia, North and South Carolina, and Georgia with his fellow New Yorker Congressman Churchill C. Cambreleng. "They are generally understood to have been electioneering, and Van Buren is now the great electioneering manager for General Jackson, as he was before the last election for Mr. Crawford." Adams, Memoirs, VII, 272.

West Chester, Pennsylvania. "At any rate, My Dear Sir, let us act as if we knew our danger, & were willing to face it."[21]

Moving on to Philadelphia, Webster reported back to Clay on his general findings. In fact for the remainder of the spring, summer, and fall he was in constant contact with Clay discussing party organization. Periodically he reported to Adams, or asked his advice, or nudged him to make a particular appointment. "If you have any general rule, in regard to Newspapers," he told the President, especially in distributing government patronage to them in the form of printing laws and notices, ". . . the giving of such a direction, would, I think be a useful thing and have a healing tendency." But if Webster thought that Adams would be guided by politics in distributing the patronage, he was sadly mistaken. Competence and honesty guided Adams, nothing more and nothing less.[22]

In Philadelphia Webster found the editors of the leading newspapers still neutral. But the Democrats had already begun "to act vigorously on the public mind." He spent three days in Philadelphia and heard again the "one continued din of complaint": distribution of the patronage by the chief executive. It was so bad, he informed Clay, "that there seems to be a feeling prevalent here, that to be active & prominent, in support of the Administration, *is the way to throw one's self out of the chance of promotion, & the sphere of regard.*" Office seekers here believe that they should "hold back, in the ranks of opposition until they shall be offered their price." Unless something is done about it, the administration is doomed.[23]

For his part Clay worked on the President at every opportunity, but no matter how hard he tried he could not convince Adams to reward their friends and dismiss their opponents. Right at the heart of the administration sat a Jacksonian, John McLean, the postmaster general. But Adams would not sack him. He was a competent, nay, excellent, postmaster general. That was all the President needed to know.[24]

Webster tried his hand with Adams. There are forty or fifty thousand Federalists in Pennsylvania, he lectured in a letter to the President, and they are crucial to our success in this state. If they are to be influenced in casting their ballots, Robert Walsh—whom Webster had once engaged to write a history of the Federalist party—must be soothed and petted. At present he is "in rather an unsatisfied mood towards the Administration." His friends have been *"neglected"* in obtaining patronage. He will be going to Washington and if you will speak to him, Mr. President, it could do much good. The appointment of Joseph Hopkinson, for example, "would gratify Mr. Walsh more than any thing else

21. DW to Miner, 24, 1827, in *PC*, II, 173–174; John W. Taylor to Edward Everett, May 18, 1827, Everett Papers, MHS.

22. DW to Adams, March 23, 1827, in *PC*, II, 172.

23. DW to Clay, March 25, 1827, ibid., II, 175–176.

24. Remini, *Clay*, pp. 288–289; Richard R. John, *Spreading the News: The American Postal System from Franklin to Morse* (Cambridge, 1995) pp. 76–109.

whatever." It would not take much. Just "some act of patronage or kindness."[25]

It was like talking to a stone wall. In a real sense the Jacksonians never had a better friend than John Quincy Adams. He helped engineer his subsequent defeat in 1828.[26]

Webster did what he could in Philadelphia, especially in raising money and talking Federalists into joining the National Republican party, before moving on to New York to perform similar tasks in the Empire State. In reckoning his party's chances in 1828, Webster calculated that all of New England, Kentucky, Ohio, Indiana, Missouri, Louisiana, most of Maryland, and perhaps all of Delaware could be gathered into the fold. They had a good chance in Pennsylvania because of the tariff issue, but they needed New York, and that state would be a difficult nut to crack, although not an impossible one. Adams had many friends within New York's business community. So too did Daniel Webster.[27]

Over the next several months Black Dan met with such success in raising money in the East, especially in New York, that in time he became a kind of unofficial party treasurer.[28] He was particularly active in Massachusetts. To help in this 1828 campaign, he turned to such Boston businessmen as Amos and Abbott Lawrence, Nathan Appleton, Thomas H. Perkins, Israel Thorndike, and David Sears. Throughout the campaign he continued raising funds and distributing them with a judicious regard for their impact on Federalists. He also enlisted the aid of various friends whom he trusted to assist him in his efforts.[29]

Henry Clay encouraged him to win not only support for Adams but also friends and advocates for tariff protection and internal improvements. "It seems to me," Clay advised, "that our friends who have the ability should contribute a fund for the purpose of aiding the cause. . . . If you coincide with these views, would it not be well for you to give an impulse to the creation of a fund for the above objects by conversation or other communication with some of our friends?"[30]

Straight off, Webster sent him $250 for the "above projects" with a promise to send more as soon as he spoke with other "friends." Thereupon Clay informed him that John Pleasants, editor of the Richmond *Whig*, needed financial help, but to send the money to the "Hon J. S. Johnston," the senator from Louisiana, who had worked so sedulously for Clay in the campaign of 1824 and had close ties with Pleasants.[31] Such a circumvention could avoid possible embarrassments in the transferral of funds.

25. DW to Adams, March 27, 1827, in *PC*, II, 179–180.

26. This is not to say he would have won in any case. But at least he could have made a stronger effort to retain his office.

27. DW to Jeremiah Mason, April 10, 1827, in *PC*, II, 184–185; Clay to Everett, November 7, 1827, Everett Papers, MHS.

28. Remini, *Election of Jackson*, p. 126.

29. Edward Everett to DW, [c. November 18, 1827], in *PC*, II, 253–254.

30. Clay to DW, October 25, 1827, Clay Papers, LC.

31. Remini, *Clay*, pp. 239, 241.

Of particular interest to Clay was the work of Charles Hammond, editor of the Cincinnati *Gazette,* who had learned about the curious circumstances of Jackson's marriage[32] and now splattered his pages with charges that Rachel Jackson was an adulteress and Jackson's mother a common prostitute. "C. Hammonds paper in Cincinnati," Clay remarked to Webster, ". . . is I think upon the whole, the efficient . . . gazette that espouses our cause. . . . I think he is very way worthy of encouragement and patronage. . . . Perhaps he might receive a present of a new set of types."[33]

Webster agreed that Hammond's *Gazette* was "certainly able & vigorously conducted" and eminently worthy of a "present." He thought he could obtain a set of types "for abt. 5 or 6 hundred Dollars" that he would ship to Cincinnati immediately. But then Clay thought of "another & perhaps a better mode of accomplishing the object in view," which he said he would discuss with Webster when next they met.[34]

The emergence of Webster as a national leader of the National Republican party necessitated his greater involvement in the local politics of surrounding states. Clay could cover the West better than anyone else, and the South as well, but Webster hoped to influence the entire New England and middle Atlantic states. He made several attempts to convince state legislatures that they should publicly endorse Adams and the American System. He badgered his brother, Ezekiel, to bring New Hampshire into line, and he instructed Zeke on what to do. "This is a time for *action,*" he insisted. "Early in the session, introduce a string of Resolutions, approving of the election of Mr. Adams—& of the general measures of the Administration—& characterizing the opposition as groundless. In support of these Resolutions, make your *speech*—print it & circulate it thro' the State. So favorable an opportunity to do good & to distinguish yourself, will never occur to you again." He explained his actions to Clay and added that if the secretary concurred, "I wish you would take occasion to suggest them to Mr [Samuel] *Bell.* His opinion would have much weight with the good people in the New Hampshire Legislature."[35]

The Massachusetts legislature of course was expected to do whatever would help its native son, but that proved more difficult than anyone supposed. Since January the two houses had been struggling without success to elect a U.S. senator for the term beginning on March 4, 1827. The lower house favored reelecting the incumbent Elijah H. Mills, an able but not very exciting senator, while the upper house, following the lead of Jacksonians, held out for John Mills

32. For full details concerning Jackson's marriage, see Robert V. Remini, *Andrew Jackson and the Course of American Empire* (New York, 1977), pp. 57–69.

33. Clay to DW, August 19, November 8, 1827, Webster Papers, LC.

34. DW to Clay, September 8, 1827, Clay Papers, LC; Clay to DW, October 17, 1827, in Clay, *Papers,* VI, 1156–1157.

35. DW to Ezekiel Webster, April 4, 1827, DW to Clay, April 14, 1827, in *PC,* II, 182–183, 190. For many years Samuel Bell served in both houses of the New Hampshire legislature. He later became a member of the state supreme court, and the governor of the state, and in 1823 he was elected to the U. S. Senate.

of Springfield. The deadlock led to a postponement of the issue until May. In the meantime Elijah Mills, the incumbent, indicated that poor health might force him to withdraw as a candidate. To add to the problem, the spring election for state representatives was approaching, and Republicans were divided between supporting and opposing the Adams administration.

Webster hoped that his amalgamation policy could resolve internal disagreements within the state, and he made an important speech to help bring it about. At a meeting called at Faneuil Hall on April 20 to oppose the election of two Jacksonian representatives he began by briefly tracing the history of Adams's election and arguing that it was the duty of everyone to acquiesce in the results of the House election. Without some forbearance in pressing for a different choice, without a degree of charity toward rivals, and without "a disposition to abstain from rancor and animosity . . . how [can] our free and popular institutions . . . be maintained?" A Massachusetts citizen was elected President; is he not "entitled to a somewhat kinder treatment than that which he [has] received"? Can the two parties of the past "unite" and "act with concert and effect," he asked, "or [are] they still to preserve towards each other an attitude of coldness and distance, if not of hostility, although their sentiments and objects were now acknowledged to be the same?" Was union ever more necessary, he went on, "or disunion more senseless?" Some argue that the differences between Federalists and Republicans of the past had gone on too long to be forgotten or reconciled. But "what was the nature of these differences?" Certainly not class differences, or differences between farmers and businessmen. "Our differences, on the contrary, have been mere differences of opinion upon questions of government, and on its public measures. The rich and poor, the learned and the unlearned, the powerful and the feeble, were found on both sides of these questions." But do these differences still exist? Most assuredly not. The French Revolution, the problems with Britain over trade leading to war: "these were the great topics on which parties had been divided."[36] They now stand resolved. Were "party feeling and party prejudice" to be revived, therefore, over the constitutional right of the House to elect the person who the members collectively believed deserved the office? He hoped the people of Massachusetts could unite behind their native son and, like Webster himself, support the efforts of the administration to "carry on wise measures for the improvement and happiness of the country." As "for reviving past heats and smothered animosities, he had no heart." Such controversies could bring no honor to the state or benefit to the nation.

Much as he valued the distinction of the office he held, Webster concluded, he would not hold it for a day if required to serve a party or recognize any master but the people, "the whole people, whom he had the honor to represent."[37]

Webster pleaded for the union of the two historic parties, Federalist and

36. If Webster really believed this, he was being terribly naive. There were many other causes for party development besides those he cited, both economic and political.
37. W&S, XIII, 24–30.

Republican, and whether he realized it or not, in this speech he stood up against the forces of political change that were currently sweeping Massachusetts and the rest of the country. The two-party system was reemerging, yet he kept pleading for amalgamation. It was a noble, valiant, but ultimately futile effort.

Still, who could not admire his call for unity? In Massachusetts he was one man both Republicans and Federalists could look to with pride, someone who continued to bring distinction and honor to his state.[38]

At this point Webster's name began to circulate in the legislature as a possible candidate for the U.S. Senate—since Elijah Mills's health had apparently eliminated him from consideration—along with the governor, Levi Lincoln. Had the election taken place at that moment, both National Republicans and Jacksonians might have agreed to support him. When he heard about it, Webster tried to convince party leaders that he did not want the post. Unquestionably his disavowal was sincere. First off, he had an established position at the forefront of the House leadership, something Massachusetts could not afford to lose. And, in addition to knowing how the House operated and conducted its business, he believed he could have a greater impact on legislation than he would if he moved to the Senate, where he would be a freshman. The House was a livelier chamber than the more sobersided upper chamber, and it was still regarded as the chief forum for legislative action. Finally, he pointed out that if he left the House, there was no one who could take his place and assume a role of leadership as he had done over the past several years.

There is no reason to doubt his sincerity in wanting to scotch the rumor of his possible nomination. He expressed his views in several letters to some of the more important policy makers of the Massachusetts legislature, and he asked them to communicate his sentiments to others. "My own feelings, I confess are very much against it," and he suggested Governor Lincoln as an alternative. He even went so far as to write Lincoln and urge him to move to the Congress as senator. "I see no way in which the public good can be so well promoted," he told the governor, "as by *your* consenting to go into the Senate. This is my own clear & decided opinion; it is the opinion, equally clear & decided, of intelligent & patriotic friends here; and I now [am] able to add, that *it is also the decided opinion of all those friends, elsewhere, whose judgment, in such matters, we should naturally regard.*" He meant of course the administration leaders in Washington.[39]

Indeed Webster had contacted Clay at the very outset of this development and once again enumerated all the reasons why he should not leave the House. "I need not say to you, My dear Sir, that both my *feelings* & my *judgement* are *against* the transfer."[40]

38. Clay congratulated Webster. "Your late Speech at Faneuil Hall," he wrote, "was all that it should have been. It presented the true condition of the existing state of things, and pointed out clearly the only correct line of policy." Clay to DW, May 14, 1827, in *PC*, II, 202.

39. DW to John Barney, April 13, DW to Lincoln, May 22, 1827, ibid., II, 187, 205.

40. DW to Clay, May 7, 1827, in ibid., II, 198.

Then a complication entered the mix. It was one that would permanently sunder the Republican party in Massachusetts: a dispute over the Charles River bridge, the connecting link between Boston and the neighboring town of Cambridge. The Jacksonians saw this toll bridge, which brought in enormous profits to its proprietors, as a privileged monopoly granted by the state legislature to enrich the few at the expense of the many. So they rammed a bill through both houses providing for the construction of a new bridge that, after the expense of building it had been paid, would be toll free.[41]

Webster regarded this legislative action as confiscatory, a violation of property rights and contrary to state and national law. He informed Henry Clay that "a little knot of Gentlemen . . . have seized on some local subjects . . . especially a taking proposition for a *free-bridge,* by means of which they hope to strengthen their ranks."[42] Their leader, William C. Jarvis, speaker of the lower house, professed friendship for Adams, but the President's real friends knew better. The Federalists agreed with Webster, as did Governor Lincoln, who promptly vetoed the bill for a new bridge.

But the Jacksonians now had an issue to take to the electorate. The people wanted a free bridge, they needed a free bridge, they deserved a free bridge, declared the Jacksonians. The wealthy few, operating under a state charter, were denying ordinary citizens what they should have by right.

The issue had such force that it helped the Jacksonians complete the structuring of their party apparatus in Massachusetts and strengthen their ties to the masses, just as Webster predicted. They called a meeting to voice their indignation and nominate their own slate of candidates for office, including governor[43] and U.S. senator. Any hope for the kind of amalgamation that Webster had argued for so ardently in his Faneuil speech now seemed doomed. The Massachusetts Democratic (Jacksonian) party had emerged.

At this juncture Webster felt obliged to accept the Senate nomination for fear that the Jacksonians would sweep all before them—that is, if his friends in the legislature agreed that he should submit. He still believed he belonged in the House and hoped that Governor Lincoln would respond to his appeal to take the office. But Webster now asked friends "whether the general good requires that I should go into the Senate." Again he queried Clay and asked him to consult Adams about it. The legislature was scheduled to meet on the last Wednesday of the month, and its first act would be the selection of a senator.[44]

Clay responded with the only advice possible. You belong in the House, he said, but if your place could be properly filled by the right person then, fine,

41. For the background of what later ended in the celebrated case before the Supreme Court *Charles River Bridge v. Warren Bridge,* see Stanley Kutler, *Privilege and Creative Destruction: The Charles River Bridge Case* (Philadelphia, 1971).

42. DW to Clay, May 7, 1827, in *PC,* II, 198.

43. They nominated Jarvis for governor, but he subsequently declined the nomination; nevertheless he received a substantial vote in the election.

44. DW to John C. Wright, April 30, DW to Clay, May 7, 1827, in *PC,* II, 196, 197–199.

move to the Senate. He asked the President about it, and Clay reported that Adams would like to see Lincoln take the office. "But if Governor Lincoln cannot be prevailed upon to accept . . . then the President decidedly prefers your coming in at the next Session."

Lincoln settled the matter when he declined to move to the Senate. In a long response to Webster's letter he explained that "under existing circumstances" he could not accept. He did not think he could do the office justice. Instead he urged Webster to take it because by his participation he could not only strengthen the power of the Senate immeasurably, which desperately needed it, but render greater assistance to the administration.[45]

This argument was seconded by Representative John C. Wright of Ohio, who frankly admitted that the Democrats had "more energetic operating talent" in the upper house "than we do. . . . We ought to have there, some of our most powerful minds." But they faced a dilemma. *"You we want in both places,"* he told Webster. Still, all things considered, the National Republicans had greater strength in the House and needed to bolster their position in the Senate. "Our men [in the House] are younger, have more elastic[it]y of mind, and . . . necessity may bring out talents & exertions equal to any emergency we shall be called to encounter." Henry Clay subsequently agreed when he heard that Lincoln could not be prevailed upon to run. "It would be expedient that you should be sent," he told Webster.[46] Needless to add, the Boston Associates—that is Cabot, Lowell, Appleton, Gorham, Thorndike, Ward, and others—were anxious to see their protégé move higher up the political ladder.

So Webster let it happen. He finally decided to leave the matter in the hands of his friends in the legislature and do whatever they thought best. He wrote to Lincoln, Nathan Appleton, and Joseph Sprague, the principal manager of this election, and announced his availability.[47] Then he took off for New York to argue a case in court. On June 7, 1827, both houses endorsed him, and he received a two-thirds vote from each.[48] In the upper house he garnered 26 votes, while John Mills won 11, Edward Everett 1, and Levi Lincoln 1. In the lower house Webster took 202 votes, Mills 82, and the remaining 44 were scattered.[49]

The news of his election probably came as no surprise to Webster, but he undoubtedly wondered whether he had made the right decision. Little did he know that his presence and participation in the upper house would help raise its power and authority as well as carve for himself a reputation as one of the greatest senators in American history.

45. Lincoln to DW, May 24, 1827, ibid., II, 205–206.

46. Wright to DW, May 24, Clay to DW, May 28, 1827, ibid., II, 208–210, 210–211.

47. His three separate letters to these men, all dated May 30, 1827, can be found ibid., II, 211–213. After his election Webster wrote to Sprague and thanked him for his help. "I beg you to be assured that I am not and shall not be insensible to the effect which your good wishes and good efforts have produced." DW to Sprague, June 20, 1827, in Webster, ed., *Private Correspondence,* I, 420.

48. Benjamin Gorham replaced Webster in the House.

49. March, *Webster,* p. 76 note.

16

"Poor Grace Has Gone to Heaven"

CONGRATULATIONS poured in on Webster, and they came from many parts of the country. Even Elijah Mills wrote, although at the last minute he had tried to restore his candidacy by claiming his health was much improved and that he now felt strong enough to undertake another term.[1] Representative Charles Miner called Webster a "pilot" who could be counted on "when the storm is up and the billows roll" to stand steadfast at the helm "until the vessel is safe."[2] One of the warmest expressions of congratulations came from Joseph Story. "I congratulate you with all my heart. . . . The vote is truly honorable to both Houses, & under all the circ[umstance]s a proud triumph of Massachusetts & national feeling."[3]

Webster returned to Boston to find Grace quite ill. She suffered an attack of erysipelas and a sudden and very bad cold, so Webster decided to take her off on a little trip. He also redoubled his efforts to help the political campaign. He spent a good deal of time encouraging his friends, including his brother, to attend the Harrisburg Convention scheduled to meet at the end of July.[4] As it so happened, Ezekiel did attend, along with Samuel Bell, Ichabod Bartlett, and others as part of the New Hampshire delegation.[5] A Boston contingent had also been chosen; it included some of the city's most notable merchants, friends of the American System, and political leaders, such as Abbott Lawrence, Edward Everett, Bezaleel Taft, and Joseph Sprague. Webster wrote to John W. Taylor of New York, Speaker of the House, citing the necessity of having New York well

1. Mills to DW, June 9, 1827, in *PC*, II, 216.

2. Charles Miner to DW, June 13, 1827, ibid., II, 219.

3. Story to DW, June 10, 1827, ibid., II, 217–218.

4. For more detailed information on the Harrisburg Convention, see *Niles' Weekly Register*, June 21, July 21, 28, 1827, and the *National Intelligencer*, June 12, 28, 1827.

5. "I am really desirous that you should go to Harrisburg," Webster wrote his brother. "It will give you an opportunity to see much of the Country, & a good many important men." DW to Ezekiel Webster, July 12, 1827, in *PC*, II, 229.

represented. The delegates need not be chosen at one general meeting, he explained. Local groups, appointing their own delegates, could serve the purpose. "I have taken the liberty to address this to you," he continued, "& similar letters to three or four others" so that they can correspond with one another and learn each others wishes and objectives for the convention.[6] It was Webster's hope that this meeting could not only express its views on the necessity of protection for certain industries and agricultural products but serve as a means of endorsing the objectives of the Adams administration. Already, in some places, a report was circulating that the administration favored "protecting & encouraging domestic manufactures etc and that this interest is to be jeopardized if Genl Jackson succeeds."[7]

More than one hundred delegates representing thirteen states attended the convention, and they took only five days to complete their business. They drew up a memorial and petition to Congress demanding "early and effectual interposition" to support the woolen industry. They proposed a duty of twenty cents per pound on raw wool, to be increased two and one-half cents annually until it reached fifty cents per pound, and for woolen cloth a 40 percent ad valorem rate with an annual increase of 5 percent until it reached 50 percent. They also asked for a one-cent-per-pound duty on hammered bar iron in addition to protection for flax, hemp, and distilled spirits. They assigned Hezekiah Niles, editor of *Niles' Weekly Register,* to compose an address to the public, and ninety-seven men signed the memorial.[8] In no way did they intend to permit Congress to duck away from addressing the tariff question. They wanted something positive done about it immediately—namely in the coming session.

Webster did not consider attending the convention if, for no other reason, the press of legal business that demanded his attention. Then the sudden death of his assistant Alexander Bliss both shocked and nearly overwhelmed him with work. For eleven years Bliss had rendered invaluable service in supervising Webster's office. "It is a dreadful calamity," Webster told Joseph Story. "I should feel that it fell heavily on me, if I did not see how it must crush others," like Bliss's wife and child. There is no doubt that Webster felt the loss keenly. "He [Bliss] was very dear to me." For a replacement Webster again turned to Portsmouth and a graduate of Dartmouth. He chose Henry Willis Kinsman, "a young Gentleman who read law with me, has been in practice two years, & whom I can recommend for fidelity & capacity." Their association lasted ten years.[9]

Webster spent the remainder of the summer and most of September at his usual retreat "on our Southern shore, to get a little quiet." Grace was not well, but the rest and relaxation, along with his constant presence, did her a tremendous amount of good. It was a great torment for her to be separated from her

6. DW to Ezekiel Webster, [June 11, 1827], DW to Taylor, June 19, 1827, ibid., II, 218, 222–223.
7. William L. Marcy to Van Buren, June 25, 1827, Van Buren Papers, LC.
8. The entire proceedings can be found in *Niles' Weekly Register,* August 11, 1827.
9. DW to Story, [July 17, 1827], DW to Samuel Jaudon, July 25, 1827, in *PC,* II, 231, 233.

husband every winter when he trudged off to Washington, to say nothing of the many trips he had to take to New York or Newport to appear in court. However, she was determined to accompany him to the capital to attend his swearing in as Massachusetts's newest senator and remain with him until the end of the session. Except for her children, her life revolved exclusively around Daniel Webster. "My Husband is the centre and the height of my ambition," she confessed to him.[10]

The three- or four-week respite did Webster much good as well. He went fishing and hunting and took long, invigorating walks to think about his future. It looked increasingly bright. Already it had been suggested to him that he run for the vice presidency on the Adams ticket. John C. Calhoun, the present Vice President, had obviously gone over to the Democrats and would probably run with Jackson. That left the second slot on the Adams ticket wide open. One man from Ohio told him that a meeting had been held in Huron County to appoint delegates to nominate electors for President and Vice President. "I would suggest the propriety of nominating Daniel Webster of Boston as a Candidate for Vice President," he wrote. "Your Character as a Representative is well known here."[11]

It was really an absurd suggestion because the ticket would then consist of two men from the same state. Politically that made no sense. How much thought Webster gave to these suggestions is not known, but it surely proved to him that he had a national reputation that might one day take him to the highest office in the country.

Webster was shaken out of his private thoughts and the peace and quiet of the southern shore by the demands of his law office.[12] He hoped to get to the capital before the session began in order to consult with Clay and others about the agenda for the year, and plan strategy for the presidential election. As he wrote to Speaker Taylor, "One reason for desiring to be early at W[ashington] was the hope of being, in some measure, useful, in the arrangements belonging to the commencement of the Session."[13]

He set off in mid-November with the entire family except Fletcher, who was attending school, and ran into such foul weather that his progress was slowed appreciably. By the time the group got to New York they knew they had to rest. Grace's condition had worsened, and Webster suffered from a bad cold and "a very painful attack of *rheumatism.*" Confined to his room, he could not rise to his feet or walk across the room without help. He notified the Speaker of his delay and suggested that "some friend" should speak to Representative John Heritage Bryan of North Carolina since all signs indicated that he might be persuaded to support the administration.[14]

10. Grace Webster to DW, January 29, 1827 in Van Tyne, ed., *Letters of Webster,* p. 567.

11. Joshua Phillips to DW, [1827], in *PC,* II, 261.

12. DW to Clay, September 28, 1827, ibid., II, 241.

13. DW to Taylor, November 30, 1827, ibid., II, 254.

14. DW to John W. Taylor, November 30, DW to Nathaniel Silsbee, December 1, 1827, ibid., II, 254, 256.

Grace was far worse off. She suffered such abdominal pains that her husband took her to the home of Dr. Cyrus Perkins, an old college friend. The pain intensified over the next few days from "her foot to her hip." Since there was abdominal swelling, Dr. Perkins called in Dr. Wright Post, a surgeon, for consultation. Both doctors agreed that Grace's condition was so serious that she ought to return home immediately. Privately they told Webster that they frankly held out little hope for her recovery.

Actually Grace had a cancerous tumor—not that the physicians recognized it—and it was slowly killing her. Webster could not and would not leave her side, yet his duty also required his presence in Congress. So he wrote to James Paige, Grace's half brother, and asked him to come to New York to help.[15]

To add to Grace's distress, the doctors administered an "unlucky application, by accident, of a blister plaister" which only "further irritated & inflamed her limb." The doctor had prescribed a "soothing anodyn plaster," but the "apothecare" blundered and sent a "very strong blister plaster." For the next several days she suffered excruciating pain. "The blister plaster, undoubtedly, did a good deal of harm," Webster moaned. It woke her during the night, and on removing it, they found that it had "produced a very great blister, which could not be healed up, for some days." Even so, she did not wish to return to Boston. She wanted to accompany her husband to Washington, where she felt certain she would recover. But her swelling abdomen looked to Webster as though the tumor were forming a head.[16]

In desperation, Webster wrote to their family physician, Dr. James Warren, and begged him to come to New York to attend Grace. He realized it was an imposition, but he appealed to Warren's "friendship & kindness." Grace thought the opinions of the New York doctors were "too *discouraging.*" She believed that Warren would "at least, try *something.*" If you could oblige her, Webster pleaded, "it would confer an obligation, never to be forgotten."

In the interim James Paige arrived to take Grace back to Boston. Reluctantly she acquiesced. The pain had left her, and she was resting more comfortably, and as soon as her condition permitted, she was prepared to return home. Webster notified Dr. Warren of the change and advised him not to come to New York. Shortly thereafter he took off for Washington together with Congressman Thomas Oakley of New York. They arrived in the capital on Sunday, December 16, and found living quarters at Mr. McIntire's house near Gadsby's Hotel.[17]

He entered the Senate the following day, and he said he felt "new & strange. . . . My habits have become conformed to the course & manner of things elsewhere; & it will require time, to enable me to feel at home, where I now am."[18]

15. DW to Paige, December 3, 5, 1827, ibid., II, 256, 257.

16. DW to Dr. John Warren, December 7, 8, 1827, ibid., II, 258, 259.

17. DW to Warren, December 8, 9, 1827, DW to Elijah Mills, December 19, 1827, ibid., II, 259, 260, 262; *Congressional Directory,* 20th Congress, 1st Session, p. 5.

18. DW to Elijah Mills, December 19, 1827, in *PC,* II, 263.

The forty-eight senators representing twenty-four states assembled on the second floor of the north wing of the Capitol. Both the House and Senate chambers were semicircular and formed like an ancient Greek theater. The upper house was smaller than the lower, seventy-five feet across, forty-five feet wide, and forty-five feet high. The dome was very flat, and a series of Ionic columns similar to those in the Temple of Minerva supported a gallery on the east side of the chamber. The walls were hung with fluted drapery. The principal light came from the east. Greek and Roman statuary and busts decorated the room, adding a peculiarly grand and elegant splendor to the place. All this provided excellent acoustics for the great oratory heard regularly in the room.

The senators' desks and chairs fanned out "in concentrated curves" from the Vice President's chair in the center and were "cut by radii," which formed the aisles. All the desks[19] were made singly of mahogany with large armchairs behind them and placed "on platforms, gradually rising one above the other."[20]

A single page, a boy of twelve or thirteen, responded to the needs of the senators, but in 1831, at Webster's insistence, a second page, Isaac Bassett, aged twelve, was appointed, and he served the upper house for the next fifty-six years, graduating to the position of messenger at the age of sixteen and elected assistant doorkeeper in 1861. Some senators objected to Bassett's appointment, but Webster argued that the majority party should have one page, and the minority party the other, a position that was ultimately agreed to by the entire house. Bassett later reported that Webster, although a great senator, could be difficult at times. "He was hard to please he was *pevish* and cross when he did not get what he

---

19. The desks, in effect, constituted the senators' offices, unlike today, when one hundred senators have three enormous office buildings for themselves and their staffs plus small hideaways in the Capitol (about seventy) for the most senior senators. Webster's desk (Desk XXIX) has become historic. In the 1830s, in order to provide each senator with additional "office" space, it was decided to mount three-inch-high mahogany writing boxes to the desks. But Webster refused the modification, supposedly on the ground that if his predecessors had made do with limited space, so could he. To match the height of the other desks, the Webster desk was therefore raised at its base. A sander and an inkwell were placed on the top front of the desk. The inkwell was made of a clear-cut glass, covered with a square, flat top that moved horizontally. At various times senators from Connecticut, Georgia, Indiana, Maine, Massachusetts, Michigan, and New Hampshire have occupied Desk XXIX. In 1974 a resolution adopted by the Senate stipulated that the Webster desk be assigned to the senior senator from New Hampshire, even though Webster had never represented that state in the Senate. See "Report on the Senate Chamber Desks," prepared by the offices of the Senate curator and historian (June 1979), pp. 4–5.

There is a tradition that Webster carved his name inside the desk. Senator Bob Smith of New Hampshire permitted me to examine the desk, and the name "D Webster" is indeed carved in the wood, after which are the names of Charles Sumner, George F. Hoar, Henry Cabot Lodge, Arthur H. Vandenberg, and thirteen other senators who sat at the desk. I confess I doubt that Webster himself carved his name in the desk, nor did any of the other senators of the nineteenth century. The tradition of senators' inscribing their desks did not begin until the twentieth century, at which time some thoughtful individual or individuals probably decided to go back and add the names of the previous occupiers of the desk, starting with Webster. I am grateful to John B. Odell of the Senate's Commission on Art for much of this information.

20. Green, *Washington*, I, 127–130; Robert Mills, *Guide to the Capitol of the United States* (Washington, 1834), pp. 43–44.

wanted. . . . He could be rude and tell people to go away when busy."[21]

"The Senate room is *transmogrified,* since last session," Webster informed the former occupant of his seat. "The V. President sits opposite the main door, & faces his former seat. The seats are crowded, &, altogether, the arrangement is not good. My place (Hobson's choice) is nearest the Chair, on its left hand. It was left by 47 wiser heads than mine, & yet I believe it the best seat in the Chamber."

It took awhile before he accustomed himself to his new position. He had become comfortable with the "course & manner" of the lower House and admitted that it would take him a little time "to feel at home." There was not much for him to do because the Democrats, after the last election, held a majority. He felt it wiser to let them exercise it. "Why should *we* be responsible for what we cannot control?"[22]

It was not long before Webster accommodated himself completely to the procedures and practices of the upper house. As a matter of fact he acquired a small room on the third floor, "just over the Senate Chamber" on the right side, that became known as Webster's Wine Room. "I had charge of it," boasted Isaac Bassett. Webster's friends sent him "hogsheads packed with the most choice wines and liquors," and what was not needed at his house he stored in the room "during the recesses of the Senate." Sometimes, Bassett admitted, "I would drop and break a bottle" and the senator would admonish me sharply. "You must be more careful, it is two preshes [precious] to spill." In no time at all the Webster Wine Room became a favorite meeting place during sessions for his colleagues and friends. There they could relax and sample excellent wines without worrying about public notice.[23]

On his entry into the Senate in 1827 Webster found such colleagues as Van Buren and Thomas Hart Benton of Missouri, both staunch Jacksonians, although Benton had supported Clay in the 1824 election; Levi Woodbury and Samuel Bell of New Hampshire, two very able men; Richard M. Johnson of Kentucky, later Vice President and the self-proclaimed killer of the Shawnee chief Tecumseh; the venerable Nathaniel Macon of North Carolina, who was to resign in November; John Tyler of Virginia, under whom Webster would serve as secretary of state in the 1840s; John H. Eaton and Hugh Lawson White of Tennessee; and Robert Y. Hayne of South Carolina.

Webster tried to busy himself with politics and the issues coming up for

21. Starting pay for a Senate page was $1.50, increased to $2 a day. At the end of the session each page received "20 gold pieces," which the secretary of the Senate sewed into their pockets. By 1888 there were fifteen pages. Bassett's papers in the Capitol include many interesting anecdotes about the senators over approximately sixty years, starting in 1830. IB Papers, Box 21, Folder E, pp. 30a–c, Box 30, Folder H, p. 6, Box 1, Folder B, p. 54.

22. DW to Elijah Mills, December 19, 1827, in *PC*, II, 263.

23. IB Papers, Box 1, Folder B, p. 78, Box 20, Folder E, p. 101. Senator Patrick J. Leahy of Vermont, who occupies the room today, renamed it the Daniel Webster Memorial Room after it had been enlarged and refurbished. New York *Times*, September 28, 1984. I am grateful to Senator Leahy for permission to inspect the room.

debate, like the abolition of imprisonment for debt, but his thoughts constantly turned toward New York and his wife's rapidly deteriorating condition, which postponed indefinitely any thought of her returning home.

Though racked with pain, Grace understood his situation. She tried to comfort him. "The first Intention of my heart is to the God who gives me strength to write—and the first of my pen to you, my best Beloved. . . . I beg you will not be too anxious about me—nor too much enhance the value of this poor life by your love for me." She seemed to sense that she was dying. Still, she tried to console him. The following day she wrote again. "I am sorry you can not get letters every day but do not, my dear Love, be too anxious about me. I think I am rather better and I felt in better spirits after Dr. Post was here. . . . I would not have you, my dear Husband, put yourself to the hardship of returning so soon . . . if I should continue as comfortable as I am now. . . . Farewell dearest and best—may Heaven bless and keep you prays your ever afft GW." The poor woman kept giving and giving, even though she had precious little left to give.[24] Christmas must have been a dreadful time for Webster, although friends tried to take his mind off his wife by inviting him to participate in their holiday festivities.

On Christmas Day he received a letter from James Paige informing him that Grace would be "glad" if it was not too inconvenient for him to return to New York in time to meet Judge Story and his wife, who would be passing through on their way to Washington. Webster replied immediately that he would certainly come but that he could not get away for possibly a week or more. His cold still bothered him, and his lungs were congested. It seemed obvious to him, he said, that if Grace's condition continued to deteriorate, he would be obliged to resign from the Senate. "I care very little about it, but wish only to fulfill the expectations of my friends."[25]

Webster did not arrive back in New York until January 3. He found his wife resting comfortably, with less pain than she had previously experienced, but noticeably thinner. He still had no idea of what troubled Grace. "The tumour, itself, has not enlarged, lately; & the parts adjacent are evidently less swelled & inflamed." He decided to return to Washington if Grace continued to feel better, but that was wishful thinking. The Storys were present but left the next day for the capital. Now that Paige had been relieved by Webster's presence, he took off for Boston to attend to some pressing business.

Two days later the pains returned, and Grace's "system" become "a little deranged," which Webster believed caused the tumor to become "rather harder." It troubled him enough to write again to Dr. Warren and ask for his help. If Warren could come, Webster felt certain the Grace would know that "all

24. Grace Webster to DW, [December 21, 22, 1827], Paige Papers, MHS.

25. DW to Paige, December 25, 28, 1827, in *PC*, II, 264, 266. Webster's friends urged him not to resign his seat. "Your resignation," wrote Jeremiah Mason, "would unquestionably be imputed to your supposed despair of success of the Administration party." Mason to DW, January 9, 1828, ibid., II, 274.

has been done, that can be done." He had not lost confidence in Dr. Perkins, whom he had known for many years, and Dr. Post enjoyed a very high reputation. A third doctor, David Hosack, had been brought in for consultation, and all three men said they would be happy to benefit from Warren's experience and knowledge. But of the three, only Perkins had ever seen such a case before, and he believed the matter was grave. The others could not be sure what troubled poor Grace. Perkins wrote out his diagnosis and sent a copy to Dr. Philip Syng Physick of Philadelphia, perhaps the most celebrated physician in the United States at that time, and another copy to Dr. Nathan Smith of New Haven and asked for their opinions and advice.[26]

Surgery was considered. But the "tumour is so large, so situated, embracing so many muscles, nerves & blood vessels," Webster informed his brother, "that an *operation* is not to be thought of. Internal remedies do not reach it, & external application have little effect." It must be left to "Providence; but you must be prepared to learn the worst."[27]

A week later Grace looked "better, & brighter," but she had difficulty breathing and felt a good bit of pressure in the chest. Her pain lessened, but she suffered from stiffness and numbness below the tumor. There were "large glandular swellings" in various parts of her body, especially about the abdomen. "The tumour looks constantly more & more like coming thro the skin." And her voice was very faint.[28]

Webster decided to bring his son Fletcher to New York. The boy knew his mother was ill, but he had no idea of her real condition. Unfortunately he arrived too late. On "Monday 1/4 past 2 o'clock" in the afternoon of January 21, 1828, Grace Fletcher Webster expired, just three days after her husband's forty-sixth birthday.[29] She was forty-seven years old, and in addition to her husband, she left behind her fourteen-year-old son, Fletcher, her daughter, Julia, just turned ten,[30] and her seven-year-old son, Edward. "Poor Grace has gone to Heaven," Webster announced to his brother. "She has just breathed her last breath."[31] Her final moment could not have been "more hopeful, cheerful, & happy," he told Story. "A heavenly smile overspread her face when she embraced us, for the last time; & pressed our faces to her cold lips."[32]

Story too had lost his first wife, and he tried to comfort his friend. "Having been a like sufferer, I can say, that the great secret of comfort must be sought . . . in employment. It requires effort and sacrifice, but it is the only specific

26. DW to Nathaniel Silsbee, January 4, 8, DW to Paige, [January 6], DW to Warren, January 6, 1828, ibid., II, 267, 268, 270, 272.

27. DW to Ezekiel Webster, January 8, 1828, ibid., II, 273.

28. DW to Story, [January 14, 1828], DW to Mason, January 15, 1828, ibid, II, 278, 279, 280.

29. DW to Ezekiel Webster, [January 21, 1828], ibid., II, 282.

30. Julia was born on January 16, 1818.

31. DW to Ezekiel Webster, [January 21, 1828], in *PC*, II, 282.

32. DW to Story, January 21, 1828, ibid., II, 283. For a loving remembrance of Grace Webster, see the sketch written by Eliza Buckminster Lee in *W&S*, XVII, 438–444.

remedy against unavailing and wasting sorrow; that canker which eats into the heart, and destroys its vitality." Return here as quickly as you can gather the strength, he advised, and resume your professional and public labors. In the meantime he would arrange Webster's business before the Supreme Court so that he would not be pressured.[33]

Webster turned to the Reverend John Gorham Palfrey of Boston, whom Grace greatly admired, for "succour and consolation" in this trial. "She died," he told the clergyman, "just as you & all Christians would have wished her to die. She died, full of good hopes, submissively, & cheerfully." As one of Grace's last requests she asked her husband to write to Palfrey and "send you her last affectionate farewell." With "suffused eyes," she said, "Ask him to remember me,—and tell him how much I have thought of him, & how often I have wished to see him, during my sickness."[34]

Religion was an integral part of Grace's life. After all she was the daughter of a clergyman. Sometimes she mildly scolded her husband because it was not integral to his. She frequently admonished him to take a greater interest and involvement in religious observances. For his part Webster had reservations about religion. "Our ancestors" in New England, he declared, those rugged Puritans whom he so much admired, possessed all the Christian virtues except charity. Their single vice? "Religious hypocrisy." It leads men to stay ten feet away from their wives when going to church as an act of merit. It leads them to forbid their daughters from attending a village dance. "External acts" then become meritorious. "I do not like creeds in religious matters," although "I verily believe . . . that creeds had something to do with the Revolution."[35]

Webster gathered his children and headed back to Boston. They took a boat to New Haven and went on to Boston by stagecoach. Paige accompanied Grace's remains to New London by boat and then went directly to Boston. Webster explained to Story that "I should not part from my wife, until I have deposited her, in the presence of our living children, by the side of those others, who have left the world before her." Although he had not yet received Story's letter of advice, he assured the justice that he would be back in Washington early in February.[36]

They reached Boston on Friday evening, January 25. On his arrival he "seemed completely broken-hearted," reported his friend George Ticknor. On Saturday, while preparing for the funeral, Ticknor noticed that Webster wore shoes unfit for the wet streets of Boston, so he asked his grief-stricken friend if he would not ride in one of the carriages.

"No," Webster replied, "my children and I must follow their mother to the grave on foot. I could swim to Charleston."

33. Story to DW, January 27, 1828, Mason to DW, January 27, 1828, in PC, II, 288, 286.

34. DW to Palfrey, January 21, 1828, ibid., II, 284–285.

35. DW to Charles B. Haddock, October 14, 1826, in W&S, XVII, 411–412.

36. DW to Story, January 21, 1828, in PC, II, 283, 284.

A few minutes later Webster took Julia and Fletcher by the hand and walked close to the hearse through the streets of Boston to St. Paul Church, where Grace's remains were committed to an underground crypt. Webster used the occasion to bring into the tomb the remains of both their daughter Grace, who had died just a little over eleven years before on January 23, 1817, and their son Charles, who had died on December 19, 1824. "My dear wife now lies with her oldest and her youngest, and I hope it may please God, when my own appointed hour comes, that I may rest by her side."[37]

Webster made no attempt to express his grief and anguish to his friends. "The sorrows, & the reflections . . . are peculiarly, for me & mine—& God grant we may improve them as we ought." Friends tried to provide solace as best they could. He and the children stayed at the home of Mrs. George Blake. His immediate problem concerned his children. Fletcher would continue to board and remain in school, but Webster could not decide immediately how to "dispose" of Julia and Edward. Mrs. Eliza Buckminster Lee, an old and dear friend who lived in Brookline, Mrs. George Ticknor, Mrs. Nathan Hale, Mrs. Nathan Appleton, and others offered to take them both for the winter. Although he hated to separate the two children, he finally decided to leave Julia with Eliza Lee, who "laid claim to Julia, of right," and have Edward stay for the winter with "Mrs. Hale's little flock." He wanted to bring them all back together when he returned from Washington, but he was inclined to let Julia stay with Mrs. Lee "or in some other family, where there is a lady. Very probably both little children may pass the summer at their uncle's [James Paige]."[38]

Webster left orders to have the furniture "put up" in his house. Then, on February 5, he headed back to Washington. "All was done that could be done," he said.[39]

37. DW to Cyrus Perkins, January 28, DW to Story, January 28, 1828, ibid., II, 288–289; Ticknor's "Reminiscences," quoted in Curtis, *Webster*, I, 314.

38. DW to Perkins, January 28, DW to Mason, January 29, 1829, in *PC*, II, 289, 290. In a letter to Paige, Webster wrote: "Edward, I am sure, is as well off as he can be, and since you cannot spare him, I am content he should remain where he is." DW to Paige, [February 6?, 1828] in *W&S*, XVII, 451.

39. DW to Mason, January 29, 1828, DW to Story, February 5, 1828, in *PC*, II, 290, 291.

17

Marriage

WEBSTER suffered a deep depression in the weeks following his return to Washington. His own illness, the wretched weather that hampered movement and frequently confined him indoors, and the devastating loss of his wife of twenty years made it difficult for him to function. Religion gave him little solace. "The love of God and of the good beings whom he has created" should be the sources of human happiness, he sighed. But "heavenly happiness" was another matter. "I am free to confess that some descriptions of heavenly happiness [in the New Testament] are so ethereal and sublimated as to fill me with a strange sort of terror." Friends and loved ones kept telling him that Grace was now like an angel of God. The very thought of it, he declared, "penetrates my soul with dreadful emotion." He hoped that like an angel, Grace enjoyed happiness and immortality, "but I would fain hope, that in kind remembrance of those she has left; in a lingering human sympathy and human love, she may yet be as God originally created her, a little lower than the angels."[1]

Webster sorely missed his beloved. He missed his children as well. He was a family man, devoted to their needs, and his loss made it increasingly difficult for him to think and work. "I have lost what mainly made home dear to me, [still] there is yet that in it which I love more than all things in the world. . . . I have a home notwithstanding the shock I have received," he explained to his brother-in-law, so "you must try to make the children write, when you cannot, so that I may hear from some of you; one every two or three days at least."[2]

Paige did his best to honor Webster's request. And the children dutifully wrote him. Julia said she had started Miss Elizabeth Palmer Peabody's school and had begun to study Latin. She asked her father whether she should undertake the study of French as well; also, he needed to tell her whether New York's City Hall was wood or marble. She thought her father had once said that it was made of wood, so she had wagered one cent with Eliza's husband, who claimed it was marble.[3]

1. DW to Charles Haddock, March 21, 1828, in *W&S*, XVII, 454.
2. DW to Paige, [February 6?], 1828, ibid., XVII, 451.
3. Julia Webster to DW, February 9, 1828, in *PC*, II, 292.

Fletcher sent his father a very good report about his progress in school. Webster glowed.

Senate Chamber,   Tuesday, February 17 [19], 1828

My Dear Son,—I have received a letter from you to-day, before I have found time to answer your last. That gave me singular pleasure, as it contained a very gratifying report from Mr. Leverett. I have nothing more at heart, my dear son, than your success and welfare, and the cultivation of your talents and virtues. You will be, in the common course of things, coming into active life, when, if I live so long, I shall be already an old man, and shall have little left in life but my children, and their hopes and happiness. In contemplation of these things, I look with the most affectionate anxiety upon your progress, considering the present as a most critical and important period in your life.

Such reports as that last received, give me good spirits; and I doubt not, my dear son, that the consciousness that your good conduct and respectable progress in your class, and among your fellows, gives me pleasure, will stimulate your affectionate heart, with other motives, to earnest and assiduous endeavors to excel. I pray Heaven to bless you and prosper you. . . .

Yours, most affectionately,
D. Webster.[4]

Webster found himself pressed on all sides after his return with responsibilities to clients, to constituents, to his family.[5] For the next several weeks he felt the pressure grow day after day. "I have been quite too much pressed," he complained to his brother-in-law. "From day light to 11 o'clock I sat here at my table; & from 11 to 5 am [P.M.] in the Court or the Senate. I shall be glad when their Honors take leave of us." He had no intention of "harassing" himself with the debates in the Senate. "Nothing very interesting is likely to arise, at present; & I feel no disposition to do more, in regard to any subject, than my duty requires.[6]

He returned to the Supreme Court to attend to his clients' interests, but he confessed he felt "very little zeal or spirit" in its proceedings. "My most strong propensity is to sit down, and sit still," he told George Ticknor, who frequently entertained the Webster children over the next few months. Even writing a letter became a burden. But, as he said, duty required him to at least "appear to take an interest in the business of the court." He admitted that his only inclination was to return home for his children's sake as well as his own. The Court finally ceased to hear arguments by the middle of March, and that gave Webster "time to look round & see where I am."[7]

One matter did cause him to pay attention to "public affairs," and that was a bill in the Senate relating to the "forms of process" in the courts that he feared was an "under cover" attempt "for annihilating the most essential parts of their

4. DW to Fletcher Webster, February 17, 1828, in *W&S*, XVII, 448–449.

5. Webster returned after the obsequies in Boston, observed President Adams, "and is now constantly engaged, either in the Senate or in arguing causes before the Supreme Court." Adams, *Memoirs*, VII, 455.

6. DW to Paige, March 13, [1828], in *PC*, II, 312.

7. DW to Ticknor, February 22, DW to Paige, March 13, [1828], ibid., II, 301, 312.

jurisdiction." It had been creeping along "sub silentio" and had arrived at its last debatable stage on the very day, Monday, February 18, that he resumed his seat. When he realized what had happened, he jumped to his feet and asked for a postponement until the next day in order to give him time to prepare a few remarks. The opposition knew what was coming but decided that it was unwise to attempt to block his request.

The following day he gave a two-hour speech and effectively brought the bill's passage to a full stop. He centered his argument principally on the fact that the bill would in effect destroy all equity process for many older states.

That did it. Senators from the older states rallied behind him, and even though Littleton W. Tazewell of Virginia and John Rowan of Kentucky tried to save the bill, it went back to committee "to be divested of its most objectionable features." Even Van Buren sided with Webster.[8]

A short time later something else intruded on his consciousness. A rumor began circulating that he would be appointed minister to Great Britain. Albert Gallatin had resigned the post and returned to the United States. Adams was inclined to offer it to Webster "if he insisted upon it." The rumor persisted throughout the spring and floated all the way up to Boston, where it was relayed back to Webster. But there were obvious problems if he "insisted" on it. His children's situation was one, and its effect on the approaching presidential election another. If he left the country, the election could be "lost or greatly lessened." Webster himself said that his "present inclination, on the whole, is *against* going," but he asked his friends, both male and female, for their advice. Eliza responded by reassuring him about the children. "The disposal of your children need not prevent it," she wrote. But Jeremiah Mason and others warned against it. Not only was he needed in the Senate to support the administration and keep the Democrats at bay, but he was indispensable to Adams's chances for reelection.[9]

As the rumor continued to circulate in Washington, the Democrats finally stepped in to decide the matter. It might have been advantageous for them to see Webster sail off to England, but all they could think about was the necessity of confirming his appointment in the Senate, and that they would not do. Not only did their majority in the upper house guarantee his rejection, but the mere suggestion of Webster's nomination provided the delicious opportunity of renewing their assault against the administration. So they launched a public attack against him by claiming that he had exacted a promise from Adams to appoint Federalists to high office in return for their votes in the House election of 1825. It was another offshoot of the "corrupt bargain" charge. The Buffalo *Republican* first made the charge, followed by the New York *Evening Post* of April 16, 1828, after which several pamphlets during the presidential campaign

8. Adams, *Memoirs*, VII, 455; *Register of Debates*, 20th Congress, 1st Session, pp. 342–343.

9. Adams, *Memoirs*, VII, 470, DW to Paige, March 13, 1828, Eliza Buckminster Lee to DW, March 2, 1828, Mason to DW, March 27, 1828, in *PC*, II, 312, 308, 322.

cited as proof of a "corrupt bargain" Webster's letter to Henry Warfield in February, 1825, which was widely known because it had been shown to several congressmen. From late spring until the conclusion of the presidential campaign Webster was vilified by the Democrats almost as often as were Clay and Adams.[10]

National Republicans repeatedly denied the charges in their own publications. The accusation, recorded Adams in his diary, had been "trumped up in fifty different shapes, and false in all, having no other foundation than casual conversations, in which Mr. Webster and others having intimated that some federalist apprehended I should pursue a system of proscription against the federalists, I disclaimed every such disposition."[11]

Obviously Webster's nomination could not go forward, whether he "insisted" on it or not. Adams noted that most of his nominations had been confirmed by the Senate, and as yet not one rejected. "I had done everything in my power to avoid a collision, and none has occurred," he said. He certainly did not intend to provoke one now. By early May "all the friends of the Administration," Adams noted, had "agreed that the political effect of the appointment of Mr. Webster would be very unfavorable." Clay also opposed it. He wanted James Barbour named to the post, thereby removing him as secretary of war and allowing the appointment of his friend and ally Peter B. Porter, who could provide the administration with additional strength in the important state of New York. So that ended that.[12]

Although Webster spoke about internal improvements in the Senate following his return and "made a very effective & earnest speech" in favor of relief for surviving officers of the Revolution,[13] what eventually stirred him back into active participation in the debates was the introduction of a tariff bill that would dramatically raise protection rates on both manufactured and raw materials. Shaped by the House Committee on Manufactures, dominated by the Democrats, it deeply troubled National Republicans. "I fear this tariff thing," warned one; "by some strange mechanical contrivance or legerdemain, it will be changed into a machine for manufacturing Presidents, instead of broadcloths, and bed blankets."[14]

Precisely. Silas Wright, Jr., Van Buren's henchman on the committee, wrote the bill, and he later explained to the Van Buren machine in New York, the Albany Regency, that he was placed on the committee in accordance with an "arrangement" with other Democrats from Pennsylvania, New York, Kentucky, and Ohio. "In order to bring our arrangement about," he wrote, "I had to consent

10. Joseph Hopkinson to DW, April 19, 1828, in *PC*, II, 335. Webster himself had shown his letter to a number of Federalists.

11. Adams, *Memoirs*, VII, 539.

12. Ibid., VII, 455–456, 525. Adams appointed Barbour minister to England and Porter secretary of war.

13. IB Papers, Box 17, Folder D, p. 2.

14. Ebenezer Sage to John W. Taylor, February 17, 1828, Taylor Papers, New-York Historical Society.

to go on it [the committee] myself." The arrangement involved a simple political formula of mutual accommodation by which the Democrats planned to adjust rates in the states where they could "buy" votes for Jackson in the presidential election. Since New England had committed itself to Adams and could not be bought, the tariff would be "adjusted" to penalize that section. The South could be a problem because it was dead set against protection yet totally committed to Jackson. Wright and his friends therefore decided that because of the southern commitment to Old Hickory, they could ignore southern demands about the tariff. The South would never turn to Adams in the election no matter how the rates were "adjusted." The President's views in favor of protection were too well known to attract its support.

That left the West and the middle Atlantic states. So Wright and his committee concocted a series of rates that levied a ten-cent-per-gallon duty on molasses; distilled spirits were raised ten cents; sail duck was established at nine cents per square yard; hemp and flax were fixed at forty-five dollars per ton, to be increased five dollars each year until it reached sixty dollars; *raw* wool would receive a charge of seven cents per pound plus a 40 percent ad valorem rate, to be increased 5 percent annually until it amounted to 50 percent; for *manufactured* wool, a burgeoning industry in New England, an involved schedule was worked out that failed to meet the minimum needs of its producers. The rationale for these various rates was simple, Wright explained. They raised the rates on "all kinds of woolen cloths" as "high as *our own friends* in Pennsylvania, Kentucky & Ohio would vote them." Then they jumped the molasses rates in order to induce westerners "to go for the woolens" schedule. The hemp, lead, and flax rates were fixed to meet the conditions of favored states, and the duty on iron was "the Sine qua non with Pennsylvania."[15]

National Republicans gasped when they read this lopsided bill. So too southerners. Debate on the bill opened on March 3 and immediately triggered a series of amendments to redress this "affront" to southern sensibilities. Most of the amendments were defeated, but one got through. By a single vote the House agreed to reduce the rate on raw wool by three cents.[16]

Webster shook his head with dismay when he read the bill. "I fear we are getting into trouble here about the *Tariff*," he worried in a letter to Joseph Sprague, his wealthy Boston friend who had attended the Harrisburg Convention. Then he posed several questions to Sprague:

"1. Can we *go* the *hemp*, iron, spirits and molasses for the sake of any woolen bill?

"2. Can we do it for a poor woolen Bill? . . .

"P. S. I think the Bill will positively *injure* the manufacturer, (though possibly the 'passing' of it may help the woolen grower—"[17]

15. Wright to Azariah C. Flagg, April 7, 1828, Michael Hoffman to Flagg, February 2, 1828, Flagg Papers, New York Public Library; Benton, *Thirty Years' View*, I, 95.

16. For the debates and voting, see *Register of Debates*, 20th Congress, 1st Session, p. 1836ff.

17. DW to Sprague, April 13, 1828, in Van Tyne, ed., *Letters of Webster*, pp. 135–136.

After a long and intense battle the tariff passed the House on April 22 by a vote of 105 to 94. All but three southerners voted against it, the West and middle Atlantic states voted solidly for it, and the New England representatives split. "We have made a few of the Yankees swallow," Wright laughingly informed the Albany Regency. The fact that a "few" New Englanders did move toward tariff protection indicated growing evidence of an important industrial trend in that section of the country.[18]

The bill went to the Senate Committee on Manufactures, which brought it to the floor for debate on May 5. Few thought it could survive the upper house because of the intense opposition by southerners, the uncertainty of the New England senators, and the fact that Vice President Calhoun sat poised to dispose of any tie votes.[19] In a long speech on May 9 Webster defended the interests of New England manufacturers by pointing out the unfair discrepancies in the bill when it jacked up rates on raw materials, like wool and hemp, but failed to provide adequate protective rates for manufactured woolens and hemp products. A tax on hemp, he said, is "a bounty on the foreign manufactured article unless that is taxed also."[20]

Senator Van Buren had "preferred to pass that Bill in the shape in which it came to us," he claimed, and although he had no desire to accommodate the wishes of New England, he realized that some change had to be made to counter the strong opposition building up against it.[21] He therefore decided to adjust the woolens schedule by raising the rate on manufactured woolens to a 40 percent ad valorem rate with a 5 percent increase each year until it reached 50 percent. On May 6 this amendment narrowly passed by the vote of twenty-four to twenty-two.

The day the amendment passed, Senator Jesse Thomas of Illinois went to see the President. "The Senate," recorded Adams in his diary, "are so nearly divided upon the bill that its passage will probably depend upon the votes of the members from Massachusetts. Mr. Thomas thinks it will depend entirely upon Mr. Webster, and, considering his vote as doubtful, came to intimate a wish to me that I would interpose to fix his indecision."

No sooner did Thomas leave the President than Webster arrived at the White House to recommend General William Henry Harrison as minister to Colombia. Whether Adams tried to "interpose" with Webster he did not inform his diary.[22] But the following day Webster returned to the White House, and he

18. Wright to Flagg, April 22, 1828, Flagg Papers, New York Public Library.

19. Michael Hoffman to Flagg, April 27, 1828, ibid.; Adams, *Memoirs*, VII, 531; Calhoun to James E. Calhoun, May 4, 1828, in American Historical Association, *Annual Report* II (1899), 265.

20. Webster's speech can be found in the *Register of Debates*, 20th Congress, 1st Session, pp. 750–765. The quotation comes from his additional remarks on page 776.

21. Van Buren, "Notes," dated May 1828, Van Buren Papers, LC.

22. Adams, *Memoirs*, VII, 531. Too frequently Adams halted his narration just at the point when he could provide important and interesting information. His conversation with Henry Clay just before the vote in the House election of 1825 is another example of his suddenly breaking off his diary entry just at a most crucial point in his narrative. Incidentally Harrison received the appointment.

himself brought up the subject of the tariff. He agreed with Thomas that passage of the bill probably depended upon his vote and that of Nathaniel Silsbee, his colleague. "He expressed some doubt how he should vote," reported Adams.[23]

Nevertheless, Massachusetts manufacturers had begun to express their opinions to their two senators, just as they had earlier when they condemned the original bill reported in the House.[24] Abbott Lawrence, for example, told Webster that "the amendments . . . to the Tariff bill in the Senate I have examined carefully and so far as Woollens are concerned the bill is very much improved and is thought by many to be now good enough. I must say I think it would do much good, and that New England would reap a great harvest by having the bill adopted as it now is."

Lawrence was someone that Webster listened to with marked respect. He was not only an important member of the Boston Associates but a man of increasing political influence. He and his brother, Amos, had been importers but in the 1820s shifted to manufacturing textiles, invested in the mills at Lowell in 1830, and later entered the China trade. He helped found the textile city that bears the family name. Born in Groton, Lawrence arrived in Boston in 1808 with less than three dollars in his pocket. He died forty-seven years later a millionaire several times over and "the most important person" in the community.[25] He loved office and power and one day was to vie with Webster for control of their party in Massachusetts. At the moment and for the next decade he was "devoted to Mr. Webster," according to John Quincy Adams, "and the main pillar of his support, both pecuniary and political."[26]

After receiving Lawrence's letter and several others,[27] Webster concluded that with this much pressure building up the bill would most likely pass. In fact, he explained to his brother-in-law, "the safe course is to expect the Bill to pass. I believe it *will* pass." How he himself would vote, particularly if final passage depended on him, he did not know, or so he said. Colleagues pleaded with him not to go on record as opposing the bill, and the *National Intelligencer* berated him for thinking solely about New England's interests and not those of the rest of the country. Still, he admitted that his inclination was to "check the amount of English Importations."[28]

On Tuesday, May 13, the moment of truth arrived, and by the count of

23. Ibid., VII, 534. Adams does not say if he tried to influence Webster one way or another.

24. Representatives were also contacted. J. B. Davis informed Representative John Bailey that he was "perfectly satisfied with the Bill as amended in the Senate." J. B. Davis to Bailey, May 21, 1828, Bailey Papers, MHS.

25. Lawrence to DW, May 7, 1828, in PC, II, 342; Samuel Babcock to Bailey, May 7, 1828, Bailey Papers, MHS; Nathan Appleton, "Memoir of Abbott Lawrence," *Collections of the Massachusetts Historical Society*, Fourth Series, IV (1858), pp. 497–498; Robert F. Dalzell, Jr., *Daniel Webster and the Trial of American Nationalism, 1843–1852* (Boston, 1973), pp. 61–62.

26. Adams, *Memoirs*, X, 43.

27. Similar letters to DW came from Samuel H. Babcock, May 7, 1828, and Israel Thorndike, April 28, 1828, in PC, II, 341, 336–338.

28. DW to Paige, [May 12, 1828], ibid., II, 345.

twenty-six to twenty-one the bill passed with Daniel Webster voting with the majority. He justified his action on the grounds of "expediency."

It is doubtful whether the interests of the country as a whole had as much influence on his vote as the fact that, as he admitted, "N.E. will, certainly, on the whole, be benefitted by it." Its defects he hoped to amend in the future. Should the bill fail this time he knew that there would not be "any chance hereafter of doing any thing for the manufacturers—& I *conscientiously* think, after what has passed, the interest of N.E. required that something should be done for them." One thing he did want to do was extend the time before the tariff would take effect. He addressed his colleagues about an extension, and the Senate agreed to it.[29]

Webster's vote for this "Tariff of Abominations," as southerners called it, marked an important turning point in his evolution as an economic and political nationalist. More and more he favored the full range of Clay's American System, including protection for manufacturers and internal improvements. More and more he championed the rising industrialism in the country. In time he became the outstanding, and the most effective, spokesman for American capitalism.

Congress adjourned on Monday, May 26. Throughout this session Webster had kept pretty much to himself. "I do not go out," he told Mrs. Ticknor, "and see nobody except in the halls of Congress." When the Ticknors arrived in Washington for a short visit, Webster arranged to have them stay next door on Pennsylvania Avenue opposite Gadsby's National Hotel, but they shared his parlor and dining facilities. "He was much out of spirits" because of his grief, observed Ticknor, and did not hesitate to admit his continuing depression. "It is true," Webster admitted. "I fear I grow more and more so. I feel a vacuum, an indifference, a want of motive, which I cannot describe."[30]

Thoughts of his children and their welfare constantly crowded into his thinking. Fortunately he had many loving friends in Boston who relieved him of his most pressing responsibility. He knew that Julia should stay with Eliza Lee. "It is my wish, my dear friend," he told Eliza, "that you should make her as much your own as your feelings prompt you to do. . . . You have a right to her, if you choose to have her, which nobody else will ever divide. You have been among our dearest friends from the day of our marriage, and, as Julia is left motherless, I know not what to do for her so well as to leave her with you. . . . I should be quite willing she should be with you most of the summer; though I hope to have her with me some of the time."[31]

With the adjournment of Congress Webster hurried home, expecting to arrive by June 1 after stopping overnight as usual in Philadelphia and New York. By that time school had closed and his children could join him. Seeing his

29. DW to Paige, [May 10, 12, 1828], in *PC*, II, 343, 345; *Register of Debates*, 20th Congress, 1st Session, p. 786; *Senate Journal*, 1827–1828, pp. 403–404; IB Papers, Box 17, Folder D, p. 3.

30. Ticknor's "Reminiscences," DW to Mrs. Ticknor, March 23, 1828, DW to Ticknor, April 18, 1828, DW to Eliza Buckminster Lee, May 28, 1828, in Curtis, *Webster*, I, 322, 323, 325.

31. DW to Eliza Lee, May 18, 1828, ibid., I, 324.

children surely buoyed his spirits and helped dispel his lingering feelings of depression. He had hoped to go up to New Hampshire for a visit, but after returning to Boston, he found that business kept him in town to argue before the state's supreme court. "That is the only professional engagement which I expect for the summer," he informed his brother, Ezekiel. "We are now in our own house, and comfortably situated." Perhaps later he would "make a little journey on to Connecticut River" and join his brother at his home, and together they would go to Cabot and Hanover for a meeting of the Dartmouth trustees. He actually did get to visit his brother and spend some time in northern New Hampshire during the latter part of July. He said he felt he "was under so urgent a necessity to get out of Town, for the sake of a little *rest*" that he left undone some political matters in connection with the approaching presidential election.[32]

Webster had another reason for visiting his brother in New Hampshire. Since March he had badgered Zeke to run for Congress and thereby strengthen the administration and help eradicate the remaining friction between the Federalists and Republicans in New Hampshire. A congressional ticket without reference to "old party distinctions" would unquestionably energize the National Republican party throughout the state. Ezekiel had no desire to serve in Washington, but Webster dismissed his objections. The senator had the disturbing habit of badgering people into doing what best served his own purpose. More than one individual turned from his own professional inclinations to enter politics at Webster's insistence. Ralph Waldo Emerson never forgave the senator for "seducing" Edward Everett from the world of letters and scholarship.

Zeke finally relented and allowed himself to be nominated by a caucus in December with the election to be held the following March. He lived to regret it.[33]

By the fall of 1828 the presidential campaign had entered its final stage. It had been one of the filthiest, if not *the* filthiest, campaign in American history. Charges of adultery, bigamy, pimping, murder, and assorted lesser crimes had been leveled at the two principal candidates.[34] But the central issue was the accusation of a "corrupt bargain" brought by the Democrats. Webster's participation in the House election of 1825 also generated a great deal of mudslinging. His activities as a campaign fund raiser,[35] as a spokesman for the administration in the House and Senate, and as a national leader of the National Republican party necessarily invited partisan attacks. He took round after round of heavy

32. DW to Fletcher Webster, May 11, DW to Ezekiel Webster, May 28, DW to Joseph Sprague, June 20, 1828, in *PC*, II, 344, 352, 355; Jeremiah Smith to DW, August 10, 1828, DW to Ezekiel Webster, June 19, 1828, in Webster, ed., *Private Correspondence*, I, 459, 458.

33. Ezekiel Webster to DW, [March 17, 1828], DW to Ezekiel Webster, March 23, 1828, in *PC*, II, 316, 321.

34. For details of this scurrilous campaign, see Remini, *Election of Andrew Jackson.*

35. Webster collected sums from John Welles, John Parker, Samuel and Nathan Appleton, Abbott Lawrence, Edward Everett, George Blake, David Sears, and Joseph Peabody, many of them bankers and merchants and all distinguished men in the community.

critical firing from the Democratic press. His about-face on the tariff also provided excellent ammunition for the assault.

But perhaps the most devastating blow was the charge of disloyalty during the War of 1812. Some said he had sympathized with secessionists who attended the Hartford Convention; others claimed that he had actually attended that convention and actively participated in its deliberations. Then, on October 29, 1828, the Boston *Jackson Republican* published an article citing a letter of Thomas Jefferson to William Branch Giles in 1825 contending that John Quincy Adams had told Jefferson that Daniel Webster had been one of the Federalist leaders in 1807 and 1808 who plotted to dissolve the Union in protest over the embargo. The author of the article, one of the owners of the newspaper, Theodore Lyman, Jr., had been Webster's close friend and associate. Lyman and his family's lofty standing in the Federalist party gave the story added credence.

Like so many other accusations in this campaign, the charge against Webster was absolutely false. Adams issued an immediate denial in the Washington *National Intelligencer*. He insisted that he had never spoken to Jefferson about such an alleged plot. He did admit writing to Giles about an open and possibly violent reaction to the embargo, but he had never mentioned Webster as being involved.

Two weeks after the article appeared Webster initiated a libel suit against Lyman brought by his lawyers Charles P. Curtis and Richard Fletcher, who obtained a grand jury indictment against Lyman. The case was tried on December 16 and 17, 1828, in the Supreme Judicial Court of Massachusetts with the chief justice, Isaac Parker, presiding. The defense argued that no libel was involved inasmuch as no malice was intended and because the article constituted a fair comment on Adams's statements. Unfortunately the jury deadlocked, with ten voting conviction and two voting for acquittal. Webster did not pursue the matter further.[36]

The senator's final contribution to the Adams campaign was an address he wrote to the voters of Massachusetts urging their support of the administration. The address did not come easily because he found it "exceedingly difficult to say any thing that has not been said before."[37] As expected, Massachusetts and the rest of New England voted for Adams and gave him fifty electoral votes.[38] Like Clay, Webster was extremely confident that Adams would get enough additional votes from Ohio, Kentucky, Indiana, Louisiana, Maryland, Delaware, and New Jersey to reelect him. Right up to the end Webster deceived himself into believing what he wanted to believe. Even when political signs indicated a different result, both he and Clay kept up their hopes. "I yet think that Mr. Adams will be re-elected," Clay wrote to Webster in late October, "but it is mortifying, and

---

36. Curtis, *Webster*, I, 329–333. See also Josiah H. Benton, Jr., *A Notable Libel Case: The Criminal Prosecution of Theodore Lyman, Jr., by Daniel Webster in the Supreme Judicial Court of Massachusetts, November Term, 1828* (Boston, 1904).

37. DW to Joseph Sprague, [August 1828], in *PC*, II, 361.

38. Maine gave one electoral vote to Jackson and eight to Adams.

sickening to the hearts of the real lovers of free Government, that the contest should be so close; and that if Heaven grants us success it will be perhaps by less than a majority of six votes."[39]

Then came the final devastating results, and Jackson overwhelmed Adams. Old Hickory won virtually everything south of the Potomac River and west of New Jersey for a total of 178 electoral votes. Adams carried New England, Delaware, New Jersey, a portion of New York, and most of Maryland for a total of 83 electoral votes. Some 1,555,340 males voted in this election, and 56 percent of them supported Jackson. The general received 647,276 popular votes to Adams's 508,064.[40]

"We are beaten," Clay moaned. But Webster said nothing. What could he say? What good would it do? So many Federalists had deserted to Jackson that Webster undoubtedly felt a sense of shame and bitterness. One thing he had tried desperately to do over the past several years was enlist what remained of the Federalist faction in support of the administration. In that he had failed. Clearly Webster was not the party leader that many believed him to be. His leadership emanated from his reputation as spokesman for the nation's pride in its past accomplishments and in its hopes for future greatness.[41]

Returning to Washington for the closing chapter of the Adams administration and witnessing the inauguration of General Jackson, Webster sounded despondent and bitter in everything he uttered and wrote. He still grieved over the loss of his wife and worried about his children. He even considered resigning from Congress and returning full-time to his law practice so that he could be with his children and take a more active role in their education and development. Loneliness beset him from the moment he left Boston, and it began to cross his mind, if it had not done so already, that he must find another wife.

In returning to Washington, Webster left his children with Achsah Pollard Webster, Ezekiel's second wife, who had come to Boston with Zeke's two daughters by his first marriage and taken up residence in Webster's house while her husband remained in Concord to attend the legislature and meet his legal obligations in court. Webster probably hoped that his brother's election to Congress in March would facilitate establishing a residence together in the capital and permit him to bring his children to Washington.[42] That prospect failed when Zeke was badly beaten in the election.

"Not much is doing in the Senate," Webster wrote after his late arrival in the capital. "I do nothing, in Congress or the Court, but what is clearly necessary; & in such cases, even my efforts 'come haltingly off.' "[43] Be that as it may, it

39. Clay to DW, October 24, 1828, in PC, II, 371.

40. Robert V. Remini, "The Election of 1828," in Schlesinger and Israel, eds., History of American Presidential Elections, I, 492.

41. Clay to DW, November 30, 1828, in PC, II, 383; DW to Ezekiel Webster, February 5, 1829, in Van Tyne, ed., Letters of Webster, p. 144.

42. DW to Ezekiel Webster, March 15, 1829, in PC, II, 406–407.

43. DW to Ezekiel Webster, January 17, 1829, DW to Achsah Pollard Webster, March 2, 1829, ibid., II, 387–388, 404.

is interesting that Salmon P. Chase, a future chief justice of the United States, thought differently. He listened in on one of the cases[44] Webster pleaded before the High Court at this time and thought that the senator stated his case "with great clearness and draws his inferences with exceeding sagacity. His language is rich and copious; his manner dignified and impressive; his voice deep and sonorous; and his sentiments high and often sublime." Chase noted that Webster argued "from general principles, seldom descending into minute analysis where intricacy is apt to embarrass and analogy to mislead." Oh, to achieve such distinction, thought Chase. "If I could . . . suppose that any degree of industry would enable me to reach his height, day and night should testify of my toils."[45]

While Webster pursued his duties in the court and the Senate, everyone else was waiting for Jackson's arrival and the inauguration of a new administration. The general was expected around the middle of February, and nobody seemed to know what he would do when he did make his appearance. Like Webster, Jackson had just lost his wife, Rachel, who had died at the moment of his electoral triumph. To the day of his death Jackson believed she had been murdered by the "vile slanderers" who accused her during the election of bigamy and adultery. Webster predicted that the President-elect would "bring a breeze with him. Which way it will blow, I cannot tell." As for Adams, he appeared to be in good health "& complains not at all of the measure meted out to him."[46]

As the day of the inauguration grew closer, "hungry friends" of the general began flooding into the capital. Office seekers arrived by the hundreds, and Webster figured that before March 3 Washington would "*overflow*" with them. Prominent among the patronage "grabbers" were "the *Typographical* Corps," as Webster called those journalists who had contributed so much to the scurrility and filth of the campaign and now expected their reward. Among them, Webster noticed Isaac Hill, the notorious editor of the *New Hampshire Patriot* who had been a particularly severe critic of Federalists in that state. Ezekiel said that Hill wanted the position of postmaster general, but Webster assured his brother that the editor would not get it. Jackson later appointed Hill the second controller of the Treasury, but even that appointment was rejected by the Senate. Others of this corps whom Webster noticed were Nathaniel Greene of the Boston *American Statesman*, Mordecai M. Noah of the New York *National Advocate,* Amos Kendall of the Frankfort, Kentucky, *Argus of Western America,* "& from every where else somebody else."[47]

Shortly after he arrived in Washington, dressed in somber black to mourn the recent passing of his wife, the white-haired, gaunt sixty-two-year-old Jackson announced his intended cabinet appointments. Washington gasped when the names were revealed. "It has set all Washington in a *buz*," reported Webster, "—

---

44. The case was *David Wilkinson v. Thomas Leland et al. National Intelligencer,* February 16, 1829.

45. John Niven et al., eds., *The Salmon P. Chase Papers, Journals, 1829–1872* (Kent, Ohio, 1993), I, 10.

46. DW to Ezekiel Webster, January 17, 1829, in *PC,* II, 387–388.

47. DW to Ezekiel Webster, February 5, 1829, Ezekiel Webster to DW, January 25, 1829, DW to Achsah Pollard Webster, February 19, 1829, ibid., II, 395, 393, 399.

friends rage, & foes *laugh*." Apart from the fact that very mediocre men decorated the list (with the exception of Martin Van Buren, chosen to head the State Department) and therefore constituted "a very *weak* Cabinet," it contained elements of dissension. "Mr Calhoun (who tho not nominally in the Cabinet [because he was the Vice President] is likely to be *near* the President) & Mr Van Buren & Mr McLean [the present and continuing postmaster general] will all be looking out for the *succession*." Fireworks, to say the very least, could well explode in Jackson's face before his four-year term ended.[48]

The inauguration on March 4, 1829, turned out to be a gorgeous springlike day, following a long cold and snowy winter. "A monstrous crowd of people" jammed the streets and the area around the east portico of the Capitol. "I never saw any thing like it before," Webster exclaimed. "Persons have come 500 miles to see Genl Jackson; & they really seem to think that the Country is rescued from some dreadful danger." Several newspapers estimated the crowd in excess of twenty thousand.

"The show," as Webster called it, lasted only half an hour. It began when the Supreme Court and foreign ministers entered the Senate chamber shortly after 11:00 A.M. Half an hour later the President-elect entered. Then Jackson, followed by the Senate and the other officials and the many ladies who had crowded into the galleries, marched through the rotunda to the portico over the east front door. But "the crowd broke in, as we were passing the Rotunda, and all became confusion."

When the officials and dignitaries finally emerged outdoors on the east portico, Jackson moved forward, read his inaugural address, and took his oath. "A great shout followed from the multitude, & in fifteen minutes, 'silence settled, deep & still.' Every body was dispersed."

As for the inaugural address, Webster could not make much of it except he thought it "*Anti-Tariff*—at least, in some degree." He surmised that Jackson's emphasis on "*reform*" meant either a "prelude to a general change in Office, or a mere *sop* to soothe the hunger, without satisfying it, of the thousand expectants for office who throng the City, & clamor all over the Country."[49]

Actually the scene was much more exciting and dramatic than Webster described.[50] After the inauguration the mob followed the President to the White House to celebrate the occasion, and they nearly wrecked the mansion. Webster did not follow, as Justice Story had. Instead he went to a bookstore and brought several books, one of which he sent to his sister-in-law, thinking it might help "to regulate matters of etiquette at Boscawen."[51]

48. DW to Ezekiel Webster, February 23, 26, 1829, ibid., II, 401, 402.

49. DW to Achsah Pollard Webster, March 4, 1829, ibid., II, 405, 406.

50. Some of the color and excitement can be found in Gaillard Hunt, ed., *The First Forty Years of Washington Society* (New York, 1906), the *United States Telegraph*, March 5, 1829, the Albany *Argus* for March 19, 1829, the Boston *Statesman*, March 12, 1829, the New York *Evening Post*, March 10, 1829, and the *Argus of Western America*, March 18, 1829.

51. DW to Achsah Pollard Webster, March 4, 1829, in *PC*, II, 406.

The inauguration of Jackson ushered in a new age that Webster found personally distasteful. The White House became a "democratically mixed public assembly." At the President's receptions and levees, according to Harriet Martineau, the sweaty and filthy shook hands with immaculately dressed diplomats, high-ranking officials, and prominent local citizens. Social boundaries were crumbling.[52]

Webster stayed on in Washington for several weeks after Congress had adjourned and then headed home early in April. No sooner did he arrive in Boston than at 3:00 in the morning he received word that his forty-nine-year-old brother had died at 4:00 P.M. on Friday, April 10, 1829, of a massive stroke or heart attack while addressing a jury. Zeke's wife was still in Boston with her eldest daughter when the news arrived and, together with Webster and his two sons, hurriedly journeyed to New Hampshire.

Zeke left behind his much younger wife, to whom he had been married for about four years, and two daughters, one fourteen, the other twelve, by his previous marriage. His death left Webster shaken. "Coming so soon after another awful stroke," he wrote to Dr. Perkins, who had attended Grace at the time of her death, it fell with "double weight. He had been my reliance, through life, and I have derived much of its happiness from his fraternal affection. I am left the sole survivor of my family," the last of a large family of brothers and sisters. Ezekiel's death, he told another, "was like tearing away one half of all that remained of myself." His death also severed Webster's still-strong ties to the place of his birth. "While my brother lived," he declared, "there was yet something to hold to; but now, the last attraction is gone. There was a large, valuable, and most pleasant farm which belonged to us, and which he [Ezekiel] had taken excellent care of for many years, but it causes me great pain now to visit it. A new generation has sprung up around it, and I see nothing interesting to me but the tombs of my parents, and my brothers and sisters." Years later Webster recalled looking at Ezekiel lying in his coffin, "a white forehead, a tinged cheek, a complexion as clear as heavenly light." He appeared to me, Webster remembered, "and so does he now seem to me, the very finest human form that I ever laid eyes on."[53]

As he admitted, his brother's death had a traumatic effect on him. Apart from tending the family estate, Ezekiel was Webster's mentor, counselor, warm supporter, devoted brother. The senator truly loved Zeke, as he had his father before him. Now he had no one close to turn to for comfort and solace.

He left Edward in Boscawen for the summer and returned to Boston. Julia wished to remain with Eliza Lee for the summer, and Fletcher expected to go to college in August.[54] The ensuing days and nights could be lonely indeed.

---

52. Larkin, *Everyday Life*, pp. 162–163.

53. DW to Cyrus Perkins, April 17, 1829, DW to Richard Peters, Jr., May 7, 1829, in *PC*, II, 409, 411; DW to Mrs. Langdon Elwyn, September 8, 1829, DW to Richard M. Blatchford, May 3, 1846, in Webster, ed., *Private Correspondence*, I, 480; II, 228.

54. DW to Jeremiah Mason, April 19, 1829 in *PC*, II, 410.

In this depressed state the senator turned for comfort to feminine companionship. But it should be stated at the outset that Daniel Webster was a passionate, romantic man all his life, however much he hid his feelings from public view. He needed female society and contact, and in this period of bereavement he appears to have developed a strong emotional bond with Sarah Goodridge, one of America's finest miniaturists, who was forty-one years of age at the time of Grace's death and six years younger than Webster. Largely self-taught at first but later instructed and encouraged by Gilbert Stuart, she learned how to paint in oils and on ivory. In 1820 she had opened a studio in Boston and soon established a reputation as an superb miniaturist. She often achieved "brilliant characterization and very fine effects of light and shadow."[55]

Sometime in the 1820s she became acquainted with Webster and painted his portrait. One portrait followed another until he had his likeness taken by her at least a dozen times over twenty years. He also engaged her to execute the portraits of his children and other members of his family. They began a correspondence, and there are presently extant forty-four letters from Webster to Goodridge, many undated, which can be found in the Massachusetts Historical Society and the Museum of Fine Arts in Boston. There are no known letters from her to Webster. Obviously they were all destroyed, probably by his heirs. His letters, which graduated from "Madam" in the beginning to "Dear Miss Goodridge" and finally to "My dear, good friend," suggest a genuine friendship, if not intimacy, between them. But they provide no proof of anything romantic. To wit: "I will not fail to come to see you, early next week"; "Mr Webster writes to inquire whether Miss Goodridge be in town & whether she will be in, at ¼ before 3 this P.M. Monday 1 oclock"; "If you are to be at home this Evening, at six or seven oclock I will call to see you"; "Mr Webster's compliments to Miss Goodridge—will call at her room this P.M. about 4 or 5 oclock." At one point he informed her that he had sent her two hundred dollars and added, "Please write me, what your present wants are, & what they will be in future & I will do all in my power to meet them." These are a few of the short notes he sent her at various times during their long relationship, all undated.[56]

As far as can be determined, Goodridge never left Boston except for an extended period in Washington during the winters of 1828–1829, 1840–1841, and perhaps 1832. Grace died on January 21, 1828, and the death possibly accounts for Sarah's first visit. During one of these trips Goodridge received this undated note: "Mr Webster presents his respects to Miss Goodridge, & hopes she has recovered from the fatigues of her journey—Mr Webster was prevented yesterday by his engagements, & today by the weather, from calling to say to her that he has spoken to a Gentleman to look out for her a suitable room for the exercise of her art."[57]

55. Dale T. Johnson, *American Portrait Miniatures in the Manney Collection* (New York, 1990), p. 125.

56. DW to Goodridge, *Microfilm Edition*, F8/9725, F4/38400, 38404, 38409.

57. Johnson, *American Portrait*, p. 125; DW to Goodridge, *Microfilm Edition*, F28/38406.

During one of the most trying periods of Webster's life, the period following Grace's death, Goodridge sent him a miniature self-portrait entitled "Beauty Revealed." It is a watercolor on ivory, measuring 2⅝ by 3⅛ inches, and shows a bare-breasted woman. It is a "strikingly realistic work" with "glowing skin tones," achieved "by the use of extremely transparent washes of color." It "shows the delicate stipple and hatching typical of Goodridge's tchnique." For a woman to present a portrait of herself with her breasts exposed was unheard of at that time. "In the United States there is no known precedent for the giving of an artistic expression of affection of this unusual, personal kind."[58]

During his "liaison" with Goodridge in 1828–1829 Webster began to acquire a reputation in Washington for "immorality." Isaac Bassett reported that "Mr Webster had a *ladies* friend her name was Ann Mitterigger" to whom the senator sent "presents and *money*" to purchase "*dresses*" for her daughter. Then, in 1832, "a coloured boy . . . came up to the Senate Chamber to see Senator Webster—he told me that Daniel Webster was his *father.*" Quite possibly this "coloured boy" was Robert Yancey, who claimed that his real name was Robert Webster, that he had been born in Gadsby's Hotel on the corner of Pennsylvania Avenue and Fourth Street on August 20, 1820, that he was the son of Daniel Webster and Charlotte Goodbrick, "a mulatto of rare beauty," whom his father had purchased and who served as his housemaid in Boston. Webster freed her, as he did several other servants he had purchased.[59]

None of these claims can be definitely proved, but over the next decade allegations about Webster's "sexual promiscuity" continued to circulate. Jane Grey Swisshelm, an editor in Pennsylvania, Minnesota, and Washington and a rabid abolitionist who relished attacking public figures, published some of the gossip in the 1850s. The first woman to obtain a seat in the press gallery of the Senate, she had been hired by Horace Greeley of the New York *Tribune,* and her "Letters" from the capital appeared frequently on the front page. After "sniffing" around Washington, to use her figure of speech, she caught a strong whiff of "moral stench," especially concerning Webster's reputation as a drunkard and the father of illegitimate mulatto children. In the Pittsburgh *Saturday Visitor* of May 4, and 25, 1850, she announced that "nearly everyone knows that [Webster] sometimes drinks to excess and his friends here say he requires to be excited by wine to make him approachable—civil. His mistresses are generally, if not always, colored women—some of them big black wenches as ugly and vulgar as himself." When the article appeared and she was identified as a correspondent for the *Tribune,* Greeley fired her for violating the unwritten rules of

58. Johnson, *American Portrait,* pp. 126–127. Gloria Manney to author, February 26, 1997. The self-portrait and Goodridge's easel and paint box were passed down by members of Webster's family and sold in 1981. "Beauty Revealed" was presented by Goodridge to Webster and inscribed "1828" on a paper backing, now lost, and shown at the Metropolitan Museum of Art in New York at an exhibition of miniatures from the Manney Collection in 1991. Members of the Webster family referred to Goodridge as Webster's fiancée. See also John Updike, "The Revealed and the Concealed," *Art and Antiques,* XV (February 1993), pp. 70–76.

59. IB Papers, Box 1, Folder B, p. 58, Box 1, Folder C, p. 82, Box 11, Folder A, p. 9.

Washington correspondents against exposing the private indiscretions of congressmen. She also lost her seat in the press gallery. But that did not stop her "exposé." A few months later she informed her readers "that the God-like statesman . . . was a great nasty beast . . . dangerous and loathsome." She claimed she "soon discovered that his whole panoply of moral power was a shell—that his life was full of rottenness." She questioned Congressman Joshua R. Giddings and Dr. Gamaliel Bailey and "they assured me of the truth of what had been told me, but advised me to keep quiet."[60]

Swisshelm never offered any proof for her charges, and she has generally been discredited, although her original article was "copied and copied" by the national press. The Lowell *American,* for example, declared: "We have never before heard that Mr. Webster's 'mistresses' were 'colored women', but the fact that he has 'mistresses' of some color is, we suppose, as notorious as any other fact concerning him."[61]

Although Swisshelm's charges can be discounted as the vindictive outpourings of an extreme abolitionist intent on destroying Webster for opposing abolitionism, other sources corroborate his reputation for moral delinquency. In his diaries James H. Hammond of South Carolina, a man of ravenous sexual appetite, admitted his own sexual waywardness and said that he deserved "great, very great condemnation." His diary entry for December 9, 1846, attempts a justification of sorts, for he notes the fact that David took Uriah's wife, that Caesar spared no woman, "that in all ages and countries down to our present day and nation the very greatest men that have lived have been addicted to loose indulgences with women. It is the besetting sin of the strong, and of the weak also, of our race. Among us now Webster and Clay are notorious for it."[62]

The distinguished New York lawyer George Templeton Strong regarded Webster as "one of the greatest intellectually, but not morally." He felt compelled to admit that Black Dan was "slightly heathenish in private life."[63]

As for Goodridge, whether Webster had any sexual involvement with her cannot be proved one way or the other, although the fact that she sent him a self-portrait with her breasts exposed raises suspicions. Indeed, in view of "Beauty Revealed," and their many encounters over the years it is not unlikely that

60. Jane Grey Swisshelm, *Crusader and Feminist: Letters of Jane Grey Swisshelm, 1858–1865,* ed. Arthur J. Larsen (St. Paul, 1935), p. 7; Swisshelm, *Half a Century* (Chicago, 1880), pp. 131–135; *Saturday Visitor,* May 25, 1850, July 5, 1851; Donald A. Ritchie, *Press Gallery: Congress and the Washington Correspondents* (Cambridge, Mass., 1991), pp. 43–44, 46, 56; Bertha-Monica Stearns, "Reform Periodicals and Female Reformers, 1830–1860," *American Historical Review,* XXXVII (July 1932), pp. 691–692. Joshua Giddings was a lawyer, a Whig congressman from 1839 to 1854, and an abolitionist, while Gamaliel Bailey was a physician, an editor, and an abolitionist. Swisshelm mistakenly believed that she was principally responsible for Webster's failure to receive the Whig nomination for President in 1852. *Half a Century,* pp. 134–135.

61. Ritchie, *Press Gallery,* p. 46. The Lowell *American* is quoted in Bartlett, *Webster,* p. 284.

62. James H. Hammond, *Secret and Sacred: The Diaries of James Henry Hammond, a Southern Slaveholder,* ed. Carol Bleser (New York, 1988), p. 172.

63. Nevins and Thomas, eds., *Diary of George Templeton Strong,* I, 225–226; II, 107.

Goodridge was Webster's mistress. Still, Webster's sexual needs are not as important as the fact that he was a very passionate man and desperately needed the close attachment and devotion of a woman. For a public figure in the 1820s only a wife could "legitimately" satisfy that need. Goodridge was a struggling spinster-artist trying to earn a living—as a matter of fact Webster borrowed over two thousand dollars from her, which he never repaid[64]—and therefore ineligible as a marital partner for Black Dan. Consequently he had to find a more suitable companion. So he looked elsewhere.

On May 15, 1829, Webster wrote a letter to the Patroon, Stephen Van Rensselaer, inviting himself for a visit. "My object," he explained to Van Rensselaer, "is no other than to express a wish to be permitted to visit you, and to cultivate an acquaintance in your family." This "acquaintance," Catherine Van Rensselaer, was a woman he hardly knew, but Webster believed she possessed "uncommon good sense, refined manner, and amiable temper; and I have the best reasons for not entertaining a doubt of domestic habits & dispositions, or of the solidity & excellence of her religious & moral principles." He had admired her character and manner from the moment he first met her. In view of the recent "change" in his "own condition," Catherine had become "the leading object of my reflections." He was about to leave for New York on business and could easily journey up to Albany. He hoped he might be welcome to visit the Van Rensselaer family. Was there "any objection to my visiting your house, & cherishing an acquaintance in your family. . . ?"[65]

Obviously Webster was shopping around, and Catherine met all the prior conditions that probably most men in the early nineteenth century looked for in a wife. In addition to everything else he cataloged in his letter, she had extraordinarily good family connections that went back to the founding of New Amsterdam by the Dutch. And she had money. Unfortunately the lady had other plans. She subsequently married G. W. Wilkins and Webster was forced to continue his search elsewhere.[66]

Webster did spend a little time in New York on business and argued several cases in Boston, in one of which, *Farnam v. Brooks,* he appeared against his occasional opponent William Wirt.[67] He also managed to get away from his work

64. DW to Goodridge, *Microfilm Edition* F23/32013, F13/16408, F10/12850, F10/12802, F10/12746. Goodridge never married.

65. DW to Van Rensselaer, May 15, 1829, in *PC,* II, 413–414.

66. He interrupted his marital search and spent much of the summer and fall in attending to his brother's affairs. He was now the sole survivor of his family and the guardian of Ezekiel's young children. The farm at Franklin became his own property, which would require his attention. Curtis, *Webster,* I, 344.

67. When the case concluded, Wirt wrote him an admiring letter. Considering Wirt's great reputation as a trial lawyer, the letter said a great deal about what other lawyers thought of Webster's legal talents. "How happy & secure you must feel with the house of your fame on its' *[sic]* everlasting rock—like the rocks that form the *substratum* of your blissful country. I wish I had been as wise all my life as you have been—gone always for substance and not for show. My show, through the earlier years of my life, was the eclipse of my substance—and the shadows of that eclipse will haunt me thro' life." Wirt to DW, July 8, 1829, in *PC,* II, 421.

to spend some time with his children and find rest in the country. He went to Brattleboro, Vermont, with Julia in July and vacationed there for several weeks. He had intended to visit Lake George, but he proceeded to Albany instead, perhaps to visit with the Van Rensselaers. In August he returned to Marshfield, "near our old shooting place at Scituate," where he spent a week reading in foul weather and "boat shooting" in fair. He also took a quick trip to New Hampshire, but the visit plainly depressed him. Once back in Boston, Julia, who had spent much of the summer at Brookline, continued her residence with Eliza Lee and received schooling from a Miss Searle, to whom Julia became quite attached. Edward stayed in the country, and Fletcher prepared to go off to Harvard.[68]

Webster himself resumed his search for a mate. Rumor had it that he had become engaged to Maria Parker, but whether unfounded or not, the lady halted the rumors by marrying Simon Adams.[69]

He had better luck on his next try. During one of his many trips to New York City he met Caroline Le Roy, the second daughter of Herman Le Roy, a wealthy merchant, whose ancestry went back to the early settlers of New York. From all reports she was not a beautiful woman and at thirty-two was fifteen years younger than Webster. Indeed, since this was her first marriage, she was a good bit older than most marriageable young ladies of that era. Nonetheless Webster found her appealing. "She is the daughter of a highly respectable Gentleman, now some years retired from the mercantile business," he wrote on November 18, his earliest statement that he had finally found a willing partner. ". . . She is amiable, discreet, prudent, with enough of personal comeliness to satisfy me"—which was hardly a compliment under the circumstances—"& of the most excellent character & principles." Edward Everett was less charitable about her looks. In a letter to his wife written two years later Everett described her as a "lady who owes much to full dress. In plain dress she is plain. . . . But what right have I to disparage her? . . . If she suits him is not that enough?"[70]

It was a courtship conducted at breakneck speed. Caroline and Daniel were married on Saturday, December 12, 1829, in the parlor of the Eastern Hotel near the Battery in New York by the Reverend Dr. Wainwright. Only Webster's daughter, Julia, and Caroline's immediate family attended the nuptials.[71]

It could hardly be called love at first sight. As a matter of fact it baffled Everett. "Mr W's being smitten so deeply, and so suddenly remains . . . a *parallelogram* to me."[72] Obviously it was a marriage of convenience—on both sides. She had money, social position, and family connections—although not as distinguished as the Van Rensselaers—and could provide him with a comfortable

68. DW to John Agg, August 10, 1829, DW to Nathan Hale, [August 1829], DW to Jeremiah Mason, August 10, 1829, DW to Elizabeth Langdon-Elwyn, September 8, 1829, ibid., II, 422, 423, 424.

69. Josiah Johnston to DW, October 19, 1829, ibid., II, 428.

70. DW to Jacob McGaw, November 18, 1829, in Van Tyne, ed, *Letters of Webster*, pp. 577–578; Everett to Mrs. Everett, January 17, 1831, Everett Papers, MHS. Everett commented, "This part of the letter pretty silly."

71. Curtis, *Webster*, I, 345; Fuess, *Webster*, I, 359–360.

72. Everett to Mrs. Everett, January 17, 1831, Everett Papers, MHS.

home and care for his children during necessary absences in Washington or on legal business in various states. Webster was intensely ambitious for higher public office, and she could bring a certain degree of luster to their social life. And not the least of it, he obtained her dowry of twenty-five thousand dollars, ten thousand of which he received on the day of the marriage, ten thousand the following July, and the remaining five thousand at Herman Le Roy's convenience. In return Webster signed over to the Le Roys, for the benefit of Caroline and her children, his house, coach house, and surrounding property on Summer Street in Boston.[73]

For her part, Caroline needed Webster. He rescued her from spinsterhood, and now that she had reached the "advanced" age of thirty-two without a husband, her life at home had become increasingly confined. She wanted and needed a larger world of social activity, something Webster could readily provide. In addition, he was a man of great fame as an orator and statesman. One of the finest lawyers in the country, he could provide the comforts of life to which she was accustomed. The speed of Webster's courtship and proposal was matched by the speed of Caroline's acceptance.

Dutifully Webster notified his son Fletcher. "The Lady who is now to bear the relation of mother to you, & Julia & Edward, I am sure will be found worthy of all your affection & regard; & I am equally certain that she will experience from all of you the utmost kindness & attachment. She insists on taking Julia with us to Washington; thinking it will be better for her, & that she will also be good company."[74]

Caroline proved to be something of a mixed blessing. She did develop cordial, indeed loving, relationships with the children, especially Fletcher. She also proved to be an asset in social situations and assisted her husband far more directly than Grace in advancing his political ambitions. But she loved beautiful, costly things, and Webster felt a great need to provide them. His increasing extravagance in their lifestyle made his search for income ever more urgent. Sometimes the pressure of his political ambition and his financial needs became too great for him to handle wisely. Also, she frequently left him to return to her family and friends in New York while he remained behind in Washington. In fact in 1841 she disregarded his pleas to return to their home, causing some to suspect that a divorce was imminent, particularly when Sarah Goodridge suddenly appeared in the capital.

Despite the relatively recent double loss of his devoted first wife and his beloved brother, Webster remarried. He married in haste, still burdened by the tragic removal from his life of the two people who meant so much to him. His motive for marrying eight months after his brother's death and a courtship of approximately one month suggests he acted because of his overwhelming need for affection and intimate human companionship. He could not properly function without a wife at his side.

73. Record of Payment from Herman Le Roy to Daniel Webster, in *PC*, III, 82. Le Roy paid the remaining five thousand dollars on July 21, 1830.

74. DW to Fletcher Webster, December 14, 1829, ibid., II, 436.

18

The Webster-Hayne Debate

CONGRATULATIONS on his marriage came from both friends and strangers, even from Sarah Goodridge. "I thank you for your congratulations, on a recent occurrence," he wrote her in reply, "& hope for an opportunity to making you & this Lady acquainted."[1]

Naturally Webster missed the opening session of the Twenty-first Congress, but he planned to arrive in Washington around the first of the new year after spending a short honeymoon in New York City with his bride. The couple remained for the Christmas holiday and then headed for the capital with Julia[2] and took lodgings with Dr. Harvey Lindsley, a Washington physician who played an active role in the American Colonization Society.

Much had transpired since the last congressional session. The Jackson administration immediately started clearing house of political opponents and replacing them with loyal Democrats. A number of these appointments required senatorial confirmation, and these new appointees had already begun to land on the Senate's calendar for action.

The appointing power took on added significance as the two emerging parties of the Jacksonian era, the Democratic and National Republican parties, sought to extend their national influence and power. Party activity during the campaign of 1828 demonstrated for all time how important patronage could be in commanding individuals to organize street rallies and barbecues, gather useful propaganda for circulation by newspapers and handbills, and work to create mass followings. "The triumph of the Jackson party," wrote a recent member of Congress from New Hampshire to Webster, ". . . has made them more insolent and overbearing than ever. All who have not gone for the *Hero* are to be forever proscribed, and would be immolated, if they had the power."[3]

Jackson himself certainly approved removal as a legitimate exercise of his

---

1. DW to Goodridge, January 11, 1830, in *PC*, III, 5–6.

2. Webster had expected to take Julia no farther than New York. She was supposed to return to Boston with her uncle James Paige. "But Mrs. Webster chose to have it otherwise, and I believe it is much better as it is. Julia seems exceedingly happy." DW to Mrs. Achsah Webster, January 17, 1830, in *W&S*, XVII, 484.

3. Joseph Healy to DW, January 18, 1829, in *PC*, III, 10.

power to institute what he called his program of *"reform."* As he explained in his first message to Congress, delivered on December 8, 1829, he believed that appointed office should be limited to four years, the equivalent of a President's first term. Each President ought to have the right to chose those individuals who could best serve the public and the chief executive. "Offices are created solely for the benefit of the people," and "no one man has any more intrinsic right to official station than another," he said.[4]

In addition to his principle of rotation of office, (subsequently called the spoils system by the National Republicans), Jackson provided other "horrors" in his message. He wanted a constitutional amendment to prevent what had happened in 1824–1825, when a minority President was elected by the House. He asked that the electoral college be abolished and that the President be chosen by a majority of the people for a single term of four or six years. *"The majority is to govern,"* he declared. It is the first principle of our political system. The people, in Jackson's view, were virtuous, intelligent, and fully capable of self-rule; they are the "sovereign power."[5] He also wished to pay off the national debt, bring about a "judicious" adjustment of the tariff schedule in order to restore harmony among the several sections of the country, alter the structure of the Bank of the United States, and remove the Indians beyond the Mississippi River so as to "protect and preserve them as nations."[6]

Any number, but not all, of these proposals to Congress worried Webster. Tampering with the United States Bank would be one. After all, he not only was a director and counsel for the BUS but had been influential in the appointment of several high officers of particular branches of the Bank. And if adjusting the tariff rates to make them more "judicious" meant lowering the rates on manufactures, then he would be obliged to fight it.

Webster also took exception to the message's highflown democratic rhetoric. He disagreed particularly with Jackson's claim that as President he had the exclusive power to control all operations of the executive branch, including removal from office. "According to the true intent & meaning of the Constitution," Webster insisted, "the President alone does not possess the power of removal from office." Such a claim, he said, is simply "hostile to the spirit of the Constitution, & dangerous to the peace, prosperity, & permanency of the Govt."[7] Clearly the message promised a lively session.

What added to the political excitement as the Twenty-first Congress got under way was the obvious rivalry for the succession that had developed between

---

4. Jackson underscored the word "reform" in his inaugural address. Both the address and his first message to Congress can be found in Richardson, *Messages and Papers,* II, 999–1001, 1011–1012.

5. After reading the President's message, the great chancellor of New York James Kent told Webster that "all theories of Government that suppose the mass of the people virtuous and able, and willing to act virtuously are plainly Utopian and *will remain so* until the return of the Saturnian age." James Kent to DW, January 21, 1830, in *PC,* III, 11–12.

6. Richardson, *Messages and Papers,* II, 1011–1012. The emphasized quotation is Jackson's.

7. DW to Joseph Hopkinson, [January 15, 1830], in *PC,* III, 8–9.

Secretary of State Van Buren and Vice President Calhoun. A factional split within the Democratic party could easily ensue unless Jackson did something to prevent it. To make matters worse, a constitutional crisis that threatened to topple the entire cabinet had developed over the summer. It started when the wives of the heads of the several departments, allegedly led by Mrs. Calhoun, refused to accept Peggy Eaton, the wife of John H. Eaton, the secretary of war, as a social equal because of her "tainted past." Instantly Jackson rushed to Peggy's defense. He saw in her something of his deceased wife, Rachel, who had been cruelly slandered during the presidential campaign and died shortly thereafter. Furthermore, rumor had it that Van Buren encouraged Jackson into believing that Calhoun had initiated the assault on poor Peggy to gain political ascendancy within the administration.[8]

As far as Webster could tell, Van Buren had "quite the lead in influence and importance. He controls all the pages on the back stairs, and flatters what seems to be at present the Aaron's serpent among the President's desires, a settled purpose of making out the lady, of whom so much has been said, a person of reputation." The consequence of this dispute, he shrewdly observed, "is producing great political effects, and may very probably determine who shall be successor to the present chief magistrate."[9]

Calhoun's standing with Jackson took a really bad turn when another rumor credited him with composing the resolutions, recently adopted by the South Carolina legislature, that enunciated the doctrine of nullification, a doctrine Jackson found altogether pernicious and dangerous. More commonly known as South Carolina's Exposition and Protest, it sought to provide a constitutional safeguard to protect the states from the abuse of power by the national government. Calhoun argued the constitutional right of the state to nullify federal legislation within its borders whenever such legislation violated its rights or sovereignty. To protect its citizens from the "tyranny of the majority," he contended, the state may "interpose" its authority and declare the offending federal legislation null and void. If the central government used force against the state to execute its laws, then the state could rightfully secede from the Union. However, Calhoun had devised his theory of nullification to obviate the necessity of secession. But if all else failed, then secession was the state's ultimate defense against injustice and tyranny.[10]

The Tariff of Abominations had provoked Calhoun into writing the Exposition. Thus, when Jackson called for a tariff revision to restore sectional harmony, everyone naturally assumed that he wished to placate South Carolina by removing the abominations and bringing the tariff schedule back to a more moderate,

8. For the complete details of the Eaton scandal, see Remini, *Jackson*, II, 203–216.

9. DW to Warren Dutton, January 15, 1830, in *W&S*, XVII, 483.

10. All of Calhoun's important political essays and writings can be conveniently found in the single volume *Union and Liberty: The Political Philosophy of John C. Calhoun* (Indianapolis, 1992), excellently edited by Ross M. Lence, who provides informative introductions to each of Calhoun's works. The Exposition runs on pp. 313–365.

"judicious" level. But the issue had become so politically sensitive that any mention of adjustment alerted and alarmed those with special interests to protect.

Webster represented some of those interests, and after learning about Calhoun's "extraordinary" claims concerning the prerogatives of the states, he knew that somewhere down the line he would have to respond to them. He had already acquired a reputation as the "Great Expounder and Defender of the Constitution" who virtually provided the Supreme Court with all the basic arguments for its major decisions. Everyone therefore expected him to set Calhoun and the other nullifiers straight about what the states and federal government could and could not do under the constitutional system.

When he returned to his seat in early January, he paid little or no attention to the Senate's proceedings and debates. He was much too busy arguing cases before the Supreme Court. He did of course take note of all the political developments that had occurred and continued to unfold. Nor did he forget his role as a leader of the National Republican party in Congress. Accordingly, he detailed what he thought should be some of his party's positions on men, issues, and the events now transpiring within the administration. In a private and confidential letter to John H. Pleasants, founder in 1824 of the Richmond *Whig,* he contended that the National Republicans must "expose the selfishness & *pretense* of the men in power" and "show ourselves uniform, & just, by acting according to our principles." As for the tariff, "we of the north must hold on where we are." The same went for internal improvements. "We, also, must go, temperately & cautiously for them also." But he favored Jackson's idea about paying the national debt. That he approved. With regard to the Calhoun–Van Buren feud he said that we must "hold ourselves absolutely aloof . . . & be ready to act for ourselves when the proper time comes—& to maintain our own men, & defend our own friends." Finally, and Webster undoubtedly thought that this had to be his party's main objective (certainly it was his), the National Republicans must "cultivate a truly national spirit—go for great ends, & hold up the necessity of the Union &c."[11]

Here, then, in just a few words, Webster summed up his central thinking about the future direction of this nation. Perhaps more than most he understood that the nation had evolved from a string of European colonies into a unified people with national pride and a belief in their destiny as a free and prosperous society. They were no longer Englishmen or Europeans, such as the Founders had been; they were Americans. A national identity had emerged. And he, more than anyone else in the country, had become the leading spokesman and historian of that identity.

Webster's committee assignments did not interfere with his legal affairs, although as a member of a special committee on roads and canals he did move consideration of a bill on mileage compensation for members of Congress and

11. DW to Pleasants, March 6, 1830, in *PC,* III, 25–26.

presented a petition for a railroad company to have the government subscribe to its capital stock. The triviality of his activities in the Senate attests to his distraction and concern for interests outside the chamber.

But events had already taken place that would suddenly command his attention, and the attention of the nation, and lead to a dramatic contest with far-reaching consequences. On December 29, 1829, two days before Webster arrived in Washington, Senator Samuel A. Foot of Connecticut had introduced a resolution that the Committee on Public Lands consider limiting the sale of public lands to those already on the market and, in addition, that the office of surveyor general be abolished. Why offer additional lands, he asked, when millions of acres still remained unsold?

Such a suggestion, especially one coming from an easterner, infuriated westerners, who saw the resolution as a dastardly attempt to restrict western migration in order to prevent low-paid laborers from leaving employment in eastern factories to go west, in effect to benefit one section of the country at the expense of another. It was the same basic argument of southerners about the tariff—namely, that northerners used their superior numbers in Congress to raise duties for their own manufactures, allowing the expense of the high rates to fall on southerners.

Senator Thomas Hart Benton of Missouri, a big, blustery Jacksonian with a powerful voice that could shake the walls, rose to condemn the resolution. Here was a former supporter of Henry Clay who had fought Jackson in a street brawl in Nashville and had moved to Missouri to escape reprisal from Jackson's "puppies" but who had reconciled with the Hero and now led the Democratic forces in the Senate.[12] In a rousing speech the day following Foot's proposal, he articulated western resentment over eastern interference in the affairs of his section. And did Foot care about the consequences of his resolution on the West? Not in the least.

As Benton spoke these words, Foot shook his head vigorously. "The Senator from Connecticut shakes his head, but he cannot shake the conviction out of my head," Benton roared, "that a check to Western emigration will be the effect of this resolution. The West is my country; not his. I know it; he does not. . . . The idea of checking emigration to the West was brought forward openly at the increase of the tariff." So said the secretary of the treasury in his annual report. The force of emigration had to be absorbed "in order to keep people in the East to work in the manufactories."[13]

If nothing else, mention of the tariff caught the immediate attention of southerners. What better way for these cotton-growing slaveholders to protect their own special interests than by joining the West in opposition to the East? A South-West alliance could both reduce the rates of protection and make western land cheap enough to attract new settlers. Benton had already advocated a

12. Remini, *Jackson*, I, 186.
13. *Register of Debates*, 21st Congress, 1st Session, pp. 4–5.

graduation bill that would reduce land prices from its present price of $1.25 an acre by twenty-five cents each year until the cost of buying public land reached a limit of twenty-five cents per acre. He therefore saw in Foot's resolution a deliberate attempt to halt the settlement of the West.

Benton renewed his attack on January 18. He denied that he purposely questioned Foot's motives in introducing his resolution. But he saw in a proposal to send the resolution to committee an attempt to suppress debate, and he had no intention of "letting it escape under a flash and a smoke." Posturing in the grand manner of the nineteenth century, he said he discriminated between "resolutions for good and for evil; the former passed, of course, the latter should be resisted. If not, the whole country may be alarmed, agitated, and enraged, with mischievous inquiries; the South about its slaves and Indians; the West about its lands; the North-east on the subject of its fisheries, its navigation, its light-houses, and its manufactories."[14] At times he became so vehement that his voice rattled the windows.

The marvelously baited invitation to the South proved irresistible to thirty-seven-year-old Robert Y. Hayne of South Carolina, and the following day he rose to the bait. When elected to the Senate in 1823, he was barely old enough to meet the age requirement set down in the Constitution. Almost ten years younger than Webster, he had no idea that his remarks would trigger one of the most celebrated debates in congressional history.

Like Benton, Hayne started off by opposing a public land policy that sought to use the land as a source of revenue and not as a means of attracting settlers. He feared that the proceeds from land sales could become a fund for corruption. Then he let fly a ringing endorsement of states' rights, a philosophy that Webster had begun to fear as inimical to the future growth, prosperity, and greatness of the nation. "The very life of our system," declared Hayne, "is the independence of the States and . . . there is no evil more to be deprecated than the consolidation of this Government."[15]

We learn from our mistakes how to feel for the sufferings of others, he continued, and surely the South has suffered in its relation to the federal government because of a system of taxation that drains off the wealth of the section to be "expended elsewhere." Hayne wanted the government to have no permanent sources of income as provided by the tariff and sale of public lands. It only "consolidates" the government and corrupts the people.[16]

Webster, who had been away from his desk, attending the Supreme Court

14. *Register of Debates*, 21st Congress, 1st Session, p. 23.

15. "Here we have an argument proceeding entirely along lines of national policy," wrote Theodore Jervey, Hayne's biographer. "Could anything be more temperate." Jervey, *Robert Y. Hayne and His Times* (New York, 1909), p. 235.

16. Hayne's speech can be found in the *Register of Debates*, 21st Congress, 1st Session, pp. 31–33. Charles March says that Hayne's "exordium was respectable in point of ability, and gave assurance of a well-prepared speech." But as he proceeded, "his tone and language became more vehement: his allusions more personal. There was an angry inflection in his voice, indicative of loss of temper." March, *Webster*, p. 118.

over a controversy between John Jacob Astor and the state of New York,[17] left the court and entered the Senate chamber "with my court papers under my arm, just to see what was passing." At that approximate moment Hayne rose to begin his speech. Unquestionably what he said, especially his remark about states' rights and the danger of a consolidated government, both shocked and annoyed Webster. "I did not like it," Webster later declared, "and my friends liked it less." Samuel Bell of New Hampshire, Ezekiel Chambers of Maryland, and Nathaniel Silsbee of Massachusetts told him that "an immediate answer to Mr. Hayne was due from him." They reminded him that back in 1825 he and McDuffie in the House expressed opinions exactly the reverse of what had now been ascribed to the South and East. Webster could not remember the occasion and looked it up. Sure enough, he found that the memory of his friends had been correct, and he decided to use it in rebuttal.[18]

In his first reply to Hayne it seems clear that Webster never intended to speak solely to the issue of public lands before the Senate. The so-called attack on the East was something he believed he must repel and denounce. More important, nullification, as espoused in South Carolina's Exposition and Protest, and the whole extreme states' rights philosophy that constricted the national identity became his real targets. He decided to use this opportunity to challenge that philosophy because he believed it perilous to the future life of the nation.[19] The "Godlike Daniel" would provide the upper house and the country at large with a powerful oration about nationalism.

He usually began his speeches slowly and quietly, sometimes with long introductions to prepare the ground and capture the undivided attention of his audience. He knew of course that his appearance—bushy eyebrows, deep-set eyes, dark complexion—and most especially his magnificent voice could produce within the first half hour a hypnotic effect on his listeners. But once he entered the main theme of his address, "all his faculties expand or take on a new character. His large black eye dilates and kindles . . . his voice ranges through all its powerful notes . . . and his gestures, frequent and sometimes violent, are accompanied with a forward fling of his body, which is more emphatic than graceful." His words then reveal a "lethal intent." His scorn, his retort, his recrimination "are hurled upon their object with a deadly skill and unsparingness almost fiendish." His smile during an oration could be "angelical," his sneer "diabolical."[20]

On January 20 he treated his audience to an uncommon display of his vaunted eloquence. He started by denying any previous intention of involving himself in the question, but in view of Hayne's remarks, he could not let the occasion pass, he said, without some reply. With respect to the issue he admitted

17. *Carver v. Jackson,* 4 Peters 1.
18. Memorandum, January 1830, DW to Warren Dutton, March 8, 1830, in *W&S,* XI, 294; XVII, 493.
19. Ibid.
20. New York *Mirror,* October 1, 1831.

his own commitment to a policy of offering the land at low prices to encourage settlement. Everyone should be able to buy good land at affordable rates. However, he did not approve "throwing" new and vast amounts of land on the market at prices "merely nominal."

Next he denied "that there has been any thing harsh or severe in the policy of the government towards the new States of the West." He traced the long history of the settlement of the West and how vast new tracts of territory had been acquired. He added that he was "struck with wonder at the success" with which it was carried out, and he looked with admiration at the wisdom and foresight that had informed the policy of distributing the public domain: how distinct republican states had been formed and then admitted as equal partners to the federal Union. "Sir, I maintain, Congress has acted wisely, and done its duty on this subject. I hope it will continue to do it."

Then, after speaking at some length on the land question, he finally got to his main objective. He reminded his audience of what Hayne had said about the government's having a fixed revenue and the fears he had expressed about consolidation and corruption.

"Consolidation!"—Webster spit out the word—"that perpetual cry both of terror and delusion,—Consolidation!" What does it mean? Does it mean "any thing more than that the union of the States will be strengthened by whatever continues or furnishes inducements to the people of the States to hold together?" He himself did not wish to see new powers acquired by the general government. "But I confess I rejoice in whatever tends to strengthen the bond that unites us, and encourages the hope that our Union may be perpetual."

Here is Webster's first public statement about his belief in the perpetuity of the Union. It was an idea that had been growing for the past fifteen years and was soon to be adopted by President Jackson and given his strong endorsement. Since the founding of the Union under the Constitution a great many men had believed that if they became dissatisfied with the workings of the system, or found that the Constitution, like the Articles of Confederation, failed to satisfy their needs or protect their special interests, they could secede and get themselves a new government. No more. That belief was moribund, as far as Webster was concerned. He looked to the day when the "Union may be perpetual."

"I know," he continued, "that there are some persons in the part of the country from which the honorable member comes, who habitually speak of the Union in terms of indifference, or even of disparagement." Not the honorable member himself, of course. But those "others" frequently declare "that it is time to calculate the value of the Union. . . . Sir, I deprecate and deplore this tone of thinking and acting." This Union "is essential to the prosperity and safety of the States. I am a unionist, and, in this sense, a national republican."

This is the first time that Webster called himself anything other than a Federalist. By these words he finally conceded that he had become a Republican, but, let it be understood, a *National* Republican.

Having made his position in the strongest terms possible, he then turned to

Hayne's presumed attack on his section of the country. Actually Hayne had not attacked the East; Benton was the culprit. By rights Webster should have responded to Benton, but he deliberately chose Hayne as his target in order to provoke a debate on the Calhoun doctrine of interposition.

"The East!" boomed Webster, "the obnoxious, the rebuked, the always reproached East!" We are charged with the crime of "a narrow and selfish policy," of attempting to restrain western migration and western interests. "And the cause of all this narrow and selfish policy, the gentleman finds in the tariff; I think he called it the accursed policy of the tariff." Webster had no difficulty in denying the charge, pointing out that New England had always opposed the tariff. In fact the first protective Tariff of 1816 was carried, he said, by southern votes. "It was truly more a Southern than an Eastern measure." He continued at some length about the unfairness of the everlasting attacks on New England. As for opposing western settlement, he reminded the Senate that in 1825, debating George McDuffie of South Carolina in the House, he had defended lower prices for land to encourage migration while McDuffie had deplored them because they would drain the population of the East.

Next he touched on a subject that he knew would explode any possibility of an alliance between the South and the West: slavery. It was a stroke of political genius. Distorting history to a certain extent to serve his purpose, he claimed that the Northwest Ordinance of 1787, by which the West could be settled and admitted as states, was "drawn" by Nathan Dane, then and now a citizen of Massachusetts.[21] The ordinance forbade slavery. It thereby "fixed for ever the character of the population in the vast regions northwest of the Ohio, by excluding from them involuntary servitude." Webster obviously implied that such a population could never ally itself with the slaveowners of the South.

The mere mention of slavery was sure to provoke a response, and as Webster shortly learned, Hayne could not wait to reply. The agitation against slavery had mounted dramatically in the last few years, and it had already begun to edge its way to the forefront of national issues. Further discussion of the subject in this chamber could usually prompt heated debate.

Webster concluded on a self-congratulatory note: "As a true representative of the State which has sent me here, it is my duty, and a duty which I shall fulfill, to place her history and her conduct, her honor and her character, in their just and proper light, so often as I think an attack, is made upon her, so respectable as to deserve to be repelled."[22]

What Webster had done in this first reply took cunning and premeditation. He deliberately switched the ground of the debate from the issue posed by the

21. Dane, among others, helped draft the Northwest Ordinance, and he introduced the article that prohibited slavery in the Northwest, but Thomas Jefferson wrote the committee report in 1784 that became the basis of the celebrated ordinance. For Dane's reaction to the speech and also to Hayne's subsequent response, see Dane's letter to Webster, March 26, 1830, in PC, III, 43–48.

22. Register of Debates, 20th Congress, 1st Session, pp. 35–41. See also Webster's Notes, in W&S, VI, 287–292.

original resolution to one that gave him the opportunity to capitalize on the growing sense of nationalism in the country and defend the honor and character of New England. It also allowed him to take several potshots at the South, slavery, and nullification that might well lead Hayne into defending that doctrine and thereby enable Webster to reassert, in even stronger terms, the supremacy of the federal Union.

Everyone in the chamber knew it would come, and Hayne did not disappoint them. The day following Webster's first reply, Hayne immediately rose to fire a few salvos of his own, but Representative Chambers asked for a postponement because Webster had to attend to some legal business before the Supreme Court and wished to be present for the entire debate. Hayne turned and saw Webster sitting at his desk, arms crossed over his chest and looking proud and haughty. In a sarcastic voice Hayne said that he presumed Webster to be present, adding that he was unwilling to agree to a postponement until he had the opportunity of replying. Certain "things" had been said, Hayne continued, "that rankled here." As he spoke these words, he dramatically pointed to his breast. Webster "had discharged his fire in the face of the Senate," he cried. I trust that the gentleman "would now afford [me] the opportunity of returning the shot."

"I am ready to receive it," Webster called out. "Let the discussion proceed."[23]

Unwilling to be excluded from what promised to be verbally historic, Senator Benton insisted on his right to speak first[24] and he harangued the Senate for more than an hour. Meanwhile Webster hurried downstairs to get a postponement of his business with the High Court.

Finally Benton sat down and Hayne took the floor. Webster watched and listened, looking defiant. Vice President Calhoun presided and clearly understood Webster's motive (Hayne knew it too) in luring the South Carolina senator into a constitutional debate on nullification. Calhoun's very presence undoubtedly encouraged Hayne, and he may or may not have passed notes to the senator to guide him in his attack.[25] In any event Hayne came well prepared to savage the New Englander.

"Little did I expect to be called upon to meet such an argument as was yesterday urged by the gentleman from Massachusetts," Hayne began. Then he rightly denied having attacked either New England or Massachusetts in his first speech. Rather he had tried to address a "great question of public policy." And

---

23. *Register of Debates*, 20th Congress, 1st Session, p. 41; IB Papers, Box 17, Folder E, p. 21.

24. Senators were surprised when Webster replied to Hayne instead of Benton so the Missourian was not out of order when he insisted on responding to Webster before Hayne.

25. Historians disagree on whether Calhoun passed notes to Hayne. Wiltse, *Calhoun*, II, 421–422, note 15, disputes it; both Fuess, *Webster*, I, p. 370, and Bartlett, *Webster*, p. 17, repeat it. The account of Calhoun's involvement can be found in March, *Webster*, pp. 118–119. "Constantly during the progress of the discussion [Calhoun] sent notes, suggestive, illustrative and advisatory to the orator, by one of the pages of the Senate." I am inclined to believe the story because it is corroborated in Sargent, *Public Men and Events*, I, 172. See John Niven, *John C. Calhoun and the Price of Union* (Baton Rouge, 1988), p. 175, for Calhoun's understanding of Webster's motives.

what was Webster's response? After mulling it all over for an entire night, the "Honorable Gentleman from Massachusetts . . . comes into this chamber to vindicate New England," and instead of answering Benton, who did criticize the East, he "pours out all the vials of his mighty wrath upon my devoted head." But the gentleman did not stop there. He deliberately assailed "the institutions and policy of the South" and called into question "the principles and conduct of" South Carolina. "When I find a gentleman of mature age and experience, of acknowledged talents and profound sagacity, pursuing a course like this . . . and making war upon the unoffending South, I must believe—I am bound to believe—he has some object in view that he has not ventured to disclose."

A splendid beginning. Right off Hayne nailed Webster for distorting the debate and introducing inflammatory inferences that were offensive to South Carolina and to the South. He then went on to score Webster for wrongly giving Nathan Dane credit as the author of the Northwest Ordinance. The only reason southerners knew Dane, Hayne sneered, was the fact that he had attended the Hartford Convention, which declared its opposition to restraining Congress from admitting new states into the Union. "So much for Nathan Dane of Beverly, Massachusetts."

Hayne quickly moved to the sensitive question of slavery, and he spoke "temperately" and "fairly" on the subject.[26] He wondered out loud whether Webster had consciously tried to enlist the prejudices of "mankind" or had used this "weakness" as an excuse to attack the South. He insisted that northern manufactures "derive greater profits from the labor of our slaves than we do ourselves."

Unfortunately, from this strong point, as he proceeded, Hayne weakened and seriously damaged his argument by attempting to demonstrate the supposed beneficial influences of slavery upon individuals and the nation as a whole. Even his friendly biographer contends that he took a position on very "slippery ground."[27]

As for the tariff, Hayne delighted in needling Webster. "The Senator from Massachusetts . . . tells us that he hears nothing but tariff! tariff! tariff!" Yet within the past ten years he has spoken eloquently and convincingly about free trade. Then, in 1828, "he was found on this floor, advocating and finally voting for the tariff of 1828—that 'bill of abomination.' " Small wonder, considering the "beautiful and enduring monument" of marble inscribed with his name that he erected before 1828, that he should now "hate the voice that should ring 'the accursed Tariff' " in his ears.

Following that assault, Hayne really struck Webster a body blow. In view of what transpired during the Hartford Convention, "that awful and melancholy period of our national history," why did the gentleman from Massachusetts— "who now manifests so great a devotion to the Union"—not "exert his great

26. Jervey, *Hayne*, p. 245. Jervey's biography, an older work, is a defensive but judicious handling of the debate from Hayne's point of view.
27. Ibid., p. 246.

talents and acknowledged influence" with his "deluded friends" in 1814 and point out to them "the value of the Union"? No, the gentleman had been silent.

Hayne must have savored every word as he spoke, and although he would not charge Webster with participation in the Hartford Convention, he did think his present and glowing effusions about the Union a bit much.

Finally, and unfortunately, Hayne fell headlong into the trap Webster had prepared so artfully and subtly. He addressed the question of nullification. And he did it badly. Here was the one great weakness of his entire speech.

If a government presumes to prescribe the limits of its own authority, he said, then the Constitution has been breached and you have a government without limitation of powers. The states necessarily would be reduced to petty "corporations," and the people placed at the government's mercy. Arguing from the Tenth Amendment to the Constitution and the Virginia and Kentucky Resolutions, Hayne defended Calhoun's theory of interposition by the states as a check on unlimited power by the central government. "In all the efforts that have been made by South Carolina to resist the unconstitutional laws which Congress has extended over them," Hayne concluded, "she has kept steadily in view the preservation of the Union, by the only means by which she believes it can be preserved—a firm, manly, and steady resistance against usurpation." Nullification did not seek to destroy the Union. On the contrary, it guaranteed its preservation.[28]

Hayne's one great mistake in invoking the doctrine of nullification—a mistake that caused Calhoun to repudiate the senator's interpretation in his Fort Hill address the following summer—was his assertion that the states and central authority acted as equals in the creation of the Constitution. The states' rights argument claimed that the states, and only the states, created the national government, that the central government is the creature of the states.

Webster rose to reply, but he yielded the floor since the hour was late. His friend Samuel Bell of New Hampshire moved adjournment, and it carried. Hayne had begun his speech on Thursday, January 21, and spoke for an hour; after an adjournment for the weekend he concluded it on Monday, January 25, speaking for about two and a half hours.[29] Without question it was a well-reasoned, graceful, eloquent, and relatively courteous speech,[30] touched with wit and occasional fire. Again and again he scored important points in presenting his case. He was, according to Edward Everett, who should know, the "foremost Southerner in debate, except Calhoun." He had done so well in fact that many friends of Webster doubted their man could adequately respond to it.[31] Even

28. Hayne's speech can be found in the *Register of Debates,* 20th Congress, 1st Session, pp. 43–58.

29. Webster, Memorandum, January 1830, in *W&S,* XI, 295; March, *Webster,* pp. 119–120, 121.

30. Charles March says that passages of Hayne's speech had "real eloquence, sparsely scattered." Unquestionably the "vehemence of the orator's language and the earnestness of his manner, produced no little effect upon his audience. They naturally begat sympathy." *Webster,* pp. 122, 123.

31. Ibid., p. 123. The "general opinion" of those who heard him, according to Isaac Bassett, agreed that he had triumphed as "the greater *Orator.*" IB Papers, Box 18, Folder D, p. 4.

Everett shared that doubt, calling Hayne's speech "a very masterly effort, and delivered with a great deal of power and with an air of triumph." He hastened to Webster's house.

"Mr. Hayne has made a speech?" said Everett.

"Yes, he has made a speech."

"You reply in the morning?"

"Yes," answered Webster, "I do not propose to let the case go by default, and without saying a word."

"Did you take notes, Mr. Webster, of Mr. Hayne's speech?"

Webster drew from his pocket a piece of paper as large as the palm of his hand. "I have it all," he responded.[32]

Justice Story also fretted. He thought Hayne's speech was an "acrimonious and disparaging tirade against New England," so he hurried to his friend's house and offered his help in looking up materials to be used in Webster's second reply to Hayne. The senator waved the offer aside with his thanks. "Give yourself no uneasiness, Judge Story," he replied. "I will grind him as fine as a pinch of snuff!"[33]

Strong words. But Webster oozed self-confidence. He had had plenty of time to prepare his second reply, working on it even before he delivered his first reply. Now all his oratorical and histrionic powers would be summoned in an exalted paean of praise to personal liberty and national sovereignty.[34]

He knew it could be the most important speech in his entire career, so he asked Joseph Gales of the *National Intelligencer,* known for his shorthand expertise, to report the speech personally. Gales later read his shorthand script to his wife, who prepared a readable manuscript that was delivered to Webster, who revised it for publication.

The excitement in Washington already generated by the first round of the debate had grown to fever pitch. Margaret Smith, the wife of Senator Samuel Smith, told her friend Mrs. Kirkpatrick that "almost everyone is thronging to the capitol to hear Mr. Webster's reply to Col. Hayne's attack on him and his party." She went on to say that "a debate on political principle would have had no such attraction. But personalities are irresistible. It is a kind of moral gladiatorship, in which characters are torn to pieces, and arrows, yes, poisoned arrows, which tho' not seen, are deeply felt, are hurled by the combatants against each other." The crowd pouring into the Capitol to hear the response wanted a killing. They

32. Harvey, *Reminiscences,* pp. 149–151. Everett did not hear Hayne's speech himself but drew his conclusions from what he was told by those who did hear the speech. On Hayne's speech, see also March, *Webster,* pp. 100–103.

33. Story to Mrs. Story, January 29, 1830, in Story, *Life and Letters,* II, 34; Harvey, *Reminiscences,* p. 156. Story's description of Hayne's speech was excessively biased.

34. And men like Calhoun and Senator James Iredell of North Carolina knew what electrifying eloquence he could evoke from the immense range of his intellect and imagination. To one of Hayne's friends, who praised the southerner's speech, Iredell responded: "He has started the lion— but wait till we hear his roar, or feel his claws." March, *Webster,* pp. 124–125.

wanted "to witness the triumph or defeat of Mr Webster."[35]

The following day, January 26, "was a day never to be forgotten by those who witnessed the scene in the Senate chamber, & a day destined to be forever memorable in the annals of the Senate." The House of Representatives was deserted, but the Senate chamber was packed, "crowded to suffocation." Every seat, every inch of ground, said Mrs. Smith, even the steps were *"compactly filled."* Senators courteously surrendered their seats to the "ladies"; there were about three hundred females in attendance, she estimated, attended by their escorts. The *"people"* jammed the two galleries and the stairways. Their presence again reminded everyone that since Jackson's inauguration the government was becoming "more and more democratic." And women too, Smith added, "are gaining more than their share of power."

Members of the House filled the lobby behind the Vice President's chair. Representative Dixon H. Lewis of Alabama eased his enormous bulk of four hundred pounds behind the painted glass partition that separated the lobby from the chamber and with his penknife scratched out a "peep hole" as large as his hand so that he could see as well as hear what Webster was about to say. The scratching sound attracted much attention, but everyone seemed to understand and approve his purpose.[36]

Party spirit "ran uncommonly high," reported Everett, as the Senate prepared to begin its proceedings. And sectional feeling even higher. Southerners, he said, seemed intent on breaking down northerners and their influence.[37]

As usual Webster sauntered into the chamber—he never strode in—and appeared absentminded, acting as if unconscious of the presence of a huge audience. Once the business of the Senate resumed, he rose, and like the gladiator in a Roman arena described by Mrs. Smith, he faced the horde of people crowded around him. The air of absentmindedness suddenly vanished and "he seemed to gradually recover perfect self-possession."

The scene has been wonderfully depicted in G. P. A. Healy's great painting now hanging in Faneuil Hall. Dressed in the revolutionary colors of blue and buff, Webster wore a brass-buttoned blue dresscoat, a buff waistcoat, and a high white cravat, "the support of his ponderous head."[38] And he spoke not to Hayne, or the ladies, or the *"people"* hanging from the galleries. He pitched his reply beyond the chamber and directly to the people of the United States. Whether he realized it or not, that speech spoke to Americans not only of his own generation but of generations to come.

35. Smith to Kirkpatrick, January 26, 1830, Hunt, ed., *First Forty Years of Washington Society*, p. 310; IB Papers, Box 17, Folder E, p. 32. It is interesting that Bassett too used the "gladiatorship" figure of speech. "In the prime of magnificent manhood, & in the zenith of his fame," wrote Bassett, "he [Webster] stood like a gladiator facing his foe." Ibid., p. 39.

36. Smith to Kirkpatrick, January 26, 1830, Hunt, ed., *First Forty Years*, p. 310; March, *Webster*, p. 133; IB Papers, Box 20, Folder C, p. 64.

37. Harvey, *Reminiscences*, p. 149.

38. Poore, *Reminiscences*, p. 116; Sargent, *Public Men and Events*, I, 172; IB Papers, Box 20, Folder A, p. 7, Box 18, Folder D, p. 4.

He began quietly. He summed up what had brought them to this point, mentioning Hayne's best "shot" and dismissing it as ineffectual. He moved on. He scored his first strike on the question of slavery. Hayne argues, he recalled, "that slavery, in the abstract, is no evil. Most assuredly I need not say I differ with him, altogether and most widely, on that point. I regard domestic slavery as one of the greatest evils, both moral and political." As for whether it be a malady and curable, Webster left to "those whose right and duty it is . . . to decide." This has been the "sentiment of the North." In other words, the abolition of slavery must come from the slaveholding states themselves. "It is their affair, not mine." Neither the central government nor Congress had any authority to emancipate the slaves.

Reversing himself on a previously held position, he also declared that he had no wish to alter the arrangement of representation in Congress, which counted the slaves as three fifths of the population. "It is the original bargain, the compact," he contended; "let it stand; let the advantage of it be fully enjoyed. . . . I go for the Constitution as it is, and for the Union as it is. But I am resolved not to submit in silence to accusations, either against myself individually or against the North, wholly unfounded and unjust."

Webster went on at considerable length to defend himself, Massachusetts, New England, and the East against Hayne's several charges of inconsistency or selfish self-interest or hostility toward other sections of the country. At one point he spoke words that every citizen in the Bay State who read them could take great pride.

Mr. President, I shall enter on no encomium upon Massachusetts; she needs none. There she is. Behold her, and judge for yourselves. There is her history; the world knows it by heart. The past, at least, is secure. There is Boston, and Concord, and Lexington, and Bunker Hill; and there they will remain for ever. The bones of her sons, falling in the great struggle for Independence, now lie mingled with the soil of every State from New England to Georgia; and there they will lie for ever. And Sir, where American Liberty raised its first voice, and where its youth was nurtured and sustained, there it still lives, in the strength of its manhood and full of its original spirit.

A group of Massachusetts men clustered in one corner of the gallery "*shed tears like girls!*" when they heard these words.[39] And after reading them in the newspapers, the people of Massachusetts also wept in the happy realization that in Webster they had a defender and spokesman without parallel.

"No one ever looked the orator, as he did,—'*os humerosque deo similis,*' in form and feature how like a god," marveled Charles March. Even his manner gave new force to the language. "As he stood swaying his right arm, like a huge tilt-hammer, up and down, his swarthy countenance lighted up with excitement, he appeared amid the smoke, the fire, the thunder of his eloquence, like Vulcan in his armory forging thoughts for the Gods!"[40]

Isaac Bassett noted that the opening section of his speech "riveted the

39. March, *Webster,* p. 142.
40. Ibid., p. 144.

attention of every one upon him, although his most zealous opponents appeared to be unconcerned & uninterested at first, one especially trying hard to read his newspaper upside down, but it was not long before friend & foe alike were carried away with the power of his eloquent oratory."[41]

Webster next proceeded to what he called "by far the most grave and important duty"—namely, to state and defend what he believed to be the "true principles of the Constitution."

First off, he affirmed the right of the people to throw off any government that becomes oppressive and intolerable. The people, that is, not the states. Governments are the creatures of the people, both national and state. "It is, Sir, the people's Constitution, the people's government, made for the people, made by the people, and answerable to the people."

Acting in their sovereign capacity, he continued, the people declared that the Constitution shall be the supreme law. The states are sovereign as long as they do not disturb the supreme law. The people conferred on the national government particular powers. The rest are reserved to the states and the people. The South Carolina doctrine, as Webster called nullification, would grant each of the twenty-four states the authority to decide which laws are legal and constitutional and which are not. "Does this not approach absurdity?" he asked. Either the laws of the central government are beyond the control of the states or we have "no constitution of general government, and are thrust back again to the days of the [Articles of] Confederation."

Then he took up the really tricky part of the problem. "Who shall interpret [the people's] will. . . . With whom do they repose this ultimate right of deciding on the powers of the government?" The people, Webster argued, have already decided that matter. They left it to "the government itself, in its appropriate branches." They wisely provided in the Constitution "a proper, suitable mode and tribunal for settling questions of constitutional law."

So that everyone would understand his meaning clearly Webster repeated his argument, this time more succinctly. "To whom lies the last appeal? This, Sir, the Constitution itself decides also, by declaring, *'that the judicial power shall extend to all cases arising under the Constitution and laws of the United States.'*" These two provisions cover the whole ground: The Constitution is the supreme law, and the Supreme Court renders the final decision in disputes involving constitutional power. "I maintain, that between submission to the decision of the constituted tribunals, and revolution, or disunion, there is no middle ground; there is no ambiguous condition, half allegiance and half rebellion."

This claim of Webster was in keeping with the thinking of many jurists and politicians, but certainly not all. Andrew Jackson absolutely disagreed that the Supreme Court rendered the *final* decision in interpreting the Constitution. He believed that the Supreme Court, the Congress, and the President each had the right to act on its understanding of the document but that the final decision lay with the people. Henry Clay also doubted the Court's ultimate authority in this

41. IB Papers, Box 17, Folder E, pp. 37–38.

area. Probably many, if not most, Americans at that time would have agreed with Jackson and Clay.

What will be the result if the Carolina doctrine is a "practical application"? Webster continued. Take the tariff, as an example. The state would declare duties null and void, then the collector would seize the goods if the duties were not paid, and finally the state would call out the militia.

"Defend yourselves with your bayonets," the leader of the nullifiers would cry to his men. If that happens, then "this is war," thundered Webster, "—civil war."

"Direct collision, therefore, between force and force, is the unavoidable result" of nullification. "To resist by force the execution of a law, generally, is treason. Can the courts of the United States take notice of the indulgence of a State to commit treason?"

He now reminded his listeners of the prosperity and honor achieved by the nation through the "preservation of our Federal Union." It is to that Union we owe our safety at home and dignity abroad. It is that Union that makes us most proud of our country. Every year brings new evidence of its blessings. "It has been to us all a copious fountain of national, social, and personal happiness."

Finally he swung into his remarkable and justly celebrated peroration.

I have not allowed myself, Sir to look beyond the Union, to see what might lie hidden in the dark recess behind. . . . While the Union lasts, we have high, exciting, gratifying prospects spread out before us, for us and our children. Beyond that I seek not to penetrate the veil. God grant that in my day, at least, that curtain may not rise! God grant that on my vision never may be opened what lies behind! When my eyes shall be turned to behold for the last time the sun in heaven, may I not see him shining on the broken and dishonored fragments of a once glorious Union; on States dissevered, discordant, belligerent; on a land rent with civil feuds, or drenched, it may be, in fraternal blood! Let their last feeble and lingering glance rather behold the gorgeous ensign of the republic, now known and honored throughout the earth, still full high advanced, its arms and trophies streaming in the original lustre, not a stripe erased or polluted, nor a single star obscured, bearing for its motto, no such miserable interrogatory as "What is all this worth?" nor those other words of delusion and folly, "Liberty first and Union afterwards"; but everywhere, spread all over in characters of living light, blazing on all its ample folds, as they float over the sea and over the land, and in every wind under the whole heavens, that other sentiment, dear to every true American heart,—Liberty *and* Union, now and for ever, one and inseparable![42]

This noble utterance was Webster's supreme gift to the American people. With poetry of language, majesty of sentiment, and sublimity of thought, he embodied in his address many of the beliefs and feelings of the American people, who, for the past two decades, had experienced a surge of nationalism they had never known before. They needed to have these new emotions properly expressed in a way that would add to their pride in the nation's glory. Webster

42. Webster's second reply can be found in the *Register of Debates,* 20th Congress, 1st Session, pp. 58–80, with his notes on pages 80–82. The version quoted here is the revised version Webster prepared for publication and can be found in *PS,* I, 287–348. The reported version can also be found ibid., pp. 349–393.

did it for them. With this oration "the Godlike" became, without exaggeration, a living legend.[43]

Those who actually heard him would never forget the swell and roll of his deep voice as he intoned the words "Liberty *and* Union, now and for ever, one and inseparable." They did not applaud; they did not shout their appreciation. They just sat as if "in a trance, all motion paralyzed."

Only the whack of the gavel and the angrily called "Order! order!" by the presiding officer, John C. Calhoun, woke the audience from its paralytic state. The crowded assembly broke up and rushed away from the hall.[44]

As Webster finished, a southern senator leaned over and said, "Mr. Webster, I think you had better die now, and rest your fame on that speech."

Hayne overheard the remark and called out, "You ought not to die: a man who can make such speeches as that ought never to die."[45]

Later someone asked him how he felt while delivering his speech. Webster replied: "I felt as if everything I had ever seen, or read, or heard, was floating before me in one great panorama, and I had little else to do than to reach up and cull a thunderbolt, and *hurl* it at him!"[46]

Webster knew, as any public speaker knows, how well he had done. "I never before spoke in the hearing of an audience so excited, so eager, and so sympathetic,"[47] he confessed, and he immediately set to work polishing his speech for publication. He worked on it for a month, selecting the words that would convey what his "gestures, modulations of voice, and changes of expression" had accomplished in the chamber, so that a reader would be "as thrilled and awed as the listening audience had been."[48]

The *National Intelligencer* published the revised version in three installments, February 23, 25, and 27, 1830, and issued it in pamphlet form. Webster had personally invited Joseph Gales to report his speech but was dissatisfied with the transcript because it lacked an emotional wallop. So the *Intelligencer*

43. For a discussion of Webster as a sectional figure and the argument that he expounded his nationalistic doctrines in a consciously divisive manner, wielding them like a weapon on the battleground of sectional politics, see Harlow W. Sheidley, "The Webster-Hayne Debate: Recasting New England's Sectionalism," *New England Quarterly*, LXVII, 1 (March 1994), pp. 5–29.

44. March, *Webster*, pp. 148–149. Calhoun interrupted Webster during the speech to ask if the speaker had stated that he, Calhoun, had changed his opinion on the subject of internal improvements. Calhoun had no right to interrupt and participate in the debate since he was not a member of the Senate. His role consisted of keeping order, recognizing senators who wished to speak, and voting in a tie. "This interruption of Mr. Calhoun," said Isaac Bassett, "was unusual & unprecedented, & while Mr. Webster let it pass with a good-humoured remark, he [Calhoun] was subsequently severely rebuked for a similar interruption by Mr. Forsyth of Ga., who in an emphatic manner pronounced it a violation of official etiquette." Calhoun never interrupted again, according to Bassett. IB Papers, Box 17, Folder E, p. 41.

45. Harvey, *Reminiscences*, p. 153. It should be remembered that Harvey was a close personal friend, but he claims that he heard this story from Webster himself.

46. Lyman, *Public and Private Life of Webster*, I, 140–141.

47. DW to Mason, February 27, 1830, in *PC*, III, 19. According to Isaac Bassett, even those who believed that Hayne was the "greater *Orator*" conceded that Webster was the "greater Statesman." IB Papers, Box 18, Folder D, p. 4.

48. Editorial note, *PS*, I, 286.

waited while he revised it. The speech was so heavily edited and rewritten that some thought "it bore little resemblance" to what Webster had actually said in the Senate.[49]

The editors printed and distributed more than forty thousand copies of this second reply to Hayne and acknowledged that twenty other printed editions appeared elsewhere. Webster and his wife themselves distributed it to friends, political figures, and influential leaders of industry and commerce. The response came immediately. People were overwhelmed by what they read. They could talk of nothing else. "It is almost the only topic of political discussion," wrote Henry Warfield, former congressman from Maryland. Even the devoted friends of Jackson "extend to you merited applause."[50] It was unbelievable. "Never have I heard such universal & ardent expressions of joy & approbation," exclaimed another.[51] Many compared it favorably with Demosthenes' oration *On the Crown*. Abbott Lawrence could hardly restrain himself. "Permit me to indulge my feelings, after the banquet I have just had in reading your speech, by expressing to you my grateful sense of obligation, for the favor conferred on me, in common with every other true son of New England, for your triumphant vindication of her character from the foul aspersions cast upon it by the South." He went on. "I thank you as a citizen of Massachusetts, of New England, of the United States, not only for myself, but for my children." The doctrines espoused in your oration are Union doctrines, and they will provide future generations with a safe and sure political guide.[52]

In a more tangible way, Lawrence demonstrated his appreciation by presenting Webster with a service of silver plate with the comment "If by any emblem or inscription on any piece of this service, referring to the circumstances of which this is a memorial, the whole will be made more acceptable, I shall be glad to have you designate what it shall be, and permit me the opportunity of adding it."[53]

People claimed that they could not remember when an event or a discovery or a new work by a popular writer had become "such a general topic of conversation." Never had a single speech caused "so much interest and pleasure." Many

49. Ritchie, *Press Gallery*, p. 23. Sometimes, as he spoke, Webster would grope for the most suitable word, trying one synonym after another. For example, "Why is it, Mr. Chairman," he said on one occasion, "that there has gathered, congregated this great number of inhabitants, dwellers, here; that these road, avenues, routes of travel, highways, converge, meet, come together, here?" When the speech was printed, all the synonyms but the best one would be left out. Hoar, *Autobiography*, I, 144.

50. Warfield to DW, March 1, 1830, in *PC*, III, 20.

51. Henry A. Dearborn to DW, February 5, 1830, in Van Tyne, ed., *Letters of Webster*, p. 147.

52. Lawrence to DW, March 3, 1830, in *W&S*, XVII, 489. See also Lawrence's letter to his son, March 30, 1830, in Lawrence, ed., *Diary and Correspondence*, p. 97, and the many letters reprinted in Curtis, *Webster*, I, 370–374, and *PC*, III, 17–20.

53. Lawrence to DW, October 23, 1830, in Lawrence, *Diary and Correspondence*, p. 102. In reply Webster simply asked that it "bear an inscription expressive of the donation." DW to Lawrence, October 23, 1830, ibid., p. 103.

compared the written text with *The Federalist Papers.*[54]

Even southerners, albeit transplanted northerners, responded favorably. "I am a son of New England," wrote one man from Columbia, South Carolina, "and proud to call you as her Champion. . . . Receive my warm acknowledgements of your able and manly defence of *my Country*—the Country of Yankees."[55]

So many of Webster's ideas and feelings about the nation perfectly matched those of Jackson—with some obvious exceptions—that the President could not help showing his approval of them.

"Been to the Capitol?" Jackson asked a close friend.

"Yes, General."

"Well, and how is Webster getting on?"

"He is delivering a most powerful speech," came the response. "I am afraid he's demolishing our friend Hayne."

"I expected it," said the delighted President.[56]

In his masterly speech Webster perhaps can be faulted on his knowledge of the events that produced the Constitution and how the document was adopted, but as he said, he chose not to look back at what lay behind. He understood something more important: that over the past forty years historical developments had produced a genuine Union of people, whether or not that was true at the beginning. Out of a triumphant past a dynamic society had emerged with a government dedicated to liberty and self-government. Only the perpetuation of that Union could safeguard freedom and ensure democratic rule.

By becoming and remaining a Union of people, said Webster, there were high, exciting hopes for the future. Otherwise he foresaw bloody, civil war.

In New Salem, Illinois, Abraham Lincoln read the speech and later told William Herndon that he "always regarded it as the grandest specimen of American oratory." More than likely the words about how the government was "made for the people, made by the people, and answerable to the people" deeply impressed the young man. Nearly thirty years later he remembered the speech and said that he planned "to consult" it as he prepared his inaugural address as President.[57]

That speech, declared Reverdy Johnson, made Webster's name "immortal." It "planted deep, deep, in every true American heart that sentiment so vital to our duty, our honor, our fame, our power, our happiness, our freedom, 'Liberty and Union, now and forever, one and inseparable.' "[58]

54. Henry Bond to DW, March 11, 1830, Joseph L. Williams to DW, April 14, [1830], in *PC*, III, 30, 52.

55. J. W. Scott to DW, February 12, 1830, in Van Tyne, ed., *Letters of Webster,* p.148.

56. Parton, *Jackson*, III, 282.

57. The reply also served in part for Lincoln's "House Divided" speech of 1858. See *Herndon's Life of Lincoln* (Cleveland and New York, 1949), pp. 386, 327. Herndon says that there is a "similarity in figure and thought in the opening lines of both speeches. In fact it may not be amiss to note that, in this instance, Webster's effort was carefully read by Lincoln and served in part as his model," p. 327.

58. Sargent, *Public Men and Events*, I, 173

19

Presidential Politics

THAT EVENING President Jackson held a levee in the White House, and both Webster and Hayne attended. The other guests were naturally anxious to see the great orator after such a brilliant performance in the Senate. He positioned himself in the middle of the East Room. A crowd completely encircled him, and many stood on tiptoe or mounted chairs in the room to catch a glimpse of him.

"Where, which is Webster?"

"There, don't you see him—that dark, swarthy man, with a great deep eye and heavy brow—that's Webster."

Hayne entered the room and immediately approached his adversary to congratulate him. As he neared, Webster extended his hand. "How are you, this evening, Col. Hayne?"

"None the better for you, sir!" came the good-natured response.[1]

Like the overwrought crowd in Washington, the entire nation soon buzzed with talk about what Webster had said. The debate in the Senate went on, of course, and did not end until May 21, when Benton—fittingly since he had started it—brought it to a close. But as far as northerners were concerned, the debate ended with the second reply, for among other things, Webster had successfully blocked the possible coalition of the South with the West, and that was extremely important.[2]

A great number of congressmen franked copies of his two replies to selected individuals at home. They in turn felt an obligation to pass them along to others. "We understand them as intended, not for our own reading only, but for the reading of as many of the community as practicable," wrote one Tennessee politician. "Accordingly, we gave them circulation. *Each* copy, by this time, has probably been read by as many as fifty different gentlemen."[3]

Several readers wrote directly to Webster and asked questions or made observations about constitutional questions that had not been covered in the

1. March, *Webster,* pp. 149–151.

2. Sydney Nathans, *Daniel Webster and Jacksonian Democracy* (Baltimore, 1973), p. 33.

3. Henry Bond to DW, March 11, 1830, Joseph L. Williams to DW, April 14, [1830], in *PC*, III, 30, 52.

reply. For example, one man did not believe a citizen who acted in conformity with a state law that had nullified and forbidden compliance with a federal law was guilty of treason. Sorry, Webster responded, "I must confess I dissent entirely from this proposition."

Also, if a state secedes, what becomes of the property of the United States within the state, like forts, and what is its relation to the other states? "It is plain to me, My Dear Sir," Webster replied, "that secession is Revolution. It may be more or less violent: it may be bloody or not bloody: but it is fundamental change of [the] political system: it is Revolution: and the constitution does not provide for Revolution. As in other cases, so in this. Revolution, if it comes, must bring its own law with it."[4]

Naturally the people of Massachusetts, especially of Boston, were ecstatic. Some wanted to give him a dinner; others a ball; still others a parade. Webster declined such demonstrations because of the jealousy and animosity it might engender among the other members of the Massachusetts delegation in Congress. He much preferred a more personal token—"say an urn or some such," with an inscription.[5] No sooner asked than granted. His many benefactors saw to that. In time he received a beautifully inscribed silver urn. Other gifts, some quite valuable, poured in on him as well.

Projects were immediately devised to publish Webster's speeches, all of them. Even the Jacksonians in Boston were delighted with his performance, and at a party meeting they expressed their feelings in the following resolution: "Resolved. That this meeting entertain a deep & grateful sense of the distinguished services of the Hon. Daniel Webster, in the Senate of the United States." One Bostonian compared the speeches with those of Edmund Burke and William Pitt. Webster's two replies, he said, "teach the citizens in general, what their relation to the federal Government is" and in such a manner that everyone not only assents in what was said but is surprised that he has not thought of it himself.[6]

With a touching sense of modesty, Webster remarked that his second reply had "made much more *talk* than it deserves, owing to the topic, & to the times. I hope it is doing some good at the South, where, I have reason to think, it is very generally circulated & read."[7]

He sent a copy to the aged James Madison, who graciously told him that it was "very powerful" and that "it crushes 'nullification,' and must hasten an abandonment of secession." In a follow-up letter Madison argued that the U.S. system of government was "so unexampled in its origin, so complex in its structure, and so peculiar in some of its features" that no political vocabulary existed that was "sufficiently distinctive & appropriate, without a detailed resort to the

4. George Hay to DW, March 10, 1830, DW to George Hay, March 12, 1830, ibid., III, 28–29, 31.

5. DW to ?, May 22, 1830, ibid., III, 72–73.

6. Jacob Hall and Samuel Austin, Jr., to DW, March 17, 1830, William Sullivan to DW, March 23, 1830, ibid., III, 34–35, 37.

7. DW to Jeremiah Mason, March 19, 1830, ibid., III, 36.

facts in the case." However, he did tell Webster in a statement that seemed to want to have it both ways that "the undisputed fact is that the Constitution was made by the people, but as embodied into the several States who were parties to it, and therefore made by the States, in their highest authoritative capacity."[8]

Henry Clay, now the undisputed candidate of the National Republican party for the presidency in 1832, congratulated Webster on "the very great addition which you have made . . . to your previous high reputation." The speeches, he declared, "are the theme of praise from every tongue; and I have shared in [that] delight."[9]

Webster's reputation reached such heights that whenever he rose in the Senate, even to offer a resolution to adjourn, everyone in the room turned to listen and "all was as still as though the hall was empty."[10]

His colleagues in the Senate showed their great admiration and respect for him when, several years later on his way to Washington, he fell ill and remained a few days in New York to recover. Unfortunately word reached Washington that his illness was serious. After a day or two, having fully recovered, Webster resumed his journey, arrived in Washington, and entered the Senate chamber unannounced. "The effect was electrical," reported one observer, "as by one spontaneous but irrepressible impulse the entire body of Senators arose to their feet and remained standing while he approached & took his seat."[11]

Although the debate over the Foot resolution dragged on through the spring, Webster had nothing more to add. In fact the rest of the session seemed to meander along into late May. "Nothing moves here, but time," he sighed, "or, rather, we all keep in motion, without making progress."[12]

But one issue did move, one that President Jackson was determine to have legislated into law: the removal of the southern tribes of Native Americans. It was the President's belief that the Indians had to be sent beyond the Mississippi River for their own safety and the safety of the nation. He wanted an Indian Removal Act, and he labored long and hard to get it.

A number of congressmen opposed the legislation introduced in both houses by the friends of the administration. Various missionary groups also objected and flooded Congress with petitions seeking protection for the Native Americans. Webster received his share of petitions and dutifully introduced them, but he took little part in the heated debate that immediately commenced when the Indian removal bill came to the floor. In the Senate Theodore Freling-

8. Madison to DW, March 15, 1830, in Webster, ed., *Private Correspondence*, I, 496; Madison to DW, May 27, 1830, in *PC*, III, 77. Madison also said that he had made a detailed statement in the matter to Edward Everett. It can be found in the *North American Review*, XXXI (August 1830), pp. 537–546.

9. Clay to DW, April 29, 1830, in *PC*, III, 62.

10. Amos A. Lawrence to his father, January 8, 1836, in "Letters of Amos A. Lawrence," *Massachusetts Historical Society Proceedings*, LIII (1919), p. 51.

11. IB Papers, Box 20, Folder I, pp. 254–255.

12. DW to Warren Dutton, May 9, 1830, in *PC*, III, 68.

huysen of New Jersey commanded the antiremoval forces and gave an impassioned speech that lasted for three days. John Forsyth of Georgia responded. Webster sat mum. The problem of the Indians did not particularly concern him, like so many Americans. He did vote for one amendment that would guarantee protection of the Indians prior to their removal, but the amendment failed. On April 26, 1830, the Senate passed the removal bill by the count of twenty-eight to nineteen along strict party lines. Webster voted with the minority.[13] In the House the President sustained a verbal battering, but the Indian removal bill eventually passed, and Jackson signed it into law on May 28, 1830.[14]

Although Webster may have thought that "nothing moves here but time," he was aware of the fact that politically a great deal of motion, or rather commotion, occurred that spring. The emotions, tensions, and heated discussion he provoked by his two replies to Hayne helped set the stage for a display of fireworks between the supporters and opponents of nullification and states' rights. The Democrats held a birthday celebration to honor Thomas Jefferson on April 13, and the "nullies" plotted to use the occasion to spout their states' rights philosophy. Word of their intention and the content of several of their proposed toasts infuriated Old Hickory and prompted the Pennsylvania delegation, in a body, to boycott the celebration.[15]

The object of this "great dinner party," Webster declared, "was to recompose & reconstruct the party, on the old Jefferson platform." Held at Brown's Hotel, the occasion attracted all the Democratic leaders, including the President, Vice President, members of the cabinet, and the Congress. Straight off Jackson fired a blast directly at the nullifiers, and some said he looked squarely at Calhoun when he gave his famous toast. "Our Union," he cried, *"It must be preserved."* Calhoun responded with: "The Union: Next to our liberty, the most dear."[16]

Jackson's toast defined his position precisely. He regarded nullification and secession as abominations.

Calhoun's priorities placed liberty ahead of Union, but Webster contended in his second reply that liberty is impossible without Union. Once the Union broke apart it would break again and again and eventually become a mass of petty states, like Germany, completely at the mercy of competing foreign powers. Its longevity and greatness as a nation, according to Webster, depended on keeping the states bound together in perpetuity.

The "great dinner" produced other political consequences. The occasion

13. *Register of Debates,* 21st Congress, 1st Session, pp. 309–320, 383. *PC,* III, 32, states that Webster's vote was not recorded. This is not true.

14. The Indian Removal Act authorized an exchange of unorganized public land in the trans-Mississippi West for Indian lands in the East. The Indians who moved would be given perpetual title to their new land, and the federal government would undertake the cost and the operation of the actual removal.

15. The Pennsylvania delegation was offended because several of the toast were strongly antitariff.

16. DW to Mason, April 14, 1830, in *PC,* III, 51; *United States Telegraph,* April 15, 17, 20, 23, 1830. For a full discussion of this "great dinner party," see Remini, *Jackson,* II, 233–236.

had been intended to give not only a states' rights but an antitariff cast to the entire Democratic party. "It was to found the party on *Southern* principles," Webster explained to Clay, "& such principles as should exclude, not only their avowed political opponents, but Mr. Van Buren's friends also." But it failed miserably. Jackson means to be reelected, Webster shrewdly commented, and has meant to do so all along. The plot to exclude Van Buren and his friends having failed, the battle royal between Van Buren and Calhoun for the succession was bound to intensify. Webster proposed to Clay that their party sit quietly while the Democrats struggled over their differences. Let the administration have its own way in legislative matters, he advised. Let it decide such issues as internal improvements, for he was certain that the decision would be so unpopular as to cause Jackson to lose the election.[17] Webster had in mind the fact that Jackson was expected to veto the Maysville extension of the National Road, which he did as soon as the Indian Removal Act was passed; furthermore, the Democrats killed the Baltimore railroad bill and Webster believed that it would "certainly *tell,* before the people."[18]

Although Webster expected Clay to win the nomination of the National Republican party without difficulty, he opposed Massachusetts's coming out with an endorsement because "it would raise the cry of *coalition revived.*" That, he insisted, had to be avoided at all costs. "Parties must, now necessarily, be sorted out, anew; & the great ground of difference will be Tariff & Int. Improvements." He really felt that a crisis had already arrived in the country.[19] But his unwillingness to have Massachusetts act on Clay's behalf began the slow, quiet, but steadily increasing resentment between the two men that developed into an unpleasant contest that ultimately injured them both.

As adjournment approached, some members of Congress considered making a formal nomination of Clay in a caucus, but Alexander H. Everett told John Quincy Adams that he thought "it was prevented by Mr. Webster, who he supposes has views upon that office for himself." Adams replied that if the senator thought he could get the nomination, he was very much mistaken. Whether or not Webster advised against the caucus nomination, the fact remained that it did not happen, most probably because a great number of Clay's friends realized that another congressional caucus might drive the final nail into Clay's presidential coffin.[20]

Webster could hardly wait for the adjournment. "I am right down homesick. I want to go to Sandwich . . . to get out of the Pennsylvania Avenue—to hear no more of bills, resolutions, & motions. I never felt more completely weary of a session. If it do not terminate soon, I shall run away & leave it."[21] And he did. Shortly before the adjournment on May 31 he took off for New York to meet up

17. DW to Clay, April 18, 1830, in *PC,* III, 58–59.
18. DW to James Barbour, May 24, 1830, ibid., III, 74–75.
19. DW to Clay, May 29, 1830, ibid., III, 78–80.
20. Adams, *Memoirs,* VIII, 231–232.
21. DW to Warren Dutton, May 9, 1830, in *PC,* III, 69.

with his wife and daughter and escort them to Boston.

In New York City he invariably stayed at the Astor Hotel, and when he took up residence, the "proprietors" of the hotel hoisted a "large white banner" on which was written, "Webster's immortal motto—'Liberty and Union, now and forever, one and inseparable,'"—in large letters "with a red stripe above and a blue strip below." Even after he died—indeed ten years after he died—the hotel still raised the "Webster Flag" every year on his birthday.[22]

Boston was anxious to get a good look at its hero's new lady when they arrived back home, and by and large it found her appropriate, even if she lacked physical beauty or the spiritual qualities that had been so outstanding in the first Mrs. Webster. A few, however, had reservations about her extravagant tastes. In view of Webster's own shortcomings in that regard, they wondered if the pairing of two profligates might not end in financial disaster for the family.

Webster, Caroline, and the children spent an all-too-brief vacation together before politics and his legal duties intruded and claimed his full attention. He spent much of the summer and autumn of 1830 engaged in the trial of John Francis ("Frank") Knapp for the brutal murder on April 7, 1830, of the eighty-two-year-old Captain Joseph White, a retired wealthy sea captain of Salem. The crime horrified and excited the public, and the trial turned out to be one of the "most remarkable criminal prosecutions on record." Webster was hired as a special prosecutor at the request of Stephen White, nephew and heir of the victim, to assist the aged attorney general of Massachusetts in the criminal prosecution of Knapp. Undoubtedly the fact that his close friend Joseph Story was White's brother-in-law contributed to Webster's decision to take case, despite the complicated legal problems involved. Undoubtedly too Story pressured him into accepting. After the trial Webster received a fee of one thousand dollars.

This was Webster's only appearance as a prosecutor in a criminal case, and the effort he put into gathering information and evidence showed, according to one contemporary, his extraordinary "capacity for toil," for "at the appointed hour, Mr. Webster was completely ready."[23]

The first trial ended in a hung jury. But in the second trial Webster won a conviction, despite conflicting and circumstantial evidence.

Webster's performance amazed the people of Salem, considering the obstacles he faced. "It would be a sad joke if the immortal Daniel," commented the *New Hampshire Patriot and States Gazette*, ". . . should not succeed in getting a culprit hanged who everybody knows deserves it." Naturally the court looked favorably on Webster's interpretation of common law and the rules of evidence, but he also bewitched the jury by his vivid and powerful presentation. They hung on every word as he described White's murder. By turns dramatic and emotional, sobersided yet eloquent, he narrated what had happened and then commented upon it:

22. Boston *Transcript*, January 20, 1862.
23. Harriet Martineau, *Retrospect of Western Travel* (London and New York, 1838), I, 278, 281.

It was a cool, desperate, concerted murder. It was neither the offspring of passion nor revenge. The murderer was seduced by no lionlike temptation; all was deliberation; all was skillful. The murderer was a cool . . . a calculating, a resolute and determined assassin. The object was money, the crime murder, the price blood.

At the blessed hour . . . he enters the house . . . ascends the stairs, arrives at the door. There is no pause. He opens it. The victim is asleep. . . . One blow, and the task is accomplished!

The jury sat wide-eyed. Like the jurors in *The Devil and Daniel Webster,* they must have watched and listened with spellbound intensity. They could hardly move. The voice. The look. The manner. He seemed almost frightening as his narration of the bloody deed unfolded.

Now mark his resolution. . . . He raises the aged arm, plunges the dagger to the heart—not once but many times—replaces the arms, replaces the bed-clothes, feels the pulse, is satisfied that his work is perfect and retires from the chamber. . . .

Gentlemen, of all the evidence you are the judges. . . . You will judge individually and collectively. His life is in your hands. All our trust is that you will remember that, while you owe him a duty, you also owe the public a duty. . . .

The kindest wish we can have for him is that he may have a devout sense that his only hope depends on the goodness of the Almighty God, and that his prayers may reach the throne of Divine Mercy.

The kindest wish we may have for you, gentlemen, is to wish that you may, by the assistance of God, be enabled to do your duty to the prisoner at the bar firmly and consistently; that you may do justice to him, and maintain the public law and the safety of the community.[24]

In the final passages of this summation he spoke in a voice and manner "less solemn," and he looked directly at the foreman.[25]

On August 20 the jury found Knapp guilty of murder in the first degree, and he was hanged. At a second trial of an accomplice the defense attorney objected to the fact that a private individual had retained counsel at a fee to aid the law officers of the state to bring about a conviction for a crime that was punishable by death. Webster immediately rose and declared that *in this case* "he appeared solely at the request of the Attorney-General, and without any pecuniary inducement." He did not mention the fact that on August 14 he had already received a fee of one thousand dollars from Stephen White in payment for his efforts in the first trial. As he said in a letter to Story, he told the court that he "had not received, and should not receive, any fee in this case; which, of course, was and is true."[26] A nice distinction that was actually true since the letter to Story was written three days before he received his fee. Also, the fee

24. Webster's summation is drawn from the two trials and is here quoted from Howard A. Bradley and James A. Winans, *Webster and the Salem Murder* (Columbia, Mo., 1956), pp. 96, 157–158.

25. Martineau, *Western Travel,* I, 282.

26. DW to Story, August 11, 1830, in *W&S,* XVII, 506. It is Maurice Baxter's belief, and mine as well, that this letter was written in November, not August, since the trial of the accomplice did not occur until November, when the question of a fee was raised by the defense attorney. Baxter, *Webster,* p. 544 note 18.

covered the Knapp trial, not that of the accomplice. But Black Dan certainly misled the court and the defense about his recompense. The court overruled the objection, and Webster won a second conviction.[27]

In addition to this difficult criminal case, Webster spent considerable time thinking about and worrying about the next presidential election. Not only did the National Republicans have to contend with an extremely popular President, but now a third party, the first in American history, had arisen that could inflict serious damage on the electoral chances of the candidates of the two major parties.

The Anti-Masonic movement developed with the disappearance and presumed murder of William Morgan, a stonemason of Batavia, New York, who threatened to reveal the secrets of the Masonic order. A fierce public outcry against Masons erupted throughout the western counties of New York because of the widespread belief that Masons controlled business, government, and the law and did not hesitate to violate the basic rights of ordinary citizens to protect their special interests. The movement seemed to reflect the democratic surge sweeping across the country at the time that asserted majority rights against the privileges of an elite minority. It spread rapidly from New York to New England and then into parts of the Old Northwest. Its members swore they would drive all Masons from elective office and positions of power and influence.[28]

The Anti-Masons turned against Jackson and Clay, the presumed candidates of the Democratic and National Republican parties, because they both were Masons. The intensity of resentment and the violence resulting from the furor frightened National Republican leaders in New York, and they begged Clay to renounce his membership in the fraternity. He refused.

Encouraged by the strength of their movement, the Anti-Masons decided to run a presidential candidate of their own, and one of the names to surface in their deliberations was Daniel Webster. He seemed perfect for their purposes. A non-Mason, a national figure, indeed a legend, a great orator, and a seasoned legislator, he had all the qualities they looked for in a candidate. And Webster himself hungered for the presidency, as they well knew. A perfect combination.

Several Anti-Masons got in touch with Webster and posed the possibility of his nomination. Black Dan could hardly resist. Even though he claimed to be a National Republican and had a near-certain belief that Henry Clay would be his party's nominee, he entertained the idea of his own nomination by the Anti-Masons. Of course he knew his acceptance would ruin his relations with Clay, to

27. Details of trial can be found in Curtis, *Webster*, I, 378–385; Baxter, *Webster*, pp. 158–161; and especially in Bradley and Winans, *Webster and the Salem Murder.*

28. On Anti-Masonry, see Michael F. Holt, "The Anti-Masonic and Know Nothing Parties," in Schlesinger and Israel, eds., *History of U.S. Political Parties*, I, 629–636, and Kathleen Smith Kutolowski, "Anti-Masonry Reexamined," *Journal of American History*, LXXI (1984), pp. 269–293. See also Paul Goodman, *Towards a Christian Republic* (New York, 1988) and William P. Vaughn, *The Antimasonic Party in the United States, 1826–1843* (Lexington, Ky., 1983).

say nothing of other National Republicans. There was also an outside possibility, though slim, that the National Republicans might turn away from Clay and accord their favor on him. After all the Kentuckian was saddled with the "corrupt bargain" charge, and Democrats had every intention of using it to bring him down.

For his part Black Dan had little confidence in Clay's ability to win the election, and he seemed convinced that when others realized it, the political situation would change rather abruptly. "Indeed, there seems to be, I am sorry to say it," he observed in a letter to Levi Lincoln, "something hollow, in Mr Clay's western support. It gives way, in the moment of trial." In any event he hesitated about giving the Anti-Masons the nod. He wanted to keep all his options open, at least for the moment. He therefore informed his Anti-Masonic contacts that any nomination at this time was inappropriate. He suggested a delay. Thus, when the Pennsylvania Anti-Masons held their state convention and endorsed the expediency of running their own candidate, William Irwin, one of Black Dan's contacts "deemed it . . . judicious to follow your advice," he informed Webster, "& therefore did not urge an immediate nomination. It also appeared to me unsafe to mention *publicly* my preference. . . . But from conversations with the members, *out of doors,* I am induced to believe that prospect is favorable" for you.[29]

Irwin and a number of other men stood ready to support Webster's nomination once he signaled them to go ahead. But the more Black Dan thought about it, the more he saw "hazard" written all over it. The offense to National Republicans and what it would do to his standing among them, especially among his Massachusetts friends, probably determined his decision. So, with some regret, he backed off, and the Anti-Masons looked for someone else.

Although Henry Clay alienated many Anti-Masons by refusing to repudiate his membership in the fraternity, there was hope that he might gain ground in the presidential race because of the continued feuding within the Jackson administration. The alienation between Jackson and Calhoun over the Peggy Eaton affair and nullification widened when the President learned that Calhoun, as secretary of war under Monroe, had argued for Jackson's arrest over his unauthorized seizure of Florida from the Spanish in 1818. Old Hickory confronted Calhoun with the evidence and demanded an explanation. The Vice President responded with "a summary answer, *that . . . was not satisfactory*" and then took his case to the public and charged Van Buren with mounting a conspiracy to destroy him. The unholy mess made for juicy gossip.

"There is much jealousy & distrust in the Cabinet," commented the delighted senator from Louisiana, Josiah S. Johnston, "& rumor speaks loud of the contemplated changes, but no one knows where the blow will fall."[30]

29. DW to Lincoln, December 25, 1830, in *PC*, III, 93, Irwin to DW, August 25, 1830 in *Microfilm Edition*, F7/8954, and Irwin to DW, September 17, 1830, in *PC*, III, 84.

30. Johnston to DW, November 6, 1830, DW to Levi Lincoln, December 25, 1830, in *PC*, III, 87, 93.

No sooner had he returned to Washington and settled in with his wife and Julia at Barnard's Mansion Hotel on Pennsylvania Avenue[31] than Webster began spreading the delightful rumors. He felt certain that Van Buren, with the aid of the still-living William H. Crawford, another member of the Monroe cabinet, and others had shaped and steered the conspiracy against Calhoun. And the intrigue and disruption of the Democratic party got worse as the winter progressed. "I doubt whether much Legislative business will be done this Session," Webster gleefully remarked, "I have never known in W. such a storm as is now raging."[32]

Nonetheless the likelihood of Clay's success in the 1832 election steadily diminished over the next few months despite the disruption among Jacksonians. The Anti-Masons had gained strength in Pennsylvania and New York, and Clay's prospects in those two states kept declining. In the West Webster thought that Clay underestimated the size and extent of the opposition. "The prospect of electing Mr Clay is, indeed, indeed, not promising," he commented. "It is far otherwise."[33]

It then occurred to him that perhaps he ought to start touring the country— not to campaign, of course. That simply was not done prior to the Civil War. But seeing the folks, letting them look at a living legend, and dazzling them with his oratory certainly could do him no harm—and who knew what might happen? The National Republicans might choose him over Clay. Fortunately this was the short session of Congress, and Webster thought that once he concluded his duties before the Supreme Court, he could leave town. So he began planning a western tour, with brief stops in Pennsylvania and New York City, before heading off for the infected Anti-Masonic regions of western New York, after which he expected to visit Ohio, Indiana, Kentucky, and Missouri and return by way of Pittsburgh and Philadelphia.[34]

At this juncture Webster began to play a very risky game to improve his chances of gaining his party's nomination. Early in the session several meetings of National Republicans decided that Webster should write an address to the people in response to the President's annual message to Congress. He readily accepted the assignment. But he did nothing, and he produced nothing. Finally, tired of waiting, a group of Clay's friends went to him and asked him to prepare a "Manifesto of some kind" giving reasons why the electorate should support the Kentuckian. They intimated "in a gentle but intelligible way" that if he refused, he would be suspected in the West of coolness toward their favorite. Having

31. His accommodations included "two rooms on the second story one pretty large one, in front, one smaller in rear, connected by a door of common size. This largest was Mrs Websters room to see her friends, and we dined there also, when we had company. The smaller room was used as a study—but we dined in it when quite alone." DW to Nathan Appleton, September 11, [1831], in Van Tyne, ed., *Letters of Webster*, p. 162.

32. DW to Lincoln, December 25, 1830, DW to Biddle, January 15, 1831, in *PC*, III, 93, 97.

33. DW to Albert Tracy, January 15, 1831, ibid., III, 97.

34. DW to Kinsman, February 25, 1831, ibid., III, 103.

little choice, Webster naturally agreed to their demands. He wrote the paper and had it published in the *National Intelligencer.* But never once did he mention Clay by name. He did not even allude to him.

Before publication Robert Letcher of Kentucky read the "Manifesto" and prevailed on Webster to add a concluding sentence in which, without naming him, "Clay is kindly alluded to." When it appeared in print, no author was cited. "It is a queer production for a party Manifesto," remarked Edward Everett, who knew its author. "Intended as a nominating document, but so faintly alluding to the person nominated" that party members could not decide who the person was.[35]

Webster's actions mark the overt beginning of his strange, conflicting, indeed ambivalent, and ultimately self-defeating feelings toward Clay. The Kentuckian was no fool. He instantly caught the drift and purpose of Webster's behavior. Friends alerted him to the New Englander's fumbling attempts at playing the double game. They repeated the general gossip in Washington that Black Dan could not be trusted.

Political leader though he might be, Webster did not have the skill to effect his goal of keeping all options open with both the Anti-Masonic and National Republican parties yet not alienate one or the other in the process. Ultimately he was the victim of his own ineptitude, and the political consequences were personally embarrassing, indeed humiliating.

He even wrote a private and confidential letter to Clay when the session ended to tell him that on his return to New York he found that the Anti-Masons were a little less vehement in their opposition to the Kentuckian, adding his conviction that they would not nominate a candidate to oppose him for the presidency.[36]

Meanwhile the situation among Democrats had grown progressively worse. Jackson rid himself of his entire cabinet, except for the postmaster general, and thereby terminated all connection with his Vice President. Van Buren had won the power struggle and was rewarded with the appointment of minister to Great Britain. "What an explosion at Washington!" Webster exclaimed on hearing the news. "It took us . . . by perfect surprise. . . . I begin to doubt whether Genl. Jackson can be re-elected."[37] It was a constitutional crisis. Never before had the government seemed close to total collapse.

Webster reacted quickly. He informed Clay that he had pretty much decided to cancel his planned expedition to the West. The advice of friends helped him make up his mind. "They say, I could not go to Kentucky, at this moment, without exposing *myself,* & what is of more consequence, my *friends,* to invidious & odious remarks, which might have a bad effect on the public mind."

35. *National Intelligencer,* March 5, 1831; Everett to Alexander H. Everett, March 10, 1831, Everett Papers, MHS.

36. DW to Clay, [April] 4, 1831, in *PC,* III, 107.

37. Donald Cole, *The Presidency of Andrew Jackson* (Lawrence, Kan., 1993), pp. 83–86; DW to Elisha Whittlesey, May 10, 1831, in *PC,* III, 112.

Among other things, he had hoped, he added, to buy land in either Ohio or Indiana for a farm for one of his sons.[38]

His regular trip to New York, following the adjournment of Congress, allowed his wife, Caroline, to visit with her family, but this year it also provided the occasion for a large public dinner given him on March 10 at the City Hotel in recognition of his "patriotic & unrivalled efforts in defence of the constitution." He expected the public notice of the dinner to attract the attention of political leaders around the country and perhaps add to his availability as a candidate. He even mentioned the dinner in a letter to Clay.[39] At the same time he kept telling friends privately that Clay could not possibly win and that the only hope for his party, indeed the *"one chance left to save the country from further & worse misrule,"* was to bring forward some man agreeable to both the National Republican and Anti-Masonic parties so that New England, New York, Pennsylvania, Ohio, New Jersey, Delaware, and Maryland could be won. He knew of course that Clay was totally unacceptable to the Anti-Masons and remarked how some men were kind enough to mention his name as that possibility. "Perhaps it may be so," he modestly commented to Charles Miner, a newspaper editor, Federalist, and former congressman from Pennsylvania. But, he continued, he sincerely doubted that he would be brought forward. And, under no circumstances, would he bring himself forward. After all, he had "little experience in public affairs," he said, and had not been long enough before the country to generate "great general confidence. My only merit is an ardent attachment to the Country, & its constitution of Government; & I am already more than paid for all my efforts, if you, & other good men, think I have done any thing to defend the Constitution, & promote the welfare of the Country."[40]

This false modesty ill became him. Any number of men claimed they would support him for higher office, and the public knew him quite well. Considering his own high opinion of his intellectual talents, it is obvious that he tried to appear unassuming. He therefore indulged his usual disclaimer about his ambitions. And he did it repeatedly.

To his credit, however, he kept up a drumbeat for the National Republicans to act as *"a Union party."*[41] The frightening signs and sounds of disunion had been struck too many times in the past dozen years, and he became increasingly concerned that some men seriously contemplated the disruption of the Union. In July Calhoun published his Fort Hill address, in which, for the first time, he publicly acknowledged his total commitment to the doctrine of nullification. All the more reason for National Republicans to reassert their belief in American nationalism.

As intended, political friends in Pennsylvania caught Webster's none-too-

38. DW to Clay, [April] 4, 1831, in *PC*, III, 107.

39. Ambrose Spencer to DW, April 19, 1831, DW to Clay [April] 4, 1831, ibid., III, 110, 107.

40. DW to [Charles Miner], August 28, 1831, ibid., III, 119–120.

41. Ibid.

subtle suggestion about finding "someone" who could unite the National Republican and Anti-Masonic parties. Unfortunately numerous National Republicans found such a union repugnant and said so openly. Naturally the friends of Clay would not support such a move. They were dead set against it. Clay himself anticipated that whomever the Anti-Masons nominated would decline in his favor. It seemed inconceivable to him that anyone would want to stand against him and General Jackson.[42]

Rejected by both major parties, the Anti-Masons held a national convention—the first in American history—on September 26, 1831, in Baltimore and nominated the former attorney general in the Monroe administration and a man who had appeared many times with Webster before the Supreme Court, William Wirt, a former Mason. They also selected Amos Ellmaker of Pennsylvania for Vice President. Supposedly an ardent National Republican, Wirt nonetheless accepted the nomination. His action surprised many who had expected the nomination to go to Justice McLean, and it outraged Clay. "I suppose the ex-Attorney General found, in the magnitude of the fee presented," Clay growled, "sufficient motives to silence all scruples as to the goodness of one cause . . . and for the desertion of another to which he stood pledged by the highest considerations of honor."[43]

Webster himself was taken aback. "For him, personally, I have the truest regard," but it will guarantee the reelection of President Jackson. "It is a pity—a great pity" that the two opposition parties could not agree on a single candidate. "May Heaven preserve us!" In writing to Clay, he deliberately passed over the convention to concentrate on what he thought should be Clay's future action. "You must be aware, My Dear Sir," he declared, "of the strong desire manifested in many parts of the Country, that you should come into the Senate." Your strong presence is needed because "we are to have an interesting & arduous session. Every thing is to be attacked." Not only the tariff but the Constitution itself. "Every thing is to be debated, as if nothing had ever been settled. . . . We need your arm, in the fight."[44]

Although Webster did not mention it in his letter, he also advised Nicholas Biddle, president of the Bank of the United States, to apply for the renewal of the Bank's charter "without delay." Although the present charter would not expire until 1836, he thought, after discussions with "a great number of persons," that if a request for renewal were delayed until after the presidential election, "there would be a poor chance for the Bank" to obtain it. Ever since his inauguration in 1829 Jackson had asked for changes in the operations of the Bank. He even went so far as to say in his first message to Congress that the BUS had "failed in the great end of establishing a uniform and sound currency."[45] He

42. Charles Miner to DW, September 8, 1831, ibid., 121; Remini, *Clay*, pp. 402–411.

43. Samuel R. Gammon, *Presidential Campaign of 1832* (Baltimore, 1922), pp. 45–52; Clay to James F. Conover, October 9, 1831, in Clay, *Papers*, VIII, 418.

44. DW to Nathaniel Williams, October 1, [1831], DW to Ambrose Spencer, November 16, 1831, in *PC*, III, 127–129, 134–135; DW to Clay, October 5, 1831, in Clay, *Papers*, VIII, 416.

45. Richardson, *Messages and Papers*, II, 1025

repeated that assertion, in various disguises, in subsequent messages. It was now time, Webster thought, to take him seriously. Once the election ended, Jackson could and surely would renew his attack against the BUS. "I am well informed," Webster continued, "that within three days, he has in conversation with several Gentlemen, reiterated his old opinions, somewhat vociferously, & declared them unchangeable." My best advice "is, that you come down here, at once, yourself, & survey the ground."[46]

Webster was not alone in urging Clay to come to the Senate. Even though it meant nudging aside his friend John Crittenden, Clay decided to take the advice because he feared, as Webster said, that the administration would strike down everything he believed important for the economic growth and prosperity of the nation. His American System would be shredded and cast aside. So he allowed his nomination to go forward, and on November 9, 1831, the Kentucky legislature duly elected him U.S. senator.[47]

But Biddle received contrary advice from Clay. If you apply for recharter when Congress reconvenes, the Kentuckian told him, "you will play into the hands" of the opposition. Wait until "the Session immediately after the next Presidential election."

Then, miraculously, Clay abruptly changed his mind. A month later, after he had arrived in Washington to take up his new senatorial duties, he reversed himself. "The friends of the Bank here, whom I have conversed"—most notably, Daniel Webster—"seem to expect the application to be made."[48]

Actually his change of heart and mind in the interim had occurred not because of discussion with friends of the BUS in Washington but for another, totally different reason.[49] On Monday, December 12, 1831, the delegates of his party opened their national convention in Baltimore and the following day unanimously nominated him for President along with Webster's friend and correspondent John Sergeant of Pennsylvania as Vice President. Now that he had in hand the nomination of his party, Clay wrote to Biddle and advised him to apply for recharter immediately. He believed he had a red-hot issue that could bury Jackson at the polls—that is, if Jackson vetoed a recharter bill.

Three weeks later, on January 6, 1832, Biddle notified Webster that "the memorial of the Bank for the renewal of its charter goes by today's mail." Nothing in the memorial was argued or discussed. It simply stated that "the charter is about to expire & that we wish it renewed."[50]

The big guns of the opposition were about to take on the President of the United States in a battle that quickly escalated into an full-scale war. As Webster had said, it would be an interesting and arduous session. He had no idea how *really* interesting and arduous it would become.

46. DW to Biddle, December 18, 1831, in McGrane, ed., *Correspondence of Biddle*, p. 146.

47. Remini, *Clay*, pp. 372–373.

48. Clay to Biddle, June 14, September 11, November 3, 1831, in Clay, *Papers*, VIII, 223–224, 264, 287–288; Clay to Biddle, December 15, 1831, Biddle Papers, LC.

49. Remini, *Clay*, pp. 379–380.

50. Biddle to DW, January 6, 1832, in *PC*, III, 140

20

Marshfield

JUST PRIOR TO his return with Caroline and Julia to Washington, Webster decided to purchase a 160-acre estate along a back road at Marshfield in the township of Green Harbor, south of Boston and not far from Plymouth. Back in 1824, when he and Grace first laid eyes on the place and spent a few days in residence at the home of the owner, Captain John Thomas, they found that they loved its closeness to the ocean and its quiet beauty, where one could hunt and fish, go boating, and relax. Each summer thereafter, when they vacationed at their summer retreat in Sandwich, they visited Captain Thomas and his wife.[1]

The property lies eleven miles from Plymouth and thirty-four miles southeast of Boston. The undulating countryside is superbly located, with the sea to the north and east. Marshlands covered with water at high tide extend several hundred acres around the area. A spring, still gushing today, is located behind the house while a small freshwater lake can be seen in the distance. Thick woods also covered part of the farm.[2]

By 1831 Thomas's financial problems had became quite burdensome. At the age of sixty-seven he found it increasingly difficult to manage his heavily mortgaged farm and provide for his wife and children. Under the circumstances he decided to sell the Marshfield property, and Webster eagerly stepped forward to buy it. They agreed on a price of thirty-five hundred dollars for the 160 acres, an earnest payment of one hundred dollars, and an arrangement whereby Thomas and his wife would retain occupancy for the remainder of their lives. At the same time Webster hired the captain's two sons, one of whom, Charles Henry Thomas, supervised operations on the farm.

On December 17, 1831, Webster sent one thousand dollars in currency and a check to Charles Henry Thomas, whom he always addressed as Henry, with instructions. For one thing, he thought the father should keep the earnest money so that the total would come to thirty-six hundred dollars. He then went on to instruct Henry on how the deed should be executed and returned to him. He said he would not put the deed on record at present or "tell more about our matters than is necessary. Let us keep our own secrets." Captain Thomas signed

1. Harvey, *Reminiscences*, pp. 264–265.

2. Oliver Bronson Capen, *Country Homes of Famous Americans* (New York, 1905), p. 59.

the conveyance on April 23, 1832, and Webster almost immediately began to enlarge the size of the property.[3]

Indeed Marshfield became an obsession. He did not choose this place because of the richness of its soil. The soil in fact was so poor that it required the frequent application of manure. He once said, "I live on the sandy seashore of Marshfield, and get along as well as I can. I am a poor farmer upon a great quantity of poor land; but my neighbors and I, by very great care . . . contrive to live on." He selected Marshfield, according to his friend Peter Harvey, because it "combined the advantages of sea and land, of running streams and quiet lakes, and presented more attractive scenery than could be found elsewhere in New England. It abounded in game of all descriptions. The land yielded animals and birds; the ocean, fishes. His tastes were therefore gratified."[4] Over time he acquired one adjoining parcel of land after another, until he had purchased 1,214 acres in twenty-three separate deed transactions. Still, he hungered for more so that by 1843 the estate had grown to 1,800 acres.[5]

He began improving his property immediately, even with the Thomases living in the house. Building and planting and raising cattle: That was what he loved to do at Marshfield. Before he died, he had constructed thirty buildings on the estate, one of them, close to the house, his so-called law office, and seven other houses for his staff. Expenditures on the entire property, both purchases and improvements, came to a little more than eighty-seven thousand dollars, a small fortune for the time.[6]

Once he took full possession of the property, he enlarged a pond near the house—called Webster's Pond today—and built a small island in its center so that his geese had a place to lay their eggs without worrying about marauding foxes. He also sailed small boats in the pond. There were three of these ponds on his property, all fed by springs of clear freshwater.

Webster's needs in working the estate required a larger and larger work force. He hired another Thomas son, Nathaniel Ray, along with housekeepers, cooks, carpenters, farmers, stable hands, gardeners, laborers, etc. for a total of more than three dozen men and women. And he planted whatever caught his eye, whether or not it could survive the Massachusetts soil and climate. Elms, pines, oaks, maples, sassafras, cedar, and many other varieties, as well as several thousand fruit trees, graced Marshfield before he was done. "There are several hundred thousands of trees here," he boasted near the end of his life, "which I have raised myself from the seeds; they are all arranged in avenues, copses, groves, long rows by the roads and fences." To young farmers he supposedly said, "Plant trees, adorn your grounds, live for the benefit of those who shall come after you." And he delighted in the attention and praise his orchards attained throughout the state. In addition, one full acre was given over to the

3. DW to Charles Henry Thomas, December 17, 1831, in *PC*, III, 137; deed, April 23, 1832, *Microfilm Edition*, F29/39770.

4. Harvey, *Reminiscences*, pp. 271–272.

5. Today only five hundred acres remain of the Webster estate.

6. Capen, *Country Homes*, p. 59.

cultivation of flowers and contained "the richest and most beautiful varieties of plants peculiar to this country."[7]

He also planted turnips, hay, corn, potatoes, oats, beets, and wheat and always tried to introduce the "best breeds of domestic animals,—cattle, sheep, swine, fowls,—the best grains, esculent roots, and fruits." A scientific farmer who constantly experimented to improve the soil and its produce, he studied all the modern literature on farming. A firm believer in the value of a blooded stock, he acquired a herd of sixty to eighty head of cattle, mostly thoroughbred, several yoke of Devon oxen, and blooded sheep and pigs.

Besides his blooded stock he began a domesticated zoo on his property. In addition to horses, sheep, chickens, and the like, several "Llamas from Peru feed in the pastures with the sheep. . . . We have also China geese, India geese, and in short, the same birds from almost every quarter of the world. As to the poultry yard, there is no end to the varieties which my man has collected. I do not keep the run of half the names and breeds." Guinea hens, peacocks, and ducks of all kinds wandered freely around the estate, the whole constituting a veritable "cattle show of no uncommon order." Webster also obtained the first Gordon setter to be introduced to the United States in 1842. It was a gift from an admirer.

Toward the end of his life Webster harvested as much as 400 tons of hay, 800 bushels of corn, 500 bushels of turnips—he placed great importance on turnips—1,000 bushels of potatoes, 500 bushels of oats, and 400 bushels of beets. To improve his agricultural produce, he transported sixty bags of guano from Peru to his estate, each bag of the fertilizer containing 150 pounds of the material.[8] "I should like to try guano at the rate of three hundred pounds to the acre, against ashes at the rate of two hundred bushels to the acre." He also used fish, kelp, and seaweed provided by the ocean nearby as fertilizer. As a matter of fact he "discovered" the value of kelp and seaweed and introduced it to his neighbors. At his own expense he laid out a road to the beach in order to harvest the fertilizer. After one storm in October 150 teams were employed to haul in "this rich manure" on to the farms adjoining Marshfield.

Not that he ever made any money from these crops. For Webster, Marshfield became a vehicle for spending money, not making it. Porter Wright, a later manager of Marshfield, once asked Webster whether he made money from the farm. "Oh, no," came the reply. Nothing. Not a penny. Although Wright never heard of Webster's selling his crops, he remembered that "he used to give them away, though."[9] However, Marshfield did provide everything that was eaten at the Webster table: meat, game, fish, vegetables, milk, and butter.

7. DW to Millard Fillmore, July 23, 1851, in W&S, XVIII, 453; Fuess, Webster, II, 324–328; Curtis, Webster, II, 217; Baxter, Webster, pp. 282–283; Harvey, Reminiscences, p. 272; Lanman, Private Life of Webster, p. 72.

8. Lanman, Private Life of Webster, p. 70.

9. Harvey, Reminiscences, p. 279; Fuess, Webster, II, 327 and note 2; Capen, Country Homes, pp. 63–64; Lanman, Private Life of Webster, pp. 70, 72; DW to Porter Wright, November 13, 1851, DW to Fillmore, July 23, 1851, in W&S, XVIII, 453, 487.

The original house on the property came in for considerable renovation and expansion as well, particularly when he moved into the residence after Captain Thomas died on July 27, 1837, at the age of seventy-three. The house, which Webster called Green Harbor because of its location near the Green Harbor River, giving him an outlet to the ocean, had been built in 1774 by Nathaniel Ray Thomas, the father of the captain. It was a basic steep-roofed, two-story structure with dormers on the third floor. From time to time Webster more than doubled its size in a haphazard fashion so that it eventually provided nine large rooms on the ground floor, all opening into one another. It had a most unusual and distinctive architectural style—"irregular" best describes it, both within and without—which may be the reason it initially appealed to him and his wife. Towering above the house were two enormous brick chimneys, crested by an array of chimney pots. Later, in 1843, his daughter, Julia, designed an extension to the west end of the building that became his Gothic-style library. This structure added another distinctive, if not unique, feature because of the curious angles of the two pairs of dormers on the second level. Each pair was constructed to form an obtuse angle with its mate. In addition, a latticed veranda ran around the entire house. In sum, the house looked like none other. It followed no known architectural style. In large measure that was its charm. It was not regarded as a beautiful house. Just a very large, imposing, and unique-looking mansion.[10]

The interior also showed an indifference to current fashion. No single plan or design appeared in the selection or arrangement of the furniture. Nothing formal could be seen in either the living or dining room. Some pieces reflected tastes of the Federal period, others of the Greek Revival. Portraits of Webster and other members of his family, Lord Ashburton, Joseph Story, a Roman girl, cattle, and marble busts of the owner and Julia were displayed in "the greatest profusion." The picture he valued most was a small silhouette, cut in black, and handsomely framed with the inscription "My Excellent Mother. D. W." According to one witness, the likeness bore a striking resemblance to Webster himself.

The furniture of the house included chairs, tables, sofas, beds, candlesticks, crockery, mirrors, carpets, curtains, clocks, paintings, engravings, glass objects, and Webster's slant-top desk, which may have been a family heirloom. Most of the furniture tended to be "heavy" in appearance, like pieces of the Victorian era. The library, with its huge, specially built "Gothic bookcase," contained volumes valued at more than forty thousand dollars and included Audubon's *Birds of America,* the *Encyclopaedia Britannica,* the best editions of Washington, Bacon, and Franklin, hundreds of poetry and history books, and "all the dictionaries that were ever heard of." It also contained the collection of thirteen silver medals voted to George Washington by Congress, which Webster had purchased from the Washington family. All the rooms were cluttered with bric-

10. Fuess, *Webster,* II, 325.

a-brac of every imaginable variety: statuary, busts, vases, and "curiosities of every description," much of it presented by admirers and all of it adding an air of extravagance, if not ostentation.[11] The citizens of Boston, for example, presented him with an enormous—two to three feet in diameter—silver vase.[12]

Webster regularly added to his collection of artworks, and Caroline Webster encouraged—indeed participated in—her husband's excesses. Unlike Grace's modest circumstances, Caroline's background reflected wealth and position. Married to a distinguished statesman, she naturally wished to impress Massachusetts society with her competence as the mistress of the Webster household. She meant her homes in Boston and Marshfield to reflect her sense of position and good taste.

The house faced south and rested on a high, grassy lawn bordering reclaimed marshland. A long avenue of elms, oaks, maples, pines, and sassafras led to the house from the main road. Webster built a small building close by as a study to house his many agricultural books.[13] It is called his law office today, although his real law office,[14] where he kept most of his lawbooks, was in Boston.[15] In addition, he built two or three dozen other structures, including outhouses, a dairyman's cottage, the fisherman's house, a residence for his chief tenant, several large barns, the gardener's house, and other lesser buildings.[16]

The mouth of the Green Harbor River lay about two miles from the mansion, and here Webster built a boathouse, where he kept his "fleet." He had his boat furniture made after his own pattern, stamped with his initials. Here, aboard his yachts *Julia*, named for his daughter, *Calypso*, given him by Stephen White, *Comet*, *Home Squadron*, or *Captain Peterson* or "a small schooner," known as the *Lapwing*, another gift from an admirer, he could truly relax and just stare at the sky and ocean, oblivious of anything or anyone around him. He forbade on board his vessels any conversation dealing with politics or business. Talk had to be confined to "natural objects."[17]

Fishing was another passion. Aboard one of his yachts, anchored in the inner roads just a few hours from Boston, his line baited and waiting for a halibut, cod, or haddock to strike, he would lose himself in contemplation as he

---

11. Lanman, *Private Life of Webster*, pp. 74–75. The Washington medals were offered to Congress in the late 1820s with the intention of having them deposited in the Library of Congress. Unfortunately a debate over the price stalled the purchase, and Webster stepped in and acquired them. Ibid., p. 77.

12. New York *Mirror*, December 5, 1835.

13. Lanman, *Private Life of Webster*, p. 75.

14. In the Boston law office Webster had five or six thousand volumes. Ibid., p. 87.

15. The "law office," a National Historic Landmark, is the only Webster building still standing. However, it has been moved from its original site to the grounds of the Isaac Winslow House nearby. It is owned by the Marshfield Historical Commission but maintained by the Winslow House Association on lease.

16. Lanman, *Private Life of Webster*, p. 74.

17. Harvey, *Reminiscences*, pp. 279–280; Robert B. Forbes to DW, May 30, 1849, in *PC*, VI, 339.

stared at the cliffs lying in the distance. "All well," he wrote to Stephen White; "spoke nothing."[18]

Besides boating and fishing, Webster loved to hunt. Across the road from the boathouse he built a "gunning shop" for his weapons. An excellent shot, he frequently visited Cohasset, Chelsea Beach, and Nantasket Beach in the summer and autumn to shoot wild fowl. Teal and coots would sit down in the water, and when they rose again, he would take aim and bring them down one after another. Once on a hot August day, when out on the marshes shooting birds, he came to the Green Harbor River and met a boatman who thought he recognized him.

"This is Daniel Webster, I believe," said the boatman.

"That is my name," replied the hunter.

"Well, now," the boatman responded, "I am told that you can make from three to five dollars a day, pleadin' cases up in Boston."

Webster allowed as how he sometimes received that amount for his services.

"Well, now," the boatman declared, "it seems to me, I declare, if I could get as much in the city, pleadin' law cases, I would not be a-wadin' over these marshes this hot weather, shootin' little birds!"[19]

Interestingly, Webster forbade the killing of any animals on his property. One day a stranger who had visited to pay his respects spotted a flock of quail running across the road. The gentleman burst out with "Oh, if I only had a gun, I could easily kill the whole flock." Then, turning to Webster, he added, "Have you not one in your house, sir?" Black Dan calmly replied that no man was ever permitted to kill a quail or any other kind of bird or a rabbit or a squirrel on his property. He then commented on "the *slaughtering* propensities of the American people." In this country, he continued, there was "an almost universal passion for killing and eating every wild animal that chanced to cross the pathway of man."[20]

Much as Webster enjoyed outdoor sports he had no taste at all for indoor amusements. He never played chess, checkers, billiards, or "ten-pins" and he was almost totally ignorant of card games, except whist, which he played with his Marshfield company after dinner for an hour or so.[21]

Webster invariably had guests at his home, sometimes as many as a dozen. He organized activities for their entertainment—fishing, yachting, hunting—and would assign someone "to take care of the ladies." He usually dined at a "late" hour, from four to six—most Americans dined at three or four while there was still light—and he rarely appeared at the dining table except in "full dress." He was very particular about the niceties of etiquette and once gently repri-

18. DW to Stephen White, August 17, 1832, in *W&S*, XVII, 523.

19. Harvey, *Reminiscences*, pp. 292–293.

20. Lanman, *Private Life of Webster*, p. 80.

21. Ibid., p. 89.

manded a guest for coming to the table in a "frock-coat."

At the dinner table he amused his friends with what seemed like an inexhaustible fund of anecdote and personal reminiscence. The subject of American history, particularly congressional history, prompted him to regale the table with amusing comments on various personalities. He loved to describe the characters of unknown persons by the meanings of their names. He also had a "keen sense of the ludicrous," appreciated "eccentric humor," and had a funny way of conjugating certain proper names. When he was inspired, his "table-talk" was fully equal to his more elaborate efforts on the Senate floor.[22]

Unfortunately Marshfield returned his love and devotion with illness and pain. The grasses growing on all sides of his estate discharged a great amount of pollen into the air in late summer and early fall, and there was simply no way anyone living in Marshfield could escape the irritant, regardless of the direction of the wind. This was particularly true where Webster lived because marshes virtually surround the entire property. Soon after moving to his new home, Webster developed a severe case of hay fever, which he called catarrh. The attacks were so severe that they frequently prostrated him. Year after year he suffered with this affliction. He consulted doctors, who prescribed all sorts of medicines, none of which worked. Even today Marshfield has a reputation as one of the worst areas in the country for allergy sufferers to live.[23]

As the Marshfield estate grew in size and possessions, Daniel Webster, Esq., and his wife played the part of the lord and lady of the manor. The farmers nearby invariably referred to him as "Squire."[24]

More and more he needed money to improve Marshfield and the old family Elms Farm at Franklin, New Hampshire. His fleet of yachts and other personal extravagances also made demands on his purse. Because of his appreciation of his great worth to many people and institutions, he had no compunction against dunning wealthier friends and companies like the Second National Bank for money, either as loans or gifts or advances on services.

Politically, this tone and style only added to a perceived belief that Squire Webster considered himself better than most. His superior attitudes toward his many endowments, topped off by this Marshfield extravaganza, seemed to prove that he could not and would not respond sympathetically to one of the main currents in American life during this Jacksonian age, the rise of popular democracy.

In no conceivable way could anyone think of Daniel Webster as a "man of the people." Much as he might try to appear as a democratic symbol of this new age, especially when presidential nominations neared, he could not pull it off. He was a thoroughgoing elitist—and he reveled in it. He had started as a Federalist, continued to believe Federalist doctrines, especially Hamiltonian notions

22. Ibid., pp. 91–92, 95.

23. The report of numerous allergists was relayed by Mrs. Betty Bates to the author, on May 16, 1995.

24. Harvey, *Reminiscences*, pp. 292–293, 274; Lyman, *Public and Private Life of Webster*, II, 98–99.

about the economy and government, and affirmed unquestionably the notion that the educated and wealthy should guide the nation's future direction. He himself said many times that he belonged "with generations that had gone by."[25] Committed to Clay's American System and now one of the strongest proponents of tariff protection, he fretted over the direction the Democratic party with its mass appeal and support would take the country. To a considerable extent Daniel Webster was out of touch with the democratic surge that swept the nation during the decades preceding the Civil War.

The establishment of such a glorified residence as Marshfield provided the final outward sign of the distance that separated Webster from the masses. Marshfield represented achievement, wealth, and the owner's pride in what he had accomplished. True, Andrew Jackson also lived in a magnificent establishment outside Nashville, Tennessee, which he called the Hermitage. He belonged to the wealthiest segment of Tennessee society. But that was not how the public at large perceived him. They saw him as their tribune, the representative of all the people. And every word he spoke or wrote in public demonstrated his sincere commitment to democracy.[26]

Webster's lifestyle also demonstrated his "aristocratic tastes and habits." Harriet Martineau, a most perceptive foreign observer of the Washington scene at this time, wrote that "Webster is a lover of ease and pleasure, and has an air of the most unaffected indolence and careless self-sufficiency." He constantly indulged his taste for fine wines and good food, and his girth had started to show their effects. "It is not often that good wine is under any roof where I am without my knowing it," he once boasted to a friend.

Martineau rightly noted that "Mr. Webster owes his rise to the institutions under which he lives,—institutions which open the race to the swift, and the battle to the strong; but there is little in him that is congenial with them. He is aristocratic in his tastes and habits: and but little republican simplicity is to be recognized in him. Neither his private conversation nor his public transactions usually convey an impression that he is in earnest."[27]

Webster's limitations, like his great talents, could be seen by most of his contemporaries during his lifetime. He could not—probably would not—disguise his true feelings about people or events. They were all there on the surface for anyone to see. When bored, he looked bored, deliberately so, especially in the Senate. His interest could be aroused only when some constitutional issue or legal point came up in which his extraordinary reasoning powers and knowledge could be brought into play. Most times he just sat slouched languidly in his seat, chewing the top of his pen or twiddling his thumbs or "bursting into

25. Speech in 1816, in W&S, XIV, 14, 76.

26. "The people are the government," Jackson said repeatedly in his state papers, "administering it by their agents; they are the Government, the sovereign power." In his first inaugural address he trumpeted his philosophic belief: "The majority is to govern." Jackson to Andrew J. Donelson, May 12, 1835, Donelson Papers, LC; Richardson, *Messages and Papers,* II, 1011.

27. Martineau, *Western Travel,* I, 277, 288; DW to Stephen White, [n.d.], in W&S, XVII, 525.

sudden and transient laughter at Colonel [Thomas Hart] Benton's oratorical absurdities."

Webster's "keen sense of the ludicrous" and dry wit surfaced not only socially when entertaining guests at Marshfield but also when speaking on the Senate floor. As one congressional observer noted, "The unequaled Webster was too wise and sensible not to enjoy humor." On one occasion during a speech the Senate clock suddenly began to strike. After it had struck continuously about fifteen times, Webster turned to the presiding officer. "The clock is out of order, sir—I have the floor." The chamber burst into laughter while he stood silent as the sergeant at arms stopped the clock from sounding.

On another occasion, just as Webster began to introduce a resolution, a man in the galleries looking like a clergyman stood up and shouted, "My friends, the country is on the brink of destruction. . . . God is looking down on you, and if you act upon correct principles you will get safely through." Then the man hastily left the chamber before the sergeant at arms could grab him. During the tumult that followed Webster stood at his place perfectly still. When order was finally restored, he said, *"As the gentleman in the gallery has concluded, I will proceed with my remarks."*

When in an exceptionally good mood he could be seen "leaning back at his ease, telling stories, cracking jokes, shaking the sofa with burst after burst of laughter." Otherwise, when not so "inspired," he just sat at his desk writing letters, "or dreaming," or mindlessly doodling so that when a vote was called, someone of his party had to poke him to "tell him that his vote is wanted." Martineau concluded that "if his moral had equalled his intellectual supremacy, if his aims had been as single as his reason is unclouded, he would long ago have carried all before him, and been the virtual monarch of the United States."[28]

Still, no one could miss the fact that this "lover of ease," this daydreamer, this distracted solon sitting at his place writing letters could in a flash spring to life and flood the chamber with the magic of his voice and the profundity of his thinking. To see his lips tremble and nostrils expand when angered, to see perspiration start from his brow as he labored to produce a convincing argument, to see him move "with anxiety and the toil of intellectual conflict"—these were the moments when a listener realized that this "pleasure-loving man" worked ferociously for his honors and material gain. To have the opportunity to see and hear Webster at his best sent mobs scrambling for seats or even standing room in any chamber or auditorium where he would perform. As soon as the doors opened, the crowd jammed its way into the hall.[29]

Usually before the Supreme Court he could be expected to demonstrate his extraordinary command of the law. "It was amusing," recorded Martineau, "to see how the Court would fill after the entrance of Webster, and empty when

28. John W. Forney, *Anecdotes of Public Men* (New York, 1873), p. 83; Poore, *Perley's Reminiscences,* I, 146; Martineau, *Western Travel,* I, 290, 243, 288–289; Lanman, *Private Life of Webster,* pp. 142–143.
29. Martineau, *Western Travel,* I, 277.

he had gone back to the Senate." He would saunter into the chamber, throw himself down in his chair, lean back against the table, all the while looking dreamy and inattentive. How could one so "dreamy and *nonchalant,*" Martineau asked herself, suddenly rouse himself to argue forcibly before the High Court? "It seemed like having a curtain lifted up."[30] Then the Court and the public came awake to the extent of his intellectual labors on behalf of his client and the extent of his knowledge of both the law and the facts in the case. When called upon to perform, he could throw off his indolent mood and summon his genius into service. "Would that Heaven had made me such a man!" enthused his wealthy friend Philip Hone, the former mayor of New York.[31]

Such a marked contrast of character in one so talented and so flawed confused many people. They recognized his natural genius, but what they did not know was that the rest came by dint of intense intellectual labor. As Martineau said, he deserved every award he ever won.

30. Ibid.
31. Hone, *Diary,* I, 117.

21

The Bank War

BIDDLE'S decision to seek a recharter of the BUS four years before its charter was due to expire touched off a titanic battle between the Congress and President Jackson. Old Hickory immediately judged the action as a deliberate ploy to convert an economic issue that he had raised at the outset of his administration into a political one to help Henry Clay in his bid to unseat him in the next election nine months hence. Jackson had asked for changes in the operation of the Bank, and Biddle had replied with a flat-out challenge to his authority and leadership. Very well, then, if Biddle would not respond to presidential requests for alterations and even refuse a proffered compromise by the secretary of the treasury, Louis McLane, he could expect nothing but all-out war.[1]

Jackson's leading advisers, the so-called Kitchen Cabinet, filled the President's ears with stinging accusations about Biddle's purposes. Francis P. Blair, the editor of Jackson's mouthpiece, the Washington *Globe*; Amos Kendall, fourth auditor of the Treasury Department and Blair's close associate; and Roger B. Taney, the attorney general, assured Jackson that the Bank president was intent on his defeat. "Now as I understand the application at the present time," wrote Taney, "it means in plain English this—the Bank says to the President, your next election is at hand—if you charter us, well—if not, beware of your power."[2]

Worse, the BUS enjoyed enormous financial and political influence in the country yet responded to the commands of only one man, Nicholas Biddle. As a central bank it controlled the expansion and contraction of currency and credit throughout the nation. Biddle wielded its vast resources, according to the Jacksonians, to "corrupt" congressmen with "loans" and such retainer fees as Webster regularly received. The BUS assisted favored politicians in their elections with financial help and punished those who challenged or questioned its actions.

---

1. John A. Munroe, *Louis McLane: Federalist and Jacksonian* (New Brunswick, N.J., 1973), pp. 304–323. On the Bank War, see Robert V. Remini, *Andrew Jackson and the Bank War* (New York, 1968), John M. McFaul, *The Politics of Jacksonian Finance* (Ithaca, N.Y., 1972), Thomas P. Govan, *Nicholas Biddle, Nationalist and Public Banker* (Chicago, 1959), and Harry Watson, *Liberty and Order* (New York, 1990).

2. Taney to Ellicott, January 25, 1832, Taney Papers, LC.

President Jackson did not need the shrill voices of Blair, Kendall, and Taney to alert him to this attack upon his leadership and what it could mean in the fall election. But he did not howl and rant as some expected. He remained calm. He quietly informed his friends that he would wait and watch. He still opposed an unmodified recharter, he said, but would take action when and if the bill passed Congress. "My friends need not fear my energy—should the Bank question come to me," he assured his old army friend and companion in arms General John Coffee, "unless the corrupting monster should be shraven of its ill gotten power, my veto will meet it frankly & fearlessly."[3]

As the new year began, Congress had not only a Bank bill to consider but a tariff measure as well. Ever since the passage of the "infamous" Tariff of Abominations in 1828 southern congressmen had demanded a revision of rates. When the Treasury Report of Secretary McLane recommended passage of a revenue tariff, rather than a protective tariff, on the assumption that the imminent extinction of the national debt would produce a mounting surplus justifying these sharp reductions, Henry Clay immediately swung into action. He asked Webster if he agreed that the opposition leaders should submit their own tariff bill. He then drew up resolutions "with the concurrence of Mr. [Nathaniel] Silsbee, yourself [Webster], Mr. [Nathan] Appleton and Mr. [John] Davis" and submitted them to the Senate on January 10. After that he met with twenty congressmen from both houses and drafted a new tariff bill. Meanwhile in the House George McDuffie, chairman of the Ways and Means Committee and a staunch free trader, reported a measure that called for sweeping reductions of the tariff rates.[4]

While the Bank and tariff bills began their slow journey through Congress, the Senate faced the immediate question of the President's nomination of his recently resigned secretary of state, Martin Van Buren, to serve as minister to Great Britain.[5] Any number of senators were out to punish the Little Magician for his past "misdeeds" by denying him the post. Since Van Buren had already left for London, the thought of bringing him back in disgrace thrilled the friends of Calhoun, who sought revenge for the Magician's role in the rupture of relations between the President and Vice President. They viewed the New Yorker as the evil force behind the administration, using his guile and cunning to manipulate Jackson to serve his own presidential ambitions. Others accused him of instigating the spoils system and engineering the breakup of the cabinet. And they delighted in the knowledge that presiding over the confirmation process was the Vice President himself.

---

3. Jackson to Coffee, February 19, 1832, Coffee Papers, Tennessee Historical Society.

4. *Executive Documents,* 22d Congress, 1st Session, Serial 216, Doc. No. 3; Adams, *Memoirs,* VIII, 445; Clay to Webster, January 8, 1832, in *PC,* III, 141; *Register of Debates,* 22d Congress, 1st Session, p. 186ff.

5. The nominations of Louis McLane as secretary of the treasury and Edward Livingston as secretary of state also came before the Senate, but they were confirmed without incident on January 12 and 13, 1832.

The debate over the nomination quickly escalated into a raging duel between Clay, Webster, Hayne, George Poindexter of Mississippi, and Stephen D. Miller of South Carolina on one side and John Forsyth of Georgia, William L. Marcy of New York, Bedford Brown of North Carolina, and Samuel Smith of Maryland on the other. Clay savaged Van Buren for "the pernicious system of party politics adopted by the present administration," while Poindexter and Miller insinuated moral delinquency in the Magician's behavior toward Peggy Eaton.[6]

Webster chose a more decorous and appropriate avenue of attack. On January 24, 1832, during the Senate's executive session, he began his speech by recognizing the seriousness of refusing confirmation of a minister who had already gone abroad and been accredited by the government to which he had been sent. But duty compelled him to discharge his constitutional responsibility, and he said he would do it "conscientiously and fearlessly." He then based his argument against confirmation on Secretary of State Van Buren's instructions regarding the negotiations of the West Indian trade to Louis McLane, the nation's minister to Great Britain at the time. By repudiating the policies of the Monroe and Adams administrations, Van Buren had, according to Webster, submitted "to the domineering tone" of the British ministry and in effect had forfeited privileges the country enjoyed under British rule "by our misbehavior in choosing rulers." Turning to the presiding officer, Webster declared: "Sir, for one, I reject all idea of holding any right of trade, or any other rights, as a privilege or a boon from the British government, or any other government."[7]

With numerous senators intent on bludgeoning Van Buren to political extinction it occurred to many of them that the pleasure of delivering the final coup ought to be conferred on the presiding officer, Vice President Calhoun, since he had suffered the most from Van Buren's machinations. So they arranged a tie when the vote on confirmation was taken on January 25. Naturally that action placed the final decision directly in the hands of John C. Calhoun.

The "cast-iron man," as Harriet Martineau called him, did not hesitate for a moment when the clerk announced that twenty-three senators had voted no to the question, and another twenty-three yes. He immediately voted against confirmation, and that killed it.

"You have broken a minister," snapped Senator Thomas Hart Benton to an opposition colleague, "and elected a Vice-President."[8]

Indeed Jackson took the rejection as a personal insult and vowed that Van Buren would be his running mate in the fall election.

"By the Eternal!" he supposedly raged when he got the news. "I'll smash them!" He immediately notified Van Buren of his decision. "The people will

6. *Register of Debates*, 22d Congress, 1st Session, p. 1341ff.

7. *W&S*, VI, 89–96.

8. Martineau, *Western Travel*, p. 243; Francis P. Blair to Van Buren, April 25, 1859, Van Buren Papers, LC; *Register of Debates*, 22d Congress, 1st Session, p. 1324; Benton, *Thirty Years' View*, I, 215.

properly resent the insult offered to the Executive, and the injury intended to our foreign relations, in your rejection, by placing you in the chair of the very man whose casting vote rejected you."[9]

For his part, Webster expressed no great elation over Van Buren's humiliating defeat, although Clay said that "our friends are in high spirits." He just mentioned in passing to Stephen White that "we are not frighten [*sic*] yet, as the consequence of our rejections of Mr VB." As for the possibility that Van Buren would join the Jackson ticket, Webster convinced himself that in such a development neither Virginia nor Pennsylvania would support him.[10]

The probability of Van Buren's nomination for Vice President added to rumors already in circulation that Calhoun would abandon the Democratic party and join Clay and Webster to form a powerful alliance against the administration. Although a true party coalition never occurred, the three men did begin to cooperate with one another to thwart Jackson's purposes and policies and thereafter were frequently spoken of as the Great Triumvirate.[11]

Calhoun's influence among southern congressmen would be important, but he certainly could not be expected to help with the tariff issue. While Clay began meeting with his friends to draft a new protective tariff, Webster tried unsuccessfully to defeat a bill for the reapportionment of representatives, mandated by the Constitution after each decennial census, that passed the House in February 1832. In the bill the middle and western states gained additional seats, but in New England the single additional seat given to Maine was offset by the loss of one seat each from Massachusetts and New Hampshire.

When the House bill arrived in the Senate, Webster moved that it be referred to a select committee of seven over which he served as chairman. After failing to convince the committee to amend the bill, he proposed a substitute on the Senate floor and delivered a very eloquent speech in its defense. Debate continued sporadically until April 26, when the Senate passed a modified version of Webster's substitute, but the House refused to concur, and eventually its version passed both houses. The struggle demonstrated once again that sectionalism had arrived in full force and would play a vital role in all subsequent issues to come before Congress.[12]

While Webster struggled to preserve Massachusetts's thirteen-member representation in the House of Representatives, Clay worked out the details of a new tariff to replace the much-despised Tariff of Abominations and spoke in

9. Henry Wikoff, *Reminiscences of an Idler* (New York, 1880), pp. 29–31; Jackson to Van Buren, February 12, 1832, Van Buren Papers, LC.

10. Clay to N. B. Beall, January 27, 1832, in Clay, *Papers*, VIII, 450; DW to White, February 12, 1832, in *PC*, III, 150.

11. See the editorials in the Washington *Globe* for January and February 1832.

12. The bill passed on May 19, and the President signed it. For various versions of Webster's speech and report, see *Register of Debates*, 22d Congress, 1st Session, pp. 1310–1386; *W&S*, VI, 102–121; and *PS*, I, 481–499. The defeat of Webster's substitute again demonstrated his inability to move legislation he personally favored through Congress.

its favor for three days, starting on February 2. In the process he adroitly managed to maneuver the bill out of the hands of the Committee on Finance to his own Committee on Manufactures, where he could better safeguard its protective features. Then, on March 10, he brought it to the floor. The bill reduced duties between five and six million dollars, but the rates on a number of articles were jacked higher than the 1828 tariff.[13]

Like everything else at this session, the new bill went through an endless round of debate. Nullifiers would have none of it, so the administration tried to find a compromise between their demands and Clay's proposals. Some of the recommendations brought cries of outrage from several of Webster's manufacturing supporters, and they promptly let him know how they felt. "The late movements in the Senate on the subject of the Tariff," wrote Harrison Gray Otis, a man with considerable interests in cotton and woolen manufacturing in Massachusetts, "have occasioned much alarm and anxiety among all classes of manufacturers in this region. . . . [y]ou must do as well as you can—but we are all afraid that some unseen power will throw you all in the wind, and that from that wind will come storms." Not satisfied with petitions, memorials, and personal letters, "a number of gentlemen, & Mr A[bbott] Lawrence among the rest, are about setting out for Washington to explain & enforce their views on the pending measure."[14]

Finally, after much maneuvering and alterations of the proposed rates between the two houses—at times frightening the New England manufacturers into such threats as joining the South and reimposing the rates of the 1816 tariff—the two houses agreed to lower the schedule by approximately 25 percent, which would reduce revenues by about five million dollars, but to retain high productive rates on woolens, iron, and cottons. The Tariff of 1832, which Jackson signed on July 14, remained a very high tariff, but at least some of the "abominations" of the 1828 law had been eliminated.

Although Webster kept abreast of developments with the tariff, informing his friends in Massachusetts how matters were proceedings and voting in favor of the final bill, he spent much of his time, when not arguing six cases before the Supreme Court, in preparing for the looming battle over the Bank bill.

Early in the session it had been agreed by the leading members of the National Republican party that Webster would leave the tariff in Clay's expert hands, and concentrate on getting the charter renewal through the Senate. Senator George M. Dallas of Pennsylvania submitted the memorial for recharter to the Senate in January, requesting at the same time that it be referred to a select committee of five members. Unprepared for this "surprise" maneuver, the Jacksonians could not block the action, and the committee was selected by ballot. Dallas received the most votes, followed by Webster, Thomas Ewing of

13. *Register of Debates,* 22d Congress, 1st Session, pp. 55, 66–75, 656–658; Remini, *Clay,* pp. 386–396.
14. Otis to DW, April 11, Jeremiah Mason to DW, May 27, 1832, in *PC,* III, 164–167, 174.

Ohio, Robert Y. Hayne, and Josiah S. Johnston. The committee was almost solidly antiadministration and pro-Bank.

On January 20, 1832, Thomas Hart Benton led off the attack for the Democrats on the Senate floor with a horrendously long speech assailing the BUS and declaring the bank drafts issued by the various branches of the institution in the leading cities to be illegal.[15] As Benton harangued the crowd, his booming voice ricocheting around the room, Webster sat quietly at his place writing letters[16] and taking notes. Benton obviously commanded the forces of the opposition, and every critical point he raised would have to be refuted.

Dallas reported from the select committee on March 13 with a favorable recommendation for recharter, and the members then began the serious business of arguing and discussing every article in the bill. Sometimes the Senate went into executive session when examining the reports and answers to inquiries requested of the Bank. Webster also kept Biddle informed of what was said and done. "I thank you for your speech in secret session," responded Biddle to one of Webster's communications, "or rather your speeches, which are worthy of you, and of the Country. We are all delighted with it here." Biddle also suggested various ideas that might be taken to strengthen the arguments favoring recharter.[17]

Both houses of Congress now had the question squarely before them. Weeks passed, but Dallas seemed reluctant to move action on the measure. Webster spoke to him, and Dallas replied that the initiative, like all money bills, ought to originate in the lower house. But George McDuffie, chairman of the House committee, told Webster that the "proceedings" should begin in the Senate, that he was giving the tariff bill top priority and holding off on the Bank bill. With Congress seemingly in a deadlock, Webster decided to summon Biddle to the capital from Philadelphia. McDuffie thinks your presence is "indispensable," and "I certainly agree with him, altogether," Webster wrote on May 14.[18]

Biddle arrived on May 20 and signaled Dallas to move ahead. Action on the recharter bill was immediately resumed in the Senate, and on May 25 Webster finally delivered his major address on the Bank bill.

Apart from Dallas's unwillingness to begin the debate, Webster's long delay in expressing his views in a public session was calculated. For one thing he wanted to hear the views of others so that he could respond to them. For another he figured the timing of his speech could be as important as what he had to say. When at last he rose and received recognition from the chair, the final round in the struggle for recharter commenced.

15. *Register of Debates,* 22d Congress, 1st Session, pp. 113–144.

16. In one of these letters he prophesied (mistakenly) that Jackson would not survive a second term in office. DW to Stephen White, January 20, [1832], in *PC,* III, 143.

17. Biddle to DW, February 2, 1832, ibid., III, 147.

18. DW to Biddle, May 14, 1832, ibid., III, 171–172.

Webster started right off by shrewdly noting that he, several other gentle-men in the room, and the presiding officer himself had been involved in the establishment of the Second National Bank back in 1816. Then, looking straight at Calhoun, he added, "I trust it will not be unbecoming the occasion if I allude to your own important agency in that transaction." You voted for the bill, he continued in an obvious ploy to entice southern votes for recharter, while I voted against it. Webster insisted that his opposition never involved the constitutional issue—he had no doubts on that score—but rather the failure of certain amend-ments that would have improved the bill.

Now the question involved a continuation of the Bank, and Webster readily acknowledged his willingness to support recharter since the BUS had greatly aided the country in establishing a sound and uniform currency. "A disordered currency is one of the greatest political evils," he argued. It wars against frugality, industry, and economy and engenders extravagance and speculation. Unless we have an efficient and well-run national bank, state banks will become the regulators of the public currency, and everyone knows where that horror leads: wildcat banking and the issuance of a deluge of worthless bank notes. Webster concluded by commenting on the assistance rendered by the BUS to the opera-tions of the Treasury in the collection and disbursement of revenues. He praised the salutary effects the Bank had had on manufactures, commerce, and agricul-ture.[19]

It is interesting to note that on this, the first of his speeches on the question, Webster did not take up the constitutional issue that Benton had raised earlier and others would pursue. But when on May 26 Gabriel Moore of Alabama introduced two amendments to the bill that would bar the BUS from establish-ing branches or discount and deposit agencies within a state without first gaining its consent and would empower the states to tax the Bank's branches and agen-cies within its borders,[20] Webster was obliged to speak again. These amendments struck at the very heart of the Bank's operations and had to be killed. Black Dan was the chosen executioner, and on May 28 he demonstrated what a skillful assassin he could be.

On this occasion Webster's temper flared from time to time to show his genuine concern. What bothered him were the lengths the opposition would go to gather support, even at the risk of inflicting constitutional injury. The Jacksoni-ans seemed determined to court the states' rights people and all those with any constitutional objection to the BUS to increase the states' taxing power without, as Webster said, "fixed limits, or any reasonable guards." What these amend-ments do, he cried, is grant the states "a power to embarrass, a power to oppose, a power to expel, a power to destroy."

With that, Webster wheeled into an extended discussion of the constitu-tionality of the BUS. He reiterated that the power was derived by implication

19. *Register of Debates*, 22d Congress, 1st Session, pp. 954–964.
20. Ibid., p. 964.

on the ground of "just necessity."[21] Furthermore, "it has already been judicially decided" by the Supreme Court that Congress may create a Bank and that states may not tax it.

Mark you, sir, he thundered, "it is the *Constitution*, not the *law*, which lays this prohibition on the States." It is therefore impossible for the Congress to relieve the states from this "constitutional prohibition." It will be, and should be, judicially struck down.[22]

None of these arguments was new, but coming from Webster, the acknowledged defender, protector, and interpreter of the Constitution, they carried additional force.

Happily a majority of the other senators agreed with him and the two amendments were defeated on June 1 by the count of twenty-six to eighteen.[23]

After a hard struggle, lasting six months, and despite the strenuous efforts of Benton and his cohorts to delay, thwart, and postpone final action, Webster called for the yeas and nays on the Bank bill on June 11. By the vote of 28 to 20 it passed the Senate. It was a tough battle, but Webster and his Senate forces, with no little help from Biddle, had won. Nearly a month later the measure rode through the lower house by the vote of 107 to 85.[24]

Nicholas Biddle let out a sigh of relief. "I congratulate our friends most cordially upon this most satisfactory result. Now for the President. My belief is that the President will veto the bill though this is not generally known or believed."[25]

He was wrong. Any number of people, including Webster, knew the President would kill the bill. *"My opinion is, the President will veto it,"* he wrote to Stephen White. "He will put it on the ground of *pre-maturity*—& say, that there is coming, seasonably, a new Congress, under a new Census, &c. But, for the present, he will *veto*. This, *I fully believe.*" Still, he also believed the Bank would ultimately win recharter. Its "inherent *popularity*" could not be so easily dismissed, not even by President Jackson.[26]

By this time, Webster, along with many other congressmen, had grown

21. A little later in this speech Webster went on to state that not only did Congress have the power to create a bank, but it also had the power to create a bank of circulation. The reason? Congress possesses constitutional control of the currency. On this point John Marshall later wrote to him that he found the idea "quite novel. . . . I however am far from undertaking to dissent from your proposition. I only say it is new, and I ponder on it." Marshall to DW, June 16, 1832, in *PC*, III, 178.

22. *Register of Debates*, 22d Congress, 1st Session, pp. 981–988.

23. *Register of Debates*, 22d Congress, 1st Session, p. 1005. As usual Webster sent copies of his speeches to political leaders around the country and received in return many glowing letters of congratulations. Not a few of these letters expressed their admiration for what they thought were new ideas about the rights and powers of the states. "I am confident no man in Ohio can be sustained, who votes to postpone the immediate consideration of the Bill," wrote Bellamy Storer to DW, June 19, 1832, in *PC*, III, 178–179.

24. *Register of Debates*, 22d Congress, 1st Session, pp. 1073, 3851–3852.

25. Biddle to Thomas Cadwalader, July 3, 1832, Biddle Papers, LC.

26. DW to White, June 28, 1832, in *PC*, III, 181.

364				DANIEL WEBSTER

weary of this long session and could not wait to finish their business and get home. Washington in June and July could be beastly hot, and sitting around all day roasting in the Capitol was very enervating. Already Webster had started to complain. "I am almost worn out—& am getting to be as thin as a hatchell—I sigh for the sea side—& for repose."[27]

But worn out or not, Webster and his colleagues had to wait for Jackson's response to the flood of legislation Congress had sent him in the past few weeks. On July 10 came the President's answer to the Bank bill. And, as expected, he vetoed it. Actually he did not simply veto it; he crucified it in a "monstrous long paper." He rained down on it with hammerblows. In a paper written mostly by Amos Kendall and in part by Roger B. Taney, Levi Woodbury, and Jackson himself, the President charged that the BUS was a monopoly granted by the government that created outrageous inequities, threatened the nation's free electoral process, and made money for foreign investors from taxes collected from all Americans. It was a "hydra," to use one of Jackson's favorite expressions when referring to the BUS, that had to be annihilated.

And it was unconstitutional! That argument by Jackson was aimed not only at Marshall and his Court but at Daniel Webster as well—intended or not. True, the High Court had declared the Bank constitutional in *McCulloch* v. *Maryland*. No matter. "To this conclusion," said Jackson in his veto, "I cannot assent." Both houses of Congress as well as the President have the right and must decide for themselves what is or is not constitutional before taking any action on a particular bill. "It is as much the duty of the House of Representatives, of the Senate, and of the President to decide upon the constitutionality of any bill or resolution which may be presented to them for passage or approval as it is of the supreme judges when it may be brought before them for judicial decision."[28] Jackson went on at length about the constitutional issue, addressing the "necessary and proper" clause that Webster and Marshall had cited in the *McCulloch* case. The President, of course, did not believe that the clause applied to such institutions as banks.

He then developed an argument that the BUS had committed gross abuses and had violated its charter. There was sufficient evidence, he contended, "to excite suspicion and alarm" and confirm the necessity of an investigation before further action on its charter be taken.

He concluded with one of the most populistic, strident, not to say shocking, statements any President has ever hurled in striking down a congressional act. "It is to be regretted," he stormed, "that the rich and powerful too often bend the acts of government to their selfish purposes." Every man is entitled to protection by law, but when the law favors the few by providing exclusive privileges and gratuities, "to make the rich richer and the potent more powerful, the

27. DW to Isaac Davis, June 30, [1832], ibid., III, 182. A hatchell is an instrument for cleaning flax or hemp. It consisted of a set of teeth fastened on a board.
28. Richardson, *Messages and Papers*, II, 1139–1140, 1144–1145.

humble members of society—the farmers, mechanics, and laborers—who have neither the time nor the means of securing like favors to themselves, have a right to complain of the injustice of their Government."[29]

Webster was seated at his desk when the veto arrived in Congress, and he immediately grabbed a pen and scratched out the following to Nicholas Biddle:

Dr Sir   ½ past 11 oclock

The *Veto* came in this morning. It is a monstrous long paper, *& goes the whole—*
It goes agt. the constitution[al]ity, in effect;

against the utility & expediency;
against the time, as premature;
against the foreign stockholders;
against refusing the taxing power
to states &c &c &c—

It contains the essence of Mr Benton & Mr Whites speech[es] about the drain of specie from west to East.

It extinguishes all hope of a reincorporation of the Bank under the present President. Yrs D. W.[30]

Webster could scarcely contain himself, so anxious was he to refute the arguments put forward in the message. News immediately circulated around the capital that he would answer the President on the following day, and hundreds in Washington planned to crowd their way into the Senate chamber to hear him.

The chamber was jammed on July 11, when the session began. Hot, muggy, and uncomfortable, the day hardly seemed appropriate to listen to a three-or-more-hour speech on the Bank. But Washingtonians cared more about hearing what surely would become a historic debate than in their personal comfort.

And the Defender of the Constitution did not disappoint them. He immediately gained the floor, so anxious was he to convince his colleagues and the American people that the veto itself was a violation of the constitutional principles on which the nation had been founded.

He eliminated any real introduction. He came immediately to the point. The President opposes the Bank, stormed Webster, indeed opposes any bank of like construct. At least now we know where he stands. "There is no longer any mystery, no longer a contest between hope and fear." And what it means is that in three years and nine months the entire Bank's operation, its custody of public deposits and transfer of public money, all loans and discounts, and all its issues of bills of circulation, must terminate. The sixty millions of loans, discounts, and promissory notes that are now out must be collected. "Now, Sir, how is it possible that this vast amount can be collected in so short a period without suffering?" In addition, the effects of this veto will be felt in the price of land, in the price of crops, in the products of labor, in the "repression of enterprise, and in embarrassment of every kind of business and occupation."

The President objects to what he calls the "favors" and "exclusive privi-

29. Ibid., II, pp. 1152–1153.
30. DW to Biddle, July 10, 1832, in *PC*, III, 186.

leges" conferred by the charter, Webster sneered, but the truth is that the powers conferred are typical of similar institutions. "If a bank charter is not to be granted, because, to some extent, it may be profitable to the stockholders, no charter can be granted. The objection lies against all banks."

But the great thrust of Webster's speech involved the President's constitutional objections to the BUS. This was what everyone waited to hear. This was Webster's forte, his specialty, his strength, his great talent.

First, he traced the long history of the BUS, going back forty-odd years, during which Congress had debated it, the Supreme Court had judged it, and every President until the incumbent had regarded the constitutional question as settled. But what does Jackson care about precedents? What does he care about opinions that differ from his own?

Obviously the President thinks little of the authority of Congress and even less of the authority of the Supreme Court.

> He asserts a right of individual judgment on constitutional questions, which is totally inconsistent with any proper administration of the government, or any regular execution of the laws. Social disorder, entire uncertainty in regard to individual rights, and individual duties, the cessation of legal authority, confusion, the dissolution of free government,—all these are the inevitable consequences of the principles adopted by the message, whenever they shall be carried to their full extent.

In the past it had been understood that constitutional questions belonged to the Supreme Court. Once Congress passed a bill and the President signed it only the High Court could judge its constitutionality. "It can be adjudged nowhere else," Webster thundered. The President may say a law is unconstitutional, "but he is not the judge." Only the judiciary "possesses this unquestionable and hitherto unquestioned right."

As a matter of actual fact there were any number of people who did not believe the Supreme Court exercised the *exclusive* right to judge the constitutionality of congressional legislation. Some questions, such as political questions, were deemed outside the Court's jurisdiction. It was Jackson's position that allowing four men—seven sat on the Court in 1832—to decide what millions of Americans could or could not do under their constitutional form was oligarchic, not republican and certainly not democratic.[31]

What the President claims, Webster continued, "is in truth nothing less, and nothing else, than the old dispensing power asserted by the kings of England, in the worst of times." Its "preposterous pretensions" culminated in the Tudor and Stuart despotisms.

> According to the doctrines put forth by the President, although Congress may have passed a law, and although the Supreme Court may have pronounced it constitutional, yet it is, nevertheless, no law at all, if he, in his good pleasure, sees fit to deny it effect; in other words, to repeal and annul it. Sir, no President and no public man ever before advanced such doctrines in the face of the nation. There never before was a moment in

31. Even Clay rejected the idea of the exclusive right of the Court.

which any President would have been tolerated in asserting such a claim to despotic power. . . . If conceded to him, it makes him at once what Louis the Fourteen proclaimed himself to be, when he said, "I am the State."

Again and again he returned to his point that precedent and the opinions of the great men of the past, including Washington and Madison, sanctioned the existence of the Bank. And for a lawyer like Webster, precedent had great meaning and value. He also discussed at length the "necessary and proper" clause and turned to logic and history to support his arguments favoring the present legislation.

Had the President rejected the bill because of policy or expediency his arguments would have been intelligible, however wrongheaded, and consistent with "first principles." But his rejection on constitutional grounds "confounds all distinctions, mixes questions of policy and questions of right together, and turns all constitutional restraints into mere matters of opinion."

He closed in a magnificent summation that included dire predictions:

> Mr. President, we have arrived at a new epoch. We are entering on experiments, with the government and the Constitution of the country, hitherto untried, and of fearful and appalling aspect. This message calls us to the contemplation of a future which little resembles the past. Its principles are at war with all that public opinion has sustained, and all which the experience of the government has sanctioned. It denies first principles; it contradicts truths, heretofore received as indisputable. It denies to the judiciary the interpretation of law, and claims to divide with Congress the power of originating statutes. It extends the grasp of executive pretension over every power of the government. But this is not all. It presents the chief magistrate of the Union in the attitude of arguing away the powers of that government over which he has been chosen to preside. . . . It appeals to every prejudice which may betray men into a mistaken view of their own interests, and to every passion which may lead them to disobey the impulses of their understanding. It urges all the specious topics of State rights. . . . It sows . . . the seeds of jealousy and ill-will against that government of which its author is the official head. . . . It affects alarm for the public freedom, when nothing endangers that freedom so much as its own unparalleled pretenses. . . . It manifestly seeks to inflame the poor against the rich. . . . If the sentiments of the message shall receive general approbation, the Constitution will have perished even earlier than the moment which its enemies originally allowed for the termination of its existence. It will not have survived to its fiftieth year.[32]

A noble effort, without question.[33] Although he misstated Jackson's argument about who judges constitutional questions—the President contended that all three branches exercised the right—and chose to regard the President's

---

32. The speech can be found in the *Register of Debates*, 22d Congress, 1st Session, pp. 1221–1248; *National Intelligencer*, September 22, 1832; *W&S*, VI, 149–180; and *PS*, I, 502–529.

33. Thurlow Weed, the anti-Jackson, anti-Regency editor of the Albany *Evening Journal*, refused to publish Webster's speech. He shrewdly pointed out that the veto contained two sentences that had enough power to carry ten presidential electors to every one that Webster's arguments might convince. Those two sentences involved the facts that a large amount of Bank stock was owned by foreigners and that the Bank "made the rich richer and the pooor poorer." Harriet A. Weed, ed., *The Autobiography of Thurlow Weed* (Boston, 1883), I, 373.

action as an unwarranted seizure of power, he scored several important points. In insisting on the Court's exclusive right to judge, he was eventually proved correct, although not until after the Civil War. He also warned against Jackson's obvious attempt at sharing with Congress the "power of originating statutes." At the time almost everyone conceded that Congress originates laws. The legislature was the centerpiece of government; its powers of originating statutes were exclusive. Today the agenda for congressional legislation is frequently determined by the President, following a tradition first asserted by Jackson.

When Henry Clay rose to continue the assault on the President and his veto, the excitement in the Senate became palpable because Clay was a verbal brawler, a gut fighter, whose personal attacks, done with panache and style, invariably delighted audiences. He feared what the veto power could lead to. "We now hear quite frequently," he declared, "the statement that the President will veto [particular legislation] urged as an objection to their passage!" With his veto Jackson can effectively force his will on Congress. This was hardly compatible with representative government. It was revolutionary, he said.[34]

Benton responded to Webster and Clay by calling them the "duplicate Senators," and chiding them for faulting Jackson's exercise of legitimate, constitutional power when the BUS corrupted officials and influenced elections through its power to control vast sums of money. His comments led to a screaming match with Clay that required all the authority of the chair to restore order.[35]

Finally on Friday, July 13, a motion to override the President's veto was called. Despite the heroic oratorical power of Webster and Clay, the friends of the Bank could not muster the necessary two-thirds vote. By the count of twenty-two to nineteen the motion went down to defeat.

Three days later both houses adjourned. The question of what would happen to the BUS now rested with the American people. In a few months most of them would vote between Jackson and Clay and in so doing would decide the fate of the BUS. Clay represented its continued existence; Jackson, its destruction.

34. Clay's speech can be found in *Register of Debates*, 22d Congress, 1st Session, pp. 1265–1274; and Henry Clay, *The Works of Henry Clay*, ed. Calvin Colton (New York, 1904), VII, 524.
35. William N. Chambers, *Old Bullion Benton: Senator from the New West* (Boston, 1956), pp. 184–186; Poore, *Perley's Reminiscences*, I, 144.

22

Nullification

I N EARLY JULY, as the Bank War neared the end of its first phase, Webster wrote to Biddle and asked for a ten-thousand- or twelve-thousand-dollar loan. And he wanted to do it without making it a Bank transaction! He was very anxious to consolidate, if not clear away, some of his many debts. He offered as collateral the notes of John Connell, a Philadelphia merchant, which came to "$5,000 certain, & probably as much more," pending the outcome of litigation conducted by Webster over Connell's claims under the French treaty signed on July 4, 1831.[1] One reason Webster gave for his request for secrecy was the need to prevent his name from appearing on the Bank's books, where congressional investigators from the House might discover it and embarrass him by making the information public. If his request could not be granted, he told Biddle, then "just tear up this letter, & throw the pieces over the side of the Boat, & say, & think nothing more of it."[2]

Coming at this time, with Biddle fighting for the life of his Bank, the request for a secret loan almost sounded like blackmail. Poor Biddle had no choice. If he refused this man, who led the forces in the Senate favoring recharter, he risked alienating him and possibly lessening his involvement in obtaining the charter. Needless to say, Biddle consented to the loan, and it did not become a Bank transaction.

Webster also owed money to the Bank for a number of past loans, and his object here was to clear his name completely from the books so that he could say, as he later did, that he had no financial involvement with the Bank. Two years later, as the Bank War entered its final phase, he wrote to Edward Everett, at the time a member of the House committee investigating the BUS, and made his disclaimer:

If, in the course of yr investigation, the Com[mitt]ee should incline to notice my name, I wish you to state, as on my authority;—
That I never had any particular or unusual accomodation from the Bank, to the amt. of a single dollar;—

1. These claims dealt with seizures of American ships and cargo by the French during the Napoleonic era.
2. DW to Biddle [c. July 4, 1832], Biddle Papers, LC.

that since I went to Boston, in 1817, I have kept my account, & done my necessary banking business at the Boston Office; & notes, bills of Exchange &c, &c, with my name on them have been collected, & discounted, &c as often as occasion required, precisely as would have been done in the case of any other person, & not otherwise. I have reports of mortgages, standing loans, &c &c between the Bank & myself, in all which there is not a single word of truth. I never gave the Bank any mortgage, & never had any standing loan, or any other accomodation, except in the way of discount of bills and notes, as at other Banks.[3]

A pretty neat and self-serving deception. In money matters Webster could play loose with facts whenever it suited his purposes. He was a poor manager of his financial assets. He speculated in real estate, stocks and bonds, and many other gambling schemes to fatten his purse, frequently with disastrous results. And despite his enormous earning power as a lawyer, his debts continued to mount on account of his unfortunate speculations and his own and Caroline's extravagances. Marshfield also produced a steady financial drain that constantly mounted over the next several decades.

Webster had hoped to get some rest after the exhausting congressional session. He really felt unwell and run-down, although, happily, he was not afflicted with the cholera that had recently broken out in Washington and other parts of the country. But the approaching presidential election and the need to alert the American people to the damage Jackson's veto of the Bank could cause the nation kept him busy throughout the summer and fall. He really got himself worked up over what the President had done and told Joseph Story that he was going to Marshfield to correct the notes of his speech and publish them as an answer to Jackson's message. "You have seen that message," he wrote. "My wish is, to give a full answer to its *trash,* on the Constitutional question. That is Taney's work.[4] The argument, you perceive, is, that some powers of the Bank are not *necessary,* & so, not Constitutional." That contention alone infuriated Webster. He went on in his letter to request a response of "close & conclusive confutation . . . of all its nonsense." You could do it in half an hour, he ventured, and please let me have it in two or three days. If you mail it by 4:00 P.M. in Boston on Monday, he said, I could get it at Marshfield the following day.[5]

At least five versions of Webster's speech of July 11 appeared in print in various forms. He convinced himself that his arguments nullified whatever Jackson had said about the constitutional issue and that the people would realize it and respond at the ballot box by registering their outrage and rejection of Jackson's "nonsensical" interpretation of the Constitution. Surely the people would recognize that Henry Clay had to replace the menace in the White House

3. DW to Everett, April 26, 1834, in *PC*, III, 342.

4. It is probable that Taney provided the constitutional arguments for the veto, but Kendall was the chief writer. See Lynn L. Marshall, "The Authorship of Jackson's Bank Veto Message," *Mississippi Valley Historical Review*, L (December 1963), pp. 466–477.

5. DW to Story, July 21, [1832], in *PC*, III, 187. It took a day for mail posted in Boston to reach Marshfield and two days from Boston to New York. Obviously, in more than 150 years the mail service in the United States has not improved over that of 1832.

if the country's institutions were to be spared irreparable harm.

Biddle was especially instrumental in distributing Webster's speech. He had it printed in Philadelphia "under my own eye," he reported, "—which I thought best. It has been reprinted largely in various papers, and the press is at work with it in the shape of a pamphlet . . . and also in numbers of the National Gazette extra. It is reported to be very effic[acious] very much sought after and very greedily devoured, and, what is important in these cholera times, easily digested." He asked Webster to see to it that the edition be widely circulated in Boston and throughout New Hampshire and Maine, suggesting as many as twenty thousand copies.[6]

Webster continued his efforts on behalf of the Bank by writing a separate piece for the Washington *National Intelligencer*, which he addressed directly "To the People of the United States." The article appeared in the October 6 issue. He also gave speeches in Worcester[7] and Albany, and they too received wide circulation.[8]

Another troubling matter to command Webster's attention was the civil strife that had broken out in South Carolina because of the new tariff and the desire of many leaders in the state to exercise the right of nullification as expounded by John C. Calhoun. Newspapers carried stories about angry verbal exchanges, duels, bloody fistfights, and riots that occurred in South Carolina in early August and September. Webster considered writing a public response to a letter written by Calhoun on August 28, 1832, to Governor James Hamilton, Jr., in which he planned to expand on and give perhaps his definitive statement on nullification, but the lack of time crowded out Webster's good intention.[9] Before he could begin its composition, the American people trooped to the polls to express their collective will.

The presidential election of 1832 ended in a disaster for Clay, the National Republican party, and Nicholas Biddle. The masses did not respond as both Webster and Clay had anticipated. The American people loved and trusted President Jackson, and they had strong doubts about Henry Clay. The final results of the election showed Jackson with 688,242 popular and 219 electoral votes; Clay garnered 473,462 popular and 49 electoral votes; and Wirt, the Anti-Masonic candidate, 101,051 popular and 7 electoral votes. Martin Van Buren easily won election to the vice presidency.[10]

6. Biddle to DW, September 27, 1832, ibid., III, 191.

7. Webster's speech at Worcester can be found in *PS*, I, 532–569. This was the only speech given at the meeting. As Edward Everett observed, there was no need "to add perfume to the violet, strength to the oak, or majesty to the thunder." *Niles' Weekly Register*, October 27, 1832.

8. *National Intelligencer*, October 23, 25, 1832.

9. *Calhoun Papers*, XI, 613–649. Calhoun's letter first appeared in the Pendleton, South Carolina, *Messenger*, September 15, 19, 1832, followed by the Charleston *Mercury*, September 26, and the Washington *United States Telegraph*, October 2, 1832. For Webster's intention to respond to this letter, see DW to James Kent, October 29, Kent to DW, October 31, 1832, in *PC*, III, 195–196.

10. Sven Petersen, *A Statistical History of American Presidential Elections* (New York, 1963), pp. 20–21. For a full discussion of this election, see Remini, *Clay*, pp. 402–411, and "The Election of

At the same time that the nation went to the polls, presumably to decide between Clay and a Bank and Jackson and no Bank, the South Carolina legislature met on October 22, in response to the governor's request, and called for a convention to meet at Columbia on November 19 to respond to the federal tariff laws. The convention met and on November 24 by a vote of 136 to 26 passed an Ordinance of Nullification that declared the tariff laws of 1828 and 1832 "null, void, and no law, nor binding" upon South Carolina, its officers or citizens. If force were employed by the federal authorities to execute the laws, South Carolina would secede and organize a new and separate government.[11]

Then, in a prearranged agreement, Robert Y. Hayne resigned as U.S. senator and Calhoun resigned as Vice President. Hayne was elected governor to succeed James Hamilton, Jr., and Calhoun took Hayne's place in the U.S. Senate. Now there was no longer any need for Webster to write his response to Calhoun's letter. The Great Defender of the Constitution could debate the Great Nullifier on the merits of interposition in an open forum on the floor of the Senate. They could have it out in public, and it would not—like the Webster-Hayne debate— be an academic contest. A real crisis existed: South Carolina had invalidated federal law within its borders, and the state threatened secession if force were employed to make it comply with the law.[12]

But President Jackson did not wait for the Congress to respond to this challenge, and on December 10 he issued his Proclamation to the people of South Carolina, cautioning them of the "dreadful consequences" should the state follow through on its threat. "Disunion by armed force is *treason*," he warned. "Are you ready to incur its guilt?" But he also tried to be conciliatory. Although he would not permit South Carolina to defy the government, he hoped the crisis could be resolved by lowering the tariff rates across the board, in effect scuttling Clay's entire system of protectionism.[13]

Because of the demands of his legal practice, Webster had not yet returned to Washington when Jackson sent his annual message to Congress and then issued his Proclamation. By delaying his return, he was able to attend a public meeting in Faneuil Hall on December 17, called to express public reaction to South Carolina's defiance and to the President's December 10 Proclamation.

1832," in Schlesinger and Israel, eds., *History of Presidential Elections*, I, 495–516. Vermont gave its seven electoral votes to Wirt.

11. *State Papers on Nullification* (Boston, 1834), pp. 29–31.

12. On the nullification crisis, see Richard E. Ellis, *The Union at Risk: Jacksonian Democracy, States' Rights and the Nullification Crisis* (New York, 1987), and William W. Freehling, *The Road to Disunion: Secessionists at Bay, 1776–1854* (New York, 1990) and his *Prelude to Civil War: The Nullification Movement in South Carolina, 1816–1836* (New York, 1966).

13. Richardson, *Messages and Papers*, II, 1217–1218. After reading the Proclamation, the general public believed it was "a manifest, but of course a very excusable, plagiarism" of Webster's second reply to Hayne, so closely did it seem to follow the argument advanced by the senator. A story was told how Webster entered an inn on his way to Washington and inquired about the news. "Sir," said another traveler, "the President has issued a proclamation against the nullifiers, taken entirely from Mr. Webster's reply to Hayne." Poore, *Perley's Reminiscences*, I, 139–140. For a different version of this story, see March, *Webster*, pp. 187–188.

Webster was convinced that matters in Charleston would eventually turn violent. "The leaders of the nullifiers," he declared in a letter to Levi Lincoln, "have placed themselves, in a situation, where retreat is impossible. They can only go forward, try the strength of their party, & the *weakness* of the Govt; & rely on the hope of drawing neighboring States into concurrence with their own measures." He had no doubt, he continued, that "both Genl. Jackson & Govr. Hamilton Jr fully expect a decision by the sword."[14]

December 17 was "a wet and dark, sloppy day" when Bostonians filled Faneuil Hall to capacity and passed resolutions in support of Jackson's position on nullification. Harrison Gray Otis, former congressman in both houses and former mayor of Boston, addressed the crowd first and sounded a democratic note in accord with prevailing sentiment in the country. "The majority must govern," Otis cried; the country was fast moving away from its republican attitudes toward more democratic perceptions. One state cannot assert its rights over the majority by defying the law.

Webster followed Otis, standing on the right-hand side of the stage, looking very intense, his face dark and a little threatening, his eyebrows bristling. He wore his usual outfit: black trousers, a buff-colored vest, a blue coat with gilt buttons. His voice rang out in a commanding tone, and he could be distinctly heard in the farthest corners of the hall. So agitated was he that he gestured constantly throughout his speech, "but vertical, up and down, not flowing from side to side" like Edward Everett and other distinguished speakers of the day, and this struck some in the audience as awkward and lacking in grace.

"When I look around me on the numbers who fill these galleries and crowd this hall," Webster began, "I thank Almighty God that I may still address them as citizens of the United States." The principles contained in Jackson's Proclamation, he announced, "are such as I entire approve. I esteem them to be the true principles of the Constitution." Nullification is nothing more than "resistance to law by force, it is disunion by force, it is secession by force: *it is civil war.*" It is the President's duty to execute the laws by lawful means, uphold the Constitution, and be slow to resort to "ultimate measures." In this crisis—and surely it was of the "utmost magnitude and the most imminent peril"—I shall give the President "my entire and cordial support." And do not believe that if one state secedes the Union may exist without it. "No sir. If the Government, on this first trial shall be found not able to keep all the States in their proper places, from that moment the whole Union is virtually dissolved." The Union must be preserved "one and entire, as it now is, or else break up, and return to the condition of separate States," each with a separate and perhaps hostile government. "I am for the Union as it is. . . . I am for the Constitution as it is." In the spirit of the resolutions now before the meeting "I say, when the standard of the Union is raised and waves over my head—the standard which Washington planted on the ramparts of the Constitution—God forbid that I should inquire whom the peo-

14. DW to Levi Lincoln, December 10, [1832], in *PC*, III, 200.

ple have commissioned to unfurl it and bear it up: I only ask in what manner, as a humble individual, I can best discharge my duty in defending it."[15]

A short speech but a splendid one, several ideas of which were picked up later by Abraham Lincoln. First, the President must execute the laws. In this he has no choice. Therefore, if a state violates the law, the President must see to it that the law is enforced, employing "lawful means," including the use of armed force. Second, the notion that one state may secede from the Union without penalty is absurd. Once the Union is broken, it will break again and again, leaving a fragmented country with various governments warring with one another and all subject to the dastardly intrigues of foreign powers. The Union must be preserved, as Jackson had said, and rebellion put down by whatever means necessary.

Many in the audience were overwhelmed by the speech. It truly gripped them. But they were also a trifle disappointed because of its brevity. Still, they came away convinced that Webster and Jackson were "great patriots" and the South Carolinians "reprobates." One young man declared, "[S]ince that day I have been a Whig and an ardent supporter of the Constitution."[16]

Webster's endorsement of Jackson's Proclamation made him, in effect, an ally of the President's in handling the nullification controversy. He could be expected to, and indeed he pledged that his voice and his vote in the Senate would, support Jackson in whatever action he felt necessary to preserve the Union. Some worried that his behavior might even presage a political alliance between the two men.

His business concerns now satisfied and his unwavering opposition to nullification publicly expounded, Webster finally headed for Washington in late December to resume his legislative duties in the Senate. When he arrived in Philadelphia, he ran into Henry Clay, who had come to the city with his son and had consulted with a group of manufacturers, including E. I. du Pont, over a possible compromise tariff that would help avert conflict with South Carolina yet provide manufacturers with enough protection for the immediate future.

While Clay sojourned in Philadelphia, the Jackson administration devised its own scheme, which would lower tariff rates by a whopping 50 percent and bring them to the level of 1816. The secretary of the treasury, Louis McLane, working with Gulian C. Verplanck of New York, the chairman of the House Ways and Means Committee, drew up the bill, and it was submitted to the House. The obvious and immediate object of the Verplanck bill was to mollify South Carolinians and thereby induce them into rescinding their Ordinance of Nullification.

Fearful of what the Jacksonians might propose and worried about the immediate effect a sharp reduction in rates would have on manufacturers, Clay had devised a scheme that he believed would satisfy South Carolinians and spare

15. Otis's speech is reported in the December 25 and Webster's in the December 26 edition of the *National Intelligence;* Boston *Daily Advertiser,* December 18, 1832, reprinted in *W&S*, XIII, 40–43.
16. *W&S*, XIII, 43 note.

manufacturers the harm of a sudden and precipitous drop in the duty rates. He proposed a very gradual reduction of rates over a ten-year period, at the end of which all protection would be annulled. Thereafter duties would be equal and levied only to meet government needs. In effect, there would be a ten-year truce on all tariff legislation, thereby removing the source of sectional discord. And to make it a real "compromise," Clay would abandon protectionism![17]

What Clay offered the manufacturers was time, time in which they could enjoy a period of security at the current high level of protection and time to cultivate popular support for their particular needs. However he managed it, Clay won the manufacturers over in support of his proposal.

Then he met Webster. They discussed the crisis facing the nation, and the Kentuckian explained what he planned to do about it. Webster was thunderstruck. Abandon protectionism! Never. He not only said he absolutely opposed the scheme but vowed to fight Clay's plan at every turn. "I opposed this bill in every stage," he later recalled, "& so did three fourths of the Tariff interest in both Houses." What the plan did, he contended, was surrender Congress's "protecting powers, & strike it out of the Constitution."[18]

Clay handed his friend a written statement of his proposal, which Webster duly copied. The preamble of the plan stated that differences of opinion existed over the policy of protecting manufactures and that when those differences threatened serious disturbances, it was time to compromise the differences. Clay would keep existing laws in force until March 3, 1840, after which they all would be repealed. Until that date no higher duties were to be laid, and what was collected would be used for governmental expenditures "without regard to the protection or encouragement of any branch of domestic industry whatever."[19]

The two men, Clay and Webster, now worked diligently to effect opposite goals: Webster to defeat the compromise, and Clay to gain its acceptance. When Webster got to Washington, he found his friends greatly alarmed over the Verplanck bill. "I never saw our friends so desponding," he reported. He tried to rally them with strong words about not surrendering the Constitution or the great interests of the Union either to nullification or proposals instigated by the fear of nullification. Still, he worried over what Clay might do and how he might invoke *"party discipline"* to force a compromise that would sacrifice the public good.[20] He was delighted to see that the "stern rebuke" by President Jackson had given the nullifiers pause, but, he added, "our more imminent danger, in my

17. For details about Clay's meeting with the manufacturers, see Epes Sargent, *The Life and Public Services of Henry Clay down to 1848* (New York, 1860), pp. 140–141; Glyndon G. Van Deusen, *The Life of Henry Clay* (Boston, 1937), p. 266; Merrill D. Peterson, *Olive Branch and Sword: The Compromise of 1833* (Baton Rouge, 1982), pp. 51–53; and Remini, *Clay*, pp. 415–417. The plan initially proposed to the manufacturers by Clay involved a seven-year truce until March 3, 1840, but he later revised his scheme to run for ten years.

18. DW to Hiram Ketchum, January 20, 1838, in *PC*, IV, 263.

19. A copy is reprinted ibid., III, 264.

20. DW to Kinsman, January 1, 1833, ibid., III, 203.

opinion, is, that seizing on the occasion, the Anti-Tariff party will prostrate the whole Tariff system." Such a catastrophe had to be prevented, so he wrote to his Massachusetts friends and urged on them the necessity of getting the legislature in Boston to issue a temperate but "firm" statement against nullification and "*on the violation of the public faith,* which would be perpetrated by this *thorough & sudden* prostration of the protective system." Obviously Webster feared tariff reduction by the passage of the Verplanck bill more than South Carolina's threat of secession.[21]

The appearance of Calhoun, Clay, and Webster in the Senate to tackle the questions of nullification and tariff duties excited Washingtonians with keen anticipation and high expectations.[22] The fact that a real crisis, not an academic argument over theory, would power the debate in the Senate added to the tension.

Calhoun glowered when he spoke, and the once-handsome features of his face now showed the scars of his many political disappointments and his growing bitterness. Webster said that the Carolinian was "highly excited" when he spoke and acted as though the whole world wished to crush him. Meanwhile Clay quietly and skillfully gathered support for his compromise among Democrats and National Republicans alike.

While these events were taking shape in Washington, the Massachusetts legislature overwhelming reelected Webster to the U.S. Senate. On January 15, 1833, the lower house cast 432 out of a total of 482 votes for Webster, and the following day the upper house unanimously endorsed his selection. His constituents heartily congratulated him on the near unanimity of his election. "In these distracting times of party," commented Charles Miner, "[it] was particularly gratifying."[23]

The same day Webster won reelection the President took action to meet South Carolina's defiance by sending a revenue collection message (more popularly known as the Force Bill message) to Congress. It was a bold measure but reasonable and devoid of bluster. The executive must execute the law, he explained, and he asked that he be authorized to close any port of entry he deemed necessary and reestablish it in some other location. He also requested a few minor changes in the federal judiciary system in order to jail lawbreaking nullifiers and protect U.S. property in the troubled area. As for military force, he counseled, the Congress need make only a few modifications of the 1792 law for the President to call out the militia and use federal ships and troops. But

---

21. DW to William Sullivan, January 3, 1833, ibid., III, 204. Interestingly enough, Webster did not think that Jackson favored passage of the Verplanck bill, and he may have been right. Jackson wanted to dispose of nullification first and then "remodel the Tariff." Ibid.

22. Nathans, *Webster and Jacksonian Democracy,* pp. 56–57, speculates that a memorandum Webster wrote to settle the crisis was intended for Jackson. Whether the President ever saw the memorandum, which called for a moratorium on tariff revision until the Supreme Court could decide on the constitutionality of protection, is uncertain. See "Principles," in *W&S,* XV, 104–105.

23. Miner to DW, February 4, 1833, in *PC,* III, 210.

force would not be used unless South Carolina initiated it.[24]

Webster totally approved of Jackson's action and said so in the Senate on February 8, after the Judiciary Committee had reported a bill on January 21 in compliance with the President's request. He reminded his colleagues that the bill was initiated by the administration. It was Jackson's bill. But, Webster continued, "I think . . . the President could not do otherwise than to recommend it to the consideration of Congress. He is not at liberty to look on and be silent, while dangers threatened the Union." Webster argued that "an unlawful combination" challenged the integrity of the nation, and "I believe the crisis calls for a mild, temperate, forbearing, but inflexibly firm execution of the laws," which was precisely what Jackson proposed. He therefore offered the administration his "hearty support."[25] It was a short speech, Webster acknowledged in a letter to Joseph Hopkinson, but it made "a little *stir* here." For one thing Andrew Jackson took notice, and Webster knew it. "I have some reason, to think, this morning, that the White House regards it as a *stone very well hone[d].*"[26]

Jackson was even more pleased when a bruising verbal clash developed in the Senate over the nature of the Union between the new senator from South Carolina, John C. Calhoun, and Daniel Webster. The two men were regarded by many as "the greatest intellects . . . of the whole country," and any contest between them guaranteed the attention of the nation.[27]

The brawl had been brewing since mid-January, but both men held off in the hope that the other would speak first and provide the advantage of rebuttal. Three weeks passed, and nothing happened. Then, on February 14, Calhoun announced he would speak the following day.

He was well prepared. To a packed gallery, despite a wintry day with fierce winds and a near-record snowfall, Calhoun provided his listeners with his first major and extended speech.[28] He stood ramrod erect at his desk, tense, nervous, and looking and sounding very angry. His dark eyes roamed the chamber constantly as though searching for Jackson personally to assault with his verbal blows. He called the President's Force Bill a "Bloody Bill," a "War Bill," an unconstitutional declaration of war against a sovereign state. He said the bill presumed to declare that the entire sovereignty of the nation belonged to the American people as though forming one community and that the states were mere "fractions or counties, and not as integral parts of the Union." His eyes now flashing, Calhoun pronounced his political creed: "I go on the ground that this constitution was made by the States; that it is a federal union of the States, in which the several States still retain their sovereignty." Sovereignty still rested with the states "while the exercise of sovereign powers is divided—a part being

24. Richardson, *Messages and Papers*, II, 1183–1184, 1192–1195.

25. *Register of Debates*, 22d Congress, 2d Session, pp. 409–413; *W&S*, XIV, 152–155.

26. DW to Joseph Hopkinson, February 9, 1833, in *PC*, III, 213.

27. March, *Webster*, p. 235.

28. Calhoun had submitted three resolutions on January 22 to challenge the constitutional argument inherent in the Force bill. *Senate Documents*, 22d Congress, 2d Session, Serial 230, Doc. No. 42.

exercised under compact, through this General Government, and the residue through the separate State Governments." He then launched into an extended discussion of his political theories, the limits of government and how liberty can best be protected. Taking aim at Jackson's famous remark that the Union must be preserved, Calhoun sneeringly retorted: "Does any man in his senses believe that [the Union] . . . can be preserved by force? . . . No, no. You cannot keep the States united in their constitutional and federal bonds by force."

Famous last words—except that they were not his last. He repeated them again and again until his death nearly twenty years later. Many remembered his words both during and at the close of the Civil War when the Union was pinned back together with a bloody bayonet.

He also spoke about the irresponsible majority, the oppressive and unequal imposition of taxes, the government's taking of money from one portion of the community and giving it to another, and the need for the concurrence of the majorities of the several states to provide justice and equality. The present contest, he concluded, is a "contest between power and liberty . . . a contest in which the weaker section, with its peculiar labor [slavery] . . . has at stake all that can be dear to freeman." It was undoubtedly the most striking and powerful address of his entire career.[29]

Webster was not impressed. "As a Constitutional argument," he explained to his friend Hopkinson, "it is too inconsiderable for an answer. Truly there is nothing in it." Webster was a little fearful that he could not better his second reply to Hayne—"nor equal it—but I will try not to show evidence of senility. *I understand the question.*" At the end of his letter he added, "I think I *begin* to understand the Constitution. My Dear Sir, 'there were giants in the earth, in those days.' This is a day of pigmies."[30]

Actually men like Jackson, Clay, Calhoun, and Webster were hardly "pigmies." Later periods of American history provide a better and wider assortment of the breed.

Webster followed Calhoun immediately.[31] He too was well prepared, although he may have been thrown off stride by the direction that Calhoun's speech took. He may have expected something more emotional and less cerebral. Still, Webster knew how to enthrall an audience, and he chose his words with that end in mind. There was a light touch now and again in his speech to brighten the prevailing mood in the overpopulated chamber and soften the frightening words being bandied back and forth about the future of the Union. His speech was a tour de force.

The cause the honorable gentleman from South Carolina espoused, Web-

29. *Register of Debates,* 22d Congress, 2d Session, pp. 519–553. A more convenient place to find Calhoun's speech is Lence, ed., *Union and Liberty,* pp. 403–460.

30. DW to Hopkinson, February 15, 1833, in *PC,* III, 214–215.

31. Like Calhoun, Webster had submitted several resolutions on the tariff in which he accepted the need for lower duties but at the same time reasserted the need for a protective system in order to guarantee American prosperity. *Debates in Congress,* 22d Congress, 2d Session, pp. 483–484.

ster began, has no basis in the Constitution, no sympathy from the people, and no huzzas from a patriotic community. "Everything beneath his feet is hollow and treacherous. . . . Sir, I love Liberty no less ardently than the gentleman himself," but "it is our established, dear-bought, peculiar American liberty, to which I am chiefly devoted," not something harking back to antiquity, the Middle Ages, or modern Europe.

Webster said he would not attempt to answer Calhoun's speech point by point since much of that speech consisted of philosophical ruminations about the general nature of political liberty and the history of free institutions. Instead he launched into an attack on two of Calhoun's most cherished beliefs: that the Constitution is a compact of states and that the states may judge violations of the Constitution.

Over against these "theories and opinions," Webster presented his own: (1) that the Constitution is a "government proper," which is founded by the people and creates direct relations between itself and the people; (2) that no state can dissolve these relations, and therefore secession is impossible without revolution; (3) that the supreme law consists of the Constitution and the acts of Congress to be interpreted by Congress or the Supreme Court;[32] (4) and that nullification is unconstitutional, a usurpation of powers of the general government and the rights of other states and therefore revolutionary.

"The people of the United States," Webster declared, "are one people. They are one in making war, and one in making peace; they are one in regulating commerce, and one in laying duties of imposts. The very end and purpose of the Constitution was, to make them one people in these particulars; and it has effectually accomplished its object."

He followed up his argument by citing the preamble to the Constitution. "We the People of the United States, do ordain and establish this Constitution." Could anything be clearer or more convincing? Webster even went so far as to state that the Constitution regards itself as "perpetual and immortal." It seeks to establish a union of people "which shall last through all time." He simply referred to the course of American history over the past half century to carry his argument. This was the fact as he saw it. In effect, he was reading back to 1787 what had occurred since that date.

Those who espouse nullification, he continued, reject the first principle of all republican liberty: "[T]he majority *must* govern. In matters of common concern, the judgment of a majority *must* stand as the judgment of the whole." To do otherwise strikes at the very heart of liberty.

Webster concluded by reassuring his listeners that there were enough South Carolinians who would stand fast by the Constitution and defend it.

I rely on no temporary expedient, on no political combinations; but I rely on the true American feeling, the genuine patriotism of the people, and the imperative decision

---

32. He said that in cases capable of and actually assuming the character of a suit the Supreme Court is the final interpreter.

of the public voice. Disorder and confusion, indeed, may arise; scenes of commotion and contest are threatened, and perhaps may come. With my whole heart, I pray for the continuance of the domestic peace and quiet of the country. I desire, most ardently, the restoration of affection and harmony to all its parts. I desire that every citizen of the whole country may look to this government with no other sentiments than those of grateful respect and attachment. But I cannot yield even to kind feelings the cause of the Constitution, the true glory of the country, and the great trust which we hold in our hands for succeeding ages. If the Constitution cannot be maintained without meeting these scenes of commotion and contest, however unwelcome, they must come. We cannot, we must not, we dare not, omit to do that which, in our judgment, the safety of the Union requires. . . . For myself, Sir . . . I shall exert every faculty I possess in aiding to prevent the Constitution from being nullified, destroyed, or impaired; and even should I see it fall, I will still, with a voice feeble, perhaps, but earnest as ever issued from human lips, and with fidelity and zeal which nothing shall extinguish, call on the PEOPLE to come to its rescue.[33]

The roar from the audience when Webster concluded his speech and sat down was deafening. "The galleries, rising to a man, gave a hearty, vociferous cheer, for 'Daniel Webster, the defender of the Constitution.' "

"Defender of the Constitution." The crowd happily confirmed the title that many had already conferred on him.

George Poindexter of Mississippi, a sinister-looking profligate in league with the nullifiers, jumped to his feet and moved adjournment. The chair ordered the galleries cleared, and then the motion was put to a vote.[34]

For many in the crowd Webster said exactly what they wanted to hear. All the themes of patriotism, nationalism, devotion to country received the majesty of language that only Webster's great talent commanded, and the crowd loved it, especially his reassurance at the end that all would be well. Not only had he spoken eloquently about the Union and patriotism, but he had affirmed the Jacksonian position that the Union was perpetual and secession preposterous. Moreover, he had joined the President in his avowal of democracy—namely, that the majority rules and anything less than that endangers the freedom of all.

True, the senator felt uncomfortable with the "masses" and worried about majority rule when it failed to give proper weight to the intelligent, experienced, and prosperous in society, but he had no doubt that legitimate government rests on the consent of all.

Jackson was beside himself when he heard what Webster had said. "Mr. Webster," he wrote to a Unionist in South Carolina, "demolished" Calhoun. "It is believed by more than one, that Mr. C. is in a state of dementation—his speech was a perfect failure; and Mr. Webster handled him as a child."[35]

Webster also labeled Calhoun's speech a failure. "It does not seem magnan-

33. *Register of Debates,* 22d Congress, 2d Session, pp., 554–587; *W&S,* VI, 182–238.
34. March, *Webster,* p. 243.
35. Jackson to Joel Poinsett, February 17, 1833, Poinsett Papers, Historical Society of Pennsylvania.

imous to underrate one's adversary, but, truly, between ourselves, I was greatly disappointed in Mr Calhoun. He has little argument;—at least, so it appeared to me."[36]

Not everyone agreed, however. Then and later some gave the palm to Calhoun, particularly for the intellectual content of his speech.[37] Webster presented theater, they argued, and his speech contained nothing new or particularly interesting. Be that as it may, Calhoun offered a states' rights philosophy that was impractical at best (concurrent majority) and invalid as a durable formula for the future. Calhoun tried to legitimize nullification and secession, and as Webster said several times in his speech, the American public rejected that contention. Nullification amounted to usurpation of power and secession to treason. What the South Carolinian would not accept was the history of the preceding half century. Like it or not, the nation was evolving into a democratic, increasingly industrial society with a strong central government able and determined when necessary, to enunciate the supreme law of the land, even if that challenged the vested rights and interests of particular states. Webster, on the other hand, rooted the legitimacy of republican government in the people, as had the Founders, and explained how the nation had actually developed, politically and constitutionally, whether or not that was the original intention of those who had established it. To Webster's great delight, no doubt, James Madison immediately wrote and told him that he agreed totally with the senator's view of the way the history of the country had evolved.[38]

Webster's address, after he had polished it, went directly into publication and appeared as early as the second week in March. It received wide circulation and praise, although it was clearly not comparable to his second reply to Hayne. Still, many regarded it as a masterpiece. One South Carolina Unionist wrote to him and said that it "tears with a giant's hand the cobwebs which the metaphysics of Mr Calhoun have thrown about the doctrine of nullification. As a constitutional argument it will ever remain as the proudest monument of intellectual exertion and power."[39]

The Webster-Calhoun debate, if it can be called such, marked the high point of the congressional controversy over the Force Bill. Webster may have made only one slip in his speech when he acknowledged that nullification might be justified if the Constitution was in fact a compact of states. Calhoun pounced on it and almost got the better of him. John Randolph, sitting close by, nodded in agreement with Calhoun, even though he thought nullification a humbug. A hat lying on a seat in front of him prevented him from getting a full view of the

36. DW to Nathan Appleton, [February 17, 1833], in *PC*, III, 216.

37. Some contemporaries thought Webster belabored the argument that the government was not a compact. "He hung his cause," criticized Adams, "upon a broken hinge." Adams, *Memoirs*, VIII, 526. For more recent critical assessments, see Freehling, *Prelude to Civil War*; Charles M. Wiltse, *John C. Calhoun, Nullifier,* (Indianapolis, 1949); and Nathans, *Webster and Jacksonian Democracy*.

38. Madison to DW, March 15, 1833, in *PC*, III, 222–223.

39. Benjamin F. Perry to DW, April 1, 1833, ibid., III, 235.

participants. "Take away that hat," he shrilled in his high, piercing voice. "I want to see Webster die, muscle by muscle."[40]

But it was not Webster's argument that was dying. Quite the contrary. For the remainder of his life Calhoun tried to convince his countrymen of the correctness of his views about the compact theory and concurrent majority. What merit they had was consumed in the flames of Civil War.

"No political occurrence has ever grieved me, like this Nullification business," confessed Webster. It not only disturbed our domestic tranquillity but "struck a deadly blow at our *character & honor abroad.*" As for Calhoun, Webster admitted that he had once entertained the highest regard for his abilities. "He appeared to me to be a true friend to his country. His recent conduct seems unaccountable." Such a pity.[41]

On February 20 the Senate passed the Force Bill by a vote of thirty-two to one. All the nullifiers left the chamber during the voting. Senator John Tyler of Virginia, who opposed both nullification and the use of force against a sovereign state, cast the single negative vote. Clay was absent because of fatigue, he said. He also did not expect a final vote to be called.[42] The House passed the bill on March 1, and Jackson signed it the following day.

At the start of the debate there was widespread talk about some extraordinary political realignments taking place in the capital. Since his arrival in Washington, Calhoun reportedly worked out an agreement with Clay to bring forward a substitute tariff that Calhoun would pronounce acceptable to South Carolina. "You have seen hints in the Newspapers," wrote Webster, "that Mr Clay & Mr Calhoun were in negotiation, to settle the Tariff question. Such is still the rumour, & I have no doubt *it is true.*"[43] It was also rumored that Jackson, in his effort to win support for the Force Bill, had dispatched Secretary of State Edward Livingston to urge Webster to come to the administration's aid with respect to nullification. Livingston and Webster were on friendly terms, and it was said that the senator frequently visited the secretary's home.[44] The rumors were true. "A number of Gen. Jacksons cabinet" had come to Webster "at his lodgings & earnestly requested him to take an active part in defence" of the Force Bill. Later "Gen Jackson took an early opportunity to thank Mr Webster personally for his support." At one point the President sent his own carriage to convey the Massachusetts senator to the Capitol. Also, Webster suddenly became a sought-after guest at the White House. "I dined at the Palace, yes, Palace, a few days since," reported Senator Tyler, "and found Mr. W. there in all his glory." Word of Webster's "dalliance" with Jackson also drifted around the country. The New York *Enquirer* "places you, I see, next [to] the President at

40. Wiltse, *Calhoun, II,* 194.

41. DW to John Ellis Wool, April 1, 1833, in *PC,* III, 234–235.

42. Clay to Philip R. Fendall, August 8, 1836, in Clay, *Papers,* VIII, 862.

43. DW to Hopkinson, February 9, 1833, in *PC,* III, 213.

44. Norman D. Brown, *Daniel Webster and the Politics of Availability* (Athens, Ga., 1969), p. 19.

dinner," wrote Charles Miner to Webster. "I earnestly hope, for my Country's sake, it may ever be so."[45]

The senator did not need any urging from the White House to challenge Calhoun's theories about the nature of the Union. And although he was wined and dined by Jackson, nothing was said about an alliance.[46] Even so, the appearance of a possible alliance between the two men caused much consternation in several political circles.[47] Vice President Van Buren was distressed because he reckoned himself Jackson's successor to the presidency, and he worried that Webster might become a rival.[48] Clay also found fault with Webster and expressed his displeasure to Nicholas Biddle: "As to your friend, Mr. W., [since] he is determined not to allow me to consider him mine, nothing I can do seems right in his eyes; whilst others can do nothing wrong."[49]

At the moment the principal irritant between Clay and Webster was the tariff, each determined to prevent the other from achieving his goal. "My wish is *to do nothing this session*" with respect to the tariff, wrote Webster, "& my determination, which will not be shaken, is, to do nothing, nor suffer any thing to be done, on the Subject of the Tariff, by a *Union of Extremes*," meaning of course a pact between Clay and Calhoun.[50]

Over several weeks Clay had indeed met privately with Calhoun and other congressmen, both northern and southern, to win support for a compromise tariff, such as the one he had discussed with Webster in Philadelphia. As he repeatedly stated, Webster was dead set against any bill that would sacrifice protection. Clay tried to assure him and other pro-tariff Senators that he himself had not abandoned protectionism, at least not immediately and not permanently. But the bill he proposed introducing would in fact do just that after a ten-year truce. Clay turned his considerable charm on Webster, but "the Godlike Daniel" would have none of it. The Kentuckian asked him to "join some of our friends at my lodgings this evening" to confer on the subject; Webster remained aloof. Clay even tried to mediate a verbal exchange that occurred in the Senate between Webster and Poindexter. Webster had made an appropriate but slightly

45. DW to Hopkinson, February 9, Miner to DW, February 4, 1833, in *PC*, III, 213, 210; Silas Wright to Azariah C. Flagg, January 14, February 2, 1833, Flagg Papers, New York Public Library; Remini, *Jackson*, III, 34–40; Webster Memorandum, HM 779, Webster Papers, Huntington Library; Tyler to John Floyd, January 22, 1833, in "Original Letters," *William and Mary College Quarterly Historical Magazine*, XXI (1912), p. 11.

46. DW to Hopkinson, [February 21, 1833], in *PC*, III, 219. Ben: Perley Poore states that "it is known to me that General Jackson personally thanked him [Webster] for his powerful aid." *Reminiscences*, I, 140. Charles March confirms this. March, *Webster*, pp. 249–250.

47. "Webster has been on the point of desertion to the admn," wrote Senator Willie P. Mangum almost ten months later. *"There is no mistake in this."* Mangum to David L. Swain, December 22, 1833, in Henry T. Shanks, ed., *The Papers of Willie Person Mangum* (Raleigh, N.C., 1950–1956), II, 55.

48. Van Buren narrates his concern and suspicions at length in his *Autobiography* (Washington, D.C., 1920), pp. 700–711.

49. Clay to Biddle, March 4, 1833, Biddle Papers, LC.

50. DW to Hopkinson, February 9, 1833, in *PC*, III, 213.

insulting allusion to Poindexter's comment about Black Dan's conduct during the War of 1812. Poindexter responded with *"I have the most perfect contempt for the Senator from Massachusetts."* He went on to accuse Webster of cowardice and deceit in supporting the Force Bill. Clay came immediately to Webster's rescue. "I learnt with surprize and regret this morning that what passed the other day between you and Mr Poindexter is likely to be made the basis of a serious proceeding. I think that ought to be prevented, and it can be prevented honorable to both parties. Do come here if you can. Your friend H. Clay."

The incident might have gotten out of hand, but Clay managed to bring them together and prevent a possible altercation. When the two men walked across the Senate floor and shook hands, everyone in the chamber sighed with relief.[51]

Finally, on February 9, Clay rose in the Senate and proposed his "compromise" tariff,[52] in which duties on imported goods would be slowly reduced over ten years until they stood at a uniform 20 percent ad valorem rate. During this ten-year period a truce would be declared against raising or lowering the tariff. According to Webster, the bill "has thrown us [National Republicans] into great confusion. I thought it necessary, in the promptest manner, to signify my dissent." Upon the motion of Felix Grundy of Tennessee, a select committee of seven Senators was chosen to consider Clay's proposal, and the seven included Webster, Calhoun, Grundy, William C. Rives of Virginia, George M. Dallas of Pennsylvania, John M. Clayton of Delaware, and Clay as chairman. Of this group only Webster and Dallas represented manufacturing states and stood solidly opposed to Clay's compromise, but others, like Clayton, demanded some form of protection to win their approval. Grundy also preferred amendments but was willing to go along with Clay if necessary. Calhoun and Rives supported the bill wholeheartedly. Clay therefore had a majority of the committee on his side, but he still sought out each of the Senators and tried to charm him into agreeing on a compromise. He held two meetings of the group, "at the first of which he [Webster] attended, and to the last he was summoned." What annoyed Webster was Clay's "mania of pacification." In his view Clay would sacrifice principle for expediency, anything to avoid a showdown with the nullifiers.[53]

Clay's "pretty little Bill," as Webster sarcastically called it, came before the Senate on February 21. By this time virtually everyone in Washington knew about the Clay-Calhoun "arrangement." It had been forcefully demonstrated just the week before, when the House elected as its printer Gales and Seaton, the editors of the Washington *National Intelligencer,* over Francis P. Blair, editor of Jackson's mouthpiece, the Washington *Globe.* The Senate immediately fol-

51. *Register of Debates,* 22d Congress, 2d Session, pp. 655–666; Sargent, *Public Men and Events,* I, 241–243; Clay to DW, February 11, March 2, 1833, in *PC,* III, 211, 221–222; Remini, *Clay,* pp. 432–433.

52. On the compromise tariff, see Peterson, *Olive Branch and Sword.*

53. DW to Nathan Appleton, [February 17, 1833], DW to Hopkinson, [February 21, 1833], in *PC,* III, 216, 220; Clay to Biddle, April 10, 1833, in Clay, *Papers,* VIII, 637.

lowed by choosing as its printer Duff Green, editor of the Washington *United States Telegraph* and a staunch Calhoun supporter. This was a double-barreled blow to the administration. The congressional printers received a substantial income to print the laws, debates, and other government documents. Two important and very lucrative patronage positions had been assigned to the friends of Clay and Calhoun.

All that now remained for the Clay-Calhoun "arrangement" was passage of the "pretty little Bill." Debate over the measure raged for several days with Webster leading the fight against it. After one speech Martin Van Buren, who disliked and distrusted the Massachusetts senator, nonetheless admired how he had "brought to its execution all the sagacity and adroitness he possessed, and in which he had no superior, to make the positions he assumed and the ideas and expressions by which he supported them convey to intelligent hearers and readers a significance beyond his words." Van Buren hit the mark exactly. Webster possessed the unique talent of making his ideas and positions convey "a significance beyond his words."[54]

It is rather remarkable that the two leading National Republicans verbally fought out their differences on the Senate floor. "The gentleman from Kentucky," rumbled Webster during one encounter, "supports the bill from one motive, others from another motive." The implication was clear, and Clay retorted that Webster "dislikes the measure because it commands the concurrence" of both himself and Calhoun. Although Webster condemns this obvious "measure of pacification," he is quick to support the administration's Force Bill, which might provoke bloodshed. "Would the Senator from Massachusetts send *his* bill[55] forth alone without this measure of conciliation?"

That was a low blow. Webster might have responded that Clay had conveniently absented himself when the vote on the Force Bill was taken, but that was not his style. So the moment of serious confrontation between the two men passed. "Mr. Webster and I came in conflict," Clay explained to his friend Francis Brooke, "and I have the satisfaction to tell you that he gained nothing. My friends flatter me, with my having completely triumphed. There is no permanent breach between us." To guarantee that their disagreement did not get worse, Clay asked Biddle to do and "say all you can to soothe him. . . . You hold a large flask of oil and know well how to pour it out." The last thing Clay wanted to do was split National Republicans or back Webster into the Democratic party.[56]

Henry Clay, Jr., visited the Capitol at this time and listened to some of the debate and then recorded in his diary his impressions, especially about Webster's style of oratory. Although he considered Webster "a great orator" with a "deep masculine voice," the senator lacked grace of movement and did not display much wit, according to young Clay. Still, he possessed a most "commanding

54. Van Buren, *Autobiography*, p. 682.

55. The Force Bill. Italics mine.

56. *Register of Debates*, 22d Congress, 2d Session, pp. 722–725, 729–742; Clay to Brooke, February 28, Clay to Biddle, March 4, 1833, in Clay, *Papers*, VIII, 628, 630.

presence." He looked grave and never smiled, but his arguments, invariably nationalistic in tone, were incontrovertible, and "his words which are pure English contain a golden meaning." Although not as quick and agile in debate as the elder Clay, Webster possessed a power of "forming original and condensed opinions which is truly remarkable." He frequently drew references from the Bible, and, said young Clay, these "are simple and affecting and often beautiful and sublime."[57]

To have heard these two men in verbal combat, however infrequently, was surely one of the great moments in American history, matched only when Webster and Calhoun tangled on the floor of the Senate.

Because President Jackson really wanted the tariff question put off this session and therefore concentrated his efforts on the Force Bill, a leadership vacuum occurred in the House of Representatives, and Clay cleverly maneuvered his tariff bill onto the floor of the House as a substitute for the Verplanck bill.[58] "It swept like a hurricane" through the chamber, reported Representative Adams.[59] On February 16 the House passed the compromise tariff by a vote of 119 to 85.[60]

Once the bill passed the House, Clay had little trouble convincing the Senate to go along and agree to this "measure of pacification." On March 1 by the vote of twenty-nine to sixteen the Compromise Tariff of 1833 passed the upper house. Both the tariff and force bills went to the President on March 2, and he signed them immediately. South Carolina repealed its Ordinance of Nullification but, to save face, or maintain its defiance, nullified the Force Bill.

Still, that did not end it. The danger signals that had flown over the nation since last summer had not been lowered by South Carolina's latest action. Webster knew, and said so repeatedly, that "the question of paramount importance in our affairs is likely to be, for some time to come, *the preservation of the Union, or its dissolution;* and no power can decide this question, but that of the People themselves. Let the question be argued—let it be discussed—give the People light, & they will decide right."[61]

Calhoun credited passage of the Force Act to the "joint influence of Webster & McLane aided by the influence of Jackson, with the express intention of establishing the doctrine of consolidation." At least, he said, "the protective system, I think, has received its death wound."[62]

Webster took his defeat over the tariff with grace. After all, protection would remain high for the next ten years, and who knew what might happen after that? As for his relations with Clay, they remained strained and uncertain.

57. Henry Clay, Jr., manuscript diary, University of Kentucky Library.

58. Remini, *Clay,* pp. 430–431.

59. Adams, *Memoirs,* VIII, 527.

60. *Register of Debates,* 22d Congress, 2d Session, pp. 697–701, 715–716.

61. DW to Joel Poinsett, May 7, 1833, in *PC,* III, 248.

62. Calhoun to Samuel D. Ingham, March 25, Calhoun to Bolling Hall, March 25, 1833, in *Calhoun Papers,* III, 148, 147.

William Plumer asked Webster about Clay's motives in advancing his compromise. "I don't talk about Mr. Clay," Black Dan snapped in response. "I have done talking about him, Mr. Plumer."[63]

Webster considered publishing his speech on the tariff, but a friend dissuaded him from it. "He said the act was done—the thing was settled—& the publication of my Speech would only prove a wider difference to exist among friends." Webster finally acquiesced, "a position which I have ever since regretted," he recorded five years later.[64]

Although Clay had unqualified respect for Webster's "great abilities," he did not "admire his general character," according to Van Buren, "and admitted that their relations had not commonly been as cordial or their intercourse as confidential as was usual between leading members of the same political party."[65] At the same time many of Jackson's friends hoped for a closer official relationship between the President and the Massachusetts senator. Secretary of State Livingston, soon to resign his office and widely known to be slated to go to France as minister, called on Webster at his lodgings to have a talk, probably at Jackson's instigation. Unfortunately he did not find the Senator home.

Webster immediately wrote to Livingston when he learned of the visit. "It is a source of regret to me" that we missed each other, he declared. "I am still desirous, however, of such an interview, &, with your permission shall seek an opportunity to meet with you, before the expiration of many months."[66]

To some it looked as though Black Dan were heading pell-mell into the Democratic party.

63. Plumer, "Reminiscences of Webster," XVII, 557.

64. DW to Hiram Ketchum, January 20, 1838, in *PC*, IV, 264.

65. Van Buren, *Autobiography*, p. 670.

66. Draft letter of DW to Livingston [March 21?, 1833], in Van Tyne, ed., *Letters of Webster*, p. 181. Van Tyne mistakenly assumes this letter was written to Clay. From internal evidence it is clear the letter was written to Livingston. See *PC*, III, 224–227.

23

On the Presidential Trail

BEFORE submitting his resignation as secretary of state and leaving Washington for France, Edward Livingston had a number of conversations with Jackson with regard to Webster's future role vis-à-vis the administration. Livingston emphasized the need for Webster's continued support, and the President supposedly "gave a favorable ear and acquiescence." Indeed the chief executive "authorized Mr. Livingston to approach Mr. Webster upon the subject."[1] But what prospect, what office could they offer the ambitious senator? Since Livingston was leaving the State Department, did that mean that Webster might take his place with the possibility of moving up to the White House in 1836? Webster might like that, but was it realistic ? Since it was already understood that Louis McLane would vacate his Treasury position and move to State, would Webster then replace McLane at Treasury? Nicholas Biddle could hardly think of a better choice,[2] but since Jackson was already preparing to remove the government's deposits from the BUS, a decision that Webster reported to Biddle as soon as he got wind of it,[3] the selection of the Massachusetts senator was absurd. Still, "the nearest friends of both parties" believed "that a seat in the cabinet was . . . proposed to Mr. Webster" by Livingston.[4]

Webster's interest in a possible alliance with Jackson may have been motivated by their similar views about the nature of the Union and, most especially, his ongoing desire for the presidency. Jackson could make an enormous difference if he designated the Massachusetts senator as his successor. No doubt Webster would have taken the Treasury, if offered, in the hope of convincing the President of the error of his ways, but Jackson was absolutely rigid on the BUS,

1. March, *Webster*, p. 250. This book was published in 1850. Webster never contradicted what March wrote, and the book went through four editions before his death.

2. Biddle wrote to Webster in mid-April and urged him to see Livingston, who would be in New York prior to his departure for Paris. "The whole question of peace or war lies in the matter of the [government's] deposits. If they are withdrawn, it is a declaration of war. It is wiser therefore to begin the work of peace before any irrevocable step is taken." Biddle to DW, April 10, 1833, in *PC*, III, 242.

3. DW to Biddle, [March 27, 28], 1833, ibid., III, 228, 234.

4. March, *Webster*, p. 251. For further discussions of this fascinating phase of Webster's life, see Brown, *Webster and the Politics of Availability*, Nathans, *Webster and Jacksonian Democracy*, Bartlett, *Webster*, and Baxter, *Webster*.

and Webster knew it. Furthermore, the idea that Black Dan could head the Treasury was ludicrous, given his notorious inability to handle his own finances sensibly and judiciously. As treasury secretary he would have been a disaster.

In fact it was this weakness that Van Buren exploited to destroy Webster as a rival in Jackson's eyes. He wrote in his *Autobiography* that Webster's "eagerness to borrow and the recklessness with which his loans were made were very generally known and his being largely in debt to the bank and, so far as that went, within its power, was undoubted. This extensive knowledge of his condition" was widely circulated "by the friends of the President."[5]

Extensive knowledge of his condition! And widely circulated. Van Buren made certain that every last critical comment about Webster's recklessness and eagerness to borrow was laid before the President. As a matter of fact Webster was presently dunning the BUS again, this time for an advance on future earnings. "In a year & a half, or two years," he explained to the cashier of the BUS in Philadelphia, "I hope to be receiving considerable sums, as comm[issio]ns on claims under the French and Neapolitan Treaties" for the recovery of money lost by Americans during the Napoleonic Wars, "to which claims I am now giving much attention. In the meantime, certain private matters render it convenient that I should anticipate these receipts. If you have no objection, therefore, I should be glad of permission to draw on you."[6] Jackson was repeatedly told, nay, warned, that the Massachusetts senator was indeed under Biddle's control.

Van Buren took up residence in the White House and "sticks as close to the President as a blistering plaster," wrote one of Webster's friends.[7] He had a position and a succession to defend, and he employed all his political skills to protect and advance them. Not for nothing was he known as the Little Magician.

Undoubtedly the possibility of a Jackson-Webster coalition that would give the succession to the senator was more a fiction in Van Buren's mind than anything else. The President and the senator might have similar nationalistic impulses, but other matters, like democracy, the Bank, and the tariff, effectively prevented any real coalition from evolving.[8] Since the presidential race of 1836 would surely include Van Buren, Webster's only real hope lay in running against him, not in place of him. By sticking with the National Republican party, he had a chance of gaining a presidential nomination, especially now that Henry Clay was discounted as a possible candidate. Already there was talk that the party would turn to Webster. "Wherever I go," one friend informed him, "the people appear pleased at the idea that you are to be substituted as a candidate for the Presidency in lieu of Mr. Clay."[9]

5. Van Buren, *Autobiography*, p. 661.

6. DW to Samuel Jaudon, April 12, 1833, in *PC*, III, 242. Naturally Webster promised to repay the money in due course. He represented claimants not only against France and Naples but against Denmark as well.

7. Eli S. Davis to DW, March 27, 1833, ibid., III, 233.

8. It is possible, indeed probable, that Jackson simply used Webster for his own purposes in the nullification crisis and never had any intention of forming a permanent alliance with him.

9. Eli S. Davis to DW, March 27, 1833 in *PC*, III, 233.

Rumors still floated around the capital about the makeup of the new cabinet, but it was soon announced that Louis McLane would definitely take the State Department but that Levi Woodbury of New Hampshire would not go to the Treasury as anticipated. It was said that some "dark-horse" would be named.[10]

Once Congress adjourned and Webster returned to Boston, he decided to take his long-delayed trip to the West in an effort to encourage popular interest in his candidacy. He arrived home about the middle of April, when he learned that President Jackson would tour the eastern states in an effort to reassure the public that the crisis with South Carolina had indeed passed. The presidential tour had been decided as early as March, and Jackson agreed to follow the route taken by President James Monroe in 1818.[11] Webster was a bit chagrined that his own absence from Boston would coincide with Jackson's arrival, so he wrote to the secretary of war, Lewis Cass, and explained his circumstances. Cass replied that the President would probably arrive in Boston around June 20, and although "I cannot ask you to postpone your intended journey . . . still, I will confess to you that the hope of meeting you . . . has dwelt upon my mind since we first conversed together on the subject." Webster responded that he felt great reluctance about leaving the city, not only because of the pleasure it would afford of seeing the President and offering him the hospitalities of his home but because his absence would be liable "to much misconstruction." And that would be unfortunate. Under the circumstances, therefore, he expected to be present when the presidential party arrived and would "abridge the extent of my travels, so as to be able to return to Boston by the 20th of June."[12]

It seems Webster was again trying to have it both ways: to keep viable his position within the National Republican party and at the same time to court the Democratic power brokers for whatever good it might do. Rumors of a coalition therefore continued to circulate.

Toward the end of May Webster finally set off on his western tour, accompanied by his wife, Caroline, his daughter, Julia, and his friend Stephen White. He expected to visit northern New York, taking the canal route, and then move into the Ohio Valley by stagecoach, with principal stops along the way at Buffalo, Columbus, and Cincinnati, before heading down to Kentucky to see Henry Clay. Newspapers carried notices of his trip so that friends and rivals had an opportunity of tracing his movements as he paraded across the country. Indeed the Washington *National Intelligencer* gave him a remarkable send-off with an editorial that may have been intended to link the tour with the next presidential election. "Great intellectual power has always commanded the attention and excited the admiration of mankind," read the piece. "We consider Mr. W. one of the most gifted and extraordinary men our country has ever produced." It

10. DW to Biddle, April 7, 1833, ibid., III, 236–237; DW to Julia Webster, March 9, 1833, in Curtis, *Webster,* I, 460.

11. For a detailed description of Jackson's tour, see Remini, *Jackson,* III, 66–83.

12. Cass to DW, April 17, DW to Cass, [c. April 21, 1833], 1833, in Curtis, *Webster,* I, 460–461.

went on to compare him with Patrick Henry, among many other great orators.[13]

Jackson also began his tour of the middle and New England states, gaining considerably more national coverage and larger crowds than Webster. But the *National Intelligencer* seemed intent on giving the Massachusetts senator greater credit for the attention he was receiving. "Curiosity and interest combine in assembling a multitude to follow the footsteps of those who are clothed with official power," began the editorial of June 15, "but it is merit only that can attract such attentions as Mr. Webster is receiving on his tour of the West."

Clay watched what was happening and may have had second thoughts about a visit from his Massachusetts colleague. In any event he warned Webster against coming to Lexington because of the cholera. It had broken out in the West and had a devastating impact on Lexington, where fifty people died within a matter of three days. The town was one of the hardest hit in the United States. Webster was well advised, said Clay, not to proceed beyond Cincinnati.[14]

The group began the journey with a pleasant visit at the home of Caroline's youngest brother, who had extensive land holdings—about eighteen hundred acres—alongside the Genesee River. After this visit Caroline and Julia returned to Boston, and Webster continued westward. Naturally party leaders in every town and city along his route extended invitations for him to speak to their people about the recent crisis. They especially wished to hear him extol the wonders of the country and the strength and stability of their government. No one could sound the nationalistic theme that Americans loved to hear with greater variations and greater imagination than "the Godlike" himself. No one knew the words and music better than he.

Most of these invitations had to be refused since he wished to get back to Boston in time to meet Jackson. But Buffalo was a major stop in the tour, and Webster agreed to give a short speech. He also agreed to participate in the launching of the steamboat *Daniel Webster.* No doubt he was pleased to see the words *"Liberty and Union,* now and for ever, one and inseparable" flying on a banner attached to the mast of the vessel. Under it was another insignia with the words "Daniel Webster." In the course of the ceremonies he responded to an address by one of the ship's proprietors. He referred back to his visit to the city eight years before, when there had been only one steamboat on the lake. Now, he had been told, there were eighteen. He congratulated the city on the "augmentation of its commercial business," and he predicted that within a short time the sugar of Louisiana, the fisheries of the East Coast, and the vegetable and mineral resources of the Northwest would "find their way hither by inland water communications." But remember, he went on, the blessings and the riches of internal commerce "are the fruits of a united government, and one general, common commercial system."

13. May 25, 1833.
14. Clay to DW, June 17, 1833, in *PC*, III, 257.

For some time in his speeches Webster had been linking capitalism and national unity to form a vision for the nation, a vision that promised such prosperity and strength as to dazzle the world. They were speeches that contained his most cherished beliefs, and he expressed them with passion and conviction.

He ended his Buffalo speech by saluting "THE COMMERCE OF THE LAKES, A NEW-DISCOVERED SOURCE OF NATIONAL PROSPERITY, AND A NEW BOND OF NATIONAL UNION."[15]

In another speech in Buffalo he addressed a different theme. At a convention of mechanics and manufacturers he spoke extensively about labor. He told his listeners that the "encouragement and protection of American manual labor" were the "just and leading object" of tariffs. Because American labor must be protected from foreign competition, he therefore favored a protective system of "prudent moderation," one that avoided extremes. The people control our institutions, he declared, and in order for them to exercise this right properly, they must "enjoy, first, the means of education, and, second, the reasonable certainty of procuring a competent livelihood by industry and labor." To be free, one must be "intelligently free"; to be independent, one must be able to secure oneself from "want," and this can be done "by sobriety and industry." Labor is vitally connected not only to the political economy but to the government and "our whole social system."[16]

For the remainder of his western trip capitalism, national unity, and the importance of labor were recurrent and important themes in his major addresses. It was probably sometime before or during this tour that Webster prepared a memorandum that outlined his personal credo regarding the several issues presently before the public. He titled the memorandum "Objects," and it almost reads like a platform for his presidential campaign. The document has no date.

First, & principal, To maintain the Union of the States, & uphold the Constitution, against the attempts of its enemies, whether attacking it, directly, by Nullification, or seeing to break it up by secession.

2. To support the Administration, fairly, in all its just & proper measures; & especially to stand by the President in his patriotic constitutional principles. . . .

3. To maintain the cause of American Capital, American industry, & more than all *American Labor,* against foreign & destructive competition by reasonable, moderate, but settled & permanent system of protective duties—

4. To preserve the general currency of the Country, in a safe state, well guarded agt. those who would speculate on the rise & fall of circulating paper; & to this end to advocate the renewal of the Bank of U.S. as the best means of promoting this end. . . .

5. To resist & oppose the oppression & tyrannical combination of [Van Buren's New York] Regency. . . .

6. I oppose, vigorously & unceasingly, all unlawful combination, all secret oaths, all

15. *National Intelligencer,* June 15, 1833. It can also be found in W&S, II, 131–133.
16. W&S, II, 133–134.

association of men, meeting in darkness & striving to obtain for themselves . . . advantages not enjoyed by other citizens of the Republic.[17]

After his New York appearances Webster took off to Ohio, and his coming was signaled by the formation of town committees to plan details for his visit. Many of committees passed resolutions expressing not so much their pleasure in his presence as their gratitude for his "explaining and sustaining the principles of the Federal Constitution," as well as "the devotion which he displayed for the stability of the Union, and the perpetuity of our free institutions."[18] The toasts at many of the dinners he attended in his honor repeated this expression of appreciation. At a dinner in Cincinnati, for example, after first toasting the President, the other branches of government, and the memory of George Washington, the guests raised their glasses to: "Our distinguished guest, the Hon. Daniel Webster: the profound expounder of the Constitution, the eloquent supporter of the Federal Union, and the uniform friend and advocate of the Western Country."

This last touch about his advocacy of the West was something Webster surely wished to hear. It would be important in any bid he might make for the presidency. Clay and Jackson had the West politically locked up, and now Webster had come to claim a share of it.

The senator replied to the toast by saluting the city of Cincinnati, and he was followed by General William Henry Harrison, the hero of the Battle of Tippecanoe in 1811, who hailed him as "the true Representative of the character and manners of his country." The endorsement of a military hero, who had defeated Indians on the frontier, like General Jackson, could provide enormous political advantage in any future presidential election. Friendly newspapers in the East noted Webster's success among these westerners. "He receives every attentions, which, unbought, unsolicited, and altogether complimentary, cannot but be grateful."[19]

In view of this success Webster might have wished to extend his western tour, but the cholera outbreak had by this time reached epidemic proportions. Under the circumstances he decided to turn back and head for home. In Columbus he alerted Clay to the possibility of his canceling his trip to Kentucky, and in Chillicothe he confirmed that he must abandon the tour. Not that he feared for his personal safety, but he did not wish to see his friend "in alarm or in affliction" over the possible consequences of his visit. He said he would return to Pittsburgh and then to New York and New England by the shortest route possible.[20]

Already the trip had taken longer than he originally intended, and now it

17. Van Tyne, ed., *Letters of Webster*, p. 183. The editor conjectures that the document was written c. June 1, 1833.

18. These resolutions were passed by the Cincinnati committee on June 17. *National Intelligencer*, June 25, 1833.

19. Ibid., July 6, 1833.

20. DW to Clay, June 10, 1833, in W&S, XVI, 231; DW to Clay, June 22, 1822, in *PC*, III, 259.

seemed certain that he would never meet the President and welcome him to Boston. It also meant missing the annual oration to be given at Harvard University by his son Fletcher, who was completing his studies at the institution. Webster wrote his son and expressed his regrets. "I have seldom felt so much concern about anything of the kind as I do upon your success upon that occasion. I pray you spare no pains."[21]

Fletcher tried valiantly to live up to his father's expectations and invariably found himself inadequate. "I hope that there is more in me than has yet appeared," he wearily wrote his father on one occasion, "for I have done nothing heretofore, and should be very sorry to think that a son of yours was wholly good for nothing; but I fear that people think there is more in me than there really is. I must do all I can to answer their expectations." The child of an illustrious parent no doubt suffers a unique disability in that he or she is always expected to perform and be better than most others of similar age because of his or her birth. It places a formidable burden on such children that they frequently cannot bear. For Fletcher the burden was ever-present.[22]

Unquestionably Webster added to the burden. He believed absolutely in the necessity of a good education. Naturally he wanted the same for his son, but he may have set standards too high for Fletcher and unduly criticized the young man when he failed to meet them. Fletcher confessed after his first term at Harvard that his performance had been below his father's expectations:

> I am very sorry indeed, that I have not done more this term, in reading those authors of whom you approved. I know I have not done enough. I will not attempt to excuse myself any more, for my negligence; but show you that I will amend for the future, and I hope to meet your approval, at the end of the second term. . . . If I apply myself as I hope to do, I may perhaps graduate higher than you seem to expect I shall, from the last term. The chief fault is, my dear father, a restlessness; I cannot stick to the same thing long, a fault of which I am as well aware, as yourself.[23]

The likelihood of his father's absence when he gave his senior oration on July 16 must have been a great disappointment to the young man, and to the father as well. Much as he might have driven the boy to greater success Webster was very fond and indeed quite proud of his son. "Do your best," he counseled, "and you will do well enough." He even suggested having the oration printed if it was well received. Unfortunately he did not expect to hear Fletcher's effort himself, although he added that he would "make every effort in my power to reach Boston in season."[24]

Webster arrived in Pittsburgh on the Fourth of July accompanied "by a numerous cavalcade of citizens." That year the Independence Day celebrations included many references to Webster, several of which specifically stated that

21. DW to Fletcher Webster, July 5, 1833, in PC, III, 259.

22. Fletcher to DW, February 25, 1832, ibid., III, 153–154.

23. Fletcher to DW, January 3, 1831, ibid., III, 95.

24. DW to Fletcher, July 5, 1833, ibid., III, 259.

the people would not forget him in future elections. A welcoming committee passed the usual resolutions and in deference to his wishes held a reception (in lieu of a public dinner), in a grove at four o'clock on the afternoon of July 8. The mayor greeted Webster by calling him "the great champion of the Constitution" and added that "to his mighty intellect, the nation, with one voice, confided its cause,—of life or death." He had annihilated "the artful sophisms of nullification," and the American people owed him a great debt.

Webster came to the reception with a prepared speech that, as he expected, received wide attention. He began straight off by discussing the "alarming moment" the nation endured during the nullification crisis, when it seemed possible that the Union would be shattered and the twenty-four states scattered into twenty-four unconnected sovereignties. Then, to the surprise of many, and no doubt the chagrin of some National Republicans, he gave President Jackson an unqualified vote of confidence in the way he had handled the crisis.

Gentlemen, the President of the United States was, as it seemed to me, at this eventful crisis, true to his duty. He comprehended and understood the case, and met it as it was proper to meet it. While I am as willing as others to admit that the President has, on other occasions, rendered important services to the country, and especially on that occasion which has given him so much military renown, I yet think the ability and decision with which he rejected the disorganized doctrines of nullification create a claim, than which he has none higher, to the gratitude of the country and the respect of prosperity.

He went on to praise the President's Proclamation of December 10, claiming it contained "the true and only true doctrines of the Constitution. They constitute the sole ground on which dismemberment can be resisted." He also admitted quite openly that he and Jackson had differed and still differed on many issues, such as the constitutional power of internal improvements, the Bank, and Jackson's reasons for vetoing the recharter. Furthermore, he differed with the President on protection and the way to distribute public lands. But not one of these differences justified opposing him at a "moment of great public exigency. I sought to take counsel of nothing but patriotism, to feel no impulse but that of duty, and to yield not a lame and hesitating, but a vigorous and cordial, support to measures which, in my conscience, I believed essential to the preservation of the Constitution. . . . It gives me the highest satisfaction to know, that, in regard to this subject, the general voice of the country does not disapprove my conduct."

It was a fitting tribute to a man who did indeed help save the Union from possible disruption as well as restore the nation's self-confidence in its ability to survive under a republican form of government. Future generations would frequently forget what Jackson's contribution meant to Americans at that time. As Webster said so often, up to that time there never was a moment of greater danger for the nation. Not only did Jackson handle it like a statesman and bring the crisis to an end, but he rescued the people from a nightmare of anxiety and fear.

By this time Jackson had abruptly ended his tour of the East because of ill health and returned to the White House. On reading the Pittsburgh speech, he felt great satisfaction not only in learning about Webster's sincere appreciation of his leadership during the nullification crisis but in knowing that the senator had publicly expressed it. Had there been no other issue separating them they might have found a way to bring about a political alliance.[25] In fact the *National Intelligencer* of July 13 commented: "Mr. Webster has wrought little less than a miracle upon the party feuds and divisions of the Western country. He has fairly extinguished the one and obliterated the other."

After concluding his remarks about nullification and the Constitution in his Pittsburgh speech, Webster referred to what he had said in Buffalo about the linkage between labor and industry and the fact that protection benefits both. He also repeated the need for education and internal improvements. It must be remembered that in all our efforts for education, both literary and religious, "we leave opinion and conscience free. Heaven grant," he concluded, "that it may be the glory of the United States to have established two great truths, of the highest importance to the whole human race; first, that an enlightened community *is* capable of self-government; and, second, that the toleration of all sects does *not* necessarily produce indifference to religion."[26]

The speech was well received by the Pittsburgh crowd, and Webster thanked it for its courtesy and hospitality and headed home via New York. He seemed satisfied with the results of his western tour; in fact he said he "rejoiced" at the receptions he had received. The "testimonials of personal respect" and the "excellent social & political spirit" he encountered pleased him tremendously. Best of all, he later told admirers, the strong pro-Union, pro-Constitution, pro-Government sentiment he witnessed was "deep, fervid, & general." The "prevailing spirit I found to be excellent—far, very far, exceeding my anticipations."[27]

Indeed the tour had been a tremendous success. "No conqueror flushed with recent victories could have had a more triumphal reception," claimed Charles March. "His progress was one ovation. Cities poured out their crowds on his approach."[28]

But what did this success mean in terms of his presidential ambitions? Webster himself said that "the great mass of Western opinion is, I think quite uncommitted." For the next presidential election several western candidates might be nominated, possibly including Associate Justice John McLean of Ohio, who had been angling for a nomination for eight years or more. Webster also expected a southern candidate to run, probably Calhoun, although here again

25. For further details on a possible merger, see Norman D. Brown, "Webster-Jackson Movement for a Constitution and Union Party in 1833," *Mid-America*, XLVI (July 1964), pp. 147–171.

26. *National Intelligencer*, July 6, 13, 1833; *W&S*, II, 137–156.

27. DW to Ezekiel Chambers, August 6, DW to Albert Trace, August 10, 1833, in *PC*, III, 260–261, 266.

28. March, *Webster*, pp. 253–254.

there might be more than one southerner put forward. As for himself, he remained cautious. He thought the National Republican party needed to "wait events" as long as possible, but not wait so long as to allow a bevy of candidates to preempt the field. He thought the matter would be discussed at length when Congress reconvened in December.[29] In that setting, and in view of the success of his western trip, Webster could hope that his party would turn to him for leadership.

As a matter of fact after his return home he was told by more than one colleague that "there is not a man in this nation young or old, who rejoices more than I do, to see this great breaking out of your fame."[30] Boston newspapers had already set up the cry for a new organization of parties based on "UNION and the CONSTITUTION." And who better than Webster to stand on such a doctrinal platform? So away with Jacksonians, National Republicans, and Anti-Masons, trumpeted the Boston *Courier* in its editorial of August 8; party reorganization "is not only desirable but necessary."

A week later Webster received a copy of a draft letter that urged his candidacy. The canvass had already begun in Virginia and other states, it said. Because Van Buren would be the Democratic nominee, someone was needed who would stand for high principles, not low politics. "From indications from Ohio Pennsylvania New York, the Union party of the Eastern States, & other parts of the country, it is evident that Mr. Webster is looked to as the Candidate who will rally the most powerful party under the battle cry of 'THE CONSTITUTION & THE UNION.' "[31] Such letters sounded enormously encouraging.

William Plumer spoke to the senator about his tour and "adverted to his being himself a candidate for the presidency. He [Webster] spoke on the subject with candor and sincerity. His friends in Ohio and Pennsylvania were, he said, of opinion that a nomination could be obtained from these states." But he cautioned them about making a nomination now. It was still too early. Better to leave the matter "to some future day."

When the conversation ended, Plumer had not the slightest doubt that Webster had his eye on 1836. "On the whole," he wrote, "it was evident that Mr. Webster had some hopes . . . of reaching the presidency at the next election."[32]

29. DW to Ezekiel Chambers, August 6, 1833, in *PC*, III, 260–261.

30. Rufus Choate to DW, August 12, 1833, ibid., III, 270.

31. Henry Dearborn to DW, August 12, 1833, with enclosure, ibid., III, 270–272.

32. Plumer, "Reminiscences of Webster," in *W&S*, XVII, 558.

24

The Great Triumvirate

WEBSTER stopped off briefly in New York on his way home from his western travels and there met Edward Livingston, who was preparing to leave for France to take up his new duties as U.S. minister. Livingston had spoken at length with the President about Webster's future. Now he was prepared to share with the Massachusetts senator what he and Jackson had discussed, part of which Webster later recorded in a memorandum.

Livingston started off by expressing Jackson's and his own deep appreciation for Webster's support over the Force Bill. He repeated this again and again in the warmest terms. Webster understood the extent of this gratitude because among other things, just before the congressional session had ended, he had been approached by a well-connected Democrat who asked him to look over a list of applicants for an important office in the East, presumably to make the final selection. But Webster had declined the invitation because "he did not wish to place himself under any obligation." Then Livingston said that the President had expressed the earnest hope that the senator would see his way clear to continue his support of the administration in the immediate future. It would be very much appreciated.

In his response Webster told Livingston that in many areas of future governmental policy there would be no great differences of opinion. Unfortunately "there was an irreconcilable difference on the great question of the currency."[1]

Indeed. As Webster knew and had informed Biddle, Jackson had decided last spring to remove the government's deposits from the BUS and place them in selected state banks. By removing government moneys from Biddle's control, the President expected to terminate the enormous authority the Bank exercised, in both financial and political circles. In effect he would kill the "monster," as he called it, not tame it, as he had originally intended.

On that issue, and that issue alone, Jackson and Webster were headed for a violent clash over constitutional interpretation. Congress, not the President, controlled the purse, argued the senator. The Constitution clearly stated that fact. And on this point Webster would speak confidently and forcefully and no doubt find ample support among his colleagues.

1. Memorandum, HM 779, Webster Papers, Huntington Library.

For his part Jackson simply presumed that he could instruct the treasury secretary to remove the government's moneys and that that would be the end of it. No congressional action was necessary, no consent required. But such a contention Webster vehemently denied.

So the hope that the two men could unite their political interests ultimately foundered on the rock of removal. Still, the suspicion of an alliance lingered for many months thereafter. Clay thought that Webster had already given himself "a fatal stab among his own friends" by his coziness with Jackson. If the Massachusetts senator pursued this course and actually deserted to the administration, "it will be with infamy."[2]

After his interview with Livingston, Webster continued his journey home and, weary and slightly ill, arrived in Boston on July 20. His family had already decamped for Marshfield, where he joined them for a restful fortnight and quickly recovered his health by fishing, farming, hunting, and relaxing in the company of his family and neighbors.

While Webster recuperated, President Jackson moved forward with his plan to remove the deposits. He had dispatched Amos Kendall, his close adviser in the matter, to identify a number of state banks into which the government's deposits could be placed. Naturally these banks had to pass muster in terms of political reliability and financial solvency. By the end of the summer of 1833 Kendall had lined up seven banks in the leading eastern cities.[3] By the fall Jackson was ready to take his final action against the "monster."

But he ran into unexpected trouble convincing his new secretary of the treasury, William Duane, that he must act as directed with respect to the deposits. Duane contended that according to the law, he must first go to Congress and inform it of his intended action, an argument Jackson totally rejected.[4]

Biddle kept Webster informed of the movements transpiring against the BUS as well as his preparations for the impending confrontation. He instructed all the branches to keep discounts at the present rate and shorten the time for which they bought bills of exchange. This, he figured, would keep the Bank strong and guard against any sudden negative decision by the administration.[5]

The matter came to a head on September 20, when, without Duane's consent, Jackson's mouthpiece, the Washington *Globe*, announced that the government's deposits would be removed. Duane reacted with defiance, and Jackson sacked him on the spot, appointing Roger Taney in his place.[6] Taney then issued an order stating that on October 1 all future government deposits would be placed in selected state banks—called pet banks by the opposition—and that for operating expenses the government would draw out its remaining funds from

2. Willie P. Mangum to David L. Swain, December 22, 1833, in Shanks, ed., *Papers of Mangum*, II, 55–56.

3. The Boston selection was the Merchant Bank of Boston, Mark Healy president.

4. Remini, *Jackson*, III, 93–94.

5. Biddle to DW, August 13, 1833, in McGrane, ed., *Correspondence of Biddle*, pp. 214–215.

6. Taney's position as attorney general was later filled by Benjamin F. Butler of New York.

the BUS until they were exhausted. Biddle responded by directing a general curtailment of loans throughout the banking system, refusing to increase discounts, and restricting discounted bills of exchange to eighty days. As a result a financial panic ensued. Business had been enjoying a period of enormous expansion, requiring credit and an abundant supply of cash. Biddle's action brought the general prosperity to a shrieking halt, and the recession threatened to deepen into a major economic collapse.[7]

Webster immediately counseled Biddle to challenge Jackson's action by bringing the matter before Congress. Biddle agreed, and as soon as Congress reconvened in early December, he submitted a memorial asking for redress and accusing Taney of violating the Bank's charter. He contended, as did Webster, that only Congress had custody of public moneys.[8]

Thus, as the first session of the Twenty-third Congress, sometimes called the Panic Session, convened, the final battle in the Bank War began. As it progressed, a new political alliance emerged of unlikely elements poised to scuttle Jackson's plan to convert the country from national to deposit banking: an alliance of Webster, Clay, and Calhoun, the "Great Triumvirate."[9] Clay, as party leader of the National Republicans, had already reached an agreement with Calhoun, leader of the nullifiers, over the Compromise Tariff. Now they, with Webster's help, intended to force the return of the deposits and kill any chance of Taney's confirmation in the Senate as secretary of the treasury. But Calhoun was different from the other two men. He *opposed* the BUS. At the same time he also opposed the removal of the deposits, and of course he ached to settle the score with Jackson.

Webster, who had clashed with Calhoun and had supported the administration's position on the Force Bill, had also parted company with Clay over the tariff. Now these three were being drawn together over the removal issue, and the person engineering this new coalition was Nicholas Biddle. "I only repeat what I have said again & again," the banker explained to Webster, "that the fate of this nation is in the hands of Mr Clay Mr Calhoun & yourself. It is in your power to save us from the misrule of these people in place, but you can only do it while you are united." You three must not be estranged from one another, he counseled. "For all our sakes, do not let [your past disagreement with Clay] grow into any difficulty. If great talents are sometimes mislead [sic] by great passions, there are fortunately still greater talents which can subdue these passions."[10]

Biddle's point was well taken. The Senate contained a majority in favor of the BUS and against removal of the deposits. To buttress that with the enormous

7. Remini, *Jackson*, III, 101–106, 108, 111. By December 13, 1833, the public funds in the BUS were virtually withdrawn, and the number of pet banks had risen to twenty-two. Ibid., p. 106.

8. DW to Biddle, October 29, 1833, in McGrane, ed., *Correspondence of Biddle*, pp. 216–217; Biddle to DW, December 9, 1833, Webster Papers, LC.

9. For a superb study of the triumvirate, see Merrill D. Peterson, *The Great Triumvirate: Webster, Clay, and Calhoun* (New York, 1987).

10. Biddle to DW, December 15, 1833, in *PC*, III, 285.

speaking and parliamentary skills of the Great Triumvirate would virtually guarantee Senate passage of a resolution requiring the restoration of the deposits. Biddle desperately wanted that action taken, as desperately as Jackson wanted to prevent it. Webster responded to Biddle's "sermon," as the Bank president himself termed his letter, by assuring him that "at present there is no coolness whatever, between those whom you would expect to see acting together."[11]

For Webster, Biddle's request posed no problem. He could cooperate with Clay and Calhoun without its bothering him one whit. He simply held himself aloof from any close contact with them. But then, although he was far from uncivil, he was never a social man in Congress, not like Clay, a hail-fellow to one and all. "He [Webster] walked to and from the Capitol," remembered Congressman John Wentworth, and had a nodding acquaintance with his fellow legislators, but "he never conversed upon personal or local politics" with them. Friendly politicians who never failed to call on Clay when visiting Washington rarely took such liberties with Webster. "But the reverse was the case with the eminent scholars, clergymen, lawyers, and especially capitalists."[12] They invariably paid their respects. Webster "had no hobby, no specialty, no ism upon which you could excite him as you could Clay, Benton, or Calhoun." Everyone treated him "with a sort of reverential awe, and had a hesitancy as to any degree of familiarity." He would "converse in the most friendly manner with all his colleagues" and usually open a conversation by quoting some abstract principle of law or "quote from the old Latin authors. But he could never fully relax with them as he could his family and intimate associates."[13]

The Great Triumvirate therefore was really never more than a glib expression about three totally different, albeit supremely gifted, personalities momentarily united to batter Jacksonianism to the ground. They represented the leadership of a working majority in the Senate. Hence the antiadministration forces were able to control the selection of committee members in the Senate and through the committees control legislation. It was important to make certain that the right people occupied positions on the essential committees, especially Finance, since that committee would deal with the central issue of this session. Clay took a seat on the Public Lands Committee while Calhoun refused any assignment. Webster, on the other hand, actively campaigned for and won the chairmanship of the Committee on Finance. He received twenty-one votes to eighteen for Silas Wright, Jr., a leading member of Van Buren's Albany Regency and an extremely able senator.[14] Added to the Finance Committee were Thomas

11. DW to Biddle, December 19, 1833, ibid., III, 286.

12. "However illiterate a man was, if he was only immensely rich, he would throw himself in Webster's way, seek an introduction, try to cultivate his intimacy, and tender the hospitalities of a magnificent home, if he should ever visit his locality. . . . Looking upon him as the grand conservator of wealth against unfavorable legislation, they did not know how soon they might need his services in the United States Court. And as Webster knew the value of rich clients . . . such manifestations could not be distasteful to him." Wentworth, "Congressional Reminiscences," p. 35.

13. Ibid., pp. 34, 35.

14. There were fives votes scattered among several other candidates.

Ewing of Ohio, Willie P. Mangum of North Carolina, John Tyler of Virginia, and William Wilkins of Pennsylvania, all save Wilkins opposed to Jackson's removal action. Webster admitted to Biddle that there had been some difficulties in arranging committee assignments, "but they were overcome, by mutual & friendly arrangements." Apparently the triumvirate had decided that cooperation, rather than resentment, would better serve their respective purposes.[15]

Webster immediately set about gathering evidence and opinions hostile to the administration's fiscal policy, especially the extent of the authority of the secretary of the treasury and the power of the President to direct the movement of government moneys. He went immediately to Justice Story and his old friend Joseph Hopkinson, both of whom allowed that the secretary had wide latitude in handling public moneys but was also subject to congressional review.[16]

At this crucial point Webster decided to take advantage of his position and obtain from Biddle a renewal of his retainer for services to the Bank. Always in need of ready cash, but mindful that the renewal might have to go before the board of the BUS and thereby attract public attention, he wrote a private letter to Biddle with an enclosure. They read as follows:

Private
Dear Sir,   [December 21, 1833]
    I have thought it proper to write the enclosed letter; to which, however, you need give no attention, if you think it more *prudent* to wait a while. I shall not undertake, professionally, agt. the Bank, whether you answer this or not. If such things have to go before the *Board*, I should prefer the subject to be *postponed.*—Will you tell me whether you apprehend any danger, from my writing to you, on account of infidelity in the P. Office—& tell me, also, if you are careful to burn *all* letters.
Yrs D. W.
[Enclosure]

Sir   Washington Decr. 21 1833
    Since I arrived here, I have had an application to be concerned, professionally, against the Bank, which I have declined, of course, although I believe my retainer has not been renewed, or *refreshed,* as usual. If it be wished that my relation to the Bank should be continued, it may be well to send me the usual retainer. Yours with regard, Danl Webster[17]

    Too much can be inferred from the enclosure. Those historians sympathetic to the administration have tended to do this.[18] It is unlikely that Webster was trying to blackmail Biddle for payment in return for his services in Congress. He had been employed by the Bank as its counsel, but Biddle had failed to indicate that he would be retained. Many of the leading, if not most, congressmen at this time were involved in what modern writers would call conflicts of interest. But

15. *Register of Debates*, 23d Congress, 1st Session, pp. 42–43; DW to Biddle, December 19, 1833, in *PC*, III, 286.

16. Story to DW, December 25, Hopkinson to DW, December 27, 1833, in *PC*, III, 292–296.

17. Ibid., III, 288.

18. Including myself.

Webster himself began putting his "own notions" on paper and arranging to have Taney's report to Congress referred to his Finance Committee for appropriate action. He immediately started work on his committee's response to the report and, in the process, solicited information and help from Biddle and others. Indeed Biddle had a hand in much of what Webster later brought forward from his committee. As a matter of fact Biddle offered his friend an overall battle strategy: Hurry a resolution, any resolution, against removal through the Senate; then send it to the House, and let the House members "talk as long as possible" until "they are forced to act by a pressure from abroad."[27]

This "pressure" would obviously come from all the traders and merchants and businessmen caught in Biddle's financial squeeze. And with each month he tightened his grip. Probably no senator felt the pressure more from his constituents than Webster. He "is the real representative of the great manufacturing and capitalist interests of New England & the North generally," commented Senator Mangum, "and judging from his representations the severe distress, and apprehension of rapidly approaching calamity in some quarters are appalling. I meet with no gentleman who seems so deeply impressed with a sense of impending general disaster."[28]

The calamity could be felt "in the *interior* no less than in the *commercial cities*." Businessmen in New York, reported Alexander Hamilton's son, "are really in very great distress nay even to the verge of General Bankruptcy."[29] Memorials and resolutions flooded into Congress about the financial panic, and delegations waited upon Jackson and pleaded for relief. To each of these delegations, as reported by Webster, the politically shrewd old President answered: "[Go] to the man who sits quietly in his armed chair in Philadelphia—he can relieve you."[30]

One set of resolutions adopted at a public meeting in Boston was read in the Senate by Webster, after which he assured his colleagues that the individuals who had attended the meeting "were neither capitalists, nor speculators, nor alarmists. They are merchants, traders, mechanics, artisans, and others engaged in the active business of life." Then he turned abruptly to Taney's action and the reasons for it. He pointed out that interest rates had risen to 12 percent, twice what they had been last September. And who felt the impact of this increase most? Labor. "Labor, that most extensive of all interests, American manual labor, feels, or will feel, the shock more sensibly, far more sensibly, than capital, or property of any kind." Reiterating a theme he had developed during his western

27. DW to Biddle, January 2, 7, Biddle to DW, January 8, 1834, in *PC*, III, 298–299, 301–302. The appropriations portion of the President's message to Congress and the Treasury report on the state of the country's finances had already been referred to the Finance Committee on December 17 and 18, 1833.

28. Mangum to Duncan Cameron, February 9, 1834, in Shanks, ed., *Papers of Mangum*, II, 75–76.

29. Levi Lincoln to DW, January 11, 1834, in *PC*, III, 306; James A. Hamilton to Van Buren, December 30, 1833, Jacob Barker to Van Buren, February 25, 1834, Jesse Hoyt to Van Buren, January 29, 1834, Van Buren Papers, LC.

30. DW to John Wallace, February 12, 1834, in *PC*, III, 320.

that is not the point. At this juncture Webster had been approached about a legal action against the Bank that he rightly declined since he was the Bank's counsel. However, if he were not going to be retained by the BUS—as was unlikely—then he would be free to take cases involving litigation against it. He simply wanted his position clarified and therefore wrote the letter with its enclosure to Biddle. Admittedly his language was crude, the inference highly suspicious. Instead of asking about his retainer, he might simply have asked if his present relations with the Bank would be continued. But he wanted the money, and since he had not heard about his status, one way or another, he asked for a clarification. No doubt Biddle simply presumed that Webster understood that his position relative to the BUS had not changed. He might even have decided that this was not a good time to talk about it in view of the Bank's present difficulties. In any event he responded as follows:

My dear Sir   Philada. Dec. 25th 1834 [1833]
I of course do not wish to see you engaged against the Bank in any case, and should therefore send the refreshment in question at once. But since you leave it to my discretion, I think it better to delay it for a short time—& for a reason which furnishes perhaps the best illustration of the necessity of abating the nuisance which now annoys us. . . . If it were done by the Board it would be in the hands of the Editor of the Globe in forty eight hours—if by the Officers of the institution, it would not be there for a week—and the fact would be either immediately announced, or it would be treasured up to be used on the first occasion, when any vote of yours gave displeasure to that gang.[19]

Webster's immediate need of cash probably prompted the retainer request. Notes came due on outstanding loans; he had bought out his brother's heirs to the family property in Salisbury, which needed repairs; and he never seemed to pause in the expansion of Marshfield.

Marshfield! It held a special place in his thinking. And it constantly made demands on his pocketbook, thereby necessitating periodic loans to repair and improve the property. "Amidst the toil of law, & the stunning din of politics," he wrote, "any thing is welcome, which calls my thoughts back to Marshfield, tho' it be only to be told which way the wind blows." Despite the scarcity of money presently available because of Biddle's financial squeeze around the country—which Webster hoped would bring down carpenters' wages—he kept improving his estate month after month. He instructed Charles Henry Thomas to go ahead with the building of the barn and shed— "for so much money, we ought to have [it] *well, & nice*." If things were not done properly and according to plan, he warned, "I fear I shall scold." He also directed the erection of a boundary wall— "dont let it be a thin thing"—and the planting of trees; in addition, he wanted certain fields enriched with sea manure such as seaweed and muscle mud dredged from the nearby ocean. To add to his financial obligations, he purchased the deed of additional land adjacent to Marshfield. He also wished to create an oyster pond down at the fish house and told Charles Henry Thomas

19. *PC*, III, 292.

to buy this property if it could be purchased cheaply.[20]

The Atlantic Ocean periodically played havoc with his estate. High tides and storms broke part of the dike protecting his property and required extensive repair. "My Dear Henry, go to work," Webster instructed, "repair, or rebuild, the dyke. If any of the trees are killed, let them die, & set out others. If the English meadow be injured, remedy the injury, as best you may; and guard, as well as you can, against future casualties. . . . Give the Atlantic, then, to understand, that hereafter you do not expect to see its unwelcome & officious waves, overflowing our meadow, interfering with our belt, & spoiling our orchard."

Yet he loved the sea. A woman once asked if he had chosen Marshfield because of its closeness to the sea.

"Yes, madam," he replied.

"And do you love the seashore?"

"Yes, I love it. . . . It seems to speak to me, and beckon to me."

The sea did speak to him, and he to it.

His constant preoccupation with Marshfield can be seen in one instruction he gave Thomas: "Do not omit writing longer than 5 or 6 days, at one time." And to each of Thomas's letters he replied immediately, usually with more instructions for beautifying the estate or improving the operations of the farm. He functioned as though the sums necessary to indulge his interests and taste would always be available to him, one way or another. When they did not readily come to hand, he dunned them from those he believed would understand his needs. "Make yourself easy about the $1000," he told Thomas at this time. "If we cannot get it from Duxbury, we can find it elsewhere."[21]

Webster's financial needs also arose from the "sacrifices" imposed on him by being a member of Congress. "My residence here [Washington] so many months every year greatly increases my expenses, & greatly reduces my income," he complained to Jeremiah Mason. "You know the charge of living here, with a family; & I cannot leave my wife & daughter at home, & come here & go into a 'mess' at 10 Dollars a week."[22]

And of course Webster speculated: in land, in business enterprises of one kind or another, even in gold mines. But his investments frequently turned sour. He brought Texas scrip issued by the Galveston Bay and Texas Land Company in a venture to promote emigration to northern Mexico. The enterprise had been arranged by a group of associates, one of whom was Samuel Swartwout, who, as collector of the Port of New York, had the rare distinction of absconding with more than a million dollars of the government's money and

20. At this time he sent three hundred trees to Marshfield, including dogwood, American limes, glutinous acacias, apple trees and many others. He wanted the various parks, paths, and driveway planted with elms, pines, sumacs, locusts, and catalpas. DW to Thomas, March 14, 25, June 9, 1834, memorandum of real estate 1825–1833, corrected to October 1833, in PC, III, 330–332, 338, 280–281, 349.

21. DW to Charles Thomas, March 25, May 6, 1834, January 5, 1835, ibid., III, 338, 346, IV, 10; Goodrich, Recollections of a Lifetime, II, 415.

22. DW to Mason, February 6, 1835, in PC, IV, 26–27.

then fleeing to Europe when his theft was discovered.[23]

Because of his never-ending financial needs, a group of Webster's wealthy Massachusetts friends periodically established "operating" funds for him to draw against. Thomas W. Ward, for example, suggested that "not less than one hundred thousand dollars" be raised not only to release Webster from the "drudgery of the Courts" so he could better attend their concerns against the expropriatory tactics of the administration but also "to sustain an independent press & circulate information & truth among the people."[24]

For Biddle the absolute need for Webster's goodwill and oratorical talents in support of his Bank forced him to accede to any and all demands from Black Dan—financial and otherwise. So when Webster asked that his retainer b refreshed, the banker responded immediately. And he received excellent servic for his money. He knew the senator would never fail him. "*You must make Speech*," he wrote early in the new year, "one of your calm, solid, stern, wor that crushes, like the block of your Quincy Granite, all that it falls on. I want t Jackson & Taney & Benton & all these people should fall by your hand. I w you to do it for my sake. I wish you to do it for your own."[25]

Clay had already begun the good work of crushing Jackson and Tane bringing to the floor of the Senate on December 26 two motions of censure against the President for his unlawful exercise of power over the Treasur other against his unconfirmed secretary of the treasury for the unsatisf reasons provided Congress on December 3 for the removal of the deposit

Now the battle had been joined, and the life of the BUS hung balance. For the next three months the upper house of Congress witnesse of the most remarkable verbal pyrotechnics in its entire history. Never be since has such an intellectual and oral feast been spread before the p was the Senate's golden age as the Great Triumvirate, in speech after tore apart the President's claim of authority over the Treasury. In the they demanded passage of the censures and the restoration of the During the debate the administration's position was ably defended by Benton and Wright, among others, Benton starting off on January 2 wit day speech that, as usual, virtually shook the walls, so vehement and was his oratory.[26]

Webster smirked as he invariably did whenever the Missouri se an extended speech. Benton, he said, "was much in his usual style. vast many things abt. the Bank—in a very round manner—whic suppose are correct, & which it is yet an infinite labor for a stranger t explain. He is infinitely laborious—always with the documents— eno[ugh] to make the most erroneous statements plausible." In t

23. DW to Edward Curtis, January 30, 1836, ibid., IV, 80. Webster probably purch 1830.

24. Ward to Edward Everett, February 18, 1834, Ward Papers, Massachusetts Hi

25. Biddle to DW, January 8, 1834, in PC, III, 302.

26. Register of Debates, 23d Congress, 1st Session, pp. 97–139.

tour, Webster cited the public works abandoned and the jobs lost as a result of the panic. Confidence had been lost, he continued, and the credit of the entire system of the currency shaken. "The public moneys are now out of the Bank of the United States. There is no law regulating their custody or fixing their place. They are at the disposal of the Secretary of the Treasury, to be kept where he pleases, as he pleases, and the places of their custody to be changed as often as he pleases." The American people, warned Webster, will never tolerate such utter confusion.

What can be done? There were a number of possibilities, he declared. Senator William C. Rives of Virginia recommended that the paper system be scrapped and the country return to an exclusively metallic currency.[31] Or the present BUS could be rechartered, or another bank established. Of course nothing could be done before 1836 unless the present Bank was rechartered, he argued. And something needed to be done. He ended his brief address by repeating that "I am in favor of renewing the charter of the present bank, *with such alterations as may be expected to meet the general sense of the country.*"[32]

Ten days later the Regency's distinguished young senator and great hope for the future Silas Wright, Jr., took the floor and presented a set of resolutions approving Taney's action that had been passed by the New York legislature. Wright's speech was especially important in persuading senators that New York did not wish to see the BUS dead in order to move the financial capital of the country from Chestnut Street in Philadelphia to Wall Street in New York. He said he opposed any bank incorporated by Congress, no matter where its location. Furthermore he contended that all the financial suffering arose not from the removal of public funds but from the murderous squeeze instituted by Biddle in retaliation.

Webster felt obligated to reply to this attack, and he quickly gained the floor and spoke for two days. "The newspapers," wrote Ralph Waldo Emerson, "say they might as well publish a thunderstorm as a report of Webster's speech in answer to Wright. His tones were like those of a commander in a battle."[33]

Webster was particularly incensed by Wright's remark that political ends had triggered the panic, that the opposition had as its prime purpose the defeat of the present administration. "Sir," he snapped, "it is a mistake to suppose that the present agitation of the country springs from mere party motives. It is a great mistake. Every body is not a politician. The mind of every man in the country is not occupied with the project of subverting one administration, and setting up another. The gentleman has done great injustice to the people." Webster was particularly concerned that without the BUS the custody and guardianship of public money would be under "the absolute power" of the chief executive, and the circulating currency left to the mercy of state banks.

31. But Webster doubted there would be much support for this suggestion.

32. *W&S*, VI, 240–249.

33. Ralph Waldo Emerson, *Journals of Ralph Waldo Emerson* (Boston and New York, 1910), III, 255–256.

He was also distressed by the frequent "boast" by Democrats *"that the poor naturally hate the rich."* Sir, he continued, "it shall not be till the last moment of my existence . . . that I will believe the people of the United States capable of being effectually deluded, cajoled, and *driven about in herds,* by such abominable frauds as this." If they do, they will be slaves, slaves to their passions, slaves to the fraud of pretended friends. To conclude his speech, he swung back to a favorite theme and tied it to the supremacy of Congress in controlling the purse:

Sir, the great interest of this great country, the producing cause of all its prosperity, is labor! labor! labor! We are a laboring community. A vast majority of us all live by industry and actual employment in some of their forms. The Constitution was made to protect this industry, to give it both encouragement and security; but, above all, security. To that very end, with that precise object in view, power was given to the Congress over the currency, and over the money system of the country.[34]

This, he thundered, was the crucial point of the controversy: Did the President or Congress have supervision of the country's monetary system? On this ground Webster chose to base his quarrel with Jackson. On this ground he would challenge the authority of the executive. And he knew exactly how to go about it.

On February 4, 1834, he moved, and it was approved, that Taney's explanation of December 3 to Congress justifying removal, along with Clay's resolution that the reasons given by Taney were unsatisfactory and insufficient, be referred to his Finance Committee. And, wonder of wonders, the following day, February 5, he had the committee's report ready to present to the full Senate. Obviously he had been working on the report since December, and he had no trouble convincing the other members of the committee to accede to his arguments. The report was entirely his.

Spectators crowded into the upper chamber to hear the report, no doubt hoping Webster would hurl "oak-cleaving thunderbolts" against the administration. The fact that he had recently provided Jackson with his only strong voice in the Senate over the force bill added to the anticipation and excitement everyone felt. The entire house hushed as he rose to speak.

Unfortunately for those who hoped for something dramatic, Webster gave the report in a straightforward manner with little or no histrionics. He was trying to present a case against the administration, and he wanted logic and facts to dominate the presentation. The report stated at the outset that the right of the secretary of the treasury to remove the deposits was unquestioned but followed it immediately with a declaration that Congress must confirm or reverse the action.

34. *W&S,* VI, 250–269. Rufus Choate was ecstatic over the speech. "Webster spoke . . . in a style of the most vehement impassioned & thrilling eloquence & argument. . . . You can never concieve *[sic]* the energy & fire with which he swept before him the Senate & a crowded audience. . . . Would to God the middling interest of the country—sending politicians to the devil—could hear such an advocate of policy & institutions so vitally essential to them." Choate to [Warwick Palfray, Jr.], January 31, 1834, in *Essex Institute Historical Collections,* LXIX (January 1933), pp. 86–87.

Taney presumes his power is absolute and unconditional, said Webster. It is not. Congress has charge of public money and has directed that it be placed in the Bank of the United States. To remove it without authority from Congress and without just cause thwarts the end and design of the law, defeats the will of Congress, and violates the contract granted the Bank by the government. The committee, Webster continued, believes that Congress never intended to give the secretary the general guardianship of the public money and that his authority is confined to the safety and proper management of the money deposited in the BUS. Taney should have waited until Congress reconvened in order to advise it of his intended action, as required by law. The committee thinks he offered no satisfactory reason for refusing to delay removal and acting so precipitously. No emergency, "no sudden occasion," nothing occurred to justify his taking immediate action.

Webster then took up the separate charges that Taney had leveled against the Bank and one by one dismissed them as untrue, vague, or unprovable. As for the contention that the Bank used public money for political purposes, Webster said it was too general to be proved or disproved. "All must see that charges of this nature are but loose and vague accusations" and can be made at any time by any person. He then hit hard when he stated that "the committee entertains no doubt that the immediate cause of the existing public distress is to be found in the removal of the public deposits, and in the manner in which that removal has been made. No other adequate cause has been suggested." In sum, then, the committee, he reported, regards the removal as "highly inexpedient and altogether unjustifiable."[35]

His listeners regretted the brevity of his remarks but agreed that the report provided as strong a case against removal as could be expected. Not that it influenced Democrats. They intended to block any action that would revive Biddle's "monster," and they expected to get some assistance from Calhoun, who, although he lambasted Jackson as a bully and dictator for removing the deposits, distrusted banks and hoped eventually to see them all eliminated. Like Jackson and Benton, he condemned paper money. To his mind, gold was the only safe and sound medium of exchange. So Calhoun could be discounted in rendering any real assistance to Clay and Webster in defending the BUS. His fury was directed toward Jackson personally, and that was about the extent of his cooperation with the other two members of the Great Triumvirate.[36]

As the debate continued in the following weeks, Webster began to suspect that only a compromise could "stop the mischief" and save the nation's banking system. Biddle's continuing squeeze was beginning to jeopardize the support of the Bank's friends in eastern cities, and Webster feared that it might boomerang on them all. One sign of it occurred in Pennsylvania, where Governor George Wolf, in a message to the legislature, blamed the BUS for the panic. And Boston

---

35. *PS*, II, 5–31.

36. Wiltse, *Calhoun*, II, 225–229. Webster and Calhoun discussed the matter privately, and Calhoun promised not to take the floor in opposition.

businessmen began to show their impatience, which even Biddle could not ignore. For a month or so Webster toyed with the suggestion by Stephen White of the Massachusetts legislature for a new national bank in which the states would have authority to regulate any branch within their borders. He finally decided that perhaps the best solution was to continue the present Bank for three, five, or six years and let Congress devise another one later on after Biddle's charter had expired.[37]

The upshot was an offer to compromise. On March 18 Webster rose on the floor and asked leave to bring in a bill to extend the BUS for six years and to refer it to the Committee on Finance, which would in due course bring it formally to the attention of the entire Senate. He then launched into a extended speech to explain what he was about. He began by praising the nation's commercial credit and the banking system. As governments rise in the scale of liberty, their progress is marked by higher degrees of security and credit, he lectured. "This undeniable truth should make well-informed men ashamed to cry out against banks and banking, as being aristocratical, oppressive to the poor, or partaking of the character of dangerous monopoly." The "history of banks," he continued, "belongs to the history of commerce and the general history of liberty."

A fascinating idea, that. Banks rightfully belong to the history of liberty? According to Webster, they do. They helped raise the middle and lower classes of society, he said, from "the iron sway of the feudal system" to a state of intelligence and property. The future security of these liberated masses of people thereafter depended on "the rule both of liberty and law." The "truth is, that banks, everywhere, and especially with us, are made for the borrowers. They are made for the good of the many, and not for the good of the few." Let us be done with the outcry against the "monster bank." A national banking system is vital to the interests of all. And what a horrible state of affairs the country will encounter when the Bank's charter expires. "Can any thing be more unconstitutional than that?"

So Webster proposed that the BUS be extended for six years but not continued beyond that time. The deposits would be restored by July 1, 1834, and the Bank would pay two hundred thousand dollars for this extension. Then Congress would create a new bank that might overlap with the old. The new bank would not issue notes of any denomination less than twenty dollars—this as a sop to Jackson, who hated paper money. He closed his speech with an impassioned appeal to the American people:

Would to God that I could speak audibly to every independent elector in the whole land! . . . I would say to them, with the sincerest conviction that ever animated man's heart, that their safety and happiness *do* require their own prompt and patriotic attention to the public concerns, their own honest devotion to the welfare of the state. . . . I would

37. *Niles' Weekly Register,* March 8, 1834; Stephen White to DW, January 9, 21, DW to Appleton, February 2, Biddle to DW, February 10, 1834, in *PC,* III, 302–303, 312–313, 318, 315.

say to them, that the Constitution and the laws, their own rights and their own happiness, all depend on themselves; and if they esteem these of any value, if they were not too dearly bought by the blood of their fathers, if they be an inheritance fit to be transmitted to their posterity, I would beseech them, I would beseech them, to come now to their salvation.[38]

This was Webster's first eloquent outburst in the removal debate, and it clearly indicated his great concern over the fearful consequences to follow the termination of national banking. Unfortunately the Senate did not respond as he had hoped. Benton, Wright, and the other anti-Bank Democrats had no intention of extending Biddle's charter, not even for a day. Calhoun went his separate way and talked philosophically about the eventual elimination of all banks. Even Biddle sounded lukewarm to Webster's proposal. He said that on the whole he was "content" with it but suggested changes that would make it more acceptable.[39] Clay, whom Webster might have expected to support his compromise, offered no help, so intent was he on bringing about Jackson's censure. In fact he considered Webster's compromise plan sheer foolishness. The central question, he informed Biddle, "is the usurpation which has convulsed the Country," not an extension of the charter. "The Bank ought to be kept in the rear; the usurpation in front." Perhaps next year would be a better time to push for recharter. So he intervened in the discussion and threatened to table if Webster persisted in going forward with his compromise. The Massachusetts senator therefore reluctantly and angrily withdrew his compromise. "Our friend wants *tone, decision,* and *courage,*" he snapped.[40]

If Clay failed to come to Webster's assistance with his Bank proposal, Webster, for his part, gave Clay precious little help in talking up the vote of censure against the President. He never directly spoke in favor of the censure resolution, although Benton believed that he "aided it incidentally in the delivery of his distress speeches," particularly when he offered memorials from various groups in the country pleading for "the prompt interposition of Congress" to end the financial panic.[41] And it was the censure motion that held the attention of the Congress and the administration. Benton and Clay each struggled to control the final outcome. In speech after speech Clay ranted against the President's wanton exercise of "ruthless, relentless, inexorable power." But Calhoun disagreed about "the usurpation of power"; he regarded Jackson's actions as an abuse, not a usurpation.[42]

Finally, on March 28, action on the censure resolutions came to a vote. Both won approval by substantial margins: The censure of Taney passed by the

38. *W&S*, VII, 82–102.

39. *Register of Debates,* 23d Congress, 1st Session, p. 1073ff; Biddle to DW, March 15, 1833, in *PC,* III, 334.

40. *Register of Debates,* 23d Congress, 1st Session, p. 1113; Remini, *Clay,* p. 455; Webster to Biddle, March 25, 1834, Biddle Papers, LC.

41. Benton, *Thirty Years' View,* I, 418–420, 423.

42. *Register of Debates,* 23d Congress, 1st Session, 718; Benton, *Thirty Years' View,* I, 413–414.

count of twenty-eight to eighteen; the censure of Jackson by the vote of twenty-six to twenty. Among those voting for censure were the Great Triumvirate and their party associates, including such nullifiers and states' rights advocates as Mangum of North Carolina, Tyler of Virginia, Preston of South Carolina, and Waggaman of Louisiana. Clay announced his victory with understandable pride and a great deal of personal satisfaction: "Our majority, on the resolutions which I offered, was as large as I ever expected."[43]

Webster's vote terminated whatever possibility once existed of his cooperating politically with Jackson and the Democratic party. The action by the Senate was personally offensive to the President, and he planned to respond to it. He blamed Clay, of course, for attempting to humiliate him publicly. As for Calhoun, he expected no better. But Webster. That must have hurt, considering his past efforts to attract the senator's support. And Jackson was not the man to take a public insult lightly.

Poor Webster. He felt abandoned by his friends. His efforts at compromise had gained him nothing. His friends, such as they were, deserted him. He felt so alone and so depressed that he left the capital in early April and took off for a short visit home and several speaking engagements in Baltimore, Philadelphia, and New York. His political future at the moment seemed bleak, at least as far as his national ambitions went. His break with Jackson was now irrevocable, and that would not sit well with a vast number of voters who idolized the Hero of New Orleans. So, like it or not, he was stuck with Clay, who had offended him once again, and Calhoun, with whom he fundamentally and philosophically disagreed.

What a group! The Great Triumvirate. Arguably the three greatest Senators in the history of the United States Congress. And they disliked one another, sometimes intensely. All three possessed extraordinary intellectual and legislative talents and had much to offer the American people. All three hungered for the presidency. Unquestionably the history of this nation would have been markedly different if any one of them had achieved it.

43. *Register of Debates,* 23d Congress, 1st Session, p. 1187; Clay to James Brown, April 1, 1834, in Clay, *Papers,* VIII, 710.

25

The Whig Party

WHILE WEBSTER was sojourning at home taking care of some business and giving short speeches about his compromise Bank bill in several places, New York City held local spring elections, in which those opposed to Jackson and his fiscal and administrative policies assumed a new name, a name Webster always insisted his friend Philip Hone invented. They called themselves Whigs. It was an appropriate name because, like their revolutionary forebears, they claimed that they stood for representative government against the autocratic rule of one man. Let the country know our purpose and motivation, declared the New York *American,* one of the first organs of this new party: "The Rescue of the Constitution from hands that are violating it—the resistance and overthrow of *Tory* prerogatives, and an Executive grasping at, and exercising, all powers—these are the aims and motives of the *Whig* party." On the other hand, the Democrats favor "unlimited support of Executive prerogatives. . . . It is therefore most appropriate that they who insist upon curtailing and controlling this prerogative of one man, should take the name of *Whigs.*"[1]

These Whigs won a stunning electoral victory in the election and called a meeting at Castle Garden on April 15 to celebrate it. Thousands were expected at attend for a "triumph second to none achieved since the days of the Whigs of 1776."[2] And who better than the Godlike Daniel to speak to them and help commemorate this stupendous success? Who else could immortalize this proud moment? So Benjamin G. Welles, the chairman of this victory celebration, wrote to Webster and invited him to participate and share his feelings and thoughts about what they had accomplished.

Black Dan declined. Theirs was a local election, he told them, and he did not feel it becoming of him to participate. Besides, "circumstances" (presumably other obligations) were such that he could not attend. However, in his letter he

1. Hone, *Diary,* I, 496, II, 629; New York *American,* April 18, 25, June 3, 20, 1834. On the Whig party, see E. Malcolm Carroll, *Origins of the Whig Party* (Durham, N.C., 1925), Glyndon G. Van Deusen, "The Whig Party," in Arthur M. Schlesinger, ed., *History of U.S. Political Parties* (New York, 1973), I, 333–496); Thomas Brown, *Politics and Statesmanship: Essays on the American Whig Party* (New York, 1985); and Daniel Walker Howe, *The Political Culture of the American Whigs* (Chicago, 1979).

2. New York *American,* May 5, 1834.

chose to state at length his fundamental political creed. "The son of a father, who acted a zealous and patriotic, though humble part, in establishing the independence of the country, I have been educated from my cradle, in the principles of the WHIGS OF 1776. Riper years have enabled me to learn, that in these principles is to be found the source of our own republican liberty, as well as of all that degree of freedom which exists on the other continent."

These principles teach us, he continued, that government is a trust to be administered for the good of all. They also teach that "all political power should be subject to constitutional and legal restraint." Legislators and magistrates are subject to the rule of law and the Constitution. "When Republicans appoint men to office, they are choosing agents, not electing masters. Miserable indeed is the condition of the community, where all power, or any unlimited power, is placed in the hands of one, in whatever form, or for whatever merits, that one may be selected.

"The principles of 1776, further teach us the indispensable necessity of maintaining, in the hands of the immediate representatives of the people, the control over the public revenues. In no country, and at no time, has there been found any other adequate security for liberty than the withholding both the right of taxation and the control of the public treasures from the Executive power."[3]

Obviously Webster's words were conditioned by the immediate political circumstances facing him and his party in the person of Andrew Jackson. In writing this letter, Webster may have remembered back to his first political essay, *An Appeal to the Old Whigs of New Hampshire,* composed anonymously in 1805, when he was twenty-three years of age.

The call to men of all political faiths to join the Whigs in their struggle with Tories attracted Bank men, high-tariff champions, some nullifiers and states' rights advocates, friends of internal improvements, and especially those who abominated Jackson, his policies, and his autocratic style of governing. Farmers, businessmen, merchants, traders, mechanics, and some laborers also embraced the party. Henry Clay in a speech on the Senate floor on April 14 acknowledged the new name for his party. "The whigs of the present day," he cried, "are opposing executive encroachment" and are contending for civil liberty, free institutions, and the supremacy of law and the Constitution.[4]

By the summer of 1834 the term had won national attention. Now all groups opposing Jacksonianism were called Whigs, even though they did not agree on every article of political faith. Some nullifiers and states' rights men like Calhoun and John Tyler might cooperate with the Whigs, vote for and with them, and, in the case of Tyler, accept nomination on the party's national ticket for Vice President, but they would part company with their colleagues on certain sensitive issues, particularly the Bank and the tariff. Obviously the Whig party from its beginning was a party of disparate elements hastily pulled together.

3. Welles's letter and Webster's reply of April 15 can be found in the *National Intelligencer,* April 24, 1834.

4. Daniel Mallory, ed., *The Life and Speeches of Henry Clay* (New York, 1843), II, 194–201.

That it lasted only twenty-odd years was virtually a foregone conclusion.

The Democrats of course jeered the new name of the supposed new party. The Washington *Globe* said the Whigs comprised none but Tories, Federalists, National Republicans, and nullifiers, and by way of "metempsychosis" the "ancient TORIES now call themselves WHIGS." But be not deceived. Their real name is WIG, "a cover for bald federalism."[5]

Webster returned to his seat in the Senate on April 21 in time to take part in the arguments that had developed over Jackson's response to the censure. With the aid of his advisers the President had prepared a Protest message, dated April 15, in which he excoriated the Senate for its insulting and unconstitutional action. He had been deeply offended by the censure, and he accused the upper house of voting on charges of impeachment that properly belonged to the House of Representatives. The Senate claimed he violated the Constitution, an impeachable offense. Such a charge should have emanated from the House, he stormed. He then went on to argue that the appointing power belonged solely to the President, that "every species of property belonging to the United States" fell under the control of officers appointed by the President and removable at his will.[6] Worse, he claimed that he was "the direct representative of the American people" and responsible to them. Unlike the members of Congress, he was elected by *all* the people and served as their tribune.[7]

No President had ever made such claims. None had ever presumed he had a special and unique relationship with the American people. None dared claim that he was the head of the nation.

The message, received by the Senate on April 17, infuriated Webster. It constituted such a monstrous assertion of executive rights and authority that he could not let it go unanswered. Unfortunately he was not present when the message arrived, but Senator George Poindexter of Mississippi rose as soon as the final sentence was spoken and moved that the Protest not be received. Frelinghuysen and Southard of New Jersey and Sprague of Maine supported the motion. Benton, of course, and William R. King of Alabama opposed it.

When Webster and Clay resumed their seats, they immediately took command of the rising vocal chorus denouncing the Protest. The impetuous Clay acted first by introducing a triple-headed motion condemning the President's assertions as a violation of the Constitution, an insult to the Senate, and unworthy to be entered in the *Journal* of the Senate. Among other things, he likened Jackson to Napoleon.[8]

But it was Webster who delivered the crushing oration against the Protest.

---

5. April 21, 22, November 8, 1834.

6. Jackson subsequently issued a supplementary message claiming he had been misunderstood on this point. "I think it proper to state that it was not my intention to deny in the said message the power and right of the legislative department to provide by law for the custody, safe-keeping, and disposition of the public money and property for the United States." Richardson, *Messages and Papers*, II, 1312–1313.

7. Ibid., II, 1289–1311.

8. *Register of Debates*, 23d Congress, 1st Session, p. 1450.

Clay's remarks, although witty and deeply felt, were hastily conceived and sounded as such. His speeches did not have the legal, constitutional, and intellectual weight that Webster could provide. But the "Great Expounder and Defender of the Constitution" needed time to assemble his facts, organize them logically, and then clothe them in oratory that would carry all before him. Webster was so disturbed by the claims of the Protest that he meant this speech to be the effort that Biddle had begged for earlier in the session, a speech that "crushes, like the block of your Quincy Granite, all that it falls on. I want that Jackson [and his minions] should fall by your hand." So Webster labored long hours to provide the crusher, and not until May 7 did he feel ready to address the Senate to deliver his response.

But he paused and thought very carefully about the tone of the speech. In choosing his words, he was constrained by his recent and very friendly relationship with the President. He did not want his crushing block to fall on Jackson personally. He took particular pains to avoid offending the chief executive. He finally decided to separate the Protest from the man. He would praise the man for his past achievements and condemn the message as the work of other men. That he thought he could get away with this appalling bit of sophistry demonstrates a political naiveté that is incredible in a man supposedly experienced in national politics.

Despite the sophistry, if it can be called that, he never spoke with more clarity, precision, and overpowering logic. The depth of strong feelings about the doctrines expounded in the message found imaginative and lively expression as he reviewed the Protest for his audience point by point. A packed chamber listened intently to each word he uttered. And his words were immediately relayed to Jackson, who found them personally insulting. The Hero took exception to any and all criticism of his actions.

Webster started his great speech by acknowledging the President's distinguished services to the country, services that rightly brought him a degree of popularity never equaled or exceeded and "whose honesty of motive and integrity of purpose are still admitted," even by those who now oppose him. Unfortunately his "interference" with the deposits has led to this Protest statement, and it cannot be treated with indifference. We can either accept it and enter it in our *Journal* or answer it, answer it "with the respect due to the chief executive."

He then reiterated the censure motion and admitted he supported it. He acknowledged that by law the secretary of the treasury could remove the deposits, but the paper read by Jackson to his cabinet stated that he took full responsibility for what Taney had done. It was the President's act, and as such it was a violation of law. "At this very moment, every dollar of the public treasure is subject, so far as respects its custody and safe-keeping, to his unlimited control. We know not where it is to-day; still less do we know where it may be to-morrow."

Now, whoever wrote this Protest, Webster continued, argues that the Senate's censure violated the Constitution. In other words, neither house may consider or decide upon official acts of the President without a view to legislation or censure. "This, I think, Sir, is pretty high-toned pretension." The President is saying in effect that the Senate may not hold an opinion or adopt a resolution or consider an act of censure dealing with the President's official conduct. "I know not who wrote this Protest . . . (I wish I did); but whoever he was" did not know what he was talking about. "I confess I am astonished, truly astonished, as well at the want of knowledge which it displays of constitutional law, as at the high and dangerous pretensions which it puts forth." All the Senate did was pass in proper legislative form a resolution giving its opinion of presidential conduct. The resolution did not impute crime, charge corruption, or propose punishment. It was not directed against the President personally but against the act. And that act was "an assumption of authority not warranted by the Constitution.

When this and the other house shall lose the freedom of speech and debate; when they shall surrender the right of publicly and freely canvassing all important measures of the executive; when they shall not be allowed to maintain their own authority and their own privileges by vote, declaration, or resolution,—they will then be no longer free representatives of a free people, but slaves themselves, and fit instruments to make slaves of others.

He followed this by repeating one of his most familiar themes: the division of political power and the need for constitutional restraints. Nothing is more deceptive, he said, or more dangerous than the claim that government must be simplified. "The simplest governments are despotisms; . . . but all republics, all governments of law, must impose numerous limitations and qualifications of authority, and give many positive and many qualified rights." Liberty is jealous of power, jealous of encroachments, jealous of man. It demands checks; it seeks safeguards; it insists on securities.

"It is strange that the writer of the Protest," whoever he was, did not understand that no one contends that *all* legislative power belongs to Congress, or *all* judicial power to the courts of the United States or *all* executive power to the President. It would be "unsafe" to do so. The writer of the Protest claims the appointing power rests absolutely in the hands of the President. "This I do not agree to."[9]

It is interesting that Webster constantly referred to the "writer of the Protest" and pretended he did not know his identity. If that is true, it is very strange because everyone else in Washington knew. Jackson had a Kitchen Cabinet, men like Van Buren, Taney, Kendall, and Blair, among others, and he frequently asked them for assistance in writing his messages. For the Protest message Jackson turned first to Taney and Kendall, but he also invited help from the man whom he had chosen to replace Taney as attorney general, Benjamin F. Butler of New York, one of Van Buren's closest friends and a member of the Albany Regency. It was generally understood that Butler, a distinguished jurist, contrib-

9. *PS*, II, 34–57. The speech can also be found in *Register of Debates*, 23d Congress, 1st Session, pp. 1663–1690, and *National Intelligencer*, June 7, 1834.

uted the greatest amount to the Protest. Jackson had taken violent exception to the censure, labeling it a vile attempt to "degrade the Executive in the minds of the people and destroy the confidence of the people in him, and thereby procure a re-charter of the Bank of the U.S." Because of his strong feelings about censure, he wanted an equally strong protest against it. And he made certain that he got it.[10]

So in thinking he could escape Jackson's displeasure by his pretense not to know the real author of the Protest, Webster was sadly mistaken, especially when he went on to attack the very heart of Jackson's extravagant claims about his relationship to the American people, something Old Hickory held very dear.

"But, Sir," Webster continued, "there is, in this paper, something even yet more strange than these extraordinary claims of power. There is a strong disposition, running through . . . [it that the President is] the peculiar protector of the public liberty. . . . Sir, I deny the proposition, and I dispute the proof." Please remember against whom the President holds his "peculiar duty." Not against a foreign foe, *"but it is against the representatives of the people and the representatives of the States!"*

Such a claim is preposterous, Webster contended. Throughout history the great enemy of liberty has been the executive power. It has always been dreaded as the chief source of danger to public liberty. "And now, Sir, who is he, so ignorant of the history of liberty . . . that declares to us, through the President's lips, that the security for freedom rests in executive authority?" Webster made it sound as though Jackson were a mere dummy, mouthing words put there by someone else.

At this point the senator seemed visibly angry. His voice grew louder. His gestures became more frequent. Who is he that charges the representatives of the people with the "insanity" or the "recklessness of putting the lamb beneath the lion's paw[?] No Sir. No, Sir," he roared. "Our security is in our watchfulness of executive power." We want an effective executive but not a dangerous one. We want one that is "efficient, independent and strong," not one that will use the military, the patronage, favors of various kinds and party to serve personal ends. "I will not trust executive power, vested in the hands of a single magistrate, to be the guardian of liberty."

Sir, we have but one executive officer. "A Briareus[11] sits in the centre of our system, and with his hundred hands [in the various departments] touches every thing, moves every thing, controls every thing. I ask, Sir, Is this republicanism? Is this a government of laws? Is this legal responsibility?"

If what the writer of this Protest says is true then, sir, "the President of the United States may well repeat from Napoleon what he repeated from Louis the Fourteenth, 'I am the state.' "

Again and again the Protest repeats that the President is responsible to the

10. Jackson to Kendall, April 1834, de Coppet Collection, Princeton University Library; Remini, *Jackson,* III, 152.

11. A hundred-handed giant in Greek mythology.

American people. For whatever he does, he assumes accountability to the people. And this is thought to be sufficient for a republican government, "an undefined, undefinable, ideal responsibility to the public judgment!"

I shall never agree to this, Webster stormed. "There is, there can be, no substantial responsibility . . . but *to the law.*"

Connected with this "airy and unreal responsibility to the public" is another sentiment: *"that the President is the direct representative of the American people."* Now, sir, this is not the language of the Constitution. Nowhere does it call him the representative of the people. He is not chosen directly by the people but by electors, some of whom are selected by the people but some of whom are appointed by state legislatures. The Constitution calls the members of the lower house of Congress representatives. It simply calls the chief executive the President of the United States. Nobody else presumes to represent *all* the people. If Jackson can call himself the "SOLE REPRESENTATIVE OF ALL THE AMERICAN PEOPLE . . . then I say, Sir, that the government . . . has already a master. I deny the sentiment, therefore, and I protest the language." Neither can be found in the Constitution. If the leading propositions put forward by the Protest message be true, then we are living in an elective monarchy.

Webster ended as he began, by exonerating Jackson from the intolerable statements in the Protest. "I have desired to say nothing that should give pain to the chief magistrate personally," he insisted. "I have not sought to fix arrows in his breast; but I believe him mistaken, altogether mistaken, in the sentiments which he has expressed." Webster knew how accurate his arrows had been in finding their mark, but he maintained throughout his speech that he meant Jackson no personal disrespect.

He concluded with another ringing declaration that brought the audience to its feet with a thunderous round of applause:

> In my judgment, the law has been disregarded, and the Constitution transgressed; the fortress of liberty has been assaulted, and circumstances have placed the Senate in the breach; and although we may perish in it, I know we shall not fly from it. But I am fearless of consequences. We shall hold on, Sir, and hold out, till the people themselves come to its defense. We shall raise the alarm, and maintain the post, till they whose right it is shall decide whether the Senate be a faction, wantonly resisting lawful power, or whether it be opposing, with firmness and patriotism, violations of liberty and inroads upon the Constitution.[12]

This splendid reaffirmation of Webster's republicanism in an oration of such conviction and logical power never achieved the popularity and renown of his other great speeches, most notably his second reply to Hayne and his Bunker Hill address. Although it is a worthy successor to these other important utterances, there are several reasons to explain why the public did not respond favorably to it. First off, despite Webster's many disclaimers, he was attacking the most popular man in America, Andrew Jackson, the Hero of the Battle of

12. *PS,* II, 58–71.

New Orleans. Also, he was denouncing principles about the headship of the government that the people had begun to accept. They liked the idea that the President served as head of government, was responsible to their will, and acted as their tribune. Through him they felt a closer relationship to government. As far as they were concerned, Webster's speech did not gloriously trumpet such important issues as the nature of the Union, nationalism, and the splendor of their republican system. It was simply an attack on a beloved President.

But those who abominated Jackson's presidential methods and claims joined Webster and echoed his criticism. They labeled Jackson a Tory despot and reveled in their new party name. "We can hardly yet believe . . . that any Chief Magistrate of this—republic?—could have dared to issue such a paper," snarled the Whig press. "Democracy now means approbation and unlimited support of Executive prerogatives. What is this then but *Toryism*, as originally understood under the Stuarts? It is therefore most appropriate that they who insist upon curtailing and controlling this prerogative of one man, should take the name of *Whigs*."[13]

But Webster's distinguished speech seemed to elevate him higher above other critics. The thirty-one-year-old Ralph Waldo Emerson declared him "a true genius. . . . Long may he live."[14] And Jackson's newspaper, the Washington *Globe* on May 12 credited him with a position and leadership role that he did not rightly deserve. "The speech of Mr. Webster against the Protest," wrote the editor, Francis P. Blair, "places him at the head of the self-named *Wig party*. He has thrown Mr. Clay and Mr. Calhoun entirely into the background. They must hereafter be considered *'the lesser lights'* in the galaxy of disinterested worthies who maintain the cause of Bank power."

The effectiveness of the many speeches by the Whig leaders, but more particularly the numerical strength of the opposition to the administration in the Senate, resulted in the approval of the motion against receiving the Protest. This "fixed majority of twenty-seven," as Benton contemptuously termed it, did not wish the Protest recorded in the Senate *Journal* because, as he said, it would provide "strong evidence against themselves" that they had in fact acted unconstitutionally. It so offended him that he swore "irrevocably" to bring about the expunging of the censure motion, no matter how long it took.[15]

The Whigs completed their string of victories over the President when at long last he submitted Taney's name to the Senate for confirmation. The following day, by the vote of twenty-eight to eighteen, the upper house rejected it.

Democrats were furious. The *Globe* claimed that the Whigs meant to *"Crucify him"* but that he would rise again. His successor, the editor predicted, will be just as steadfast in opposing the Bank as Taney, for the President will entrust the department to *"none other."* Almost immediately Jackson forwarded the

13. New York *American*, April 18, 22, 25, June 3, 20, 1834.
14. Emerson, *Journals*, III, 308–309.
15. Benton, *Thirty Years' View*, I, 427–433.

name of Levi Woodbury of New Hampshire to take Taney's place, and the Senate unanimously confirmed him on June 29.[16]

Although the Whigs scored much-needed but useless triumphs over Jackson in censuring him, refusing to accept his Protest, and rejecting Taney as secretary of the treasury, the Democrats in the House of Representatives, where they held a majority, fielded victory after victory in the war against the BUS. On April 4 they passed a series of resolutions stating that the Bank ought not to be rechartered, or the deposits restored, and that the state (pet) banks should continue to receive the government's money. In addition, they called for an investigation of the BUS, chose a committee that included Edward Everett,[17] and charged it to find out whether it had deliberately triggered the financial panic.[18] Webster immediately wrote to Everett and said that "if, in the course of your investigations, the committee should incline to notice my name," please assure the members "on my authority, that I never had any particular or unusual accommodation from the bank to the amount of a single dollar." Webster felt vulnerable on this point, as indeed he should have, and he begged his friend to protect him.[19]

Fortunately for Black Dan, Biddle defiantly refused to testify before the House investigating committee or permit access to the Bank's books or its correspondence with members of Congress relating to personal loans. "Of one thing I am certain," he told Webster, "that if nothing is done this session, we shall have a summer and fall such as have not often been experienced. The B.U.S. will be able to stand the squall—but I really fear that the country will suffer deeply— you and I have done what we can to prevent it & therefore will have nothing to reproach ourselves with."[20]

The subsequent report of the committee concluded that the Bank was guilty of precipitating the panic, a conclusion that drove the final nail in the BUS coffin. "The Bank is dead," declared the new attorney general. Indeed. The board of directors of the Bank then ordered Biddle to end his financial squeeze, and he reluctantly complied.

Biddle's very ruthlessness killed the institution. He succeeded in convincing the American people that he exercised irresponsible financial power. He proved to the people, said Senator William C. Rives of Virginia, "never again to give themselves such a master." Even the business community turned against him. And Jackson gloated. "I have obtained a glorious triumph," he gleefully informed his friend John Coffee.[21]

16. *Globe*, June 24, 25, 30, 1834.

17. Of the seven-man committee, two were Whigs: Edward Everett and William W. Ellsworth of Connecticut.

18. *Register of Debates*, 23d Congress, 1st Session, pp. 3474–3477.

19. DW to Everett, April 26, 1834, in *W&S*, XVIII, 6.

20. Biddle to DW, May 15, 1834, in *PC*, III, 347.

21. Rives to Levi Woodbury, May 26, 1834, Woodbury Papers, LC; Jackson to John Coffee, April 6, 1834, Coffee Papers, Tennessee Historical Society.

The Senate undertook a separate investigation. On June 30 Senator Samuel L. Southard of New Jersey introduced a motion that the Finance Committee continue to sit during the summer and fall and find out whether the Bank had in fact violated its charter and instigated the panic. The resolution passed, twenty to twelve, with the investigating team consisting of Webster as chairman and Ewing, Mangum, Tyler, and Wilkins. The committee spent some time in Philadelphia, but Webster hardly participated. He was known publicly as a very active friend of the Bank, so he tried to keep a low profile. Still, he did help shape the final report, written mostly by Tyler, which naturally approved both the operations and policy of the BUS. It was submitted at the next session of Congress in December, but its effect was virtually nil. It influenced no one and changed nothing.[22]

Webster's long association with the Bank began to produce rumbles that could have a disastrous effect on his presidential plans. Stories were reported and quotations manufactured that put the senator in an extremely unfavorable light. One expression attributed to him was regularly repeated and would not go away, and the Portland *Argus* decided to print it. Said Webster, according to the *Argus:* "Let Congress take care of the Rich, and the Rich will take care of the poor."[23]

James Brooks immediately relayed the news report to Webster who promptly replied to it. It is an "utter falsehood," he assured Brooks. Claiming he had no idea about its origin, he swore that he had never said anything remotely like it, publicly or privately, or anything that might give "the least countenance or color to such an imputation." He then proceeded to state his precise position.

. . . For the last twenty years, on all suitable occasions, I have endeavored to maintain, as great and leading political truths, that Republican Constitutions are established for the benefit of the whole People, and that all measures of government ought to be adopted with strict regard to the greatest good of the greater number; that the Laws should favor the distribution of property to the end that the number of the very rich, and the number of the very poor, may both be diminished, as far as practicable, consistently with the rights of industry and property; and that all legislation in this country is especially bound to pay particular respect to the *earnings of labor;* labor being the source of comfort and independence to far the greatest portion of our people.[24]

Webster had genuine concern for labor. Whenever he spoke about maintaining "the cause of American Capital, American industry," he always followed up by insisting that "more than all *American labor*" needed protection.[25]

With his reputation among Whigs expanding daily with the circulation of his response to Jackson's Protest message, Webster did not need this kind of story to circulate as the time grew near for his party to begin thinking of its

22. *Senate Journal* 23d Congress, 1st Session, Serial 237, pp. 391–392.

23. *National Intelligencer,* August 16, 1834.

24. DW to James Brooks, August 5, 1834, in *PC*, III, 359.

25. See, for example, his undated memorandum in Van Tyne, ed., *Letters of Webster,* p. 183.

nominee for the next presidential election. So he had the Washington *National Intelligencer* print his letter to Brooks in its August 16 issue.

The expression attributed to Webster is undoubtedly a fabrication. But the sense behind it was real enough to cause many people to believe it. At heart Webster believed that property must be protected at all costs, and he no doubt relied on the beneficence of the wealthy to do their Christian and moral duty by the poor. His statement to Brooks when published may have had some effect among Whigs, certainly not among Democrats. But the expression periodically popped up to haunt him for the rest of his life.

One other tricky financial matter awaited the Finance Committee before the adjournment of Congress, and that involved the coinage of money. Jackson's hard-money policy—he wanted only gold and silver specie to circulate—had two strong advocates in Benton and Calhoun. But the amount of gold in the country had been depleted because of an unfavorable ratio with silver. A number of Boston and New York businessmen petitioned Webster to do something about it. The House passed a gold coinage bill on May 28, Webster reported it out of his committee, with some amendments, on June 14, and it passed easily on June 28. But Clay opposed the bill and with six others voted against it, while both Webster and Calhoun voted for it. The Gold Coinage Act of 1834 essentially changed the ratio of gold to silver from fifteen to one to sixteen to one which the Jacksonians hoped would usher in a currency consisting entirely of hard money. Webster knew better, but he decided that prudence dictated that he not get in the way.[26]

With the congressional session rapidly drawing to an end, Webster was anxious to get back to Marshfield. He had hoped to get home in time to escort his thirteen-year-old son, Edward, to Exeter, where he would begin his new studies. Unfortunately the length of the session—it did not end until June 30—kept Webster in Washington, and he passed on the chore to Fletcher. "It is high time he was at school," the father wrote. He asked Fletcher to take the trouble to attend to Ned's "personal cleanliness." Enjoin on him, he instructed, the importance of "exact & steady habits." Give him a little pocket money, and tell him that an allowance will be sent each month. Stay in town with him a few days "until he has been at school once or twice, & begins to feel a little at home."[27]

To date Ned's performance in school had been less than satisfactory. On one occasion he brought home a report card with "23 marks for *misdemeanors,*" Caroline Webster informed her husband, and she had "given him a long lecture. He says that his marks are for trifles."[28]

Now the boy was headed out of state to continue his studies and the father decided to give him a lecture of his own.

26. Benton, *Thirty Years' View,* I, 469.

27. DW to Fletcher Webster, June 5, 1834, in *PC,* III, 348.

28. Caroline Webster to DW, December 31, 1832, in Van Tyne, ed., *Letters of Webster,* p. 584.

You are now at a most important period of your life, my dear son, soon growing up to be a young man and a boy no longer, and I feel a great anxiety for your success and happiness.

I beseech you to be attentive to all your duties, and to fulfill every obligation with cheerfulness and punctuality. Above all, remember your moral and religious concerns. Be constant at church, and prayers, and every opportunity for worship. There can be no solid character and no true happiness which are not founded on a sense of religious duty. Avoid all evil company and every temptation, and consider that you have now left your father's house and gone forth to improve your own character,—to prepare your own mind for the part you are to lead in life. All that can be done for you by others will amount to nothing unless you do much for yourself. Cherish all the good counsel which your dear mother used to give you, and let those of us who are yet alive have the pleasure of seeing you come forward as one who gives promise of virtue, usefulness, and distinction. I fervently commend you to the blessing of our Heavenly Father. . . . Your affectionate father, Daniel Webster[29]

Webster also had advice for Fletcher, who, having completed his work at Harvard, was now studying law with Samuel B. Walcott and was subsequently admitted to the bar in 1836. At your age, the father informed his son, "I . . . studied nothing but law and politics. I wish you to take the same course." Also, you should "cultivate liberal knowledge; it will turn to account, even practically." He then explained the meaning of "honest quackery" and how valuable it could be. On almost any subject, he added, "I wish I had more knowledge than I possess, seeing that I could produce it, if not for use, yet for effect."[30]

When the congressional session finally ended, Webster was detained in the capital because he still had legal business with commissioners dealing with American claims of his various clients against foreign nations. Then other financial matters delayed him in Philadelphia and New York so that by the time he reached home in Boston—around the middle of July—he was fairly exhausted. He remained in Boston for a good part of the summer thinking and planning the ways in which he might win the nomination of the Whig party for President of the United States. He truly hoped—indeed he had every expectation—that the moment of triumph he had desired for years was imminent.

29. DW to Edward Webster, June 23, 1834, in PC, III, 351–352.
30. DW to Fletcher Webster, January 15, 1836, in ibid., IV, 75–76.

26

The Presidential Nomination

D URING the summer of 1834 several of Webster's friends started serious work on building an organization to support his developing candidacy for the presidency. Caleb Cushing, a state representative from Newburyport, and Rufus Choate, congressman from Salem, began negotiations with John Sargent to purchase control of the Boston *Atlas* and convert it into Webster's mouthpiece for the direction of Whig politics in Massachusetts. The senator needed the kind of publicity and attention that only a first-rate, intelligently edited newspaper could provide, and both Cushing and Choate believed they had the man who could do the job in the associate editor, John O. Sargent, who would replace the more independently minded Richard Hildreth. "He is young, but manly," Cushing assured Webster, "intelligent, & in every respect, as it seems to me, such as we could desire. . . . He enters, heart & soul, into all our hopes & wishes." With Choate's concurrence, Cushing continued: "I pledged our friends to two things: 1. indemnity. 2. any requisite intellectual aid, without limitation of quantity or form." We will settle the matter in late August.[1]

To help Webster provide this press with all the material necessary for a campaign, Cushing offered whatever service his friend thought would help advance his candidacy. "Please consider my pen at your command, for whatever may be deemed within my competency," he declared. He was particularly concerned about the *Atlas*'s past opposition to candidates enjoying Anti-Masonic support, especially Edward Everett, and he hoped Webster would approve his action in remedying the situation.[2]

Webster replied that he "rejoiced" to know that his friends had begun a campaign on his behalf, urging that Cushing and Choate "carry thro' the arrangement" of acquiring the *Atlas,* placing Sargent "as the effective head, hereafter," and approving their actions in putting the paper "under new influences" with respect to Everett. "I could not, & would not, unjustly disregard his feelings, for the sake of any object, political or person[al]." Webster felt it absolutely necessary that the Anti-Masons and Whigs join forces in opposition to the

1. Cushing to DW, August 9, 1834, in *PC,* III, 361; Claude M. Fuess, *Caleb Cushing* (Hamden, Conn., 1965), I, 168–171.
2. Cushing to DW, August 10, 1834, in *PC,* III, 361–362.

Democrats, and he wanted no action taken that could jeopardize such a union. He told John Quincy Adams that "his own impressions upon Masonry . . . had always been unfavorable; said his father had always disliked the institution, and had brought him up in the dislike of it." He even wrote the governor, John Davis, and expressed the hope that the Anti-Masons would support his [Davis's] reelection since he had supported the law to abolish future secret oaths.[3]

So the arrangements were carried forward, the money was obtained—the Boston Associates had committed themselves to supporting Webster for the presidency as early as 1834[4]—and the *Atlas* became the first important beam in the Webster campaign structure. The next step necessitated acquiring additional newspaper support by winning commitments from Whig editors of the several states in all the sections of the country. A good place to start was Ohio and Pennsylvania because of Webster's recent tour, so on August 20, 1834, Edward Everett, Abbott Lawrence, Rufus Choate, Warren Dutton, and Franklin Dexter addressed a circular letter to John Woods, the Whig editor of the Hamilton, Ohio, *Intelligencer*, inviting him, as a "defender of the Constitution," to come out in favor of Webster's candidacy. They also solicited aid from other Whig editors in Ohio and Pennsylvania. Later Webster himself prodded his friends about working up support in Pennsylvania. In particular he asked Edward Everett to write to Elihu Chauncey, an influential Philadelphia financier and lawyer, "to see if he cannot move the Pa. *press*, more or less, to be breaking ground."[5]

James Watson Webb, editor of the New York *Courier and Enquirer*, found himself in deep financial debt and asked Webster for assistance, offering in return his newspaper's endorsement of the senator's candidacy. Webster agreed to help if Webb could not raise money any other way. Not much later the editor received assistance from Roswell L. Colt, a New York banker, a director of a Baltimore bank, and Webster's close friend. By the following February the *Courier and Enquirer* was actively engaged in advancing the senator's candidacy.[6]

One supporter in Alabama wrote Webster directly and urged him to tour the South in the fall. " Things in this quarter," he said, "promise the happiest results from such a step." Many in the South strongly favored the Union and were "ashamed of Jackson misrule" but could never vote for Clay because of the "Bargain & Sale" charge. They also could not abide Van Buren, the supposed Democratic candidate because of his reputation as a devious and unscrupulous politician. That left Webster. But southerners did not know the Massachusetts senator, the writer explained, despite his reputation "as the first among American Senators." A "visit from you at the present juncture would stir public opinion & occurrence would spring a breeze and a strong and lasting one in your

3. DW to Cushing, August 13, 1834, DW to Davis, August 14, 1834, in *W&S*, III, 362, XVI, 242; Adams, *Memoirs*, IX, 71.

4. Dalzell, *Enterprising Elite*, p. 180.

5. DW to Everett, [January 7, 1835], in *PC*, IV, 12.

6. Webb to DW, January 20, DW to Webb, January 22, Webb to DW, January 25, 1835, *Microfilm Edition*, F10/12235, 12241, 12251.

favour."[7] Unfortunately Webster's legal commitments kept him from taking another tour. Besides, it might appear as campaigning, and that would never do.

But Webster did accept an invitation in September from his native state to attend a dinner to honor Senator Samuel Bell. If he could consolidate the votes of Massachusetts and New Hampshire, it would form a solid base from which to obtain the votes of all the other New England states. "I do not know how it is," he remarked to one friend, "but the older I grow, the stronger are my attachments to the place of my nativity. I would do more to set New Hampshire right than to change twice her number of votes in any other state."[8]

The possibility of building a electoral majority in 1836 appeared brighter to Webster when Maryland, in the fall state elections, provided the Whigs with a stunning victory. Unfortunately this early success was not repeated in other middle Atlantic states. Still, Webster kept up his hopes, particularly when he heard from supporters in the West that his recent tour had produced a strong hold on "the confidence and affections of the People." His Cincinnati speech was "spoken of as a master piece." One westerner wrote: "My first and most ardent wishes are for your success—next the defeat & overthrow of the Heir *adopted* [Van Buren]."[9]

But some states in the West had already started looking at another candidate. With Clay seemingly out of contention—and he made no move to solicit a nomination—the associate justice of the Supreme Court John McLean of Ohio indicated his willingness to become a candidate. This was not the first time he had appeared ready to run, only to step aside at the last minute. At this juncture he seemed prepared to go the distance, and before the end of the year a rump caucus in Ohio officially nominated him.

Other sections besides the West suddenly became politically active. In Tennessee a group led by "John Bell, Davy Crockett and Company," in open defiance of the President's wishes that Van Buren obtain the Democratic nomination, put forward a favorite son, Hugh Lawson White, one of Jackson's old friends and confidants who had recently broken with the President. The Whigs of course encouraged this rebellion in order to strip Van Buren of southern support. "The idea that he [White] is popular in the south," admitted Major Andrew Jackson Donelson, the President's ward and private secretary, ". . . was well suited to the taste of Whigs and Nullifiers."[10]

It soon appeared that a great number of Whigs had suddenly decided on pursuing the self-defeating "strategy" of encouraging as many states as possible to nominate favorite sons in order to throw the election to the House, where they presumed they had a better chance of winning the presidency. It would mean that the race could become a three-way or four-way contest and end up,

7. Edward Gazzam to DW, September 20, 1834, in *PC*, III, 364–366.

8. Plumer, "Reminiscences of Webster," in *W&S*, XVII, 559.

9. John Barney to DW, December 7, 1834, in *PC*, III, 373–374.

10. Donelson to Edward Livingston, April 13, 1835, Livingston Papers, Princeton University Library.

like 1824, in the House of Representatives. And because of this so-called strategy, they opposed holding a Whig national nominating convention.[11] Besides, they feared a free-for-all among the friends of Clay, Calhoun, and Webster at a convention that could tear the party apart. "We are commencing a singular schism," said the bemused Churchill C. Cambreleng, a New York congressman and one of Van Buren's closest allies: "—the prostrated condition of the opposition—. . . they must now I think divide—Clay and Calhoun will try and keep together and Webster will probably hang himself on his own hook—They are talking of Judge White or of any body against Van Buren but its idle work—the battle has been fought and won, thanks to the able tactics of the triumvirate."[12]

All this, but especially the decision not to hold a convention, guaranteed defeat for the Whigs. The party could not hold at the center. In fact it was not a national party at all, at least not yet.[13]

The fact that southern Whigs began uniting behind Senator White caused Webster considerable anguish. "Another Richmond is in the field . . . in the person of Hugh Lawson White," he complained. "This worthy senator has been so true to his chief, in all & singular his measures, ends & aims, that report goes that it perplexes the occupant of the White House to decide between the Rival claims." He told Edward Everett that "howsoever the Jackson jugglers may conduct their own nomination, the duty of Whigs is plain." They must support a Whig, a genuine Whig, not a Democrat soured on the President. Webster also thought that those newspapers favoring his nomination ought to make this point absolutely clear to the public: that Whigs "will support a Whig, & none but a Whig."[14]

The initial thrust in proposing Webster's candidacy came in the August issue of the *New England Magazine,* which carried an unsigned article written by Joseph Story entitled "Statesmen—Their Rareness and Importance." In the article Story provided a glowing account of Webster's political career, and the implication was clear that in Webster the nation would find a President who was a true statesman.[15]

But not until December 17, 1834, when the *Atlas* declared formally in his favor, did the earliest organized presidential propaganda on his behalf begin to appear. The people had become impatient, the paper editorialized, for a genuine antiadministration candidate, "the BEST AND STRONGEST CHAMPION OF THEIR PRINCIPLES," one who was committed to the cause of the Constitution "in its original purity" and would fight the battles of the Constitution. The paper

11. For details, see Remini, *Jackson,* III, 182, 252ff, 272, 331.

12. Cambreleng to Livingston, December 11, 1834, Livingston Papers, Princeton University Library. See also Henry W. Kinsman to DW, January 18, 1835, Webster Papers, New Hampshire Historical Society.

13. Richard P. McCormick answers his own question "Was There a 'Whig Strategy' in 1836?," *Journal of the Early Republic,* IV (Spring 1984), pp. 47–70, by arguing that there was no strategy because there was no national Whig party.

14. DW to Edward Everett, [December 8, 1834], DW to Everett, [December 8, 1834], in *PC,* III, 374–375.

15. Story, *Life and Letters,* II, 171–172.

dismissed all the other possible candidates: White and Calhoun could hardly call themselves Whigs, McLean lacked national support, and Clay had had his chance in 1832 and muffed it.

On whom then shall the choice fall? Who, under all the circumstances should be the candidate of the great WHIG PARTY ? We answer without a thought of hesitation—that man is DANIEL WEBSTER. He stands before the country with the highest claims in its favor and rewards. He stands before the friends of the Constitution, as the ablest expounder and champion of that sacred charter. He stands before the friends of free principles, as the advocate of liberal opinions—as the ardent zealous, consistent advocate of freedom—at home and abroad—in the struggling nations of Europe—in the devoted republics of South America—wherever Liberty could get a foothold, and raise her voice and banner to the people. . . .

Why then may we not unite, in the support of a man like WEBSTER, the full strength of the friends of the Constitution? It is time that the Whig candidate should take the field. Why should the friends of Mr. Webster throughout the country delay any longer to present his claims to his fellow citizens?

Sargent notified Webster of his declaration. "We have taken the field," he said, and high time. It was advisable to do this before the Massachusetts legislature convened in order to pressure it into nominating the senator. "We propose to follow up this matter immediately; and are desirous to communicate by letter with such of your friends as you may designate in other parts of the country."[16]

So the campaign for Webster's election to the presidency began. And it was a tough, uphill battle all the way. Already there was talk of a fourth candidate to oppose Van Buren: General William Henry Harrison, who had won the Battle of Tippecanoe over the Shawnee Indians in 1811. As it turned out, he, rather than McLean, became the favorite western candidate now that Clay was out of the picture. And despite what some of his correspondents told him, Webster was not popular among westerners. He was simply not their sort. Not democratic enough, too elitist in sentiment. Although Clay preferred Black Dan over the other possible candidates, he too recognized that his quondam friend and ally lacked substantial support in his section of the country. Westerners might very well go for Harrison, Clay declared. "He is weak, vain, and far inferior to Webster, but I believe him to be honest and of good intentions." That plus his military record made the big difference among westerners.[17]

Clay finally decided that there had to be two Whig candidates for President, one to win northern and western votes, the other to capture southern votes. Only White could embody "southern views, interests and feelings," and it galled Clay to think that the Whig party would have to rely on him instead of someone with more orthodox Whig views. To win northern and western states, on the other hand, one of the candidates had to be Harrison, maybe Webster, or possibly McLean. In the long run Clay thought that Pennsylvania would decide among these three who would be the so-called northern-western candidate. It

16. Sargent to DW, December 17, 1834, in *PC*, III, 380.

17. Clay to Southard, April 12, July 31, 1835, Clay to Christopher Hughes, August 25, 1835, in Clay, *Papers*, VIII, 778–779, 782–784.

was the "keystone state," he said. As it turned out, the Pennsylvania Whig convention endorsed Harrison.[18]

By the beginning of the new year it had become obvious to everyone, especially Webster, that Massachusetts had to put his name forward immediately. On January 1 he wrote to his friend Jeremiah Mason, and although he feigned disinterest—"I cannot say that I have any personal wishes about it"—he stated emphatically "that if Massachusetts is to act at all, *the time has come.*" Not only should it be done "as soon as practicable," but "in the mean time notice of the intention should be given to friends in the neighboring States, and especially in New York, that they may prepare for it."[19]

There was of course strong support in the Massachusetts legislature to vote a nomination, but there were some who feared that Webster might be a weak candidate and who therefore believed they should hold off and see who all the other candidates might be and then make a final selection. Some even hoped that Clay would change his mind and run, but on December 26 the Kentuckian asked that his name be withdrawn from all consideration. As Caleb Cushing said, the Massachusetts legislature would definitely and "cordially make a nomination." Even so, he wanted to be sure it was done "handsomely and con amore." Abbott Lawrence agreed, but he worried that Webster might then resign his Senate seat. He personally opposed such a move—"it would be unequivocally a national calamity"—and strongly implied that if money was a problem to keep the senator in place, another fund could be raised by his friends. Jeremiah Mason also wanted Webster to stay put and told him that a resignation would look like "false delicacy." Besides, "if the election is to be finally determined in the House of Representatives, the presence of a candidate at Washington, without exerting any improper influence, will be advantageous."[20]

Webster had no intention of resigning. He just wanted his friends to get on with his nomination. "There has been some impatience here," he snorted, to hear what is going on in Boston so that our "friends in other quarters" might know how to proceed.[21]

As a matter of fact Webster's friends in the legislature were proceeding with as much dispatch as prudence would allow. They checked with Governor John Davis and found him totally supportive; letters were written to the Whig members of the Massachusetts delegation in Congress for their consent, although Mason did not think they could wait for a reply since that might entail an interminable delay. Also, a preliminary meeting of legislators was held on January 16 to be sure the nomination would not run into any last-minute hitch. Only one member objected to calling a general meeting on January 21 to make the nomination.[22]

18. Remini, *Clay,* p. 479.

19. DW to Mason, January 1, 1835, in *PC,* IV, 5.

20. Cushing to DW, January 3, Lawrence to DW, January 5, Mason to DW, January 8, 1835, ibid., IV, 8–9, 11, 13–14.

21. DW to Mason, January 22, 1835, ibid., IV, 17.

22. Mason to DW, January 8, Cushing to DW, January 16, 1835, ibid., IV, 13, 14.

Finally on the scheduled day a caucus of the Massachusetts legislature unanimously nominated Daniel Webster to run for the presidency of the United States. Notices went out to the press and the leading politicians in Congress. The Boston *Advertiser,* edited by Nathan Hale, immediately announced its support along with other important Whig journals. The impatient Webster breathed more easily when he received the news, and of course he hoped that it would inspire other Whig candidates to step out of the way and produce a national "outbreak" of support on his behalf. He also anticipated an endorsement from Clay.

None of these things occurred. All the announced candidates remained in place, Clay said nothing, and the nation at large failed to respond as he had expected. If anything, the opponents of Democratic rule throughout the country seemed intent on having the election decided in the House of Representatives.

Still, Webster and his friends kept hoping for the best. After all, compared with the other announced candidates, White, McLean, and Harrison, Webster clearly possessed superior intellect, talents, and experience. Obviously he was a statesman. None of the others could claim that distinction.

In addition, it was anticipated that New England, if not most of the East, would support him. Pennsylvania and New York were considered vital. Surely Pennsylvania would remember his labors during the Bank War, and New York, despite the Van Buren influence, had regularly shown enthusiasm for him whenever he spoke in the state. Besides, his wife's family had many connections in the Empire State and could exercise valuable influence among important Whigs. Maryland was also presumed to be a sure bet for his candidacy. It could provide 10 electoral votes, New York 42, and Pennsylvania 30 for a total of 82. Adding Massachusetts would raise it to 96. The rest of New England had 36 electoral votes, which could bring the total to 132, with 147 votes necessary for election. If he swept New England—"Pray remember the importance of R.I.," Webster instructed one friend[23]—and these other states, he would still be shy 15 votes. He would have to pick them up from other middle Atlantic states or the West. Little hope existed for winning southern votes. Finding the 15 votes in the West was a long shot at best, but Webster thought he must try. "The *Schism* in the Jackson party proceeds. It appears [to] me, that nothing is likely to stop its progress. If we *Whigs* had union & energy, we have now before us a prospect, no way discouraging."[24]

Although everyone took pains to express his admiration for Webster's enormous talents and services to the nation, a great many Whigs had their doubts about his ability to win the election. And they said so openly. Democrats agreed.

Indeed, even before he was nominated, the Democratic press, sensing his imminent nomination, had begun to attack. The Albany *Argus,* the organ of the

23. DW to Everett, May 1, 1835, in *PC,* IV, 44.
24. DW to Jeremiah Mason, January 22, 1835, in ibid., IV, 17.

Regency, led off on December 10 by printing an anonymously written letter from Washington in which Webster was accused of having a financial interest in an important measure pending before Congress.

The charge claimed that the senator had received twenty thousand dollars from an agent involving payment of claims for French spoliations prior to 1800. But the bill then before Congress was a request from President Jackson for passage of a law authorizing reprisals against French property in the United States if France continued to stall on paying claims arising during the Napoleonic Wars[25] as stipulated in a convention between the two countries signed on July 4, 1831—in other words, claims that occurred much later than 1800. What the senator had received had nothing to do with what Congress debated after it reconvened in early December.

Webster had already returned to Washington for the start of the short session of the Twenty-third Congress when the anonymously written letter appeared in the *Argus*. The New York *Evening Post* reprinted the charge, which fueled popular belief that Webster cared nothing for ordinary citizens and consorted only with the rich and those who could financially benefit him. James H. Causten, the agent mentioned in the accusation, immediately wrote a letter to Gales and Seaton, the editors of the *National Intelligencer*, and stated unequivocally that "no such arrangement, nor any other arrangement has been made between Mr Webster & myself. . . . I feel it a duty, not only to Mr W & myself, but to the claimants also, thus to declare the falsehood of the statement in the Albany & N York Papers." Interestingly this letter was written in Webster's hand. The editors published it on December 18, 1834. Meanwhile Webster asked an intermediary to query the editor, Edwin Croswell, about who had written the anonymous letter. Croswell refused to identify the writer but confirmed that he was a member of Congress (possibly Cambreleng?). Causten surmised in his diary that the culprit was Senator Benton.[26]

Not satisfied with Causten's first letter, Webster asked him to write a second, and he did. Causten claimed he wanted "to shield Mr. Webster and to shield myself." But Webster returned it with the remark that it was "too long." He enclosed a draft of the kind of letter he wanted, which Causten dutifully copied and signed. But the draft was "made to shield himself only," complained Causten, "leaving myself and the cause without notice. It was a selfish and heartless act on his part—and I take no credit to myself for yielding to the modification. It was not my judgement, but sound policy that thus yielded."[27]

Incidents like this added to Webster's growing reputation as one who used people for his own purposes and did not hesitate to discard them if necessary. In awkward or embarrassing situations he could not be trusted to protect his friends or supporters.

25. Mainly claims resulting from Napoleon's Berlin and Milan decrees.

26. Causten to Gales and Seaton, December 16, 1834, DW to Daniel Barnard, December 19, 1834, in *PC*, III, 377–378, 383.

27. Causten to DW, January 1, 1835, DW to [Causten], no date, ibid., IV, 6–8 with notes.

On January 12, 1835, Webster spoke in support of a bill for payment of claims for French spoliations *prior* to 1800 but prefaced his remarks with a denunciatory attack on the charges brought against him, labeling them "false and malicious." The *Argus* subsequently apologized to Webster and admitted that the author of the anonymous letter had confused claims prior to 1800 with those covered under the Convention Treaty of 1831.[28]

The new bill for claims prior to 1800, for which Webster spoke so ardently, reignited charges from the opposition that he and Causten were speculating in the claims. No doubt the charges were true in part, but Webster denied them. Most probably he expected to get a hefty piece of the legal action should the bill be approved.

As it turned out, when the French finally paid twenty-five million francs in spoliation claims for property taken or destroyed during the Napoleonic period,[29] Webster represented many American claimants before the Spoliations Commission. These claims ran in excess of one hundred thousand dollars for which he received 5 percent as an average commission.[30]

His connection with spoliation claims, his speculations, his financial dealings of one kind or another, his association with banking interests, and his presumed involvement in the Hartford Convention during the War of 1812 all came to the attention of the public through the obliging agency of the Democratic press. To counter these accusations, friends in Massachusetts undertook the task of writing replies and corrections. Webster himself was asked to help in the endeavor. He told his old college friend James Bingham that with respect to the Hartford Convention "I had no hand or part whatever." It was true, he conceded, that he advised the then governor that it would be unwise to appoint delegates to the convention, a statement that could not be documented. "Further than this I have no recollection of interfering in the matter. At the same time, it is true that I did not regard the proposed convention as seditious or treasonable."[31]

Not unexpectedly, Webster was also asked for his opinion on slavery. In response to the steady increase of antislavery feeling in the North, the American Anti-Slavery Society had been established in 1833. In addition, race riots broke out and became a frequent occurrence in the Jacksonian era. In August 1835

28. *Register of Debates* 23d Congress, 2d Session, pp. 162–178; *Niles' Weekly Register*, January 31, 1835.

29. It took warlike threats from Jackson and his statement that he did not intend to threaten the French to bring about a settlement and avert possible conflict. A full account of the crisis with France can be found in Remini, *Jackson*, II, 286–289, III, 201ff, 230ff, 274ff. Webster identified three separate groups on the "French question": the "very warlike," such as Jackson; the southern anti-Jackson men, who "speak of the whole matter as a *debt*, and recommend an action of assumpsit, instead of war"; and "then there is the rest of us, who desire to say & do nothing to encourage France, in her neglect of our rights, & who are not willing, nevertheless, to hazard the peace of the Country, without absolute necessity." DW to William Sullivan, February 23, 1835, in *PC*, IV, 32.

30. Editor's note, in *PC*, IV, 6.

31. DW to Bingham, August 24, 1835, in ibid., IV, 50.

rioting occurred in the nation's capital, and Washington verged on total disorder.[32]

Early on Webster publicly revealed his position on slavery, which *Niles' Weekly Register* had published on June 29, 1833.

In my opinion, the domestic slavery of the southern states is a subject within the exclusive control of the states themselves; and, this, I am sure, is the opinion of the whole north. Congress has no authority to interfere in the emancipation of slaves, or in the treatment of them in any of the states. . . . The servitude of so great a portion of the population of the south, is, undoubtedly regarded at the north, as a great evil, moral and political; and the discussions upon it, which have recently taken place in the legislatures of several of the slave-holding states, have been read with very deep interest. But it is regarded, nevertheless, as an evil, the remedy for which lies with those legislatures themselves, to be provided and applied according to *their* own sense of policy and duty. The imputations which . . . are constantly made against the north, are, in my opinion, entirely destitute of any just foundation. I have endeavored to repel them, so far as has been in my power, on all proper occasions.

Now in 1835 Webster was being asked again to state his views on the subject, and he carefully referred inquirers to his 1833 letter and his remarks in Congress during his debate with Senator Robert Y. Hayne in 1830.[33] But for many abolitionists his statements sounded tame and conventional and not at all what they expected from the Godlike Daniel.

Senator William C. Preston, perhaps as a jest, toasted Webster as "A Northern man with Southern principles!" Webster turned the accusation aside with the light stroke of humor. "Well, sir, I was born in New Hampshire, and therefore I am a northern man. . . . And if what the people say of us be true, it is equally certain that I am a man of southern principles. Sir, do I ever leave a heeltap in my glass? Do I ever pay my debts? Don't I always prefer challenging a man who won't fight?"[34]

Caleb Cushing, soon to begin his own congressional career, perhaps worked hardest in providing propaganda on all manner of subjects for the Webster candidacy. "I am collecting material for a magazine analysis & possibly pamphlet, on your speeches &c during & connected with the war," he informed Webster. "Mr Mason has told me that there was a proceeding of yours in New Hampshire in reference to this matter, advantageous to be used; & this prompted me to ask you, at your leisure, to indicate to Mr [Richard] Fletcher or to me, where to find any particulars to my purpose." In the meantime Cushing had prepared a laudatory article entitled "Mr. Webster," which appeared in the March 1835 issue of the *New England Magazine.*[35]

32. See Michael Feldberg, *The Turbulent Era: Riot and Disorder in Jacksonian America* (New York, 1980) and Leonard L. Richards, *"Gentlemen of Property and Standing": Anti-Abolition Mobs in Jacksonian America* (New York, 1970).

33. DW to James Longue, November 21, 1835, in *PC*, IV, 65–66.

34. Goodrich, *Recollections of a Lifetime*, II, 417–418.

35. Cushing to DW, January 16, 1835, in *PC*, IV, 15. Cushing may have been referring to a document issued by the Portsmouth Committee of Defense, which Webster chaired.

From Washington Webster did his best to encourage his friends, provide them with important, relevant material for their propaganda, seek support in other states, and spur the Democrats into developing their *"Schism."* He also regularly attended the Supreme Court. He infuriated Jackson when he led the opposition to the President's nomination of Roger Taney for a seat on the Court, replacing Associate Justice Gabriel Duvall of Maryland, who had resigned. It is possible that Webster himself might have been nominated to the place had he not veered away from an alliance with Jackson. Now he stood in the Senate prepared to block Taney's confirmation.

"I am busy in the Court,"[36] he informed Jeremiah Mason. "Mr. Taney is yet before us. *Probably* will not be confirmed; but that is not certain." What Webster planned to do was introduce a judiciary bill that would unite Delaware with Maryland and attach them to Justice Henry Baldwin's Third Circuit Court and then create a new circuit in the West, presumably with a new western judge. "Five Judges will do very well for the Atlantic States," he noted.

He hoped this scheme would attract favorable attention in the West and needed support for his candidacy.[37] Furthermore, to advance his search for western backing, he considered another tour "as far at least as Ken. & Indiana. I am fully persuaded it would be a highly useful thing." His friends, he said, urged him to do it, and the only difficulty was his reluctance to devote six weeks to it once the session ended.[38]

While involved in these behind-the-scenes and eventually unsuccessful manipulations to establish a new circuit court, Webster also involved himself in the election of Massachusetts Governor John Davis to the Senate seat being vacated by Nathaniel Silsbee, who had chosen not to run again. It was important to Webster that his colleague in the upper house follow his direction, and Davis seemed to be a man he could rely on. Despite strong support for John Quincy Adams in the lower house of the Massachusetts legislature, Webster derailed Adams's election through his many contacts among the most important legislators. As a result Davis took Silsbee's seat and Edward Everett, endorsed by both Whigs and Anti-Masons, was elected governor. It pleased Webster that the *Atlas* gave Everett strong support in the election. Everett reciprocated by helping line up the remnants of the Anti-Masonic party in the country, especially Pennsylvania, behind Webster's presidential campaign.[39]

But Webster's "connivance" in the Senatorial race totally fractured his relations with Adams. "The difference between Mr. A. and Mr. W. is very unfortu-

36. He was busy with *Charles River Bridge v. Warren Bridge.*

37. DW to Mason, January 22, February 1, 1825, DW to Warren Dutton, January 30, 1835, in *PC*, IV, 17, 24, 26. Jackson nominated Taney on January 15.

38. DW to Mason, February 6, 1835, ibid., 27. He also considered a tour of the South.

39. Samuel F. Bemis, *John Quincy Adams and the Union* (New York, 1956), pp. 313–314; Darling, *Political Changes in Massachusetts*, pp. 184–185; Fuess, *Webster*, II, 40–41; Private and Confidential Letterbook of Edward Everett, MHS. Everett later regretted that he had ever allowed Webster to talk him into involving himself in the "coarse violence" of "party contests." But he did it now and later, when Webster asked him to become U.S. minister to England, in order to "promote Your [Webster's] Service." Everett to DW, July 6, 1846, in Van Tyne, ed., *Letters of Webster*, p. 332.

nate," wrote Everett. "It originated in misinformation and exaggeration; was aggravated by third persons, who had private griefs to gratify against Mr. Webster. . . . Mr. A's feelings toward him are, I fear, irrecoverably alienated."[40]

While his friends in Boston worked out the details of winning Davis's election to the Senate, Webster kept trying to generate national interest in his candidacy. He worked hard to convince the electorate that he was the candidate who could best defend the Constitution against corruption and was its "ablest expounder and champion." To that end he was determined to defeat Taney's nomination to the High Court. He also regularly participated in Senate business and conducted his usual legal duties a floor below in the Supreme Court. He was so busy in the final months of the short session that when asked about taking on additional casework, he swore he would have to "leave off saying 'Mr President,' [in the Senate] or leave off saying 'May it please your Honors.' "[41] He simply could not keep up doing both.

On January 6, 1835, Calhoun offered a resolution to inquire into the extent of executive privilege, and the Senate passed it. A committee was formed with Calhoun as chairman and Webster and Thomas Hart Benton as members. A month later the committee reported its findings, and not unexpectedly it uncovered practices and problems that outraged many senators. As a result legislation was proposed to limit executive authority. Calhoun and Benton clashed repeatedly on the floor in a two-day debate, and then on February 16 Webster added his sentiments.

"Mr. President," he began, "the professed object of this bill is the reduction of executive influence and patronage. I concur in the propriety of that object." The extent of the President's power of appointment and removal was so great, he continued, "that it brings a dangerous mass of private and personal interest into operation in all great public elections and public questions. This is a mischief which has reached, already, an alarming height." Under Jackson the power of the executive branch had been increased to such an alarming extent that unless Congress exercised its powers of control, the President would function, to all intent and purposes, as a dictator. See what happened when Jackson dismissed the secretary of the treasury for refusing to remove the deposits in accordance with the presidential will. The country was beset with crisis and turmoil. This house had tried to block the action but could not. Under Jackson the President had assumed unconstitutional powers and even claimed to be the sole representative of all the people.

Webster then attempted to prove through a logical progression that the Founders of the nation had intended to link the Senate with the removal power. It was a stunning intellectual exercise. He was heroic in his efforts, however much he failed to achieve his goal. "Sir," he said, "I think the whole matter is sufficiently plain. Nothing is said in the Constitution about the power of removal,

40. Everett to H. Denny, October 20, 1835, in Private and Confidential Letterbook of Edward Everett, MHS.
41. DW to William Sullivan, February 23, 1835, in PC, IV, 32–33.

because it is not a separate and distinct power. It is part of the power of appointment. . . . It belongs to it, is attached to it, forms a part of it, or results from it.

If this be true, the inference is manifest. If the power of removal, when not otherwise regulated by the Constitution or law, be part and parcel of the power of appointment, or a necessary incident to it, then whoever holds the power of appointment holds also the power of removal. But it is the President and the Senate, and not the President alone, who hold the power of appointment; and therefore, according to the true construction of the Constitution, it should be the President and Senate, and not the President alone, who hold the power of removal.[42]

Much as Webster was respected for his knowledge and defense of the Constitution "in its purity," the American people in the long run would not accept this limitation on their popular President. Jackson continued to exercise the sole power of removal and established the practice, once and for all, that the power resides exclusively in the executive office. The Senate was totally cut off from it.

Although Webster's speech impressed many Americans—Emerson said it was "a fine, wise, oratorical scream" with "real passion"—Representative John Quincy Adams thought his "reasonings so utterly ignorant or unprincipled, that they provoked my anger, and I answer them with cutting sarcasm." Clearly Adams had been deeply hurt by what Webster had done to him, and at this session and in the following Congress he rose on several occasions in the House to heap "sarcasm" on something Webster had said in the Senate. He was intent on revenge, however petty, for Black Dan's interference in the Senatorial election.[43]

To annoy President Jackson even more, the Senate killed the Taney nomination. It waited until the last day of the session—March 3—to take any action. So great was Jackson's anticipation that he sat in an antechamber in the Capitol until 1:00 A.M. on Wednesday, March 4, to sign last-minute bills being hurried through Congress. The Senate postponed Taney's confirmation, an act tantamount to rejection, by passing a bill reducing the size of the Supreme Court from seven to six members. But the House refused to go along, and the bill failed. When the secretary of the Senate brought the President word of what the upper house had done, Jackson threw down his pen, muttering that it was past midnight and that he would sign no more legislation from a gang of scoundrels. He rose from his chair and stormed out of the building.[44]

So the session ended on a quarrelsome note. Webster relayed all this to the editors of the *National Intelligencer,* who used it for an article that appeared on March 10.

Webster remained in Washington a few additional days after the session ended to attend to his court case. Then he went on a short campaign swing through western Pennsylvania, a state he absolutely had to win if he expected to

42. *Register of Debates,* 23d Congress, 2d Session, pp. 458–470.

43. Emerson, *Journals,* III, 455; Adams, *Memoirs,* IX, 226.

44. Carl Swisher, *Roger B. Taney* (New York, 1935), p. 314; *National Intelligencer,* March 10, 1835; DW to [Gales and Seaton], [March 8, 1835], in *PC,* IV, 36.

gain the White House. He canceled the idea of a western trip as well as one to the South. He wooed the Pennsylvania state legislators in Harrisburg and party leaders in Lancaster, where he was tendered a public dinner. He also huddled with Biddle and other supporters in Philadelphia, trying to figure the best strategy to win the state's favor. "Friends in Philadelphia," he advised Everett, "suggested the importance of the expression of opinions, by local meetings, as often as convenient; as such things usually get into circulation, and are more ready than mere paragraphs. . . . I have seen a meeting called in Franklin Co., Mass; & it has occurred to me that it might be well for you to write a line to Mr. [George] Grennell," the local Whig congressman.[45]

He briefly stopped off in New York, where his newfound publisher friend James Watson Webb assured him that "I have embarked in the contest with all the ardour necessary for success, and under the fullest persuasion that if New England and the Middle states & part of the West will as truly discharge their duty to you and the Country, as the South & South-west will to Judge *White* Van Buren can never succeed."[46]

On his return to Boston in mid-April Webster continued to solicit support by attending a celebration to honor the Battle of Lexington and hear Everett orate at length on the sixtieth anniversary of the great event. Ralph Waldo Emerson, who heard the oration and pronounced it a good one, observed that Everett "is not content to be Edward Everett, but would be Daniel Webster. This is his mortal distemper. . . . Daniel Webster, Nature's own child, sat there all day and drew all eyes. . . . Webster spoke at the table few and simple words, but from the old immoveable basis of simplicity and common natural emotion to which he instinctively and consciously adheres."[47] At the same time Perkins, Marvin and Company published a two-volume edition of the senator's *Speeches and Forensic Arguments*, which was carefully distributed throughout the state.

In May his wealthy friends presented him with a fifteen-hundred-dollar vase in appreciation for his many services to the nation, state, and community—as well as to their personal interests.[48] Then, in the fall, the citizens of Boston gave him a massive silver vase for his efforts over the years in defending the Constitution.[49] There was no doubt that he had Massachusetts's vote locked up, but the rest of the country remained in serious doubt. "In truth," he admitted to Senator Southard of New Jersey, "we are rather waiting for manifestations elsewhere. Friends here are ready to act, with as much zeal & spirit as their neighbours; but they think there is a want of *decision*, in other quarters."[50]

What particularly disturbed him was the candidacy of Hugh Lawson White, who by this time was running as a Whig candidate and receiving consid-

45. DW to [Everett], April 2, 1835, ibid., IV, 38–39.
46. Webb to DW, April, 1835, ibid., IV, 42.
47. Emerson, *Journals*, III, 471.
48. *Niles' Weekly Register*, May 23, 1835.
49. The proceedings of the presentation can be found in Webster, *Works*, I, 319–336.
50. DW to Southard, April 28, 1835, in *PC*, IV, 42–43.

erable support from southern Whigs and nullifiers. White's candidacy convinced Webster that Van Buren would be elected President, and "by a vast majority." The Richmond *Whig* and the *United States Telegraph*, edited by Calhoun's close friend Duff Green, "have endeavored to persuade the People that the question is narrowed down to a choice between Judge White & Mr. Van Buren," as though Webster counted for nothing, not to mention General Harrison and Justice McLean. And the Washington *National Intelligencer* chose not to declare for any candidate. The editors might at least "preach the necessity of supporting *a* Whig Candidate—*some* Whig Candidate," grumbled Webster. The paper ought to be "our natural field marshall [*sic*]." Unfortunately it seems at present to be without "object, end, or aim." "For my part, I confess, it looks to me as if the whole Whig strength in the Country was either to be frittered away, or melt into the support of Mr V. Buren." And how can the country be spared this disaster? "If the Country is to be saved, My Dear Sir," he told Southard, "it must be by an undeviating adherence to the Constitution. . . . We must go for the *whole* Constitution, & for men who will support the *whole* Constitution."[51]

Webster and his friends hoped eventually to work up a ticket of himself as the presidential candidate and General Harrison as the vice presidential candidate. But these efforts—newspaper articles calling for such a ticket and Fourth of July toasts to the Webster-Harrison combination in various Massachusetts towns—failed to ignite any interest in the Harrison camp.

Webster also headed for Maine to argue a case before the U.S. circuit court and find supporters for his presidential bid. The citizens of Bangor naturally tendered this distinguished celebrity a large public dinner, where he exhibited once again his extraordinary speaking talents. It is doubtful, however, that his speech gained him many votes. People loved to hear him orate, but they chose to cast their votes for someone else.[52]

Then Webster's candidacy received a mortal blow when Pennsylvania Whigs refused to endorse him. Webster and Everett had been working assiduously in winning over the Pennsylvania Anti-Masons, especially those who agreed with Webster that Anti-Masons should unite with Whigs to defeat the Democratic ticket.[53] But they failed in their efforts. Ironically they won over a faction of Anti-Masons known as Exclusives, like Thaddeus Stevens,[54] who wanted to remain independent of the two major parties. But the rest of the Pennsylvania Anti-Masons, who favored cooperation with the Whigs, known as Coalitionists, opted for Harrison, and at a joint caucus held in mid-December they cleverly arranged the overwhelming nomination of General Harrison. Old

51. DW to Southard, April 28, DW to Biddle, May 9, 12, 1835, ibid., IV, 42–43, 44–45.

52. His short address on the occasion can be found in Webster, *Works*, I, 311–315.

53. See Harmar Denny to DW, November 5, 11, DW to Denny et al., November 20, 1835, in *PC*, IV, 57–60, 61–62, 64.

54. At first Stevens opposed Webster, but he reversed himself when he read several statements by Webster supporting Anti-masonic principles. Unfortunately Stevens's support caused Governor-elect Joseph Ritner to throw his influence behind Harrison since Stevens had opposed Ritner's nomination for governor. Henry Clay may also have urged Ritner to support the general. Brown, *Webster and the Politics of Availability*, pp. 140–141.

Hickory had proved the value of military glory in a political campaign, and the Whigs and Coalitionists of Pennsylvania chose Tippecanoe in the hope that he could repeat Jackson's triumph.[55] Even Biddle deserted "the Godlike." And as Clay had said earlier, as Pennsylvania goes, so goes the northern Whig nomination.

None of this made any sense to Webster. His reputation as a statesman far outdistanced anything Harrison had achieved, on or off the battlefield. As recently as December 2 the *National Intelligencer* had published Caleb Cushing's flattering biography of him, which highlighted all of the senator's great achievements, paying special attention to his role in the War of 1812, his skill in the *Dartmouth College* case, and his magnificent defense of nationalism against nullification in the Webster-Hayne debate. Furthermore, Webster had achieved a far superior record on Anti-Masonry than his rival. As a matter of fact Harrison had foolishly written a letter to the chairman of the state Anti-Masonic committee declaring that he was "not informed of the principles which govern the anti-masonic party of Pennsylvania, otherwise than that they are opposed to masonry." Anti-Masons found the letter offensive, and it should have done him in.[56] But it did not, and the action baffled and troubled poor Webster when the Anti-Masons nominated his rival. The senator could not understand that local politicians did not see in him a candidate who could attract the votes of the masses. Quite the contrary, he was viewed as aristocratic and antidemocratic. With Webster they would lose both the local and national elections. With Harrison they had a fighting chance to win.[57]

Webster had returned to Washington for the start of the Twenty-fourth Congress when he received the devastating report from Pennsylvania. The news left him shakened and embittered. Then and there he should have thanked his friends and notified the Massachusetts legislature that he had decided to withdraw from the contest.

But he did not. He could not. Instead he decided to stick it out. He desperately wanted to be Jackson's successor.

Nor did his friends wish him to withdraw. "Some of Mr. Webster's friends in Massachusetts are mad," commented Duff Green's *United States Telegraph,* "mad with man worship; mad with slavish devotion to the 'god-like man.' "[58]

---

55. Charles Snyder, *The Jacksonian Heritage: Pennsylvania Politics, 1833–1848* (Harrisburg, 1958), pp. 65–70; Nathans, *Daniel Webster and Jacksonian Democracy,* pp. 97–98; Brown, *Webster and the Politics of Availability,* p. 140.

56. *Niles' Weekly Register,* November 14, 1835.

57. One delegate tried to explain to Webster what had happened. "All agree," he wrote, " 'Mr. Webster is my first choice,' but we cannot carry him. Why? It seems strange that he who is the *first choice* of every one should be *less* popular than the man who is only the *second choice,* & confessedly his inferior. Ah, but he was a Federalist? Damning sin! Never to be forgiven. But he was opposed to the war! Let no statesman or patriot hereafter, dare to interpose his voice to save his Country from the Horrors of war!" Charles Miner to DW, December 17, 1835, in *PC,* IV, 73–75.

58. Quoted in Joel Silbey's, "The Election of 1836," in Schlesinger, and Israel, eds., *History of Presidential Elections,* I, 585–586.

27

A Humiliating Defeat

WEBSTER and his New Hampshire friend William Plumer were walking together one moonlit night around the Capitol building, enjoying each other's company and conversation, when suddenly Webster burst into an impassioned monologue about his "aspiration after glory." Without glory, he said, life was "not worth possessing." Petty struggles of the day did not particularly interest him, he went on, except when they provided "the opportunity of saying or doing something, which would be remembered in after time."

Plumer listened and smiled.

"You laugh at me, Plumer!" Webster remarked. "Your quiet way of looking at things may be the best, after all; but I have sometimes such glorious dreams! And sometimes too, I half believe that they will one day wake into glorious realities."

They continued walking—"he musing on schemes of ambition, and labors of immortality—I on the duties of a humbler, but not unhappy life."[1]

This conversation had occurred several years earlier, but Plumer recorded them during the 1836 presidential election. Webster's ambition for the presidency reminded Plumer of their walk and conversation. Webster did indeed have glorious dreams, but like those of many people, they were mostly for and about himself and his passion for immortality.

The action of the Pennsylvania Whigs pretty much convinced him that his glorious dreams would not become reality at this time, particularly after the Maryland Whigs also nominated Harrison in late December. He sat in his Senate seat brooding about his "bad luck." He spoke little in debate, declined invitations for supper, and just sat by the fire at night, trying to comprehend the course of events. His wife, Caroline, had chosen to remain in Boston during this session, and her absence and that of his daughter, Julia, did not help his spirits. "I have not been out—have invited no company—& occupy myself with common Congress matters," he told his wife, "& with some preparation for the Court— . . . though in the Court, I have not a great deal to do this year, & wish I had less." On top of everything else he caught a bad cold that lingered for more than a month. "My cold is getting better," he reported in early February, "so that I go

1. Plumer, "Reminiscences of Webster," in *W&S*, XVII, 560.

[to] the Senate, in fair weather, but I am obliged to be very careful. I have not been to an evening party, this winter—& only once to dine."[2]

Then on January 22 he suffered a brutal personal attack on the floor of the House from his earlier ally former President John Quincy Adams. Webster had opposed an appropriation for a fortifications bill on January 14 because there was no real danger of war and because it would place a large sum of unrestricted money in the President's hands. Even if the enemy had landed on our shores, he said, and were battering down the walls of the Capitol, he would vote against the bill. The preservation of the Constitution meant more to him than forty Capitols.[3]

It was a stupid speech and indicates his distressed, not to say disturbed, mental condition at the time. He left himself wide open for the drubbing he received a few days later.

And Adams administered it. He had the opportunity he had long been waiting for, and he savored every minute of the three hours it took him to deliver his "deadly thrust." Several times he was interrupted by the chair for his references to the actions of the upper house, but the Democrats cheered him on. Then he closed in for the kill. Only one step more was necessary, he declared, for the men who refused an appropriation if the enemy were at the gates of the Capitol. *"I say, there was only one step more, and that a natural and an easy one—to join the enemy in battering down these walls."*[4]

The House went wild. Shouts, whistles, applause, and hisses echoed around the chamber. The Whigs sat stunned by the vehemence of Adams's attack. The Democrats laughed and applauded and told the dour New Englander what a splendid speech it was. A great many others thought it a notable effort by a man not generally credited for his oratory. Thereafter he was known as "Old Man Eloquent."[5]

Adams took great satisfaction in noting in his diary how he "demolished the speech of Webster, drove him from the field, and whipped him." To his mind Black Dan had delivered "a desperate and furious, yet insidious and crafty, onset upon my character."[6]

Webster was shocked. "The House, I understand was disgracefully disorderly, on Friday," he wrote his wife, "& when Mr Adams abused *me* well, some of the members, I believe principally those from the State of New York, *clapped him*—& then the galleries hissed." Webster told the recently inaugurated Governor Everett that the Massachusetts delegation in the House demonstrated feelings "of *the deepest indignation*." Adams will now become, he predicted, a

2. DW to Caroline Webster, December 23, [1835], February 9, [1836], in Van Tyne, ed., *Letters of Webster*, pp. 197, 203.

3. *Register of Debates*, 24th Congress, 1st Session, pp. 148–163.

4. *Register of Debates*, 24th Congress, 1st Session, p. 2270; Bemis, *John Quincy Adams and the Union*, pp. 322–323.

5. *Register of Debates*, 24th Congress, 1st Session, p. 323.

6. Adams, *Memoirs*, IX, 339.

"political vagrant," wandering from party to party, seeking a place to settle. "But you will think I, too, am angry, & warm. Not so. I keep cool. I certainly feel great contempt for Mr Adams, & have been obliged to form very bad opinions of the qualities of his heart, but I do not intend to be betrayed into any warmth. . . . I will leave him, in other hands, at least for the present."[7]

To top off all these unpleasant incidents and disappointments, President Jackson, on December 28, 1835, formally nominated Roger B. Taney to succeed Chief Justice John Marshall, who had died on July 6, 1835.

Taney chief justice! What a wretched appointment for such an important office! What an affront to the Senate! Well, Taney might be nominated, but that did not spell confirmation. Not while Webster could prevent it. Then, when Jackson nominated Philip P. Barbour of Virginia to succeed Justice Gabriel Duvall of Maryland, who had resigned, it became clear that an entirely new, "Jacksonian," court was in the offing. If confirmed, Taney and Barbour would be the fourth and fifth justices to be appointed by Jackson, in a court of seven. And if McLean persisted in his presidential candidacy, he might provide Jackson with a sixth appointment. What a disaster that would be! Although not a member of the Judiciary Committee, Webster had to prevent these nominations from winning Senate approval. To help him, the Senate Judiciary Committee, on January 5, 1836, recommended that the nominations lie on the table.

What made the possibility of killing these appointments problematical at this time, despite the action of the Judiciary Committee, was the fact that the political complexion of the Senate had changed since the last Congress. The administration's numerical strength had grown in the upper house as a result of state elections. Connecticut, Illinois, and Louisiana replaced three senators who had died or resigned, and each of the new senators proved unswervingly loyal to the administration. In Mississippi the Democrats took over both houses and promptly elected Robert J. Walker, a fellow Democrat, to the U.S. Senate. Then, when John Tyler resigned his seat rather than obey instructions from the Virginia legislature that both its senators vote to expunge the censure of Jackson, he was replaced by William C. Rives, Jackson's former minister to France and (at this time) a loyal Democrat.

Rives took his seat on March 14, and the Democrats, sensing victory, prepared for a showdown. The Whigs tried to move adjournment to stall the process of confirmation and failed. On March 15 the Senate took up and approved Taney's nomination as chief justice by a vote of twenty-nine to fifteen. Webster, Clay, Calhoun, and the "stool pigeon," as Jackson called Senator White, voted against confirmation. But to the surprise of many, John Davis, Webster's colleague, voted in favor. The disappointed Webster simply shrugged it off. What else could he do? "I have been asked for the reason for your vote," Webster informed Davis, and ". . . have always said, that having lost our majority in the Senate, there was no hope of defeating the nomination." Also, there was the real

7. DW to Caroline Webster, January 24, DW to Everett, January 27, 1836, in *PC*, IV, 77, 78.

possibility that they might get a worse nominee if Taney were rejected. But I "am now rather sorry that you did not go with a majority of friends in the Senate."[8]

When Barbour's nomination came up, Webster moved to postpone action until the House had voted on a judiciary bill that would rearrange the circuit courts and increase the membership of the Supreme Court from seven to nine. But the Democrats, confident of their strength, defeated the motion, and Barbour was confirmed by the vote of thirty to eleven.[9]

Eventually Jackson got to appoint six justices before he left office,[10] and then poor Webster faced a Court totally out of sympathy with his "Federalist" views. After a number of defeats in presenting his arguments before them over the next several years, he joked about it. While standing before the Court during one case, Webster noted the changes in the personnel that had taken place since he first appeared before it as counsel. "It has been my duty to pass upon the question of the confirmation of every member of the Bench," he said to the present members, "and I may say that I treated your honors with entire impartiality, for I voted against every one of you."[11]

With so many defeats for Webster in the space of a few months it is small wonder that the man who loved parties and dinners with friends stayed confined to his room. He said he did "not go out at all, & for a month have asked nobody to my rooms." Just the thought of facing a chief justice whom he had actively tried to defeat and whose censure by the Senate he had approved gave him pause. With a Democratic Court and a Democratic Senate in place the future looked dismal indeed.

At long last Webster seriously considered withdrawing from the presidential race and resigning from Congress. Whether he meant to abandon his political career at this time or not, he certainly went about deciding the wrong way. He would not—perhaps he could not—make the decision himself. He passed it along to others. Instead of consulting his family and close friends and then deciding for himself, he asked the Massachusetts legislature to do it for him. He wrote to his legal associate Henry Kinsman and told him that in view of the "state of things at present existing in the country," he personally believed he should withdraw from the presidential contest. "I do not wish to receive the votes of one or two States, as a mere matter of respect, or proof of confidence." That would be humiliating. What stopped him, he continued, was the fear that such action would injure the Whig cause in Massachusetts. He therefore asked Kinsman to consult his friends and get their reaction. If they decide that "our common principles and common cause" dictate that he stand pat and do nothing,

8. DW to Davis, April 7, 1836, ibid., IV, 100–101.

9. *Senate Executive Journal*, IV, 520–522.

10. John McLean, Henry Baldwin, James M. Wayne, Roger B. Taney, Philip P. Barbour, and John Catron.

11. Hoar, *Autobiography*, I, 141.

then "I shall cheerfully abide by their determination."[12]

At a Whig meeting of the Massachusetts legislature on March 24 Webster's letter was read, whereupon the Whigs unanimously adopted resolutions against his withdrawing from the race or resigning his seat. Governor Everett said that "we had nothing to hope, now or at any time, either from the South or the West, in his opinion. The general feeling seemed to be that Massachusetts must stand alone, if she stand at all."[13]

A meeting of the Massachusetts delegation of Whigs in Congress—Webster and Adams not attending—also concurred in this decision.[14]

So Webster stuck it out, no doubt knowing full well that he faced a crushing rejection by the people in the fall presidential election. Although he remained a viable candidate and tried to exude a degree of confidence to his Massachusetts constituents, all the enthusiasm, zest, and interest he had once had for the election drained away. For the remainder of the campaign he paid it little attention. Instead he became extremely active in land speculation, especially lots in Michigan, Ohio, Indiana, Illinois, and the Wisconsin Territory. He contacted several speculators in these areas and invested tens of thousands of dollars in an effort to make a quick profit. By and large he left the selection of sites to the speculators. "We leave the choice of places to your discretion," he commented to them, "looking to safety, & to the hopes of profit." He sent his son Fletcher out west to assist in the selection and purchases of the property, and Webster asked his speculators to include him in their negotiations. After several months in the saddle, riding from town to town across the prairie, the young man proudly reported to his father that "I can drink whiskey of a morning, steer across the prairie by a compass, follow an Indian Trail in the Woods & sleep on the floor of a log Cabin, with my saddle for a pillow."[15]

Several western newspapers took notice of the sudden craze for western land by eastern speculators. "If the capitalists who are buying up the public lands could increase agricultural, manufacturing and mercantile population of the United States at their pleasure," editorialized the Detroit *Daily Advertiser*, "they would be masters of an almost unlimited wealth."[16] The frenzy of land purchases grew so speedily and involved so much paper money in circulation—"land continues to be taken with great rapidity," said Webster—that Jackson issued a Specie Circular, requiring specie, not paper, for the purchase of government land. But it did not slow Webster one whit. Hardly a week went by during the summer and spring of 1836 without his pouring more money into his land

12. DW to Kinsman, February 27, 29, 1836, in *PC*, IV, 88–89, 90. A week before, Webster had authorized Kinsman to deny that he had declined the presidential nomination. DW to Kinsman, February 20, 1836, ibid., IV, 88.

13. DW to Davis, April 7, 1836, ibid., IV, 100.

14. Memorandum by Levi Lincoln, February 19, 1836, ibid., IV, 87–88.

15. DW to Phineas Davis, May 16, DW to Fisher Harding, May 16, Harding to DW, May 4, Fletcher Webster to DW, July 1, 1836, ibid., IV, 107, 110–112, 112–113, 144.

16. August 24, 1836.

deals.[17] When all else failed to empty his pockets, he had Marshfield to absorb his attention and extra cash. At the same time he started improvements on the Elms Farm in Franklin, New Hampshire, which he had purchased outright from his brother's heirs, and hired John Taylor, Jr., to manage it for him in his absence.[18]

Webster left Washington midway during the session and returned home for a brief visit. He probably needed a change of scenery and a respite from politics. Caroline had developed pleurisy, and he felt obliged to be at her side. He informed John Davis that he expected to start back for Washington on April 8, "although to tell the truth, I have had more than half a mind not to return at all. I see no good to be done, & there is little, either in or out of Congress, to encourage effort."[19]

Whether or not he wanted to return to the capital there were constant demands on his time and services as a speaker and congressman. One of the most important occurred when Texans proclaimed their independence from Mexico on March 2, 1836, and seven weeks later, on April 21, defeated the Mexican Army at the Battle of San Jacinto and captured General Antonio López de Santa Anna, the president of the Mexican Republic. Straightaway they expected immediate recognition and eventual annexation by the United States, and Samuel P. Carson, the secretary of state of Texas, wrote to Webster and pleaded for his help. "To a mind *like Yours*," he declared, "I need only say we wish the countenance, and cheering *recognition* of our dear mother country. . . . By all those holy feelings then, and by all the considerations, which make *liberty*, with her glorious train of attributes, dear to man; allow me to invoke Your aid in obtaining an immediate *recognition* of our Independence. What may not be done for '*millions* Yet unborn' by the voice, Yes Sir the *mighty* voice of Daniel Webster? and who can estimate the loss, if that voice is withheld?"[20]

Webster spoke briefly on the Texas question several times after his return to Washington, none of it coming anywhere near what the Texans wished to hear. On May 9 he said that he, like everyone else, sympathized with those seeking liberty but added that this was no time for Congress to do anything about Texas beyond preserving U.S. neutrality. He also warned against personally attacking Santa Anna and calling him a barbarian on the floor of Congress since the United States had recently signed a treaty with him. In a letter to Everett the senator frankly admitted that "we are in a peck of troubles here. . . . My greatest fear, at present, is of a war about Texas." The issue could bring into "our politics new causes of embarrassment, & new tendencies to dismemberment." On May 23 he spoke again in Congress and allowed that if Texans had established a government de facto, then it was the duty of the United States to

17. Joseph Williams to DW, May 4, 1836, in *PC,* IV, 108. For a more complete picture of Webster's land speculations, see ibid., IV, 114ff.

18. Agreement between Daniel Webster and John Taylor, Jr., September 14, 1835, ibid., IV, 51–52.

19. DW to Davis, April 7, 1836, ibid., IV, 100.

20. Carson to DW, March 30, 1836, ibid., IV, 99.

acknowledge their independence. The timing and the manner in which it was done, he added, call for "grave and mature consideration." He ended his remarks by referring to the Monroe Doctrine and expressing the belief that attempts would be made by some European powers to obtain a "cession of Texas from the Government of Mexico."[21]

That last remark caught the attention of many people, both North and South. There was a particular concern that Britain would attempt to "gain a footing in Texas" or be drawn into the Texan War and thereby jeopardize the security of the United States. Mexico might become another India.[22] Pressure therefore mounted around the country to force recognition of Texan independence and then to annex the territory.

But Jackson resisted the pressure. He did not want to jeopardize Van Buren's election in the fall, and he feared the slave question might poison any negotiations involving annexation.[23]

Another messy problem involved the Cherokee Indians. In a treaty of removal signed on December 28, 1835, the Cherokee Nation had agreed to cede its remaining lands east of the Mississippi River to the United States for a sum of $4.5 million and take up permanent residence west of the Mississippi in an area that later became the state of Oklahoma. But the ratifying process among the Native Americans was a fraud. Fewer than a hundred Indians participated, and thousands of Cherokees protested the removal in petitions to Congress. Despite these protests, Jackson went right ahead and submitted the treaty to the Senate for its approval. The Whigs resisted and put up a strong effort to defeat the treaty. Webster, Clay, Henry Wise, and others delivered long and fervent appeals against ratification.

Whigs are "worn out and exhausted" trying to win justice for the Indians, Webster scolded. The Democrats, no matter where they come from, have "no concern for Indian rights, so far as I can perceive." He later asked a friend whether he ought to "do some act to clear myself from the shame and sin of the treaty." He said he fought the treaty for a week, and he and other members of the opposition came close to rejecting it and would have done so had not Robert Goldsborough of Maryland suddenly changed his vote. "We relied on him as a man of honor and religion; but he voted for the treaty, and turned the scale— mortified some of his friends severely." The two-thirds vote required for the treaty passed on May 18, 1836, by a single vote, thirty-one in favor, fifteen against. Goldsborough went home and never returned. He died five months later. Jackson immediately added his signature and proclaimed the Treaty of New Echota in force. Removal of the Cherokees was to take place within two years—that is, by May 23, 1838.[24]

---

21. *Register of Debates*, 24th Congress, 1st Session, pp. 1415–1416, 1527–1528; DW to Everett, May 7, 1836, in *PC*, IV, 110.

22. John Catron to DW, June 12, 1836, in *PC*, IV, 131–133.

23. Remini, *Jackson*, III, 358ff.

24. DW to Hiram Ketchum, May 12, 1838, in Curtis, *Webster*, I, 576; *Journal of Executive Proceedings of the Senate*, IV, 546.

By this time Webster felt uneasy about continuing as a presidential candidate. It had become a source of unending embarrassments for him. Delegates at the Whig convention in New Jersey first passed a resolution that said, "We entertain the highest opinion of the eminent abilities and patriotism of the Hon Daniel Webster," and then proceeded to nominate William Henry Harrison unanimously.

By early May the senator realized he had made a mistake in allowing his name to remain as a presidential candidate. "I should have withdrawn from the canvass altogether," he admitted to James Watson Webb, editor of the *Courier and Enquirer.* Now it was too late. His friends and the "state of affairs in Massachusetts" obliged him to stick it out, however much that meant a defeat in the fall that could be personally humiliating. He therefore asked Webb to follow a course that "you think duty & honor point out. I have certainly no desire that any effort should be made for me, under circumstances which leave no hope that good would be produced by such effort." Act, he added, for the good of the country "and the cause."[25]

A disillusioned, disappointed, and emotionally weary senator returned to his home in Boston when this interminable and boring session ended in early July. "We have nothing very interesting," he told Fletcher. "It has been, on the whole, a dull & barren session."[26] The only important piece of legislation to win congressional and presidential approval was the Deposit Act of 1836. As chairman of the Senate Finance Committee, again elected over Silas Wright at the beginning of the session, Webster had a hand, but not a terribly important one, in its final passage. The act required those banks receiving government funds to redeem all their notes in specie on demand and to issue no notes for less than five dollars after July 4. Later that amount would be raised first to ten and then to twenty dollars. Part of this bill involved the distribution of the surplus in the Treasury, which had been mounting because of the high tariff rates and the tremendous number of land sales. The distribution section of the Deposit Act stated that all money in the Treasury in excess of five million dollars as of January 1, 1837, would be turned over to the states in proportion to their representation in Congress.[27]

On returning home, Webster had no difficulty in keeping his mind off the approaching election. Newspapers around the country hardly noticed his candidacy. To all intents and purposes, as far as they were concerned, he had withdrawn from the race. Justice McLean also saw the futility of his own candidacy and had the good sense to withdraw and remain on the Supreme Court. Northern Whig newspapers concentrated their attention on Harrison and took note of his attendance at rallies and dinners, especially when he traveled to Virginia, Pennsylvania, and New York. They seemed to view the contest as a Van

25. Joseph Scott to DW, June 6, 1836, DW to Webb, May 6, 1836, in *PC*, IV, 126, 109.
26. DW to Fletcher Webster, June 12, 1836, ibid., IV, 130.
27. 5 *U.S. Statutes at Large*, 55–56.

Buren–Harrison race, but in the South they reported the race as a Van Buren–White or Van Buren–Anti-Van Buren contest. The poor Whigs were so disorganized and leaderless that despite southern dislike of Van Buren and some concern in many parts of the country about his reputation as a political manipulator, he seemed likely to win election by a large margin. He had the President's total support, and the American people trusted Jackson and his policies enough to take their chances with the Little Magician. There could be little doubt that Van Buren would pursue the goals of his predecessor, while a Whig would unquestionably call for another national bank, federally sponsored internal improvements, and the maintenance of such tariff duties as would protect the interests of the manufacturing community.

The Democratic party unanimously nominated Van Buren for the presidency at its convention in Baltimore held on May 23, 1836. Although the defection of White attracted southern Democrats as well as southern Whigs, the party remained strong in most sections of the country. Even in New England it produced moderate gains in state and local elections.[28]

Throughout November, on various days in various states, voters went to the polls to cast their ballots for electors who would choose the next President and Vice President. Massachusetts held its election on November 15. Webster knew that it was "highly probable" that his electors would be chosen and consequently wrote to one of them, his former colleague in the Senate Nathaniel Silsbee, and asked him to inform the other electors on the ticket that in view of what had already happened and was about to happen in other states, it was his "earnest wish that they should act with entire freedom from all considerations merely personal to myself; and that they should give the vote of the State in the manner they think most likely to be useful in supporting the constitution and laws of the country, the union of the States, the perpetuity of our republican institutions, and the important interests of the whole country; and in maintaining the character of Massachusetts for integrity, honor, national patriotism, and fidelity to the constitution."[29]

His letter was laid before the other electors and was "*well received* by all of them." After a brief consultation the electors of Massachusetts chosen by the people cast all fourteen of their electoral votes for Daniel Webster as President.[30] Who better to support the Constitution and the Union of states? Who better to maintain Massachusetts's character for integrity, honor, and patriotism? Unfortunately the rest of the country did not agree. Even New Hampshire, his native state, preferred another. It conferred its electoral votes on Van Buren, as did Maine, Rhode Island, and Connecticut. That surely must have been a blow to Webster. Vermont opted for Harrison.

As New Hampshire went, so did the rest of the country. Van Buren won a

28. Silbey, "Election of 1836," p. 596.
29. DW to Silsbee, November 15, 1836, in *PC*, IV, 161–162.
30. Silsbee to DW, December 27, 1836, ibid., IV, 169–170.

majority of 170 electoral votes, Harrison 73, White 26, and Webster 14. Van Buren took New York, Pennsylvania, Illinois, Michigan, Missouri, and all of the South except Tennessee and Georgia, which went to White. Harrison captured the border and the other western states.[31]

All the candidates save Webster won two or more states. Only Black Dan's vote revealed a total lack of national, much less regional, support. All he had to show for his efforts was Massachusetts. It was a humiliating defeat.

William Plumer spoke to his friend about the election and found that "Webster felt sore at his own ill success in the canvass; and imputed some part of his apparent unpopularity to Clay." The senator felt "depressed and gloomy" and said he was tired of life and did not care what happened to him. Because of his ambition, he wanted "nothing short of the highest." He had fame but no power, Plumer remarked, at least not to the extent he desired. "He has long served under men whom he does not like and whom he considers his inferiors in mental power."[32]

Plumer wished that his friend would write a book on the law and government. Webster's vast knowledge of both subjects would bring him a more durable reputation if he attempted such a work. Instead, Plumer predicted, he will probably "fritter away" the few remaining years of his life in a "vain struggle for the presidency which he can never reach." He will give more political speeches and some powerful legal arguments, "but I wish he might add to his character of lawyer, orator, and statesman, that of the author of a standard work on law and government. . . . He is capable of doing this; and it would crown the climax of his glory with a wreath of enduring fame."[33]

There were of course specific reasons why so many people dismissed his candidacy. The western vote especially disappointed him, given his recent trip and his speech in 1825, when he advocated cheap land for settlers. But as one transplanted and "highly prejudiced" New Englander pointed out, the West "acknowledged the distinguished ability of Mr. Webster, & his undoubted fitness for the station yet his *availibility* [sic] is doubted. The *name* of Federalist and Hartford Conventionist (it being almost impossible to eradicate from the public mind, his immediate connection with the latter) are [sic] strong weapons in the hands of our opponents, which they wield with powerful effect." Moreover, his political principles "are of a comparatively dry, cold & formal nature, nor can he wind himself around the affections of the people like Mr. Clay."[34] In the South one man suggested that southern Whigs would never vote for him because of "his late declarations concerning Texas." Some regarded his ties to bankers and

31. Schlesinger and Israel, eds., *History of Presidential Elections*, I, 640. Richard M. Johnson, Van Buren's running mate, failed to win a majority of electoral votes for Vice President, so the Senate, as mandated by the Constitution, elected him to the office on February 8, 1837, by a vote of thirty-three to sixteen. Silbey, "Election of 1836," p. 600.

32. Plumer, "Reminiscences of Webster," in *W&S*, XVII, 559–560.

33. Ibid., XVII, 561–562.

34. N. S. Howe to Caleb Cushing, February 18, 1838, Cushing Papers, LC.

other capitalists as disabling. But the presidency was forever closed to Daniel Webster because basically he was disconnected from his own age. He was not a man of the people, and the electorate knew it. The public never really took to him as a presidential candidate, although his speeches moved them deeply. His speeches were heroic, but he himself was not. He lacked mass appeal. He could not "wind himself around the affections of the people." Besides, he was no leader. Clay was the leader, said Rufus Choate, Webster "the philosopher." Webster could write state and diplomatic papers and legal opinions for an administration, but he could never implement them. So the people instinctively looked elsewhere for leadership.

Also, he personified New England with all its virtues and failings. He "got a set of cold New England manners," Choate continued, "and had thoroughly conformed himself for home consumption."[35] His "imperious and arrogant bearing" and "haughtiness of manner" were admitted by both friend and critic.[36] His tastes, style, and pursuits were confined to those of the privileged class. As a matter of fact he distrusted democratic rule, although he appreciated that legitimate government must be rooted in the consent of the majority. According to Webster, merit, education, and position in society had value, and should be heeded in the councils of government.

Thus, in an age increasingly characterized by raucous egalitarianism, such a man could not expect to find favor with common folk, certainly not in sufficient numbers to ensure election.

Unfortunately there was nothing Webster could do to change public perception. To begin with, he had not the faintest idea how to go about accomplishing it. Nor did he fully recognize how the people felt about him, how they admired and revered him but did not love or trust him. He preferred to blame Clay for his unpopularity rather than seek the cause in his own personal deficiencies. To his great misfortune Daniel Webster was "cursed" with superior legal skills, exceptional oratorical powers, and driving political ambition that were all spiked by an undemocratic air, a superior attitude, and an overbearing demeanor.

Daniel Webster simply was not a man of this Jacksonian age, and never could be. He belonged in an earlier era. He was and always remained a Federalist.

35. Parker, *Reminiscences of Choate*, p. 238.
36. Hoar, *Autobiography*, I, 135, 137.

28

The Charles River Bridge *Case*

PERHAPS it said something about his emotional state at this time, but Webster wrote out his last will and testament and appointed his wife and eldest son coexecutors. He was fifty-four. Perhaps he felt his age more keenly when his twenty-three-year-old son, Fletcher, married Caroline Story White, the daughter of Stephen and Harriet White, and a niece of Joseph Story, on November 27, 1837. Or perhaps his disappointment over the election influenced his decision. Whatever the reason, Webster deemed it important at this time to make one out.[1]

After the marriage Fletcher returned to Detroit with his bride in an effort to establish a lucrative law practice and continue as his father's agent in acquiring land and stock in the West. He managed to infect his father with his enthusiasm for the possibility of vast financial returns from western lands and investments, not that Webster himself needed much urging. Fletcher soon involved him in speculative ventures extending from Michigan to Wisconsin, and Webster was named a director of the Clamorgan Land Association, a risky enterprise that claimed almost half a million acres of land in Missouri and Arkansas on the basis of a dubious Spanish grant. Before long Webster had invested upward of one hundred thousand dollars, often providing promissory notes since he did not have the ready cash. Jackson's Specie Circular, requiring specie for the purchase of land, frequently forced Webster to scramble for the money. At one point he had promised to pay sixty thousand dollars for the purchase of land in Rock Island City, Illinois, and he simply could not meet his obligation. But when really hard pressed, he could always find help from Nicholas Biddle and his Philadelphia bank or some other friendly bank or wealthy patron. And Webster did not hesitate to use privileged information to instruct his son about future purchases.

There is now *some* probability, that both the land bill, & the bill rescinding, in effect, the Treasury [Specie Circular] Order, may pass. Should that be the case, there will be a scramble for Govt. lands, till May 1st. when the land bill will go into operation, & stop the sales. If you have any knowledge, or can obtain any, of good lands, at Govt. prices, it

1. Webster's First Will, November 1836, in Van Tyne, ed., *Letters of Webster,* pp. 593–595.

will be well to be prepared. It will be a week, after you receive this, before you will know the fate of the bills. Should both pass, & should you know lands, which could be entered, with prospect of a handsome profit, you may lay out 2,000 Dlls for me, & draw on me for the money. I will give you due notice.[2]

Fletcher shot right back that he could buy five thousand acres of government land for $6,250. If he could then sell it for $10 per acre, "you see the profit would be immense." A "little fortune" could be made, he enthused, "& not much trouble about it."[3]

Not surprisingly, since Webster's object was immediate profit, some of his speculations involved enormous risk. And not a few times these speculations ended disastrously. For example, Fletcher was obliged to tell his father that Phineas Davis, the secretary-treasurer of the Gibraltar Land Company, near Detroit, in which Webster had bought one eighth of the company's stock and been assured of a 1,000 percent profit, had acted "improperly." The bookkeeping, if it could be called that, "was careless or worse."[4] In fact "in some of his dealings . . . he has not behaved very honourably." Fletcher also discovered that one tract of land in Michigan proved to be totally underwater. And it had cost him two thousand dollars![5] Webster involved himself with so many stock and land agents that his financial arrangements became hopelessly tangled and even today cannot be untangled.[6]

To say the very least, by the beginning of 1837 Webster had overextended himself in his speculations, probably in the hundreds of thousands of dollars; in addition, his personal finances were so disordered that he seriously considered resigning from Congress to bring them under control. He was also still despondent over his poor showing in the late election and suffered several "indispositions" in the succeeding months. He felt he needed rest. He thought travel to the West might help, both physically and financially. He could inspect his various properties and oversee pending transactions. He also considered a trip to Europe, where he might find the relaxation and diversion he so desperately needed. Within two months of his defeat at the polls he made up his mind to resign at the end of the session. Accordingly he announced his intention to several Massachusetts friends. "I feel," he wrote, "as deeply as man can feel, my obligations, high & solemn, to the People of Massachusetts. But I really need an interval, at least,—a temporary cessation—of my duties here. For fourteen

2. DW to Fletcher Webster, February 24, 1837, in *PC*, IV, 199.

3. Fletcher Webster to DW, March 14, 1837, ibid., IV, 207.

4. Baxter, *Webster*, p. 287.

5. Fletcher Webster to DW, March 2, 1837, in *PC*, IV, 202.

6. Despite the amount of documentation available to a modern biographer, these financial dealings cannot be fully explained or understood, and no attempt will be made here to do so. Webster's business papers, records, and financial transactions can be found in Webster, *Microfilm Edition*, reel 29. See also his many letters concerning his financial operations to Fletcher and his agents and from them, PC, IV, passim. Maurice Baxter in his biography of Webster makes a valiant and largely successful attempt to sort out some of Webster's many transactions. See pp. 285–298.

years, I have had no leisure, not enough even to travel thro. my own Country. I want a year or two."

Not unexpectedly the reaction from friends and Whig members of the Massachusetts legislature was overwhelmingly opposed to his resignation. It would be used everywhere "as a surrender of all hope" for the Whig party, they chorused. The Whig influence would be "greatly impaired." At this moment you "constitute the hope & strength of that Party—future prospects personally & Publicly depend on your remaining."[7]

So he agreed to stay—at least until the fall. In the meantime he made plans when the short congressional session ended in early March 1837 to travel West. He wrote his son and informed him that he planned to leave home around the end of April and proceed by way of Pittsburgh, Lexington, and Louisville and then come north to Detroit to meet Fletcher and his wife, arriving around June 10 or 15.[8]

To make him feel even more despondent, when Webster arrived in Washington, he found the Senate controlled by the Democrats and, under Benton's leadership, preparing to rescind the censure of Jackson passed on March 28, 1834. On December 26 Benton moved that the censure be expunged from the *Senate Journal,* but the formal debate on the resolution did not begin until three weeks later.

Of the Great Triumvirate, Calhoun spoke first, accusing Jackson of employing "patronage and power" to coerce members of the Senate into "a gross and palpable violation of the constitution." Clay spoke next, berating the Democrats for what they were about to do. The censure will be expunged, he admitted, and when "you have perpetrated it, go home to the people, and tell them what glorious honors you have achieved for our common country. Tell them that you have extinguished one of the brightest and purest lights that ever burnt at the altar of civil liberty."[9]

Webster spoke last. On January 16, 1837, he rose slowly from his chair, as though physically burdened by what he felt compelled to say. He was, remembered Benton, less passionate than Calhoun or Clay, having a "temperament less ardent, and he delivered himself with comparative moderation" since he had no "personal griefs" against the President. Simply but sincerely he expressed his "grief and mortification" at what was about to happen.[10] "I speak in my own behalf," he declared, and "solemnly PROTEST this whole proceeding." The Constitution decrees that a record of our proceedings shall be kept, but the resolution declares that it shall be expunged, and that which is expunged is no record at all. Webster insisted that other senators had no authority to deprive the

7. DW to Robert Winthrop, January 27, DW to Hiram Ketchum, January 28, DW to [Edward Everett], January 31, 1837, Henry Shaw to DW, February 8, 182, Robert Winthrop et all to DW, February 15, 1837, in *PC,* IV, 182, 183, 185–186, 187, 194.

8. DW to Fletcher Webster, February 20, 1837, ibid., IV, 195.

9. *Register of Debates,* 24th Congress, 2d Session, pp. 429–440.

10. Benton, *Thirty Years' View,* I, 728–730.

minority of their "personal rights," secured by the Constitution, "either by expunging, obliterating or mutilating, or defacing the record of our votes." We watch in silence, he continued, while a scene will be enacted that will "be little elevated above the character of a contemptible farce.

Having made this PROTEST, our duty is performed. We rescue our own names, character, and honor from all participation in this matter; and whatever the wayward character of the times, the headlong and plunging spirit of party devotion, or the fear or the love of power . . . we desire to thank God that they have not, as yet, overcome the love of liberty, fidelity to true republican principles, and a sacred regard for the Constitution.[11]

Webster sat down. No one rose to speak again. Dead silence. "Question," someone shouted. The roll was called. Forty-three senators were present, five absent. When the vote was concluded, it showed that twenty-four favored expunging the censure and nineteen were opposed, including Calhoun, Clay, and Webster. So the record of the Senate in 1834 was taken from the shelf and opened to the page with the censure. Then broad black lines were drawn around it amid a storm of hisses and boos. As the secretary of the Senate performed this act, the Whig senators walked out of the chamber to demonstrate their disapproval.[12]

Webster received numerous requests for copies of his speech. Biddle told him "how delighted" he was with it. From Massachusetts came many congratulatory notes, particularly since he had referred to his state in glowing terms during the speech. Robert Winthrop, who had studied law in Webster's office, said it was received "with great enthusiasm. Great as the effect of it seems to have been in the Senate Chamber, it seems to be calculated to produce even greater effect among the People of the Commonwealth." Winthrop suggested that copies be sent to every member of the state legislature and as many other leaders as soon as possible.[13]

For Webster personally the passage of Benton's resolution was a fearful blow to the constitutional system. Jackson willed the expunging of the censure; once the votes became available, Benton implemented that will, using the power, prestige, and patronage of the administration and setting the Constitution aside in the process.

Webster endured one more personal blow before the string of his recent defeats was completely played out, and that involved the celebrated *Charles River Bridge* case, presently before the Supreme Court. The case extended as far back as the last century and involved years of litigation.

In 1785 the state of Massachusetts granted a forty-year charter to a group of investors to build and operate a bridge across the Charles River between

11. *W&S*, VIII, 30–35.
12. Benton, *Thirty Years' View*, I, 731.
13. Biddle to DW, January 20, Winthrop to DW, January 21, 1837, in *PC*, IV, 174, 175–176.

Boston and Charlestown and collect tolls. Because a ferry operating across the river, whose receipts went to Harvard College, would lose income on completion of the bridge, the state required the Charles River Bridge Company to pay an annual fee to Harvard as compensation. The success of the bridge encouraged the state to consider chartering a second bridge in 1792, but when the Charles River Bridge Company protested, the legislature abandoned plans for another bridge and extended the charter of the existing bridge seventy years. Therein lay the beginning of the later dispute.[14]

The enormous growth of Boston following the War of 1812 brought demands and petitions to the legislature by merchants and townspeople for a newer and better bridge, one that was toll-free. With the advent of democratic rule throughout the nation, the people of Boston naturally resented the privileged position of the Charles River Bridge Company and its claim to monopoly rights because of the original charter. Bostonians believed that their rights took precedence over the company's rights. Federalists and National Republicans tended to defend the claims of the Charles River Bridge Company, and Jacksonians to oppose them.

Responding to popular demand, the state chartered the Warren Bridge Company in 1828 to build a new bridge a mere 260 feet from the Charles River Bridge. The new bridge could charge tolls for six years—or however long it took to recover the cost of construction—but at the end of that time the structure would belong to the state and become a free bridge. On December 25, 1828, the Warren Bridge opened for business. The stockholders of the first bridge again protested, claiming exclusive rights and demanding compensation for the loss of their business. How could their toll bridge possibly compete against a free bridge?[15]

Seeking the best legal assistance they could find, the proprietors of the Charles River Bridge hired Webster and the state's future chief justice Lemuel Shaw, who immediately sought an injunction against the Warren Bridge. They contended that the property rights of their clients had been violated. But the Massachusetts court ultimately decided against them, and the case went to the U.S. Supreme Court, where it was argued on March 7–11, 1831, by Webster and Warren Dutton against William Wirt and Walter Jones.[16] But the Court deadlocked and directed a reargument.[17]

Because of illnesses and vacancies, the case took longer than expected to

14. An excellent account of this case can be found in Stanley I. Kutler, *Privilege and Creative Destruction: The Charles River Bridge Case* (Philadelphia, 1971).

15. Baxter, *Webster and the Supreme Court,* pp. 120–122.

16. For the complete documentation of this case, see *PLFP,* III, part I, 398ff.

17. Stanley Kutler believes that Marshall, Baldwin, and McLean favored the Warren Bridge, and Story, Thompson, and Johnson the Charles River Bridge. Justice Duvall did not attend the argument. Kutler, *Privilege and Creative Destruction,* pp. 172–179. But Maurice Baxter, following Charles Warren's lead, claims that Marshall, Story, and Thompson favored the Charles River Bridge, while Baldwin dissented, and McLean and Johnson were undecided. Baxter, *Webster and the Supreme Court,* p. 123.

be reargued. In the interim the President placed several new members on the High Court, including Chief Justice Taney, who distrusted monopolistic charters with respect to transportation because they prevented future legislatures from effecting changes when required by public necessity.[18]

Webster, on the other hand, believed that property rights could not be abrogated once a contract had been drawn. Economic progress depended on such a guarantee. For Webster, the *Charles River Bridge* case was simply a dispute between two private litigants. They were not public enterprises. And both companies had appealed to the state for legal protection of their property rights. For him, political liberty could not exist without property rights, protected by law. Therefore the charter granted by Massachusetts to the Charles River Bridge Company, in which the funds for construction were provided by the company, constituted a contract and could not by subsequent legislation be altered without the consent of the company. For the government to step in and violate those rights, according to Webster, invalidated what had been achieved by the American Revolution.

As an observer and participant in the politics of the Jacksonian era he surely must have recognized that the political atmosphere had changed dramatically since the Revolution and that such things as egalitarianism and democracy now held full sway in the political thinking of the masses and their leaders. But according to Webster, the Jackson attack on monopoly as a threat to the common good revealed a future direction that could cripple the economy and the country. He feared that the contract clause of the Constitution would be further eroded by legislative action unless the courts could stem the Jacksonian tide that demanded economic egalitarianism and an end to monopolies. The large concentration of wealth in the hands of the few did not particularly trouble Webster as it did Jackson and many Democrats. He reckoned it natural and inevitable, a sociological fact of life.

Thus, once Marshall died and Taney took his place, making the Democrats the majority on the Supreme Court, Webster's fears became ever more real, and he urged his clients to seek a compromise with their opponents.[19] Unfortunately it was too late for that. By 1837, when the case was reargued, the toll-less Warren Bridge had become state property. And now Chief Justice Roger Brooke Taney, one of the principal authors of Jackson's Bank veto, presided.

Taney was descended from a well-to-do Maryland tobacco-raising tidewater family. He had graduated from Dickinson College in Pennsylvania in 1795 at the age of fifteen. The class valedictorian, he then studied law, won election to the Maryland assembly, became an ardent Jacksonian and received appointment as attorney general in the cabinet in 1831, and proved to be one of the President's closest advisers. Sharp-featured, with a long, narrow face and a small mouth, and highly intelligent, he was expected by many Democrats to support state

18. *Niles' Weekly Register,* November 2, 1833.
19. Ibid.

prerogatives and dismantle John Marshall's program of "constitutional national-ism" and "national capitalism."

Taney certainly was different from his predecessor. Where Marshall wore "knee breeches," for example, Taney preferred trousers reaching down to his shoes. Still, although the new Chief Justice, in the course of his long career on the bench, modified some aspects of Marshall's program and attempted to apply Jacksonian reform wherever possible, he did maintain the fundamental author-ity of the central government under the Constitution developed during Mar-shall's tenure over the previous thirty-four years.[20]

On January 19 Dutton opened for the Charles River Bridge Company before an immense crowd of lawyers, congressmen, and foreign ministers and "a large circle of ladies, of the highest fashion, and taste, and intelligence."[21] The size and character of the crowd obviously indicated that in the major constitu-tional contest about to transpire important economic and political questions would be addressed and ruled upon.

After Dutton had concluded his arguments, Harvard law professor Simon Greenleaf and Massachusetts Senator John Davis followed for the defendants. Greenleaf was particularly skillful in insisting that the case involved a public versus a private right. He also pleaded Massachusetts's power of eminent do-main. Story was quite taken with his performance. "Our friend Greenleaf's argument was excellent,—full of ability, point, learning, condensed thought, and strong illustration,—delivered with great presence of mind, modestly, calmly, and resolutely."[22]

Webster responded on January 24. But his performance was not up to speed. For one thing, he rambled. For another, he repeated himself to no point. For a third, he resorted to what amounted to personal "abuse" when referring to Greenleaf.[23] The disappointments of the past few months showed in his manner, behavior, and speech. He seemed to know he would lose and could not quite put his heart into his effort. One observer said that he appeared "to be very uneasy and moody." He spoke about an hour "on general and mis-cellaneous topics in the cause" and took all the next day to complete his presentation.[24] Webster himself admitted to his son that it was all very "laborious."[25] His friend Justice Story tried to find merit in what he heard,

20. Frank O. Gatell, "Roger B. Taney, 1777–1864," in Friedman and Israel, eds., *Justices of the United States Supreme Court*, I, 635–655. See also Swisher, *Roger B. Taney* and Walker Lewis, *Without Fear or Favor: A Biography of Chief Justice Roger B. Taney* (Boston, 1965).

21. Joseph Story to Charles Sumner, January 25, 1837, in Story, *Life and Letters*, II, 266.

22. Ibid.

23. Greenleaf to Charles Sumner, January 24, 1837, Sumner Papers, MHS. Webster never liked to be contradicted, in or out of court, and several times he tangled with judges and opposing attorneys when he disliked what they had ruled or said. It was not uncommon when he behaved badly for the judge to rebuke him sharply. Hoar, *Autobiography*, I, 137.

24. Greenleaf to Charles Sumner, January 24, 1837, Sumner Papers, MHS.

25. DW to Fletcher Webster, February 12, 1837, in *PC*, IV, 190.

but he surely knew that Webster had performed badly.[26]

Webster started off by presenting a history of the dispute and arguing the inviolability of contract. Then he got down to an important point: the "clamor about monopoly!" He addressed the question of the rights of the public to "break up the monopoly" and to a free bridge. "The rights of the plaintiffs are no monopoly," he declared. "They are the enjoyments of the property for which they had paid in advance; and which, by contract made by law, they were entitled to enjoy for twenty years yet to come. They are called rapacious monopolists, when they claim to hold what they have purchased." They hold not a monopoly, he continued, but a franchise. The only question to be decided is whether the defendants have infringed the rights of the plaintiffs and violated the Constitution of the United States. The state is not a party to the cause. Forget the state. The suit is against the persons who built the Warren Bridge, and it is from them that relief is sought.

Throughout his argument Webster tried to drive across the point that only when capitalists believe their investments are secure will they make private funds available for economic growth. The future prosperity and development of this country, he insisted, demand that the state safeguard these investments.

As for eminent domain, it resides in the "sovereign—in the people. What portion of it is granted to the legislature belongs to them; what portion is not granted remains with the people. Taking public or private property for public benefit, by the state, is an exercise of the power of the state over its eminent domain. But granting a franchise is not an exercise of that power." The legislature may grant franchises, but it may do "just what it is limited to do, and nothing more." It is restrained by the state's constitution. And "in the constitution it is expressly declared, that property shall not be taken by the public without its being paid for." Thus eminent domain did not apply in this case, for once a state granted an exclusive franchise it could not under any circumstance plead eminent domain in order to rescind that franchise by issuing another franchise.

Webster closed with a pointed reference to past decisions of the High Court:

> The plaintiffs have placed their reliance upon the precedents and authority established by this honorable Court, in the course of the last thirty years, in support of that constitution which secured individual property against legislative assumption and that they now asked the enlightened conscience of this tribunal, if they have not succeeded in sustaining their complaint upon legal and constitutional grounds: if not, they must, as good citizens of this republic, remain satisfied with the decision of the Court.[27]

Webster concluded his argument on January 26, and the Court took the matter under review. But he knew that he had lost. Politics had defeated him.

---

26. "Webster's closing reply was in his best manner," Story wrote, "but with a little too much of *fierté* here and there. He had manifestly studied it with great care and sobriety of spirit." Joseph Story to Charles Sumner, January 25, 1837, in Story, *Life and Letters*, II, 266.

27. *W&S*, XV, 322–347.

Not the law. Not a true interpretation of the Constitution. "It will be decided tomorrow," he wrote his son on February 12, "& we shall *lose* it. The fact is, *political* opinion has got on to the Bench, & it is in vain to deny. The old judges will be one way; the new ones (a majority) the other."[28] To his old friend Jeremiah Mason, he was more detailed in his comments and more critical. The bridge case will be "decided wrong." The three old judges—Story, McLean, and Thompson—will declare for the plaintiffs; the four new ones—Taney, Baldwin, Wayne, and Barbour—for the defendants. He thought McLean had doubts about jurisdiction, doubts "nobody else entertains."

The Court, he complained, "is revolutionized." To his mind "Taney is smooth & plausible, but cunning & Jesuitical [he was a Catholic] & as thorough going a party judge" as ever sat on the bench. Taney believes in " protecting his friends, & punishing his enemies." Baldwin, on the other hand, "is naturally a confused & wrong-headed creature, opinionated, & intriguing." Wayne "is a gentlemanly man, naturally fair enough and would follow Marshall and Story" when they "had the power of giving the lead." Unfortunately he "is not of great fame" and on constitutional questions will heed the lead of his friends. Barbour "is honest, & conscientious; & he is certainly intelligent" but is devoted to states' rights and fears the power of the central government. "The Constitution is now in these hands; & God only knows what is to save it from destruction."[29]

On February 14, three weeks after Webster concluded his argument, the Court, in a four to three vote, handed down its decision. Speaking for the majority, Chief Justice Taney invoked a states' rights interpretation and ruled against the Charles River Bridge and in favor of the Warren Bridge. The older bridge, he said, did not have a monopoly, nor had the state granted an exclusive franchise, and any question about the meaning of a charter or grant should be interpreted in favor of the public authority that issued the charter, not the private company that received it. Community rights must not be lost by implication. In ruling on such matters, he continued, the courts should be careful about deciding in favor of property holders if they encroach upon the rights reserved to the states. They must never presume that the states have surrendered their rights in awarding grants unless they explicitly say so.

In addition, Taney clearly enunciated the need to open the economy to competition. The old must give way to the new in the modern world. If older companies can claim implied monopolies over transportation routes and demand protection by the courts, "we shall be thrown back to the improvements of the last century and stand still, until the claims of the . . . [old companies] shall be satisfied, and they shall consent to permit these States to avail themselves of the lights of modern science" that can add to the wealth and prosperity of the nation. While the rights of private property were sacred, he allowed, "we must not forget that the community also have rights, and that the happiness and well

28. DW to Fletcher Webster, February 12, 1837, in *PC*, IV, 190.
29. DW to Mason, February 13, 1837, ibid., IV, 191–192.

being of every citizen depends on their faithful preservation."[30]

Story and Thompson dissented, and McLean denied the Court's jurisdiction, although he favored the plaintiff's rights. Story argued the necessity of protecting investments when these investments increase public comforts and conveniences. If the state means to invite citizens to invest in such an enterprise, "there must be some pledge that the property will be safe" and that the success of the enterprise will not be the signal "of a general combination to overthrow its rights, and take away its profits."[31]

The decision upset Webster terribly. It was another personal humiliation and, in his mind, a constitutional disaster. In effect, he believed that the contract clause of the Constitution had been virtually annulled, although Taney had made it clear that he was not undermining the basic principle of the *Dartmouth College* case. Webster wrote to Story and told him that his, Story's, opinion was "the ablest, and best written opinion, I ever heard you deliver. It is close, searching, and scrutinizing." It satisfied him to believe that Taney's opinion "had not a foot nor an inch, of ground to stand on."[32]

Despite Webster's jaundiced opinion, the *Charles River Bridge* decision is a milestone in American constitutional history. In recognizing the claims of the community against large property holders, it marked another advance in the continuing development of democracy in the United States. Its positive response to changing economic conditions and its understanding of the necessity of balancing competing interests showed an acute awareness of what the American people expected of their government. Regardless of its apparent anticorporate sentiments, the decision actually aided the growth of industry by denying monopolistic claims of older companies whose charters implied or were believed to have granted exclusive privileges. The decision reflected the direction the nation was taking in its rise toward a fully developed industrial society. It reflected the ongoing evolution of Jacksonian Democracy.

The decision also reflected how far Webster stood from his countrymen in this age of advancing democracy. Property rights, not community rights, best revealed his true interests. The champion of American capitalism, the great advocate of the Constitution "as it is established," the recognized spokesman for conservative values, he had represented business interests for far too long to be considered by the public as a proponent of its collective rights.

The country had changed over the past few decades, and now the High Court had changed too. Webster stayed behind.

30. 11 Peters 420ff.
31. 11 Peters 608.
32. DW to Story, n.d., in *PLFP*, part I, III, 643

29

Panic!

THE *Charles River Bridge* decision was handed down just as Andrew Jackson prepared to leave the White House and turn the country and government over to his successor, Martin Van Buren. Jackson might be gone, but the democracy that bore his name remained a vigorous force, one that Webster increasingly feared would pick up steam and head in a direction that endangered sound constitutional principles and the rule of law.

He had tried to assert in his argument before the High Court what he regarded as a fundamental truth growing out of the American Revolution about property rights. Having failed to win his case in court, he felt compelled to speak directly to the public and reiterate what he had said and offer it as a set of guiding principles for the Whig party. With an eye to the presidential election of 1840 he wanted to enunciate his personal views and perhaps articulate what might become his party's platform.

At the time when he still considered resigning from the Senate his friend Hiram Ketchum, an attorney and leader of the Webster Whigs in New York City, had suggested that he make a speech before submitting his resignation. "Now, would it not be better," he responded to Ketchum, "that some occasion should be found for my making a *Speech in N. York?*" Not only was New York essential to his insatiable political ambitions, despite his defeat, but its large business community guaranteed a friendly response to what he wanted to say.[1]

Webster's suggestion immediately produced an invitation. A group of prominent New York Whigs asked him to address them as soon as Congress adjourned. He would be given a public welcome and assured a large and responsive audience. Webster accepted and on March 15 arrived in Amboy, New Jersey, where a select committee greeted him. Flags were hoisted in his honor as he boarded the steamboat to take him to the Battery. There he was met by an immense crowd standing on the docks, rooftops, and sheds. He entered a barouche with three leading Whig stalwarts, including Philip Hone, his wealthy New York friend, and together they paraded up Broadway to the cheers of

1. DW to Ketchum, February 11, 1837, in *PC*, IV, 189.

thousands of spectators. At the American Hotel he addressed the crowd briefly from a front window. At six o'clock he appeared at Niblo's Saloon before an audience of four or five thousand and gave a two-and-a-half-hour speech that Hone said was "one of those glorious exhibitions of talent for which he stands unrivaled."[2]

He never spoke better. "I am proud," he trumpeted, that we enjoy an identity of principles and objectives. "You are for the Constitution of the country; so am I." You are for Union; so am I. You are for equal laws and equal rights, for "constitutional and just restraints of power"; so am I. "In glowing and animated terms," he went on to castigate the Jackson administration for the derangement of the currency, the illegal Treasury orders, and the many other fiscal evils that had fallen "on the industrious and commercial classes of the community." Already there had been loss of business confidence, disorder, and bankruptcies. The price of cotton had fallen to one half its value. Unemployment had risen, and it appeared that a full-scale financial panic was in the offing.

"I predicted all this from the beginning," Webster boomed, "and from before the beginning." I have come here "to speak my sentiments freely. . . . I have nothing to conceal, and shall therefore conceal nothing." There is "nothing in my heart which I am ashamed of; I shall throw it all open, therefore, to you, and to all men."

The crowd erupted. One man shouted: "That's right; let us have it, with no non-committal"—an obvious reference to President Van Buren's reputation for being noncommittal.

"Yes, my friend," Webster responded, "without non-committal or evasion, without barren generalities or empty phrase, without *if* or *but.*"

He had hit his stride. The audience was with him, and he reveled in it. He immediately announced his decision not to resign from the Senate, after which he proclaimed his fervent belief that the government was national, not consolidated, that it did not embrace all power. "On the contrary," he declared, "it is delegated, restrained, strictly limited."

He turned to the administration's public land policy and declared his unalterable opposition to ceding public lands to the states. Because they constitute "the common property of all the people of all the States, I shall never consent to give them away to particular States." They should be sold "at a low price," and portions should be used for internal improvements. "I desire the growth and prosperity of the West, and the fullest development of its vast and extraordinary resources." The revenue from the sale of land, however, should be turned over to the states. "The States need the money. The government of the United States does not." Westerners applauded his efforts on their behalf and increasingly regarded him as their friend and advocate.[3]

Webster then condemned extravagant government expenditures, the un-

2. Hone, *Diary,* I, 247–248.

3. For Webster's advocacy of western rights, see Peter J. Parish, "Daniel Webster, New England, and the West," *Journal of American History,* LIV (December 1967), pp. 524–549.

necessary surplus that the Jackson administration had acquired. Revenue should be kept, he said, at the "just and reasonable" needs of the government.

"I am in favor of protecting American industry and labor," he went on, not only in large manufactures but especially as employed "in the various mechanic arts, carried on by persons of small capitals." If duties were abolished on hats, boots, shoes, on fabricated articles of brass, tin, and iron, on ready-made clothes, on carriages and furniture, etc., thousands of laborers would be immediately thrown out of work in this city and other cities in the nation. Protection of labor against the "cheaper, ill-paid, half-fed, and pauper labor of Europe" is a "duty" this government owes its citizens.

Next, he turned to foreign affairs, in particular the independence of Texas, which the United States had recently recognized. Straight off he admitted that there existed "insurmountable objections to the annexation of Texas." He saw no need for it, unlike the acquisitions of Louisiana and Florida. "I am altogether at a loss to conceive what possible benefit any part of this country can expect to derive from such annexation." Moreover, "Texas is likely to be a slave-holding country; and I frankly avow my entire unwillingness to do any thing that shall extend the slavery of the African race on this continent, or add other slave-holding States to the Union." Personally, he declared, "I regard slavery in itself as a great moral, social, and political evil." Slavery already exists in the country, and the Constitution gave it "solemn guarantees," which we all are bound "in honor, in justice" to respect. But he said he would do nothing "to favor or encourage its further extension." Slavery in the states where it exists is beyond the reach of Congress. "I shall concur, therefore, in no act, no measure, no menace, no indication of purpose, which shall interfere or threaten to interfere with the exclusive authority of the several States over the subject of slavery as it exists within their respective limits."[4]

All things considered, then, Webster maintained that there was no political necessity for or any advantage to be obtained from annexation, although he recognized that a great many people in the country favored it. He believed it "to be for the interest and happiness of the whole Union to remain as it is, without diminution and without addition."

He then addressed Jackson's extraordinary increase in the powers of the executive branch. This development truly offended him. The presidential power must be brought back "within its constitutional limits," he cried in sharp, ringing tones. He listed the spoils system, the Specie Circular, Jackson's assertion that he was "the *representative of the whole American people*, the war against the BUS and the unholy mess that it had inflicted on the nation's currency and exchange. Jackson came to power " on professions of reform," but look, look, he stormed, what his administration has brought us. As for the President's hard money schemes, Webster allowed that he too was " a *bullionist*." He favored a

4. Webster's views on slavery had been expressed many times before and widely circulated. For example, a letter he had written to John Bolton in 1833 had been published in *Niles' Weekly Register* for June 29, 1833. DW to Bolton, May 17, 1833, in *PC*, III, 252–253.

solid specie basis for American currency, but " I believe, also, that an exclusive gold and silver circulation is an utter impossibility in the present state of this country and of the world." It was downright foolish. States will charter banks, which will issue paper, and the longer the government fails to regulate the currency properly, the greater the amount of paper in circulation. "Gentlemen, I hold . . . this derangement . . . this violation of the currency, to be one of the most unpardonable of political faults." He expected the early signs of economic distress in the country beginning to be felt to get even worse. " I greatly fear, even, that the worst is not yet. I look for severer distresses; for extreme difficulties in exchange . . . and for a sudden fall in prices." One thing the government can do, he announced, is repeal the Specie Circular.

You gentlemen, Webster concluded, living in this great city, have a special duty and responsibility that you cannot escape:

> You must live and act . . . either for good or for evil to your country. You cannot shrink from your public duties. . . . In the common welfare, in the common prosperity, in the common glory of Americans, you have a stake of value not to be calculated. . . . Shall we not, by this friendly meeting, refresh our patriotism, rekindle our love of constitutional liberty, and strengthen our resolutions of public duty? Shall we not . . . here, to-night, pledge our mutual faith to hold on to the last to our professed principles, to the doctrines of true liberty, and to the Constitution of the country . . . ? Whigs of New York! I meet you in advance, and give you my pledge for my own performance of these duties, without qualification and without reserve.

The crowd, "delighted and instructed," listened with rapt attention to every word he spoke, "unconscious that they had been standing in one position for nearly four hours."[5] It was quite a performance!

The following day Webster took up a position in the governor's room at City Hall, where, from noon until 2:00 P.M., he met his friends and admirers. "A constant stream of orderly, well-behaved citizens," reported Hone, "visited and tendered the city's welcome to the man whom all (without regard to party) acknowledge as the eloquent and patriotic expounder and supporter of the Constitution."[6]

Later Hone gave a dinner party in Webster's honor with a select company of important Whigs, and the senator found himself in his element. "He was talkative, cheerful, full of anecdote," Hone confided to his diary, "and appeared to enjoy himself as much as he caused others to, and made a very gay termination of an exceedingly sorrowful sort of week."

Hone was referring to the "troubles of Wall Street." For on March 17, two days after Webster had given his speech, much of what he predicted occurred. I. and L. Joseph of New York, one of the largest dealers in domestic exchange with connections to a variety of commercial and mercantile enterprises and

5. They had been standing for four hours, although Webster spoke for only two and a half hours.
6. Hone, *Diary*, I, 248; *National Intelligencer*, April 29, May 2, 1837; *Niles' Weekly Register*, May 6, 1837. See also *W&S*, III, 132–173, and *PS*, II, 118–152.

banks, closed its doors, triggered by the price collapse of cotton in New Orleans. The closing touched off a chain reaction, and a number of exchange companies went bankrupt. The price of specie rose sharply and created a run on the banks. Then, on May 10, all the New York banks agreed to suspend the payment of their notes in specie. Boston followed the next day, and soon every bank in the nation was forced to suspend specie payments. Many of them failed with losses totaling tens of millions of dollars. It seemed the nation verged on complete economic collapse.

"I certainly never saw such hard times as the present," Webster remarked in early April to his son Fletcher, "especially in New York." There had been many failures, and "money is too scarce, & times too *really distressing*, here, to think of raising any more at present for western operations." Actually he himself was in grave financial straits. In his enthusiasm for making a quick profit from land and stock speculations, Webster had failed to foresee the financial direction of the country until it was too late. His speculations in February 1837 alone exceeded one hundred thousand dollars, virtually all purchased on credit, and he found it impossible to meet his financial obligations when they came due. He naturally called on friends, like Caleb Cushing, for help, and they usually obliged him. To creditors he begged for time. "I do not see that it is *possible* for me to meet [my obligation]," he explained to one banker. "I hope to be able to pay a part, say 1/3rd. . . . I have not the means of taking it up. No money can be raised here, by any means within my command. . . . If any securities I have will be useful to you, to the amount of ten thousand Dollars, I will readily loan them to you." Because of his name and reputation, creditors did not wish to embarrass him, but they still demanded payment. The indebtedness he had amassed in 1836 and the first two months of 1837 were never to be completely liquidated. These debts, and others he acquired in the ensuing years, plagued him for the rest of his life.[7]

Although Webster, like virtually all Whigs, blamed Jackson's fiscal policies for the Panic of 1837, those policies really had little to do with causing it. Actually a worldwide depression brought about the debacle, no doubt provoked by the Bank of England's sudden restriction of loans to the United States and the subsequent reduction of British purchases of cotton.[8] But the Whigs thought differently, and with the distress mounting each month they realized that they now had a political weapon with which to bludgeon the Democrats in the press and at the polls. Surely, whomever they nominated in 1840 would win the presidency overwhelmingly.

Webster, who had been thinking of another trip to the West to inspect his land purchases and visit his son, now realized that such a trip made a great deal of political sense. It would allow him to reestablish contact with this most

7. DW to Fletcher Webster, April 9, DW to Cushing, April 10, 13, DW to William Bradley, April 27, 1837, in *PC*, IV, 211, 213–214, 222.

8. For an excellent analysis of the causes of the panic, see Peter Temin, *The Jacksonian Economy* (New York, 1969).

important section of the country. He had informed Fletcher as early as February that he expected to make the journey in April and visit Louisville and St. Louis and then work his way north to Detroit.

Because of business duties, his financial difficulties and the need to borrow several thousand dollars to make the trip, Webster, Caroline, and Julia did not set out on their tour until early May. He had invited his godson William Pitt Fessenden to join him, and the young man caught up with the Websters at Harrisburg. Fessenden found Caroline Webster "very sociable and agreeable" and Julia "bashful, but possessed of a very intelligent face and good conversational accomplishments."[9]

Except for eleven miles, the group crossed Pennsylvania all the way by canal or railroad. The excursion provided ample proof, if any was needed, of the worth of internal improvements. They descended the Ohio River by riverboat and stopped off at Wheeling, Virginia, where Webster was honored with a public dinner and gave a speech on current conditions in the country and how Jacksonian economics had caused the depression. News of the suspension of specie payments by banks had just reached Wheeling, and Webster in his speech likened the financial disaster in the eastern states to war and pestilence. He proposed a toast, saluting: *"Our Country—our free Government.—*Never to be despaired of, never to be deserted."[10]

They next stopped at Maysville, Kentucky, where they debarked, attended a reception, and rode overland to Lexington, escorted by a committee, to visit Henry Clay and his family. "Mr. Webster meets with so warm a reception all along the shore that what with guns, dinners, speeches, and the like, one is continually excited," Fessenden reported. Naturally at Clay's home they were entertained royally and did a great deal of drinking, dancing, gambling and horse racing. Young Fessenden was rather shocked by the antics of the western Whigs. Clay and his friends, he wrote, were "talking as loudly, betting as freely, drinking as deeply, and swearing as excessively as the jockeys themselves."[11]

The party then visited Frankfort, Versailles, and Louisville, where Webster was enthusiastically received. But in Louisville the reception "was something akin to idolatry." At the barbecue held in Webster's honor no less than twenty sheep, twenty-five calves, thirty shoats, sixty bacon hams, and several heifers were prepared. A crowd estimated at four thousand took part in the feast, after which Webster gave a two-hour speech. His reception "was enthusiastic beyond description," exclaimed one journalist. There were "loud and long-continued thunder-peals of applause, that followed the vivid flashes of his eloquence."[12]

Webster wisely decided to visit General William Henry Harrison at his home in Ohio. Harrison had done surprisingly well in the last presidential race

9. Francis Fessenden, *Life and Public Services of William Pitt Fessenden* (Boston and New York, 1907), I, 12.

10. *National Intelligencer,* May 20, 1837.

11. Fessenden, *Life,* I, 13.

12. Ibid., I, 15; *National Intelligencer,* June 10, 1837.

and had single-handedly (and without lifting a finger to do it) knocked Webster out of the contest. A friendly call on "Tippecanoe" would surely do no harm and might do the Massachusetts senator considerable good in the future. So the party ascended the Ohio River, landed at North Bend, and paid General Harrison a short visit. From there the group traveled to Madison, Indiana, to meet Webster's colleague Senator William Hendricks. His arrival was signaled by an artillery salute, and then Webster, seated next to Hendricks in an open barouche, led a long procession to the town square, which was decorated with flowers, shrubbery, evergreens, flags, and banners, one of which read, "Liberty and Union, Now and Forever, One and Inseparable." Webster obliged the crowd with an hourlong speech, much of it on "free school education—common school education," which he wholeheartedly endorsed.[13]

Moving on to Cincinnati, where he met Salmon P. Chase, a future secretary of the treasury and chief justice of the Supreme Court, Webster was introduced to the awaiting crowd by General Harrison. This show of unity between two rival Whigs for the nomination encouraged some party members to believe that the winning presidential ticket stood before them: Harrison and Webster. Harrison gave a short address both before and *after* Webster spoke, thereby getting in the last word. Then the party turned around and by private carriage rode across Ohio, Indiana, and Illinois, boarded a steamer, and sailed down the Mississippi to St. Louis, where they arrived on June 9.

The anticipated crowd waited onshore to greet Webster, and he responded by removing and waving his hat, triggering another explosion of enthusiasm. He entered a coach while a band played "Hail to the Chief." He paraded up Market Street to his hotel, all the while "windows lined, handkerchiefs waving, boys huzzaing, dogs barking, noses glowing, with four or five Indian chiefs following in the rear, each of whom in turn seized Mr. Webster in his arms and kissed his cheek." Again there was a grand reception, dinner, and another speech, this one lighthearted and informal. "No man, whether from the West or the East, the North or the South," commented one newspaper, "has ever met with so warm a reception in the west bank of the Mississippi—without parade or ostentation, it is true, but honest, heartfelt, and disinterested."

By this time some members of the party had begun to wilt. "Mrs. Webster and daughter are sick and tired with glory," Fessenden jokingly remarked; "their fatigue must be excessive, and, as to the show, Mrs. Webster, though proud of her husband, has little taste for it, and poor Julia none at all." But Fletcher's arrival in St. Louis helped restore everyone's spirits.[14]

Fletcher's presence gave Webster an opportunity to learn more about his recent land and stock speculations. The party now sailed up the Mississippi to Alton, headed east to Springfield, where Webster met the local leader of the Whig party, Abraham Lincoln, and moved on to northern Illinois to inspect his

13. Fuess, *Webster*, II, 63; *National Intelligencer,* July 15, 1837.

14. *National Intelligencer,* June 14, 24, 1837; Fessenden, *Life*, I, 15–16.

property holdings in Peru and Chicago. In Illinois, Fessenden, who had himself grown weary of the "noise and glory," parted from the group, happy to get away. Before he left, however, he recorded something interesting. "So far as gaining friends was concerned," he observed, "Mr. Webster might well, if not better, have stayed at home and left his fame and public service to speak for him." At another time Fessenden noted Webster's lack of warmth when meeting people. The senator "would never gain popularity by personal intercourse—to strangers he appeared repellent." Still another time: "[I]f Daniel was but half as winning as either his wife or daughter, I would give more for his chances."[15] Clearly Webster did not have the charisma necessary to attract the kind of support so essential to electoral success. True, he could be congenial and very amusing, laughing, drinking, conversing, telling stories, and enjoying simple pleasures among his peers. And he could enthrall a crowd with his oratory. Westerners genuinely and rightly considered him their friend and advocate. But too often they saw only eastern "refinement" and intellectual arrogance, much as he might try to hide his true character. Too often he appeared "repellent," as Fessenden said. In addition, his long ties with business, especially his relations with Biddle's Bank, convinced many people that Daniel Webster was too closely allied with the wealthy to represent them as President.

Still, despite these limitations and despite the debacle of a year ago, Webster felt he deserved the presidency, and he continued to pursue it relentlessly. Henry Clay, another relentless pursuer, could scarcely believe that Webster would undertake this tour to win backing for another run for the nomination. "Ambition has a powerful blinding effect," Clay declared. "And I think Mr. Websters case is a shocking proof of it. Within less than six months after it had been demonstrated that he could get the vote of but one of 26 States against not a very popular Candidate, he commences a long and arduous tour with the evident purpose of becoming a Candidate again." It will not work. "The cordial and distinguished reception of Mr. Webster at the West (with which I have been greatly rejoiced) ought to be viewed as homage to his acknowledged ability rather than as indicating any general disposition to support him as a Candidate for the Presidency."[16] In this regard Clay was absolutely correct.

The Webster party left Chicago, crossed Lake Michigan to Michigan City, and then went by land to Toledo and Detroit. At Buffalo they attended a splendid steamboat regatta on Lake Erie, organized in Webster's honor, and on July 20 he gave the last of this long series of western speeches at Rochester, New York. The group reached New York City on July 26 and spent a few days recuperating before heading back to Massachusetts and the country retreat at Marshfield.

Webster glowed. As far as he was concerned, the trip had been a smashing success. Showered with gifts, praised to the heavens before thousands of people,

---

15. Fessenden, *Life,* I, 12, 15; Charles A. Jellison, *Fessenden of Maine: Civil War Senator* (New York, 1962), p. 27; *National Intelligencer,* September 20, 1837.

16. Clay to Waddy Thompson, Jr., July 8, Clay to Matthew L. Davis, July 3, 1837, in Clay, *Papers,* IX, 58, 55.

kissed, embraced, wined, dined, and entertained with parades, regattas, and barbecues, he reckoned that this tour would place him up front among Whig candidates for the presidential nomination in 1840. Newspapers had carried accounts of his travels and how the crowds had received him so enthusiastically. His speeches were reported, although they contained little more than what he had said in New York back on March 15. In addition, he had inspected some of his property in Illinois, Ohio, and Michigan and had conferred with several of his agents, who escorted him on his tour. It no doubt pleased him to hear, after he had returned home, that at a local election in Michigan there was a great parade with "Bands of music, Stage Coaches, Flags—a ship on wheels, the Constitution, filled with Sailors & covered with ensigns, one of them bearing in noble capitals 'Daniel Webster & the Constitution.' "[17] Although he deluded himself totally, he had great hopes for the future, political as well as financial.

While he was inspecting his property in Illinois, word reached him that President Van Buren had called Congress into special session on September 4 to deal with the financial crisis facing the nation. Webster was therefore obliged to cut short his tour[18] and, of necessity, limit his respite at Marshfield.

He was slightly delayed in returning to Washington because of the need to negotiate his debts, gain extensions of time—he usually "asked 6 & 12 months indulgence"—and collect funds due him. He was deeply troubled by not only his own affairs but those of some of his agents. In one or two instances his creditors hinted at instituting legal action if he did not meet his obligations. Despite these fiscal woes, Webster actually considered more improvements for Marshfield. "I must have a fish pond," he told Charles Thomas, and he suggested raising the dam and building an embankment in order to accommodate such a pond.[19]

At the same time Fletcher wanted his permission to move to Peru, Illinois, and manage Webster's 160-acre farm called Salisbury. He had returned to Detroit, where his wife gave birth to a girl, Grace Fletcher—making Webster a grandfather for the first time[20]—but where he had little success in the practice of law and found prices much too high. "I thought that by taking charge of your farm & other property thereabouts," he explained, ". . . that I should be sure of a living besides what I could get from the Law and any operations that I might be able to make." Webster had doubts, but he agreed to let Fletcher move. "He is a noble fellow," the senator proudly wrote, ". . . [and] I am very much attached

17. Fletcher Webster to DW, August 28, 1837, in *PC*, IV, 234.

18. DW to George Jones, June 24, 1837, ibid., IV, 224.

19. See, for example, Ramsay Crooks to DW, September 23, 1837, DW to Crooks, January 2, February 24, 26, May 12, 1838, in *Microfilm Edition*, F11/14424, F12/14556, 14677, 14693, 14927. DW to Thomas, December 11, 1837, in *PC*, IV, 253.

20. Grace Fletcher Webster was born on August 28, 1837. Fletcher said his daughter "has blue eyes & light hair & takes after the Story's in appearance. I can see nothing that gives her a claim to Webster blood. I thought at first she had red hair, but was agreeably disappointed. Poor Caroline suffered extremely & the child hardly lived—but thank God! both are now doing well." Fletcher to DW, September 1, 1837, in *PC*, IV, 236.

to him." However, to take care of Salisbury and his other western investments, he subsequently hired Nathaniel Ray Thomas, the brother of Charles Henry Thomas.[21]

Webster took his seat in the Senate on September 8. President Van Buren had already sent down his message, in which he called on Congress to enact a series of bills to meet the ongoing and deepening financial crisis. He recommended withholding the fourth installment of the Treasury surplus, due to be distributed on October 1 under the provisions of the Deposit-Distribution Act of 1836. He also proposed a uniform bankruptcy law and the issuance of ten million dollars of Treasury notes to meet the emergency. He opposed the enactment of another national bank and suggested the divorce of the Treasury from the deposit banks. In effect, he wanted an "independent treasury system" with subtreasuries located in the leading cities to receive and disburse government revenues. Paper issued by state banks would not be acceptable in payment of obligations to the government.[22]

Van Buren was caught between two wings of the Democratic party, between hard-money Radicals, like Benton, and soft-money Conservatives like William C. Rives of Virginia and Nathaniel P. Tallmadge of New York. Hard-money Radicals were sometimes referred to as locofocos.[23] By recommending the issuance of Treasury notes yet refusing to accept paper money from state banks, Van Buren hoped to keep both sides of his party satisfied. It amused Webster to think that the party of Andrew Jackson would sponsor a bill to issue millions of dollars in paper.

Bills to implement Van Buren's suggestions were put forward by Senator Silas Wright, as chairman of the Senate Finance Committee, of which Webster was now a minority member. Webster, like Clay and other Whigs, argued against postponing the fourth installment of the revenue surplus on the grounds that the states needed the money and the loss of it would cause them much "inconvenience." The Senate rejected the argument and passed the suspension of payments by the vote of twenty-eight to seventeen. It then passed the bill to issue ten million dollars in Treasury notes in denominations of no less than one hundred dollars. As a swipe at the Whigs and to end all speculation on the matter, the Senate also passed a resolution against the establishment of another national bank. The vote was thirty-one to fifteen.[24]

In the debate over the independent treasury, or subtreasury or divorce bill, as it was variously called, John C. Calhoun came out in favor of the Van Buren

21. Fletcher to DW, September 1; DW to Henry Kinney, August 24, DW to Franklin Haven, October 2, 1837; DW to Nathaniel Thomas, March 5, 1838, ibid., IV, 236, 230, 242 note 2, 282–284.

22. Richardson, *Messages and Papers*, II, 1541–1563.

23. This was a radical New York movement within the Democratic party. It developed when a group of radical Democrats used "locofoco" matches to light candles at a meeting in New York City on October 29, 1835, after the more conservative Democrats had turned off the lights. Locofocos supported the elimination of all paper money, free trade, and the abolition of monopolies or subsidies to private business.

24. *Register of Debates*, 25th Congress, 1st Session, pp. 45–47, 1372.

proposal, thus signaling an end to his cooperation with the Whigs in opposing the policies and practices of the administration. He genuinely favored the scheme but offered an amendment that would permit the government to accept both specie and the paper of specie-paying banks until 1840, after which only specie would be accepted.[25]

Webster's major speech on the subtreasury bill came on September 28, and he started right off by announcing his opposition to the doctrines put forward in the President's message, the bill itself, and the amendment advanced by Calhoun. "In all these, I see nothing for the relief of the country," he said. He then launched into an extended history of the currency in the United States to show that despite differences of opinion from various factions and parties, starting with the Founding Fathers, it had always been understood that the government had an obligation to provide a sound circulating media of exchange. President Jackson inaugurated his "experiment" in currency with the promise that it would provide the nation with sounder money. But what had resulted? The system proved "radically vicious," "inconvenient," "clumsy, and wholly inadequate to the proposed ends." Sooner or later there had to be an "explosion." And it had occurred. Without mentioning the subtreasury, Webster then argued the constitutional obligation of the government to maintain a "proper"—that is, a "uniform"—currency, not merely regulate the coinage rates for gold and silver. He cited President Madison, whose message to Congress in December 1815 emphatically stated that Congress must provide a national currency—namely, a paper currency as a substitute for specie, one that would win the confidence and accommodate the needs of the American people. And what did Congress do? It enacted a National Bank in 1816, one sponsored and largely written by John C. Calhoun, then a member of the House.[26]

Calhoun quickly responded and in effect repudiated his earlier position on the Bank. He no longer thought that Congress had the constitutional power to enact one. He also said that government had no right to interfere with the financial operations of individuals. Moreover, banking was a private affair, and therefore government had no authority to place restrictions of any kind upon it because it constituted private property.[27]

Webster came right back at him. But he did it in a playful manner. No right to place restrictions on private property? But that is exactly why governments are formed, Webster responded. "Government does interfere and place restrictions in a thousand ways upon every kind of individual property," and it is done for the good of the community. But if the honorable senator from South Carolina wants a system of private individual banking, he need not stir from his seat. All he need do is look around and he will see all the blessings of such a system of

25. Wiltse, *Calhoun, Nullifier*, pp. 342–356; *Register of Debates*, 25th Congress, 1st Session, pp. 50–66.

26. *PS*, II, 155–184.

27. *Calhoun Papers*, XIII, 592–615.

"individual irresponsible banking." "If this is the currency which the government seeks to give us, we have got it!"

But what Webster really objected to in the administration's proposal was its attempt to create two currencies: specie for the government; "depreciated paper" for the people. We want the government to make this *"bad money of the people better.* We want an equality; that both government and people may share the same fate, and use the same money, and that the government may perform its duty of rendering the money, the currency of the people, sound and good."[28]

Despite the efforts of the Whigs, supported by some Conservative Democrats, the Senate passed the independent treasury bill on October 4 by a vote of 26 to 20 with Calhoun's amendment attached. But the House tabled it on October 14 by a vote of 120 to 107, with the Conservatives joining the Whigs to prevent its passage.[29]

With the end of the special session Webster returned home to await the results of the fall elections, which everyone predicted would result in a sweep for the Whigs. Actually they were spectacular. Clay likened the results to the victories at Yorktown and Waterloo. The people, he said, had rescued the country. "God bless them," he wrote. "God bless them forever!" The New York results, in particular, truly surprised everyone. Van Buren's home state was "revolutionized."[30]

The chairman of the Suffolk County Whig convention invited Webster to attend a celebration to honor the victory in Massachusetts and give a speech. The senator replied that he would "cheerfully" attend. "Let us remember, that this great and unprecedented success has been obtained clearly and distinctly on Whig grounds. It has been the result of no yielding, no compromise, no abandonment of our principles."[31] Unfortunately because of the great number of Whig meetings, the Suffolk County celebration was "deferred." However, Webster did attend, along with several other notable Whigs from around the country, a victory rally held in Faneuil Hall on November 10.[32]

In New York City he attended a Whig dinner for about 220 guests at the Astor House that began at seven-thirty and lasted all night. There were at least a dozen speeches from such worthies as John Bell of Tennessee, William Graves of Kentucky, Samuel Southard of New Jersey, and John P. Kennedy of Maryland. Webster's turn did not come until two o'clock in the morning! He promised to be brief, given the lateness of the hour, but the audience would not hear of it. So he "kept on in a strain of unwearied and unwearying eloquence until *four o'clock.*" Not another speaker on the globe "could thus have fixed their attention at such an unseasonable hour," reported Philip Hone. Several times during the

28. *PS*, II, 184–192.

29. *Register of Debates*, 25th Congress, 1st Session, p. 511.

30. Quoted in Remini, *Clay*, pp. 505–506.

31. DW to Henry Edwards et al., November 16, 1837, in *PC*, IV, 249.

32. *National Intelligencer*, November 16, 1837.

speech Hone looked around "and I verily believe not a person left the room while he was speaking."[33]

When Webster returned to Washington to take his seat on December 29—late as usual—he found Congress embroiled not in financial problems but in slavery and abolition. The antislavery feeling in the country had grown steadily throughout the decade and now intruded in Congress in the form of petitions demanding its termination and the elimination of the slave trade in the District of Columbia. The House had already reacted to the demand by passing a gag rule the previous May in which all antislavery petitions were simply laid on the table without debate or comment. In the Senate, the day before Webster arrived, Calhoun had introduced a set of resolutions encompassing the entire question of slavery and the nature of the Union. In the resolutions he restated his compact theory of the Constitution, emphasized the right of the states to manage their own institutions, declared slavery a fact of life that could not be touched, rejected demands for the abolition of slavery in the District of Columbia, and insisted that any opposition to territorial expansion based on abolitionism would threaten the life of the Union. Clay countered with several resolutions of his own. A slaveholder yet strongly opposed to slavery, Clay proposed that slavery be left to the exclusive control of slaveholding states, that petitions about slavery in the states be rejected by the Senate, that the abolition of slavery in the District required the consent of Virginia and Maryland because they had ceded the land constituting the District, and that the Constitution provided no power to prohibit the slave trade between slaveholding states.[34]

Clay and Calhoun engaged in several heated exchanges over these resolutions, no doubt exacerbated by Clay's anger over the South Carolinian's recent desertion of his friends in the Whig party. For his part Webster said little about the essential question of whether Congress should or should not abolish slavery in the District. The legalist, the constitutionalist in him focused on whether or not Congress had the power to enact such legislation. And on that score he had no doubt. So, on January 10, 1838, he rose in the Senate and stated his position.

"The words of the Constitution are clear and plain," he insisted. Congress has exclusive jurisdiction over ceded territory "in all cases whatsoever."[35] The acts of cession by Virginia and Maryland contained no limitation or condition; therefore nothing is clearer than that both states expected Congress to exercise total jurisdiction as the Constitution mandates. There is nothing in the acts of cession, nothing in the Constitution, nothing in the history of the transaction, and nothing in any other transaction remotely suggesting any limitation on the authority of Congress. Would Congress, he asked, have accepted the cession had there been any restraint on its constitutional power? "I think not." All the parties to the transaction knew what they were doing, all knew that both states

33. Hone, *Diary*, I, 289.

34. *Congressional Globe*, 25th Congress, 2d Session, p. 55, appendix, pp. 57–60.

35. Presumably, then, Webster held that Congress could legislate slavery in such territories as the Florida Territory and those territories remaining from the Louisiana Territory.

had surrendered all jurisdiction, and all knew that Congress had acquired total jurisdiction. Therefore Congress had full authority to regulate slavery within the District.

However, in stating his position, Webster was quick to assert his belief that slavery in the states was another matter. It is a "subject belonging absolutely and exclusively to the States themselves."[36]

Webster amplified his remarks in a letter to Luther Peck, a Whig congressman from New York, written a day after he gave this speech. Congress may not only abolish slavery in the District whenever "humanity and true policy may require it," he wrote, but it may also regulate or restrain the purchase and sale of slaves in the District in any manner it deems "just and expedient." Furthermore, citizens have the unquestioned right to petition Congress for the restraint or abolition of slavery in the District, and these petitions must be "read, referred and considered" without reproach or rebuke to the signers of such petitions. "The right of petition, free, unqualified, and untrammelled, I hold to be of the very substance and essence of civil liberty." A free government cannot exist without it.[37]

The very fact that Congress could consider passage of a gag resolution or relinquish its right to abolish slavery in the District enraged Webster. "Mr Clay & Mr Calhoun, in my judgment, have attempted in 1838, what they attempted in 1833, *to make a new Constitution,*" he told his friend Hiram Ketchum. Webster could foresee real problems ahead for Congress because "the Anti Slavery feeling is growing stronger & stronger, every day; & while we must be careful to countenance nothing, which violates the Constitution, or invades the rights of others, it is our policy, in my opinion, most clearly, not to yield the substantial truth, for the sake of conciliating those whom we never can conciliate, at the expense of the loss of the friendship & support of those great masses of good men, who are interested in the Anti Slavery cause."[38]

After much quarreling, haggling, and amending, the Senate finally adopted Calhoun's resolutions, except for the one that stated any opposition to territorial expansion based on abolitionism would threaten the Union. That one it tabled. And Clay's resolution regarding slavery in the District also passed. Webster voted against both.[39]

As these three titans of the Senate tore up what remained of their grand coalition, they treated their audience to one of the great debates in American history. Never before had there been such a debate, one so personal, so dramatic, so portentous. The crowds that packed the galleries, the corridors, and

36. *PS,* II, 198–203. Webster's speech "inspired Abolitionists with the hope that [he] would become the leader of the crusade against slavery. . . . This was noticed by the Southern leaders, who began to tempt him with promises of support for the Presidency—promises which were subsequently broken again and again." Poore, *Perley's Reminiscences,* I, 212–213.

37. DW to Peck, January 11, 1838, in *PC,* IV, 261–262.

38. DW to Ketchum, January 15, DW to Benjamin Silliman, January 29, 1838, ibid., IV, 262, 265.

39. *Congressional Globe,* 25th Congress, 2d Session, appendix, pp. 60–62, 63, 65.

the floor itself heard Clay's "glowing rhetoric," Calhoun's "nervous logic," and Webster's "overshadowing majesty."[40] Clay and Webster castigated Calhoun for his apostasy, and the once Great Triumvirate dissected, analyzed, and debated momentous national issues for the next several weeks and months, issues such as slavery, abolition, territorial expansion, finance, banking, depression, public lands, and the nature of the Union. The weeks and months in which these three giants harangued their audience about these issues are among the supreme moments in the history of the U.S. Senate. Unfortunately the splendor of it could not be accurately recorded; only the memory of it has been preserved.

Once he had given his speech on slavery in the District, Webster turned back to a major speech on the subtreasury that he was preparing and that he gave on March 12 and 13.[41] He spoke for five hours the first day and four hours the second! The subtreasury bill had been reintroduced by the Finance Committee chairman, and Calhoun became active again on its behalf. Webster paid close attention to the construction of his speech as he prepared it.

It was ingeniously contrived. He wove together an economic analysis of the banking system (repeating much of what he had said earlier and demonstrating that the administration's bill guaranteed further financial disaster) with a brief against Calhoun to discredit him by reviewing his past political inconsistencies. Webster himself had several inconsistencies to his "credit" that Calhoun exploited in his rebuttal. But Webster's speech was hailed by the partisan Whig press as the greatest display of eloquence, "greater even than his reply to General Hayne." It became the standard text for any opponent of the subtreasury.[42]

Webster's attack on Calhoun cut deep, although it was done with style, wit, and grace. Unlike Clay, he maintained his dignity throughout.

Finally, the honorable member [Calhoun] declares that he shall now march off, under the banner of States rights! March off from whom? March off from what? We have been contending for great principles. We have been struggling to maintain the liberty and to restore the prosperity of the country; we have made these struggles here, in the national councils, with the old flag, the true American flag, the Eagle, and the Stars and Stripes, waving over the chamber in which we sit. He now tells us, however, that he marches off under the State-rights banner!

Let him go. I remain. I am where I ever have been, and ever mean to be. Here, standing on the platform of the general Constitution, a platform broad enough and firm enough to uphold every interest of the whole country, I shall be found.[43]

Ten days later Calhoun replied. It always took him time to prepare his rejoinders. He needed time to assemble his thoughts, sharpen his arguments, select his words. And when he spoke, he looked, said Harriet Martineau, as if he

40. Henry Stanton, *Random Recollections* (New York, 1887), p. 84.

41. Webster also spoke on the subtreasury on January 31, 1838. It can be found in *W&S*, VIII, 140–161.

42. Hone, *Diary*, I, 311; *W&S*, VIII, 162–237.

43. Ibid., VIII, 236.

had never been born and could never be extinguished.[44] One congressman later said that "Calhoun spoke like a college professor demonstrating to his class."[45]

Because Webster had been careful to express his personal regard for Calhoun, explaining that his attack on Calhoun's record was political, not personal, the South Carolinian responded in kind. He acknowledged that no personal difference ever existed between them, not even a word that could give offense. But they had deep political differences, and he went on to defend his record and his alleged "desertion" of the Whig party. He also examined Webster's record, which was not exactly free of inconsistencies, referring to the Bank, the tariff, the War of 1812, and even Webster's defense of Jackson during the nullification controversy. Webster by his "consolidated doctrines," said Calhoun, would sweep away every vestige of the rights of states with a single blow and reduce them to petty and impotent corporations.[46]

Webster naturally felt obliged to respond to Calhoun's rejoinder and gave what many considered the funniest, if not the best, speech of his life. It was truly magnificent. He started by saying that he happened to meet a friend who informed him that he ought to hasten his steps because "the war was to be carried into Africa" and Webster would be "annihilated." Under the circumstances what could I do? he asked his audience with a straight face. "I lost no time in following the advice, Sir, since it would be awkward for one to be annihilated without knowing any thing about it."

He continued. When Scipio decided to carry the war into Africa, "Hannibal was not at home. Now, Sir, I am very little like Hannibal, but I am at home; and when Scipio Africanus South-Caroliniensis brings the war into my territories, I shall not leave their defence to Asdrubal, nor Syphax, nor any body else. I meet him on the shore, at his landing."

The audience punctuated that last sally with loud guffaws.

On the subject of slavery, Webster continued, Calhoun says I am no friend of the South. "Why, Sir, the only proof is, that I did not vote for his resolutions."

Calhoun also stated that he had always belonged to the states' rights party. "Sir . . . I sat here the other day, and held my breath" while he said it. "Sir, if the honorable member ever belonged, until very lately, to the State-rights party, the connection was very much like a secret marriage. And never was secret better kept." Calhoun's nationalistic activities in Congress following the War of 1812 were very well known by many in this chamber. "Sir, is there a man in my hearing . . . who ever heard, supposed, or dreamed that the honorable member belonged to the State-rights party before the year 1825?"

Webster also referred to Calhoun's opposition to a measure during the War of 1812 to create another bank. "Well, Sir, I agreed with him. It was a mere

44. Martineau, *Western Travel*, I, 149.

45. Wentworth, "Congressional Reminiscences," p. 21.

46. *Congressional Globe*, 25th Congress, 2d Session, appendix, 632–641. "Clay & Webster," said Calhoun, have tried "to break me down," but "I did not come out second best." Clay to Samuel D. Ingham, April 13, 1838, in *Calhoun Papers*, XIV, 258.

paper bank," a means of circulating irredeemable paper. "But, Sir, I say again that the gentleman himself took the lead against this measure, this darling measure of the administration. I followed him; if I was seduced into error, or into unjustifiable opposition, there sits my seducer."[47]

In all his speeches during this session Webster exhibited powers totally unlike anything that he had demonstrated on the Senate floor before and for which he never had credit. He showed that his wit was as keen as his logic was conclusive and that he could see the ridiculous. His wit had a acid flavor, wrote one: tart but pleasant and free from bitterness that "comes from an overflow of gall and provokes revenge rather than pleasant laughter." Even Calhoun laughed at some of Webster's jabs.

At one point the Massachusetts senator referred to an English play that ridiculed the sentimentality in certain schools of German literature. Two strangers meet at an inn.

"A sudden thought strikes me," says one stranger to the other. "Let us swear eternal friendship!" The offer is immediately accepted.

Calhoun is like that, said Webster. He and the Whigs have been engaged in a contest against the Democratic administration and when victory seems at hand, Calhoun suddenly cries out: "Halloo! a sudden thought strikes me. I abandon my allies! They have always been my oppressors! Let you and I swear eternal friendship."

The audience howled, despite the gaveling of the presiding officer, Vice President Richard M. Johnson. What made the humor even more irresistible in the minds of many was the fact that it emanated from the grave, dignified, and Godlike Daniel, whose face never betrayed anything more than a smile.[48]

Despite the efforts of the Whigs and Conservative Democrats, they could not win passage of an amendment, proposed by Senator Rives, to substitute state banks for the subtreasury.[49] But they did manage to kill Calhoun's amendment to discontinue bank notes gradually for debts owed the government.

Webster was more successful with his amendment. He proposed, and the Senate adopted, his proposal that directed the secretary of the treasury not to discriminate between hard and soft money in collecting debts owed the government. With this amendment, the subtreasury or independent treasury

47. W&S, VIII, 238–260. Webster's "bold denial," wrote Calhoun, "of the part he took in the late war has surprised every body. . . . His course during that period is so deeply fixed in the opinion of nine-tenths of the people, that all he can say, or do cannot alter the verdict of the publick." Calhoun to George Bancroft, April 14, 1838, in Calhoun Papers, XIV, 261.

48. Sargent, Public Men and Events, pp. 49–50.

49. During the early debates on the independent treasury the Democratic newspaper organ, the Washington Globe, attacked Webster for contributing to a Boston bank's insolvency because of his failure to repay loans for his speculative ventures in the amounts of tens of thousands of dollars. Webster denied his indebtedness to the bank, whereupon Francis Blair, the editor, published a letter from Webster himself to substantiate his accusation. The controversy did Webster's reputation little good among the masses of voters, who continued to see him as untrustworthy when it came to money. Globe, January 20, 23, February 2, 1838; DW to Nathaniel Thomas, May 11, 1838, in PC, IV, 296.

to let you take care of yourself hereafter. But your letter shows an apparent spirit of repentance, & if I were sure that I could trust *that,* I might be induced to overlook the enormity of your misconduct. But how can I be sure that you have *now* told me the whole truth? How can I trust your present statements? Besides, how was this debt created? Was it by gaming, or other immoral habits,—or by mere thoughtlessness, & folly? . . . I want to know more about the manner of contracting this debt; & I expect the whole truth. I would not expose you to public reproach, nor cast you off, for slight cause; but with all my affection, I will not excuse misconduct, and especially, I will not put up with any degree or particle of misrepresentation, or concealment of the truth. On the receipt of this, you will immediately write to me, directed to Boston, & when I receive your letter, I shall determine what course to pursue.

Your affectionate, but distressed Father.[6]

Ned responded immediately. He swore he was repentant, had "never gambled for a cent" in his entire life, and was telling "the *truth* now." The money was spent "for such things as nuts & raisins, crockerey, cigars, candy pantaloons chess men backgammon boards knifes and some *wine* a very little of which I can say with a clear conscience I drank my self, riding on horse back and other ways for pleasure." The wine was the "*only* immoral thing" he purchased. The "silly boys" who got him into this trouble had graduated "so that there would not be the same temptations" in the future. He did not wish to leave school, but if his father so decreed, he would abide by his decision. "I remain my dear Father your most affectional [*sic*] and *deeply* penitent son."[7]

Webster forgave him. He would pay the debts and allow him to continue his studies, but he expected him to be truthful and to hear "nothing of you, hereafter, except what may be gratifying." The father explained that he owed "a good deal of money, & am at present receiving but a small income from my profession." If he could get Edward through Dartmouth, that would be as much as he could afford to do. Then he offered more advice: "If you intend yourself for the *Bar,* you must begin, early, to contract a habit of diligent & ambitious study. You must be emulous of excellence. An ordinary lawyer is not an enviable character. I believe, verily, that you have sense and ability enough to make you quite respectable, & I pray you, My Dear Son, keep your attention steadily directed to your progress in your studies."

Webster enclosed three checks totaling $250, but he asked his son not to cash them all until October 1 or 5, when presumably he would cover them.[8]

During the summer Webster also came to terms with his craving for the presidency. Winning the nomination of the Whig party almost guaranteed election in 1840, given the state of the nation's economy. But he realistically evaluated his personal chances. He rightly concluded that both Clay and General Harrison had greater support among Whigs, and Clay seemed hell-bent on winning the nomination. In fact Abbott Lawrence, one of the Boston Associates

6. DW to Edward Webster, September 8, 1838, in Van Tyne, ed., *Letters of Webster,* pp. 597–598.

7. Edward Webster to DW, September 13, 1838, in *PC,* IV, 326–327.

8. DW to Edward Webster, September 21, 1838, ibid., IV, 327–328.

who had been very supportive of Webster throughout his career, flatly informed him that his chances for winning the presidency were virtually nonexistent. Why, then, should the party continue to waste its efforts on him?[9] And just before the congressional session ended, Clay had contacted him in a faintly veiled effort to convince Webster that his candidacy was hopeless, that it only guaranteed a quarrel between their respective friends, and that such a quarrel could split the Whig party. Clay of course hoped his rival would withdraw in his favor. It was "a long & friendly interview," and the Kentuckian tried to put his comments gently, "of course not in the form of advice, but of suggestion."

Webster just listened. After a moment or two he spoke as politely and as gently as possible and told the Kentuckian that he "did not clearly see that he should abandon his position." He chose to disregard the impertinence of Clay's suggestion and in the ensuing months avoided any visible display of his irritation and displeasure.[10]

But facing the reality of his situation and recollecting what Thurlow Weed had said to him, Webster knew that when the Whigs held their convention in December 1839, there was little chance they would turn to him to head their ticket. They needed a popular candidate, one with charisma, one "who will poll the most votes," and Webster simply did not measure up to that standard.[11] So, wisely, he made no effort to start a national campaign. He seemed resigned to the fact that he would not receive serious consideration. Massachusetts would support him, of course, but that was probably as far as it would go.

Under the circumstances he started thinking of other possibilities. He could return to private life and try to get his finances in order, a thought that regularly intruded on his thinking. He might also take a trip to Europe. As an ardent, indeed rabid Anglophile, with numerous correspondents and friends in Britain whom he had known in America, such as Sir Charles Bagot, Sir Stratford Canning, Sir Charles Vaughan, Lord Stanley, John Denison, and others, Webster yearned to visit England. He might also be able to unload his western properties on English investors. That in itself was reason to go.

One problem stared him in the face: the cost. How would he pay for such a trip, particularly since he intended to bring his wife and daughter? Well, he could borrow the money and put up his lands and stock as collateral, and his friends always seemed ready to oblige. The more he thought about it and discussed it with his wife and daughter, the more his enthusiasm for such an adventure mounted. He finally decided to write his friend Samuel Jaudon, the cashier of the old BUS and presently living in England, and asked what the prospects were for the sale of western lands in Great Britain. "I have a great desire to see England," he explained, "& if that desire be ever gratified, it must

9. Everett to Robert Winthrop, May 21, 1838, Winthrop Papers, MHS; Dalzell, *Enterprising Elite*, p. 278 note 93.

10. Clay to Otis, July 7, 1838, in Clay, *Papers*, IX, 212–213. "It is best for *him*, and best for the common cause," Clay arrogantly told Otis. "It would be regarded as a measure of great magnanimity and his praises would be generally sounded." Remini, *Clay*, 524.

11. Barnes, *Memoir of Weed*, II, 76.

be done without much longer delay." He spelled out the lands and stock he had for sale and indicated that it would not be worth his while to go abroad "for a less sum than $100,000."[12]

While he waited for a response, Webster returned to his congressional duties, arriving a month and a half late. He excused himself, after a fashion, by claiming that Congress had done nothing of consequence, except to amuse itself by debating abolitionism. Nor was business before the Supreme Court very demanding, "nor is the Court itself what it has been." He had two or three "old causes to dispose of, but have not recd retainers, for new causes, for some time past."[13] Things were bad all over.

At least the Massachusetts legislature reelected him to the Senate, unanimously in the upper house and in the lower by a vote of 330 to 65, although he said: "[W]hether I shall ever take a seat, under that election, is uncertain." He left his wife and daughter behind and boarded at Miss Polk's with several other congressmen, including Hugh Lawson White. His daughter, Julia, now a young lady of twenty-one, had consented to marry Samuel Appleton Appleton, the son of Eben Appleton, and a business partner of both his uncle, Nathan Appleton, and Julia's uncle, James W. Paige. "Julia has consented to be mine," Appleton wrote to his prospective father-in-law, "and it only remains for me to prove by my conduct through life how sincerely and devotedly I love her."[14]

When Jaudon finally responded to Webster's letter, he offered little encouragement about selling property in England. Indeed his words placed a pall over the entire prospect of a trip abroad.[15]

Even so, Webster passionately longed to go. He loved the country he had never seen, its institutions, its people, its literature, its law and legal precedents, its traditions, its regal tone, and he simply could not give up his plans to visit it, despite the financial problems it posed. So he turned to other possibilities. Even before he heard from Jaudon, he thought of a scheme that would solve his problem: become a special minister to England to arbitrate the rising conflict over territory between Canada and the United States.

This particular quarrel centered on the dispute over the northeastern boundary separating Canada from the United States as defined by the Treaty of Paris in 1783, which officially ended the American Revolution. Some twelve thousand square miles of land were involved, and Americans claimed it all. The dispute quickly escalated, and fighting broke out in 1839 between lumbermen in Maine and New Brunswick along the Aroostook River—the so-called Aroostook War—and threatened to spread to other areas.[16]

The possibility of a special mission inspired Webster into drawing up a

12. DW to Jaudon, January 12, 1839, in *PC*, IV, 338–340.

13. DW to Jaudon, January 13, 1839, ibid., IV, 340.

14. DW to Jaudon, January 13, Appleton to DW, February 17, 1839, ibid., IV, 340, 345.

15. "I do not take quite courage enough, from what you say, to set forth for England," Webster wrote Jaudon on March 29, 1839, ibid., IV, 354.

16. For the Aroostook War, see Howard Jones, *To the Webster-Ashburton Treaty: A Study in Anglo-American Relations, 1783–1843* (Chapel Hill, N.C., 1977).

fourteen-point memorandum on the boundary question. His proposals had nothing startling in them, but they were basically sound and reasonable, certainly not belligerent. He also heard that Joel Poinsett, the secretary of war, had suggested him for such a mission to President Van Buren. "I therefore called on Mr P—told him what I had heard" and gave an opinion on the course a minister should pursue. Webster also read his memorandum to the President.[17]

Courteous as always, Van Buren listened, expressed his pleasure with the suggestions, and asked for a copy of the memorandum. But he had no intention at all of sending a leading Whig on this important mission. He chose not to send anyone. It certainly did not help that David B. Ogden, a New York lawyer, publicly accused Webster of suggesting that if the disputed territory was not settled by July 4, the United States should seize it. Webster emphatically denied the accusation, but it about killed any possibility of his representing his country abroad.[18]

So Webster had to look elsewhere for financial support. Naturally he turned to his friends and the banks. First, he wrote to Samuel Ruggles, a New York banker, and requested a loan of fifty thousand dollars (but said he could get along with forty thousand), offering his western lands as collateral. He told Ruggles, "I think I can do something useful to myself, in England, and it is possible I might also be in some measure useful to my friends."[19] Ruggles's bank finally agreed to twenty-eight thousand dollars as a two-year loan, payable with interest semiannually, for which Webster put up his lands in Ohio, Indiana, Michigan, Illinois, and Wisconsin.[20] In addition, his friends in Boston got up a subscription on his behalf when they heard that he was putting up his Summer Street properties for sale to pay for the trip. "The Subscribers in consideration of Mr Websters public services are desirous to lessen the loss to him which must be considerable on the Sale of his Estate and to enable him with more ease to complete his arrangements for his visit to England which they think will be useful to the Country." Any number of these friends put up five hundred dollars apiece. Even Nicholas Biddle contributed—as a separate donation—by placing "something in your way that will help pay your expenses &c &c."[21]

Thomas W. Ward, the American agent of the Baring Brothers banking firm in England, informed the brothers of Webster's projected visit and guessed that what had been raised in Boston and Philadelphia matched what New York had provided. Ward himself said that he had withheld his "esteem & confidence" because of the senator's "disregard to his moral obligation and a recklessness in

17. Memorandum on the Northeastern Boundary Negotiations and Memorandum of Proposal for Special Mission to England, in *PC*, IV, 346–349, 350.

18. *National Intelligencer*, March 9, 19, 1839. See also Webster's Senate speech on the boundary dispute, in *W&S*, XIV, 271–274.

19. DW to Ruggles, March 2, 25, 1839, in *PC*, IV, 346, 353.

20. Receipt for loan, ibid., IV, 361–362.

21. Subscription list, May 1, 1839, ibid., 359–361; Biddle to DW, May 5, 1839, in *Microfilm Edition*, F12/15493.

pecuniary matters." Still, he admitted that Black Dan was "by far the greatest man we have" and can "bring more power of mind in an argument on great questions ... than any man now living." Ward then suggested that Baring's would do well to assist him financially in England. "It will be easy to have him in your Books if you desire it, but whatever he may owe you I think you will be very safe in writing off to Profits & Loss."[22]

Besides having a burning desire to visit England for personal reasons, both emotional and financial, Webster genuinely believed his visit could help his country. He thought he could smooth relations between the two rivals if he had the opportunity to meet important British statesmen and discuss with them their mutual concerns.[23]

With the problem of expense off his mind, Webster set about placing those properties not conveyed as collateral in trust to protect them from seizure by creditors. He also arranged his passage and that of his wife, Caroline, his daughter, Julia (who wanted to be married in London, the birthplace of her intended husband), and his sister-in-law Harriette Story Paige, aboard the steamship *Liverpool,* scheduled to depart New York on May 18. It was agreed that Appleton would follow them to England, where the wedding would take place, and that Ned would join them at the same time.

But before Webster left, he repaid Henry Clay for his failure to support him in the election of 1836. Recognizing that his own candidacy was out of the question, Webster opted not to give Clay or anyone else his support, which Clay expected and desperately needed. His revenge—if it can be called that—had begun the previous fall, when he instructed or strongly indicated to the editor of the Boston *Atlas* that Clay should be faulted for the recent electoral defeat in Maine. Shortly thereafter the *Atlas* declared that the Whig party should abandon those candidates who could not appeal to the masses and turn their support to General Harrison.[24] Supposedly the Kentuckian's lack of popularity had caused the defeat in Maine.

Clay choked back his anger when he heard what the *Atlas* had printed. "I am mortified—shocked—disgusted with the course of some men," he raged. "I had hoped for better things of them." He suspected that Webster had become Harrison's promoter, and these suspicions were heightened when the Anti-Masonic National Convention meeting in November in Philadelphia nominated Harrison for President and Webster for Vice President. All signs indicated, Clay declared, that the two men were conspiring to deprive him of the nomination. To Clay's mind, further proof of a conspiracy developed when Webster's friends

22. Ward to the Baring Brothers, April 29, 1839, Baring Papers, Public Archives, Ottawa, Ontario.

23. Charles M. Wiltse, "Daniel Webster and the British Experience," *Proceedings of the Massachusetts Historical Society,* LXXXV (1974), p. 67.

24. Harrison Gray Otis to Clay, September 14, 1838, Clay to Francis Brooke, November 3, 1838, in Clay, *Papers,* IX, 229–230, 245; Jellison, *Fessenden,* p. 28. John Quincy Adams spoke with Abbott Lawrence, who told the former President that he thought Webster had coalesced with Harrison against Clay. Lawrence himself preferred Clay. Adams, *Memoirs,* X, 43.

in New York, under Weed's direction, rallied behind General Winfield Scott, who had been sent by the President to restore peace along the Canadian border and succeeded in terminating the Aroostook War.[25]

As the time approached for his departure for Europe, Webster had to make up his mind about whether or not to endorse anyone. He chose to remain silent. "Our Whig prospects are none of the best," he informed Samuel Jaudon, "owing to our irreconcilable difference, as to men. My opinion at present is, that our only chance is with Genl. Harrison, & that is not a very good one."[26] After he had arrived in London, he instructed John Healy to publish a letter to the people of Massachusetts in which he formally announced his withdrawal from the presidential race. He said nothing about the other candidates. He would let Clay, Harrison, and Scott fight it out among themselves. For Clay, it was a stinging rebuke in view of their long association and regard for each other's abilities.[27]

Having cut himself loose from mounting Whig rivalry, the fifty-eight-year-old Webster set sail for his only trip to the European continent. He could hardly wait to leave the country.

Crossing the North Atlantic Ocean at any time of the year can be harrowing, but according to Caroline Webster, they had "a delightful voyage—not a single storm, or gale of wind during the passage." She did suffer seasickness for the first ten days, as did Mrs. Paige. Julia did well; so too Webster, "with the exception of one day, when the sea & other causes laid me up." Otherwise he "was fit for duty the whole voyage."

They arrived in Liverpool on Sunday, June 2, at 10:00 A.M. and went to the Adelphi Hotel, where they stayed for four days to recover from the two-week trip. They had many visitors on the day they arrived and attended a large dinner party in the evening, all of which signaled what was to come during their entire stay abroad: one caller after another, one dinner or breakfast or soiree or theater and opera engagement after another.[28] Webster was well known in Great Britain, and his arrival was duly noted in the *Times*. "Whether in the councils of his country or at the bar," stated the newspaper, "he has few rivals and no superiors."[29] The *Gazette* also took notice. "We cordially welcome to our shores this great and good man, and accept him as a fit representative of all the great and good qualities of our trans-Atlantic brethren."[30] His reputation as America's supreme orator had been documented by the publication of his most notable

25. Clay to Harrison Gray Otis, September 24, December 13, 1838, in Clay, *Papers*, IX, 233; Weed to William H. Seward, August 10, 15, 1839, Seward Papers, University of Rochester; Vaughn, *Antimasonic Party in the United States*, pp. 180–181.

26. DW to Jaudon, March 29, 1839, in *PC*, IV, 355.

27. DW to John Healy, with enclosure, June 12, 1839, ibid., IV, 370; Remini, *Clay*, p. 531.

28. Caroline Le Roy Webster, *Mr. W. & I: Being the Authentic Diary of Caroline Le Roy Webster* (Binghamton, N.Y., 1942), p. 1; DW to Charles Henry, June 9, 1839, in *PC*, IV, 366.

29. *Times* of London, June 4, 1839, quoted in Wiltse, "Webster and the British Experience," p. 68.

30. Quoted in Curtis, *Webster*, II, 8.

speeches, and the leaders of British society and politics wanted to get a closer look. He was so sought after that he was obliged to decline numerous invitations that he wished he had had the time to accept.[31]

On Wednesday the Websters headed straight for London, stopping frequently to sight-see—they did a great deal of sight-seeing when social obligations allowed—and visiting various lords and ladies along the way. They went first to Chester and then boarded the railroad to London. The usual two-hundred-mile run from Liverpool to London, said Webster, took ten and one-half hours. As he crossed the countryside, he was struck by two things: first the "agricultural beauty and richness of the Country" and second, the ancient ecclesiastical architecture of England, which he pronounced "most magnificent & grand spectacles."[32]

They arrived in London on Thursday evening and were greeted by Jaudon and his wife, with whom they stayed until they could find their own quarters. The presence of Parliament filled the city to capacity, making lodgings extremely difficult to come by. It was the middle of what was called the Season. Finally, rooms at the Brunswick Hotel, Regent Street, Hanover Square became available, and the Websters took possession on Saturday, June 8.[33]

His friend John Denison, who was the Viscount Ossington and a member of Parliament, could not welcome him to England because of his absence in Paris to attend his wife's ailing uncle, but he placed at Webster's disposal his coach and horses, coachman, and postilion along with the services of his highly placed brothers and brothers-in-law, who were divided "among all professions." They would see to Webster's needs and comfort until he, Denison, returned later in the summer. "I am sure there will be a universal desire throughout the world of London to pay the fullest tribute of respect to your well known name."[34]

So began the whirlwind of engagements. Over the next several days they "met all the *Lions*," including "Poets, Historians, Novelists, Counts, Naval Officers, &c. &c." "Our heads are rather turned at present," Caroline gushed. In addition, Webster visited the Inns of Court to hear how the British conducted their legal proceedings. "They are vastly better *trained* than we are," he admitted. "They speak short. They get up, begin immediately—& leave off when they have done. Their manner is more like that of a school boy, who gets up to say his lesson, goes right through it, & then sits down, than it is like our more leisurely & elaborate habit."

Webster was less impressed with the debates in Parliament. "Some of their ablest men are far from being fluent speakers," he told John J. Crittenden of Kentucky. "In fact they hold in no high repute the mere faculty of ready speak-

31. "Lord Fitzwilliam has the first volume of your speeches in his library," Charles Sumner wrote to Webster, "and he told me with what pleasure he had read your discourse at Plymouth." June 24, 1839, in Van Tyne, ed., *Letters of Webster*, p. 219.

32. DW to Charles Thomas, June 9, Edward Curtis, June 12, 1837, in *PC*, IV, 366, 369.

33. Caroline Webster, *Mr. W. & I*, pp. 2–4; DW to Isaac Davis, June 24, 1839, in *PC*, IV, 374.

34. Denison to DW, June 5, June 10, 1839, in *PC*, IV, 363, 368.

ing, at least not so high as it is held in other places. They are universally men of business." They do not have twenty-six legislative bodies as in the United States "to take part of the law-making off their hands." Since there is so much to be done, it is imperative that "less should be *said*. Their debates, therefore, are often little more than conversations across the table." He was especially disappointed in Thomas Babington Macaulay, the distinguished historian, but he convinced himself that the speech he heard was no doubt below Macaulay's "ordinary efforts."[35]

Webster dazzled the British when they met him. What a specimen exclaimed Thomas Carlyle. What a "magnificent specimen. You might say to all the world, 'This is your Yankee Englishman; such limbs *we* make in Yankee-land!' As a logic-fencer, advocate, or parliamentary Hercules, one would incline to back him at first sight against all the extant world."[36] On the whole, the British found him dignified, not loquacious, a "perfectly-bred man, though not English in breeding; a man worthy of the best reception among us, and meeting such, I understand." On a visit to the British Museum a young artist followed Webster around "with admiring eyes." One of the Webster group turned to the artist and said, "Well—how do you like *our* head?"

"Glorious, magnificent, one of Nature's noblest works," the enraptured artist responded. "How I should like to paint that head."[37]

Webster spent some time just "poking around *incog.*" Nobody recognized him as he wandered about, and that, he said, "is a queer feeling." He found that a "stranger in London is in the most perfect solitude in the world. He can touch every body, but can speak to nobody. I like much these strolls by myself."[38]

Except for these solitary strolls, the Websters kept up a dizzy pace of activity, for they were much sought after. "I can truly say that your distinguished name has gone before you," Charles Sumner wrote him from Rome, "and that you will find large numbers of the best people who will be anxious to make your acquaintance." One of these, Alexander Baring, Lord Ashburton, the celebrated financier of the house of Baring Brothers, whose friendship was so important later on, invited him to dine on very short notice so that he could meet the lord chancellor, Henry Brougham. The senator readily accepted and was delighted to find that "I am already asked whether I will have a conversation with those in high places, on the subjects of common interest to the two countries." Perhaps he could prove useful to his country after all, with or without a formal appointment by the President.[39]

35. Caroline Webster, *Mr. W. & I*, p. 6; DW to Edward Curtis, June 12, DW to Healy, June 9, DW to Crittenden, July 31, DW to Isaac Davis, June 24, 1839, in *PC*, IV, 369, 364, 384–385, 374.

36. Thomas Carlyle to a friend, June 24, 1839, quoted in Curtis, *Webster*, II, 21.

37. Harriette Story Paige, *Daniel Webster in England: Journal of Harriette Story Paige, 1839* (Boston and New York, 1917), pp. 18–19.

38. DW to Charles Thomas, June 9, 1839, in *PC*, IV, 367.

39. Sumner to DW, June 24, 1839, in Van Tyne, ed., *Letters of Webster*, p. 219; Ashburton to DW, June 12, DW to Edward Curtis, June 12, 1839, in *PC*, IV, 370–371, 369.

Some indication of his notoriety can be seen in the fact that Queen Victoria invited the Websters to a ball even before they were officially presented at court. It was an honor neither Webster nor Caroline expected. Lord Palmerston, the foreign secretary, had suggested to the queen that court etiquette be relaxed since Webster was "a person upon whom an act of civility would be usefully bestowed."[40] Indeed. So the invitation went forward, and the Websters attended the ball with the U.S. minister to Great Britain, Andrew Stevenson, and his wife, Sarah. Webster had to admit that the Stevensons had "received and treated me with great propriety and kindness," even though the senator had voted against the minister's confirmation.[41]

The queen's invitation required special dress, and the party got themselves appropriately rigged. And what a sight they were! Webster wore a court dress consisting of "smallclothes, white silk stockings, diamond knee and shoe buckles; a coat of the fashion of the last century, lined with white satin, with a white satin vest, embroidered in colours, and ornamental steel buttons, of the same fashion as the coat, point-lace shirt ruffles, and lace frills over the hands." Ribbons were attached to the back of the coat collar, giving the appearance of the "bag-wig of former times." Harriette Paige thought his outfit "exceedingly becoming." It was the costume worn by every gentleman attending the ball. Caroline wore an embroidered pink silk dress, Julia white tulle over her satin gown, and Harriette Paige a rose-colored silk dress. The cost of buying so many clothes for all the functions required of them seemed very extravagant, especially to Caroline. "I shall be *ruined* if I stay here any longer, with buying dresses &c. &c.," she exclaimed. Not that that realization stopped her for a moment.[42]

Only two weeks after their arrival in London, and outfitted in the best refinery that their money would allow, the Websters made their way to Buckingham Palace to attend the most important ball of the Season. They arrived at the palace shortly after ten o'clock on June 17 and waited in the saloon with all the other guests. Caroline thought that all the nobility of Europe was present. Shortly thereafter Queen Victoria entered, preceded by her chamberlains, who carried "long gold sticks, walking backward, facing the Queen." According to Caroline, Victoria looked very young; Harriette Paige thought her short with grayish blue eyes and not very pretty. The queen ascended her throne, and Sarah Stevenson introduced the ladies while Andrew Stevenson did the honors for Webster. They then adjourned to a dining room where they enjoyed a superb supper. The gold on the sideboard dazzled the Americans. They left at four the next day, just as the sun rose. They needed their rest because they had a dinner engagement that night with the duke of Wellington, followed by a performance at the opera.[43]

40. Palmerston to Victoria, June 15, 1839, quoted in Herbert C. F. Bell, *Lord Palmerston* (New York, 1936), I, 247.

41. DW to Curtis, June 12, 1839, in *PC*, IV, 369.

42. Paige, *Webster in England* p. 28; Caroline Webster, *Mr. W. & I*, p. 16.

43. Paige, *Webster in England*, p. 29; Caroline Webster, *Mr. W. & I*, pp. 19–20.

Usually the Websters rose to have breakfast at nine, unless they had a breakfast date. British breakfasts started at ten and lasted until noon. After breakfast they would sight-see; at four in the afternoon Webster would go to Parliament to hear the debates and stay until six while the ladies went shopping or to a picture gallery. They would then dress and go to dinner at the home of some nobleman, writer, or well-to-do Londoner, which usually absorbed most of evening. At ten o'clock they would attend a concert or musical event at someone's home. They would stay until midnight or one o'clock. It was a crowded schedule, a hectic schedule, but Webster loved every moment of it.[44]

After two months he boasted that "we have had an opportunity of seeing almost every body, whom we had a desire to see," not only the nobility and leading statesmen but such literary lights as Dickens, Carlyle, Wordsworth, Southey, Macaulay, and others. Webster also thoroughly enjoyed the city itself. "London is striking," he wrote, "by its immense extent; by its manifestation of the enormous accumulation of wealth; by its Cathedrals, Churches, Hospitals, & Bridges; by the splendor & number of Equipages, met in every street; by its numerous large & beautiful parks & squares, in the midst of the City, as it were; and by its admirable regularity, & good government. Nothing can be better than the system of police, which here keeps 2 millions of people in good order."[45]

The people he met showed him "unbounded" hospitality. Contrary to his expectations, he found "nothing cold or stiff in their manners." Unfortunately, however, "the thing in England most prejudiced agt. U. S. is the *Press*. It's [sic] ignorance of us is shocking, & it is increased by such absurdities as the travellers publish," like Captain Frederick Marryat's *A Diary in America*. Later Webster declared that "the only unkind feeling" he brought back from Europe was

no small degree of indignation at the injustice and arrogance of certain European journals, whenever they speak of American credit, or the responsibility and integrity of the governments of the American States. It has appeared to me that there must be lurking at the bottom of all this a strong desire to disparage free institutions, by representing them as unworthy of reliance, on the part of foreigners, and unsteady to the sacred obligations of public faith. . . . I wish we could find more leisure, from our domestic controversies, to direct the public attention, as it ought to be directed, against these foreign misrepresentations.[46]

Webster thought that the British Whigs knew more about and thought better of the United States than the Tories did. Since American Whigs liked to consider themselves the counterparts of British Whigs, this observation was not unremarkable.[47]

Webster exercised extreme caution when speaking with the men and

44. Webster to Curtis, July 4, 1839, in Curtis, *Webster,* II, 12–13. "In the Even'g, we all went to a concert at Prince Esterhazy's—where were assembled the general society of London." Memorandum, July 10, 1839, in Van Tyne, ed., *Letters of Webster,* p. 220.

45. DW to Samuel Frothingham, July 30, 1839, in *PC,* IV, 383–384.

46. DW to Biddle, August 3, 1840, *The Daily Chronicle and General Advertiser,* September 1, 1840, in the Biddle Family Papers at Andalusia on microfilm, LC.

47. DW to Hiram Ketchum, July 23, 1839, in *PC,* IV, 381.

the school and its library and watch the boys playing on the grounds. They also stopped off to inspect Windsor Castle. At Windsor Kenyon asked Webster for an autograph to keep as a souvenir of their trip. Delighted to oblige, Webster wrote:

> When you and I are dead and gone,
> This busy world will still jog on,
> And laugh and sing, and be as hearty
> As if we still were of the party.
>
> *John Kenyon*
> *Daniel Webster*

Windsor Castle Inn, July 19, 1839[57]

The group then returned to London. It was a grand trip, and if Webster had any complaint after several months in Britain, it was the weather. It rained constantly, and the family groaned under its depressing influence. "The last 30 days," grumbled Webster, "the weather has been very wet, & still continues so." "Clouds, mist, & pouring rain, have constituted the succession of atmospheric operation." Paige noted in her journal that it rained eleven straight days.[58]

Still, they managed to keep up a steady pace of sight-seeing, fox hunting, theatergoing, and partying. At the invitation of the archbishop of Canterbury Webster even attended the consecration of two Anglican bishops at Lambert Palace. Then, on August 5, the Websters, Mrs. Paige, and about twenty-eight others were invited to dine with the queen. They arrived at Buckingham Palace promptly at 7:30 P.M., and after a short wait in the saloon the queen arrived with her train. Caroline noted that the "table furniture" was made of gold and silver. "The room full of mirrors, fine paintings, side tables covered with gold." She declared the dinner "superb" and not at all formal. After dinner they retired to the drawing room for coffee. The queen spoke at length to Webster, who, during dinner, sat nearly at the foot of the table, "two distinguished persons on each side of him." Webster thought the queen "intelligent and agreeable," while Caroline said that she liked "the Queen much—she has fine spirits, laughed and was very animated." Caroline left the party after the first dance, but Webster, Julia, and Harriette did not get home until 1:00 A.M. Everyone agreed it was "a very splendid party."[59]

The next day the Websters took off on a tour of England, Wales, and Scotland by coach and railroad, leaving at half past one in the afternoon after everyone had recovered from the previous evening's festivities. They headed first for Coventry, visited Stratford-on-Avon to view Shakespeare's birthplace, and journeyed on to Worcester, Gloucester, Bath, Bristol, and Liverpool. They then proceeded into Scotland, where on August 17 they learned from the Liv-

57. Ibid., II, 25.

58. DW to Samuel Frothingham, July 30, DW to George Ticknor, August 21, 1839, in *PC*, IV, 384, 390; Paige, *Webster in England*, p. 163.

59. Caroline Webster, *Mr. W. & I*, pp. 69–72; Paige, *Webster in England*, pp. 175–179.

erpool papers that Edward and Appleton had arrived in England aboard *The British Queen*. The two men joined the group in Glasgow on August 26, and their presence helped vary each day's schedule. Julia and Appleton took frequent walks together, and Edward and his father inspected livestock and farming equipment. The group then went to Edinburgh before heading back to London.

Although it was a rather quick six-week tour of Britain, in which they could not stay very long in any given place or get "much below the surface of things," still, "the agriculture, & the general [aspect?] of things—in England & Scotland, I have looked at, pretty attentively. Taken together, England exhibits a high wrought, exact, elaborate system of art & industry. Every productive power is carried to the utmost extent of skill, & maintained in the most unceasing activity." He thought the prices of produce as well as the rents were high. The average rent for "good land in England," he claimed, ran about seven, ten, or fifteen dollars. But each acre yields about forty bushels of wheat and fifty or sixty of oats. "I think I have learned something," he told his manager at Marshfield, Charles Thomas. "The English are better farmers than we are. *Turnips have revolutionized English Agriculture.* The sheep are as thick as flies, and mutton is dear. But all these things remain to be talked over."[60]

After their return to London the group immediately began making preparations for Julia's wedding. The marriage took place at 11:30 A.M. on Tuesday, September 24, at St. George's, Hanover Square, with the Reverend Philip Scofield officiating and Edward serving as groomsman. Invitations went out to forty friends. The ceremony lasted only ten minutes or so, after which the guests numbering about twenty attended a *déjeuner* at the hotel. When it ended, the newlyweds and Mrs. Paige took off for Hartford for a short honeymoon in Cambridge; they returned two days later.[61]

With the wedding safely over the family began thinking about a tour of the Continent. Shortly after his arrival in England, Webster had received a letter from Lewis Cass, the U.S. minister to France, inviting him to visit Paris and offering to serve as guide. "I am sure you will not regret the little time, which an excursion into France will cost you," he added.[62] Webster finally decided to send his wife, son, daughter, and son-in-law ahead while he stayed behind and tried to unload some of his American properties on British investors. He accompanied the family to the steamer on September 29 to wave good-bye as they took off for the Netherlands, Belgium, a trip down the Rhine, Switzerland, and then France.

Selling western land and speculative stocks in America to the British proved to be a daunting task. "My dear friend," he informed Senator John J. Crittenden, "I fear it will be very many years before American credit shall be restored to the state it was in at the time the late administration began its experiments on the

60. DW to John Healy?, September 20, DW to Thomas, October 14, 1839, in *PC*, IV, 393, 403; Paige, *Webster in Britain*, pp. 208, 216.

61. Caroline Webster, *Mr. W. & I*, pp. 150–153; Paige, *Webster in England*, pp. 350–351. Harriette said that Julia insisted she accompany her. Ibid., p. 351.

62. Cass to DW, June 23, 1839, in *PC*, IV, 373.

country." All this made it impossible for Webster to divest himself of any but a small amount of his property. "Money matters have been in a most horrid state here all summer. Everything American, stocks and lands, are perfectly flat. Nothing can possibly be sold. By great exertions, I have done enough to pay expenses, so as to go home no poorer than I came, & that is about all."[63]

At this point the Baring Brothers banking company contacted Webster and asked for his opinion on certain constitutional questions involving individual American states. Naturally they would pay him handsomely. They wanted to know whether these states had the right to contract loans at home and abroad. "We are happy to be able to avail ourselves of your visit to this country to refer the point (on which we never entertained a doubt) to you, and to ask your legal opinion on the subject." Webster, who knew Alexander Baring, Lord Ashburton, quite well, responded immediately. The incident later caused a minor sensation in the United States when he was accused of acting as "the *legal* counsellor of the Chancellor of the British Exchequer."

In his response to the Baring Brothers Webster said the states most definitely had this power. He then offered a short lesson in American civics. "Every state is an independent, sovereign, political community." Certain powers, however, are reserved to the general government. "This general government is a limited government. Its powers are specific and enumerated." The Constitution contains no prohibition or restraint on state legislatures in regard to making loans. However, states may not emit bills of credit, but bonds and other securities given for borrowed money are not bills of credit. What are bills of credit? In two words, paper money. Thus "the several states possess the power of borrowing money for their own internal occasions of expenditure," which the Congress has fully recognized. Webster went on to express what he called an opinion of a more general nature. "It is, that I believe the citizens of the U. States, like all honest men, regard debts, whether public or private, and whether existing at home or abroad, to be of moral as well as legal obligation." The "great mass of the American people" would never tolerate any state's violating "the faith solemnly pledged for her pecuniary engagements."[64]

Having satisfied himself that he had done everything possible to sell some of his American properties, Webster joined his family in Paris, arriving on October 19 with Colonel James Henderson, the minister from the independent republic of Texas. Edward remained in Geneva, where he was to continue his studies for nine months in the care of a Monsieur de Bort. "I believe he destines himself to the law," Webster ventured, "but . . . will of course attend to literature and general knowledge, and I hope make progress in modern languages, especially French." Actually Edward Everett, then touring Europe with his wife,

63. DW to Crittenden, July 31, DW to Charles Thomas, October 14, DW to Everett, October 16, ibid., IV, 385, 402–403, 408.
64. Baring Brothers to DW, October 12, DW to Baring Brothers, October 16, 1839, ibid., IV, 401–402, 404–406; Ralph W. Hidy, *The House of Baring in American Trade and Finance: English Merchant Banks at Work, 1763–1861* (Cambridge, Mass., 1949), pp. 283–284.

served as Edward's guardian and adviser. In early June 1841 young Webster returned to the United States, resumed his studies at Dartmouth, and was graduated with the class of 1841.[65]

When he arrived in Paris, Webster found that his wife had been doing a good bit of shopping—she could hardly resist all the "superb" shops she visited—and had bought dozens of items, not only for herself but for friends and relatives.[66] As usual they went sight-seeing, and at the monument of Casimir Périer the guide pointed to the figure on the monument and said: "Very many people observed a likeness to the great orator, Danl Webster, of America."

He then looked at Caroline. "You have heard of such a great man?"

"Yes," Caroline responded quietly.

"He is in London," the guide continued, "and they say he is coming here; I should like to see him."[67]

They toured Versailles and dined with the king and queen at St. Cloud, Webster sitting on one side of the queen, Lewis Cass, the U.S. minister, on the other. Caroline pronounced the "dinner very superb." Gold platters, silver plates, and forks abounded, and "as you use one fork another is placed at your side. . . . Every kind of wine handed you, first claret, then sherry, then burgundy, then champagne, then malmsey &c &c." Webster must have been ecstatic. Few appreciated good wine and food as much as the Massachusetts senator. "Everything so nice," Caroline enthused. "Finger bowls await you on resting; the servant stands behind you and holds it" while you cleanse your fingers and rinse your mouth in mint-flavored water.[68]

King Louis Philippe had lived in the United States following the French Revolution and told Caroline that he had been to New York long before she was born. He reminisced a good bit about his experiences in America, inquiring after old friends. He must have enjoyed the Websters very much because he invited them to use the royal box at the Théâtre Français to witness a performance by a local favorite, Mlle. Mars, a woman in her sixties who played juveniles.[69]

The Websters departed Paris on November 2 to return to London. They all experienced seasickness crossing the Channel because of rough seas that delayed their return. They also ran into trouble with customs over several items in their possession, but since they planned to sail for America directly, the customs agent let them through. Many prominent men and women came to bid them farewell and express their disappointment that they would not stay through the winter. The duke of Rutland was particularly kind and visited them several times. "He is a very gentlemanly nice person," declared Caroline.[70]

65. Paige, *Webster in England*, p. 351; DW to Jaudon, August 21, 1839, in *W&S*, XVIII, 62; DW to Everett, May 24, 1840, in Webster, ed., *Private Correspondence*, II, 81.

66. Caroline Webster, *Mr. W. & I*, pp. 169–170.

67. Ibid., p. 171. Apparently she did not tell the guide who she was or that his wish was gratified.

68. Ibid., pp. 195–196.

69. Ibid., pp. 192, 197–198, 200.

70. Ibid., pp. 212–224.

During one of his meetings with the duke, Webster thanked him for his "just and liberal sentiments" regarding relations between Britain and the United States. In a letter he assured Rutland that every intelligent American sees not only the evils that would ensue from any "interruption of the harmony existing between the two countries" but the "embarrassments" that would be felt in the United States whenever any disasters occurred that could "derange the general prosperous course of trade and business in England." Our commercial and trade relations are so intimately entwined, he said, that what affects one nation affects the other. "Let us hope, my dear Duke, that between two Christian nations speaking the same language, having the same origin, enjoying the same litera- ture, and connected by these mutual ties of interest, nothing may ever exist but peace and harmony, and the noble rivalship of accomplishing most for the general improvement and happiness of mankind."[71]

Unfortunately the situation in America had worsened over the past several months. Although the border dispute between Canada and the United States had quieted, thanks to the efforts of General Winfield Scott, the seizure of the ship *Caroline* by the British, which resulted in the death of one American, had provoked further incidents. Canadian revolutionaries had recruited American supporters who joined Hunters' Lodges and called themselves Patriots.[72] They obtained a small steamboat, the *Caroline,* to ferry supplies to the rebels. Then a small British-Canadian party surprised the steamer's crew, towed it to the middle of the Niagara River, set it ablaze, and sank it. During the brief struggle one American, Amos Durfee, was killed. This attack infuriated Americans, especially along the New York frontier, and they demanded that the murderer be captured and put on trial. Throughout most of 1838 and 1839 New York authorities arrested several Canadians for the murder, but all of them were subsequently released for lack of evidence. In turn these actions enraged the British because they regarded the seizure as a military action carrying out government orders.

Webster's concern had been heightened when he heard that Lord Palmer- ston had informed Andrew Stevenson that "if the American Govt. does not repress or punish these outrages, the British Government will." He went out of his way to remind Stevenson how the Monroe administration had sent General Jackson to invade Florida in 1818 in pursuit of Seminole Indians because Spain had failed to stop Indian raids along the American frontier. During the invasion Jackson had executed two British subjects, Alexander Arbuthnot and Robert Ambrister. Apparently that incident still rankled.

Webster considered remaining in London through the winter in the hope that it might serve a useful purpose in helping to resolve the conflict, but "things have not favored that desire." Besides, "I now feel a strong wish to get home. I feel that my place is not here." He longed to get back to Marshfield. "Poor old

71. DW to duke of Rutland, November 16, 1839, in *PC*, IV, 409–410.

72. On the Patriots, see Oscar A. Kinchen, *The Rise and Fall of the Patriot Hunters* (New York, 1956) and Kenneth R. Stevens, *Border Diplomacy: The Caroline and McLeod Affairs in Anglo-American-Canadian Relations, 1837–1842* (Tuscaloosa, Ala., 1989), pp. 8–10, 36–38.

barren sea beaten Marshfield! Lowther Castle or Belvoir or Windsor—neither of them is Marshfield." So he and the family went down to Portsmouth and on November 22 boarded the sailing vessel *Mediator* and headed for home.[73]

The crossing took a little more than five weeks and proved rough, tedious, and frightening, especially toward the end. They ran out of brandy, whiskey, oil, lemons, molasses, and nearly all the candles. Daniel and Caroline celebrated their tenth wedding anniversary as well as Christmas on the stormy sea. At times the raging water reminded Caroline of the "foaming of Niagara." She said she "never felt more deeply sensible of our dependence on a merciful Providence, and I trust I shall ever feel grateful for his mercies." But "the ship took care of us," Webster reported, and after some difficulty approaching land because of a thick fog, they arrived safely in New York Harbor on the evening of December 28.[74]

It was the only trip Webster ever took to the Continent. But it subsequently proved to be very beneficial for his country.

73. DW to Everett, October 16, 1839, in *PC*, IV, 408. The group had expected to leave England on November 17, but because of fog and the lack of ballast on board, their departure was delayed until November 22.

74. Caroline Webster, *Mr. W. & I*, pp. 226–238; DW to John Healy, December 29, 1839, in *PC*, IV, 412. Caroline later said that this trip was "the most pleasant period of my life." IB Papers, Box 20, Folder 38, Papers K and L.

31

Secretary of State

EVEN BEFORE Webster disembarked from the ship, he had learned of the action taken by the Whig National Convention at Harrisburg, Pennsylvania: that instead of Henry Clay, the delegates nominated General William Henry Harrison for President despite his modest career. The Whigs chose him on account of his showing in the 1836 election and, most especially, the fact that he was a certified general and hero, just like Andrew Jackson.

Born in Virginia, Harrison achieved fame in 1811 by virtue of his victory over the Shawnee Indians at Tippecanoe Creek in Indiana. He settled in Ohio, won election at different times to both houses of Congress, and was appointed minister to Colombia. That was it, except for his remarkable electoral showing at the last presidential contest.[1]

But the convention pulled another surprise. Instead of Daniel Webster as its candidate for the vice presidency, as the Pennsylvania Whigs and Anti-Masons had preferred,[2] the convention chose a former Democrat, John Tyler of Virginia. Had Webster in any way encouraged Thurlow Weed to advance his candidacy for second place, it is conceivable that he would have been nominated and elected.

Webster may have taken some malicious satisfaction with Harrison's nomination. At least it kept Clay, the two-time loser, from getting it. And Clay was so incensed by what the Whigs had done that he virtually lost control of himself when the news reached him. He raved and ranted at those within earshot. Like everyone else, he knew that the Whigs would triumph in 1840, and triumph big, no matter whom they chose. That the party had turned him aside in favor of someone less worthy nearly overwhelmed him. He raged at this catastrophic defeat.[3]

Webster could claim a measure of credit for Harrison's victory. He was a

---

1. *Proceedings of the Democratic Whig National Convention* . . . (Harrisburg, 1839), p. 18. These proceedings are reprinted in Schlesinger and Israel., eds., *History of Presidential Elections*, I, 700–713.

2. "The nomination of Mr Tyler has placed some of your friends in Penna. in rather an embarrassed position," wrote Harmar Denny to Webster. "Some of our papers have not yet lowered the Harrison & *Webster* flag, for that of Harrison & Tyler." Denny to DW, January 31, 1840, in *PC*, V, 8.

3. Remini, *Clay*, pp. 545–560.

major figure in the Whig party whose opinion was much respected, and he had made it abundantly clear before leaving for England that he preferred Harrison. Not that he came out publicly in support of the general. That would have been too risky in case Clay won the nomination. Nonetheless the Kentuckian took exception to Webster's failure to endorse him and reckoned it an important factor in Harrison's victory.

Harrison did too. Within a month of his arrival home, Webster received a letter from Harrison in which the general credited the senator with providing him strong Massachusetts backing. The state, Harrison observed, "supported me without wavering from the beginning to the end. . . . It has, I am satisfied made a strong impression in Pennsylvania, Ohio & Indiana, & I trust that no one who knows me will think that it was lost upon me." He went on to congratulate Webster on his safe return, adding, "I have no doubt that your trip my dear sir will prove advantageous to our Country." He ended his long letter by asking for financial assistance, something Webster could not possibly provide. Although it was now almost three years since the panic first struck, financial conditions had hardly improved. "Times are here so hard," Harrison complained, and ". . . almost every body feels the pressure & no one out of mercantile business more that I do."[4]

Webster felt the pressure just as much, for he had no sooner arrived at his home in Boston than creditors began hounding him for payment.[5] Like other Whigs, he hoped that Harrison's election would bring better times, and not just financially. "The tendency of the times is to the lowest radicalism [locofocoism]. The war is agt. property, & industry, & good character, by the needy, the lazy, & the vicious." "No man can rejoice in [Harrison's coming election] more than I do; for I think the preservation of interests, most valuable to the Country, entirely depend upon it." Unfortunately "a very bad & reckless spirit" has engulfed the nation: "a spirit of disorganization, of hostility to property, of disregard to engagements & contracts; & a spirit quite too indifferent to the obligations of morality & religion."[6]

But "a political revolution is in progress," and Harrison will win and help restore patriotism, Webster prophesied; he always qualified this opinion by adding, "if he lives." At sixty-seven (an age considered "far advanced in years" in the 1840s)[7] Harrison would be the oldest President in the country's short history if elected. In several letters written in the early months of 1840 Webster repeated his concern about Harrison's possible longevity—as if he feared his immediate demise before November and the subsequent triumph once more of Jacksonian radicalism. Something had to happen, he added, to stay "the rage of party" and bring a "return to the doctrines & the feelings of *honest politics,* and

4. Harrison to DW, January 25, 1840, in *PC*, V, 4–6.

5. Herman Le Roy, Jr., to DW, January 25, George W. Jones to DW, January 27, 1840, ibid., V, 6–7.

6. DW to Caroline Webster, [March 22], DW to Nathaniel Williams, March 24, 1840, ibid., V, 22–23.

7. "Recollections of an Old Stager," in *Harper's New Monthly Magazine,* XLVII (June–November 1873), p. 753.

true patriotism." If Harrison survives to November and the party triumphs overwhelmingly, the Whigs can undo all the horrors of the last two administrations. "Our *locofocoism,* the spirit of which has too much invaded the Govt. itself, is not a whit better than your *socialism,*" Webster informed an English friend. "We need a *Conservative* party more than you do." A Whig administration under Harrison can provide it, for "Genl Harrison is an honest man, & an amiable man; & would be likely, I think, to bring good men about him; & if he should be elected, tho' he has something of the self respect of an old soldier, will exhibit nothing of the obstinacy & ignorant presumption, of his *penult* predecessor [Jackson]."[8]

Webster returned to Washington as soon as he could put his affairs in order in Boston and deliver an address to members of the state legislature and other interested farmers on his observations concerning the state of British agriculture.[9] He did not arrive in the capital until January 27, four days after the Senate had passed, by a vote of twenty-four to eighteen, the subtreasury bill, which would finally become law when the House agreed to it in late June and the President signed it on July 4, 1840.

Caroline did not accompany him to Washington but remained in New York visiting with her father. So for the next two months Webster fended for himself. "I have become snugly settled here," he told Harriette Paige "in a room as big as a closet, a good wood fire, Charles,[10] my French books, my law books, &c. &c."[11] Nothing of consequence was happening in Congress, he said. "I am here, doing nothing, and among others who do nothing, of any use or importance, in these sad times."[12]

Actually he was extremely busy arguing six cases before the Supreme Court, and lonely for the company of his wife, he kept pestering her to join him. He got rather testy when she did not appear and did not write to explain her prolonged absence. "What in the world has become of you," he wrote her. "I am really out of all patience, & full of anxiety. If you are sick, why do not friends write? If you are well, why do you not write yourself."[13]

Still no reply. Finally, in early March, a letter arrived that said nothing about joining him. It was as though she meant to defy him. Webster finally lost patience. "If you had wished to mortify me, you could not have taken a better course. I care nothing of the things about which you write. *Are you coming here, or are you not?* My Dear Wife, what possesses you, to act as you do? . . . I am disappointed—ashamed—mortified. . . . I say to every body, that I am looking for you, every day. *This must be explained.*" He wrote to her almost every day

8. DW to Fletcher Webster, February 7, DW to Nathaniel F. Williams, March 24, DW to Joshua Bates, March 26, 1840, in *PC,* V, 10, 22, 24.

9. The address can be found in *W&S,* II, 293–307.

10. His servant.

11. DW to Harriette Paige, February 2, 1840, in *W&S,* XVIII, 73.

12. DW to Joshua Bates, March 26, 1840, in *PC,* V, 23.

13. DW to Caroline Webster, March 4, 1840, ibid., V, 17.

throughout March, but she did not join him or explain her reasons. The strain in the marriage began to be noticed. Finally, his patience gone, his nerves frazzled, he shot up to New York and brought her back with him to Washington himself.[14]

Webster did have one piece of good news, the arrival on February 10, 1840, of his first grandson in Peru, Illinois. "I am almost afraid to give you joy on the birth of a son," Webster wrote to Fletcher, "such little things being in their first days so delicate and fragile. . . . And now for a name. As he has dark hair and eyes, you may give him mine if you please." He went on to say that he credited a large portion of the "little sense and character" the family possessed to his father's mother, Susannah Bachelder, a woman of "uncommon strength of understanding." If he had had many sons, Webster continued, he would have named one of them Bachelder. But mothers generally name sons, he added, and no doubt she has already chosen one. As it turned out, the child was named Daniel Fletcher Webster, Jr., and while the infant's father called him Dan, his grandfather called him Daniel Webster, Jr.[15]

Unfortunately the situation for Fletcher and his family had deteriorated rather badly in the past few months because the Illinois legislature had halted construction on the Michigan and Illinois Canal, making Webster's property in Peru far less valuable. "In this state of things, & while it lasts," Webster explained to his wife, "Peru will be nothing, & it will be impossible that there should be any business there, by which F. could support his family." Fletcher confirmed that "we all feel discouraged." His wife wished to return to the East with their children, and Fletcher hoped to relocate in New York. "I was unfortunate in coming here," the young man confessed. "I came on an *ebb tide* and things have been going backward every since."[16] True, just like his father's investments.

The distractions of his wife's absence, the death in Washington of Nathaniel Ray Thomas, his agent for his western investments, whose funeral arrangements the senator had to supervise, the birth of his grandson, and the financial problems he and his son faced kept Webster's mind focused mainly on family affairs. He did give several speeches in Congress during this session, but his principal speeches during the spring and summer occurred outside Congress and involved the approaching presidential election.[17]

14. DW to Caroline Webster, March 7, 1840, ibid., V, 19. "Julia received a letter from Mrs Webster," Samuel Appleton wrote his father-in-law, "who speaks of her joining you in Washington as very uncertain." Appleton to DW, February 29, 1840, ibid., V, 17. Probably Caroline simply wished to remain with her New York family after the long sojourn in Europe and could not bring herself to explain her wishes and needs in a letter.

15. DW to Fletcher Webster, March 5, 1840, in Webster, ed., *Private Correspondence*, II, 76–77. Later that year Julia Webster Appleton, gave birth to her first child, Caroline Le Roy Appleton.

16. DW to Caroline Webster, March ?, Fletcher Webster to DW, April 8, 1840, in *PC*, V, 27–28; Fletcher Webster to DW, April 16, 1840, in *Microfilm Edition*, F13/16632. Fletcher returned to the East in January 1841.

17. For Webster's speech on March 3 in response to Calhoun's speech on the effects of protectionism, and his speech on March 30 on the Treasury note bill, see *W&S*, VIII, 266–277, 278–296.

Whigs everywhere begged him to attend their meetings and address them on the problems facing the nation and the need for a change of administration. But they had already initiated a different kind of campaign from that which they had practiced in the past. Imitating the antics of Democrats, they served up a campaign consisting of parades, songs, log cabins, rolling balls, hard cider, barbecues, and every other imaginable gimmick to excite the masses into shouting their approval for "Tippecanoe and Tyler, Too." No statement of principles or policies had been issued by the Whig nominating convention, even though the Democrats had endorsed an extensive statement when they nominated Van Buren at their convention in Baltimore. The people preferred hoopla to discourse, said cynical Whig politicians, and they provided it to vulgar excess. When the Democrats sneered at Harrison as someone who would gladly sit in his log cabin on a pension of two thousand dollars a year, consuming a barrel of hard cider, the Whigs reveled in the charge and pronounced Harrison the "Log Cabin and Hard Cider" candidate, a man of simplicity, frugality, and common sense, and denounced Van Buren as the candidate of the rich who drank wine from silver coolers while lounging on his cushioned settee.

> Old Tip he wears a homespun suit,
> He has no ruffled shirt—wirt—wirt.
> But Mat he has the golden plate
> And he's a little squirt—wirt—wirt.[18]

To an extent even Webster adapted his style of public oratory to the new mode of political campaigning. Hoopla and ballyhoo and political shenanigans became all the rage in every section of the country during this log cabin campaign. In part it helped people forget the financial misery that still plagued the nation.

But Webster genuinely lamented this drift into song, slogan, and claptrap to elect a President. In several of his speeches he struggled to insert a semblance of reasoned argument about important national issues, but even he occasionally could not resist the temptation to resort to rabble-rousing demagoguery.[19]

Webster could not accept invitations at great distances from Washington during the congressional session, but he did attend rallies, meetings, and conventions close by. One of the most important occurred in Baltimore in early May, when he and Clay rode in separate barouches during a "Grand National Procession." To all outward appearances the two men appeared friendly and totally supportive of the Harrison-Tyler ticket. In his speech at the convention Webster told the thousands attending that the time had come for a change. "Every breeze says change. Every interest in the country demands it." And it will come, "come to give joy to the many, and sorrow only to the few." Still, we are called to accomplish not a temporary change but one that will last half a

18. Robert Gunderson, *The Log-Cabin Campaign* (Lexington, Ky., 1957), pp. 107, 121.

19. Nathans, *Webster and Jacksonian Democracy*, pp. 130–131; Richard Current, *Webster and Rise of National Conservatism* (New York, 1955), pp. 113–114.

century. The coming revolution will last for years, and its benefits "felt forever."[20]

The following month he spoke at a Whig Festival in Alexandria, Virginia, just across the Potomac River from the capital. Again, a huge gathering from the surrounding area of Maryland, Virginia, and the District of Columbia appeared, and at 3:00 P.M. the activities began with Webster giving the first speech, followed by other notable Whigs.[21] The last speech ended at 10:00 P.M.[22]

In his address Webster expressed his appreciation to be able to speak before a southern audience on subjects common to Americans both North and South. We are Whigs, he said; you are Virginians, and I am a Massachusetts man. "But our enemies shall not separate the Whigs of the old Bay State from the Whigs of the Old Dominion." The audience erupted with three loud cheers. He assured them that the North contemplated no harm to the South. "We of New England are bound to you by our sacred compact, the Constitution of the United States. . . . And I tell you, for one, that not one jot or tittle of that compact shall ever be violated with my consent." Can you believe that General Harrison, a child of Virginia with the blood of the Revolution coursing through his veins, would ever "lay ruthless hands on the institutions among which he was born and educated?"

"No! no!" the people cried.

"I say No, too," Webster shouted back at them.

He went on to castigate the Democratic administration for the plight of the country, but it is interesting that he took pains to exonerate Jackson publicly from the nation's present economic woes, even though privately he denounced him. General Jackson was "an extraordinary man," he cried, but his measures were carried out by "very ordinary men." Only with Harrison and a Whig administration could the country regain "our lost prosperity."[23]

So active did Webster become in campaigning for Harrison that he even left Congress before the session ended to deliver speeches in Massachusetts and Vermont. He seemed determined to ensure the electoral votes of every New England state for Tippecanoe.

The event on July 7 at Stratton Mountain, Vermont, went particularly well. "We had a time—& a scene, on the mountains, not to be described," he reported. "Only think of 3000 men, encamped for two days, on the very top of the ridge of the G. mountains. Nothing but a Naushon Hunt can come up to it, in grandeur and heroism." He had other triumphs in Bellows Falls on July 8 and in Keene on July 9. The receptions he received to his remarks about undoing the financial bungling of the Democrats were truly "extraordinary—marvelous—

20. W&S, III, 108–109.

21. National Intelligencer, June 13, 1840.

22. It is instructive that the people of this antebellum period relished political discourse, even speeches that lasted for hours. Frequently during his speeches Webster would pause and say he was cutting his speech short because of the lack of time, and the people would shout back at him, "No, no! Go on, go on!" It is a sad commentary on American political life today that political discourse is no longer popular or respected. W&S, III, 33.

23. Ibid., III, 110–113.

unprecedented. We are either on the high road to the accomplishment of the greatest civil revolution ever yet achieved in this country," he told Charles Warren, "or else we are in enchanted ground, surrounded by fairies, fancies, phantoms, & dreams."[24]

In all these speeches Webster displayed a distinct change of speaking style. With remarkable skill he seemed to transform himself into a relaxed and appealing public speaker. He was witty, folksy, and direct in his manner. Gone were the oratorical flourishes, the classical illusions, the evidence of great learning. "The man that says I am an aristocrat—is a liar," he roared on one occasion, a statement that must have caused Democrats apoplexy.[25]

Webster also invaded New York—always a state of paramount importance because of its huge electoral vote—where a "grand gathering of the merchants" turned out at the Exchange "to hear the Almighty Daniel Webster discourse on . . . the Subtreasury and General Harrison." George Templeton Strong, a young lawyer soon to achieve distinction at the bar, came away dazzled by what he had seen and heard. "Webster certainly has intellect stamped on his face in clearer characters than any man I ever saw."[26]

Webster also spoke in Saratoga on August 19 for three and a half hours before an audience estimated by the Albany *Advertiser* at more than seven thousand. He gave a glowing oration on "the great subject of *American labor.*" The laborers of the United States *are* the United States, he said. Strike them from this country, and the population is reduced from sixteen to one million. The American laborer, he lectured, deserves "a comfortable home, decent though frugal living, and to be able to clothe and educate his children, to qualify them to take part . . . in the political affairs and government of their country. Can this be said of any European laborer?" He also spoke of the log cabin, "half hidden in snow drifts in New Hampshire," that his father had built with his own hands. He described how his father had struggled to give him an education so that he could better himself in a changing world. It was a moving tribute to his humble origins and his father's profound influence, and the *Advertiser* said it wished "that every elector of the Union had been at Saratoga, and within the reach of Mr. Webster's voice." He emphasized the "revolution" currently taking place and delved into a detailed history of the Bank; but "perhaps the chief beauty of the speech was its perfect adaptation to the intellect of every man who heard him." In addition, there were "touches of true oratory as ever sprang from human lips."[27]

Webster socialized a good bit during his New York tour. He invited himself to James Kent's home for dinner, and Kent had a few critical comments to make about his guest in his diary: "He is 57 years old, and looks worn and furrowed;

24. DW to Charles Warren, July 12, 1840, in *PC*, V, 47.

25. *W&S*, XIII, 114–142.

26. Allan Nevins and Milton Halsey Thomas, eds., *The Diary of George Templeton Strong* (New York, 1952), I, 147. The entry date is September 28, 1840.

27. Quoted in *National Intelligencer*, August 27, 1840. The full speech, as edited, corrected, and shortened by Webster, can be found in *W&S*, III, 5–36.

his belly becomes protuberant, and his eyes deep in his head. I sympathize with his condition. He has been too free a liver. He ate but little, and drank wine freely."[28]

Indeed Webster loved to imbibe, much to the detriment of his health. Many observers commented on his drinking habits, but few ever saw him publicly inebriated. Because he had drunk so much over so many years, he had acquired that rare ability to appear sober even after a long night of imbibing. His drunkenness never became generally known to the public, except on a few occasions. The amount of his drinking steadily increased over the next few years, particularly after political setbacks, until, toward the end of his life, he developed cirrhosis of the liver. Once, perhaps facetiously, he said that the temperance movement in the United States "has done infinite good. The moral influences of the Temperance associations has been everywhere felt, and always with beneficial results."[29] Unfortunately the "moral influences" of the temperance movement never touched Webster himself, and his heavy drinking shortened his life dramatically.

The climax of Webster's efforts to produce a great Whig victory throughout New England came on September 10, when he presided over the General Convention of the Whigs of New England at a gathering on Bunker Hill. He presented the party's Declaration of Principles and Purposes, which the convention adopted and he signed. Whig newspapers around the country immediately reprinted the declaration, which added to Webster's personal standing within the party. The document affirmed Whig belief in the Constitution, freedom of speech and the press, popular education, "man's capacity for self-government," and the "benign influence of religious feeling and moral instruction on the social [and] individual happiness of man." It condemned the banking and hard-money policies of the Democrats, the disregard for judicial pronouncements, and especially the worshiping at the shrine of party. As a result, the document stated, "the history of the last twelve years has been but the history of broken promises and disappointed hopes. . . . Men thus false to their own professions, false to the principles of the Constitution, false to the interests of the people, and false to the highest honor of their country, are unfit to be the rulers of this republic."[30] Nothing was said in this document about tariffs or internal improvements. Such subjects seemed mundane and irrelevant compared with the lofty principles delineated in his declaration.[31]

Webster did not confine his electioneering solely to New England and New

28. Kent's diary, August 22, 1840, quoted in Van Tyne, ed., *Letters of Webster,* pp. 744–745.

29. DW to F. D. Anderson et al; October 8, 1851, ibid., p. 748. Similarly, he told those involved in the sabbatarian movement of the great good they accomplished. "The longer I live, the more highly do I estimate the importance of a proper observance of the Christian Sabbath, and the more grateful do I feel towards those who take pains to impress a sense of this importance on the community." DW to Charles W. Ridgely, March 3, 1845, ibid., pp. 745–746.

30. *National Intelligencer,* September 17, 1840.

31. An excellent account of this meeting and celebration can be found in Hone, *Diary,* I, 494–498. Hone had been invited to attend by Webster, and he also gave a short address.

York;[32] he also visited Richmond, Virginia,[33] to attend the Whig convention on October 5 and speak at a public reception to the ladies of Richmond at the "Log Cabin."[34] Some fifteen thousand attended the convention, and Webster's speech made quite a hit,[35] so much so that Thomas Ritchie, the editor of the Richmond *Enquirer* and a Van Buren associate, responded with a vicious attack on Webster's past Federalist association, especially his supposed participation in the Hartford Convention.[36]

Webster did not restrict his activities to speechmaking. When Harrison's military career was ridiculed by the opposition, the senator wrote to General James Miller, who had been associated with Harrison in the army, and asked him for an endorsement of the candidate's military prowess. Miller willingly obliged, and the Whig press printed their correspondence extensively. An exchange of letters between Webster and Nicholas Biddle on American credit at home and abroad that criticized Democratic fiscal policies was also published.[37]

Webster pretty nearly exhausted himself in his efforts to bring about a Whig victory. He spoke at an Essex County Whig convention in Newburyport, Massachusetts, for his friend Caleb Cushing, who was seeking reelection to Congress, but few heard him because his voice failed. Still, he continued his furious pace. Concerned about his native state of New Hampshire,[38] which had gone Democratic in the last two presidential elections, he decided to make a brief tour of the state in late October. "They carried me," he reported, "from Nashua to Francistown & from Francistown to Oxford," where after giving numerous speeches, he was forced to summon a doctor, who gave him "a powerful emetic." By this time he verged on collapse. So he instructed John P. Healy, his law associate, "to inform all inquirers, that I shall make no more speeches any where, or under any circumstances."[39]

No further speeches were needed. He had served his party and General

32. He gave a speech in Patchogue, Long Island, on September 22 and another to a meeting of merchants on Wall Street on September 28. See *W&S*, III, 55–79, 114–142. The Patchogue speech proved Webster to be a most effective practitioner of the new style of campaigning. Benjamin Butler, an attorney general under Jackson and a member of the Albany Regency, said the speech sounded like the utterance of a "vulgar demagogue," not the Godlike Daniel. Nathans, *Webster and Jacksonian Democracy*, pp. 142–143.

33. Webster spent three days speaking in Richmond "day and night." It "did me up," he said. He was exhausted and was obliged to rely on sleeping potions. DW to Curtis, October 10, 1840, in *W&S*, XVIII, 89.

34. Ibid., III, 83–102, 105–108.

35. *Niles' Weekly Register,* October 17, 1840; John J. Crittenden to DW, October 27, 1840, in *PC,* V, 60.

36. *National Intelligencer,* October 3, 1840.

37. DW to Miller, June 29, Miller to DW, June 30, 1840, in *National Intelligencer,* July 11, 1840. The Webster-Biddle exchange can be found ibid., September 17, 1840.

38. "It would be peculiarly gratifying to me, I confess, if I might indulge the hope that New Hampshire, would be found among his [Harrison's] supporters." DW to Coffin, June 11, 1840, in Webster, ed., *Private Correspondence,* II, 85.

39. DW to Caroline Webster, October 26, 1840, in *PC,* V, 58–59.

Harrison faithfully and well and had become the candidate's principal spokes-man in the East. Perhaps no other party leader had done as much. By compari-son, Henry Clay did precious little. A few speeches but nothing spectacular or out of the ordinary.[40] Harrison owed Webster a great debt, and he fully intended to honor it.

As the campaign drew to an end, the wild, sometimes uncontrolled exuber-ance of the people in demonstrating their allegiance to the Whig party foretold a smashing victory in November. "Since the World began," noted Senator Crit-tenden, "there was never before . . . such a glorious excitement & uproar among the people. It is a sort of Popular Insurrection."[41]

And what an insurrection it was. A record number of people marched to the polls in 1840 and trounced both Van Buren and the Democratic party. Harrison received 52.9 percent of the popular vote, or 1,275,612, against 46.8 percent for Van Buren, or 1,130,033. A Liberty party advocating the abolition of slavery garnered 0.3 percent, or 7,053 votes, for its candidate, James G. Birney. Harrison took nineteen states, for 234 electoral votes, to Van Buren's seven states with 60 electoral votes. Van Buren won Alabama, Arkansas, Illinois, Mis-souri, New Hampshire,[42] South Carolina, and Virginia. Harrison carried the rest. The Whigs also captured Congress, now holding 28 of the 50 seats in the Senate and 133 seats to the Democrats' 102 in the House. In the short history of the Whig party from 1834 to 1854 this was its greatest electoral triumph. Nation-ally it was to win the presidency again in 1848, the Senate in 1842, and the House in 1846.[43] And that was the extent of its victories.

"Well! My Dear Sir," Webster enthused in a letter to Nathaniel Williams, "we have lived to see a great revolution accomplished. I now pause, to reflect—to be grateful—so to contemplate the dangers we have escaped, & the new prospects which are now before us." To John M. Clayton, he said that "the revolution is so extensive, so complete, & so over whelming, that I can scarcely realize it." He also admitted that he was exhausted, needed rest, and intended to keep quiet until he returned to Washington. But already he knew that greater things lay ahead for him. Congratulations poured in on him. His contribution to the overwhelming victory was attested by all. "To you Sir, more than any other man," wrote the former senator from Louisiana, George Waggaman, "is due the Credit of having broken down the political Monster that has well nigh destroyed

40. Remini, *Clay*, p. 561.

41. Crittenden to DW, October 27, 1840, in *PC*, V, 60.

42. "For my part," Webster wrote a few months earlier, "I shall continue to love her [New Hamp-shire's] white-topped hills, her clear running streams, her beautiful lakes, and her deep shady forests, as long as I live, whatever part she may act in public affairs. I find myself arrived at a period of life when these scenes begin to return, bringing with them the fresh remembrance of juvenile years. I shall not renounce my parent, nor be ashamed of her, however long she may continue in what I think political error." DW to Coffin, June 11, 1840, in *W&S*, XVIII, 86.

43. William Nesbit Chambers, "Election of 1840," Schlesinger and Israel, eds. *History of Presiden-tial Elections*, I, 680–682, 690. See also Michael F. Holt, "The Election of 1840, Voter Mobilization, and the Emergence of the Second American Party System: A Reappraisal of Jacksonian Voting Behavior," in William J. Cooper et al., *A Master's Due: Essays in Honor of David Herbert Donald*, (Baton Rouge, 1985).

the energies and morals of the American people." The people will not be satisfied, he continued, "unless you be the first and foremost in official Station" when the new administration is organized.[44]

Harrison had every intention of appointing Webster to high office. He thought he would ask Clay to take the State Department and Webster the Treasury Department. But Clay took himself out of contention by announcing to the President-elect in several face-to-face meetings they had in Kentucky that he wished to remain in the Senate, where he could best guide the Whig program into law. Naturally he assumed that his program—that is, the American System—would constitute the administration's program. He went on to say to Harrison that since he would remain in Congress, he expected Webster to take the State Department. He had no problem with such an appointment but he candidly revealed to the President-elect his feelings about and past relations with Webster. He admitted that his confidence in the man had been badly shaken in the past few years, but he allowed that Webster's appointment as secretary of state "would not diminish the interest I felt in the success of his administration, nor my zeal in its support" so long as the principles "which I believe would govern it." He also said that he understood that many of Webster's friends wanted him to take the Treasury Department, but Clay rightly attacked that suggestion because Webster "had not the requisite qualifications for that office."[45] He knew that Black Dan owed Biddle's bank more than one hundred thousand dollars and suggested that Harrison look elsewhere for the treasury secretary.

The President-elect had hoped that Webster would take the Treasury because it would be very difficult to fill, certainly more difficult than finding a secretary of state. Undoubtedly the Whigs in Congress—and Clay most certainly—would wish to dismantle the entire Jacksonian economic program. The secretary of the treasury therefore would play a far more important role in shaping the direction of the Harrison administration than any other officer in the cabinet. So, immediately following his interviews with Clay, Harrison wrote to Webster and invited him to join his administration. "Since I was first a candidate for the presidency, I had determined, if successful, to solicit your able assistance in conducting the Administration, and I now ask you to accept the State or Treasury Department." He also asked for recommendations for the posts if like Clay, he had decided to remain in the Senate.[46]

For his part, Webster received the invitation with a sense of genuine gratitude. For some time he had been seriously considering resigning from the upper house, where he felt bored and impotent.[47] He figured he could better spend his time rebuilding his law practice and working off his debts. He would even

44. DW to Williams, November 7, DW to Clayton, November 16, Waggaman to DW, November 8, 1840, in *PC*, V, 61, 62.

45. Clay to Francis Brooke, December 8, 1840, Clay to Porter, December 8, 1840, in Clay, *Papers*, IX, 458, 459.

46. Harrison to DW, December 1, 1840, in Curtis, *Webster*, II, 48.

47. DW to Jaudon, June 30, 1840, in Webster, ed., *Private Correspondence*, II, 87.

have accepted appointment as minister to Great Britain, if it had been offered, but interestingly he would not consider a judicial appointment. "There never was a time when I would have taken the office of Chief Justice of the United States, or any other judicial station," he told his friend Hiram Ketchum. He said that he had mixed up politics and the law too much to feel comfortable on the bench. He did not believe he had all the "accuracy and precision of knowledge which the bench requires."[48]

Now he had exactly what he wanted, and the invitation spared him the necessity of separating himself from government and gave him the highest administrative rank in Washington after the President. For a man as ambitious for honors and place as Webster the invitation was impossible to refuse. Besides, his friends strongly urged him to accept it and promised to give him full support. "The impression which I have," Biddle wrote him, is "that the coming administration will be in fact your administration."[49]

Webster responded to Harrison from Washington, where he had just arrived on December 11, and told him he very much appreciated his confidence and friendship and would accept the office of secretary of state. As for Treasury, he offered no names but thought that the "all important questions of revenue, finance, and currency, properly belonging to the Executive, should be Cabinet questions; that every member of the Cabinet should give them his best consideration" in order to promote "union and efficiency of action." As for the daily details of running that department, "I do not think myself to be particularly well qualified." In addition, he knew that Clay would undoubtedly expect to have the controlling hand in financial matters, and Webster had no desire to compete with or take direction from him. But to keep his options open—indicating his enormous desire to be a part of the administration—Webster told Harrison that if he, Harrison, should change his mind and decide to offer State to someone else, he would be open to another invitation to take the Treasury.[50]

A few days later Webster wrote again to Harrison with suggestions for the other places in the cabinet. The President-elect had reservations about one of the suggestions but decided to put off naming the remaining members until he arrived in Washington in late January or February.[51] He ultimately assigned to the Treasury post Thomas Ewing of Ohio, whom Clay opposed for this particular office, John Bell of Tennessee as secretary of war, one of Clay's friends, George Badger of North Carolina, as secretary of the navy, and Francis Granger of New York, an ally of Thurlow Weed's and therefore a Webster supporter, as postmaster general. Clay's close friend and colleague in the Senate John J. Crittenden had been named earlier as attorney general.

No sooner did Webster receive his appointment than he decided he must rid himself of his indebtedness, especially to the Pennsylvania Bank of the

48. DW to Hiram Ketchum, December 18, 1840, ibid., II, 96.

49. Biddle to DW, December 13, 1840, in McGrane, ed., Correspondence of Biddle, pp. 337.

50. DW to Harrison, December 11, 1840, in Curtis, Webster, II, 50–51.

51. Harrison to DW, December 27, 1840, ibid., II, 52.

United States, the old BUS. "It is quite impossible for me to go into office here, with the matter unadjusted," he told Biddle. Earlier Biddle had bought up Webster's outstanding notes, amounting to $114,000, but he was no longer the president of the bank, and Webster was obliged to deal with the new officers of the institution. Even so, Biddle asserted his considerable influence with these officers, and after several months of negotiations Webster and the bank agreed that he should transfer to the bank with clear titles most of his western properties in exchange for the cancellation of his debt. He retained 1,120 acres of land in Illinois, his farm near Peru, property in Rock Island, and approximately 850 acres of mineral lands in Wisconsin. Unfortunately Webster did not have a clear title to the lands in every instance. Some titles were unrecorded; others were held jointly by him and other persons; still other titles had been improperly or inaccurately registered. So for nearly his entire term as secretary of state Webster was engaged in trying to obtain clear title to his property. He ultimately succeeded in clearing most, not all, of them, but he was forced to use his official position to achieve it. Not to put too fine a point on it, he sold diplomatic appointments. For example, he appointed Washington Irving minister to Spain, and as a consequence, Irving's brother-in-law, Moses Grinnell, and Grinnell's associates returned to Webster clear title to some lands previously mortgaged to them.

Webster also accepted cash. The nomination of Alexander Powell as consul at Rio de Janeiro had to be withdrawn by the President because of the rumor that Powell had paid Black Dan for the position. Webster also received money as a loan from Isaac Jackson, a wealthy merchant in Philadelphia, to purchase a house in Washington. "I must have a *House*. I am not in a condition to buy one." He figured a good one might cost around fifteen thousand dollars. As an alternative scheme he suggested that Jackson could buy a house as an investment "& let me occupy it." All this he wanted Jackson to keep *"religiously private."* As it turned out, Jackson loaned him the money and was promptly appointed the chargé to Denmark. With the loan Webster purchased the Swann house facing President's Square (later named Lafayette Square). "Money, public and private," as John Quincy Adams noted in his diary, "is the insuperable obstacle to his [Webster's] progress, and will finally, at no distant day, turn him out upon the world, and prove the ruin of this Administration, as it did of the last."[52]

On returning to Washington for the start of the final (short) session of the Twenty-sixth Congress on December 9, Webster left Caroline in New York until

52. DW to Biddle, [February 1841], Grinnell to DW, [February 10, 1842], James Doty to Biddle, March 25, 1841, Webster to Caroline Webster, March 31, 1841, in *PC*, V, 94, 87–88, 97, 103, 189; DW to Jackson, February 12, March 19, Jackson to DW, February 15, March 17, 20, 1841, in *PD*, I, 13–15; *Journal of the Executive Proceedings of the Senate* (Washington, 1887), VI, 47–48. "We are all highly delighted at the nomination of Mr. Irving," wrote Moses Grinnell to Webster. "And now my dear friend, permit me to say, that you have gratified me *beyond measure*. Yes, I am happy, and *you* have the thanks of my whole heart for this generous act of yours. [Richard M.] Blatchford has got the Deeds all made out, and they are under [Samuel B.] Ruggles examination." Grinnell to DW, [February 10, 1842], in *PC*, V, 189; Adams, *Memoirs*, XI, 47–48.

he could find suitable quarters for their extended stay in Washington. In the interim William W. Seaton, editor of the *National Intelligencer* and recently elected mayor of the District, invited Webster to stay at his house, where he would be less bothered by jobseekers. The senator readily accepted. Since he knew how busy he would be with the details of his new office, presuming he would be confirmed, he submitted his resignation from the Senate to the Vice President on February 22, 1841. His colleague John Davis also resigned to assume the governorship of the state, and the Massachusetts legislature replaced both men with Rufus Choate and Isaac C. Bates respectively.[53]

In mid-February, on a stormy afternoon, Harrison arrived at the capital and walked from the railroad station on Pennsylvania Avenue to City Hall. Tall, thin, with a long face and nose and a sloping forehead, he carried himself with military bearing, holding his hat in his hand and bowing to the crowd that lined the streets to welcome him. He loved classical literature, frequently quoting it in his conversation and correspondence. He likened his trip from his home in Ohio to Washington to the return of Cicero to Rome.[54]

No sooner did Harrison arrive than Webster attached himself to the general and soon developed such a close relationship that the President-elect consulted him regularly on both appointments and the writing of his inaugural address. For the first weeks after Harrison's arrival the two men conferred every day from early morning to the dinner hour, six o'clock. Said Senator Willie P. Mangum: "Mr. Webster's influence is predominant" with regard to appointments. One reason for Harrison's willingness to draw Webster into his confidence was his growing concern about the attitude and activities of Henry Clay. The Kentucky senator had no regard, with good reason, for Harrison's intellectual abilities, let alone knowledge of or interest in Whig principles. He simply presumed that he would direct Whig legislation in Congress, but he did it in such a defiant manner as to offend Harrison. For one thing he demanded that a special session of Congress be called immediately on Harrison's taking office so that the legislative process could begin promptly after the cabinet had been confirmed. He simply took it for granted that this would be done. In addition, he planned to enact legislation to limit the President's appointment, dismissal, and veto powers as well as reduce the executive's tenure to a single term and bring the Treasury exclusively under the control of Congress. He appeared to be acting out of spite for failing to win the presidential nomination. His arrogance, his presumption, his impetuosity, and his cavalier manner of treating the President-elect gave promise of an early rupture in their relations.

And with Black Dan as well. "I fear," wrote Mangum, "for widening of the breach between Clay & Webster."[55]

53. Harvey, *Reminiscences*, pp. 160–161. Abbott Lawrence had coveted Webster's seat and the loss deeply offended him.

54. Poore, *Perley's Reminiscences*, I, 245–246.

55. Mangum to William A. Graham, March 27, 1841, in Shanks, ed., *Papers of Mangum*, III, 128–129. See also Calhoun to Virgil Maxcy, February 19, 1841, in *Calhoun Papers*, XV, 508.

It came soon enough, and it began over appointments. Clay wanted his friend John Clayton of Delaware,[56] not Thomas Ewing, appointed secretary of the treasury. He even went to Harrison and insisted upon Clayton's appointment, and then he wrote to Ewing and told him he should expect the office of postmaster general. "And you had better conform to that indication," he decreed.

Harrison handed the senator a double defeat when he not only gave Ewing the Treasury post but denied Clayton any place in the cabinet at all. Clay took the rebuke as a sure sign that Webster's sly hand lay behind it.[57]

A more important defeat for the Kentuckian occurred over the appointment of the collector of the Port of New York, a powerful position because it controlled hundreds of jobs and millions in revenue. The Whig governor of New York, William H. Seward, and his political mentor and ally, Thurlow Weed, had decided on Edward Curtis for the post, and Webster enthusiastically supported their choice.[58] Clay vigorously opposed it. Not only had Curtis actively participated in denying Clay the Whig presidential nomination in 1839, but as a partisan political operator he would use the collector's office to advance the interests of Clay's enemies. He "is Mr. W.'s *factotum*," claimed William L. Marcy, former governor and senator of New York. Furious, Clay confronted Harrison and labeled Curtis "faithless and perfidious and in my judgment unworthy of the place."

"Mr. Clay," Harrison retorted, "you forget that I am President."[59] Curtis's appointment went forward, although Clay managed to delay confirmation until the following September.

The Democrats exulted. "Webster has prevailed," chortled Marcy; "the distresses of the victors begins to be laughably amusing to the vanquished." It suddenly appeared that an "implacable war" had broken out between the friends of Clay and Webster, not because of principles or policy but because of political partisanship. And Webster had Harrison's ear, as everyone could readily see.

During one of their conferences Webster, in as delicate a manner as possible, informed Harrison that he had presumed to write an inaugural address. Too bad, the President-elect responded. He had already written one. Webster asked to see it and gave Harrison his version to read.

Webster was appalled by what was handed him. A more inappropriate address he could not imagine. Harrison had written mostly about the ancient world, especially the history of Rome. The document repeated the word "proconsul" so many times that Webster lost count. And the address went on intermi-

---

56. Clay worked with Clayton in winning passage of the Compromise Tariff of 1833, a tariff Webster disapproved of wholeheartedly.

57. Remini, *Clay*, pp. 571–572.

58. DW to Curtis, May 25, June 10, 1841, in *PC*, V, 122–123.

59. Marcy to P. M. Wetmore, January 17, February 6, 21, 22, March 18, 1841, Marcy Papers, LC; Clay to Peter B. Porter, January 8, Clay to Harrison, March 15, 1841, in Clay, *Papers*, IX, 473, 517; Tyler, *Letters*, II, 10, note 4.

nably. It was to set a record for length, a record not equaled for the rest of the nineteenth century and all of the twentieth. As it stood, reported Webster, it had no more to do with the United States "than a chapter in the Koran." Apparently Harrison was trying to prove to the American people that he had a classical education.

Not surprisingly, therefore, after reading Webster's efforts, which said nothing about Rome or proconsuls, Harrison rejected it. Besides, he said, if he read it at his inaugural, everyone would know that Webster had written it and that he had not. Carefully and gingerly Webster then asked permission to insert a few "modifications" in the address Harrison had composed and the President-elect reluctantly agreed.

Webster spent the entire next day inserting his modifications. It took him so much time that he arrived late for supper at the Seatons'.

"I am sorry to see you looking so worried and tired," said the alarmed Mrs. Seaton. "I hope nothing has gone wrong. I really hope nothing has happened."

"You would think that something had happened," Webster replied, "if you knew what I have done. I have killed *seventeen Roman proconsuls* as dead as smelts, every one of them!"[60]

So began the short-lived administration of President William Henry Harrison. On March 4 a "showy-shabby" procession of students, Tippecanoe clubs, floats of log cabins, civilians, militia companies, veterans of the War of 1812, and military cavalcades, with General Harrison on a "mean-looking white horse," wearing a plain frock coat and bowing and waving with his top hat to the people, marched up Pennsylvania Avenue to the inauguration at the Capitol. Not only did Harrison take more than an hour and a half to read his misbegotten address, but he also caught a bad cold, one that steadily worsened with each passing day and finally developed into pneumonia. However, in the inaugural he did say that he intended to arrest the concentration of power in the hands of the executive. He also renewed an earlier pledge to serve only one term, promised to use the veto with caution, and vowed to inform the Congress of his reasons for removing officeholders, especially the secretary of the treasury, and to leave legislation completely in the hands of Congress. It would appear that he intended to wipe away all of Jackson's "abominations" as President.

For their part, Clay and the Whigs in Congress apparently intended to reduce him to a mere figurehead.[61]

The fifty-nine-year-old Webster was unanimously confirmed by the Senate on March 5 and began his duties the following day. Setting up his office in the State Department building at Pennsylvania Avenue and Fifteenth Street, a two-story building of brick with a modest colonnade in the Greek Revival style, he promptly went to work, usually putting in a twelve-hour day. He rose early in

60. Harvey, *Reminiscences*, pp. 161–163.

61. Freeman Cleaves, *Old Tippecanoe: William Henry Harrison and His Time* (New York, 1939), p. 336; Adams, *Memoirs*, X, 439; Leonard D. White, *The Jacksonians: A Study in Administrative History, 1829–1861* (New York, 1954), p. 47.

the morning—about four or five o'clock—and was known to be the first to arrive at the department and the last to leave.

Webster had to get settled in not only his office but his new house as well.[62] After all, as secretary of state he would have to do a great deal of entertaining, and do it immediately. Once the purchase of the Swann house had been arranged and the rooms repaired and painted (requiring several months to complete before he and Caroline could occupy it), the dinner parties commenced, and they were done lavishly. Webster did much of the marketing for these dinners and liked to go in the early morning. Invariably wearing "a large, broad-brimmed, soft felt hat, with his favorite blue coat and bright buttons, a buff cassimere waistcoat and black trousers," he strolled from stall to stall, followed by his servant carrying a large basket. He regularly joked with the butchers, fishmongers, and grocery store proprietors "with a grave drollery." He always liked company at dinner and would say to his friends, "Come and dine with me tomorrow. I purchased a noble saddle of Valley of Virginia mutton in market last week, and I think you will enjoy it." Or he might entice them with "I received some fine cod-fish from Boston today, sir; will you dine with me at five o'clock and taste them?" Or, "I found a famous possum in market this morning, sir, and left orders with Monica, my cook, to have it baked in the real old Virginia style, with stuffing of chestnuts and surrounded by baked sweet potatoes. It will be a dish fit for the gods. Come and taste it." Monica's famed soft-shell crabs, terrapin, fried oysters, and roasted canvasback ducks "have never been surpassed in Washington," said one. Webster especially liked her Cape Cod chowder, roast Rhode Island turkey, and old-fashioned New Hampshire boiled dinner—all topped off with the finest wines and liquors. He did like to dine well, and his waistline and pocketbook showed it.[63]

These dinners also served a useful purpose for Webster in pursuing his duties as secretary of state. Although he never conducted state business at these gatherings, they helped enormously to improve his relationships with the various ministers because of the "gay spirits" and lighthearted mood they engendered. Former congressional colleagues, friends, and the diplomatic corps soon vied for invitations to these sumptuous affairs.

One party the Websters gave was deemed "the crowning entertainment of the season." Eight rooms of the mansion were thrown open, each "dazzlingly lighted"—a rare event in most American homes at the time. The President, all the foreign ministers, and most of the diplomatic corps attended, as well as judges of the Supreme Court and members of Congress. Webster received his guests with the "dignity and courtesy" characteristic of him in his brighter

---

62. "As to the new house. Things go on there very well. The painter has finished the upper stories and is getting down fast. The cellar and kitchen are all in nice order, and the big table, &c. all in place. All outside is done, except repairing the steps and taking up the pavements round about the front door. On the whole all looks well" DW to Caroline Webster, August 8, 1841, in *W&S,* XVIII, 107.

63. Poore, *Perley's Reminiscences,* I, 264–265, 384.

moods. There was no music, no dancing, but "plenty of lively conversation, promenades, eating of ices and sipping of rich wines, with the usual spice of flirtation."[64]

Surrounded at the dinner table by his close friends and confidants, Webster sparkled. At one such dinner Philip Hone commented: "I have never seen him so agreeable, for five hours he was the life of the company; cheerful, gay, full of anecdotes, and entirely free from a sort of gloomy abstraction in which I have sometimes seen him, as it were, envelop himself." Rather than serious political talk, he "preferred the light gossip in which he delights to pass the social hours." Frequently the evening ended with Webster leading his guests in song, his own voice louder and more exuberant than the others. At another party in New York, Hone said that "we sat until 11 o'clock and broke up after a grand chorus of 'Auld Lang Syne.' "[65]

Besides providing the setting for improving relationships with the foreign ministers, these parties allowed Webster to relax and escape the serious and increasingly dangerous problems confronting him as secretary of state. And indeed there were grave difficulties facing him at the very outset of his tenure, the most critical of which involved the British.

Not only had the Aroostook War, the seizure of the ship *Caroline,* and the continued incursions of the members of the Patriots and Hunters' Lodges[66] along the entire northern border jeopardized relations between the two countries, but now another incident had arisen that brought both nations to the brink of war.

While visiting New York, Alexander McLeod, a bibulous and boastful Scottish-Canadian deputy sheriff, bragged about his role in the *Caroline* incident that had resulted in the death of one American. He was promptly arrested on November 12, 1840, and indicted for murder and arson. The *Caroline* incident, as far as Americans were concerned, involved the violation of U.S. territorial sovereignty, the destruction of American property, and murder.

The British government responded that the sinking of the *Caroline* was a "public act," committed under government orders, and therefore the participants could not be held accountable. Furthermore, it threatened that if McLeod were executed, war would result. Henry Fox, the British minister to the United States, was instructed to ask for his passports if McLeod was executed. A real fear existed that even if McLeod were found innocent, he would be lynched. Andrew Stevenson, the American minister in London, reported that there seemed "to be a general impression that war is inevitable." Americans, incensed by British arrogance and brutal disregard of U.S. sovereignty, demanded war, while Britons, determined to teach upstart Yankees a lesson, commanded that

64. Ibid., 297–298.

65. Hone, *Diary,* I, 185, 379; II, 628–630.

66. On the Hunters' Lodges and other societies, see DW to Tyler, July, 1841, in *W&S,* XVI, 343–344. On their efforts to disrupt the later negotiations between Webster and Ashburton, see Kinchen, *Rise and Fall of Patriot Hunters,* pp. 117–123.

McLeod be rescued or revenged. By the opening weeks of 1841 the possibility of war was very real. Even the duke of Wellington thought it likely.[67]

The Van Buren administration, at the time of McLeod's arrest, found itself caught in an untenable position. Repudiated by the people, about to depart from power in a matter of months, and reluctant to take any action that would rupture his relations with his fellow New Yorkers, President Van Buren did nothing, arguing that the federal government could not interfere in the legal processes of the state. Better, he thought, to leave the unholy mess in the hands of his Whig successor, William Henry Harrison.[68]

The mess remained when Webster took office as the new secretary of state, for as late as February 9, 1841, Lord Palmerston had threatened a war of retaliation and revenge if the authorities in New York dared execute McLeod. But Webster's arrival at State immediately changed the climate between the British and American governments. The British believed they could get a sympathetic hearing from him, could negotiate with him, and, they hoped, bring the issue to a speedy conclusion. Webster was rightly regarded as an intense Anglophile who considered any conflict between the two countries an unmitigated disaster. But his even more intense nationalism guaranteed that he could not and would not be cajoled or bullied into sacrificing American rights. However, in the McLeod case he agreed with the British that the participants in the *Caroline* incident had acted under the orders of the British government and that therefore the issue properly belonged to the federal government, not the state government, to resolve. Webster hoped to secure McLeod's release with a writ of habeas corpus and have the case transferred to the Supreme Court. He even asked a friend and Utica lawyer, Joshua Spencer, to serve as McLeod's counsel. Unfortunately the Whig governor of New York, William H. Seward, had no intention of cooperating with Webster and thereby risking his political future by turning McLeod over to federal authorities.

With the President's consent, Webster sent Attorney General John Crittenden to Albany to try to persuade the governor to issue a nolle prosequi for McLeod's release. But nothing could change Seward's mind, and several unfortunate letters, both private and public, traveled between Albany and Washington. McLeod was brought to trial on October 4, 1841.[69]

While Webster worked to restore friendlier relations between the United States and Great Britain and bring McLeod under federal jurisdiction, his attention was continually distracted by the intrusion of job seekers, some of whom

67. Muriel E. Cunningham, *Lord Aberdeen: A Political Biography* (London and New York, 1983), p. 312; Senate Executive Documents, 28th Congress, 1st Session, vol. 27, doc. 341; Jones, *To the Webster-Ashburton Treaty*, pp. 20–32, 48–52.

68. John Niven, *Martin Van Buren: The Romantic Age of American Politics* (New York, 1983), p. 474; Jones, *Webster-Ashburton Treaty*, p. 50.

69. Seward informed Webster that neither the state nor federal government could settle the McLeod case. Only the courts could settle it. He said further that he never considered the possibility of a nolle prosequi. Seward to DW, March 22, 1841, *Microfilm Edition*, F14/18455; Stevens, *Border Diplomacy*, p. 95.

were highly placed. Indeed the opening weeks of his term required more attention to the business of dispensing available jobs and fending off unwanted patronage hounds. As it turned out, he had the controlling hand in the awarding of consulates abroad and federal judgeships at home.[70] He had the unpleasant obligation of refusing Biddle's request to be named minister to Austria, which, happily, did not impair their close relationship. The more important post of minister to Great Britain went to his good and learned friend and former governor of Massachusetts Edward Everett, who had in the past frequently helped raise funds for Webster.[71] Closer to home he appointed his jobless son Fletcher to the important post of chief clerk of the State Department.[72]

Stepping outside his area of responsibility, Webster also tried to get one of his supporters, General James Wilson of New Hampshire, appointed territorial governor of Iowa and Harrison was obliged to teach him the same lesson he had taught Henry Clay. Webster had recommended Wilson for the post, and Harrison told him that it had already been promised to Colonel John Chambers of Kentucky, his former aide-de-camp and presently his acting secretary. Thereupon Webster had the temerity to tell Chambers, with "sour sternness [and] a cloud gathering on his massive brow," that he "must not take that position, for I have promised it to my friend, General Wilson."

Shocked and outraged, Chambers replied: "Mr. Webster, I shall accept the place, and I tell you, sir, not to undertake to dragoon me!"[73]

Apparently Webster took up the matter with the other members of the cabinet, who all agreed that General Wilson would be the better choice. At the next cabinet meeting Webster informed the President that the members assembled had decided that Wilson, not Chambers, should be the territorial governor of Iowa.

"Ah! that is the decision, then, is it?" responded Harrison. Without saying another word, he wrote a few words on a piece of paper, handed it to Webster, and instructed him to read it out loud.

Webster glanced at it, paled, and finally read, "William Henry Harrison, President of the United States. . . ." But he got no further, for Harrison rose to his feet and in a loud voice exclaimed, "William Henry Harrison, President of the United States, tell you, gentlemen, that, by ----, John Chambers

70. Baxter, *Webster,* p. 300.

71. Everett's nomination, he was told by Webster, was opposed in the Senate by southerners, whose "objection was, that we were in danger of constant controversies with England, upon the subject of slaves, & that on that point your views were not such as the Southern Gentlemen approved." Clay supported Everett's nomination "very strongly . . . which I mention the more readily, as his general course, thro the extra session, has not been such as I would cordially approve." After a long and heated debate Everett was confirmed on September 11, 1841. DW to Everett, November 20, 1841, in *PD,* I, 21.

72. For appointments and requests for appointments, see *Microfilm Edition,* reels 38, 39, and 40. John Quincy Adams found Fletcher "bloated with self-sufficiency," "impertinent," "ignorant," and "insolent." "Into what hands have the Presidency, the Departments of State and of the Treasury, fallen!" growled the former President. Adams, *Memoirs,* XI, 249.

73. Poore, *Perley's Reminiscences,* I, 258.

shall be Governor of Iowa." And that ended the matter.[74]

Because so many removals from office were expected, a horde of hungry politicians, with raccoon tails in their hats (the raccoon had become something of a Whig symbol in the 1840 election) and dozens of recommendations in their sweaty hands descended on Washington, formed a steady line at Harrison's front door at the White House, and drove the poor ailing man to distraction with their appeals. The President finally instructed Webster to issue a circular to department heads and others in key positions that neither officers of the government nor the patronage were to be used to influence elections, nor could government money be expended for political purposes.[75]

But the circular did not stem the flood of job seekers who expected a reward for their party services. Long out of office and favor, these Whigs meant to do to the Democrats what had been done to them. And not only was the bedraggled Harrison harassed by office seekers, but Henry Clay kept hounding him to call a special session in Congress to address the nation's financial crisis. Clay finally sent him a rough draft of a proclamation recalling Congress, but it served only to infuriate Harrison for its presumptuousness. He responded with a letter that the highly sensitive and impetuous Clay misread as an order for him to stay away from the White House. Henceforth communicate only by mail, was Clay's interpretation.[76]

It is quite possible that Harrison had every intention of calling a special session eventually, but not at Clay's direction. He would issue the call in his own sweet time. But when he learned from Secretary Ewing that the country verged on insolvency, he realized that something had to be done immediately about the government's revenue. So he finally sent out the summons on March 17, directing Congress to reconvene on May 31.

It proved to be his last important act as President. The cold he had contracted during the inaugural festivities worsened with each succeeding week, and at twenty minutes before one o'clock on the morning of April 4, 1841, exactly one month after taking office, William Henry Harrison died from pneumonia. The first President to die in office, he was succeeded by the Vice President, the fifty-one-year-old John Tyler of Virginia, a slaveowner, a former Democrat who had deserted to the opposition during the nullification crisis, and a zealous advocate of states' rights. John Quincy Adams said that Tyler had "all the interests and passions and vices of slavery rooted in his moral and political constitution—with talents not above mediocrity." He called him the "Acting President."[77]

As the highest-ranking official in Washington, Webster had the "most painful duty" to notify Tyler, the department heads, and the entire diplomatic corps

74. "Recollections of an Old Stager," p. 754.

75. Circular, March 20, 1841, in *PC*, V, 96–97.

76. Harrison to Clay, March 13, 1841, in Clay, *Papers*, IX, 514; Remini, *Clay*, pp. 575–576.

77. Adams, *Memoirs*, X, 457.

of the President's demise. Until Tyler's arrival in the capital on April 6 the secretary of state was in fact the acting President.[78]

When he sent out this doleful announcement, it surely must have crossed Webster's mind more than once that if he had taken Thurlow Weed's advice and the Whig nominating convention in Harrisburg had named him for the second slot, as the Massachusetts delegates had proposed, he, not Tyler, would now be sitting in the White House as the President of the United States.[79]

78. DW to Thomas Carr, April 4, 1841, in *PC,* V, 104. Webster sent Fletcher to deliver the formal message to Tyler.

79. "We did not elect Mr Tyler-that was the work of the Whigs-especially of Mr C's friends," Webster wrote a few months later, "who made an effort, at Harrisburg, & succeeded in it, to put Mr T. on the Ticket instead [of] D.W. proposed by Mass." DW to Hiram Ketchum, July 12, 1841, ibid., V, 134.

32

"I Will Stay Where I Am"

WEBSTER had gotten along with Harrison extremely well during the past month, despite their minor difference over the Chambers appointment. How he, a leading nationalist, would now interact with a rigid states' rights President had everyone guessing. Some even conjectured that he would be replaced. One extreme states' righter, Thomas W. Gilmer of Virginia, wanted Webster "put into some dark corner, or thrown overboard entirely," calling him "a federalist of the worst die, a blackguard & vulgar debauchee," a man who, "but for his splendid talents, would be in jail or on some dunghill."[1] But Tyler knew he could not move that precipitously and expect cooperation from the Whig Congress, so he decided to keep the cabinet. "Among ourselves," commented Webster two weeks later, "we are quite harmonious, & get on without jarring."[2]

Tyler was not only a former Democrat but a former governor and former senator. As a staunch advocate of the old states' rights Republican school he had broken with Jackson over the Bank War and the Proclamation to South Carolina in 1832. Courtly, tall, standing over six feet, rather gaunt-looking, with a high "retreating forehead," he reputedly possessed all the "features of the best Grecian model." His most prominent feature was his sharply defined aquiline nose.[3]

From the start, as the secretary of state said, the President and Webster did indeed get along rather well, and they managed to work together as a team. After all, the two men had at least one thing in common from the start: Both had an intense dislike of Henry Clay.

Within a matter of months the dislike between Tyler and Clay turned into a ferocious hatred. Clay had every intention of enacting the Whig program of economic reform as speedily as possible, starting with another national bank.

1. Gilmer to Frank Minor, January 1, 1841, Tyler Papers, College of William and Mary, quoted in Norma Peterson, *The Presidencies of William Henry Harrison & John Tyler* (Lawrence, Kan., 1989), pp. 51–52.

2. Webster gave Tyler the benefit of the doubt. "My *hope* is, that he will consider himself *instructed,* not by one single state, but by the *Country.* In the matter of a Bank, my opinion is, he will sign whatever Congress may agree upon." DW to John Davis, April 16, 1841, in *PC,* V, 108.

3. Anne Royall, *Letters from Alabama on Various Subjects* (Washington, D.C., 1830), I, 550, note; Oliver P. Chitwood, *John Tyler: Champion of the Old South* (New York, 1964), p. 253.

On his return to Washington for the special session he wasted little time in making his purposes known to everyone, including Tyler. Within moments of their first interview in the White House they got into a shouting match. Clay demanded a new bank *now*. Tyler preferred to wait. After all, he had little time to prepare for the special session and wished to have the question postponed. Clay would not budge, and Tyler lost his patience. Do your duty to the country as you think proper, the President snapped at the senator, and "so help me God, I shall do mine."[4]

So began the Clay-Tyler feud that nearly wrecked the Whig party in 1841. Angry and bitter, Clay stormed out of the White House and immediately set to work to demonstrate his complete dominance of Congress. He directed committee memberships, making himself chairman of the Senate Finance Committee, and began laying out the legislative program. "He predominates over the Whig Party with despotic sway," declared the New York *Herald* on July 30, 1841. "Old Hickory himself never lorded it over his followers with authority more undisputed, or more supreme." Soon the members began calling him the Dictator.[5]

First on Clay's agenda was the repeal of the subtreasury system, a bill that passed both houses with relative ease and that Tyler signed on August 13. Then he called on Secretary of the Treasury Ewing to provide Congress with a draft of a new Bank charter, a move the President supported since it allowed him a controlling voice. As presented by Ewing on June 12, the plan set forth a Fiscal Bank incorporated in the District of Columbia, to be capitalized at thirty million dollars, and authorized to establish branches in the various cities, provided it obtained the consent of the state in which the branches would be located. This branching provision and the location of the bank had been carefully drawn to avoid Tyler's constitutional reservations. In devising the plan so that it would also conform to "the business interests of the country," Ewing had Webster's help.[6]

Webster strongly endorsed the Ewing plan and, without revealing his identity, wrote a series of editorials that appeared in the Washington *National Intelligencer* for June 15, 16, and 17. In these editorials he pleaded for passage of this Fiscal Bank even though it might not meet all the expectations of each member of Congress. Unlike Clay, Webster argued for compromise, knowing the President had serious doubts about a national bank. But the Clay faction positively hated Ewing's proposal because of the branching provision. Even so, it was probably the best that could be enacted under the circumstances, wrote Webster. But whatever happened, he pleaded, the Whigs must remain united and

4. Lyon G. Tyler, *The Letters and Times of the Tylers* (New York, 1970), II, 33–34. Mordecai M. Noah, editor of the New York *Evening Star* and a rabid supporter of Clay, disliked Webster but admitted that the secretary's "influence appears to be paramount at Washington. . . [;] the people never intended by the election of Harrison & Tyler to bring Daniel Webster into power." Noah to D. Lambert, July 18, 1841, in Shanks, ed., *Papers of Mangum*, III, 201.

5. Remini, *Clay*, pp. 578–599.

6. Tyler, ed., *Letters*, II, 45.

not allow division to split their ranks. "UNION is first. If we will but UNITE, we can form decisive purposes and summon up our energies. . . . There is but one remedy for the urgent necessities of the country, but one *hope* of the salvation of the Whig party—it is *union,* immediate UNION. Let us try such a bank as we can agree upon and can establish." If it fails, we can always revise it.

Webster repeated his theme of union in his letters to his friends throughout the entire special session, and he tried desperately to remind the Whigs of the fate that awaited them and the country if they did not heed his plea for compromise. He begged friends to use their influence with the press, claiming the Ewing bill conceded enough "to State rights & Constitutional scruples" to win Tyler's approval.[7]

But Clay refused to listen. His committee brought forward a bill with the branching authority fully restored. Then, when an amendment was offered to require state consent to branching and Rufus Choate, who had succeeded Webster in the Senate, spoke in favor of the amendment and predicted a presidential veto without it, Clay demanded to know who had told him that Tyler would veto, assuming rightly that Webster had been the source. If so, Clay wanted that fact openly acknowledged. He wanted the country to understand "that not only the Palace but the Department of State was in the field against him."

Answer, Clay cried. Choate refused. "I want a direct answer," shouted the infuriated Kentuckian. After a good deal of badgering back and forth the chair finally called both men to order. Clay was labeled by some a "sublime blackguard," and certain Whig newspapers denounced "the tyrannical insolence of Mr. Clay," whose "bullying disposition . . . causes him to forget himself sometimes." The Democrats could scarcely mask their pleasure, watching the Whigs destroy themselves. "Our friends are in the highest spirits," said a snickering William Marcy, "—they think they see the certain & speedy dissolution of the Whig party." The Democrats took particular pleasure in knowing that Webster had obviously joined Tyler "to embarrass the cause of Mr. Clay."[8]

"Clay and Webster are now openly hostile," announced Representative Henry Wise of Virginia. "The former is ready to quarrel with the latter, and will seek occasion to do so."[9]

For his part, Tyler felt trapped, surrounded as he was by "Clay-men, Webster-men, anti-Masons, original Harrisonians, old Whigs and new Whigs—each jealous of the others, and all struggling for the offices."[10]

If Clay was judged harshly for his intransigence on a national bank, Webster also took fire for what some Whig newspapers termed an abandonment of "those

7. Fletcher Webster to Ketchum, July 28, 1841, in *PC,* V, 139.

8. Marcy to Wetmore, July 3, 1841, Marcy Papers, LC; *Congressional Globe,* 27th Congress, 1st Session, pp. 140–145; Poore, *Perley's Reminiscences,* I, 275; New York *Herald,* quoted in George Poage, *Henry Clay and the Whig Party* (Chapel Hill, N.C., 1936), p. 56 note.

9. Wise to Judge Tucker, May 29, 1841, in Tyler, ed., *Letters,* II, 34. Mordecai M. Noah said that the Whig party "cannot be kept together a day, an hour, under Daniel Webster." The secretary "is the origin of all the trouble" in Washington. Noah to Mangum, n.d., Noah to Lambert, July 19, 1841, in Shanks, ed., *Papers of Mangum,* III, 233, 201.

10. Tyler to Tucker, July 28, 1841, in Tyler, ed., *Letters,* II, 53.

great constitutional landmarks with which his name and fame are so intimately interwoven." Clay had been condemned by Webster for abandoning principle in concocting the Compromise Tariff of 1833; now it was the secretary's turn to take the same kind of criticism.[11] But he rightly feared the consequences of a deadlock. If the amended bill passes Congress, as expected, and Tyler vetoes it, as expected, he wrote, "I know not what will become of our Administration." But if Tyler signs it, "we shall go on swimmingly."[12]

His worst fears were realized. The "Dictator" demonstrated his muscle in Congress by introducing another amendment to the Fiscal Bank bill that would allow the Bank to override any objection by a state to branching by claiming its action was " necessary and proper." Although Senator Rives called the amendment a trick, it narrowly passed, and the following day the Fiscal Bank bill won Senate approval. On August 6 the House also gave its approval and sent it to the President. All of which convinced Tyler that Clay was scheming to force a veto and then "get all the credit" for supposedly proposing a "compromise."[13]

Webster groaned. "I fear we shall have a *Veto*. . . . Prepare for the blow. My notion is, to preach moderation, & forbearance—let the papers urge the Whigs to hold together." Talk already started building that with the possible exception of Webster the cabinet would resign if Tyler vetoed, and Clay predicted that a veto would bring about "the separation of the President from the Whigs."[14]

By this time Webster had thrown in his lot with Tyler completely, exerting his considerable influence and assistance. "I am with the President a good deal," he informed Caroline. "He seems quite kind, but is evidently much agitated. I am nearly worn down with labor & care." But Tyler's closest friends kept Webster at arm's length. "As to Webster," Henry Wise wrote Beverley Tucker, "I . . . will act towards him as you will—without trusting him, will accept his aid."[15] Wise repeated the same criticism that had been heard for years: Daniel Webster could not be trusted.

Tyler waited his full constitutional time of ten days before sending down his veto message. He objected not only to the branching provision but to the Bank's authority to discount notes. Three days later the Senate failed to override.[16]

The Democrats could hardly believe their good fortune. "We should get

11. *National Intelligencer*, July 24, 1841. "You can have no idea of the horror and indignation felt towards the Webster administration of thirty days," wrote David Lambert. "They gave to it the worst name that of tyranny, insolence and proscription could possibly give." Lambert to Mangum, May 7, 1841, in Shanks, ed., *Papers of Mangum*, III, 154.

12. DW to Everett, July 28, 1841, in *PC*, V, 138–139.

13. Wise to Tucker, July 11, 1841, in Tyler, ed., *Letters*, II, 52; Marcy to Newell [?], June 25, 1841, Marcy to Wetmore, July 24, 1841, Marcy Papers, LC; Poage, *Clay and Whig Party*, p. 63.

14. Webster to Ketchum [?], August 13, 1841, in *PC*, V, 140; New York *Tribune*, August 11, 16, 1841, Clay to Peter B. Porter, August 8, Clay to Thomas Hart Clay, August 15, 1841, in Clay, *Papers*, IX, 581, 584.

15. DW to Caroline Webster, [August 21, 1841], in *PC*, V, 145; Wise to Tucker, June 18, 1841, in Tyler, ed., *Letters*, II, 46.

16. Richardson, *Messages and Papers*, III, 1918–1921.

the North Bend Glee Club to sing 'Tippecanoe & Tyler too," laughed one. But Whigs reacted angrily, and a group of them, staggeringly drunk, grouped themselves around the White House at 2:00 A. M., and beat drums, blew trumpets, and shouted, "Huzza for Clay!" and "A Bank! A Bank! Down with the Veto!" Poor Webster held a "carousal" at his house, got gloriously drunk, and "swore he would stay in office."[17]

Having determined to keep his office, Webster put as good a face on the events in Washington as possible. The Bank was only one issue, he protested. The Whigs must hold together for the sake of other measures and not lose them too. A bankruptcy bill, a land bill, and a duty bill to authorize a government loan hung in the balance. "Why should all these be lost" on account of *"one measure"*?[18]

On August 17 Representative John Sergeant of Pennsylvania and Senator John M. Berrien of Georgia came to see the President as delegates from a Whig caucus in Congress to learn if they could fashion another Bank or fiscal agent that would be acceptable to Tyler. Knowing the great desire of Whigs to have some form of national banking, the President declared that he had no objection to a Bank in the District with agents in the states to handle the government's fiscal business. But he strongly objected to its making local discounts. The next day, Wednesday, the usual meeting day of the cabinet, Tyler consulted with the members about his discussion with Berrien and Sergeant. Webster cited constitutional reasons for agreeing with the President and thought the stock of such a Bank, as proposed, would be acceptable to businessmen. Thereupon Tyler asked Webster and Ewing to see to it that an acceptable plan was shown to Sergeant, but he warned them against committing him in any way. Webster himself actually went to the Capitol and spoke with Berrien and Sergeant about "provisions & modifications which I supposed would ensure the Presidents signature." For a brief period it looked as though the impasse had been broken and a new Bank could be chartered. But in deference to the President's constitutional sensitivities Webster suggested (and it was agreed) to dispense with the word "bank" and call the agency the Fiscal Corporation of the United States.[19]

The Fiscal Corporation bill sped through the House with a minimum of debate on August 23 in the hope of winning passage before Tyler changed his mind. Unfortunately in the Senate Clay again managed to offend the President by describing Tyler's close advisers as a *"corporal's guard."* Clay had in mind such men as Henry Wise, Thomas W. Gilmer, George H. Proffit, W. W. Irwin, Francis Mallory, and Caleb Cushing, Webster's close friend and financial sup-

17. Remini, *Clay*, pp. 590–591; Marcy to Wetmore, August 18, 1841, Marcy Papers, LC. Charles Sumner of Massachusetts predicted that the veto "will be the beginning of a great schism in the Whig ranks. Indeed, this is silently beginning; at present it is like a crack, under ground, which has not become externally visible." Sumner to George Hillard, June 30, 1841, Sumner Papers, LC.

18. DW to [Ketchum?], August 13, 1841, in *PC*, V, 140.

19. "Diary of Thomas Ewing, August and September, 1841," *American Historical Review*, XVIII (1912), pp. 98–102; "Memorandum on the Banking Bills and the Vetoes," in *PC*, V, 177–178.

porter. The remark prompted Representative John M. Botts of Virginia to publish a letter in which he accused Tyler of treachery toward the Whigs and forming a third party with states' righters and other friendly Democrats to get himself elected in 1844. But, continued Botts, the Whigs would *"Head*[20] *Captain Tyler, or die."*[21]

The attempt to ridicule Tyler into obeying the dictates of his party produced the opposite effect. He grew angrier with each Whig thrust, and he finally decided to abandon the Bank plan he had so recently agreed to sanction.[22]

At the cabinet meeting on August 25 Tyler seemed "gloomy and depressed." He had decided to veto the Fiscal Corporation bill and urged the members to get final passage postponed. He may also have decided to rid himself of his cabinet, knowing that a second veto would surely trigger resignations. "We are on the eve of a cabinet rupture," wrote his close friend Henry Wise. "With some of them we want to part friendly. We can part friendly with Webster by sending him to England." Another close friend, Abel P. Upshur, said that Webster would stick to the President "till he kills Clay, and no longer." The others will "sacrifice him to Clay."[23]

As Tyler had requested, Webster and Ewing worked particularly hard with their friends to win a postponement. Webster spoke to Rives, who told him that Clay had given notice that he intended to bring up the Bank bill on September 1. All hope of a postponement now seemed futile. Two days later Ewing went to see Webster, and they had a long conversation together. They both now anticipated a dissolution of the cabinet. Webster revealed that "he could not sleep well of nights, for thinking of it—said if he were rich he would not mind it personally, but that he felt great unwillingness at his age to return to the Bar."[24]

On September 3 the Senate passed the Fiscal Corporation bill by an almost strict party vote of twenty-seven to twenty-two. Six days later Tyler vetoed it, whereupon Ewing informed Webster that he intended to resign. "Indeed I could not feel that my reputation as a man of truth and candor was safe, while I attempted to represent him [the President]," the treasury secretary declared. It seemed extremely likely that the other members of the cabinet—Crittenden, Badger, and Bell—would resign at the same time.[25]

Only Webster held back. Granger, the postmaster general, hesitated momentarily but was finally induced to go along with the others. Badger gave a dinner on Thursday, September 9, to which all the members of the cabinet were invited. Clay also attended. During the meal pressure was brought to bear on

20. To check him.

21. Remini, *Clay*, pp. 593–594.

22. "Memorandum on Banking Bills and Vetoes," in *PC*, V, 179.

23. Wise to Tucker, August 29, Upshur to Tyler, July 28, 1841, in Tyler, ed., *Letters*, II, 90, 115.

24. "Diary of Ewing," pp. 104, 109; Ewing to Samson H. Mason, May 8, 1842, in Shanks, ed., *Papers of Mangum*, III, 330.

25. "Diary of Ewing," p. 111.

Webster to complete the mass exodus. "It was declared to him," Tyler later revealed, "that if he would resign I would necessarily have to vacate the government by Saturday and thus Whig rule be thoroughly reestablished.[26] He had too much sagacity not to see that the rule sought to be established was *Clay rule* only, and nothing more."[27] Webster responded by telling the group that he thought "they had acted rashly," that it would look "too much like a combination between a Whig cabinet and a Whig Senate." What he did not say, because the man was sitting in their midst, was that he believed it would also appear as though Henry Clay were the prime mover.[28]

For the moment, then, Webster refused to commit himself and withdrew from Badger's supper. He called a meeting at his home of the Massachusetts delegation in Congress on Friday, September 10, and informed the group that the resignations of the other cabinet members would be presented to Tyler the following day at 11 o'clock. He then asked for advice on what he himself should do. Webster claimed that it was a matter of supreme indifference to him whether he stayed or went, a declaration, observed John Quincy Adams, "which it is possible he believed when he made it." Webster had gotten such a reputation of untrustworthiness that it was difficult at times for his colleagues to tell whether he believed what he said was the truth or not. He did admit that he saw no good reason to justify his resignation. The President, he continued, had always treated him with respect, and he thought Tyler wished him to remain. He added that the Fiscal Corporation bill would have been signed had Botts not published that stupid letter. He concluded by stating that "the joint resignation of the four heads of Departments together was a Clay movement, to make up an issue before the people against Mr. Tyler." Adams asked about the reasons given for the resignations of the other four cabinet members, and Webster ticked them off: the President's want of confidence in the advice given, his use of the veto, a member's personal friendship with Clay, and "other & preexisting causes." He said nothing of course about Ewing's sense of honor about being known as "a man of truth and candor" that he did not want challenged.

When the discussion ended, the Massachusetts delegation agreed unanimously that Webster would not be justified in quitting his office at this time. "But we all felt that the hour for the requiem of the Whig party was at hand."[29]

At half past twelve o'clock on September 11 the first cabinet resignation

---

26. Congress was scheduled to adjourn on Monday, leaving no time to confirm the members of a new cabinet. In 1841 it was assumed that a vacancy requiring Senate confirmation must be filled before Congress adjourned or remain vacant until it reconvened.

27. Tyler to Alexander Gardiner, May 6, 1845, in Tyler, ed., *Letters,* II, 97.

28. DW to Ketchum, September 10, 1841, in *W&S,* XVIII, 110. In this letter he added: "I will not throw the great foreign concerns of the country into disorder or danger, by any abrupt party proceeding."

29. John Tyler, Jr., to Lyon Tyler, January 29,1883, in Tyler, ed., *Letters,* II, 121 note; Adams, *Memoirs,* XI, 13–14; *Madisonian,* September 25, 1841, quoted in Van Tyne, ed., *Letters of Webster,* p. 239.

was submitted, followed shortly thereafter by the others. When Ewing's letter arrived at the President's desk, Webster asked Tyler, before the seal was broken, to entrust it to his care for a few moments. Tyler handed him the letter.[30] Back in his office Webster asked Ewing to see him and tried to persuade him to withdraw his letter, promising him his "choice of Foreign Missions." But Ewing refused. His sense of honor and duty forbade it.[31]

Webster returned the letter to Tyler in silence. Then in his "deep-toned voice" he exclaimed: *Where am I to go, Mr. President?*

"You must decide that for yourself, Mr. Webster," Tyler responded.

"If you leave it to me, Mr. President, I will stay where I am."

As Webster spoke these words, Tyler rose from his desk, stretched out his hand to Webster, and warmly expressed his gratitude. *"Give me your hand on that, and now I will say to you that Henry Clay is a doomed man from this hour."*[32]

Tyler's closest friends had hoped to see the entire cabinet replaced, and probably the President did too. They all knew that Webster had no great personal regard for Tyler or his abilities and would follow whatever course seemed to him most advantageous. "The plan is to give [the London mission] to Webster," declared Abel Upshur, "which rids Tyler of him as S. of State." But the President was genuinely moved by Webster's decision to stick, and he was anxious to prevent any more "jarring," as he put it. Besides, he needed him in his ongoing battle with Clay and his friends in Congress. And Webster was a power in the North that could provide needed support if Tyler decided to seek the presidential nomination in 1844. Also, Webster's continuing efforts in resolving the conflict with Great Britain dictated his retention. So Tyler built a new cabinet around Webster, replacing Ewing with the incompetent Walter Forward of Pennsylvania; Bell with John Spencer,[33] the New York secretary of state, who had the strong support of Governor William H. Seward and Thurlow Weed; Badger with Upshur; Crittenden with Hugh S. Legaré of South Carolina, a state's rights Whig who had once called Calhoun a demagogue; and Granger with Charles A. Wickliffe, a former Kentucky legislator and governor, whom Clay hated with a passion. "Like myself," Tyler explained, "they are all original Jackson men, and mean to act upon Republican principles."[34]

Tyler hurriedly assembled his new cabinet and submitted their names to Congress on Monday, September 13, the last day of the congressional session. All were confirmed. Clay absented himself.

30. John Tyler, Jr., to Lyon Tyler, January 29, 1883, in Tyler, ed., *Letters*, II, 121 note. John Tyler, Jr., was the President's private secretary and was present during the resignation proceedings.

31. "Diary of Ewing," p. 112.

32. John Tyler, Jr., to Lyon Tyler, January 29, 1883, in Tyler, ed., *Letters*, II, 122, note.

33. Initially Tyler offered the post to Associate Justice John McLean, who declined it as beneath him.

34. John Tyler, Jr., to Lyon Tyler, January 29, 1883, Upshur to Tucker, September 7, Tyler to Thomas A. Cooper, October 8, 1841, in Tyler, ed., *Letters*, II, 121–123 note, 122, 125.

That same day a caucus of sixty or seventy Whigs met and issued an address to the American people by which they formally expelled John Tyler from the Whig party.[35]

The following day the Washington *National Intelligencer* published a letter sent to the editors by Daniel Webster. In it he gave his reasons for declining to submit his resignation. He understood that the differences that existed between the President and Congress had triggered the crisis, but he did not see how mass resignations could resolve them. On the contrary, the only remedy for these "evils has been, and is, on union, conciliation, and perseverance of the whole Whig party." Furthermore, he believed he could render valuable service to the public by retaining his post. He and the President concurred on all matters pertaining to foreign relations, and he did not want to run the risk of "embarrassing the Executive, in regard to subjects and questions now immediately pending," and which could affect the preservation of peace. Moreover, if he had had good reason to resign, he would not have done so without giving the President ample notice and enough time to choose his successor.[36]

The letter did not please Tyler's friends. They thought it should have commented further on the "betrayal" of the President by the other members of the cabinet. Webster "is made out a sort of martyr, for remaining in the cabinet, to the high and important calls of his country. And this is history!" The letter did nothing more than attempt to conciliate the Whigs and pronounce himself indispensable for attaining peace with Great Britain. But the most important reason he refused to step aside was that he knew that the resignations were meant to establish the *"Clay rule"* and he would not submit to it. By standing his ground, he hoped to undercut Clay's domination of the Whig party.[37]

All these factors, those stated by Webster himself as well as by his critics, influenced his decision. Of course he did not mention that he enjoyed being the secretary of state. How could he? But he loved the importance, authority, the patronage, and the glamour of the office. It provided intellectual excitement almost every day. And it swelled his sense of pride in what he had achieved with his life.

As it turned out, the new cabinet got along famously. "The members of the cabinet are perfectly harmonious on all the great subjects before us," reported Upshur two months later, "and none of us have yet differed in our views very materially from the President."[38]

But Webster's relations with the Clay faction of the Whig party continued to deteriorate. In fact the pace of that deterioration quickened. Clay himself

35. The address was written by Senators Berrien of Georgia, Nathaniel P. Tallmadge of New York, and Oliver H. Smith of Indiana and Representatives Horace Everett of Vermont, Samson Mason of Ohio, John P. Kennedy of Maryland, John C. Clark of New York, and Kenneth Rayner of North Carolina.

36. September 16, 1841.

37. Tyler, ed., *Letters*, II, 119.

38. Upshur to Tucker, November 2, 1841, in Tyler, ed., *Letters*, II, 125.

thought that Webster's continuance in the cabinet "must injure him to an extent that he will find it difficult ever to repair." Then, with a presumptuousness so characteristic of the man, Clay went to Webster and told him to his face what he thought his fate would be if he continued in office. "I then said to him 'If you mean to continue in Mr. Tyler's Admon for the purpose of closing any incomplete business to which your attention and service are necessary, the public will approve your conduct. But if you identify yourself with it and remain indefinitely the public will condemn you.' " Webster just gritted his teeth and said nothing.[39]

The Whig party appeared to be splitting apart,[40] torn between Webster's followers, who enjoyed the patronage that their leader increasingly made available to them, and the Clay men, whose anger toward the secretary bordered on the violent. One New York Whig declared that "Webster is doomed." His followers are "the tools of a tool, we can never trust them"; as for Webster himself, "no lucky chance can now save him from general execration."[41]

In facing all these events and deciding his course of action, Webster did not have the presence and comforting help of his wife, Caroline. She remained in New York but was undecided about her next move: whether to stay in New York with her family (her father had died on March 18, 1841) or to go to Boston or Marshfield. For the first few months the Swann house at Lafayette Square, which was still being painted and repaired, was not ready to receive her. Without any consideration for her husband's difficult situation she pestered him with her dilemma and asked him to join her.

Webster snapped at her in response: "What can I do?—I really feel embarrassed, & distressed.—It is impossible for me to leave Washington at present. Congress sits longer than was expected—we are in the midst of most important matters—& my leav'g here for some time to come, is out of all question. I am perplexed. Between your uneasiness where you are, & your indecision where to go, & the critical & harassing state of th'gs here—I find noth'g to solace me." Not even Fletcher's presence helped. To add to Webster's misery the poor man suffered a riding accident that truly frightened him. He had been out for a drive in a wagon when the harness broke and the horse took him on a wild ride. "We were in no small danger," Webster reported. The horse rounded three sides of Capitol Square "at full speed" before the wagon hit a post that broke the axle and threw Webster to the ground. He escaped with minor bruises but admitted that he did "not wish another such drive."[42]

39. Clay to John M. Clayton, November 1, 1841, Clay to John O. Sargent, July 29, 1843, in Clay, Papers, IX, 620, 841; Remini, Clay, p. 598.

40. "The whig party is now divided into two hostile sections," wrote Calhoun. "They are very hostile. I regard the entire defeat and dissolution of the party as certain." Calhoun to Virgil Maxcy, December 26, 1841, in Calhoun Papers, XVI, 21.

41. Nicholas Carroll to Mangum, October 28, 1841, in Shanks, ed., Papers of Mangum, III, 248. "The whigs assault . . . especially Webster, with great bitterness." Calhoun to Thomas G. Clemson, December 31, 1841, in Calhoun Papers, XVI, 27.

42. DW to Caroline Webster, August 22, 1841, in Van Tyne, ed., Letters of Webster, p. 601; DW to Caroline Webster, August 8, 1841, in Webster, ed., Private Correspondence, II, 107.

In his misery and loneliness he sighed for home. "Oh, Marshfield! and the Sea, the Sea!"[43]

Again Washington began to gossip that his marriage was in trouble. "It is understood here that Mrs W is about to separate from Mr. W."[44] No wonder. At this time Sarah Goodridge, the miniaturist, came to Washington and visited the lonely man. No wonder too that at this time Representative Gilmer called the secretary "a vulgar debauchee."

Another matter to set gossipy tongues wagging was the fact that Caroline's father had left her a "large slice of property" upon his death but arranged that in "no case" would it "revert to her husband. This has aroused his [Webster's] ire & produced a breach between the Le Roy family & Mr. W." To make matters worse, Webster's friends had refused him any further financial aid, and in desperation he "turned out the contents of his wine cellar to supply a pressing emergency." Presumably he sold it. "You can see at once how strongly a *public* separation and blazoning his private misconduct will operate upon the position of the Secy. It is possible that 'the separation' may be avoided, but his embarrassments cannot." However, when Goodridge departed and Caroline finally arrived in Washington in late November—the house was now ready for occupancy—the couple began to entertain again, and the gossip slowly subsided.[45]

They entertained lavishly. Caroline opened a dozen rooms of their mansion, all "magnificently furnished," for the enjoyment of their guests, and she presided over sumptuous meals "looking like a queen." Even the unfailingly critical former President Adams, after attending one of her dinner parties, acknowledged that "Mrs. Webster was very amiable." To the astonishment of many guests, as they entered the house, portraits of Queen Victoria, Lord Melbourne, and the duke of Wellington hung in the vestibule of the mansion! Lord Morpeth, the earl of Carlisle, presently touring the country, called Webster a "very gracious" host.[46]

When the special or first session of the Twenty-seventh Congress finally adjourned on September 13, Webster started making plans for a brief visit home. Although Congress failed to enact a new Bank bill after repealing the Independent Treasury Act, it did pass a bankruptcy bill, a land bill, and a duties bill, which Tyler signed on August 19, September 4, and 11 respectively. It was a very respectable record for the Whigs, accomplished unfortunately at the expense of party unity.

Despite a howling gale that pummeled the Massachusetts shoreline, Webster finally left the turmoil of Washington for the peace and quiet of Marshfield. He took off by railroad on September 27 and with only short stops along the way reached home on October 4. He found his property had sustained considerable

43. DW to Harriette Paige, August 22, 1941, in Webster, ed., *Private Correspondence*, II, 108.

44. Nicholas Carroll to Willie P. Mangum, October 28, 1841, in Shanks, ed., *Papers of Mangum* III, 248.

45. Ibid.

46. Ibid.; Peterson, *Great Triumvirate*, p. 325; Adams, *Memoirs*, XI, 139.

damage: trees downed, fences gone, crops ruined. "I believe there is not an apple or pear on any tree, this side of Boston," he sighed.[47] But as always Marshfield provided the rest and comfort and peace of mind that restored his strength and vigor. And he needed all the strength and vigor he could possibly muster to face the difficult problems that lay ahead.

47. DW to Edward Curtis, October 5, [1841], in *PC*, V, 163–164.

33

The Webster-Ashburton Treaty

As secretary of state Webster could hardly expect to escape for very long from his responsibilities as a government official by resting at Marshfield, particularly in view of the never-ending dispute with Great Britain over the Maine boundary line and the seizure of McLeod following the *Caroline* incident.

Less troublesome but a factor in the continuing deterioration of Anglo-American relations was the financial crisis resulting from the Panic of 1837. Three of the seven "American Banking Houses" in London failed to meet their financial obligations, and even the renowned Baring Brothers barely escaped fiscal disaster. Worse, several American states where British capital had been invested, including Pennsylvania, repudiated their debts.[1]

To complicate matters even further, British soldiers on the night of September 19, 1841, kidnaped a forty-seven-year-old American by the name of James W. Grogan in Alburg, Vermont, on suspicion of arson and carted him off to Canada, where he was imprisoned, apparently in retaliation for the McLeod capture. It struck Americans as an implied threat that Grogan's fate rested on whether or not McLeod was found guilty at his trial in Utica, New York, which commenced on October 4, the day Webster arrived at Marshfield. In his father's absence Fletcher Webster, the chief clerk and acting secretary of state, sent a strong letter of protest to the British minister, Henry S. Fox. By early November he urged his father not to "delay much longer" his return to Washington.[2]

During the fall the Democrats in Congress mounted a spirited assault on Webster's handling of the McLeod case. Faulted for not writing an angry retort over Britain's demand for McLeod's release, Webster was accused by one House member, Samuel S. Bowne of New York, of "servile cringing to British power [which had] brought shame and dishonor on our country." Charles J. Ingersoll of Pennsylvania, who hated the secretary because Webster had once headed a

---

1. Muriel E. Chamberlain, *Lord Aberdeen: A Political Biography* (London and New York, 1983), p. 310.

2. Fletcher Webster to Fox, September 28, 1841, Sworn Deposition of James W. Grogan, [October 13, 1841], in *PD*, I, 152–160; Fletcher Webster to DW, October 9, 1841, in *Microfilm Edition*, F16/20522; Fletcher Webster to DW, November 7, 1841, in *PC*, V, 170; Stevens, *Border Diplomacy*, pp. 138–143.

Senate committee that investigated Ingersoll's supposed acceptance of a bribe when serving as a U.S. district attorney, joined in introducing a resolution in the House demanding to know whether Webster had informed Fox that he could expect McLeod's release.[3]

This time the Whigs, most notably John Quincy Adams, came to Webster's defense. The former President modestly claimed that his speech "has given him [Webster] the means of saving himself from ruin, and his country from a most disastrous war. My reward from him will be professions of respect and esteem, speeches of approbation and regard for me to my friends, knowing that they will be reported to me, secret and deep-laid intrigues against me. . . . Such is human nature, in the gigantic intellect, the envious temper, the ravenous ambition, and the rotten heart of Daniel Webster."[4] The resolution was quashed.

Then, suddenly, the deteriorating relations between the United States and Great Britain dramatically changed. It began on October 12. The jury found McLeod not guilty since he had an airtight alibi. Four witnesses swore he was at their home the night of the attack on the *Caroline*. It took the jurors half an hour to reach their verdict. Nevertheless it was suspected, although never proved, that the federal government (Webster?) was responsible for the absence of several vital prosecution witnesses. To avoid the possibility of a lynching, McLeod was speedily and safely transported back across the Niagara River; he received a tumultuous greeting in Montreal.[5]

A month before this verdict was reached an important political change also took place in Britain when Sir Robert Peel,[6] leader of the Conservatives, became prime minister, replacing Lord Melbourne. At the same time the more amiable Lord Aberdeen took over as foreign secretary in place of Palmerston. A man of unusual features with some resemblance to his kinsman Lord Byron, Aberdeen had "remarkably high cheek bones" and dark, curly hair. Melbourne thought he possessed a "beautiful magnificent expression; a sweet expression." He had a perfect horror of war and revolution and regarded France as the greatest threat to world stability and peace. As foreign secretary, therefore, he had a great desire to bring about an amicable settlement of the American crisis.[7]

It also helped that Edward Everett assumed the post of U.S. minister to Great Britain, replacing the quarrelsome and tedious Andrew Stevenson. The Peel government was very anxious to repair the rifts that had threatened war between the two governments and saw in Webster a kindred spirit who could help in the process. Also helpful was the fact that the Peel ministry investigated

3. *Congressional Globe*, 27th Congress, 1st Session, appendix, 75, 153–155; Kenneth R. Stevens, "The Webster-Ingersoll Feud: Politics and Personality in the New Nation," *Historical New Hampshire*, XXXVII , (Summer–Fall, 1982), pp. 174–192.

4. Adams, *Memoirs*, XI, 20.

5. Jones, *To the Webster-Ashburton Treaty*, pp. 63–65; Cunningham, *Aberdeen*, p. 312.

6. Webster is reputed to have said that "Sir Robert Peel is head and shoulders above any man I ever saw in my life." Lyman, *Public and Private Life of Webster*, II, 104.

7. Cunningham, *Aberdeen*, pp. 6–8.

the Grogan matter, directed his release, and provided compensation. In addition, when the McLeod trial ended favorably, the Peel government did not press the United States for reparation for McLeod's eleven-month incarceration in a New York prison.[8]

In a wise and statesmanlike action Webster immediately took the McLeod incident one step further and drafted a proposal which Tyler submitted to Congress in his first annual message of December 7, 1841, that would permit the federal government in the future to take jurisdiction away from the states of persons accused of a crime while acting under the authority of a foreign power.[9] Senator John M. Berrien of Georgia, chairman of the Judiciary Committee, confidentially asked Webster to draft such a bill, and the secretary did. Congress passed this legislation on August 29, 1842.[10]

Webster made another important contribution to international law—namely, the conditions under which an attack by one country on another can be justified in the name of self-defense. In a letter dated April 24, 1841, to the British minister in Washington, Henry Fox, he stated his position. His knowledge of both common law and international law, resulting from forty years of study and practice before state and federal courts dealing with settlements of claims of merchants and traders, amply prepared him for the task. To convince the British of his argument, he needed all the skills he had acquired over the years. The question involved the attack on the *Caroline* by British authorities for which no individual could be held personally responsible in a court of law. In his letter to Fox, Webster argued that Great Britain in this case could not plead self-defense under the laws of nations. It would be necessary, he contended, for Britain to show "a necessity of self-defence, instant, overwhelming, leaving no choice of means, and no moment for deliberation." It would be necessary to show that local authorities in Canada did nothing unreasonable or excessive, that appeals to the persons on board the *Caroline* were impracticable or would be unavailing, that they could not wait for daylight, that no discrimination between the innocent and guilty could be made, and that it would not have been enough to seize or detain the vessel. Rather it must be shown "that there was a necessity, present and inevitable, for attacking her, in the darkness of the night . . . killing some . . . and then drawing her into the current . . . [and] setting her on fire" without regard to the innocent or guilty, the living or the dead. "All this, the Government of the United States cannot believe to have existed."[11]

Webster's tightly reasoned doctrine of self-defense has achieved an im-

8. The United States never paid McLeod for his incarceration but in 1855 the British awarded him an annual pension of two hundred pounds. Stevens, *Border Diplomacy*, p. 170.

9. Richardson, ed., *Messages and Papers*, III, 1927–1942. Peel characterized the President's message as "ambiguous, concealing peaceful desires and intentions under blustering words." But he liked Everett's accompanying note and termed it "conciliatory." Peel to Aberdeen, December 30, 1841, Aberdeen Papers, BM 43,061.

10. Berrien to DW, January 10, 1842, in *PD*, I, 706–707; *U.S. Statutes at Large*, V, 539.

11. DW to Fox, April 24, 1841, in *PD*, I, 58–68.

portant position in international law and diplomacy. It was expressly endorsed by the Nuremberg Tribunal in 1945–1946 at the trial proceedings of Nazi leaders, and the Israelis applied it to justify their raid in 1976 on the Entebbe airport in Uganda, quoting what they called Webster's "classic formulation" of the right of self-defense in his letter to Fox.[12] The opinionated and hypercritical Charles Sumner was much impressed by the letter. "His letter to Fox," Sumner wrote to George Hillard, "was truly a masterly production, argumentative, eloquent & true." Sumner thought that where Webster "reads the British Govt. a lecture in the common law, is truly delicate & admirable; & then the homily on the preservation of neutrality is dexterous & amusing."[13]

Another example of Webster's creative statesmanship developed out of his handling of the boundary dispute between Maine and New Brunswick that had provoked the Aroostook War. Maine took the position that the disputed territory, roughly twelve thousand square miles, belonged to it. Canadians on the other side naturally disputed this claim, and although Britain now seemed disposed to compromise, Maine resisted, just as it had resisted all efforts in the past to settle the matter that did not accede completely to its demands.

The dispute had originated at the end of the American Revolution, when England and its colonies signed a peace treaty and agreed on a boundary line that ran north from the source of the St. Croix River to the "highlands" separating the tributaries of the St. Lawrence River from those that emptied into the Atlantic Ocean. Using a 1755 map drawn by the respected scientist John Mitchell, the peace commissioners failed to attach the map, or any other map, to the treaty itself. As a result the language of the treaty and the actual geographical locations of specified points mentioned in the treaty did not coincide. Nor was there agreement about the meaning of "highlands."[14] So both countries claimed the larger share of the twelve thousand square miles. At the time Maine was part of Massachusetts, and the two did not separate until the passage of the Missouri Compromise in 1820. Therefore any settlement of the disputed area involved two states as well as the United States and Great Britain.

In compliance with the terms of the Treaty of Ghent, which ended the War of 1812, the boundary dispute was submitted to the king of the Netherlands, William I, for arbitration, and in 1831 he advised the two nations to compromise their differences since he found it impossible to locate the highlands. Britain seemed prepared to accept his solution, but both Maine and the Senate rejected it. The Aroostook War exacerbated the problem, and relations between the two countries continued to deteriorate.

Obviously the state of Maine constituted a major stumbling block to any attempt at a reasonable solution to the problem. Then, in May 1841, Francis

12. *PD*, I, 31–32.

13. Sumner to Hillard, June 30, 1841, Sumner Papers, LC.

14. The British argued that the highlands referred to noticeable elevations, while the Americans claimed it meant a watershed.

O. J. Smith, an influential lawyer, newspaper publisher, entrepreneur, and former representative and senator from Maine, called on Webster at his home with an unusual but interesting proposition. He suggested that past diplomatic efforts had failed because the negotiations were directed *"at the wrong end of the dispute."* The difficulty lay, he said, between the people of Maine and New Brunswick, not the federal and British governments. No wonder the negotiations failed. Maine and New Brunswick had to be convinced of the necessity of compromise. "Now my plan is" to bring public sentiment in Maine around by "enlisting certain leading men of both political parties . . . and through them, at a proper time hereafter, guiding aright the public press." Once the press and the political leaders had been brought around "the same work could be accomplished in much less time among the citizens of the interested provinces." In brief, he suggested a propaganda campaign of unprecedented proportions to convince the people of Maine that what they had rejected in the past was in reality good for them and good for the country. "A few thousand dollars expended upon such an agency," he claimed, "will accomplish more than hundreds of thousands expended through the formalities and delays of ordinary diplomatic negotiations & surveys." And just think what war would cost.

It was a breathtakingly novel idea. But how would Smith go about accomplishing this feat? First, he and his associates would fan out over Maine and enlist the services of "a few judicious co-operators" and through them, steadily but "silently," draw in the "men of influence of both political parties" without exciting the interests or prejudices of any group or class. He would make "certain assurances" to these individuals "in order to adjust the tone and direction of the party presses, and through them, of public sentiment." Articles and commentaries in strategically placed religious journals would appear throughout the state. Such a newspaper campaign, when properly conducted, could bring results that years of negotiations could never accomplish. After the electorate had been properly prepared, the legislature would be petitioned by *"our own people"* to settle the boundary dispute and include provisions for limited navigation of the St. John River and an indemnity for lost territory.

For himself, as compensation, Smith asked for thirty-five hundred dollars per annum plus incidental and traveling expenses and postage to be paid by the government. And if he succeeded in his campaign, he also expected an "allowance of a liberal commission as disbursing agent" on whatever sums the negotiation might ultimately involve. Success, he pointed out, "would warrant almost any expenditure."[15]

Webster loved Smith's idea. Himself a master of propaganda, he recognized immediately the possibilities the scheme might provide. And he knew that Smith was not some lunatic with a lamebrained idea. Here was a successful businessman and politician, a man who later made a fortune as a shareholder in Samuel

15. *House Reports*, 29th Congress, 1st Session, Serial 490, no. 684; Smith to DW, [June 1841?], July 2, November 20, 1841, in Webster, *PD*, I, 94–96, 97, 161–162. Smith had originally suggested his idea to President Van Buren, but it had not been acted upon.

Morse's magnetic telegraph and as a contractor for the telegraph line constructed between Washington to Baltimore in 1843 and 1844. More important, Smith knew his way around Maine politics and could "divest a subject of
party interest, and *party* excitement" to make it a matter for "every body's business."[16]

Webster took the proposal to Tyler, who approved it. At first the President
had his doubts because it meant meddling in Maine's internal affairs, which
violated his states' rights beliefs, but Webster easily convinced him that the
possibility of war posed a threat to the safety of all the people, and surely
that transcended any local or state consideration. However, the problem of
compensation gave the two men pause. In view of Tyler's difficulties with Congress, as well as the need for moving "silently" in convincing "men of influence,"
it did not seem wise or feasible to take the Smith project to the legislature.
Instead Tyler and Webster agreed to draw upon the President's secret service
fund, a fund authorized by Congress in 1810 for "contingent expenses" involved
in negotiations with foreign nations.[17]

Thus, as it subsequently developed, Webster employed Smith as a secret
agent of the State Department and drew up a proposed boundary settlement
and had Smith publish it in the Portland *Christian Mirror,* a politically neutral
but widely read religious newspaper in New England. Three editorials, dated
November 18, December 2, and February 3, signed "Agricola," and entitled
"NORTHEASTERN BOUNDARY—WHY NOT SETTLE IT?" appeared in the *Mirror*
and argued that without compromise, war was inevitable. The articles urged the
people of Maine to do the following: petition the state legislature to assert
Maine's title to the territory as projected by Webster in his proposed settlement,
demand free navigation of the St. John for fifty years, compensate the state for
its past defense of the territory, obtain British indemnity to Massachusetts and
Maine for giving up their claim to some of the territory, and grant Britain
ownership of land needed for a military road.[18]

The editorials were immediately picked up and reprinted in other journals
throughout the country. The Portland *Eastern Argus,* the Chicago *American,*
and Richmond *Enquirer* were a few such newspapers, and the *Eastern Argus,*
the most influential of Maine's sheets, slowly moved to full support of a compromise boundary.[19] For his part, Webster deftly dovetailed Smith's propaganda
with that of his own. He dispatched Peleg Sprague, a former senator, and Albert
Smith, a retiring congressman, both from Maine, to evaluate the political climate

16. Jones, *To the Webster-Ashburton Treaty,* p. 91; Smith to DW, November 20, 1841, in *PD,* I, 162.

17. Frederick Merk, *Fruits of Propaganda in the Tyler Administration* (Cambridge, Mass., 1971)
pp. 8–9, 63; Peterson, *Presidencies of Harrison & Tyler,* pp. 119–120. A special committee of the
House of Representatives in 1846 investigated Webster's use of the secret fund. See *Congressional
Globe,* 29th Congress, 1st Session, p. 636ff, reprinted in Merk, *Fruits of Propaganda,* pp. 180–220.

18. The articles are reprinted in *House Reports,* 29th Congress, 1st Session, Serial 490, no. 684, pp.
26–35; Merk, *Fruits of Propaganda,* pp. 158–172; Jones, *To the Webster-Ashburton Treaty,* pp. 91–
92. See also *Congressional Globe,* 29th Congress, 1st Session, p. 636ff.

19. Smith to DW, April 16, 1842, in *PC,* V, 200; Jones, *To the Webster-Ashburton Treaty,* p. 93.

in their state about the possibility of compromise. Their findings suggested that a settlement was indeed possible, although they learned that politicians in both parties feared saying so publicly. In addition, Webster periodically wrote unsigned editorials for the Washington *National Intelligencer*, which were reprinted in other important journals. With consummate skill, these editorials argued the need for compromise.[20]

But now another and potentially more dangerous problem arose that threatened the peace process. The America brig *Creole* sailed for New Orleans from Hampton Roads, Virginia, in late October 1841 with a cargo of merchandise, principally tobacco, and 135 slaves and 6 white passengers. On November 7, off Great Abaco Island in the Bahamas, 19 slaves revolted, killing a passenger named Howell, the owner of 39 slaves on board, and wounding the ship's captain, the first mate, and 2 of the crew. In the melee, 2 blacks were seriously injured, 1 of whom later died. The slaves ordered the crew to sail the brig to Nassau, a British possession, where the attorney general declared those slaves who had not participated in the mutiny free under the British Emancipation Act of 1833. The mutineers were imprisoned while officials awaited further instructions from London.

The "outrage" echoing throughout the South when the *Creole* finally arrived in New Orleans on December 2, 1841, added to the still-smoldering outrages over the boundary and *Caroline* incidents and threatened to provoke Northern and Southern congressmen into a declaration of war against Great Britain. Resolutions demanding restitution for the loss of the slaves passed the Louisiana, Virginia, and Mississippi legislatures in January, February, and March respectively, while the press throughout the country shrilled condemnation of Great Britain. In the Senate, Clay, Calhoun, Benton, and other Whig and Democratic leaders put aside their differences to excoriate the British for this latest example of their disdain for this country's sovereignty and national honor.[21] As unlikely as it sounds today, Americans living at the time actually believed that the United States and Great Britain verged on a third war. The fiery James Henry Hammond of South Carolina believed the country was "ready for it. . . . With such a stupid imbecile as Tyler at the head of Affairs and such an unprincipled and cowardly Sect of State as Webster" the situation could hardly be worse. Tyler and Webster, who "is in the pay of the great English Bankers, the Barings," seem "bent on peace."[22]

On January 29, 1842, through the American minister to London, Edward Everett, Webster protested the British action, insisting that the vessel was en

20. Richard N. Current, "Webster's Propaganda and the Ashburton Treaty," *Mississippi Valley Historical Review*, XXXIV (September 1947), pp. 187–191; Jones, *To the Webster-Ashburton Treaty*, p. 93.

21. Benton, *Thirty Years' View*, II, 409–413; Richard K. Crallé, ed., *The Works of John C. Calhoun* (New York, 1853–1855), III, 560–583; Jones, *To the Webster-Ashburton Treaty*, pp. 77–78. For the resolutions passed by the Mississippi legislature, see *PD*, I, 519–521.

22. Carol Bleser, ed., *Secret and Sacred: The Diaries of James Henry Hammond, a Southern Slaveholder* (New York, 1988), pp. 88–89.

route from one American port to another in a lawful manner with slaves aboard recognized by the Constitution as property in those states where slavery existed. The vessel was "forcibly and violently" taken to Nassau against the master's will, Webster declared, and control of the ship should have been immediately returned to the master and crew. Although the two countries had no agreement on extradition, he demanded the surrender of the mutineers and murderers and their return to this country to stand trial for their crimes.[23] There was no violation of British law, nor any infringement of the principles of the law of nations. It was *not* a matter of British law that was involved here, Webster added, but "the comity, and the usages of Nations." Make it clear to the British, he instructed Everett, that without the exercise to the fullest extent "of the doctrine of non-interference, and mutual abstinence from any thing affecting each other's domestic regulations, the peace of the two countries . . . will always be in danger."

This excellent diplomatic paper brought Webster much praise when printed on February 23 by order of the Senate. As a matter of fact, at Clay's suggestion, one thousand extra copies were made available. It pleased the secretary to know that "the 'Creole' paper is well recd—& there are those who knash their teeth, at that *fact*."[24]

But there were critics as well. Abolitionists objected to Webster's language about how the Constitution recognized slavery as property in states where the institution existed and began to have serious doubts about his friendship for their cause.[25]

Just as this latest misfortune took shape, the British informed Washington in late December that they wished to appoint a special mission to the United States to attempt a settlement of the problems between the two countries and that the mission would be headed by Alexander Baring, Lord Ashburton, the retired head of the banking firm of Baring Brothers. Now sixty-seven years of age, Ashburton had visited the United States in 1795, had business connections in America, owned more than a million acres of land in Maine, none of which was currently in dispute, had married the daughter of William Bingham, a Philadelphia banker and former senator, and was a prominent supporter of Anglo-American reconciliation.[26] The Peel government had more pressing

23. Webster said that "we have not considered as fugitives from justice slaves who were concerned in the mutiny, or those who were not, and therefore have made no demand for the delivery up of either. . . . I did not choose to demand it" because "I did not wish . . . to weaken our claim for compensation for the rest of the slaves." He asked Story for a legal opinion; the justice, who the year before had delivered the Supreme Court's majority opinion in the famous *Amistad* case, which freed mutinous slaves, disagreed with Webster's statement that under international law Britain must return the slaves. It was a matter of "comity and discretion" with the sovereign states, he said. DW to Story, March 17, Story to DW, March 26, 1842, in *PD*, I, 524–527.

24. DW to Everett, January 29, 1842 in *PD*, I, 177–185; DW to Edward Curtis, February 24, 1842, in *PC*, V, 191; *Congressional Globe*, 27th Congress, 2d Session, p. 256.

25. Peterson, *Great Triumvirate*, p. 322.

26. Merk, *Fruits of Propaganda*, p. 59. Lady Ashburton, the former Maria Matilda Bingham, was the senator's only daughter and came into a large inheritance that allowed Alexander Baring to obtain a partnership in the House of Baring Brothers on his return to England. She had divorced

Caroline LeRoy Webster, the second wife of Daniel Webster, was not a beautiful woman from all reports. At the time of her marriage she was thirty-two, fifteen years younger than her husband. Portrait attributed to John Wesley Jarvis. (From the collection of the Lamont Gallery, Phillips Exeter Academy, Exeter, New Hampshire)

This portrait of Webster by Francis Alexander was completed in December 1835 for Dartmouth College. It captures much of the character of its subject, resembling a "thunder storm in July," said Jeremiah Mason. (Courtesy of Hood Museum of Art, Dartmouth College, gift of Dr. George C. Shattuck)

An engraving of Webster's estate at Marshfield. (Courtesy of the New York Public Library)

Photograph of Colonel Daniel Fletcher Webster of the Twelfth Massachusetts Infantry in his Civil War uniform. The only child of five to survive his father, he was killed at the age of forty-nine on August 30, 1862, at the Second Battle of Bull Run. (Courtesy of the Marshfield Historical Commission)

Webster's direct descendants living today come through his daughter Julia Webster Appleton, wife of Samuel Appleton. Of her five children, four were living at the time of Webster's death. Portrait by Chester Harding. (From the collection of the New Britain Museum of American Art, Connecticut, John Butler Talcott Fund)

Major Edward Webster of the Massachusetts Volunteers in his Mexican War uniform. He died at the age of twenty-seven in San Angel, eight miles from Mexico City on the evening of January 23, 1848, of typhoid fever. Painted by George P. A. Healy. (Courtesy of the Hood Museum of Art, Dartmouth College, gift of Mrs. Ashley K. Hardy)

The Hone Club of New York, organized in 1838 by Philip Hone and ten other wealthy men, commissioned George P. A. Healy to paint this splendid portrait of their "divinity." It was presented to the club on April 25, 1846, and cost $500 with the frame. (Courtesy of the National Portrait Gallery, Washington, D.C.)

Above: This detail of "Webster's Reply to Hayne" is part of an enormous composition by George P. A. Healy, measuring 16 by 30 feet and crowded with more than a hundred notable Americans, many of whom were painted from life. (Courtesy of the Library of Congress)

Below: At the age of seventy-four the quintessential New York politician Martin Van Buren sat for this daguerreotype by Mathew Brady. (Courtesy of the National Portrait Gallery, Washington, D.C.)

Unlike Webster, who refused to consider the second slot on the Whig ticket in the election of 1840, John Tyler accepted it and succeeded to the presidency one month after Harrison's inauguration. Portrait by George P. A. Healy. (Courtesy of the National Portrait Gallery, Washington, D.C.)

This oil painting by Albert Gallatin Hoit of William Henry Harrison, the first Whig president, was completed shortly before Harrison's death from pneumonia in 1841. (Courtesy of the National Portrait Gallery, Washington, D.C.)

Alexander Baring, Lord Ashburton, the retired head of the banking firm of Baring Brothers, agreed to come out of retirement and serve as a "special messenger of peace" to resolve the conflicts between Great Britain and the United States. An engraved likeness after a painting by George P. A. Healy. (Courtesy of the Library of Congress)

Henry Temple, third Viscount Palmerston, foreign secretary in the ministry of William Lamb, second Viscount Lord Melbourne, exacerbated the Anglo-American crisis that almost led to a third war between the two nations. He later condemned the Webster-Ashburton Treaty as a *"capitulation."* Portrait by Francis Cruikshank. (Courtesy of the National Portrait Gallery, London, England)

George Hamilton Gordon, fourth Earl of Aberdeen was foreign secretary in the Robert Peel ministry and helped initiate the peace mission of Lord Ashburton in an effort to bring about an amicable settlement of the American crisis. Portrait by John Partridge. (Courtesy of the National Portrait Gallery, London, England)

Daguerreotype by Albert S. Southworth of Daniel Webster looking stern, solemn, and states-manlike. The picture was taken around the time that Webster was charged with official misconduct for "corruption and embezzlement" in his handling of funds as secretary of state. (Courtesy of the National Portrait Gallery, Washington, D.C.)

President James K. Polk's victory over Henry Clay in the election of 1844 stunned Webster. "It mortifies my pride of Country to see how the great office of President may be disposed of," he said. Nathaniel Currier's lithograph after a daguerreotype by John Plumbe, Jr. (Courtesy of the National Portrait Gallery, Washington, D.C.)

Edward Everett gave up a life of scholarship and learning, according to Ralph Waldo Emerson, because Webster had "seduced" him from his natural calling to pursue a political career. Mezzotint on steel by John Sartain. (Courtesy of the National Portrait Gallery, Washington, D.C.)

General Zachary Taylor "means well, but he knows little of public affairs, and less of public men," said Webster. Oil painting on canvas attributed to James R. Lambdin about the time of Taylor's election as president. (Courtesy of the National Portrait Gallery, Washington, D.C.)

The Compromise of 1850 debates in the Senate. Clay is addressing Vice President Millard Fillmore on the dais and Webster is seated with his head resting on his left hand. (Courtesy of the National Portrait Gallery, Washington, D.C.)

Abbott Lawrence, one of Webster's chief financial benefactors until their split in 1840, expected to run as vice president on the Whig ticket with Zachary Taylor. He and his friends wrongly blamed Webster for preventing it. (Courtesy of the Massachusetts Historical Society)

President Millard Fillmore was obliged to intervene in foreign affairs when Webster could no longer function effectively as secretary of state because of failing health. (Courtesy of the National Portrait Gallery, Washington, D.C.)

Daniel in the Lion's Den.

Daguerreotype of Black Dan around the last two years of his life.

Webster's blundering diplomacy and his heavy drinking are here satirized in this widely published political cartoon. (Courtesy of the New York Public Library)

A close-up photograph of Webster's house at Marshfield in which the curious shape of the two pairs of dormers on the second level are plainly visible. Each pair was constructed to form an obtuse angle with its mate. (Courtesy of the Marshfield Historical Commission)

This idealized rendering of Webster's final hours at Marshfield shows his son Fletcher, standing immediately to Webster's right, with Peter Harvey standing behind Fletcher. Fletcher's wife sits to the right of the picture with her three children close by her side, and Drs. John Jeffries and J. Mason Warren stand behind Webster's bed. (Courtesy of the Marshfield Historical Commission)

The Webster plot at the Winslow Cemetery at Marshfield where Webster, his first wife, and five children are buried. (Courtesy of the Marshfield Historical Commission)

problems in Europe and Asia to be constantly bothered by the possibility of war with the United States and thought that the unfortunate events of the past few years could be amicably resolved. At least it was worth a try. Lord Aberdeen mentioned to Everett that Ashburton's well "known friendly relations" with Webster "were among the chief inducements to select" him.[27]

Ashburton "suffered himself to be persuaded" to come out of retirement[28] and serve as "a special messenger of peace" because he knew that in Webster he would find a kindred spirit who, like himself, believed that the interests of both countries dictated the immediate reestablishment of friendly relations, and he felt confident that they could hammer out a successful and equitable settlement. There could not have been a better choice for the mission.

For his part, Webster was delighted with this sudden turn of events. Sending out "so distinguished a man, nay, the sending of a special Minister at all," provided "strong proof" of Britain's desire to sign a treaty restoring friendship between the two countries. He knew Lord and Lady Ashburton quite well and liked them enormously.[29]

Ashburton wrote to Webster to announce his coming. He even agreed to cross the Atlantic "at this stormy season of the year" to begin the "good work" as soon as possible.[30] He had the confidence and "full powers" of his government in this important service and anticipated success, "meeting as I am sure I shall with a corresponding disposition with the existing enlightened Government of America."

Ashburton arrived in Annapolis aboard the British frigate *Warspite* on April 2, 1842, after his ship had been blown off course from New York. Three secretaries, five servants, a carriage, three horses, and numerous trunks accom-

---

her first husband, Count de Tilly, who had married her for her money. Poore, *Perley's Reminiscences,* p. 283.

27. Everett to DW, January 3, 1842, in *PD,* I, 488.

28. Ashburton had served as minister of trade in Peel's first ministry for several months in 1834–1835.

29. Everett to DW, December 31, 1841, DW to Everett, January 29, 1842, Everett to DW, January 3, 1842 in *PD,* I, 173–176, 177–185, 488–489.

30. Ashburton was so anxious to leave that his instructions, dated February 8, 1842, were "prepared under great pressure" and were not ready in their final form when he left England. After Peel had approved the instructions, they were forwarded to Ashburton with an indication that they might be modified later after the duke of Wellington had studied them from a military point of view. Memorandum, February 14, 1842, Aberdeen Papers, BM 43,123. Wellington wanted enough land to build a military road to New Brunswick and around Prince Edward Island. Memorandum, February 8, 1842, ibid. Aberdeen also consulted Sir James Kempt, Sir Howard Douglas, Lord Seaton, and Sir George Murray, asking their opinions with respect to security and defense in case of war. Kempt and the others agreed that "the whole country between the Right Bank of the St. Lawrence, and the *South West Branch of the St. Johns River*" must be retained. Aberdeen to Kempt, et al., February 24, 1842, Kempt et al. to Aberdeen, March 1, 1842, ibid. These suggestions were sent by Aberdeen to Ashburton on April 1, 1842, FO881/259, PRO. On March 3 Aberdeen told Ashburton to discuss the boundary question "in general terms" only "without coming to any decision or making any specific proposition" until he received the final instructions. Aberdeen Papers, BM 43,123. Aberdeen sent his final instructions to Ashburton on March 31, 1842. FO881/259, PRO.

panied him. Unfortunately Lady Ashburton remained at home because of health and "domestic duties." He brought with him "full powers to make a final settlement of everything." Webster could hardly wait to greet the envoy and extend to him every hospitality possible to make him comfortable and feel welcome. He boasted to Philip Hone that now "he had the fullest confidence in being able to settle *all* the differences with England before the first of September."[31]

"All" the differences? That would be quite an accomplishment if true. For "all" the differences included: the northeastern boundary problem and the area between Lake Superior and the Lake of the Woods in the Old Northwest, the *Caroline* and *Creole* incidents, and the Oregon country, which Britain and the United States had jointly occupied since 1824 when the Russian boundary of Alaska was established at 54°40′. In addition, the right of search and seizure of ships on the high seas was certain to be discussed. This question still outraged Americans because of British impressment of seamen before and during the War of 1812, and now Lord Aberdeen invited the United States to join the alliance of Austria, France, Prussia, Russia, and Britain (the Quintuple Treaty of December 20, 1841) in an agreement to grant one another the mutual right of search to suppress the slave trade and declare the slave trade piracy. The United States had banned the slave trade in 1808 but could not adequately enforce it. With the Emancipation Act of 1833 abolishing slavery, Great Britain used its superior naval force to board and search "slavers" operating off the coast of Africa. Everett rather naively asked Webster whether there could be any objection to joining this alliance. Surely there could be "nothing derogatory to our honor, in making common cause with them in this way."[32]

Unfortunately, passionate Anglophobes, such as Lewis Cass, the holdover minister to France, and Henry Wheaton, another holdover minister to Denmark, deluged Americans with pamphlets[33] and letters protesting against participation in the alliance. No doubt, as Webster surmised, Cass had his eye on a presidential nomination[34] and intended to use the issue to convince slaveowners in the United States that Britain really wanted to bring about universal emancipation.[35] Webster regretted that Cass and Wheaton had meddled in this matter.

31. Ashburton to DW, January 2, 1842, Everett to DW, December 31, 1841, January 3, 1842, DW to Everett, January 29, 1842, in *PD*, I, 173, 486–488, 488, 496. In his instructions to Ashburton, Aberdeen insisted on a land passage from Montreal to the Atlantic Ocean and would accept no less than the award limits of the king of the Netherlands in 1831. Aberdeen to Ashburton, February 8, March 31, 1842, FO881/259, PRO. Hone, *Diary*, II, 594–595; Jones, *To the Webster-Ashburton Treaty*, p. 113.

32. Everett to DW, January 3, DW to Everett, April 26, 1842, in *PD*, I, 488–489.

33. Lewis Cass, *The Right of Search* . . . (Paris, 1842); Henry Wheaton, *Enquiry into the Validity of the British Claim to a Right of Visitation and Search* . . . (London, 1842).

34. Adams, *Memoirs*, XI, 243; Frank B. Woodford, *Lewis Cass: The Last Jeffersonian* (New Brunswick, N.J., 1950), p. 215ff.

35. Later, after the treaty had been completed and published but not ratified, Cass objected vehemently to Article VIII, the joint cruising article, because, he said, it implied American consent to the British practice of search. The controversy continued from August 1842 to March 1843 with

As Story pointed out, "they have a tendency to embarrass our negotiations; and I am surprized that they should write without orders, and thus inflame, if not misdirect the public mind." Cass would have been recalled immediately "but for the fear of making a martyr of him" among Democrats. Offended that his recommendations and suggestions had been disregarded and his authority undermined, he wrote to Webster on September 17, 1842, and requested permission to resign as minister to France and return to the United States. He returned in late 1842.

The propaganda of Cass and Wheaton did not neglect to mention the humiliations suffered when American seamen had been impressed during the late war allegedly on the grounds that they had not lost their British citizenship. Not even naturalization in another country could erase their former status, according to the British. It was deemed indelible and perpetual. Subjects owed the crown lifetime allegiance, a policy the Peel government could not and would not renounce. Cass was so persistent in his efforts that he helped convince the French Chamber of Deputies to reject the Quintuple Treaty. But the other nations ratified.[36]

So, with the arrival of Ashburton in early April, Webster gave himself approximately six months to settle problems that were as old as the Republic itself. Without question, he set an impossible deadline.

But he counted on several factors to bring it off. First, of course, was the obvious desire of the Peel government to conclude a treaty and its choice of Ashburton as special minister to negotiate with Webster. No two men were better suited to conduct the negotiations. Second, Webster had the complete confidence and cooperation of President Tyler. Over the past six months, since the cabinet resignations, they had grown closer. They both were, in different ways, ostracized by the Whig party. They needed and depended on each other, and with greater frequency, Tyler relied on Webster for advice and assistance on a whole range of issues, treating him as the head of the cabinet. They saw each other every day, dined together often, and kept each other informed of their thoughts and expectations. As Webster reported to Everett, he and Tyler "got along very well so far as the affairs of my own Department, except that he has felt himself obliged to make some appointments, which were very bad." Finally,

---

Cass faulting the treaty as a departure from the traditional policy of avoiding entangling alliances and because it failed to obtain an explicit disavowal by the British of the right to search American ships. Webster responded to the charges in a letter of November 14, 1842, in which he characterized Cass's analysis as a "tissue of mistakes." Cass published the correspondence together with a lengthy defense dated March 7, 1843, in the *Globe* and the *National Intelligencer.* See Cass to DW, September 17, October 3, 11, 1842, March 7, 1843, DW to Cass, August 29, November 14, December 20, 1842, in *PD,* I, 714–721, 724–775; *National Intelligencer,* March 18, 21, 23, 28, 1843.

36. DW to Everett, April 26, Story to DW, April 19, 1842, Cass to DW, March 5, 15, 1841, February 15, September 17, 1842, in *PD,* I, 543–544, 538, 37–38, 44–45, 502–513, 716; Ashburton to Aberdeen, April 26, 1842, Aberdeen Papers, BM 43,123; Cass to DW, January 24, February 13, 1842, Wheaton to DW, January 29, February 15, March 12, in *Microfilm Edition,* F16/21375, 21552, 21441, 21590, 21849; Peterson, *Presidencies of Harrison & Tyler,* pp. 127–128.

Webster conceived what he called "a grand stroke," proposing something never attempted before, something incredibly novel. Faced with the problem of Maine's intransigence toward any compromise and the need to satisfy Massachusetts's claims and faced with the constitutional problem that no state could negotiate a treaty with a foreign power to fix a boundary, he decided to invite both states to send commissioners to Washington to meet with him and Ashburton to work out a boundary settlement. The President, avidly states' rights in his thinking, gladly gave his consent. Webster hoped that his ploy would eliminate the two constitutional and political problems. Actually it almost wrecked the negotiations.[37]

Webster also turned to a number of contemporary authorities, particularly Joseph Story, for help and guidance on such matters as legal, diplomatic, geographic, and strategic issues in devising his compromises and arguments. And because the final results of the negotiations were so creditable to the nation, the secretary did not hesitate to acknowledge the enormous assistance he had received from them.[38]

Within weeks of Ashburton's departure for America, Webster began his negotiations to have the state commissioners made available in Washington. He contacted Reuel Williams, a senator from Maine and regular critic of the Tyler administration, and made his proposal, asking him to confer with Governor John Fairfield of Maine and other responsible officials about its feasibility. Of course, he said, any treaty signed by the United States and Britain would be submitted for ratification to the Senate, but no agreement on a boundary line would be adopted without Maine's consent.[39]

With the arrival of Lord Ashburton in this country and with his consent to the idea of state representation in the proceedings, Webster directly contacted Governor Fairfield and Governor John Davis of Massachusetts and asked them to appoint commissioners empowered to treat with "the authorities of this Government." Furthermore, he promised that no line would be drawn without the *unanimous* consent of these commissioners. As agreed by the Maine legislature, four commissioners were subsequently appointed: Edward Kavanagh, Edward Kent, William Pitt Preble,[40] and John Otis, the first two Democrats, the others

---

37. DW to Everett, August 25, 1842, DW to Sparks, March 11, 1843, in *PD*, I, 696, 786.

38. Story to DW, March 26, 1842, in Van Tyne, ed., *Letters of Webster*, pp. 263–266; DW to Bell and Paine, April 30, DW to George Coffin, May 28, James Renwick to DW, June 11, DW to John Spencer, August 10, James Abert to Spencer, August 15, 1842, in *PD*, I, 547–548, 567–568, 574, 681, 683–689.

39. DW to Reuel Williams, February 2, Williams to DW, February 12, DW to Williams, February 18, 1842, in Van Tyne, ed., *Letters of Webster*, pp. 256–261; DW to Williams, February 9, 1842, in *Microfilm Edition*, F16/21521.

40. Preble proved to be particularly difficult during the entire negotiating process. He stubbornly argued for all the claims put forward by Maine. All these individuals, save Preble, "are, I believe, reasonable men," wrote Ashburton to Aberdeen. Preble "was the American agent at The Hague . . . who caused by his protest the arbitration to be rejected." Ashburton to Aberdeen, May 29, 1842, FO881/259, PRO.

Whigs. The Massachusetts commissioners included Charles Allen, Abbott Lawrence, and John Mills, all Whigs.[41]

At the same time that Webster wrote the governors he alerted his propaganda agent, Francis Smith, of his action. "It is a moment, likely to produce important results," he declared, "& I must therefore pray your attention to the subject. . . . I verily believe the time has come for a vigorous effort for ending [the boundary] controversy." Smith intensified his efforts as Webster directed, and between them they slowly nudged the sympathies of the leaders and people of Maine and Massachusetts toward a better regard for the secretary's policy of compromise.[42]

It can be imagined with what anticipation and pleasure Webster greeted his friend Ashburton in Washington. He had taken great pains to be sure that wherever his lordship landed—New York, Annapolis, or Norfolk—the collectors at these ports would see to it that the "immediate landing of his baggage and effects, and those of his suite," would be handled "without the charge of duties of course, and also without search or examination." He also arranged to rent for Ashburton a mansion owned by Matthew St. Clair on Lafayette Square near his own home at a cost of twelve thousand dollars for ten months and an additional thousand as insurance against damages.

On April 6, two days after reaching Washington, Ashburton met with President Tyler, presented his credentials, and then accompanied Webster on a tour of the Capitol and the Library of Congress.[43] He was affable to all; even the suspicious Senator Thomas Hart Benton conceded that. He went out of his way to charm Webster, and they enjoyed a very pleasant initial visit.[44] Ashburton referred to the secretary in his dispatches to Aberdeen as Tyler's "real efficient prime minister."[45] The goodwill that Ashburton exuded seemed so pervasive that the prospects for peace glowed brighter. Webster gushed his affection for all things British, and that could not help but please the six-foot-tall envoy. Their mutual interests and tastes made their many encounters both pleasant and productive.[46]

The two men not only thought alike but to some extent even looked alike. Both had large heads, high foreheads, and piercing dark eyes with heavy brows.

41. DW to Fairfield and Davis, April 11, 1842, in *PD*, I, 534–537; Jones, *To the Webster-Ashburton Treaty*, p. 114.

42. DW to Smith, April 10, 1842, in *PD*, I, 533–534; Merk, *Fruits of Propaganda*, pp. 63–65.

43. Ashburton to Aberdeen, April 8, 1842, in FO881/259, PRO.

44. "From all quarters," Aberdeen wrote Ashburton, "we hear of your personal popularity; and I feel certain that this must lead greatly to increase the probability of a favourable result." Aberdeen to Ashburton, June 18, 1842, Aberdeen Papers, BM 43,123.

45. Ashburton to Aberdeen, April 25, 1842, dispatch no. 5, FO881/259, PRO. However, he wrote, "it must not be forgotten that in this country though you treat nominally with the Secretary of State you treat substantially with the people who intrude bodily into every thing." Ashburton to Aberdeen, June 14, 1842, Aberdeen Papers, BM 43,123.

46. It is an interesting fact that Fletcher Webster named his second son Ashburton.

Ashburton's complexion, however, was "clear red and white," Webster's a dark, dusky hue.[47]

Webster dined his guest frequently and lavishly. He served American favorites in the American (he did not like "French" dishes) style: Maine salmon, Massachusetts mackerel, New Jersey oysters, Florida shad, Kentucky beef, Illinois prairie chickens, Virginia mutton and terrapin, Maryland crabs, Delaware canvasback ducks, and South Carolina ricebirds, all cooked by his black servant Monica and served in a style that made Ashburton admit "their superiority to the potages, sauces, entremets, ragouts, and desserts of his Parisian white-capped manipulator of casse-roles." Ashburton reciprocated, of course, offering his guests "the cream of culinary perfection and the gastronomic art, with the rarest wines." There never had been, Webster informed his British friend John Denison, "a pair of more friendly negotiators" to "put their heads together."[48]

The two men commenced their work immediately and concentrated their talks on the boundary question as the most difficult and the most pressing. It did not take Ashburton long to read the political climate in America, and his sometimes acute observations on what was happening in the country helped in the negotiations.[49] "I would further discharge my duty," he warned Aberdeen almost two months after his arrival, "by cautioning you not to mistake or undervalue the *power* of this country. You will be told that it is a mass of ungovernable & unmanageable anarchy, and so it is in many respects." For example, bankrupt finances, "bad administration & jobbing in every department—a loose ill connected mass of conflicting interests." But do not be mistaken. "With all these disadvantages I believe that the energies & power of the country would be found to be immense in the case of war and that the jarring elements would unite for that purpose."[50]

One thing Webster did not mention to Ashburton as the talks got under way was the information that a map had been discovered that seemed to prove the British claim about the boundary line. Jared Sparks, a professor of history at Harvard, a biographer of Washington, a diligent investigator, and a highly respected scholar, wrote to Webster and informed him that while researching the archives of Paris for his multivolume edition of the diplomatic correspondence of the American Revolution, he discovered a 1783 letter from Benjamin Frank-

47. Poore, *Perley's Reminiscences*, I, 288.

48. Curtis, *Webster*, II, 219; Poore, *Perley's Reminiscences*, I, 283–285; DW to Denison, April 26, 1842, in *PC*, V, 201.

49. Ashburton to Aberdeen, April 25, 1842, dispatch no. 5, FO881/259, PRO. Dispatch no. 6 of the same date dealt exclusively with the Maine boundary. "My difficulties are not with the President or his Chief Minister. The disposition of both are favorable, but in the singular state of parties here, which makes them powerless, I am not always sure of being much advanced when I have agreed with them." Ashburton to Aberdeen, April 26, 1842, Aberdeen Papers, BM 43,123. A month later he mentioned Stevenson as one of those characters who "is in league with old Cass in France who is as busy as he can be in endeavouring to keep up hostile feelings on every point between the two countries." Ashburton to Aberdeen, May 29, 1842, Aberdeen Papers, BM 43,123.

50. Ashburton to Aberdeen, May 29, 1842, Aberdeen Papers, BM 43,123.

lin, one of the commissioners in the peace negotiations, to the French foreign minister. The letter mentioned a map that had "a strong red line" drawn on it, showing the "limits of the United States as settled in the preliminaries between the British & American plenipotentiaries." Sparks immediately began searching for the map in the well-indexed catalog of sixty thousand maps in the archive's collection. What he found was a 1746 map by the French cartographer Jean-Baptiste d'Anville, on which "was drawn a *strong red-line* throughout the entire boundary of the United States, answering precisely to Franklin's description." Unfortunately the demarcation totally supported British claims.[51]

Webster was not surprised. He himself had made an identical discovery three years earlier of a Mitchell map belonging to General von Steuben that corresponded exactly to what Sparks had found. He had purchased it in 1838 from a Steuben heir and had sold it to C. S. Daveis, an agent in Maine working in Washington. So there were at least two maps with strong red lines justifying the British claim. Under the circumstances Webster decided to suppress this information. Instead he got Daveis to sell the map to the State Department for two hundred dollars. He also recruited him as an agent, along with Sparks, to assist in dealing with Maine. Both men joined Peleg Sprague and Francis Smith in convincing the state to accept a compromise boundary, and all four were paid out of the President's secret fund.[52] When Daveis and Sparks went to Augusta, the capital, they brought with them copies of their maps. So overwhelming was the evidence they presented that a number of Maine's politicians agreed to accept a compromise line, and Sparks immediately relayed this information to Webster.[53]

But there were more than two maps floating around with "strong red lines" marking the boundary, one of which Lord Palmerston discovered in 1839 in the British Museum and hid in the Foreign Office, telling no one. He hid it because it supported the American claim! It was the so-called King George III map.[54] Considering the number of maps in existence that supposedly had been used by the commissioners in 1783, no single map with red lines would be acceptable to both sides. Besides, as Franklin had said, the map represented only a "preliminary" settlement, not one that had been "adopted" by the peace-

51. Sparks to DW, February 15, 1842, in *PD*, I, 513–516.

52. Later there was a congressional investigation of Webster's handling of these funds. Granted Webster used the secret fund in questionable ways, still the argument advanced by Samuel Flagg Bemis in his biography of John Quincy Adams, *John Quincy Adams and the Foundations of American Foreign Policy* (New York, 1949), pp. 479–481, that Webster and Sparks received money from Ashburton to persuade Maine to give up its claim to the disputed territory has been fully refuted by Jones, *To the Webster-Ashburton Treaty*, pp. 127–132, and will not be repeated here. Bemis's comment that "Webster achieved a diplomatic triumph—against his own country" by the treaty is gratuitous and undeserving of reply in light of the overwhelming and contradictory evidence.

53. DW to Sparks, March 4, 1842, in *PD*, I, 523; Merk, *Fruits of Propaganda*, pp. 10, 65 and note 51, 66, 71, 179; Sparks to DW, May 19, 1842, in Curtis, *Webster*, II, 100–102.

54. Details of this "war of the maps" can be found in Jones, *To the Webster-Ashburton Treaty*, pp. 102–113.

makers in the Treaty of 1783. A final boundary line had been left for future negotiations.[55]

When the discussions began, Ashburton, who knew nothing of the King George and d'Anville maps, insisted straight off that the commissioners operate through Webster, not directly with him. As early as April 1 he had been warned by Aberdeen that Maine could be a problem and that he would need to work around it. "You must have some means, therefore, of carrying that State with you in the negotiation with the general government." Aberdeen thought that certain members of Congress, "in concert with Webster," could help in winning Maine's consent to whatever was decided.[56]

Webster kept the commissioners informed of all developments. Indeed he consulted quite regularly with them.[57] He had full authority in conducting these negotiations and hoped to move through all the unresolved issues as speedily as possible. Unfortunately Ashburton's instructions changed from time to time. Those he brought with him had been flexible. Originally Aberdeen regarded the entire disputed territory as lacking in real value and therefore ought to be split down the middle. He did think, however, that the Madawaska settlements along the St. John River ought to be British since they were already under Canadian civil jurisdiction. He also wanted the navigation of the St. John protected because of its importance to the timber trade. Curiously, these original instructions did not mention two of Britain's historic strategic objectives, the safeguarding of the only decent land route between Halifax and Quebec and the dislodging of American settlements from the highlands just south of Quebec.[58]

But this changed. Shortly thereafter, in keeping with the angry demands of the duke of Wellington, Ashburton was instructed to obtain a particular rectangular slice of land, one larger than the Americans could be expected to accept, that would provide security for the Halifax–Quebec military road. The envoy protested this sudden change of instruction. He said he felt himself "crippled."[59] At the same time Ashburton consulted with Lieutenant Governor William Colebrooke of New Brunswick without telling Peel or Aberdeen or Webster. Later a secret delegation, which had the full knowledge of the British ministry, came

---

55. Webster later took the position that none of the maps was conclusive. DW to William B. Lawrence, April 24, 1843, in *PD*, I, 794.

56. Aberdeen to Ashburton, April 1, 1842, Aberdeen Papers, BM 43,123.

57. Adams, *Memoirs*, XI, 127.

58. Cunningham, *Aberdeen*, p. 321.

59. Memorandum, February 14, 1842, Aberdeen to Ashburton, February 9, March 3, May 16, 1842, Aberdeen Papers, BM 43,123; Aberdeen to Ashburton, March 31, 1842, FO881/259, PRO. "If I leave this country," Ashburton wrote Aberdeen on April 25, 1842, "throwing all our relations with it into confusion, because I had insisted on a larger portion of this Disputed Territory than we had at one period of our negotiations been willing to accept, and which our adversary had always refused to give, the consequence could not fail to be that the whole Union would indignantly take part with Maine, and we should pass for a Power having trifled with and insulted the country." FO881/259, PRO. Aberdeen protested that Ashburton's powers had not been crippled. "On the contrary, they have been extended." Aberdeen to Ashburton, July 2, 1842, Aberdeen Papers, BM 43,123.

from New Brunswick to Washington to advise Ashburton.[60] All of which delayed the reaching of final decisions.

The talks quickly bogged down over the respective claims of the two nations. The commissioners bombarded Webster with objections, and the Brunswick delegation made demands on Ashburton. "So many difficulties arise," Webster reported to Everett, "not only between us and England, but between us and the commissioners, and the commissioners of the two States themselves." He worried that they were approaching an impasse. Aberdeen too was concerned. To head off a breakdown in the negotiations, he told Ashburton that if a rupture appeared certain, "you are authorized to accept the award of the King of the Netherlands *in all its parts*."[61]

In addition to the boundary dispute, the *Creole* incident almost deadlocked the talks.[62] To make matters worse, Webster had to contend with his and the President's deteriorating relationship with the controlling Whig party in Congress. The Whigs kept pressuring the secretary to resign and took added offense when he kept refusing; worse, they plotted to impeach Tyler. "I hardly know what to say to you of the state of our affairs here," Webster wrote in despair to Everett in late June, "except that it is bad enough, & at present not growing better." Naturally he saw the not-so-subtle presence of Henry Clay behind it all. "The truth is," Webster continued, "the friends of Mr Clay, some of them, seek to embarrass the President, in all things, to the extent of their power. This causes resentment in him; & between their factious spirits & his resentment . . . no one can tell what may happen to the public interest."[63]

On top of everything else, the heat and humidity of Washington had become oppressive. In April Ashburton had complained that the "thermometer is at 80 and my nerves begin to give me warning." By June his nerves were frazzled, and by July he could hardly bear it. "I must throw myself on your compassion," he pleaded with Webster, "to contrive some how or other to get me released. I contrive to crawl about in these heats by day & pass my nights in a sleepless fever. In short I shall positively not outlive this affair if it is to be much prolonged."[64]

Webster grew testy as well, and sometimes his "unreasonable, ungracious

---

60. The different instructions sent to Ashburton are discussed in E. D. Adams, "Lord Ashburton and the Treaty of Washington," *American Historical Association*, XVII (July 1912), pp. 764–782; Ashburton to Aberdeen, April 26, June 14, 1842, Aberdeen Papers, BM 43,123; Jones, *To the Webster-Ashburton Treaty*, pp. 121–122.

61. DW to Everett, June 28, 1842, in Webster, *PD*, I, 592; Ashburton to Aberdeen, June 29, 1842, FO881/259, PRO; Aberdeen to Ashburton, May, n.d., 1842, Aberdeen Papers, BM 43,123. Later Aberdeen said, "The Award of the King of the Netherlands was always our *ne plus ultra* with respect to territory." Aberdeen to Ashburton, July 2, 1842, Aberdeen Papers, BM 43,123.

62. "My real difficulty here," wrote Ashburton, "is with the Creole case. . . . The President, as a Virginian, has a strong opinion about Creole case, and is not a little disposed to be obstinate on the subject." Ashburton to Aberdeen, June 29, 1842, Aberdeen Papers, BM 43,123.

63. DW to Everett, June 28, 1842, in Webster, *PD*, I, 592.

64. Ashburton to Aberdeen, April 26, 1842, Aberdeen Papers, BM 43,123; Ashburton to DW, July 1, 1842, in *PD*, I, 604.

and difficult moods" nearly provoked a quarrel with his foreign visitor. It reached the point where Ashburton announced he could not stay in the United States much longer and would have to return home.[65]

Despair gripped Webster. President Tyler then stepped in and asked to see Ashburton.

"My lord," said Tyler during his interview with the envoy, "I cannot suppose that a man of your lordship's age and personal position, retired into the bosom of your family after a long and successful life, would have crossed the Atlantic on so arduous a mission, unless you had truly come with the most painful desire to close the unhappy controversies that now threaten the peace of the two countries. Your lordship could have felt none of the ordinary diplomatic temptations, and if you cannot settle them, what man in England can?"

Indeed. The point hit Ashburton with particular force.

"Well! well!" blurted Ashburton in response. "Mr. President, we must try again."[66]

Webster himself felt he had to relax and clear his mind before trying again. He decided to break away and return for a short visit to Marshfield,[67] where he could renew his strength before resuming negotiations. "Marshfield never looked so well," he reported when he reached home. To him his estate was "something like an ecstasy. . . . Superficial observers see nothing in Marshfield but rocks, and sands, and desolation . . . a grim and melancholy looking thing. . . . But these are malignant persons and not to be believed."[68]

He spent more than a week at Marshfield "fishing and trout-catching." He also stopped off in Boston to confer with Jared Sparks about strategy. They studied several old maps together, and after agreeing on how they were to be used, Webster returned to Washington.[69]

By this time Ashburton had informed Aberdeen that he had an inkling that Webster had "discovered some evidence, known at present to nobody, but favorable to our claims, and that he is using it with the Commissioners. I have some clue to this fact and hope to get at it." Meanwhile he felt it "neces-

65. Tyler, ed., *Letters of Tyler*, II, 216. But the British were very anxious to reach a settlement. "If the Americans are now disposed to adopt his [the king of the Netherlands'] award in all its parts, exactly as he pronounced it," Aberdeen wrote to Ashburton, "I think we must submit, rather than incur the imminent danger of war by the failure of your mission." Aberdeen to Ashburton, May 16, 1842, Aberdeen Papers, BM 43,123.

66. Tyler, ed., *Letters of Tyler*, II, 218.

67. The relentlessly critical John Quincy Adams said Webster had "gone to Marshfield to shoot snipes and fish for trout, and to patch up some shameful rents in his private finances." Adams, *Memoirs*, XI, 249.

68. DW to Fletcher Webster, May 21, 1842, DW to Mrs. Edward Curtis, May 26, 1842, in Curtis, *Webster*, II, 108, 109–111. Webster also conducted some private business in Boston during this sojourn.

69. DW to Sparks, May 14, 1842, in *PD*, I, 556–557. Ashburton noted Webster's departure in his dispatch to Aberdeen, adding that "with Massachusetts he [Webster] has great influence, but not so with the dominant party in Maine." May 12, 1842, FO881/259, PRO.

sary" to "assist the Secretary with his Commissioners."[70]

With the resumption of talks in Washington the Maine delegation presented Webster with a note in which it refused any line west of the northern line from the St. Croix River and south of the St. John River, and although it would accept Britain's request for land for a military road between Halifax and Quebec, it rejected Ashburton's demand for the Madawaska settlements without territorial compensation.[71] Webster explained Maine's demand about southern Madawaska to Ashburton and the need for locating the northwestern boundary line along the highlands above the St. John with permission to navigate the river. Ashburton had offered to allow U.S. retention of Rouse's Point, even though it lay north of the forty-fifth parallel—the northern boundary of New York and Vermont established by the peace treaty of 1783—but he said nothing about the highlands.[72] Webster reminded Ashburton that without Maine's consent—he had promised nothing less—no agreement was possible, leaving both nations again facing the threat of war.

Ashburton was particularly worried about the state of domestic politics in the United States, which he said "is becoming critical" and could affect the negotiations. "The President is very weak," he confided to Aberdeen, and he might surrender to the demands of men in both parties "to get rid of Webster," and that in many respects would be "threatening to my business." So on June 28 he went directly to Webster himself to learn the truth. The secretary readily admitted "the confused disordered state of things, thought the President could not do without him, and would certainly not move before my affairs were settled, in as far as they are capable of settlement, but he added that it would be prudent to lose no time."[73]

In Ashburton's mind Webster's position had been so seriously undermined by the political turmoil that the secretary was unequal to the task of bringing about a speedy conclusion to their negotiations. He found Webster "so weak & timid and irresolute that he is frightened by every body and at last does nothing." Webster even reversed himself and joined with the Maine commissioners on a point that had already been decided. "With remarkable talents," Ashburton told Aberdeen, "he does not face the slightest opposition and neither commands nor leads any body." Had he just a little "firmness of character I should settle with Maine, but I must use my materials as I find them and get on as well as I can." It will mean, he declared, that "I shall be forced nearer to the utmost bounds of my instructions than I like."[74]

70. Ashburton to Aberdeen, June 14, 1842, Aberdeen Papers, BM 43,123.

71. Maine delegates to DW, June 29, 1842, in *PD*, I, 592–603; Ashburton to Aberdeen, May 29, 1842, Aberdeen Papers, BM 43,123; Ashburton to Aberdeen, June 29, 1842, FO881/259, PRO.

72. Aberdeen to Ashburton, May 26, 1842, dispatch no. 9, FO881/259, PRO; Ashburton to Aberdeen, June 12, 1842, Aberdeen Papers, BM 43,123.

73. Webster momentarily calmed Ashburton's worst fears, and the envoy reported to Aberdeen in late June that "my expectation still is that the Secretary of State will remain where he is long enough for our purpose." Ashburton to Aberdeen, June 29, 1842, Aberdeen Papers, BM 43,123.

74. Ashburton to Aberdeen, July 13, 1842, ibid.

Aberdeen responded immediately. "You are uneasy about the stability of the govt, & the position of Webster," he wrote, but since "all parties seem now disposed to hasten the settlement of their differences with us, I trust that nothing can happen to shake what you may already have done."[75]

With Ashburton desperately anxious to conclude the negotiations successfully[76] but still doubtful about Webster's "command of others," he agreed to sit down with the secretary and resume their informal discussions on a one-to-one basis. And he was much more willing to yield on earlier demands. He offered important concessions, such as trading off the Madawaska settlements for American concessions in the Old Northwest. Undoubtedly the determination of the Maine commissioners to obtain Madawaska ultimately wore down his resistance. "I shall probably give up after a little fight my cherished Madawaska settlements," he admitted to Aberdeen. "I shall do so, as you might suppose, with regret, but . . . it [is] expedient to press forward." The giving up of the Madawaska settlements, confessed Ashburton, was "my important move." For his part Webster too wished to hurry the negotiations along before time ran out on him. "Let me repeat," he wrote to Everett, "that the great object is to show mutual concession."[77]

This intense spirit of conciliation, fueled by the apprehension of war, helped break the stalemate on the boundary question. Within four days they worked out a mutually acceptable compromise.

Webster conveyed the results of this compromise to the Maine delegation on July 15.[78] In his letter he explained that the line agreed upon would divide 12,027 square miles, or 7,697,280 acres, between the two countries. Of this total, the United States would receive 7,015 square miles, or 4,489,600 acres, and Britain 5,012 square miles, or 3,207,680 acres.[79] He pointed out that what the

75. Aberdeen to Ashburton, July 18, 1842, ibid.

76. Aberdeen too was anxious for success in the negotiations. "I wish only say that the importance of a successful result is so great, as almost to justify any sacrifice compatible with the safety of our N. American Provinces." Aberdeen to Ashburton, July 2, 1842, ibid.

77. Ashburton to Aberdeen, June 29, 1842, ibid.; Ashburton to Aberdeen, July 13, 1842, FO881/259, PRO. Aberdeen knew the Madawaska settlements would be difficult to obtain and said so in a dispatch to Ashburton. It was much too "valuable and in every respect more important for the United States to possess" than the "upper part of the St. John and the St. Lawrence." Aberdeen to Ashburton, May 16, 1842, Aberdeen Papers, BM 43,123. But he thought the proposed Maine boundary "ought to be satisfactory to the Public here. . . . The Madawaska settlement . . . will be regretted." Aberdeen to Ashburton, July 18, 1842, ibid.; DW to Everett, June 14, 1842, in PD, I, 581.

78 . There is a delightful but no doubt apocryphal story told by citizens of Maine to the effect that the boundary of the St. Croix River was decided upon when an inebriated Webster traveled down the river and veered too far south to where the river empties into the Bay of Fundy. As a result Campobello Island became part of New Brunswick, not Maine. Eric B. Kinsman to author, November 21, 1994. However, Webster's son Edward served as secretary of the joint commission for running and marking the boundary as designated by the Webster-Ashburton Treaty. Could this have been the Webster in question? DW to Edward Webster, March 21, 1843, in Webster, ed., Private Correspondence, II, 171.

79. DW to Maine commissioners, July 15, 1842, in PD, I, 620–624.

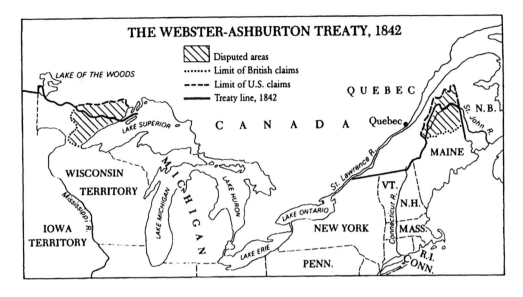

United States conceded was "supposed to be of no value for cultivation or settlement," while the land conceded by the British embraced "without doubt, all the valuable land south of the St. Francis and west of the St. John." Furthermore southern Madawaska and the free navigation of St. John River for Maine lumbermen had been acquired.[80] Although the award recommended by the king of the Netherlands in 1831 was territorially larger than what Britain now conceded, the land obtained by the United States by this agreement was far superior in value. What the United States received, although only seven twelfths of the disputed territory, was in value "at least four-fifths of the whole." In addition, the compromise awarded $125,000 to both Maine and Massachusetts from the federal government,[81] and Maine was to be reimbursed for past surveys of the land and maintaining the civil posse. Ashburton also conceded Rouses

80. With respect to the St. John they drew a line starting from the source of the St. Croix north to a point where it intersected the St. John. The line then followed to the mouth of the St. Francis River, the outlet of Lake Pohenagamook, and curved southwesterly to a point where it touches the northwest branch of the St. John. The line then continued down in a southwestern direction to the forty-fifth parallel.

81. "My expectation is that after all the bluster about not selling their country, the Maine people will very soon come to want money, but I shall put myself on the defensive and take care that the demand comes from them." Ashburton to Aberdeen, May 29, 1842, Aberdeen Papers, BM 43,123. A few weeks later Ashburton received a dispatch that anticipated this demand. "I am confirmed in the notion," wrote Aberdeen, "that it will be inexpedient for you to have recourse to any payment of money in your negotiation, and that our sacrifice had better be of another description." Aberdeen to Ashburton, May 20, 1842, ibid. In a follow-up letter he said that the House of Commons would be "little disposed" to grant any money. But if the Americans should offer it, "I do not know that it ought to be rejected." Aberdeen to Ashburton, June 18, 1842, ibid.

Point, which gave the United States the forty-fifth parallel it wanted and control of more than 200 miles of lake coast in New York and Vermont.[82]

The British government liked the compromise. Aberdeen told Peel that the line drawn was an improvement over that suggested by the king of the Netherlands. The 1831 recommendation, said Aberdeen, brought the line within twenty or thirty miles of Quebec and the St. Lawrence, and that "would scarcely be tolerated in this country." The present compromise does "not come nearer than fifty. This was the important territory in a military view, though utterly worthless in every other." What is more, as Ashburton had said in his dispatch of July 28, a general settlement was the most important thing, "and I am well pleased that we end by driving the Enemy off the crest of the highlands so much coveted at the War office." As for the "concessions made to us in the more remote parts of the line," Aberdeen declared, they "are of little consequence."[83]

Arguably, although it cannot be proved absolutely, the United States deserved the entire twelve thousand square miles, but arguably too, the British had an equally valid claim.[84] Neither side would concede the legitimacy of the other's claim. The only possible resolution to the problem was compromise.

The Massachusetts delegation also received the details of the compromise and responded almost immediately that it would accept the settlement if the navigation of the St. John River were open to both grain and lumber and if the compensation were increased to $150,000.[85] Webster and Ashburton agreed without hesitation.

The Maine commissioners proved more difficult, and Ashburton claimed that he was forced—"somewhat irregularly"—to step in since Webster "had no influence with them." For a day or two "I was in doubt whether I might not fail altogether, but at last Preble yielded and after signing he went off to his wilds in Maine as sulky as a Bear."[86]

Taking the position that they were surrendering "a portion of the birthright of the People of their State, and prized by them because it is their birthright," the commissioners nevertheless overcame their objections to the proposal because of "the spirit of attachment and patriotic devotion of the State to

82. DW to Maine commissioners, July 15, 1842, in *PD*, I, 620–624; Jones, *To the Webster-Ashburton Treaty*, pp. 136–137.

83. Aberdeen to Ashburton, May 16, Aberdeen to Peel, August 15, 1842, Aberdeen Papers, BM 43,062, Ashburton to Aberdeen, July 28, 1842, Aberdeen Papers, BM 43,123. Aberdeen received Ashburton's dispatch no. 26 informing him of the compromise on August 14. Aberdeen also said that the settlement of differences with the United States "will greatly improve our relations with France, which are now rather uncomfortable." Aberdeen to Ashburton, June 18, 1842, ibid.

84. Aberdeen later admitted that he had less faith in the justice of the British claim. Cunningham, *Aberdeen*, p. 326.

85. Massachusetts commissioners to DW, July 20, 1842, in William R. Manning, ed., *Diplomatic Correspondence of the United States*, (Washington, D.C., 1940–1945), III, 758.

86. Ashburton to Aberdeen, July 28, 1842, Aberdeen Papers, BM 43,123.

the Union, and being willing to yield to the deliberate convictions of her Sister-States to the path of duty." In addition to Ashburton's irregular efforts and willingness to surrender southern Madawaska, they were no doubt influenced to a considerable extent by the effect the powerful propaganda campaign unleashed by Webster, Smith, and company had had upon the people of Maine and by the evidence of the Sparks and Daveis maps. However, they enclosed a memorandum asking New Brunswick to pay the amount of the fines assessed by the province for timber illegally cut in the disputed territory to be divided equally between Maine and Massachusetts.[87] Again, Webster and Ashburton agreed.

With that final concession the secretary breathed a sigh of relief. The most difficult obstacle to a peace treaty had now been cleared. By comparison, the rest of the disagreements over boundaries between the two countries seemed relatively simple. Ashburton was especially pleased with the results "because I was sure that if we failed we should come very soon to collision." He also rejoiced in the possibility of escaping Washington immediately. "The heat of this place," he told Aberdeen, "is beyond all description and I am sitting with my pen in one hand and a fan in the other. . . . Webster does not look as if he would much outlive our treaty . . . but I am much more comfortable since Preble is gone back to Maine."[88]

The two men settled their differences over the area from Lake Superior to the Lake of the Woods very quickly, with Ashburton yielding St. George's Island, a particularly fertile land of about twenty-six thousand acres. They ran a line from Pigeon River and the Grand Portage to Rainy Lake and the Lake of the Woods, giving the United States part of Vermilion and the rich Mesabi Range, a fact neither man knew at the time. Mutual rights of navigation were included where appropriate.[89]

Of the thousands of square miles acquired by Webster in this compromise agreement much of it contained important iron deposits. Indeed the final settlement brought the United States more land in quantity and quality than the British. For his part, Ashburton obtained five thousand square miles of land, including the fertile area north of the St. John and adjacent to the Madawaska River as well as enough property for a military road between Quebec and the Bay of Fundy. These territorial negotiations were finally concluded in early August.[90]

87. Maine commissioners to DW, July 22, 1842 in Manning, ed., *Diplomatic Correspondence*, III, 760, 765 note 1. New Brunswick ultimately paid Maine and Massachusetts $14,893.45 according to a settlement reached in September 1846. Jones, *To the Webster-Ashburton Treaty*, p. 212 note 27.

88. Ashburton to Aberdeen, July 28, 1842, Aberdeen Papers, BM 43,123. He also said that "Webster is in weak health and his office not well organized" for getting "the treaty into shape."

89. Ashburton to DW, July 16, 29, 1842, DW to Ashburton, July 27, 1842, in *PD*, I, 624–627, 645–649; Ashburton to Aberdeen, July 16, 1842, FO5/380, PRO; Ashburton to Aberdeen, July 28, August 9, 1842, FO881/259, PRO; Jones, *To the Webster-Ashburton Treaty*, pp. 133–138; Baxter, *Webster*, pp. 347–348.

90. Ashburton to Aberdeen, July 28, August 9, 1842, FO881/259, PRO.

As for the Oregon country, the two negotiators discussed it, got nowhere, and decided to leave it alone since it was not an immediate problem.[91]

A more troubling issue was the *Creole* incident, which had the potential of terminating the negotiations because of the strong emotions it aroused around the country about slavery.[92] At the time Congress argued incessantly over "the peculiar institution," and tempers flared during the debates over the right of petition and a gag resolution. Black murderers and mutineers have to be brought to justice, shouted southerners; otherwise slave uprisings will become common occurrences, and property rights in human chattel will be jeopardized.

Ashburton, knowing his government would never surrender the *Creole* slaves, wanted to conciliate and considered offering reparations, even though he had no authority to do so. He also saw the reasonableness of the fears of southerners that they could not sail safely along their own coastline with slave property abroad. But he misjudged Webster's position on the slavery question. The secretary had not asked for the return of the freed slaves and had no intention of doing so. He knew of course that the Peel government would never accede to the demand. He regarded slaves in the South as legitimate property, and he simply wanted compensation for the *Creole* losses, relying on the law of nations to compel British compliance. Although his position won the applause of southerners, it brought down on his head the outrage of abolitionists. They denounced him for his moral failure to understand the wickedness and evil of slavery.[93]

With no resolution possible and the danger of jeopardizing the boundary settlement—"my great plague was the Creole," Ashburton lamented to Aberdeen[94]—Webster and Ashburton finally agreed through an exchange of notes that the British government would instruct colonial governors to avoid in the future "official interference" with vessels driven by storm, accident, or violence into British ports. An unsatisfactory solution, given the fact that this assurance

---

91. Ashburton had instructions to offer the United States a boundary consisting of the forty-ninth parallel to the Columbia River and thence to the ocean. Webster tried to acquire an adequate harbor for the United States on the Pacific to aid the whaling and trading companies of the country and promote access to Asian markets. According to Frederick Merk, *The Oregon Question: Essays in Anglo-American Diplomacy and Politics* (Cambridge, Mass., 1967), pp. 211–215, Ashburton's instructions made it impossible to resolve the Oregon question. As a last resort Aberdeen hoped that the United States would renew the convention by which the status quo "would be prolonged for a time." And if the Americans proposed to take possession of San Francisco Harbor, "they will scarce object to our occupation of the North Bank of the mouth of the Columbia River, & to retaining Juan de Fuca." Aberdeen to Ashburton, July 18, 1842, Aberdeen Papers, BM 43,123.

92. Tyler had a personal conference with Ashburton and suggested setting the *Creole* matter aside until a later time. That would mean extending Ashburton's stay in the country, and the envoy was reluctant to agree. Ashburton to Aberdeen, June 29, 1842, Aberdeen Papers, BM 43,123.

93. Ashburton to DW, inclosure no. 1 to dispatch 22, in Ashburton to Aberdeen, June 29, 1842, Ashburton to Aberdeen, May 10, 1842, FO881/259, PRO.

94. Ashburton to Aberdeen, August 9, 1842, Aberdeen Papers, BM 43,123. "Only yesterday a quarrelous foolish letter [came] from the President to Webster which made me fear we might at last sink fast, and if it were not that the general object of the mission is popular in the country I think this would have been the case."

lacked full authorization from the British government, it nevertheless avoided an impasse and referred the matter back to London. "I was . . . principally moved to this change," Ashburton informed Aberdeen, "by the confidential opinion of members of the Senate's committee on foreign relations."[95] In addition, it had Tyler's approval. And in the final treaty Webster managed to include a provision for the future extradition of those accused of the "crime of murder, or assault with intent to commit murder, or Piracy, or arson, or robbery, or Forgery, or the utterance of forged paper, committed within the jurisdiction of either" country.[96] Ashburton said that the day they finally signed the treaty, August 9, 1842, was "not one of the most happy of my life," because of the *Creole* "plague," but on balance he thought that "the Secretary of State behaved well & liberally throughout."[97]

Not until 1853 was the *Creole* case finally settled. An Anglo-American claims commission awarded $110,330 to the owners of the freed slaves, accepting Webster's argument that the vessel had not violated any law and that the island officials had violated international law by boarding a ship of another nation with armed force.[98]

With respect to the mutineers, when the U.S. consul, Timothy Darling, attempted to bring the "mutineers and murderers to trial, as pirates," the chief justice of the Bahama Islands in Nassau declared that the slaves "had a natural and inalienable right to regain their freedom in the manner they did," a decision Edward Everett called "absolutely ferocious."[99]

As for the *Caroline* matter, the demand by the United States for reparation had been flatly refused by the Melbourne government, and because Webster regarded the incident as involving the sovereignty, dignity, and independence of the nation, it proved as difficult to write into the treaty as the *Creole* controversy. Webster told Ashburton that it constituted a violation of America's "soil and territory—a wrong for which, to this day, no atonement, or even apology, has been made by Her Majesty's Government."[100] So, Britain could either admit that a state of war existed or pay a reparation. Ashburton refused either alternative. But he understood this country's sensitivity about its honor and dignity and admitted in a note that Palmerston should have offered an explanation and

95. Ashburton to Aberdeen, August 13, 1842, ibid.

96. Ashburton to DW, July 31, August 6, DW to Ashburton, August 1, 1842, in *PD*, I, 657–669; Article X, Webster-Ashburton Treaty, in *W&S*, XII, 30–39. The crimes of "piracy, robbery, and the utterance of forged paper" were first suggested by Aberdeen. However, he told Ashburton that the British government objected to Webster's inclusion of "mutiny and revolt on board ship," and it was omitted. Aberdeen to Ashburton, June 3, 1842, FO881/259, PRO. Later Webster also signed extradition treaties with France and Prussia. *PD*, I, 976–802; II, 187–193.

97. Ashburton to Aberdeen, August 9, 1842, Aberdeen Papers, 43,123.

98. Jones, *To the Webster-Ashburton Treaty*, pp. 150–152.

99. Everett to DW, May 16, 1842, in *PD*, I, 561,; DW to Ashburton, May 4, 1842, with Darling's letter of April 16, 1842, enclosed, in FO5/379, PRO.

100. DW to Ashburton, July 27, 1842, in *PD*, I, 650.

apology immediately following the *Caroline's* destruction. The tone and substance of this note clearly indicated Ashburton's intention that his words be taken as an apology.[101] Both Tyler and Webster accepted it as such, especially when the British government swore that no disrespect had been intended at the time of the incident. But since the *Caroline* was involved in illegal acts, no compensation would be awarded.[102] The latter provision particularly pleased Aberdeen. In a note to Peel he specifically pointed out that the final treaty no longer demanded *"indemnification & redress."*[103]

Webster later revealed that it had taken him two days to get Ashburton to consent to use the word "apology." Such an expression of regret did not come easily to this crusty old Englishman.[104]

At the very beginning of the negotiations President Tyler suggested to Webster that "it would add lustre" to any settlement if Britain could be induced "to abandon the claim to impress seamen in time of war from American ships."[105] In the minds of many Americans, this issue, and this issue alone, had precipitated the War of 1812. The British claim to a right of impressment during wartime infuriated Americans. It also infuriated Webster because it violated freedom of the seas. But to date it had been impossible to "induce" the British government to renounce the right.[106]

Ashburton had absolutely no authority to discuss this issue officially[107] and knew what the reaction in Britain would be if he did, although again he was sympathetic to the American position, which was seen, he said, as "undeniable tyranny" by foreigners. Privately he conceded that the resumption of impressment in the future seemed quite remote.[108] Both Ashburton and Webster felt uncomfortable in attempting to include the question in their talks because of its political ramifications, so they agreed to keep it out of the treaty but include it in an exchange of notes. This would allow Webster the opportunity of writing a

101. Ashburton to DW, July 28, 1842, ibid., I, 651–656; Stevens, *Border Diplomacy*, pp. 165, 203 note 32. Jones, *To the Webster-Ashburton Treaty*, pp. 153–154, for a slightly different interpretation. Jones says it was something *close* to an apology. But Peel obviously regarded it as an apology.

102. Ashburton to DW, July 28, DW to Ashburton, August 6, 1842, in *PD*, I, 651–656, 669–671.

103. Aberdeen to Peel, August 25, 1842, Aberdeen Papers, BM 43,062.

104. Curtis, *Webster*, II, 121 note 1.

105. Tyler to DW, May 10, 1842, in *PD*, I, 550.

106. DW to Ashburton, August 8, 1842, ibid., I, 673.

107. "I stand here unfortunately as a person able to *settle* a great many things, and in truth I can *settle* very few, and those not the particular things which most interest the great masses." Ashburton to Aberdeen, June 29, 1842, Aberdeen Papers, BM 43,123.

108. Aberdeen agreed totally with Ashburton on this point. "But you will at once see that it is a very different thing to abstain from exercising a Right we possess, and officially to abandon this Right. Our legal doctrine of the indelible character of the allegiance of the Queen's Subjects must be maintained; in whatever manner we may think it expedient to enforce this doctrine, or not." He called it "our *Droit de Visite.*" Aberdeen to Ashburton, June 3, July 18, 1842, Aberdeen Papers, BM 43,123.

strong statement setting forward the American position, which, when published, he hoped would appease popular resentment.[109]

In his long, detailed, closely argued, and well-written note to Ashburton, dated August 8, Webster stated emphatically that "the practice of impressing seamen from American vessels cannot hereafter be allowed to take place." It is "the simplest, and best, but the only rule, which can be adopted" consistent "with the rights and honor of the United States and the security of their citizens." Henceforth the crew of every American merchant vessel "will find their protection in the flag which is over them." This statement, said Webster, was intended to extinguish the flames of past conflicts, not reignite them. "I persuade myself that you will do justice to this frank and sincere avowal of motives."[110]

Ashburton responded the very next day. His government would give Webster's note "the deliberate attention which its importance deserves. . . . I have much reason to hope that a satisfactory arrangement respecting it [impressment] may be made . . . [for] my government [will] favorably . . . consider all matters having for their object the promoting and maintaining undisturbed kind and friendly feelings with the United States."[111] For all practical purposes Ashburton conceded everything Webster had said and in effect agreed that the practice would never be resumed.[112]

Aberdeen dismissed the exchange as so much hot air. "Webster has taken the opportunity," he told Peel, ". . . of addressing a very elaborate note to Ashburton on the subject of impressment. This is to produce some effect in Congress & could scarcely be expected to lead to any practical result."[113]

At Tyler's suggestion, Webster also took up the African slave trade problem, a problem that bedeviled the United States because it did not have the naval strength to enforce its own ban on the importation of slaves passed by Congress in 1808. Britain used its warships to seize "slavers" off the coast of Africa and keep them from exporting their cargo to its colonies. This practice naturally brought up the additional question of the right of visit and search. Southerners got it into their heads—largely through the propaganda of Cass and Wheaton— that British frigates might search and seize any suspicious-looking ship, even those carrying the American flag. To prevent such a possibility from causing future problems between the two nations, Webster borrowed an idea from a

---

109. Ashburton to Aberdeen, May 12, 1842, FO881/259, PRO. "The simple stipulation that sailors shall not be taken from ships on the high seas," wrote Ashburton, "seems to me to evade conveniently the decision of the more general principle which would otherwise obtrude itself." Ibid. Ashburton did try to offer to the British ministry a possible solution to the problem in time of war, but Aberdeen informed him that "there are obstacles in the way of adopting the scheme suggested by your Lordship, which, at the present moment, appear to Her Majesty's Government insurmountable." Aberdeen to Ashburton, June 3, 1842, ibid.

110. DW to Ashburton, August 8, 1842, in *W&S*, XI, 318–326.

111. Ashburton to DW, August 9, 1842, ibid., XI, 326–328.

112. Cunningham, *Aberdeen*, p. 320.

113. Aberdeen to Peel, August 25, 1842, Aberdeen Papers, BM 43,062.

former secretary of state, John Quincy Adams, and suggested that Britain and the United States establish a "joint-cruising" operation consisting of pairs of warships to patrol the west African coastline.[114] Tyler made a few alterations in the proposal to prevent the United States from becoming entangled in British involvements with other countries, and when Ashburton wholeheartedly endorsed the idea, the two negotiators included it in Article VIII of the final treaty. It stipulated that each nation, acting independently of the other, would maintain a naval squadron of not less than eighty guns "to enforce, separately and respectively, the laws, rights, and obligations of each of the two countries, for the suppression of the slave-trade." Unfortunately the United States never lived up to the requirements of the treaty. Until the outbreak of the Civil War all but one secretary of the navy was a southerner or sympathized with the southern position on slavery, and they did not adequately enforce Article VIII. In addition, Congress severely cut the appropriations for the cruising operation. Still, the treaty constituted an important step in advancing mutual understanding between Britain and the United States.[115] As Ashburton told Aberdeen, they had laid "the groundwork of a more cordial general conciliation than has ever existed since the revolutionary war."[116]

Thus, after four long, grueling, hot, and exhausting months, in which the discussions and notes on all the issues constantly crossed and recrossed one another, Webster and Ashburton completed their negotiations on the boundary question, and on Saturday, July 30, the secretary gave a splendid dinner at his Washington mansion to celebrate the occasion. Besides the two negotiators, the President, the entire cabinet, the commissioners from Maine and Massachusetts, those engaged in the northeastern boundary surveys, and a few select senators attended. As the host, Webster gave the first toast: "Queen Victoria! long may she continue to reign over a prosperous and happy people."

114. They also proposed a clause "pledging the two countries jointly to remonstrate with Brazil & Spain & to press strongly upon them to take effectual measures to prevent the importation of African slaves." The fact that Great Britain and the United States were acting "in concert in this matter will do great good," said Ashburton. Ashburton to Aberdeen, June 14, 1842, ibid. Aberdeen responded: "Your joint remonstrance to Brazil & Spain is good, and you are right in taking it for granted that you cannot go too far in that direction." Aberdeen to Ashburton, July 2, 1842, ibid.

115. Tyler to Robert Tyler, August 29, 1858, in Tyler, ed., *Letters*, II, 240; Jones, *To the Webster-Ashburton Treaty*, p. 142; DW to Everett, April 26, in *PD*, I, 543–544; Ashburton to Aberdeen, April 26, 1842, Aberdeen Papers, BM 43,123; Ashburton to Aberdeen, May 12, and enclosure no. 1, June 14, 1842, FO881/259, PRO; Jones, *To the Webster-Ashburton Treaty*, pp. 144–145. It should be stated clearly, however, that Article VIII really evaded, it did not solve, the visit and search controversy. Webster later clarified the U.S. position to the British in a superb analysis of the law of nations in which while restating his country's position, he argued that the purpose of Article VIII was to avoid differences over visit and search by permitting both nations to act concurrently in suppressing the slave trade. However, the British did not formally renounce the right of visit until 1858. DW to Everett, March 28, 1843, in *PD*, I, 807–817. Hugh G. Soulsby, *The Right of Search and the Slave Trade in Anglo-American Relations* (Baltimore, 1933) calls Webster's statement "definitive" in explaining American's position on the right of visit. P. 100.

116. Ashburton to Aberdeen, June 14, 1842, Aberdeen Papers, BM 43,123.

Ashburton followed with: "The President! perpetuity to the institutions of the United States."

Then came Tyler, who probably gave the best toast of all: "The Commissioners! blessed are the peacemakers."[117]

Ten days later, on August 9, 1842,[118] the two negotiators signed the Treaty of Washington, as it was known by contemporaries. Then, in 1871, the Atlantic nations signed another treaty by the same name, and the earlier settlement became known as the Webster-Ashburton Treaty.[119]

Just prior to signing the treaty, Ashburton obtained a copy of one of Sparks's letters, along with the map, and conveyed the information contained in them to Aberdeen in a letter marked *"private & confidential."* This "extraordinary evidence," he wrote, proves the validity of the British claim and places our case "beyond all possible doubt, and if I had known it before I *agreed* to sign I should have asked your order." The information that came to him "was strictly confidential and *then* communicated because I *had* agreed to sign." Had he known "the secret earlier," he would have "made my stand on the upper St. John & probably at the Madawaska settlements." But he also realized that if he had known and used the information, he would have had "to let the public into this *secret*" and Maine might then have refused the settlement. Ashburton's "informant" figured that without the Sparks map "Maine would never have yielded," and that at least eased the envoy's mind about having agreed to sign. To him and to Aberdeen it was far more important that the two countries resolve their problems than struggle over a few thousand square miles of territory. "[A]s to the Aroostook, which is the only part of the territory of any value," we would never have obtained it "without fighting for it. . . . I think you may now confidently reckon on peace with this country for some time barring any extraordinary accidents."[120]

Five months later Ashburton wrote to Webster: "What we may, I believe, really boast of, my dear Sir, is that we have done a work of peace which, to the

117. *National Intelligencer,* August 2, 1842. Tyler gave Ashburton a farewell dinner on August 17 that delayed the envoy's departure until the end of the month. Ashburton to Aberdeen, August 13, 1842, Aberdeen Papers, BM 43,123.

118. Initially Webster and Ashburton signed a treaty dealing with the boundary questions and a separate convention for the slave trade. Tyler preferred a single treaty, so the boundary agreements became Articles I–VII, and the slave trade Articles VIII–XI. Tyler to DW, August 8, 1842, in *PC* I, 679–680.

119. Jones, *To the Webster-Ashburton Treaty,* p. 216 note 1.

120. Ashburton to Aberdeen, August 9, 1842, Aberdeen Papers, BM 43,123. There are two letters of this date, both of which are marked "private." Ashburton was amazed at how many people had known the "secret" without its being leaked to him earlier. But there is evidence as well that Ashburton did in fact know about the map and relayed the information to Aberdeen on June 14, 1842. Ashburton also "compensated" Sparks. Money was provided to the American to help him convince the governors of Maine and Massachusetts to accept the treaty. Cunningham, *Aberdeen,* p. 325.

extent of our power, we must endeavor to prevent folly or malevolence from spoiling."[121]

Webster agreed totally. Terminating all the various irritants that had jeopardized friendly relations with Great Britain was vitally important to him, and he took enormous pride in what they had accomplished. It was indeed a stunning diplomatic triumph.

121. Ashburton to DW, January 2, 1843, in W&S, XVIII, 163. To Aberdeen, he wrote: "Upon the whole looking back with some leisure upon the past, I am satisfied with what I have done in this matter of some delicacy." Ashburton to Aberdeen, August 13, 1842, Aberdeen Papers, BM 43,123.

34

Formulating Foreign Policy

THE SPLENDID success of the negotiations that everyone recognized had spared the country from a possible third war with Great Britain resulted from the determined efforts not merely of Webster and Ashburton but of the many individuals called upon by the negotiators to render assistance. They included commissioners and propagandists, historians, specialists of the law and geography, and members of the Senate Foreign Relations Committee and the cabinet. But none did more than President John Tyler. Webster knew it and acknowledged it.[1]

More than anything else, the treaty cleared away most of the disputes that had plagued relations between the two countries for decades. Only Oregon remained, and Webster hoped to head a special mission to resolve that problem after he stepped down as secretary of state. The treaty marked the beginning of the end to the feelings of intense hostility that had always characterized American attitudes toward the former mother country. It prepared the two countries for a rapprochement that was to last from that time forward.[2]

It "reflects credit," commented the *National Intelligencer,* "upon those who have conducted the negotiations and gives the fullest measure that the National honor has been maintained. . . . Let us hail it as the welcome harbinger of better times." *Niles' Weekly Register* agreed. "Sincerely do we congratulate the country upon the final settlement. America would be mad were she willing to precipitate

1. "I shall never speak of this negotiation, my dear Sir, which I believe is destined to make some figure in the history of the country, without doing you justice. Your steady support and confidence, your anxious and intelligent attention to what was in progress, and your exceedingly obliging and pleasant intercourse, both with the British minister and the commissioners of the States, have given every possible facility to my agency in this transaction." DW to Tyler, August 24, 1842, in *W&S,* XVIII, 146–147.

2. Andrew Jackson in 1844 took exception to what Webster had accomplished. "Had Mr. Webster had an ounce of American feeling in him, when negotiating on the North Eastern boundary, he would have put this matter [of Oregon] to rest, when Ashburton proposed to stop the line at the Rockey [sic] Mountains." If he had said, "No Sir, we carry it out to the Pacific agreable to the Treaty of 1783, or our negotiation is at an end," Britain would have capitulated because of its involvement with China, the Afghans, and the Irish. It has therefore kept Oregon "as a nest egg" to provoke war with the United States whenever it suits its purpose. Jackson to William B. Lewis, September 17, 1844, Jackson-Lewis Papers, New York Public Library.

a contest" with Great Britain. And because of our growing size and strength, "Great Britain would be still more craz'd were she to hasten a result which such a contest would almost inevitably bring upon her." Both newspapers of course gave Webster the lion's share of the praise. "Those who have been most opposed to Mr. Webster's remaining in the Cabinet are understood to admit that it was fortunate for the country that he was there at this important juncture. We doubt whether any other citizen would have had in his power to bring the affair to so happy an issue." He has proved himself "wise in counsel, and resolute in action." Even John Quincy Adams, that supreme diplomat and at the time chairman of the House Committee on Foreign Affairs, a man who never stopped whining about the "rotten heart of Daniel Webster," told his constituents that "there is perhaps no other citizen who could have brought the negotiation to a favorable termination, and saved us from being plunged into a war with England."[3]

To show its gratitude, the nation now awarded him a new title to add to that of "Defender of the Constitution": "Daniel Webster, Defender of Peace."[4]

But the Senate had to ratify the document, and Webster had great fears over what might happen. As Ashburton had said, "folly or malevolence" might try to spoil our accomplishment. And that possibility really troubled the secretary. "It is quite uncertain whether Congress will do any thing," Webster worried. "The Treaty will be acted upon, this week. No doubt it will be assailed, as would any Treaty, and as ratification requires two thirds, [its] fate is not absolutely certain."[5]

The Whigs controlled the Senate and had cast out the President. In their eyes Webster was almost as bad. Would they now approve the handiwork of these two outcasts?

What Webster did next proved again his mastery of propaganda. He summoned his paid henchmen and friends in Maine and Massachusetts to come out in written and vocal support of the treaty and convince the nation that the terms agreed upon were most favorable to the United States. And their efforts succeeded brilliantly. Despite some opposition from Senator Reuel Williams and a few other politicians, the people of Maine reacted favorably to the treaty. So too the citizens of Massachusetts.[6] More important, after the President had forwarded the treaty to the Senate on August 11, Webster contacted Senator William C. Rives of Virginia, chairman of the Committee on Foreign Relations, and revealed to him the existence of the Sparks map that supported British claims. Rives shared this information with other committee members, and it was presented to the full Senate meeting in executive session. Democrats who opposed ratification howled over Webster's deception, calling his action despica-

3. *National Intelligencer,* August 23, September 28, 1842; *Niles' Weekly Register,* August 27, 1842; Adams, *Memoirs,* XI, 20.

4. Charles Sumner, *Works* (Boston, 1870), I, 304–316.

5. DW to John Healy, August 17, 1842, in *PD,* I, 691.

6. Edward Kent to Edward Kavanagh, August 16, John Otis to DW, January 17, 1843, ibid., I, 690–691, 703–704.

ble and dishonorable. Thomas Hart Benton took particular delight in pillorying the secretary. He called Webster "the champion of the British Government." Of course he knew that the Sparks information had been brought forward at this time and passed around among "Senators to alarm them into prompt action." Senator James Buchanan of Pennsylvania joined in the general attack. Not only had the secretary's inept diplomacy lost territory and failed to gain reparations for the *Creole* and *Caroline* incidents, Buchanan contended, but he had also failed to force Britain to abandon its impressment policy.

But other senators, notably John C. Calhoun, realized that if the treaty was rejected and the matter brought before an independent arbiter, the Sparks map could be awfully damaging. In his speech on the Senate floor he rebuked Benton and Buchanan for failing to see that the treaty was more beneficial to the United States than the award in 1831.[7] He himself wrote a number of unsigned editorials that Gales and Seaton very accommodatingly printed in the *National Intelligencer*, along with editorials from other friendly newspapers, such as the Portland *Eastern Argus*. All these found a receptive audience.[8]

The editorials, plus Calhoun's strong support, the Sparks map, and the concern over the possibility of conflict with Great Britain if the boundary was not immediately settled, brought a quick and surprising result. Despite all the criticism—and more was to follow in the future when Webster's use of secret service money surfaced—the Senate ratified the treaty on Saturday, August 20, at nine o'clock in the evening, after only four days of debate, by the overwhelming margin of thirty-nine to nine. Never had a treaty of the United States received such a large majority.[9]

Webster could hardly believe it. "I did not look for a majority quite so large," he rejoiced. "I am truly thankful that the thing is done." He was bursting with gratitude. He thanked Rives for guiding the treaty through the Senate with such a sure and skillful hand. He also wrote his thanks to Edward Everett in London. He may even have thanked Calhoun. The secretary then sent one of his clerks, William S. Derrick, to receive the treaty, after Tyler had signed it, and take it to England for ratification.[10]

Unfortunately, and much to Webster's regret, the Senate removed the secrecy of its proceedings, and the nation and Great Britain learned of Sparks's map. And it nearly brought down the Peel government. In a series of unsigned articles in the *Morning Chronicle* Lord Palmerston excoriated Webster for his

7. *Congressional Globe*, 27th Congress, 3d Session, Appendix, pp. 1–21, 49–53, 59–67.

8. Jones, *To the Webster-Ashburton Treaty*, p. 164.

9. The lone Whig to vote against the treaty was Charles Conrad of Louisiana, a former Jacksonian. Senator Reuel Williams offered a resolution directing the President to seize the disputed territory if ratification failed, but it was rejected, thirty-one to eight.

10. DW to Mason, August 21, 1842, in *W&S*, XVIII; 146, DW to Rives, [August 21, 1842], in *PD*, I, 692; DW to Everett, August 22, 1842, in *W&S*, XIV, 405. It is interesting that Ashburton had an inkling that the treaty would be confirmed, but then he was in consultation with members of the Senate Foreign Relations Committee. Ashburton to Aberdeen, August 13, 1842, Aberdeen Papers, BM 43,123.

dishonorable action in not informing Ashburton of the map's existence, and he lambasted Ashburton for falling victim to the deception. "Lord Ashburton's *capitulation*," he called it, and he proposed writing in red letters across the face of the treaty the word "shame."[11]

He might have gotten away with this hypocrisy if Peel had not been told that Palmerston had hidden away the so-called King George III map that upheld the American territorial claim. He told no one of its existence except a special agent, George W. Featherstonhaugh, who subsequently shared the information with Peel. As Peel rightly noted in the debate in Parliament, nothing could be more fallacious than arguing a claim from a contemporary map unless the negotiators had adopted it. Palmerston backed down, and the Parliament ratified the treaty. "The truth is," Ashburton explained to Webster, "that the desire of all here is peace, and more especially with your country." On October 13 Edward Everett, the U.S. minister, and Lord Aberdeen exchanged ratifications that put the treaty immediately into operation.[12]

The news of Parliament's action arrived in New York Harbor in early November and was hailed in Battery Park, Peck Slip, the Navy Yard, Brooklyn Heights, and Jersey City with a one-hundred-gun salute. Webster happened to be in New York at the time, and he received "several thousand citizens" in the governor's room in City Hall. For two hours they paraded past him to thank him and shake his hand. He then favored them with a brief speech on the merits of the treaty.[13]

The Webster-Ashburton Treaty, no matter how questionable the means of bringing it to fruition, benefited both countries enormously. The American people, including those in Maine, understood and appreciated its importance.[14] But the revelations about the means Webster employed to achieve this result did his reputation much harm. It reinforced the perception by Americans that he could not be trusted, not with money and certainly not with the affairs of the nation as chief executive.

His reputation took another savage blow when George Prentice, Clay's biographer[15] and the editor of the Louisville *Daily Journal*, the leading Whig

11. Jones, *To the Webster-Ashburton Treaty*, p. 170; Merk, *Fruits of Propaganda*, p. 79. Webster noticed Palmerston's remark about "capitulation" but did not comment further. DW to Fletcher Webster, October 19, 1842, in *PC*, V, 246. "I am not afraid [of the critics]," Ashburton wrote Webster, "and though I have not your power of destroying an adversary . . . I have a right to be heard." Ashburton to DW, January 2, 1843, in *W&S*, XVIII, 162.

12. Ashburton to DW, January 2, 1843, in *W&S*, XVIII, 163; Hunter Miller, ed., *Treaties and Other International Acts of the United States of America* (Washington, D.C., 1931–1948), IV, 408–410; Curtis, *Webster*, II, 147.

13. *National Intelligencer*, November 9, 1842.

14. Calhoun expressed what a great many Americans believed at the time. "We *ratified* the treaty yesterday, which will give us time & leisure to settle our domestick troubles, without any from abroad; a thing most desirable." Calhoun to Thomas G. Clemson, August 22, 1842, in *Calhoun Papers*, XVI, 418.

15. George D. Prentice, *Biography of Henry Clay* (Hartford, Conn., 1831).

newspaper in Kentucky, published an article, "Anecdote of Daniel Webster," on January 26, 1842, in which he accused the secretary of the attempted rape of the wife of a poor clerk in his department when she came to him looking for employment. Webster had allegedly pounced on her, declaring, "This, my dear, is one of the prerogatives of my office." He was about to commit some "lascivious" act when her screams brought rescuers, who saved her from "dishonor."

Webster vehemently denied the charge, took an oath attesting to his "chastity" before a justice of the peace, and Prentice was obliged to retract the story. But the Clay press could not resist it. And the Democrats enjoyed it almost as much. "I hope the world is convinced of his chastity," chortled George Bancroft to Van Buren, "now that he has made oath. . . . All English annals show nothing so humiliating."[16]

Few could really believe such a malicious and disgusting story about Webster. Indeed there is absolutely no evidence to document it. But the implications, as the Clay press clearly intimated, suggested a deficiency of character that in Calhoun's opinion had made Webster "almost universally odious. There is no confidence in him. His integrity is questioned by almost all of every party." As a consequence, Calhoun declared, Clay had been able to "detach the almost entire body of the whigs from the administration."[17]

Webster sustained a dreadful pounding by Whigs over the next several months because he would not respond to their renewed demands that he quit his office now that the treaty had been concluded and no other major issue needed his attention as secretary of state. Resign, counseled Abbott Lawrence, one of the most prominent Whig leaders in Massachusetts. Lawrence, once Webster's most ardent supporter and now a staunch advocate for Clay, had begun to challenge Webster's preeminent position within the state party. "*Now* is the *accepted* time to quit, with honor, your present *responsible* but *disagreeable* position," he lectured. Even Webster's close friend Jeremiah Mason advised him to go. Tyler, he said, "is almost universally detested" by Whigs, "as deep & thorough as their contempt for his weakness & folly." Leave now, he continued. "Your friends doubt whether you can with safety to your own character & honor act under, or with such a man."[18] Some Whigs even held a convention and passed resolutions urging him to resign. The calls grew louder when Tyler vetoed— Senator Preston called it "his veto of the month"—a new tariff bill now that the Compromise Tariff of 1833 had expired. And he did it against Webster's recommendation. "I would give almost my right hand if you could be persuaded

16. Bancroft to Van Buren, February 21, 1842, "Van Buren-Bancroft Correspondence, 1830–1845," *Massachusetts Historical Society Proceedings* 2d serial, V, XLII (1909) p. 391; Peterson, *Great Triumvirate*, p. 331.

17. Calhoun to Thomas G. Clemson, April 3, 1842, in *Calhoun Papers*, XVI, 213.

18. Lawrence to DW, July 30, Mason to DW, August 28, 1842, in *PC*, V, 232, 239–240. See also Mason to DW, August 28, 1842, in *Microfilm Edition*, F17/23021. Some of Webster's friends urged him to remain, however. See, for example, John Mills to DW, July 28, 1842, in *PC*, V, 231–232. See also Kinley J. Brauer, "The Webster-Lawrence Feud: A Study in Politics and Ambitions," *Historian*, XXIX (November 1966), pp. 34–59.

to sign the bill," the secretary wrote him. But Tyler would not yield. "How deeply do I regret that I cannot have your full concurrence in this procedure," he responded.[19] Not until late August 1842 did Congress pass a tariff that Tyler approved. The Tariff of 1842 in effect returned the general level of duties to those of 1832.[20]

What made this latest disagreement so ironic was that Tyler himself would not have minded terribly much if Webster had resigned. For some time he had cast his eye on Texas and the possibility that it could be annexed. But his secretary of state resisted this reach for such a grand prize. To Webster and others it had "hazard" written all over it. Mexico would surely object, and the possibility of war with that country was too frightening to contemplate.

Still, Webster would not give up his office. He reveled in the power and the prestige and the glory it provided him. "He loves office," observed George Bancroft. "Having been without it all his life, he has a fondness for it, of which you can have no conception."[21] Jealousy also motivated the secretary. He knew that Clay, now busily working to win the Whig nomination for 1844, wanted him out, and for that reason alone he would not go. The thought that Massachusetts Whigs scheduled to meet the following month might nominate Clay for the presidency gnawed at Webster. It was one thing for the Whigs to pass a resolution saying they would support him if nominated, but it was quite another to "endeavor to *pledge* the Whigs of the State for him." It would be "little short of insanity," Webster insisted. *"He has no degree of reasonable prospect of being elected."*[22]

But the Massachusetts convention meeting on September 14 paid no attention to Webster's advice. Under Lawrence's adroit management it nominated Clay and its governor, John Davis, for Vice President. The delegates also passed a resolution in which they declared "their full and final separation" from the present administration. Webster was confronted with the implicit call for his resignation. He could resign or face the consequences.[23]

Then Webster committed an act of incredible folly. He was invited to a reception to be given at Boston's Faneuil Hall on September 30 to celebrate his triumph in concluding the treaty with Great Britain. In view of the results of the recent convention, he remarked to Charles Curtis, "I perceive it is quite impossible for me to enter into the discussion of material questions, & express my own opinions, without giving offence."[24]

19. Resolution of Maryland Whigs, August 22, 1842, DW to Tyler, August 8, Tyler to DW, August 8, 1842, in *PC*, V, 236–237, 236, 235.

20. Daniel Walker Howe, *Political Culture of the Whigs*, (Chicago, 1979), p. 220; Stanwood, *American Tariff Controversies* (Boston and New York, 1903), II, 28–30.

21. Bancroft to Van Buren, February 21, 1842, "Van Buren-Bancroft Correspondence," p. 391.

22. DW to John Healy, August 26, 1842, in *PC*, V, 239.

23. Brauer, "The Webster-Lawrence Feud," pp. 37–38; Curtis, *Webster*, II, 141 note; Hamilton A. Hill, *Memoir of Abbott Lawrence* (Boston, 1883), pp. 73–74.

24. DW to Curtis, September 15, 1842, in *PC*, V, 243.

He seemed to be looking for trouble, and he found it. He walked to Faneuil Hall with his friends Jeremiah Mason, Harrison Gray Otis, Josiah Quincy, and others. He arrived at eleven o'clock to face an audience of three thousand jammed into every available space in the building. Dressed as usual in his blue coat with brass buttons, looking rested from a month's sojourn at Marshfield, he mounted the podium and stood before the "mob," as Mason called the audience, and faced down their obvious disapproval. He "looked like Coriolanus." As he stared at them, "his deep calm eyes" glanced from one end of the room to the other. As he did so, "every head in the hall was instantly uncovered. If that audience had come to cavil, it was already awed into respectful attention."[25]

Mayor Jonathan Chapman introduced him in a long but eloquent speech and expressed the public's gratitude for the great service he had rendered the country. Everyone in the hall then expected the great man to flood the hall with nationalistic and patriotic oratory extolling the merits of his treaty-making endeavors, but what they heard "was bitter as wormwood to nearly the whole of the Whig party," Adams recorded in his diary: "boastful, cunning, jesuitical, fawning, and insolent; . . . dealing open blows at the late Whig Convention for their resolution of total severance from John Tyler, and sly stabs at Clay and me, without naming either of us."[26]

Immediately upon commencing his speech, Webster made plain what he intended to do. Speaking of his role in negotiating the treaty, he said, "I take great pleasure in acknowledging here, as I will acknowledge everywhere, my obligation to [the President] for the unbroken and steady confidence reposed in me . . . and infinitely important to my own reputation." He acknowledged that "many persons" demanded that he resign from the cabinet. But "I give no pledges, I make no intimations, one way or the other; and I will be as free, when this day closes, to act as duty calls. . . . I am, Gentlemen, a little hard to coax, but as to being driven, that is out of the question." He had listened, he declared, to his own judgment, which directed him to remain at a post where he could serve his country, and he asked his listeners, he asked the country, to say whether the nation was better off today because he had stayed.

The recently held Whig convention, he continued, had been "inconsiderate and hasty," a direct slap at Abbott Lawrence, who had masterminded the convention. In separating from the President, the members had a right to speak for themselves. But not for others. Not for me. "I am a Whig, I always have been a Whig, and I always will be one; and if there are any who would turn me out of the pale of that communion, let them see who will get out first. I am a Massachusetts Whig, a Faneuil Hall Whig, having breathed this air for five-and-twenty years, and meaning to breathe it, as long as my life is spared." If Tyler should make changes of benefit to our mercantile trade, "are the Whigs of Massachu-

---

25. Hale, *Memoir of Lawrence*, p. 74; Curtis, *Webster*, II, 142–143. Curtis was in the hall.

26. Adams, *Memoirs*, XI, 256. What Webster hoped to do in giving this speech, said Adams, was "to split up the Whigs and out of the two fragments to make a Tyler party." Ibid.

setts to give him neither aid nor succor?" And what about me? "If I choose to remain in the President's councils, do these gentlemen mean to say that I cease to be a Massachusetts Whig? I am quite ready to put that question to the people of Massachusetts."

There was silence in the hall as he continued. "Generally, when a divorce takes place, the parents divide the children. I should be glad to know where I am to go."

It was a blistering attack. Stamped with Websterian power, which frequently elicited great applause when he spoke about the treaty, it also demonstrated such "ill temper from beginning to end" that Lawrence and the other Whig leaders could barely contain their anger. Webster "laid about him as if determined that his blows should be felt." The attack on the Massachusetts Whig convention was justified, the secretary later insisted, because it had been "aimed against me. Its object was, to destroy my standing & character, politically, with the Whigs. This object, I determined to defeat, at all hazards, & all consequences; & thank God I did defeat it."

In defending Tyler's banking plan during the speech, he declared that if adopted, it would have been "the most beneficial measure of any sort ever adopted in this country, the Constitution only excepted." To the Whigs listening in the audience, this was utter nonsense. He then compounded this foolishness by declaring that the action of Congress, in rejecting the President's plan, failed to consider the real needs of the people. Although he did not mention Clay by name, it was obvious to everyone in the room who he thought was the principal culprit in blocking this "most beneficial measure."[27]

The speech cost him dearly.[28] He alienated many of his loyal followers, including Congressman Robert Winthrop, his former law student. It was the last straw for John Davis and Harrison Gray Otis, who deserted him and joined forces with Abbott Lawrence.

The distress of the Whig members of his audience was echoed in many Whig newspapers around the country when they reprinted his speech in full. The *National Intelligencer* sadly observed that the speech "overboils with ill-concealed rancor towards" Henry Clay. The Portland *Advertiser* printed it with "disappointment and dissatisfaction," and the New York *American* wondered if any "man of honor and self-respect" could now "hold a seat in the Cabinet of Mr. Tyler." The Alexandria, Virginia, *Gazette* laughingly thought the speech gave great satisfaction to the locofocos. The Albany *Evening Journal* said it was "discourteous," but Thurlow Weed, its editor, privately contended that when Webster asked where he was to go, it "was a matter of little or no importance." From that moment, Weed continued, Black Dan "ceased to be a power in the

---

27. Sargent, *Public Men and Events,* II, 191; DW to Robert Letcher, October 23, 1843, in *PC,* V, 316; Winthrop to Everett, October 15, 1843, Everett Papers, MHS; Otis to George Harrison, October 25, 1842, Otis Papers, MHS. The entire speech is in *W&S,* III, 117–140.

28. Charles Sumner said that in the hall the speech "was not received with any warmth. The applause seemed to be led off by some *claqueurs,* or fuglemen, and in rapture and spontaneousness was very unlike the echoes he has excited in the same hall at other times." Quoted in Hill, *Memoirs of Lawrence,* pp. 74–75.

land." Even the Boston *Atlas,* Webster's own mouthpiece in Massachusetts, declared that although the audience heard "the outpourings of a powerful intellect," Webster's remarks in relation to the Whig convention were most unfortunate.[29]

Philip Hone, who regarded Webster as something of a deity, read the accounts of the speech with disbelief. The torrents of support, he recorded, that had set in so irresistibly for Clay to head the Whig ticket "can never convey Mr. Webster to its bosom to personal honor or political distinction. These two eminent men are undeniably rivals and . . . whatever simulated expressions of good will may pass between them, it is impossible they should be friends." It is a great misfortune that the party has two such giants in its ranks, he regretfully concluded.[30]

Most southern Whigs regard Webster as " 'down among the dead men,' ever since his Faneuil Hall speech," according to Benjamin Leigh, a former Virginia senator. "I really grieve for Webster" to see how his passions and vices have "perverted" the "very highest abilities which God can endow mere mortal man." No one can put confidence in Daniel Webster's "virtue." He is "wanting in moral courage." Lately, Leigh added, he had heard "some stories impeaching his [Webster's] integrity and honor which have shocked me." If they are true, "twere better that he had been born a dog."[31]

Webster shrugged off the criticisms. "You see what a dust my speech has raised," he wrote his son Fletcher. "It is no more than I anticipated. I am sorry the Intelligencer acts so foolishly; but that is its own affair." He planned to have the speech printed in pamphlet form and "widely distributed." Naturally he made a point of sending a copy to Tyler.[32]

But many in Boston heartily disagreed with the criticisms of their "mighty Pan," as George Ticknor called him. Ticknor and Jeremiah Mason were "filled with admiration. So was everybody, down to my tailor, bookseller, and bookbinder," Ticknor asserted. It took courage for Webster to speak as he did. "He was every moment upon the brink of all his audience hated, and it is a wonder how he got through without being mobbed." Forget the criticism. "Webster, I think, is looked on as a greater man to-day in Boston that he ever was before."[33]

Nevertheless the criticism mounted, especially in the halls of Congress. And it blistered the secretary. Representative Thomas Arnold of Tennessee launched into "a vehement and unmeasured inventive" against the mighty Pan, "whose enquiry in his Faneuil Hall speech, 'What will you do with me?' he most unmercifully scourged." Western and southern representatives, especially Arnold, Garrett Davis of Kentucky, John Minor Botts of Virginia, and Kenneth

29. *Intelligencer,* October 5; *Advertiser,* October 3; *American,* October 1; *Gazette,* October 6; *Evening Journal,* October 4; Weed, *Autobiography,* II, 482; *Atlas,* October 1.

30. Hone, *Diary,* II, 621–622.

31. Leigh to Mangum, March 28, 1844, in Shanks, ed., *Papers of Mangum,* IV, 81–82.

32. DW to Fletcher Webster, October 15, 1842, in Van Tyne, ed., *Letters of Webster,* p. 280. See also DW to Fletcher Webster, October 2, 1842, in *W&S,* XVIII, 150.

33. Ticknor to Hugh S. Legaré, October 2, 21, 1842, in Ticknor, *Life,* II, 210–211.

Rayner of North Carolina, "insisted on keeping up a daily attack upon him. You must have seen," Robert Winthrop wrote to Nathan Hale, "the extreme to which they carried their vituperative epithets," calling him "disgraced and degraded." And for the rest of the congressional session that began in early December 1842, each time Webster's name was mentioned or some action was required that the secretary had requested, several representatives took the opportunity to attack and "revile" him. It therefore became more and more difficult for him to make a graceful exit from the cabinet. Like it or not, he had to stay put.[34]

One possible escape for Webster lay in completing the boundary problem left unresolved with Great Britain. The Oregon territory had to be settled between the two nations, something Webster wanted to do with Ashburton but could not because the envoy lacked full authority to concede anything north of the Columbia River. U.S. claims to the area rested on the discoveries of Robert Gray, Lewis and Clark, the settlement of John Jacob Astor's American Fur Company at Astoria at the mouth of the Columbia River, and the claims of Spain that had been surrendered to the United States under the terms of the Adams-Onís Treaty of 1819. Aside from settlements by trappers, British claims to the Oregon territory arose from the many expeditions of such explorers as Captain James Cook, George Vancouver, and Sir Alexander Mackenzie. Webster himself did not think very highly of the area. "I believe Oregon to be a poor country," he told Everett, ". . . and of very little consequence to the United States."[35]

At the moment the two nations had agreed to joint occupation of the area, roughly the territory between the forty-second and 54°40' parallels and between the Rocky Mountains and the Pacific Ocean. Both countries were willing to split the territory at the forty-ninth parallel, but Britain insisted that when the line reached the Columbia River, it should follow down the river to the Pacific Ocean. The United States rejected this proposal. It had to have a deepwater port on the Pacific, and none was available except the area from the Strait of Juan de Fuca to Puget Sound, north of the Columbia River. "All the good harbors between the Russian Settlements [north of 54°40'] & California," Webster argued, can be found in "the Straits of St Juan de Fuca, & the inland waters with which they communicate."[36] For a man like Webster, with his strong New England sense of the importance of mercantile trade, a deepwater harbor on the Pacific had to be acquired to facilitate access to the markets of Asia. He desperately wanted a "window" to the East in order to advance the nation's trade around the world. Something like the ports of Boston or New York City.[37] And Webster believed he was the man who could convince the British that the forty-ninth parallel should be run straight across from the Rocky Mountains to the Pacific, thereby making Puget Sound American.

34. Adams, *Memoirs*, XI, 281, 325; Winthrop to Hale, January 11, February, 1843, Hale Papers, LC; Nathans, *Webster and Jacksonian Democracy*, p. 202.

35. DW to Everett, January 29, 1844, in *W&S*, XVIII, 179.

36. DW to Everett, November 28, 1842, in *PD*, I, 834.

37. On this point see Norman A. Graebner, *Empire on the Pacific: A Study in American Continental Expansion* (New York, 1955), pp. 131, 220.

The more he thought about it, the more Webster liked the idea of returning to England on a special mission to settle the question. It would permit him to resign from the cabinet without being forced out, it would quiet the clamor of Whigs, it would return him to a country and people he genuinely loved, and if successful, it would provide the crowning achievement to his diplomatic career. The President favored the idea as well because it would allow him to find another secretary who might help him satisfy his expansionist craving for Texas.

Webster therefore developed the so-called tripartite plan to accomplish his objective. It was as visionary and unrealistic, not to say ridiculous, as his hope that the Whigs would accept Tyler back into their ranks. During his negotiations with Ashburton he proposed that if Great Britain could persuade Mexico to sell San Francisco to this country, the United States would concede the boundary at the Columbia River. As Webster's plan finally evolved over the next several months, he further proposed that Mexico sell Upper California to the United States, the money to be used to repay both American and British claims against Mexico. In addition, he resurrected a plan first put forward in 1826 by Foreign Secretary George Canning, in which the Oregon Territory would be divided along the forty-ninth parallel to the Columbia River and Britain would surrender to the United States a quadrilateral tract of land adjoining the Strait of Juan de Fuca, known today as the Olympic Peninsula. The complete tripartite plan would, if implemented, provide the United States with two deepwater harbors, one from Mexico and the other from Britain.[38]

Despite British reluctance to become involved in the further dismemberment of Mexico—although a voluntary cession by Mexico would not pose a problem—Webster thought he could persuade them to participate in the plan if he himself returned to England either at the head of a special mission or as Everett's replacement. But Everett thought he was perfectly capable of negotiating a settlement and believed the forty-ninth parallel from the Rockies straight to the ocean could be achieved. Besides, like Webster, he was much admired by the British for his learning, his agreeable disposition—in marked contrast with his predecessor—and his obvious appreciation of British life and society. Why bother with a special mission or, what was worse, with replacing him?

For the secretary to cast Everett aside for his own benefit seemed unconscionable. But when it came to self-interest, Webster could sacrifice even his closest friends. "I have some reason to think," Everett admitted to Peter C. Brooks, "there is an intention to disgust and drive me from my place. Our great men are terribly selfish; and . . . I am fearful not only that Mr. W. has thoughts of supplanting me, but of discrediting me."[39] Even among his devoted friends, Webster had now acquired a reputation for deceit and duplicity. Whatever served his own self-interest was all that seemed to matter to Black Dan.

John Quincy Adams insisted that Daniel Webster "treats his friends as Goldsmith says Garrick did his—

38. DW to Everett, November 28, 1842, January 29, 1843, in *PD*, I, 826–828, 834–838, 841–844.

39. Everett to Brooks, November 3, 1842, quoted in Paul Revere Frothingham, *Edward Everett: Orator and Statesman* (Boston and New York, 1925), p. 229.

"He cast off his friends as a huntsman his pack,
For he knew when he pleased he could whistle them back."[40]

Right from the start the tripartite plan was an idiotic idea. The British did not care for it or for a special mission, and Mexico had no intention of selling California. It certainly did not help the American cause when Commodore Thomas ap Catesby Jones, in command of a naval squadron, captured Monterey on October 19, 1842, and hoisted the American flag in the mistaken belief that war had broken out between the United States and Mexico. When he discovered his mistake, he apologized and surrendered the town. This action only intensified Mexican fears about the ultimate intentions of the United States.[41]

Relations between the two countries further deteriorated on account of the many raids by Texans into Mexico and the capture by Mexican authorities in the fall of 1841 of approximately 350 settlers in Santa Fe, 200 of them Americans. These settlers had been sent by President Mirabeau Lamar of Texas to Santa Fe to open trade relations and encourage the inhabitants of New Mexico to join the Texans in their ongoing struggle against Mexico. The Santa Fe prisoners suffered a horrible winter march to Mexico City; some were executed along the way; others were confined to leper prisons or chained and forced to work on public roads. One of Webster's most notable diplomatic achievements was his superb handling of this issue, resulting finally in the liberation of the American and Texan captives in the summer of 1842.[42]

These episodes doomed any hope for the tripartite plan, but Webster had been encouraged to pursue it by the American minister to Mexico, Waddy Thompson, who assured President Tyler that "this Government would cede to us Texas and the Californias" in order to extinguish its debt. In his enthusiasm for the plan he predicted that the harbors of California would "secure [for the United States] the trade of India & the whole Pacific Ocean. In addition to which California is destined to be the granary of the Pacific."[43]

Driving ahead with his hope for a special mission, Webster wrote confidentially to Caleb Cushing, a member of the House Committee on Foreign Affairs, asking him to consult with the chairman, John Quincy Adams, to see if the committee would recommend the appropriation of funds to finance the special mission. Cushing readily obliged. Adams also went along, and he presented a motion to his committee that he be instructed to move an amendment to the

40. Adams, *Memoirs*, X, 43.

41. Merk, *Oregon Question*, pp. 189–215. John Quincy Adams was certain the administration plotted a war "for conquest and plunder from Mexico," but Webster assured him that he "was wrong in all this." Adams thanked the secretary for the information, but in his diary he wrote, "what an abîme of duplicity." *Memoirs*, XI, 346–347.

42. Leslie Combs to John Tyler, December 19, 1841, DW to Powhatan Ellis, January 3, 6, February 26, DW to Balie Peyton, January 6, Powhatan Ellis to DW, February 17, April 28, DW to Waddy Thompson, April 5, June 2, 27, July 8, Thompson to DW, April 29, June 20, 1842, in *PD*, I, 378–458. The son of Senator John J. Crittenden of Kentucky was among the prisoners, and Webster made a special effort to win his release. DW to Thompson, February 7, 1843, in *W&S*, XVIII, 165–166.

43. Thompson to Tyler, April 29, 1842, in *PC*, I, 420.

civil and diplomatic appropriation bill to provide a special minister to Great Britain. But it was so clear to the other members that the mission was intended for Webster's benefit that they voted the motion down, six to three.[44] That ended that.

With the mission gone Webster turned his attention to replacing Everett as minister to England, despite Everett's reluctance. He thought he had an easy method of dislodging the minister when Tyler, on December 30, 1842, in a message to Congress written by Webster, recommended that a mission be sent to China. Edward Everett would head it. In view of Britain's latest imposed treaty on the Chinese, following the Opium War, which opened several ports to trade, a mission would have as its object the acquisition of similar privileges for the United States, thereby widening this nation's commercial involvement in Asia. On March 3, 1843, Congress approved the mission and appropriated forty thousand dollars to carry it out. The Senate also confirmed Edward Everett as commissioner. This action initiated the first U.S. foreign policy toward China.[45]

Webster really thought that Everett would make the ideal person to head the mission,[46] and at the same time he could take Everett's place in London. When he learned of Webster's proposal, Adams, like many others,[47] immediately saw through the secretary's scheme and labeled it "the back door by which Webster skillfully secures to himself a safe retreat from the Tyler Cabinet."[48] But he had to admit to the secretary that he was "much gratified" by the China idea, "deeming the mission of transcendent importance" and declaring Everett "by his character and attainments peculiarly well suited for it." Webster was so delighted with these unsolicited remarks that he asked Adams to write Everett and repeat what he had said.[49] Tyler too had readily agreed with the proposal, not only because of Everett's suitability for this important undertaking but as a means of getting rid of Webster. By this time the secretary knew he had to retire gracefully from the cabinet or get pushed. An added factor was Tyler's continuing attempt to gain favor with Democrats in the hope of possibly winning their nomination in 1844, especially if he acquired Texas.[50]

44. DW to Cushing, February 24, 1843, in *PD,* I, 844–845; Adams, *Memoirs,* XI, 329–330. Cushing, Adams, and Isaac Holmes of South Carolina voted for the mission.

45. Richardson, *Messages and Papers,* III, 2066–2067; DW to Everett, March 10, 1843, in *PD,* I, 878, 896.

46. Everett discusses at length the situation in China in his letter to DW, November 29, 1842, in *PD,* I, 890–894.

47. Thomas Hart Benton opposed the mission as "a studied fraud . . . to enable a gentleman, who loves to travel in Europe and Asia, to extend his travels to the Celestial Empire at the expense of the United State, and to write a book. . . . I repeat this mission is not created for the country, but invented for a man; and he is now waiting to take it, and to go and bump his head nineteen times against the ground, in order to purchase the privilege of standing up before his Celestial Majesty." *Congressional Globe,* 27th Congress, 3d Session, pp. 391–392.

48. Adams's disgust seemed to boil over. "Webster's political profligacy is gigantic," he declared. Adams, *Memoirs,* XI, 335, 337, 340.

49. Ibid, XI, 335, 337.

50. Tyler, ed., *Letters,* II, 247–255.

Adams wrote his letter to Everett, which Webster dispatched via a diplomatic pouch. The secretary also wrote Everett to tell him of his reassignment. "The appointment gives, I think, universal pleasure." He followed this up by referring to rumors circulating in Washington and in the newspapers that "the object of nominating you to China, is to make way for your humble servant to go to London." Then, without batting an eye, he disclaimed any desire for the post. "In the present state of things, I have no wish to go to England," he lied, "—not the slightest." Even if the place were vacant, he continued, "I would not accept an appointment to fill it, unless I saw that something might be done.... At present I see little or no prospect of accomplishing any great objects."[51]

Everett equivocated for a short time but then declined the appointment. Fortunately this unpleasant episode did not rupture the relationship between the two men. Everett chose to excuse Webster for being "terribly selfish" and entertaining ideas "of supplanting me" and "discrediting me." He apparently believed that genius can be forgiven anything, even treachery.[52]

The administration then turned to another Webster friend, Caleb Cushing, who had been rejected three times by the Senate as secretary of the treasury.[53] Cushing was named after Congress had adjourned, so he received a recess appointment. Fletcher Webster was made secretary to the mission to provide another position now that his father was about to leave office.

Actually Webster thought more of the China mission than just a means of getting himself back to England. "I consider it a more important mission than ever proceeded from this Country," he told Thomas Curtis, "& the more important than any other, likely to succeed it, in our days."[54] And it is clear from his subsequent actions that he meant what he said. He issued a circular on March 20, 1843, asking those persons familiar with China to provide the State Department with information and advice about ways in which friendly relations and "commercial intercourse between the two countries" could be advanced.[55]

He incorporated many of the recommendations and suggestions he received into the May 8, 1843, instructions for Cushing. These instructions reminded the commissioner that his mission was "to produce a full conviction on the minds of the Government and the people that your Mission is entirely pacific." But the "leading object of the Mission ... is to secure the entry of

51. DW to Everett, March 10, 1843, in *PD*, I, 897. Webster repeated his disclaimer to others, insisting he was "too poor" to accept the appointment, unless called upon to "make sacrifices" out a "a high sense of duty" to his country. DW to Robert Letcher, February 21, 1843, in *PC*, V, 274.

"Is there an escroc [swindler] in a penitentiary who could match that for prevarication?" wrote John Quincy Adams in his diary about another of Black Dan's controversies at this time. Adams, *Memoirs*, XI, 337.

52. Everett to DW, April 3, 18, 1843, in *PC*, I, 905–907, 910–912.

53. Tyler nominated Cushing for secretary of the treasury on March 3, 1843, and the Senate rejected it, twenty-seven to nineteen. Tyler then resubmitted the nomination twice on the same day. Each time it was rejected, twenty-seven to ten, and twenty-nine to two. *Journal of the Executive Proceedings of the Senate*, pp. 178, 179, 186, 187.

54. DW to Curtis, March 12, 1843, in *PC*, I, 900.

55. Circular, March 20, 1843, ibid., I, 901–902.

American ships and cargoes into these ports ["Amoy, Ning-po, Shang-hai, and Fow-chow-fow"], on terms as favorable as those which are enjoyed by English merchants." You will at all times maintain "the equality and independence of our own country." You are not to kowtow; be respectful toward Chinese officials, but make them aware that you are a "peace bearer from a great and powerful Nation. Finally, you will signify, in decided terms, and a positive manner, that the Government of the United States would find it impossible to remain on terms of friendship and regard with the Emperor, if greater privileges, or commercial facilities, should be allowed to the subjects of any other Government, than should be granted to citizens of the United States."[56]

These instructions established the first important American policy toward China and became a "cornerstone" for the Open Door doctrine of 1899–1900. It led immediately to the signing of the Treaty of Wanghia on July 3, 1844, which provided the United States with a most-favored-nation guarantee. In achieving this treaty, Caleb Cushing proved to be an excellent diplomat, another wise choice on the part of the President and the secretary.

Webster's instructions to Cushing, along with the Tyler Doctrine, which he wrote in 1842, have justly merited him recognition as a "pioneer" in establishing American foreign policy toward East Asia and the Pacific.[57]

The Tyler Doctrine set down for the first time this nation's foreign policy toward the Pacific region and especially toward the Hawaiian Islands that ultimately led to their annexation in 1898. Not much attention had been paid to these islands, known at the time as the Sandwich Islands, although a treaty of friendship, a treaty that was never submitted to the Senate for ratification, had been signed by Commodore Thomas ap Catesby Jones with local chieftains in 1826. But New England merchants and traders, along with missionaries, enlarged American interest in the islands over the following twenty years. By the time Webster assumed the headship of the State Department, Americans had come to dominate the economic life of the islands, centering their interests on whaling, essential imports, sugar, and sandalwood. The islands also had obvious strategic value for the Alaskan and China trade.

In March 1842 King Kamehameha III wrote a letter to President Tyler requesting his aid in establishing a convention with Britain and France that would recognize the independence of the Hawaiian kingdom. The Reverend William Richards and Timoteo Haalilio, a native chieftain and private secretary to the king, carried the letter to the President, arriving in Washington on December 5, 1842. Three days later, December 7, they met with Webster. Richards reported that the secretary not only seemed cold—Webster frequently behaved this way with unwanted visitors—but "appeared to know little about the Islands or Mr. [Peter A.] Brinsmade," an earlier emissary of the king's who had informed the secretary about the "numerous and obvious" benefits to be gained in Hawaii.

---

56. For examples of the advice Webster received, see Thomas Perkins to DW, April 3, Edwin Leis to DW, April 20, and John Forbes et al. to DW, April 29, 1843, ibid., I, 903–904, 912–915, 917–921; DW to Cushing, May 8, 1843, ibid., I, 922–926.

57. *PD*, I, 884.

But Webster was wary of making any commitment or getting involved. He purposely approached the issue very cautiously and so put them off.[58] Adams later suggested to the envoys that Webster's behavior could be explained by the fact "that they are black" men, which was a deliberate and malicious smear.[59]

Webster's attitude changed completely when the two envoys declared that if they failed to secure recognition for Hawaiian independence, they would place the islands under the formal protection of Great Britain.

That did it. In an instant the secretary became more accommodating. An interview with the President, which he had earlier backed away from, was quickly arranged, and the two men met with not only Tyler but the entire cabinet. Richards described the interview in his journal as "pleasant free and full."[60]

Between December 7 and 29 Webster met seven times with the envoys and asked them to place their request in writing, as they did on December 14. At a subsequent meeting with them on December 29 the secretary read a letter of response that Richards characterized as "not quite what I wanted," but he conceded that "others think it is well."[61] However, since Webster now whole-heartedly approved of Hawaiian independence, he promised to assist the two men in every way possible. Adams pointed out that the letter, which he regarded as "in language not very explicit, evades a direct acknowledgement [of Hawaiian independence], and declines the negotiation of a treaty, but argues the right of the Sandwich Islands to be recognized as an independent State, and against the right of any European power to colonize or take possession of them." Adams summed up the letter precisely.

This letter contained the kernel of what came to be called the Tyler Doctrine, a foreign policy statement that can be found in Tyler's message to Congress, written by Webster and delivered on December 30, 1842, which also spelled out U.S. policy toward China. The message presented an elaborate and able argument for the recognition of the Sandwich Islands government and for the purposes of the mission to China. Taken as a whole, it centered on the question of American interests in the entire Pacific region.

The sections on Hawaii and China dealt with specific concerns involving those two areas. The Hawaiian section came first, and Webster repeated much of the wording of the letter he read to Richards and Haalilio. But the message went on to note the overall importance of the islands to American interests, declaring that it "could not but create dissatisfaction on the part of the United States at any attempt by another power, should such attempt be threatened or feared, to take possession of the islands, colonize them, and subvert the native

58. "Journal of William Richards," December 7, 1842, in Harold Whitman Bradley, *The American Frontier in Hawaii: The Pioneers, 1789–1843* (Stanford, Calif., 1942), pp. 407, 441; Brinsmade to DW, April 8, 1842, in *PD,* I, 858–865.

59. Adams, *Memoirs,* XI, 275. Besides, Richards was white.

60. "Journal of Richards," December 7, 1842, pp. 442–443.

61. Haalilio and Richards to DW, December 14, 1842, DW to Haalilio and Richards, December 19, 1842, *PD,* I, 866–871; "Journal of Richards," December 30, 1842, p. 443; Adams, *Memoirs,* XI, 284.

Government." This Tyler Doctrine was awkwardly worded in part and not as potent as the Monroe Doctrine in describing the American attitude toward any attempt at colonization; still, it got its point across quite well. The message went on to say that the United States desired "no peculiar advantages, no exclusive control over the Hawaiian Government, but is content with its independent existence and anxiously wishes for its security and prosperity." Should "an opposite policy by any other power" be adopted, the United States would be justified "in making a decided remonstrance." In effect, this message extended to the Hawaiian Islands the noncolonization, nonintervention principles of the Monroe Doctrine, principles that remained in effect until the islands were annexed in 1898.[62] But not until 1844 did the United States recognize the independence of Hawaii, following the lead of France and Great Britain.

Caution best characterizes Webster's approach to the issue of Hawaiian independence. More than anything else, he wished to protect the interests of American merchants, whalers, entrepreneurs, and missionaries. But he was leery of going beyond that. So he crafted the Tyler Doctrine to safeguard these interests and prevent foreign powers from abrogating them.

As for China, he did not expect the immediate establishment of full "diplomatic functionaries" in that country, but he thought the Congress should appropriate funds for a commissioner "to reside in China to exercise a watchful care over the concerns of American citizens and for the protection of their persons and property."[63]

In the message Webster noticed the presence of American missionaries in the Pacific area but dealt more specifically with their problems abroad when he was asked to address incidents occurring in the Ottoman Empire and Denmark.

The retired naval officer Commodore David Porter, a hero of the War of 1812, served as the U.S. representative to the Ottoman Empire. Like all previous diplomats abroad, he tended to regard American citizens living in the empire as merchants, nothing else. But missionaries were very active in the Middle East, so much so that the patriarch of the Maronite Church in Syria begged the sultan to expel them. The government of the empire asked Porter to aid in the removal, citing the terms of the commercial treaty the United States had signed with Turkey in 1830. The missionaries objected and demanded of Porter "the rights common to all American citizens"; however, the commodore insisted there was nothing he could do.[64]

The nonsectarian American Board of Commissioners for Foreign Missions then took the problem to Webster. Writing for the board, of which he was a member, Samuel Armstrong[65] stated that Porter had construed the treaty of

---

62. Richardson, *Messages and Papers*, III, 2064–2065.

63. Ibid., III, 2067.

64. Eli Smith et al. to Jasper Chasseaud, July 20, Porter to Chasseaud, October 14, 1841, in *PD*, I, 272–279.

65. Armstrong was a Whig, a wealthy publisher of religious works, and a former mayor of Boston and governor of Massachusetts whom Webster had opposed in 1835, calling him a self-made man "of the common people." He ran as an independent against Edward Everett. Boston *Morning Post*,

1830 with Turkey as strictly commercial and did not extend the "customary patronage and protection . . . to our missionaries" that are bestowed on merchants. They are therefore "denationalized" and must go to the British for protection. Please help us.[66]

Webster readily complied. For the first time in American diplomatic history he issued a formal declaration, via a letter to Porter, in which he instructed the commodore "to extend [to missionaries] all proper succor and attentions, of which they may stand in need, in the same manner that you would to other citizens of the United States, who, as merchants, visit or dwell in Turkey." In the future "this Government expects from its representatives abroad" full "aid and protection . . . in all cases, where citizens of the U. States are concerned." Happily the missionaries were not expelled.[67]

The Denmark situation developed from the persecution of American Baptists in that country. Responding to an appeal from the Baptist General Convention for Foreign Missions, based in Boston, Webster instructed the U.S. minister to Denmark, Isaac Jackson, to provide "your official intervention to shield" two representatives sent by the board of the Baptist Convention to intercede with the Danish government on behalf of their fellow Baptists. Webster expected Jackson to protect them "from any oppressive treatment to which they may be subjected in the discharge of their duties."[68]

Both these incidents generated considerable excitement in the United States. Separation of church and state was one thing; denial of basic American rights abroad was quite something else. As secretary of state Webster inaugurated the policy that thereafter extended official protection to American missionaries serving in foreign lands.

The Webster-Ashburton Treaty, the Tyler Doctrine, the instructions to Cushing, the policy of self-defense, the release of the Santa Fe prisoners, the formulation of the "McLeod law" concerning federal jurisdiction in matters dealing with foreign affairs, the insistence on upholding the rights of Americans traveling abroad, and the repeated attempts to foster the opening of trade relations with all nations so as to gain international respect for the United States and foster the nation's economic growth—all these constitute Webster's enduring achievements as secretary of state.

But Webster himself believed that his greatest achievement had been the preservation of "the peace of the world" by eliminating the dangerous irritants in the relations between Great Britain and the United States.[69] And he was correct. He earned and deserved the title of peacemaker.

January 15, 1836. Interestingly, James Richards, the older brother of William Richards, the envoy of King Kamehameha, helped found the ABCFM.

66. Armstrong to DW, January 31, 1842, in *PD*, I, 279–280.

67. DW to Porter, February 2, 1842, ibid., I, 280–281.

68. DW to Jackson, April 12, 1842, ibid., I, 264–265. Webster succeeded in convincing the Danish government, like the governments of Britain and Sweden-Norway, to reduce the fee it imposed on vessels passing through the sound, the main entrance to the Baltic Sea, on their way to Russia.

69. DW to Everett, April 27, 1843, in ibid., I, 930.

35

"The Return of the Prodigal Son"

IN VIEW OF his many accomplishments for the nation as secretary of state, Webster had made the right decision in refusing to resign in 1841. But he had paid a huge personal and political price. And it had now become unbearable. With Tyler moving ever closer to the Democrats for advice and support, with his increased determination to pursue a policy of annexing Texas, which his secretary of state strongly opposed,[1] and with the Whigs unrelenting in their demands for his resignation, Webster finally decided he must go. Each day he watched how his influence with Tyler waned. For example, on March 3, 1843, he urged the President *not to sign the bill*" repealing the bankruptcy law. Tyler signed it anyway.[2] He also vetoed the new tariff bill against Webster's strong appeal. There then began a systemic effort on the part of the President to "compel him to resign out of sheer self-respect; make him feel that he was in the way; treat him coldly; never consult him, and pay little or no attention to what at any time he might propose or bring before the council-board; give him a cold shoulder and averted looks." There followed periods when the two men hardly spoke to each other. The secretary surely did not deserve this cowardly treatment, considering his services to the administration, but "as Mr. Webster could not be trusted [with respect to Texas], he must be got rid of."[3]

Another factor in deciding Webster's course of action was the state of the nation's economy. The depression triggered by the Panic of 1837 had not yet run its course. The opening months of 1843 recorded the low point in the depression. It had been Webster's hope that as an important official of the administration he could use his influence and authority to help restore the nation to economic health. His correspondence during the two years of his tenure as

1. The Texas chargé d'affaires to the United States, Isaac Van Zandt, said that Webster stood in the way of annexation. Van Zandt to Anson Jones, March 15, 1843, in Tyler, ed., *Letters*, III, 129.

2. DW to Tyler, March 3, 1843, in *PC*, V, 277–278.

3. Sargent, *Public Men and Events*, II, 199; John Pendleton Kennedy to Winthrop, April 30, 1843, Winthrop Papers, MHS.

secretary of state suggests "something like a pledge to the business and banking communities" that he would remain in office until prosperity returned. He realized now the "futility of failure of his efforts." The only sensible course was to submit his resignation.[4]

Naturally some of his business and banking friends, as well as his wife, urged him to remain in office. "If you go," wrote Nicholas Biddle, "who is to take your place? . . . Some cobweb spinner.—So stay—stay."[5]All of which was very kind and friendly. But it did not help. As he said many times, his resignation was "inevitable." On May 8, 1843, he placed it in Tyler's hands. And the President responded most graciously. He thanked Webster for "the zeal and ability" with which he had discharged "the most delicate and important negotiations." Moreover, "you have manifested powers of intellect of the highest order, and in all things a true American heart."[6]

Unfortunately the administration's mouthpiece, the *Madisonian,* reported that the President had given Webster *"permission to retire."* When they read this notice, some Whigs blanched. "O Gog and Magog!" snorted Philip Hone. "John Tyler pleased to grant Daniel Webster permission to retire from office! Daniel Webster, the personification of pure Whig principles, consorting with treachery and corruption—a giant shrinking before a dwarf—Daniel Webster standing, cap in hand, before John Tyler, like a hard-pressed schoolboy, asking from the pedagogue permission to *go out.*" Quite possibly, Hone added, necessity "may have something to do with the humiliation of intellectual greatness."[7]

Webster left his office knowing that his political influence and position in his party had been totally shattered. "Popularity seems to fall from him," wrote Harrison Gray Otis, "like the dew from the wings of a duck."[8] He had gained so much political influence because of the enormous assistance he had provided Harrison in the election of 1840, only to lose it all serving Tyler. "Frozen out," a pariah to his fellow Whigs, he was as broken down a politician as his bitterest enemy could wish.[9]

For that reason his friend William W. Seaton, in an attempt to bring about a reconciliation between Webster and the Whigs, decided to give one of his famous "stag" supper parties and invited a large number of congressmen. The festivities had just begun when Webster entered, looking very dignified. He glanced around the room. At that a southern senator called out: "Gentlemen, I have a sentiment to propose—the health of our eminent citizen, the negotiator of the Ashburton Treaty."

4. *PC,* V, 265.

5. Biddle to DW, February 27, 1843, in McGrane, ed., *Correspondence of Biddle,* pp. 344–345.

6. DW to Tyler, May 8, Tyler to DW, May 8, 1843, in Curtis, *Webster,* II, 211–212. The department was taken over on an interim basis by Attorney General Hugh S. Legaré. Later Tyler appointed Abel P. Upshur to the post.

7. Hone, *Diary,* II, 652.

8. Otis to George Harrison, September 9, 1842, Otis Papers, MHS.

9. Abbott Lawrence to Everett, October 3, 1843, Everett papers, MHS.

Webster instantly responded: "I have also a sentiment for you,—The Senate of the United States, without which the Ashburton Treaty would have been nothing, and the negotiator of that treaty less than nothing."

The group applauded enthusiastically. His quick and appropriate response "banished every doubtful or unfriendly feeling." The evening turned into a love feast.[10]

But this was only a beginning. It would take time before Whigs would forget that he had turned his back on them, that he had countenanced and sustained "the treachery of John Tyler." Still, they also remembered his great services to the party: "the overshadowing majesty" of his speeches on the Bank, removal of the deposits, and Jackson's vetoes. Nor could they forget that he was the incomparable "expounder of constitutional doctrines held by them." Given time to reflect, both the Whigs and Webster would recognize that they needed each other. Almost immediately the former secretary of state showed that he understood what was expected of him. "No imperiousness marked his bearing, but rather the humility of the prodigal son."[11]

But this prodigal son harbored deep resentments. The first and greatest of them harkened back to 1836, when he had run for the presidency. "There was no Kentucky candidate before the People; there was a Massachusetts candidate. *How did Kentucky act?*" Eight years later he still remembered, and it gnawed at him. "I have some degree of self-respect, & some pride; & shall certainly submit to no sort or degree of ill treatment. And such, I must confess, I think I have recd." Furthermore, he had worked for months to complete a treaty with Great Britain and prevent a war nobody wanted. And "it never recd. a word of commendation, from certain leading Whigs." No one is obliged to praise, he granted. Commendation must be voluntary. "But, then, if to withhold approbation be no injury, to be complained of, gross abuse, personal & political, is such an injury; & you know how freely that has been bestowed on me. I have been attacked & vilified by such men as Garrett Davis, [John Minor] Botts [of Virginia], Jno. C. Clark [of New York], [Kenneth] Rayner, & many others, in Congress, all of them being most especial friends of Mr Clay."

Still, he knew that a continued feud could do irreparable damage. "Much consideration, wisdom, & conciliation" must be exercised. "We must have a hearty *union,* or the prospect [for the next election] is hopeless. That, we must all be convinced of." For his part he wished "well to the Whig cause, & am ready to make all reasonable sacrifices to insure its success." He could never abandon Whig principles. "I am as willing, now, as I ever was, to exert my faculties for the continued support, & further diffusion, of those principles. . . . I must live & die, as I was born, a 'Whig.' "[12]

10. Poore, *Perley's Reminiscences,* II, 311.

11. Sargent, *Public Men and Events,* II, 200.

12. DW to Robert Letcher, October 23, 1843, in *PC,* V, 315–317. Robert C. Winthrop said Davis, Botts, and Rayner kept up a "daily attack" on the former secretary. Winthrop to Nathan Hale, February 1843, Hale Family Papers, LC.

So Webster bade his friends in Washington farewell, packed his belongings, and leased his house for three years to the new British minister, Richard Pakenham, for twelve hundred dollars. Pakenham also agreed to purchase an unspecified amount of furniture. What the minister did not buy was auctioned, and the remainder shipped to Marshfield. "It is an awful business, this breaking up," Webster moaned.[13] He notified Seth Weston, one of his employees at Marshfield, of his homecoming and gave specific instructions about his needs and expectations. He wanted all the boats, sails, and oars placed in good order, especially *The Julia*, which had leaked a good deal on his last visit. That said, it was time for him to depart the Washington arena. "It is high time for me to catch a fish or two."[14]

On May 15, 1843, he headed home. He had no particular plans at the moment except to rest, fish, shoot, farm, and build a room for a library. "The change is something," he commented, "but not altogether disagreeable." In time he would resume a more active law practice, and he fully expected to return to Washington to plead before the Supreme Court, although he had to confess that around the Capitol "I always thought ex-Congressmen, ex Secretaries &c. doleful images." At the age of sixty-one Webster sometimes wallowed in self-pity, but he retained his sense of humor, and that helped him ease past the worst of it.[15]

Life at Marshfield also helped. There he usually rose at three or four o'clock in the morning—he needed only six hours of sleep—and believed it was the most "attractive" part of the day. He often described the morning as "sweet and fresh and delightful." The stillness especially appealed to him. He liked to be alone, and he would sit and watch the sun rise. Then he would inspect his cattle, both "foreign and domestic," which by this time had grown to a sizable number. Their "sleek sides," noted one visitor, "bear the comfortable signs of milk, butter, and cheese." Or he might examine all the vegetables he grew from "diminutive bean up to the unwieldy pumpkin." After that he went to his library to write letters before breakfast. Later he might plow a field or go hunting or fishing. But his passion was the sea. He loved to sail and always maintained "a well-appointed fishing-boat." Many times Webster, rigged out in a loose coat and trousers and wearing a slouched hat, set sail before dawn and stayed out until long after dark. Otherwise he had dinner at four or four-thirty, played whist in the evening, and generally retired no later than ten o'clock.[16]

And he entertained—again lavishly. His great friend Philip Hone reported that he "is the very perfection of a host. At one moment instructive and eloquent, he delights his guests with the charms of his conversation . . . sings snatches of songs, tells entertaining stories, and makes bad puns." Here was the Webster

13. Richard Smith to DW, February 27, DW to Edward Curtis, March 8, 1844, in *PC*, VI, 33, 35.

14. DW to Weston, March 12, 1843, in Webster, ed., *Private Correspondence*, II, 169–170.

15. DW to Everett, May 12, November 30, 1843, in *PC*, V, 303–304, 321–322.

16. Curtis, *Webster*, II, 216–222; Hone, *Diary*, II, 737, 739.

only intimates saw. "There were few gayer or more valued associates on a fishing or sailing party," said Hone. Outsiders, on the other hand, generally thought him "cold, grave and stern." At dinner, according to Hone, Webster presided at the table "with the grace and elegance of high breeding." Needless to add, the food and wine were superb.[17]

Webster made very few speeches for the remainder of 1843—four in all. He gave a Bunker Hill speech (his second) on June 17,[18] a speech on agriculture in Rochester, New York, on September 20 and 21,[19] and an address on the "Landing of the Pilgrims" before the New England Society of New York on December 22.[20] Then, when the Whigs of Essex County invited him to address their convention, which was to meet in Andover on November 9[21]—his Bunker Hill oration[22] proved to them once again how much they needed and relied on his great talents—he readily accepted.[23] By accepting such invitations, he hoped to make his way back into the good graces of both the Massachusetts and New England Whigs. In his speech at the convention he reaffirmed his commitment to the party and its principles concerning the tariff and banking. But he did not apologize for his previous statements and actions; in fact he defended them. He protested his steadfast loyalty as a Whig.[24]

This initial process of "rehabilitation" gathered momentum when a group of New Hampshire Whigs asked his permission to present his name as a candidate for the presidency when the national party held its nominating convention in May 1844. Webster did not have a ghost of chance, and he knew it. Everyone conceded that Clay would get the nod. But the request demonstrated that his hold on the affections of a large segment of New England Whigs had not weakened. He naturally declined, but he did it gently and in delicately phrased language. The opinion of others, he said, "is generally and strongly set in another direction," he declared, and therefore he asked his supporters "not to oppose . . . the leading wishes of political friends." Both the invitation—signed by more

17. Hone, *Diary*, II, 736–740; Greeley, *Recollections*, p. 250.

18. *W&S*, I, 259–283.

19. Ibid., XIII, 172–195.

20. Ibid., III, 201–216.

21. Ibid., III, 159–185.

22. The President and his cabinet attended. "And there was the immortal Dan," the newspapers reported, "the orator of the day, who added the brightest and the greenest leaf to the chaplet which adorns his brow, by the oration with which he invested with the *toga virilis* the monument, the offspring of New England patriotism, in strains of eloquence bright and impressive as those in which he announced its birth. . . . No praise can do it justice, no extract can be fairly made, no passage can be selected as unequaled, while all are unsurpassed in the same great oration." Hone, *Diary*, II, 661–662. John Quincy Adams thought otherwise. "What a name in the annals of mankind is Bunker Hill! what a day was the 17th of June, 1775! and what a burlesque upon them both is an oration upon them by Daniel Webster, and a pilgrimage of John Tyler, and his Cabinet of slave-drivers, to desecrate the solemnity by their presence! . . . Daniel Webster is a heartless traitor to the cause of human freedom." Adams, *Memoirs*, XI, 383–384.

23. Stephen Phillips to DW, October 15, 1843, in *PC*, V, 314–315.

24. *W&S*, III, 159–200.

than a thousand New Hampshire Whigs—and his response were widely circulated, and they greatly aided Webster's full return to the good graces of the party establishment.[25]

That fact became more evident when the Massachusetts Whigs turned to him as their candidate to replace Rufus Choate in the Senate.[26] Choate had replaced Webster in 1841 but now wanted desperately to return to private life. So David Sears sounded out the fallen idol. "You were the Peace-maker of the Nation," Sears wrote. "Will you not again come forward . . . and regardless of personal considerations gain for us a second time the objects of our struggle?" One compelling reason why Sears and others wanted Webster back was the fact that the tariff would soon come up for revision, and they needed his powerful voice and intellect in Washington to protect their interests.[27]

Webster hesitated, citing "weighty private reasons." He pointed out to Sears that in returning to the bar, "I am now earning and receiving fifteen thousand dollars a year," which he would have to sacrifice if he returned. Perhaps "after this Congress," I will know better if "I could possibly afford it," and, if still wanted, I could be persuaded to accept. To put it another way, his friends would have to guarantee financial support once more if they wanted him back in Washington. They did, of course, but it was all the Whigs could do to persuade Choate to fill out his term until this Congress adjourned.[28]

The invitation reinforced Webster's feelings that his long sojourn with Tyler was forgiven and (maybe) forgotten. It also helped that upon his return to Washington to argue for the plaintiff in *Vidal v. Girard's Executors* [29] he repaired his relationship with several Whigs outside New England. Up to this time that relationship had not been good, especially in the capital. Indeed anytime he appeared in Washington "few or none of the prominent Whigs called on him. He felt the neglect: he was uncomfortably isolated." And when Senator Choate of Massachusetts tried to tell his colleagues what Webster thought about certain issues, he got a frigid look. In fact on one occasion Henry Clay supposedly responded, "Who cares a d--n about what Webster thinks?"

On this particular visit to Washington by Webster, Choate tried to bring about a reconciliation with John Minor Botts, Willie P. Mangum, Alexander Barrow, James F. Simmons, William S. Archer, Nathan Sargent, James T. Morehead, and a few others. "The return of the prodigal son" was to be achieved through "a feast of Southdown mutton." It turned into quite an affair. At first there was a chilly reception when Webster walked into the room, but the New Englander made himself as agreeable as possible. He drank wine with each man,

25. John Haven et al. to DW, September ?, 1843 in *Microfilm Edition* F19/25356; DW to Haven et al., January 3, 1844, in *PC*, VI, 4–6.

26. Perhaps with Webster's own connivance. See Nathans, *Webster and Jacksonian Democracy*, pp. 218–220.

27. Sears to DW, January 27, 1844, in Curtis, *Webster*, II, 238–239.

28. DW to Sears, February 5, 1844, ibid., II, 239–240.

29. 2 Howard 127ff.

taking pains "to conciliate his old friends and restore old feelings." Finally, "as the night wore away and the bottle circulated, cold obstructions wore away, and hearts were warmed into genial conviviality." Webster pronounced the mutton fit for an emperor, and a better judge "probably could not be found on the continent." The evening ended with Webster "once more a *Whig* in full communion with, and good standing in, the party." The former secretary admitted that he had indeed "buried hatchets, &c. &c. I think there is a returning feeling of kindness." In fact some Whigs thought a Clay-Webster ticket would not only permanently heal the breach between the two men but provide the party with an unbeatable combination. Philip Hone now referred to him as "the great man of the East."[30]

His argument in the *Girard* case before the Supreme Court[31] also helped Webster's cause by obtaining for him yet another title: "Defender of the Christian religion"! A wealthy banker, Stephen Girard, had left a sizable fortune to the city of Philadelphia for the founding of a charitable school for poor white male orphans, but he stipulated that religion must be excluded from its curriculum and governance.[32] Webster argued for the heirs, who wanted to break the will on the ground that the bequest was derogatory of the Christian religion and therefore invalid. He spoke for three days, but instead of providing legal arguments, he gave an extended sermon. He narrowed his case to the will's provision excluding clergymen from the school.

> I maintain that, in any institution for the instruction of youth, where the authority of God is disowned, and the duties of Christianity derided and despised, and the ministers shut out from all participation in its proceedings, there can no more be charity, true charity, found to exist, than evil can spring out of the Bible, error out of truth, or hatred and animosity come forth from the bosom of perfect love. No, Sir! No, Sir! If charity . . . turns infidel to the great doctrines of the Christian religion, if it turns unbeliever, it is no longer charity! . . . I . . . do insist, that there is no such thing in the history of religion, no such thing in the history of human law, as a charity, a school of instruction for children, from which the Christian religion and Christian teachers are excluded, as unsafe and unworthy intruders.[33]

One congressman, John Wentworth of Illinois, remembered a member's rushing from the Supreme Court chamber into the House of Representatives shouting, "Preaching is played out. There is no use for ministers now. Daniel Webster is down in the Supreme Court room eclipsing them all by a defence of the Christian religion. Hereafter we are to have the gospel according to Webster."

---

30. Sargent, *Public Men and Events,* II, 209–210; Stanton, *Random Recollections,* p. 151; DW to Edward Curtis, January 11, Biddle to DW, January 9, 1844, in *PC,* VI, 9; Hone, *Diary,* II, 697.

31. According to John Quincy Adams, who had no way of knowing, Webster was to receive "fifty thousand dollars for his share of the plunder" of the estate as his fee. *Memoirs,* XI, 510.

32. John Quincy Adams called it "the infidel provision in Stephen Girard's will." Ibid., XI, 507.

33. *W&S,* XI, 143–144.

Curious to find out what was going on, Wentworth hurried down to the courtroom along with a number of other congressmen. As he walked into the room, he heard Webster say, "Suffer little *children* to come unto Me," accenting the word "children." He repeated the words, only this time he emphasized *"little."* Then, rolling his eyes heavenward and extending his arms, he repeated it a third time. "Suffer little children to come unto *Me.* Unto *Me*—unto *Me*, suffer little children to come."

The audience sat transfixed. "I have heard such stalwarts in the American pulpit as Lyman Beecher, Robert J. Breckinridge, Hosea Ballou, William Ellery Channing, and Alexander Campbell," commented Wentworth, "but Webster overshadowed them all." The former secretary reminded him "of Paul at Mars Hill." At one point in the "sermon" the audience burst into applause, the only time Wentworth ever heard such a demonstration in the Supreme Court.[34]

Why Webster, a reputable lawyer who despised those who practiced law and harangued a court with everything but legal arguments, could deliver this "sermon" is incomprehensible. Was it for political effect to help win his return to the good graces of Whigs? Some thought so. He himself probably thought it a perfectly legitimate and incontestable argument. Whatever the reason it failed to move the Court.

In a unanimous vote the Court found against him and in favor of the validity of the charity. As a matter of fact Story, sitting in place of the absent Taney, was downright contemptuous of Webster's performance.[35]

But not all lawyers found fault with Webster's "sermon." The young George Templeton Strong, a future founder of the law school at Columbia University, could hardly contain his enthusiasm for what Webster had preached. "Have been reading with delight and astonishment," he recorded in his diary on February 15, 1844, "the argument in the Supreme Court of the United States in the Girard will case delivered by—(silence for two minutes and a half, followed by a flourish of trumpets and three claps of thunder in G-sharp)—DANIEL WEBSTER!" Could any one of our "quacking flock of 'statesmen' and politicians" have said anything to equal it? "Though the immortal Daniel is said to be slightly heathenish in private life, and though it is but a forensic argument after all," it gives one hope "to find a man wide awake" who will venture beyond "legal technicalities and deal with a subject in the light of realities and truths."[36]

More important, the clergy reveled in what he had preached. A group of them, representing several denominations, held a meeting in Washington and asked permission to publish his remarks, which they intended to circulate throughout the nation. "The powerful and eloquent argument of Mr. Webster," wrote H. L. Ellsworth, chairman of the meeting, ". . . demonstrates the vital

34. John Wentworth, "Congressional Reminiscences," pp. 35–36. Wentworth attended all three days of Webster's preaching. The first day he had no trouble getting a seat. With difficulty the second day. "But on the third I scarcely found standing-room." Ibid.

35. "Mr. Webster did his best for the other side, but it seemed to me, altogether, an address to the prejudices of the clergy." Story to James Kent, August 31, 1844, in Story, *Life and Letters,* II, 469.

36. Strong, *Diary,* I, 225–226.

importance of Christianity to the success of our free institutions, and its necessity as the basis of all useful moral education; and that the general diffusion of that argument among the people of the United States is a matter of deep public interest."[37]

Webster readily consented. Suddenly he had become "the man for the clergy, and all the clergy of the country."[38] "It is not known when he will 'take orders,' " guffawed the *Pennsylvanian* on February 14.

This outpouring of clerical approval of Webster's performance helped restore his popularity in the country, which the Whig leaders did not fail to notice. But before granting him full pardon for his past sins, many of them wanted to know his position on what had become the leading topic of political discussion—namely, the annexation of Texas. Once Tyler rid himself of Webster the President had moved very rapidly toward annexation, and by 1844 the issue had taken top priority on the national agenda. However, it also involved the question of slavery. The admission of Texas would add another slave state to the Union, and an active, zealous, and rapidly growing number of abolitionists, especially in New England, vehemently opposed the "peculiar institution" and its extension. The Liberty party, formed four years earlier, had met in Buffalo, New York, on August 30, 1843, and nominated James G. Birney to run for President in the next election on a platform that opposed the extension of slavery.

Now, then, where did Webster stand? Abijah Bigelow and others asked him. What were his opinions on annexation, slavery, and the consequences should Texas be admitted? What did he have to say that might help enlighten the public mind?

Webster responded in a letter dated January 23, 1844. He began by reciting what he had said in 1837 when first asked these questions. He had opposed annexation then, and he still opposed it on constitutional, moral, and political grounds. "I regard slavery in itself as a great moral, social, and political evil." He added that he would do nothing "to favor or encourage its further extension."[39] A little later he wrote an even stronger statement.

All wise men & good men regret the existence of Slavery. They think its existence with us, a great blot, in our system, and they hope that the prevalence of humanity, religion, moral improvement, & better notions of what the good of society actually requires, will hasten on the day, without bloodshed or violence, when the whole system shall be abolished. Reason, Religion, Humanity, & a sincere love of Universal Liberty, are the true agents to produce this great & so desirable result.[40]

Continuing his letter to Bigelow, he said he still questioned the constitutionality of admitting Texas. "We have a Republic, Gentlemen, of vast extent & unequalled natural advantages. . . . Instead of aiming to enlarge its resources,

37. Ellsworth to DW, February 13, 1844, in *W&S*, XI, 134.

38. Ketchum to DW, February 21, 1844, quoted in Baxter, *Webster*, p. 166.

39. Abijah Bigelow et al. to DW, January 23, 1844, in *Microfilm Edition* F19/25597; DW to Bigelow et al., January 23, 1844, in *PC*, VI, 12–20.

40. DW to Anthony Colby, May 20, 1844, in *PC*, VI, 160.

let us, rather, to strengthen its Union, to draw out its resources, to maintain & improve its institutions of Religion & Liberty, & thus to push it forward in its career of prosperity & glory."[41]

Not until March was the letter published, and although Webster was not a presidential candidate, nor likely to become one, his letter provided the country with the first and most unequivocal statement about Texas in the 1844 campaign. It "made the President very angry," and rumor had it, Webster wrote, that "I am to be punished, by inflicting blows on my friends." All of which, even if untrue, redounded to Webster's credit among Whigs.[42] Two months later both Van Buren and Clay, the intended presidential candidates of their respective parties, issued statements against annexation.[43]

Although Webster continued to make steady progress in winning favor with the Whigs, he visited Tyler in the White House and was courteously received. But he was disheartened by the removal of many of his own patronage appointees, and his more recent recommendations for appointments were rarely followed, although Tyler assured him that when it happened, it was done "with pain at my inability to oblige you."[44]

Then came really tragic news. His favorite granddaughter, Grace Fletcher Webster, the oldest daughter of his son Fletcher, now in China with Cushing, died on February 7. She was six and a half years old. "Nothing since the death of your mother, & my brother," Webster wrote to Fletcher, "has affected me so deeply as the loss of dear little Grace. There were causes, beside her sweetness & loveliness, which tied her very close to my heart."[45] Remarkably, the day following the child's death, his own daughter, Julia, gave birth to her second daughter, Julia Fletcher Appleton.[46]

Another tragedy of national significance occurred on February 28, 1844, when a gun, the Peacemaker, exploded aboard the battleship *Princeton*. At the time the President and his cabinet, along with a number of distinguished guests, were aboard. Fortunately the President had gone to a cabin when the explosion occurred, but the secretary of state, Abel P. Upshur, the secretary of the navy, Thomas W. Gilmer, and Virgil Maxcy and others were killed, and many were injured. Senator Benton was knocked unconscious and suffered a burst ear-

---

41. DW to Bigelow et al., January 23, 1844, in *PC*, VI, 12–20.

42. DW to Everett, April 1, 1844, in *PC*, VI, 41.

43. For Van Buren's Hammet letter, see Washington *Globe*, April 27, 1844, and for Clay's Raleigh letter, see *National Intelligencer*, April 27, 1844.

44. Tyler to DW, [February 27, 1844,] in *PC*, VI, 33–34.

45. DW to Fletcher Webster, April 1, 1844, in *PC*, VI, 42. Fletcher had two remaining children: Daniel Fletcher Webster, Jr. (1840–1865), and Harriette Paige Webster, born on September 9, 1843, and died on March 2, 1845. To the child's mother, Webster wrote: "This blow came wholly unexpected, and gives me great grief. . . . Grace has been greatly beloved by me, and I had hoped to live, myself, to see her grow up. . . . We can do nothing, my dear daughter, but commend you . . . and ourselves to the mercy of God." DW to Mrs. Fletcher Webster, February 5, 1844, in *W&S*, XVIII, 181–182.

46. Julia now had three children: Caroline Le Roy Appleton, Samuel Appleton, Jr., and Julia Fletcher Appleton.

drum. His escape from serious harm seemed so providential that he subsequently made peace with all his old political enemies, including Daniel Webster, who jokingly called him the "Lord Palmerston of America."[47]

Tyler then named John C. Calhoun to replace Upshur, and between them they arranged a treaty annexing Texas to the United States.[48] Calhoun's appointment alarmed Webster even before the treaty became public knowledge. "We have no doubt the annexation of Texas, (& therefore the extension of slavery, & the establishment, forever, of a predominance of the slave holding interest,) is a matter of active negotiation, at this moment. . . . Mr. Calhoun's appointment . . . is another very fearful omen, in regard to Texas. We hope New England, & all the North, will rise up, like one man, to oppose this abominable project."[49]

The treaty, signed by Tyler and Sam Houston, president of the Texas Republic, was submitted to the Senate, along with several other documents, including Calhoun's letter to the British minister, Richard Pakenham. In the letter Calhoun claimed that the treaty would protect American slavery from British attempts to interfere in Texas to bring about universal emancipation.

That admission convulsed northern abolitionists. Webster said the letter made "sensible people ashamed of their Country. Never did I see such reprehensible sentiment, & unsurpassed nonsense, united. I am utterly astonished at Mr Calhoun."[50]

The Pakenham letter killed the treaty. On June 8, to hardly anyone's surprise, the Senate rejected the treaty by the vote of thirty-five to sixteen. The Whigs and Van Buren Democrats united against it. "The Texas treaty is killed," Webster gleefully commented. "Texas stock will go down to the bottom. But I believe that these recent events may bring Texas into a more respectable condition. If I had means I should buy a little of her stock & lay it by."[51]

In the interim the Whigs held their national convention in Baltimore on May 1 and unanimously nominated Clay for President and Theodore Frelinghuysen of New Jersey for Vice President. The party platform said nothing about Texas.[52] The attempt by some Whigs to propose Webster for second place had been vetoed six months earlier by Clay himself. Publicly Clay said nothing, but privately he warned his friends that Webster could not be trusted. To nominate him "would be shocking to the moral sense of our friends," he said. But the Webster movement found little general support and soon died. It "had a still birth," snickered Clay, "and that without any aid from me."[53]

The day after the nominating convention a Young Men's Ratifying Conven-

47. Chambers, *Old Bullion Benton*, pp. 272–273; DW to Everett, January 28, 1846, in *PC*, VI, 117.

48. The negotiations had been virtually completed by Upshur before his death.

49. DW to Charles Allen, March 13, 1844, in *PC*, VI, 37.

50. DW to Robert Winthrop, April 28, 1844, ibid., VI, 46.

51. DW to Samuel Jaudon, June 11, 1844, ibid., VI, 51.

52. Schlesinger and Israel, eds., *History of Presidential Elections*, I, 807.

53. Clay to Peter B. Porter, October 3, Clay to John Lawrence, October 5, Clay to John M. Clayton, October 10, Clay to John M. Berrien, October 27, 1843, in Clay, *Papers*, IX, 864, 865–866, 868–869, 873.

tion met in Baltimore. A number of Whigs had begged Webster to attend to show "his adhesion to the nominations . . . and to assume the lofty rank among Whigs from which some have thought he was inclined to swerve." Of course he consented.[54] The meeting was presided over by John M. Clayton, and the delegates "by unanimous acclamation" called for Webster to address them. The prodigal son gave an excellent speech, approving the nominations without the least reservation and pledging himself and receiving the pledges of all in his hearing "to an unwavering, united, and zealous support of the people's candidate."[55]

In his speech Webster acknowledged his differences with Clay, but he added, "I know of no great national constitutional question; I know of no great interest of the country, still less . . . in which there is any difference between the distinguished leader of the Whig party and myself. (Tremendous cheering) . . . he is a Whig . . . I am a Whig, and that with regard to the part which I am to act, there is no more doubt, I trust, of my disposition than there is of my duty." We have a name "of lofty renown, a renown that must never be sullied, a name won amid wounds, and scars, and blood, denoting great and self-sacrificing patriotism." We must "preserve the Constitution." Let us so conduct ourselves that if "that grand constitutional structure, the great work of the world, that noble achievement of our fathers shall be destroyed, there shall be no record which shall justly ascribe that catastrophe to Whig violence, Whig misrule, or Whig ambition."[56]

After hearing him speak, the Whigs, in one enormous shout, welcomed the Godlike Daniel back into the fold. As he left the podium, he "was met and shaken by the hand by many of the prominent men on the platform."[57]

Some ten thousand individuals came to this ratifying convention, and as part of the celebration they formed a procession by state, each under its proper banner. Then, with flags, patriotic emblems, badges, "and the weapons of peace," they marched through the streets and passed through triumphal arches, with wreaths and bouquets thrown at their feet, and "cheered on by the bright eyes of the prettiest young women in the world." The "display of banners &c was superb," reported Hezekiah Niles, publisher of *Niles' Weekly Register.* A

54. Webster arrived in Baltimore late in the evening and could not get a room, so he was taken to Philip Hone's room. Hone had already retired when he was awakened "by a man who stood erect and silent at my bedside." At first he thought it was a constable on official business, but with a "rub of my eyes, I perceived the dark brows of *Daniel Webster* hanging over me." Instantly Hone removed his nightcap, "and I sat uncovered in the presence of the great man of the East." Hone, *Diary,* II, 697–698.

55. *Niles' Weekly Register,* May 4, 1844.

56. The speech, "The Nomination of Clay," can be found in *W&S,* XIII, 196–202. Webster also spoke glowingly of Frelinghuysen. "There is not in the country a man of purer character, of a more sober temperament, of more accessible manners, of more fine, unflinching, unbending Whig principles, than Theodore Frelinghuysen." Ibid.

57. Sargent, *Public Men and Events,* II, 224. Reunited at last, Clay said that he and Webster had had no correspondence, "direct or indirect," since 1841. Clay to Nathaniel Beverley Tucker, January 11, 1845, in Clay, *Papers,* X, 189.

prize was given to the state with the largest number of delegates in proportion to its congressional representation. Delaware won with 992.[58]

It quickly became evident in Washington and around the country that Webster's "presence & aid at Baltimore" had brought "great benefits" to the Whig party. It now expected Webster to employ his "presence & aid" in active support of the candidates in the coming campaign.[59]

The Democrats, meeting in the same city on May 27, snubbed Tyler, dumped Van Buren because of his anti-Texas stand, and nominated a dark horse, James Knox Polk of Tennessee, an ardent expansionist—"I was exceedingly surprised at the nomination of Mr. Polk," exclaimed Webster[60]—along with George M. Dallas of Pennsylvania as his running mate. The party platform called for the "reoccupation of Oregon and the reannexation of Texas at the earliest practical period."[61]

With the spirit of "Manifest Destiny"—that is, a belief that "Providence" had given the nation a right to possess "the whole continent" and extend the blessings of liberty and self-government to everyone under its governance[62]— sweeping the country, Clay found it necessary to "reinterpret" his position on Texas. In his Alabama letter of July 1, written in response to a newspaper editorial in the Tuscaloosa *Monitor,* he declared that he personally had "no objection to the annexation of Texas, but I certainly would be unwilling to see the existing Union dissolved or seriously jeoparded for the sake of acquiring Texas."[63]

The letter shocked and outraged many northern Whigs. "Mr Clays letter has caused much depression, & some consternation, among his friends," noted Webster, "& great exultation among his enemies." Then he added, "I feel pretty tolerable angry." It was, commented another, "Mr Clay's political death-warrant."[64] The Kentuckian responded by issuing a second Alabama letter, on July 27, this time to the editors of the Tuscumbia *North Alabamian,*[65] but it only made the situation worse. Democrats accused him of waffling.

58. Hone, *Diary,* II, 697–698.

59. "I ascribe to your influence & wisdom much of the propriety & dignity which marked the proceedings of the Convention," wrote Judge Ambrose Spencer of New York, the father of John C. Spencer, former secretary of war and recently resigned secretary of the treasury because of his opposition to the annexation of Texas. Spencer to DW, June 8, 1844, in *PC,* VI, 50.

60. DW to Robert Letcher, July 5, 1844, ibid., VI, 52.

61. Schlesinger and Israel, eds., *History of Presidential Elections,* I, 799–801.

62. On Manifest Destiny, see Albert K. Winberg, *Manifest Destiny* (Baltimore, 1935), Frederick Merk, *Manifest Destiny and Mission in American History* (New York, 1963), Thomas R. Hietala, *Manifest Design: Anxious Aggrandizement in the Later Jacksonian America* (Ithaca, N.Y., 1985), and Reginald Horsman, *Race and Manifest Destiny: The Origins of American Racial Anglo-Saxonism* (Cambridge, Mass., 1981).

63. Clay to Stephen F. Miller, July 1, 1844, in Calvin Colton, ed., *The Works of Henry Clay* (New York, 1857), IV, 490–491.

64. DW to Edward Curtis, September 1, 1844, in *PC,* VI, 53; Sargent, *Public Men and Events,* II, 244.

65. Remini, *Clay,* p. 660; Poage, *Clay and Whig Party,* pp. 143–144.

He wires in and wires out,
And leaves the people still in doubt,
Whether the snake that made the track
Was going South, or coming back[66]

Webster tried to lend his "presence & aid" to the campaign as much as possible. He called a conference with Whig leaders of New York, headed by Thurlow Weed, to plan strategy. But "Mr Weed is quite desponding," reported Webster. He himself had to be careful what he said in view of his past feud with Clay. "For myself, I shall be dumb," he wrote.[67]

But he gave numerous speeches, all in the East. One event in Albany, New York, drew an estimated fifty thousand people. It began with a procession in front of the courthouse at noon and moved along the main streets to a raised stage in a large, open area to accommodate the crowd. Webster was introduced by the chairman, Samuel Stevens, not as Daniel Webster from Massachusetts "but Daniel Webster of the United States."

And he spoke for three hours! Political discourse really meant something to the American electorate in 1844, and the crowd listened with rapt attention to every word Webster spoke. "I was unfortunately one of the tens of thousands who could not get near enough to enjoy this intellectual banquet," Philip Hone recorded in his diary, "but I witnessed from a distance the commanding figure of the orator, and occasionally caught the sound of his deep sonorous voice." Later Hone read the speech in the newspapers and pronounced it "the best he ever made on such an occasion. It is a clear, sound, uncontrovertible argument in favor of the Whig doctrines of the present day. On the subject of American industry it is glorious. It carries even me beyond the highest point of conviction to which I had ever reached."[68]

In his speech Webster spoke glowingly about the achievements of Washington, Hamilton, and Madison.[69] He discussed the tariff, internal improvements, the needs of farmers and manufacturers around the country, and of course the annexation of Texas. He asserted as a "moral proposition" that the agricultural interest of New York and the adjoining western and southern states "is materially, substantially, and beyond measure benefited by the existence of manufac-

---

66. Quoted in Poage, *Clay and Whig Party*, p. 147.

67. DW to Edward Curtis, September 1, 1844, in *PC*, VI, 53.

68. Hone, *Diary*, II, 712–714.

69. It is interesting that the generation following the revolutionary generation tended to regard James Madison as the great man after Washington. Because of the *Federalist Papers* and later his notes on the *Debates in the Federal Convention of 1787*, he was seen as the most important individual responsible for the establishment of the American system of government, which, as Webster repeatedly argued, was one of the political wonders of the world. Although Thomas Jefferson was given credit as the principal author of the Declaration of Independence, too often he was judged as a political partisan, especially among Whigs. It is a great pity that Americans today do not have the same regard for Madison as did the men and women of the antebellum era. Henry Clay always insisted he was a "Madisonian Republican." Remini, *Clay*, pp. 13, 136, 158, 180, 370 note 17, 402, 436 note 12, 462 note 11, 592.

tures of the North. . . . Sure I am, as sure as I am of any principle, moral or political, that, if there is such a thing as benefiting the agriculture of the country, it is to be accomplished by urging forward manufactures and the mechanical arts. This will multiply the number of consumers, and thus the prices of what they consume."[70]

The spokesman of American industry Daniel Webster was now the darling of the overwhelming number of conservative gentleman of means in the country, who regarded him as America's most eminent champion of capitalism. He particularly praised corporate expansion, arguing that the larger the corporation, the better because more people would benefit from it. These corporations applied capital for the benefit of all. They tended "not only to increase property, but to equalize it, to diffuse it, to scatter its advantages among the many, and to give content, cheerfulness, and animation to all classes of the social system."[71]

Webster repeated this performance in Portsmouth, Trenton, Boston, Springfield, Taunton and Pepperell, Massachusetts, Valley Forge, Philadelphia, and New York City, ending up in Faneuil Hall on November 8. He also presided at numerous meetings, one of which included Whigs "from all the New England States."[72] In many, not all, of his formal addresses at mass gatherings he failed to mention Clay by name, much to the annoyance of Clay's closest friends and allies. Mostly he talked about government, constitutional issues, and Whig principles and policies. At these "great mass-meetings (as they are called) in all parts of the country,"[73] he provided his listeners with a good bit of colonial and revolutionary American history—he fully understood the importance of history to a statesman—and of the great destiny that lay in store for the nation if it remained true to its heritage. The speeches frequently glowed with lyric beauty about the greatness of the country and the advances it had made in just half a century. Americans, both those who heard him and those who read the printed versions of his addresses in the newspapers or pamphlets, savored every word. They were even taught and memorized in schools. Nobody could now accuse him of failing in his duty to the party or its nominees. He had atoned for his dalliance with the "traitor." But never once in all his speeches did he apologize for having remained in Tyler's cabinet. He had served his country, and served it well. Why should he apologize? He stood his ground proudly and defied anyone to deny him his honors.

He also helped deliver his state in the election. Massachusetts gave Clay a whooping twenty-five thousand majority, more than the aggregate ma-

70. *W&S,* III, 219–248.

71. Webster had repeated this message in countless speeches over the past ten years. See, for example, his "Lecture before the Society for the Diffusion of Useful Knowledge," given in Boston on November 11, 1836. *W&S,* XIII, 62–78. See also Melvyn Dubofsky, "Daniel Webster and the Whig Theory of Economic Growth, 1828–1848," *New England Quarterly,* XLII (December 1969), pp. 551–572.

72. All these addresses can be found in *W&S,* XIII, 203–306; DW to Messrs. Bellas et al., August 30, 1844, in Webster, ed., *Private Correspondence,* II, 193.

73. Hone, *Diary,* II, 714.

jority for Polk in New York, Pennsylvania, and Virginia.

"*All Hail Massachusetts,*" cried one prominent Whig. "Glorious old Massachusetts, the cradle of American liberty, the last refuge of good principles."[74]

When Webster spoke in Faneuil Hall on November 8, news indicating Clay's defeat had already begun to arrive. But who could believe it? A third-rate politician from Tennessee, a nobody, a dark horse beating the greatest statesman in the nation! Still, it was true. By a mere 1.4 percent of the popular vote, or 1,337,243 to 1,299,062, James K. Polk had been elected President of the United States. James Birney, the Liberty party candidate, received 62,300 votes. But the electoral vote showed a much wider gap between Polk's 170 and Clay's 105.[75]

Webster could scarcely believe it. "It mortifies my pride of Country to see how the great office of President may be disposed of," he told Everett. It had always been his opinion that "Clay could never be President" after his popularity had been tried and found wanting in 1832, but this time "I thought his election highly probable, & he certainly came near success." He could have triumphed too, Webster argued, "but for two causes;—his Alabama letter,—& a general feeling throughout many parts of the Country, & especially in Western N.Y.—that his temper was bad—resentful, violent, & unforgiving."[76]

In some respects this description fits Webster himself—that is, the part about being resentful and unforgiving. In many ways Clay and Webster had similar characteristics, two of which prevented either of them from becoming President. First, the electorate did not trust them, and second, in temperament and disposition both men were unsympathetic toward the democratic spirit that had evolved in the country over the past several decades. For Webster it was something he had always understood. As he said many times, he did not belong to this generation. Many of his contemporaries shared this understanding. He is "a man of the past," explained Emerson.[77]

Webster tried not to despair. He really believed that "all is not lost. . . . Our cause, the cause of our country, of our common weal, of our common truth is still the same." He then tried to sort out what he regarded were the immediate duties of every Whig in the nation:

To maintain the identity of the Whig party, & the integrity of the Whig cause, to endeavor, as *Whigs* . . . to avoid, at the same time, any change of flag, or the adoption of any new party organization; to reason public questions, through & through, before the people, but without acrimony, reproach, or abuse, to act, in short, on the presumption that the People are reasonable, capable of being enlightened, & of being brought to see & to embrace the truth,—these seem to me to be the heads, in general, of the duties which are now before us.[78]

74. Ibid., II, 720.

75. Schlesinger and Israel, eds., *History of Presidential Elections*, I, 861.

76. DW to Everett, December 15, 1844, in *PC*, VI, 63–64. For a full discussion of the reasons for Clay's defeat, see Remini, *Clay*, pp. 658–667.

77. *W&S*, XIV, 76; Emerson, *Complete Works*, XI, 202, 204.

78. Speech in Faneuil Hall, November 8, 1844, in *W&S*, XIII, 301; DW to David Hall, November 26, 1844, in *PC*, VI, 58.

Webster also mentioned the election frauds and the need for revision of the naturalization laws. The recent sharp rise in foreign immigration, especially among Germans and Irish, produced a growing antiforeign and anti-Catholic prejudice in several states in the early 1830s and 1840s, and it needed to be addressed.

The outbreak of Catholic-Protestant riots in Philadelphia gave birth in June 1843 in New York and Pennsylvania to an organized American Republican party, a nativist association, which demanded stiffer naturalization laws. Whigs in the two states sided with the "Natives." Philip Hone said that the "Whigs abandoned all their local candidates and went en masse for the Native Americans." The existence of this party played a major role in Clay's defeat in New York and Pennsylvania. In Boston, after eight elections that had ended inconclusively, the "Native American," Thomas Aspinwall, was finally chosen mayor. Nativism was a growing political force, and Webster joined the demand for "an efficient reformation of the naturalization laws" to prevent recent emigrants in this country from being marched, on arrival, "to the polls, and to give their votes for the highest offices in the national and state elections." He sincerely believed that these fraudulent votes had contributed substantially to Clay's defeat. But as many Whigs noted, it was "the defection of the Abolitionists," who supported Birney, as well as the Native Americans, that brought about their electoral failure.[79]

The unexpected political deluge that engulfed the Whigs in 1844 and the likely consequences to ensue with a rabid expansionist in the White House convinced Whigs that they must put their best men in Congress in order to block the expected "villainies" that were sure to follow. In Massachusetts that meant returning Webster to the Senate, where his knowledge, leadership, and stature could be put to use. Rufus Choate had refused to stand for reelection, and that made this task easier. The Massachusetts legislature was scheduled to elect the new senator in January 1845, and as far as the Whigs were concerned, there could be no other to replace Choate but the "Godlike Daniel."[80]

But Webster had shown no enthusiasm for resuming life in Washington. For one thing, he still had his financial house to put in order. However, a year before he had let it be known that he might be available, "say March, 1845," if his friends thought that "I should enter the next Congress." He frankly admitted that "I should prefer suitable public employment, to returning to the bar at my age. I have seen enough of courts of law, to desire to be in and among them no more. But my affairs require attention, and the means of living, you know, must be had." He pointedly added that he earned fifteen thousand dollars a year from his profession.[81]

79. Tyler Anbinder, *Nativism and Slavery: The Northern Know Nothings and the Politics of the 1850s* (New York, 1992), pp. 7–13; Remini, *Clay*, pp. 653–654, 663–664; Hone, *Diary*, II, 719; speech in Faneuil Hall, November 8, 1844, in *W&S*, XIII, 301–305.

80. James Schouler, "The Whig Party in Massachusetts," *Massachusetts Historical Society Proceedings*, L (October 1916–June 1917), p. 46.

81. DW to David Sears, February 4, 1844, in *W&S*, XVIII, 182–183.

Shortly after the debacle of 1844, in fact a week after Congress had reconvened in December, the Whigs got a taste of what lay in store for the country under Democratic rule. On December 10 George McDuffie of South Carolina in the Senate and Charles J. Ingersoll of Pennsylvania in the House introduced a joint resolution calling for the annexation of Texas!

Webster was aghast. Apart from the question of Texas itself, such a joint resolution violated the Constitution. A treaty annexing Texas constitutionally required Senate action, not action by the Congress. "I . . . maintain that the Two Houses cannot, by majorities ratify *Treaties,*" he stormed, "because Treaty-making power belongs, exclusively, to the President & Senate." But he understood the motive behind the action. Senate ratification required a two-thirds vote, while a joint resolution required only a simple majority. It was easier to get a simple majority in two houses than two thirds in one. Besides, the Senate had already demonstrated that a two-thirds vote was impossible when it had rejected a Texas treaty the previous June. "Truly," Webster groaned, "our condition is most discouraging. I feel sick at heart, to see the depths of disgrace in which we are sinking. This free Country, this model Republic, disturbing its own peace, & perhaps the peace of the world, by its greediness for more slave Territory, & for the greater increase of Slavery!"[82]

Well, then, would Webster allow his name to go forward as a candidate for the Senate? "I feel little inclination to return to that area of strife," he confessed. But what was his alternative? Some other "suitable public employment"? And what would that be? Or a return to the bar and more legal cases and the drudgery of attending to his fiscal problems? Still, much as he might loathe facing these money problems, they could not be avoided indefinitely. He owed $41,024 to various individuals, which "must be paid in full." Then there were substantial amounts owed to others who could be put off or ignored because they were close friends, such as Caleb Cushing, to whom he owed $9,000. And there were other debts, many he could hardly remember. But Webster had to admit that the necessity of toiling for the next several years to pay off these everlasting obligations really offended him. "I find a still stronger objection, in the necessity of attending to my own affairs." National politics was in his blood. The country seemed headed toward "disgrace." He was needed.[83]

But the money he would sacrifice by limiting his law practice in order to return to the Senate had to be provided. He had made that quite clear the year before. Twice before his wealthy friends had gotten up a subscription to ease the financial pain of "public employment." So he again invited their help with a promise to provide "certain property" holdings he had in his possession as security for a loan of twenty-five thousand dollars. Remarkably, his friends[84] chose to

82. DW to Robert Winthrop, December 13, 21, 1844, in *PC*, VI, 62, 64. Representative Winthrop of Massachusetts had denounced the resolution. *Congressional Globe,* 2d Session, p. 16ff.

83. DW to Everett, December 15, 1844, in *PC*, VI, 64; undated list of Webster's debts, ibid., VI, 86–87.

84. Some of these men included the Appletons, the Lowells, the Quincys, the Cabots, the Lymans, the Perkinses, David Sears, George Shattuck, John Murray Forbes, Francis Skinner, William W.

be more generous and waved his offer aside. They raised a hundred thousand dollars, mostly through subscription in Boston and New York: sixty thousand in Boston, forty thousand in New York. The Barings, for whom Webster had provided legal advice in the past, were also solicited. Thomas W. Ward, the company's representative in Boston and a member of the Boston Associates, informed Joshua Bates, the present head of the firm in England, that this was a "prelude to an application by and to [Webster's] friends." Ward regarded the former secretary "as a sort of public property. He uses his great powers on the side of the public faith, peace, and good government, and must be sustained, with all his failings. I know what you have done, and the House [of Baring], and in the future I shall conform entirely to the wishes of the House in doing anything for him."

To start, a thirty-seven-thousand-dollar annuity was immediately established in Webster's name with the Massachusetts Hospital Life Insurance Company supervised by David Sears, William Amory, and Ignatius Sargent. It brought in an average income of one thousand dollars, which were directed semiannually to Webster's account. "This Fund," Sears informed him on March 21, 1846, "has been created freely and cheerfully by your friends in evidence of their grateful sense of the valuable services you have rendered your whole country. They have done it without your sanction or knowledge." The income raised was "to be paid over half yearly . . . on [Webster's] demand." When not demanded, the income would form part of a new capital of the annuity and settled on him and his wife for life.[85]

A few disgruntled Whigs, such as Abbott Lawrence[86] and Harrison Gray Otis, still angered by Webster's feud with Clay, would not subscribe, even though they wanted him back in Congress. The subscription reminded Otis of a story he had heard about a similar subscription raised for Charles Fox, British foreign secretary under Lord Grenville. Some questioned the delicacy of providing this money and wondered how Fox would take it. "Take it," responded one wag, "quarterly to be sure!"[87]

Webster had not the slightest problem with this financial arrangement. He simply reasoned that if the wealthy men of Boston and New York wished him to serve in the Senate, they could jolly well pay for it, considering the professional

---

Stone, William Amory, and William Winchester. With few exceptions, the list included all the leading Boston bankers, manufacturers, lawyers, and merchants.

85. DW to David Sears, February 4, 1844, in *W&S*, XVIII, 182–183; DW to David Sears et al., April 24, 1845, in *PC*, VI, 85; Agreement regarding the Webster Annuity, January 5, 1846, ibid., VI, 106–108; Ward to Bates, January 15, 1846, Thomas W. Ward Papers, MHS; David Sears to DW, March 21, DW to Sears, March 26, 1846, in *PC*, VI, 130–131, 137–138. Curtis, *Webster,* II, 286, claims the annuity never amounted to more than $1,135 per annum and ordinarily brought in only $950.

86. Lawrence had stopped contributing to the Webster fund after 1839. Lawrence to Thomas W. Ward, April 29, 1839, Ward Papers, MHS.

87. Otis to George Harrison, February 7, 1845, in Samuel Eliot Morison, *The Life and Letters of Harrison Gray Otis, Federalist, 1765–1848* (Boston and New York, 1913), II, 303–304. At the time he wrote his letter Otis said the subscription was almost filled. See also Darling, *Political Changes in Massachusetts,* pp. 325–326.

income he would necessarily sacrifice. "The contribution which you now make known to me," he wrote to David Sears, "must be placed, entirely, to the account of the friendship and generosity of yourself & the other Gentlemen. Expressions of thanks, however warm & earnest, would, in a case like this, be feeble. I must rest, therefore in the persuasion, that all who have borne a part in this transactions, will believe that it has deeply & profoundly impressed me with the sentiments & emotions, justly belonging to the occasion."[88]

One of the subscribers, John Murray Forbes, a prominent Boston merchant, later wrote that the hundred-thousand-dollar fund "was largely influential in preventing Webster's reaching the presidency by putting him in the position of a candidate subsidized by rich men." He went on to say that political subscriptions "in those days" were "on a small scale and would make a very poor show compared with modern times."[89] Indeed.A southerner sneered that "he [Webster] has never been a Statesman, but a feed advocate all his life."[90]

With Webster's needs satisfied, the Massachusetts upper house on January 16, 1845, unanimously elected him U.S. senator. The previous day the lower house had chosen him over his Democratic rival, Marcus Morton, former governor of the state, by a vote of 186 to 84.[91]

"The Country is yet worth saving," Webster declared. "The Whig party is strong, but it wants good direction. The mere hangers-on upon it—persons without character, or influence, of their own—have really caused it its chief misfortunes. We need your counsel," he told Edward Everett, "& we need your pen."[92]

The party and the country also needed Daniel Webster.

88. DW to Sears, March 26, 1846, in Curtis, *Webster,* II, 287–288.

89. The writer lived until 1890. John Murray Forbes, *Letters and Recollections of John Murray Forbes* (Boston and New York, 1900), I, 118.

90. John R. Mathewes to Calhoun, December 1, 1844, in *Calhoun Papers,* XX, 437.

91. *PC,* VI, 70.

92. DW to Everett, December 15, 1844, ibid., VI, 64.

36

Charges of Official Misconduct

ALTHOUGH still burdened by an oppressive debt—even John James Audubon had to beg him to pay what he owed for three volumes of a double elephant folio of *Birds of America* Webster had purchased in 1836[1]—the newly elected senator felt much relieved by the large subscription (which sold out in a matter of weeks) and the knowledge that it would allow him to maintain his normal standard of living. He had "seen enough of courts of law," he said, and now he could take a case or two if he wished, or if the money involved proved attractive, or if "the rich men" who subsidized him needed his help.

The refusal of Abbott Lawrence to become a subscriber bothered Webster particularly. They had been friends for many years, and Lawrence had been one of his original financial backers, practically from the time of his arrival in Boston. Their relationship had been strained in the election of 1840, when they disagreed over the presidential nomination, but the real split came after the ratification of the Webster-Ashburton Treaty, when Webster remained in Tyler's cabinet and after Black Dan's defiant speech in Faneuil Hall on September 30, 1842. Now the new senator wished to repair the rift, but it was Nathan Appleton who initiated the action. Appleton was related to Webster through marriage, but he was also a close friend and business associate of Abbott Lawrence's. It was an awkward, not to say disagreeable, situation for him, so he wrote to Webster and suggested that he (Webster) write a letter indicating a willingness "to let byegones be bye-gones." Appleton even helped in the composition of the letter, suggesting changes after Webster had submitted it to him to ensure that it would "receive a cordial response from Mr. Lawrence." And the letter worked—at least to some extent. The "intimate and cordial personal relations" were restored, "but it is very apparent that confidence between them never can be restored," claimed John Quincy Adams, who had been shown the correspondence by Lawrence in his "counting-house." Lawrence no longer trusted Webster, that

---

1. The price of the Audubon work was eight hundred dollars, to be paid in four installments. Webster had paid only two hundred when this letter was written. "I . . . am sadly in want of money to assist in the defraying of my expenses," Audubon pleaded, "and I wish you would oblige me by sending me the balance of your account." Webster sent him another two hundred dollars. Audubon to DW, February 3, 1843, in *PC*, V, 268.

was clear. "All Webster's political systems are interwoven with the explorations of a gold-mine for himself," Adams continued, "and all his confidential intimacies with Lawrence have been devices to screw from him, or, by his agency, from others, money by the fifty or hundred thousand dollars at a time."[2]

So the breach was repaired, and a year and a half later Webster wrote to Lawrence from Washington and said, "[I]f I can do any thing for you here, or send you any thing acceptable, it will afford me much pleasure to do so."[3]

Webster would not take his seat in Congress until March 4, 1845, with the inauguration of President Polk, but he headed south shortly after his election to attend business in New York and argue several cases before the Supreme Court in Washington.[4] While in New York he visited with several of the "rich men who subsidized" his return to public office, among them Philip Hone. Hone was very fastidious and believed that "great men, statesmen, divines, eminent lawyers, physicians, and magistrates should dress well." It had an important effect on their fellowmen, he argued. Black was "safest" and never went out of style. "But in this matter of dress one of our great men (than whom there is none greater), Mr. Webster, has a strange fancy. He is not slovenly, but on the contrary tawdry, fond of a variety of colors." Hone could not remember having seen Webster in black, "the only dress in which he should appear." He was rather amused when he met his friend on Wall Street at noon one day and found him wearing "a bright blue satin vest, sprigged with gold flowers, a costume as incongruous for Daniel Webster as ostrich feathers for a sister of charity."[5]

Webster took time out from his visits with his patrons to write to his five-year-old grandson and namesake, Daniel Fletcher Webster, Jr. From the perspective of a man who had just celebrated his sixty-third birthday he offered the child some grandfatherly advice.

> Your mother and father . . . are anxious about your health [ever since Grace died the year before]; but more anxious that you should grow up to be a good man. You bear my name. My friends will all be kind to you, if you behave well. You must love and obey your parents; strive to learn; be kind and gentle to all; do nothing which you think to be wrong; always speak the truth; and remember your Creator in the days of your youth . . . and always treat all members of the family kindly.[6]

Webster returned to Washington to argue a particularly sensitive issue that could have political repercussions since it involved the selling of alcoholic

2. Appleton to DW, August 4, 1845, Appleton Papers, MHS; DW to Appleton, [August 8, 1845], with enclosure, September 11, 1845, Appleton to DW, September 11, 1845, in Van Tyne, ed., *Letters of Webster*, pp. 630–631; Adams, *Memoirs*, XII, 214.

3. DW to Lawrence, February 25, 1846, in *PC*, VI, 125.

4. He argued the Passenger Cases and the License Cases. He also provided a constitutional opinion for Brigham Young and elders of the Mormon Church regarding a charter they had received from the legislature of Illinois four years before and that the current legislature had repealed. Young et al. to DW, February 1, DW to Young et al., March 3, 1845, ibid., VI, 72, 76.

5. Hone, *Diary*, II, 728–729.

6. DW to Daniel Fletcher Webster, Jr., February 10, 1845, in Webster, ed., *Private Correspondence*, II, 198.

beverages and grew out of the temperance reform movement. The case, *Thurlow* v. *Massachusetts,* centered on a law requiring a license for the sale of liquor in quantities less than twenty-eight gallons. Samuel Thurlow was indicted for violating this law and hired Webster to plead his case. "I sincerely hope the license law may be repealed," Webster wrote. "We are attacked about here from all quarters, and by all sorts of weapons; of which the most annoying are laughter and ridicule."[7] On the ground that the Massachusetts law, and similar laws from Rhode Island and New Hampshire, violated the commerce clause of the Constitution they were appealed to the Supreme Court and, taken together, were known as the License Cases.[8]

Since the state licensing law meant the virtual termination of the retail liquor trade and since imported liquor generated tariff revenue, federal and state law collided, Webster argued, and therefore the state law must be voided. He rested his case on the commerce and the supremacy clauses of the Constitution.

The Court disagreed, as he knew it would. "My own opinion," he told his son, "is; That the License laws will be sustained."[9] Unanimously! The Court, in a decision handed down on March 6, 1847, agreed with counsel for the three states that the laws represented a lawful exercise of the state police power.[10]

Webster had better luck when he argued the so-called Passenger Cases in December 1848. These involved laws passed by New York and Massachusetts that levied taxes on passengers arriving in their respective ports, including immigrants, in order to raise money—in the case of New York for a marine hospital and in the case of Massachusetts to prevent the landing of any "lunatic, idiot, maimed, aged, or infirm person."[11] The state courts in both cases upheld the statutes, despite the commerce clause of the Constitution.

Webster shook his head in dismay. "The Massachusetts law levying a tax on passengers, is now under discussion in the Supreme Court," he informed Fletcher. "It is strange to me how any Legislature of Massachusetts could pass such a law. In the days of Marshall & Story it could not have stood one moment. The present Judges, I fear, are quite too much inclined to find apologies for irregular & dangerous acts of State Legislation."[12] It was very discouraging. The protection of property rights, restraints on state legislatures, and the supremacy of federal law clearly enunciated by the Marshall Court, which Webster himself had helped construct, had been muddied by the Taney Court. Now the Court seemed inclined to excuse and encourage the states in their foolhardy and dangerous mischief. The decision in the License Cases only intensified Web-

7. DW to Everett, January 17, 1839, in *W&S,* XVIII, 43. Rufus Choate and Benjamin F. Hallett were Webster's associates in the case.

8. 5 Howard 504. *Thurlow* v. *Massachusetts, Fletcher* v. *Rhode Island,* and *Pierce* v. *New Hampshire.*

9. DW to Fletcher Webster, [January 1848?], in *W&S,* XVI, 490.

10. Six justices, out of nine, wrote separate opinions. Only the issue of slavery, raised by the Rhode Island counsel, kept the judges from agreeing on the reasons for their decision.

11. *Smith* v. *Turner, Norris* v. *Boston.* 7 Howard 283.

12. DW to Fletcher Webster, February 1847, in *PC,* VI, 208.

ster's disillusionment. "I am tired of these Constitutional questions," he grumbled. "There is no Court for them."[13]

In the Passenger Cases Webster concentrated on the commerce clause and tried to remind the judges of the *Gibbons* decision, which he had argued so successfully before Marshall. The Taney Court, in Webster's mind, concerned itself too much with social issues like abolitionism, temperance, and nativism, issues that had generated state legislation that Webster believed conflicted with national interest.[14] He hoped to coax the Court back from the position it had taken in 1837 in the case *New York* v. *Miln,* which sanctioned the use of police power by a state and diminished the effectiveness of the commerce clause as a restraint upon local legislatures.[15] The present situation did not involve a legitimate exercise of police power, Webster contended, but an interference with foreign commerce. The Marshall Court had decided that commerce was an exclusive power of Congress, and the present Court ought to recognize "the sanctity of [past] decisions." "The early decisions of this court were in some measure inherent to the constitution itself," he insisted. "They were, indeed, a part of the constitution." He also made reference to slavery, recognized by the Constitution, especially the restrictions placed on black seamen by southern states. He said that he did not wish to disturb the "peculiar institution," "nor should he lift his finger to do so. It belonged not to him, but to those alone who had power over it."[16]

Webster believed that the decision in this case would be more important to the country than any decision since the *Steamboat* case. He thought that his efforts in the two cases had "done something toward explaining and upholding the just powers of the Government of the United States on the subject of commerce." And this time Webster had a better feeling about how the Court might decide. *"We shall succeed in the cause,"* he ventured. "The passenger law of Mass will *not* be sustained." He sensed that several of the judges might be sensitive to the connection with slavery, which is why he mentioned the subject in his argument.[17]

In a five to four decision the Court invalidated the laws of New York and Massachusetts, just as Webster had predicted. Taney and three other justices dissented. The majority had different reasons for nullifying the laws, Justice McLean reaffirming that Congress had exclusive power to regulate commerce. But the decision resulted in no useful doctrine and showed how divided the Court was over the authority of the states with respect to slavery and over issues raised by the commerce clause.

13. DW to Fletcher Webster, December 29, 1847, in *PLFP,* p. 716.

14. *PLFP,* p. 682.

15. 11 Peters 102

16. *W&S,* XV, 403–404.

17. DW to Blatchford, February 3, 1849, in Curtis, *Webster,* II, 373; DW to [Edward Curtis], January 3, 1849, in *PLFP,* p. 725; DW to Fletcher Webster, [January 1848], in *W&S,* XVI, 490; Baxter, *Webster and the Supreme Court,* pp. 219–220.

Webster had labored long and hard on the Passenger Cases and was happy when the Court finally rendered its decision. "This will probably be and I am content it should be my last" argument over a constitutional question. "I am willing to confess to the vanity of thinking that my efforts in these two cases have done something towards explaining and upholding the just powers of the government of the United States, on the great subject of commerce."[18] Since he was sixty-six years of age when he wrote this letter, he took it for granted "that people begin to say, 'He is not the man he was.' In some respects that is certainly true; perhaps in many."[19]

By the time Webster finally found a moment to take his seat in Congress and consider other issues facing the nation, the joint resolution to bring Texas into the Union by law instead of treaty had passed both houses on February 28 and had been signed by Tyler on March 1, just three days before he was scheduled to leave office. But that did not end the grasping for territorial expansion. In his inaugural address on March 4, 1845, President Polk declared that the United States had a "clear and unquestionable" title to Oregon. During the campaign the Democrats had demanded the "reoccupation of Oregon," right up to the 54°40' parallel. If Polk went ahead with this apparent threat to end joint occupation of the territory, it would constitute the first step in declaring war against Great Britain.

Congress adjourned before Webster could attempt anything like reversing the action on Texas. He would have to wait until the following December, when the new Congress was to assemble, and perhaps he could then find fault with whatever constitution Texas put forward and thereby block its admission as a state. It was a long shot, but he had no other alternative.

He returned to Marshfield, where he spent the summer, interrupted only to eulogize Andrew Jackson, who died on June 8, 1845, at the age of seventy-eight, and his great friend, counselor, and collaborator Associate Justice Joseph Story, who died on September 10, 1845, at the age of sixty-six.[20] Although Webster had disagreed and quarreled with Jackson on a number of issues, especially the BUS, he had given the Old Hero unstinting support in the struggle with the South Carolina nullifiers.[21] They both loved the Union and sought to make it strong.

Story's death was a deep personal loss. The two men had been very close, and they worked together many times to frame legislation and develop legal arguments touching a variety of issues. Critics then and later complained that

---

18. DW to R. M. Blatchford, February 3, 1849, in *W&S*, XVIII, 295.

19. DW to Fletcher Webster, January 29, 1848, ibid., XVIII, 267.

20. He eulogized Jackson before the New York Historical Society and Story before the Suffolk County bar in Boston. These eulogies can be found in *Niles' Weekly Register*, July 5, 1845, for Jackson, and *W&S*, III, 297–302, for Story.

21. Philip Hone wished Webster "had left this duty to be performed by some one else. It was uphill work, not by any means a labor of love, and is very likely to be misunderstood or misrepresented." Hone, *Diary*, II, 733.

Webster never acknowledged completely the debt he owed Justice Story. He used Story, as he did others, and took credit for what did not belong to him. Unfortunately the eulogy for the great jurist did not live up to expectations, perhaps reflecting their differences of opinion in the *Girard* case, perhaps the depth of his own personal feeling. In any event it was a sad ending.

When Webster first returned to Congress, he and Caroline rented a furnished house "about as big as two pigeon-boxes" in a quiet neighborhood on Louisiana Avenue next to the Unitarian church. "The ringing of the bell on Sunday," he said, "is all that we hear from it." Hone thought it a charming place "in one of the back streets." But at least he lived in his own house "as a gentleman should." Webster entertained lavishly, as a gentleman should, and at a dinner Hone attended he served "pickled pork, a quarter of a lamb, fried chicken and nice vegetables, and cool wine. This was a treat, and the more so because our host was in the most exuberant spirits."[22]

When Webster took his seat in the Senate for the start of the Twenty-ninth Congress, in December 1845, momentous changes had taken place. Most important of all was the arrival of a whole new generation of legislators. Still present were Webster, Clay, and several others who represented the second generation, the one that had followed the Founding Fathers in conducting the affairs of the nation. Now a third generation had appeared, one imbued with the slogans and aggressiveness of Manifest Destiny. Expansionists among them greedily looked westward toward the Pacific and greeted with enthusiasm the two new senators from Texas, Sam Houston and Thomas J. Rusk. Webster tried to block the admission of Texas as a state and spoke in the Senate on December 22, 1845, against the joint resolution. He cited many reasons, one of which dealt with the constitution of Texas that prevented the legislature from abolishing slavery. The resolution passed over his objections, as he knew it would, and Texas became the newest slave state in the Union.[23]

Other new arrivals in the Senate included Simon Cameron of Pennsylvania, replacing James Buchanan, who had been appointed secretary of state, Daniel S. Dickinson and John A. Dix of New York, Reverdy Johnson of Maryland, and Thomas Corwin of Ohio. To be sure, any number of second-generation legislators were also present. Returning like Webster to his former seat was John C. Calhoun, replacing Daniel E. Huger, who had resigned. And there were John J. Crittenden from Kentucky, John M. Berrien from Georgia and the onetime attorney general under President Jackson, Lewis Cass of Michigan and recently returned as minister to France, Thomas Hart Benton of Missouri, John M. Clayton of Delaware, and Willie P. Mangum of North Carolina.

Many of the "eagle-screamers of Manifest Destiny"—or "the 54 40s," as Webster called them—rattled the walls around them with cries that sounded

22. DW to George Ticknor, January 24, 1846, in *W&S*, XVI, 442; *Congressional Directory*, 28th Congress, 1st Session, p. 23; Hone, *Diary*, II, 766–767.
23. *W&S*, IX, 55–59.

bold and frightening. In the House a debate began on a joint resolution advising the President to notify Britain that the United States was giving a year's notice that it intended to terminate joint occupation of the territory. A "ruffian spirit" seemed to have emerged in the lower chamber, but Webster believed the Senate, where more "sober feelings" prevailed, would reject any such joint resolution.

The "ruffian spirit" in the House was also reflected in the administration, according to Webster. Secretary of State James Buchanan was "cold, stern, repulsive, & not very gentle," while Polk was "nettled & a little excited." The President seemed to think "his antagonists sharp, captious, & not always quite respectful."[24]

Happily, with each passing week, the revulsion against the possibility of war, which giving notice to terminate the joint occupation could easily precipitate, seemed to grow "in favor of *Arbitration*." The principal *"war feeling,"* said Webster, came from the Northwest. "Those new states, full of enterprise, & fast becoming full of people," have nothing to lose and "look upon war as a pleasant excitement, or recreation." They have no ships, no cotton, no exportable goods and think that war would increase employment, raise the price of their commodities, "& scatter money." Most of the Whigs in Congress said nothing about Oregon and seemed to agree with John C. Calhoun, who favored negotiating a settlement along the forty-ninth parallel, excluding the island of Vancouver. Nevertheless a conciliatory version of the joint resolution passed both the House and the Senate, and Polk signed it on April 29.[25]

Fortunately the British preferred arbitration to conflict, largely because it wished to import needed American grain once the Corn Laws had been repealed. "This is likely to distress our patriots," said Webster. "They cannot get up a fight." He then alerted his friend John Denison, a member of Parliament, that "every good man in the United States would deprecate a War between us & England for . . . [this] poor cold country [Oregon]." Sadly, "we have not an elevated, or able Executive Govt.," and Polk is only known "as a man of mediocrity." Webster expressed the hope that Lord Aberdeen, the foreign secretary, would "keep cool, avoid sharp points, not stand on matters of punctiliousness, nor be quick to find cause of offence, or even of retort." Naturally Denison showed Webster's letter to Aberdeen.[26] What effect or influence it had cannot be determined, but Buchanan and the British minister to the United States, Richard Pakenham, subsequently signed a treaty that divided the disputed terri-

24. Peterson, *Great Triumvirate*, p. 415; DW to Nathan Appleton, January 12, 1846, in *PC*, VI, 110–111.

25. DW to David Sears, January 17, 1846, ibid., VI, 112.

26. DW to George Ticknor, February 21, DW to Denison, February 26, Denison to Aberdeen, March 24, 1846, ibid., VI, 123, 126–127. At approximately the same time that Aberdeen read his letter, Webster delivered an impassioned speech in the Senate attacking the administration's belligerency and calling for a settlement at the forty-ninth parallel. *Congressional Globe*, 29th Congress, 1st Session, pp. 567–596.

tory at the forty-ninth parallel. Polk submitted it to the Senate, which passed it on June 15, 1846, by a vote of forty-one to fourteen. "We have done a *good* days work," Webster gleefully informed a friend. That evening he dined with the British minister and was served "a beautiful dinner: good wine, good taste, and good manners."[27]

During the debates on the joint resolution Representative Charles Jared Ingersoll of Pennsylvania, Webster's old nemesis and the chairman of the House Committee on Foreign Affairs, gave a speech on February 9 criticizing Webster's handling of foreign affairs while serving as secretary of state. He denounced the Webster-Ashburton Treaty as a giveaway of American territory and condemned the proceedings affecting the McLeod and *Caroline* affairs. He also derided the secretary's failure to get the British to repudiate their right of visit and search. If Webster had conducted the negotiations over the Maine boundary properly, Ingersoll said, there would now be no problem over Oregon.[28]

The speech was immediately published in all the leading newspapers. Then, on February 29, in Webster's very presence, Senator Daniel S. Dickinson of New York repeated several of these charges, especially one point about McLeod's attorney's being paid by the American government. Of course he did not know this as a fact himself, since he was citing Ingersoll as his authority, but he hoped it was false.

"It is wholly false." The deep, resonant voice of Webster rang out.

Would Webster care to explain himself? Not at this time, came the reply.[29]

Not until April 6 and 7 did the former secretary reply in a lengthy speech in which he defended his treaty and, according to Ingersoll's grandson, "indulged in such a coarse tirade upon Mr. Ingersoll as has rarely been heard in an elevated body."[30] No question about it, the speech was a dandy.

The first day Webster gave a clear, closely reasoned, and extremely able defense of the treaty itself, complete with a long history of the negotiations, quotations from various documents, dispatches and letters, and the speeches of several individuals. No wonder it took him so long to respond. The research and writing involved in the undertaking were staggering in their scope and thoroughness.

On the second day Webster let Ingersoll have it with both barrels.

Well, now, sir, I say that a series of more direct, unalloyed falsehoods—absolute, unqualified, entire—never appeared in any publication in Christendom. Every allegation here made—every one, would entirely justify the use of that expressive monosylable [sic], which some people are base enough and low enough to deserve to have thrown in their teeth, but which a gentleman does not often like to utter. Every one of them, from beginning to end, is false. . . . [And] this is stated by a man, or a thing, that has a seat in

27. *Congressional Globe*, 29th Congress, 1st Session, p. 1223; Hone, *Diary*, II, 767.

28. *Congressional Globe*, 29th Congress, 1st Session, Appendix, pp. 284–286.

29. *Ibid.*, Appendix, p. 326.

30. William M. Meigs, *The Life of Charles Jared Ingersoll* (Philadelphia, 1900), p. 280.

one of the houses of Congress. . . . Sir, it would be natural to ask, what can account for all this apparent malice? Sir, I am not certain there is any malice in it. I think it proceeds rather from a moral obtuseness, a native want of discrimination between truth and falsehood. . . .

Sir, this person's mind is so grotesque, so *bizarre*—it is rather the caricature of a mind, than a mind. When we see a man of some knowledge, and some talent, who is yet incapable of producing any thing true, or useful, we sometimes apply to him a phrase borrowed from the mechanics. We say, there is a screw loose, somewhere. In this case, the screws are loose all over. The whole machine is out of order, disjointed, rickety, crazy, creaking, as often upside down as upside up . . . and generally incapable of any thing, but bungling and mischief.

Webster then tore into Dickinson, but gently, less fiercely. "I always thought him a man of courteous manners and kind feelings," he continued, "but it cannot be expected I shall sit here and listen to statements such as the honorable member has made on this question, and not answer them." What Webster objected to was Dickinson's repeated insistence that he was being true to the history of the past and wished to tell the truth but then uttered one falsehood after another. If this was how he researched after truth, Webster declared, a collection of his researches "would be a very amusing compilation." If he put them together, "I undertake to say they would sell well. The Harpers [publisher] would make a fortune out of them." People would pay well for "a good hearty laugh."

Webster said that he had told Dickinson right here on the floor that his one remark about McLeod's attorney was false. And what did he do? "Yes, miserable, calumnious, and scandalous as it was, he snatched at it eagerly," repeated it the following day, inserted it into the newspapers, and used his frank to distribute the speech in all parts of New York—enough "to fill a small barn; and pretty bad fodder it would be."

Dickinson protested that what he said was "documentary history" because it was "printed and went to the public from an official source."

"Indeed," Webster responded. "So any falsehood, any vile calumny, that is raked up, no matter what it is, if printed, is 'documentary history.' The gentleman's own speech, according to that, is already documentary history!"[31]

Webster's harangue was as thorough a job of demolition as ever heard in the Senate. He squelched Ingersoll and Dickinson so thoroughly and so devastatingly that future critics in Congress took him on at their own risk when challenging anything he had done or said. He not only had provided a stinging rebuke to his accusers but, more important, had laid out as irrefutable and as forceful a defense of the treaty as could possibly have been made.

Vice President George M. Dallas, who presided while Webster delivered this blast, could scarcely believe what he heard or the ferocity with which the senator spoke. He told his wife that the speech "would have overwhelmed and perhaps disgusted you." Webster attacked Ingersoll "with the savage and

31. "Defense of the Treaty of Washington," in *PS*, II, 364–433.

mangling ferocity of a tiger." For at least half an hour "he grit his teeth, scowled, stamped, and roared forth the very worst and most abusive language I have ever heard uttered in the Senate." Do get a copy of the speech, Dallas advised, and read that portion relating to Ingersoll.[32]

Webster rushed it into print. Unlike his usual method of revision and polishing before publication, this speech went immediately to the public to counter Ingersoll's accusations. Newspapers gobbled it up, filling almost twenty columns, starting on page one.

Years later Webster mellowed. When Edward Everett began preparing Webster's *Works* for publication, the senator asked Everett to tone down his defense of the treaty speech with respect to Ingersoll. "It is not very easy to make a triphammer strike a little more softly," Everett responded, "but I will do what I can."[33]

Of course Ingersoll had no intention of letting Webster get away with his assault. He began an investigation to prove malfeasance by Webster while serving as secretary of state. Edward Stubbs, the disbursing agent for the Department of State, was "the original mover of the mischief," Webster later revealed. Stubbs went to Ingersoll and gave him some information relative to the McLeod case, "not then intending to disclose secret papers." But Ingersoll was subsequently "let loose among all the vouchers & papers touching Secret Service money &c. &c. &c." and discovered material that seemed to prove that the secretary had embezzled public money and was delinquent in the settlement of accounts. He also found a letter of F. O. J. Smith to Webster about "adjusting" the "tone and direction" of party presses in Maine.[34]

On April 9, two days after Webster had flattened him, Ingersoll rose in the House and delivered what appeared to be a scorching rebuttal. He said "that Mr. Webster while Secretary corruptly took the public moneys, applied them as well to corrupt the party press as to procure the release of McLeod and was guilty of impeachable misdemeanors in office." He was, Ingersoll thundered, "a defaulter when he left the office, having used the secret service fund for his own purposes, and only repaid it about a year ago." Ingersoll based his accusation, he declared, on "information" he had in his "possession." He then introduced a resolution asking President Polk to deliver documents about the use of the secret service fund and any relevant letters dealing with the treaty. After an extended and acrimonious debate the resolution passed 136 to 28. "So you see," Dallas wrote his wife, "the fight is furious."[35]

32. Dallas to Sophie Dallas, April 7, 1846, in *Pennsylvania Magazine of History and Biography*, LXXIII (1949), p. 375. Said Representative William L. Yancey, "Mr. Ingersoll caught hell in the castigation Mr. W. gave him." *Congressional Globe*, 29th Congress, 1st Session, p. 653.

33. Everett to DW, August 25, DW to Everett, August 26, 1851, in *Microfilm Edition*, F25/34628, 34633. In the *Works* Everett deleted the personal attacks on both Ingersoll and Dickinson.

34. DW to Fletcher Webster, May 20, 1846, in *PC*, VI, 161 and Van Tyne, ed., *Letters of Webster*, pp. 326–327; Meigs, *Ingersoll*, pp. 282–284.

35. Dallas to Mrs. Dallas, April 9, 1846, *Pennsylvania Magazine of History and Biography*, LXXIII (1949), p. 375; *Congressional Globe*, 29th Congress, 1st Session, pp. 636–640, 734.

Quite so. Representative William L. Yancey of Alabama rose in the House on April 10 and savaged Webster with such intensity that he permanently fixed in the public mind a description of the senator's true character. After linking Webster with northern "rich men" and implying that he had served them as a paid lackey, Yancey summed up with a particularly brutal characterization of the man. "Of Daniel Webster I know nothing," he declared, "save what the public records disclose. That history, thus disclosed, has given me a loathing of his public character." His "infatuated admirers" have named him the "Godlike," but there is "another familiar appellation, and I must think a true one—'*Black Dan!*'" Webster "has two characters," Yancey stormed, "which Proteus-like he can assume, as his interests or necessities demand—the 'God-like' and the 'Hell-like'—the 'God-like Daniel,' and '*Black Dan!*'"[36]

This interpretation has been repeated by critics and historians down to the present. It points up the real fact that in Daniel Webster resided two distinct personalities, one cold, proud, untrustworthy, power- and money-mad; the other heroic, majestic in mind and speech, truth-seeking and statesmanlike.

Quite properly Polk refused Ingersoll's request for a disclosure of diplomatic documents. Thereupon, on April 27, in an even more heated exchange with certain House members, Ingersoll formally accused Webster of "corruption and embezzlement," having "required [public] money to be directed *to himself*." In passing he also mentioned that Webster had adopted "a *new mode*" of diplomacy by corrupting the press. In all, there were three specific charges: the use of secret service funds without President Tyler's knowledge, the use of this money "to corrupt party presses," and the existence of a balance of $2,290 in Webster's possession when he resigned as secretary of state.[37]

Representative George Ashmun of Massachusetts responded to these charges with a defense of Webster and was "grossly insulted by foul language of charges of lying and cowardice from Ingersoll." A wild exchange ensued with the Speaker refusing to interfere. "This discreditable scene closed" with a resolution to appoint one committee to investigate Webster and another to investigate how, and in what manner, and by whom Ingersoll had obtained secret documents from the State Department's files. Both resolutions passed. John Pettit of Indiana, the mover of the resolution to look into Ingersoll's charges against Webster, did so "with the avowed purpose of impeachment against Mr. Webster." He did not expect any impeachable matter to result from the committee's investigation, but he did believe "that the publication of the secret papers would operate injuriously upon the reputation of Webster in the public mind." This entire "transaction," said John Quincy Adams, demonstrates the

36. *Congressional Globe*, 29th Congress, 1st Session, p. 653.

37. *Congressional Globe*, 29th Congress, 1st Session, pp. 729–735; Adams, *Diary*, XII, 260; "Official Misconduct of the Late Secretary of State, June 9," Reports of Committees, *Congressional Globe*, 29th Congress, 1st Session, vol. III, serial 490, report 684, pp. 1–3, 6–8. For Webster's response to these charges, see "Memorandum on the Ingersoll Charges," in Van Tyne, ed., *Letters of Webster*, pp. 319–321.

"malicious personal enmities" that existed in the Congress at that time.[38]

The Webster committee, as finally chosen, consisted of Jefferson Davis of Mississippi, a Democrat, Jacob Brinkerhoff of Ohio, a Democrat, Daniel P. King of Massachusetts, a Whig, Seaborn Jones of Georgia, a Democrat, and Samuel F. Vinton of Ohio, a Whig, who was chosen to served as chairman—three Democrats and two Whigs, not an encouraging prospect for Webster.[39]

As soon as the committee met, Brinkerhoff moved that the members choose a Democrat as chairman, instead of Vinton, because it was a " 'party Comee' & ought to have a party man, at its head." When the vote was taken, Jefferson Davis voted to keep Vinton as chairman. Said Webster: "This Mr Davis, whom I do not know, appears to be an honorable man." Obviously the senator received periodic reports of the committee's proceedings, probably from King.[40]

Webster immediately wrote to Tyler and solicited his aid in rebutting Ingersoll's charges. The former President agreed and added that he had read Webster's speech "with much satisfaction." The committee called Tyler to testify, and he totally supported everything his former secretary of state had said and done. For his part, Webster believed that when the committee learned that "every expenditure was sanctioned by the President, then that fact should be reported, and the inquiry should stop there. The manner of the expenditure cannot be material; nor can its object be inquired into" because the President had absolute discretion in its dispersal.

Webster probably was concerned about an investigation into the charge of corrupting the press. If so, his concern was groundless because F. O. J. Smith contacted him and said, "I write now only *to assure you,* that I am ready to bear testimony, if need be, in the fullest manner to your vindication, & explain, in a way to put your assailants to shame, all that concerns my agency as to the Boundary question."[41]

But the committee decided to pursue all three charges. Webster felt very uncomfortable remaining in Washington while this investigation proceeded, so he took off for Boston. "I should prefer remaining away from Washington, if I can, for the present," he told Representative Robert C. Winthrop of Massachusetts, with whom he had been reconciled since their falling-out in 1842. If the committee did not require his presence, he continued, then "I shall stay where I am." However, he wanted Winthrop to inform the committee that if it needed some explanation from him, "I will present myself immediately." While in Bos-

38. Adams, *Memoirs,* XII, 260, 263.

39. *Congressional Globe,* 29th Congress, 1st Session, pp. 730–731, 735. Originally John Pettit had been chosen to chair the committee, but when the House refused to honor his request for a clerk, he resigned. Adams, *Memoirs,* XII, 263.

40. DW to Fletcher Webster, May 20, 1846, in *PC,* VI, 161; DW to Fletcher Webster, May 17, 25, 31, 1846, in Van Tyne, ed., *Letters of Webster,* pp. 326–329.

41. Webster also thought the committee should content itself with a general report "that nothing illegal or reprehensible has been done." Tyler to DW, April 21, DW to Winthrop with enclosure, May 2, 1846, in *PC,* VI, 146–147, 148–149; Smith to DW, April 30, 1846, in Van Tyne, ed., *Letters of Webster,* p. 318.

ton he spoke to Smith, who assured him that "everything is properly *straight.*" He then took a short trip to Franklin to check on his farm, the Elms, and see if the house needed to be moved because of the proposed route of the Northern Railroad to stretch from Concord, New Hampshire, to White River Junction, Vermont. After his inspection he decided the house could remain where it was.

During this visit to New Hampshire he reminisced frequently about his early life and his family. On a beautiful, sunny afternoon he looked out over the rich and level field to the east at the end of which he saw "plain marble gravestones, designating the places where repose my father, my mother, my brother Joseph, and my sisters Mehitable, Abigail and Sarah, good scripture names, inherited from their Puritan ancestors." He sighed as he wrote. "My father, Ebenezer Webster!" Ah, there was a man.[42]

While in Boston Webster also attended the installation of his friend Edward Everett, former minister to Great Britain, who had been appointed president of Harvard.[43] But it was Black Dan, not the Godlike Daniel, who showed up. He did not arrive on time for the ceremonies but waited until the moment when Everett, having just been invested and given the keys and charter, rose to make his inaugural speech. Of course it is entirely possible that the time of his late arrival was completely accidental. Whatever the fact, at the precise moment Everett started to speak Webster entered the stage from a side door, and when he did, the entire assembly rose to greet him. "It seemed as if the cheering and the clapping of hands and the waving of handkerchiefs would never leave off. The tears gushed down the cheeks of women and young men and old. Everything was forgotten but the one magnificent personality." The reception robbed poor Everett of the attention due him. "The whole genial current of feeling flowing towards [Edwards]," Ralph Waldo Emerson recorded in his journal, "was arrested, and the old Titanic-Earth-Son was alone seen. The house shook with new and prolonged applause, and Everett sat down, to give free course to the sentiment."[44]

Daniel Webster never had a better friend than Edward Everett, yet he abused him terribly. Emerson said that Webster's "evil genius" did Everett "incalculable harm" by steering him away from learning and scholarship, his natural bent, into the polluted world of politics. But Everett, an "infatuated admirer," like so many others, was totally devoted to the Godlike Daniel and forgave him over and over for any and every lapse into Black Dan.

While Webster dawdled in Massachusetts and New Hampshire, the committee examined numerous witness, including Stubbs[45] and F. O. J. Smith.

42. DW to Winthrop, May 2, DW to Caroline Webster, May 3, 1846, in *PC*, VI, 148, 150; DW to Curtis, May 9, 1846, in Van Tyne, ed., *Letters of Webster*, p. 325; DW to Blatchford, May 3, 1846, in Webster, ed., *Private Correspondence*, II, 225–228.

43. Everett said his job at Harvard consisted of "being that of an usher and a police magistrate combined." Everett to DW, July 6, 1846, in Van Tyne, ed., *Letters of Webster*, p. 332.

44. Hoar, *Autobiography*, I, 143; Emerson, *Journal*, VII, 166–167.

45. Webster suspected Stubbs did "not behave as he ought." DW to Fletcher Webster, May 17, 1846, in Van Tyne, ed., *Letters of Webster*, p. 326.

Stubbs was "thoroughly examined," according to Webster, and "has been compelled to do me justice."[46] Not until June 9 did the committee complete and report its work.

In regard to the first charge Tyler testified that he had known about and sanctioned the dispersal of the secret service funds, so the committee dismissed it. As for the second charge, Smith denied giving bribes and removed "every foundation for a belief, or even a suspicion, that the public money was used, or attempted to be used, to corrupt the party presses."[47] The charge was dismissed. On the third charge the committee discovered that many of the vouchers had been submitted after Webster had left the cabinet, some of them a full year after he had resigned. The supposed balance of $2,290, after all the vouchers had been accounted for, was reduced to $40. It was also discovered that Webster had put up his own money when necessary, perhaps as much as $1,000. Peleg Sprague also provided evidence that he had received $200 from Webster to represent the secretary's views before the Maine legislature, and while he had not submitted a receipt for the money, he had acknowledged it in a note to the secretary. This final charge was also dismissed, and then by a vote of four to one the committee declared that there was "no proof in relation to any of the charges, to impeach Mr. Webster's integrity or the purity of his motives in the discharge of the duties of his office."[48]

Brinkerhoff voted against the motion and wrote a minority report in which he basically argued that the evidence exonerating the former secretary was inconclusive. Webster called his report "poor, weak, & contemptible—& can do no harm."[49] Both the majority and minority reports were brought to the full House on June 9. Jefferson Davis was largely responsible for the majority report, for which Ingersoll never entirely forgave him.[50] After the reading of the majority report Representative Winthrop moved that the minority report not be read, but the House overruled him. After a long discussion, and by a vote of 158 to 16, both reports were ordered to be printed.[51]

The committee looking into Ingersoll's method of gathering information

46. DW to Fletcher Webster, May 20, 1846, ibid., p. 327.

47. Reports of Committees, *Congressional Globe,* 29th Congress, 1st Session, vol. III, serial 490, report 684, p. 15.

48. Ibid., pp. 2–4; Peleg Sprague, memorandum, May 27, 1846, in Van Tyne, ed., *Letters of Webster,* pp. 318–319. This memorandum had been solicited by Webster. See DW to Fletcher Webster, May 25, 1846, ibid., p. 328. There was an effort on the part of Representatives Henry D. Foster of Pennsylvania, Thomas Butler King of Georgia, and Robert C. Schenck of Ohio to bring about a reconciliation between Webster and Ingersoll. Apparently both men were willing to make public statements retracting what they had said previously, but Ingersoll insisted that Webster take the first step, and this the senator refused to do. See "A Proposed Retraction by Mr. Ingersoll," ibid., pp. 322–324.

49. DW to Fletcher Webster, June 10, 1846, in Van Tyne, ed., *Letters of Webster,* p. 330.

50. To the end Ingersoll believed "the absolute truth of the charges" he had brought against Webster. Meigs, *Ingersoll,* pp. 288–289.

51. *Congressional Globe,* 29th Congress, 1st Session, pp. 945–956.

reported on June 12 and expressed no opinion except to suggest that subordinate officers of the State Department had taken questionable actions. Webster said that "Stubbs' conduct appears so bad, that if Mr. Buchanan has any sense of justice, he will turn him out of office." As for Ingersoll, the evidence will satisfy the public of his "rascality, both in his charges, & in his mode of rumaging *[sic]* for evidence."[52]

The Ingersoll controversy ended with Webster's complete vindication. The majority report "negatives all Ingersoll's charges," he wrote.[53] In judgment, legal argument, method of obtaining evidence, and evaluation of evidence, Ingersoll did not impress or convince his colleagues that he had a sound case. Probably they did not want to believe it because they resented the attack on a treaty that had their full approbation. Still, Webster's reputation of playing fast and loose with public money and the fact that the secret service money did not really require full accountability and that therefore no one could probably ever discover what he might have done with it left doubts in people's minds. Webster did not pocket public funds. That seems certain. If anything, he spent his own money in advancing the proceedings of the treaty.

But what Ingersoll and other critics did not know was that a story circulated in London to the effect that Lord Ashburton "had given Daniel Webster a cheque for £10,000, on Webster's own suggestion, to help the passage of the treaty through the Senate," which Ashburton "paid out of his own pocket." After the treaty was passed, "Ld A heard no more of the money. . . . But he always believed afterwards that the Senate had been a pretext, and that the money had gone into Webster's own pocket."[54]

This story, involving a staggering amount of money, did not come directly from Ashburton. Rather it was told to Edward Stanley, earl of Derby and foreign secretary in the 1860s and 1870s, by Samuel Wilberforce, the bishop of Winchester, who presumably got it directly from Ashburton.[55] It is all hearsay, very circumstantial, and recorded in Derby's diary thirty years after the fact. It must be evaluated in that light. But it is certain that Ashburton did inform Aberdeen on August 9, 1842, when the treaty was signed, that Webster had "prepared a voluminous budget for popular impression to go to the Senate. I am not apprehensive about the fate of both the Treaty and Convention. The former I think quite safe."[56] Certainly Webster did not think the treaty was "quite safe"[57]; did Ashburton think so because of all the money he had contributed to win

52. Curtis, *Webster,* II, 283; DW to Fletcher Webster, May 31, in Van Tyne, ed., *Letters of Webster,* p. 329.

53. DW to Fletcher Webster, May 31, in Van Tyne, ed., *Letters of Webster,* p. 329.

54. John Vincent, ed., *The Diaries of Edward Henry Stanley, 15th Earl of Derby, 1826–1893* (London, 1994), IV, 110. The date of the diary entry is July 4, 1872. I am grateful to Professor James Sack of the University of Illinois at Chicago, who brought this diary to my attention.

55. Ibid.

56. Ashburton to Aberdeen, August 9, 1842, in *PD,* II, 680.

57. DW to John Healy, August 17, 1842, ibid., 691.

passage? And did the word "budget" mean a summary of income and expenditures? More likely the minister used the word in its original sense—that is, a portfolio filled with documents. It is known, however, that in another dispatch to Aberdeen on August 9, Ashburton told the foreign secretary that he had drawn on the secret service fund for £2,998, to compensate Jared Sparks and send him to meet with the governors of Maine and Massachusetts to gain their support. "Without this stimulant Maine would never have yielded," he argued in justifying his action.[58] Unquestionably, British money was being doled out to obtain passage of the treaty. But the question remains: Did Webster pocket any of it, as Ashburton assumed, according to the story attributed to Bishop Wilberforce? For such an enormous amount of money, as mentioned by Derby, is it not reasonable to suppose that some of it would have appeared in Webster's subsequent financial dealings over the next ten years of his life? He might have paid off some of his indebtedness, although that was not his usual style, or put it into more elaborate improvements at Marshfield. There is simply no way to reach a definite conclusion. All of which is to say that wrongdoing on Webster's part with respect to the British money cannot be proved or disproved. But taken as a whole, it constituted evidence that some people later considered highly suspicious.

Vindicated and convinced that the majority report by the House committee would persuade the public of his innocence, Webster put the controversy completely out of his mind. More important events had occurred in the interim.

The United States had declared war on Mexico.

58. Ashburton to Aberdeen, August 9, 1842, Aberdeen Papers, BM 43,123

37

A Tour of the South

WITH the annexation of Texas, Mexico broke off diplomatic relations with the United States. Polk worsened the deteriorating situation by offering thirty million dollars for California, New Mexico, and acceptance of the Rio Grande as the Texas boundary, terms that Mexico summarily rejected. Then Polk ordered General Zachary Taylor to advance his troops into a disputed area between the Nueces River and the Rio Grande. Not surprisingly, these troops skirmished with Mexican troops, and in the action sixteen American soldiers were killed or wounded. No sooner did Polk receive this information than on May 11, 1846, he asked Congress for a declaration of war, "not in direct terms, but by circumlocution." The following day the Senate voted in favor, 40 to 2, with Webster absent in Cambridge attending Everett's inauguration and Calhoun present but not voting. But the South Carolina senator made a frightening prediction: "Mexico is to us the forbidden fruit; the penalty of eating it [is] to subject our institutions to political death." The House passed the measure on May 13 by a vote of 117 to 50, with many Whigs, including John Quincy Adams, voting no.[1]

"I begin to feel quite alarmed for the state of the Country," Webster declared. He worried particularly about relations with Great Britain if the American squadron in the Pacific took possession of the California ports. He thought the war should be supported only if waged for national defense and public rights, not for ambition, aggrandizement, or acquisition of territory. He worried most of all about the consequences of the war.[2]

A third worry involved the financing of this bloodbath. "Will the People of the United States support an expensive & bloody war, merely for conquest, &

---

1. *Congressional Globe,* 29th Congress, 1st Session, pp. 795–804, 810; Adams, *Memoirs,* XII, 261; Calhoun to Henry Conner, May 15, 1846, quoted in Peterson, *Great Triumvirate,* p. 423. For the war itself, see Justin Smith, *War with Mexico* (New York, 1919), K. Jack Bauer, *The Mexican War, 1846–1848* (New York, 1974), Seymour V. Conner and Odie B. Faulk, *North America Divided: The Mexican War, 1846–1848* (New York, 1971), and John S. D. Eisenhower, *So Far from God: The War with Mexico, 1846–1848* (New York, 1988).

2. DW to Peter Harvey, May 18, DW to Fletcher Webster, May 20, DW to Charles Thomas, May 22, 1846, in *PC,* VI, 158, 162, 163; DW to Fletcher Webster, June 1, 1846, in Van Tyne, ed., *Letters of Webster,* p. 330.

aggrandizement?" he asked. *"Will the money hold out?"*[3] Greater revenue was needed, and raising the tariff offered the best way to obtain it. But Polk and the Democrats opposed any such raise, and many of them favored a policy of free trade. Secretary of the Treasury Robert J. Walker proposed a plan that essentially asked for no greater revenue than the government absolutely needed. The program of systematic protection for particular industries and raw materials was eliminated. All minimum and specific duties would be abolished, and ad valorem duties substituted in their place. A bill to this effect was introduced in the House in mid-April but, because of the Oregon and Mexican business, was not seriously debated until mid-June.

Webster took violent exception to the plan because the fairly high Tariff of 1842—which generally restored duties to the level of 1832—was perfectly satisfactory. Ad valorem principles, he said, were "absurd" and would destroy or injure "interests" that must be protected and preserved. So he started organizing an opposition to the Walker proposal almost immediately.[4] "Our especial interests," he informed his friends and supporters, "as it seems to me, is to look to the preservation of the great industrial interests of the country."[5] And only protection could provide that preservation.

He set to work by contacting his business friends in Boston and New York and inviting them to come to Washington for "the next ten days" and urge upon Whigs the necessity of uniting in opposition to the plan. *"Information,"* he told them, "on many subjects will be very much needed." The ad valorem principle must be materially altered. Failing that, and he really gave it little hope, "our best chance of killing the Bill is, to put [it] to the vote, *just as it is."*[6]

Unfortunately Webster organized an opposition *outside* Congress when he should have been working *inside* on representatives and senators close at hand. Henry Clay had resigned from the Senate in 1842 and could not provide the necessary leadership. That task fell to Webster's close friends and allies John Clayton, John J. Crittenden, Willie Mangum, and others. Webster did not consult with these men. He waited too long. He waited until he faced a crisis. His actions demonstrated how halting and feeble his leadership could be. He knew what he wanted to do—which was to preserve the rates of the Tariff of 1842 by killing the proposed bill—but he took the less effective means to achieve his purpose. One observer claimed that Webster had "no ambition to lead," that he could not rouse himself sufficiently until the last moment. On this occasion he

3. DW to Ambrose Spencer, May 28, 1846, in *PC*, VI, 165; DW to Fletcher Webster, August 6, 1846, in Van Tyne, ed., *Letters of Webster*, p. 343.

4. DW to Nathan Appleton, July 8, 1846, in *PC*, VI, 175. As a matter of fact Webster had been organizing an opposition to a proposed revision of the tariff since 1845, when he asked manufacturers to form a committee and write a "View or Statement" to Walker explaining the benefits of the Tariff of 1842 and indicating where it might be altered "without injury. I am sure he would receive such a communication very kindly." DW to Fletcher Webster, May 12, 1845, in *W&S*, XVI, 431–432.

5. DW to James K. Mills, July 24, 1846, in *W&S*, XIII, 231.

6. DW to Nathan Appleton, July 8, Appleton to DW, July 10?, 1846, in *PC*, VI, 175–176, 177–179.

delayed doing anything useful in Congress until the bill passed the House by a vote of 114 to 95 and arrived in the Senate.[7]

It arrived on July 13 and was generally called the Walker tariff. Because of an evenly divided upper chamber, Whigs and Democrats scrambled to pass or kill it. Webster polled the members regularly in order to gauge his strategy. Informed that Senator Spencer A. Jarnagin of Tennessee, a Whig, had been instructed by his state legislature to vote in favor of tariff reduction, Webster tried to dissuade him from obeying the instruction and convince him to follow his own inclinations against the bill. "I was supposed [to have] as much influence with him, as any body, & I exerted it, as far as I could." Webster wrote two private letters to him, and all the Whig members from Tennessee called on him. Finally Jarnagin agreed that the bill had to be killed, but he wanted to force the presiding Vice President, George Dallas, to cast the deciding vote. To humor him, Webster even worked out a scenario[8] that Jarnigan agreed to follow. According to this plan, Webster would move to strike out a part of the ninth section of the bill, and Jarnigan would vote for it. Then, on a motion to engross the bill, the Tennessean would not vote, forcing Dallas to break the resulting tie. Then, if Dallas voted for the bill, Jarnagin would move to lay it on the table, thus killing it. Everything depended on Jarnagin. If he followed the scenario, said Webster, and "brought to act against the Bill, its fate was sealed."[9]

But he still worried that it might pass despite his efforts unless it was altered—that is, "alter its *ad valorem* principle materially." That seemed impossible, so with the help of his friend and adviser Edward Curtis, the former collector of customs in New York who now practiced law in Washington, Webster concocted a substitute bill, which he sent to James K. Mills, a prominent Boston merchant and banker, and a number of manufacturers for their approval. "I do not wish to make any important movement on this subject of the tariff, against the judgment of those most interested in it," he wrote. He proposed to reduce all duties, "whether specific or *ad valorem*," by 25 percent (later revised to 20 percent) and at the end of five years reduce it further by 8½ percent. He knew some Whigs would oppose his substitute, calling it a compromise, and several of them warned him that it would damage his "popularity" and standing within the party. "My wish is to do good, & save the country," he explained to Mills. "I care nothing for consequences to my own popularity. If I can defeat this infamous Bill, & retain the principle, & the principal provisions of 1842, it is glory enough for me." So "you & your friends & my friends must look these things over *& say what is best.*"[10]

Actually Webster regarded his proposal not as a compromise but as a substitute that would retain all the principles of the Tariff of 1842 and that offered

7. Quoted in Peterson, *Great Triumvirate*, p. 393.

8. Memorandum, no date, in Van Tyne, ed., *Letters of Webster*, pp. 341–342.

9. DW to Fletcher Webster, July 26, 1846, in *W&S*, XVI, 459–464.

10. DW to Mills, [July 19, 1846,] in *PC*, VI, 184–185; DW to Mills, July 21, 1846, two letters, in *W& S*, XVI, 457–458; DW to Mills, July 24, 1846, in Webster, ed., *Private Correspondence*, II, 230.

reductions which would leave "the protected interests safe and satisfied." He
even hoped it would "quiet a great deal of clamor."[11]

At first his business consultants in Boston and New York took a dim view of
his "compromise," but as the possibility of the Walker bill's passing became more
apparent, they finally came around. "Every man of business here—Whig or
loco—. . . all are *for* the proposal," Webster insisted. But many Whigs members
in Congress *"are agt it, . . . on political grounds."*[12]

On Saturday, July 25, Webster began a speech against the Walker bill that
concluded on Monday, July 27. Every interest, shipping, mercantile, manufacturing, agricultural, "all, all, were opposed to it." Who proposed it? he asked.
"The people? No." "King Party" was the culprit. He especially objected to the
ad valorem schedule in the bill, which not only was susceptible to fraud but
could seriously jeopardize the movement of raw materials to manufacturers. He
thought labor would suffer as well. Free trade in Europe meant cheap bread,
but in the United States a protective tariff helped laborers "improve their lot"
and live a more comfortable life. He believed implicitly that America's working
class aspired to become entrepreneurs. Labor and capital were synonymous
because each at different times and in different ways created the other. "Labor
everywhere mixed itself with capital," he declared. He provided numerous figures, charts of foreign manufactured articles, such as silk, wool, cotton, iron,
cigars, and clothing, and foreign articles for consumption, such as coffee, tea,
wines, molasses, and fish, all provided by his business friends to document his
case.[13]

Webster curtailed his speech on the second day so that the debate could be
brought to a close "before accidents should turn up." Then something unexpected developed. Senator Clayton of Delaware, one of Clay's staunchest allies,
moved that the Walker bill be recommitted to the Finance Committee with
instructions to remove the duties imposed by the bill where foreign raw materials were taxed to the prejudice of "mechanics or manufacturers" so that no
higher duty would be collected on raw materials than provided by the Tariff
of 1842. This was a "useless" motion, according to Webster, and "led to fatal
consequences." Still, the Whigs, including Jarnagin, could not vote against it,
and the motion passed by a single vote. It meant putting off a showdown for
another day, and that was the "fatal" consequence.

Webster wrote Jarnagin a third letter, a very strong one, "beseeching" him
not to waver. But none of Jarnagin's Whig friends who went looking for him that
evening could find him. Then word reached Webster that the Tennessean had
been spotted at the White House. That spelled disaster. "At the meeting at the

11. DW to Fletcher Webster, July 27, 1846, in Webster, ed., *Private Correspondence*, II, 231.

12. DW to Mills, July 21, 1846, in *W&S*, XVI, 457; Mills to DW, July 23, 25, 1846, Joseph Balch to
DW, July 25, 1846, in *PC*, VI, 189–190, 192–193.

13. *W&S*, IX, 161–235; XIV, 312–314; Sargent, *Public Men and Events*, II, 286.

Presidents," Webster believed, ". . . means were found to fix Mr Jarnagin's vote for the Bill."[14]

The next day, Tuesday, July 28, at nine o'clock, Webster received a response to his third letter to Jarnagin in which the Tennessean declared that "after a patient examination of all the circumstances with which I am surrounded . . . it is with pain I have to say . . . I cannot concur" with our friends. He would refuse to vote upon the engrossment of the bill and leave its fate to Dallas, "but I cannot vote to postpone it."[15]

After receiving this response, Webster knew "that all ground of reliance on his vote was now taken away." Then the chairman of the Finance Committee reported the bill back without alteration and asked that his committee be discharged from further consideration of Clayton's resolution. The decision gave Webster the opportunity to move to strike out one section of the bill, which could permit fraudulent valuation by importers, and it passed. Not by Jarnagin's vote—he did not vote—but by that of Thomas Hart Benton, who believed the section unconstitutional. Thus amended, the bill was engrossed by the casting vote of the Vice President, Jarnagin not voting. Jarnagin did not ask that it be laid on the table, and on the final vote it squeezed through the Senate by the vote of twenty-eight to twenty-seven, Jarnagin voting with the majority.[16]

Senator Simon Cameron of Pennsylvania then moved Webster's compromise, but it lost. "I will not impute any corrupt motive to Mr Jarnagin," said Webster. In politics there are "means of influence" that are not "generally esteemed positively corrupt" but can produce "great effects." Nevertheless Jarnagin "falsified his promises, & has thoroughly disgraced himself, forever." If he had kept his word, "I have no doubt the Bill would have been defeated." But Webster placed even greater blame on Clayton, Crittenden, and the other friends of Clay who preferred killing the Walker bill over passing his substitute in order to take the tariff question to the electorate as a campaign issue in the presidential election of 1848.[17]

Worn out, disgusted, and distressed, Webster knew what would happen next. The amended bill went back to the House, more "means of influence" were exerted, and the Walker Tariff of 1846 passed. Polk signed it on July 30. This tariff moderated protection on many articles and reduced rates to about 25 percent. Webster found some hope in the belief that the falling off of revenues would impact on the prosecution of the war so that the tariff would have to be revised the following year. "By that time, also, I trust some of our Whig friends will have come to their senses." But the Walker Tariff actually brought in consid-

14. *W&S*, IX, 236; DW to Fletcher Webster, July 29, 1846, in Van Tyne, ed., *Letters of Webster,* pp. 338, 339.

15. Jarnagin to DW, [July 1846], in Van Tyne, ed., *Letters of Webster,* p. 342.

16. DW to Fletcher Webster, July 29, 1846, ibid., pp. 339–340; *Congressional Globe,* 29th Congress, 1st Session, p. 1158.

17. John W. Davis to Clayton, August 22, 1848, Clayton Papers, LC; DW to Fletcher Webster, July 29, 1846, in Van Tyne, ed., *Letters of Webster,* p. 339.

erable revenue because of the economic prosperity that returned to the country after 1844. Only the woolens industry was seriously injured by it.[18]

Congress then reenacted the independent treasury, passed in the Van Buren administration and repealed in the Tyler administration. Convinced that "its strange, un-American character" had been fully exposed, Webster spoke against it on August 1. "I frankly confess," he admitted, "that I did not expect that this sub-treasury scheme would ever be revived. I had heard of 'Polk, Dallas, and the tariff of 1842,' but I really never did expect to hear of 'Polk, Dallas, and the old dead sub-treasury.' "[19]

On August 8, two days before the scheduled adjournment of Congress, David Wilmot of Pennsylvania introduced an amendment to a two-million-dollar appropriations bill to assist in arranging the boundary with Mexico, a clear indication by Polk that he expected to acquire additional territory. The amendment, known thereafter as the Wilmot Proviso, stated that slavery must never exist in any territory to be acquired from Mexico. The House passed both the bill and the proviso, but it died in the Senate, thanks to a filibuster by Webster's Massachusetts colleague John Davis.[20]

Webster returned home after Congress had adjourned on August 10, but the problems plaguing the nation could not be forgotten or kept in abeyance. The war constantly commanded attention, and more and more the question of slavery and its extension intruded into everyone's thoughts and conversations. It divided the nation, North and South, something Webster dreaded. Unity of the country, unity among Whigs, unity of national purpose were articles of faith to him. He shuddered to think about the consequences should the nation fall apart. And now, because of the war and the likelihood that a military victory might mean the acquisition of a vast new territory, the Whig party seemed to be dividing over the question of slavery. Increasingly, northern Whigs favored terminating slavery, and they proudly declared themselves Conscience Whigs, while those who were pro-slavery or more cautious about freeing slaves because it would antagonize their southern Whig brethren and thereby endanger the Union called themselves Cotton Whigs. In Massachusetts those Whigs who regarded the safety of the Union and the protective tariff as having priority before abolition were sometimes referred to as Commercial Whigs. Within the state men like Charles Sumner, Charles Francis Adams, the son of former President John Quincy Adams, Stephen C. Phillips, Henry Wilson, and John Palfrey declared themselves Conscience Whigs, while Nathan Appleton, Abbott Lawrence, Robert C. Winthrop, and Leverett Saltonstall were Cotton or Commercial Whigs.[21]

18. DW to Fletcher Webster, July 29, 1846, ibid., p. 339; DW to [Franklin Haven?], August 5, 1846, in PC, VI, 194; Peterson, Great Triumvirate, p. 422.

19. W&S, IX, 244–251.

20. Charles B. Going, David Wilmot, Free Soiler (New York, 1924), pp. 94–105, 159–201.

21. Kinley J. Brauer, Cotton versus Conscience: Massachusetts Whig Politics and Southwestern Expansion, 1843–1848 (Lexington, Ky., 1967), p. 2.

At the Whig State Convention on September 23, 1846, the young, strikingly handsome, highly talented Charles Sumner gave a speech on the "Anti-slavery Duties of the Whig Party." In an eloquent appeal he denounced slavery as a moral evil. He concluded by begging Webster to join the Conscience Whigs and add to his titles of "Defender of the Constitution" and "Defender of Peace" another and even greater title, *"Defender of Humanity."* When the resolutions committee reported without including opposition to slavery as a political duty, a floor fight ensued.

Webster was summoned from his dinner. When he entered the hall, learning on the arms of Abbott Lawrence and Robert C. Winthrop, thereby publicly confirming his reconciliation with both men, a shout went up from the floor: "Webster!" It was followed by three cheers. He proceeded majestically toward the platform, the delegates parting as he approached. He took his seat on the platform, presumably as a spectator. But prolonged applause and loud cheers from both the Conscience and Cotton Whigs echoed around the hall, urging him to address the delegates. He had not expected to speak but under the circumstances felt obliged to say a few words to warn his Whig brethren against introducing questions on which the national party could not unite. Obviously he sided with the Cotton Whigs.

His first words were "I like to meet the Whigs of Massachusetts in State Convention assembled, because their proceedings always breathe the spirit of"—here he paused several seconds for dramatic effect before he let the word explode from his mouth—" Liberty." When he finally uttered the word, "it seemed to weigh ten pounds," according to one observer. "It was a shot right between wind and water."

The crowd erupted as he completed his sentence. Shouts, applause, the cry "Webster, Webster" filled the hall. When the noise abated, he started again but spoke only five minutes. Still, something he said struck everyone most forcefully. In his opinion, the "hopes of the country" rested on only one thing. "I see in the dark and troubled night which is now upon us, no star above the horizon, but the intelligent, patriotic, *united* Whig party of the United States."[22]

The next day Sumner wrote to Webster in an attempt to prod him into joining the Conscience Whigs, "believing that there now lie before you fields of usefulness & glory, which you have not yet entered." Webster's response was typical when faced with a politically sensitive issue. He dodged it. He assured Sumner that while they differed on some questions and took different views about "the line of duty" to obtain "all the good" possible, he would not allow these differences to "interfere with personal regard" or his personal good wishes.[23] Did that mean he differed with Sumner on slavery? Without saying it

22. Sumner, *Works*, I, 304–316; David Donald, *Charles Sumner and the Coming of the Civil War* (New York, 1960), pp.147–148; Boston *Courier*, September 24, 1846; Stanton, *Random Recollections*, p. 150; W&S, XIII, 327–329.

23. Sumner to DW, September 25, 1846, in *PC*, VI, 195; DW to Sumner, October 5, 1846, in W&S, XVI, 464.

directly, he most assuredly did—but without personal rancor or loss of "personal regard."

At a preelection rally in Faneuil Hall on November 6, Webster pursued the theme of Whig unity, but he also condemned the Mexican War as "universally odious throughout the United States" and accused Polk of instigating the conflict. It "was a Presidential war," he cried. As such, "in my judgment it is an impeachable offence." Throughout, he said nothing about slavery or the Wilmot Proviso.[24]

In response Democrats accused him of disloyalty, of aiding the Mexican cause. He was, they said, the *"Prince of traitors."*[25]

At a more nationally visible setting, a public dinner given in his honor at the Museum Building in Philadelphia on December 2, he repeated these condemnations, but because he blasted the Polk administration on every issue raised in the past two years, especially the tariff, he appeared to be signaling his own availability for a presidential nomination in 1848. He spoke for four hours—an extraordinary length of time at a dinner, even for 1846—to an estimated crowd of twelve hundred. Philip Hone pronounced his address "clear, luminous, and powerful," but the New Yorker said nothing about its exciting any interest in Webster's presidential prospects.[26]

The "presidential war" took on a more personal color for Webster when his son Edward resigned his position as secretary for the American commission to survey the boundary under the Webster-Ashburton Treaty, a post secured for him by his father, and helped organize a company of Massachusetts volunteers to fight the war. Elected captain by the company, the twenty-six-year-old Edward had hoped to become regimental commander, but the officers wisely chose Caleb Cushing, who was nearly twice Edward's age. Edward ran a distant third behind both Cushing and Isaac Wright. Not surprisingly, the loving father thought "that Edward has been badly treated" because the important role he had played in gathering the regiment together had been overlooked. "Some miserable & dirty political & radical motives prevented it," he contended, even though the post had gone to his very close friend and financial supporter. He asked his son to write every day before sailing and immediately after he touched land. "I am afraid of no unbecoming conduct, no fear, on one side, & foolish recklessness on the other." What Webster did fear were the "accidents of war . . . [and] the *climate.* Pray study to guard agt the effects of climate, in every possible form."

When Edward finally took off with his troops, he sailed to the Brazos and headed for Matamoros. He purposely left home with a letter in his pocket from George Curson (who had carried dispatches to Mexico during Webster's tenure as secretary of state) to General Juan Nepomuceno Almonte, former Mexican

24. *W&S*, XIII, 327–341.

25. Quoted in Joel Silbey, *The American Political Nation, 1838–1893* (Stanford, Calif., 1991), p. 98.

26. Hone, *Diary*, II, 780–781. Webster's speech can be found in *W&S*, IV, 7–56.

minister to the United States and presently Mexico's minister of war. Webster instructed his son to get rid of it. "An American officer should not have in his pocket a letter to one of the enemy."[27]

When President Polk appointed Cushing a brigadier general, thereby vacating the position of regimental commander, Webster immediately wrote Cushing and asked him to use his good offices to advance his son. "A father's judgment is not to be trusted," Webster cheerfully admitted, "but I doubt whether, when you leave the Regiment, any body is left in it fitter to be at [its] head." Then his fears for his son's safety surfaced, and he begged Cushing to help provide his son with protection: "Could Edward be put on the Staff, at or near Head Quarters?"[28]

As for the question of the position of regimental commander, it was an elective one, as Webster knew full well, and the officers chose Isaac Wright. Edward had to make do with a promotion to the rank of major.

Edward contracted a severe illness after reaching Mexico and returned home in poor health. Once he had recovered he insisted on rejoining his regiment and returned with the ever-faithful Henry Pleasants at his side. Henry had been a slave with a Washington family and cruelly treated. Webster had purchased Henry for five hundred dollars and then given him his freedom. After an extended residence with the Webster family Henry had married and returned to Washington. When Edward asked him to accompany him to Mexico, Henry, without "a moment's hesitation," replied, "I will go with you, Master Edward, to the ends of the earth."[29]

The Mexican War crowded out all other issues when Congress reconvened in December. The increasing likelihood of acquiring additional territory from Mexico heightened the fears of some and the expectations of others. David Wilmot again attached his Proviso to an appropriations bill, the so-called Three Million Bill to help bring the war to a speedy conclusion, and it passed. In the Senate Webster read resolutions adopted by the Massachusetts House of Representatives condemning slavery and supporting the Wilmot Proviso. Actually he himself believed that the Proviso would only generate "contention, strife, and agitation." He favored the basic idea of the Proviso—indeed he claimed he had favored it since 1838—but thought it impolitic and mischievous in the present situation. Any treaty ending the war, he declared, would be opposed by northern senators if it included additional slave territory. He much preferred the amendment submitted by Senator Berrien that declared the war must not be prosecuted with a view toward dismembering Mexico. He warned that "we

27. DW to Fletcher Webster, January 27, DW to Edward Webster, February 5, 22, DW to General John Wool, April 7, 1847, in *PC*, VI, 205, 206–207, 210–211, 223; Edward Webster to DW, March 17, 1847, in Van Tyne, ed., *Letters of Webster*, p. 354.

28. DW to Cushing, April 15, 1847, in *PC*, VI, 226. Webster also wrote to General John E. Wool and asked if Edward might join Wool's staff "as a volunteer aid. . . . He is enterprising, ambitious, & full of activity, without bluster." DW to Wool, April 7, 1847, ibid., VI, 223.

29. Curtis, *Webster*, II, 329–330.

appear to be rushing upon perils headlong, and with our eyes wide open." The result could threaten the existence of the Union.[30]

This fear for the safety and continuance of the Republic under its present constitutional form runs through many of Webster's most important speeches at this time, even though he always ended them, as he did this speech, on an optimistic note: "I put my trust in Providence, and in that good sense and patriotism of the people, which will yet, I hope, be awakened before it is too late."

What made him especially apprehensive now was the knowledge of what war often does to divide and destroy a nation. He expanded on this theme in a letter to Fletcher, now in the state legislature after his return from China, in which he reminded his son about the duty Americans have during such crises. It was guidance applicable to every generation, not simply the generation facing the possibility of civil war.

We may think a war unnecessary or unjust; but if a majority think otherwise, we must submit, because we have agreed that a majority shall govern. We may oppose the counsels which lead to war, or to the continuance of war. All this is constitutional and just. But we may not seek to obstruct the proceedings of Government, in carrying on a war, merely because we disapprove the war itself. Whether the war was brought on by our own acts, or by the acts of others . . . our political duties must be the same. . . . There may be an unjust war, and there may be an unjust peace, in the opinion of the minority. But in these, as in other cases, the minority must yield to the majority, unless it means to break up the government.

We can and should write, speak, argue, and vote against measures we oppose when they are under discussion, he continued. But when the popular will has been constitutionally expressed by constitutionally chosen individuals, and these individuals adopt by majority vote measures we dislike, those measures "are to be regarded as law, just as much as if we had ourselves concurred in them, and as laws they must be obeyed. And snarling and grumbling, and all attempts to sever one's self from what the Country has decided upon, are but the effusions of narrow feelings. They produce no effect, on the public counsels, and only gratify pique, and spleen."[31]

This was probably one of the strongest statements Daniel Webster ever wrote affirming his belief in the democratic process. Although he "belonged to another age" and his political views remained "federalist" and "elitist," he recognized that majority rule was basic to the preservation of the American Republic under the Constitution.

In the present situation the Mexican War could produce disastrous consequences if more territory than needed were acquired by the United States. Better, said Webster, to forgo increasing the geographic size of the country than to seize more territory and thereby destroy ourselves over the slavery question. But the Berrien amendment against dismembering Mexico failed to win a ma-

30. W&S, IX, 253–261.

31. DW to Fletcher Webster, April 24, 1847, in PC, VI, 229–230.

jority, and Webster was obliged to vote for the Wilmot Proviso, which also failed. The central question had been ducked, but it would return and bring in its train all the consequences Webster dreaded. Having successfully avoided the central question, the Senate then passed the Three Million Bill.

When this short session of Congress concluded, Webster planned to take a tour of the South, something he had wanted to do and certainly something he needed to do if he expected to win southern support for any future presidential bid. After all, he was hardly more than a name to southerners, a very distinguished name, to be sure, but in these days of increasingly democratic pretensions it had become mandatory for the electorate to fix a face and a real presence to a name. By touring the South and then swinging up North via the "Western country," he could advance his presidential stature throughout the nation without appearing to be campaigning.

After disposing of some pressing legal business that kept him in Washington until late April, Webster, in company with his wife, Caroline, Josephine Seaton, the daughter of his friend and coowner of the *National Intelligencer* William W. Seaton, and several others, finally set out "on his long-projected tour through the Southern States to New Orleans," stopping off at all the principal cities along the way. Actually he had decided to skip New Orleans, "with regret and tears," intending to make "a flying trip to it next November." Instead he would head for Charleston, Savannah, Columbia, and Augusta, then travel over the Allegheny Mountains into Tennessee, and return home by way of Cincinnati, Columbus, and Cleveland. As much as possible he planned to take railroads, or the cars, as they were almost universally called, in order to see the countryside. Hundreds of miles by railroad, crisscrossing from city to city, could appreciably cut down the amount of time necessary to complete the tour.[32]

The group arrived in Richmond on April 28. At this first stop a pattern developed that was repeated in every city and town they visited. An appointed committee surrounded by a large crowd met the Webster party at the cars and after an official ceremony of welcome escorted them to their hotel. Invariably Webster responded with something appropriate for the occasion and place. Frequently another reception awaited them at the hotel, and that evening a public dinner was held to honor the distinguished guest. Large crowds usually turned out to see this miracle from New England, and they paid him all the attention and respect he craved.

At the dinner in Richmond Webster was introduced as the man committed to "advance the fame of the country, perpetuate the Union, and multiply the securities of national happiness and prosperity." The reporter for the Richmond *Whig* said he did not have the skill or daring to reproduce the Webster response except to say that at the end of it the senator admitted that he would like the

---

32. *National Intelligencer*, April 29, 1847; DW to Fletcher Webster, April 25, DW to Harriette Paige, May 9, 1847, in *W&S*, XVIII, 238–239, 245. New Orleans had to be skipped because of his delay in leaving Washington. DW to Fletcher Webster, April 21, 1847, in Van Tyne, ed., *Letters of Webster*, p. 357.

following words written on his tombstone: "Here lies one who wished well to the Constitution of his Country."[33]

Webster found Richmond a lovely city, especially in the morning, when the air, he said, was sweet, & fresh & delightful." He became quite lyrical in describing it to his friend Harriette Paige. Most people, he believed, know nothing of the morning, except that it comes along with a cup of coffee, a beef steak, and a piece of toast. " With them, morning is not a new issuing of light; a new bursting forth of the sun; a new waking up, of all that has life, from a sort of temporary death, to behold, again the works of God, the Heavens & the Earth." Most people think of it as part of the domestic day, belonging to breakfast, to reading the newspapers, to answering letters, to sending children to school, and to giving orders for dinner. "I know the morning; I am acquainted with it, & I love it, fresh and sweet as it is, a daily new creation, breaking forth, and calling all that have life, and breath, & being, to new adoration, new enjoyments, & new gratitude."[34]

This lyrical mood frequently asserted itself during the trip, even to describing how turpentine was extracted and tar made. The countryside delighted Webster, although during May the mounting heat and humidity bothered him and he felt generally fatigued. The party moved on to Raleigh, where they stayed with the governor and enjoyed his hospitality. The weather turned cold with gale-force wind as they headed to Goldsboro, Wilmington, Charleston, Columbia, Augusta, and Savannah.

Charleston reminded Webster a bit of Boston, especially the way the Ashley River wound around the city. He was impressed by the size of the "palace-looking" houses, the regularity in the squares with which the streets had been laid out, the many piazzas, and the "great hospitality and great splendor" in which some families like the Pinckneys, Sumpters, and Hugers lived. He noted that the abolition of primogeniture had broken "the whole old fashioned aristocratic system of Southern life" in Charleston and its surrounding countryside. "Slave labor, and rice and cotton cultivation, work in badly with democratic subdivisions of property."[35]

He took a little excursion on a steamboat to see a rice plantation, and it fascinated him. "It is a beautiful crop," he declared. At the moment the rice rose to six or eight inches "of a beautiful soft, light green, like the color of a gosling's wing, and the vast fields are all laid off in squares." But it needs freshwater and a tide to let the water in and then to draw it off, for rice must be grown half the time underwater and half above. Unfortunately this produces "an unhealthy climate." "If it were not for the sickliness of climate in summer, [this area] would be a very desirable place." The water kills all the weeds, so little hoeing is needed, and very little plowing. Some acres, he said, produce as much as ninety bushels a crop, each bushel worth about $1.15.

On this tour he spotted alligators snoozing along the banks. "I had a little

33. April 30, 1847.
34. DW to Paige, April 29, 1847, in W&S, XVIII, 240–241.
35. DW to Harriette Paige, May 9, 1847, ibid., XVIII, 244–245.

gun on board, with two buck shot in the barrel . . . and I put these two shot in the neck of one of the fellows." He also traveled upcountry to see a cotton plantation. At that time of the year the plants were only up three or four inches. "The fields are pretty, but are said to be exceedingly beautiful, when the plant is in blossom." He learned how cotton got its name,[36] and he shared the information with his carpenter at Marshfield, Seth Weston. "There! I do not believe there is a man in all Marshfield but you and me, who knows why this plant is called 'cotton.' "[37]

He remained in Charleston for a week and then moved on by railroad to Columbia, where the students of the college formed a torchlight procession through the campus to the home of his friend William C. Preston, president of the college. He dined at Wade Hampton's plantation, Millwood, even though Hampton himself was away. The daughters of the house did the honors. He also dined with the governor and attended "an elegant *fête*" at Professor Francis Lieber's residence, along with a Citizen's Ball, "given in homage to his greatness and worth."[38]

In Augusta, Georgia, his next stop, the *Chronicle and Sentinel* on May 19 hailed his coming with a salute that made the grueling trip all worthwhile. "We of the South," it read, "have a right to claim Mr. Webster, as we do, as one of the bright stars of our common country. Even political prejudices vanish at his coming among us."

At Augusta, where he arrived on May 21, the first noticeable signs of physical distress appeared, forcing him to cancel several appearances. The weather, fatigue, and a severe attack of his "catarrh" exhausted him. "My attack was bilious and feverish," he informed Fletcher. He said that these attacks began in 1836 and made a regular appearance "on the 23d of August, seldom varying a day."[39] He still hoped to go to Savannah for two days, then take the railroad four hundred miles west and north. But his spirit, like his health, sagged, for despite the excellent crowds, the enthusiastic responses, the adulation, and the glowing editorial tributes he received, the tour had not produced the one thing he desperately wished to hear: He failed to elicit any serious mention of his prospects as a presidential candidate in 1848. After all, Henry Clay had politically annihilated himself in 1844 by losing to a "third-rate" nobody. And after Clay, who but the Godlike Daniel possessed the stature, the greatness, the talents, and the experience to serve as President of the United States?

Throughout the tour Webster had said nothing about slavery or its extension, the Wilmot Proviso, or anything else that could disturb or annoy southern-

36. "The word 'cotton' originally meant a thin, light cloth, made in England out of wool and linen; and when the uses of this plant were found out, and people learned to make a similar light cloth out of it, they called its product 'cotton wool.' "

37. DW to Weston, May 10, 1847 in *W&S*, XVIII, 246–248. A full description of cultivating cotton can be found in DW to Paige, May 15, 1847, in ibid., XVIII, 252–254.

38. *National Intelligencer*, May 20, 1847; DW to Fletcher Webster, May 5, DW to Edward Curtis, May 6, 1847, in *W&S*, XVIII, 242–243.

39. The newspapers explained that he was suffering from a cold and fatigue. DW to Fletcher Webster, May 10, 1847, in *W&S*, XVIII, 245–246, DW to Robert B Croes, July 22, 1851, in *PC*, VII, 268.

ers. He tended to apotheosize the Constitution—the late John Marshall was a natural in Virginia—the Union, the common heritage of southerners and New Englanders, and the great promise of American life.[40] Yet with all the cheers and applause he received the crowds failed to shout back their hope to make him their next President. Instead of his name, all he heard was the name of General Zachary Taylor, America's latest hero, who had won the Battle of Buena Vista over the Mexicans in late February 1847 against almost impossible odds. Americans loved military heroes, just as they had loved Jackson and Harrison before him and many others to follow. But for southerners Taylor held a special attraction. He was a Louisiana planter and slaveholder. People soon started to call him by his nickname, Old Rough and Ready.

When Webster first heard about Taylor's great victory back in Washington, he attempted to use the general's influence to Edward's advantage. For help in this endeavor he wrote to Senator Crittenden, whose son Webster had helped rescue from the Mexicans when he served as secretary of state. "My own acquaintance with Genl Taylor is slight," Webster admitted to Crittenden, "& I have thought that you might be willing to enclose to Edward a note of introduction, to be presented to Genl. Taylor, when he shall meet him," and perhaps he could be transferred to the general's command, where he would be safe. Webster said he had great regard for Taylor. "I admire his prudence, judgment, & modesty, as much as his coolness & bravery."[41]

It surely galled Webster, as he paraded from one southern town and city to another, to listen to the excited expectations of Whigs who believed they had found another General Harrison who could lead them to electoral victory, presuming of course that Taylor was a Whig. Several southern Whigs whom the senator had known intimately in Congress and whom he counted on to help him win a nomination told him that they intended to nominate the general at their state convention.[42] The experience could only have alerted him to the fact that 1848 would be yet another year in which his presidential ambition would be thwarted.

Actually he had been fully aware of Taylor's rising popularity even before he left on his tour. When word of the victory at Buena Vista reached Washington, rumor insisted that the general would receive the Whig nomination. "Genl Taylor's popularity seems to spread like wild fire," Webster wrote to Fletcher on April 18. "They say it is likely to break down party division entirely, in the south and west."[43] On April 27 the National Whig, a Washington newspaper, proclaimed "Taylor for President. The Hero of Palo Alto, Resace de La Palma, Monterey." Webster seemed to have accepted the idea as inevitable when he told Fletcher that "the probability now is, that General Taylor will come in as President with a general rush. He would, certainly, were the election now to

40. The few surviving speeches he gave during this tour can be found in W&S, IV, 71–103.
41. DW to Crittenden, April 6, 1847, in PC, VI, 221–222.
42. John Berrien to DW, June 21, 1847, ibid., VI, 237.
43. DW to Fletcher Webster, April 18, 1847, in Van Tyne, ed., Letters of Webster, p. 356.

come on. It is in the nature of mankind to carry their favor towards military achievement. No people yet have ever been found to resist that tendency."[44]

Still, he undertook the southern tour because he was not ready to give up his own ambition for another shot at the presidency in 1848. But the reaction he encountered throughout the South depressed him, depressed him because he knew the reason for it. "I know that they say I am no politician," he confided to Peter Harvey, "and know nothing about the feeling of the masses of men. 'Mr Webster is,' they say, 'a great man, an able man, but he has no sympathies with the people; the people know nothing about him, and their wants he knows nothing about.' " That is not true, the senator continued. "I do know a great deal more about the temper of the American people than they give me credit for, and a great deal more than they know." Be that as it may, the perception the people had of him could not be denied. And it remained fixed to the end of his life.[45]

Why then go on with this charade when he felt miserable and longed for the bliss and comfort of Marshfield? His allergies troubled him constantly throughout the trip. The tedium of processions and welcoming committees and dinners and speeches wore him down—first the cold and then the heat and humidity, the intensity of which he had never really experienced before, despite his many years in Washington. He needed to get back home. He needed to rest at his refuge in Marshfield.

In Savannah, his next stop, he spoke at the Greene and Pulaski Monument and attended a dinner, but by this time he had decided to terminate his tour. "Most of the West I have seen already, and care less about visiting it now," he haughtily remarked.[46]

Most southerners were disappointed by his decision but could appreciate that his health necessitated it. "The weather was so unfavorable during your stay," they admitted.[47] Webster learned that the steamer *Southerner* bound for New York would be leaving Charleston toward the end of the month, so he turned around and headed back to that city, where he arrived on the afternoon of May 29. He embarked the same evening and reached New York on June 1.[48]

Webster had no sooner returned to Marshfield than his good friend Representative George Ashmun advised him about what had been happening during his absence. "The Taylor fever has been spreading far & wide," he reported. He did not say so directly, but he clearly implied that Webster's nomination at the national convention, much to his regret, did not look promising. The masses will always choose a military hero over a statesman to serve as their President, no matter how threadbare his credentials. "The world gets crazy so easily! & there is no suitable Asylum for a whole people suddenly grown insane."[49]

44. *W&S*, XVIII, 239.

45. Harvey, *Reminiscences*, p. 199.

46. DW to Fletcher Webster, May 23, 1847, in *W&S*, XVIII, 254.

47. John Berrien to DW, June 21, 1847, in *PC*, VI, 237.

48. *National Intelligencer*, June 3, 5, 1847.

49. Ashmun to DW, June 14, 1847, in *PC*, VI, 235–236.

38

A Double Tragedy

WEAK, exhausted, and still suffering from his hay fever, Webster returned home around June 10. A week at Marshfield did him a world of good. "Think of us at Marshfield," he wrote to William W. Seaton, "—on our piazza, with now and then a grandchild with us, a pond near, where 'cows may drink and geese may swim.' " There "is such a chance for rest and for a good long visit from 'Tired Nature's sweet restorer.' " In fact there is green grass "more than we saw in all the South."[1]

But that green grass was making him miserable. It contributed to the severe allergic reactions he suffered throughout the summer. It got so that he could predict the onset of his "annual catarrh." He told Edward Curtis, "In seven days, I shall begin to sneeze and blow my nose; the first week this catarrh is usually most severe." Finally he consulted Dr. Samuel Jackson of Philadelphia. Dr. Jackson supposedly had great success in treating "catarrh" as a nervous affliction that "simulates an inflammatory disease." After examining his patient in the fall, the good doctor declared "that a depleting, debilitating treatment, aggravated and prolonged" his condition. He prescribed a "generous and substantial" diet, as substantial as "the digestive organs will bear," along with a tonic for two or three weeks and "the inhalation of pure sulphuric ether." He did not think a change of climate would have much influence although Webster usually found relief "by passing from an inland to an ocean atmosphere." Webster pursued this prescription, on and off, for the rest of his life. To say the least, it did nothing for his waistline, but the intake of "pure sulphuric ether" surely cleared his nasal passages.

At this time Webster's rheumatism also kicked up, but despite its annoyance, he had grown rather accustomed to it.[2]

To his great chagrin, on inspecting the Marshfield grounds, he found that his fish baskets, book of flies and hooks, several rods, and all the tops of the red rod that had been given him by William Edgar had disappeared. Then, to his complete surprise and delight, he found an unopened box—nobody knew when

1. DW to Seaton, June 21, 1847, in *W&S*, XVI, 487.

2. DW to Cushing, June 18, 1847, in *PC*, VI, 236–237; DW to Curtis, August 15, 1849, in Webster, ed., *Private Correspondence*, p. 338; Curtis, *Webster*, II, 312

or from whom it came—and discovered inside "the most splendid angling apparatus you can imagine. There are three complete rods, all silver mounted, with my name engraved; beautiful reels, and books of flies and hooks, and quantities of other equipments." With it was the maker's card, a man by the name of Welch. In his letter of appreciation to the donor, Webster waxed rhapsodic. "I never saw . . . such a rich and elegant apparatus for angling." Such exquisite workmanship, such rich mountings, such beautiful flies! "Poor Isaak Walton! Little did he think . . . that any unworthy disciple of his would ever be so gorgeously fitted out, with all that art and taste can accomplish for the pursuit of his favorite sport. . . . If my warmest thanks may be made acceptable to the source to which I owe this extraordinary and elegant outfit for angling, I pray you to present them with cordiality and earnestness."[3]

While resting at home and indulging his "favorite sport," Webster had to forgo one important event: a Rivers and Harbors Convention held in Chicago on July 5.[4] It appeared to be a sectional response to a convention, held the previous year in Memphis and presided over by Calhoun, that had proposed a federally sponsored program of public works aimed at providing outlets in southern port cities for western products. If successful, such a program would reactivate the old South-West political alliance. A bill to implement it passed Congress, but Polk vetoed it. Now, in Chicago, northern commercial interests meant to counteract this challenge by proposing internal improvements that would draw the western economic interests into the eastern orbit. Accordingly, the country's major politicians from both parties were invited to attend, but only Whigs, Wilmot Proviso Democrats, and Barnburners (the radical wing of the New York Democratic party, which supposedly opposed slavery so vehemently that it would even burn down the barn to get rid of the rats)[5] showed up. Philip Hone, who attended, said some ten thousand visitors, of whom six thousand were delegates, crowded into the city. Abbott Lawrence, still distrustful of Webster and himself grasping after political power, led the Massachusetts delegation. No building could hold this human mass, so the delegates sat under an enormous marquee on the courthouse grounds. Webster had intended to make an appearance but was forced to decline after he had canceled the northern and western portions of his tour. Still, he sent a letter of encouragement in which he declared that "I never entertained a particle of doubt" concerning the power of the government to appropriate funds for clearing rivers and building harbors. This power "is not partial, limited, obscure," or discriminatory, as had been suggested at the Memphis convention. "In my opinion, the authority of the Government in this respect, rests directly on the grant of the Commercial power of Congress; and this has been so understood from the beginning, by the wisest and best men"

3. DW to Fletcher Webster, June 12, DW to Welch, June 10, 1847, in *W&S*, XVIII, 255–257.

4. For an excellent discussion of this convention, see Mentor Williams, "The Chicago River and Harbor Convention, 1847," *Mississippi Valley Historical Review*, XXXV (March 1949), XV, pp. 607–622.

5. Barnburners were allied with locofocos.

in the country. The letter was read to the delegates just before the convention adjourned on July 7. It received three cheers and was ordered to be entered into the minutes.[6]

Westerners were genuinely disappointed by Webster's absence, for they regarded him as something of a champion of their interests. His record on the public lands issue especially pleased them because he favored providing cheap or even free land to settlers. He opposed using the land to provide revenue; it should be made readily available to those who would cultivate it. "The great object of government, in respect to these lands," he said as early as 1825, "was not so much the money derived from their sale, as it was the getting of them settled."[7] He also espoused preemption—that is, the right of squatters to buy the land they occupied without competition when it was put up for purchase.

New Englanders and many Whigs took exception to his position on public lands, fearing its consequence to their special interests. When Caleb Cushing gave a speech in Congress favoring preemption, John Quincy Adams stated flatly that their constituents opposed it. The crusty former President also recognized who had prompted Cushing's speech. He "takes his cue from Webster and hazards opinions unpopular now in our State and section."[8]

The opposition of New England to preemption and the other "presumptions" of western demands were spelled out in a speech by Webster's colleague Senator John Davis of Massachusetts on February 9, 1837.[9] But Webster recognized that continued opposition to western needs would be self-defeating. The future belonged to the West. He, like Cushing, knew that preemption would "prevail" in Congress, said Adams, and "against which he sees that all resistance is vain."[10] Rather than opposition he preached cooperation and compromise between the two sections. He endeavored to do this by his advocacy of a liberal public lands policy as well as support for internal improvements and a favorable adjustment of certain tariff rates to benefit western farmers.[11] Ultimately he succeeded. Lawrence's presence at the Chicago convention was one indication of his success.

Webster's congressional record from 1825 (his first important speech on advocating settlement over revenue with regard to the West) until 1850 (when he introduced a homestead resolution) clearly established "his claim," in the words of one historian, "to be regarded as a pioneer in the recasting of New England's attitude toward the West." He "blazed the pro-western trail," which others subsequently followed.[12]

6. Hone, *Diary*, II, 801, 811; DW to Samuel Smith et al., June 26, 1847, in *PC*, VI, 239–240.

7. *Register of Debates*, 18th Congress, 2d Session, p. 252.

8. Adams, *Memoirs*, X, 18.

9. *Congressional Globe*, 24th Congress, 2d Session, Appendix, pp. 313–317.

10. Adams, *Memoirs*, X, 18.

11. *Niles' Weekly Register*, June 3, 1843.

12. Peter J. Parish, "Daniel Webster, New England, and the West," *Journal of American History* LIV (December 1967), pp. 525, 546.

Although Webster had expected to attend this Chicago convention and thereby further improve his presidential prospects among westerners, his absence spared him the discomfort of hearing the delegates discuss possible Whig presidential candidates and learning of "the spreading fire" of enthusiasm among them for Zachary Taylor. But could anyone be sure that the general was a Whig, a bona fide Whig, not just some military opportunist seeking a nomination? Rumor had it that Taylor had responded to an editorial in a Cincinnati newspaper by stating that he had not acquainted himself with the leading issues of the day. When pressed, he declared himself a Whig or a "democrat of the Jeffersonian school" and said he would have voted for Clay had he voted at all in 1844. His statement, when reprinted, startled a good many Whigs, including Webster. "If Genl Taylor did that letter, then . . . we cannot support him." Webster's newspaper, the Boston *Atlas*, for which he wrote many unsigned articles, carried an editorial advising against a Whig nomination of Taylor. Later Taylor labeled himself a "no-party" Whig—whatever that meant.[13]

All this put a new spin on presidential politics. Clay, in retirement at his home in Lexington, Kentucky, stirred himself and arranged to have his friend John J. Crittenden eased out of the Senate and into the governor's mansion so that the Great Pacificator could take his place in Congress and start the process of campaigning for another bid for the presidency. To complicate matters more, a second military hero appeared on the scene. In a combined land-sea operation General Winfield Scott, perhaps the finest general in American history, led the first amphibious landing expedition and captured Veracruz. By mid-April he had reached the plateau leading directly to Mexico City by defeating General Santa Anna in battle at the pass of Cerro Gordo. Now the Whigs had two certified heroes as possible presidential candidate. Unfortunately for Scott, he had no support among westerners, or so Clay said. His published letters to Secretary of War William L. Marcy subjected him to ridicule as something of a scold. "Old Fuss and Feathers," many laughingly referred to him.[14]

It soon became clear to Webster that with Scott out of the way and Taylor a dubious Whig he had a real opportunity to win the nomination, that his only possible rival for the nomination was Clay. And Clay was a three-time loser. Would the Whig party actually put him forward for a fourth run when Daniel Webster, the "Defender of the Constitution" and "Defender of Peace," was available? Conscience Whigs might not cotton to him, but would Taylor or Clay, each a slaveowner, be preferable?

Webster and his friends then decided to try to win an endorsement from

13. Taylor wrote a good many impolitic letters during this campaign. In responding to the Cincinnati *Morning Signal*, he seemed to advocate applying the Northwest Ordinance against slavery to the Southwest, thereby outraging southern Whigs. Holman Hamilton, *Zachary Taylor: Soldier in the White House* (Indianapolis and New York, 1951), pp. 42–43; DW to Fletcher Webster, July 5, 1847, in *PC*, VI, 241; *Atlas*, July 3, 1847. There are at least fifteen unsigned articles opposing the acquisition of territory from Mexico in the *Atlas* for 1847, most, if not all, of which sound as though they were written by Webster.

14. Remini, *Clay*, pp. 687–699.

the Massachusetts Whig convention when it met in September. The Defender of Peace knew that the Lawrence faction would oppose him, despite his apparent reconciliation with its leader. Besides, the state's Cotton Whigs preferred Taylor and hoped to form a ticket with the general at the top and Abbott Lawrence as his running mate.

The Lawrence group guessed what the Websterites were up to and hoped to strengthen their position by winning support from the Conscience Whigs. Men like Adams, Sumner, Phillips, Wilson, Palfrey, and their friends found themselves in the enviable position of holding the balance between the two rival factions and were amused, if not delighted, to be courted by both.[15]

When the convention met in Springfield on September 29, the friends of Webster seemed to have the upper hand. What they wanted was a unanimous endorsement of the senator. They therefore showed the Conscience Whigs great latitude in voicing their opposition to slavery. But "by prearrangement" at a preconvention caucus, and with the tacit approval of the Cotton Whigs, the Conscience Whigs planned to offer a motion declaring that it was "inexpedient" to recommend the nomination of candidates for the national ticket. It was their intention to block the naming of Webster as the state's "favorite son" and then get the convention to pledge itself in favor of the Wilmot Proviso and against any candidate who would not take a definite stand against slavery. This plan, they calculated, would attract both the Lawrence Whigs because it denied Webster a nomination and the Websterites because it would prevent the Massachusetts delegation at the national convention from supporting Taylor.[16]

But the plan failed. Although the motion that would block Webster's selection, proposed by Stephen Phillips, caught the chairman, George Ashmun, by surprise, George T. Curtis immediately moved to table it. The tabling motion passed by a vote of 242 to 232 and rescued the Websterites from a public embarrassment. The resolution against supporting any candidate unwilling to pledge himself against slavery also failed. In desperation the Websterites on the platform committee rushed to draw up a set of resolutions acceptable to the Conscience Whigs, hoping that might appease them.

Just then Webster mounted the platform in an effort to save his nomination. "I am here, ready to express my opinion . . . [and] thank God, there is nothing I shrink from." With his eye glued to the door through which the committee would return with its amended resolutions he talked and talked and talked. He would not relinquish the floor until the committee returned. It was, in the opinion of one historian, "one of the most remarkable and agile speeches of his career." He immediately proceeded to condemn the Mexican War as unnecessary and unjustified. Some "think that violence is strength," he cried. "That I hold to be a mistake. Violent counsels are weak counsels; violent conduct is weak

15. Donald, *Sumner and the Coming of the Civil War,* pp. 156–157; Brauer, *Cotton versus Conscience,* p. 213.

16. For details of this preconvention planning, see Brauer, *Cotton versus Conscience Whigs,* pp. 213–217; Martin B. Duberman, *Charles Francis Adams, 1807–1886* (Boston, 1960), pp. 110–116, and Donald, *Sumner,* p. 158.

conduct; violent language is always weak language." Unless the President of the United States can make a case to prove that the war is being prosecuted for the safety of the Union and the just rights of the American people, he declared, "then Congress ought to pass resolutions against the prosecution of the war, and grant no further supplies."

As he continued, his antislavery rhetoric escalated and grew more intense. He even claimed credit for the Wilmot Proviso! "We hear much, just now, of a panacea for the danger and evils of slavery and slave annexation, which they call the Wilmot Proviso. . . . Did I not commit myself in 1838 to the whole doctrine, fully, entirely? And I must be permitted to say that I cannot quite consent that more recent discoverers should claim the merit, and take out a patent. I deny the priority of their invention. Allow me to say, sir, it is not their thunder."[17]

By the time he finished this speech he had performed a miracle, according to the *Liberator*, William Lloyd Garrison's radical antislavery newspaper. "He who had gone up, as men thought, the Oldest of the Old Whigs, came down again younger than the Youngest! His youth was renewed like the eagle's. . . . He had never been an Old Whig at all. He had always indulged in a Conscience. The Wilmot Proviso was not Mr. Wilmot's, after all, but Mr. Webster's thunder."[18]

The speech worked. At least the convention went on to endorse Webster, although at the expense of party unity, something the senator dreaded and constantly preached against. But the Lawrence Whigs also achieved their purpose. They had forced Webster into making statements against slavery that would surely cost him southern votes, and they had demonstrated that in Massachusetts Webster's availability was anything but supported with unity. Besides, they had kept the convention from excluding Taylor as a possible presidential candidate. As for the endorsement of Webster they regarded that action as an empty courtesy.[19]

Once Webster had what he wanted he again came forward and offered "a few generalities intended as a soother," but several Conscience Whigs would have none of it. Charles Francis Adams, for example, had learned from his father that Daniel Webster could not be trusted and would do or say whatever he believed the occasion required.[20]

The Conscience Whigs looked around at the wreckage that their plan had provoked. They had pretty much scuttled Webster's national chances for the nomination, even though he was the only antislavery candidate available, but they had also failed to bind the Massachusetts delegation against Taylor's nomination. Dejected and angry, they left the hall protesting that they would never attend another Whig convention.[21]

Webster returned to Marshfield to prepare for the approaching session of

17. Donald, *Sumner*, p. 158; *W&S*, XIII, 345–358.

18. *Liberator* (October 8, 1847), quoted in Donald, *Sumner*, p. 158.

19. Dalzell, *Webster and American Nationalism*, pp. 138–141.

20. Adams diary, September 23, 1846, quoted in Duberman, *Adams*, p. 118.

21. Donald, *Sumner*, pp. 158–159.

Congress. He hated the idea of giving up the pleasures of his home for "toilsome law and wrangling politics." Among other things he would miss the music of the ocean. "I hear the sea, very strong and loud at the North . . . the deep, hollow-sounding, half-groaning, or loud wailing voice of the ocean, uttered as if a resentment of its violent disturbance by the winds." But he had to leave and so set about readying Marshfield for winter quarters. Luckily his barns were full, he reported, with three thousand bushels of corn, three thousand of turnips, seven or eight hundred of beets, and a barnful of hay.[22]

He arrived late in Washington, as usual, presented petitions to end the war, but spent most his time during this session arguing an important case, *Luther v. Borden,* before the Supreme Court. The case resulted from a revolt in Rhode Island in 1842 that shocked and frightened the nation.[23] Thomas W. Dorr led an armed uprising against the state's franchise law of 1724, which restricted the suffrage to property holders. By the early 1840s the state's disfranchised adult white males outnumbered legal voters. Dorr and his supporters framed a People's Constitution that abolished limited franchise and set up a new government with Dorr as governor. State officials under the original colonial charter decreed martial law, and the governor, Samuel Ward King, asked President Tyler for federal troops to assist in putting down the rebellion. Tyler responded that he would interfere only if the insurrection got beyond the power of the state to deal with it. Eventually the charter government crushed the rebellion, seized Dorr, sentenced him to life imprisonment, but released him after a year and enacted electoral reforms to provide a more equitable suffrage.

One of Dorr's followers, Martin Luther, brought suit against Luther M. Borden, a state militiaman, and other members of the state militia, who had entered his house wrongfully, he contended, under authority of the state's proclamation of martial law. After review in lower courts the case reached the Supreme Court on appeal in January 1848, with Benjamin F. Hallett and Attorney General Nathan Clifford arguing for Luther and the Dorr government and John Whipple and Webster for Borden and the charter government. Hallett contended that the people of Rhode Island, much like the colonists at the time of the Revolution, had met in convention and acting in their sovereign capacity had adopted a new, more democratic constitution, and therefore the charter government had been superseded and had no authority to declare martial law.

Webster, like everyone else, understood the larger political implications of the situation. It was 1848, a presidential election year, and the Dorrites had aligned themselves with the Jacksonian party. This case therefore was seen as a contest between Whigs and Democrats.

Webster argued this case, unlike the *Girard* case, brilliantly. He worked hard on its preparation. He always said that doing the necessary research for the brief, preparing his arguments, and looking up precedents were never tedious

22. DW to Blatchford, December 7, 1847, in Curtis, *Webster,* II, 314.

23. For details of the Dorr Rebellion, see Marvin E. Gettleman, *The Dorr Rebellion* (New York, 1973) and George M. Dennison, *The Dorr Rebellion* (Lexington, Ky., 1976).

and unrewarding. What he did find mind-numbing was having to sit hour after hour listening to and taking notes of the arguments advanced by the opposition, arguments that frequently were idiotic and devoid of constitutional or legal validity. And in this case, as in so many other cases he had argued before the Supreme Court since the deaths of John Marshall and Joseph Story, he faced a hostile court, one unsympathetic with his particular, Federalist, view of the Constitution.[24]

What Webster did was simply apply the rule of law to Hallett's premise of popular sovereignty. Colonists at the time of the Revolution, he argued, established representative government that protected liberty and property and established a specific process for changing government. Legitimate power resides with the people, he agreed, but they do "not exercise it in masses or *per capita.*" They exercise it through their elected representatives. The charter government of Rhode Island had exercised and did exercise the means of making constitutional revisions and political changes. And a Rhode Island court had so conceded. The so-called People's Constitution, therefore, had no legal or political legitimacy. Did any man under the authority of the Dorr constitution exercise a particle of official power? he asked. Did any officer ever make an arrest? Did any man ever bring a suit? "Never. It never performed one single act of government. It never did a thing in the world. All was patriotism, and all was paper; and with patriotism and with paper it went out on the 4th of May, admitting itself to be, as all must regard it, a contemptible *sham!*"

The Supreme Court, Webster concluded, should not involve itself in a purely political decision, one already settled by the legitimate state legislature.[25]

Since it was a presidential election year, the Court held the case over before handing down its decision. Then, beginning in its January 1849 term, after the election, the Court ruled in Webster's favor.

Chief Justice Taney gave the majority decision, which set forth the limitations of judicial power. This case involved a political, not a judicial, matter, he declared. Between two governments claiming legitimacy the Court did not have jurisdiction. Since a Rhode Island court had already ruled in favor of the charter government, that decision bound the federal courts. Besides, Congress under the authority of the Constitution had authorized the President to act to preserve domestic tranquillity. And as Webster had indicated in his argument, President Tyler had been prepared to assist the charter government if needed. Thus, both the legislative and executive branches of the federal government had performed their necessary and respective functions. It was not up to the Court to presume to know better about what was purely a political consideration.[26]

Webster took great comfort in the decision. Perhaps there was some hope

24. DW to Fletcher Webster, February 7, 1847, in *PC,* VI, 208.

25. 7 Howard, 3ff; *W&S,* XI, 217–242; *PLFP,* 747, 749–750, 751; Baxter, *Webster and Supreme Court,* pp. 58–64. For Webster's notes for his oral argument, see *PLFP,* pp. 751–764.

26. In his decision Taney agreed that the sovereignty of each state resides in the people and "is a political question to be settled by the political power." 7 Howard 34–48.

for this Court after all. Reason, common sense, and the law had been respected and reaffirmed.

All the while Webster spent attending the Supreme Court and the Senate during the winter months of 1847–1848 his thoughts constantly turned to his children. Edward wrote him regularly, but he and his regiment had moved to within striking distance of the battlefield of Contreras, about seven miles from Mexico City, which had been captured by Scott the previous September. Edward thought the city "is not so superb as I had anticipated, although there are numerous elegant churches."

Webster not only worried about Edward and what might happen to him in Mexico but in January became concerned about the health of his daughter, Julia. She had contracted tuberculosis, and suddenly her condition had deteriorated alarmingly. So much so that he planned to go to Boston in January 1848 and bring her back with him to Washington, where the weather was milder and he could watch over her and tend to her needs. "She may bring as many or as few of the children as she pleases," he said.

In her letters to her father Julia made light of her condition. She had a cold that worsened because of the damp days they had had in Boston. "I am now to stay in my room, until I get rid of it," she explained. She seemed far more concerned about her father's winning the Whig nomination. Webster assured her that he wished only to be "the first farmer in Marshfield, South Parish, and I am content with this, unless I should be called to be first, elsewhere, where I can do more good." Fletcher kept him informed of Julia's condition. But with the new year his letters sounded ominous. "I am infinitely concerned about Julia," the father replied. Webster was not an emotionally demonstrative man, but he was sincerely and deeply devoted to his family.[27]

In the midst of his concern about Julia, Webster received the shattering news on February 21 that his son Edward had died in San Angel, eight miles from Mexico City on the evening of January 23, 1848, of typhoid fever after an illness of seventeen days. He died in his sleep. At about the same time Webster also received a letter dated January 12 from Henry Pleasants, the former servant who had accompanied Edward to Mexico. Pleasants described how Edward had been exposed to rain and cold that brought on "an atact [attack] the Same as he had at Matamoras [sic] . . . I myself think he is improveing very fast for i have been up with him the last ten nights and his rest is much Better now than it has been."[28] Eleven days later Edward succumbed.

"I hardly know how I shall bear up under this blow," Webster wept. "It almost crushed us." Addressing this letter to "My dear and only Son," he told

27. Edward Webster to DW, December 20, 1847, DW to Fletcher Webster, January 29, February 4, 1848, Julia Appleton to DW, December 27, 1847, DW to Julia Appleton, February 14, 1848, in W&S, XVIII, 264, 265, 267, 268, 269.

28. Timothy Childs to DW, March 6, Pleasants to DW, January 12, 1848, in PC, VI, 264, 273. Childs was the attending physician and "witnessed the patience with which he [Edward] bore his illness and the calm resignation with which he met his fate."

Fletcher of the pain he endured on learning of Edward's death. Edward, the black sheep of the family, the boy he had once threatened to disown, dead at the age of twenty-seven. "I have always regarded it as a great misfortune to outlive my children; but I feel now, but more intensely, as when Grace and Charles died. But the will of Heaven be done in all things!" He asked George Healy, the eminent artist who had painted Webster many times, to execute "a beautiful picture of dear Edward. I shall take it home and keep it before my eyes as long as I live."[29]

Julia was informed of Edward's death by her husband. "Dear little Neddy!" she sobbed. "I cannot believe you are gone!" He died in a "wicked & cruel war . . . without one friend to smooth his dying pillow." At least his hands were not stained with Mexican blood. She recognized that it "was God's will, & 'God's will be done'—but *now* I feel nothing but what my brother in the flower of his youth, was a useless sacrifice—to what?—ambition & vainglory. May God in his mercy, sanctify this great affliction to us all."[30]

When she wrote these words, Julia herself was dying. Webster knew it but could barely think about it. "Another event is approaching," he admitted, "which goes to the very bottom of my heart. I cannot trust myself to speak of it, or to write about it." Julia also knew. "May we all prepare to follow him [Edward], through him Who is the Way, the Truth and the Life, and through whom alone we can find acceptance with God," she wrote her father in a remarkable display of Christian resignation.[31] On April 28, with her father at her side, along with the other members of her family, she died of consumption at the age of thirty. Her last words were "Let me go, for the day breaketh."[32]

The following day, Saturday, at 8:00 A.M., Webster recorded her passing.

It is over. Mrs. Appleton died last evening at a quarter past eight o'clock. She suffered a good deal at times during the day from difficulty of respiration, but finally expired, calmly, without a struggle, and without pain. She retained all her faculties to the last moment in a most remarkable degree. Her mind was never brighter, and she conversed as much as her strength would allow. During her suffering moments she seemed impatient to be gone, but generally exhibited perfect resignation, and the most assured Christian faith. I have never seen a death so calm and serene, and attended with such perfect soundness and strength of mind.[33]

29. DW to Fletcher Webster, February 23, March 15, DW to Mrs. Ticknor, March 13, 1848, in W& S, XVIII, 271, 274, 275.

30. Julia Appleton to DW, [February 23, 1848], in *PC*, VI, 272–273. Three days later she wrote: "It is indeed a sad affliction; but, thank God! I feel such perfect trust in His mercy and love, and know so well that 'He doth not willingly afflict or grieve the children of men,' that I feel assured it was for Edward's good and happiness, as well as for ours, that he was taken away." Julia Appleton to DW, February 26, 1848, in W&S, XVIII, 271.

31. DW to Hiram Ketchum, April 3, 1848, in *PC*, VI, 282; Julia Appleton to DW, February 26, 1848, in W&S, XVIII, 271.

32. Curtis, *Webster*, II, 326. A year following Julia's death her daughter Constance Mary Appleton, born May 30, 1847, died on March 15, 1849, and was later buried at Marshfield. Ibid., II, 332.

33. DW to Charles Thomas, [April 29, 1848], in *PC*, VI, 284.

"Poor Mr. Webster!" Philip Hone recorded in his diary. "My heart bleeds for him." The deaths of Julia and Edward "will wring their parents' hearts, and bring a sympathizing tear into the eye of many a friend."[34]

The loss of two children in a matter of three months devastated Webster as he struggled to find the strength to endure this latest affliction. The funeral took place on Monday, May 1, and the Episcopal service was conducted by Bishop Eastburn. The body was laid to rest in the Webster tomb under St. Paul's Church in Boston.

Edward's remains had been returned to the father on May 1, the very day of Julia's funeral. Henry Pleasants accompanied the body, bringing with it Edward's effects and favorite horse. "I paid five hundred dollars for Henry," the senator said, "and it was the best spent money I ever laid out in my life." As he spoke, tears flowed freely down his face.

Major Webster, with full military honors, was buried three days later alongside his mother and brother Charles and sisters Grace and Julia. Twice within a week, the father said, he looked upon the coffins of "the mother and four out of five of her children," all buried in the same tomb.

It was an agony. "May God enable me to sustain these overwhelming sorrows, and still always to bless His most Holy name."[35]

34. Hone, *Diary,* II, 839.

35. DW to Samuel Jaudon, April 15, 1848, in *PC,* VI, 283; DW to Mrs. Eliza Buckminster Lee, May 8, 1848, in *W&S,* XVIII, 277; Curtis, *Webster,* II, 330

39

"I Am Old, and Poor, and Proud"

WEBSTER spent the week following the burial of his children at Marshfield, where he began preparing the final resting place for his first wife and deceased children. Later the remains of his family were transported to Marshfield, where three monuments for Julia, Edward, and Grace, chosen earlier by Julia, had been erected in their memory. They stood four feet high on granite bases, capped with marble. The monument for their mother was "rather larger, so as to bear the names of Grace and Charles." Webster personally planted two weeping elms on the lawn in front of the house as a living reminder of his two recent losses. When he finished, he handed the shovel to Fletcher and said, *"My son, protect these trees after I am gone; let them ever remind you of Julia and Edward."* He wanted the trees to be called "The Brother and Sister."[1]

After returning to Washington, Webster hardly functioned, laboring as he did "under deep depression." On March 17, toward the end of the session, he managed to speak against the administration's ten regiment bill to raise an additional $16 million for the support of forces in Mexico. Despite his efforts, the bill passed later that day. But the same messenger who brought Webster the news of his son's death on February 21 also brought word that Nicholas Trist, a State Department employee sent to Mexico on a secret mission, had disobeyed orders to return to the United States and negotiated at Guadalupe Hidalgo an unauthorized treaty of peace in which Mexico ceded California and New Mexico to the United States and accepted the Rio Grande as the Texas boundary in return for $15 million and an additional $3.25 million for American claims against Mexico. Despite Trist's unauthorized action, the treaty had everything Polk wanted, especially California, so he accepted it and submitted it to the Senate for ratification.[2]

1. DW to Fletcher Webster, June 2, 1852, in W&S, XVIII, 533; Curtis, *Webster,* II, 330–331; Lanman, *Private Life of Webster,* p. 76.

2. *Congressional Globe,* 30th Congress, 1st Session, pp. 484–490; DW to Caleb Cushing, March 12, 1848, in *PC,* VI, 273–274.

The sudden death of John Quincy Adams, stricken in the House on February 21 and dying two days later, held up action on the treaty in the upper house. One of Webster's sharpest and most unrelenting critics had passed from the scene. At the funeral ceremonies held in the House the silver-mounted coffin bore an inscription written by Webster at the request of the Massachusetts delegation to Congress. "Having served his country for half a century, and enjoyed its highest honors," it read in part, John Quincy Adams died on February 23. Adams's biographer says that Adams must have been content with the inscription, "if not with the hand that wrote it."[3]

A little more than two weeks later, on March 10, 1848, the Senate ratified the Treaty of Guadalupe Hidalgo, Webster voting in opposition.[4]

Despite several political setbacks and despite his depression, Webster felt compelled to deliver a denunciation of the Mexican War, this fiendish struggle that had taken from him his beloved son. He wanted, and needed, to go on record attacking the war as an unconstitutional exercise of executive authority. He also wished to advertise the fact that the peace was unconstitutionally negotiated, provided unwanted territory, except for San Francisco, and would perpetuate African slavery in this country and threaten the life of the Union. As the "especial guardian of the Constitution," to use Hiram Ketchum's expression, he had an obligation to speak out, however delayed, and warn the people of the fraud that Polk and his administration had perpetrated against them and their institutions.[5]

Because he waited for the arrival in Washington of Henry J. Raymond, managing editor of the New York *Courier and Enquirer* and later founder of the *New York Times,* who had expertly reported his argument in the *Luther* v. *Borden* case, Webster did not give his Mexican War speech in the Senate until Thursday, March 23.[6] When all was ready, he blasted the administration, lacing his speech with sarcasm, wit, and his vast knowledge of history and the constitutional requirements for legitimacy in any action taken in as momentous an event as a national war.

Normally we negotiate a treaty first, then ratify it, he declared. But this administration has chosen to reverse the process. "We ratify first, and negotiate afterwards. . . . It strikes me that the course we have adopted is strange, is even *grotesque.*"

3. The full inscription reads: "JOHN QUINCY ADAMS BORN an inhabitant of Massachusetts July 11, 1767 DIED a citizen of the United States, in the Capitol, at Washington, February 23, 1848, Having served his country for half a century, And enjoyed its highest honors." Bemis, *Adams,* II, 539.

4. *Senate Executive Documents,* 30th Congress, 1st Session, serial 509, document 52; *National Intelligencer,* June 10, 1848. Webster voted against the treaty "because it contained these cessations of territory, and brought under the authority of the United States, with a pledge of future admission into the Union, the great, vast, and almost unknown countries of New Mexico and California." *PS,* II, 508.

5. Ketchum to DW, March 20, 1848, in *PC,* VI, 280.

6. DW to Raymond, March 15, 1848, ibid., VI, 274.

This war was waged for one thing: to create new states on the southern frontier. "I have opposed this object. I am against all accessions of territory to form new States. . . . If I were asked to-day whether, for the sake of peace, I would take a treaty for adding two new States to the Union on our southern border, I would say, *No!* distinctly, No! And I wish every man in the United States to understand that to be my judgment and my purpose."

We hear it said that "we must have some territory, the people demand it. I deny it; at least, I see no proof of it whatever. . . . But it is said we must take territory for the sake of peace. We must take territory. It is the will of the President. If we do not now take what he offers, we may fare worse. Mr. Polk will take no less, that he is fixed upon. He is immovable. He—has—put—down—his—foot! Well, Sir, he put it down upon 'fifty-four forty,' but it didn't stay."

That last remark hit its intended target with telling effect. I mean no disrespect, Webster went on, but "who and what is Mr. Polk?" We are on the eve of a presidential election, and Polk has decided not to run for reelection. A new man will assume his office. What then? "Why, then Mr. Polk becomes as absolutely insignificant as . . . you or I; and, as far as I am concerned that certainly is little enough."

We propose to take New Mexico. The people in this desolate place "are infinitely less elevated, in morals and condition, than the people of the Sandwich Islands [Hawaii]." The Cherokees, Choctaws, Pawnees, and Flatfeet Indians are far superior to these "*Digging* Indians" in New Mexico. Have they any notion of popular government? Free government? "Not the slightest! Not the slightest on earth!" Between New Mexico and California "I hold they are not worth a dollar; and we pay for them vast sums of money!" Along California's coastline there are villages, ports, and settlements, but to the "rear all is wilderness and barrenness, and Indian country." And to this wasteland, this " monstrosity," this " disfiguration," this " enormity," we propose to bring the Constitution and its frame of government.

Little did Webster know that just two months earlier in California a transplanted New Jersey carpenter by the name of James Marshall had discovered gold in the millrace he had built in partnership with John Sutter, a Swiss immigrant, on the American River. Word of the discovery had not yet reached the East, but when it did, it sent some ninety thousand seekers hurrying across and around the continent in a wild scramble for what was possibly the greatest lode of undiscovered placer gold in history.

Webster concluded his speech by acknowledging that many would disagree with him. But whether "supported or unsupported, by the blessing of God, I shall do my duty."[7]

---

7. *W&S*, X, 3–33. In editing Webster's speeches and writing, Edward Everett called this speech "Objects of the Mexican War," but the *National Intelligencer* of March 25, 1848, entitled it "Mr. Webster's Speech on the War with Mexico," a most fitting title.

Henry Raymond hurriedly printed the speech in the March 27 issue of his newspaper. It soon appeared in newspapers around the country and was later published in a Boston pamphlet. It helped stimulate interest in Webster as a possible presidential candidate and was so intended by its author.[8] His New York friend Hiram Ketchum wrote two articles that appeared in the New York *Tribune* on March 24 and April 1 under the heading "The Presidency—Daniel Webster," which were also widely reprinted.

These stirrings excited Webster into believing that his turn to win a formal nomination by his party had at last arrived. True, Taylor's popularity had not waned, but his remarks in a letter to Peter Sken Smith on January 30, 1848, that he would accept any nomination, provided it had been made "entirely independent of party considerations," disturbed many Whigs. He followed up that astounding announcement with a response to a "no-party" political meeting that had nominated him in Montgomery County, Alabama, that he would not oppose the use of his name, provided it was "independent of party distinction."[9]

A no-party candidate! What kind of Whig was that? Did the Whigs really want another John Tyler to head the government? Zachary Taylor had not held a single civilian position, had not even voted in his entire life! Did Whigs want such a nonentity to sit in the White House? Webster himself wrote to his friends and argued that "there are hundreds and thousands of Whigs who are sober-minded and religious, who will not vote for a candidate, brought forward only because of his successful fighting in this war against Mexico." Many of Webster's friends subsequently began to drum up support for his nomination.[10]

But what about Henry Clay, the other possible candidate? Prince Hal, as some dubbed him, had begun another campaign and on April 10 announced his willingness to undertake a fifth try for the presidency.[11] Probably the most popular political figure in the country, Clay attracted an army of supporters who would fight hard to win him the nomination.

Webster sighed. As things stood, he informed his friends, "when the convention comes, there will be no leading candidate but Mr. Clay and General Taylor; and unless the latter should, in the mean time, come out clearly and distinctly, with an avowal of Whig principles, which, I think, he is not likely to do, Mr. Clay will, most certainly, be nominated."[12]

Apart from the fact that he was a proved loser, Henry Clay was a slaveowner. Worse, he would not state publicly that he opposed the extension of slavery into

8. DW to Ketchum, April 2, 1848, in *PC*, VI, 282.

9. *PC*, VI, 281, note 3; Lexington *Observer and Kentucky Reporter,* March 4, April 8, 1848; Taylor to William B. Preston, March 28, 1848, Taylor Papers, Virginia Historical Society, Richmond; Hamilton, *Taylor,* II, pp. 66–72; K. Jack Bauer, *Zachary Taylor: Soldier, Planter, Statesman of the Old Southwest* (Baton Rouge, 1985), pp. 215–238.

10. DW to Richard M. Blatchford, January 30, DW to Ketchum, April 3, 1848, in *PC*, VI, 269, 282.

11. Remini, *Clay,* pp. 687–705. Clay ran for the presidency in 1824, 1832, and 1844. He also tried but failed to win a nomination from the Whig party in 1840 and 1848.

12. DW to Richard M. Blatchford, January 30, 1848, in *PC*, VI, 269.

the territories.[13] Could Conscience Whigs in the North support him? Obviously not. It therefore followed in the minds of Webster and his friends that if the Whigs could not unite behind Clay and did not want another Tyler to contend with, the only alternative was the Godlike Daniel. In their minds it was conceivable that the Clay and Taylor forces at the Whig convention, scheduled for June 7 in Philadelphia, would deadlock. Then, in order to defeat the other, they would turn to Webster, who would overwhelmingly win nomination.

A beautiful, fanciful, but hopelessly unrealistic dream. If Clay was a proved loser, so was the Massachusetts senator. He could barely carry his own state, much less New England, and certainly not the West or the South. Besides, neither he nor his supporters had the political skills to pull off a plan such as they had imagined.

Recognizing the necessity of building political support outside New England, Webster sought to encourage help in New York, where his family connections and long association with its business and political leaders made it a likely place for recruitment. He wrote to several possibilities, including Millard Fillmore, formerly a representative and now the comptroller of New York, in which he acknowledged that relations between them had been "rather cool" in the past because of a misunderstanding when Webster headed the State Department. He wanted Fillmore to know that he entertained "the highest & warmest regard for you."

Fillmore had absolutely no recollection of any "misunderstanding" between them but was happy to receive Webster's letter and good wishes for his future success.[14]

Webster's personal involvement in the campaign for a nomination centered on reminding Whigs that they must be just toward the North, the core of their political strength. And who among the three possible candidates best represented that section? He also let it be known that he could not support Taylor. Webster's involvement in the campaign, naturally, was done through his most loyal followers, men like Edward Everett, Hiram Ketchum, George Ashmun, and William W. Seaton, among others. To Everett, he wrote: "You and Mr. H K can, I am quite sure, get up something which will *tell*" at the convention. Once we have laid the case before the southern Whigs, he added, "& *propose* a Northern Candidate" in whom they have confidence and would support, then "I think we should have a chance for a Whig President."[15]

13. "We cannot carry Ohio for you," wrote Thomas B. Stevenson to Clay, "unless you take ground satisfactorily against extending slavery in new territories, or, in less exceptionable phrase, *for free soil remaining free.*" Stevenson to Clay, April 8, 1848, Clay Papers, LC. In his statement Clay made no mention of slavery in the territories, as his northern supporters had begged him to do. He thought that a politically charged announcement would be inappropriate. Remini, *Clay*, p. 703.

14. DW to Fillmore, April 24, 1848, in *PC*, VI, 283–284; Fillmore to DW, May 2, 1848, in *Microfilm Edition*, F21/28592. Fillmore had attacked Webster in 1842 over the latter's refusal to resign from Tyler's cabinet.

15. DW to Everett, May 22, 29, Anson Burlingame to James Wilson, May 27, 1848, in *PC*, VI, 286–287, 288, 290.

Webster's concern that a northern man be nominated not only revealed his own craving for the honor but also reflected the mood of most Conscience Whigs, who opposed Taylor because he was a slaveholder who would represent the southern agricultural wing of the Whig party, as opposed to the northern wing, which emphasized support of manufactures and commerce.[16]

In the midst of this maneuvering the Democrats held their convention in Baltimore on May 22 and nominated the senator from Michigan, General Lewis Cass, who had also served as minister to France and had publicly quarreled with Webster over the joint cruising convention of the Webster-Ashburton Treaty.[17] Cass supported the doctrine of squatter sovereignty, or popular sovereignty, which contended that local government in the territories should decide the question of slavery. For political and sectional balance, General William O. Butler, a Kentucky slaveholder, was chosen for Vice President. The New York representation at the convention consisted of two delegations: the conservative Hunkers, who supposedly "hunkered" after spoils, and the radical Barnburners, who opposed slavery and supported the Wilmot Proviso. Cass's selection caused the Barnburners to walk out of the convention, thereby splitting the party and increasing the possibility of a Whig victory in the fall.[18]

Webster had nothing but contempt for the Cass nomination. "I regard Genl Cass," he told Everett, "as the most likely man in the Country to embroil us with foreign nations. He loves war, & commotion; &, besides, he utterly hates England, & every thing English."[19]

As the time for the Whig convention drew closer, some Whigs seriously considered naming a ticket consisting of Taylor *and* Webster. But Webster assumed that if Taylor were nominated, Abbott Lawrence, the general's ardent supporter, would be nominated with him. Other Whigs, however, wanted Webster for the top spot—if, and only if, he would first give assurances that he would not support Taylor under any circumstances. Henry Wilson, a Massachusetts delegate to the national convention, assured Webster that "we want just such a man as you are to lead us. . . . The people would rally around you as no man of our time ever saw men rally." He promised to vote for Webster in the convention, and in return "I *want the assurance that you nor your friends do not in any event intend to aid directly or indirectly the nomination of Taylor.*"[20]

Two weeks before the Whigs met in national convention Taylor issued a

16. Anson Burlingame to James Wilson, May 27, 1848, ibid., VI, 288.

17. See chapter 33, note 35.

18. H. D. A. Donovan, *Barnburners* (New York, 1925), pp. 98–109; John Mayfield, *Rehearsal for Republicanism: Free Soil and the Politics of Antislavery* (Port Washington, N.Y., 1980), pp. 101–125. See also Robert G. Rayback, *Free Soil: The Election of 1848* (Lexington, Ky., 1970) and Richard H. Seward, *Ballots for Freedom: Antislavery Politics in the United States, 1837–1860* (New York, 1976).

19. DW to Everett, May 29, 1848, in *PC*, VI, 290.

20. James Watson Webb to DW, June 2, Henry Wilson to DW, May 31, DW to Richard M. Blatchford, June 10, 1848, ibid., VI, 291–293.

letter, written by others and published in the New Orleans *Picayune*, in which he professed to be "a Whig but not an ultra Whig."[21] Presumably the letter was intended to calm the fears of those who worried about his political orthodoxy. And when the Whigs finally met in Philadelphia, the Louisiana delegation brought with them a letter from Taylor in which he promised to abide by the decision of the convention and to withdraw from the campaign if someone else was chosen.[22]

Philadelphia "was overflowing with people from all parts of the Union" when the Whig National Nominating Convention met. The day before the convention began rallies (the newspapers called them public meetings) were held for Clay, Scott, and Taylor to demonstrate the relative strength of each of the leading candidates, and all were fully attended. Significantly, there was no rally for Webster. It was a sure sign that his candidacy was not being taken seriously by the national party.[23]

On June 7 some 279 delegates crowded into the saloon of the Chinese Museum to select their candidate and chose the former governor of North Carolina John M. Morehead as president of the convention. The Massachusetts delegation of twelve included such Webster friends and associates as Rufus Choate, Henry Wilson, and George Ashmun.

On the following day a Louisiana delegate was granted permission to read Taylor's letter, after which the balloting began. Nomination required 140 votes. When the first ballot ended, the chair announced that Taylor had received 111 votes, followed by Clay with 97, Scott with 43, Webster with 22, and 4 for John Clayton and 2 for Associate Justice John McLean. Webster had received 3 votes from Maine, 6 from New Hampshire, 12 from Massachusetts, and 1 from New York. On the second ballot Clay lost 11, Taylor picked up 7, Scott gained 6, Webster and Clayton remained in place, but McLean lost 2 and dropped out.[24]

Clay's supporters forced an adjournment, so the balloting did not resume until June 9. On the third ballot Connecticut, which had cast all its votes for Clay, now split them evenly with Taylor. The saloon erupted. Applause, hisses, and cries of "Order! gentlemen! order! rap! knock!" echoed around the room. Then 3 more Clay votes switched to Taylor; Webster and Clayton lost 3 apiece, but Scott gained another 5. When the balloting ended, Taylor had 133, Clay 74, Scott 54, Webster 19, and Clayton 1.

With a bandwagon starting to roll for Old Rough and Ready the delegates proceeded to cast their fourth ballot and finally produced a nominee. Taylor received 171 votes, Clay slumped to 32, Scott kept gaining and had 63, but Webster fell to 14. Webster lost 2 Maine votes to Scott and 2 New Hampshire

21. Bauer, *Taylor*, pp. 222–223; Hamilton, *Taylor*, II, 74–75; Remini, *Clay*, pp. 704–709.

22. Schlesinger, ed.,"Whig National Convention of 1848," *History of U.S. Political Parties*, I, 433–439.

23. *National Intelligencer*, June 8, 1848.

24. Schlesinger, ed., "Whig National Convention of 1848," I, 433–437. Taylor had 118, Clay 86, Webster 22, Scott 49, Clayton 4.

votes to Taylor. Massachusetts awarded him only 9 votes and gave 2 to Scott and 1 to Taylor.

In the contest for Vice President, again the delegates needed two ballots to decide a winner. In the first go-round Abbott Lawrence, the heavy favorite when the convention began, took 109 votes, but Millard Fillmore captured 115, with 50 votes scattered among twelve other candidates. On the second ballot Fillmore won the nomination with 173 votes while Lawrence dropped to 87.[25]

A suspicion immediately arose that Webster had scuttled Lawrence's chances for the nomination so that he might increase his "chance of getting into President Taylor's Cabinet,"[26] a charge Black Dan vehemently denied. "This is contemptible," he snorted. Supposedly he had written to various delegates to influence their votes. But "I have written no such letter," he insisted. In what can only be considered a fabrication, he added, "I have no doubt" Lawrence "heartily desired that I might succeed, in the nomination for the Presidency." When that failed, "it was perfectly right, that he should permit his friends to propose him for the V. Presidency." Webster was also sure that Lawrence "is too just, either to harbor suspicions against me, which are wholly without foundation, or to be offended or dissatisfied with me, on account of any indiscreet remarks . . . made by others." This letter was passed along to Nathan Appleton, who showed it to Lawrence.[27]

Despite the fabrication that Lawrence "heartily desired" his nomination, Webster surely made no attempt to decide the vice presidential nomination. Not only did he lack the skill, will, interest, determination, or subtlety of maneuver to pull it off, but he had always expected Lawrence to win the second slot—and said so many times—if Taylor were chosen to head the ticket. In fact he could no more engineer Lawrence's defeat than he could his own nomination.

The actual culprit was a Conscience Whig, Charles Allen of Massachusetts. After Taylor had won the nomination, Allen took the floor and objected to a proposal to make it unanimous. "We spurn the nominee," he cried, because he "will continue the rule of slavery for another four years." Suddenly there were cries of "sit down, order, knock, hear him, go on."[28] Then, referring ever so obliquely to Lawrence's prospects for the vice presidency, he stormed: "Massachusetts will spurn the bribe. . . . I say that the Whig party of the United States is . . . dissolved."

25. *National Intelligencer,* June 10, 1848; Schlesinger, ed., "Whig National Convention of 1848," I, 437–444. Horace Greeley claimed that "evidences of dissatisfaction induced the managers to take him [Lawrence] off, and let Mr. Fillmore be nominated." *Recollections,* p. 213.

26. Apparently Lawrence himself believed that the "supporters of Mr. Webster" deprived him of the nomination. Hill, *Memoir of Lawrence,* p. 78.

27. DW to Richard Blatchford, June 10, 16, 1848, in *PC,* VI, 293–294, 296–297; Blatchford to Appleton, June 12, 1848, Appleton Papers, MHS. Whether Lawrence was offended or harbored suspicions he did not say, but he was deeply disappointed by his defeat. He had come, said Appleton, within six votes of winning the nomination, and that fact rankled. Appleton, "Memoir of Abbott Lawrence," *Collections of Massachusetts Historical Society,* Fourth Series (1858), IV, 500.

28. Schlesinger, ed., "Whig National Convention of 1848," I, 441.

A chorus of hisses and boos "and great excitement among the Southern members" greeted that announcement, but Samuel Galloway of Ohio really worsened the situation by proposing that Taylor be supported only if he agreed to the principle of "no extension of Slavery over territory now free."

"No! No!" the delegates roared. "Withdraw it!"

The chairman, John M. Morehead, declared the motion out of order, and despite the general confusion of the scene, the convention proceeded to nominate Millard Fillmore. Lawrence had been upended by his own state delegation.[29]

Webster knew that Allen had killed Lawrence's nomination and said so. What really bothered him of course was his own failure to obtain the nomination for President. He thought the conduct of Maine, Rhode Island, Connecticut, and Vermont "abominable. While N.Y. & Ohio have hardly acted better." As far as he was concerned, "nobody has showed any pluck, except Mass—How can she stand alone?" Why, then, he asked, should the South be expected to yield its candidate when the North would not *demand* its candidate? He had placed "unbounded trust, personal and political," in his New York friends, he informed Thurlow Weed a few years later. Their switch to Taylor "gave me dissatisfaction and uneasiness." They had rejected a man genuinely committed to party principles, for one who seemed devoid of principles, if not brains. "The whole subject is a painful & mortifying one, to me," he added.[30]

Webster had let it be known that he could not support Taylor. That was prior to the convention. Would he support him now? His first inclination was to "stand quite aloof." But he soon realized that he had little choice in the matter. "I can see no way, but acquiescence in Taylor's nomination; not enthusiastic support, nor zealous approbation; but acquiescence, or forbearance from opposition." Hardly an attitude or position to recommend him to the general or the general's friends. If Taylor won the election in November, Webster could expect to exercise little influence in the new administration. Not that he cared. As for Webster's situation if Taylor were elected, he wrote to Fletcher, "[I]t is quite indifferent. I have, for myself, no object whatever." But he always said things like that. A few days later he had another change of heart respecting his relationship to Taylor. "I see no way, but to *fall in,* & acquiesce. The run is all that way. We can do no good by holding out. We shall only isolate ourselves."[31]

Webster did not encourage his friends to organize an opposition, even though the Conscience Whigs had clearly severed relations with Taylor and with the Whig party and wanted Webster to head a third party. But he would have none of it. "What wd. it all come to?" he asked. Another humilia-

29. Quoted in Hamilton, *Taylor,* II, 95–97.

30. DW to Blatchford, June 10, DW to Hiram Ketchum, June 11, DW to Samuel Phelps Lyman, June 11, 1848, in *PC,* VI, 294–295; DW to Weed, June 9, 1851, ibid., VII, 255.

31. DW to Fletcher Webster, June 10, 16, 19, 1848, in *W&S,* XVI, 495–497. Friends like Edward Everett tried to encourage him to make peace with Taylor so that he could provide "a wise direction to affairs at home & abroad" as secretary of state. Everett to DW, June 26, 1848, in *PC,* VI, 300.

tion, like the one in 1836? No, thank you, not again.[32]

So the Conscience Whigs decided to join the Barnburners of New York, who had met in Utica on June 22 and endorsed the Wilmot Proviso and nominated former President Martin Van Buren. A subsequent meeting in Buffalo on August 9 united the Barnburners with the Conscience Whigs and the remnants of the old Liberty party to form the Free Soil party. They nominated Van Buren and Charles Francis Adams, son of the late President, for Vice President, adopting a program of "free soil, free speech, free labor, and free men."[33]

The formation of this third party eventually forced Webster into publicly stating his preference, however cool, for Taylor. "It is utterly impossible for me to support the Buffalo nomination," he admitted to Ebenezer Hoar. "I have no confidence in Mr. Van Buren, not the slightest. I would much rather trust Genl. Taylor than Mr. Van Buren even on this very question of slavery, for I believe that Genl. Taylor is an honest man," while Van Buren has been on the wrong side of slavery and all the other great issues that have faced the nation for the last fifteen years.[34]

The country had been waiting to hear what Webster would do with respect to the presidential candidates, and his long silence worried both Cotton and Conscience Whigs. He told Hiram Ketchum that he had nothing new to say. Besides, "I am so much disgusted with our Northern politicians, Whigs and all, that I am out of all humor of making further effort." But as the weeks rolled by, he realized that "I must say *something, somewhere,* soon," or else it would be said for him by others.[35]

When the congressional session ended, he finally decided on a course of action.[36] On September 1, at the invitation of neighbors and friends, he addressed the citizens of Marshfield and visiting reporters in the crowded ballroom of the Winslow House to talk about the approaching presidential election. To start, he admitted that if the Whig candidate chosen in Philadelphia were "entirely satisfactory to the people of Massachusetts and to us, our duty would be plain." But it is not! Taylor is a military man, he said, with no experience or training in civil affairs. He may be a gallant soldier, honest and upright, and probably holds to the main doctrines of the Whig party, but that hardly qualifies him to be the President of the United States. His was "the nomination not fit to be made." Why, then, was he nominated? "That sagacious, wise, far-seeing

32. DW to Fletcher Webster, June 19, 1848, in PC, VI, 299.

33. Mayfield, *Rehearsal for Republicanism,* pp. 101–125; Frederick J. Blue, *The Free Soilers: Third Party Politics* (Urbana, Ill., 1973), pp. 70–80. See also Rayback, *Free Soil* and Seward, *Ballots for Freedom.*

34. DW to Hoar, August 23, 1848, in PC, VI, 303.

35. DW to Ketchum, July 21, 1848, in Curtis, *Webster,* II, 342; DW to Fletcher Webster, no date [June 1848?], in W&S, XIV, 497.

36. As the session neared its end, Webster gave a short speech on August 12 in the Senate on a bill to organize the Oregon Territory in which he said unequivocally "that under no circumstances will I consent to the further extension of the area of slavery in the United States, or to the further increase of slave representation in the House of Representatives." PS, II, 479–487.

doctrine of availability lies at the bottom of the whole matter," Webster lamented. So what should we do? We can vote for Taylor, Cass, or Van Buren or not vote at all.

Then Webster dissected Van Buren and Cass. Of Van Buren he said that the Little Magician was "the soul and centre" of opposition during John Quincy Adams's administration. "He did more to prevent Mr. Adams's reelection in 1828, and to obtain General Jackson's election, than any other man—yes, than any *ten* other men in the country." Webster followed that up by listing Van Buren's many other failings, especially his actions when he served as Jackson's secretary of state. Of Cass, Webster declared, "I hold him, I confess, in the present state of the country, to be the most dangerous man on whom the powers of the executive chief magistracy could well be conferred." Cass believes that through wars, invasions, and vast armies we can "establish a great, powerful, domineering government over all this continent." And he believes that the Wilmot Proviso should not be applied to the territories. But what about Taylor?

I profess to feel a strong attachment to the liberty of the United States, to the Constitution and free institutions of this country, to the honor, and I may say the glory, of my native land. I feel every injury inflicted upon it, almost as a personal injury. I blush for every fault which I think I see committed in its public councils, as if they were faults or mistakes of my own. I know that, at this moment, there is no object upon earth so much attracting the gaze of the intelligent and civilized nations of the earth as this great republic. All men look at us, all men examine our course, all good men are anxious for a favorable result to this great experiment of republican liberty. We are on a hill and cannot be hid. . . . They see us as that star of empire which half a century ago was represented as making its way westward. I wish they may see it as a mild, placid, though brilliant orb, moving athwart the whole heavens to the enlightening and cheering of mankind; and not as a meteor of fire and blood, terrifying the nations.[37]

This was hardly an endorsement of Taylor. It was also later reported that Webster had received "a considerable sum of money, to make the speech in favor of the ticket."[38] His reputation concerning money allowed any and all accusations to circulate freely, and a great number of men believed them. This address, however, was obviously not paid for since it hardly constituted an endorsement. But at least he had made clear his utter revulsion at the thought of either Cass or Van Buren occupying the White House. The friends of Old Rough and Ready could take some comfort from that. What he had tried to do, he explained to Richard M. Blatchford, was to make a clear case for all Whigs to vote for Taylor, to assume a position of complete independence from the general's subsequent failure or success, and finally "to show the preposterous conduct" of those Free Soil Whigs who had seceded from the party and "take service under Mr. Van Buren."[39] He himself ultimately voted for Taylor, even though he

37. *PS*, II, 491–512.
38. Poore, *Perley's Reminiscences*, p. 346.
39. DW to Blatchford, September 18, 1848, in Curtis, *Webster*, II, 347.

"did not believe in it." He later said he regretted that vote.[40]

Webster believed that the real battleground of the election would occur in Pennsylvania. That state had gone Democratic in 1844, but slumping iron prices and the price of manufactures, which Pennsylvanians blamed on the Walker Tariff, brought about a political switch in 1848, and as a result Taylor carried the state in the November election. He also won New York—in large measure because of Van Buren's candidacy, which took votes away from Cass—along with four New England and six southern states for a total of 163 electoral votes, more than enough to elect him President. The West went solidly for Cass, and he picked up five southern and southwestern states, giving him 127 electoral votes. Van Buren received no electoral votes, but he attracted 291,263, or 10 percent of the total popular vote. Taylor had 1,360,099, and Cass 1,220,544 popular votes.[41]

Having given what many regarded at best as a very tepid endorsement of Taylor during the campaign—as a matter of fact some said that the senator and his friends had "lent a strong hand to the work of party insubordination"[42]— Webster did not expect to share the spoils of victory, although he was anxious to obtain something for Fletcher. He said he had only "two wishes, respecting myself & mine." First, he wanted to retire from Congress, if his friends would agree, and second, he wished "that some place be given to Fletcher Webster— by which he can earn his bread."[43]

His desire to retire had been building for months, if not years. "I am tired of Congress," he complained to Edward Everett. "The long sessions wear me down, with their tediousness, as much as with their toil." He was "burnt out" and knew it. What he really wanted to do, and should have done, was something that had "engaged my contemplation for many years, 'A History of the Constitution of the United States, and President Washington's Administration.'" The idea had been stirring in his mind for a long time, and had he not "frittered or wasted" his time with politics and professional and personal duties he might have done it.[44]

He had all the makings of a scholar. He studied for hours and read voraciously on a wide range of subjects. He loved literature, both ancient and modern, and sometimes tried his hand at writing poetry. Interestingly he also loved science and kept track of all the research and progress being made in the field. He read Dr. Holland's medical volume and found that this eminent London physician had "some excellent chapters upon the effect of the mental affections

40. Millard Fillmore claimed Webster gave him this information shortly before his death. Interview with Fillmore that appeared in the New York *Herald*, September 16, 1873, in Frank H. Severance, ed., *Millard Fillmore Papers, Publications of the Buffalo Historical Society*, volume XI, II, 135.

41. DW to Cushing, October 14, 1848, in *PC*, VI, 306–307; Schlesinger and Israel, eds., *History of Presidential Elections*, II, 918.

42. George W. Julian, *Political Recollections, 1840 to 1872* (Westport, Conn., 1970), p. 71.

43. DW to Ketchum, November 27, 1848, in *PC*, VI, 307.

44. DW to Everett, November 28, 1848, in *W&S*, XVIII, 289–290.

upon the corporal system, its diseases, &c. But I knew all this before Dr. Holland," he boasted. "Any man can learn it by observation." If you complain about the heat, mosquito bites, the annoyance of flies, of course you will feel ill and out of sorts. But if you turn your mind to other things, "either of reading or writing, you will disregard the flies, never hear the buzz of the mosquitos, nor care about heat, until it fires the zodiac. There! there is a piece of common sense, worth remembering and acting upon."

His knowledge of geology, according to Professor Felton, "was extensive and exact," and he studied the principal works on the subject. He especially enjoyed reading and meditating on man's relation to the environment. His farm, the raising of animals and produce may have stimulated his initial interest in the subject, but as he grew older, his attention to environmental matters broadened. He became very aware of and intrigued by the different species in the animal and vegetable world. Among the books he revered was Humboldt's *Kosmos*. He not only read and meditated on the book but often quoted from it. And of course history and geography were also particular favorites.

Webster knew or corresponded with many of the literary and scientific figures of his age. He regretted that he had not been able to enjoy their fellowship more. "I have kept very bad company," he noted. "I have lived among lawyers, and judges, and jurymen, and politicians, when I should have lived with Nature, and in the company of the students of Nature."

In the seven volumes of the record of books lent by the Library of Congress to congressmen between 1815 and 1853, Webster is listed as having borrowed hundreds of books, and the list documents the extraordinary range and depth of his interests, particularly in his later years. These books include history, biography, art, philosophy, fiction, drama, poetry, and such works as Audubon's *Ornithology*, Pascal's *Thoughts*, Bacon's *Works*, Boswell's *Johnson*, Soyer's *Cookery*, Defoe's *Memoirs*, Campbell's *Lives of the Lord Chancellors*, Dryden's *Virgil*, Macaulay's *Essays*, Ranke's *History of the Popes*, McGregor's *History of the Sikks*, Dryden's *Virgil*, Burton's *Anatomy of Melancholy*, Smith's *Life of Pocahontas*, Elme's *Dictionary of the Fine Arts*, and Moore's *Epicurus*. In August 1852, during the last weeks of his life in Washington, he read *Works of Dr. Watts*, *Bible Cyclopedia*, Fazer's *Pagan Idolatry*, Barnes's *Notes on Isaiah*, and *Translation of the Prophets*.[45] And it is amazing how much knowledge he retained from reading these books.

After examining Campbell's book on the lord chancellors, he advised his son to read it as well. "You will imbibe a new love for legal studies." He often reread masterworks of literature, sometimes to learn what the "notes of the recent editions" had to say because they invariably contained "new and interesting matter." Frequently he held long discussions on literary works with his friends that were "quite agreeable to me. We talked of Shakespeare, and the

45. Library of Congress, Receipt Ledgers. Seven volumes cover Webster's periods of service as a member of Congress and as secretary of state.

Players' edition of his plays; and, if I mistake not, settled the question whether shoes were made right and left in Shakespeare's time, by referring to the passage in 'King John.' "[46] The great literary men of Webster's time always recorded him as a kindred soul. After all, three volumes of his speeches and one volume of his diplomatic papers had been published to critical success. Other than his orations, his own attempts at literature are not overly distinguished. But his major orations are masterworks.[47]

His second wish concerned Fletcher and his future and that of his family. From the moment he returned to Washington he began soliciting patronage for his son from the President-elect's closest advisers, and he was bitterly disappointed in Taylor's refusal to appoint Fletcher to the position of U.S. district attorney for Massachusetts. The post went to George Lunt, who, as a delegate to the Whig convention, had switched his vote from Webster to Taylor. Lunt had then become an active campaigner for the general in the national election.[48]

Webster's devoted friends hoped that Taylor would overlook the recent past and appoint the Massachusetts senator secretary of state. Undoubtedly Webster would have jumped at the chance had Taylor offered it to him. But the President-elect had other ideas. His closest advisers were John J. Crittenden, recently elected governor of Kentucky, who would have been chosen secretary of state but declined any cabinet post for himself, and William H. Seward, the newly elected senator from New York who felt unfairly treated as governor by the Tyler administration over the McLeod affair. "He is a contemptible fellow," was Webster's judgment of Seward at the time.[49]

When Webster returned to Washington, the new senator from Illinois, Stephen A. Douglas, introduced on December 11 a bill to create a single state from the entire Mexican cession. At the same time the people of New Mexico petitioned the Senate to establish over them a territorial government that would exclude slavery. Then, on February 22, 1848, Webster offered an amendment to an appropriations bill authorizing a temporary military government in New Mexico and California in which existing laws—meaning Mexican law abolishing slavery—would remain in effect until such time as a regular territorial govern-

46. *King John*, Act IV, Scene 2, the passage in which the tailor says:

> Standing on slippers which his nimble haste
> Had falsely thrust upon contrary feet.

47. DW to Fletcher Webster, April 24, 1852, in *W&S*, XVIII, 526; DW to John H. B. Latrobe, July 10, 1851, ibid., XVI, 621; Curtis, *Webster*, II, 670; Peterson, *Great Triumvirate*, p. 400; DW to Fletcher Webster, December 26, 1848, in *W&S*, XIV, 509; DW to Richard Blatchford, February 4, 1849, ibid., XVIII, 295. For his published works, see *Speeches and Forensic Arguments* (Boston, 1830, 1835, 1843) and *Diplomatic and Official Papers* (Boston, 1848); Everett to DW, January 9, 1850, in *PC*, VII, 4.

48. DW to Fletcher Webster, March 26, 1849, in *PC*, VI, 322–323. "I went back, alone, & spoke to the President," Webster told Fletcher; "expressed my regret, & disappointment; & added, that in my opinion Mr. Lunt was not fit for the office." DW to Fletcher Webster, [March 29, 1849], in Van Tyne, ed., *Letters of Webster*, p. 377.

49. DW to Ketchum, July 1841, in *Microfilm Edition*, F15/19836.

ment was formed. Calhoun objected, contending that the exclusion of slavery would violate the Constitution. Does the Constitution extend to the territories or not? he asked. Is it not the supreme law of the land?

"What land?" Webster called out.

"The land; the Territories of the United States are a part of the land," Calhoun retorted.

The Constitution does indeed extend over the territories, Webster responded, but "how does it get there?" Does the Constitution of itself settle titles to land, regulate the rights of property, fix relations between parent and child? Obviously not. These require legislative enactments. "The Constitution and the laws of Congress passed under it shall be the supreme law of the land."

What Webster was saying was that Congress had total control of the territories and could exclude slavery or not as it chose.[50] But the Senate did not agree to this amendment, and the appropriations bill passed without it.

Just before the Senate concluded its session and a few days before his inauguration, Taylor finally completed his cabinet appointments. On February 24 Webster made a courtesy call on the President-elect and came away with a somewhat favorable impression. He was not "disagreeable looking," Webster related, and seemed "social enough, & talks with propriety." They conversed in generalities for half an hour and made no mention of cabinet appointments. "General Taylor means well," he reported, "but he knows little of public affairs, and less of public men." As Webster had suspected, the cabinet, as finally chosen, lacked real distinction, with the possible exception of the secretary of state, John M. Clayton of Delaware. For a time Abbott Lawrence had been considered for the Treasury post but instead was sent as minister to Great Britain. Even so, there was little doubt that Lawrence, not Daniel Webster, would have the controlling voice in the distribution of the patronage throughout the state of Massachusetts.[51]

Except for his exchange with Calhoun over his amendment to an appropriation bill Webster just sat in the Senate, taking little part in the proceedings. "I am overwhelmed with labor; obliged to study from five to eleven A.M.; be in court from eleven to three; and all the rest of the day in the Senate till ten o'clock."[52]

After Congress had adjourned, he spent the next several months petitioning those now in power, including the President, the cabinet, and other influential members of Congress,[53] to find a suitable position for his son. He even procured a case of Madeira, his favorite wine, and presented it to Taylor in order "to make

50. *W&S*, XIV, 317–335.

51. DW to Franklin Haven, February 25, 1849, in Curtis, *Webster*, II, 358; Dalzell, *Webster and American Nationalism*, p. 159.

52. DW to Blatchford, February 27, 1849, in Curtis, *Webster*, II, 359.

53. Including Senator William H. Seward, a valued adviser to Taylor. Webster now said that Seward was "very thoroughly friendly, & Persevering" in pushing Fletcher's case to the President. DW to Fletcher Webster, [March 29, 1849], in Van Tyne, ed., *Letters of Webster*, p. 378.

a favorable impression." He got nowhere, and it was a wicked blow to his pride. "This business of Fletcher's, I confess, has wounded me. No disappointment to myself could come half so near my heart." Quite possibly the deaths of his two children a little more than a year before had something to do with it. "Of five children," he kept reminding himself, "only one now remains."[54] In soliciting help, he wrote one letter after another, exaggerating Fletcher's talents and demeaning rivals.[55] It was only by his dogged persistence and determination and a desire by the administration to get rid of him, rather than any sense of acknowledgment for his past services to the country, that in late February 1850 the position of surveyor of the port of Boston was finally granted to his son. Fletcher held the appointment until President Lincoln removed him in 1861.[56]

During the spring and summer of 1849 the few appointments that had Webster's endorsement and were accepted by the Taylor administration were minor. For the most part the President turned over the executive patronage to his department heads and stood idly by while Whigs from around the country scrambled and connived for office. But only "particular favorites, or particular cliques" controlled the patronage. They "govern every thing," sighed Webster, and he did not belong.[57]

When not worrying about Fletcher's future, Webster had his own enduring indebtedness to fret over. "I am old, and poor, and proud," he dejectedly admitted.[58] What is so ironic is that he made "money with ease," lots of it. Over his entire career he probably made "a dozen fortunes," but he spent them as fast as they came in. He "spent it without reflection." He gave away hundreds and thousands of dollars. One of his private secretaries remembered how often he sent money to the poor. On six successive days he donated from fifty to one hundred dollars to men and women whom he did not know but who had written him pathetic and pleading letters. He had many accounts in various banks, but he kept no record of his deposits. Once in a while he would make a note and slip it into his pocket, where it was forgotten. When a secretary drew a check for several thousand dollars, he would sign it without looking at it, as though it were "so much waste paper." His checks were rarely protested, but when they were, "they caused him an immense deal of mental anxiety." Toward the end of his life

54. The death of his two-year-old granddaughter Constance Mary Appleton, Julia's daughter, on March 15, 1849, may also have accelerated his drive to take care of Fletcher and his family.

55. DW to Fletcher Webster, [March 29, 1849], in Van Tyne, ed., Letters of Webster, p. 377.

56. DW to Edward Curtis, April 3, [1849], in PC, VI, 328; DW to Jeremiah Mason, May 8, 1848, in Curtis, Webster, II, 328–329; DW to Charles March, February 5, 1849, in W&S, XVIII, 297. The Webster correspondence in the Library of Congress and other archives for 1849 contain the vast collection of correspondence by the senator on behalf of his son, all of them available in the Microfilm Edition, reel 21. See, for example, DW to Fletcher Webster, March 26, 27, 28, 29, April 1, 2, 6, etc., 1849, in PC, VI, 322ff. "I wish it had been a different office," Webster wrote after Fletcher had been confirmed as surveyor by the Senate, "but under the circumstances it is right for him to take it." DW to Peter Harvey, [March 1, 1850], ibid., VI, 19.

57. DW to ?, June 24, 1849, in PC, VI, 345.

58. DW to Blatchford, December 5, 1848, in Curtis, Webster, II, 351.

creditors became more insistent about payment. By this time he found himself hard pressed to meet his obligations.[59]

To repay his debt of nine thousand dollars to Caleb Cushing, he finally deeded all the land he held in Rock Island, Illinois, land for which he originally paid the exorbitant price of sixty thousand dollars. As it turned out, some of the titles were flawed, some sold for taxes, and some may have been conveyed to the Pennsylvania Bank in 1841. It was a pulverizing burden that never seemed to end. Despite his renowned law practice and the fact that he was now involved in arguing claims for his clients before the Mexican Claims Commission—" I have earned a good deal of money, within the last year," he confessed—nothing really changed. "It has all been paid away" for either mortgages or old debts. He finally acknowledged that he could not see "that I shall ever be able to pay my debts." Indeed, to the day he died, the Rock Island lands still awaited final settlement.[60]

He chalked it up to fate and bad luck. "I am afraid my luck is always bad, and I fear is always to be so." At the beginning of his career friends regularly tried to induce him into investing in one business scheme or another until he learned at last that he had no head for business and was fated to lose money. He finally realized that to avoid bankruptcy, he must say to those men who approached him about investing in their schemes, "Gentlemen, if you have any projects for money-making, I pray you keep me out of them; my singular destiny mars every thing of that sort, and would be sure to overwhelm your own better fortunes."

He "was never destined to be rich," he lamented. "No such star presided over his birth."[61]

59. Lanman, *Private Life of Webster*, p. 90.

60. Property deed to Caleb Cushing, [November 27, 1849], in *PC*, VI, 359–360; DW to Fletcher Webster, January 25, 1850, in *W&S*, XVI, 530; DW to Cushing, September 20, 1850, in *Microfilm Edition*, F22/31165.

61. DW to General Lyman, January 15, 1849, in *W&S*, XIV, 510–511.

40

The Seventh of March Speech

O N AVERAGE during the course of a year Webster received hundreds of
invitations to dinners, anniversaries, and celebrations of one kind or
another, the majority of which he had to decline, particularly in the late summer
or early fall, when his "annual catarrh" took hold and left him wheezing and
coughing and feeling generally miserable. At the age of sixty-seven he felt old
and tired. Despite his indisposition, he did attend the anniversary dinner in
October 1849 commemorating the *"Embarkation,"* not the landing, of the
Pilgrims, and N. P. Willis, reporting for the New York *Tribune,* described the
dinner as attended by a hundred "mostly rich men," but also "smart men," and
presided over by Webster, who was dressed with "that courtly particularity
which becomes him." These rich men would usually arrive early to his "performances" and "bribe officers" to give them the best seats in the room. Together
they would nod in assent "to his most profound sentences and Latin quotations,
which they neither understood, nor could they spell or write the words they
contained."

In this "Embarkation" speech, Webster, "in a strain of narrative eloquence
that . . . showed the great master," ranged over history, current events, and the
great men of the early seventeenth century, quoting Milton, Shakespeare, and
Bacon in the process. But Willis thought he looked "really ill—much thinner
than I had ever seen him." During the speech the orator appeared "so debilitated
that, in his least emphatic sentences, the more difficult words failed of complete
utterance." His face, though genial and kindly, seemed somber and "unlighted
with health or impulse." Yet "the eyes so cavernous and dark, the eyelids so livid,
eyebrows so heavy and black, and the features so habitually grave" still projected
the appearance of a great man. "It is all majestic, all expansive and generous."[1]

His health kept him from accepting an invitation to attend the anniversary
dinner of the Hebrew Benevolent and the German Hebrew Benevolent Societies in New York. In his response Webster conveyed his genuine regard for the
Jewish religion:

I feel, and have ever felt respect and sympathy for all that remains of that extraordi-

---

1. Reprinted in the *National Intelligencer,* October 9, 1849; Wentworth, "Congressional Reminiscences," p. 35.

nary people who preserved, through the darkness and idolatry of so many centuries, the knowledge of one supreme spiritual Being, the Maker of Heaven and Earth, and the Creator of Man in his own image; and whose canonical writings comprise such productions as the books of Moses and the Decalogue, the prophecies of Isaiah, the psalms of David, the Book of Job, and Solomon's prayer at the Dedication of the Temple. The Hebrew Scriptures I regard as the fountain from which we draw all we know of the world around us, and of our own character and destiny as intelligent, moral, and responsible beings.[2]

By the time Webster returned to Congress for the start of the Thirty-first Congress he felt much better since the catarrh had subsided. And he needed all the energy and physical strength he could muster for what turned out to be a tumultuous session. So strong was the sentiment for disunion in the South that a call had gone out for a convention of slave states to meet in Nashville to promote southern unity and demand their rights, especially their rights as slaveowners.[3] "The feeling for disunion," commented Henry Clay as he returned to the Senate, "is stronger than I supposed it could be."[4] It took weeks before Congress could get down to serious business because of the sectional wrangling over the speakership. Not until December 22, after sixty-three ballots, was Howell Cobb of Georgia elected Speaker over the Whig Robert C. Winthrop of Massachusetts by a vote of 102 to 99.[5]

The question of the status of California and New Mexico faced Congress, and because of the discovery of gold and the wild rush to the goldfields in 1849, California had swelled in population and now petitioned for admission as a state in the Union. In his first annual message President Taylor endorsed the petition. He also expected New Mexico to apply in the near future and said he would favor its admission as well. Both areas excluded slavery under Mexican rule, and both presumably would enter the Union as free states, totally disrupting the balance presently existing between slave and free states. Southern congressmen took a dim view of that prospect and could be expected to fight it, threatening secession if it succeeded. The Constitution followed the flag, they argued, meaning that slavery was protected in the newly acquired territories.

"There is so much excitement & inflammation on the subjects of Slavery, Dissolution, &c.," fretted Webster on his arrival in Washington, "as that it overwhelms, or threatens to overwhelm, all really important measures." But he made light of its seriousness. He completely misinterpreted it. "All this agitation, I think, will subside, without serious result, but still it is mischievous, and creates heart burnings. But the Union is not in danger." Things will "cool off," he thought, California would be admitted and New Mexico "postponed. No bones will be broken."

Under the circumstances he saw no need to enter the brouhaha. He would

2. DW to Mordecai M. Noah, November 9, 1849, in *W&S*, XVIII, 347

3. For this convention, see Thelma Jennings, *The Nashville Convention* (Memphis, 1980).

4. Clay to Leslie Combs, December 22, 1849, in Clay, *Papers*, 635.

5. *Congressional Globe*, 31st Congress, 1st Session, pp. 61–67.

remain silent, he said, unless something happened "by way of attempting to carry evil purposes into effect," in which case "I shall have something to say."[6]

What amazed him, he explained in a response to William Furness's impassioned plea that he league himself with abolitionists, was to hear slavery condemned on scriptural grounds. After all, the Jews practiced it, and nothing Jesus or Paul said indicated that it violated divine law. But Christianity preaches love, kindness, mercy, and personal holiness, and as such it "discountenances slavery" and everything else that is oppressive or unjust.

The true objection to slavery is its injustice. It is opposed to the natural equality of mankind. It is founded only in the power of the strong over the weak. Superior force is its origin. And, therefore, even if it were a useful social institution, it could not be defended. But, in other cases, so in this, that which is unjust cannot, on the whole, be useful. Slavery has proved itself, every where, a great social & political evil. Its influence is as bad on the master, as on the slave; and often worse. It blunts the moral feelings, inspires a false sense of superiority, & insensibly hardens the heart.

Once slavery has become part of the social and political system, he declared, it hardly ever can be extricated by "violent eradication." We must remain calm, "wait for events, & the orderings of Providence, who often 'shapes our ends, rough hew them how we will.' "

In the letter to William Furness, Webster said that he had opposed slavery from his earliest youth. Any pretense of defending it "on the ground of difference of races, I have ever condemned. I have ever said that if the black race is weaker, that is a reason against, not for, its subjection & oppression." But to combat it with violence, bloodshed, and civil war "would only rivet the chains of slavery the more strongly." We must rely on "the mild influences of Christianity," not on the storms and tempests of heated controversy, to "dissolve the iron fetters by which man is made the slave of man." After all, it has taken two thousand years for "the regeneration & redemption of mankind." So it will come to pass that slavery too will be abolished "while we give to it our fervent prayers." It "seems to me, we must leave both the progress & the result in His hands who sees the end from the beginning, & in whose sight a thousand years are but a single day."[7] Simply put, leave slavery to heaven, a solution no partisan on either side would accept.

This astonishing statement demonstrates how far from many of his constituents Webster stood on the issue. He remained steadfast in his views and attitudes about noninterference while a swelling number of northerners wanted something done to stop the spread of slavery and bring about its eventual abolition. As such he risked becoming irrelevant. Indeed some Whigs had al-

6. DW to Franklin Haven, January 13, 1850, in PC, VII, 5; DW to Peter Harvey, February 13, 1850, in Van Tyne, ed., Letters of Webster, p. 392.

7. DW to Samuel Lothrop, February 12, DW to William H. Furness, February 15, 1850, in PC, VII, 9–10, 11–12. Webster said he did believe that Jesus and the apostles regarded slavery as "an evil, an injustice to be overcome." DW to Reverend Dr. Calvin Hitchcock, March 17, 1850, in Microfilm Edition, F22/30022.

ready begun to dismiss him as a relic of a bygone age.

With each day and each week the atmosphere in Congress became more heated and violent. Still, Webster assured his friends there was no danger and asked them to spread the word. He tended to support Taylor's position and thought that California would be admitted as a free state "by a large majority of the House" and "two thirds of the Senate." He could not, would not believe that a secession crisis faced the nation. "Let the North keep cool," he counseled. He also urged his friends to try to prevent Massachusetts from sending petitions to Congress. They will do no good and only incite the firebrands.[8]

While Webster sojourned in this fantasy world, Henry Clay set about developing a plan by which all the issues involved in precipitating the present crisis could be resolved and peace restored. What he had in mind was a "comprehensive scheme" that would satisfy both northern and southern interests. He subsequently drew up a compromise or "series of resolutions" in which California would be admitted as a state without mention of slavery, territorial governments would be organized in the remaining portion of the Mexican cession without any congressional restriction or condition on the subject of slavery, the Texas boundary would be settled by the United States' assuming the Texas debt acquired before annexation, and a more effective fugitive slave law would be passed. Another resolution declared that it would be "inexpedient" to abolish slavery in the District of Columbia without the consent of Maryland and the residents of the District and compensation for the slaveholders. Still another pronounced it "expedient" to abolish the slave trade in the District and forbid the sale of slaves or their transportation to other markets outside Washington. The final resolution stated that Congress had no power to interfere in the interstate slave trade.[9]

Before presenting these eight resolutions to Congress, Clay paid Webster a visit at his home on Monday, January 21, 1850. It was a cold, miserable evening, and Clay looked "very feeble" when he showed up unannounced at 7:00 P.M. Throughout the hourlong interview Clay coughed continuously, and he was totally exhausted by the time the meeting ended. He had come to secure Webster's support for his compromise and explained at length each of the eight resolutions. Webster liked what he heard and agreed in substance to the proposal. As for the Wilmot Proviso, which caused so much dissension between the North and South, Webster said "that was no shibboleth for him." He added that if New Mexico were left alone, it would "no more have slavery than California." Though drained by his exertions in explaining his compromise, Clay came away exhilarated by his sense of accomplishment. At least two of the three members of the Great Triumvirate would support his peace plan.[10]

8. DW to Peter Harvey, February 14, 1850, in *PC*, VII, 10.

9. Remini, *Clay*, pp. 732–733.

10. The interview was recorded by a "gentleman" visiting Webster at the time and can be found in Curtis, *Webster*, II, 397–398. Undoubtedly the "gentleman" was Curtis himself.

Relations between the two men had never been close and at times verged on open rupture. For the past ten years they had treated each other with courtesy, but "their intercourse had been only formal." The great tragedy of their relationship is that they could have been so useful to each other, and that would have greatly benefited the nation at large. All the Clay Whigs, commented John J. Crittenden, "desired to see Clay and Webster elected to the Presidency, and we felt that to accomplish this object it was necessary that Mr. Clay should come first, but we were never able to make Webster and his personal friends see this, and therefore neither of them won the prize."[11]

Given their great talents and services to the country, both men should have occupied the White House, but neither of them ever totally enjoyed the people's confidence. Neither man was trusted. And in that democratic age they really belonged "with generations that had gone by."[12] Worse, the electorate understood this. As the former Democratic senator from Illinois Sidney Breese told Webster, "How unfortunate for the Country that you adopted opinions adverse to the democracy! Had you not, you would have been President."[13]

On Tuesday, January 29, Clay presented his resolutions to the Senate, but not until February 5 did he deliver his first major address on his compromise. He ended with a plea for the Union. The debate on the proposals opened on February 11 and extended to March 27, with all the powerful voices on both sides giving vent to their interests and passions.

Shortly after Clay had introduced his resolutions, Robert Winthrop went to Webster with a message from a group of southern congressmen headed by Edward Stanly of North Carolina. If the Senate would endorse Taylor's plan, not Clay's, these southerners were "prepared to do their best to make him [Webster] the next President" on a "moderate platform." No doubt elated at the prospect, Webster assured Winthrop that he had not "pledged himself" to support the resolutions and was turning the matter over in his mind. "In short," he declared, "I am substantially with the President, and you can tell Mr. Stanly so." There the matter rested for the next several weeks while Winthrop returned to Boston to attend a dangerously ill relative.[14]

When the debate on Clay's resolutions began, Webster was still optimistic about what would happen, but as the rancor and discord escalated with each speaker, he began to have his doubts. For one thing, he came to realize that the southerners were serious about leaving the Union if their demands were not met. They were not bluffing. For another he knew that his passive participation in senatorial proceedings would hinder the efforts of those, like Clay, who were trying to avert catastrophe. A secession crisis existed, whether he appreciated it

11. Stanton, *Random Recollections*, p. 151.

12. *W&S*, XIV, 76.

13. Breese to DW, March 16, 1850, in *PC*, VII, 34.

14. Robert Winthrop, Jr., *A Memoir of Robert C. Winthrop* (Boston, 1897), pp. 110, 111; Winthrop to Everett, March 3, 1850, Everett Papers, MHS.

or not, and Webster finally began to understand that he could not remain silent.[15] On February 24 he wrote his son and told him that he planned to speak. At the moment he did not know what he could say "to beat down the Northern and the Southern follies, now raging in equal extremes." With obligations to his clients and appearances before the Supreme Court he was hard pressed to find the necessary time required for this effort. "I am nearly broken down with labor and anxiety," he groaned. But for the next week he devoted himself heart and mind to what became one of the most important speeches of his entire life.[16]

In preparing his address, he consulted a number of friends, although he kept his own counsel and did not reveal what position he would take. He even went to see Calhoun on March 2 and spent two hours with the old nullifier. For thirty years they had differed, but "good feelings have always subsisted between us," Webster insisted. Like Clay, Calhoun was desperately ill, weak and growing more feeble by the day. He too had decided to deliver a speech in the Senate but was so debilitated that he asked Senator James Mason of Virginia to read it for him. The unfortunate man would not live out the month, but he was determined that the Senate and the nation should hear him once more.

Calhoun gave Webster a summary of that speech during their meeting and it no doubt helped the Massachusetts senator focus more sharply on what he needed to say.[17] Still defiant, Calhoun would adopt his usual "dogmatical assertion, & violent denunciations of the North," reported Webster. "Alas! poor man he will speak in the Senate, I fear no more." As for himself, "I mean to make a *Union* Speech, and discharge a clear conscience."[18]

On Monday, March 4, Calhoun, wrapped in a black cloak and looking like a ghostly apparition, listened in the Senate while Mason read his anticompromise speech. Without offering any plan of his own, this "cast-iron man" blamed the North for the nation's present misfortunes and warned that disunion was the only alternative left to the South if its interests and institutions continued to be scorned and attacked. He held out no hand of conciliation. He simply made demands on the North: Reject the Wilmot Proviso and popular sovereignty, protect southern rights to take slavery to all the territories, and restore the balance between sections. He swore his everlasting allegiance to the Union, but it came at a price. He died on March 31.[19]

Contemporaries frequently compared Calhoun with Webster on such qualities as integrity, deportment, intellectual power, knowledge, and service to the

15. For a different point of view, see Dalzell, *Webster and American Nationalism*, pp. 190–192.

16. DW to Fletcher Webster, February 24, 1850, in *PC*, VII, 16.

17. DW to Charles Henry Warren, March 1, 1850, in *W&S*, XVI, 534; Wiltse, *Calhoun*, III, 459–460. Wiltse quotes from the New York *Tribune* of March 8, 1850, which described this interview at length.

18. DW to Harvey, [March 1, 1850], in *PC*, VII, 19.

19. *Congressional Globe*, 31st Congress, 1st Session, pp. 451–455. Webster paid eloquent tribute to his old antagonist on April 2, 1850. See ibid., p. 625ff. Calhoun's biographer says that Webster spoke with "deeper emotion" than he had ever done before in the Senate. Wiltse, *Calhoun*, III, 476.

nation. A highly prejudiced individual, Philip Hone, acknowledged that they both had talents of the highest order but where Webster "goes for the country," Calhoun would sacrifice everything for South Carolina. "The first is a statesman in the broadest sense, the last was the *man of a State.*"[20]

By early March Webster had let it be known that he planned to deliver a major address, and whether it be "good or bad," he declared, "nobody will care a fig about it a month hence" if peace is restored to the country.[21] The possibility that his speech might be another reply to Hayne struck almost everyone. The second reply "was a turning point in your life," wrote Benjamin Silliman, a lawyer and Whig politician. "Your speech this week may be the turning point in the life of this nation." The nation seemed to plead with him for another eloquent barrage to disperse the threatening storm. "Do it, Mr. Webster; as you can do it, like a bold and gifted Statesman and Patriot," begged one Democrat. "Reconcile the North and South, and *preserve the Union.*" He was assured that he would be greater than George Washington if he could pull it off. Washington secured our liberty, but *"Whoever preserved the Union, secures the Liberties of the world."* Philip Hone recognized that his idol's "position is extremely delicate and embarrassing, even to a man like him, of iron nerves."[22]

General James Hamilton of South Carolina repeated a conversation he had had with Calhoun on the day Calhoun's address was read to the Senate. Suppose Webster does succeed in resolving the issue, Hamilton asked, "what shall we of the South do for him"?

"Make him President Sir," Calhoun responded, "for he will deserve it for that single act. Besides his eloquence genius and his great public services Mr Webster possesses many noble qualities. I shall most probably never recover my health but if I do I would not only not allow my name used against him but would regard it as a sacred duty to support him."[23]

Abraham Venable also related a conversation with Calhoun in which the South Carolinian acknowledged his great respect for the senator. "Mr. Webster has as high a standard of truth as any statesman with whom I have met in debate."[24]

On the evening prior to his great speech Webster held a long conference with his closest advisers, Peter Harvey, Edward Curtis, a director of the Bank of Commerce in New York, and his son, Fletcher, "questioning and doubting how it would go."[25] He made extensive notes, far more than usual, and he kept worrying about how it would turn out, whether "good or bad."

20. Hone, *Diary*, II, 890.

21. DW to Charles Henry Warren, March 1, 1850, in *W&S*, XVI, 535.

22. Silliman to DW, March 5, R. B. Barker to DW, March 4, 1850, in *PC*, VII, 21, 22; Hone, *Diary*, II, 887.

23. Waddy Thompson to DW, March 2, 1850, in *PC*, VII, 21.

24. Venable to DW, June 7, 1850, in *W&S*, XVIII, 371.

25. DW to Harvey, April 7, 1850, in *PC*, VII, 54.

Later that evening Robert Winthrop returned from Boston and went to see Webster. He found him "in the last agonies of preparation."

"What say our friends in Boston?" Webster inquired.

They are perfectly satisfied with Taylor's policy and do not wish to see matters pressed to a "dangerous pass" over the Wilmot Proviso, came the reply.

"I have not told a human being what I am going to say to-morrow, but as you are here at the last moment, I will say to you that I don't mean to have anything to do with the proviso," Webster responded. And on that note Winthrop left, still convinced that the senator would support the President's plan.[26]

There were many in the country who believed that of all the men in Congress, Webster had the power to save the Union by his invocation of everything Americans held dear, and in Washington people knew that March 7 might indeed be a "turning point in the life of the nation," so they swarmed into the Senate chamber early in the morning to stand witness to the great event. "We have never, we think, on any former occasion," reported one Washington newspaper, "seen the Senate Chamber so crammed with human beings as it was yesterday by the multitudes of both sexes who were attracted thither by an eager desire to hear Mr. Webster's speech." Even the senators were "crowded out of their seats," relinquishing them to the women in the audience. Though gravely ill, John C. Calhoun rose from his deathbed and entered the room to hear what Webster had to say. The excitement, anticipations, and expectations of the crowd soared. Tension in the room became so palpable that it put everyone on edge.[27]

At noon the Senate was convened. Isaac Walker of Wisconsin had the floor to finish his remarks of the previous day, but he gallantly yielded to Webster, who was, he said, "the one man, in my opinion, who can assemble such an audience."[28] Webster rose and thanked Walker. He looked solemn and purposeful as he shuffled his notes in his hands. In the opinion of one man "Webster's far-seeing mind was doubtless troubled by the prospects of a bloody civil war, with the breaking up of the Union he loved so well." His demeanor signaled what he was about to say.[29]

He began with a powerful statement that has echoed through the years. "I wish to speak to-day, not as a Massachusetts man, nor as a Northern man, but as an American, and a member of the Senate of the United States. . . . I speak to-day for the preservation of the Union. 'Hear me for my cause.' "

After that opening the crowd knew that Webster would not fail them and would deliver a heroic oration.

We live in the midst of violent agitation, he continued, surrounded by great dangers to our institutions and government. "The imprisoned winds are let

26. Winthrop, *Memoir*, pp. 111–112; Winthrop to John Clifford, March 4, 1852, Winthrop Papers, MHS.

27. *National Intelligencer*, March 9, 1850.

28. *Congressional Globe*, 31st Congress, 1st Session, p. 476.

29. Poore, *Perley's Reminiscences*, I, 365. For the notes of this speech, see Van Tyne, ed., *Letters of Webster*, pp. 393–397.

loose." The East, North, and "stormy South" combine to throw the sea into commotion and "toss its billows to the skies," disclosing "its profoundest depths." I do not presume to hold the helm in this combat, "but I have a duty to perform, and I mean to perform it with fidelity, not without a sense of existing dangers, but not without hope." He now launched into an extended history of how the nation had arrived at this crisis. With slavery he went back to the ancients and followed the course of that "peculiar institution" after its introduction to America, repeating much of what he had said in his letter of a few weeks before to William Furness. He contended that colonial southerners regarded slavery as "an evil, a blight, a scourge, and a curse."

"But soon a change began." The North became more hostile to slavery, the South more vocal in its support. In that section it became a cherished institution, "no evil, no scourge, but a great religious, social, and moral blessing." No doubt the sudden expansion of the plantation system accounted for this phenomenon.

When he arrived at the territorial questions, he said that if a bill to establish a government for New Mexico included a provision for the prohibition of slavery, "I would not vote for it." Nor would he vote for "the Wilmot," as he derisively referred to the Proviso, a remark that "was never forgiven" by Free Soilers.[30] He would not wound the pride of southerners. "They would think it a taunt, an indignity." Northern Whigs in the room no doubt were startled by that unexpected remark. Obviously he was reaching out to southerners in a gesture of conciliation.

What followed then did not merely startle northern Whigs; it angered and revolted them. With respect to fugitive slaves, "the South, in my judgment is right, and the North is wrong." Wrong in that they will not perform their constitutional duties to return slaves who have escaped into the free states. They enact personal liberty laws to harass and prevent southerners from regaining their legitimate property. He said he would support a new fugitive slave bill, "and I desire to call the attention of all sober-minded men at the North, of all conscientious men, of all men who are not carried away by some fanatical idea or some false impression, to their constitutional obligations."[31] It is a matter of morals and conscience and law, he declared. What right do northerners have to get around the Constitution and "embarrass" southerners whose slaves have escaped? "None at all; none at all," he stormed. Here are legitimate grounds for complaint that ought to be removed. Make no mistake, the South has been injured.

He went further in his attempt at conciliation and forever damned himself in the minds of many of his own constituents. He said he would not receive from the Massachusetts legislature any petitions "whatever on the subject of slavery,

30. Sargent, *Public Men and Events*, II, 362.

31. Article IV, Section 1, paragraph 3 of the Constitution states: "No Person held to Service or Labour in one State, under the Laws thereof, escaping into another, shall, in Consequence of any Law or Regulation therein, be discharged from such Service or Labour, but shall be delivered up on Claim of the Party to whom such Service or Labour may be due."

as it exists at the present moment in the States." As for abolition societies, "I do not think them useful. I think their operations for the last twenty years have produced nothing good or valuable." He did admit, however, that many of their members were honest, good, and well-meaning. But mischief attends their activities as they arouse great agitation in the North against southern slavery. Extremists exist in both sections of the country, especially in the press, and they "are violent."

Then he switched the thrust of his speech into an extended effort to placate the North. If the South has a grievance against the North—and there was really only one—the North has several complaints against the South. First off, northerners never expected the south to change from hating slavery and regarding it as an evil, "an evil which all hoped would be extinguished gradually," to cherishing, preserving, and extending it. They also resent contrasting the slaves of the South with laborers in the North, "giving the preference, in all points of condition, and comfort, and happiness, to the slaves of the South." These northern laboring men are "freeholders, educated men, independent men" who till their own farms with their own hands. Five sixths of the entire property of the North, he contended, was in the hands of these laborers. If they are not freeholders, they earn wages that they accumulate and turn into capital. Eventually they themselves become "small capitalists." Webster also objected to the way free blacks employed on northern ships as cooks and stewards were imprisoned when these ships docked at southern ports and kept there until the ships departed. These imprisonments were illegal and unconstitutional, he declared.

What troubled Webster throughout the debate on Clay's resolutions was the repeated threat of secession, even from the lips of so-called patriots.

Secession! Peaceable secession! Sir, your eyes and mine are never destined to see that miracle. The dismemberment of this vast country without convulsion! . . . There can be no such thing as a peaceable secession. Peaceable secession is an utter impossibility. Is the great Constitution under which we live, covering this whole country, is it to be thawed and melted away by secession, as the snows on the mountain melt under the influence of a vernal sun, disappear almost unobserved, and run off? No, Sir! No, Sir! I will not state what might produce the disruption of the Union, but, Sir, I see as plain as I see the sun in heaven what that disruption itself must produce; I see that it must produce war, and such a war as I will not describe, *in its twofold character.*

Think of what our ancestors, our fathers, and our grandfathers would say if secession occurred. They would "rebuke and reproach us" if we dishonored what their heroism and labor had produced. He found the very thought of it repugnant. He said he was ashamed to have to pursue this line of argument. "I have an utter disgust for it. I would rather hear of natural blasts and mildews, war, pestilence, and famine, than to hear gentlemen talk of secession."

He refused to believe that men would deliberately destroy something unique and wonderful in the world. It just could not happen. Finally, as though his words had the power to command, he bellowed: "There will be no secession! Gentlemen are not serious when they talk of secession."

As for the Nashville Convention, scheduled to meet in early June, he reminded those who planned to attend that they were to meet close to where "the bones of Andrew Jackson" lay buried. Could they desecrate his grave with secession?

He hurried to his close. It was a stunning peroration and echoed the close of the second reply to Hayne, but it lacked the grandeur of the earlier work:

> We have a great, popular, constitutional government, guarded by law and by judicature, and defended by the affections of the whole people. No monarchical throne presses these States together, no iron chain of military power encircles them; they live and stand under a government popular in its form, representative in its character, founded upon principles of equality, and so constructed, we hope, as to last for ever. In its history it has been beneficent; it has trodden down no man's liberty; it has crushed no State. Its daily respiration is liberty and patriotism; its yet youthful veins are full of enterprise, courage, and honorable love of glory and renown. Large before, the country has now, by recent events, become vastly larger. This republic now extends, with a vast breadth, across the whole continent.[32]

He concluded by quoting from the *Iliad,* in the Alexander Pope translation, and conjured up the image of a shining nation, washed on either shore by two great oceans, and looking as beautiful, as magnificent, as complete as the ornamental border of Achilles' silver buckler.[33]

Taken as a whole, this speech was meant to convey the simple statement that the North and South were destroying the Union, and the blame rested squarely on the shoulders of both. As *oratory* it was not one of Webster's greatest efforts, but as the cry of a patriot, pleading for the life of his country, it was a magnificent outburst.

Throughout its delivery Webster frequently paused. Indeed not only did he speak with "very unusual deliberation," but his sentences "were broken into the oddest fragments." He spoke slowly, but his enunciation was "very distinct." His voice only occasionally rose to a pitch indicating excitement. When the idea of possible secession came into his mind, "his eyes appeared like two balls of fire, and his gesticulation indicated the strength of his patriotic impulses." Great drops of perspiration stood out on his face, especially toward the end of his address. Throughout he stood erect with his "burning eyes" fixed on Calhoun. One hostile listener suggested that it might be a "greatly troubled conscience on his final act of apostasy from his early New England faith." Or could it be a "very recent and heavy dinner?" he sneered. More likely the former, he allowed.[34]

32. *PS,* II, 515–551.

33.   Now, the broad shield complete, the artist crowned
                             With his last hand, and poured the ocean round;
                             In living silver seemed the waves to roll,
                             And beat the buckler's verge, and bound the whole.
                                  in Homer, Iliad (1806), Book XVIII.

34. Lyman, *Public and Private Life of Webster,* II, 158; Julian, *Political Recollections,* p. 86.

In effect the speech sounded as though Webster supported Clay's resolutions, even though he did not mention them by name—or the President's plan. He actually preferred to start off by admitting California, following the administration's lead, and then enacting the other compromise measures. He was reaching out to both the Clay and Taylor supporters, but not because of his presidential pretensions, although they surely appeared then and later to have been his motive; rather he sincerely feared for the continuance of the Union unless the two sides could be harmonized, and this was his contribution to a final resolution. He said nothing essentially new in his remarks, but the emotional appeal of a man speaking as an American who loved his country with a passion moved his audience deeply. They could see on his face and the movement of his body how committed he was to the fundamental message he wanted to convey. Unlike Calhoun, he did not name one section as the culprit. Blame belonged on both sides. He set aside his regional pride and prejudices—and they were many—because for him a greater region held his principal allegiance. He was an American first, then a Massachusetts man and a New Englander.

"Union is his paramount motive," Hone recorded in his diary, "the Constitution the star by which he steers." Even before he read the speech, Hone figured that in order to "preserve these, he will probably concede more to the South than the fiery politicians (Whigs even) of the North may think expedient."[35]

Webster called his address "The Constitution and the Union," or "Speech for the Union and the Constitution, March 7, 1850," and he wanted the word "Union" "in some form" included in references to it. But it became better known simply as the Seventh of March speech. In importance and impact on the country it is rivaled only by the second reply. And because of the frightening crisis facing the nation, it took on additional power. In the entire history of the Senate few other speeches aroused as much controversy.

Initially the response was rapturous. The *National Intelligencer* rushed it into print, unedited and uncorrected, in its issue of March 9. Samuel Morse's recent invention of the telegraph also helped deliver it to the nation. A copy was telegraphed to Boston the morning after it had been delivered, and the Boston *Atlas* brought it out five days later in Webster's own revised version. At least two hundred thousand copies were distributed from Washington alone, after a first printing of twenty thousand, and either given away to important individuals or sold for a pittance.[36] Webster himself drafted long lists of names of influential men to whom he sent pamphlet copies. "One hundred & twenty thousand have gone off," he informed his son. "I am sending a handsome copy to each member of the [Massachusetts] Legislature, & shall send the Speech also pretty general[ly] to the Clergy of Mass."

35. Hone, *Diary,* II, 887.

36. Edward Curtis to Peter Harvey, March 28, [1850], in Van Tyne, ed., *Letters of Webster,* p. 407; DW to Harvey, April 7, 1850 in *PC,* VII, 54.

In preparing a published version of his address to be dedicated to the people of Massachusetts, he wanted to preface it with a "motto" of some sort. He preferred a Latin quotation and searched through Cicero but found nothing satisfactory. Milton's Latin poems came close but did not hit the mark. Finally he asked Winthrop, who was "strong in classical quotation," to find something suitable. "I would give ingots of gold—ingots of gold—for" something appropriate. Winthrop remembered some excerpts from Livy and suggested *"Vera Pro Gratis,"* roughly meaning that he must say, "What is true in preference to what is agreeable."

"Just the thing," Webster responded. He liked it so much that he adopted it as his own personal motto. Several months later he sent Winthrop a "massive seal-ring" with *Vera pro gratis* inscribed on the stone and the words "Daniel Webster to R. C. Winthrop, 1850" written on the ring itself.[37]

No sooner did the speech circulate than words of praise gushed from all segments and sections of the country. The *National Intelligencer* declared that it added "fresh lustre to the fame of the great orator, and gave fresh proofs of his truly national and patriotic spirit." In the South the praise was particularly effusive. The Charleston *Mercury* said that it did not always agree with Webster on every point, "but nowhere has he urged his opinions offensively; and when he reaches the true grounds of the present controversy he marks his way so clearly, and treads so loyally on the plain track of the constitution and pledges of the Government, that the difficulty is not to agree but to disagree with him." Now, for the first time since the opening of Congress, continued the *Mercury,* "we feel . . . a hope that [the controversy] may be adjusted." The Boston *Daily Advertiser* and Boston *Courier* agreed, claiming that Webster's constitutional argument was "impregnable, unassailable, irrefutable; it is the true argument, the whole argument, and the only argument."[38]

Individuals from around the country joined the chorus of appreciation and gratitude. "The exordium of this speech is in every man's mouth," said one. Webster had stood up for the "stability, prosperity & glory of the Republic" by soundly rebuking the fanatics and demagogues on both sides of the issues whose mad and treasonable efforts sought to "shatter the massive pillars of the UNION" and spin the nation into *"Civil War."* If George Washington were to rise from his tomb and address the Senate, "he would have uttered the words of your speech," one Philadelphia merchant assured him. A group of New Yorkers conferred on him yet another new title the "Advocate and Preserver of the Union." Most important of all, wrote another admirer, you have " created new hope" that the crisis can be terminated and peace restored to the land. Ordinary citizens expressed their thanks, and northern merchants and businessmen, because of

37. DW to Fletcher Webster, March 31, Everett to DW, April 3, 1850, in *PC,* VII, 48, 52; Curtis, *Webster,* II, 409, note 1; Winthrop, *Memoir,* p. 114; Winthrop to Everett, March 17, 1850, Everett Papers, MHS. Winthrop felt very proud about "hunting up a bit of Latin" for Webster. "I doubt whether *you* could have done better," he boasted to Everett.

38. *National Intelligencer,* March 9, 19, 1850.

their considerable financial involvement with southern planters, also applauded.[39]

Democrats seemed especially happy with Webster's address. Even Isaac Hill, one the earliest and most strident Democratic editors and the senator's longtime New Hampshire adversary, told a prominent New England minister that he regarded Webster's "effort as the crowning act" of his life. It placed Webster "immeasurably before any man who had acted in public life since Washington—& that it was 20 years in advance of any other public man." Hill wrote to Webster directly, expressing his gratitude for "the great principles" of his speech. The senator graciously responded that Hill's letter was "a gratifying incident in the history of my life."[40]

Webster himself felt very proud of what he had accomplished, although he told George Ticknor that he took comfort in the fact that "if its fate should be to go to the bottom, it has no cargo of value, and only one passenger will be drowned." He later said that he regarded his speech as "probably the most important effort of my life, and as likely as any other to be often referred to." Edward Everett also allowed that it was "as important a speech probably as you have ever made."[41]

But hard on the heels of the praise came howling criticism, especially from Massachusetts. Webster got an initial whiff of it when the Boston *Atlas*, once his mouthpiece but now extremely hostile to his conciliatory approach, came out bluntly on March 11 and asserted that "his sentiments are not our sentiments." Only half a dozen Whig journals in New England supported what Webster had said, the *Atlas* claimed, while more than seventy papers opposed it. Thereafter the *Atlas* kept up a steady barrage of censure and reproach, so critical in fact that Webster felt compelled to undertake a campaign in Massachusetts to offset it. He wrote letters that furnished suggestions for articles to be carried in the Boston *Courier* and other friendly newspapers. But the senator's loyal friend Edward Everett, who liked the power of the speech, had to admit that he had reservations about some parts of it. He told Webster that in Boston there was "a good deal of dissatisfaction" expressed "at the ground you have taken." Almost the entire Massachusetts delegation in Congress, including Webster's colleague in the Senate John Davis, divorced itself from his position. Only George Ashmun refused to condemn him. The former secretary of the Massachusetts Board of

39. Hone, *Diary*, II, 888; Henry A. S. Dearborn to DW, March 11, John Pendleton to DW, March 12, William Winder to DW, March 12, Nathaniel Pendleton to DW, March 21, Citizens of New York to DW, April 10, 1850, in *PC*, VII, 25, 32, 33–34, 39–40, 65; Samuel Armstrong to DW, March 12, 1850, in *W&S*, XVIII, 357. "Your speech has disarmed—has quieted the South," wrote one Tennessean, "—we have nothing more to ask and will pledge unbroken fraternity—everlasting fellowship and ceaseless efforts to preserve 'the Union of our Ancestors.' " H. J. Anderson to DW, April 8, 1850, in *PC*, VII, 55–56.

40. John O. Choules to DW, March 18, Hill to DW, April 17, DW to Hill, April 20, 1850, in *PC*, VII, 37, 69–71, 72–73.

41. DW to Ticknor, March 17, DW to Everett, September 27, 1851, in *W&S*, XVIII, 359, 473; Everett to DW, April 3, 1850, in *PC*, VII, 51.

Education and now the Free Soil representative from the West Newton district Horace Mann called Webster a "fallen star" who tried to settle by geography "and not by the Ten Commandments, a great question of human duty." He vowed "that the Northern Members would . . . endeavor to undo the influence of the Speech." Representative Robert Winthrop of the Boston district admitted to Everett that "I cannot help wishing . . . most heartily, that he had taken other advice & made a different speech." By a "few omissions & a few additions & a few qualifications, [he could] have left us a safe New England platform." Had President Taylor "said the same things precisely in his Message, we should all have said—'so much for having a Southern President' & W. himself would have led off in denouncing him." As for the conclusion, it "is, to my mind, quite atrocious. 'Better disunion, a civil or a servile war, &c &c than an extension of the *boundaries* &c &c.' "[42]

In Massachusetts the so-called "conservative portion of the community" took "exceptions to your course," wrote Linus Child, a Lowell attorney and an agent for several large manufacturing companies. Abolitionists naturally condemned a great many things he had said. It infuriated them that he could charge the North with wronging the South over the elimination of a moral evil. Free Soilers were also angered by his rejection of the Wilmot Proviso. And Webster's approval of a more stringent fugitive slave law generally disgusted those Whigs less vehement in their antislavery views, some of whom deserted to the Free Soil party. "We surrendered to the slave-owners," moaned John Murray Forbes. The "scales fell from my eyes and I gave up the Whig party." After that speech, in Forbes's opinion, Webster "would not have had the vote of one third of his own party for any office in the gift of the people of his adopted State, Massachusetts."[43]

Critics claimed to understand the senator's motives. There was only one way to account for it, lectured the great abolitionist minister Theodore Parker: "as a bid for the Presidency." He pandered to "certain political brokers," a majority of whom are "slaveholders or pro-slavery men." Parker cited the lure and craving for the presidency as the evil that had brought about Webster's spiritual degradation. He charged Black Dan with a lack of moral principles, an absence of moral conviction.[44]

Another criticism, as could be expected, involved Webster's close association with the wealthy of New England. He served the elite of the North, the "lords of the cotton looms," not ordinary citizens. His moral defects deafened

42. Duberman, *Charles Francis Adams*, p. 167; DW to George Ticknor, June 1, 3, 13, 14, 1850, in *W&S*, XVI, 542–546; Horace Mann, *Slavery: Letters and Speeches* (Boston, 1851), p. 251; Winthrop to Everett, March 17, 1850, Everett Papers, MHS; Everett to DW, March 12, 22, John Choules to DW, March 18, 1850, in *PC*, VII, 27–31, 37, 40–41. Webster's argument from "*Nature*, too," said Winthrop, "is, at the best, pretty loose, & is much less satisfactory to our friends." Winthrop to Everett, March 17, 1850, Everett Papers, MHS.

43. Child to DW, April 1, 1850, in *PC*, VII, 49; Forbes, *Letters and Recollections*, I, 171, 142.

44. Frances Power Cobbe, ed., *The Collected Works of Theodore Parker* (London, 1863), p. 228.

him to the cries of the oppressed. Clergymen in Massachusetts were particularly vicious in their assault. They called him a traitor. "I know of no deed in American history, done by a son of New England, to which I can compare this" Parker cried, "but the act of Benedict Arnold." Ralph Waldo Emerson spoke of "Mr. Webster's treachery" and said that Black Dan's frequent mention of the word "liberty" in the speech revolted him. " 'Liberty! liberty!' Pho! Let Mr Webster for decency's sake shut his lips once & forever on this word. The word *liberty* in the mouth of Mr Webster sounds like the word *love* in the mouth of a courtezan."

But the most stinging and enduring condemnation came from the pen of the Quaker abolitionist John Greenleaf Whittier in his poem "Ichabod". Describing his reading of the speech as "one of the saddest moment of my life," he immediately sat down and wrote the poem.

> So fallen! so lost! the light withdrawn
> Which once he wore!
> The glory from his gray hairs gone
> Forevermore!
>
> Revile him not, the Tempter hath
> A snare for all;
> And pitying tears, not scorn and wrath,
> Befit his fall!
>
> Oh, dumb be passion's stormy rage,
> When he who might
> Have lighted up and led his age,
> Falls back in night. . . .
>
> Let not the land once proud of him
> Insult him now,
> Nor brand with deeper shame his dim,
> Dishonored brow. . . .
>
> All else is gone; from those great eyes
> The soul has fled:
> When faith is lost, when honor dies,
> The man is dead!
>
> Then, pay the reverence of old days
> To his dead fame;
> Walk backward, with averted gaze,
> And hide the shame![45]

Horace Mann read this mournful "dirge" to the full House of Representatives. He also used the *Atlas* in a series of articles to convey his outrage over

45. James Freeman Clarke, *Anti-Slavery Days* (Westport, Conn., 1883), p. 137; Cobbe, ed., *Works of Parker*, p. 231. Emerson, *Works*, XI, 181; Emerson, *Journals*, XI, 345–346; John Greenleaf Whittier, *The Complete Poetical Works of John Greenleaf Whittier* (Boston and New York, 1894), pp. 186–187. "Mr. Webster is a man who lives by his memory, a man of the past, not a man of faith or of hope," declared Emerson. "He looks at the Union as an estate." Emerson, *Works*, XI, 202, 204.

Webster's abandonment of human rights. His long public address to his constituents dealt especially with the fugitive slave issue, the one issue that particularly
distressed northerners, and Mann's letter truly nettled Webster. So much so, in
fact, that he wrote a public response to the citizens of Newburyport defending
his position. In it he denied that the Constitution required a trial by jury for
fugitive slaves.[46]

By and large the critics scored one important point: The speech argued
geography, politics, history, and constitutional law to make its case but said
nothing of moral principles. Human beings were involved, and Daniel Webster
did not pause for a moment in his speech to consider their plight or their rights.

His character and reputation repeatedly and thoroughly thrashed by this
devastating criticism, Webster counterattacked with the assistance of some of
his staunch friends. He directed them to send copies of his speech to "every
man that reads the Atlas" and to "all the towns of Mass" and throughout New
England as well as New York, Pennsylvania, and Ohio. He supervised newspaper
rejoinders against particular critics, like Mann, the preparation of antiabolition-
ist tracts by distinguished New Englander professionals and businessmen, and
the publication of a letter of support signed by eight hundred prominent Massachusetts men, such as Rufus Choate, Nathan Hale, Jr., Oliver Wendell Holmes,
George Ticknor, Joseph Quincy, and Jared Sparks. This letter was published in
the April 3, and again in the April 15, editions of the Boston *Courier* and
Boston *Advertiser* as well as the Washington *National Intelligencer.* Webster
also pledged to "take the stump in every village in New England" if necessary.
"We will put the disorganizers down, *if we can,*" he cried.[47]

Between directing this defense and attending his legal business before the
Supreme Court, Webster had little time to help Clay find the necessary majority
to win approval of the compromise proposals in Congress. But he did what he
could. Frightened for the safety of the Union, he linked the defense of his
speech with the need for passage of the compromise measures—all of them,
including a fugitive slave law.

Almost immediately after Webster had delivered his speech, William H.
Seward spoke on March 11 and expressed his faith in an unshakable Union,
virtually sneering at those who needed compromises to rescue it. In seeking

46. Clarke, *Anti-Slavery Days,* p. 139; Mann, *Slavery,* pp. 263–281; DW to Edward Rand et al.,
May 15, 1850, in *PC,* VII, 85—95. Emerson said that Webster was "the life and soul" of the fugitive
slave bill, even though he was not its author. Emerson, *Works,* XI, 219. Henry Thoreau in *Walden
Pond* refers to "the passage of Webster's Fugitive Slave Bill" in the chapter "Higher Laws."

47. DW to Everett, March 10, DW to Franklin Haven, March 12, Choules to DW, March 18,
Everett to DW, March 22, DW to Fletcher Webster, March 31, 1850, in *PC,* VII, 24, 27, 37, 40–41,
48; *National Intelligencer,* April 6, 1850; T. H. Perkins et al. to DW, March 25, Edward Curtis to
Peter Harvey, March 15, 28, April 12, DW to Harvey, May 11, June 2, 3, 1850, in Van Tyne, ed.,
Letters of Webster, pp. 404, 406, 407, 408, 412, 415–417. Never "a day so painful occurred in
Boston," commented Emerson, "as the letter with 800 signatures to Webster. The siege of Boston
was a day of glory. This was a day of petticoats, a day of imbecilities, the day of the old woman *La
Veille [sic].*" Among the eight hundred were names of "ideots *[sic];* of aged & infirm people, who
have outlived everything but their night cap." Emerson, *Journals,* XI, 249.

justification for forbidding the extension of slavery into the territories, he invoked "a higher law than the Constitution," a phrase that delighted the most violent opponents of slavery. He would follow Taylor's plan and vote for California's admission, he said, "without conditions, without qualifications, and without compromise."[48]

The New York senator believed that Webster's support of the compromise provided Seward with the unique opportunity to take total command of the northern Whig party by promoting the President's position on strong antislavery grounds. Webster's course, he told Weed, "has rendered of little value the little moderation I can practice in regard to the other portion of the Union."[49]

Senator Henry Foote of Mississippi then proposed the formation of a select committee of thirteen to prepare a solution to their problems. Clay thought it unlikely to succeed but was willing to try it.[50] Webster not only opposed the idea but spoke against it. It would be a waste of time, he declared. He feared that the committee would only bring forward more amendments and instructions that would lengthen the debate and would needlessly delay and possibly kill any chance of resolving the dispute. He wanted to get on with a vote on the compromise so that Congress could return to other matters, like a tariff revision. Everyone "speaks to defend himself, & to gratify his constituents," he complained. "No one inquires how the Union is to be preserved, & the peace of the Country restored." In the course of the ensuing debate Henry Foote and Thomas Hart Benton, who wanted the admission of California separated from the other issues, got into a shouting match that ended when Foote drew a pistol and Benton screamed, "Let the assassin fire."[51]

Despite Webster's objections, Foote's proposal carried. And, to his annoyance, Webster was placed on the special committee along with Henry Clay, who served as chairman.[52] The regard the senators had for Webster in placing him on the committee was expressed by Willie P. Mangum of North Carolina, also a member of the committee, who told him, "*Upon you, the safety of the Country depends.*"[53]

But Webster responded badly. He showed his annoyance by taking little

---

48. *Congressional Globe*, 31st Congress, 1st Session, appendix, pp. 260–269. John Hale, the Free Soil senator from New Hampshire, agreed with Seward and in the midst of his remarks accused Webster of abandoning his earlier antislavery commitment. Webster vehemently denied the charge, insisting that no inconsistency existed between his feelings and position now and what they had been earlier. Ibid., appendix, pp. 591–592.

49. Seward to Weed, March 11, 15, 1850, quoted in Michael F. Holt, *The Political Crisis of the 1850s* (New York, 1978), p. 85.

50. Remini, *Clay*, p. 744.

51. DW to Franklin Haven, May 18, 1850, in *PC*, VII, 100; *Congressional Globe*, 31st Congress, 1st Session, pp. 721–722, 760–763.

52. The committee consisted of Clay, Webster, Samuel S. Phelps, James Cooper, Willie P. Mangum, John Bell, John M. Berrien, Lewis Cass, Daniel S. Dickinson, Jesse D. Bright, William R. King, James M. Mason, and Solomon W. Downs.

53. Mangum to DW, April 11, 1850, in *PC*, VII, 65.

part in the committee's deliberations and even leaving Washington in late April for home. He needed to confront his constituents and learn first hand, not through outside interpreters, how they regarded his speech.

On his arrival in Boston he was driven to Revere House on Bowdoin Square, where an estimated five thousand people had gathered to greet him. Standing in his carriage, he saluted the crowd with a brief speech in which he defended his position on fugitive slaves and declared that it was time for Massachusetts to "conquer her own prejudices." The enthusiastic reception he received convinced him that his reputation in the state among the electorate was as lofty as ever. His efforts over the past two months in explaining and defending his speech had apparently paid off. Another indication of his continuing popularity and political muscle at home came during his visit when he helped block a resolution in the legislature criticizing his speech and instructing him to vote against the extension of slavery.[54]

Several days before Webster's return to Washington, Clay presented the select committee's report to the Senate in the form of a single package, an omnibus bill, that linked together the admission of California as a free state, establishment of territorial governments for New Mexico and Utah without a provision to legislate on slavery, and adjustment of the boundary of Texas with compensation. As a separate item the report called for a fugitive slave law and the abolition of the slave trade in the District of Columbia. These recommendations were almost identical to those first proposed by Clay in late January.[55]

Webster had problems with the idea of an omnibus bill. "In my opinion it is unfortunate that the measures were all put together. When I left the committee to go home, it was agreed that they should not be, but that vote was rescinded in my absence." Nevertheless he favored passage of the bill but expressed a fear that showed remarkable prescience—namely, that "there is an unquestionable majority of votes in the Senate, in favor of *every one of the propositions contained* in the Bill perhaps with some amendments, & yet I have fears that no majority will be found for them, all together." As a package the bill was all or nothing, but when it was separated into its several parts, senators could vote for one item they approved and against another they disapproved. Still, despite this shifting back and forth, as Webster said, a majority existed in favor of every one of the propositions.[56]

Convinced that this compromise would restore peace to the Union, Webster began a diligent campaign through the newspapers and his contacts with political and business leaders to win northern support for it. He encouraged and directed the gathering of signatures for petitions to congressmen to vote in favor of it. Once the compromise passed, he reckoned, Congress could turn to other urgent matters, such as the tariff, for "it is just as I knew it would be, with Whig

54. Boston *Advertiser*, April 30, 1850; *W&S*, XIII, 386–389; Poore, *Perley's Reminiscences*, p. 365.
55. *Congressional Globe*, 31st Congress, 1st Session, pp. 944–951.
56. DW to Franklin Haven, May 18, 1850, in *PC*, VII, 100.

Senators of the South. They will not give a single vote for the Tariff until this Slavery business is settled."[57]

The existence of a fugitive slave bill in the compromise proved to be an enormous stumbling block for northerners. The existing statute of 1793 fundamentally relied on the states for enforcement. As a consequence many northern states passed so-called personal liberty laws to hinder and prevent the execution of the law within their boundaries. However, in the case *Prigg* v. *Pennsylvania* in 1842 the Supreme Court had struck down Pennsylvania's personal liberty law and by extension all similar state laws. It had declared that the execution of the law belonged to the federal government. Under the circumstances Webster decided to offer an amendment to the fugitive slave bill. His proposal provided for a jury trial for those slaves accused of running away from their owners. Unfortunately he did not speak to it or explain it. He simply proposed it and let it just sit. Few noticed it, and it soon faded from view.[58]

Had Webster given a strong speech in its favor, had he tried to show some compassion for fugitives, had he demonstrated some moral conviction about the institution he genuinely hated, he might have deflected a great deal of the condemnation he endured then and later. Instead he remained silent. He acted and spoke out of concern for the Union, not the plight of slaves.

The moral judgment against him hounded him for the rest of his life. In the final hour, said Emerson four years after Webster's death, he came down on "the side of abuse and oppression and chaos, not the side of humanity and justice."[59]

57. DW to Harvey, May 29, June 2, DW to Dudley Hall et al., June 3, DW to Samuel Lawrence, June 10, 1850, ibid., VII, 102–103, 107–109, 114.

58. Webster consulted with Associate Justice McLean on his amendment. McLean to DW, April 6, 1850, in *Microfilm Edition*, F22/30187; *Congressional Globe*, 31st Congress, 1st Session, p. 1111. Samuel Eliot complemented Webster on his amendment. It "removed the only real impediment to a cordial support of the doctrines of the [Seventh of March] speech." Eliot to DW, June 12, 1850 in *PC*, VII, 115.

59. Emerson, *Works*, XI, 226.

41

"*Union, Union, Union Now and forever!*"

WEBSTER invited Willie Mangum, his wife, and his daughter for "tea" at his home, after which they attended the opera. He imbibed "rather freely" during the evening and was drunk by the time they started for the theater, but he showed no signs of it. Unfortunately the heat of the theater finally got to him. Suddenly, in the middle of the performance, he jumped to his feet and began singing "Hail Columbia, Happy Land" at the top of his lungs. Caroline was mortified, but the rest of the audience found his antics hilarious. Finally she grabbed hold of his coattails and pulled him down into his seat. "He remained quiet during the remainder of the evening."[1]

By this time of his life Webster's drinking had become a serious problem, one that had undoubtedly developed in large measure because of his many disappointments and frustrations in not obtaining the single goal he prized above all others, the presidency. The humiliation of the 1836 defeat embittered him. As he grew older, he slowly came to realize that his chances of gaining national popular support were almost nil. Although to the end of his life he strove to win a nomination from his party, he surely guessed that it would never happen. He desired public life to the very depth of his being, but with each frustrated attempt to advance to the presidency and the humiliation that accompanied it, he talked about abandoning politics and returning to the law full-time. But that alternative only deepened his frustration and increased his drinking.

There are other factors that may account for his alcoholism: his unsatisfactory relations with his wife—the public gossip of impending divorce occurred several times over the years—plus the many personal tragedies he suffered with the loss of his beloved first wife and four of his five children. And he probably despaired that Fletcher would ever amount to much. The young man had encountered one failure after another—with no letup.

Not only was Webster making a public spectacle of himself during the final

---

1. "Recollections of Mangum Turner," in Shanks, ed., *Papers of Mangum*, V, 751.

years of his life because of his drinking, but he was destroying his health. Yet it is remarkable that with all his heavy imbibing he always managed to appear sober, unless, as happened occasionally, he suddenly engaged in some unseemly act at a most inappropriate time and place, such as occurred at the opera. But the heavy drinking destroyed his liver. He was slowly killing himself.

The nation, too, seemed to be killing itself. With the national crisis over slavery deepening, with Clay, Webster, and their supporters urging conciliation and compromise, with the President, jealous of Clay's leadership, threatening a veto of the omnibus bill and demanding the immediate admission of California and New Mexico as states to circumvent the Wilmot Proviso, and with the delegates of the Nashville Convention awaiting the results of the debates in Congress before taking any action, many despaired for the life of the Union. Then an unforeseen event completely altered the direction of national affairs. President Taylor died on July 9, 1850. After attending a July Fourth celebration on a blisteringly hot and muggy day and consuming large quantities of raw fruit and vegetables, washed down with ice water, he became ill and died five days later, probably of acute gastroenteritis. Webster, his voice "full of emotion," announced "the appalling news" of Taylor's imminent demise to the Senate, delivered a brief eulogy in the upper house on July 10, and served as one of the pallbearers during the funeral on July 13.[2]

This was the second time a Whig President had been struck down. Millard Fillmore, a New York politician who had risen from relative obscurity by winning the vice presidential nomination over Abbott Lawrence, now held the office both Webster and Clay had sought all their mature lives. Big-framed and strikingly handsome, with an air of quiet dignity about him, Fillmore at the time of his accession favored the Taylor plan as an alternative to the Wilmot Proviso in the belief that it would reconcile discordant views involving public policy.[3] He detested Thurlow Weed and Senator William H. Seward, New York's ruling political clique, whose friends, at their instigation, had pushed resolutions through the New York legislature demanding imposition of the Proviso[4] and whose enormous influence on Taylor[5] over the past two years had clearly exacerbated the crisis.

Fillmore met with Webster the very day of his inauguration and assured the senator that he would accept any reasonable compromise solution to end the crisis and restore peace in the country. He obviously looked to his friends Webster and Clay for assistance in shaping his administration and bringing the

2. *National Intelligencer,* July 9, 1850; Hamilton, *Taylor,* II, 389, 391–392; W&S, X, 140–143.

3. Robert J. Rayback, *Millard Fillmore: Biography of a President* (New York, 1959), pp. 1, 36, 38, 51.

4. For this information I am indebted to Professor Michael Holt of the University of Virginia, who is presently writing a history of the Whig party.

5. Fillmore protested to Taylor that his appointments in New York, in accordance with the suggestions of Seward and Weed, were destroying his (Fillmore's) influence in his home state. Elbert B. Smith, *The Presidencies of Zachary Taylor & Millard Fillmore* (Lawrence, Kan., 1988), pp. 162–163.

nation out of the crisis. Within a week he flushed out the cabinet[6] and decided to build another with Webster as secretary of state.

Any number of Whigs wrote to the new President and recommended Webster for the position of secretary of state because he had "the confidence & affection of the North" and the "confidence of the South." The Boston *Daily Advertiser* in an editorial on July 15 urged his appointment on the grounds of his qualifications and present popularity. Even Clay supported the idea, although Fletcher Webster cautioned, "I am afraid of the kisses of an enemy." Naturally "there were *some* N.E. Whigs who expressed a wish to the President, that I might not be appointed," Webster admitted to his Boston banker friend Franklin Haven, "as my appointment would appear to be an approval of my recent course in Congress."[7]

That was not the only reason opponents of his appointment gave to Fillmore. One Whig argued that Webster "is a prostitute in morals and something worse in politics. . . . Loose in money matters, tainted with fraud, fixed in profligacy, he is a living ulcer and infection. . . . Give us a *pure* Cabinet for God's sake—not *Whores* like Webster."[8]

At first Fillmore hesitated about offering the position to the senator, not only because of the "unsavory" gossip that always seemed to surround the man but because Webster favored Clay's compromise, not the Taylor plan. He seriously considered offering it to Representative Robert C. Winthrop, Webster's former law student and former Speaker of the House. But when word of his possible appointment came to him "in a way to admit of no mistake," Winthrop "went to the President, & declared his unalterable purpose not to accept a Cabinet office. He took occasion, also, to add . . . [that] he was still in favor of Mr. W's being placed at the head of Affairs."[9]

6. Actually Taylor's cabinet assisted the process by resigning the day following the President's death. Fillmore had asked them to stay for a month while he reorganized the government, but they all resigned within a week. Rayback, *Fillmore*, p. 242.

7. Daniel D. Barnard, July 11, James K. Mills to DW, July 17, DW to Haven, July 21, 1850, in *PC*, VII, 124–125, 128, 130; Fletcher Webster to Harvey, July 15, 1850, in Van Tyne, ed., *Letters of Webster*, p. 420.

8. "A True Friend" to Fillmore, July 16, 1850, Fillmore Papers, Buffalo and Erie County Historical Society. I am very grateful to Professor Michael Holt, who provided me with a copy of this letter.

9. In his letter Winthrop refers to himself in the third person and then switches to the first person. "It was by no means true," he wrote, "that the State Department had been offered to Mr. Webster. . . . He [Fillmore] has hesitated long on the subject, &, if he decided to give it to Webster, it will rather be *in spite* of Mr. W's recent speeches [because he favored the Compromise, not Taylor's plan], than on account of them. . . . The truth is, that Mr. Fillmore had been wavering between Webster & a Massts man [Winthrop] every way his inferior." Winthrop to Everett, July 19, 1850, Everett Papers, MHS. Again, I am grateful to Professor Holt for alerting me to this letter. Fletcher Webster confirms that Winthrop was the "Massts man," declaring he had heard that Fillmore preferred Winthrop to Webster. See Fletcher Webster to Peter Harvey, July 15, 1850 in Van Tyne, ed., *Letters of Webster*, p. 420.

Winthrop related his discussion with the President to Webster, or so he said in his letter to Everett, and Webster somewhat confirmed it when he told Franklin Haven that "you will be glad to know that Mr Winthrop acted in the most friendly, open, & decided manner. He behaved like a man, throughout." DW to Haven, July 21, 1850, in *PC*, VII, 130.

Sometime during the week following Taylor's demise Fillmore switched from the Taylor plan to the compromise. Most probably it occurred when he learned that the governor of Texas, Peter H. Bell, had written a letter on June 14 to Taylor—which reached Washington after Taylor's death—threatening to send an army to Santa Fe if Congress did not return to his state all the territory north and east of the Rio Grande. The threat of immediate armed conflict made the difference. And once Fillmore opted for the compromise he signaled his switch by appointing Webster. That action clearly announced where he presently stood on the question.

In selecting his cabinet, Fillmore later said that he wanted to appoint "trusted men, in whom the country had confidence. I placed Mr. Webster at the head of the State Department, because he was a man of considerable experience in the matters of State, and because he was known and respected by the people both for his diplomacy and the public services he had rendered." The senator "possessed those sterling qualities of the head and the heart that gave us all entire confidence in him."[10]

But to assume the office of secretary of state once again gave Webster pause. He worried, naturally, about money, the everlasting, ever-present need for money. And just as in 1841 he thought he must refuse the offer unless this difficulty could be resolved. Accepting the appointment would mean giving up some twenty important cases presently before the Supreme Court and other legal business and sacrificing an income of nearly twenty thousand dollars a year, give or take a few thousand depending on his case load, for a "paltry" annual salary of six thousand dollars. As he explained to Haven, "nobody can well be Secretary of State, who has not a fortune, unless he is a Bachelor. The Secretary of State is the head of the Administration, & he must have a house, sometimes to receive guests in."[11]

Once again his business friends in Boston and New York were approached, and once again they responded enthusiastically. Since they deemed Webster's appointment of primary importance to the country and to their commercial interests, they willingly set about raising a twenty-thousand-dollar fund for his benefit. Directed in part by Edward Curtis, a Bank of Commerce director, and Richard M. Blatchford, Webster's close friend and business agent (Thomas Ward, a agent of Baring Brothers and Company, called them Webster's "Ministers of Finance"), a group of forty financiers and businessmen agreed to contribute five hundred dollars (although some contributed one thousand dollars and more) "for the benefit of the Hon. Daniel Webster."[12] The banking interests of

10. Interview with Fillmore that appeared in the New York *Herald*, September 16, 1873, 135. Webster spoke on March 13, April 4, 11, 17, June 3, 7, 17, 1851.
11. DW to Haven, July 12, 1850, in *PC*, VII, 125.
12. Thomas Curtis to David Sears, with enclosure of names of subscribers, October 26, Griswold to DW, with enclosure of names of subscribers, August 1, 1850, ibid., VII, 167–169, 194–195. Some of the subscribers included J. K. Mills & Co., F. Skinner & Co., Robert G. Shaw & Sons, G. S. Robbins & Son, William, Nathan, and Samuel Appleton, John A. Lowell, John P. Cushing, Samuel

the Barings, Corcoran & Riggs, and Howland & Aspinwall were well represented in this group. As it turned out, according to Edward Curtis, "the rich" got
their money's worth. "If they were here to see how incessantly Mr. W. labors,"
how "conciliation & internal peace are distinctly the result of his exertions, &
how cheerfully he gives up Marshfield for the hot rooms of his small dwelling
house at Washington, they would feel that they can never pay for such services."[13]

Several months later Charles Allen, the Free Soil representative of Massachusetts, publicly charged that during the summer Webster had demanded and
received a gift of fifty thousand dollars, making him a "stipendiary of the bankers
and brokers" who stood to make a handsome profit from the transfer of funds to
Mexico as part of the Treaty of Guadalupe Hidalgo. Allen based his charge on
hearsay evidence circulated by Representative John Otis of Maine, a former
commissioner in the Webster-Ashburton negotiations. The accusation "was so
utterly disgusting to the House [of Representatives], and treated with so much
scorn and indignation," George Ashmun informed Webster, that a resolution to
investigate the charges was overwhelmingly rejected, 119 to 35. No real evidence could ever be found at the time to substantiate the charge.[14] But unfortunately the stigma of corruption that had already attached itself to Black Dan
intensified and it endured to the end of his life.

But there were other factors besides money that troubled the senator.
Fiercely, almost obsessively concerned about the safety of the Union and the
need in Congress for his strong voice and vote to help win passage of the
compromise, he fretted over resigning his seat and redirecting his energies
toward foreign affairs. He feared that a Free Soiler might be appointed by
Governor George Briggs to replace him. But that obstacle was overcome when
Webster and Fillmore applied "extreme pressure" on the governor to name
Robert Winthrop to the position. And it came as a unexpected gift when Boston
elected Samuel A. Eliot, an ardent champion of compromise, to take Winthrop's
place in the House. Eliot overwhelmingly defeated the Free Soil candidate,
Charles Sumner.

"Boston, ever true & glorious Boston, has helped us immensely," Webster
enthused on hearing the news. "Mr Eliots triumphant Election awakened entirely new hopes." It proved that "I was not a dead man." Beyond doubt, "that
election was a clear and convincing proof that there was breaking out a new

---

Lawrence, Thomas W. Ward, William B. Astor, Gouverneur Morris, Henry Chauncey, and Warren
Delano, Jr., George Griswold, Jonathan Sturges, Morris Ketchum, John L. and William H. Aspinwall, J. Prescott Hall, Edward Curtis, and Samuel Jaudon.

13. Curtis to Harvey, August 10, [1850], in Van Tyne, ed., *Letters of Webster,* p. 426.

14. *Congressional Globe,* 31st Congress, 1st Session, pp, 686–687; Robert Schenck to DW, February
26, Ashmun to DW, March 1, Haven to DW, February 28, 1851, in Curtis, *Webster,* II, 492–494;
DW to Haven, March 2, 1851, in *PC,* VII, 211. Both George Ashmun and Henry W. Hilliard, an
Alabama Whig, defended Webster. Hilliard at the time was seeking a diplomatic post. Ibid., VII,
209. The "liberal contribution from a number of his personal and political friends," said Hone, was
"equally honorable to the donors and the recipient, and disgraceful to his vilifier." *Diary,* II, 914.

fountain of brilliant light in the East." Webster could hardly contain himself in his happiness because it confirmed in his mind that he had a political future after all. "Ever intelligent, ever patriotic, ever glorious Boston."[15]

The election was a relief, and the more he thought about it, the more he convinced himself that as secretary of state he might be in an even better position—considering his influence with the President and the patronage he would employ—to influence national affairs. In other words, he could use the "office and foreign policy to promote national unity."[16]

Another consideration was his health and the amount of work that would be involved in his return to the State Department. But once the money problem dissolved and he convinced himself that he might better serve his country in its present peril by accepting the post, Webster set aside the thoughts of health, work, and the awful heat and humidity of Washington during the late spring and summer and decided to accept the appointment. "I yielded, to what has been suggested on so many sides," he wrote, "& gave my own wishes to the wishes & opinions of my friends. I must leave myself in their hands." He worried about the amount of drudgery and anxiety involved; still, "I was persuaded to think it was my duty, in the present crisis, to accept a seat in the Cabinet, but it made my heart ache to think of it."[17]

No doubt he also had less elevated reasons for giving his consent. The power, prestige, and patronage of the office always excited him. Moreover, in the not-too-distant past the office of secretary of state had led immediately to the presidency, and already Black Dan was giving very serious thought to running in 1852—that is, if Fillmore decided to retire.

The President delayed offering the position for two weeks while he mulled over whether he really wanted Webster in view of his "unsavory" reputation and the fact that the appointment would "create some little shock among some of our Free State Whigs in New York & New England."[18] Fillmore "is exceedingly cautious," the senator fussed, "& takes time for consideration; but he is not wanting in firmness, I think, & is a thorough conservative Whig." Furthermore, he "is a sensible man" "& not likely to be in favor of any *isms.*" Most important of all, unlike Zachary Taylor, President Fillmore was now deeply committed to Clay's compromise.[19]

The President probably offered the position to Webster on July 19. It came via another member of the Senate. Following his formal acceptance, Webster was nominated and confirmed on July 20, commissioned on July 22, and at 10:00 A.M. on July 23 assumed his new duties as secretary of state. He immediately

15. Rayback, *Fillmore*, p. 243; DW to Harvey, September 10, DW to Haven, September 12, 1850, in *PC*, VII, 143, 145.

16. This point is argued very effectively by Kenneth E. Shewmaker, "Daniel Webster and the Politics of Foreign Policy, 1850–1852," *Journal of American History*, LXIII (1976), pp. 303–315.

17. DW to Harvey, July 21, 1850, in *PD*, II, 9.

18. Winthrop to Everett, July 16, 1850, Everett Papers, MHS.

19. DW to Haven, July 12, 21, 1850, in *PC*, VII, 125, 130.

dispatched telegraph messages to his political and financial supporters, informing them of his action.[20]

Webster made his last address as a senator in the upper house on July 17, delayed a week in consideration of Taylor's death. In the speech he pleaded once again for the passage of the omnibus bill. "The question is," he declared, "whether we have the true patriotism, the Americanism, necessary to carry us through" this ordeal. "For myself, I propose, Sir, to abide by the principles and the purposes which I have avowed. I shall stand by the Union, and by all who stand by it. . . . I mean to stand upon the Constitution. I need no other platform. I shall know but one country. . . . I was born an American; I will live an American; I shall die an American."[21]

Just as he sought peace in the country as a whole, in leaving the Senate, Webster decided the time had come to make peace with several of his verbal combatants in the upper chamber. "It is impossible that I should entertain hostile feelings, or political acrimony towards" Lewis Cass, Daniel S. Dickinson, James Shields, Jesse Bright, Thomas J. Rusk, "&c &c in the Senate," he told Peter Harvey. "We have agreed, that as we are never likely to be called on to act in a matter of so much moment to the Country, again, so we will not mar the joy, or the honor of the past by any unnecessary quarrels for the future."[22]

It was a gracious and fitting way to depart, and the other senators gladly accepted his outstretched hand. They wished him well as he began his new assignment.

Two weeks later, on July 31, what Webster most feared occurred in the Senate chamber: The omnibus bill went down to defeat. One after the other the various parts of the bill were killed, with only the Utah Territory provision surviving. "All gone but Utah," cried the jubilant Thomas Hart Benton. "*He* had routed *Clay! He* had smashed his Omnibus to atoms." Seward danced around the room like a little top. The "Mormons alone got thru' living," commented Elizabeth Lee; "the Christians all jumped out."[23]

As Webster had feared, the omnibus as a single package had too many enemies. Fortunately Senator Stephen A. Douglas of Illinois, chairman of the Committee on Territories, immediately set about repairing the damage. Since a single package was unacceptable, he separated the various parts of Clay's compromise and wrote each into an individual bill. As separate measures each had a better chance at passage, or so he believed.[24] But it

20. *Executive Register of the United States, 1789–1902* (Washington, 1905), p. 150; DW to Fletcher Webster, July 23, 1850, in *W&S*, XVIII, 379; DW to Harvey, July 21, in *PD*, II, 9; DW to Harvey, July 21, 1850, in Curtis, *Webster*, II, 465 note. Webster submitted his resignation from the Senate on July 22, and Winthrop took his place on July 30.

21. *W&S*, X, 144–170.

22. DW to Harvey, October 2, 1850, in *PC*, VII, 155.

23. *Congressional Globe*, 31st Congress, 1st Session, pp. 1449, 1458–1459, 1473–1474, 1504, appendix, pp. 1482–1485; Elizabeth Blair Lee to Samuel Phillips Lee, August 1, 1850, quoted in Elbert Smith, *Francis Preston Blair* (New York, 1980), p. 206; *National Intelligencer,* August 1, 1850.

24. Robert W. Johannsen, *Stephen A. Douglas* (New York, 1973), pp. 294–296; Smith, *Presidencies of Taylor and Fillmore*, pp. 179–180.

would take months before each bill could be acted on.

In the meantime Webster fully intended to use his new office to advance in every possible way the efforts of the compromisers to resolve the difficulties blocking the resolution of the crisis and threatening the disruption of the Union.

In appointing Webster his secretary of state, Fillmore deserves credit for selecting a man with a far greater national reputation than his own, a man in obvious and constant pursuit of the presidency, and a man who would surely use his position to further his own personal agenda and ambition. Also, Webster had a reputation for "mishandling" money that could lead to trouble. But Fillmore was willing to risk all that because he needed Webster's national stature to bolster, if not legitimize, his administration among Whigs and because Webster had diplomatic experience and might well eclipse his outstanding record as secretary under Tyler. Still, the conduct of foreign affairs, as well he knew, rested completely with him, and although he generally gave Webster full support and encouragement and indeed relied on him and followed his suggestions, he also became an active participant in the conduct of the State Department.

The appointment was a vindication for the New Englander. He had taken considerable abuse recently, and to him, returning to the State Department meant that his talents and past services had not been unappreciated or forgotten. Caleb Cushing congratulated him and added that "it must be a proud triumph to step at once over the heads of your enemies, and be giving orders to Mr [Abbott] Lawrence and the rest." Lawrence, whom Webster made a special point to retain as minister to England, told Everett: "Whatever differences of opinion may have existed between us, I am free to say, that no man in the Union is more competent to discharge the duties of Secretary of State than Mr Webster."[25]

The President immediately asked Webster for recommendations for the other cabinet positions. The secretary provided a list of worthy Whigs, and from it Fillmore appointed John J. Crittenden attorney general, Charles M. Conrad secretary of war, and William A. Graham secretary of the navy. Other appointees not on the list included Thomas Corwin, secretary of the treasury, Nathan K. Hall, the postmaster general, and Alexander H. H. Stuart, secretary of the interior. Webster thought they were "all sound men, of fair and upright character, sober minds, and national views." They in turn looked to him as a leader. "Mr. Webster appears among them, like a father teaching his listening children," observed Edward Curtis, who watched the cabinet members react to him at a dinner party.[26]

Besides favoring his friends in his recommendations to the President, Webster assisted his financial supporters in their operations whenever they inter-

25. Cushing to DW, September 14, Lawrence to Everett, [August 16, 1850] in *PC*, VII, 149, 148. Lawrence reported that the British also found the appointment "highly satisfactory."

26. DW to Fillmore, [c. July 18, 1850], in *PC*, VII, 129; DW to Stuart, August 10, 1850, in *W&S*, XVIII, 383; Edward Curtis to Peter Harvey, August 16, [1850], in Van Tyne, ed., *Letters of Webster*, p. 426. Two men on Webster's list of recommendations, Edward Bates and James A. Pearce, received appointments from Fillmore but turned them down. Rayback, *Fillmore*, pp. 245–246.

sected with foreign affairs. The indemnity paid in four annual installments of three million dollars to Mexico by the United States under the treaty terms that ended the Mexican War is one instance. Loans on money in advance of payment dates and the indemnity transfer fees were attractive exchange operations. Webster "collaborated" with William W. Corcoran, a Washington banker, and his Baring Brothers associates in their Mexican operations. Corcoran had already canceled more than five thousand dollars of Webster's notes after the senator had delivered his Seventh of March speech, as well as provided him with an outright gift of one thousand dollars. According to one extremely critical historian, the new secretary of state asked "no particular quid pro quo other than a bribe."[27] Actually Webster was not after a bribe. True, he took care of his friends, but he always tried to do what he could to advance American business and commercial interests because he believed that such efforts would promote the prosperity of the entire nation. As he said repeatedly, not only did capitalism increase property, but its advantages were scattered "among the many."[28] As for the Baring Brothers, he did indeed have "connections" with them. But he was also biased toward Great Britain. A passionate Anglophile, he admired what Britain had accomplished and wished to see his own country emulate those achievements.

In becoming the secretary of state a second time—thereby holding the unique distinction of serving in that office under three Presidents—Webster had several things in his favor: He had the complete confidence and support of the President, he was a skillful and hardworking administrator, and, most important of all, he knew precisely what he wanted to accomplish as secretary. He was determined to use foreign policy in every way possible to promote national unity and help banish forever any thought of disunion.[29] Under his direction foreign policy served the needs of domestic political goals. It meant that on occasion he resorted to bombast, chauvinistic flag-waving, bluffs, threats, insults, and intimidation, but he believed they were worth the risk. Sometimes his actions backfired, but those mishaps mostly occurred toward the end of his tenure, when age and illness sharply diminished his judgment and diplomatic skills.

It is interesting that the three greatest men of this age—Calhoun, Clay, and Webster—each in his own way devoted their remaining years to the achievement of one objective: saving the Union and preventing civil war. Calhoun offered nullification and the current majority theories, Clay offered compromise, but Webster offered something more ephemeral: inspiration. Webster

---

27. Webster to Corcoran, March 7, 9, 1850, in *Microfilm Edition*, F22/29878, 29929; Henry Cohen, *Business and Politics in America from the Age of Jackson to the Civil War* (Westport, Conn., 1971), p. 91.

28. W&S, XIII, 74.

29. Of course he also wanted to advance the American economy by gaining trade advantages, and to this end he believed that the nation's business interests had to be fostered and kept clearly in mind whenever commercial arrangements with foreign countries were made.

constantly used his position as secretary of state to preach the message of promise, the promise that the Union is the "greatest benefit" and "main hope" for the
future prosperity and happiness of all the American people, both North and
South. What would the future be like without union? An unthinkable possibility.
A frightening thought.[30]

The first few weeks of his tenure centered on two matters: reacquainting
himself with the operation of the State Department, and helping win passage of
the separate compromise bills that Douglas had drawn up and presented to
Congress. As he had in the Harrison-Tyler administrations, Webster was the first
to arrive at the department. He often said that "what little I have accomplished
has been done early in the morning." Upon arrival in his office he first attended
to his mail, frequently writing more than twenty letters a day, this in addition to
his official correspondence. There were also official documents to sign. One
complete day normally had to be devoted to nothing but signing passports and
certificates and other such documents to "let the world know, at home & abroad,
that I am Sec. of State. This you know is a necessary, but a tedious business."

With the mail he attentively read only official letters and disposed of them
immediately. Political letters were merely glanced at and filed away for future
consideration, personal and private letters were answered the following morning, and anonymous mail was simply thrown in the wastepaper basket.

He usually kept two clerks taking his dictation at the same time. As he
paced the floor, he would dictate a diplomatic dispatch to his chief clerk in one
room and letters to his private secretary in another. Although Charles Lanman[31]
was his private secretary, "his especial favorite" was George J. Abbot, an accomplished classical scholar, who frequently hunted up appropriate Latin quotations
for his public documents. William C. Zantzinger was another valuable clerk.
Webster worked them hard, but they respected him for it. "His generous and
considerate treatment of the clerks," noted one observer, "won their affection."

After concluding the correspondence and document signing, he received
callers—diplomats, friends, acquaintances, visitors to the city, and patronage
seekers. He regularly met with the President, attended cabinet meetings, and
kept contact with friends in Congress each day to learn what was happening.[32]

During these first few weeks Webster involved himself rather significantly
in helping Douglas win passage of the compromise bills. Although the Illinois
senator performed wonders in rounding up support for the separate measures,
there was real danger that the New Mexico boundary question might fail. Gover-

30. *W&S*, X, 169.

31. Lanman was in his middle thirties, well educated, a skillful artist who sketched Webster's house
in Franklin, "of a literary taste, & fond of employing both his pen, & his pencil." He married the
daughter of a rich Georgetown merchant and was financially independent. Webster found him "of
unbounded devotion, and Enthusiasm," and in September 1851 he invited Lanman to become his
private secretary. DW to Everett, September 27, 1851, in *PC*, VII, 274.

32. Lanman, *Private Life of Webster*, pp. 83–86; Poore, *Perley's Reminiscences*, pp. 382–383; DW to
?, September 15, 1850, in *PC*, VII, 150; DW to Fletcher Webster, [July 24, 1850], in *W&S*, XVIII,
554.

nor Bell of Texas had called a special session of the Texas legislature to give him the mandate to send an army to Santa Fe. That action could kill the bill, and if the New Mexico bill failed, it could pull down all the others.

Webster immediately came to the rescue. Fillmore had asked him to draft a response to Governor Bell's letter to Taylor. Webster agreed, but as he was writing, "a thought struck me like a shot, that here was a case for a [special] message" to Congress. The President went along and directed him to prepare both the message and an answer to the letter.

It took Webster a day, Sunday, August 4, and two nights to write both. Then he had Curtis and Ashmun examine the message, after which Ashmun showed it to a half dozen senators and twice as many representatives and asked for their approval. Ashmun "travelled over the whole City in the burning heat on Sunday to *consult* with these Gentlemen. This gratified them." On Monday the message was read to the President. "It will be well, I think," said Webster, "to put in as many soft words as we can to soothe the irritation of Texas." Further corrections and changes were made until both Fillmore and members of the cabinet were satisfied. "Monday night I kept the Clerks up, to make out the necessary number of copies, &c," Webster reported. On Tuesday morning, August 6, he labored between 5:00 and 7:00, going over "every paper again" until he thought "that all was right." He took the finished product back to Fillmore at 9:00 A.M., "& before eleven [the President] signed them & sent them off." The entire operation went so well that an exhausted Webster had nothing but praise for the President. "He is a man of business, & a man of intelligence, & wide awake," he declared.[33]

The President's message to Congress bluntly warned Texas that if it resorted to arms, it would be met with force by the central government. Taking a page from Andrew Jackson's Proclamation to the citizens of South Carolina in 1832, Webster wrote that Fillmore had no choice but to act in accordance with his obligation under the Constitution. Then, in soothing tones, the President said that he "hoped I shall not be regarded as stepping outside from the line of my duty . . . if I express my deep and earnest conviction of the importance of an immediate decision or arrangement or settlement of the question" by the Congress.[34] And not only this question but all the questions "which have now for a long time agitated the country" and monopolized Congress's time to the exclusion of everything else. In case anyone still wondered where Fillmore stood, this message made it abundantly clear that he not only supported the compromise but would sign legislation to bring it about.

The message, as Webster expected, had its intended impact. As though shaken awake from a six-month slumber by the President's call to action, the Senate passed the boundary bill on August 9. The bill conceded 33,333 more square miles of territory to Texas along with ten million dollars. Over the next week and a half the Senate then agreed to admit California, abolish the slave trade in the District of Columbia, organize the New Mexico territory, and en-

33. DW to Fillmore, July 30, DW to Haven, August 10, 1850, in *PC*, VII, 132, 135–136.
34. Richardson, *Messages and Papers*, IV, 2603–2609.

dorse the fugitive slave bill. With that action, all the essential features of Clay's original compromise plan had been passed. Once the Senate approved the bills the House quickly followed suit. By September 6 the first bill had passed, and Fillmore immediately signed it. Others followed, and by September 20 Clay's Compromise of 1850 had become law.[35]

Washington virtually collapsed with relief and happiness. Public buildings were illuminated, and impromptu parades, dinners, bonfires, barbecues, and other demonstrations erupted throughout the city, starting with the passage of the California and Utah bills in the House. "Hail Liberty and Union, and Domestic Peace!" trumpeted the *National Intelligencer.* "Hail the return of Government from its long aberration back to its just sphere of action and usefulness." One group of festive revelers hurried to the two-story brick house where Webster lived on Louisiana Avenue and sent up round after round of cheers and huzzas. The secretary rose from a dinner party and greeted the mob at his front door. "A work has been accomplished," he shouted over the din around him, "which dissipates doubts and alarms, puts an end to angry controversies, fortifies the Constitution of the country, and strengthens the bonds of the Union." The crowd loved it, even though most of them heard nothing but the continuing noise of rejoicing from the throats of those present. Later a large contingent of congressmen came to serenade him. Webster emerged from his home in a dressing gown with a friend on either side of him holding a candle. "Now is the summer," he began, "—no! Now is the winter of our discontent made glorious summer by this son of York."

"It is a day of rejoicing here," Webster happily wrote a few days later, "such as I never witnessed. The face of everything seems changed. You would suppose nobody had ever thought of disunion." But he had to admit it was a close call. "I feel relieved." Since March 7 there had not been an hour in which he had not felt "a 'crushing' weight of anxiety & responsibility." He had slept badly and "sat down to no breakfast, or dinner" with an easy mind. But now he had found relief. "It is over. My part is acted, & I am satisfied."[36]

Senator Henry S. Foote of Mississippi, who first proposed the idea of an omnibus bill, declared that next to Clay the secretary of state "signalized himself in this ever-memorable conflict, and from the day when he had delivered his celebrated 7th of March speech he had been receiving every hour, in one form or another, the tokens of public gratitude. This was perhaps the most happy moment of his life." Moreover, he "risked his own popularity in that contest, perhaps more seriously than any other man."[37]

Webster's "great soul was full of gladness and gratitude," and in a burst of

---

35. Holman Hamilton, "Domestic Senate Leadership and the Compromise of 1850," *Mississippi Valley Historical Review,* XLI (December 1954), pp. 407–412. See also Holman Hamilton, *Prologue to Conflict: The Crisis and Compromise of 1850* (Lexington, Ky.; 1964), pp. 133–144.

36. *National Intelligencer,* August 10, September 9, 1850; Poore, *Perley's Reminiscences,* pp. 384–385; DW to Harvey, September 10, 1850, in *PC,* VII, 143; Dalzell, *Webster and American Nationalism,* pp. 208–210.

37. Henry S. Foote, *Casket of Reminiscences* (New York, 1968), p. 8.

exuberance and good cheer he decided to attend a concert being given one evening by the Swedish Nightingale, Jenny Lind. He entered the opera house "in his grandest manner" and slowly passed down the center aisle. As it happened, Mlle. Lind was about to sing the national anthem to begin the program. As soon as the audience spotted Webster, it "spontaneously broke forth with tempestuous applause," as though "recognizing the remarkable coincidence that the renowned defender of the Constitution should have happened" to enter "at the very moment that the sacred emblem of the nation's liberty and union was on the eve of being rapturously apostrophized in song." Then, after the audience had settled itself and the first number on the program began, Webster, probably drunk and oblivious of everything and everyone around him, audibly hummed in unison with the Swedish Nightingale. All the "enthusiasm of his soul" and "all his patriotic pride," remembered Foote, "had evidently been kindled into flame." His "whole moral nature appeared to have been 'touched and inspired' by the seraphic sounds" emanating from the diva's throat. When the song ended, Webster bounded to his feet, as though obliged on behalf of the nation to offer the lady a "formal tribute of respect." He strode to a "central position" between the audience and the platform and "made her one of the most honoring and majestic bows I ever beheld." What Lind thought of this intrusion into her recital anyone can guess, but she responded to the bow with a graceful and gracious curtsy. The audience loved it and "gave vent to their delight in most vociferous applause." Not satisfied, Webster bowed again with similar results. When he bowed a third time, the lady fled from the stage.[38]

"Men are a great deal happier than they were six months ago," claimed Webster, "and crimination and recrimination, are no longer the order of the day." The country, he said, "has had a providential escape from very considerable dangers."[39]

One development that might take place in the near future as a result of the passage of the compromise, he thought, was the possible "remodelling of Parties." Divisions like the Cotton and Conscience Whigs and between northern and southern Democrats might make a new alignment of parties unavoidable. "There must be a Union Party, & an opposing Party under some name," Webster contended. Now that the compromise had become law, our Whig friends must "resist all further attempts at agitation & disturbance." Those who talk "about Wilmot Provisos" and violate or seek repeal of the Fugitive Slave Law "will have no right to consider themselves either as Whigs, or as friends to this Administration." With respect to questions of constitutional law and public policy "we must all be of one faith" and not espouse doctrines and utter sentiments hostile to the just and constitutional rights of the South. A healthier, more productive political climate, he insisted, could be brought about with such a realignment. Surely it was in the best interests of the country. So he tried to

38. Ibid., pp. 9–11; Poore, *Perley's Reminiscences*, p. 388; Hone, *Diary*, II, 909–910.

39. DW to ?, September 15, 1850, in *PC*, VII, 151; DW to Haven, September 12, 1850, in *W&S*, XVIII, 386.

implement this possible "remodelling" by purging from federal office all those who opposed the compromise—with mixed results.[40] It took several years before a realignment came about. But the gradual disappearance of the Whig party and the rise of the Republican party unfortunately did not erase sectional differences, as Webster had hoped and expected.

In assisting the final passage of the Compromise of 1850, the new secretary wielded the patronage ax with gusto. Appointments of diplomatic personnel and newspapers designated to publish the laws, resolutions, and related documents fell under his authority as secretary of state. His increasingly close relationship with the President also meant that executive patronage could be employed to assist the cause. And he showed less reluctance than Fillmore in exercising the power. The recommendations by friends of the compromise in the Congress received preferential treatment. Wherever possible their wishes were followed. As for the printing patronage, Webster withdrew this privilege from any hostile or suspected editor. He reappointed only forty-two editors out of a possible sixty-eight—and he made twenty-five additional changes in the next congressional session. His removals constituted a 60 percent turnover during his short tenure as secretary. The "startling number" of replacements caused one historian to suggest rightly that in addition to building support for the compromise, he was building support for himself for a presidential bid in 1852. "I will immediately see to the matter [of the printing patronage]," he informed Solomon George Haven, a former collector of the New York customs, "and the [Albany] Evening Journal [Thurlow Weed's paper] shall not be forgotten, while it holds a decided, bold constitutional course. You may hint this matter any way you please." Webster subsequently transferred the patronage from Weed's paper to the *New York State Register* in Albany.[41]

Steady pressure to ensure the implementation of each part of the compromise became necessary because large segments of the North, particularly in New England, took violent exception to the Fugitive Slave Law. Many Whigs and Free Soilers blamed Webster for its passage[42] and swore they would prevent its enforcement. The secretary therefore regularly intruded his presence to guarantee enforcement of the law in Massachusetts.

On one occasion Theodore Parker led a vigilance committee and attempted the rescue of two captured fugitive slaves, William and Ellen Craft, whose owner sent agents to Boston in November 1850 to arrange their return. The agents were not only harassed upon their arrival but thrown into jail. Webster intervened to speed the judicial prosecution of the Crafts and have them restored to their master—"for two days I have been endeavoring to do something to put this

40. DW to Harvey, October 2, DW to Thomas Corwin, November 13, 1850, in *PC*, VII, 155, 180; Holt, *Political Crisis of the 1850s*, p. 91.

41. DW to Fillmore, December 20, 1851, DW to Haven, April 29, 1852, in *PC*, VII, 9–10; Culver H. Smith, *The Press, Politics, and Patronage: The American Government's Use of Newspapers* (Athens, Ga., 1977), pp. 184–185; Holt, *Political Crisis of the 1850s*, pp. 94–95.

42. Emerson, *Journals*, XI, 345–346.

business of the attempt to arrest Crafts into a better shape," he notified the President—but the couple was rescued and spirited off to England before the court could act.[43]

No sooner did the furor over the Crafts' escape recede when a fugitive slave, Frederick Jenkins, known as Shadrach, was arrested in Boston on February 15, 1851, but hustled away to Canada before he could be returned to his owner. "Was it by conivence [sic] or by absolute force?" Webster telegramed Peter Harvey. "[D]id the Marshal do his duty. Answer." This second flagrant violation of the law provoked a presidential proclamation, written by Webster, calling for public obedience to the law and the apprehension and prosecution of those involved in "this outrage." He also wrote a public letter in connection with a celebration of George Washington's birthday in which he expressed his anger at the lawless behavior of some of his Massachusetts compatriots. Eight men were subsequently indicted for their part in Shadrach's escape, but a hung jury resulted in their release.[44]

Hard on the heels of that incident, at a time when Webster was visiting in Boston, another fugitive, Thomas Sims, was captured on April 3, 1851. This time the secretary stepped in personally to supervise arrangements for the slave's return to his master. Mobs formed and rallies were held that denounced both the law and its chief defender, Black Dan. The vigilance committee again planned another rescue, but before it could act, Sims, surrounded by hundreds of policemen and armed personnel, was spirited aboard the ship, *Acorn,* at four in the morning of April 12 and, at a cost of twenty thousand dollars, shipped back to his owner in Savannah, Georgia, where he was publicly flogged.[45]

Defiance of the law infuriated the secretary, no matter the reason. The law must be obeyed, he lectured, whether an individual approves or disapproves. He told the President that the "abolitionists & free soilers . . . are insane, but it is an angry & vindictive insanity." No matter, Fillmore responded. Sims has been returned. "I congratulate you and the country upon the triumph of law in Boston. She has done nobly. She has wiped out the stain of the former rescue." Judges petitioned the President for authority to send in federal troops if necessary to enforce the law, and Fillmore, after consulting his cabinet, decided to gave the authority to marshals and their deputies when a federal judge deemed it necessary.[46]

---

43. DW to Fillmore, November 5, 15, 1850, in *PC*, VII, 177–178, 180–181. Parker married the couple and explained and defended his actions to Webster, December 12, 1850, ibid., VII, 189–190.

44. DW to Harvey, February 17, DW to Henry Dearborn, February 23, 1851, a proclamation, February 18, 1851, ibid., VII, 204, 206–208; *Microfilm Edition,* February 20, 1851, F23/32591.

45. DW to George Lunt, April 4, 1851, DW to Fillmore, April 6, 9, 11, 13, 1851, in *PC*, VII, 180–181, 226–227, 229–233; Leonard Levy, "Sims' Case: The Fugitive Slave Law in Boston," *Journal of Negro History,* XXXV (January 1951), pp. 39–74. On April 3 Fletcher Webster tried to prevent what he thought was an attempted rescue of Sims and got into a "tussle" with the town watchman. He was briefly jailed for assaulting the watchman, but the charge was quickly dropped. Fletcher Webster to DW, April 4, 1851, in *PC*, VII, 228; Boston *Daily Advertiser,* April 5, 1851.

46. DW to Fillmore, October 29, 1850, DW to Fillmore, April 13, Fillmore to DW, April 16, 1851, in *PC*, VII, 173–174, 232–233, 237.

Unquestionably the vigor of the enforcement of the compromise measures, especially the Fugitive Slave Act, helped ease sectional tension in the South and stave off the efforts of radicals to drive that section out of the Union. The Nashville Convention had adjourned without taking any action, and efforts in other states like Georgia, Mississippi, and South Carolina to provoke a confrontation were successfully blocked. As for the North, it took time but the intense furor over the Fugitive Slave Act slowly subsided.

Still, Webster suffered years of abuse by Free Soilers and abolitionists before the merit of his seventh of March speech and the necessity of his actions as secretary of state were properly recognized and appreciated. The bitter resentment some Bostonians, but not a majority, felt toward him flared into the open when the Board of Aldermen denied the use of Faneuil Hall for a public reception to honor him on the ground that it had recently refused a similar request by abolitionists. "I feel that either I am disgraced or Boston is," Webster snapped when he learned of it. Friends gasped when they heard what had happened. "The 'cradle of the Revolution' refused to its favorite child! . . . Webster ostracized in Boston!" Unthinkable![47]

At the time the Board of Aldermen acted Webster happened to be residing in the Revere House in Bowdoin Square in Boston. The apologetic Common Council, reflecting the opinion of a majority of the city's citizens who approved his position on the Fugitive Slave Law, tried to undo the mischief of the aldermen by passing resolutions that expressed their deep regret. They cited the action taken by the aldermen as "unprecedented and injudicious,—calculated to increase rather than diminish the public excitement." They further asked Webster to meet with them in Faneuil Hall.

Dressed as usual in his "revolutionary" outfit, the secretary met a committee sent by the Common Council to extend the invitation. The chairman of the committee started to approach Webster, but the secretary's "manner was very forbidding." The secretary just stared at him, the black eyes threatening and intimidating. The poor man realized "he was on dangerous ground." He stopped dead in his tracks and simply read the resolutions of the Common Council and handed them to the secretary. In a curt voice Webster responded, "I will answer the committee in writing; good morning, gentlemen," and walked away.

His note to the council was also curt, stating that it was "inconvenient" for him to meet with them in Faneuil Hall. "What I have done, within the last year, to maintain the Union," he fumed several days later to Francis Brinley, president of the Common Council, ". . . has not been done in a corner; and I shall not go into a corner to perform what may remain to be done. Nor shall I enter Faneuil Hall, till its gates shall be thrown open, wide open, not 'with impetuous recoil—grating harsh thunder,' but with 'harmonious sound, on gold hinges moving,' to let in, freely and to overflowing, you and your fellow-citizens, and all men, of all parties, who are true to the Union as well as to Liberty."

47. Resolutions of Boston Common Council, April 17, 1851, in Van Tyne, ed., *Letters of Webster,* pp. 471–472; DW to Everett, April 23, 1851, in *Microfilm Edition,* F24/33332; Hone, *Diary,* II, 916.

During this visit a large crowd congregated before his hotel to cheer his presence and demonstrate their approval of his stand on the much despised law. Webster came out and gave a short speech of appreciation, ending with a ringing plea: *"Union,* UNION, UNION now and forever!"[48]

For the remaining years of his life Webster "preached" this message. To northerners he warned against violating the law; to southerners he appealed to their sense of kinship and tried to stir within them "emotional chords of loyalty."[49]

That overwhelming concern for the Union also permeated his actions in directing foreign affairs. He deliberately manipulated foreign policy for domestic political purposes—shamelessly. One such incident involved the Austrian chargé d'affaires, Chevalier Johann Georg Hülsemann.[50]

The Hungarian uprising for liberation from Austria, led by Louis Kossuth in 1848, had brought an immediate and an overwhelmingly enthusiastic response from the American people. The secretary of state, John M. Clayton, had instructed A. Dudley Mann to undertake a mission to Austria with the idea of rendering assistance by recognizing any regime established by Kossuth. But the revolution failed when Russia intervened and helped Austria to crush it. At a public celebration of the Sons of New Hampshire held in Boston on November 4, 1849, Webster declared that "we have all had our sympathies much enlisted in the Hungarian effort for liberty. We have all wept at its failure."[51]

"By skillful espionage," Austria procured a copy of Mann's instructions and naturally took exception to the mission, instructing its chargé in America to protest. Although Webster initially tried to discourage any further notice of the matter, Hülsemann insisted on following his instructions. On September 30, 1850, he submitted to the secretary a letter in which he described Mann's instructions as "offensive" and "hostile." He characterized the actions of the United States as an unwarranted and improper "interference in the internal affairs of [Austria's] government." Moreover he threatened "acts of retaliation" if the United States attempted to take part in the "political movements of Europe." Webster notified the President of the letter and added an ominous comment: "We shall have a quarrel with Austria."[52]

Then it occurred to Webster that he had an ideal instrument to turn an

48. Harvey, *Reminiscences,* pp. 190–192; DW to Francis Brinley, April 19, 1851, in Curtis, *Webster,* II, 500. In his letter to Brinley, Webster is here quoting from *Paradise Lost;* DW to Fillmore, April 15, Rufus Choate to DW, [April 15, 1851], in *PC,* VII, 235–236; Boston *Courier,* April 23, 1851, in *W&S,* XIII, 405–407.

49. "My object has been, & is, to preserve the Institutions of our Fathers; & I feel, deeply, that those institutions can only be preserved by conciliation, & the cultivation of friendly sentiments between the different parts of the country." DW to William Prescott, November 7, 1850, in Van Tyne, ed., *Letters of Webster,* p. 440. See also the letters and editorial comments in *PC,* VII, 182–191.

50. See Merle Curti, *Austria and the United States, 1848–1852: A Study in Diplomatic Relations* (Northampton, Mass., 1926).

51. Curtis, *Webster,* II, 558.

52. Rayback, *Fillmore,* p. 327; Hülsemann to DW, September 30, 1850, in *PD,* II, 43–46; DW to Fillmore, October 3, 1850, in *W&S,* XVIII, 394.

incident in foreign relations to domestic purpose. He could have dismissed Hülsemann's charges with a few deft jabs. Instead he decided to write a response—this is "a favorable opportunity," he declared—to reach out to the American people and stir their national pride as well as their resentment over the utter gall of the Austrian government to criticize the actions of American elected officials. He said he wanted "to show the world, the difference between the fundamental principles of our Government, and those of the arbitrary monarchies of Eastern Europe."

Webster spent weeks turning out draft after draft, while fighting off illness and his annual catarrh. He spent more time on this single letter than on any other state paper during his two terms as secretary of state. His clerk, William Hunter, Jr., and Edward Everett prepared preliminary drafts for him. He consulted with friends, family, and the President and reworked it at least a dozen times before he was satisfied.[53]

Dated December 31, 1850, the letter dismissed Hülsemann's complaint, commenting that it was "somewhat strange" that the Austrian government did not perceive that by its instructions to Hülsemann, "it was itself interfering with the domestic concerns of a foreign state; the very thing, which is the ground of its complaint against the United States." He boasted of the power of the Republic, which at "the present moment is spread over a region, one of the richest and most fertile on the Globe," with a population already more than twenty-five million. Compared with the United States, "the possessions of the House of Hapsburg, are but as a patch on the earth's surface." That jab delighted Americans when they read it.

Had the United States, he went on, recognized the independence of Hungary (as it did not), it would still not have violated international law. Hülsemann misstated the purpose of Mann's "errand," Webster continued, which was one of "enquiry." It was "wholly unobjectionably and strictly within the rule of the Law of Nations." Had Mann been arrested and treated as a spy, "the Spirit of the People of this Country, would have demanded immediate hostilities, to be waged by the utmost exertion of the Power of the Republic, military and naval." As for the threatened "acts of retaliation" mentioned in Hülsemann's letter, Webster said the United States was indifferent to what Austria might do. The American people "are quite willing to take their chances, and abide their destiny," he scoffed. But be aware that "nothing will deter, either the Government or the people of the United States, from exercising, at their own discretion, the rights belonging to them as an independent nation." Many of the great principles of the Constitution have already taken root in Austria, and we "cherish a sincere wish that they may produce the same happy effects throughout His Austrian Majesty's extensive dominions, that they have done in the United States."[54]

It was quite a polemic, and the American people cherished every word of

---

53. DW to Fillmore, October 3, November 13, Fillmore to DW, December 20, DW to Everett, October 20, 1850, in *PD*, II, editorial note 33, 46–49. Poore, *Perley's Reminiscences*, I, 403, claims that Hunter wrote the letter, but he is mistaken.

54. DW to Hülsemann, December 21, 1850, in *PD*, II, 49–61.

it. It was like a Fourth of July oration, and they felt inspired and proud, just as Webster intended. They delighted not only in Webster's cunning trick of turning the Austrian complaint on its head but in his "cleverness" in reiterating and demonstrating anew the superiority of this country and its institutions over those of Europe. Walter Forward said it was one of the "most *heartily American* state papers that ever emanated from the foreign department of the government." The celebrated inventor Samuel F. B. Morse congratulated the secretary for "your admirable rebuke to the insolent but impotent Austrian." Abbott Lawrence, minister to Great Britain, thought so well of it that he had copies printed in pamphlet form and distributed to "every Government in Europe."[55]

It may have been *"heartily American,"* but it was no state paper. Rather it was a political tract, a rallying cry for unity, a shout of praise for the greatness of American institutions, and a salute to a magnificent compromise that had unified the nation. It was his intention, Webster told George Ticknor, " to speak out and tell the people of Europe who and what we are, and awaken them to a just sense of the unparalleled growth of this country" and one that would " touch the national pride, and make a man feel *sheepish* and look *silly* who should speak of disunion." In this he succeeded brilliantly.[56]

Fortunately his letter did not rupture the relationship between the two countries, but Webster continued to make political and nationalistic capital out of the Hungarian uprising. When the abortive revolt ended in failure, Kossuth and his close associates fled to Turkey. Austria and Russia demanded their extradition, but the sultan refused and instead had the exiles interned. Webster now attempted to secure their release. And he used the first official mission from the Ottoman Empire to the United States to help bring it about.

Amin Bey, a grave-looking Turkish naval officer representing the empire, arrived in New York on September 12, 1850, and from all sides heard warm words of praise and gratitude for his country's kindness in protecting Kossuth and refusing to turn the Hungarian exiles over to the Austrians. Once Amin Bey reached the capital, Webster treated him as the nation's invited guest and won an appropriation of ten thousand dollars from Congress to defray the diplomat's expenses. He escorted the visitor to the Capitol, introduced him to members of Congress (so that they could look at "his red cap"), presented him to the President, and even entertained him at his home in Marshfield, although it was difficult since Webster could not exchange a single word in normal conversation with the foreign diplomat. Still, he attended to his guest's needs dutifully, making certain that "all swine's flesh [was kept] out of his sight." Instead he fed him beef, poultry, rice, and plenty of coffee. At every public occasion Webster used the opportunity to address the people about how this country had won the respect of foreign nations by remaining *"united* citizens of a *united* states." Amin

55. Forward to DW, February 12, Morse to DW, January 20, Lawrence to DW, January 27, 1851, ibid., II, 66, 64, 65.

56. DW to Ticknor, January 16, 1851, ibid., II, 64. Ticknor thought the Hülsemann letter "boastful and rough." Ibid.

Bey came here, he declared, as the guest of the United States, "not as the guest of a faction . . . not as the guest of a dissevered and broken country, but the guest of the *United* States of America."[57]

Congress meanwhile decided to take advantage of Turkey's gratitude for the cordial reception its representative had received and requested that the President seek the release of the Hungarian rebels and bring them to America. Upon executive direction, Webster instructed George P. Marsh, the U.S. minister to Turkey, to begin the negotiations with the Sublime Porte. Inform the Turkish government, read the instructions, that if it accedes to this request, the government and people of the United States will regard the action "as a friendly recognition of their intercession, & as a proof of National Good Will & regard."[58]

The negotiations succeeded, and on September 10 Kossuth and fifty associates with their families boarded the USS *Mississippi* and were taken to England, where Kossuth toured for three weeks before taking passage to the United States aboard the Cunard liner *Humboldt*. To the frenzied cheers of Americans waiting onshore to greet them, the exiles arrived in New York on December 5, 1851.

Pandemonium best describes the hysterical reception the rebels received as they paraded up Broadway from the Bowery to Central Park. The thought that this nation on its own had brought about the release of these "champions for liberty" excited the imagination and pride not only of New Yorkers but of the entire country. "The land of the free" had come into its own.[59]

Kossuth marveled at what he saw and heard. Standing five feet eight inches, handsome, bearded, intelligent, dignified, and "amiable and graceful in his manners," he frequently wore a military uniform with the steel scabbard of his sword trailing on the ground behind him as he walked. He recognized instantly that a splendid opportunity had suddenly opened up to him. Here in America, in this "cradle of liberty," could be found the encouragement and support he desperately needed for the liberation of Hungary. Americans, he thought, would provide money, men, and supplies for him to renew his war against the Austrian Empire.

And he had a ready-made climate awaiting him on his arrival. A "new" mood in the country had produced the Young America movement aimed at actively involving the United States in all revolutionary causes to overthrow despots and advance the rights of oppressed peoples everywhere.[60] But it horrified Webster. "It is evident that a new issue, or a new topic is rising in our political discussions," he noted. Various newspapers, such as the Washington

57. DW to Fillmore, September 19, 1850, in *W&S*, XVIII, 390; John Porter Brown to DW, September 16, DW to Fillmore, September 19, DW to Amin Bey, [March] 1851, in *PD*, II, 71–74, 36; DW to Fillmore, October 14, 1850, in *PC*, VII, 160.

58. DW to Marsh, February 21, 1851, in *PC*, II, 74–78.

59. Marsh to DW, September 18, 1851, in *PD*, II, 78–79. Donald S. Spencer, *Louis Kossuth and Young America: A Study of Sectionalism and Foreign Policy* (Columbia, Mo., 1977), pp. 4–9.

60. Spencer, *Kossuth*, pp. 11–47.

Union, had come out boldly in favor of reversing "our established policy" of global neutrality (unless our rights were transgressed) and replacing it with "the doctrine of intervention," in effect of launching a program of "propagation of our own opinions and forms of government" around the world.[61]

For those who desired an abandonment of isolationism, Kossuth became a symbol of intervention. Webster and Fillmore now found themselves in the awkward position of having helped arrange the liberation of revolutionists and by so doing endangering one of the most cherished ideals of American foreign policy.

So, as Kossuth began visiting the great cities of the country, pursuing his own revolutionary agenda, Webster realized he would have to exercise extreme caution in dealing with the Hungarians and the sympathies aroused among Americans for their plight. He had to keep clear "both of Scylla and Charybdis." Kossuth's popularity alone necessitated care and judicious concern for every word he said and action he took. Webster could ill afford to offend the electorate by some discourtesy or offense toward Kossuth, not if his presidential ambition still glowed as intensely as ever—and it did. Still, he had no intention of abandoning the traditional policy of isolationism. "I shall treat him," Webster explained to his friend Richard Blatchford, "with all personal and individual respect, but if he should speak to me of the policy of 'intervention,' I shall 'have ears more deaf than adders.' "[62]

Webster's strategy was cunningly laid out. He would praise the striving for liberty as it arose in other parts of the world, giving it vocal encouragement, but deny that this nation had any responsibility for materially assisting its realization. In a speech delivered in the Pennsylvania House of Representatives in Harrisburg, presented in appreciation for the formal vote of thanks tendered him by the legislature for his Hülsemann letter, the secretary articulated precisely what he meant:

> We, the descendants of those who achieved the Independence and established the Constitution of this country, are bound to speak out to the whole world of mankind and bear testimony to the cause of popular republican government. Let other governments do as they will: it is not our duty to traverse the earth and make proselytes. Our business is to make proselytes by our example, to convert man to republicanism by showing what republicanism can do in promoting the true ends of government. . . . We will place in the political firmament a sun, bright-glowing and cheering, the warming influence of which all shall feel and know.[63]

Kossuth arrived in Washington in late December, and Webster presented him to the President. Fillmore received the visitor with "great propriety" but backed away from pledging any support. "Sympathy, personal respect and kindness but no departure from our established policy."[64]

61. DW to Everett, November 12, 1850, in *PD,* II, 90.

62. DW to Haven, December 23, 1851, in *W&S,* XVIII, 497; DW to Blatchford, [December 30, 1851], in *PC,* VII, 96.

63. Speech given on April 1, 1851, in *W&S,* XIII, 401–404.

64. DW to Blatchford, December 31, 1851, in Webster, ed., *Private Correspondence,* II, p. 502.

Not content with following the President's lead, Webster proceeded to commit a major diplomatic blunder. At a formal congressional banquet held in Kossuth's honor at the National Hotel in Washington on January 7, 1852, the secretary pulled out all stops in launching what seemed to be a mindless campaign for the presidential nomination by playing on the Hungarian's national popularity. He began by saluting Kossuth for "his part in the great struggle for Hungarian national independence." Although "our principles and our sentiments" are "generally disliked" or unknown beyond the ocean, he exclaimed, yet they go forth "on all the winds of heaven" toward those sons of Hungarian liberation who have "most distinguished themselves in that struggle." No throne is safe from "the progress of opinion" by the just and intelligent. "Depend upon it, gentlemen, that between these two rival powers,—the autocratic power, maintained by arms and force, and the popular power, maintained by opinion,— the former is constantly decreasing, and, thank God, the latter is constantly increasing." Then he shamelessly, and at length, reminded everyone of his letter to Hülsemann and his letter to the U.S. minister in Turkey and said he would stand by the principles expressed in those letters "while the sun and moon endure, and while I can see the light of the sun and the moon." He also referred to the address on Greek independence that he had given nearly forty years before. This self-congratulatory section of his speech prefaced what can only be described as a gratuitous and insulting discourse on the relations between Hungary and Austria.

No nation, he declared, can be happy living in a "country belonging to somebody else." Hungarians "are distinct from the Austrians," and "they are an *enlightened* nation" with their own history and traditions. With respect to "free institutions, constitutional government, and an hereditary love of liberty," Hungary stands far above all its neighbors. Then Webster had the effrontery to state that the emperor of Austria would accept no petition for peace "unless it be founded on the utter extermination of the nationality of Hungary." Let me add, he continued, "what I am sure will not sound well upon the Upper Danube, and that is that, in my humble judgment . . . Austria would be a better and stronger government to-morrow if she confined the limits of her power to her hereditary and German domains. . . . Of course, all of you, like myself, would be glad to see her [Hungary] when she becomes independent, embrace that system of government which is most acceptable to ourselves. We shall rejoice to see our American model upon the Lower Danube and on the mountains of Hungary." Our "first prayer shall be that Hungary may become independent of all foreign power."

Finally Webster raised his glass and gave a toast: "*Hungarian Independence*—Hungarian control of her own destinies; and Hungary as a distinct nationality among all the nations of Europe."[65]

It was shocking. It was blatant. And it was stupid. Disregarding the fact that he represented the American government in its relations with foreign countries

65. *W&S*, XIII, 452–462.

and should have been more discreet in what he said, Webster deliberately courted popular approval with cheap, strident, nationalistic clichés to promote his presidential ambitions. In giving this speech, he told his advisers that as one objective he wanted to be sure that his political opponents "shall have no well-founded charge against us for coolness in the cause of liberty." To put a happier spin on his remarks, it has been suggested that he wanted to prevent revolution in this country by praising it abroad.[66] Perhaps.

Not unexpectedly, the Austrian government was outraged. Hülsemann completely bypassed Webster (a snub that the secretary resented) and wrote directly to Fillmore requesting an audience. The President waived protocol, and Hülsemann formally registered his country's protest. Moreover, he told Fillmore straight out that if Webster continued as secretary of state, he would suspend official diplomatic relations between the two nations and leave his post. The President icily tried to turn the complaint aside by assuring Hülsemann that Webster had not spoken for the administration. But the prickly chargé would have none of it. Nor would he accept the secretary's nonsensical excuse that he had spoken not as secretary of state but as a private citizen and therefore had a perfect right to air his personal opinions. Not wishing to see, much less to speak, to Webster again, Hülsemann took off on a trip to the South and Cuba.[67]

Prince Felix Schwarzenberg, the Austrian minister of foreign affairs, was so incensed by the speech that relations between the two countries teetered dangerously toward a serious break. Daniel Barnard, the U.S. minister to Prussia, subsequently notified the department that the Prussian foreign minister, Baron Anton Prokesch von Osten, told him that Schwarzenberg "*would not receive any person whatever representing the country or government of the United States.*"[68]

Webster had created a diplomatic mess, although his hope that the American people would revel in his bombastic effusion apparently succeeded. The New York *Herald* of January 15 thought that his remarks had heroically endorsed the Hungarian cause, while Horace Greeley's *Tribune* believed he had elevated the administration in the public's estimation.[69]

In this one speech Webster had bungled his primary job of maintaining cordial relations with foreign nations. And the rupture of Austrian-American relations seriously detracted from his reputation as a statesman. Fortunately the fracture lasted only a few months. Schwarzenberg died in April, and Webster's death six months after that cleared the path for a rapprochement. The new foreign minister, Count Karl Ferdinand Buol-Schauenstein, and the new secretary of state, Edward Everett, patched up their differences and resumed regular

66. DW to Blatchford, [January 11, 1852], in *PD*, II, 106; Current, *Webster and the Rise of National Conservatism*, p. 176.

67. Hülsemann to Fillmore, January 8, 1852, quoted in Spencer, *Kossuth*, p. 91; DW to Charles McCurdy, January 15, 1852, in *PD*, II, 109–112.

68. Daniel Benard to DW, February 10, 1852, in *PD*, II, 113–117.

69. Spencer, *Kossuth*, p. 91.

diplomatic relations. Hülsemann returned to his post, but he had the last word. "The hostile proceedings of the Secretary of State" and the "revolutionary address in which he openly held out encouragement to Hungary, spurring her on to a new rebellion," he declared, were the direct cause of the breach between the two countries.[70]

While Webster fumbled along as best he could in running the State Department during the remaining months of his life, necessitating greater presidential involvement in foreign affairs, Kossuth took off on a grand tour of the United States. But the longer he stayed, and the more he appealed for intervention in the affairs of Europe, the more the American people wearied of his entreaties and cooled in their enthusiasm for him and his cause. They continued to give him verbal support, but nothing more. The anti-interventionists reminded the electorate of Washington's Farewell Address and his warning against entangling alliances. The Young America crusade slowly wound down. And any number of people, particularly the leading public men, were disgusted by Kossuth's "assumption and arrogance." General Winfield Scott regarded him "as a gigantic humbug."

When Kossuth ended his tour and returned to Washington, he was virtually ignored. Senator Seward said that "Hungary and Kossuth have passed from the memory of all men here." On July 14, 1852, using the aliases "Mr. and Mrs. Alexander Smith," the Hungarian and his wife boarded the liner *Africa* and quietly left the United States.[71]

By and large Webster had handled the Amin visit and the Hülsemann letter with consummate skill, but in the Kossuth dinner speech he seriously jeopardized national interest.[72]

70. Hülsemann to DW, April 29, 1852, in *PD*, II, 117–119.

71. Spencer, *Kossuth*, pp. 145–151,168; Poore, *Perley's Reminiscences*, p. 405.

72. *PC*, II, 43.

42

Exploring New Channels for Commerce

DISASTER also attended Webster's efforts to control and direct the political situation in Massachusetts. With the 1850 fall elections approaching the secretary decided to make the compromise, including the Fugitive Slave Act, a test of legitimate Whiggery. "For my part," he wrote the President, "I much prefer to see a respectable Democrat elected to Congress, than a professed Whig, tainted with any degree of Free Soil doctrines, or abolitionism." Men who act on principles, however wrong they may be, show a "consistency of conduct; and they are therefore, less dangerous than those who are looking for nothing but increased power, and influence, and who act simply, on what seems expedient, for their purposes, at the moment." That meant, to Webster's way of thinking, that Free Soil separatists could not return to the Whig fold, creating in effect three parties in Massachusetts.[1]

The fall election involved the naming of a new governor, a U.S. senator to replace Winthrop, whose term would expire, members of the House of Representatives, and a number of lesser state officers. And the results were a disaster for Webster. The Free Soilers and Democrats together won a majority—even Horace Mann was reelected to Congress, much to Webster's distress—and they decided to share the spoils controlled by the legislature, with the governorship going to a Democrat, George S. Boutwell, and the six-year U.S. Senate seat commencing March 4, formerly held by Webster, going to the Free Soilers. To add insult to injury, the Democratic–Free Soil coalition agreed on Charles Sumner for senator.

Cries of "corrupt bargain" rang throughout Massachusetts as the coalition proceeded to elect Boutwell on January 11. The Webster Whigs put Winthrop

1. DW to Fillmore, September 19, 1850, in Van Tyne, ed., *Letters of Webster,* p. 432; Donald, *Sumner,* p. 185. "The politics of Massachusetts are in a state of utter confusion," Webster said. "Many Whigs . . . act a most mean part, in their courtship of abolitionism." DW to Fillmore, October 24, 1850, in *PC,* VII, 165. Philip Hone believed that the same sentiment was true in New York. "Parties are so broken up, mixed up, and scattered, that nobody knows what the result may be," he wrote the day before the election. Hone, *Diary,* II, 907.

forward for the Senate seat, but Webster himself dismissed Winthrop as a candidate for failing to endorse the Fugitive Slave Act and for his apparent drift toward abolitionism. He preferred Samuel Eliot. By ruthlessly purging from federal office all dissenters, Webster hoped to form a new "Union party" of Whigs and Democrats. "I repeat my earnest opinion," he pleaded, "that the true course for the Whigs in the Massachusetts legislature is to join the Conservative Democrats, if by so doing they can elect a decided Union man of that party." But Conservative Democrats would not support Eliot, and his candidacy evaporated. "Webster's idea, if it be his, of getting Eliot elected," commented John Clifford, "is upon a par with the infatuation which has *been the 'source of all our woes,'* that he can be elected himself to the Presidency. Indeed, in my judgment the latter would be more easy of accomplishment than the former."[2]

The reshuffling of party allegiances in both Democratic and Whig ranks caused such turmoil that the balloting between Sumner and Winthrop dragged on from January to late April. Not until the twenty-sixth ballot cast on April 24, and by a majority of a single vote, did the legislature finally chose Charles Sumner.[3]

It devastated Webster, despite his feelings toward Winthrop. It was an emphatic and personal blow to his pride and influence in Massachusetts. It followed by ten days the action of the Board of Aldermen to close Faneuil Hall to him. Outraged, he told Peter Harvey that henceforth "I am quite resolved not to commit any interest of mine to the management of the Whig State Committee of Massachusetts. The leading object of that Committee will be . . . to sacrifice high national considerations, and to court, as they have courted, free soilers, and semi-free soilers, abolitionists, and semi-abolitionists." In the South "Union Whigs, Tariff Whigs, Internal Improvement Whigs" refuse to cooperate with Massachusetts Whigs, claiming rightly that they could expect more from Massachusetts Democrats. It was clear to him and to others, Webster declared, "that the present organization of the Whig Party can not be continued throughout the United States."[4]

He despaired for the future. The country had abandoned its moral values, its religious underpinnings. "Religious instruction has hitherto been very well supported in the Country, under the voluntary system; but the laxity of morals, & the perverseness of sentiment, prevalent in these times casts a deep cloud over the future." What the country needed was the teaching and preaching of "the law & the gospel."[5]

His gloom dissipated somewhat when a group of New York businessmen collected twenty-five hundred dollars and purchased a "state carriage" for his

2. DW to Thomas Curtis, January 24, 1851, in *PC*, VII, 196; Clifford to Winthrop, January 3, 1851, Winthrop Papers, MHS.

3. Donald, *Sumner*, pp. 191–202; Dalzell, *Webster and American Nationalism*, pp. 228–229.

4. DW to Harvey, May 4, 1851, in *W&S*, XVI, 611.

5. DW to Thomas Curtis, January 20, 1851, in *PC*, VII, 196.

use. Custom-made in the English style in dark green wood, this "close quarter coach" boasted mountings in pure silver, lamps and the hub in heavy silver plate, "cherry colored *broce telte*" trimmed with silk lace for the interior, and best of all, Webster's crest, a horse's head, attached to the door with his motto *Vera pro gratis.* Also presented were "a span of horses, harness &c." "The carriage is the most beautiful thing of the kind we have ever seen," commented the New York *Express,* which reported the gift. It was truly regal, and Webster gushed his appreciation after it had been presented to him in Washington by Charles B. Wood, whose firm, Wood, Tomlinson, and Company, manufactured the carriage. It is "as elegant as any ever seen in the country," he enthused. Of "exquisite workmanship," rich but not gaudy, commodious, with "pleasant and agreeable" motion, it really "is too splendid and superb for a plain farmer of Marshfield," he protested, but "I accept it with all thankfulness, and shall always regard it as the measure . . . of your bounty and munificence."[6]

Month after month he was showered with hundreds of gifts from people all over the country in appreciation for his efforts to seek peace, and he accepted them as expressions of the popular will to preserve the Union. "Yes, Gentlemen! the Constitution and the Union! I place them together: If they stand, they stand together; if they fall, they fall together." He wrote this to the businessmen who had provided the state carriage, but they were sentiments he conveyed to all at every opportunity.

Portraits, drawings, prints, lithographs, and busts of Webster appeared in many public places. His first portrait had been painted when he was twenty-two. Later Gilbert Stuart had executed several likenesses, and Hiram Powers did a bust in the classic style. The secretary was also photographed in the relatively new daguerreotype process by several important artists, including Mathew Brady. His massive head, majestic brow, the black eyes, and "crag-like face" captivated artists of every style and technique of portraiture. Although he hated sitting for his portrait—he "looked upon us as so many horseflies," complained George P. A. Healy—he probably sat more than any other man of his age, with the possible exception of John Quincy Adams and Andrew Jackson.

When Healy first returned to the United States from Paris to execute a commission of King Louis Philippe of France to paint a picture of the Webster-Hayne debate, he was invited by the Hone Club, organized by Philip Hone in 1838, and ten other wealthy men who "cherished [Webster] as a divinity," to render a portrait of their idol. On April 25, 1846, Healy presented the results of his work to the president of the club, Hone. It depicted a seated Webster looking sober, benign, and statesmanlike, a globe in the foreground to acknowledge his international involvements as secretary of state, a quill pen lying on a table to denote his literary skills, a statue of a whippet to show his love of animals, and a small bust and a sheaf of paper in the background. It cost the club five hundred

6. DW to William M. Richards et al., March 21, 1851, in *PC,* VII, 217–218; an illustration of "Mr. Webster's State Carriage," along with the report of the New York *Express,* can be found in *PC,* VII in the illustration section following page 198.

dollars with the frame. Hone judged it "a great picture,—the best by far that has been done." At their next meeting the members viewed the portrait with great pleasure and satisfaction, and several of the members brought bottles of their best wine to celebrate. Together they drank to the health of their divinity "with three times three."[7]

But Healy's most famous picture was his fanciful rendering of "Webster's Reply to Hayne." It took him until the spring of 1851, a total of four years, to complete the canvas. An enormous composition, measuring sixteen by thirty feet, it is crowded with more than a hundred notable Americans, many of whom were painted from life.[8] Healy thought that for the "centre ornament at the top of the frame" he would place the "Arms of the U.S.A. with the words The defence of the Constitution, & for the centre of the bottom, a space for carved letters into the frame, large enough for the three or four concluding sentences of the great speech itself." Unfortunately by the time Healy completed his monumental canvas Louis Philippe had been deposed, and he needed to find a new buyer. He wanted ten thousand dollars for the work, a rather steep price, and figured that Massachusetts was the most likely place to look. "The proposition is," editorialized the Boston *Evening Transcript*, "that if one half the purchase money can be raised by private subscription, of which there is no longer any doubt, the remaining half shall be subscribed by the city, with a view to securing a work of art, that will be so interesting, for centuries to come to all Americans."

Eventually, in December 1852, the city of Boston purchased the work, and it now hangs in Faneuil Hall.[9] It was first shown in the Athenaeum on Monday, September 8, 1851, and tickets were required for admission. Viewers gasped when they looked at it for the first time. "There he stands!" exclaimed one admirer. "It is Daniel Webster as he appears in his moments of forensic power," reported the Boston *Transcript*, "sternly collected,—confident, determined; conscious of the effect of what he has said and clearly certain of what he is about to say." In October and November the painting went on tour and was displayed first at the National Academy of Design in New York City. On Saturday, February 21, 1852, it was shown in Washington in the Common Council Room at City

---

7. Hone, *Diary*, II, 749, 760–761, 765–766.

8. For a complete list of the individuals represented, including the ladies and gentlemen in the gallery, see the Boston *Transcript*, September 10, 1851. The mesdames Webster, Polk, Otis, Paige, McLean, and Benton are shown, along with such notables as John Quincy Adams, Alexis de Tocqueville, General Winfield Scott, Philip Hone, Harrison Gray Otis, and Henry Wadsworth Longfellow. In the picture Webster is seen standing with the weight of his body on his right foot, his left hand resting on the desk and his right arm hanging by his side. Calhoun is presiding, John M. Clayton sits to Webster's right, his right arm leaning on the desk. Hayne can be seen behind Senator Jacob Burnet of Ohio "eyeing the God-like in a calm manner. Down his back stream a few silvery curling locks." *Bulletin of the American Art-Nation* (October 1851), p. 113.

9. Boston *Evening Transcript*, December 18, 1852. In making the purchase the Boston mayor and aldermen required some changes in the painting. They did not stipulate publicly what those changes were, but it was assumed that they wanted "the portraits of their board introduced." New York *Evening Post*, January 5, 1853.

Hall. It cost 25 cents to view the masterwork.[10] Webster attended the initial showing and, like everyone else, judged it a great work of art. It took everyone by surprise, wrote one critic, "the expectation falling far short of the reality."[11]

But as magnificent as Healy's picture is, the portrait that never fails to have a powerful impact on first viewing is Francis Alexander's work, completed in December 1835 for Dartmouth College. It is Black Dan gazing "as if from a wind-swept height." It captures the impression that Webster so often made on his contemporaries, one dark, brooding, and a little frightening. It resembled "a thunder storm in July," marveled Jeremiah Mason, "sudden, portentous, sweeping all before it."[12]

Black Dan. Unfortunately the dark side of Daniel Webster seemed to predominate during the final years of his life. He frequently drank to excess, a complaint that went back at least a decade but that escalated after the Free Soilers and abolitionists had savaged him unmercifully. Bitterness and frustration surfaced in his words and actions as one disappointment followed another, and they were sometimes reflected in the photographs taken of him as secretary of state.

Illness added to his discomfort. In August 1851 Webster had gone to Franklin to escape his annual catarrh, which usually lasted until October 1. While in New Hampshire he suffered a severe attack of the gout, principally in the large toes. Finally, on September 9, he went to Boston and placed himself under the care of Dr. John Jeffries, who was to attend him until his death. The doctor found his complexion sallow, his eyes red, his pulse quick, and his "countenance indicative of great uneasiness." Webster had lost weight, suffered constant thirst, and "although without appetite, he was consuming food without restraint" and imbibing "stimulating drinks freely." He was "taking iodide of iron with hydriodate of potash and minute doses of oxide of arsenic as a preventive of catarrh." With some difficulty, the doctor prevailed on him to give up all these medicines and restrict himself to the simplest food.[13]

Still, there were a few notable achievements among the disappointments during his final years. One diplomatic project he helped initiate that had enormous significance for the United States in the future and culminated successfully during the following administration was the opening of Japan.

In an effort to build upon the Tyler Doctrine and his instructions that led to the Treaty of Wanghia with China, Webster capped these achievements by further strengthening the nation's role and position in the Pacific area. This had become particularly important because of the long stretch of coastline with four

10. *National Intelligencer,* February 23, 1852.

11. Charles Henry Hart, "Life Portraits of Daniel Webster," *McClure's Magazine,* IX (1897), pp. 619–630; Peterson, *Great Triumvirate,* pp. 390–391; Hone, *Diary,* II, 749, 760, 765; Healy to DW, April 29, 1851, in *PC,* VII, 240–241; James Barber and Frederick Voss, *The Godlike Black Dan* (Washington, 1982), pp. 40, 42.

12. Barber and Voss, *Black Dan,* p. 36; Fuess, *Webster,* I, 91.

13. John Jeffries, "An Account of the Last Illness of the Honourable Daniel Webster," *American Journal of the Medical Sciences,* New Series, XXV (January 1853), pp. 110–111.

deepwater ports (Seattle, Portland, San Francisco, and San Diego) that the nation now possessed that fronted the Pacific. His understanding of the national power that had been acquired over the past decade undergirded his diplomacy and resulted in the opening of Japan to American commerce.

The decision to take the preliminary steps toward that goal came in the spring of 1851. Japan had resisted all earlier efforts to break through its isolation. Only the Dutch enjoyed a very limited trade operating out of an island in the Nagasaki harbor. Efforts by Presidents Jackson and Polk to win concessions had failed. Aaron H. Palmer, a merchant and director of the American and Foreign Agency of New York, first approached Presidents Taylor and Fillmore about winning commercial concessions from the Japanese, and he held numerous conferences with Webster in early 1851. But it was Captain James Glynn who put forward a plan that really propelled the administration's efforts to bring about a diplomatic breakthrough.[14] What particularly attracted Webster to the basic idea was the opportunity it provided to expand American commercial and trading interests beyond what he had already accomplished in Hawaii and China under President Tyler. Or, as Webster himself put it, to forge "the last link in the chain of oceanic steam-navigation," one that would extend

from China and the East Indies to Egypt, thence through the Mediterranean and the Atlantic Ocean to England, then again to our happy shores and other parts of this great Continent, from our own ports to the Southernmost part of the Isthmus, that connects the two Western Continents; and from its Pacific coast, north- and southward, as far as civilization has spread,—the steamers of other nations and of our own, carry intelligence, the wealth of the world, and thousands of travelers.[15]

The pride of national achievement, such as prying open a market that the great nations of Europe had failed to accomplish, might also serve to quell sectional antagonisms, something that Webster kept uppermost in his mind.

The opportunity for initiating the project came with the decision to transport back to Japan seventeen rescued Japanese sailors picked up at sea and held in San Francisco. After numerous discussions with the President and Glynn, and the weighing of various means of implementing this opportunity, Webster on May 9, 1851 informed the secretary of the navy, William A. Graham, that Captain John H. Aulick, who had already been chosen to assume command of the U.S. East India squadron, would head a mission to Japan to return the Japanese sailors and carry instructions to negotiate, if possible, a treaty that would inaugurate "commercial relations with the Empire of Japan, or at least of placing our intercourse with that island upon a more easy footing." Providing "an imposing naval force" to accompany Aulick, Webster said, "would be most auspicious for the accomplishment of the more important objects of [his] mission."[16]

The following day Webster completed and countersigned a letter from

14. Aaron Haight Palmer, *Documents and Facts Illustrating the Origin of the Mission to Japan* (Washington, D.C., 1857), pp. 11–20; Glynn to Fillmore, June 10, 1851, in *PD*, II, 292–297 and editorial introduction, pp. 253–254.

15. DW to John H. Aulick, June 10, 1851, in *PD*, II, 289–290.

16. DW to Graham, May 9, 1851, ibid., II, 288.

President Fillmore to the emperor of Japan. He addressed the emperor as "Great & Good Friend." He then denied that Aulick came as a "missionary of religion." He informed this "Great & Good Friend," in case he had not heard, "that the United States of America now extend from sea to sea" on account of the recent acquisitions of California and Oregon (which are "rich in gold & silver & precious stones") and that "our steamers can reach the shores of your happy land in less than twenty days." In reaching China, their ultimate destination, these steamers may be wrecked on your shores by storms and winds, "and we ask & expect from your friendship & your greatness, kindness for our men & protection for our property." We ask for trading rights with your people and promise that we will not break any of your laws. "Our object is friendly commercial intercourse, and nothing more. You have many productions, which we should be glad to buy, & we have productions which might suit your people."

Webster then singled out the specific product that he wished to obtain. "Your Empire has a great abundance of coal," he said, and this our steamers must use to ply the China trade. They would be "glad" if you would appoint a harbor where the coal could be brought and purchased. Consider how these interests have brought "our two countries so near together; and what purposes of friendship, amity & intercourse they ought to inspire into the breasts of those who govern both countries."[17]

No threats of any kind, as Aaron Palmer had once suggested, intruded into this letter. No mention of past mistreatment of shipwrecked American seamen.[18] Nothing but "friendly commercial intercourse" had prompted the mission.

Webster then prepared his instructions to Aulick. They were quite explicit. The President, he declared, invested the captain "with full power to negotiate & sign a treaty of Amity and Commerce between the United States and the Empire of Japan." Secure, if you can, rights for our vessels to enter one or more ports where they could sell or barter their cargoes without having to pay "extravagant port-charges." He emphasized the importance of obtaining coal. But if the Japanese persisted in their isolation, "you might perhaps induce them" to consent to bringing the coal to a neighboring island where the steamers could purchase it. Furthermore, he stressed the importance of assuring the Japanese that the United States had no intention of interfering with the religion of other countries. But most important of all, Japan must "bind itself to protect American sailors and property" when shipwrecked on its shores. Finally, because of the great distance between the United States and Japan, ratifications of any treaty should be fixed at three years.[19]

Unfortunately Aulick had to be relieved of this assignment because of alleged misconduct in his dealings with the Brazilian minister to the United States, Sergio T. de Macedo.[20] In his place Fillmore decided to send Commo-

17. Fillmore to the Emperor of Japan, May 10, 1851, ibid., II, 289.

18. Palmer, *Mission to Japan*, pp. 11–13.

19. DW to Aulick, June 10, 1851, in *PD*, II, 289–292.

20. Aulick led Macedo to believe that the expense of conveying him to Rio had been provided for by the captain himself although this was not true.

dore Matthew C. Perry, who was given the same instructions as those originally directed to Aulick. James Watson Webb, who served as an intermediary,[21] later remarked that Webster gave Perry "full and discretionary powers" for the "proceedings," but that the commodore was to "be held to a strict responsibility." To forestall trouble with the Dutch, who might take exception to the United States' intruding on their monopoly, Webster instructed George Folsom, the American chargé d'affaires at The Hague, to ask the Dutch to instruct their "Superintendent of the Dutch Factory of Dezima" off Nagasaki to assist in the successful completion of Perry's mission so that both countries could benefit. If the Dutch refused, he continued, Folsom should tell them that "Commodore Perry will not deem himself under any obligation to protect or to regard the interests of Hollanders in Japan." Fortunately the Dutch not only agreed to the request and informed the governor-general of the Dutch East Indies of the action but provided maps and charts to assist the mission.[22]

Perry set sail from Norfolk, Virginia, in November 1852 and arrived in Tokyo Bay the following July. He signed the Treaty of Kanagawa with the Japanese, which opened two ports to American trade, after which he returned to the United States in March 1854.

The ultimate success of the Perry mission belong, both to the commodore and the Franklin Pierce administration, which guided it to completion, and to Fillmore and Webster, who initiated it. Although Perry's instructions were somewhat modified later, Webster provided the basic direction, purpose, and goals of the expedition. Together with his earlier successes with China and Hawaii, Webster pioneered the establishment of a genuine American policy toward the Far East and the Pacific. He also materially advanced the expansion of U.S. commerce around the world. As one historian has declared, Daniel Webster "deserved to be known as the architect of American foreign policy toward East Asia and the Pacific."[23]

At the same time that Webster sought to open up Japan he had to fend off the troublesome French, who created a minor irritation for him in Hawaii.[24]

The problem arose because the Hawaiian government discriminated against French liquor and Catholic schools, and Napoleon III used this as an excuse to seize Honolulu. The United States protested, and the French backed off. But further threats by the French to "cannonade Honolulu" if "certain unjust and ridiculous demands" were not met prompted Webster to instruct William C. Rives, U.S. minister to France, to notify Napoleon in forceful terms that France "shall not take possession of these Islands, nor shall she by military power, reduce them to the necessity of accepting degrading terms." The United

21. Perry sought greater discretionary power and approached Webster through Webb, who was a mutual friend.

22. Webb to Perry, May 1, 1857, Fillmore to DW, January 12, 1852, DW to Folsolm, January 27, June 14, Folsom to DW, March 20, June 14, July 20, 1852, in *PD*, II, 298–305.

23. Ibid., II, 258–259.

24. See Ralph S. Kuykendall, *The Hawaiian Kingdom, 1778–1854: Foundation and Transformation* (Honolulu, 1938).

States would never consent to see either Britain or France seize Hawaii. This country, he said, would use its naval power to preserve "the honor and dignity of the United States, and the safety of the government of the Hawaiian Islands." Meanwhile King Kamehameha III signed a proclamation transferring sovereignty of the islands to the United States in the event of a French attack, a proclamation apparently suggested by Luther Severance, the U.S. commissioner to Hawaii. Although Severance did not think the islands should be taken by "virtue of the 'manifest destiny' principle," on the other hand, "can we not accept their voluntary offer?"[25]

Webster lacked any real desire to annex Hawaii—Manifest Destiny never affected his policy—and in a confidential letter on July 4 he instructed Severance to return the document transferring sovereignty of the islands to the United States and to assure the king that this administration was committed to preserving Hawaiian independence. The French, on the other hand, took exception to Rives's note on the subject and not only disclaimed any intention of annexing Hawaii but protested American interference in a dispute that involved Hawaii and France alone. Despite this rebuke, Webster not only had gained the gratitude of the Hawaiian government but had forced France to state unequivocally that it would respect Hawaiian sovereignty.[26]

In his ongoing efforts to promote American economic interests around the world, Webster noticed that the Amazon River had been little used as a vehicle of commerce and, as a friendly gesture, pointed out that fact to the Brazilian minister. You see, he wrote, "the government of the United States strongly favors all enterprizes and all political arrangements designed to explore new channels for commerce, and to increase the intercourse of nations."[27]

Indeed it was with this thought in mind that he took a serious look at opening up additional U.S. trade within the Western Hemisphere, particularly with Latin America. In his global mercantile vision, increasing the number of interoceanic routes offered a certain means of creating new markets and goods. For that reason he began exploring the possibility of some form of transit across Central America, through Panama or Nicaragua or Mexico, to shorten the distance between the Pacific coast and the eastern seaboard of the United States. Because of recent developments, such as the vast migration of Americans to California in search of gold and "the increase of commerce on both shores bounding this country, the plans for various lines of communication across the [isthmus] by rail roads and canals from sea to sea have given the whole region a new importance."[28] In 1849 Cornelius Vanderbilt and his associates the Accessory Transit Company, a subsidiary of the American Atlantic and Pacific

25. DW to Severance, July 14, Severance to DW, March 17, 1851, in PD, II, 277, 268.

26. DW to Severance, July 14, Severance to DW, October 14, 1851, Eugène de Sartiges to William S. Derrick, September 20, Pierre Jules Baroche to Eugène de Sartiges, October 15, 1851, ibid., II, 275–279, 281–286; Rives to DW, July 8, 22, Baroche to Rives, July 17, 1851, RG 59, NA.

27. DW to Macedo, May 7, 1851, in PD, II, 659.

28. DW to Ignacio Gómez, February 7, 1851, ibid., II, 451.

Ship Canal Company, obtained a grant from Nicaragua to build a ship canal or road-and-water route across its territory.

But the presence of Great Britain in Belize, the Mosquito Coast, and the Bay Islands required that it be included in any transit development in Central America, especially after it seized the Atlantic port town of San Juan del Norte from Nicaragua in 1848, renamed it Greytown, and attached the port to its Mosquito Coast protectorate.

Negotiations between Great Britain and the United States resulted in the Clayton-Bulwer Treaty of April 19, 1850. This treaty provided that the two nations would encourage the building of a neutral and unfortified interoceanic canal across Central America but that neither country would seek its exclusive control. They also agreed not "to occupy, or fortify, or colonize, or assume, or exercise any dominion over Nicaragua, Costa Rica, the Mosquito Coast or any part of Central America." Unfortunately the treaty was ambiguously worded and later created a number of controversies that lasted until 1901.[29] For one thing, Britain insisted that it applied to future and not present possessions in Central America.[30]

Webster refused to recognize British or Mosquito control of Greytown, and in January 1851 Britain declared it a free port. Nevertheless in May the local government instituted a system of harbor fees, an action that immediately led to trouble.

In August 1851 the Vanderbilt group completed its road-and-water transit (railroads and canals) and opened the route to business. Then, on November 21, a British man-of-war fired upon one of Vanderbilt's steamers, the *Prometheus,* that operated on the Atlantic side of the Nicaragua route, to collect the port fee of $123, which the captain of the steamer initially refused to pay because, he insisted, it violated the Clayton-Bulwer Treaty. A few days later another Vanderbilt ship, ironically named the *Daniel Webster,* was also forced to pay the harbor duty.[31]

This "outrage" brought demands that the United States send a warship to protect American interests and property. Webster agreed and advised Fillmore to look upon the incident as "serious and likely to produce excitement. . . . I deem some Naval Force . . . to be essentially necessary, in order to suppress violences and to preserve the peace." At the same time he instructed Abbott Lawrence, U.S. minister to Great Britain, to discover whether the action against the *Prometheus* was authorized by the British government, and, if so, to inform Lord Palmerston, the foreign secretary, that the United States regarded it as a violation of the Clayton-Bulwer Treaty. After a delay caused by Palmerston's

29. Wilbur D. Jones, *The American Problem in British Diplomacy, 1841–1861* (Athens, Ga., 1974), p. 86.

30. Henry Lytton Bulwer to DW, August 17, 1851, RG 59, NA.

31. Joseph L. White to DW, December 2, 1851, in *PD,* II, 466–467. White, a former Indiana congressman, was the counsel for Vanderbilt's company. See David I. Folkman, Jr., *The Nicaragua Route* (Salt Lake City, 1972).

resignation, his successor, Lord Granville, not only assured Lawrence that there had been no authorization for the "act of violence" by the British war vessel but formally disavowed it. He offered an "ample apology" for "the infraction of Treaty engagements." To his credit, despite the urgings of his supporters to make political capital of the incident, Webster did not attempt to use the national excitement over the *Prometheus* affair to advance his own presidential prospects. "The outrage upon the Prometheus by the English Brig skillfully managed will 'bring down the house' in your favor," wrote his friend Charles March. "There is deep excitement on the subject here among all classes."[32]

This happy conclusion to what could have been a "serious" breach in Anglo-American relations led immediately to a convention on April 30, 1852, negotiated by Webster and James F. Crampton, Bulwer's successor as British minister to the United States. The Webster-Crampton Convention attempted to resolve several problems in the Central American area involving Nicaragua, Costa Rica, Britain, and the United States. Webster of course was concerned about protecting the interests of the Vanderbilt company. In effect he hoped that the convention would result in a quadripartite treaty that would implement the Clayton-Bulwer Treaty. Unfortunately Nicaragua rejected the convention for several reasons: past wrongs "perpetrated by England," a degree of hostility toward Vanderbilt's company, and a desire for better terms. It "was, in fact, a mere matter of dollars & cents, the general good of the world being a mere feather in the balance against any violation of the eminent domain of Nicaragua." The "idea, to which they would cling here," John Kerr, the first U.S. chargé d'affaires to Nicaragua, reported to Webster, "is, that out of a jealousy, natural in their view, to two great maritime nations, something, sooner or later, may be elicited for the advantage of Nicaragua."[33]

So months and years of exhausting work in attempting what could have been a significant advance in the ultimate building of a canal across Nicaragua and the settling of a variety of boundary disputes and territorial rights ended in frustration and defeat.

Webster also failed in his attempts to obtain transit rights across the isthmus of Tehuantepec in Mexico. Water routes from the Gulf of Mexico to the Pacific Ocean were possible across Panama and Nicaragua, but Tehuantepec, the narrowest part of Mexico, could serve for a transcontinental railroad. The Mexicans had first awarded a grant to develop a means of transportation across the isthmus in 1842 to José de Garay, who sold it to British entrepreneurs, who in turn, sold it in 1849 to two New York businessmen, Peter and Louis Hargous. The brothers and their associates formed the New Orleans Tehuantepec Company, which

32. DW to Fillmore, December 3, DW to Lawrence, December 3, 1851, Lawrence to DW, January 14, with enclosures, Granville to Lawrence, January 10, Lawrence to Granville, January 13, 1852, in *PD*, II, 467–473; March to DW, December 2, 1851, in Van Tyne, ed., *Letters of Webster,* p. 505.

33. DW to Felipe Molina, April 8, 15, DW to Fillmore, April 22, DW to Robert Walsh, April 29, DW to Kerr, April 30, Kerr to DW, July 28, 1852, in *PD*, II, 480–506. See also Great Britain, *Correspondence with the United States Respecting Central America* (London, 1856).

planned to construct a railroad across the two-hundred-mile length of the isthmus. To protect their investment, they convinced the American government to negotiate, and sign in 1850, a convention with Mexico that allowed the United States to intervene under certain circumstances to safeguard the construction of the railroad.[34]

But the Hargous brothers wanted further concessions, whereupon Webster committed a colossal error by instructing the U.S. minister to Mexico, Robert P. Letcher, to seek amendments to the convention that would in effect make Tehuantepec an American protectorate. He also foolishly authorized Letcher to "hint" that the money owed Mexico under the terms of the Treaty of Guadalupe Hidalgo would be withheld if the amendments were not accepted. Meanwhile the U.S. Senate approved the convention on March 7, 1851.[35]

Outraged, Mexico rejected the amendments. Fearing another Texas annexation, Mexico restricted the activities of the New Orleans company. Furthermore, its minister to the United States, Luis de la Rosa, asked Webster, as a condition to ratifying the convention treaty, to consider it and the Garay grant as separate issues. Attempting to bluff the Mexicans, Webster refused and on April 30 in a strongly worded note to Rosa threatened "serious embarrassments which may result if the treaty should be rejected."[36]

Mexico promptly called Webster's bluff. Its Senate nullified the Garay grant on May 22, 1851, and ordered the suspension of construction on the isthmus and, if necessary, the expulsion of laborers. Rosa further registered his country's fury by informing Webster that his language in the note of April 30 suggested "nothing else than a war between the two nations."[37]

War! The last thing the Fillmore administration needed over an inconsequential matter at a time of domestic crisis. Webster then compounded his mistakes. In several notes, one more astounding than the next, he chided Rosa for assigning motives to the United States that were "neither quite respectful of the Government of the United States nor entirely compatible with the existing treaties between the two governments."[38] Meanwhile Judah P. Benjamin, one of the associates of the New Orleans company, went to see Fillmore and told him that his company would send five hundred men to protect its interests and "resist any attempt to drive them off." Such a collision, Fillmore cautioned Webster, would force "this government either to sustain its own citizens" or "unite with Mexico in punishing them."[39]

The secretary protested the action of the Mexican Senate as unconstitu-

34. J. Fred Rippy, *The United State and Mexico* (New York, 1926), pp. 48–67.

35. Peter Hargous to DW, August 12, 24, DW to Letcher, August 24, Mariano Arista to DW, October 22, DW to Letcher, December 4, 1850, in *PD*, II, 523–524, 526–537, 538–540.

36. Judah P. Benjamin to DW, April 15, DW to Rosa, April 30, 1851, ibid., II, 544–547, 547–556; Rosa to DW, March 7, 1851, cited in Rippy, *United States and Mexico*, pp. 56–57.

37. Rippy, *United States and Mexico*, p. 59; Rosa to DW, June 25, 1851, in *PD*, II, 511.

38. DW to Rosa, August 25, 1851, ibid., II, 583–586.

39. Fillmore to DW, July 19, 1851, ibid., II, 567–568.

tional and instructed Letcher to use every effort possible to obtain the ratification of the convention. He also advised Letcher that "if the Treaty is not ratified . . . serious consequences will result." Mexico, he insisted, "must be persuaded to act promptly."[40]

But Mexico did not. The Mexican legislature waited until April 7, 1852, and then rejected the Tehuantepec convention by a vote of seventy-one to one.

Webster had bungled the matter from start to finish. And he blamed Mexico for the fiasco. "Our great trouble is Mexico," he wrote the President. "The Government of that country seems to act, as if it intended to provoke the United States, to take another slice of its territory."[41] But the fault lay squarely on his shoulders. His hard-line policy in protecting the American holders of the Garay grant and his failure to appreciate Mexican fears about American intentions, to say nothing of his insulting notes, almost provoked a serious confrontation between the two countries.

When Webster took charge of the State Department, he tried to accomplish three major objectives with Mexico: obtain transit rights across the isthmus of Tehuantepec, prevent incursions of Indians from Mexico into this country, and discourage the activities of filibusters from the United States in Mexico. All three of his Mexican objectives ended in failure, but the Tehuantepec failure was the most notable.

His concern and interest in Central and South America also led to an entanglement with France and Great Britain over the ongoing hostilities between Haiti and the Dominican Republic, despite the traditional U.S. policy of avoiding any alliances or agreements with foreign countries. Webster tended to favor the Dominican Republic, which had declared its independence from Haiti in 1844, in part because of racial prejudice and in part because of his sympathy for a nation struggling to maintain its independence. The British and French ministers to the United States, Bulwer and Ernest de Boislecomte, wanted to force Haiti into accepting a permanent peace or a truce of not less than ten years or face a naval blockade of its major port cities. Webster moved cautiously. Anxious to maintain American interests in the Caribbean—several New York commercial houses specialized in Santo Domingo trade—he nevertheless felt constrained by his regard for the constitutional limitations on the government's war powers. He stated quite frankly that the administration was prepared to endorse a tripartite blockade, provided Congress approved, and an appeal for peace. Then, in August 1851, Britain and France blockaded Port-au-Prince and Cap-Haïtien when the Haitian government refused to promise not to renew hostilities against the Dominican Republic. The U.S. Navy "cooperated" in the operation without employing "actual coercion." The Haitian government conceded, and the blockade was lifted.[42]

40. Rippy, *United States and Mexico*, pp. 59–60; DW to Letcher, August 18, December 23, 1851, in *PD*, II, 574–576, 599.

41. DW to Fillmore, May 19, 1852, in *PC*, VII, 326.

42. Bulwer to DW, August 17, DW to Bulwer, August 20, 1850, DW to Robert M. Walsh, January 18, three notes, DW to Bulwer, July 5, two notes, 1851, in *PD*, II, 315–316, 317–318, 325–330, 333–

Webster himself regarded U.S. participation as a departure from its traditional policy of isolation, although no actual treaty was involved. He moved rather deftly through the two years of negotiations, maintaining American influence in the area and supporting the sovereignty of the Dominican Republic. He and Fillmore did not exactly violate the principles of the Monroe Doctrine, but according to the leading historian of that Doctrine, their approval of the blockade had "dangerous implications."[43]

Even more important to the United States because of its strategic location was Cuba. "The southern Atlantic States want Cuba," Webster informed the President, just as "California covets the Sandwich [Hawaiian] Islands; and both covet Mexico." As for Cuba, "it is, indeed, obvious enough what danger there would be to us, if a great naval power [such as Britain] were to possess this key to the Gulf of Mexico and the Caribbean sea." That had always been true—and still is. Andrew Jackson had offered to invade and capture the island after seizing Florida from the Spanish in 1818, but President Monroe would not agree to it. Then President Polk unsuccessfully offered the Spanish one hundred million dollars for the island. To complicate matters, filibustering expeditions by Americans became all the rage in the 1850s.[44]

One of the most notorious filibusterers, a man who caused Webster considerable trouble, was the Venezuelan-born Narciso López, who operated out of New Orleans and led an attack of more than 400 men against Cuba on August 3, 1851. It was not his first violation of Cuban sovereignty. The Spanish swiftly crushed the invasion, publicly garroted López, and shot 50 other filibusterers, including William L. Crittenden, the nephew of Attorney General John J. Crittenden. Some 162 other adventurers were sentenced to work the Spanish quicksilver mines.[45]

The executions of Crittenden and his followers, along with the imprisonment of the other "lawless people," as Webster called them, provoked a storm of protest in the United States and violent demonstrations in Key West, Mobile, and New Orleans. The Spanish consulate in New Orleans was invaded, the consul assaulted, and property destroyed. Poor Fillmore and Webster were bombarded not only with appeals by the relatives of the unfortunate prisoners to rescue their kinsmen but with demands from around the country for apologies and reparations from the Spanish. There were also fears that the Anglo-French naval force cruising in the Caribbean in connection with the Haitian problem

---

334. See also Rayford W. Logan, *Haiti and the Dominican Republic* (New York, 1968) and *The Diplomatic Relations of the United States with Haiti, 1776–1891* (Chapel Hill, N.C., 1941).

43. Dexter Perkins, *The Monroe Doctrine, 1826–1867* (Baltimore, 1933), pp. 266–267; Logan, *Diplomatic Relations,* p. 275.

44. DW to Fillmore, July 13, 1852, in *W&S*, XVIII, 536; DW to Fillmore, [April 25,], October 4, 1851, in *PD*, II, 385. On filibustering, see Charles H. Brown, *Agents of Manifest Destiny: The Lives and Times of the Filibusters* (Chapel Hill, N.C., 1980).

45. Allen Owen to DW, September 5, 1851, in *PD*, II, 374, 379–382; Philip S. Foner, *A History of Cuba and Its Relations with the United States* (New York, 1963), II, 50–59. Owen was U.S. consul in Havana.

might be ordered to stop American ships to search for adventurers. If that happened, Webster advised Fillmore, "the first attempt to execute those orders by visiting an American Ship, or in any other way interrupting our Commerce would lead to immediate war."[46]

But the Anglo-French force chose not to interfere. Then, risking the fury of American anger over the fate of the filibusterers and reversing the approach he employed in the Austrian brouhaha, Webster rather adroitly couched an apology to the Spanish with an implied plea for clemency for the remaining prisoners working in the mines. The note must have been singularly difficult to write: to apologize and extricate the country from an embarrassment, but not to do it abjectly and jeopardize American strategic interests in the Caribbean.

Webster did it magnificently. "The Executive Government of the United States," he explained to Angel Calderón de la Barca, the Spanish minister in Washington, "regards these outrages not only as unjustifiable, but as disgraceful acts, and a flagrant breach of duty & property; and . . . it disapproves them as seriously, and regrets them as deeply, as either Mr. Calderón or his Government can possibly do."[47] Webster also agreed to an indemnity for the consul and the Spanish citizens who had suffered property losses in New Orleans and Key West, which Congress allowed in a bill passed on August 31, 1852, granting an indemnity of twenty-five thousand dollars.

Then the secretary wrote to Daniel Barringer, U.S. minister to Spain, and directed him to seek the release of the prisoners. "May not the sword of justice be now sheathed without danger, and the voice of Christian humanity be allowed to be heard?" Even if the Spanish government can feel no compassion for the prisoners themselves, "is it not highly just & proper to consider that they have friends and families, distressed fathers & mothers, weeping brothers & sisters, all of them unoffending?"[48] Webster told Fillmore that "I have spent the morning in composing a letter to Mr Barringer, in behalf of the prisoners in Spain. . . . If this has not been a religious duty, it has been at least a work of mercy."[49]

Webster's note to Calderón pleased Queen Isabella II because of its sincerity and obvious willingness to placate the honor of Spain, so she accepted the apology. "Her Majesty had declared herself satisfied with the terms of the aforesaid note," Calderón informed Webster, "being pleased to recognize in it, the friendly and high-toned sentiments of the illustrious President of the Republic and of his Secretary of State." She also agreed that the insulting violence that had occurred in New Orleans had been duly and properly expiated. Thereupon, in a "spontaneous act of her Royal clemency," she pardoned all the prisoners.[50]

46. Peter Hamilton to DW, September 8, with enclosure, Edward Cook to DW, September 12, Angel Calderón de la Barca to William S. Derrick, with enclosure, September 5, DW to Fillmore, December 8, 1851, in *PD*, II, 375–382, 411–412.

47. DW to Calderón, November 13, 1851, ibid., II, 396–401.

48. DW to Barringer, November 26, 1851, ibid., II, 404–408.

49. DW to Fillmore, November 27, 1851, ibid., II, 408.

50. Calderón to DW, January 13, 1852, in ibid., II, 417–418.

When Webster's note to Calderón was published in the United States, it brought down on his head a great deal of criticism,[51] but he long ago decided to risk it as "a work of mercy." Britain and France suggested that the United States join them in a tripartite convention and forswear any desire to acquire Cuba from Spain, but Webster, much as he might agree with their purpose, kept putting them off. Not until he had died did the administration reject the proposal and inform the other nations that the United States regarded Cuba as a purely American problem—a problem that would bedevil American foreign policy well into the next century.[52]

51. Criticism of another kind developed over his handling of the treaty with the Swiss Confederation negotiated by the Taylor administration. This treaty granted most-favored-nation status to the United States, but it stipulated that only Christians would enjoy guaranteed privileges under the treaty. When the agreement came before Webster, he approved it because of his desire to promote and extend American commerce throughout the world. But American Jews naturally protested. Mordecai M. Noah, the distinguished and politically influential New York newspaper editor, led the attack and petitioned Webster to strike out the offending provision. Webster noted the objections and referred them to the Senate, which deleted them. The treaty was then ratified and signed by the President on March 12, 1851, although the Swiss found ways to continue discriminating against Jews. DW to Fillmore, January 7, Joseph Abraham et al. to DW, February 25, DW to Abraham, March 5, 1851, in *PD*, II, 167–169. See also Heinz K. Meier, *The United States and Switzerland in the Nineteenth Century* (The Hague, 1963).

52. Crampton to DW, with enclosures, April 23, DW to Crampton, April 29, 1852, in *PD*, II, 348, 428–432.

43

"A Disappointed, Heart-Stricken Man"

DESPITE several misadventures in Latin America that sullied his second stint as secretary of state,[1] Webster did enjoy a few diplomatic successes in the region. On July 10, 1851, Webster and Felipe Molina, the Costa Rican minister to the United States, negotiated a treaty of amity and commerce between their two countries. In addition, tension between Venezuela and the United States over claims cases ended with the signing of a convention in 1852. Isaac N. Steele, U.S. minister to Venezuela, gave Webster full credit for making the agreement possible.[2]

The secretary also tried to gain commercial access to the extensive river systems of South America. He "had watched our commercial interests more closely and acted more promptly," declared Samuel Jaudon, a Philadelphia banker, "than our merchants themselves." Although he failed to get the free navigation of the Amazon, Webster did play a significant role in opening up the Río de la Plata to international commerce. The U.S. minister to Brazil Robert C. Schenck and the U.S. minister to Argentina John S. Pendleton were instructed to negotiate a series of treaties that would make trade on the Plata and its tributaries accessible to commercial ships of all nations. The ministers succeeded in obtaining agreements with Uruguay and Paraguay, but they were never implemented. Still, the first treaty of amity and commerce with Argentina was successfully negotiated, and the accord signed on July 27, 1853, guaranteed reciprocal freedom of commerce.[3]

1. In addition to those incidents already covered in the previous chapter, the boarding of the vessel *Addison*, a New Bedford whaler, and the removal of four seamen by the maritime governor of Valparaiso, plus the granting of asylum to a rebel leader in Chile by Balie Peyton, the U.S. minister, were poorly handled. These were referred to Webster for guidance. The secretary's "response of July 2, 1851 was not one of his more thoughtfully crafted papers." He misunderstood the *Addison* situation. However he did order Peyton to end the asylum for the Cuban leader. See *PD*, II, 633–635, 651–661. See also Roderick Sherman, *The Diplomatic and Commercial Relations of the United States, 1820–1914* (Boston, 1926).

2. Steele to DW, May 8, 1852, in *PD*, II, 649–651.

3. Steele to DW, May 8, June 9, 1851, Jaudon to DW, May 7, DW to Schenck, April 29, 1852, in *PD*, II, 464–465, 646–651, 667, 664–666.

One of the secretary's minor diplomatic successes was the way he handled a long-standing quarrel with Portugal involving American claims against that nation for shipping losses suffered during the War of 1812. The Taylor administration took a hard line and demanded full compensation in the amount of $223,327. But the Portuguese offered to pay only the smaller claims in full; for the larger one, and apparently there was only one, it refused to pay anything unless a third-party arbiter decided that the full amount was fair and equitable. The Taylor administration would not agree to arbitration and actually came close to breaking off diplomatic relations.

With Webster's arrival in the State Department the dispute was swiftly settled. "I have come to the conclusion," he told the Portuguese minister, Joaquím César de Figanière e Morão, "that, as your Government has offered to pay the small claims & leave [the larger one] to arbitration, we may as well settle it that way: this is my personal opinion, but have not had time to confer with the President—the arbitration to be agreed to hereafter."[4]

Delighted with this change of attitude, the minister agreed to sit down with Webster and work out the details. On February 26, 1851, the two men signed the Convention for the Settlement of Claims that finally concluded what had been an interminable and bitter diplomatic dispute. Webster recommended Louis Napoleon as the third-party arbiter, and, on November 30, 1852, the French monarch decided that no indemnity should be paid by the Portuguese.[5]

Webster also brought to a successful conclusion with Prussia a treaty for extradition that originated during his first term as secretary of state. Both France and Prussia had requested such agreements following the model set down in Article X of the Webster-Ashburton Treaty. The United States had already signed an extradition convention with the French in 1844, but the Prussian convention ran into problems. Anxious to put the matter behind him, Webster began talks with Baron Friedrich von Gerolt, the Prussian minister to the United States. After yielding to all of Webster's demands, Gerolt and the secretary of state signed the Convention for the Mutual Delivery of Criminals on June 16, 1852, making this the third such convention (after Great Britain and France) that Webster had helped negotiate.[6]

These few modest diplomatic successes, especially his now-famous Hülsemann letter, encouraged Webster to think very seriously once again about winning the Whig nomination for President in 1852. Fillmore had told him repeatedly that he would not be a candidate, leaving the secretary free to pursue

4. Interview between DW and Figanière, [August 14, 1850], in *PD*, II, 150–152.

5. DW to Figanière, September 5, 1850, ibid., II, 147–150, 152–154. The Senate ratified the treaty on March 7, 1851. James Clay, son of Henry Clay, had been chargé d'affaires in Lisbon in the Taylor administration and resigned because the Portuguese would not agree to the full amount demanded by the United States. Webster replaced him with Charles B. Haddock, the son of Webster's older sister Abigail.

6. Fillmore to DW, "Memo of Treaty with Prussia," Gerolt to DW, June 23, 1851, January 16, 1852, DW to Fillmore, July 9, 1851, ibid., II, 187–193.

his own presidential ambitions. Thus, when the opportunity developed to take a five-hundred-mile tour of New York with Fillmore and the entire cabinet on the occasion of the completion of the Erie Railroad from New York to Dunkirk on Lake Erie that would provide maximum exposure without the appearance of campaigning, Webster jumped at it, although he told friends he was reluctant to go and confessed that it posed "some danger to health." He foresaw "four elements of distress in it: 1. Heat. 2. Crowds. 3. Limestone-water. 4. The necessity of speech-making."[7] Still, he joined the tour, gave speeches, and thoroughly enjoyed the attention and adulation lavished on him by the crowds.

There was another good reason for taking the trip. The North was still howling its anger over the Fugitive Slave Law, and this five-hundred-mile journey across the very center of abolitionist territory would give him and the President a vast audience to preach the message of compromise, Union, and obedience to the law.

On the morning of May 12, the presidential party departed from New York City and headed north and then west, stopping at one rural town after another. At each stop the President spoke, indicating to some observers that he might have changed his mind about not running for reelection. Webster also spoke, but his major efforts occurred on the return trip after he had left the presidential party. These speeches were given in Albany, Syracuse, and Buffalo, but he also addressed large crowds in other towns, such as Rochester, Canandaigua, Auburn, the hometown of William H. Seward—"where everybody there, I suppose," said Webster, "is a Free-soiler, or nearly everybody." He frequently joked with the crowd and drew laughter, friendly vocal responses to his questions, cheers, and applause. He defended his Seventh of March speech and denounced Seward's doctrine of the "higher law." The "policy of courting the Abolitionists has been long enough practised," he complained, especially by Whigs. And "it has always failed." In Syracuse, "that laboratory of abolitionism, libel, and treason," he came right out and condemned those people who "set up themselves over the Constitution, above the law, and above the decisions of the highest tribunals, and who say [the Fugitive Slave Law] shall not be carried into effect." They have "pledged their lives, their fortunes, and *sacred honor!*—for what? For the violation of the law, for the committal of treason to the country; for it is treason, and nothing else."[8] They pledge their sacred honor to violate the Constitution.

At Dunkirk, his son Fletcher, who had accompanied him, suddenly fell ill and frightened the father half out of his mind. In the middle of the night Fletcher was seized by a "violent inflammation of the throat" and could not breathe. A physician arrived within twenty minutes and bled the patient, gave

7. DW to Blatchford, May 11, 1851, in Curtis, *Webster,* II, 502.

8. DW to Blatchford, May 25, 1851, in *PC,* VII, 250; DW to Harvey, June 3, 1851, in *W&S,* XVI, 614. The Syracuse speech can be found ibid., XIII, 408–421. A convention of radical abolitionists gathered in Syracuse in early May 1851, and Webster referred to them as an "assemblage of insane persons." *PS,* II, 587.

him a "powerful emetic, applied mustard-plasters, etc. etc." The worst symptoms passed, and within a few days Fletcher had completely recovered. Because of his son's illness, Webster separated from the presidential party as it continued on the tour, and he later followed behind as best he could. "I was terribly frightened," he informed Harriette Paige. At the time "it seemed to me highly probable that I should be childless, before morning. God, in his mercy, averted that calamity."[9]

Speaking in Buffalo in a pouring rain on Thursday, May 22, Webster addressed himself to the central question of the last several decades: "Can we preserve the union of the States, not by coercion, not by military power, not by angry controversies . . . but by the silken cords of mutual, fraternal, patriotic affection? That is the question, and no other."

But the problem was slavery, he reminded them, and that seemed insurmountable. He said he would never consent to adding "one foot of slave territory beyond what the old thirteen States had at the time of the formation of the Union. Never, never." Also, it was his unshakable opinion "that it was not within the scope or design of the Constitution to admit new States out of foreign territory." He had had nothing to do with the acquisition of Florida, and he had opposed the annexation of Texas, but those who had voted for it now proclaimed themselves "the champions of liberty, crying up their Free Soil creed, and using it for selfish and deceptive purposes." So "you may thank them" for adding five or six more slave states to the Union. "Do not blame me for it."

He reminded everyone that he had voted against the treaty with Mexico. "I wanted none of her territory, neither California, New Mexico, nor Utah."

Now, Gentlemen, I wish I had ten thousand voices. I wish I could draw around me the whole people of the United States, and I wish I could make them all hear what I now declare on my conscience as my solemn belief, before the Power who sits on high, and who will judge you and me hereafter, that, if [the Compromise of 1850 had not passed] civil war would have ensued; blood, American blood, would have been shed; and who can tell what would have been the consequences? . . . But I cannot express the horror I feel at the shedding of blood in a controversy between one of these States and the government of the United States, because I see in it a total and entire disruption of all those ties that make us a great and happy people.

Still, slavery does exist in the southern states. Unfortunately Congress can do nothing about it. "It must be obvious to every intelligent person that, if Congress possessed power over slavery as it exists in the Southern States, any attempt to exercise such power would break up the Union just as surely as would an attempt to introduce slavery in Massachusetts."

Turning to the Fugitive Slave Law, he acknowledged that on account of it he had been vilified as an apostate from liberty, a hypocrite, and a liar. "But it

9. DW to Blatchford, May 17, 1851, in Curtis, *Webster,* II, 503; DW to Paige, [June 1, 1851], in *PC,* VII, 251.

does not disturb me . . . Is not the Constitution libeled and abused. Do not some people call it a covenant with hell?"[10] He believed it his duty to stand up for what he thought just and right and "to exert any power I had to keep that country together. I cared for nothing, I was afraid of nothing, but I meant to do my duty. And, Gentlemen, allow me to say here to-day, that if the fate of John Rogers[11] had stared me in the face, if I had seen the stake, if I had heard the faggots already crackling, by the blessing of Almighty God I would have gone on and discharged the duty which I thought my country called upon to perform. I would have become a martyr to save that country."[12]

A bit of bombastic self-praise and bravado to conclude the speech, spiced throughout with self-justification, but a courageous reaffirmation of his principles in the face of stiff and vocal abolitionist and Free Soil opposition to them.

Webster was rather pleased with what he had said in Buffalo, and indeed the entire tour seemed to reinvigorate him. He spoke on May 28 to the young men of Albany and urged them to sustain the cause of Union. "Go on, young men of Albany! Go on, young men of the United States! . . . Go, then; uphold the institutions under which you were born. . . . For I yet believe firmly that this Union, once broken, is utterly incapable, according to all human experience, of being reconstructed in its original character, of being re-cemented by any chemistry, or art, or effort, or skill of man."[13]

Webster edited his Buffalo, Syracuse, and Albany speeches and had them published.[14] He clearly intended them as propaganda for his presidential campaign. He also worked closely with Edward Everett to bring out his works in 1851, for the exact same purpose.[15] This six-volume publication included previously published papers and a long biographical sketch of Webster by Everett.[16] It was hoped and believed that the sketch and the various addresses and papers would serve as campaign material for both the convention and the election thereafter.

After retracing his steps back to New York City, Webster continued on to Washington, where he arrived during the evening of June 3, 1851. By this time he believed that he might have a possible rival for the Whig nomination in Millard Fillmore. "I have no doubt Mr Fillmores friends urge him constantly to be a candidate; and altho' he has often said to me, & others, that he should not, I think he has been inclined, lately, to change his purpose. I infer this, partly

10. William Lloyd Garrison in his *Liberator* called the Constitution "a covenant with death, and an agreement with hell."

11. Rogers was a colonial New Englander and a much-persecuted nonconformist who died of smallpox, not at the stake, as Webster implied.

12. *PS*, II, 580–600; DW to John M. Botts, June 3, 1851, in *W&S*, XVI, 615.

13. *W&S*, IV, 267–290.

14. *Mr. Webster's Speeches at Buffalo, Syracuse, and Albany, May, 1851* (New York, 1851).

15. Everett, ed., *The Works of Daniel Webster* (Boston, 1851). 6 vols.

16. Webster gave Everett instructions on how he wanted the biographical material written. DW to Everett, January 8, 1851, in Webster, ed., *Private Correspondence*, II, 411.

from some appointments, which he has made, & partly" from his behavior during the tour as he went about greeting the people and consulting with local political leaders.[17] Despite this, both men continued to treat the other with all the respect they had previously shown each other. It did not affect their working relationship, and Webster made a particular point not to do anything that might embarrass or distress the President. "My deep and sincere regard for the President," he wrote, "as well as my official relations to him, would make it exceedingly painful to me, if any thing should occur, in which my name should be concerned, however remotely, manifesting disrespect to him or the slightest want of kindness, or delicacy towards his feelings." As for Fillmore, he kept silent about his own plans well into the winter of 1851–1852 but assured several of Webster's friends that he would leave the field open for his secretary of state. George Ashmun spoke to him, *"& he thinks the coast will be clear."*[18] So Webster went straight ahead with his plans to win the nomination when the Whigs met in national convention the following year.

As he well knew, he needed an organization if he expected to achieve his goal, and he also knew he could not rely on the regular Massachusetts Whig state committee. "I am quite resolved not to commit any interest of mine" to it. "The leading object of that Committee will be to re-establish a Whig government in Mass., and, if we may judge by the past, we may fear that to effect this object they will be ready to sacrifice high national considerations, and to court, as they have courted, free soilers, and semi free soilers, abolitionists, and semi-abolitionists."[19]

So he decided to operate outside that body—but discreetly. He said he wanted a "meeting of Union men of all parties," and he encouraged the formation of a "Central Committee" of such worthies as Edward Everett, Rufus Choate, Peter Harvey, Franklin Haven, George Ashmun, Joshua T. Stevenson, George T. Curtis, and twelve others, who met in Boston on June 5 to inaugurate his campaign. Everett suggested circulating nominating petitions in every Massachusetts school district with a cover letter signed by the nineteen. The committee drew up the petition, and Haven subsequently informed Webster that their arrangements had gone very well.[20] Everett claimed that the "individual subscriptions to a nomination" had been "eminently successful." More than seven thousand names were obtained in Boston alone, "& the country towns are coming in strong," so much so that he entertained high hopes that the Whig convention in November would place Webster's name in nomination without difficulty. The Central Committee, especially Choate, Ashmun, and Stevenson, worked hard for its "divinity," and Webster told Harvey that he could never thank

17. DW to Haven, June 11, 1851, in *PC*, VII, 257.

18. DW to Harvey, September 13, DW to Haven, December 14, 1851, ibid., VII, 274, 297.

19. DW to Harvey, May 4, 1851, in *W&S*, XVI, 611.

20. DW to Everett, June 6, Ashmun to DW, [June 5,] 1851, in *Microfilm Edition*, F24/33783, 34039; DW to Haven, June 11, 1851, in *PC*, VII, 256–257; Dalzell, *Webster and Nationalism*, pp. 230–232.

them enough. "They tower above all thanks of mine."[21]

Once his campaign caught fire in other states, as he believed it would, Webster thought he ought to resign his office, especially if Fillmore became a declared candidate. In the meantime he decided to lie low and attend to his health.[22]

On July 4 the cornerstone of the new addition to the Capitol building was laid by President Fillmore, who asked Webster specifically to give the principal address. Standing before the audience, a little unsteadily and clearly showing his age of sixty-nine years, the Godlike Daniel did not perform as well as expected. He stood erect, and his voice was still strong and vibrant, but now great hollows showed in both cheeks, and his eyes had lost some of their luster.

In his speech, a copy of which had been deposited under the cornerstone, Webster traced the course of liberty in this country since Washington laid the foundation stone of the original Capitol building in 1793. "Our inheritance is an inheritance of American liberty," he exclaimed. "But by the WANT OF UNION that liberty can be lost." Also, "another most important part of the great fabric of American liberty is, that there shall be written constitutions," founded on the authority of the people and "regulating and restraining all the powers conferred upon government, whether legislative, executive or judicial."

In the middle of the speech Webster paused to read a short statement he had written that had been placed separately beneath the cornerstone by the President. It described the proceedings of the day and concluded with: "all here assembled, whether belonging to public life or to private life . . . unite in sincere and fervent prayers that this deposit, and the walls and arches, the domes and towers, the columns and entablatures, now to be erected over it, may endure forever! GOD SAVE THE UNITED STATES OF AMERICA! Daniel Webster, Secretary of State of the United States."[23]

Many in the crowd who heard him thought the oration decidedly below par. In fact the speaker appeared to be drunk. "He exhibited considerable weakness," commented Isaac Bassett. "He has resorted to stimulants."[24] But knowing Webster's inclinations, Bassett probably jumped to this conclusion. More likely is the fact that the secretary's declining health accounts for his substandard performance.

Shortly after the laying of the cornerstone Webster returned to Marshfield and then to his home in Franklin, where he spent the summer trying to renew his strength after a long and arduous winter and spring at the State Department. As he approached the age of seventy, he realized that his physical powers were in rapid decline. In addition to his annual catarrh, he now found that he could

21. DW to Haven, June 11, Everett to DW, June 26, DW to Harvey, November 27, 1851, in *PC*, VII, 256–257, 260, 289. For the glowing address to the people written by Everett, see Curtis, *Webster*, II, 579–581.

22. DW to Haven, June 11, 1851, in *PC*, VII, 257.

23. *PS*, II, 602–626.

24. IB Papers, Box 1, Folder B, p. 52.

not "get rid of that tendency to diarrhoea, which I contracted in [Harrisburg] Pennsylvania, in April,"[25] when he spoke to the members of the state legislature. Then he developed a "violent pain" in one foot, which the doctor diagnosed as gout. "The physicians say it will do my constitution a great deal of good, and go off in good time." The intense heat that summer also affected his eyes. Then he caught a heavy cold. He dieted, and for the catarrh, Dr. Jackson of Philadelphia prescribed "iodate of iron to the hydriodate of potash," but his health showed little improvement. The "effort connected with the 4th of July may well enough account for this," he told the President. Between the dieting, "the catarrh and the Harrisburg diarrhoea, I am a good deal reduced."[26]

During the summer of 1851, as Webster rested, the regular Massachusetts Whig Central Committee pretty much decided to endorse Robert C. Winthrop for governor despite the fact that his nomination was unacceptable to Webster. Angered, the secretary told Everett, who had been invited to preside as chairman of the annual fall convention in Springfield, not to go. "A Convention which shall nominate me, for one high office, and Mr Winthrop for another would be an inconsistency, I think."[27]

Winthrop captured a decided plurality of votes in the November election, but because he failed to win a majority, the final choice of governor went to the legislature, where a coalition of Democrats and Free Soilers reelected George Boutwell. "The late election has turned out *precisely* right," gloated Charles March. "It removes from your friends the opprobrium of a connection with free-soilism, will excite the Whigs to a glorious triumph next year." Fletcher told his father that he rejoiced that "your name was not connected with his [Winthrop's] at Springfield."

Webster's personal Central Committee then held a huge rally to launch his presidential campaign in Faneuil Hall on November 25. It "was every thing that could be wished: thronged, orderly, enthusiastic." Rufus Choate gave the main address, in which he delighted in pointing out that the doors of Faneuil Hall "were at length opened," harking back to the earlier controversy when the city authorities refused to permit a gathering of Webster's friends.[28]

25. At the time of Webster's death Dr. John Jeffries stated that his patient had been plagued with diarrhea *"for the past eighteen or twenty years,"* but only since Harrisburg had it become persistent. To combat it and the catarrh, Webster used opiates, generally in the form of a sulfate of morphia and the compound spirits of sulfuric ether. Jeffries, "An Account of the Last Illness," p. 110.

26. DW to Fillmore, August 5, 1851, in Webster, ed., *Private Correspondence*, II, 459; DW to Fillmore, July 20, 1851, in Curtis, *Webster*, II, 525. On August 27 he again wrote the President and said, "Thus far the catarrh holds off. It was due the 23d, but, as yet, does not show itself. But I dare not have confidence, for some days yet, that it will not come on in force." It did. One day, he reported, he was "quite sick." The catarrh attacked "the head, eyes, nose, etc., with great violence." DW to Fillmore, August 27, September 8, 28, DW to Blatchford, September 15, 1851, ibid., II, 527–528.

27. DW to Everett, September 4, 3, [1851], PC, VII, 271, 270. Everett on his own had already decided not to go. Everett to DW, September 3, 1851, ibid., VII, 271.

28. March to DW, December 2, Fletcher Webster to DW, November 17, 1851, in ibid., VII, 292, 285; Blue, *The Free Soilers*, pp. 226–228.

But other possible presidential Whig candidates emerged during the fall. Of course Clay's name always came up, but the poor man was in dreadful health and finally resigned his Senate seat in December to take effect the following September. He died on June 29, 1852, in a hotel room in Washington.[29]

Much more serious was the candidacy of General Winfield Scott, announced at a public dinner in Wilmington, Delaware, on November 16. The fact that Seward and Weed sparked the drive for the general made the nomination absolutely anathema to Fillmore. But Scott enjoyed a number of advantages: He was a war hero like Andrew Jackson, William Henry Harrison, and Zachary Taylor and therefore very likely to attract large numbers of popular votes, and he gave a strong performance at the Whig convention in 1848, gaining votes during the balloting when everyone else, including Clay and Webster, steadily lost them. "Genl Scott is fairly in the pool," observed one active New York Whig businessman, "and is daily making capital."[30]

For Webster, facing either a military hero or a President with the federal patronage at his disposal, should Fillmore choose to run, could prove impossibly daunting. Still, he of all the candidates best represented "the Compromise, the Union and the Constitution," which were what he believed the American people wanted their President to espouse and defend. But because campaigning had changed considerably with the rise of democracy, bringing many more voters to the polls, the great masses of ordinary citizens who read the penny press, not the more intellectually stimulating journals in which Webster's three-hour speeches and learned articles appeared, found his "aloofness and aristocratic airs" decidedly unappealing. Judge Thomas M. Key, an Ohio lawyer, active in Democratic politics, and "a man of talent, young, ardent, and idolizing Mr. Webster," visited the secretary in Washington, bringing with him a letter of introduction. He was politely but "coolly" received. The great man had no time to waste with him. So Judge Key "took his leave & never went back again. Judge Key is perhaps the most popular young man in Ohio & withal, one of the most shrewd. A half dozen kind words from Mr. Webster, would have made him his Champion."[31] That kind of behavior could never pass muster among Whig leaders or delegates at the convention in 1852. They wanted a candidate with charisma who could meet and charm ordinary citizens with a congenial personality, and Daniel Webster simply did not qualify.

Toward the end of the year, while he toiled over foreign problems and started preparing the case he would argue in March 1852 before the district court in Trenton, New Jersey, defending Charles Goodyear's patent for vulcan-

29. Remini, *Clay*, p. 774ff.

30. Simeon Draper to DW, [c. November–December 1851], in *PC*, VII, 291.

31. Elisha Mills Huntington to ?, enclosed in Fletcher Webster to DW, November 28, 1851, ibid., VII, 289–290.

ized rubber[32]—the so-called *India Rubber* case—both of which took a great deal of his time and energy, Webster wanted Ashmun, Haven, Harvey, Everett, Stevenson, Ketchum, Blatchford, Curtis, and a few others (several of whom were members of his Central Committee) to come to Washington to form a *"council"* and consult with "Northern, Western, & Southern Gentlemen" and make future plans for the campaign. But more than a month later his council had not yet been formed. There is "good feeling here" in Washington, he fretted, "but there seems to be nobody to give it direction, or to form any organization among friends." There was no "follow up" to the Massachusetts effort. "We are fast losing the golden moments of opportunity."[33] Southerners seemed more inclined toward Fillmore now that the fears for the safety of the Union had greatly diminished, and Scott kept picking up delegate support. At the same time Fillmore refused either to declare himself a candidate or to withdraw from the race.

James Watson Webb, Webster's longtime supporter in New York, planned a rally in March to endorse the secretary but warned his candidate not "to *write* or *speak* until after the nomination." Unfortunately Webster had already obligated himself to give a lecture on February 23 to the New-York Historical Society at Niblo's Saloon on "The Dignity and Importance of History," but he assured Webb that it dealt with literary matters and would not "contain a word upon any passing political subject." He told a friend, "If I make a poor figure in this intended address, no matter; everybody knows that I know nothing but law and politics."

The New York rally took place on March 5, and Webster was again hailed as the "Great Defender of the Constitution and the Union." But the Whig legislative caucus meeting on April 8 overwhelmingly endorsed General Scott.[34]

Webster spent considerable time away from his duties in Washington during the first quarter of 1852, escaping to Boston or Marshfield whenever possi-

32. *Goodyear v. Day* was Webster's last important legal case. Goodyear hired Webster to plead for him by offering ten thousand dollars, and five thousand dollars more if the decision was favorable. "Really I do not see how I can forego the fee," said Webster. "This fee I must have, for it will pay fifteen thousand dollars of my debts." Webster won the case. "Three or four more such windfalls as that will let me die a free man," he told his friend Peter Harvey, "and that is all I live to do." Interestingly, no man holding the position of secretary of state had ever before taken a fee and gone to court. Baxter, *Webster and the Supreme Court*, pp. 153–154; Harvey, *Reminiscences*, pp. 103–104. For the case itself, see *Federal Cases*, X, and *PLBP*, III. Webster argued his last case before the Supreme Court, *Gaines v. Relf*, on February 3, 1852.

33. DW to Haven, February 6, 1852, two letters, in *PC*, VII, 301–302.

34. Webb to DW, February 8, DW to Webb, February 11, 1852, ibid., VII, 303, 304; Curtis, *Webster*, II, 591. In the speech for the New-York Historical Society, which drew an audience of more than three thousand, some of whom paid as much as fifty dollars for a ticket, Webster said that history is philosophy that is taught by example but does not tell us all its variations and possibilities. History should explain the development of knowledge and the arts and the changes taking place over time in society. History is also an artistic expression, and he cited some of the great historians of the past. As for American history, he thought it was divided into three parts: the colonial era, the Revolution through establishment of the nation under the Constitution, and the period from 1789 to the present. See *PS*, II, 629–666.

ble, passing a week in New York seeing friends, partying, giving the New-York Historical Society speech, and then arguing the *India Rubber* case in Trenton, where he stayed from March 20 to April 2.

As the date of the Whig National Convention drew closer, Webster's prospects for a nomination grew increasingly dim. To begin with, he had no organization, at least not one up to 1852 standards. In the city of Washington, "the place of all others where there should be some concerted plan of action," there was none. "There ought to be money," complained Alexander H. Lawrence, a Washington lawyer, "there ought to be printed matter—and more than all *now,* there ought to be *men, true men,* who will seek out those who come here and exert themselves in Mr Webster's cause." A upsurge of "Union Whigs" acting in his favor had simply not materialized. "All is *apathy,*" moaned one of his friends, "both in Congress & out." Within a few more weeks Webster himself began to sense that defeat was in the offing. "It seems to me, with great deference," he admitted to his son, "that things are not in a good way. Nobody does any thing on our side."[35]

Having exhausted himself laboring twelve and more hours at the State Department, Webster and his wife departed Washington for Boston and home in late April. A few weeks later, on May 8, in the hope of finding relaxation and recreation, he and his private secretary, Charles Lanman, decided to go fishing for trout. They left Marshfield early in the morning and headed for a Plymouth pond, about ten or twelve miles from the house. Their large buggy, an old-fashioned phaeton, open in front and very high from the ground, was drawn by two horses.

Lanman held the reins while Webster, sitting beside him, talked about the hardships endured by the Pilgrims. As they rode along, suddenly the "king-bolt, or transom bolt" snapped, and the body of the carriage fell to the ground, throwing the seventy-year-old Webster, encumbered by a robe stretched across his legs, headlong to the ground "with some violence," along with his companion. They were ascending a hill and were traveling at a slow speed; otherwise, said Webster, we would not "have escaped with our lives." In falling he threw his hands forward to protect his head, and "this brought the whole weight of the body upon the hands and arms, turning back the hands, and very much spraining the wrists." His head hit the ground "with much force,"[36] and he sustained a small flesh wound near the right temple. The joints of both wrists were injured, the left more so, without any apparent fracture, although at the time Webster thought he might have broken one bone of the left wrist. Both hands were considerably swollen for the next several weeks, and he "suffered frequent severe paroxysm of pain through the joint."

Lenman picked the statesman up off the ground, "blood streaming down his dome-like forehead," and helped him to a neighboring house, where he lay

35. Lawrence to George Abbot, May 5, 1852, DW to Fletcher Webster, [June 11, 1852], in *PC*, VII, 321–322, 328.

36. Lanman, *Private Life of Webster,* pp. 173–174; Jeffries, "Account of the Last Illness," p. 111.

down until a doctor could be summoned. He suffered chills that made his teeth "chatter, and caused a shivering of the whole body . . . and then for a moment my eyes swam, and I felt dizzy." An eighty-year-old man tended him until the doctor arrived. *"Thank God, he has his reason!"* the old man exclaimed as he wiped away the tears in his eyes.[37]

When the doctor was summoned, he was informed that Webster was "nearly dead." When he arrived, he found his patient's forehead "much contused and somewhat lacerated." He dressed the wound and tried to make his patient as comfortable as possible.[38] After four hours Webster felt well enough to travel, and he and Lenman got another carriage and returned to Marshfield.

The accident "disturbed the bile of the system, and gave a yellow tinge to the skin and eyes," Webster reported. His left arm was black and blue from the wrist almost to the shoulder, so he put splints on his arm and used a sling to keep it motionless. He also regularly bathed it in cold water to bring down the swelling. On May 20 he visited Drs. J. Mason Warren and John Jeffries for consultation and assured the doctors he had "no complaint of uneasiness in the head." They agreed that he had "made too many applications, of ice-water, liniments, poultices &c &c, and they recommend an abstinence from everything of that kind." They ordered him to rest as much as possible and keep his left arm in a sling. He acted strangely by walking about his mansion and peering into a closet or a trunk, and "twenty times a day" he visited the various apartments where his servants had congregated. He had a speaking engagement in Faneuil Hall on May 22 that he insisted on keeping, even though he was "suffering under great general debility." He removed the sling from his arm to deliver his speech, and "it gave me a troubled night." He seemed unsteady on his feet, and it was later charged that he was intoxicated, a story that many people naturally believed. Jeffries came to his immediate defense with the statement "that the charge was entirely untrue."

What had happened escaped the doctor's notice. Webster had suffered a subdural hematoma[39] in the fall that no one recognized at the time. It accounted for his dizziness.

Following the accident, his disposition soured and he sometimes acted out

37. Lanman, *Private Life of Webster*, p. 174; in his account of the accident to Fillmore he wrote that the man said, "Your mind is clear, and your life is safe." DW to Fillmore, May 12, 1852, in *W&S*, XVIII, 530.

38. Harvey, *Reminiscences*, pp. 424–425.

39. A subdural hematoma is a hemorrhage caused by a head injury in the underside of the dura mater or membranous layers that cover the brain. The blood is usually clotted or partly clotted. It can cause dizziness, confusion, nausea, headaches, and other symptoms that may come and go. The clot gets larger if untreated by surgical procedures and leads to death. Such surgical procedures were not available in 1852.

In making the statement that Webster suffered a subdural hematoma as a result of the accident, I have had the benefit of the medical opinion of Dr. Bernard H. Adelson of Winnetka, Illinois, senior attending physician and chief of the geriatric service of Evanston Hospital, Illinois, a professor of clinical medicine at the Northwestern University, and one of the Midwest's leading diagnosticians, who studied the details provided by the autopsy report completed after Webster's death. I am very grateful to Dr. Adelson for his invaluable assistance and opinion in this matter.

of character. In the speech in Boston he noticed with contempt a petition signed by some of the city's leading merchants and businessmen. With soaring sarcasm he described the burden of having to carry around such petitions and the relief he felt on finding he was not asked to give any money. "Oh, yes, I'll sign—I'll sign," he gleefully responded to the appeal. Then, incredibly, he read out the names of the businessmen who had signed the petition, one after another. When he finished, he threw down the petition with disdain, and the long sheet fell and unrolled upon the floor. George F. Hoar, a future U.S. senator from Massachusetts, who reported the incident, excused Webster's behavior as the consequence of age.

Over the next several weeks the effects of the accident became even more apparent as the statesman's physical and mental faculties showed a marked decline. His legs swelled, but he would not report it to his physician or his family. More and more President Fillmore was obliged to assume the duties of the secretary of state.[40]

Webster took another severe blow, this time emotional, when the Whig National Convention met at the Mechanics' Institute in Baltimore on June 16 to choose its presidential candidate. Two weeks earlier, in the same city, the Democrats had nominated the little-known brevetted Brigadier General Franklin Pierce of New Hampshire for President on the forty-ninth ballot, along with William R. King of Alabama for Vice President on a platform supporting the compromise measures of 1850. What had begun with General Andrew Jackson's election in 1828 had now become the essential fact of political life—namely, that a military reputation backed by a well-oiled and functioning party organization spelled electoral victory. Hardly anything else mattered. And Webster had neither.

When the Whig convention met on Wednesday, June 16, Francis Granger, former postmaster general in the administrations of Harrison and Tyler and a veteran politician, watched the Webster delegates operate and shook his head in disbelief. Many of the secretary's friends, he told Fillmore, "were Scott men at heart. The rest, Choate included, seemed to me to act like a parcel of school boys, waiting for the sky to fall, that they might catch larks. Such another collection, of very respectable, out of place gentlemen, was never seen."

That said it all: respectable gentleman, completely out of their depth and totally disconnected from the modern political world.[41]

Some 294 Whig delegates to the convention gathered in the Mechanics' Institute, where 3,000 spectators crowded into every space available to watch the proceedings. Over the speakers' platform hung a large transparency with the

40. DW to Fillmore, May 12, 1852, in W&S, XVIII, 530; Jeffries, "An Account of the Last Illness," p. 111; DW to Fillmore, May 9, 19, 1852, in W&S, XVIII, 528–532; DW to Fillmore, May 24, 1852, in Webster, ed., *Private Correspondence,* II, 532; Lanman, *Private Life of Webster,* pp. 174–175; Jeffries to Sleeper, November 20, 1852, in Van Tyne, ed., *Letters of Webster,* pp. 750–752; Harvey, *Reminiscences,* pp. 425–426; Hoar, *Autobiography,* I, 144. For Webster's speech in Faneuil Hall on May 22, see W&S, XIII, 510–522.

41. Granger to Fillmore, June 30, 1852, Fillmore Papers, Buffalo Historical Society.

words "Liberty and Union Now and Forever, One and Inseparable." It took the delegates two days to adopt an essentially conservative platform, much of it taken from a platform drawn up the evening before by southern delegates, which pledged the party to the principle that the central government was "of a limited character, and it is confined to exercise the powers expressly granted by the Constitution." It also affirmed the rights of the states, "the palladium of our liberties," the fundamental policies set down in Washington's Farewell Address, the necessity of obedience to the Constitution and the laws, strict economy in federal expenditures, and the importance of internal improvements. It specifically endorsed the compromise measures adopted in 1850, including the Fugitive Slave Law, hailing them as a "settlement in principle and substance of the dangerous and exciting questions which they embrace." The platform was adopted by the vote of 227 to 66, all the dissenters being northern Seward-Scott men. In view of this action, Webster's floor managers hoped to convince the delegates that only their candidate best represented this platform.

Suddenly, with the adoption of the platform, there arose a shout for "Choate! Choate!" Rufus Choate, probably the most outstanding orator in the hall, came forward and addressed the delegates, delivering a rousing speech in which he praised the "finality of the Compromise." "In the language of Daniel Webster," he said to shouts and applause, " 'Sink or swim, live or die, survive or perish, I am for that very declaration.' " The crowd loved every word and applauded wildly. After several more speeches by half a dozen delegates the balloting began late Friday evening, June 18.[42]

Fillmore, now endorsed by the dying Clay[43] but still reluctant to come out openly and fight for the nomination, had given his floor manager, George Babcock of New York, a letter of withdrawal to be used "whenever you may deem it proper." He relied on Babcock's "prudence and wisdom" in making the decision but warned him to "guard against any premature act or disclosure, which might embarrass my friends . . . you will not suffer my name to be dragged into a contest for a nomination, which I have never sought: do not now seek."[44]

The Scott forces, led by Seward (Weed, perhaps convinced that the Whigs faced a debacle in the fall election, had conveniently left for Europe) gathered momentum as the balloting began and did not hide the fact that they disapproved the Fugitive Slave Law, many of them having voted against the adoption of the platform. For southerners that meant Scott had to be defeated, and because Fillmore had signed all the compromise measures, they rallied behind him. At one point Babcock took an informal poll of his friends and found that they did not wish to abandon Fillmore, so he decided against withdrawing him. One of the President's floor managers then approached Choate and suggested

42. *National Intelligencer*, June 17, 19, 1852; Rayback, *Fillmore*, pp. 356–357.

43. Webster was "especially wounded when he was informed that Mr. Clay had advised the Southern delegates to support Mr. Fillmore." Poore, *Perley's Reminiscences*, I, 418. "It wounded me very much," Webster told a friend. Harvey, *Reminiscences*, p. 216.

44. Fillmore to Babcock, June 12, 1852, Fillmore Papers, Buffalo Historical Society.

that the Webster delegates swing to Fillmore. Unfortunately nothing came of it.[45]

On the first ballot, with 147 votes needed to nominate, the combined Fillmore and Webster forces showed their strength by taking a total of 162 votes to 131 for Scott. Of the 162, Fillmore took 133 and Webster a paltry 29.[46] The President captured all but 1 southern vote and received 1 vote each from Rhode Island, Connecticut, Vermont, Pennsylvania, Ohio, Wisconsin, and California; 7 from New York City; and 4 from Iowa. Webster had 11 votes from Massachusetts (2 went to Scott); 4 from New Hampshire", 3 each from Vermont, Connecticut, and Wisconsin; 2 from Rhode Island and New York; and 1 from California. Not a single vote from the South. Fillmore locked it up, and that hurt Webster deeply. It was in fact "mortifying to him." It "cut him to the soul." Scott took much of the West and the North. After six ballots in which nothing really changed the convention adjourned.

Had an agreement of some kind been worked out Fillmore would have taken the nomination on the next ballot. But nothing happened. "My friends will stand firm," Webster declared.[47]

He should have yielded. By standing "firm," he ensured Fillmore's defeat, as well as his own, and Scott's victory. A switch of 29 votes was infinitely easier to accomplish than a switch of 133. In actual fact any number of Fillmore delegates were more likely to vote for Scott once they were released. "I have the names of 14 others who are prepared to vote for Genl Scott the moment your name is withdrawn," wrote John Barney, representative from Maryland, to the President, "or any indication of an attempt to transfer your votes to Mr Webster." In Granger's opinion, "never more than 94 of the southern votes which sustained you, that could have been given to him [Webster]." Scott's floor managers had already approached several southern delegates with a promise that their candidate would accept the platform, and this, combined with Webster's perceived inability to win in the fall election, made a switch to the general far more reasonable.[48]

On Saturday the convention reconvened and after forty-six ballots without a decision adjourned until Monday. At this point a number of Fillmore's southern supporters, possibly including Robert Toombs and Alexander H. Stephens of Georgia, both Webster admirers, met the secretary's delegates "by special invitation" and made two proposals: "[B]ring Mr Webster, after one or two ballots, with a sufficient vote to the Maryland line"—that is, win forty additional votes from the North—and they, the southern delegates for Fillmore, would

45. Rayback, *Fillmore*, p. 358.

46. *National Intelligencer,* June 19, 1852.

47. *National Intelligencer,* June 19, 1852; DW to Daniel Jenifer, [June 19, 1852], in *Microfilm Edition,* F26/37083; Sargent, *Public Men and Events,* II, 389, 390.

48. Barney to Fillmore, June 20, 1852, Granger to Fillmore, June 30, 1852, Fillmore Papers, Buffalo Historical Society. Granger went on to say that "there was never a moment, when the withdrawal of your name could have been done, without creating a feeling of unkindness towards you." Fuess, *Webster,* II, 287–288, states that only 106 of Fillmore's strength of 130 could be counted as safe for Webster if the President were withdrawn from the race.

"promptly move" to Webster and provide the support necessary for nomination; if, however, Webster's friends could not get the added votes, then his managers would transfer his delegates to Fillmore.

Choate, Childs, Grinnell, Webb, and others readily accepted the first proposition, "but they did *not* say that they would meet us on the other proposition," reported Joseph Cobb. "This . . . gave offence to some" of the southerners and "caused them, I fear, to be too obstinate in afterwards withholding a complimentary vote for Mr Webster.[49]

The Webster delegates did what they could to find the additional votes, repeating again and again that Webster represented what the people wanted in their candidate. But none of the northerners would budge. New York and Maine, where the Webster men thought they could best find the additional votes, held fast to Scott. In desperation Webster's friends turned back to southerners for help. But not even an elaborate dinner or the impassioned appeals by Choate could move them.[50]

Devastated by the voting to date—he received the results via the telegraph—Webster denounced Fillmore's supporters for failing to understand that the safety of the Union and the perpetuation of the Constitution, "in its original character," depended on his nomination. Nor, obviously, did they appreciate his merits or service to the Union over four decades. It was they, not his supporters, who should yield. If the Union crumbled as a consequence, the fault would be theirs.

Critics contended that in not yielding to Fillmore, Webster had deserted his principles and ultimately helped destroy his party "out of spite."[51] But the criticism is groundless. He neither deserted his principles nor acted out of spite. Fillmore did not want the nomination, had not sought it, as he said, and had even asked Barney to tell his delegates to switch to Webster. He had triumph enough in the passage of the Whig platform, approving and confirming his actions with regard to the compromise. He felt vindicated. But to his request to withdraw his name, his friends "said no."[52] They believed that since the Webster managers had failed to bring their candidate to the "Maryland line," "the south could not dare to change its vote."[53]

Webster, on the other hand, lusted after the nomination. He had served his country long and well and in a very human way believed the nomination was due him. He should have known better and yielded, but by standing fast, at least for the first several days of the convention, he devoutly hoped that ultimately his worth and importance to the party would be acknowledged and result in his nomination.

49. Joseph Cobb to Fillmore, June 28, 1852, Fillmore Papers, Buffalo Historical Society.

50. Fuess, *Webster*, II, 288; Dalzell, *Webster and Nationalism*, pp. 269–274; Baxter, *Webster*, pp. 490–492.

51. DW to Daniel Jenifer, [June 19, 1852], in *Microfilm Edition*, F26/37083; Sargent, *Public Men and Events*, II, 389; Dalzell, *Webster and Nationalism*, p. 273.

52. Rayback, *Fillmore*, p. 357.

53. Cobb to Fillmore, June 28, 1852, Fillmore Papers, Buffalo Historical Society.

On Saturday, June 19, after the convention had adjourned, Barney returned to Washington and went to see Webster. Quite frankly he explained to the secretary that he could not be nominated, given his pitiful showing in the balloting, and that he must "instruct his friends to vote for [Fillmore] otherwise Genl Scott will be nominated."

Webster sat and listened. He "seemed overwhelmed by the humiliating position in which he stood before the World." Finally he spoke. After "40 years devoted to the public service," he groaned, and all he had to show for it was barely more than two dozen votes out of over 290 cast. How mortifying.

"He is prostrate," Barney said. He desires nothing more than to remain in his present position. "You are by nature generous," Barney told the President, "& can now afford to be magnanimous."

After a moment Webster turned to his visitor and burst out with, "All I ask is a decent vote that I may retire without disgrace." Thereupon Barney struck back with a stinging " 'It was a fearful responsibility you are about to assume of defeating the *true* Whig party by delaying action.' "

No friend advised me "to act forthwith," came the response.

"You have no other friends," answered the delegate. And with that Barney departed, leaving Webster "wounded & offended."[54]

Alone, defeated, and humiliated, the secretary slowly concluded that continuing to stand "firm" only guaranteed further insult. He consulted with his son; his brother-in-law, James Paige; George Abbot, a friend who clerked in the State Department; and one or two others and finally decided to concede. As Fletcher boarded the "cars" on Monday, June 21, to return to Baltimore with his father's concession, Webster wrote to Fillmore, explaining his actions. "I have sent a communication to Baltimore, this morning to have an end put to the pending controversy. I think it most probable you will be nominated before 1 o'clock. But this is opinion merely. Yrs. D.W."[55]

Fillmore responded the same day. "I had intimated to my friends, who left last evening and this morning, a strong desire to have my name withdrawn, which I assume will be done unless the knowledge of your communication, shall prevent it."[56]

It all seemed so absurd. A clear majority of delegates who had approved the Compromise of 1850 could not control the convention and by default allowed it to slip away to those who preached a "higher law," even if it might mean the end of the Union as they knew it, one never to be "reconstructed in its original character."

"It's a trial of endurance," commented George Templeton Strong, "between the Websterites and the Fillmoreites, and it is like to end by the faction that's soonest worn out going over to the other side." With all the "intriguing, caucusing, bragging, and betting" going on and wearing everyone out, Strong

54. Barney to Fillmore, June 25, 1852, Fillmore Papers, Buffalo Historical Society.

55. DW to Fillmore, June [1852], in *W&S*, XVI, 647.

56. Fillmore to DW, June 21, [1852], in *PC*, VII, 332.

could not understand how the two factions were able to hold out so long in ninety-degree temperatures.[57]

On Monday, June 21, as the delegates resumed voting with their forty-seventh ballot, Webster showed no gain. He remained locked in position, although he gained 1 vote on the forty-eighth and forty-ninth ballots. Neither the Fillmore nor the Webster delegates would yield to the other. A stalemate. On the fifty-second ballot Webster lost 3 votes, which went to Scott, and that brought on the final disaster. The Pennsylvania delegates switched from Fillmore to Scott and on the very next vote the general was nominated. He received 158 votes, Fillmore 114, and Webster 21. The convention then nominated William A. Graham of North Carolina for Vice President.[58]

Southerners later stated that they were willing to give Webster "a complimentary vote," on account of his past services. "He is very dear to the hearts of our people. . . . But his friends are responsible both for the nomination (if Gen Scott is unwelcome to their constituents) and for the absence of a complimentary vote to Mr Webster."[59]

Before the delegates adjourned, Duncan of Louisiana offered a resolution:

Resolved, That second, and only second, to the illustrious Clay, in the estimation of the Whigs of Louisiana and the Union of the United States, in his connection with the past struggles of their party and with the Compromise measures, stands the name of Daniel Webster; whose fame fills the Union; whose patriotism embraces the length and breadth of the land; whose pure self-devotion . . . proved that he knew no North, no South; and who will at all times be named with praise in every land and on every sea in which the banner of the Union may be unfurled.

"Prolonged and hearty cheering" echoed around the hall when Duncan completed his reading. Then Starkie of Mississippi rose and provided the delegates with "a brief but eloquent eulogium on the character and services of Mr. Webster." He concluded by introducing Mississippi's resolution, which expressed the abiding confidence of the Whigs in "his [Webster's] wisdom, patriotism, and integrity, and pledging to him the everlasting gratitude of the American people." This was also greeted with prolonged cheers, and both resolutions were adopted by acclamation.[60]

If the resolutions were meant as a consolation prize for failing to nominate him, Webster wanted none of it. That evening a group of well-lubricated Whigs marched to Webster's residence in Washington to serenade him. "The crowd was dense; the music delicious; the cheers inspiring." Some time elapsed before the secretary, wearing a long dressing gown, appeared. The brokenhearted Webster looked "sad and weary," like "another Coriolanus." He mumbled a few words, said nothing about Scott, and ended by muttering that he would sleep well that evening and rise like the lark in the morning. "There was an inexpress-

57. Strong, *Diary*, II, 96–97.

58. Joseph B. Cobb to Fillmore, June 28, 1852, Fillmore Papers, Buffalo Historical Society; Schlesinger, ed., *History of U.S. Political Parties*, I, 485–487, 490.

59. Joseph B. Cobb to Fillmore, June 28, 1852, Fillmore Papers, Buffalo Historical Society.

60. Schlesinger, ed., *History of U.S. Political Parties*, I, 490.

ible sadness in his words." The serenaders thought they had heard "a funeral sermon preached to them. Thenceforth Mr. Webster was a disappointed, heart-stricken man, and he retired to Marshfield profoundly disgusted with the insincerity of politicians."[61]

It was sad to see what the convention did to Webster. It showed on his face, in his voice, in his behavior. It showed "in the lessened interest he took in public affairs." It showed in his "general depression of spirits." And he made no attempt to hide his feelings. He felt rejected and defeated.[62]

A friend from New York, Charles A. Statson, saw Webster standing alone shortly after the convention and looking "feeble and very unwell." He walked up to the secretary, put his hand on Webster's breast, and said, "I hope all is right here."

"Yes, sir," came the reply. "I am too near God to have a single heart burning against a human creature on the earth, but I have a chagrin as profound as my entire nature, and it is that after having performed my duty to my southern brethren, *they had neither the courage or kindness to place me on the record of that convention.* I do not say I did not want the nomination, but I would rather have had *their record* than the nomination."[63]

Over the next several weeks he thanked his many campaign workers for "their unparalleled efforts" on his behalf. But the bitterness always peeked through his letters of appreciation. "The result of the Baltimore convention is certainly bad enough. It shows a great deal of folly, and a great deal of infidelity."[64]

His friend Edward Everett tried to put it into proper perspective for him, even though he could not do it himself. Even if you had won the nomination and the election, Everett said, "what could the Presidency add to your happiness or fame?" Consider all the "second rate and wholly incompetent persons" who have held the office, and then remember James Madison. "The example of Mr Madison shows that even repeated election to the office is of very little moment to a great constitutional statesman."[65]

In retrospect it is obvious that Webster could never have attained the presidency on his own. Only by running for the vice presidency with Harrison would he have won the prize he so desperately craved. And it could have been his. But unlike Theodore Roosevelt and Lyndon Johnson, he refused to accept second place to a man he regarded as his inferior. His sense of pride and self-worth barred any possibility of his acceding first place to Tippecanoe—or Old Rough and Ready, for that matter. He was a victim of his all-consuming pride.

61. Poore, *Perley's Reminiscences*, I, 418; Forney, *Anecdotes of Public Men*, pp. 11–12; Curtis, *Webster*, II, 622.

62. Sargent, *Public Men and Events*, II, 391.

63. Account of an interview with DW by Stetson, June 1852, in Van Tyne, ed., *Letters of Webster*, pp. 531–532.

64. DW to Webb, June 22, in *PC*, VII, 332–333; DW to Blatchford, June 22, 1852, in *W&S*, XVI, 657.

65. Everett to DW, June 22, 1852, in *PC*, VII, 333.

44

"That Voice, Alas! We Shall Hear No More Forever"

WEARY, ILL, heartbroken, and burdened by self-pity, Webster left Washington on July 6, after attending the funeral services in the Capitol for Henry Clay, who had died on June 29, and returned to his Elms Farm in the small town of Franklin, where he had been born, "a spot of absolute quiet." "I cannot think of remaining in Washington through August and September," he confessed. Along the way a number of Whigs assured him of their undying loyalty and swore they would never support Scott. They had already considered forming a third, a "Union," party, and expressed a hope that he would consent to be their candidate. Edward Curtis told him that if the Massachusetts delegates openly charged the Baltimore convention with deception or fraud, "it would not then be unfit for *yourself* to lead us all to a proclamation of opposition to Scott."[1]

Still bitter and angry, Webster refused to commit himself. Instead he praised the Democratic candidate from New Hampshire, Franklin Pierce. A great many people wondered whether he would publicly declare against Scott and, if he did, whether the Whig party would survive.

To help dispel some of Webster's gloom, Curtis gave him some very good news when he said that "a gentleman of considerable wealth and influence" asked him "privately" how much it would take "to put Mr. Webster *out of debt*," that "he would like to take a part in an effort to relieve you." Curtis replied that he did not know but would ask Webster to supply the answer by "*return* mail." It is not known what the secretary said in response, but by October some thirty-one hundred dollars were obtained and turned over to him.[2]

The wretched man returned to Franklin by way of Philadelphia, New York, and Boston. When he reached Boston, something extraordinary happened: a

---

1. DW to Fillmore, July 13, 1852, in Webster, ed., *Private Correspondence,* II, 535; DW to James Paige, July 14, Curtis to DW, July 12, 1852, in *PC,* VII, 337, 336.

2. Curtis to DW, July 12, 1852, in *PC,* VII, 336–337 and editorial note.

public outpouring of devotion and veneration to demonstrate that no matter what had happened in Baltimore, he remained their Godlike Daniel. With a sense of resignation he consented to attend a reception in his honor on July 9, and it proved to be "by far the most impressive and touching demonstration ever made by that people toward Mr. Webster."[3]

Virtually the entire city turned out to greet him. A procession was formed as an escort, and the streets were brightly decorated with flags and buntings and transparencies. A military contingent, "larger than ever before appeared in New England," formed without being asked or invited. Every shop and store closed, and Boston "put on the garb of a national holiday." All the streets and thoroughfares were thronged with people, "multitudes of whom were strangers." The railroad brought in hundreds of visitors, who had come to witness the gala event. Busts and portraits of Webster were displayed on balconies and on the walls of houses fronting the parade route. Every form of visual representation of the great man was proudly shown, as though the people were professing a religious faith. And in the heat and humidity of an unusually hot summer day they waited for him.

Webster had stopped off in Roxbury to visit his friend Samuel H. Walley. There, at half past three o'clock, he entered a barouche drawn by six gray horses. Accompanied by the arrangements committee in two separate carriages and escorted by the National Lancers, he headed toward Boston. A cannon announced his departure, followed by fieldpieces stationed in Roxbury. At the same moment the bells of Roxbury and Boston began to peal.

When the entourage reached Boston, General Tyler, the chief marshal, and General Edmands greeted the secretary. Then they headed for the Common,[4] passing the thousands lined along the streets, in doorways, on balconies, and at windows. The masses had "come forth," cheering and screaming and showering him with bouquets and garlands "as if to bestow an unwonted and unparalleled ovation upon one who deserved the purest feelings of their hearts." The natural reserve of New Englanders had totally disappeared. Women held up their infants "that they might say, in after-life, they had seen the Defender of the Constitution on his triumphal entry into Boston."

A continuous roar of voices and the fluttering of handkerchiefs marked every step along the way. Not until seven o'clock did the procession reach the Common, entering the Charles Street gate at the foot of Beacon Street. Webster and his escort alighted from their carriages and took their places on a platform specially erected for the occasion. The troops were drawn up on the parade ground at the base of the hill and provided a salute. Barriers were removed, and the crowd poured in and surrounded the platform. J. Thomas Stevenson gave an appropriate tribute to the hero, linking him to George Washington and

---

3. Curtis, *Webster,* II, 628.

4. The route in Boston went through Washington, Tremont, West, Bedford, Summer, Washington, State, Commercial, Cornhill, Court, Tremont, and Beacon streets to the Common.

recounting the tremendous public services he had rendered the nation. "We welcome you to the heart of hearts of a Commonwealth which knows you. . . . And, as we welcome you, it is 'an hundred thousand welcomes.' "

Deeply moved and with tears in his eyes, Webster responded with a gracious and poignant speech in which he extolled Massachusetts and its unique contributions to liberty, the Constitution, and the Union. He had known John Adams, Robert Treat Paine, Elbridge Gerry, and other great men of the revolutionary period, he said, but he regrettably "never saw John Hancock or Samuel Adams or James Otis." He relived some of the moments when he first came to Boston in 1804. He had found nothing but rewards and honors. If his years of service as a congressman "be satisfactory to this great and ancient and glorious State of Massachusetts—whether in riches or in poverty, or in health or in sickness—I am rewarded." Massachusetts had honored him by calling him to its service. And "I honored her, and still honor her, if not as the first among the first of all the true, patriotic Union States. . . . If she did not go before all others, I aver no others went before her." He ended by thanking all for what they had done this day. As for himself, he "was nothing but a pains-taking, hard-working civilian, giving my life and my health and my strength to the maintenance of the Constitution; and the upholding, according to the best of my ability, under the providence of God, the liberties of my country."[5]

This outpouring of devotion and respect buoyed Webster's spirits tremendously. It helped ease some of the sting of the Baltimore rejection. He needed this reassurance of his worth and importance to the people of his state. Unfortunately it was never matched in other states of the country.

But this demonstration gave "regular" Whigs supporting Scott some concern. They feared it could lead to a "National Union Convention" to nominate Webster.[6] Never fear, the *National Intelligencer* and other Whig papers assured their readers, the secretary's speech was meant "to cause the fire of liberty and patriotism and a hearty loyalty to the Union to burn brighter than ever in the throbbing hearts before him." He said nothing about the presidency, the paper reported, and any effort to call a Union convention "meets no favor from true Whigs of the North, nor of any other section."[7]

5. An official account, published by the committee of arrangements, in Curtis, *Webster*, II, 629–639.

6. Any number of Whigs had written to him expressing their dissatisfaction with the nominations of the two parties and requesting that he permit his name to be offered by an "opposition Convention." John L. Stephens to DW, August 3, 1952, in *PC*, VII, 341. Stephens was the half brother of Alexander H. Stephens. One man suggested the following ticket:

Union Constitutional Candidate for President
Daniel Webster of Massachusetts

for vice president
Alexander Stevens [*sic*] of Georgia

Charles Fletcher to DW, August 17, 1852, ibid., VII, 347. See also Richard J. Mapes to DW, October 10, 1852, in Van Tyne, ed., *Letters of Webster*, pp. 539–540.

7. July 13, 17, 1852.

But that was the problem, the Scott adherents angrily responded. Webster said nothing about the presidency, and by his silence was slowly but surely destroying Scott's candidacy and with it the entire Whig party. They demanded that he speak out and declare his unwavering support for the national ticket. But he did not. He kept his silence.

Following the celebration, Webster left for Franklin, where he thought seriously about resigning his office and possibly going abroad. There were "so many causes of vexation, & humiliation, growing out of the events connected with the convention, that I am pretty much decided & determined, to leave the Department early in August." As he looked over the valley lying in the bend of the river and enjoyed the green fields of his farm, shaded with elms and maples and ringed with high ranges of hills on both sides of the river, he reveled in the peace and contentment of this rural life. He looked out at the site of one of the last forts built on the northern frontier to protect the settlers from the attacks of Indians, and he remembered the story of Mrs. Call and how she died and how his father had purchased the Call residence. "Mrs. Call's murder by the Indians, a hundred years ago," he wrote the President, "has little to do with legislation or diplomacy." But it was amid these "scenes of memory I am apt to talk, when there is anybody present to talk to, and to write when alone." Why return to Washington, where he knew his diplomatic efforts were proving fruitless? Why not "go abroad, or into obscurity"?[8]

Throughout July Webster pondered the idea of going abroad. He reckoned it would improve his health and possibly "avoid my annual catarrh." Prior to his departure from Washington the President, knowing how he felt and keenly aware of the decline in his ability to conduct the affairs of his department, had offered him the mission to England since Abbott Lawrence had resigned on May 14 to take effect on October 1. But once he had the offer he had second thoughts. He felt disinclined to brave the Atlantic Ocean in late fall or early winter. Besides, "I have been some years in a position to give instructions on Diplomatic matters, not to receive them." Also, as an unsuccessful candidate for the presidency "I did not feel like taking employment, or seeking shelter to any other employment." And, it was certain, anyone who took the post would be recalled in a matter of months when Fillmore stepped down on March 4, 1853. "The Party will demand this, whatever may be the personal inclinations of the incoming President." Finally he had a personal reason, the opposition of his wife. So he thanked the President for the offer but politely declined.[9]

Nor did Webster relish the idea of returning to Washington in the fall to

8. DW to Fillmore, July 13, 1852, in Webster, ed., *Private Correspondence*, II, 535–536; DW to Fletcher Webster, July 4, 1852, in *PC*, VII, 334.

9. DW to Everett, August 14, 1852, in *PC*, VII, 343; DW to Fillmore, July 25, 1852, in *Microfilm Edition*, F27/37352. Fillmore subsequently appointed Joseph R. Ingersoll to the post. Webster had begun thinking about retirement and again contemplated writing a history of the Constitution and the Washington administration. Abbot to Everett, April 12, [1854], and outline of a history of Washington's administration in Van Tyne, ed., *Letters of Webster*, pp. 702–708.

"live there as a private man for the Winter," although he knew that his absence from his post " would no doubt be complained of," as indeed it was. The thought occurred to him that he might conduct the department from Boston. At least he would be " nearer my Kith & Kin." The idea itself showed how disturbed and confused his thinking had become in the past few months. Conducting State Department business from Boston! It was preposterous.[10]

Frequently he lapsed into reverie. More and more he contemplated his own mortality. His state of mind is revealed somewhat in what he said at a dinner party he gave in the Astor House for some of his New York friends. Ill, weary, and morose, he sat silently until one of the men said to him: "Mr. Webster, I want you to tell me what was the most important thought that ever occupied your mind."

The great man stirred from his reverie, passed his hand over his forehead, and in a low tone replied: "The most important thought that ever occupied my mind was that of my individual responsibility to God!"[11]

The steady decline of Webster's ability to function as secretary of state became even more evident with the final diplomatic issues he had to face. Ironically and unhappily, one of them involved a fisheries dispute with Great Britain, and his diplomacy can only be described as disastrous.

The difficulty over fishing rights went back to the first treaty the United States ever signed with Great Britain. It came up again during the negotiations of the treaty concluding the War of 1812. Then a convention of 1818 compounded the problem by giving the United States various fishing rights around the coasts, bays, and creeks of certain parts of Newfoundland and Labrador. In return the United States renounced any right to fish or cure fish within a three-mile limit of the coasts, bays, creeks, and harbors of British North America except for the specified areas.

In September 1850 the British complained about the need to establish a reciprocal trade agreement between Canada and the United States, but Webster shrugged it off. Such reciprocity "seems much more advantageous to Canada than to us," he sniffed. Perhaps Congress "may take a different view."[12]

Congress of course did nothing. Thereupon the British offered to open the St. Lawrence River to American navigation and allow American fishermen access to the coasts of Nova Scotia and New Brunswick in exchange for a "free interchange of all natural productions, not only between Canada and the United States, but between the United States and all Her Majesty's North American Provinces."[13]

The secretary did not respond. Then, on July 5, 1852, while he vacationed in Franklin and pondered Fillmore's offer of the mission to England, the British

10. DW to James Paige, July 14, 1852, in *PC*, VII, 337.

11. Harvey, *Reminiscences*, pp. 403–404.

12. DW to Henry L. Bulwer, September 14, 1850, in *PD*, II, 683.

13. Butler to DW, June 24, 1851, ibid., II, 683–685.

minister to the United States, John F. Crampton, abruptly informed Webster that his government had stationed a naval force to protect Canadian fishing grounds from encroachment by American fishermen.[14] Furthermore, the British interpreted the three-mile coastal limitation as extending from "Headland to Headland," effectively excluding American fishermen from the Bay of Fundy and Chaleur Bay, which were more than six miles wide from their mouths.[15] The United States insisted that the three-mile limit should follow a line around all the curves, inlets, recesses, and indentations of the coast, not headland to headland. Obviously the British meant the move as a means of provoking the Americans into breaking the stalemate over the reciprocal trade matter.

For Webster, personally, any interference with fishing rights directly involved New Englanders. He asked Crampton to meet with him in Boston, rather than in Washington, a request that provoked critical comment, and he informed the President that he had prepared "a paper which will appear" in the Boston *Courier* and in the Washington *National Intelligencer* to explain the American position. "I hope you will approve of it." He stressed that this was "a very serious business," but incredibly, he did not wait to receive the President's approval for his "paper" before rushing it into print.[16]

Anyone but Fillmore would have dismissed him immediately or administered a proper tongue-lashing. But the President understood his secretary's mental state, so he said nothing. However, when Webster's "paper" appeared in Boston, Washington, New York and elsewhere, it staggered Fillmore.

In an editorial preceding his paper, the secretary stated that "the process of seizing American fishermen" had "already begun, and all who venture within the waters covered by the new pretensions of the British Cabinet, will be captured and condemned." But "fortunately for our country, it has not *yet* been deprived of the invaluable services of Mr. Webster."

After that self-congratulatory bit of foolishness came the official "paper." In it he explained that a recent change of ministry accounted for the new British policy. "Vessels of war" were expected along the coast of British North America "when, no doubt, seizure will begin to be made."

Not content with this undiplomatic approach, he proceeded to commit an even more incredible blunder. "It was undoubtedly an oversight in the Convention of 1818, to make so large a concession to England, since the United States had usually considered that those vast inlets or recesses of the ocean ought to be open to American fishermen, as freely as the sea itself, to within three marine miles of the shore." This action by the British of cutting off "valuable fall fishing to American fishermen . . . may end in the destruction of human life, in the

14. Crampton to DW, July 5, 1852, ibid., II, 685–686; Wilbur D. Jones, *The American Problem in British Diplomacy, 1841–1861* (Athens, Ga., 1974), p. 109ff.

15. Lord Malmesbury to Crampton, August 10, 1852, in *PD*, II, 706–711.

16. DW to Fillmore, July 17, 1852, ibid., II, 687.

involvement of the government in questions of a very serious nature, threatening the peace of the two countries."[17]

What he had done was concede the British position! And he threatened retaliation.

The publication caused a firestorm of criticism and controversy, particularly in Congress. Such Anglophobes as Senator Lewis Cass denounced the "paper." It "is a mistake," he thundered. "It is in fact saying to the fishermen, 'There is great doubt in regard to this question. Take care how you go there until that doubt is removed.' This is not the way to meet such a question as this. It is not proper to meet it by throwing out doubts to the country and to the world." Obviously, said Senator Andrew P. Butler of South Carolina, "Great Britain has done this with a view to bring this subject to a negotiation; I confess this it is a singular form, in which they have proceeded, to reach that result." Senator Solon Borland of Arkansas angrily rebuked Webster for making "the matter one of newspaper publication and popular discussion. Now I ask if this subject . . . be of sufficient importance to call forth the Secretary of State in public proclamations to warn the people of impending danger . . . what has withheld his hand from communicating all his information in regard to it to the two Houses of Congress, who alone are competent to deal with the question?" He reminded his colleagues that during the War of 1812 "the present distinguished Secretary of State, then a member of the other House, denounced and opposed the war, and used terms of reproach against those who were engaged in it and . . . uttered that notable exclamation, 'Let them starve and freeze!' " Isaac Toucey of Connecticut insisted that Webster should have sent a naval force instead of a public notice, adding that the secretary had abjectly surrendered American rights to the British. Within the Senate several fire-eating patriots spoke about using armed force to maintain American rights, contending that there had not been a worse confrontation with the British since the War of 1812. "Our fleet ought to be sent there—and it can be sent with but one object," Senator Thomas G. Pratt of Maryland cried, "—with instructions . . . precisely similar to those sent on the part of Great Britain."[18]

But Webster had his defenders. Surprisingly Seward was one of the strongest. Since Borland and others wanted to draw their attacks from Webster's past, he declared, just remember that the secretary also upheld American maritime rights for years, most notably in 1842, and his record of achievement had been "spread over every page of your annals for near half a century."

What senators found most difficult to dismiss or forgive was that Webster had granted Britain's contention about the three-mile limit from headland to headland. "Here the whole is surrendered," roared Senator Pierre Soulé of Louisiana; "there is no escape from the admission. IT WAS AN OVERSIGHT TO MAKE SO LARGE A CONCESSION TO ENGLAND!" Webster had indeed written

17. Editorial on the fisheries question, July 19, 1852, ibid., II, 689–694.

18. *Congressional Globe*, 32d Congress, 1st Session, pp. 1890–1897.

hastily and rashly, and his concession would plague American foreign policy for many years to come.[19]

Outside the walls of this angry Senate, calmer voices could be heard. "To suppose *a war* upon such a question," editorialized the *National Intelligencer,* "would be to suppose that the rulers of both nations had parted with their senses."[20]

It was bad enough that Webster remained in Franklin to compose important state papers without the benefit and advice of the President or of the cabinet, bad enough that he proposed conducting negotiations with the British minister in Boston, and worse that Fillmore had been obliged to appoint William S. Hunter, Jr., acting secretary of state during Webster's absence, but for him to suggest, as he did, that the President send a naval force to Newfoundland "to look after the disturbances among the fishermen" and do it through Hunter showed he no longer commanded the ability to serve as secretary of state.

The President felt obliged to rebuke him, but he did it gently, very gently. When you meet with Crampton in Boston, he wrote, I trust you will reach an agreement that will "allay the present excitement and prevent any bloodshed. I would suggest that you unite in a publication in which you should express your regrets that any misunderstanding had arisen between our fishermen . . . and the colonial subjects of Great Britain." Your publication in the *Courier* has been "misunderstood, and has consequently created unnecessary alarm." He said that he would wait until the secretary and Crampton had reached some agreement from which proper instructions might be drawn before he "ordered the vessel [the *Mississippi* steam frigate] to proceed to that destination [Newfoundland]."[21]

Fillmore's cabinet members insisted that Webster must return to Washington at once. Exchanging letters and telegrams was hardly the way to conduct the nation's foreign affairs. Convinced that he must take a stronger hand, Fillmore wrote Webster again and stated flatly that "it was impossible to settle these matters by telegraph, and though I regretted to trouble you, I thought the whole matter ought at once to be transferred to the seat of government . . . without delay."[22]

Webster already understood the general criticism about his absence, and after meeting with Crampton, "who is disposed to do anything to keep the peace," and then bringing him to Marshfield for a visit, he wrote the President before receiving Fillmore's last letter, stating that he intended "to proceed to Washington, just as soon as I shall have health and strength enough to encounter the journey and the heat."[23]

---

19. *Ibid.,* appendix, 905, 913–917; editorial note, *PD,* II, 675. "I have been informed of the flare-up in the Senate, yesterday respecting the Fisheries," Webster wrote the President. "I have very considerable alarm on this subject." DW to Fillmore, August 4, 1852, in Van Tyne, ed., *Letters of Webster,* p. 535.

20. July 22, 1852.

21. Fillmore to DW, July 20, 1852, in *PD,* II, 694–696.

22. Fillmore to DW, July 25, 1852, ibid., II, 697.

23. DW to Fillmore, July 24, 1852, ibid., II, 696.

Webster and Crampton left for Marshfield on July 25, and when the train reached Kingston, about nine miles from his home, they found thousands of people waiting to greet and escort them to his estate. For miles on either side of the road, women and children shouted their greetings. "Garlands without number were scattered along his pathway." Most of the men joined the procession of more than 150 vehicles riding behind Webster and Crampton. When they arrived at his home, Seth Sprague, who headed the welcoming committee, gave a speech in which he thanked his neighbor for what he had done for agriculture, "the science of cultivating the earth," for the "valuable animals you have . . . imported and raised to improve our flocks and herds." You have taught us to appreciate the importance of science to the farmer, and "we hope that you may live long to teach us the art of using the ploughshare instead of the sword, and the pruning-hook rather than the spear."

Webster delighted in this unexpected expression of appreciation and affection from his neighbors and thanked them "from the bottom of my heart." He said his years at Marshfield among friends and neighbors had been happy ones. "I know not of an unkind thing done, or word spoken to me or mine, or to any one near or dear to me." He would soon be retiring from public life, he declared, and since his life had been devoted to upholding the Constitution and liberty and the rights of his country, he assured the crowd that he would protect the rights of fishermen in the present controversy with Great Britain. This despite the presence of Crampton. "To use a Marblehead phrase, they shall be protected hook and line, and bob and sinker." The United States will not "allow our vessels to be seized. . . . No, no, no!" He regretted that his health did not permit his presence in Washington, but he needed relaxation, and as soon as his strength had been restored, he would return to his post.

Everyone present agreed that the affair at Marshfield "was grand and enthusiastic beyond description." They thought his speech was "beautiful and appropriate," but some sensed a "tone of sadness in all he uttered." It was the last speech Daniel Webster ever gave in public.

After the crowd had gone, Webster entered his house totally exhausted. He threw himself into his favorite chair, the so-called Garibaldi chair,[24] and "for a moment his head fell upon his breast, as if completely overcome." He looked up and glanced at a portrait of his daughter Julia. Suddenly he broke down in tears "like one whose heart was broken." *O, I am so thankful to be here! If I could only have my will, never, never would I again leave this home.*[25]

While at Marshfield, Crampton had several discussions with Webster, and although they did not resolve the problem, the British minister agreed to write the provincial authorities in Canada "to desist from all annoyance of American Fisherman, until further advice." Webster informed the President of this break-

---

24. It was an ornate walnut chair with a tooled leather back and seat said to have been given him by Garibaldi.

25. Curtis, *Webster,* II, 643–647.

through and added, "I do not know that there is anything else which we can do at present."[26]

The President was not altogether happy with Webster's "hook- line, bob-and-sinker" speech at Marshfield, but he did decide to send the frigate *Mississippi* to the fishing grounds "to give protection to our fishermen."[27]

Webster finally left Marshfield and arrived in Washington on August 9, but he stayed less than a month. Although sunburned, he clearly showed both a physical and mental decline. But if his behavior during this unfortunate affair showed haste, carelessness, and poor judgment, the British had also acted precipitously and foolishly in trying to break the stalemate.

Concerned about the unfavorable reaction in America, the ministry underwent a complete change of heart, and Lord Malmesbury, the foreign secretary, instructed Crampton to inform Webster that British action had never been intended to give offense. The instructions also strongly implied that the headland position would not be enforced and American fishermen would not be excluded from the bays beyond the three marine miles from shore. In short, the ministry abandoned the position taken on July 5.[28] Nevertheless the problem did rise again in the future to disturb Anglo-American relations, and Webster's unfortunate *Courier* "paper" in conceding the British position was used by them with telling effect.

But if he mishandled the fisheries issue, he truly bungled his negotiations with Peru over the Lobos Islands.[29] And it all centered on the problem of the nitrogen-rich dung from sea birds.

Guano became the fertilizer of choice throughout the United States in the 1840s, and the trade brought Peru, which controlled its extraction and sale, approximately forty million dollars a year. It was found principally on several islands, the Chincha and Lobos Islands, well off the coast of Peru, and was sold in the United States on consignment from the Felipe Barreda & Brothers Company. This fertilizer became so popular that Americans, annoyed at the monopoly held by the Peruvian government and the high prices charged for it, urged Congress and the State Department to secure better terms.[30]

Webster, who used guano extensively on his Marshfield property, became actively involved in the problem when Captain James C. Jewett of the *Philomela*, involved in the guano trade with a silent partner, Alfred G. Benson, a New York merchant, contacted the State Department and asked whether the Lobos Islands could be exploited by American citizens since they lay well beyond the

---

26. DW to Fillmore, July 25, 1852, in *PD*, II, 696–697; Curtis, *Webster*, II, 649–650.

27. Fillmore to DW, July 29, 1852, in *PD*, II, 702.

28. Malmesbury to Crampton, August 10, Malmesbury to Abbott Lawrence, August 13, 1852, ibid., II, 706–711.

29. See Kenneth E. Shewmaker, " 'Untaught Diplomacy': Daniel Webster and the Lobos Islands Controversy," *Diplomatic History*, I (Fall 1977), pp. 321–340.

30. *PD*, II, 713–715.

three-mile limit. In responding to this letter, and with Fillmore's knowledge and approval, Webster committed a colossal error because of his ignorance of the history of the region. He stated that his department was not aware that the islands "were either discovered or occupied by Spain or by Peru," that their distance from the continents was "greater than is necessary to make them a dependency," and that "it is quite probable that Benjamin Morrell, Junior, who, as Master of the Schooner Wasp, of New York, visited those Islands in September, 1823, may justly claim to have been their discoverer." Under the circumstances Webster believed it "the duty of this government to protect citizens of the United States who may visit the Lobos Islands for the purpose of obtaining guano." Furthermore he would suggest to the secretary of the navy that "a vessel of war" be sent to the islands to protect American citizens who wish to obtain the guano from "molestation."[31]

Webster's near-mental and physical collapse accounts for this appallingly witless letter. Secretary of the Navy William A. Graham not only issued the necessary order but assured Jewett personally that the navy would protect him. Benson and Jewett then proceeded to outfit a veritable fleet of ships, equipped and manned by more than a hundred workers, with the lead ship, *Sarah Chase,* prepared for battle (four nine-pound cannons, small arms, cutlasses, and a large quantity of canister, round shot, and powder), if necessary.

Then, on August 21, Webster completely reversed himself. He wrote Jewett again and said that since his last letter he had been informed that the Peruvian government claimed jurisdiction over the islands and in 1842 had issued two decrees forbidding foreign vessels, "on pain of confiscation," from removing any guano without a license. Your ships, Webster continued, must not use their arms to resist the Peruvians. Such would be a "private war which can never be countenanced by this Government." Accordingly the naval commander of the Pacific will be directed to abstain from protecting any American vessels that violate the Peruvian decrees. Placing the blame on Jewett, Webster concluded by stating that the captain's original letter "had a tendency to mislead us."[32]

Just prior to sending this letter, Webster had received a strongly worded protest from Juan Ygnacio de Osma, Peruvian minister to the United States, who had heard of Jewett's expedition and denounced it as "a clear violation" of international law. Morrell had not discovered the islands, as Webster supposed. They had always been part of Peru, going back to the ancient Incas. Osma then declared that his government was prepared to resist any attempt to violate its rights and laws, and he protested U.S. encouragement and protection of the

---

31. Jewett to DW, June 2, DW to Fillmore, June 5, DW to Jewett, June 5, 1852, in *PC*, II, 736–738. Fillmore later said that he could not remember having approved the letter. Fillmore to DW, September 19, 1852, ibid., II, 775–777.

32. Jewett to DW, August 16, with enclosure, DW to Jewett, August 21, 1852, in *PD*, II, 756–760; Graham to Commodore Charles S. McCauley, June 16, 1852, in *Senate Documents*, serial 621, no. 109, part 2, p. 2.

Jewett expedition "as an attack on the sovereignty of Peru and as an act of unjustifiable hostility against said Republic."[33]

Finally Fillmore took a hand in the dispute. After receiving a copy of one of Osma's earlier notes, the President had already begun to have doubts about the position Webster had adopted. He informed Webster that he wanted "to take no position on the subject that shall be either unjust before the world, or from which I may be compelled to recede hereafter."[34] Defensive on hearing that the President would "consider the subject further," the secretary thrashed about to find evidence to support his contentions and enlisted the aid of his friend Hiram Ketchum, who had offered to obtain testimony in New London, New Bedford, Nantucket, and Sag Harbor to prove that American citizens had "undisputed possession" of the islands for the last fifty years. In desperation Webster pleaded: "If there is any proof of that, for Mercy's sake let us have it." Unfortunately for him no such proof existed.[35]

Meanwhile Webster tried to hold off Osma by asserting that the sovereignty over the Lobos Islands had yet to be decided. However, he added that the United States was "prepared to give due consideration to all facts tending to show possession" by Peru and was willing to continue negotiations on the matter until the case could be proved one way or another. Under the circumstances, the U.S. chargé d'affaires in Lima and the naval forces of the Pacific would be informed to take whatever action necessary "to prevent collision" between the two countries. "No countenance," he assured Osma, would be given any American enterprise that undertakes to defend itself in obtaining guano from the Lobos Islands. Such acts constitute private war, and as such their authors would "forfeit the protection of their own Government."[36]

Joaquin José de Osma, the older brother of the minister, who had arrived in the United States as a special envoy, responded to Webster's last note to his brother and completely demolished every claim, every historical fact, every legal argument that Webster had advanced. Pizarro, not Morrell, had discovered the Lobos Islands, and he defied the secretary to present any evidence that American ships had visited the islands after 1833.[37]

It was devastating, but Webster had no one to blame but himself, although he tried to palm off his misjudgments on Jewett and William S. Hunter, Jr., who had recently served as acting head of the State Department. Even John Randolph Clay, the U.S. minister to Peru, wrote Webster as early as June 24 insisting

33. Osma to DW, August 9, 1852, in PD, II, 751–755. This protest also makes clear that Webster had an interview with Osma on July 2, when he refused to recognize the sovereignty of Peru over the islands and claimed that Morrell had discovered them.

34. Fillmore to DW, July 8, 1852, ibid., II, 742–743.

35. Ketchum to DW, August 12, DW to Ketchum, August 14, 1852, ibid., II, 755.

36. DW to Osma, August 21, ibid., II, 761–768.

37. Osma to DW, October 7, 1852, RG 59, notes from foreign legations, Peru, NA.

"that the right of property in [the islands] was *incontestably* vested in the Peruvian Nation."[38]

When all these facts came together before President Fillmore, he finally recognized that Webster could no longer function adequately as secretary of state, although he magnanimously allowed that "in the hurry of business you relied too much upon Mr. Hunter & Capt. Jewett," as he himself had relied "wholly and entirely upon you." The situation with Peru had reached a point of "imminent danger of a collision, and it will be almost a miracle if the orders to our fleet countermanding those issued in June, should reach Commodore [Charles S.] McCauley in time to prevent it, but I sincerely hope they may."[39]

Fortunately, nothing irrevocable occurred, and the Lobos affair was brought to a timely end on November 16, when Edward Everett, Webster's successor, withdrew his predecessor's claims and formally recognized Peruvian sovereignty over the Lobos Islands. Moreover, no "protection or countenance," Everett assured the Peruvian minister, would be given any U.S. citizen engaged in proceedings "inconsistent with this acknowledgement."[40]

The Lobos affair was a sad, sad ending to Webster's otherwise distinguished diplomatic career, one totally unworthy of him and one that would never have happened had he had full command of his faculties. Toward the end he admitted that his original letter to Jewett "may have been a wrong step, or a hasty step," taken "in a hurried moment." Although he had relied on Hunter and Jewett for his information, it in no way excused him. "What I wish, more particularly, to say, now," he wrote to Fillmore, "is, that the measure was mine, & I am responsible for it."[41]

His illness accounts for most of what happened. The rejection by the Whig convention caused him to drink more heavily, and by the spring of 1852 he was suffering from an advanced case of cirrhosis of the liver. In addition to alcohol, arsenic might have been a complicating cause of Webster's cirrhosis since that drug, in small quantities, had been prescribed by his physician to combat his catarrh.[42] For a number of years he had been regularly taking "iodide of iron with hydriodate of potash and minute doses of oxide of arsenic."[43] Mental symptoms of cirrhosis include an inability to concentrate and an impairment of memory. But the severe blow to his head in early May, causing a subdural hematoma, undoubtedly constituted the most important factor in Webster's rapid mental decline.

38. Clay to DW, June 24, Fillmore to DW, September 19, in *PD*, II, 723, 739–742, 775–777.

39. Fillmore to DW, September 19, 1852, ibid., II, 775–776.

40. Everett to Joaquin José de Osma, November 16, 1852, in *PD*, II, 785–787. See also Shewmaker, " 'Untaught Diplomacy,' " pp. 321–340.

41. DW to Fillmore, September 15, 1852, in *PD*, II, 774.

42. Jeffries, "An Account of the Last Illness," p. 113. Here again I have had the benefit of the medical advice of Dr. Bernard H. Adelson.

43. Ibid., pp. 110–111.

By the end of the summer of 1852 Webster was frequently "quite sick nearly all day" and "unable to sit up." During these spells he stayed in bed, never leaving it for more than five minutes. The catarrh descended upon him "in its various forms, alternating, as usual, but as yet not so severe and heavy as on former occasions." Bright sunlight affected his eyesight and kept him indoors except when he was at home—he returned to Marshfield in September 1852— and the sea was calm and he could go fishing on his yacht, protected by an awning. Sometimes his feet swelled, and he experienced "short paroxisms of pain." Still plagued by a serious diarrhea condition, loss of appetite, and the swelling of his stomach and bowels accompanied by "great pain," weakness, and fatigue, he began to suspect he might never return to Washington. Becoming increasingly feeble, he consulted doctors in Boston "for further medical advice & direction," but they provided little real relief. "The Doctors say, I shall get along with patience and care, & recommend entire quiet, and strict regimen." He was finally reduced to eating a "bowl of gruel" each day with a glass of brandy and water. He read little and wrote not at all, except to sign his name. When he took medicine to stop the diarrhea, he became constipated, "making matters still worse."[44]

He first realized the seriousness of his condition on his return to Marshfield from Washington. He had lost weight, his tongue had acquired a light brown coat, and his complexion had turned "pale with a peculiar sallowness; but there was no jaundice at this or any other time." He had lost his appetite and endured constant thirst. His doctor reported that he had "the aspect of a very sick man."[45]

At a dinner party in Marshfield honoring Thomas Baring, then visiting the United States, Webster was too ill to dine but said he would drop in during the evening. The guests were visibly shocked when they saw the great man. "If a ghost had come among us, it could hardly have startled us more," reported George Ticknor. "He looked dreadfully, but he had his usual stately air and bearing."[46]

To add to his miseries, creditors hounded him constantly. "I must beg you, therefore to relieve me from the loathsome task of continual solicitation as to this thing, year after year, & month after month," Caleb Cushing wrote him, "& to dispose of now at once." But Webster could not and did not comply, apart from offering a token payment, a request for patience, and a promise to repay all *"if I live."* Yet at the exact same time he was purchasing another fifty acres of land near Marshfield and drawing on his banker friend Franklin Haven for a thousand dollars. Long ago he had stopped trying to make restitution for what he owed. Although he earned a great deal of money—millions by present-day standards—he gave it away and spent it on himself and his family to live in style and luxury; he also lost thousands, possibly hundreds of thousands, in bad

44. DW to Fillmore, September 12, 22, 28, 1852, in *PC*, VII, 349–352; Curtis, *Webster*, II, 674.

45. Jeffries, "An Account of the Last Illness," p. 111.

46. Ticknor, "Reminiscences," quoted in Curtis, *Webster*, II, 671.

investments. But more than anything else, he was constitutionally opposed to or incapable of meeting his financial obligations.[47]

The Scott Whigs also annoyed him with requests that he publicly declare his support of the general, but he steadfastly refused. In fact he privately deprecated the nominee and praised Pierce. He even predicted an overwhelming defeat for Scott and the likelihood of the Whig party's becoming "a Northern sectional organization." At the same time his friends and supporters kept urging him to allow a third-party nomination on his behalf, despite the discouragement from such Webster Whigs as Edward Everett, Rufus Choate, and George Ashmun. But he said he would not "encourage or invite any movements designed to make him an independent candidate for the presidency," nor would he "interfere to prevent any portion of the people from casting their votes for him." It almost sounded as though he relished the thought of drawing votes from the other candidates. Nevertheless in a last-ditch effort Moses Grinnell, James Watson Webb, William M. Evarts, and other New York Whigs begged him to reconsider.[48]

But he simply could not do it. If he did, "it would gratify not only you and your friends, but that great body of implacable enemies, who have prevented me from being elected President of the United States," Webster replied. They would call me a traitor or worse. How can you ask me "to perform any act of humiliation for their gratification, or the promotion of their purposes?"

Letting off steam this way about his frustration at failing to achieve his one major goal in life made him feel better. He also took the opportunity to savage the Whig convention. "No earthly consideration could enduce me to say anything or do anything from which it might be inferred directly or indirectly that I concur in the Baltimore nomination, or that, I should give it, in any way the sanction of my approbation." If I did, "I should feel my cheeks already scorched with shame by the reproaches of posterity." As for the suggestion by Grinnell and company, "I encourage nothing. I discourage nothing. I leave them entirely free to judge of their own course."[49]

The depth of the anger and frustration he felt, as well as his own moral weaknesses, was amply demonstrated by his willingness to sacrifice the Whig party by not repudiating this "Union" party movement and by his praising the Democratic nominee, Franklin Pierce. At this crucial moment in history he effectively undermined the presidential candidate of his own party. Years later, after the Whig party had in fact collapsed and disappeared from the political scene, some men pointed at Daniel Webster—Black Dan—and bitterly accused

47. Cushing to DW, September 11, DW to Cushing, September 30, 1852, in *PC*, VII, 349, 352, and editorial note, 348; DW to Haven, September 29, 1852, in *W&S*, XVI, 665.

48. DW to Fillmore, October 18, 1852, Grinnell to DW, October 9 with an enclosure, DW to Grinnell, October 12, 1852, with an enclosure, in *PC*, VII, 365, 356–358; Curtis, *Webster*, II, 651–652.

49. DW to Grinnell, October 12, 1852, with an enclosure, in *PC*, VII, 357–358.

him of single-handedly smashing their party. Their accusation still finds advocates today.

Webster's health declined rapidly in September, and his Boston physician, John Jeffries, visited him for several days and conferred with a local doctor, John Porter. They decided that Webster's condition warranted bringing in "a medical man of high national reputation," either Dr. J. Mason Warren or Dr. James Jackson of Boston. They were particularly concerned about the inflammation and distension in his stomach and lower bowel and had applied leeches liberally. After Dr. Jackson had examined Webster on October 6, he told Ticknor privately that his patient "had a mortal disease in some one of the great organs of the abdomen, but that, after the most careful examination, he could not tell in which of them it was, with any considerable degree of confidence." Later he surmised that the affected organ was the liver. He also said that Webster should be encouraged to prepare his will.[50]

Webster had begun to suspect he was dying and therefore directed one of his small boats, the one he called "the Home Squadron," which had a mast and flag, be moved to a large pond close by where he could see it. He also sent instructions that as long as he lived, a ship lantern at the top of the mast be lighted at six o' clock every night and extinguished in the morning. "My light shall burn & my flag shall fly as long as my life lasts." Then he asked to have his cattle driven up the lane in front of the house so he could watch them as they were girted. He delighted in guessing what the measurements would be.[51]

He wanted to write a letter to try to reconcile two friends who were involved in a bitter lawsuit. He dictated it to Abbot, after which his son raised him up in his bed so that he could sign the letter and envelope. Later he asked his secretary to read from the ninth chapter of St. Mark's Gospel, the passage in which a sick child had been brought to Jesus to be cured, and Jesus said, "If you canst believe, all things are possible to him that believeth; and straightaway the father of the child cried out, with tears, Lord, I believe, help Thou mine unbelief." After that Webster requested the tenth chapter of St. John's Gospel, which says, "And many believed on Him there."[52]

By the middle of October Webster was sinking fast. Attended daily by his two doctors, Jeffries and Warren, he acknowledged that "I have been in great danger, & am in danger now." Although he could sit at a table and do a little writing—even sign his name—"I dont foresee the result. I am in the hands of God."[53]

On Friday, October 15, he sent his manservant William Johnson to fetch

50. DW to Fillmore, October 4, 1852, ibid., VII, 353–354; Curtis, *Webster,* II, 682.

51. DW to Thomas D. Hatch, [c. October 1, 1852], in *W&S*, XVI, 668; Harvey, *Reminiscences,* p. 440.

52. Abbot to a friend, October 10, 1852, in Curtis, *Webster,* II, 683–684.

53. DW to Fillmore, October 15, 1852, in *PC*, VII, 360–361.

Edward Curtis. When Curtis arrived, he handed him an inscription for his grave. It read:

"Lord, I believe; help Thou mine unbelief."
Philosophical argument, especially that drawn from the vastness of the universe in comparison with the apparent insignificance of this Globe, has sometimes shaken my reason for the faith that is in me; but my heart has assured, and reassured me, that the Gospel of Jesus Christ must be a Divine Reality.
The Sermon on the Mount cannot be a merely human production. This belief enters into the very depth of my conscience. The whole history of man proves it.

Dan'l Webster

He then turned to Abbot and said that in writing this inscription, he wanted "to leave somewhere a declaration of my belief in Christianity. I do not wish to go into any doctrinal distinctions in regard to the person of Jesus, but I wish to express my belief in His divine mission."[54]

"The disease makes progress," reported Dr. Jeffries in mid-October. "The seat of the disease now enlarges. It is a sub acute inflammation of the peritoneum."

On one occasion, while Harriette Paige, his sister-in-law, was shampooing his hair, he picked up a strand that had fallen from his head, stared at it for a moment, and murmured, "See how the thread of my life is spinning out." Turning to Mrs. Paige and his wife, family, and staff, he added, "My heart is full, I have many things to say to you all, but I cannot." Then he burst into tears.

But the tears disturbed him, and he shook off the intensity of his feelings with the remark "I will be brave & manly, I will die firm."

The "effusion," as Dr. Jeffries called it, grew each day, and Webster measured one inch more around his abdomen. Every so often his mood changed, and he joked or provided Sarah, his nurse, or his wife with "a rhyme or two."[55]

On October 17 Webster suffered "an excessively painful attack, which cost Dr. Jeffries, with his oil, morphine, & squills,[56] two hours to subdue." He complained that the doctors "measure me, like an ox, & find, that there is a small, but positive diminution of the distension of the stomach & bowels." It raised his hopes.[57]

Even so, Webster thought the time had come to submit his resignation as secretary of state. "My Dear Sir," he wrote the President on October 18, "I should love to pass the last months of your Administration, with you, around

---

54. Memorandum by Edward Curtis, October 15, 1852, ibid., VII, 361–362; Curtis, *Webster*, II, 864.

55. Abbot to a friend, October 15, 1852, in *PC*, VII, 362–363, and note 1, 363–364; Abbot to Harvey, October 11, 1852, in Van Tyne, ed., *Letters of Webster*, pp. 540–541. Once he said he felt "easy, & strong, & as if I could go into the Senate, & make a speech!" DW to Fillmore, October 18, 1852, in *PC*, VII, 364.

56. Squills induce vomiting.

57. DW to Fillmore, October 17, 1852, in *PC*, VII, 364.

your Council Board. But let not this embarrass you. Consider my Resignation as always before you, to be accepted, any moment you please. I hope God, in his mercy, may preserve me; but his will be done!"

It was the last letter Webster ever wrote. Three days later he took a turn for the worse. He vomited, "always with blood," which "continued very profusely." And he was in agony. The doctors decided his case was hopeless.[58]

For several days he had been preparing his will. Caroline's marriage settlement gave her a claim on Marshfield that he hoped she would surrender by accepting a transfer to her of the annuity provided him by his many financial benefactors. He asked Edward Curtis to arrange it, if possible. Both Caroline and the subscribers subsequently agreed to go along with his proposal. But despite the generosity of his friends and his substantial income from legal fees, his debts exceeded his assets. He also asked the trustees of his property—his brother-in-law James Paige, Franklin Haven, and Edward Curtis[59]—to manage his real estates in Marshfield and Franklin so as to provide Caroline a yearly income of five hundred dollars. Furthermore he directed that she should reside in Marshfield as long as she wished.[60] Webster wanted his estates to remain "in the blood and name of my own family" and asked the trustees to manage it for Fletcher's use and his male descendants. After Fletcher he wanted his grandson Daniel Fletcher Webster, Jr., to take one of the properties and Ashburton Webster to take the other.[61]

To the trustees he bequeathed as trusts for the use of his heirs all his books,

58. DW to Fillmore, October 18, Abbot to Fillmore, October 21, 1852, ibid., VII, 364–365 and note; Harvey, *Reminiscences*, p. 441; Jeffries, "An Account of the Last Illness," p. 113.

59. Caroline, Fletcher, and Richard Blatchford were designated executors of the will, and he asked that they always consult Franklin Haven in matters of money, Charles and George Curtis on legal matters, and Charles Thomas on matters respecting Marshfield, which had a mortgage of twenty-five hundred dollars, held by Samuel Frothingham. Under her marriage settlement, Caroline's trustees had a mortage on Marshfield "for her whole separate fortune; and he had no means of compensating them from personal estate, for the surrender of her rights," which was why he wanted the subscribers of his annuity to continue it with Caroline after his death. In this way he could get them to surrender her rights to Marshfield for the benefit of his male descendants. Curtis, *Webster*, II, 690. He also asked the executors of his will to consult with John Taylor respecting his Franklin property, which was clear of any incumbrance. In addition, he appointed Edward Everett, George Ticknor, Cornelius C. Felton, and George Curtis his literary executors.

60. Two years after Webster died, Caroline moved to New York City, where she resided until her death in New Rochelle on February 26, 1882, at the age of eighty-five. Marshfield burned in 1878, the barn in 1870. Mrs. Daniel Fletcher Webster sold the estate in 1884 to Walton Hall.

61. Daniel Fletcher Webster, a colonel of the Twelfth Massachusetts Infantry, was killed at the Second Battle of Bull Run on August 30, 1862. He was buried in Marshfield on September 9, 1862. He was forty-nine years of age at the time of his death. Fuess, *Webster*, II, 360 and note 3. He had six children, of whom three girls died at young ages. The fourth daughter, Caroline, died at the age of thirty-six. His older son, Daniel Fletcher Webster, Jr., was wounded in the Civil War, contracted tuberculosis, and died on September 2, 1865. Ashburton Webster died of tuberculosis on July 23, 1879. Neither Daniel Jr. nor Ashburton married so that in less than twenty-seven years after Webster's death, the male line of descendants had ended. Webster's direct descendants living today come through his daughter Julia Webster Appleton. Of her five children—Caroline Le Roy, Samuel, Julia Frances, Daniel Webster, and Constance Mary—four were living at the time of Webster's death. Constance Mary Appleton died on March 16, 1849. Ibid., II, 360–361.

plate, pictures, statuary, furniture, etc., with certain exceptions, such as the property Caroline brought with her on their marriage and his lawbooks, which he gave to Fletcher. To his son-in-law Samuel Appleton Appleton he left his California gold watch and chain; to his granddaughter Caroline Le Roy Appleton, his portrait by Healy; to his grandson Samuel Appleton, his gold snuffbox and all his guns and fishing equipment; to his grandson Daniel Webster Appleton, his Washington medals; to his granddaughter Julia Webster Appleton, a clock belonging to Grace. He further directed that his servant William Johnson should not repay any portion of the six hundred dollars that Webster had paid for his freedom. He also declared his black servants, Monica McCarty, Sarah Smith, and Ann Bean, "all free."[62]

At 8:45 P.M. on Thursday, October 21, Webster summoned Paige, Jeffries, Abbot, and Charles Henry Thomas, son of the man who had sold Marshfield to Webster and who now supervised the grounds on the estate, to join George and Edward Curtis and to witness his will.

"Come here," he said to Paige and George and Edward Curtis, "do you say on your honor as Gentlemen, that my Wife approves the Will?"

"She does approve it, I know it," Edward Curtis responded.

"Ask her to come & kiss me & tell me that she approves it."

Caroline entered, supported by Paige and "in great distress." She knelt by Webster's side and stared frightenedly at his face, creased by pain. He asked her if she had read and approved the will, and she responded affirmatively.

"Where is Fletcher? Where is Fletcher?" he suddenly called out.

"Here I am Father."

"My Son, do you know & approve my Will[?]"

"Entirely," Fletcher responded.

Then, said Webster, "this is my last Will & Testament."

His seal was affixed, and the papers were prepared for signing.

"Now raise me up," he commanded. Thomas helped him. "Hold the paper a little squarer, Brother Curtis," Webster commanded. "You are not accustomed to hold papers to sick men." Then he signed his name in a bold hand, bolder than usual, and Abbot, Jeffries, and Thomas affixed their signatures as witnesses.

Clasping his hands together, he muttered, "Thank God, for strength to [do] a sensible act." He then raised both hands and with great solemnity, added: "Oh, God! I thank Thee for all Thy mercies."[63]

"Have I, on this occasion, said any thing unworthy of Daniel Webster?"

"No, no, dear sir," came the unanimous response.

Bursting into tears, Caroline threw her arms around his neck. He tried to calm her, but she was so distraught that she had to retire to her room.

---

62. Webster's last will and testament, [October 21, 1852], in *PC*, VII, 367–371; Curtis, *Webster*, II, 690, 692.

63. Notes by Abbot, October 21, 1852, in *PC*, VII, 365–366; Curtis, *Webster*, II, 697. He followed these remarks with a short discourse in which he thanked God for his children, His mercies, and "for all His care." Ibid., II, 697–698.

After she left, Webster "fell into a kind of doze" from which he later roused himself in a "state of great exhaustion." With each passing day he grew more feeble, his condition worsened, and he began vomiting, which greatly reduced his strength.

His longtime friend Peter Harvey arrived and approached the bed. Webster held out both hands to him, put his arms around Harvey's neck, and kissed him.

Then he said: "Kiss me. . . . I shall be dead tomorrow. . . . God bless you, faithful friend."[64]

That evening, Saturday, October 23, in a semiconscious condition, he repeated indistinctly the words "Poet, poetry; Gray, Gray."

Fletcher recited the first line of Gray's "Elegy" to him. "The curfew tolls the knell of parting day."

"That's it, that's it," Webster cried.

Someone brought in a copy of the poem and read it to him. He smiled. He remained in a semiconscious state for the next few hours, but he was restless.

Dr. Jeffries read to him, "Though I walk through the valley of the shadow of death I will fear no evil, for thou art with me; thy rod and thy staff they comfort me."[65]

"The fact—the fact!" Webster called out. "That is what I want! Thy rod—thy rod! thy staff—thy staff!"

He craved stimulants, and Dr. Jeffries reportedly ordered a "spoonful of brandy in fifteen minutes, another in half an hour, and another in three quarters of an hour, if he still lives."

Sometime past midnight on Sunday, October 24, Webster suddenly roused himself.

"I still live!" he exclaimed. Then he fell silent. They were his last words.

After 1:00 A.M. he seemed to lose consciousness, and he started "sinking gradually, without convulsion, cold sweat, or haze of the eye." His family, except for Caroline, who could not bear to watch and remained in her room, gathered around him with the domestics and his "personal attendants."[66] They took up a deathwatch.

An eerie silence filled the room. No one wept; no one moved. Only the sighing of the wind, the sound of the clock in the hall below, and the deep breathing of the dying man could be heard. At thirty-five minutes after two o'clock on the morning of Sunday, October 24, 1852, Daniel Webster, aged seventy years, nine months, and six days, stopped breathing.

Jeffries felt the pulse, waited a few moments before gently releasing the

64. Harvey, *Reminiscences*, pp. 442–443.

65. Samuel Lyman says that at one point Webster said, "Heavenly Father, forgive my sins, and receive me to thyself, through Christ Jesus." Lyman, *Public and Private Life of Webster*, II, 279.

66. Those present included Fletcher and his wife, Paige and his wife, Samuel Appleton Appleton, George and Edward Curtis, Miss Downes, Mr. Le Roy, Peter Harvey, Charles H. Thomas, George Abbot, and William Zantzinger of the State Department, and Drs. Jeffries and Warren. *National Intelligencer*, October 28, 1852; Poore, *Perley's Reminiscences*, I, 421.

arm, and said, "Dead." The immediate cause of death, he later acknowledged, was bleeding of the stomach and bowels, resulting from cirrhosis of the liver.[67]

Webster did indeed have cirrhosis of the liver, but that is not what killed him. He died from the subdural hematoma from his fall the previous May. That fall caused a hemorrhage beneath his skull and onto the surface of the brain. The hemorrhage was in part due to the trauma of the fall and in part a bleeding tendency caused by his chronic liver disorder.

The bleeding onto the brain surface is likely to have spontaneously ceased within a few hours of the trauma. The blood ultimately formed a clot that over a period of weeks or months slowly swelled and enlarged, pressing upon his brain, probably causing changes in his cognition and personality, and ultimately killing him.[68]

The word of Webster's demise spread rapidly from Marshfield and environs to Boston. Mournful church bells—the traditional signal of death—sounded wildly. Then three times three strokes to indicate a male, followed by seventy strokes tolled slowly to denote the age of the deceased. It was Sunday, but people instantly knew what they meant, for everyone in the community had been apprized of Webster's condition for the past several weeks, and such a sound only meant that the Godlike Daniel was dead.[69] The tolling of the bells was picked up by one village and passed to the next so that by 8:00 A.M., only hours after he had died, church bells sounded in Boston and one hundred minute guns were fired from the Common. Flags were lowered to half-mast. The governor ordered the closing of all public buildings. A hush seemed to come over the city. Soon the dreadful news reached New York, Philadelphia, Baltimore, and Washington, and the entire nation went into deep mourning. A month later European newspapers "were filled with details of the event," and several hundred Americans in Paris held a meeting to pay homage to his memory. President Fillmore notified his cabinet and instructed them to wear "the usual badges of mourning for thirty days." The "fame of our illustrious statesman belongs to his country," he wrote, "the admiration of it to the world." He further ordered all flags to be lowered and public buildings draped in mourning.[70]

A single thought struck everyone as soon as he heard of Webster's passing:

67. *National Intelligencer,* October 28, Boston *Courier,* October 26, 1852, Curtis, *Webster,* II, 701; Jeffries, "An Account of the Last Illness," p. 114. Curtis gives the time at twenty-three before three o'clock, but Jeffries says it was 2:35 a.m. There is also some confusion about what were Webster's last words, whether it was something about poetry or "I still live." I think the evidence supports the latter. See Abbot to Fillmore, October 25, 1852, in *W&S,* XVIII, 562.

68. Jeffries, "An Account of the Last Illness," p. 113; Dr. Adelson to author, June 16, 1995, and discussion with Dr. Adelson on May 2, 5, June 27, August 8, 1995.

69. The bells of the First Baptist Church of Marshfield were to remain motionless because the members disapproved of Webster's drinking habits. But a ten-year-old boy, Asa Sherman, defied his elders and set the bells ringing in unison with those of all the other Marshfield churches. Betty Bates to author, May 16, 1995. Ms. Bates is the coauthor of the history of Marshfield.

70. Goodrich, *Recollections,* II, 504; Fillmore to members of the cabinet, October 25, 1852, in *PC,* VII, 372–373.

"Calhoun, Clay and Webster are gone; the mighty pillars of the State are swept away." First Calhoun in 1850, then Clay just a few months ago, and now Webster. How dreadful for the country. And who could possibly replace them at this time of national need?[71] They are, said James Henry Hammond, "the last links of the chain of the Union."[72]

Some had trouble accepting Webster's death. "He is gone! he is gone! How difficult, how almost impossible, to realize it," preached the Reverend Orville Dewey in Washington to his congregation. "He was so a part of this nation and of this nation's life and history, that the very world, that American world, feels a shock in this disruption of his ties to it. He is gone! Daniel Webster is dead! That vast space which he occupied is darkened; that great and majestic presence has passed away."[73]

George Templeton Strong said it was "the ending of one of the greatest men of this time; one of the greatest intellectually, not morally."[74]

Emerson happened to be at the beach in Plymouth on Sunday staring across the hazy water as he thought about Daniel Webster. "The sea, the rocks, the woods, gave no sign that America and the world had lost the completest man. Nature had not in our days, or not since Napoleon, cut out such a masterpiece. . . . He was a statesman, and not the semblance of one." He taught legislators, "style and eloquence," said Emerson. He raised popular discourse "out of rant and out of declamation to history and good sense."[75]

On Wednesday, October 27, a meeting of the mayor of Boston and distinguished citizens was held in Faneuil Hall to plan a fitting memorial for the great man. Edward Everett, appointed by Fillmore to succeed Webster as secretary of state, spoke, and from his words no one could miss the enormous personal loss he felt. We are here to consider a memorial to him, he said, but he left in his "works" his greatest memorial. "As a repository of political truth and practical wisdom applied to the affairs of Government, I know not where we shall find their equal." But we will miss the sound of his great voice. "That Voice, alas!" he cried, "we shall hear no more forever." He is gone. But what better way to leave this world than his final utterance, "I still live."[76]

Speaking to students, faculty, and alumni at Dartmouth many months later, Rufus Choate, in a series of questions, summed up the core of Webster's life.

Who better than he has grasped and displayed the advancing tendencies and enlarging duties of America? Who has caught—whose eloquence, whose genius, whose coun-

71. New York *Express*, October 25, 1852. "From the old heroic race to which Webster and Clay and Calhoun belonged down to the rising race of Sewards and Douglases and [Hamilton] Fishes is a dismal descent," mourned George Templeton Strong. Strong, *Diary*, II, 107.

72. Hammond, *Secret and Sacred*, p. 199.

73. *National Intelligencer*, October 26, 1852.

74. Strong, *Diary*, II, 107.

75. Emerson, *Journals*, VIII, 335–336.

76. *National Intelligencer*, October 30, 1852.

sels, have caught more adequately the genuine inspiration of our destiny? Who has better expounded by what moral and prudential policy, by what improved culture of heart and reason, by what true worship of God, by what good faith to all other nations, the dangers of that destiny may be disarmed, and its large promise laid hold on? . . . He sought to preserve, and to set forward to her glory [America—]our America.[77]

Dr. J. B. S. Jackson performed an autopsy thirty two-hours after Webster died, with six doctors in attendance, including Jeffries, Jackson, Porter, and Warren. They found the stomach distended and containing a half pint of blood, and blood was found throughout the intestines "in very considerable quantity." They therefore decided that "the immediate cause of death was hemorrhage from the stomach and bowels." Dr. Jeffries examined the cranial cavity and brain. "The cranial capacity was very unusual," he reported, "the largest which has yet been recorded." And "the membranes of the brain were most remarkably diseased."[78]

The funeral took place on Friday, October 29. Boston completely shut down to honor him. Nearly every building was draped in mourning. "All Boston and the region around is [sic] in mourning," reported one newspaper. "Nothing of the kind has ever before equalled the testimonials of respect which are exhibited this day." Said George Ticknor: "In my time, Boston has never been so saddened before." Special trains, cars, wagons, boats, "and every conveyance that could be had were crowded with mourners going to Marshfield." A steady steam of humanity sorrowfully trudged its way to his estate. More than two thousand carriages parked on the estate.

At noon the gates of Marshfield were opened so that all who wished to view the majestic form might do so. The open coffin was placed on the lawn under a tree in front of the house as more than ten thousand people filled the grounds and passed slowly around the bier.[79] Each person took a moment to look at the ravaged specimen, dressed as always in his blue coat with brass buttons, white vest and tie, gloves, and black pants. Franklin Pierce, Everett, Choate, the governor, the mayor of Boston, and hundreds of farmers, fishermen, and laborers attended.

The coffin was returned to the house, where a religious service in "the primitive manner of New England" was conducted before friends and relatives by the Reverend Ebenezer Alden, pastor of the Congregational Church of Marshfield. It consisted of a prayer, a scriptural reading, and a brief eulogy. Six neighboring farmers then bore the coffin to a low platform carriage, which was drawn by two black horses to the gravesite a mile away. A crowd, stretching about half a mile, followed "through a line of saddened forms and faces on

77. Speech delivered on July 27, 1853, in Samuel Gilman Brown, ed., *The Works of Rufus Choate* (Boston, 1862), I, 492–558.

78. Jeffries, "An Account of the Last Illness," pp. 114, 115, 116, 118.

79. Initially the coffin rested in a large room in the house, but the main beam of the floor could not support all the people who wanted to view the remains, so it was moved outdoors.

each side." A prayer was offered by the officiating clergyman, and then Daniel Webster was laid to rest in Marshfield within earshot of the sea he loved so much. The family had declined the offers from the President and governor for a state funeral. He was "buried simply as a Marshfield man, with Marshfield pall-bearers; his kin—and servants, chiefly black." Nothing "was ever equal to this moral display of the feeling of a whole people; no ceremonies ordained by imperial power could ever so strike on the hearts of men."[80]

The tremendous sorrow felt in Boston showed "a touch of repentance in it for the injustice that had been done" to Webster because of his stand on the compromise measures, especially the enforcement of the Fugitive Slave Law. But Theodore Parker, the clergyman and abolitionist, showed no repentance at all and had the "temerity" to preach a "sermon" to his congregation in which he denounced the statesman for wickedness and corruption. It shocked Boston. It shocked the nation. Newspapers around the country, almost with a single voice, condemned Parker for this "outrage."

Preachers in New England rushed to extol Webster in their sermons. "The number of those delivered is quite enormous," commented Ticknor, and the number published "in New England is getting to be very great."[81]

Politicians echoed these sentiments. Even Democrats lauded the man. Franklin Pierce, the Democratic candidate running against Scott, said in Concord, New Hampshire, "I have no heart to speak, or to contemplate the extent of the loss we have sustained." Throughout November, while the electoral returns started to roll into the offices of newspapers, the tributes to Webster from public and private men continued without interruption. As the returns spelled out the devastating defeat suffered by General Scott and the Whig party—he lost the presidency by winning only four states for a total of 42 electoral votes while Pierce took twenty-seven states for a total of 254—Daniel Webster, who had predicted the defeat, received the unconditional approval and adulation of the nation.[82]

Shortly before he died, Webster, quoting Octavius Caesar, had jokingly asked people to applaud if they thought he had lived his life well. In 1852 the American people applauded rapturously. Nearly 150 years later they have not stopped—and rightfully so.

He still lives.

80. Boston *Courier* quoted in *National Intelligencer*, October 30, 1852; Ticknor to C. S. Daveis, October 30, 1852, in Ticknor, *Life*, II, 283; Curtis, *Webster*, II, 703–704.

81. Ticknor to Everett, November 20, 1852, in Ticknor, *Life*, II, 284; *National Intelligencer*, November 16, 1852.

82. *National Intelligencer*, November 4, 13, 16, 185.

Bibliographical Essay

THE DOCUMENTARY basis of this book is derived from *The Papers of Daniel Webster*, expertly edited by an old and lamentably departed friend, Charles M. Wiltse. In my opinion, these books constitute one of the very finest examples of the collecting, collating, editing, and publishing projects presently under way at many universities and historical repositories to make available to the American public the important works of the men and women who have shaped our history. Beginning in 1974,the Webster Project at Dartmouth College eventually issued seven volumes of correspondence, two volumes of speeches and formal writings, two volumes of diplomatic papers, and three volumes of legal documents (the New Hampshire, the Boston, and the federal practices), for a total of fourteen volumes, along with a general index. Earlier a *Guide and Index to the Microfilm of the Papers of Daniel Webster,* (Hanover, N.H., 1971), along with forty-one reels of film, was published and constitutes the entire corpus of Webster's papers extant at the time of publication. Collectively these works stand as a magnificent tribute to the great man.

One of the earliest multivolume collections of Webster's works that included a fair sample of his correspondence, major speeches, and some legal and diplomatic papers was the National Edition of his *Writings and Speeches* (Boston, 1903), eighteen volumes, edited by James W. McIntyre. Other collections include Edward Everett, ed., *The Works of Daniel Webster* (Boston, 1851), six volumes; Fletcher Webster, ed., *The Private Correspondence of Daniel Webster* (Boston, 1857), two volumes; and Claude H. Van Tyne, ed., *The Letters of Daniel Webster, from Documents Owned Principally by the New Hampshire Historical Society* (New York, 1902).

Another completed project of documentary material of a major figure of this period, Henry Clay, is that of James F. Hopkins et al., eds., *The Papers of Henry Clay* (Lexington, Ky., 1959–1992), ten volumes and a supplement.

There are also comprehensive publication projects under way for all the leading figures of the antebellum era, with the single exception of Martin Van Buren. The Jackson Papers project consists at present of five published volumes. The period covered by these five volumes extends from 1770 through 1824. A microfilm edition of the entire corpus of Jackson Papers exists on thirty-nine reels with a *Guide and Index to the Microfilm Editions* (Wilmington, Del., 1987), prepared by the director of the Jackson Papers project, Harold Moser. For students and scholars, the *Correspondence of Andrew Jackson* (Washington, D.C., 1926–1935), edited in six volumes by John Spencer Bassett, remains an indispensable source, and it contains many of the best letters from several collections of Jackson manuscripts.

Two other projects currently in progress and highly important for any study of this period are the Calhoun Papers and the Polk Correspondence. The publication of these papers have progressed farther along than the Jackson Papers project. For the Calhoun documents, see W. Edwin Hamphill et al., eds., *The Papers of John C. Calhoun* (Columbia, S.C., 1959–   ), twenty-two volumes, reaching to 1846. For the Polk correspondence, see Herbert Weaver et al., eds., *Correspondence of James K. Polk* (Nashville, 1969–   ), eight volumes, covering the years 1817 through 1844.

Other published primary sources essential to this work include: Charles Francis Adams, ed., *Memoirs of John Quincy Adams* (Philadelphia, 1874–1877), twelve volumes; Thomas Hart Benton, *Thirty Years' View* (New York, 1865), two volumes; Allan Nevins, ed., *The Diary of Philip Hone, 1828–1851* (New York, 1927), two volumes; Lyon G. Tyler, *The Letters and Times of the Tylers* (New York, 1896, 1970), three volumes; and John C. Fitzpatrick, ed., *Autobiography of Martin Van Buren* (Washington, D.C., 1920).

Of the many personal reminiscences provided by Webster's contemporaries, I found Peter Harvey, *Reminiscences and Anecdotes of Daniel Webster* (Boston, 1877); Charles Lanman, *Private Life of Daniel Webster* (New York, 1852); Samuel P. Lyman, *The Public and Private Life of Daniel Webster* (Philadelphia, 1852); Charles March, *Daniel Webster and His Contemporaries* (New York, 1852); Harriette Story Paige, *Daniel Webster in England* (Boston and New York, 1917); and Caroline Le Roy Webster, *Mr. W. and I* (New York, 1942) very useful, particularly for anecdotal material and insights into Webster's character and personality.

Of published Webster material, the Library of Congress presently holds 445 individual titles, some of them biographies or partial biographies, but many reminiscences, eulogies, speeches, poems, short stories, and a folk opera. Among the earliest biographies the most informative and still valuable is George Ticknor Curtis, *Life of Daniel Webster* (New York, 1870), two volumes. In the modern period Irving H. Bartlett, *Daniel Webster* (New York, 1978); Maurice G. Baxter, *One and Inseparable: Daniel Webster and the Union* (Cambridge, Mass., and London, 1984); Richard Current, *Daniel Webster and the Rise of National Conservatism* (Boston, 1955); and Claude Moore Fuess, *Daniel Webster* (Boston, 1930), two volumes, each contributed in differing ways to my understanding of Black Dan.

Studies that focus on particular aspects of Webster's career or certain time periods that add important details about his life include Maurice Baxter, *Daniel Webster and the Supreme Court* (Amherst, Mass., 1966); Norman Brown, *Dan-*

iel Webster and the Politics of Availability (Athens, Ga., 1969); Robert Dalzell, Jr., *Daniel Webster and the Trial of American Nationalism, 1843–1852* (Boston, 1973); Howard Jones, *To the Webster-Ashburton Treaty: A Study in Anglo-American Relations, 1783–1843* (Chapel Hill, N.C., 1977); Sydney Nathans, *Daniel Webster and Jacksonian Democracy* (Baltimore and London, 1973); and Kenneth R. Stevens, *Border Diplomacy: The Caroline and McLeod Affairs in Anglo-American–Canadian Relations, 1837–1842* (Tuscaloosa, Ala., and London, 1989).

The other two members of the Great Triumvirate have been handsomely served by historians over the past few decades. Charles M. Wiltse's massive three-volume *John C. Calhoun* (Indianapolis and New York, 1944–1951) is excellent, but for an in-depth treatment of Calhoun's character and personality, consult John Niven, *John C. Calhoun and the Price of Union* (Baton Rouge, 1983). Another excellent treatment is the Pulitzer Prize-winning study by Margaret L. Coit, *John C. Calhoun, American Portrait* (Boston, 1950).

For Clay, my own *Henry Clay: Statesman for the Union* (New York, 1991) is the most recent. But see also Calvin Colton, *The Life and Times of Henry Clay* (New York, 1842), two volumes, which the author concluded with *The Last Seven Years of the Life of Henry Clay* (New York, 1856); Carl Schurz,*Henry Clay* (Boston, 1887), two volumes; Bernard Mayo, *Henry Clay, Spokesman of the New West* (Boston, 1937); George R. Poage, *Henry Clay and the Whig Party* (Chapel Hill, N.C., 1936); and Glyndon G. Van Deusen, *The Life of Henry Clay* (Boston, 1937).

Biographies of other important individuals of the antebellum period include: my own *Andrew Jackson and the Course of American Empire, 1767–1821* (New York, 1977), *Andrew Jackson and the Course of American Freedom, 1822–1832* (New York, 1981), and *Andrew Jackson and the Course of American Democracy, 1833–1845* (New York, 1984), along with a one-volume condensation of this three-volume study entitled *The Life of Andrew Jackson* (New York, 1988); John Niven, *Martin Van Buren and the Romantic Age of American Politics* (New York, 1983); Donald B. Cole, *Martin Van Buren and the American Political System* (Princeton, 1984); William N. Chambers, *Old Bullion Benton, Senator from the New West* (Boston, 1956); Samuel F. Bemis, *John Quincy Adams and the Foundations of American Foreign Policy* and *John Quincy Adams and the Union* (New York, 1949, 1956), two volumes; Harry Ammon, *James Monroe: The Quest for National Identity* (New York, 1971); the unfinished biography of James K. Polk by Charles G. Sellers, Jr., *James K. Polk, Jacksonian, 1795–1843* (Princeton, 1957), and *James K. Polk, Continentalist, 1843–1846* (Princeton, 1966); Thomas P. Govan, *Nicholas Biddle, Nationalist and Public Banker* (Chicago, 1959); Albert J. Beveridge, *The Life of John Marshall* (Boston and New York, 1919), R. Kent Newmyer, *Supreme Court Justice: Joseph Story, Statesman of the Old Republic* (New York, 1985); Carl B. Swisher, *Roger B. Taney* (New York, 1935); Albert D. Kirwan, *John J. Crittenden: The Struggle for the Union* (Lexington, Ky., 1962); Ann Mary Butler Coleman, *Life of John J.*

768

BIBLIOGRAPHICAL ESSAY

Crittenden (Philadelphia, 1871), two volumes; Robert Seager II, *And Tyler Too: A Biography of John and Julia Gardiner Tyler* (New York, 1963); Oliver Perry Chitwood, *John Tyler: Champion of the Old South* (New York, 1939); Freeman Cleaves, *Old Tippecanoe: William Henry Harrison and His Time* (New York, 1939); Holman Hamilton, *Zachary Taylor* (Indianapolis and New York, 1941, 1951), two volumes; K. Jack Bauer, *Zachary Taylor* (Baton Rouge, 1986); Robert J. Rayback, *Millard Fillmore* (Buffalo, 1959); and Robert W. Johannsen, *Stephen A. Douglas* (New York, 1973). In addition to his life of Clay, Glyndon G. Van Deusen has written biographies of three other notable Whigs: *Horace Greeley: Nineteenth Century Crusader* (New York, 1953), *Thurlow Weed: Wizard of the Lobby* (New York, 1947), and *William Henry Seward* (New York, 1967). Of special merit is Merrill D. Peterson, *The Great Triumvirate: Webster, Clay, and Calhoun* (New York, 1987).

For the history of the Supreme Court and Webster's importance in its development, I relied heavily on Maurice Baxter's *Webster and the Supreme Court,* cited above. In addition, I found most helpful G. Edward White, *The Marshall Court and Cultural Change, 1815–1835* (New York, 1988), George L. Haskins and Herbert A. Johnson, *Foundations of Power: John Marshall, 1801–1815* (New York, 1981), Francis N. Stites, *Private Interest and Public Gain: The Dartmouth College Case, 1819* (Amherst, Mass., 1972), Stanley I. Kutler, *Privilege and Creative Destruction: The Charles River Bridge Case* (Philadelphia, 1971), Morton J. Horwitz, *The Transformation of American Law, 1780–1860* (New York, 1977), Carl B. Swisher, *The Taney Period, 1836–1864* (New York, 1972), James W. Hurst, *The Growth of American Law: The Law Makers* (Boston, 1950), and Robert G. McCloskey, *The American Supreme Court* (New York, 1994).

Daniel Walker Howe, *The Political Culture of the American Whigs* (Chicago, 1979) and Howe's edition, *The American Whigs: An Anthology* (New York, 1973), along with Thomas Brown, *Politics and Statesmanship: Essays on the American Whig Party* (New York, 1985) and Glyndon G. Van Deusen's article "Some Aspects of Whig Thought and Theory in the Jacksonian Period," *American Historical Review,* LXIII (1958), pp. 305–322, are essential for an understanding of Whig political thought. In addition, see Rush Welter, *The Mind of America, 1830–1860* (New York, 1975); Fred Somkin, *Unquiet Eagle: Memory and Desire in the Life of American Freedom, 1815–1860* (New York, 1967); John Ashworth, *"Agrarians & Aristocrats": Party Ideology in the United States, 1837–1846* (London, 1983) and *Slavery, Capitalism, and Politics in the Antebellum Republic,* vol. I, *Commerce and Compromise, 1820–1850,* (Cambridge, Mass., 1995); Jack Larkin, *The Reshaping of Everyday Life, 1790–1840* (New York, 1988); Robert F. Dalzell, Jr., *Enterprising Elite: The Boston Associates and the World They Made* (Cambridge, Mass., 1987); and Arthur A. Ekirch, Jr., *The Idea of Progress in America, 1815–1860* (New York, 1969). See Maurice G. Baxter, *Henry Clay and the American System* (Lexington, Ky., 1995) for Clay's American System and other aspects of his economic thinking. Major L. Wilson, *Space,*

Time, and Freedom: The Quest for Nationality and the Irrepressible Conflict (Westport, Conn., 1974) provides interesting contrasts in the goals and purposes of the Whigs and Democrats. For the Democrats, consult Jean H. Baker, *Affairs of Party* (Ithaca, N.Y., 1983), Marvin Meyers's classic study *The Jacksonian Persuasion* (Stanford, Calif., 1957), and especially Harry L. Watson, *Liberty and Power: The Politics of Jacksonian America* (New York, 1990).

The market revolution that embraced the many economic changes occurring in the nation following the War of 1812 can be traced in Charles Sellers, *The Market Revolution* (New York, 1995). For specific economic problems or concerns of the antebellum period, see Murray Rothbard, *The Panic of 1819* (New York, 1962), Reginald C. McGrane, *The Panic of 1837: Some Financial Problems of the Jacksonian Era* (Chicago, 1924), Peter Temin, *The Jacksonian Economy* (New York, 1969), Ralph C. H. Catterall, *The Second Bank of the United States* (Chicago, 1902), Bray Hammond, *Banks and Politics in America from the Revolution to the Civil War* (Princeton, 1957), Larry Schweikart, *Banking in the American South from the Age of Jackson to Reconstruction* (Baton Rouge, 1987), Malcolm J. Rohrbough, *The Land Office Business* (New York, 1968), Daniel Feller, *Public Lands and Jacksonian Politics* (Madison, Wis., 1984), Stephen Hahn, *The Roots of Southern Populism* (New York, 1983), Frank W. Taussig, *The Tariff History of the United States* (New York, 1893), and Sean Wilentz, *Chants Democratic: New York City and the Rise of the American Working Class, 1788–1850* (New York, 1984).

My own *Martin Van Buren and the Making of the Democratic Party* (New York, 1959) was the first to recognize the Magician's unique contribution to the structuring of the Democratic party and the motivation behind it. Richard Hofstadter, *The Idea of a Party System* (Berkeley, Calif., 1972) pursued the entire concept of party development and the drastic changes in attitude from the end of the eighteenth through the beginning of the nineteenth century. The thesis was further developed in Michael Wallace, "Changing Concepts of Party in the United States: New York, 1815–1825," *American Historical Review,* LXXIV (1968), pp. 453–491. Other important studies of party activity and evolution include Ralph Katcham, *Presidents Above Party* (Chapel Hill, N.C., 1984) and Richard P. McCormick's two books, *The Second American Party System: Party Formation in the Jacksonian Era* (Chapel Hill, N.C., 1966) and *The Presidential Game: The Origins of American Presidential Politics* (New York, 1982). On the Federalists, Shaw Livermore, Jr., *The Twilight of Federalism: The Disintegration of the Federalist Party, 1815–1830* (Princeton, 1962) is excellent. For all the presidential elections in this antebellum period, see Arthur M. Schlesinger, Jr., and Fred J. Israel, eds., *History of American Presidential Elections, 1789–1968* (New York, 1971), four volumes.

All secondary sources treating the Jacksonian era begin with Arthur M. Schlesinger, Jr., *The Age of Jackson* (New York, 1945), a brilliantly written landmark in Jacksonian scholarship. From Clay's point of view, see Glyndon G. Van Deusen, *The Jacksonian Era, 1828–1848* (New York, 1959). Other more recent studies of Whig and Democratic ideology and politics include Robert Kelley, *The Cultural Pattern in American Politics: The First Century* (New York, 1979), Richard L. McCormick, *The Party Period from the Age of Jackson to the Progressive Era* (New York, 1986), Ronald P. Formisano, *The Transformation of Political Culture: Massachusetts Parties, 1790s–1840s* (New York, 1983), Roy Nichols, *The Invention of the American Political Parties* (New York, 1967), and Joel Silbey, *The Partisan Imperative: The Dynamics of American Politics before the Civil War* (New York, 1985) and *The American Political Nation, 1838–1893* (Stanford, Calif., 1991).

There are two splendid accounts of the Jackson presidency: Richard B. Latner, *The Presidency of Andrew Jackson* (Athens, Ga., 1979) and the more recent Donald R. Cole *The Presidency of Andrew Jackson* (Lawrence, Kan., 1993).

On the nullification crisis and the Compromise Tariff of 1833, the most recent account is Richard B. Ellis, *The Union at Risk: Jacksonian Democracy, States' Rights and the Nullification Crisis* (New York, 1987). See also William W. Freehling, *Prelude to Civil War: The Nullification Movement in South Carolina, 1816–1836* (New York, 1966) and Merrill D. Peterson, *The Olive Branch and Sword: The Compromise of 1833* (Baton Rouge, 1982). Freehling's excellent study of the secession movement, *The Road to Disunion: Secessionists at Bay, 1776–1854* (New York, 1990), is particularly informative.

For a general survey of the Bank War, see my own *Andrew Jackson and the Bank War* (New York, 1968). And Watson's *Liberty and Power*, previously cited, is detailed and insightful. Also useful are John M. McFaul, *The Politics of Jacksonian Finance* (Ithaca, N.Y., 1972) and James Roger Sharp, *The Jacksonians versus the Banks: Politics in the States after the Panic of 1837* (New York, 1970).

Paul Goodman, *Towards a Christian Republic: Antimasonry and the Great Transition in New England, 1826–1836* (New York, 1988) and William P. Vaughn, *The Antimasonic Party in the United States, 1826–1843* (Lexington, Ky., 1983) explain this extraordinary phenomenon in American history.

On the Whig party, two older works are still useful: E. Malcolm Carroll, *Origins of the Whig Party* (Durham, N.C., 1925) and Arthur C. Cole, *The Whig Party in the South* (Washington, D.C., 1913). More recent articles on various aspects of the party include Charles G. Sellers, Jr., "Who Were the Southern Whigs?" *American Historical Review*, LIX (January 1954), pp. 341–346; Thomas Brown, "Southern Whigs and the Politics of Statesmanship, 1833–41," *Journal of Southern History*, XLVI (August 1980), pp. 361–380; Lynn L. Marshall, "The Strange Stillbirth of the Whig Party," *American Historical Review*, LXXII (January 1967), pp. 445–468; William S. Stokes, "Whig Conceptions of Executive Power," *Presidential Studies Quarterly*, VI (Winter 1976), pp. 16–35; and Glyndon G. Van Deusen, "The Whig Party," *History of U.S. Political Parties*, cited previously, I, 333–496.

Major L. Wilson, *The Presidency of Martin Van Buren* (Lawrence, Kan., 1984) is the most useful study of its subject. I particularly like Robert Gray

Gunderson, *The Log Cabin Campaign* (Lexington, Ky., 1957), which captures all the fun and nonsense of the campaign of 1840. For the economic issues involved in the campaign, see Michael F. Holt, "The Election of 1840, Voter Mobilization and the Emergence of Jacksonian Voting Behavior," in William J. Cooper, Jr., et al., eds., *A Master's Due* (Baton Rouge, 1985), pp. 16–58. The remarkable surge of party partisanship in this period is discussed and analyzed in Joel Silbey, *The Shrine of Party: Congressional Voting Behavior, 1841–1852* (Pittsburgh, 1967).

The individual presidencies of Harrison, Tyler, Polk, and Taylor are extensively covered in the American Presidencies Series published by the University of Kansas Press. These include Norma Lois Peterson, *The Presidencies of William Henry Harrison & John Tyler* (Lawrence, Kan., 1989), Paul Bergeron, *The Presidency of James K. Polk* (Lawrence, Kan., 1987), and Elbert B. Smith, *The Presidencies of Zachary Taylor and Millard Fillmore* (Lawrence, Kan., 1989). Robert J. Morgan, *A Whig Embattled: The Presidency under John Tyler* (Lincoln, Neb., 1954) is fair and balanced. For Polk, see also Charles A. McCoy, *Polk and the Presidency* (Austin, Texas, 1960).

Albert K. Weinberg, *Manifest Destiny* (Baltimore, 1935) and two works by Frederick Merk, *Manifest Destiny and Mission in American History* (New York, 1963), and *The Oregon Question: Essays in Anglo-American Diplomacy and Politics* (Cambridge, Mass., 1967), trace the background, goals, and purposes of the "eagle-screamers." Norman A. Graebner, *Empire on the Pacific: A Study in American Continental Expansion* (New York, 1955) is particularly enlightening, and Dexter Perkins, *The Monroe Doctrine, 1826–1867* (Baltimore, 1933) is the classic study on that subject.

For a modern account of the Mexican War, consult K. Jack Bauer, *The Mexican-American War, 1846–1848* (New York, 1974), although Justin H. Smith, *The War with Mexico* (New York, 1919), two volumes, remains the most detailed account available. Robert W. Johannsen explains the popular enthusiasm for the war in *To the Halls of the Montezumas: The War with Mexico in the American Imagination* (New York, 1985), while John H. Schroeder, *Mr. Polk's War: American Opposition and Dissent, 1846–1848* (Madison, Wis., 1973) analyzes the strong opposition to it by Whigs.

An especially good introduction to the slavery question is Peter Kolchin, *American Slavery, 1619–1877* (New York, 1993). See also Kenneth M. Stampp, *The Peculiar Institution: Slavery in the Ante-Bellum South* (New York, 1956). James Oakes, *The Ruling Race: A History of American Slaveholders* (New York, 1982) is both provocative and compelling.

Although more than thirty years old, Louis Filler, *The Crusade against Slavery, 1830–1860* (New York, 1960) is still a good place to start for the abolition movement. See also Gilbert H. Barnes, *The Antislavery Impulse, 1830–1844* (New York, 1933), Dwight Dumond, *Antislavery: The Crusade for Freedom in America* (Ann Arbor, Mich., 1961), Carleton Mabee, *Black Freedom: The Nonviolent Abolitionists from 1830 through the Civil War* (New York, 1970),

Thomas D. Morris, *Free Men All: The Personal Liberty Laws of the North, 1780–1861* (Baltimore, 1974), Richard H. Sewall, *Ballots for Freedom: Antislavery Politics in the United States, 1837–1860* (New York, 1976), Theodore C. Smith, *The Liberty and Free Soil Parties in the Northwest* (New York, 1897), and James Brewer Stewart, *Holy Warriors: The Abolitionists and American Slavery* (New York, 1976).

Michael F. Holt, *The Political Crisis of the 1850s* (New York, 1978) is indispensable for political developments of the decade prior to the outbreak of the Civil War. But still valuable are Allan Nevins, *Ordeal of the Union* (New York, 1947), two volumes, and David Potter, *The Impending Crisis 1848–1861* (New York, 1976). Eric Foner, *Free Soil, Free Labor, Free Men: The Ideology of the Republican Party before the Civil War* (New York, 1970) is excellent on the Free Soil movement, and Joseph G. Rayback, *Free Soil: The Election of 1848* (Lexington, Ky., 1970) and Frederick J. Blue, *The Free Soilers: Third Party Politics 1848–1854* (Urbana, Ill., 1964) provided me with valuable information. On the Compromise of 1850, see Holman Hamilton, *Prologue to Conflict: The Crisis and Compromise of 1850* (Lexington, Ky., 1964). The criticism Webster sustained over his role in the enforcement of the Fugitive Slave Law is expertly analyzed in Stanley W. Campbell, *The Slave Catchers: Enforcement of the Fugitive Slave Law 1850–1860* (Chapel Hill, N.C., 1970). See also Thomas D. Morris, *Free Men All: The Personal Liberty Laws of the North 1780–1861* (Baltimore, 1974).

Other sources, such as manuscript collections that are too numerous to list here, and works of reminiscences and anecdotes by contemporaries for the early nineteenth century can be found in the footnotes.

Index